CONSTITUTIONAL LAW

THIRTY-FIRST EDITION

STEVEN L. EMANUEL

Founder & Editor-in-Chief, *Emanuel Law Outlines* and
Emanuel Bar Review
Harvard Law School, J.D. 1976
Member, NY, CT, MD and VA bars

The *Emanuel® Law Outlines* Series

Wolters Kluwer
Law & Business

This book is intended as a general review of a legal subject. It is not intended as a source of advice for the solution of legal matters or problems. For advice on legal matters, the reader should consult an attorney.

About Wolters Kluwer Law & Business

Wolters Kluwer Law & Business is a leading global provider of intelligent information and digital solutions for legal and business professionals in key specialty areas, and respected educational resources for professors and law students. Wolters Kluwer Law & Business connects legal and business professionals as well as those in the education market with timely, specialized authoritative content and information-enabled solutions to support success through productivity, accuracy and mobility.

Serving customers worldwide, Wolters Kluwer Law & Business products include those under the Aspen Publishers, CCH, Kluwer Law International, Loislaw, ftwilliam.com and MediRegs family of products.

CCH products have been a trusted resource since 1913, and are highly regarded resources for legal, securities, antitrust and trade regulation, government contracting, banking, pension, payroll, employment and labor, and healthcare reimbursement and compliance professionals.

Aspen Publishers products provide essential information to attorneys, business professionals and law students. Written by preeminent authorities, the product line offers analytical and practical information in a range of specialty practice areas from securities law and intellectual property to mergers and acquisitions and pension/benefits. Aspen's trusted legal education resources provide professors and students with high-quality, up-to-date and effective resources for successful instruction and study in all areas of the law.

Kluwer Law International products provide the global business community with reliable international legal information in English. Legal practitioners, corporate counsel and business executives around the world rely on Kluwer Law journals, looseleafs, books, and electronic products for comprehensive information in many areas of international legal practice.

Loislaw is a comprehensive online legal research product providing legal content to law firm practitioners of various specializations. Loislaw provides attorneys with the ability to quickly and efficiently find the necessary legal information they need, when and where they need it, by facilitating access to primary law as well as state-specific law, records, forms and treatises.

ftwilliam.com offers employee benefits professionals the highest quality plan documents (retirement, welfare and non-qualified) and government forms (5500/PBGC, 1099 and IRS) software at highly competitive prices.

MediRegs products provide integrated health care compliance content and software solutions for professionals in healthcare, higher education and life sciences, including professionals in accounting, law and consulting.

Wolters Kluwer Law & Business, a division of Wolters Kluwer, is headquartered in New York. Wolters Kluwer is a market-leading global information services company focused on professionals.

Dedication

To Jeffrey Howard Emanuel,

No longer even close to being
the littlest Emanuel

Abbreviations Used in Text

CASEBOOKS

Chemerinsky — Erwin Chemerinsky, *Constitutional Law* (Wolters Kluwer, 4th Ed. 2013)

Sullivan & Gunther — Kathleen Sullivan & Gerald Gunther, *Constitutional Law* (Foundation Press, 17th Ed., 2010). (Where earlier editions are referenced, the edition number is indicated.)

L,K,&C — Lockhart, Kamisar, Choper, Shiffrin & Fallon, *Constitutional Law — Cases, Comments, Questions* (West Publ., 8th Ed., 1996)

S,S,S,T&K — Stone, Seidman, Sunstein, Tushnet & Karlan, *Constitutional Law* (Wolters Kluwer, 7th Ed., 2013)

HORNBOOKS AND OTHER AUTHORITIES

Chemerinsky Hnbk — Erwin Chemerinksy, *Constitutional Law: Principles and Policies* (Wolters Kluwer, 4th Ed. 2011)

Ely — John Ely, *Democracy and Distrust* (Harvard Univ. Press, 1980)

Engdahl — David Engdahl, *Constitutional Power: Federal and State* (West Publ., Nutshell Series, 1974)

N&R — Nowak & Rotunda, *Constitutional Law* (West Publ., 5th Ed., 1995)

Schwartz — Bernard Schwartz, *Constitutional Law: A Textbook* (MacMillan Publ., 2nd Ed., 1979)

Tribe — Lawrence Tribe, *American Constitutional Law* (Foundation Press, 2nd Ed., 1988)

SUMMARY OF CONTENTS

Preface xxv

Casebook Correlation Chart xxvii

Capsule Summary C-1

1. INTRODUCTION 1

2. THE SUPREME COURT'S AUTHORITY 7

3. FEDERALISM AND FEDERAL POWER GENERALLY 19

4. THE FEDERAL COMMERCE POWER 27

5. OTHER NATIONAL POWERS 65

6. TWO LIMITS ON STATE POWER: THE DORMANT COMMERCE CLAUSE
   AND CONGRESSIONAL ACTION 83

7. INTERGOVERNMENTAL IMMUNITIES AND INTERSTATE RELATIONS . . 115

8. SEPARATION OF POWERS 127

9. DUE PROCESS OF LAW 159

10. EQUAL PROTECTION 247

11. MISCELLANEOUS CLAUSES: 14TH AM. PRIVILEGES OR IMMUNITIES;
    TAKING; CONTRACT; RIGHT TO BEAR ARMS; EX POST FACTO;
    BILLS OF ATTAINDER 411

12. STATE ACTION 449

13. CONGRESSIONAL ENFORCEMENT OF CIVIL RIGHTS 469

14. FREEDOM OF EXPRESSION 499

15. FREEDOM OF RELIGION 655

16. JUSTICIABILITY 707

Essay Exam Questions and Answers 749

Table of Cases 757

Subject Matter Index 765

TABLE OF CONTENTS

Preface xxv

Casebook Correlation Chart xxvii

Capsule Summary C-1

Chapter 1

INTRODUCTION

I. ROADMAP OF CONSTITUTIONAL LAW 1

II. THREE STANDARDS OF REVIEW 2
   A. Three standards 2
   B. Consequences of choice 3
   C. When used 3

Chapter 2

THE SUPREME COURT'S AUTHORITY

I. REVIEW OF ACTS OF CONGRESS (*MARBURY v. MADISON*) 8

II. REVIEW OF STATE COURT DECISIONS 10
   A. General principles of review 10
   B. *Martin v. Hunter's Lessee* 10
   C. Recent state challenges to Supreme Court authority 11
   D. Independent and adequate state grounds 11

III. CONGRESS' CONTROL OF FEDERAL COURT JURISDICTION 12
   A. The problem generally 12
   B. *McCardle* case 13
   C. Limits on congressional power 14
   D. Modern congressional controls on federal jurisdiction 14

IV. THE SUPREME COURT'S JURISDICTION TODAY 15
   A. Limited scope of discussion 15
   B. *Certiorari* 15

Quiz Yourself on
THE SUPREME COURT'S AUTHORITY (ENTIRE CHAPTER) 15

Exam Tips on
THE SUPREME COURT'S AUTHORITY 16

Chapter 3

FEDERALISM AND FEDERAL POWER GENERALLY

I.   THE CONCEPT OF FEDERALISM 19
  A. Nature of federalism 19
  B. Federal government has limited powers 19
  C. Specific powers 20

II. *McCULLOCH v. MARYLAND* 21
  A. Doctrine of implied powers 21
  B. *McCulloch* and the "Necessary and Proper" Clause 21

III. THE "TERM LIMITS" PROBLEM 24

Quiz Yourself on
FEDERALISM AND FEDERAL POWER (ENTIRE CHAPTER)............. 25

Exam Tips on
FEDERALISM AND FEDERAL POWER GENERALLY 26

Chapter 4

THE FEDERAL COMMERCE POWER

I.   THE COMMERCE CLAUSE GENERALLY 27
  A. Introduction 27
  B. Limitation on states vs. limitation on Congress 27
  C. Chronological approach 27

II. CASES PRIOR TO 1933 28
  A. The groundwork — *Gibbons v. Ogden* 28
  B. Inactive 29
  C. Economic regulation 29
  D. "Police power" regulations and the commerce-prohibiting technique .. 30

III. COURT BARRIERS TO THE NEW DEAL 31
  A. The New Deal threatened 31
  B. The *Schechter Poultry* ("Sick Chicken") case 31
  C. The *Carter Coal* case 32
  D. The Court-packing plan 32

IV. THE POST-NEW-DEAL TREND 33
  A. The post-New-Deal trend generally 33
  B. Expanded "substantial economic effect" 33
  C. The "cumulative effect" theory 34

    D. The commerce-prohibiting technique (police power regulations) 35

    E. Civil rights legislation 36

V. SOME MODERN LIMITS ON THE COMMERCE POWER 38

    A. Some limits still exist 38

    B. Can't ban "guns near schools" (*U.S. v. Lopez*) 38

    C. Violence against women (*Morrison*) 41

    D. Regulation of non-commercial activity as part of broader regulatory scheme 42

    E. Forcing someone to buy a product (*N.F.I.B. v. Sebelius*) 44

    F. Summary of the modern limits on the Commerce power 51

    G. Summary of modern view 52

VI. THE TENTH AMENDMENT AS A LIMIT ON CONGRESS' POWER ... 53

    A. Apparent irrelevance of Tenth Amendment 53

    B. Once again irrelevant 54

    C. Overruling of *National League of Cities* 54

    D. Significance of case 56

    E. Use of state's lawmaking mechanisms 56

Quiz Yourself on
THE FEDERAL COMMERCE POWER (ENTIRE CHAPTER) 59

Exam Tips on
THE FEDERAL COMMERCE POWER 62

Chapter 5

OTHER NATIONAL POWERS

I. THE TAXING POWER 65

    A. Several provisions on tax 65

    B. Special rules on taxes 66

    C. Regulatory effect 66

        1. Disguised regulation 66

        2. Modern rules 67

        3. Effect of calling a measure a "penalty" (the Affordable Care case) 67

II. THE SPENDING POWER 70

    A. The spending power generally 70

    B. Not limited to enumerated powers 70

    C. Achievement of otherwise disallowed objectives 71

    D. Spending program can't "coerce" the states (*N.F.I.B.* case) 72

    E. "General welfare" still required 77

III. THE WAR, TREATY AND FOREIGN AFFAIRS POWERS 77

IV. OTHER POWERS 79

Quiz Yourself on
OTHER NATIONAL POWERS (ENTIRE CHAPTER) 80

Exam Tips on
OTHER NATIONAL POWERS 81

Chapter 6

TWO LIMITS ON STATE POWER: THE DORMANT COMMERCE CLAUSE AND CONGRESSIONAL ACTION

I. THE DORMANT COMMERCE CLAUSE — REGULATION 84
   A. Negative implications of federal power 84
   B. Negative implications of the Commerce Clause 84
   C. Traditional approach 84
   D. Early interpretations 85
   E. Rise of the "local" vs. "national" distinction 86
   F. Modern approach 88
   G. Application of the test 88
   H. Regulation of transportation 89
   I. State barriers to incoming trade 91
      1. Protection of economy 92
      2. Health and safety regulations 92
      3. *Baldwin* case 92
      4. Valid health objective not sufficient 92
      5. Intentional discrimination (the *Washington Apple* case) 93
      6. Discrimination by city against out-of-towners 94
      7. Facially neutral statutes and the meaning of "discrimination" 94
      8. Personal mobility 95
   J. State barriers to outgoing trade 95
   K. Local-processing requirements 96
   L. Environmental regulation 98
   M. State as purchaser or subsidizer 100

II. STATE TAXATION OF INTERSTATE COMMERCE 102

III. CONGRESSIONAL ACTION — PREEMPTION AND CONSENT 104

Quiz Yourself on
TWO LIMITS ON STATE POWER (ENTIRE CHAPTER) 109

Exam Tips on
TWO LIMITS ON STATE POWER 112

Chapter 7

INTERGOVERNMENTAL IMMUNITIES AND INTERSTATE RELATIONS

I. TAX IMMUNITIES 115

II. FEDERAL IMMUNITY FROM STATE REGULATION 117

III. STATE IMMUNITY FROM FEDERAL REGULATION 117

IV. INTERSTATE RELATIONSHIPS 118

Quiz Yourself on
INTERGOVERNMENTAL IMMUNITIES & INTERSTATE RELATIONS
(ENTIRE CHAPTER). 121

Exam Tips on
INTERGOVERNMENTAL IMMUNITIES AND
INTERSTATE RELATIONS. 122

Chapter 8

SEPARATION OF POWERS

I. DOMESTIC POLICY AND THE SEPARATION OF POWERS 128
   A. General problem 128
   B. No right to "make laws" 128
   C. President's veto power 130
      1. The "pocket veto" 130
      2. The "line item" veto 131
      3. The legislative veto 132
   D. Special prosecutor 134
   E. Interference with, or undue delegation to, the Judicial Branch 135

II. FOREIGN AFFAIRS AND THE WAR POWERS 135
   A. Special presidential role in foreign affairs 135
   B. The war powers 136
      1. Commitment of the armed forces abroad 137
      2. Habeas corpus, and the rights of enemy combatants to it (*Boumediene*) 138

III. APPOINTMENT AND REMOVAL OF EXECUTIVE PERSONNEL 141
   A. The President's power of appointment 141
   B. *Buckley v. Valeo* **(the Election Law Case)** 143
   C. The President's right to remove appointees 143
   D. Removal by Congress 146
   E. Impeachment 147

IV. LEGISLATIVE AND EXECUTIVE IMMUNITY 148

A. Scope of discussion 148
B. Congress and the Speech and Debate Clause 149
C. Executive immunity 149
D. "Executive privilege" 150

Quiz Yourself on
SEPARATION OF POWERS (ENTIRE CHAPTER) 153

Exam Tips on
SEPARATION OF POWERS 155

Chapter 9

DUE PROCESS OF LAW

I. THE BILL OF RIGHTS AND THE STATES 161
   A. The Bill of Rights generally 161
   B. Enactment of the Civil War Amendments 162
   C. Due process of law and "incorporation" 162
   D. The Fifth Amendment's Due Process Clause 164

II. SUBSTANTIVE DUE PROCESS — BEFORE 1934 164
   A. Introduction 164
   B. Early history of substantive due process 165
   C. Lochner and its aftermath 166

**III. SUBSTANTIVE DUE PROCESS — THE MODERN APPROACH
    TO ECONOMIC AND SOCIAL-WELFARE REGULATION** 168
   A. Initial decline of Lochnerism 168
   B. Judicial abdication in economic cases 169
   C. Summary of modern approach 170

Quiz Yourself on
SUBSTANTIVE DUE PROCESS — ECONOMIC AND SOCIAL-WELFARE
REGULATION 171

**IV. SUBSTANTIVE DUE PROCESS — PROTECTION OF NON-ECONOMIC
    RIGHTS, INCLUDING "FUNDAMENTAL" RIGHTS** 172
   A. Overview 172
   B. The early non-economic cases 173
   C. Birth control (the *Griswold* case) 174
   D. Post-*Griswold* contraceptive law 176
   E. Abortion generally 176
   F. *Roe v. Wade* 176
   G. The modification of *Roe* by *Casey* 178
   H. Post-*Roe* developments, generally 184
   I. Consent 184

J. Public funding of abortions 186
K. Types of abortion allowable 188
L. Future of abortion regulation 195
M. Post-Roe regulation of contraception (*Carey* case) 196
N. Family relations 197
O. Sexuality, including homosexuality 200
P. The "right to die" 205
Q. Other assorted autonomy issues 213
    1. Autonomy of mental processes 213
    2. Rights of committed mentally retarded 213
    3. Prohibition of risk-taking 213
    4. The right to travel 214
    5. Right to occupation 214
R. No right to be protected from privately-imposed harm 214
S. Looking back on the "fundamental value" approach 216

Quiz Yourself on
SUBSTANTIVE DUE PROCESS — PROTECTION OF
NON-ECONOMIC RIGHTS 217

V. PROCEDURAL DUE PROCESS 222
A. Introduction 222
B. "Liberty" and "property" before 1970 223
C. Growth in the '70s of "entitlements" 224
D. Narrowing of "entitlements" theory 224
E. The tenure cases (*Roth* and *Perry*) 224
F. Breadth of injury is weighed 226
G. Freedom from arbitrary procedures 226
H. Narrowing of protected "liberty" interests 226
I. Rights of students 226
J. What process is due 227

Quiz Yourself on
PROCEDURAL DUE PROCESS 237

Exam Tips on
DUE PROCESS OF LAW 240

Chapter 10

EQUAL PROTECTION

I. INTRODUCTION 249
A. Historical overview 249
B. Operation of the Clause 251

Chapter 11

MISCELLANEOUS CLAUSES:
14TH AM. PRIVILEGES OR IMMUNITIES; TAKING; CONTRACTS; RIGHT TO BEAR ARMS; EX POST FACTO; BILLS OF ATTAINDER

I.   THE 14TH AMENDMENT'S PRIVILEGES OR IMMUNITIES
     CLAUSE 412

II. THE "TAKING" CLAUSE 414
     A. The Taking Clause generally 414
     B. The taking/regulation distinction 415
     C. Requirement of "public" use 425

III. THE "CONTRACT" CLAUSE 427
     A. The "Contract" Clause generally 427
     B. Protection of public agreements 428
     C. Protection of private contracts 428
     D. More deferential standard 431
     E. Incidental effect on contracts 431
     F. Other retroactivity issues 432

IV. THE SECOND AMENDMENT "RIGHT TO BEAR ARMS" 432

V.   EX POST FACTO LAWS 440

VI. BILLS OF ATTAINDER 441

     Quiz Yourself on
     MISCELLANEOUS CLAUSES (ENTIRE CHAPTER) 442

     Exam Tips on
     MISCELLANEOUS CLAUSES 446

Chapter 12

STATE ACTION

I.   INTRODUCTION 449

II. THE "PUBLIC FUNCTION" APPROACH 453
     A. The "public function" approach generally 453
     B. The *White Primary* Cases 453
     C. Company towns and shopping centers 453
     D. Parks and recreation 455
     E. The requirement of state "exclusivity" 455
     F. Future of "public function" doctrine 457

III. "NEXUS" — THE SIGNIFICANCE OF STATE INVOLVEMENT 457
- A. The "nexus" theory generally 457
- B. "Commandment" 457
- C. "Encouragement" by the state 459
- D. "Symbiosis" between state and private actor 460
- E. Involvement or "entanglement" by state 461

Quiz Yourself on
STATE ACTION (ENTIRE CHAPTER) 465

Exam Tips on
STATE ACTION 467

Chapter 13

CONGRESSIONAL ENFORCEMENT OF CIVIL RIGHTS

I. INTRODUCTION 469

II. CONGRESS' POWER TO REACH PRIVATE CONDUCT 471
- A. Purely private conduct 471
- B. Early decision 471
- C. The *Guest* case 472
- D. *Morrison* wipes out the expansive interpretation of *Guest* 473
- E. Current state of the law 473
- F. The Thirteenth Amendment and private conduct 474
- G. Violation of other constitutional rights 476

III. CONGRESS' POWER TO REMEDY VIOLATIONS OF THE CIVIL WAR AMENDMENTS 476
- A. General problem 476
- B. Congress' broad "remedial" powers 477
- C. The Voting Rights Act 478
  - 1. Historical background of the V.R.A. 478
  - 2. Voting Rights Act of 1965 478
  - 3. Upheld in *South Carolina v. Katzenbach* 478
  - 4. Obligation to rely on current data (*Shelby County v. Holder*) 479

IV. CONGRESS' POWER TO REDEFINE THE MEANING AND SCOPE OF CONSTITUTIONAL GUARANTEES 486
- A. Substantive modifications 486

V. CONGRESS' POWER TO ABROGATE THE ELEVENTH AMENDMENT, AND THUS AUTHORIZE PRIVATE DAMAGE SUITS AGAINST THE STATES FOR DISCRIMINATION 489
- A. Private money-damage suits against states for discrimination 489
- B. The Eleventh Amendment 489

C. Age and disability discrimination 490

D. Significance of standard of review 492

E. Right to allow damages for actual constitutional violations 493

F. 3-step analysis 493

Quiz Yourself on
CONGRESSIONAL ENFORCEMENT OF
CIVIL RIGHTS (ENTIRE CHAPTER) 494

Exam Tips on
CONGRESSIONAL ENFORCEMENT OF CIVIL RIGHTS 495

Chapter 14

FREEDOM OF EXPRESSION

I.   GENERAL THEMES 502

A. Text of First Amendment 502

B. Two broad classes 502

C. Analysis of "track one" cases 504

D. Analysis of "track two" cases 507

E. Regulation of "pure conduct" 508

F. Unprotected categories 508

II. ADVOCACY OF ILLEGAL CONDUCT 509

A. Introduction 509

B. The "clear and present danger" test 510

C. The Learned Hand test 512

D. Statutes directly proscribing speech 513

E. Threat of communism and the Smith Act 514

F. The modern standard 515

III. OVERBREADTH AND VAGUENESS 519

A. Overbreadth 519

B. Vagueness 522

Quiz Yourself on
FREEDOM OF EXPRESSION — GENERAL THEMES; ADVOCACY OF
ILLEGAL CONDUCT; OVERBREADTH AND VAGUENESS 522

IV. REGULATION OF CONTEXT — "TIME, PLACE AND MANNER" . . 526

A. Context regulations generally 526

B. Meaning of "narrowly tailored" 528

C. "Leave open alternative channels" requirement 529

D. Licensing 529

E. Intrusive speakers vs. right to be left alone 531

F. Canvassing and soliciting 532

    G. **The hostile audience and "fighting words"** 533
    H. **Offensive words and the sensitive audience** 536
    I. **Regulation of "hate speech"** 540
    J. **All speech not necessarily created equal (the disfavoring of indecent speech)** 544
    K. **Regulation of indecency in media** 546
    L. **The public forum** 549
    M. **Right of access to private places** 557

V. SYMBOLIC EXPRESSION 557
    A. **Problem generally** 557
    B. **Flag desecration** 560

Quiz Yourself on
"TIME, PLACE AND MANNER" RESTRICTIONS;
SYMBOLIC EXPRESSION 562

VI. DEFAMATION, INTENTIONAL INFLICTION OF EMOTIONAL DISTRESS, AND THE BANNING OF "FALSE SPEECH" 569
    A. **Regulation of defamatory and other false speech** 569
    B. **Initially no protection** 569
    C. ***New York Times v. Sullivan*** 569
    D. **Extension to "public figures"** 570
    E. **Private figures** 571
    F. **Non-media defendants** 572
    G. **Statements of no "public interest"** 572
    H. **Statements of opinion** 573
    I. **Intentional infliction of emotional distress** 573
    J. **False statements of fact outside the defamation context** 574

VII. OBSCENITY 576
    A. **Generally unprotected** 576
    B. ***Miller*** 578
    C. **Private possession by adults** 579
    D. **Protection of children** 579
    E. **Protection of animals, and the "animal crush video" issue** 580
    F. **Other issues** 581

VIII. COMMERCIAL SPEECH 582
    A. **Overview** 582
    B. **The *Virginia Pharmacy* revolution** 582
    C. **Regulation of lawyers** 584
    D. **Commercial speech doctrine curtailed** 585
    E. **Current status** 586

Quiz Yourself on
DEFAMATION, OBSCENITY AND COMMERCIAL SPEECH   590

IX. **REGULATION IN THE CONTEXT OF POLITICAL CAMPAIGNS**   . . .   592
     A. **Money in political campaigns, generally**   592
     B. ***Buckley v Valeo***   593
     C. **Contributions to Political Action Committees**   597
     D. **"Soft money" and pre-election "issue ads" (*McConnell,*
         Wisconsin Right to Life and *Citizens United*)**   597
     E. **Campaign spending by political parties**   603
     F. **How low can limits be set**   604
     G. **Corporate and judicial expression during campaigns**   604

X.   **SOME SPECIAL CONTEXTS**   605
     A. **Scope**   605
     B. **Schools**   605
     C. **Furnishing of legal services by lay groups**   609
     D. **Government as speaker or as funder of speech**   610

XI. **FREEDOM OF ASSOCIATION, DENIAL OF PUBLIC JOBS
     OR BENEFITS, AND UNCONSTITUTIONAL CONDITIONS**   613
     A. **Freedom of association generally**   613
     B. **Right not to associate**   614
     C. **Ways of interfering with right**   618
     D. **Illegal membership**   618
     E. **Denial of public job or benefit**   618
     F. **Compulsory disclosure**   622
     G. **The bar membership cases**   623
     H. **Unconstitutional conditions**   624

XII. **SPECIAL PROBLEMS CONCERNING THE MEDIA**   627
     A. **Summary of issues**   627
     B. **Special role for the press**   627
     C. **Prior restraints**   629
     D. **Governmental demands for information held by press**   634
     E. **Disclosure of confidential or illegally-obtained information**   636
     F. **Right of access to government-held information**   638
     G. **Regulation of broadcast media**   640

Quiz Yourself on
FREEDOM OF ASSOCIATION; DENIAL OF PUBLIC JOBS OR BENEFITS;
SPECIAL PROBLEMS OF THE MEDIA   642

Exam Tips on
FREEDOM OF EXPRESSION   645

Chapter 15

FREEDOM OF RELIGION

I. INTRODUCTION 656

II. THE ESTABLISHMENT CLAUSE 657

   A. Background 657

   B. Religion and the public schools 658

      1. Religious instruction 658

      2. Prayer reading 661

      3. Modification of curriculum 664

   C. Sunday closing laws 666

   D. Property-tax exemptions for churches 667

   E. Military and prison chaplains 667

   F. Helping religious groups spread their message 668

   G. The "excessive entanglement prong" 668

   H. Entanglement by church involvement in government affairs 670

   I. Ceremonies and displays 671

      1. Ceremonies 671

      2. Religious displays 672

   J. No preference for one sect over others 678

   K. Financial aid to religious schools 680

      1. Three-prong test 680

      2. Broad themes 681

      3. Particular programs 681

      4. Transportation 681

      5. Textbooks and other materials 682

      6. Salary supplements 682

      7. Furnishing of teachers 683

      8. Services 683

      9. Tuition vouchers 684

      10. Scholarships for religious study 687

      11. Aid to higher education 688

III. THE FREE EXERCISE CLAUSE 688

   A. Introduction 688

   B. Intent to interfere with religion 689

   C. Incidental burdensome effect, and required accommodations 691

      1. 1990 shift 691

      2. Pre-1990 law 691

      3. The 1990 "generally-applicable rule" case (*Employment Div. v. Smith*) 694

      4. Anti-discrimination laws, and a group's right to pick its "ministers" ... 695

   D. Military service and conscientious objection 696

   E. Public health 696

   F. What constitutes a "religious belief" 697

Quiz Yourself on
FREEDOM OF RELIGION (ENTIRE CHAPTER) 698

Exam Tips on
FREEDOM OF RELIGION 703

Chapter 16

JUSTICIABILITY

I. INTRODUCTION 708

II. ADVISORY OPINIONS 708

III. STANDING 709
    A. Nature of "standing" generally 709
    B. Federal taxpayer and citizen suits 711
    C. Standing not based on taxpayer or citizen status 713
    D. The "injury in fact" requirement 713
        1. Non-economic harms 714
        2. Must be "actual or imminent," not "speculative" 714
    E. Harm suffered by many 715
    F. Causation 716
    G. Special deference when plaintiff is a state acting for its citizens 718
    H. Third-party standing 719
    I. "Prudential" standing 719

IV. MOOTNESS 720

V. RIPENESS 721

VI. THE 11TH AMENDMENT, AND SUITS AGAINST STATES 722

VII. POLITICAL QUESTIONS 727

Quiz Yourself on
JUSTICIABILITY (ENTIRE CHAPTER) 734

Exam Tips on
JUSTICIABILITY 739

ESSAY EXAM QUESTIONS AND ANSWERS 745

TABLE OF CASES 753

SUBJECT MATTER INDEX 761

Preface

Thank you for buying this book.

This new edition includes full coverage of the Supreme Court's term that ended in June 2013. It features extensive coverage of several cases that have generated national attention, including:

- ❑ *U.S. v. Windsor*, where the Court invalidated, apparently on both equal protection and substantive due process grounds, the federal **Defense of Marriage Act's** ban on federal recognition of state-sanctioned **same-sex marriages**

- ❑ *Fisher v. Univ. of Texas*, where the Court said that **race-conscious admissions systems** at public universities **violate Equal Protection** unless the university proves that there are **"no workable race-neutral alternative methods"** that could achieve the compelling goal of "educational diversity," and that courts **must not give deference to the university's own judgment** about whether such race-neutral alternatives exist and would work.

- ❑ *Shelby County v. Holder*, where the Court invalidated a key part of **the Voting Rights Act of 1965**, by holding that the Act's **"preclearance"** requirement — compelling certain states to get advance federal approval for even small changes to their voting methods — went beyond Congress' Fifteenth Amendment enforcement powers because Congress' choice of covered states was **based on 40-year-old data.**

Here are some of this book's special features:

- ◼ **"Casebook Correlation Chart"** — This chart, located just after this Preface, correlates each section of the main Outline with the pages covering the same topic in the five leading Constitutional Law casebooks.

- ◼ **"Capsule Summary"** — This is a 110-page summary of the key concepts of Constitutional Law, specially designed for use in the last week or so before your final exam.

- ◼ **"Quiz Yourself"** — Either at the end of the chapter, or after major sections of a chapter, I give you short-answer questions so that you can exercise your analytical muscles. There are over 100 of these questions, each written by me.

- ◼ **"Exam Tips"** — These alert you to what issues repeatedly pop up on real-life Constitutional Law exams, and what factual patterns are commonly used to test those issues. I created these Tips by looking at literally hundreds of multiple-choice and essay questions asked by law professors and bar examiners. You'd be surprised at how predictable the issues and fact-patterns chosen by professors really are!

I intend for you to use this book both throughout the semester and for exam preparation. Here are some suggestions about how to use it:[1]

1. The book seems (and is) *big*. But don't panic. The actual text includes over 60 pages of *Quiz Your-*

---

1. The suggestions below relate only to this book. I don't talk about taking or reviewing class notes, using hornbooks or other study aids, joining a study group, or anything else. This doesn't mean I don't think these other steps are important — it's just that in this Preface I've chosen to focus on how I think you can use this outline.

self short-answer questions, plus lots of *Exam Tips*. Anyway, you don't have to read everything in the book — there are lots of special features that you may or may not decide to take advantage of.

2. During the semester, use the book in preparing each night for the next day's class. To do this, first read your casebook. Then, use the *Casebook Correlation Chart* to get an idea of what part of the outline to read. Reading the outline will give you a sense of how the particular cases you've just read in your casebook fit into the overall structure of the subject. You may want to use a yellow highlighter to mark key portions of the *Emanuel®*.

3. If you make your own outline for the course, use the *Emanuel®* to give you a structure, and to supply black letter principles. You may want to rely especially on the *Capsule Summary* for this purpose. You are hereby authorized to copy small portions of the *Emanuel®* into your own outline, provided that your outline will be used only by you or your study group, and provided that you are the owner of the *Emanuel®*.

4. When you first start studying for exams, read the *Capsule Summary* to get an overview. This will probably take you about one day.

5. Either during exam study or earlier in the semester, do some or all of the *Quiz Yourself* short-answer questions. You can find these quickly by looking for *Quiz Yourself* entries in the Table of Contents. When you do these questions: (1) record your short "answer" on the small blank line provided after the question, but also: (2) try to write out a "mini essay" on a separate piece of paper. Remember that the only way to get good at writing essays is to write essays.

6. Three or four days before the exam, review the *Exam Tips* that appear at the end of each chapter. You may want to combine this step with step **5**, so that you use the Tips to help you spot the issues in the short-answer questions. You'll also probably want to follow up from many of the Tips to the main Outline's discussion of the topic.

7. The night before the exam: (1) do some *Quiz Yourself* questions, just to get your thinking and writing juices flowing and (2) re-scan the *Exam Tips* (spending about 2-3 hours).

My deepest thanks go to two of my colleages at Wolters Kluwer, Barbara Lasoff and Barbara Roth, who have helped greatly to assure the reliability and readability of this and my other books for many years.

Good luck in your ConLaw course. If you'd like any other Wolters Kluwer publication, you can find it at your bookstore or at **www.aspenlaw.com**. If you'd like to contact me, you can email me at **semanuel@westnet.com**.

Steve Emanuel

Larchmont NY

August 23, 2013

CASEBOOK CORRELATION CHART

(**Note:** general sections of the outline are omitted from this chart. **NC** = not directly covered by this casebook.)

Emanuel's Constitutional Law Outline *(by chapter and section heading)*	Sullivan & Feldman **Constitutional Law** (18th ed. 2013)	Stone, Seidman, Sunstein, Tushnet & Karlan **Constitutional Law** (7th ed. 2013)	Rotunda, **Modern Constitutional Law** (10th ed. 2012)	Varat, Cohen & Amar **Constitutional Law** (14th ed. 2013)	Chemerinsky, **Constitutional Law** (4th ed. 2013)
CHAPTER 2 **THE SUPREME COURT'S AUTHORITY**					
I. Review of Acts of Congress (*Marbury v. Madison*)	1-16	25-38	1-9	25-37	1-9
II. Review of State Court Decisions	16-20	38-48	9-28	45-55	10-11
III. Congress' Control of Federal Court Jurisdiction	29-32	69-81	28-38	37-43	33-40
IV. The Supreme Court's Jurisdiction Today	NC	155-158	28-29	NC	NC
CHAPTER 3 **FEDERALISM AND FEDERAL POWER GENERALLY**					
I. The Concept of Federalism	73-74	159-179	NC	105-110	115-116, 126-158
II. *McCulloch v. Maryland*	74-90	53-65	70-81	110-126	116-126
III. State Oversight of the Federal Government — Term Limits	90-96	NC	462-478	NC	NC
CHAPTER 4 **THE FEDERAL COMMERCE POWER**					
I. The Commerce Clause Gen'ly	109-110	179-180	174-289	127-139	158, 161-169
II. Cases Prior to 1933	110-118	180-185	174-191	139-142	158-163
III. Court Barriers to the New Deal	118-124	185-193	192-198	142-143	163-165
IV. The Post-New-Deal Trend	125-136	193-202	198-209, 226-237	143-151	169-182
V. Some Modern Limits	136-164	202-240	237-255	151-189	190-220
V. The Tenth Amendment as a Limit on Congress' Power	164-179	346-365	256-289	223-244	220-241
CHAPTER 5 **OTHER NATIONAL POWERS**					
I. The Taxing Power	187-196	294-301	209-214	189-196	241-245
II. The Spending Power	196-217	301-322	214-226	196-206	245-250
III. The War, Treaty, and Foreign Affairs Powers	399-405	322-325	290-368	207-217	NC
CHAPTER 6 **TWO LIMITS ON STATE POWER: THE DORMANT COMMERCE CLAUSE AND CONGRESSIONAL ACTION**					
I. The Dormant Commerce Clause —Regulation	219-273	240-280	82-144	256-306	455-496, 498-504
II. State Taxation of Interstate Commerce	293	281-282	163-172	252-256	NC
III. Congressional Action - Preemption and Consent	281-293	283-292	154-163	314-333	432-455, 496-498

CASEBOOK CORRELATION CHART (continued)

Emanuel's Constitutional Law Outline *(by chapter and section heading)*	Sullivan & Feldman **Constitutional Law** (18th ed. 2013)	Stone, Seidman, Sunstein, Tushnet & Karlan **Constitutional Law** (7th ed. 2013)	Rotunda, **Modern Constitutional Law** (10th ed. 2012)	Varat, Cohen & Amar **Constitutional Law** (14th ed. 2013)	Chemerinsky, **Constitutional Law** (4th ed. 2013)
CHAPTER 7					
INTERGOVERNMENTAL IMMUNITIES AND INTERSTATE RELATIONS					
I. **Tax Immunities**	294-295	NC	78-81	NC	NC
II. **Federal Immunity from State Regulation**	295	NC	NC	NC	NC
III. **State Immunity from Federal Regulation**	295	NC	NC	223-244	NC
IV. **Interstate Relationships**	295-296	NC	144-153	NC	NC
CHAPTER 8					
SEPARATION OF POWERS					
I. **Domestic Policy and the Separation of Powers**	297-308	367-381, 424-448	296-303, 359-368, 424-437	335-340, 368-384	317-358
II. **Foreign Affairs and the War Powers**	308-367	382-411	290-342	340-368	369-418
III. **Appointment and Removal of Executive Personnel (Including Impeachment)**	383-399	420-424, 448-451	437-461	384-395	358-369
IV. **Legislative and Executive Immunity**	405-424	412-420	383-423	395-404	419-429
CHAPTER 9					
DUE PROCESS OF LAW					
I. **The Bill of Rights and the States**	425-465	739-750	498-503	407-465	518-548
II. **Substantive Due Process — Before 1934**	467-482	750-766	479-494	466-477	603-621
III. **Substantive Due Process — The Modern Approach to Economic and Social-Welfare Regulation**	482-491	766-776	494-498	477-489	621-646
IV. **Substantive Due Process — Protection of Non-Economic Rights**					
Early non-economic cases	492-493	841-842	843-846	533-535	968-970
Griswold v. Connecticut	493-503	842-853	846-854	535-541	970-979
Roe v. Wade	503-415	854-873	854-862	565-575	979-988
Modification of *Roe* by *Casey*	515-526	873-893	865-882	576-591	988-1000
Post-*Roe* developments	526-528	893-909	852-854, 862-865, 882-886	591-600	1000-1030
Family Relations	529-535	909-920	853-854	541-565	939-967
Sexuality, Incl. Homosexuality	535-550	920-937	887-902	600-609	1046-1058
The Right to Die	550-562	937-951	902-915	609-620	1030-1046
Rights of the Mentally Retarded	549-550	NC	784	NC	NC
V. **Procedural Due Process**	562-568	953-973	311-341, 503-534	977-1010	1142-1196

CASEBOOK CORRELATION CHART (continued)

Emanuel's Constitutional Law Outline *(by chapter and section heading)*	Sullivan & Feldman **Constitutional Law** (18th ed. 2013)	Stone, Seidman, Sunstein, Tushnet & Karlan **Constitutional Law** (7th ed. 2013)	Rotunda, **Modern Constitutional Law** (10th ed. 2012)	Varat, Cohen & Amar **Constitutional Law** (14th ed. 2013)	Chemerinsky, **Constitutional Law** (4th ed. 2013)
CHAPTER 10					
EQUAL PROTECTION					
I. Introduction	601-602	NC	NC	635-641	711-717
II. Economic and Social Laws — The "Mere-Rationality" Test	602-616	497-520	657-663	641-656, 835-843	717-740
III. Suspect Classifications, Especially Race	616-650	453-496, 520-574	664-698	656-691, 730-752	740-838
IV. Affirmative Action and "Benign" Discrimination	650-709	574-598, 608-629	698-737, 944-954	752-813	838-866
V. Classifications Based on Sex	709-756	629-696	756-775	691-730	866-905
VI. Classifications Based on Alienage	756-761	696-707	737-750	813-822	905-921
VII. Illegitimacy	NC	NC	750-756	822-828	921-924
VIII. Mental Retardation and Mental Illness	761-766	505-506, 714-717	784-785	829-835	928-929
IX. General Principles of Middle-Level Scrutiny	709-715	NC	NC	NC	NC
X. Unequal Treatment of Gays, and the Banning of Same-Sex Marriage	535-550	934-937	NC	NC	946, 1046
XI. Fundamental Rights	766-809	776-841	775-843	843-975	1062-1142
CHAPTER 11					
MISCELLANEOUS CLAUSES					
I. The 14th Amendment's Privileges or Immunities Clause	439-440	729-738	479-485, 836	423	522-528, 1062-1068
II. The "Taking Clause"	568-594	986-1026	552-570	501-533	658-710
III. The "Contract Clause"	594-600	973-986	541-552	489-501	646-658
IV. The Second Amendment "Right to Bear Arms"	454-458	48-52, 741-750	570-595	621-634	13-33
V. *Ex Post Facto* Laws	426	65-66	NC	NC	NC
VI. Bills of Attainder	426	NC	534-541	NC	NC
CHAPTER 12					
STATE ACTION					
I. Introduction	812-814	1555-1556	596-603	1011-1018	548-551
II. The "Public Function" Approach	814-821	1559-1568, 1597-1608	603-613	1018-1024	553-567
III. "Nexus" — The Significance of State Involvement	821-835	1568-1597	614-656	1025-1058	567-600
CHAPTER 13					
CONGRESSIONAL ENFORCEMENT OF CIVIL RIGHTS					
II. Congress' Power to Reach Private Conduct	835-846	344-346, 1556-1559	932-939	1062-1075	NC
III.-IV. Congress' Power to Remedy Constitutional Violations, or to Modify Constitutional Rights	846-883	325-344	916-931, 940-954	1075-1115	251-266, 269-316

CASEBOOK CORRELATION CHART (continued)

Emanuel's Constitutional Law Outline (by chapter and section heading)	Sullivan & Feldman Constitutional Law (18th ed. 2013)	Stone, Seidman, Sunstein, Tushnet & Karlan Constitutional Law (7th ed. 2013)	Rotunda, Modern Constitutional Law (10th ed. 2012)	Varat, Cohen & Amar Constitutional Law (14th ed. 2013)	Chemerinsky, Constitutional Law (4th ed. 2013)
CHAPTER 14 **FREEDOM OF EXPRESSION**					
I. General Themes	885-898	1027-1038	NC	1117-1126	1197-1235, 1273-1290
II. Advocacy of Illegal Conduct	899-955	1038-1083	955-976	1126-1169	1304-1337
III. Overbreadth and Vagueness	1277-1295	1116-1124	1456-1458	1169-1180	1235-1243
IV. Regulation of Context — "Time, Place and Manner"	1111-1123, 1143-1277	1083-1100, 1214-1420	991-1024, 1048-1067	1268-1287, 1329-1379	1337-1365, 1399- 1427, 1545-1616
V. Symbolic Expression	955-978, 1123-1143	1337-1357	1067-1070, 1195-1217	1435-1452	1489-1544
VI. Defamation, Intentional Infliction of Emotional Distress, Banning of False Speech	978-1009	1135-1165	1115-1146	1192-1220, 1317-1328	1461-1489
VII. Obscenity	1009-1053	1183-1201	1260-1306	1220-1268	1365-1399
VIII. Commercial Speech	1084-1110	1165-1183	1098-1115	1288-1317	1427-1460
IX. Regulation in the Context of Political Campaigns	1383-1433	1357-1405	1218-1260	1485-1557	1501-1544
X. Some Special Contexts	1229-1254	1317-1337	1024-1048	1379-1433	1590-1609
XI. Freedom of Association, Denial of Public Jobs or Benefits, and Unconstitutional Conditions	1344-1383	1410-1419	1147-1195	1452-1485, 1557-1583	1290-1303 1616-1637
XII. Special Problems Concerning the Media	1433-1475	1420-1452	976-991, 1067-1098	1585-1614	1637-1672
CHAPTER 15 **FREEDOM OF RELIGION**					
II. The Establishment Clause	1526-1604	1470-1521	1307-1381, 1391-1393	1615-1701	1708-1808
III. The Free Exercise Clause	1489-1526	1521-1554	1381-1409	1702-1727	1683-1708
CHAPTER 16 **JUSTICIABILITY**					
II. Advisory Opinions	34-35	83-84	38-44	56-59	42-45
III. Standing	35-53	85-121	1421-1477	60-77	45-80
IV. Mootness	52-53	153-155	1414-1421	77-80	86-91
V. Ripeness	53-54	153-155	1410-1414	80-85	81-86
VI. The 11th Amendment, and Suits Against States	164-186	336-344	44-46	244-250	266-269
VII. Political Questions	53-69	121-153	46-69, 350-354, 791-802	85-96	91-113

CAPSULE SUMMARY

This Capsule Summary is intended for review at the end of the semester. Reading it is not a substitute for mastering the material in the main outline. Numbers in brackets refer to the pages in the main outline where the topic is discussed. The order of topics is occasionally somewhat different from that in the main outline.

CHAPTER 1

INTRODUCTION

I. THREE STANDARDS OF REVIEW

A. Three standards: There are three key *standards of review* which reappear constantly throughout Constitutional Law. When a court reviews the constitutionality of government action, it is likely to be choosing from among one of these three standards of review: (1) the *mere-rationality* standard; (2) the *strict scrutiny* standard; and (3) the *middle-level review* standard. [2]

1. **Mere-rationality standard:** Of the three standards, the easiest one to satisfy is the *"mere-rationality"* standard. When the court applies this "mere-rationality" standard, the court will *uphold* the governmental action so long as two requirements are met:

   a. **Legitimate state objective:** First, the government must be pursuing a *legitimate governmental objective*. This is a very broad concept — practically any type of health, safety or "general welfare" goal will be found to be "legitimate."

   b. **Rational relation:** Second, there has to be a *"minimally rational relation"* between the means chosen by the government and the state objective. This requirement, too, is extremely easy to satisfy: only if the government has acted in a completely *"arbitrary and irrational"* way will this rational link between means and end not be found.

2. **Strict scrutiny:** At the other end of the spectrum, the standard that is hardest to satisfy is the *"strict scrutiny"* standard of review. This standard will only be satisfied if the governmental act satisfies two very tough requirements:

   a. **Compelling objective:** First, the *objective* being pursued by the government must be *"compelling"* (not just "legitimate," as for the "mere-rationality" standard); and

   b. **Necessary means:** Second, the *means* chosen by the government must be *"necessary"* to achieve that compelling end. In other words, the "fit" between the means and the end must be extremely tight. (It's not enough that there's a "rational relation" between the means and the end, which is enough under the "mere-rationality" standard.)

      i. **No less restrictive alternatives:** In practice, this requirement that the means be "necessary" means that there must not be any *less restrictive* means that would accomplish the government's objective just as well.

3. **Middle-level review:** In between these two review standards is so-called *"middle-level"* review.

   a. **"Important" objective:** Here, the governmental objective has to be *"important"* (half way between "legitimate" and "compelling").

b. "Substantially related" means: And, the means chosen by the government must be *"substantially related"* to the important government objective. (This "substantially related" standard is half way between "rationally related" and "necessary").

B. Consequences of choice: The court's choice of one of these standards of review has two important consequences: [3]

1. Burden of persuasion: First, the choice will make a big difference as to who has the *burden of persuasion*.

   a. Mere-rationality standard: Where the governmental action is subject to the "mere-rationality" standard, the *individual* who is attacking the government action will generally bear the burden of persuading the court that the action is unconstitutional.

   b. Strict scrutiny: By contrast, if the court applies "strict scrutiny," then the *governmental body* whose act is being attacked has the burden of persuading the court that its action is constitutional.

   c. Middle-level review: Where "middle level" scrutiny is used, it's not certain how the court will assign the burden of persuasion, but the burden will usually be placed on the government.

2. Effect on outcome: Second, the choice of review standard has a very powerful effect on the *actual outcome*. Where the "mere-rationality" standard is applied, the governmental action will *almost always be upheld*. Where "strict scrutiny" is used, the governmental action will *almost always be struck down*. (For instance, the Supreme Court applies strict scrutiny to any classification based on race, and has upheld only one such strictly scrutinized racial classification in the last 50 years.) Where middle-level scrutiny is used, there's roughly a 50-50 chance that the governmental action will be struck down.

   a. Exam Tip: So when you're writing an exam answer, you've got to concentrate exceptionally hard on choosing the correct standard of review. Once you've determined that a particular standard would be applied, then you might as well go further and make a prediction about the outcome: if you've decided that "mere-rationality" review applies, you might write something like, "Therefore, the court will almost certainly uphold the governmental action." If you've chosen strict scrutiny, you should write something like, "Therefore, the governmental action is very likely to be struck down."

C. When used: Here is a quick overview of the entire body of Constitutional Law, to see where each of these review standards gets used: [3]

1. Mere-rationality standard: Here are the main places where the "mere-rationality" standard gets applied (and therefore, the places where it's very hard for the person attacking the governmental action to get it struck down on constitutional grounds):

   a. Dormant Commerce Clause: First, the "mere-rationality" test is the main test to determine whether a state regulation that affects interstate commerce violates the *"dormant Commerce Clause."* The state regulation has to pursue a legitimate state end, and be rationally related to that end. (But there's a second test which we'll review in greater detail later: the state's interest in enforcing its regulation must also outweigh any *burden* imposed on interstate commerce, and any discrimination against interstate commerce.)

   b. Substantive due process: Next comes *substantive due process*. So long as no "fundamental right" is affected, the test for determining whether a governmental act violates substantive due process is, again, the "mere-rationality" standard. In other words, if the state is pursuing a legitimate objective, and using means that are rationally related to that objective, the state will not be found to have violated the substantive Due Process Clause. So the vast bulk of *eco-*

nomic regulations (since these don't affect fundamental rights) will be tested by the mere-rationality standard and almost certainly upheld.

    c. **Equal protection:** Then, we move on to the *equal protection* area. Here, "mere-rationality" review is used so long as: (1) *no suspect* or *quasi-suspect classification* is being used; and (2) *no fundamental right* is being impaired. This still leaves us with a large number of classifications which will be judged based on the mere-rationality standard, including: (1) almost all economic regulations; (2) some classifications based on alienage; and (3) rights that are not "fundamental" even though they are very important, such as food, housing, and free public education. In all of these areas, the classification will be reviewed under the "mere-rationality" standard, and will therefore almost certainly be upheld.

    d. **Contracts Clause:** Lastly, we find "mere-rationality" review in some aspects of the *"Obligation of Contracts"* Clause.

2. **Strict scrutiny:** Here are the various contexts in which the court applies *strict scrutiny*: [4]

    a. **Substantive due process/fundamental rights:** First, where a governmental action affects *fundamental rights*, and the plaintiff claims that his *substantive due process* rights are being violated, the court will use strict scrutiny. So when the state impairs rights falling in the *"privacy"* cluster of marriage, child-bearing, and child-rearing, the court will use strict scrutiny (and will therefore probably invalidate the governmental restriction). For instance, government restrictions that impair the right to use contraceptives receive this kind of strict scrutiny.

    b. **Equal protection review:** Next, the court uses strict scrutiny to review a claim that a classification violates the plaintiff's *equal protection* rights, if the classification relates either to a *suspect classification* or a *fundamental right*. "Suspect classifications" include *race*, *national origin*, and (sometimes) *alienage*. "Fundamental rights" for this purpose include the right to *vote*, to be a *candidate*, to have access to the *courts*, and to *travel interstate*. So classifications that either involve any of these suspect classifications or impair any of these fundamental rights will be strictly scrutinized and will probably be struck down.

    c. **Freedom of expression:** Next, we move to the area of *freedom of expression*. If the government is impairing free expression in a *content-based way*, then the court will use strict scrutiny and will almost certainly strike down the regulation. In other words, if the government is restricting some speech but not others, based on the *content of the messages*, then this suppression of expression will only be allowed if necessary to achieve a compelling purpose (a standard which is rarely found to be satisfied in the First Amendment area). Similarly, any interference with the right of *free association* will be strictly scrutinized.

    d. **Freedom of religion/Free Exercise Clause:** Lastly, the court will use strict scrutiny to evaluate any impairment with a person's *free exercise* of religion. Even if the government does *not intend* to impair a person's free exercise of his religion, if it substantially burdens his exercise of religion the government will have to give him an *exemption* from the otherwise-applicable regulation unless denial of an exemption is necessary to achieve a compelling governmental interest.

3. **Middle-level review:** Finally, here are the relatively small number of contexts in which the court uses middle-level review: [4]

    a. **Equal protection/semi-suspect:** First, middle-level review will be used to judge an *equal protection* claim, where the classification being challenged involves a *semi-suspect* trait. The two traits which are considered semi-suspect for this purpose are: (1) *gender*; and (2) *illegitimacy*. So any government classification based on gender or illegitimacy will have to be "substantially related" to the achievement of some "important" governmental interest.

    b. **Contracts Clause:** Second, certain conduct attacked under the Obligation of Contracts Clause will be judged by the middle-level standard of review.

    c. **Free expression/non-content-based:** Finally, in the First Amendment area we use a standard similar (though not identical) to the middle-level review standard to judge government action that impairs expression, but does so in a ***non-content-based*** manner. This is true, for instance, of any content-neutral ***"time, place and manner"*** regulation.

CHAPTER 2
THE SUPREME COURT'S AUTHORITY AND THE FEDERAL JUDICIAL POWER

I. THE SUPREME COURT'S AUTHORITY AND THE FEDERAL JUDICIAL POWER

A. ***Marbury*** **principle:** Under *Marbury v. Madison*, it is the Supreme Court, not Congress, which has the authority and duty to declare a congressional statute unconstitutional if the Court thinks it violates the Constitution. [8-9]

B. **Supreme Court review of state court decision:** The Supreme Court may review state court opinions, but only to the extent that the decision was decided ***based on federal law.*** [10-11]

    1. **"Independent and adequate state grounds":** Even if there is a federal question in the state court case, the Supreme Court may not review the case if there is an ***"independent and adequate"*** state ground for the state court's decision. That is, if the same result would be reached even had the state court made a different decision on the federal question, the Supreme Court may not decide the case. This is because its opinion would in effect be an "advisory" one. [11]

        a. **Violations of state and federal constitutions:** If a state action violates the ***same clause*** of both state and federal constitutions (e.g., the Equal Protection Clause of each), the state court decision may or may not be based on an "independent" state ground. If the state court is saying, "This state action would violate our state constitution whether or not it violated the federal constitution," that's "independent." But if the state court is saying, "Based on our reading of the constitutional provision (which we think has the same meaning under both the state and federal constitutions), this state action violates both constitutions," this is ***not*** "independent," so the Supreme Court may review the state court decision. [12]

    2. **Review limited to decisions of highest state court:** Federal statutes limit Supreme Court review to decisions of the ***highest state court available***. But this does not mean that the top-ranking state court must have ruled on the ***merits*** of the case in order for the Supreme Court to review it. All that is required is that the case be heard by the highest state court ***available*** to the petitioner. (*Example:* A state trial court finds a particular state statute to be valid under the federal Equal Protection Clause. An intermediate appellate court in the state affirms; the highest state court refuses to hear an appeal from the affirmance. As a matter of both the federal judicial power and federal statutes, the Supreme Court may hear this case, because the intermediate appellate court was the highest court "available" to the petitioner.)

C. **Federal judicial power:** Article III, Section 2 sets out the federal judicial power. This includes, among other things: (a) cases arising under the ***Constitution*** or the ***"laws of the U.S."*** (i.e., cases posing a "federal question"); (b) cases of ***admiralty***; (c) cases between ***two or more states***; (d) cases between ***citizens of different states***; and (e) cases between a state or its citizens and a ***foreign country or foreign citizen***. Note that this does ***not*** include cases where both parties are citizens (i.e., residents) of the same state, and no federal question is raised. [12]

II. CONGRESS' CONTROL OF FEDERAL JUDICIAL POWER

A. Congress' power to decide: *Congress* has the general power to ***decide what types of cases the Supreme Court may hear***, so long as it doesn't expand the Supreme Court's jurisdiction beyond the federal judicial power (as listed in the prior paragraph). [*Ex parte McCardle*] [13-14]

B. Lower courts: Congress also may decide what ***lower federal courts*** there should be, and what cases they may hear. Again, the outer bound of this power is that Congress can't allow the federal courts to hear a case that is not within the federal judicial power. [14]

> **Example 1:** Congress may cut back the jurisdiction of the lower federal courts pretty much whenever and however it wishes. Thus Congress could constitutionally eliminate diversity jurisdiction (i.e., suits between citizens of different states), even though such suits are clearly listed in the Constitution as being within the federal judicial power.

> **Example 2:** But Congress could not give the lower federal courts jurisdiction over cases between two citizens of the same state, where no federal issue is posed. The handling of such a case by the federal courts would simply go beyond the federal judicial power as recited in the Constitution.

CHAPTER 3

FEDERALISM AND FEDERAL POWER GENERALLY

I. THE CONCEPT OF FEDERALISM

A. The federalist system: We have a *"federalist"* system. In other words, the national government and the state governments co-exist. Therefore, you always have to watch whether some power being asserted by the federal government is in fact allowed under the Constitution, and you must also watch whether some power asserted by the states is limited in favor of federal power. [19]

B. Federal government has limited powers: The most important principle in this whole area is that the federal government is one of ***limited, enumerated powers***. In other words, the three federal branches (Congress, the executive branch, and the federal courts) can only assert powers ***specifically granted*** to them by the United States Constitution. So any time Congress passes a statute, or the President issues, say, an Executive Order, or the federal courts decide a case, you've got to ask: What is the enumerated, specified power in the U.S. Constitution that gives the federal branch the right to do what it has just done? (This is very different from what our Constitution says about the powers of *state* governments: state governments can do whatever they want as far as the U.S. Constitution is concerned, unless what they are doing is ***expressly forbidden*** by the Constitution.) [19]

     1. No general police power: The most dramatic illustration of this state/federal difference is the general *"police power."* Each state has a general police power, i.e., the ability to regulate solely on the basis that the regulation would enhance the welfare of the citizenry. But there is ***no general federal police power***, i.e., no right of the federal government to regulate for the health, safety or general welfare of the citizenry. Instead, each act of federal legislation or regulation must come within one of the very specific, enumerated powers (e.g., the Commerce Clause, the power to tax and spend, etc.).

         a. Tax and spend for general welfare: Congress *does* have the right to "lay and collect taxes … to pay the debts and provide for the … general welfare of the United States. … " (Article I, Section 8.) But the phrase "provide for the … general welfare" in this sentence modifies "lay and collect taxes … to pay the debts. … " In other words, the power to tax and spend is subject to the requirement that the general welfare be served; there is no ***independent*** federal power to provide for the general welfare.

C. **"Necessary and Proper" Clause:**   In addition to the very specific powers given to Congress by the Constitution, Congress is given the power to "make all laws which shall be ***necessary and proper*** for carrying into execution" the specific powers.

    1. **Rational-relation test:** The "Necessary and Proper" Clause is easy for Congress to satisfy: if Congress is seeking an ***objective*** that is within the specifically enumerated powers, then Congress can use ***any means*** that is: (1) ***rationally related*** to the objective Congress is trying to achieve; and (2) is not specifically forbidden by the Constitution. [21]

        a. **Broad reading given to Clause:**   Congress gives a very ***broad and deferential reading*** to Congress' powers under the Clause. [23]

        Example: Congress passes a statute to civilly commit certain sexually-dangerous federal prisoners at the end of their prison sentences. The prisoners attack the statute as being beyond Congress' powers.

        Held: Congress acted properly. The Necessary and Proper Clause grants Congress broad authority. Congress is entitled to large discretion in choosing the particular means to carry out a given enumerated power — all that's required is that Congress chooses a means that's *rationally related* to the implementation of some constitutionally-enumerated power. Here, Congress has the power to define federal crimes, and to run a prison system housing those who commit such crimes. Allowing the Federal Bureau of Prisons to maintain custody of prisoners who would be dangerous to others if released is a rational method of carrying out the federal power to incarcerate those who commit federal crimes. [*U.S. v. Comstock*] [23]

D. **Can't violate specific constitutional provision:**   Even where congressional action appears to fall within a specific grant of power, the federal action may not, of course, violate some ***other*** specific constitutional guarantee. In other words, congressional (or other federal) action must satisfy ***two*** tests to be constitutional: (1) it must fall within some specific grant of power under the Constitution; and (2) it must not violate any specific constitutional provision. [20]

CHAPTERS 4, 5 AND 8
POWERS OF THE FEDERAL GOVERNMENT; THE SEPARATION OF POWERS

I.   POWERS OF THE THREE FEDERAL BRANCHES

A. **Powers of the three branches:**   Here is a summary of the powers of the ***three branches*** of the federal government:

    1. **Congress:**   Here are the main powers given to Congress [20]:

        a. **Interstate commerce:**   Congress has the power to ***regulate interstate commerce***, as well as foreign commerce.

        b. **Taxing and spending:**   Congress has the power to ***tax*** and the power to ***spend***.

        c. **DC:**   Congress can regulate the ***District of Columbia***.

        d. **Federal property:**   Congress has power to regulate and dispose of ***federal property***.

        e. **War and defense:**   Congress can ***declare war***, and can establish and fund the armed forces.

f. **Enforcement of Civil War amendments:** Congress can *enforce* the *post-Civil War amendments*. (For instance, under its power to enforce the Thirteenth Amendment's abolition of slavery, Congress can ban even private intrastate non-commercial conduct.)

2. **President:** Here are the main powers of the President:

   a. **Execution of laws:** The President holds the *"executive power."* That is, he *carries out* the laws made by Congress. It is his obligation to make sure the laws are "faithfully executed."

   b. **Commander in Chief:** He is *Commander in Chief* of the armed forces. So he directs and leads our armed forces (but he cannot declare war — only Congress can do this).

   c. **Treaty and foreign affairs:** The President can make *treaties* with foreign nations (but only if two-thirds of the Senate approves). He appoints *ambassadors.* Also, he effectively controls our *foreign policy* — some of this power over foreign policy stems from his right to appoint ambassadors, but much is simply *implied* from the nation's need to speak with a single voice in foreign affairs (so that congressional involvement in the details of foreign affairs will generally not be appropriate).

   d. **Appointment of federal officers:** The President appoints all *federal officers.* These include *cabinet members*, *federal judges* and *ambassadors.* (But the Senate must approve all such federal officers by majority vote.) As to *"inferior* [federal] officers," it's up to Congress to decide whether these should be appointed by the President, by the judicial branch, or by the "heads of departments" (i.e., cabinet members). (But Congress can't make these lower-level appointments itself; it may merely decide who *can* make these appointments.)

   e. **Pardons:** The President can issue *pardons*, but only for federal offenses. (Also, he can't pardon anyone who has been impeached and convicted.)

   f. **Veto:** The President may *veto* any law passed by both houses (though this veto may be *overridden* by a 2-3's majority of each house). If the President doesn't veto the bill within 10 days after receiving it, it becomes law (unless Congress has adjourned by the 10th day after it sent him the bill — this is the so-called "pocket veto").

3. **Judiciary:** The federal *judiciary* may decide "cases" or "controversies" that fall within the federal judicial power. See the section on "Federal Judicial Power" in the chapter called "The Supreme Court's Authority and the Federal Judicial Power," above.

II. THE FEDERAL COMMERCE POWER

A. **Summary:** Probably Congress' most important power is the power to *"regulate Commerce* ... among the several states." (Art. I, §8.) This is the "Commerce power." [27]

> **Exam Tip:** Any time you have a test question in which Congress is doing something, first ask yourself, "Can what Congress is doing be justified as an exercise of the commerce power?" Most of the time the answer will be "yes."

B. **Summary of modern view:** There seem to be *four broad categories* of activities which Congress can constitutionally regulate under the Commerce power:

1. **Channels:** First, Congress can regulate the use of the *"channels"* of interstate commerce. Thus Congress can regulate in a way that is reasonably related to highways, waterways, and air traffic. Presumably Congress can do so even though the activity in question in the particular case is completely intrastate. [52]

2. **Instrumentalities:** Second, Congress can regulate the *"instrumentalities"* of interstate commerce, even though the particular activities being regulated are completely intrastate. This category refers

to people, machines, and other "things" used in carrying out commerce. [52]

> **Example:** Probably Congress could say that every truck must have a specific safety device, even if the particular truck in question was made and used exclusively within a single state.

3. **Articles moving in interstate commerce:** Third, Congress can regulate *articles moving* in interstate commerce. [52]

> **Example:** The states and private parties keep information about the identities of drivers. Since this information gets exchanged across state lines (e.g., from states to companies that want to sell cars), the information is an article in interstate commerce and Congress may regulate how it's used. [*Reno v. Condon*]

4. **"Substantially affecting" commerce:** Finally, the biggest (and most interesting) category is that Congress may regulate those activities having a *"substantial effect"* on interstate commerce. [*U.S. v. Lopez.*] As to this category, the following rules now seem to apply: [53]

   a. **Activity is commercial:** If the activity itself is arguably *"commercial,"* then it doesn't seem to matter whether the *particular instance* of the activity directly affects interstate commerce, as long as the instance is part of a general class of activities that, *collectively*, substantially affect interstate commerce. So even purely intrastate activities can be regulated if they're directly "commercial." This is especially true where Congress regulates the intrastate commercial activities as part of a *broad scheme* to regulate interstate commerce in the same activity. [53]

   > **Example:** In the federal Controlled Substances Act (CSA), Congress outlaws all distribution and possession of marijuana. California then makes it legal under state law for a Californian to cultivate marijuana for her own personal medicinal use. The U.S. seeks to prevent P, a Californian, from taking advantage of this state-law loophole. P asserts that the application of the CSA to bar P from personally cultivating marijuana for her own personal medical use is beyond Congress' Commerce powers.
   >
   > *Held*, Congress' Commerce powers extend to this regulation of P's own cultivation and use. Marijuana is a commercial commodity, and the CSA is regulating interstate commerce in that commodity. Congress reasonably feared that if it exempted personal — and thus "intrastate" — cultivation and use of marijuana for medical purposes, some of the marijuana so cultivated would be illegally drawn into the interstate market, jeopardizing Congress' overall scheme of banning the drug. So the private cultivation of marijuana by people like P, even though purely an intrastate activity, falls within Congress' Commerce power. [*Gonzales v. Raich*] [42]

   b. **Activity is not commercial:** But if the activity itself is *not "commercial,"* then there will apparently have to be a *pretty obvious connection* between the activity and interstate commerce. [53]

   > **Example 1:** Congress makes it a federal crime to possess a firearm in or near a school. The act applies even if the particular gun never moved in (or affected) interstate commerce. *Held*, in enacting this statute Congress went beyond its Commerce power. To fall within the Commerce power, the activity being regulated must have a "substantial effect" on interstate commerce. The link between gun-possession in a school and interstate commerce is too tenuous to qualify as a "substantial effect," because if it did, there would be essentially no limit to Congress' Commerce power. [*U.S. v. Lopez*]
   >
   > **Example 2:** Congress says that any woman who is the victim of a violent gender-based crime may bring a civil suit against the perpetrator in federal court. *Held*, Congress went beyond its Commerce power. Although it may be true that some women's fear of gender-based violence

dissuades them from working or traveling interstate, gender-based violence is not itself a commercial activity, and the connection between gender-based violence and interstate commerce is too attenuated for the violence to have a "substantial effect" on commerce. [*U.S. v. Morrison*]

    i.   **Jurisdictional hook:** But where the congressional act applies only to particular activities each of which has a direct link to interstate commerce, then the act will probably be within the Commerce power. Thus the use of a *"jurisdictional hook"* will probably suffice. (*Example*: Suppose the statute in *Lopez* by its terms applied only to in-school gun possession if the ***particular gun had previously moved in interstate commerce.*** This would be enough of a connection to interstate commerce to qualify.) [52]

c.   **Little deference to Congress:** The Court ***won't*** give much ***deference*** (as it used to) to the fact that Congress ***believed*** that the activity has the requisite "substantial effect" on interstate commerce. The Court will basically decide this issue for itself, from scratch. It certainly will no longer be enough that Congress had a ***"rational basis"*** for believing that the requisite effect existed — the effect must *in fact* exist to the Court's own independent satisfaction. [*Lopez*.] [53]

d.   **Traditional domain of states:** If what's being regulated is an activity the regulation of which has ***traditionally*** been the ***domain of the states***, and as to which the states have expertise, the Court is less likely to find that Congress is acting within its Commerce power. Thus ***education, family law*** and ***general criminal law*** are areas where the court is likely to be especially suspicious of congressional "interference." [53]

    i.   **National solution:** However, the fact that the activity has traditionally fallen within the states' domain can be ***outweighed*** by a showing that a ***national solution*** is needed. This would be so, for instance, where one state's choice heavily affects other states. Regulation of the ***environment*** is an example, since air and water pollution migrate across state boundaries. The same would be true of regulation of ***drug trafficking*** (e.g., Congress can regulate forbid cultivation of marijuana, because otherwise, Congress' national ban on the drug might be undermined; see *Gonzales v. Raich*). [42]

e.   **Forcing someone to buy or sell a product:** Congress may not use its Commerce powers to require that a person ***not presently in the marketplace*** for a particular type of product to ***buy that product***. That's true even if many individuals' combined failure to purchase the product significantly affects interstate commerce in the product. [***Nat'l Fed. of Indep. Bus. v. Sebelius*** (2012)] [44]

    i.   **Health insurance:** So, for instance, Congress can't use its Commerce powers to require otherwise-uninsured citizens to ***purchase health insurance*** or pay a penalty, even though the uninsureds' failure to have insurance has a substantial effect on the interstate health-insurance market by making everyone else's insurance costs higher. [*N.F.I.B. v. Sebelius*, *supra*.]

Example: Congress, in an attempt to greatly broaden the availability of health-care insurance, enacts the 2010 Affordable Care Act ("ACA"). Because pre-ACA there have been millions of uninsured individuals, and these individuals have been receiving government-mandated emergency health care paid for by higher taxes and higher insurance premiums charged to everyone else, the ACA imposes an "individual mandate." Under the individual mandate, most uninsured individuals are required to buy a specified level of health insurance. If an individual doesn't buy qualifying insurance, he is required to make a "shared-responsibility payment" to the Internal Revenue Service, which the ACA refers to as a "penalty." (The payment to the IRS is typically much less than the cost of qualifying insurance.) In Congress' view, the individual mandate and the shared-responsibility payment system fall within the Commerce power, because these measures are simply a means of regulating how and when people will pay (via insurance) for a product (health care) that they would inevitably consume even without regulation. Twenty-six states claim that the mandate goes beyond the Commerce power.

Held, 5-4, for the state plaintiffs on this point: the individual mandate is not authorized by the Commerce power. The Commerce Clause allows Congress to regulate "*existing commercial activity.*" But it does not allow Congress to "compel[] individuals to *become* active in commerce by purchasing a product, on the ground that their failure to do so affects interstate commerce." Allowing Congress to regulate based on the effect of *inaction* on commerce "would bring countless decisions an individual could potentially make within the scope of federal regulation[.]" For instance, many Americans do not eat a balanced diet, and therefore become obese. Obese people have higher health costs, which are borne in part by other Americans. Under Congress' theory, therefore, "Congress could address the diet problem by ordering everyone to buy vegetables." But giving Congress the power to "regulate what we do not do [would] fundamentally chang[e] the relation between the citizen and the Federal Government," in a way the drafters of the Commerce power never intended.

Four dissenters claim that the individual mandate falls within the Commerce power, because virtually all uninsured persons will eventually consume health care, and 90% will do so within any 5-year period. Therefore, all Congress is doing is regulating the terms by which individuals *pay* for an interstate good they already consume: "Persons subject to the mandate must now pay for medical care *in advance* (instead of at the point of service) and *through insurance* (instead of out-of-pocket). ... Establishing payment terms for goods in or affecting interstate commerce is *quintessential economic regulation.*" [*N.F.I.B. v. Sebelius, supra*] [44]

Note: But by a different 5-4 majority, the Court in *N.F.I.B.* sustained the individual mandate as an exercise of Congress *taxing* power. See *infra*, p. C-11.

C. **The Tenth Amendment as a limit on Congress' power:** The ***Tenth Amendment*** provides that "the powers not delegated to the United States by the Constitution, nor prohibited by it to the States, are reserved to the States respectively, or to the People." This Amendment today seems to place a small but possibly significant limit on Congress' ability to use its commerce power to ***regulate the states***. [53-59]

1. **Generally-applicable law:** If Congress passes a ***generally applicable law***, the fact that the regulation ***affects the states*** has virtually no practical significance, and the Tenth Amendment never comes into play. If the regulation would be valid if applied to a private party, it is also valid as to the state. [56]

   Example: Congress passes minimum-wage and overtime provisions, which are made applicable to all businesses of a certain size. The statute contains no exemption for employees of state-owned mass transit systems. *Held*, the regulation even of state employees here is a constitutional exercise of the commerce power, and is not forbidden by the Tenth Amendment. [*Garcia v. San Antonio Metropolitan Transit Authority*]

2. **Use of state's law-making mechanisms:** But the Tenth Amendment ***does*** prevent Congress from interfering in certain ways with a state's ***law-making processes***. Congress may not simply "***commandeer*** the legislative processes of the states by directly ***compelling them to enact and enforce a federal regulatory program.***" [*New York v. United States*] [56-59]

   Example: Congress provides that each state must arrange for the disposal of toxic waste generated within its borders, or else be deemed to "take title" to the waste and thereby become liable for tort damages stemming from it. *Held*, the congressional scheme violates the Tenth Amendment. Congress may not force a state to enact and enforce a federal regulatory program, and this is in effect what Congress has tried to do here. *New York v. United States, supra*.

a. **Administrative actions:** Similarly, Congress may not compel a state or local government's *executive branch* to perform functions, even ones that are easy-to-do and involve no discretion.

Example: Congress can't order local sheriffs to perform background checks on applicants for handgun permits. [*Printz v. U.S.*] [58]

III. THE TAXING AND SPENDING POWERS

A. **Taxing power:** Congress has the power to "*lay and collect taxes.*" (Art. I, §8.) This is an independent source of congressional power, so it can be used to reach conduct that might be beyond the other sources of congressional power, like the Commerce Clause. [65]

1. **Regulation:** Congress can probably *regulate* under the guise of taxing, so long as there's some real revenue produced. [66-70]

2. **Limits on taxing power:** There are a few *limits* which the Constitution places upon the taxing power:

   a. **Direct taxes:** "Direct taxes" must be allocated among the states in proportion to population. This provision is of little practical importance today.

   b. **Customs duties and excise taxes must be uniform:** All *customs duties* and *excise taxes* must be *uniform* throughout the United States. (*Example:* Congress may not place a $.10 per-gallon federal excise tax on gasoline sales that take place in New Jersey, and a $.15 per-gallon tax on those that take place in Oklahoma.) [66]

   c. **No export taxes:** Congress may not tax any *exports* from any state. (*Example:* Congress may not place a tax on all computers which are exported from any state to foreign countries.) [66]

3. **Effect of calling a measure a "penalty":** The fact that Congress labels a measure as a "*penalty*" does *not* prevent the measure from being upheld as a valid tax, as long as the measure actually functions in a way that resembles a tax. [*N.F.I.B. v. Sebelius* (2012)] [67]

   Example: In the 2010 Affordable Care Act ("ACA"), Congress requires most individuals to purchase health insurance, even if they have previously chosen to "self-insure." (This requirement is called the "individual mandate.") If a covered person doesn't make the required insurance purchase, she must pay the IRS at tax-filing time a "*shared-responsibility payment,*" a payment that the Act repeatedly characterizes as a "*penalty*" rather than as a tax. If a person doesn't make the shared-responsibility payment, the IRS can use some of its standard tax-collection methods, but cannot bring a *criminal prosecution.*

   Held, by a 5-4 vote, the individual mandate and shared-responsibility payment scheme is a valid exercise of Congress' taxing power. If a federal statute would be unconstitutional unless found to be a valid tax, the Court will treat it as a tax as long as that interpretation is a "fairly possible" one. The process here "yields the essential feature of any tax: it *produces at least some revenue* for the Government." And the fact that Congress called this a "penalty" rather than a "tax" is not dispositive, because the Court will look at the reality of how the scheme operates, not the label used by Congress. Here, the payment to the IRS would typically be far less than the price of insurance, making it look more like a tax (which a rational person might voluntarily choose to pay instead of buying insurance) than a penalty for unlawful conduct. Also, by prohibiting criminal prosecutions for non-payment (and by not referring to the failure to buy insurance as "unlawful"), Congress has again made the payment seem more like a tax than a penalty for wrongdoing.

The four dissenters would hold that where Congress designates a payment as a "penalty" rather than a "tax," that should by itself be enough to prevent the scheme from being authorized by the tax-and-spend power. [*N.F.I.B. v. Sebelius, supra.*] [67]

B. Spending power: Congress also has the power to "pay the debts and provide for the common defense and general welfare of the United States." (Art. I, §8.) This is the *"spending"* power. [70]

   1. Independent power: This is an independent power, just like the Commerce power. So Congress could spend to achieve a purely local benefit, even one that it couldn't achieve by regulating under the Commerce power.

   2. Use of conditions: Congress may generally place ***conditions*** upon use of its spending power, even if the congressional purpose is in effect to regulate. Conditions placed upon the doling out of federal funds are usually justified under the "Necessary and Proper" Clause (which lets Congress use any means to seek an objective falling within the specifically-enumerated powers, as long as the means is rationally related to the objective, and is not specifically forbidden by the Constitution). [71]

      Example: Suppose Congress makes available to the states certain funds that are to be used for improving the states' highway systems. Congress provides, however, a state will lose 5% of these funds unless the state passes a statute imposing a speed limit of no higher than 55 mph on all state roads. Even without reference to the Commerce Clause, this is a valid use of congressional power. That's because by the combination of the spending power and the "Necessary and Proper" Clause, Congress is permitted to impose conditions (even ones motivated solely by regulatory objectives) on the use of federal funds. [*South Dakota v. Dole*] [72]

      a. Conditions can't amount to "coercion": But there is a ***limit*** to how much pressure Congress can bring to bear on the states when it sets conditions on a new program that relies on the spending power. Pressure that amounts to ***"coercion"*** will cause the new program to go beyond the spending power.

         i. Loss of pre-existing federal funding: So far, this "coercion" problem has arisen only where Congress tells the states that if they don't agree to participate in a new federally-funded program, they will lose ***major federal funding*** associated with an independent ***pre-existing program***. In this situation, the Court will ask whether Congress has left the states ***"no real option but to acquiesce"*** in the new program and its conditions. If the answer is "yes," the Court will conclude that Congress has coerced the states, and that this coercion ***goes beyond the scope of Congress' spending power.*** (Only one case — set forth in the following Example — has found that Congress used such unconstitutional coercion.)

         Example: Every state has for decades participated in Medicaid, a federal-state program under which the states provide health care for certain classes of poor people, and Congress pays most of the costs. In the 2010 Affordable Care Act (ACA), Congress dramatically expands the Medicaid program by means of the "Medicaid Expansion." Under the Medicaid Expansion, each participating state must now give Medicaid coverage to *every adult under 65* with income up to 133% of the federal poverty level (whereas far fewer people have been covered by most states under the pre-Expansion version of Medicaid). Congress promises to pay all or nearly all of the costs (depending on the year) of the Expansion. If a state declines to participate in the Expansion, it will lose ***all*** Medicaid funding, not just the "extra" funding to cover the newly-eligible recipients. An average state that declines to agree to the Expansion will lose, in addition to the funds to cover the Expansion itself, more than 10% of its total budget. Twenty-six states claim that the threatened loss of all existing Medicaid funding is so coercive that the Medicaid Expansion goes beyond Congress' spending power.

Held (by a 7-2 vote), for the plaintiff states. Congress is entitled to impose conditions on the use of money it provides to states. But the Court will give closer scrutiny to those situations in which Congress, in connection with *one* federally-financed program, imposes conditions that take the form of threats to terminate a state's participation in *another* significant federally-funded program. Here, Congress has held "a gun to the head" of the states: a state that rejects the Medicaid Expansion (essentially a new program) will lose all funding for "old" Medicaid, typically over 10% of the state's overall budget. This is "economic dragooning that leaves the states with *no real option but to acquiesce"* in the Medicaid Expansion. Such compulsion goes beyond Congress' spending power.[1] [*N.F.I.B. v. Sebelius* (2012)] (other aspects of which are discussed *supra*, C-10 and C-11). [72]

C. **"General Welfare" Clause:** Although, as noted above, Congress can "provide for the common defense and general welfare of the United States," the reference to "general welfare" does *not* confer any independent source of congressional power. In other words, no statute is valid solely because Congress is trying to bring about the "general welfare." Instead, the phrase "for the general welfare" describes the circumstances under which Congress may use its "taxing and spending" power. So if Congress is *regulating* (rather than taxing and spending), it must find a specific grant of power (like the Commerce Clause), and it's not enough that the regulation will promote the general welfare. [71]

IV. THE SEPARATION OF POWERS

A. **Separation of powers generally:** Let's now review some of the major practical consequences that come from the fact that each federal branch gets its own set of powers. These practical consequences are collectively referred to as *"separation of powers"* problems. [128-135]

1. **President can't make the laws:** The most important single separation of powers principle to remember is that the *President cannot make the laws*. All he can do is to *carry out the laws* made by Congress. [128]

   Example: During the Korean War, Pres. Truman wants to avert a strike in the nation's steel mills. He therefore issues an "executive order" directing the Secretary of Commerce to seize the mills and operate them under federal direction. The President does not ask Congress to approve the seizure. *Held*, the seizure order is an unconstitutional exercise of the lawmaking authority reserved to Congress. [*Youngstown Sheet & Tube v. Sawyer*]

   a. **Line Item Veto:** The principle that the President can't make the laws means that the President can't be given a *"line item veto."* That is, if Congress tries to give the President the right to veto individual portions of a statute (e.g., particular expenditures), this will violate the Presentment Clause. (The Presentment Clause says that bills are enacted into law by being passed by both Houses, then being presented to the President and signed by him.) [*Clinton v. City of New York*] [131]

   b. **Congress' acquiescence:** But the scope of the President's powers may be at least somewhat expanded by *Congress' acquiescence* to his exercise of the power. This congressional acquiescence will never be *dispositive*, but in a close case, the fact that Congress acquiesced in the President's conduct may be enough to tip the balance, and to convince the Court that the President is merely carrying out the laws rather than making them. [129]

---

1. But the Court held that the rest of the ACA could be *severed* from the unconstitutional condition. So each state got to choose whether to participate in the Medicaid Expansion, or instead just keep its pre-existing Medicaid rights and funding. [76]

    c. **Implied powers:** Recall that Congress' powers are somewhat expanded by the "Necessary & Proper" clause — Congress can pass any laws reasonably related to the exercise of any enumerated power. There's no comparable "Necessary & Proper" clause for the President. But the effect is the same, because of the inherent vagueness of the phrase "shall take care that the laws be faithfully executed..." The Constitution does specifically enumerate some of the President's powers (e.g., the pardon power, the commander-in-chief power, etc.), but this specific list is not supposed to be exclusive. Instead of giving a complete list of the President's powers (as is done for Congress), the Constitution gives the President this general "executive" or "law carrying out" power.

        i. **Consequence:** Consequently, so long as the President's act seems reasonably related to carrying out the laws made by Congress, the Court won't strike that act merely because it doesn't fall within any narrow, enumerated Presidential power. (*Example:* Nothing in the Constitution expressly gives the President prosecutorial discretion (the power to decide whom to prosecute), yet he clearly has this power, because it's part of the broader job of "carrying out the law.")

    d. **Delegation:** Congress may ***delegate*** some of its power to the President or the executive branch. This is how federal agencies (which are usually part of the executive branch) get the right to formulate ***regulations*** for interpreting and enforcing congressional statutes. If Congress delegates ***excessively*** to federal agencies (by not giving appropriate standards), the delegation can be struck down — but this is very rare.

2. **War powers:** Be alert for separation-of-powers issues when the President's ***war-related powers*** are at stake.

    a. **Can't declare war:** The President is the Commander-in-Chief of the armed forces. But ***only Congress, not the President, can declare war.*** The President can commit our armed forces to repel a sudden attack, but he cannot fight a long-term engagement without a congressional declaration of war. [137]

    b. **Habeas corpus:** The constitutional right of prisoners — including foreign prisoners of war — to make a ***habeas corpus petition*** reflects separation-of-powers principles. Under the ***"Suspension Clause"*** of Art. I, § 9, cl. 2, the government (i.e., the executive branch) may not suspend habeas corpus — the right of a state or federal prisoner to prove to a federal judge that the prisoner is being held in violation of the constitution or federal law — except "when in Cases of Rebellion or Invasion the public Safety may require it." [138]

        Example: At the President's urging after 9/11, Congress passes a law that foreigners held by the military as enemy combatants at the U.S. base in Guantanamo Bay, Cuba may not use a habeas corpus petition to a federal district judge to contest the legality of their imprisonment. (Instead, such prisoners are required to appeal to the federal Court of Appeals for the D.C. Circuit, but that court is limited to reviewing the record of the military tribunal that made the enemy-combatant classification, and can't examine newly-discovered evidence.) The Ps, foreigners captured abroad, held at Guantanamo and classified as enemy combatants, seek a ruling that the law unconstitutionally takes away their right to show by habeas petition that they were misclassified as an enemy combatant.

        Held, for the Ps. The law violates the Suspension Clause, because the appeal procedure in the law is not an adequate substitute for habeas corpus, and even foreigners imprisoned by the U.S. have habeas rights. Separation-of-powers principles make it vital that the judicial branch keep the power to hear habeas challenges to the executive branch's authority to imprison a person. [*Boumediene v. Bush*] [139]

3. **Treaties and executive agreements:** As noted, the President has the power to enter into a ***treaty*** with foreign nations, but only if two-thirds of the Senate approves. Additionally, the Court has held that the Constitution implicitly gives the President, as an adjunct of his foreign affairs power, the right to enter into an ***"executive agreement"*** with a foreign nation, without first getting express congressional consent. [78]

4. **Appointment and removal of executive personnel:** The President, not Congress, is given the power to ***appoint federal executive officers***. This is the ***"Appointments" Clause.*** [141-143]

   a. **Text of Clause:** The Clause (Article II, §2) says that the President shall "***nominate***, and by and with the ***Advice and Consent of the Senate***, shall appoint ***Ambassadors ... Judges*** of the Supreme Court, and all other ***Officers of the United States***. ..." The Clause then goes on to provide that "the Congress may by Law vest the Appointment of such ***inferior Officers***, as they think proper, in the President alone, in the Courts of Law, or in the Heads of Departments."

   b. **Interpretation:** The Clause means, in the most general sense, that ***Congress may not appoint executive-branch or judicial-branch federal officials***.

   c. **Top-level ("principal") officers:** In the case of ***"principal"*** officers of the United States (i.e., ***top-level*** officers), the President nominates a candidate, and the Senate must, as a constitutional matter, decide whether to approve the nomination. As to such officers, Congress ***may not take away or limit*** the President's right of appointment. [141]

      i. **Cabinet members:** "Principal" executive-branch officers are people who have ***no boss*** except for the President. ***Members of the Cabinet*** and ***ambassadors*** are the main examples of such officers.

      Example: Congress may not appoint a Secretary of Defense — it must wait for the President to nominate the Secretary, at which point the Senate can choose to consent or reject the nomination.

   d. **Lower-level ("inferior") officers:** In the case of ***lower-level*** federal officials (the ones the Appointments Clause calls ***"inferior"*** officers), Congress *does* have the right to limit the President's right of appointment (because the final sentence of the Clause says that "Congress may by Law vest the Appointment of such ***inferior*** Officers, as they think proper, in the ***President alone***, in the ***Courts of Law***, or in the ***Heads of Departments***)."

      i. **Three possible appointers:** So although Congress cannot itself *make* appointments of inferior officers, it has the right to choose, on a position-by-position basis, to confer the power of appointment on ***any*** of the following: (1) the ***President***; (2) the ***federal judiciary***; or (3) the ***"heads of departments"*** (e.g., Cabinet members). [142]

      Example 1: Congress creates the post of Deputy Secretary of State, and says that the person occupying this post must be appointed by the Secretary of State. There is no Appointments Clause problem with this statute, since (1) the Secretary of State is a cabinet member and is thus automatically a "head of [a] department"; and (2) the Deputy Secretary is an "inferior" federal officer, the power to appoint whom Congress may therefore confer (by authority of Article II, § 2, final sentence) on the head of the department in which the Deputy will serve.

      Example 2: Congress creates the post of *Assistant* Deputy Secretary of State, and gives the power of appointment for this post to the Deputy Secretary of State. This statute *is* a violation of the final portion (the "inferior officers" part) of the Appointments Clause, assuming that the post is senior enough that the person who holds it exercises "significant authority." (Significant authority is required for a person to be an inferior federal officer at all, as opposed to a rank-and-file federal employee who is not even an inferior officer.)

Why is this a violation? Because although Congress can limit the President's power to make appointment of an inferior federal officer, Congress must give this appointment power either to the President, the judiciary, or a "head of department" (typically, a Cabinet member). The Deputy Secretary of State does not fall into any of these three categories, so Congress can't constitutionally grant her the power to appoint an inferior federal officer.

e. **Congress can't appoint federal executives:**   The most important single thing to remember about the appointment of federal officers is that *Congress has no power to directly appoint federal executive officers,* whether they're *top-level* (i.e. "principal" officers) or *lower-level* ("inferior" officers). [143]

Example: Congress establishes the Federal Election Commission, which enforces federal campaign laws. The Commission has power to bring civil actions against violators. The statute establishing the Commission allows Congress to appoint a majority of the Commission's members. *Held*, the tasks performed by the Commission are primarily executive, and its members are "officers of the United States." Therefore, the members must be appointed by the President, not Congress. [*Buckley v. Valeo*]

f. **Removal of federal officers:**   The power to *remove* federal officers similarly rests mainly with the *President*.

i. **General rule:** The general rule (subject to exceptions discussed below) is that the President *may remove* any presidential or executive-branch appointee *without cause*.

ii. **High-level ("principal") federal officers:** Thus Congress may not limit in any way the President's right to remove a *high-level* ("principal") purely-executive-branch appointee, such as a *Cabinet member* or *ambassador*.

Example: The President may remove the Secretary of State)at any time, without cause. Congress may not limit this right by saying, for instance, "The President may remove the Secretary of State only for good cause."

iii. **Lower-level and independent:** But Congress has more freedom to limit the way that both high-level and lower-level officers at *"independent"* federal agencies, and *lower-level* (*"inferior"*) executive-branch officers, may be removed. In general, Congress may say that these officers may be removed by the President or his subordinate *only for cause*.

(1) **Independent agency-heads:**   Thus suppose an appointee performs a *judicial* or *quasi-judicial* function, such as the head of an independent agency created by Congress. Congress may, in order to guard against interference from the Executive Branch, say that the officer shall be removed only for cause. [144]

Example: Congress creates the Federal Reserve. This agency is an "independent" quasi-legislative agency rather than a purely-executive-branch agency (i.e., it doesn't exist just to carry out the law; by means of the rule-making authority delegated to it by Congress it also "makes" the law). Therefore, Congress may say that (i) the Chairman (who is a "principal federal officer," i.e., someone who has no boss) shall serve a fixed term of 6 years; and (ii) the President may not remove a sitting Chairman except for cause.

(2) **Lower-level ("inferior") officers:**   Similarly, in the case of an *"inferior"* federal officer (i.e., one who has a boss, such as someone who reports to the head of a cabinet department), Congress may say that the officer shall serve a fixed term, and may

be removed only for cause. And that's true even if the officer is a pure executive-branch employee.

Example: Congress may say that a Special Prosecutor who is to investigate possible Executive-Branch wrongdoing — an "inferior" executive officer — may only be removed by the Executive Branch for "good cause" or other inability to perform his duties. [*Morrison v. Olson*]) [145]

Note: But Congress *can't* confer *two levels* of good-cause protection, even for the benefit of officers who work in independent agencies. So Congress can say that the Chairman of the Federal Election Commission may be removed by the President only for cause, but Congress can't then say, "there shall be a Deputy FEC Commissioner, who may be removed by the Chairman only for cause." Such a provision would unduly limit the President's ability to discharge his power to appoint federal officers. [*Free Enterprise Fund v. Public Co. Accounting Oversight Bd.*] [144]

    iv. **Impeachment:** Separately, Congress may remove any federal executive officer by *impeachment*, discussed immediately below.

  g. **Impeachment:** Congress can remove any "officer" of the U.S. (President, Vice President, Cabinet members, federal judges, etc.) by *impeachment*. The House must vote by a *majority* to impeach (which is like an indictment). Then, the Senate conducts the trial; a two-thirds vote of the Senators present is required to convict. Conviction can be for treason, bribery, and other "high crimes and misdemeanors." Probably only serious crimes, and serious non-criminal abuses of power, fall within the phrase "high crimes and misdemeanors." [147]

5. Removal of federal judges: Federal *judges* cannot be removed by *either* Congress or the President. Article III provides that federal judges shall hold their office during "good behavior." This has been held to mean that so long as a judge does not act improperly, she may not be removed from office. The only way to remove a sitting federal judge is by formal *impeachment* proceedings, as noted above.

  a. **Non-Article III judges:** However, the above "life tenure" rule applies only to garden-variety federal judges who hold their positions directly under *Article III*. Congress is always free to establish what are essentially *administrative* judgeships, and as to these, lifetime tenure is not constitutionally required.

B. Legislative and executive immunity:

1. Speech and Debate Clause: Members of Congress are given a quite broad immunity by the "Speech and Debate" Clause: "For any speech or debate in either house, [members of Congress] shall not be questioned in any other place." This clause shields members of Congress from: (1) civil or criminal suits relating to their legislative actions; and (2) grand jury investigations relating to those actions. [149]

2. Executive immunity: There's no executive branch immunity expressly written into the Constitution. But courts have recognized an implied executive immunity based on separation of powers concepts. [149-150]

  a. **Absolute for President:** The President has *absolute* immunity from civil liability for his *official* acts. [*Nixon v. Fitzgerald*] [149] (There's *no* immunity for the President's *unofficial* acts, including those he committed before taking office. [*Clinton v. Jones*])

  b. **Qualified for others:** But all other federal officials, including presidential aides, receive only *qualified* immunity for their official acts. (They lose this immunity if they violate a "clearly established" right, whether intentionally or negligently.) [*Harlow v. Fitzgerald*] [149]

3. **Executive privilege:** Presidents have a qualified right to refuse to disclose confidential information relating to their performance of their duties. This is called "*executive privilege*." [150-153]

   a. **Outweighed:** Since the privilege is qualified, it may be outweighed by other compelling governmental interests. For instance, the need for the President's evidence in a *criminal trial* will generally outweigh the President's vague need to keep information confidential. [*U.S. v. Nixon*] [150-153]

CHAPTER 6

TWO LIMITS ON STATE POWER: THE DORMANT COMMERCE CLAUSE AND CONGRESSIONAL ACTION

I.   THE DORMANT COMMERCE CLAUSE

A. **Dormant Commerce Clause generally:**   The *mere existence* of the federal commerce power *restricts the states* from *discriminating against*, or *unduly burdening*, interstate commerce. This restriction is called the *"dormant Commerce Clause."* [84]

1. **Three part test:**   A state regulation which affects interstate commerce must satisfy *each* of the following three requirements in order to avoid violating the dormant Commerce Clause:

   a. The regulation must pursue a *legitimate state end*;

   b. The regulation must be *rationally related* to that legitimate state end; and

   c. The regulatory *burden* imposed by the state on interstate commerce must be *outweighed* by the state's interest in enforcing its regulation.

   d. **Summary:**   So to summarize this test, it's both a *"mere-rationality"* test (in that the regulation must be rationally related to fulfilling a legitimate state end) plus a separate *balancing test* (in that the benefits to the state from the regulation must outweigh the burdens on interstate commerce). [88]

2. **Discrimination against out-of-staters:**   Above all else, be on the lookout for *intentional discrimination against out-of-staters*. If the state is promoting its residents' *own economic interests*, this will not be a legitimate state objective, so the regulation will virtually automatically violate the Commerce Clause.

   Example: New York refuses to let a Massachusetts wholesaler set up a receiving station in New York, from which he can buy New York milk to sell it to Massachusetts residents. New York is worried that this will deprive New Yorkers of enough milk. *Held*, this restriction violates the dormant Commerce Clause — New York is protecting its own citizens' economic interests at the expense of out-of-staters, and this is an illegitimate objective. [*H.P. Hood & Sons v. DuMond*]

3. **Health/safety/welfare regulations:**   Regulations that are truly addressed to the state's *health, safety and welfare* objectives are usually "legitimate." (But again, this cannot be used as a smokescreen for protecting residents' own economic interests at the expense of out-of-staters.)

4. **Balancing test:**   When you perform the balancing part of the test (to see whether the benefits to the state from its regulation outweigh the unintentional burdens to commerce), pay special attention to whether there are *less restrictive means* available to the state: if the state could accomplish

its objective as well (or even almost as well) while burdening commerce less, then it probably has to do so. [89]

> **Example**: Wisconsin can't ban all out of state milk, even to promote the legitimate objective of avoiding adulterated milk — this is because the less restrictive means of conducting regular health inspections would accomplish the state's safety goal just as well. [*Dean Milk Co. v. Madison*]

    a. Lack of uniformity: A measure that leads to a *lack of uniformity* is likely to constitute a big burden on interstate commerce. For instance, if various states' regulations are *in conflict*, the Court will probably strike the minority regulation, on the grounds that it creates a lack of uniformity that substantially burdens commerce without a sufficiently great corresponding benefit to the state.

5. Some contexts: The most standard illustrations of forbidden protectionism are where the state says, *"You can't bring your goods into our state,"* or *"You can't take goods out of our state into your state."* Here are some other contexts where dormant Commerce Clause analysis may be important:

    a. Embargo of natural resources: Laws that prevent *scarce natural resources* from moving out of the state where they are found are closely scrutinized. Often, this is just protectionism (e.g., a state charges higher taxes on oil destined for out-of-state than for in-state use.) But even if the state's interest is *conservation* or *ecology*, the measure will probably be struck down if *less-discriminatory alternatives* are available. [96]

    b. Environmental regulations: Similarly, the states may not *protect their environment* at the expense of their neighbors, unless there is no less-discriminatory way to achieve the same result. (*Example:* New Jersey prohibits the importing of most solid or liquid waste into the state. *Held*, this violates the Commerce Clause. Even if the state's purpose was to protect the state's environment or its inhabitants' health and safety, the state may not accomplish these objectives by discriminating against out-of-staters. [*Philadelphia v. New Jersey*]) [98-100]

    c. "Do the work in our state": Statutes that pressure out-of-state businesses to *perform certain operations* within the state are likely to be found violative of the dormant Commerce Clause. Such statutes will probably be found to unduly burden interstate commerce. [96-97]

6. Discrimination by city against out-of-towners: The dormant Commerce Clause also prevents a *city or county* from protecting its own local economic interests by discriminating against both out-of-state and out-of-town (but in-state) producers. (*Example:* Michigan allows each county to decide that it will not allow solid wastes generated outside the county to be disposed of in the county. County X responds by barring both non-Michigan waste and waste generated in Michigan by counties other than X. *Held*, this scheme violates the dormant Commerce Clause because it is an attempt to protect local interests against non-local interests. The regulation is not saved merely because it discriminates against in-state but out-of-county waste producers as well as out-of-state producers. [*Fort Gratiot Sanitary Landfill v. Mich. Dept. of Nat. Res.*] [94]

7. Market participant exception: But there is one key *exception* to the dormant Commerce Clause rules: if the state acts as a *market participant*, it *may* favor local over out-of-state interests. (*Example:* South Dakota owns a cement plant. It favors in-state customers during shortages. *Held*, this does not violate the Commerce Clause, because the state is acting as a market participant. [*Reeves v. Stake*]) [100-102]

B. State taxation of interstate commerce: Just as state regulation may be found to unduly burden (or discriminate against) interstate commerce, so state *taxation* may be found to unduly burden or discriminate against interstate commerce, and thus violate the Commerce Clause. To strike a state tax as violative of the Commerce Clause, the challenger must generally show either: [102-104]

1. **Discrimination:** That the state is *discriminating* against interstate commerce, by taxing in a way that unjustifiably benefits local commerce at the expense of out-of-state commerce. [103]

2. **Burdensome:** Or, that the state's taxing scheme (perhaps taken in conjunction with other states' taxing schemes) unfairly *burdens* interstate commerce even though it doesn't discriminate on its face. One way this can happen is if the tax leads to *unfair cumulative taxation*. The test is whether, if every state applied the same tax, commerce would be unduly burdened.

   Example: North Dakota requires every out-of-state mail order vendor who sends mail into the state to collect N.D. use tax on any sales made to N.D. buyers, even if the vendor has no in-state employees. *Held*, this taxing scheme violates the Commerce Clause, because it unduly burdens interstate commerce. If this scheme were allowable, all 6,000 taxing jurisdictions in the U.S. could impose local-tax-collection requirements on all out-of-state vendors, making compliance virtually impossible. [*Quill Corp. v. North Dakota*] [103]

II. CONGRESSIONAL ACTION — PREEMPTION AND CONSENT

A. **Federal preemption generally:** The discussion above relates only to the "dormant" Commerce Clause, i.e., the situation in which Congress has not attempted to *exercise* its commerce power in a particular area. Now, we consider what happens when Congress *does* take action in a particular area of commerce.

   1. **Supremacy Clause:** If there is a *conflict* between *federal law and state law*, the *state law is simply invalid*. The *Supremacy Clause* of the Constitution (Article VI Clause 2) says that "This Constitution, and the Laws of the United States which shall be made in Pursuance thereof ... shall be the supreme Law of the Land. ... " So if federal and state law conflict, the Supremacy Clause means that *state law must yield to federal law*. In that event, federal law is said to have "*preempted*" state law. [104]

   2. **Express vs implied preemption:** Federal preemption of state law falls into two main categories: *"express"* preemption and *"implied"* preemption [104]:

      [1] *Express* preemption occurs when a federal law *specifically* (i.e., "expressly") says that it preempts state or local law.

      [2] *Implied* preemption occurs when Congress does *not* expressly state that it intends to preempt state or local law, but *manifests an intent* to do so.

B. **Express preemption:** Congress sometimes, in enacting a statute, takes the trouble to state explicitly that the statute is intended to preempt some area of state or local law. That is, Congress says, "In the area of [X], the only governing law shall be federal law." This is *"express preemption."* As long as the federal statute is validly enacted (e.g., it falls within one of Congress' enumerated powers, such as the commerce power), any state or local law that falls *within the zone* intended by Congress to be *exclusively federal* will be *invalid* under the Supremacy Clause. [104]

   Example: The federal Employee Retirement Income Security Act (ERISA) says that it "supersede[s] any and all State laws insofar as they ... relate to any employee benefit plan[.]" If a state purports to regulate some aspect of an employee benefit plan, the state regulation will be valid as a violation of the Supremacy Cause. That's true even though the state regulation may be perfectly consistent with ERISA.

C. **Implied preemption:** Most preemption cases involve *"implied preemption,"* i.e., situations in which Congress has not explicitly said that it intends to preempt state or local law, but in which the *structure or purpose* of the congressional action suggests that Congress intended to displace non-federal law.

There are *two main types* of implied preemption:

[1] "*field* preemption" and

[2] "*conflicts* preemption"

[*Gade v. National Solid Wastes Management*] [105]

1. **"Field preemption":** **"Field preemption"** occurs "where the scheme of federal regulation is *so pervasive* as to make reasonable the inference that Congress *left no room* for the states to supplement it." *Gade, supra.* In other words, field preemption occurs where Congress has indicated that it intends to *"occupy the entire field"* in question. [105]

> **Example:** In 1940, Congress passes the Alien Registration Act, which requires aliens 14 and over to register with the federal Immigration and Naturalization Service, be finger-printed, and obey other restrictions. The prior year, Pennsylvania passed a state alien registration act which required all aliens to register with a state agency, and to receive and carry a state-issued alien identification card.
>
> *Held*, the state alien registration law is preempted by the federal one. The federal government's special role in immigration and foreign relations, and Congress' decision to enact a single integrated system for alien registration, make it clear that Congress intended to displace any state requirements that aliens register. [*Hines v. Davidowitz*]

   a. **Congressional intent is paramount:** In field preemption, as with other preemption categories, the issue is always one of *congressional intent.* [105]

   i. **Broad federal coverage of area:** Where the existing federal regulatory scheme is *broad*, and *covers most of the subject area*, the Court is much more likely to find federal field-preemption than where the federal scheme is less comprehensive.

   ii. **Field traditionally left to states:** Subject matter areas *traditionally left to the states* are *less likely* to be found to be the subject of federal field-preemption. This means that if the subject area is usually viewed as "*local*" rather than "national," preemption is unlikely to be found. This is especially true in cases involving *health* and *safety* regulations.

   iii. **National matters:** Conversely, areas *traditionally left to federal control*, such as foreign relations, bankruptcy, patent and trademark, admiralty, immigration, etc., will normally be found to be federally preempted. Registration of aliens, at issue in *Hines, supra*, is an illustration.

2. **"Conflicts preemption":** **"Conflicts preemption"** applies to two situations: first, where compliance with both federal and state regulations is a *physical impossibility*; and second, where state law is inconsistent with the *purposes and objectives* of federal law.

   a. **Direct physical conflict:** Occasionally, federal and state regulations are drafted in such a way that it is *physically impossible for a person to obey the federal and state regulations simultaneously.* When this happens, the state regulation is of course invalid. *Labelling regulations* sometimes fall into this category. [106]

> **Example:** Wisconsin's syrup-labeling rules are written in such a way that if out-of-state syrup is labeled so as to comply with the federal Food and Drug Act, the syrup will be

2. **Two-prong test:** Even if a state does impair an out-of-stater's exercise of a right fundamental to national unity, the state impairment is not necessarily invalid. But the state will lose unless it satisfies a two-pronged test:

    a. **"Peculiar source of evil":** First, the state must show that out-of-staters are a *"peculiar source of the evil"* the statute was enacted to rectify. [119]

    b. **Substantial relation to state objective:** Second, the state must show that its solution (the discriminatory statute) is *"substantially related"* to this "peculiar evil" the out-of-staters represent. Generally, to meet this prong the state must show that there are no *less discriminatory alternatives* that would adequately address the problem. (For instance, in *Alaska Hire*, had Alaska been able to show that there was no other way to combat unemployment than to absolutely prefer in-staters, it would have met this prong.) [119]

3. **No "market participant" exception:** Recall that a state is immune from Commerce Clause violations if it's acting as a *market participant*. But there's *no* such market participant exception for the Privileges & Immunities Clause. (Thus even if, in the *Alaska Hire* case, Alaska had been hiring the workers itself, its absolute preference for residents would have violated the clause.) [119-121]

4. **Distinguished from Equal Protection:** When a non-resident is discriminated against, he may also have an Equal Protection claim. But there are two key differences:

    a. **Aliens and corporations:** The Equal Protection Clause can apply to *corporations* and to *aliens*; the Privileges & Immunities Clause can't. [120]

    b. **Strict scrutiny:** Conversely, the level of scrutiny given to the state's action is much tougher under Privileges & Immunities Clause than under Equal Protection Clause. Under Equal Protection, non-residency isn't a suspect classification, and therefore the discrimination must just meet the "mere-rationality" standard. Under the Privileges & Immunities Clause, by contrast, the statute must survive what amounts to *strict scrutiny* — the non-residents must be a "peculiar source of the evil," and there must not be less-discriminatory alternatives available. [121]

    c. **Tactical tip:** Wherever possible, couch the attack as Privileges & Immunities, rather than Equal Protection, since the level of scrutiny usually makes a dispositive difference.

CHAPTER 9

THE DUE PROCESS CLAUSE

I. INTRODUCTION

A. **Two major principles:** For the rest of this outline, we'll be talking about rights guaranteed to individuals by the Constitution. Before we get into the individual rights, there are two general principles that are crucial to remember: [161-162]

1. **Protected against the government:** First, practically all of the individual rights conferred by the Constitution upon individuals *protect only against government action*. They do *not* protect a person against acts by other private individuals. (*Example:* Suppose P is a woman who's two months pregnant, and none of the private hospitals in her state will perform an abortion. P's substantive due process right to an abortion has not been violated, because the government has not interfered with that right.)

    Note: The only exception to the "government action only" rule is the Thirteenth Amendment's ban on slavery, which *does* apply to private conduct.

2. **Not directly applicable to states:** The other general principle to remember is the central role of the Fourteenth Amendment's *Due Process* Clause. Many of the important individual guarantees are given by the Bill of Rights (the first ten amendments). For instance, the First Amendment rights of free expression and freedom of religion fall into this category. But the Bill of Rights does *not directly* apply to the states. However, the Fourteenth Amendment's Due Process Clause (which does apply to the states) has been interpreted to make nearly all of the Bill of Rights guarantees applicable to the states — these individual guarantees are "incorporated" into the Bill of Rights. "Incorporation" is discussed further below.

II. THE 14TH AMENDMENT GENERALLY

A. **Text of 14th Amendment:** Section 1 of the 14th Amendment provides, in full, that: "All persons born or naturalized in the United States, and subject to the jurisdiction hereof, are citizens of the United States and of the State wherein they reside. No State shall make or enforce any law which shall abridge the privileges or immunities of citizens of the United States; nor shall any State deprive any person of life, liberty, or property, without due process of law; nor deny to any person within its jurisdiction the equal protection of the laws." [162]

1. **Three rights:** So in one sentence we have three major rights: (1) the right to due process; (2) the right to equal protection; and (3) the right to the privileges or immunities of national citizenship.

B. **The Bill of Rights and the states:** One of the major functions of the 14th Amendment's Due Process Clause is to make the *Bill of Rights* — that is, the first 10 amendments — applicable to the states. [161]

1. **Not directly applicable to states:** The Bill of Rights is not *directly* applicable to the States. The Supreme Court held early on (in 1833) that the Bill of Rights limited only the federal government, not state or municipal governments. [162]

2. **Effect of due process clause:** But enactment of the 14th Amendment in 1868 effectively changed this. The 14th Amendment directly imposes on the states (and local governments as well) the requirement that they not deprive anyone of "life, liberty or property" without due process. Nearly all the guarantees of the Bill of Rights have been interpreted by the Supreme Court as being so important that if a state denies these rights, it has in effect taken away an aspect of "liberty."

3. **Application of Bill of Rights to states:** The Supreme Court has never said that due process requires the states to honor the Bill of Rights as a whole. Instead, the Court uses an approach called *"selective incorporation."* Under this approach, each right in the Bill of Rights is examined to see whether it is of *"fundamental"* importance. If so, that right is "selectively incorporated" into the meaning of "due process" under the 14th Amendment, and is thus made binding on the states. [162-164]

4. **Nearly all rights incorporated:** By now, nearly *all rights contained in the Bill of Rights* have been incorporated, one by one, into the meaning of "due process" (and thus made applicable to the states). [163] The only major Bill of Rights guarantees *not* incorporated are:

   a. **Grand jury:** The 5th Amendment's right not to be subject to a criminal trial without a *grand jury indictment* (so that a state may begin proceedings by an "information," as some states do); and

   b. **Right to jury in civil cases:** The 7th Amendment's right to a *jury trial* in *civil* cases.

   c. **Excessive fines:** The 8th Amendment's prohibition on *excessive fines*. (But that Amendment's prohibition on excessive *bail* does apply to the states.)

5. **"Jot-for-jot" incorporation:** Once a given Bill of Rights guarantee is made applicable to the states, the *scope* of that guarantee is interpreted the *same way* for the states as for the federal government. The Court has rejected "the notion that the 14th Amendment applies to the states only a 'watered-down' ... version of the individual guarantees of the Bill of Rights." [*Malloy v. Hogan*] [163-164]

> **Example:** The 4th Amendment right not to be subject to an unreasonable search or seizure is interpreted the same way whether the case involves federal or state police — thus if on a given set of facts the FBI would be found to have violated the 4th Amendment, so would local police.

C. **The federal Due Process Clause:** We'll generally be discussing the *14th* Amendment's due process clause, which binds the states. But keep in mind that there is also a due process clause in the *5th* Amendment, that is binding on the *federal* government. Both clauses have been interpreted the same way, so that any state action that would be forbidden by the 14th Amendment Due Process Clause is also forbidden to the federal government via the 5th Amendment Due Process Clause. (For instance, exactly the same limits apply to federal and state regulations that impair the right to have an abortion.)[164]

III. SUBSTANTIVE DUE PROCESS — ECONOMIC AND SOCIAL WELFARE REGULATION

A. **Substantive due process generally:**   There are two quite different functions that the Due Process Clause serves. Most obviously, it imposes certain *procedural* requirements on governments when they impair life, liberty, or property. (We'll be talking about this "procedural due process" area below.) But the Due Process Clause also limits the *substantive power* of the states to regulate certain areas of human life. This "substantive" component of the Due Process Clause derives mainly from the interpretation of the term *"liberty"* — certain types of state limits on human conduct have been held to so unreasonably interfere with important human rights that they amount to an unreasonable (and unconstitutional) denial of "liberty." [164]

> **Exam Tip:** Any time your fact pattern suggests that a state or federal government is *taking away* some thing or value that could be considered "life," "liberty," or "property," then entirely apart from the issue of whether the government has used proper procedures, you must ask the question: Has the government by carrying out this taking violated the individual's *substantive* interest in life, liberty, or property?

1. **Non-fundamental rights:**   There's an absolutely critical distinction that you must make right at the outset, when you're analyzing a substantive due process problem. That's the distinction between *fundamental* and *non-fundamental* rights. If a right or value is found to be "non-fundamental," then the state action that impairs that right only has to meet the easy *"mere-rationality"* test. In other words, it just has to be the case that the state is pursuing a *legitimate governmental objective*, and is doing so with a means that is *rationally related* to that objective.

    a. **Economic regulation:**   Nearly all *economic* regulation (and most *"social welfare"* regulation) will turn out to implicate only non-fundamental rights, and will almost certainly be upheld under this easy-to-satisfy mere-rationality standard. So anytime you can't find a fundamental right being impaired, you should presume that the measure does not violate substantive due process.

2. **Fundamental rights:**   But if a state or federal government is impairing a *"fundamental"* right, then it's a different ball game entirely: here, the court uses *strict scrutiny*. Only if the governmental

had no "fundamental right" to live together, and in *Moore* the Court pointed out that families' rights to live together were different, and much stronger.

2. **Upbringing and education:** Similarly, a parent's right to direct the **upbringing** and **education** of his children is "fundamental."

> **Example 1:** The state may not require parents to send their children to public schools. Parents have a fundamental right to determine how their children will be educated. [*Pierce v. Soc. of Sisters*] [173]

> **Example 2:** A parent has a fundamental interest in deciding who will spend time with the child. Therefore, the state may not award visitation rights to a child's grandparents over the objection of the child's fit custodial parent, unless the state first gives "special weight" to the parent's wishes. [*Troxel v. Granville*]

   a. **Right to continue parenting:** There's also probably a fundamental right to **continue parenting** — so the state can't take away your child just because it thinks a foster home would be "better" for the child. (Even if there's child abuse, the parent still has a fundamental right to parent, but here the state's interest in protecting the child would be "compelling," so putting the child in foster care would probably satisfy strict scrutiny.)

   b. **No relationship:** If a parent has **never married** the other parent, and has never **developed a relationship** with the child (e.g., they have never lived together), then there is probably **not** a fundamental right to continue to be a parent. (So the state may, for instance, deny the non-custodial unwed parent who has never participated in the child's upbringing the right to block an adoption of the child. [*Quilloin v. Walcott*] [200]

3. **Right to marry:** The **right to marry** — at least marry a person of the opposite sex — is also fundamental, so again the state can only interfere with this right by passing strict scrutiny. (*Example:* A state may not forbid anyone from remarrying unless he is not current on all support payments from his prior marriage. [*Zablocki v. Redhail*]) [199]

   a. **Same-sex marriage:** Although conventional marriage is "fundamental," as *Zablocki* shows, the right of persons of the **same sex** to marry, or to enter some other socially-recognized ceremony of commitment, has so far **not** been classified by the Court as fundamental. However, in *Windsor v. U.S.* (2013) [C-52] the Court struck down Congress's refusal to recognize for federal-law purposes same-sex marriages that had been validly performed under state law. For more about what *Windsor* means for the status of same-sex marriage, see Par. (E)(1)(b) *infra*, p. C-32.

E. **Adult sex:** There is no general fundamental right to engage in **adult consensual sexual activity**. Therefore, the Court will generally review restrictions on adult consensual sexual activity under the **mere-rationality** test.

1. **Rational-relation review "with bite":** However, although the Court purports to use the mere-rationality standard to review restrictions on adult sexual activity, the Court will sometimes **strike down** the regulation on the grounds that it interferes with people's sexual autonomy. In doing so, the Court has seemed to use mere-rationality review **"with bite"** — i.e., without the usual amount of **deference** to the legislature — especially in cases involving **gay rights.** [201]

   a. **Homosexual sodomy:** Thus the Court has **struck down** all state laws that **criminalize homosexual sodomy**, on the grounds that such laws **"demean the lives of homosexual persons,"** and thereby violate their substantive due process rights. [*Lawrence v. Texas.*] In *Lawrence*, the Court said that gays have "the full right to engage in their [homosexual] conduct without intervention of the government."

      i.   **Not a "fundamental" right:** But the Court in *Lawrence* stopped short of calling the adult sex a "fundamental right" for substantive due process purposes; the Court purported to use mere-rationality review, but did so "with bite," i.e., with unusual rigor. [204]

    b. **Same-sex marriage:** Related to the "homosexual sodomy" issue is the issue of ***same-sex marriage.*** The Court decided in *Windsor v. U.S.* (*infra*, p. C-52) that Congress could not constitutionally refuse to ***recognize same-sex marriages that have been validly performed under state law.*** *Windsor* seems to have been based in part on substantive due process theory (as well as on equal protection theory). The decision also seems to have given Congress much less than the usual ***deference*** paid to the legislature in cases of mere-rationality review (i.e., cases where there is no "fundamental" substantive due process right at issue). [368-378]

      i.   **Significance:** Therefore, although *Windsor* does not recognize a *general* right to same-sex marriage, fundamental or otherwise (it merely forces the federal government to recognize state-consecrated same-sex marriages), the case seems like a large step towards the Court's eventual recognition of such a right. But as in *Lawrence*, the Court may ultimately find such a state-law due process right to same-sex marriage not by calling the right "fundamental," but by applying unusual demanding mere-rationality review.

F. **The "right to die," and the right to decline unwanted medical procedures:** The law of "right to die" and "right to pull the plug" is developing. Here's what we know already:

   1. **Can't be forced to undergo unwanted procedures:** A competent adult has a 14th Amendment liberty interest in ***not being forced to undergo unwanted medical procedures***, including artificial life-sustaining measures. It's not clear whether this is a "fundamental" interest. (*Example:* P, dying of stomach cancer, has a liberty interest in refusing to let the hospital feed him through a feeding tube.) [205]

   2. **State's interest in preserving life:** The state has an important ***countervailing interest in preserving life.***

   3. **"Clear and convincing evidence" standard:** In the case of a now-incompetent patient, the state's interest in preserving life entitles it to say that it won't allow the "plug" to be "pulled" unless there is ***"clear and convincing evidence"*** that the patient would have voluntarily declined the life-sustaining measures. [*Cruzan v. Missouri*] [205]

      Example: P is comatose, hospitalized, being fed through a tube, and kept breathing through a respirator. P's parents want the hospital to discontinue the tube-feeding and respirator. *Held,* the state may insist that if the parents can't show "clear and convincing evidence" that during her conscious life P showed a desire not to be kept alive by such artificial measures, the measures must be continued. [*Cruzan, supra*]

    a. **Living wills and health-care proxies:** But probably the states must honor a ***"living will"*** and a ***"health-care proxy."*** In a living will, the signer gives direct instructions. In a health-care proxy, the signer appoints someone else to make health-care decisions. [207]

   4. **No "right to commit suicide":** Terminally-ill patients do ***not*** have a general liberty interest in ***"committing suicide."*** Nor do they have the constitutional right to ***recruit a third person*** to help them commit suicide. [*Washington v. Glucksberg*] [209-213]

      Example: A state may make it a felony for a physician to knowingly prescribe a fatal dose of drugs for the purpose of helping the patient commit suicide.

G. **Other possible places:** Here are a couple of other areas where there might be a fundamental right.

   1. **Reading:** You probably have a fundamental right to ***read what you want***. (*Example*: A state cannot forbid you from reading pornography in the privacy of your own home, even though it can make it criminal for someone to sell you that pornography.) [*Stanley v. Georgia*] [213]

2. **Physical appearance:** You may have a fundamental right to control your ***personal appearance***. (*Example:* If the public school which you are required to attend forces you to cut your hair to a length of no more two inches for boys and four inches for girls, this might violate a "fundamental right." But this is not clear.) [205]

H. Final word: Deciding whether the right in question is "fundamental" is, as noted, the key to substantive due process analysis. But it's not the end of the story. Even if you decide that the right is "fundamental" you've still got to carry out the strict scrutiny analysis: it might turn out that the state's countervailing interest is indeed "compelling" and the means chosen is "necessary" to achieve that interest. (*Example:* A state has a compelling interest in taking a child away from an abusive parent and putting him into foster care.)

1. **Non-fundamental:** Conversely, even if the right is not "fundamental," you've still got to apply the "mere-rationality" standard, and you might decide that the state is being so completely irrational that the state action is a violation of substantive due process anyway.

V. PROCEDURAL DUE PROCESS

A. Introduction: We turn now to the other main aspect of the 14th Amendment's Due Process Clause: this is the requirement that the state act with adequate or fair ***procedures*** when it deprives a person of life, liberty or property. Here, the emphasis is on the particular case presented by the particular person — has the government handled his particular situation fairly? Our discussion is divided into two main questions: (1) has the individual's life, liberty or property been "taken"?; and, if so, (2) what process was "due" him prior to this taking?

1. **Life, liberty or property:** The most important single thing to remember about procedural due process is that there cannot be a procedural due process problem unless government is taking a person's ***life***, ***liberty*** or ***property***. In other words, there is ***no general interest in having the government behave with fair procedures.*** (*Example:* A city hires for an opening on its police force. The city can be as arbitrary and random as it wants, because as we'll see, an applicant for a job has no liberty or property interest in obtaining the job. Therefore, the city doesn't have to give the applicant a hearing, a statement of reasons why she didn't get the job, a systematic test of her credentials, or any other aspect of procedural fairness.) [222]

2. **Distinction between substance and procedure:** Always distinguish between "substantive" due process and "procedural" due process. Procedural due process applies only where ***individual determinations*** are being made.

> **Example:** Suppose a state passes a law that says that no person with child support may marry. This statute raises an issue of substantive due process — unless this means of enforcing child support payments is necessary to achieve a compelling state interest, the state may not use that method at all, against anyone. Separately, even if this "ban on marriage" could pass this substantive due process hurdle (which it apparently can't, based on past Supreme Court cases like *Zablocki v. Redhail*) the state still must use *adequate procedures* before enforcing the ban *against a particular person.* For instance, the state must probably provide a person with ***notice*** that the ban will be applied, and a ***hearing*** at which he can show that the ban shouldn't apply to him because (for instance) he's fully paid up. The obligation to use fair procedures always applies ***"one case at a time,"*** and governs the application of government action to a particular person in a particular situation.

B. Liberty: Remember that ***"liberty"*** is one of the things the government cannot take without procedural due process. What *is* "liberty" for due process purposes? [223]

1. **Physical liberty:** First, we have the interest in "***physical***" liberty. This liberty interest is violated if you are ***imprisoned***, or even if you are placed in some other situation where you do not have physical freedom of movement (e.g., juvenile and/or civil commitment).

2. **Intangible rights:** Also, a person has a liberty interest in being able to do certain intangible things not related to physical freedom of movement. There's no complete catalog of what interests fall within this "intangible" aspect of liberty. Here are some examples, however: (1) the right to drive; (2) the right to practice one's profession; (3) the right to raise one's family. But one's interest in having a ***good reputation*** is not "liberty" (so the state can call you a crook without giving you due process — see *Paul v. Davis*). [226]

C. Property: The government also can't take "***property***" without procedural due process. Here are the things that may be "property" for procedural due process purposes: [223]

1. **Conventional property:** First, of course, we have "conventional" property (i.e., personal and real property). Thus the government cannot impose a monetary fine against a person, or declare a person's car forfeited, without complying with procedural due process.

    a. **Debt collection:** Certain kinds of ***debt collection*** devices involve "property." For instance, if the state lets private creditors ***attach*** a person's bank account prior to trial (which means that the owner can't get at the funds), even that temporary blockage is a "taking" of property. Similarly, if the state lets a private creditor ***garnish*** a person's wages, that's a taking of property. On the other hand, if the state simply passes a law that lets creditors use ***self-help*** to repossess goods, there's no governmental taking of property when the creditor repossesses. (The due process requirement applies only where it is *government* that does, or at least is involved in, the taking of liberty or property.)

2. **Government benefits:** ***Government benefits*** may or may not constitute "property" rights. Generally, if one is just ***applying*** for benefits and hasn't yet been receiving them, one does ***not*** have a property interest in those benefits. (*Example:* If P applies for welfare, and has never gotten it before, the government does not have to comply with procedural due process when it turns P down. Therefore, the government doesn't have to give P a statement of reasons, a hearing, etc.)

    a. **Already getting benefits:** But if a person has ***already been getting the benefits***, it's probably the case that he's got a property interest in ***continuing*** to get them, so that the government cannot ***terminate*** those benefits without giving him procedural due process. [*Goldberg v. Kelly*] [224] (But state law can change even this — for instance, if the state statute governing welfare benefits says that "benefits may be cut off at any time," you probably don't have a property interest in continuing to get those benefits, so you have no claim to due process.)

3. **Government employment:** A government ***job*** is similar to government benefits.

    a. **Applicant:** If you're just ***applying*** for the job, you clearly do ***not*** have a property interest in it.

    b. **Already have job:** If you already have the job, then the court looks to ***state law*** to determine whether you had a property interest in the job.

        i. **Ordinarily at-will:** Ordinarily, under state law a job is ***terminable at will***; if so, the jobholder has no property right to it, so he may be fired without due process. [225]

        ii. **Legitimate claim of entitlement:** If either a statute or the public employer's ***practices*** give a person a "***legitimate claim of entitlement***" to keep the job, then she's got a property interest. (*Example*: If a public university follows the publicized custom of never firing anybody from a non-tenured position without cause except on one year's notice, then a non-tenured teacher has a property right to hold his non-tenured job for a year following notice. [*Perry v. Sindermann*]) [225]

D. Process required: If a person's interest in property or liberty is being impaired, then she is entitled to due process. But *what procedures* does the person get? There is no simple answer. [227]

1. **Traditional civil litigation:** When a person's property is at stake in a traditional *civil lawsuit*, the range of procedural protections required by due process is broad. The litigant probably has a due process right to a *hearing*, the right to *call witnesses*, the right to *counsel*, and the right to a *fair and objective trial*. [228]

   a. **Punitive damages:** In some circumstances the award of *punitive damages* may violate the defendant's due process rights. [229]

      i. **Ratio of actual to punitive:** A punitive damages award will violate due process if it is *"grossly excessive."* [*BMW of North America v. Gore*]

         (1) **Ratio of punitive to compensatory:** One of the most important factors in whether an award of punitive damages is grossly excessive is the *ratio* of the *punitive damages* to the *actual damages.* A punitive award that is *more than nine times* the compensatory award probably won't satisfy due process. [State *Farm Mut. Automobile Insur. Co. v. Campbell*].

      ii. **Reprehensibility:** Another of the key factors in the due process analysis is the *reprehensibility* of the defendant's conduct — the more reprehensible the conduct, the higher the amount of punitive damages that may be awarded without violating due process.

      iii. **Conduct vis a vis strangers to the litigation:** Only the defendant's conduct *towards the plaintiff*, not its conduct towards *strangers to the litigation,* may be taken into account by the jury in setting the amount of punitive damages. [*Philip Morris USA v. Williams*].

   b. **Judicial bias:** A litigant also has a procedural due process right to be free of a *large risk of bias on the part of the judge hearing the case*. [230-231]

      i. **Standard:** Removal of the judge is required where "a person with a personal stake in a particular case had a *significant and disproportionate influence in placing the judge on the case* by *raising funds or directing the judge's election campaign* when the case was pending or imminent." [*Caperton v. A.T. Massey Coal Co.*]

      ii. **Campaign contributions:** So in states that *elect judges*, *large judicial campaign contributions* by one party in a pending case can give the other party a procedural due process right to have the judge in question *removed from the case*. [*Caperton, supra*]

2. **Criminal defendants and prisoners:** *Criminal defendants* receive the broadest procedural due process protections during the course of their trial (e.g., right to counsel, right to present witnesses, right to confront opposing witnesses, etc.). [231-233]

   a. **Convicted prisoners:** Once the criminal defendant has been *convicted*, he gets dramatically *less* procedural due process protection. Thus prison officials who give extra punishment to a prisoner or change his terms of confinement won't commit a substantive due process violation, and don't need to observe procedural due process protections during their decision-making process, so long as their action doesn't "impose[] *atypical and significant hardship* on the inmate in relation to the *ordinary incidents of prison life*." [*Sandin v. Conner*] [231]

   Example: A prisoner who is charged with disobeying prison regulations is not entitled by due process to *present witnesses* during the disciplinary hearing, even if the hearing leads to his being put in solitary confinement for 30 days. [*Sandin*]

      i. **Access to DNA testing:** A prisoner has no independent liberty interest in being given access to *DNA evidence to prove his innocence*. [*District Attorney's Office for the Third Judicial District v. Osborne.*] So as long as the state's overall procedures for allowing a prisoner to use newly-discovered evidence to show his innocence are not "fundamentally unfair" (which they will rarely be), the prisoner has no due process post-conviction right to test the prosecution's crime-scene samples, even at his own expense, to see if the samples match his DNA. [*Osborne, supra*] [232-233]

3. **Non-judicial proceeding:** Where the property or liberty interest is being impaired in something *other* than a judicial proceeding, the state does *not* have to give the individual the full range of procedural safeguards that would be needed for a court proceeding. Instead, for any particular procedural safeguard that the plaintiff says she should get (e.g., the right to a hearing), the court conducts a *balancing* test: the strength of the plaintiff's interest in receiving the procedural safeguard is weighed against the government's interest in avoiding extra burdens. [*Mathews v. Eldridge*] [227-228]

   Examples: If *A* has been receiving welfare benefits, these benefits may not be terminated without giving *A* an evidentiary hearing, because a wrongful termination of welfare benefits, even temporarily, is likely to lead to extreme hardship, without a large countervailing benefit to the government. [*Goldberg v. Kelly*] By contrast, a tenured employee who is being fired from a government job gets fewer procedural safeguards — he gets notice of the charges and an opportunity to present some evidence, but not a full adversarial evidentiary hearing with right to counsel; this is because the government's interest in being able to fire unsatisfactory employees quickly is factored into the balance. [*Cleveland Board of Ed. v. Loudermill*]

   a. **School suspensions:** Where a *public-school student* is *suspended* for disciplinary reasons for more than a trivial period, due process requires that he be given at least *oral notice* of the charges against him and, if he denies them, an *explanation of the evidence* the authorities have and an *opportunity to present his side of the story*. [*Goss v. Lopez*] But the student is *not* constitutionally entitled to *written notice, a formal hearing,* the right to have *counsel present,* or the right to *call and examine witnesses.* [237]

CHAPTER 10

EQUAL PROTECTION

I. EQUAL PROTECTION GENERALLY

A. **Text of clause:** The Equal Protection Clause is part of the 14th Amendment. It provides that "[n]o state shall make or enforce any law which shall ... deny to any person within its jurisdiction the equal protection of the laws." [249]

   1. **General usage:** The Clause, like all parts of the 13th, 14th and 15th Amendments, was enacted shortly after the Civil War, and its primary goal was to attain free and equal treatment for ex-slaves. But it has always been interpreted as imposing a *general* restraint on the governmental use of classifications, not just classifications based on race but also those based on sex, alienage, illegitimacy, wealth, or any other characteristic.

   2. **State and federal:** The direct text of the Clause, of course, applies only to state governments. But the federal government is also bound by the same rules of equal protection — this happens by the indirect means of the Fifth Amendment's Due Process Clause. So if a given action would be a violation of Equal Protection for a state, that same action would be unconstitutional if done by the federal government (though in this situation, if you wanted to be scrupulously correct, you would call it a violation of the Fifth Amendment's Due Process Clause). [251]

a. Government action only: The Equal Protection Clause, and the Fifth Amendment's Due Process Clause, apply *only to government action*, not to action by private citizens. This is commonly referred to as the requirement of *"state action,"* and is discussed further below.

Example: D, a large private university, refuses to admit African American students. No government participates in this decision. The university's conduct cannot be a violation of the Equal Protection Clause, because there is no "state action."

3. Making of classes: The Equal Protection Clause is only implicated where the government *makes a classification*. It's not implicated where the government merely decides which of two classes a particular person falls into. (For instance, if Congress says that you don't receive Social Security if you work more than 1,000 hours per year, then it's made a classification that distinguishes between those who work more than 1,000 hours and those who work less — this classification can be attacked under the Equal Protection Clause. But an administrative determination that a particular person did or did not work 1,000 hours is not a classification, and cannot be attacked under the Equal Protection Clause, only the Due Process Clause.) [251]

4. "As applied" vs. "facial": Here is some nomenclature: If P attacks a classification that is clearly written into the statute or regulation, he is claiming that Equal Protection is violated by the statute or regulation *"on its face."* If P's claim is that the statute does not make a classification on its face, but is being *administered* in a purposefully discriminatory way, then he is claiming that the statute or regulation is a violation of equal protection *"as applied."* (*Example:* A statute that says "you must be a citizen to vote" creates a classification scheme "on its face" — citizens vs. non-citizens. But if P claims that in actual administration, blacks are required to prove citizenship but whites are not, then his equal protection claim would be on the statute "as applied.")

a. Same standards for both: Either kind of attack — facial or "as applied," — may be made. Both follow essentially the same principles. For instance, if no suspect classification or fundamental right is involved, the classification scheme will violate the Equal Protection Clause if it's not rationally related to a legitimate state objective, whether the scheme is on the face of the statute or merely in the way the statute is applied.

5. What the Clause guarantees: The Clause in essence guarantees that *people who are similarly situated will be treated similarly.* [252]

Example: Consider racial segregation in the public schools. Such segregation gives a different treatment to two groups that are similarly situated, African Americans and whites. Therefore, it violates the Equal Protection rights of African Americans. (Of course, this reflects a judgment that there are no meaningful differences between blacks and whites that relate to public education. If the issue were, say, compulsory medical screening for sickle cell anemia, blacks and whites might not be similarly situated.)

a. Dissimilar: The Equal Protection Clause also guarantees that people who are *not* similarly situated will not be treated similarly. But this aspect is rarely of practical importance, because courts are rarely convinced that differences in situation require differences in treatment by the government.

6. Three levels of review: Recall that in our discussion of substantive due process, we saw that depending on the circumstances, one of two sharply different standards of review of governmental action was used, the easy "rational relation" test or the very demanding "strict scrutiny" standard. In the Equal Protection context, we have two tests that are virtually the same as these two, plus a third "middle level" of scrutiny. Let's consider each of the three types of review: [255]

a. Ordinary "mere-rationality" review: The easiest-to-satisfy standard of review applies to statutes that: (1) are *not based on a "suspect classification"*; (2) do not involve a *"quasi-sus-*

pect" category that the Court has implicitly recognized (principally gender and illegitimacy); and (3) don't impair a *"fundamental right."* This is the so-called *"mere-rationality"* standard. Almost every *economic regulation* will be reviewed under this easy-to-satisfy standard. (This is similar to the ease with which economic regulation passes muster under the substantive due process clause.) Under this easiest "mere-rationality" standard, the Court asks only "whether it is conceivable that the classification bears a rational relationship to an end of government which is not prohibited by the Constitution." [255]

   i.   Standard summarized: So where "mere-rationality" review is applied, the classification must satisfy two easy tests: (1) government must be pursuing a *legitimate governmental objective*; and (2) there must be a *rational relation* between the classification and that objective. Furthermore, it's not necessary that the court believe that these two requirements are satisfied; it's enough that the court concludes that it's *"conceivable"* that they're satisfied.

b. Strict scrutiny: At the other end of the spectrum, the Court will give *"strict scrutiny"* to any statute which is based on a *"suspect classification"* or which impairs a *"fundamental right."* (We'll be discussing below the meaning of these two terms, "suspect classification" and "fundamental right.") A classification based on *race* is a classic example of a "suspect class"; the right to *vote* is an example of a fundamental right. [255]

   i.   Standard: Where strict scrutiny is invoked, the classification will be upheld only if it is *necessary* to promote a *compelling* governmental interest. Thus not only must the objective be an extremely important one, but the "fit" between the means and the end must be extremely tight. This strict scrutiny test is the same as for substantive due process when a "fundamental right" (e.g., the right to privacy) is involved.

c. Middle-level review: In a few contexts, the Court uses a *middle level* of scrutiny, more probing than "mere-rationality" review but less demanding than "strict scrutiny." This middle level is mainly used for cases involving classifications based on *gender* and *illegitimacy*. [256]

   i.   Standard: This middle-level test is usually stated as follows: the means chosen by the legislature (i.e., the classification) must be *substantially related* to an *important governmental objective*. So the legislative objective must be *"important"* (but not necessarily "compelling," as for strict scrutiny), and means and end must be *"substantially related"* (easier to satisfy than the almost perfect "necessary" fit between means and end in strict scrutiny situations).

7. **Importance:** Con Law essay exams very frequently test the Equal Protection Clause because: (1) it's open-ended, so it applies to a lot of different situations; (2) there are often no clear right or wrong answers under it, so it gives the student a good chance to show how well she can articulate arguments on either side; and (3) it's one of the two or three most important single limitations on what government can do to individuals.

   a.   Test tip: Therefore, any time you're asked to give an opinion about whether a particular governmental action is constitutional, make sure to check for an equal protection violation.

II. ECONOMIC AND SOCIAL LAWS — THE "MERE-RATIONALITY" STANDARD OF REVIEW

A. Non-suspect, non-fundamental rights (economic and social legislation): First, let's examine the treatment of classifications that do *not* involve either a *suspect class* or a *fundamental right*. Most *economic* and *social-welfare* legislation falls into this category. [256]

1. **Mere-rationality standard:**   Here, as noted, courts use the "mere-rationality" standard. In other words, as long as there is some *rational relation* between the classification drawn by the legislature and some *legitimate legislative objective*, the classification scheme will not violate the Equal Protection Clause. [256]

   Example: Suppose the Muni City Council, in order to cope with a budget deficit, increases the fares on all city-operated buses from $1 to $2. Statistical evidence shows that 80% of people who ride the Muni bus system on a typical day have incomes below the city-wide median. At the same time the City Council increases the bus fares, it refuses to raise the annual automobile inspection fee; car owners on average have higher-than-median incomes. P, a bus passenger, sues Muni, arguing that it is a violation of his equal protection rights for the city to increase bus fares for the poor while not increasing inspection fees for the affluent.

   A court would apply the "mere-rationality" standard to this regulation, because poverty is not a suspect class, and no fundamental right is at issue here. Since the City Council could rationally have believed that Muni's deficit would be better handled by raising bus fares, and because the Council could rationally have decided to tackle its deficit problem one phase at a time, the constitutional challenge will almost certainly lose.

   a. **Need not be actual objective:**   One thing this "mere-rationality" standard means is that the "legitimate government objective" part of the test is satisfied even if the statute's defenders come up with merely a *"hypothetical"* objective that the legislature "might have" been pursuing. The government does not have to show that the objective it's pointing to was the one that *actually motivated* the legislature. [258-259]

   b. **No empirical link:**   Also, there does not have to in fact be even a "rational relation" between the means chosen and the end — all that's required is that the legislature *"could have rationally believed"* that there was a link between the means and the end.

   c. **Loose fit:**   Finally, a very *loose fit* between means and end will still be O.K.

2. **Conclusion:**   Therefore, if you decide that a particular government classification does not involve a suspect category or a fundamental right, and should thus be subjected to "mere-rationality" review, you should almost always conclude that the classification survives equal protection attack. (But see the discussion of "mere-rationality with bite" immediately below, for an important exception to this rule.)

3. **Review "with bite" for laws motived by "animus" towards the unpopular:**   But if the Court finds that a law has been motivated solely by *"animus"* or *"hostility"* towards a *politically-unpopular group*, the Court has generally been willing to *strike down* such legislation even though only "mere-rationality" review is supposedly being used. In so doing, the Court has said that the *desire to harm an unpopular group* cannot be a *"legitimate governmental objective."* These cases are frequently described as involving mere-rationality review *"with bite,"* i.e., review without the customary *extreme deference* to the legislature that made the challenged classification. [260]

   a. **"Hippies"**   For instance, where the Court found that a federal statute was motivated solely by congressional animus against "hippies," it invalidated the statute. [*U.S. Dep't of Agric. v. Moreno*] [260]

   Example: Congress changes the Food Stamp program to exclude any household that had two or more unrelated members. The Supreme Court later concludes that the change "was intended to *prevent so-called 'hippies' and 'hippie communes' from participating"* in the program.

   Held, this change did not even satisfy mere-rationality review. If equal protection means anything, "it must at the very least mean that *a bare congressional desire to harm a politically unpopular group cannot constitute a legitimate governmental interest."* Therefore, the change here flunks mere-rationality review because it does not meet the requirement of a legitimate governmental interest. [*Moreno, supra.*] [260]

b. Gays and same-sex marriage: Similarly, the Court has been quick to find that legislation disadvantaging *gays* and/or *same-sex marriage* was motivated solely by "animus," and to strike down such legislation even while purporting to use mere-rationality review.

> **Example:** Colorado amends its constitution to prohibit any state or local law that protects homosexuals against discrimination on the basis of their sexual orientation or conduct. *Held*, this amendment violates gays' equal protection rights — it's not even minimally rational, and is motivated solely by animus towards gays. [*Romer v. Evans*] [366]

i. *Windsor* and DOMA: Similarly, the Court invalidated a federal statute (the Defense of Marriage Act, or DOMA) in which Congress defined *marriage* in such a way as to refuse to recognize same-sex marriages entered into under state law. [*U.S. v. Windsor, infra*, p. C-52.] The Court seems to have concluded in *Windsor* that Congress was motivated solely by animus towards gays and same-sex marriage. The case also seems to hold that DOMA did not satisfy even mere-rationality review, though the Court's review of the statute seems to have been conducted "with bite," i.e., with much less than the deference to the legislature that is usually applied in mere-rationality cases. [368]

4. Non-suspect classes: Here is a partial list of classifications that have been held *not* to involve a suspect or quasi-suspect class:

a. Age: Classifications based on *age*.

> **Example:** Suppose that a state requires all state troopers over 50 to retire, in order preserve a physically fit police force. Because age is not a suspect or quasi-suspect classification, the "mere-rationality" test will be used. Because there is some slight overall relation between age and fitness, this requirement is satisfied, so the retirement rule does not violate equal protection. [*Mass. Board of Retirement v. Murgia*] [263]

b. Wealth: Classifications based upon *wealth*.

> **Example:** Suppose that a state provides that no low-income housing project may be built in any community unless a majority of the voters approve it in a popular referendum. A resident who would like to live in the low-income housing that would be built if allowed challenges the statute on equal protection grounds. Even if P shows that the statute was motivated by a desire to discriminate against the poor, P's constitutional challenge will probably fail. Because wealth is not a suspect or quasi-suspect class, the court will use "mere-rationality" review, and will uphold the statute if it finds that the legislature could reasonably have believed that its statute might help achieve some legitimate state objective, perhaps letting communities avoid the greater governmental cost that arguably accompanies concentrations of low-income residents.

c. Mental condition: Classifications based upon *mental illness* or *mental retardation*.

> **Example:** A city makes it harder for group homes for the mentally retarded to achieve zoning permission than for other group living arrangements to do so. This classification, based upon mental status, will not be treated as suspect or quasi-suspect, and will thus be subject only to "mere-rationality" review. (However, such a zoning procedure was found to violate even "mere-rationality," in [*City of Cleburne v. Cleburne Living Center*].)

d. Sexual orientation: Classifications based on *sexual orientation.* Thus governments, at least historically, have faced only mere-rationality review when they have treated *homosexuals* differently from heterosexuals. (But as noted *supra*, the Court now seems to apply mere-rationality review *"with bite"* to what it perceives as anti-gay legislation, even though gays still don't have suspect or semi-suspect status. [260])

III. SUSPECT CLASSIFICATIONS, ESPECIALLY RACE

A. Suspect classifications: At the other end of the spectrum, we apply *strict scrutiny* for any classification that involves a *"suspect class."* [265]

    1. Race and national origin: There are only three suspect classes generally recognized by the Supreme Court: (1) *race*; (2) *national origin*; and (3) for some purposes, *alienage*. So be on the lookout for a classification based on race, national origin, or alienage. For other classifications, you can safely assume that these are not suspect. [265]

    2. Purposeful: One of the most important things to remember about strict scrutiny of suspect classifications is that this strict scrutiny will only be applied where the differential treatment of the class is *intentional* on the part of the government. If the government enacts a statute or regulation that merely has the unintended incidental *effect* of burdening, say, African Americans worse than whites, the court will *not* use strict scrutiny. [*Washington v. Davis*] *This is probably the most frequently-tested aspect of suspect classifications.* [266-271]

        Example: Suppose a city gives a standardized test to all applicants for the local police force. The city and the test designers do not intend to make it harder for African Americans than for whites to pass the test. But it turns out that a lot fewer African Americans pass than whites, even though the applicant pools otherwise seem identical. This differential will not trigger strict scrutiny, because the government did not intend to treat African Americans differently from whites.

        a. Circumstantial evidence: However, remember that an intent to classify based on a suspect class can be proven by *circumstantial*, not just direct, evidence. For instance, if a particular police force picks new officers based on a personal interview conducted by the police chief, and over five years it turns out that only 1% of African American applicants receive jobs but 25% of whites do (and there is no apparent objective difference in the black versus white applicant pools), this statistical disparity could furnish circumstantial evidence of purposeful discrimination, which would then allow a court to apply strict scrutiny to the selection procedures.

    3. Invidious: In addition to the requirement that the discrimination be "purposeful," it must also be *"invidious,"* i.e., based on prejudice or tending to denigrate the disfavored class. This requirement is what has caused race, national origin, and (for some purposes) alienage to be the only suspect classes — these involve the only minorities against whom *popular prejudice is sufficiently deep.* [271]

        a. Rationale: Why do we give especially close scrutiny to governmental action that disadvantages very unpopular minorities? Because ordinarily, groups will protect themselves through use of the *political process*, but: (1) these particular groups don't usually have very much political power, because the past discrimination against them has included keeping them out of the voting system; and (2) even if the minority votes in proportion to its numbers, the majority is very likely to vote as a block against it, because of the minority's extreme unpopularity.

        b. "Discrete and insular" minority: A famous phrase to express this concept, from a footnote in a Supreme Court opinion, is *"discrete and insular minorities"* — discrete and insular minorities are ones that are so disfavored and out of the political mainstream that the courts must make extra efforts to protect them, because the political system won't. [271]

    c. Traits showing suspectness: Here are some traits which probably make it more likely that a court will find that a particular class is suspect:

        i. Immutability: If the class is based on an ***immutable*** or unchangeable trait, this makes a finding of suspectness more likely. Race and national origin qualify; wealth does not. The idea seems to be that if you can't change the trait, it's especially unfair to have it be the basis of discrimination. [271]

        ii. Stereotypes: If the class or trait is one as to which there's a prevalence of false and disparaging ***stereotypes***, this makes a finding of suspectness more likely. Again, race, national origin and alienage seem to qualify, at least somewhat better than, say, wealth. [272]

        iii. Political powerlessness: If the class is ***politically powerless***, or has been subjected to ***widespread discrimination*** (especially official discrimination) historically, this makes it more likely to be suspect.

    d. "Separate but equal" as invidious: Even if a classification involves a group that has frequently been discriminated against, the classification's defenders may argue that their particular use of the classification is not "invidious" because it's not intended to disadvantage the class. ***Affirmative action*** is one example where this argument might be raised. Another context in which the requirement that the discrimination be "invidious" arises is the ***"separate but equal"*** situation; in this context, the defenders of the classification claim that although both classes are treated differently, the unpopular class is being treated no "worse." In general, the Court now seems to hold that discrimination based on race or national origin is ***"per se" invidious***; for instance, the argument that the races are being treated "separately but equally" will almost never serve as a successful defense to an Equal Protection problem. [274]

    Example: Virginia forbids interracial marriage. It claims that blacks aren't disfavored, because whites are blocked from marrying blacks just as much as blacks are blocked from marrying whites. *Held*, the statute's legislative history shows that it was enacted to protect the "racial purity" of whites, so the classification is invidious and violates Equal Protection. [*Loving v. Virginia*]

4. Strict equals fatal: Once the court does decide that a suspect classification is involved, and that strict scrutiny must be used, that scrutiny is almost always ***fatal*** to the classification scheme. For instance, no purposeful racial or ethnic classification has survived strict scrutiny since 1944. [273]

    a. "Necessary" prong: Sometimes, this is because the state cannot show that it is pursuing a "compelling" objective. But more often, it's because the means chosen is not shown to be ***"necessary"*** to achieve that compelling objective. A means is only "necessary" for achieving the particular objective if there are ***no less discriminatory alternatives*** that will accomplish the goal as well, or almost as well.

    Example: Suppose Pearl Harbor occurred today, and the U.S. government once again put any citizen of Japanese ancestry into an internment camp. Presumably this would not be a "necessary" means of dealing with the danger of treason and sabotage, because less discriminatory alternatives like frequent document inspections and/or loyalty oaths would be almost as effective as virtual imprisonment.

5. Some examples: Here are two contexts in which claims have been made (and in most instances accepted) that a suspect class has been intentionally discriminated against in violation of Equal Protection:

    a. Child custody and adoption: Some notion of "racial compatibility" or "racial purity" may motivate state officials to differentiate based on race in ***child custody*** and ***adoption*** proceedings. In general, the practical rule is that the state may not impose flat rules that handle child custody and adoption differently based solely on the race of the child and parents. [276]

Example: Mother and Father are divorced, and Mother is given custody of Child. All are white. Mother then marries Husband, who is African American. The family court transfers custody to Father, on the grounds that Child will be socially stigmatized if she grows up in an interracial family. *Held*, this custody decision can't survive strict scrutiny — government may not bow to private racial prejudices. [*Palmore v. Sidoti*]

    b. Political process: Actions taken by government that relate to the ***political process***, and that are intended to disadvantage racial or ethnic minorities, often run afoul of Equal Protection. [275]

Example: A state requires that in every election, each candidate's race must appear on the ballot. *Held*, this violates Equal Protection because it was motivated by a desire to keep African Americans out of office. [*Anderson v. Martin*]

6. Segregation: The clearest example of a classification involving a suspect class and thus requiring strict scrutiny is ***segregation***, the maintenance of physical separation between the races.

    a. General rule: Official, intentional segregation based on race or national origin is a violation of the Equal Protection Clause. As the result of *Brown v. Board of Education*, even if the government were to maintain truly "separate but equal" facilities (in the sense that, say, a school for blacks had as nice a building, as qualified teachers, etc., as a school for whites), the intentional maintenance of separate facilities ***per se*** violates the Equal Protection Clause. [277-280]

    b. Education and housing: The two areas where official segregation is most often found are ***education*** and ***housing***.

        i. Education: Thus if a school board establishes attendance zones for the purpose of making one school heavily African American and/or Hispanic, and another school heavily white, this would violate Equal Protection.

        ii. Housing: Similarly, government may not intentionally segregate in housing. For example, it's a violation of Equal Protection for a city to do its ***zoning*** in such a way that all ***government-subsidized housing*** is built in the heavily black part of town, if the intent of this zoning practice is to maintain racial segregation.

    c. Must be *de jure*: But it's critical to remember that there is a violation of equal protection only where the segregation is the result of ***intentional government action***. In other words, the segregation must be ***"de jure,"*** not merely ***"de facto."*** [280]

Example: School district lines are drawn by officials who have no desire to separate students based on race. Over time, due to housing choices made by private individuals, one district becomes fully African American, and the other all-white. Even though the schools are no longer racially balanced, there has been no equal protection violation, because there was no act of intentional separation on the part of the government. *Cf. Bd. of Ed. v. Dowell*. [281]

    d. Wide remedies: If a court finds that there has been intentional segregation, it has a wide range of ***remedies*** to choose from. For instance, it can bus students to a non-neighborhood school, or order the redrawing of district boundaries. But whatever remedy the court chooses, the remedy must ***stop*** once the effects of the original intentional discrimination have been eradicated. (Then, if because of housing patterns or other non-government action, the schools become resegregated, the court may ***not*** reinstitute its remedies.)

IV. RACE-CONSCIOUS AFFIRMATIVE ACTION

A. Race-conscious affirmative action: You're more likely to get an exam question about race-conscious *affirmative action* than about official discrimination against racial minorities. If you see a question in which government is trying to help racial or ethnic minorities by giving them some sort of preference, you should immediately think "equal protection" and you should think "strict scrutiny." [285]

1. Public entity: Be sure to remember that there can only be a violation of equal protection if there's *state action*, that is, action by the federal government or by a state or municipality. In general, the use of affirmative action by private entities does *not* raise any constitutional issue (except perhaps where a judge orders a private employer to implement a race-conscious plan). But any time you have a fact pattern in which a police department, school district, public university, or other governmental entity seems to be intentionally preferring one racial group over another, that's when you know you have a potential equal protection problem.

2. Strict scrutiny: It is now the case that *any affirmative action program that classifies on the basis of race will be strictly scrutinized.* [*Richmond v. Croson*] So a race-conscious affirmative action plan, whether it's in the area of employment, college admissions, voting rights or anywhere else, must be adopted for the purpose of furthering some "compelling" governmental interest, and the racial classification must be "necessary" to achieve that compelling governmental interest. [290]

    a. Past discrimination: Since a race-conscious affirmative action plan will have to be in pursuit of a "compelling" governmental interest, probably the only interests that are likely to qualify are: (1) the government's interest in *redressing past discrimination*; and (2) a *university's* interest in *student-body diversity*. So if the government is merely trying to get a *racially-balanced work force*, to make African Americans *more economically successful*, or any other objective that is not closely tied to one of these two objectives, you should immediately be able to say, "The government interest is not compelling, and the measure flunks the strict scrutiny test." [290-291]

    b. Clear evidence: Even if the government's trying to redress past discrimination, there's got to be *clear evidence* that this discrimination in fact occurred.

        i. Societal discrimination: Redressing past discrimination "*by society* as a whole" will *not* suffice. There must be past discrimination closely related to the problem, typically discrimination *by government*. [291]

    c. Quotas: One device that is especially vulnerable to Equal Protection attack is the racially-based *quota*. A racially-based quota is an inflexible number of admissions slots, dollar amounts, or other "goodies" set aside for minorities. For instance, it's a quota if the state says that 1/2 of all new hires in the police department must be African American, or if it says that 20% of all seats in the public university's law school class will be set aside for African Americans and Hispanics. Probably *virtually all racially-based quotas will be struck down even where the government is trying to eradicate the effects of past discrimination* — the Court will probably say that a quota is not "necessary" to remedy discrimination, because more flexible "goals" can do the job. [291]

    d. Congress: It doesn't make any (or at least much) difference that the affirmation action program was enacted by *Congress* rather than by a state or local government. Here, too, the Court will apply strict scrutiny if the program is race-conscious. [*Adarand Constructors, Inc. v. Pena*].

    i. **Possibly greater deference:** However, the Court might give slightly greater *deference* to a congressional finding that official discrimination had existed in a particular domain, or that a particular race-conscious remedy was required, than it would to a comparable finding by a state or local government. (We don't know yet whether this greater deference would occur.)

B. **Preferential admissions in higher education:** Any scheme which gives a preference to one racial group for *admission* to a *public university* must be *strictly scrutinized*. However, such preferences will not necessarily be *invalidated* as the result of this strict scrutiny.

    1. **Main principles:** Here are what seem to be the main principles governing affirmative action in public-university admissions, as the result of two 2003 cases involving the University of Michigan and one 2013 case involving the University of Texas: [293]

        [a] Race-conscious admissions measures will *receive strict scrutiny*, and thus must be narrowly-tailored to achieve a compelling objective.

        [b] The pursuit of *"educational diversity" in the student body* can be a *compelling objective*. (But mere *"racial balancing,"* in which the sole object is to make the student body reflect the percentage of racial or ethnic minorities in some other population, like the state's body of just-graduating high school seniors, is *not* a compelling objective.)

        [c] A *one-student-at-a-time evaluation* in which the student's race is merely one factor among various ones considered may well be *sufficiently narrowly-tailored* to achieving the goal of having an "educationally diverse" student body.

        [d] Mechanical approaches resembling *quotas*, such as automatically awarding an applicant a fixed number of *points* towards admission based on his race, are *not narrowly-tailored* and therefore violate equal protection.

        [e] Even where a race-conscious method is not quota-like, the court will find the method to be sufficiently narrowly-tailored to the achievement of educational diversity *only* if the university carries the burden of showing that *"no workable race-neutral alternatives"* would achieve the educational benefits of diversity *as well or "about as well"* as the race-conscious method actually chosen.

        [f] In deciding whether the university has carried its burden of showing that its race-conscious admissions scheme is narrowly tailored (in [e] above), the university is *not entitled to any judicial deference* to its conclusion that there were "no workable race-neutral alternatives." That is, the court must examine *from scratch* what plausible race-neutral methods of selecting a class existed for that university, and whether these methods would have been administratively workable (e.g., cost-effective) and would have achieved the same, or almost the same, "educational diversity."

    2. **Three key cases:** Here is a brief summary of the three key Supreme Court cases on race-conscious university admissions policies, and of how each illustrates one or more of the above six principles.

        a. **Illustration of valid plan:** The following case illustrates principles [a], [b] and [c] above (plan is *upheld* despite strict scrutiny, because it pursues the compelling goal of educational diversity, and does so in a sufficiently narrowly-tailored way):

        Example (valid plan): The University of Michigan Law School evaluates each applicant's entire file, weighing such variables as undergraduate GPA, LSAT scores, and the contribution the applicant will make to diversity in the student body. The school treats as a major "plus" factor an applicant's membership in one of three historically-discriminated-against groups, blacks, Hispanics and Native Americans. The school does so to create a "critical mass" of these minority students, so that they will participate without feeling isolated.

Held (by a 5-4 vote), this form of affirmative-action is constitutional. The interest in a diverse student body is a compelling one, and the approach here — in that it relies on an individualized, non-mechanical evaluation of each applicant — is narrowly tailored to achieve that interest. [*Grutter v. Bollinger*] [295]

Note: It's not certain that *Grutter* would be decided the same way today, now that Justice O'Connor (who voted with the majority there) has been replaced by Alito (who is far more hostile to race-conscious government action in the name of affirmative action). At the least, *Fisher v. Univ. of Texas*, discussed *infra* in Par. (c), shows that if the plan upheld in *Grutter* were before the present Court, the University of Michigan Law School would bear a heavy burden of showing that there were "no workable race-neutral alternatives" available to it, a burden which the *Grutter* Court recited but seems not to have rigorously applied.

b. Illustration of invalid plan: The following case illustrates principles [a], [b], and [d] above (plan is *invalidated* after strict scrutiny; although it pursues the compelling goal of educational diversity, it does not do so in a sufficiently narrowly-tailored way, because it is a mechanical approach resembling a quota):

Example (invalid plan): The University of Michigan undergraduate college awards pre-measured "points" to applicants for various attributes (e.g., up to 5 points for being an outstanding artist or student leader). Every black or Hispanic applicant automatically gets 20 points for diversity. 100 points are needed for admission. The extra 20 points for minority-group status has the effect that virtually every minimally-qualified black or Hispanic applicant is admitted, whereas many well-qualified non-minority applicants are rejected.

Held (by 6-3), this form of affirmative action is unconstitutional, because it is not narrowly-tailored to the achievement of the compelling interest in student-body diversity. The scheme here is a mechanical one that is equivalent to a quota, not an individualized-evaluation scheme like the one approved in *Grutter, supra*. And the fact that "near-misses" can be flagged for individualized review does not save the scheme. [*Gratz v. Bollinger*] [298]

c. Illustration of narrow-tailoring requirement: The following case (which is more recent than the above two) illustrates principles [a], [b], [e] and [f] (plan *remanded* for strict scrutiny to be applied again to it; although the plan pursues the compelling goal of educational diversity, the university must show that there were "no workable race-neutral alternatives," and the university will not be entitled to any deference from the court on the issue of whether such alternatives existed):

Example: The University of Texas reserves about 75% of its admissions slots for a race-neutral "Top Ten Percent" program, under which any student who finishes in the top 10% of her in-state public high school class is guaranteed admission. The remaining 25% of slots are then filled by the use of a "holistic review" method, which has recently been modified so that race and ethnicity (particularly being black or Hispanic) will be expressly considered as a plus factor, but is just one factor among many. The University decides to use add race-consciousness to its pre-existing holistic method because "seminar" classes at the school (i.e., those containing between five and 24 students) rarely contain a "critical mass" of black and Hispanic students. P, who is white, narrowly misses qualifying under either program. She sues the University, claiming that its use of race in the holistic method prevented her from gaining admission under that method, and violated her equal protection rights. The lower courts reject her claim, while giving great deference to the University's conclusion that the plan's race-conscious aspect is the only feasible way to bring about the compelling goal of educational diversity in the entering case.

Held, case remanded for the lower courts to re-apply strict scrutiny. The University must bear the burden of proving that race-consciousness is ***"necessary"*** for achieving the educational diversity that's being sought. Strict scrutiny "require[s the] court to examine with care, and ***not defer to***, a university's 'serious, good faith consideration of ***workable race-neutral alternatives.***'" If a race-neutral approach could promote the interest in diversity even "about as well" as the selected race-conscious method, and would do so "at tolerable administrative expense," then the university may not consider race. [*Fisher v. Univ. of Texas* (2013)] [300]

Note: Fisher seems to mean that courts' determination of whether the means-end fit is sufficiently tight in admissions cases will be very ***context-specific*** — the same race-conscious plan might pass muster in one university, program or state and not in another. For instance, on remand in *Fisher* itself, the apparent-workability of the Top Ten Percent plan in filling 75% of the U. Texas class (workable mainly because of Texas' heavily racially-segregated public high schools) would likely work *against* the University, whereas such a race-neutral plan might be found *not* "workable" in another context (e.g., in an undergraduate program in a state with less-segregated public high schools, or in a graduate or professional program). [304]

C. Other affirmative action contexts:

    1. Admissions to public schools by race-conscious means: *No individual student's race may be considered in making that student's public high-school or elementary school assignment,* if the district is not combating prior official segregation. ***Parents Involved in Community Schools v. Seattle School District No. 1*** (2007). [306]

        Example: The Seattle school system adopts a "tiebreaker" plan for allocating spaces to incoming ninth graders who want to attend certain racially-imbalanced oversubscribed high schools. One of the tiebreakers is that as between a white and nonwhite student seeking admission to the same oversubscribed high school, the one who will lessen the target school's degree of racial imbalance (compared with district-wide percentages) will get the slot. Thus a black student will be selected over a white student if the target school already has a materially higher percentage of white students in it than the overall district white percentage. Seattle has never been found to have officially practiced school segregation; racial imbalance in the target schools schools is due to racially-imbalanced residential housing patterns.

        Held, the race-conscious plan here must be strictly scrutinized, and will be struck down. Five members of the Court believe that it is not narrowly-tailored to meet any governmental objective. The decisive fifth member of the Court (Kennedy) believes that reducing school-by-school racial imbalance and increasing diversity in the student population are compelling governmental interests, but that the plan here — based on labelling each student as "white" or "non-white" — is not necessary to achieve those interests, because the district has not shown that methods not involving the "crude" binary racial classification of each students (e.g., race-conscious drawing of school-attendance zones) cannot adequately achieve these same objectives. *Parents Involved in Community Schools v. Seattle School District No. 1, supra.*

    2. Minority set-asides: *Minority set-asides*, by which some percentage of publicly-funded contracts are reserved for minority-owned businesses, will be subjected to scrutiny and generally struck down. That's true whether the set-aside is enacted by Congress or by a state/local government. [313-323]

    3. Employment: Anytime a public ***employer*** gives an intentional preference to one racial group, strict scrutiny will probably be called for. [323]

        a. Layoffs: If the employer intentionally prefers blacks over whites when it administers ***layoffs***, that preference will almost certainly be unconstitutional. [*Wygant v. Jackson Bd. of Ed.*] [325]

        b. Hiring: A racial preference in ***hiring*** is almost as hard to justify (though it might pass muster if that particular public employer had clearly discriminated against African Americans in the past, and there seemed to be no way short of a racial preference in hiring to redress that past discrimination).

   c. **Promotions:** A race-based scheme of awarding *promotions* to cure past discrimination (so that African Americans eventually get promoted to the levels that they would have been at had there not been any discrimination in the first place) is the easiest to justify, since it damages the expectations of whites the least. But even this will have to satisfy strict scrutiny. [326]

4. **Drawing of election districts:** A *voter* who thinks she has been disadvantaged by the drawing of *electoral districts* in a race-conscious (or other "group-conscious") way may bring an equal protection suit against the government body that drew the district lines. But the plaintiff must show either: (1) that the lines were drawn with the *purpose* and *effect* of *disadvantaging the group* of which P is a part; or (2) that *race* was the *"predominant factor"* in how the district lines were drawn. [326-331]

   a. **"Partisan gerrymander" claims almost impossible to win:** The first of these types of claims — "my group has been systematically disadvantaged" — is used to attack *"partisan gerrymanders,"* gerrymanders based on political factors rather than racial factors. These claims are *almost impossible to win.* [*Vieth v. Jubelirer*] [328-328]

      i.   **Lack of political power over many elections:** For one thing, the mere fact that in one or two election cycles the plaintiff group does not get nearly the same percentage of seats as it has of the total electorate can never by itself suffice to win an Equal Protection challenge to a partisan gerrymander. At the very least, the Ps must show that they lack political power, and have been *fenced out of the political process*, over *many elections.*

      ii. **Never successful:** *No partisan-gerrymander claim has ever succeeded.* See, e.g., *League of United Latin Amer. Citizens v. Perry*, where a congressional-district gerrymander was upheld even though the lower court found (and the Supreme Court agreed) that "the single-minded purpose of the [party ruling the state legislature] in enacting the [gerrymander] was to *gain partisan advantage."* [328]

   b. **Race as predominant factor:** But the second type of attack — "race was the predominant factor in drawing district lines" — has a *much better chance of success.* If the court concludes that *race* was indeed the *predominate factor* in how the electoral district lines were drawn, the court will *strictly scrutinize* the lines, and probably strike them down. Legislatures may "take account" of race in drawing district lines (just as they take account of ethnic groups, precinct lines, and many other factors), but they may not make race the predominant factor, unless they can show that using race in this way is necessary to achieve a compelling governmental interest (e.g., eradication of prior official voting-rights discrimination). The desire to create the maximum number of "majority black" districts will not by itself be a "compelling" interest. [*Miller v. Johnson*] [331]

5. **Law enforcement and other operational areas:** Even where government's own *operational needs* are arguably aided by a race-conscious policy, the Court will strictly scrutinize this use of race. Thus race-conscious government decisions in such operational areas as *law enforcement, prison administration* and the *military* will be strictly scrutinized.

   Example: A state prison system racially segregates new prisoners in cell assignments, believing that this cuts down on gang-related violence. *Held*, the race-conscious policy must be strictly scrutinized, even though the state believes that its policy does not prefer one race over another. [*Johnson v. California*] [333]

V. MIDDLE-LEVEL REVIEW (GENDER, ILLEGITIMACY AND ALIENAGE)

A. Middle-level review generally: A few types of classifications are subjected to "middle-level" review, easier to satisfy than strict scrutiny but tougher than "mere-rationality" review. [335]

    1. Standard: Where we apply the middle-level standard, the government objective must be *"important,"* and the means must be *"substantially related"* to that objective.

        a. No hypothetical objective: One important respect in which mid-level review differs from "mere-rationality" review concerns the state *objectives* that the Court will consider. Recall that in the case of the easy "mere-rationality" review, the Court will consider virtually *any objective that might have conceivably motivated* the legislature, regardless of whether there's any evidence that that objective was in fact in the legislature's mind. But with "intermediate-level" review, the Court will *not* hypothesize objectives; it will consider only those objectives that are shown to have *actually motivated the legislature.*

    2. What classes: There are two main types of classifications that get middle-level review: (1) *gender*; and (2) *illegitimacy*. We also consider *alienage* here, because it has aspects of both strict scrutiny and mere-rationality review, so it's kind of a hybrid.

B. Gender: The most important single rule to remember in the entire area of middle-level scrutiny is that *sex-based classifications get middle-level review.* [*Craig v. Boren*] So if government intentionally classifies on the basis of sex, it's got to show that it's pursuing an important objective, and that the sex-based classification scheme is substantially related to that objective. [336-337]

> **Example:** City sets the mandatory retirement age for male public school teachers at 65, and for female teachers at 62. Because this classification is based upon gender, it must satisfy middle-level review: City must show that its sex-based classification is substantially related to the achievement of an important governmental objective. In this case, it is unlikely that City can make this showing.

    1. Benign as well as invidious: The same standard of review is used whether the sex-based classification is *"invidious"* (intended to harm women) or *"benign"* (intended to help women, or even intended to redress past discrimination against them). [271]

    2. Male or female plaintiff: This means that where government classifies based on sex, the scheme can be attacked either by a *male* or by a *female*, and either gender will get the benefit of mid-level review.

> **Example:** Oklahoma forbids the sale of low-alcohol beer to males under the age of 21, and to females under the age of 18. *Held*, this statute violates the equal protection rights of males aged 18 to 20, because it is not substantially related to the achievement of important governmental objectives. [*Craig v. Boren*] [336-337]

    3. Purpose: Sex-based classifications will only be subjected to middle-level review if the legislature has *intentionally* discriminated against one sex in favor of the other. (This is similar to the requirement for strict scrutiny in race-based cases.) If, as the result of some governmental act, one sex happens to suffer an *unintended burden* greater than the other sex suffers, that's not enough for mid-level review.

> **Example:** Massachusetts gives an absolute preference to veterans for civil service jobs. It happens that 98% of veterans are male. *Held*, this preference does not have to satisfy mid-level review because the unfavorable impact on women was not intended by the legislature. Therefore, the preference does not violate equal protection, since it satisfies the easier "mere-rationality" standard. [*Personnel Admin. of Mass. v. Feeney*]

4. **Stereotypes:** Be on the lookout for *stereotypes*: if the legislature has made a sex-based classification that seems to reinforce stereotypes about the "proper place" of women, it probably cannot survive middle-level review. (*Example:* Virginia maintains Virginia Military Institute as an all-male college, because of the state's view that only men can handle the school's harsh, militaristic method of producing "citizen soldiers." *Held*, this sex-based scheme does not satisfy mid-level review, because it stems from traditional ways of thinking about gender roles; there are clearly *some* women who are qualified for and would benefit from the VMI approach, and these women may not be deprived of the opportunity to attend VMI. [*U.S. v. Virginia*]) [339-342]

5. **"Exceedingly persuasive justification":** Although the Supreme Court still gives gender-based classifications only mid-level, not strict, scrutiny, the Court now applies that scrutiny in a very tough way. The Court now says that it will require an *"exceedingly persuasive justification"* for any gender-based classification, and will review it with *"skeptical scrutiny."* [*U.S. v. Virginia, supra.*] [335]

C. **Illegitimacy:** Classifications disadvantaging *illegitimate children* are "semi-suspect" and therefore get middle-level review. [359]

1. **Claims can't be flatly barred:** Therefore, the state can't simply bar unacknowledged illegitimate children from bringing wrongful death actions, from having any chance to inherit, etc. Such children must be given at least *some reasonable opportunity* to obtain a *judicial declaration of paternity* (e.g., in a suit brought by their mother). Once they obtain such a declaration, they must be *treated equivalently to children born legitimate.*

   > **Example:** Pennsylvania passes a statute of limitations saying that no action for child support may be brought on behalf of an out-of-wedlock child unless the action is brought before the child turns 6. *Held*, the statute violates the child's equal protection rights. Since the classification is based on out-of-wedlock status, it will be upheld only if it is substantially related to an important governmental objective. Concededly, Pennsylvania has an interest in avoiding the litigation of stale or fraudulent claims. But the 6-year statute of limitations is not "substantially related" to the achievement of that interest. [*Clark v. Jeter*]

D. **Alienage:** Alienage might be thought of as a "semi-suspect" category. In fact, though, alienage classifications, depending on the circumstances, will be subjected either to *strict scrutiny* or to *mere-rationality* review (so there's only middle-level review as a kind of "average").

1. **Distinguished from national origin:** Be careful to distinguish "alienage" from "national origin": if a person is discriminated against because he is *not yet a United States citizen,* that's "alienage" discrimination. If, on the other hand, he's discriminated against because he is a naturalized citizen who originally came from Mexico (or whose ancestors came from Mexico), that's discrimination based on "national origin." Remember that national origin always triggers strict scrutiny, whereas alienage does not necessarily do so.

2. **General rule:** Subject to one large exception covered below, discrimination against aliens is subject to *strict scrutiny*. [354]

   > **Example 1:** A state cannot deny welfare benefits to aliens, because such a classification based on alienage cannot be shown to be necessary to the achievement of a compelling state interest. [*Graham v. Richardson*]

   > **Example 2:** A state cannot prevent resident aliens from practicing law, because such a classification cannot survive strict scrutiny. [*In re Griffiths*]

3. **"Representative government" exception:** But the major exception is that strict scrutiny does not apply where the discrimination against aliens relates to a *"function at the heart of representative government."* Basically, this means that if the alien is applying for a *government job*, and the performance of this job is *closely tied in with politics, justice or public policy*, we use only *"mere-rationality"* review. So government may discriminate against aliens with respect to posts like *state trooper*, *public school teacher*, or *probation officer*. See, e.g., [*Ambach v. Norwick*]. [355]

     a. **Low-level government jobs:** But don't make the mistake of thinking that because what's involved is a government job, strict scrutiny automatically fails to apply. If the job is *not* closely tied in with politics, justice or public policy — something that is true of most *low-level jobs* — then strict scrutiny applies.

     Example: Strict scrutiny would almost certainly be applied to a city ordinance that said that no resident alien may work for the city government as a sanitation worker.

4. **Education of illegal aliens:** A last quirky rule in the area of alienage is that if a state denies *free public education* to *illegal aliens*, this will be subjected to intermediate-level review, and probably struck down. [*Plyler v. Doe*] (But this comes from a combination of the fact that the plaintiffs were aliens and also that they were children. If a state discriminates against *adult* illegal aliens, we don't know whether something higher than middle-level review will be applied.) [356-359]

E. **Other unpopular groups:** Discrimination against *other unpopular groups* might conceivably be subjected to middle-level review. For instance, discrimination against the *elderly* or the *disabled* might possibly trigger mid-level review, but the Court has not addressed this question. (This would be a good gray area for an exam question — you could argue both the pros and the cons of applying mid-level review to these unpopular, frequently-discriminated-against groups.)

F. **Congressional affirmative action plans:** Finally, remember that there's one other area where the Court uses mid-level review: affirmative action programs established by *Congress*.

VI. UNEQUAL TREATMENT OF GAYS, AND THE BANNING OF SAME-SEX MARRIAGE — ENHANCED "MERE-RATIONALITY" REVIEW

A. **Sexual orientation classifications generally:** The Court has decided *three cases* since 1996 in which legislatures seemed to classify based on *sexual orientation*. Two of the three have been basically equal protection cases. In those cases, the Court has been *unwilling* to treat classifications that are based on sexual orientation — and that seemed to have the purpose of disadvantaging gays — as having official *"semi-suspect"* or *"suspect"* status.

1. **Mere-rationality review:** Therefore, when the Court hears a challenge to a classification based on sexual orientation, the Court purports to use easy-to-satisfy *"mere-rationality"* review, not mid-level review or strict scrutiny.

     a. **Mere-rationality review "with bite":** However, the gay *plaintiffs* have *prevailed* in their constitutional challenge in both of these equal protection cases (as well as in the one substantive due process case, *Lawrence v. Texas*, *supra*, p. C-31). That has occurred, in major part, because although the Court has purported to apply mere-rationality review, it has in fact given *much less deference* to the legislature's sexual-orientation-based classification system than is typically applied in mere-rationality cases. The level of review used can fairly be described as "mere-rationality review *with bite.*"

2. **Animus towards unpopular minority:** A persistent theme in these three decisions has been the majority's conclusion that legislative classifications based on sexual orientation have historically

been *based solely on animus towards a disfavored minority*, and that such animus *cannot be a "legitimate governmental interest."* Therefore, the Court concludes, the classification system fails mere-rationality review because of the lack of a legitimate interest. (See also *supra*, p. C-39, for more about the Court's treatment of legislative actions that seemed to be motivated solely by animus towards disfavored minorities.)

B. Singling out of gays because of animus: In a 1996 case, the Court *struck down* a Colorado state-constitutional amendment that would have *prevented the state or any of its cities from giving certain protections to gays or lesbians*. The Court found that the measure flunked even "mere-rationality" review. [*Romer v. Evans*] [366]

    1. Rationale: The majority concluded that the Colorado amendment was "inexplicable by anything but *animus toward the class that it affects*" (gays and lesbians). And, the majority said, "a *bare ... desire to harm a politically unpopular group cannot constitute a legitimate governmental interest.*" The lack of a legitimate governmental objective meant that the amendment was a violation of equal protection, even though the Court used only mere-rationality review.

C. Same-sex marriage: The biggest debate in the area of gay rights currently is whether and when gay and lesbian couples have a constitutional right to *enter into same-sex marriages*.

    1. *Windsor* case: So far, the Supreme Court has decided only one case relating to same-sex marriage, *U.S. v. Windsor* (2013). There, the Court decided that *when a same-sex couple has been married under the law of a state*, the federal government *may not treat the couple any differently* than it would treat a *heterosexual couple* married under that same state's law. [368]

        a. DOMA statute: The *Windsor* decision invalidated, apparently mainly on equal protection grounds, part of a 1996 federal statute called the *Defense of Marriage Act* (DOMA). The part of DOMA at issue said that the federal government *didn't have to recognize a same-sex couple as being married* — even if they were married under state law — for purposes of any *federal benefits* or *regulations*. The facts and holdings are set forth in the following example.

        Example: Two women, Windsor and Spyer, are a gay couple who have lived together for decades in New York City. At the time Spyer dies in 2009, New York views the two women as married under New York law (on account of a marriage they entered into in Canada while living in New York). Under the federal estate tax's "marital exemption," when one married spouse dies, any property left to the other passes free of estate tax. But DOMA, by preventing the federal government from recognizing any same-sex couple as being married, deprives Spyer's estate of the deduction, costing the estate (and therefore Windsor as beneficiary) a large amount of tax. Windsor sues the federal government, contending that DOMA violates her equal protection and due process rights.

        Held (5-4), for Windsor. The federal government has a long tradition of "recognizing and accepting state definitions of marriage[.]" DOMA is an "unusual deviation" from this tradition. This unusual deviation is "strong evidence of a law having the purpose and effect of disapproval" of the class of same-sex married couples; the law places "a *stigma*" on every married same-sex couple. The statute's legislative history shows that its purpose was to express "*moral disapproval* of homosexuality[.]" This purpose of injuring and disparaging those whom a state has "sought to protect in personhood and dignity" is *not a legitimate purpose*, and the statute has no other purpose. Therefore, the statute violates equal protection principles, as incorporated into the obligation of due process that the Fifth Amendment imposes on the federal government. [*U.S. v. Windsor, supra.*] [368-378]

        Note: The majority opinion in *Windsor* is ambiguous on a couple of points. First, it's not clear whether the holding is based mainly on equal protection principles or on substantive due process ones; but it's pretty clear that equal protection is at least one of the principles underlying the Court's opinion. Second, it's not clear what ***standard of review*** the majority applied in striking down the DOMA provision. My best guess, based on the majority's language and citations, is that the Court is applying only ***mere-rationality*** review, but that it is doing so ***"with bite,"*** by giving virtually no deference to various objectives (beyond simple anti-gay animus) that did motivate or might have motivated some members of the congressional majority who voted for the statute. [378]

b. **State's right to ban same-sex marriage:** *Windsor* does not decide whether a ***state*** violates equal protection (or for that matter substantive due process) if it ***refuses to allow same-sex marriage.*** As we go to press (August 2013), 34 states have some sort of "mini-DOMA," i.e., either a statutory or state-constitutional provision limiting marriage to opposite-sex couples. The constitutionality of such state laws is almost certain to come before the Court within the next few years. [376]

   i. **Prediction:** My prediction is that if the issue comes before the Court as presently constituted, the five-member *Windsor* majority will decide that ***yes***, a state's refusal to permit same-sex marriage is a ***denial of equal protection*** (and perhaps ***substantive due process*** as well).

      (1) **Rationale:** Here's my rationale for this prediction: The majority concludes that Congress in enacting DOMA was motivated solely by animus towards gays, and that DOMA violates the "personhood and dignity" of gay couples that have actually married. Given this perspective, that same majority is likely to find that any randomly-selected state mini-DOMA that comes before the Court was enacted for similar reasons of animus towards gays, and similarly violates gay couples' "personhood and dignity" by refusing them the same right to marry as the state confers on opposite-sex couples. [376]

      (2) **Justice Scalia's view:** Justice Scalia, in dissent in *Windsor*, makes the same prediction, based on a similar analysis of the majority's reasoning. [376]

VII. FUNDAMENTAL RIGHTS

A. **Fundamental rights generally:** Now, let's look at the second way strict scrutiny can be triggered in equal protection cases: there will be strict scrutiny not only when a "suspect classification" is used, but also when a ***"fundamental right"*** is burdened by the classification the government has selected. Whenever a classification burdens a "fundamental right" or "fundamental interest," the classification will be subjected to strict scrutiny ***even though the people who are burdened are not members of a suspect class.*** [379]

   1. **"Fundamental" defined:** "Fundamental" means something absolutely different in this Equal Protection context than it means in the Substantive Due Process context. Remember that in due process, the fundamental rights are ones related to privacy. Here, the fundamental rights are related to a variety of other interests protected by the Constitution, but generally having nothing to do with privacy. [379]

   2. **List:** The short list of rights that are "fundamental" for equal protection strict scrutiny purposes is as follows: (1) the right to ***vote***; (2) maybe the right to be a ***political candidate***; (3) the right to have access to the ***courts*** for certain kinds of proceedings; and (4) the right to ***migrate interstate.*** [359]

B. **Voting rights:** The right to ***vote*** in state and local elections is "fundamental," so any classification that burdens that substantially burdens right to vote is often strictly scrutinized. [383- 390]

1. **Duration of residence:** This mainly means that if the state imposes a substantial *waiting period* on newly-arrived residents, before they can receive some *vital governmental benefit*, this will be strictly scrutinized.

> **Example:** Pennsylvania denies welfare benefits to any resident who has not resided in the state for at least a year. *Held*, this one-year waiting period impairs the "fundamental right of interstate movement" so it must be strictly scrutinized, and in fact invalidated. [*Shapiro v. Thompson*]. [397-398]

2. **Vital government benefit:** But the key phrase here is *"vital government benefit"* — if the benefit is *not* vital, then the state may impose a substantial waiting period. (*Example:* A one-year waiting period before a student can qualify for low in-state tuition at the public university probably does not burden a fundamental right, and thus does not need to be strictly scrutinized.)

F. Necessities: The right to *"necessities"* is *not* fundamental. So if the state distributes necessities in a way that treats different people differently (or if it distributes the money to be used to buy these things differentially), there will be no strict scrutiny because there is no fundamental right. [399]

1. **Education:** For instance, one does not have a fundamental right to a *public school education*. Therefore, the state may allow or even foster inequalities in the distribution of that public school education, without violating any fundamental right, and thus without having to pass strict scrutiny. [*San Antonio School Dist. v. Rodriguez*] [380-383]

> **Example:** The Ps claim that Texas' system of financing public education violates equal protection, because districts with a high property tax base per pupil consistently spend more on education than those with a low base are able to do.
>
> *Held*, education is not a fundamental right. Therefore, Texas' scheme merely has to undergo "rational relation" review. Because the use of property taxes to finance education is a rational way of achieving the legitimate state goal of giving each local school district a large measure of control over the education its residents get, this "mere-rationality" standard is satisfied. *San Antonio School Dist. v. Rodriguez, supra.*

    a. **Complete deprivation:** Actually, it's still possible that a *complete deprivation* of public education might be held to be a violation of a "fundamental" right. If a state simply refused to give any public education *at all* to some groups of residents, this might be such a large deprivation that it would amount to a violation of a fundamental right, and thus be subject to strict scrutiny. [381]

2. **Food, shelter:** There is no fundamental right to the material *"necessities of life."* Thus *food*, *shelter*, and *medical care* are not "fundamental" for equal protection purposes. Therefore, the state may distribute these things unevenly. Similarly, the state may give some people but not others money for these things without having to survive strict scrutiny. (*Example:* The state can give a smaller per capita welfare payment to big families than small families, without having the scheme subjected to strict scrutiny. This is because the food and shelter for which the payments are used are not "fundamental rights." [*Dandridge v. Williams*]) [399]

CHAPTER 11

MISCELLANEOUS CLAUSES

I. FOURTEENTH AMENDMENT PRIVILEGES OR IMMUNITIES

A. Privileges or Immunities Clause Generally: The Fourteenth Amendment has its own "Privileges or Immunities" Clause: "No state shall make or enforce any law which shall abridge the privileges or immunities of citizens of the United States." [412]

1. **National rights only:** But this clause is very narrowly interpreted: it only protects the individual from state interference with his rights of *"national"* citizenship. The most important of these rights of "national" citizenship are: (1) the right to *travel from state to state* (which as we saw is also protected by the Equal Protection Clause); and (2) the right to *vote in national elections*.

2. **Right to change state of residence:** The clause is most relevant where a state treats *newly-arrived residents less favorably* than those who have resided in-state for a longer time: this violates the "right to travel," protected by the clause. (*Example:* If a state gives newly-arrived residents lower welfare payments than ones who have been residents longer, this is a violation of the "right to travel" protected by the 14th Amendment P&I clause. [*Saenz v. Roe*]) [413]

3. **Strict scrutiny:** The Court gives *strict scrutiny* to state laws that interfere with the rights of national citizenship. [*Saenz v. Roe*]

II. THE "TAKING" CLAUSE

A. **The "Taking" Clause Generally:** The Fifth Amendment contains the "Taking" Clause: *"[N]or shall private property be taken for public use, without just compensation."*

1. **General meaning:** The gist of the Taking Clause is that the government may take private property under its "power of eminent domain," but if it does take private property, it must *pay a fair price*. This is true even if the property is taken to serve a compelling governmental interest. [414]

2. **Taking vs. regulation:** The government (whether it's federal or state) must pay for any property that it "takes." On the other hand, if it merely *"regulates"* property under its police power, then it does not need to pay (even if the owner's use of his property, or its value, is substantially diminished). [415-424]

   a. **Land use regulations:** Usually the problem of distinguishing between a compensable "taking" and a non-compensable "regulation" occurs in the context of *land-use regulation*.

   b. **Guidelines:** Here are some guidelines about when a land-use regulation will avoid being a taking:

      i. **No denial of economically viable use:** A land-use regulation must not "deny an owner *economically viable use* of his land," or it will be considered a taking. However, few land use regulations are likely to be found to deny the owner all economically viable use of his land. For instance, if a particular 3-story building is made a landmark, the fact that the owner can't tear down the building to build a skyscraper doesn't deprive him of "all economically viable use." But if the state were to *permanently* deny the owner the right to *build any dwelling* on the land, this *would* probably constitute a denial of all economically viable use. [416]

      Example: The state of South Carolina, in order to protect against coastal erosion, prohibits landowners from building any permanent habitable structure at all on certain parcels. P owns 2 vacant parcels (for which he paid $1 million), on which the building ban applies. *Held*, by the Supreme Court, if this regulation indeed prevents P from making any "economically viable use" of the parcels (something for the state court to decide on remand), there has been a "taking" for which the state must pay compensation, even if the state was just trying to protect the health and safety of its citizens. [*Lucas v. South Carolina Coastal Council*] [417]

Note 1: Most zoning, environmental laws and landmark-preservation laws will satisfy this don't-deny-all-economically-viable-uses rule, and will thus *not* be takings, merely non-compensable regulations.

Note 2: If a land-use law merely *temporarily* prevents all economically viable use of a parcel, this will not necessarily constitute a taking — *all surrounding circumstances* must be considered to determine whether the interference with use is significant enough to constitute a taking. For instance, a 2- or 3-year *moratorium on development* of a particular parcel, until a permanent land-use scheme can be enacted by government, might not constitute a taking even though for that period an affected owner can't make any economically viable use of her parcel. [*Tahoe-Sierra Preservation Council v. Tahoe Regional Planning Agency*] [417-418]

ii. **Permanent physical occupation:** If the government makes or authorizes a *permanent physical occupation* of the property, this will *automatically* be found to constitute a taking, no matter how minor the interference with the owner's use and no matter how important the countervailing governmental interests. (*Example:* The state requires landlords to permit cable TV companies to install their cable facilities in the landlord's buildings. *Held*, this compulsory cabling was a taking because it was a permanent physical occupation, even though it didn't really restrict the owner's use of his property or reduce its value. [*Loretto v. Teleprompter*]) [415]

iii. **Diminution in value:** The more drastic the *reduction in value* of the owner's property, the more likely a taking is to be found. But a very drastic diminution in value (almost certainly much more than 50%) is required. [416]

iv. **Landmark:** *Landmark preservation schemes*, just like zoning and environmental regulations, will rarely be found to constitute a taking. This is especially true where the designation of a particular building to landmark status occurs as part of a *comprehensive* city-wide preservation scheme. (*Example:* New York City didn't carry out a taking when it designated Grand Central Station as a landmark; this was true even though this designation prevented the owner from constructing a 55-story office building above the Terminal. [*Penn Central v. New York City*]) [420]

3. **Requirement of "public" use:** The Taking Clause says that private property shall not be taken *"for public use"* unless just compensation is paid. This language has been interpreted by the Supreme Court as prohibiting the taking of private property for *private use, even if just compensation is made.* Thus the government cannot simply take private property from one person, and give it to another, without any public purpose.

a. **"Public use" construed broadly:** However, the Supreme Court has construed the requirement of a "public use" quite *broadly*. Here are two principles illustrating just how broadly the Court stretches the phrase:

❏ So long as the state's use of its eminent domain power is *"rationally related* to a *conceivable public purpose,"* the public use requirement is satisfied. *Hawaii Housing Authority v. Midkiff.* [425]

❏ The property *need not be open to the general public after the taking.* Therefore, the fact that the property is *turned over to some private user* does not prevent the use from being a public one as long as the public can be expected to derive some benefit (e.g., economic development) from the use. [425]

Example: The City of New London, as part of an economic-development plan for the City's waterfront area, condemns 15 houses owned by the Ps. The properties are not blighted. The plan contemplates turning the properties over to private developers. The Ps claim that this is not a "public use," and thus violates their rights under the Fifth Amendment even if "just compensation" is paid.

Held, for the City. Even though the properties are being turned over to private developers (not made available to the public), and even though the properties were not blighted, this is still a "public use" as the term is used in the Fifth Amendment. [*Kelo v. New London*] [426]

III. THE "CONTRACT" CLAUSE

A. The "Contract" Clause: The so-called "Contract" Clause (Art. I, §10) provides that "no state shall … pass any … law impairing the obligation of contracts." The clause effectively applies to both federal and state governments. The Clause has a different meaning depending on whether the government is impairing its own contracts or contracts between private parties. [427]

  1. Public contracts: If the state is trying to escape from its *own financial obligations*, then the Court will *closely scrutinize* this attempt. Here, the state attempt to "weasel" will be struck down unless the modification is "*reasonable* and *necessary* to support an *important* public purpose" (basically *middle-level review*). [428]

  2. Private contracts: But when the state is re-writing contracts made by *private parties*, the judicial review is not so stringent. Here, even a *substantial* modification to contracts between private parties will be allowed so long as the state is acting "*reasonably*" in pursuit of a "legitimate public purpose." So we apply what is basically "mere-rationality" review in this situation. (*Example:* If a state's economy is in shambles with widespread home mortgage foreclosures, the state probably may temporarily order a lower interest rate on home mortgages, or impose a moratorium on mortgage repayments, without violating the Contract Clause.) [428-430]

   a. Incidental effect on contracts: Even this "mere-rationality" standard applies only where the state takes an action that is *specifically directed* at contractual obligations. If the state applies a *"generally applicable rule of conduct"* that has the *incidental by-product* of impairing contractual obligations, the Contract Clause *does not apply at all*. [431]

   Example: Suppose Manco, a manufacturing company located outside the state of Texahoma, contracts with Disposal Corp., which operates a toxic waste disposal facility within Texahoma. The contract runs through the year 2100, and allows Manco to deliver up to 1,000 tons of toxic waste per year to the dump. The Texahoma legislature then enacts a statute that, effective immediately, prohibits anyone from disposing of any additional toxic wastes within the state. Even though this enactment has an effect on the Manco-Disposal contract, it does not trigger Contract Clause review at all, because the statute affects contracts as an incidental by-product, rather than being specifically directed at contractual obligations.

IV. THE SECOND AMENDMENT "RIGHT TO BEAR ARMS"

A. Text of the Amendment: The Second Amendment provides: "A well regulated Militia, being necessary to the security of a free State, the right of the people to *keep and bear Arms*, shall *not be infringed*." [432]

B. Applicable to private individuals: The *Amendment* confers on *private individuals* a right to keep basic firearms, including handguns, *at home for self-defense*. [*District of Columbia v. Heller* (2008)] [432]

Example: Washington D.C. makes it a crime to keep any type of handgun at home. It also makes it a crime to keep a non-gun (e.g., a rifle) at home unless the weapon is kept unloaded and inoperable (e.g., by a trigger lock). *Held*, both provisions violate the Second Amendment right of private individuals to keep at home operable firearms of the type that were kept by private citizens for self-defense in 1791. [*Heller, supra.*] [433-437]

1. **Applies to states and cities:** The Second Amendment *applies the same way to state and local governments* as to the federal government. [*McDonald v. City of Chicago*] [437]

   a. **Selectively incorporated:** This result is due to the Supreme Court's conclusion in *McDonald* that the Second Amendment should be deemed to be *selectively incorporated* into the 14th Amendment's *Due Process Clause*, and thereby made applicable to the states. (The Court believed that the right to bear arms in self-defense is "*fundamental to our scheme of ordered liberty*," the test for whether any Bill of Rights guarantee should be deemed incorporated into the 14th Amendment guarantee of due process and thus made applicable to the states.) [437]

2. **Review standard to be used:** It's unclear what *standard* the court will use for reviewing governmental restrictions that impair Second Amendment rights (*Heller* and *McDonald* didn't decide this). The most likely outcome is that *mid-level review*, under which the question is whether the means chosen by government is "*substantially related*" to the achievement of an "*important*" governmental interest, will ultimately be used. [438]

3. **Some regulation allowed:** It seems likely that despite the broad reading of the Second Amendment in *Heller* and *McDonald* , all governments will be allowed to exercise *substantial regulation of gun possession.* So, for example:

   a. **Licensing requirements:** *Licensing requirements* will probably *not* be found to violate the Second Amendment as long as the procedures for obtaining a license are not unreasonably burdensome, and are directed towards keeping guns out of the hands of people who do not have a Second Amendment right to possess them. [439]

      Example: Licensing requirements that deny gun permits to felons and the mentally ill — and that give government a reasonable amount of time to check whether the applicant falls into these categories — are probably valid even after *Heller* and *McDonald*.

   b. **Concealed-carry permits:** Similarly, the Amendment will probably be found not to prohibit governments from banning the *carrying of concealed weapons in public places.* [439]

   c. **Modern weapons:** Probably the Amendment won't be found to block governments from banning the possession of *modern weapons* that are much more *advanced and dangerous* than those existing in 1791. So *machine guns, assault rifles* and *sawed-off shotguns* probably may still be banned. [439]

V. *EX POST FACTO* LAWS

A. **Constitutional prohibition:** Article I prohibits both state and federal governments from passing any "ex post facto" law. An *ex post facto* law is a law which has a *retroactive punitive effect*. So government may not *impose a punishment* for conduct which, at the time it occurred, was *not punishable*. Also, government may not *increase* the punishment for an offense over what was on the books at the time of the act. [440]

   Example: On June 1, Joe smokes a cigarette in a public building. On June 10, the state legislature makes it a crime, for the first time, to smoke in a public building. Because of the ban on *ex post facto* laws, Joe cannot be convicted of the June 1 smoking, since it was not a crime at the time he did it. The same would be true if the legislature on June 15 increased the penalty for such smoking over what it was on June 1.

1. **Criminal only:** The ban on *ex post facto* laws applies only to measures that are *"criminal"* or *"penal,"* not to those that are civil. Basically, this means that only measures calling for *imprisonment* will come within the *ex post facto* ban (so a measure that imposes, say, *disbarment*, or one that imposes *deportation*, can be made retroactive, since these sanctions are civil). See, e.g., *Galvan v. Press*.

VI. BILLS OF ATTAINDER

A. **Generally:** Art. I prohibits both the federal government and the states from passing any *"bill of attainder."* A bill of attainder is a legislative act which "applies either to named individuals or to easily ascertainable members of a group in such a way as to *punish* them without a *judicial trial.*" (*Example:* Congress prohibits the payment of salaries to three named federal agency employees, on the grounds that they are engaged in subversive activities. This is an invalid bill of attainder, since it applies to named or easily-identified individuals, and punishes them without a judicial trial. [*U.S. v. Lovett*]) [441]

CHAPTERS 12 AND 13

THE "STATE ACTION" REQUIREMENT; CONGRESSIONAL ENFORCEMENT OF CIVIL RIGHTS

I. STATE ACTION

A. **State action generally:** Virtually all of the rights and liberties guaranteed by the Constitution to individuals are protected only against interference by the government. We summarize this rule by referring to the requirement of *"state action."* But sometimes, even a *private individual's act* will be found to be "state action" that must comply with the Constitution. There are two main doctrines that may lead a private act to be classified as state action; if *either* of these doctrines applies, then the private action is "state action" even if the other doctrine would not apply. The two doctrines are the *"public function"* doctrine and the *"state involvement"* doctrine. [449-452]

B. **"Public function" doctrine:** Under the *"public function"* approach to state action, if a private individual (or group) is entrusted by the state to perform functions that are *governmental in nature*, the private individual becomes an *agent of the state*, and his acts constitute state action. [453-457]

1. **Political system:** The *electoral process* is a "public function," and is thus state action. Therefore, the carrying out of *primary elections* is state action, even if the acts are directly carried out by "private" political parties. (*Example:* A state convention of Democrats (in essence, a "private" political party) rules that only whites may vote in the Texas Democratic Primary. *Held*, this racial restriction is "state action," and therefore violates the 15th Amendment. The primary is an integral part of the election scheme, and the running of elections is traditionally a "public function," so the running of the primary is state action even though it is directly carried out by private groups. [*Smith v. Allwright*]) [453]

   a. **Company town:** Similarly, operation of a *"company town"* is a "public function," and thus is state action, because towns are usually operated by the government. [453-454]

      i. **Shopping centers not a public function:** But operation of a *shopping center* is *not* the equivalent of operating a company town, so a person does not have any First Amendment rights in the shopping center. [*Hudgens v. NLRB*] [454]

    b. **Parks:** Operation of a ***park*** is usually deemed a governmental function, so generally the operation of a park will constitute "state action" under the "public function" doctrine. Therefore, even if the park is being operated by private persons, it must still obey constitutional constraints (e.g., it can't be operated for whites only). [*Evans v. Newton*]. [455]

2. **The "exclusively public" requirement:** Apparently, the function must be one that traditionally has been ***"exclusively"*** a public function, in order for the "public function" doctrine to apply. [455-457]

    Example: A warehouseman has a warehouseman's lien on goods stored with him, to cover unpaid storage charges. He sells the goods pursuant to the warehouseman's lien, and the owner claims that due process was required because the resolution of disputes is a "public function." *Held*, the warehouseman's lien and sale was not a "public function" because the resolution of disputes between private individuals is not traditionally an "exclusively" governmental activity — for instance, the parties might have agreed to private arbitration. [*Flagg Bros. v. Brooks*]. [456]

C. **"State involvement" doctrine:** Even if the private individual is not doing something that's traditionally a "public function," his conduct may constitute state action if the state is ***heavily involved*** in his activities. This is the ***"state involvement"*** branch of state-action doctrine. Here are some of the ways in which the state and private actor can be so closely involved that the private person's acts become state action: [457]

1. **Commandment:** The state may become responsible for the private party's actions because it ***commanded***, i.e., required, the private party to act in that way. (*Example:* The state enforces a private agreement among neighbors that none will sell his house to a black. Because the state has lent its state judicial enforcement mechanism to this otherwise private contract, the combination of enforcement and private discrimination violates equal protection. [*Shelley v. Kraemer*] [457-459]

2. **Encouragement:** If the state ***"encourages"*** the private party's actions, then the private action will be converted into state action. (*Example:* The voters of California amend their constitution to prohibit the state government from interfering with any private individual's right to discriminate when he sells or leases residential real estate. This amendment immediately results in the repeal of two state Fair Housing statutes. *Held*, this state-constitutional amendment amounts to governmental "encouragement" of private discrimination. Therefore, the resulting private discrimination will be imputed to the state, and the state constitutional provision violates the 14th Amendment. [*Reitman v. Mulkey*]) [459]

3. **Symbiosis:** There is state action if there exists between the state and private actor a ***"symbiotic"*** relationship, i.e., a relation between the two that is ***mutually beneficial***. (*Example:* A Wilmington, Delaware city agency owns and runs a parking garage complex. The agency gives a 20 year lease to a privately-operated restaurant located in the complex. The restaurant refuses to serve African Americans. *Held*, African Americans who are refused service have had their equal protection rights violated. The relation between the restaurant and the publicly-run garage was so close and symbiotic — the garage wouldn't have been able to operate viably without rents from the restaurant — that the restaurant's actions must be imputed to the state, and therefore constitute state action. [*Burton v. Wilmington Parking Authority*]) [460-461]

4. **Entanglement or entwinement:** State action may arise from the fact that the state is so ***"entangled"*** or ***"entwined"*** with a private actor that even though the state might not directly benefit from the private actor's conduct, the conduct will still be treated as state action. This is true where the state and the private party ***act together*** to carry out the action being challenged. [461-463]

Example 1: A state allows a private litigant — either a civil litigant or a defendant in a criminal case — to use peremptory challenges to exclude jurors on racial grounds. This conduct constitutes state action, and therefore violates the Equal Protection Clause. [*Edmondson v. Leesville Concrete Co.*; *Georgia v. McCollum*] [463]

Example 2: A state recognizes a private association of high schools as being the regulator of high school interscholastic sports. Most members of the association are public high schools within the state, and these schools are active in the association affairs as part of the schools' official business of running athletic programs. Because the association's activities are deeply entwined with state affairs, the association's conduct is state action. [*Brentwood Academy v. Tenn. Secondary School Athl. Assoc.*] [463]

    a. Mere acquiescence not enough: But if the state merely *acquiesces* in the private party's discrimination, this won't be enough of a state involvement to convert the private actor's conduct into state action. [464]

    Example: The state regulates all utilities. A private utility cuts off plaintiff's service without notice or a hearing, and this fact is known to the state, which does not object. *Held*, the utility's conduct was not state action, because the state merely acquiesced in that conduct, rather than actively participating in it. [*Jackson v. Metropolitan Edison Co.*]

    b. Licensing: Similarly, the fact that the state has *licensed* a private person is generally not enough to convert the private person's conduct into state action. [461-461]

    Example: A private club refuses to serve African Americans. Even though the state has given the club one of a limited number of liquor licenses, this act of licensing is not enough to turn the club's action into state action. [*Moose Lodge v. Irvis*]

II. CONGRESSIONAL ENFORCEMENT OF CIVIL RIGHTS

A. Congressional enforcement of civil rights: Congress has special powers to enforce the post-Civil War amendments, i.e., the Thirteenth, Fourteenth, and Fifteenth Amendments. [469-471]

    1. 13th Amendment: The Thirteenth Amendment *abolishes "slavery"* and *"involuntary servitude."*

    2. 14th Amendment: The Fourteenth Amendment requires the states to give *"due process," "equal protection,"* and *"privileges and immunities."*

    3. 15th Amendment: The Fifteenth Amendment bars the states from denying *voting rights* on the basis of race, color or previous condition of servitude.

B. Congress' power to reach private conduct: The special enforcement powers let Congress reach a lot of *private conduct* that it could not reach by means of any other congressional power. [471-476]

    1. 14th and 15th Amendments: When Congress enforces the Fourteenth and Fifteenth Amendments, it has some, but not unlimited, power to reach private conduct. So Congress could, for instance, make it a crime for somebody to *interfere with a state official* who is trying to guarantee another person's equal protection rights or voting rights. (*Example:* Congress can make it a crime for D to prevent a school principal from allowing African Americans to enroll in an all white school.) [471-474]

    a. Can't reach purely private discrimination: But Congress under the Fourteenth Amendment *cannot* simply make it a crime for one private person to practice ordinary racial discrimination against another. [471] (Congress would instead have to use its power to regulate interstate commerce; this is the basis on which the 1964 Civil Rights Act, forbidding racial discrimination in places of public accommodation, was upheld. [*Katzenbach v. McClung*])

2. **13th Amendment:** But the *13th* Amendment is different. §1 of the 13th Amendment provides that "neither slavery nor involuntary servitude, except as a punishment for crime … shall exist within the United States." §2 gives Congress the power to "enforce this [amendment] by appropriate legislation." The 13th Amendment, unlike the 14th and 15th, is *not explicitly limited to governmental action.* Indeed, that's the most important thing to remember about the 13th Amendment, and its principal use today — it's practically the only clause in the entire Constitution that prevents one private citizen from doing something to another. So the 13th Amendment gives Congress important authority to reach certain private conduct that it couldn't reach through the 14th and 15th Amendments. [474-476]

   a. **"Badges of slavery":** If the 13th Amendment only meant that Congress could take special action to ensure that slavery itself, in its most literal sense, shall be wiped out, the Amendment wouldn't be of much practical use today. But instead, the Supreme Court has held that the Amendment allows Congress also to stamp out the *"badges and incidents"* of slavery. In fact, Congress has the power to determine what the "badges and incidents of slavery" are, so long as it acts rationally — once Congress defines these "badges and incidents," it can then forbid them. [474-476]

      Example: In 1866, Congress passes a statute, 42 U.S.C. §1982, which provides that "all citizens of the United States shall have the same right, in every state and Territory, as is enjoyed by white citizens thereof to inherit, purchase, lease, sell, hold and convey real and personal property." In a modern case, the Ps argue that the statute prevents D (a private developer) from refusing to sell them a house solely because they are African American.

      Held, this statute applies to block discrimination by D, a private citizen. Furthermore, the statute is constitutional under the 13th Amendment. §2 of the 13th Amendment, which gives Congress enforcement powers under that amendment, gives Congress the power to make a rational determination of *what the badges and incidents of slavery are.* Here, Congress could have rationally concluded that barriers to enjoyment of real estate, and discrimination in housing, are relics of slavery. [*Jones v. Alfred H. Mayer Co.*] [474-476]

   b. **Ancestry, ethnic discrimination:** As we've just seen, the 13th Amendment clearly lets Congress prevent private discrimination against African Americans, on the grounds that it's a "badge or incident" of slavery. *All other racial minorities are also protected* — Congress could probably even bar private racial discrimination against *whites* based on the 13th Amendment (though the Court has never explicitly decided this). But it's not clear whether private discrimination based on *non-racial grounds* (e.g., *ancestry*, *ethnic background*, religion, sex, etc.) can be barred by Congress acting pursuant to the 13th Amendment. [475]

   c. **Must have statute:** The application of the 13th Amendment to a broad range of "badges and incidents of slavery" applies only where Congress has used its *enforcement* powers by passing a *statute* that relies on the Amendment. If private citizen A discriminates against B on the basis of race, but the type of discrimination is not one that Congress has outlawed, then the 13th Amendment's "naked" or "self-executing" scope *won't* be enough to reach that discrimination. Probably actual *peonage* — the keeping of a person as a slave — is the only type of private racial discrimination that is directly barred by the 13th Amendment in the absence of a congressional statute. [475]

C. **Congress' remedial powers:** The Thirteenth, Fourteenth and Fifteenth Amendments all have specific provisions giving Congress the power to *"enforce"* that amendment. See, e.g., §5 of the Fourteenth Amendment, giving Congress the power to enforce the amendment *"by appropriate legislation."*

1. **Remedial powers:** Under this enforcement power, Congress may ***prohibit*** certain actions that ***don't directly violate*** these amendments, if it reasonably believes that these actions would or might ***lead*** to violations of the amendments. That is, Congress has ***broad "remedial" or "prophylactic" powers.*** [486]

   Example: Congress may use its 15th Amendment remedial powers to forbid, in the Voting Rights Act (further discussed below), any voter literacy test or character test in states with a history of voting rights violations. That's true even though such tests aren't themselves necessarily unconstitutional — Congress' 15th Amendment remedial powers are triggered by Congress's reasonable fears that such tests ***may lead*** to violations of the 15th Amendment. [*South Carolina v. Katzenbach*]

2. **Reference to "Necessary and Proper" clause:** Congress' power to enforce the Civil War Amendments is to be judged generally by reference to the ***"Necessary and Proper"*** clause (*supra*, p. C-6). That is, as long as the ***means*** chosen by Congress are ***"rationally related"*** to achieving an objective that one of these Amendments is designed to fulfill, Congress has not exceeded its enforcement authority. (But as we'll see below, there is one important limitation on this principle, the special "congruent and proportional" standard for judging Congress's exercise of its Fourteenth Amendment enforcement powers; see *City of Boerne v. Flores*, *infra*, p. C-67.)

   a. **Easy "rationally related" review standard:** This easy-to-satisfy "rationally related" standard means that if Congress reasonably fears that the ***effect*** of a state law will include interferences with a right guaranteed by one of these three Amendments, Congress can prohibit the state law from being enforced. That's true even if it's clear that the members of the state legislature did not, when they enacted the law, have a ***purpose*** of promoting violations of any of the Amendments. [477]

3. **Obligation to rely on current data (*Shelby County v. Holder*):** Cases like *South Carolina v. Katzenbach*, *supra*, giving a broad reading to Congress' remedial powers under the Fifteenth Amendment, were decided when massive official racial discrimination against minority voters in many southern states — and Congress' response — were both relatively ***recent*** phenomena. But recent decades have seen large reductions in such overt racial discrimination in voting. So the question arises, may Congress continue to single out for more-burdensome federal regulation of voting practices certain states based solely on these states' 1960s and 1970s histories of official racial discrimination in voting?

   The answer according to a recent (2013) case is ***"no."*** If in the present era Congress wants to use its Fifteenth Amendment enforcement powers to prevent future violations of the Amendment — rather than punish past violations — Congress must ***adjust the measures it uses*** to reflect ***current rather than historical voting circumstances***. [479]

   > **Example:** In the most recent version of the Voting Rights Act (enacted in 2006), Congress continues to use its Fifteenth Amendment remedial powers to set certain criteria that the Justice Department is to use to compile a list of states and local governments that will be deemed to have had a history of intentional discrimination in voting (this is the "coverage formula"). Congress then says that any jurisdiction on the list must get federal pre-approval ("preclearance") before making any major or minor change to the jurisdiction's voting regulations (e.g., imposition of new Voter ID methods, different voting hours, or redrawing of electoral districts). The coverage formula (and thus the list of covered jurisdiction) is based solely on voter-registration and turnout data from the 1972 elections or earlier. Shelby County, which is covered because it's in a state (Alabama) that's on the list, challenges the constitutionality of Congress' assertion of this power.
   >
   > *Held* (5-4), for the county: the formula for compiling the list of jurisdictions exceeds Congress' Fifteenth Amendment powers. There is a ***"fundamental principle of equal sovereignty"***

among the states. If Congress is going to "divide the States" (as it has done here by means of the coverage formula), this equal-sovereignty principle requires Congress to design the coverage formula on a "*basis that makes sense in light of current conditions.*" Given the large amount of progress the covered states have made since 1972 (including the fact that black and Hispanic registration and turnout percentages are actually higher than for whites in five of the six states covered on account of 1972 data), Congress' failure to use any data from later than 1972 fails this "make sense" standard. Therefore, the coverage formula may not be enforced (though the decision does not prevent Congress from applying preclearance to jurisdictions if Congress enacts a *new* coverage formula based on current conditions). [*Shelby County v. Holder* (2013)] [479-486]

III. CONGRESS' POWER TO REDEFINE THE MEANING AND SCOPE OF CONSTITUTIONAL GUARANTEES

A. Congressional power to redefine the scope of constitutional rights:　Congress does *not* have the power to *redefine the scope* of the rights protected by the Civil War amendments in a way that is different from the way the Supreme Court would define their scope. [486-487]

　　1. No power to redefine scope: This is true whether Congress is trying to *expand* or *contract* the right.

　　　　Example: The Supreme Court issues a decision defining the First Amendment Establishment Clause more narrowly than the Court had previously defined that clause. Congress doesn't like this decision. It therefore passes the "Religious Freedom Restoration Act," which in effect says that all state and local governments must refrain from any action that would have violated the Establishment Clause under the earlier, now-overruled, cases. *Held*, Congress has no power to either expand or contract the scope of constitutional rights, so the Act is an unconstitutional exercise of congressional power. [*Boerne v. Flores*] [487-489]

IV. CONGRESS' POWER TO ABROGATE THE ELEVENTH AMENDMENT AND THUS AUTHORIZE DAMAGE SUITS AGAINST THE STATES FOR DISCRIMINATION

A. Private money-damage suits against states for discrimination:　Congress often prohibits a certain type of discrimination, and then attempts to make *state and local governments*, not just private individuals, obey the prohibition. Sometimes, Congress goes even further, and attempts to *give private individuals the right to bring private actions* for *money damages* against a *state or local government* that commits the prohibited discrimination.

　　1. Significance of Eleventh Amendment:　But because of the existence of the *Eleventh Amendment*, it will often turn out that Congress *has overstepped its boundaries* by such an attempt to let private individuals sue state and local governments for discrimination.

　　2. The Eleventh Amendment: The Eleventh Amendment says, in brief, that the *states are immune* from being sued for *money damages by private citizens in federal court*. We discuss the Amendment in much greater detail below (see p. C-106).

　　　　a. Abrogation of amendment: It's always been clear, however, that Congress has in some circumstances the power to *abrogate* the states' Eleventh Amendment immunity from private suits. But the Court's view of how and when Congress can do so has changed over the years.

　　b.　**Use of Commerce powers:**　Originally, nearly everyone thought that Congress could use its extremely broad *Commerce Clause* powers to abrogate the states' Eleventh Amendment immunity. That is, it was thought that Congress could *ban a particular type of discrimination* by use of its Commerce powers, and under those same powers (i) require the states to comply with the ban, and (ii) *strip their Eleventh Amendment immunity* so that private citizens could sue the state for violation of the federal ban.

　　　　i.　**Use of Commerce powers disallowed:**　But in *Seminole Tribe of Florida v. Florida* (discussed in more detail *infra*, p. C-107), the Court held that the Commerce powers *cannot* serve as the basis for a congressional abrogation of the Eleventh Amendment, and thus as the basis for letting private individuals sue a state for damages for violating a federal ban on some sort of discrimination.

　　　　ii.　**Use of Civil-War-Amendment powers:**　On the other hand, it's always been clear that Congress *may* rely on its *Civil-War-Amendment remedial powers* as the source of authority for a general anti-discrimination statute. And under those powers (unlike the Commerce power), Congress can not only ban discrimination that would violate the Civil War amendments, but can subject state governments to the ban, and *abrogate the states' Eleventh Amendment immunity,* so as to let private victims sue a discriminating state for damages.

　　　　　　(1)　**Restrictions:**　But as we'll discuss immediately below (in Par. (B)), the Court has placed a special "congruent and proportional" restriction on Congress' powers to enforce the Civil War amendments. This restriction, when coupled with the above-described ban on Congress' use of its Commerce powers to abrogate states' Eleventh Amendment immunity, significantly limits Congress' ability to let private citizens sue state governments for discrimination.

B.　**"Congruent and proportional":**　When Congress purports to use its enforcement powers to prohibit acts that it fears might lead to constitutional violations, Congress' action must be *"congruent and proportional"* to the threatened violation. If not, the congressional action is *invalid* under the enforcement powers. [*Boerne v. Flores*] [488-489]

　　1.　**Significance:**　The most important consequence of this principle is that if Congress wants to let private individuals *sue the states* in federal district court for money *damages* for state violations of a federal anti-discrimination statute, two conditions must be satisfied:

　　　　[1]　Congress must ordinarily have before it evidence of *widespread past constitutional violations by the states* of the sort that Congress is trying to prevent; and

　　　　[2]　the *remedy* picked by Congress must be *"congruent and proportional"* to the state violations that Congress is trying to prevent.

　　Otherwise, Congress' action cannot be justified by its Civil-War-Amendments enforcement powers. And only those powers (not, say, the Commerce power) are sufficient to let Congress overcome states' *Eleventh Amendment immunity from private federal-court damage suits.* [489-490]

　　　　Example:　In the Age Discrimination in Employment Act (ADEA) Congress makes the states, when they act as employers, obey the same age-discrimination rules as private employers. And Congress authorizes state employees to sue the states in federal court for money damages for ADEA violations committed by the state. Congress says it has acted under authority of its 14th Amendment §5 remedial powers, to prevent violations by the states of older state employees' equal protection rights.

　　　　Held, Congress went beyond the scope of its §5 remedial powers, because there was no evidence that the states routinely violated older workers' equal protection rights. Therefore, Congress' regulation was not a "congruent and proportional" response to any threatened constitutional violations, making the regulation not authorized under Congress' §5 remedial powers. Consequently, the states are free to assert their Eleventh Amendment immunity from private damage suits (which immunity can properly be overcome only by Congress' use of its §5 remedial powers, not by its use of other powers like the Commerce power). [*Kimel v. Fla. Bd. of Regents*] [490-491]

a. **Area receiving heightened scrutiny:** But if the federal statute that creates the right of the plaintiff to sue a state for damages deals with an area that involves *either a suspect or semi-suspect class or a fundamental right, Congress has more freedom.* Since the Court applies some form of *heightened scrutiny* to these areas, the Court will be much more likely to find that Congress' decision to allow a damages suit *meets the "congruent and proportional" requirement* and is thus constitutional. [492-493]

   Example: Title II of the Americans with Disabilities Act (ADA) requires states (as well as private citizens) to accommodate disabled persons' access to certain public facilities, including courthouses. The Ps are paraplegics who seek damages from the state of Tennessee because they do not have adequate access to court services. (One P, for instance, has been required to crawl up stairs to answer criminal charges, because the county courthouse has no elevator.)

   Held, for the Ps. Congress has power to allow damages for violations of ADA Title II, at least in the court-access area. The right of access to courts is subject to *"more searching judicial review"* than the rational-relation review used in ADA Title I disability-discrimination-in-employment cases (as to which the Court has held that Congress does *not* have power to subject the states to money-damage awards, because of lack of evidence that the states as employers have systematically discriminated against disabled employees). [*Tennessee v. Lane*]

b. **Right to prohibit direct constitutional violations:** Also, if the state conduct that the plaintiff is complaining of was an *actual violation* by the state of the plaintiff's *constitutional rights,* Congress can grant the plaintiff the right to recover damages against the state in federal court without worrying about whether the federal statute is congruent-and-proportional to the overall pattern of constitutional violations that Congress was trying to prevent.

   Example: Congress may allow P, a wheel-chair-bound prisoner, to sue a state for actual damages caused to him when his disability was not accommodated. (His cell was too small for him to turn his wheelchair around in it.) Because P's suit is premised on an *actual violation* of his 14th Amendment liberty interest (not merely based on a federal statute that was enacted out of a general fear that states or private citizens would discriminate), the Court will not consider whether the ADA statute is "congruent and proportional" to the constitutional violations feared by Congress. [*U.S. v. Georgia*] [493]

CHAPTER 14

FREEDOM OF EXPRESSION

I. GENERAL THEMES

A. **Text of First Amendment:** The First Amendment provides, in part, that "Congress shall make no law ... abridging the *freedom of speech*, or of the press; or the right of the people peaceably to assemble, and to petition the Government for a redress of grievances." [502]

   1. **Related rights:** There are thus several distinct rights which may be grouped under the category "freedom of expression": freedom of *speech*, of the *press*, of *assembly*, and of *petition*. Additionally, there is a well-recognized "freedom of *association*" which, although it is not specifically mentioned in the First Amendment, is derived from individuals' rights of speech and assembly.

B. Two broad classes: Whenever you consider governmental action that seems to infringe upon the freedom of expression, there's one key question that you must always ask before you ask anything else. That question is, "Is this governmental action intentionally '***content-based***' or '***content-neutral***'?" If the action is "content-based," the government's action will generally be subjected to strict scrutiny, and the action will rarely be sustained. On the other hand, if the action is "content-neutral," the government's action is subjected to a much less demanding standard, and is thus much more likely to be upheld. [502-504]

1. **Classifying:** A governmental action that burdens a person's expression is "content-based" if the government is aiming at the ***"communicative impact"*** of the expression. By contrast, if the government is aiming at something other than the communicative impact of the expression, the government action is "content-neutral," even though it may have the *effect* of burdening the expression.

   Example 1 (content-based): Under Maryland tort law, if a speaker (D) intentionally makes outrageous statements attacking another person (P), P may be able to recover against D for intentional infliction of emotional distress (IIED). In a federal-court diversity case based on Maryland tort law, a jury grants P (the father of a Marine killed in Iraq) a civil judgment for IIED against the Ds, who are members of a church that thinks God punishes the U.S. military for tolerating homosexuality. The IIED consists of the Ds' having carried, during and nearby the Marine's funeral, picket signs attributing the Marine's death to God's desire to punish the military for not rooting out homosexuality.

   Maryland's common law of IIED is "content based." That's because the "outrageousness" of the Ds' messages on the picket signs results solely from the content of those messages. [*Snyder v. Phelps*] [538]

   Example 2 (content-neutral): A city forbids the distribution of all leaflets, because it wishes to prevent littering. This ban is "content neutral" — the government is banning all leaflets, regardless of their content, and the harm sought to be avoided (littering) would exist to the same extent regardless of the message in the leaflets. Therefore, the government action is subject to less rigid review — more or less "intermediate level review" (though it was still struck down on these facts). [*Schneider v. State*] [504]

   a. **Tip:** Here's a tip to help you decide whether a given governmental action is content-based or not: would the harm the government is trying to prevent exist to the same degree if the listeners/readers ***didn't understand English***? If the answer is "no," the action is probably content-based.

      Example: Suppose a funeral attendee in *Snyder v. Phelps* (Example 1 *supra*) didn't speak English. He wouldn't suffer the harm the state was trying to prevent — being emotionally harmed by the statements on the picketers' signs — even if he saw or read the signs, so it's clearly the content of the communication that the state is objecting to. But in the case of the ban on littering, even a whole city of non-English-speakers would suffer the same harm — littered streets — so the ban is content-neutral.

   b. **Motive counts:** When a court decides whether a regulation is content-based or content-neutral, ***motives*** count for everything — the question is what the state really ***intends*** to do. If the court believes that the state intends to inhibit certain speech because of its message, the court will treat the statute as content-based (and strictly scrutinize it) even though it is neutral on its face.

C. Analysis of content-based government action: Once we've determined that a particular government action impairing expression is "content-based," we then have to determine whether the expression falls within a category that is ***protected*** by the First Amendment.

1. **Unprotected category:** If the speech falls into certain pre-defined ***unprotected categories***, then the government can basically ***ban that expression completely*** based on its content, without any interference at all from the First Amendment. [506]

   a. **List of categories:** Here is a list of these unprotected categories, as the Supreme Court has recognized them: [508]

   [1] ***"Incitement."*** This category includes advocacy of ***imminent lawless behavior***, as well as the utterance of ***"fighting words,"*** i.e., words that are likely to precipitate an immediate physical conflict;

   [2] ***Obscenity***;

   [3] ***Misleading or deceptive speech (i.e., fraud)***;

   [4] Speech ***integral to criminal conduct***, such as speech that is part of a ***conspiracy*** to commit a crime or speech ***proposing an illegal transaction***; and

   [5] ***Defamation***.

   b. **Not totally unprotected:** But even speech falling within an "unprotected category" receives one small First Amendment protection: government must regulate in a basically ***viewpoint-neutral*** way. That is, it can exclude certain subjects entirely, but it can't single out certain viewpoints for less favorable treatment. [506]

   Example: The state may ban all "fighting words." But it may not choose to ban just those fighting words directed at the listener's race, religion, or other enumerated traits. [*R.A.V. v. City of St. Paul*]

2. **Protected category:** All expression not falling into one of these five pre-defined categories is "protected." If expression is protected, then any government ban or restriction on it based on its content will be ***presumed to be unconstitutional***. The Court will subject any content-based regulation of protected speech to ***strict scrutiny*** — the regulation will be sustained only if it (1) serves a ***compelling governmental objective***; and (2) is ***"necessary,"*** i.e., drawn as ***narrowly as possible*** to achieve that objective (since a broader-than-needed restriction wouldn't be a "necessary" means). [505-506]

   Example: A District of Columbia statute bans the display of any sign within 500 feet of a foreign embassy, if the sign would bring the foreign government into "public disrepute." *Held*, this regulation is content-based, since a sign is prohibited or not prohibited based on what the sign says. Therefore, the regulation must be strictly scrutinized, and cannot be upheld. Even if the government's interest in protecting the dignity of foreign diplomats is compelling — which it may or may not be — the statute is not "necessary" to achieve that interest, since a narrower statute that only banned the intimidation, coercion or threatening of diplomats would do the trick. [*Boos v. Barry*] [506]

   a. **Religious speech gets equal protection:** The requirement of content-neutrality is now so strong that it seems to take precedence over the ***Establishment Clause*** (which protects separation of church and state). Thus if the government allows private speech in a particular forum, it may not treat ***religiously-oriented*** speech ***less favorably*** than non-religiously-oriented speech.

   Example: If a public university gives funding for student publications on various topics, the requirement of content-neutrality means that the university must give the same funding to a student publication whose mission is to proselytize for Christianity. [*Rosenberger v. Univ. of Virginia*]

D. **Analyzing content-neutral regulations:** Now, let's go back to the beginning, and assume that the government restriction is ***content-neutral***.

1. **Three-part test:** Here, we have a ***three-part test*** that the government must satisfy before its regulation will be sustained if that regulation substantially impairs expression [507-508]:

    a. **Significant governmental interest:** First, the regulation must serve a ***significant governmental interest.***

    b. **Narrowly tailored:** Second, the regulation must be ***narrowly tailored*** to serve that governmental interest. So if there's a somewhat ***less restrictive*** way to accomplish the same result, the government must use that less-intrusive way. (*Example:* Preventing littering is a significant governmental interest. But the government can't completely ban the distribution of handbills to avoid littering, because the littering problem could be solved by the less restrictive method of simply punishing those who drop a handbill on the street. [*Schneider v. State*])

    c. **Alternative channels:** Finally, the state must ***"leave open alternative channels"*** for communicating the information. (*Example:* Suppose a city wants to ban all billboards. If a political advertiser can show that there's no other low-cost way to get his message across to local motorists, this billboard ban might run afoul of the "alternative channels" requirement.)

2. **Mid-level review:** This three-part test basically boils down to ***mid-level*** review for content-neutral restrictions that significantly impair expression (as opposed to strict scrutiny for content-based restrictions).

E. **Overbreadth:** The doctrine of ***overbreadth*** is very important in determining whether a governmental regulation of speech violates the First Amendment. A statute is "overbroad" if it bans speech which could constitutionally be forbidden but *also* bans speech which is protected by the First Amendment. [519-522]

1. **Standing:** To see why the overbreadth doctrine is important, let's first consider how a litigant attacks the constitutionality of a statute *outside* the First Amendment area. Here, the litigant can only get a statute declared unconstitutional if he can show that it's unconstitutional in its ***application to him.***

    a. **Lets P assert third-party rights:** But the overbreadth doctrine lets a litigant prevail if he can show that the statute, applied according to its terms, would violate the First Amendment rights of ***persons not now before the court.*** So overbreadth is really an exception to the usual rule of "*standing*" — under the usual standing rules, a person is not normally allowed to assert the constitutional rights of others, only his own.

2. **"Substantial" overbreadth:** In cases where the statute is aimed at ***conduct*** that has expressive content (rather than aimed against pure speech), the overbreadth doctrine will only be applied if the overbreadth would be ***"substantial."*** In other words, the potential unconstitutional applications of the statute must be reasonably ***numerous*** compared with the constitutional applications. [520-522]

F. **Vagueness:** There is a second important First Amendment doctrine: ***vagueness.*** A statute is unconstitutionally vague if the conduct forbidden by it is so ***unclearly defined*** that a reasonable person would have to ***guess at its meaning***. [522]

1. **Distinguish from overbreadth:** Be careful to ***distinguish vagueness from overbreadth:*** they both leave the citizen uncertain about which applications of a statute may constitutionally be imposed. But in overbreadth, the uncertainty is hidden or "latent," and in vagueness the uncertainty is easily apparent. [522]

    Example: Statute I prohibits anyone from "burning a U.S. flag as a symbol of opposition to organized government." Statute II prohibits anyone from "burning a U.S. flag for any purpose whatsoever." Statute I is probably unconstitutionally vague, because there's no way to tell what the statute means by "symbols of opposition to organized government." Statutue II is unconstitutionally overbroad — it's obviously not vague, since it's perfectly clear that it bans *all* flag burning. But since by its terms it appears to apply to constitutionally-protected conduct (e.g., burning that's intended as a political expression), and since there's no easy way to separate out the constitutional from unconstitutional applications, it's overbroad.

II. ADVOCACY OF ILLEGAL CONDUCT

A. Advocacy of illegal conduct: Remember that one of our "unprotected categories" is the ***advocacy of imminent illegal conduct***. The government can ban speech that advocates crime or the use of force if (but only if) it shows that two requirements are met:

[1] The advocacy must be ***intended*** to incite or produce "imminent lawless action"; and

[2] The advocacy must in fact be ***likely*** to incite or produce that imminent lawless action.

[*Brandenburg v. Ohio* (1969)] [515]

1. Mere membership not enough: M*ere knowing membership* in a group — even a very dangerous and subversive group — cannot be forbidden. Membership in a group can be punished only if the member is an *active* (not passive) member who ***specifically intends to further the organization's illegal ends.*** [*Scales v. U.S.* (1961)] [517]

     a. Active support by intangible means: On the other hand, the government *can* constitutionally prohibit virtually any kind of ***active support*** of an illegal organization, even support that is intended to further the organization's *legal* aims. [517]

     Example: Congress makes it a crime to provide "material support" to a designated foreign terrorist organization, and defines "material support" broadly to include such things as training the group's members to use legal methods of accomplishing their objectives. *Held*, Congress did not violate the First Amendment — even support of a terrorist organization's ***legitimate*** aims can be harmful (e.g., by "free[ing] up other resources within the organization that may be put to violent ends, and "lend[ing] legitimacy" to the group). Therefore, government may forbid such support. [*Holder v. Humanitarian Law Project* [517]]

III. TIME, PLACE AND MANNER REGULATIONS

A. Time, place and manner generally: Let's now focus on regulations covering the ***"time, place and manner"*** of expression. This is probably the area of Freedom of Expression on which you are most likely to be tested, since these kinds of regulations are quite often found in real life. When we give you the rules for analyzing "time, place and manner" restrictions below, assume that the speech that is being restricted is taking place in a ***public forum***. (If it's not, then the government has a somewhat easier time of getting its regulation sustained; we'll be talking about these non-public forum situations later.) [526]

1. Three-part test: A "time, place and manner" regulation of public-forum speech has to pass a ***three-part test*** to avoid being a violation of the First Amendment [527]:

     a. Content-neutral: First, it has to be ***content-neutral***. In other words, the government can't really be trying to regulate content under the guise of regulating "time, place and manner."

     Example: City enacts an ordinance allowing parades or demonstrations "to protest governmental policies" to be conducted only between 10 a.m. and 4 p.m. No such restrictions are placed on other kinds of parades or demonstrations. Even though this restriction is ostensibly merely a "time, place and manner" restriction, it violates the requirement of content-neutrality, because the restriction applies to some expressive conduct but not others, based on the content of the speech.

b. Narrowly tailored for significant governmental interest: Second, it's got to be ***narrowly tailored*** to serve a ***significant governmental interest***. (We saw this above when we were talking more generally about the analysis of all content-neutral restrictions on speech.) This basically means that not only must the government be pursuing an important interest, but there must not be some significantly ***less intrusive*** way that government could achieve its objective.

Example: Suppose the government wants to prevent littering on the streets. Even though prevention of littering is an important governmental objective, the government may not simply ban all distribution of handbills, because there is a significantly less restrictive means of achieving this objective — a direct ban on littering — so the ban on handbills is not "narrowly tailored" to achieving the anti-littering objective.

c. Alternative channels: Finally, the state must "leave open ***alternative channels***" for communicating the information.

Example: City is a medium-sized city, with six public parks and many streets. City enacts an ordinance stating that any parade or demonstration, no matter what the content of the message, shall take place only in Central Park or on Main Street. City argues that its limited budget for police security, and the greater ease of handling crowds in these two places than in other places, justify the ordinance. Even though this time, place and manner restriction is apparently content-neutral and is arguably narrowly tailored for a significant governmental interest, it probably violates the "leave open alternative channels" requirement because it puts off limits for parades and demonstrations the vast majority of locations within City.

2. Application to conduct: These rules on when the state may regulate the "time, place and manner" of expression apply where what is being regulated is pure speech. But much more importantly, these rules apply where the state is regulating ***"conduct"*** that has an expressive component. ***So the state can never defend on the grounds that "We're not regulating speech, we're just regulating conduct."*** [528]

Example: It's "conduct" to hand out handbills, or to form a crowd that marches down the street as part of a political demonstration. But since both of these activities have a major expressive component, the state cannot restrict the conduct unless its satisfies the three-part test described above, i.e., the restriction is content neutral, it's narrowly tailored to achieve a significant governmental interest, and it leaves open alternative channels.

3. "Facial" vs. "as applied": A "time, place and manner" regulation, like any other regulation impinging upon First Amendment rights, may be attacked as being either invalid ***"on its face"*** or invalid ***"as applied."*** Thus even a time, place and manner restriction that has been very carefully worded to as to satisfy all three requirements listed above may become unconstitutional ***as applied to a particular plaintiff***. [519]

Example: A City ordinance provides that any parade or demonstration participated in by more than five people shall be held only after the purchase of a permit, which shall be issued by the City Manager for free to any applicant upon two days notice. The City Manager normally issues such permits without inquiring into the nature of the demonstration planned by the applicant. P, who is known locally as an agitator who opposes the current city government, applies for a permit. The City Manager denies the permit, saying, "I don't like the rabble rousing you've been doing." Even though the ordinance on its face is probably a valid time, place and manner restriction, the application of the ordinance to P's own permit request ("as applied to P") violates P's First Amendment rights, because that application is not being carried out in a content-neutral manner. P's "as applied" attack will succeed.

B. Licensing: Be especially skeptical of governmental attempts to require a *license* or *permit* before expressive conduct takes place. [529-531]

    1. Content-neutral: Obviously, any permit requirement must be applied in a ***content-neutral*** way. (*Example:* Local officials give permits for speeches made for purposes of raising money for non-controversial charities, but decline to give permits for demonstrations to protest the racism of local officials. The requirement of content neutrality in the licensing scheme is not being satisfied, and the scheme will be automatically struck down.) [529]

    2. No excess discretion: Also, the licensing scheme must set forth the grounds for denying a permit ***narrowly*** and ***specifically***, so that the discretion of local officials will be curtailed. (*Example*: A municipal ordinance cannot require a permit for every newspaper vending machine where the permit is to be granted on "terms and conditions deemed necessary by the mayor" — the grounds for denying a permit must be set forth much more specifically, to curb the official's discretion. [*Lakewood v. Plain Dealer Publ. Co.*]) [530]

    3. Narrow means-end tailoring: Finally, the permit ***mechanism*** must be ***closely tailored*** to the ***objective*** that the government is trying to achieve.

    4. Reasonable means of maintaining order: But if these three requirements — content-neutral application, limited administrative discretion and close means-end fit — are satisfied, the permit requirement will be ***upheld*** if it is a ***reasonable means of ensuring that public order is maintained.*** [530]

        Example: A requirement that a permit be obtained before a large group of people may march would probably be upheld as a reasonable way of maintaining order, if the requirement is applied in a content-neutral way and is drafted so as to apply without exception to *all* large marches.

    5. Right to ignore requirement: Assuming that a permit requirement is unconstitutional, must the speaker apply, be rejected, and then sue? Or may he simply speak without the permit, and then raise the unconstitutionality as a defense to a criminal charge for violating the permit requirement? The answer depends on whether the permit is unconstitutional on its face or merely as applied. [531]

        a. Facially invalid: If the permit requirement is unconstitutional *on its face*, the speaker is ***not*** required to apply for a permit. He may decline to apply, speak, and then defend (and avoid conviction) on the grounds of the permit requirement's unconstitutionality.

        b. As applied: But where the permit requirement is not facially invalid, but only unconstitutional ***as applied to the speaker***, the speaker generally does ***not*** have the right to ignore the requirement — he must apply for the permit and then seek prompt judicial review, rather than speaking and raising the unconstitutionality-as-applied as a defense. (However, an exception to this rule exists where the applicant shows that ***sufficiently prompt judicial review*** of the denial was ***not available***.)

C. Right to be left alone: People have no strong ***right to be left alone***, and the government therefore can't regulate broadly to protect that right. As a general rule, it's ***up to the unwilling listener*** (or viewer) ***to avoid the undesired expression.*** [531]

    Example: A city can't make it a misdemeanor to walk up and down the street handing advertising brochures to people without the recipient's express consent. (It's up to the recipient to decline the handbill.)

    1. Captive audience: But if the audience is ***"captive"*** (unable to avert their eyes and ears), this makes it ***more likely*** that a fair degree of content-neutral regulation ***will be allowed***. (However, the fact that the audience is captive is just one factor in measuring the strength of the state interest in regulating.) [531]

> **Example:** A state may make it a crime to approach close to a woman who is entering an abortion clinic, if the approacher's purpose is to orally "counsel or educate" the woman and the woman does not consent to the approach. [*Hill v. Colorado*]

D. Canvassing: A speaker's right to *canvass*, that is, to go around ringing doorbells or giving out handbills, receives substantial protection. [532]

   1. Homeowner can say "no": The individual listener (e.g., the homeowner), is always free to say, "No, I don't want to speak to you about becoming (say), a Jehovah's Witness." The city can then make it a crime for the speaker to persist.

   2. City can't give blanket prohibition: But the *government* cannot say "No" *in advance* on behalf of its homeowners or other listeners. [533]

> **Example:** A city passes an ordinance providing that "All doorbell ringing for the purpose of handing out handbills is hereby forbidden." *Held*, such an ordinance violates the First Amendment, even if (as the city claims) it is a content-neutral ordinance designed to protect unwilling listeners, such as those who work nights and sleep days. The most the city can do is to provide that once the individual homeowner makes it clear he doesn't want to be spoken to, the speaker must honor that request. [*Martin v. Struthers*]

   3. Time, place & manner: But the authorities may impose "time, place & manner" limits on canvassing, if these limits: (1) are content-neutral; (2) serve a significant governmental interest; and (3) leave open adequate other channels for communication. (*Example:* A town might prohibit canvassing after 6:00 PM, if its policy is truly content-neutral (e.g., it wasn't enacted for the purpose of silencing Jehovah's Witnesses), is enacted to protect homeowners' night-time tranquility, and allows solicitation to take place at other times.)

E. Fighting words: One of our other "unprotected categories" consists of *"fighting words."* "Fighting words" are words which are likely to make the person to whom they are addressed commit an *act of violence*, probably against the speaker. Expression that falls within the "fighting words" category can be flatly banned or punished by the state. [*Chaplinsky v. New Hampshire*] [533-535]

> **Example**: D picks out one member of his audience and calls him a liar, racist and crook. D can be arrested for this speech, because these are words which might well provoke a reasonable person to whom they are addressed into physically attacking D.

   1. Limits: But the "fighting words" doctrine is tightly limited:

      a. Anger not enough: It's not enough that the speaker has made the crowd angry; they must be so angry that they are *likely to fight*. [534]

      b. Crowd control: The police must *control* the angry crowd instead of arresting the speaker if they've got the physical ability to do so. (In other words, the police can't grant the hostile crowd a "heckler's veto.") [534]

      c. Dislike of speaker's identity: The doctrine doesn't apply where it's the mere *identity* or *lawful acts* of the speaker, rather than his threatening words, that moves the crowd to anger. (*Example*: If D is a black civil rights worker speaking in a small southern town with a history of racial violence, the fact that members of the audience are ready to attack D because they hate all black civil rights activists will not suffice to make D's speech "fighting words" — here the anger is not really coming from the speaker's particular threatening words, but from his identity and his lawful advocacy of change.) [535]

F. Offensive language: Language that is *"offensive"* is nonetheless protected by the First Amendment. [536-540]

  1. **Profanity:** This means that even language that is *profane* may not be banned from public places. (*Example*: D wears a jacket saying "Fuck the Draft" in the L.A. County Courthouse. D cannot be convicted for breaching the peace. The state may not ban language merely because it is "offensive," even if profane. [*Cohen v. Calif.*]) [536-537]

      a. **Sexually-oriented non-obscene language:** This protection of "offensive" material also means that messages or images that are *sexually-oriented* but not obscene are, similarly, protected.

          Example: Congress bans the use of the Internet to display any "indecent" language or images which may be accessed by minors. *Held*, this statute is unconstitutional, because it restricts the First Amendment rights of adults to receive indecent-but-not-obscene material. [*Reno v. ACLU*] [547]

  2. **Racial or religious hatred:** Similarly, this means that messages preaching *racial or religious hatred* are protected (at least if they don't incite imminent violence or come within the "fighting words" doctrine). (*Example*: A member of the American Nazi Party tells a predominantly-Jewish audience, "Jews are the scum of the earth and should be eliminated." D cannot be punished for, or even restricted from, saying these words.) [540]

  3. **Limits:** But offensive language *can* be prohibited or punished if: (1) the audience is a *"captive"* one (e.g., the speech occurs on a city bus or subway); or (2) the language is *"obscene,"* under the formal legal definition of this term (lewd and without socially redeeming value).

G. Regulation of "hate speech": Government efforts to regulate *"hate speech"* — for instance, speech attacking racial minorities, women, homosexuals, or other traditionally disfavored groups — may run afoul of the First Amendment for being content-based. [540-544]

  1. **Three rules:** Here are the general rules about how a state may go about banning hate speech:

      General ban: A ban on speech or conduct intended or likely to incite anger or violence based solely on *particular listed topics or motives* — such as race, color, religion or gender hatred — is *impermissibly content-based.* That's true even if all the speech/conduct banned falls within an *"unprotected"* category such as, here, *"fighting words."* [*R.A.V. v. St. Paul*] [541]

      Example: City bans only those "fighting words" that evoke hatred or conflict based on race, ethnicity or gender (not fighting words based on, say, the listeners' political affiliation). This enactment is content-based, in that it selects speech for proscription based on its content. Therefore, the statute will be strictly scrutinized, and struck down for not being sufficiently narrowly-tailored to achieve the compelling state interest in avoiding dangerous physical conflict. (However, a state could ban *all* fighting words — it just can't select fighting words based only on certain types of hatred.) [*R.A.V.*] [541]

      Worst examples: However, a state *may* impose a content-based ban on *particular instances* of unprotected speech if the ban forbids *only the very worst examples* illustrating *the very reason the particular class of speech is unprotected.*

      Example: The state may choose to criminalize just the very most dangerous "fighting words," just the very most obscene obscene images, etc. [*R.A.V.*]

      Penalty-enhancement statutes: Also, a state may identify particular generally-applicable criminal proscriptions, and may then choose to punish *more severely* those criminal acts that happen to be motivated by hate than those not motivated by hate. This is called the *"penalty enhancement"* approach. [*Wisconsin v. Mitchell*] [543]

Example: For instance, from within the overall class of acts that constitute arson (all of which are defined as crimes), the state may punish arson more seriously if it's motivated by bias against particular groups.

All intimidating acts: Finally, a state may select a particular type of expressive act (e.g., cross-burning), and punish *all instances* where that act is done with a purpose of *intimidating or threatening* someone, even though the state doesn't punish other types of intimidating or threatening acts. [*Virginia v. Black*] [544]

Example: A state may choose to ban all cross-burnings that are done with intent to intimidate another. That's true even if the state chooses not to criminalize other types of expressive activity that are done with intent to intimidate another (e.g., burning that other in effigy).

H. Injunctions against expressive conduct: Where the restriction on expression is in the form of an *injunction* issued by a judge, there is a special standard of review. When a court issues an injunction that serves as a kind of "time, place and manner" restriction, the injunction will be subjected to slightly *more stringent* review than would a generally-applicable statute or regulation with the same substance: the injunction must "*burden no more speech than necessary* to serve a significant governmental interest." [*Madsen v. Women's Health Center, Inc.*] [544]

I. The public forum: Let's turn now to the concept of the *"public forum."* [549-557]

1. Rules: Here are the rules concerning when the fact that speech occurs in a public forum makes a difference, and how: [549]

a. Content-based: If a regulation is *content-based*, it makes no difference whether the expression is or is not in a public forum: strict scrutiny will be given to the regulation, and it will almost never be upheld.

b. Neutral "time, place & manner": It's where a regulation is *content-neutral* that the existence of a public forum makes a difference; especially regulations on "time, place & manner" are less likely to be upheld where the expression takes place in a public forum. [549]

i. Non-public forum: When expression takes place in a *non-public forum*, the regulation merely has to be *rationally related* to some *legitimate governmental objective*, as long as equally effective alternative channels for the expression are available.

ii. Public forum: When the expression takes place in a *public forum*, by contrast, the regulation has to be *narrowly drawn* to achieve a *significant governmental interest* (roughly *intermediate-level* review). It is necessary, but not sufficient, that the government also leaves alternative channels available. [549]

Example 1 (public forum speech): A city says, "No political campaign messages may be presented in handbills distributed on city streets." Since this rule impairs communications in a public forum (city streets), the city will have to show that its ordinance is necessary to achieve a significant governmental interest, which it probably can't do (anti-littering won't be enough, for instance). The city can't say, "Well, TV or radio ads will let the same message be given" — the existence of alternative channels for the communication is necessary, but is not enough, when the expression takes place in a public forum.

Example 2 (non-public forum speech): A city says, "No political campaign messages may be displayed on privately-owned billboards, even with the consent of the owner." Here, no public forum is involved. Therefore, as long as adequate alternative channels are available (which they probably are, e.g., radio & TV ads), the city only has to show that its regulation is rationally related to some legitimate governmental objective. The city can probably meet this burden (e.g., by pointing to the objective of beautifying the city).

2. **What are public forums:** What places, then, are public forums?

   a. **"True" or "traditional" public forums:** First, there are *"true"* or *"traditional"* public forums. These are areas that are public forums by custom and tradition, not by virtue of any particular government policy. The classic examples are: (1) *streets;* (2) *sidewalks*; and (3) *parks*. [551]

   b. **"Designated" public forums:** There's a second type of public forum: places that the government has *decided to open up* to a broad range of expressive conduct.

   Some possible examples:

   [1] places where *government meetings* take place that the government has decided to open to the public at large (e.g., a school board meeting held in a school auditorium);

   [2] places that government has decided may be *used by a broad range of people or groups* (e.g., school classrooms after hours, under a policy that lets pretty much any group use them, or a municipal theater that any group may rent).

   These are called *"designated"* public forums. [552]

   i. **Same rules:** The *same rules* apply to designated public forums as apply to true public forums, except that government can *change its mind* and remove the designation (in which case the place becomes a non-public forum that can be subjected to much broader viewpoint-neutral regulation, as described below).

   c. **Non-public-forums:** Still other public places are not at all associated with expression traditionally, so they can be treated as *non-public forums* (also sometimes called *"limited public forums"*).

   i. **Illustrations of non-public-forums:** Here are some illustrations of facilities that, even though they are owned by the government, are not public forums: *airport terminals*, *jails*, *military bases*, the insides of *courthouses*, and *governmental workplaces*. [555-557]

   ii. **Rules for non-public forums:** In a non-public forum, the government regulation just has to be:

   [1] *reasonable* in light of the *purpose served* by the forum; and

   [2] *viewpoint neutral*.

   [*Int'l Soc. for Krishna Consciousness, Inc. v. Lee* (1992)] [552]

   iii. **Reasonableness:** The above requirement of *"reasonableness"* has relatively little bite here, as in the due process and equal protection areas. Government may limit speech in the non-public forum even if *less restrictive alternatives are readily available*, and even if the restriction chosen is not the *"most reasonable."* [552]

   (1) **All expression banned:** Often, even a regulation that completely *bans* expression in a particular non-public forum will be found to satisfy this "mere-rationality" test. Or, the government can choose entirely to forbid discussion of *certain subjects* (but *can't* forbid just certain *viewpoints*).

   Example: A publicly-owned airport terminal is not a public forum. Therefore, the government may ban face-to-face solicitation of funds in the terminal, because such a ban is rationally related to the legitimate governmental objectives of reducing congestion and combatting fraud. (However, a total ban even on literature distribution will not be upheld, because this ban does not even satisfy the "mere-rationality" standard.) [*Int'l Soc. for Krishna Consciousness v. Lee*]

    iv. Viewpoint neutrality: But the requirement of *viewpoint neutrality* has a real impact in these non-public-forum cases. The government can restrict speech across the board in these forums, but it can't restrict speech by *preferring some messages or perspectives over others.* [553]

        (1) Can't bar religious viewpoint, even if it involves worship: The requirement of viewpoint-neutrality for non-public forums means that when a school district allows after-hours use of *school facilities* by various (even though not all) community groups, *religious groups* must be given *equal access.* [553]

        Example: A school district allows an elementary school to be used after hours by any community group that wishes to put on a program about current affairs. However, the district says that "programs of primarily religious content" are excluded. The Good Christians Club wants to hold a discussion of how practicing Christians should view recent events in the Middle East, to be followed by a prayer for peace in that region.

        Held, for the Club. The district's program is a non-public forum (or as the Court calls it, a "limited public forum"). Since the program proposed by the Club concerns the appropriate topic (current affairs), the school district cannot exclude it on the grounds of its religious orientation, because that would be illegal viewpoint-discrimination. [Cf. *Good News Club*] [553]

J. Access to private property: In general, a speaker does not have any First Amendment right of *access* to another person's *private property* to deliver his message.

    1. Shopping centers: Most significantly, a person does not have a First Amendment right to speak in *shopping centers.* [*Hudgens v. NLRB*] (*Example:* State trespass laws may be used to prevent a person from conducting an anti-war demonstration or a religious proselytizing campaign at her local privately-owned shopping center.) [557]

IV. REGULATION OF SYMBOLIC EXPRESSION

A. Symbolic expression: Let's consider *"symbolic expression,"* i.e., expression that consists solely of *non-verbal* actions. [557-562]

    1. Standard: We use essentially the same rules to analyze restrictions on symbolic expression as we do for restrictions that apply to verbal speech, or to verbal speech coupled with conduct. Thus: (1) any attempt by government to restrict symbolic expression because of the *content* of the message will be strictly scrutinized and almost certainly struck down; (2) any restriction on the *time, place or manner* of symbolic expression will have to be *narrowly tailored* to a *significant governmental objective* and will have to *leave open alternative channels*. [558]

        Example: The Ds (high school students) wear armbands to school, in the face of a school policy forbidding students from wearing such armbands. Because school officials were motivated by a desire to suppress particular messages — anti-war messages — the ban must be strictly scrutinized, and is struck down. [*Tinker v. Des Moines Schl. Dist.*] [559]

    2. Flag desecration: The most interesting example of government regulation of symbolic expression is *flag desecration* statutes. The main thing to remember is that if a statute bans flag desecration or mutilation, and either on the statute's face or as it is applied, the statute is directed only at particular *messages*, it will be invalid. (*Examples:* Both the Texas and federal flag burning statutes have been struck down by the Supreme Court. In the case of the federal statute, the Court concluded that Congress was trying to preserve the flag as a "symbol of national unity." The statute was therefore content-based, so the Court struck it down. [*U.S. v. Eichman*]) [562]

V. DEFAMATION, INTENTIONAL INFLICTION OF EMOTIONAL DISTRESS, AND THE BANNING OF "FALSE SPEECH"

A. Defamation: The First Amendment places limits on the extent to which a plaintiff may recover tort damages for *defamation.* [569]

1. *New York Times v. Sullivan* **test:** Most importantly, under the rule of *New York Times v. Sullivan*, 376 U.S. 254 (1964), where P is a *public official*, he may only win a defamation suit against D for a statement relating to P's official conduct if P can prove that D's statement was made either "with *knowledge* that it was false" or with *"reckless disregard"* of whether it was true or false. These two mental states are usually collectively referred to as the *"actual malice"* requirement. [569-571]

> **Example**: The *New York Times* runs an ad saying that P — the Montgomery, Alabama police commissioner — has terrorized Dr. Martin Luther King by repeatedly arresting him. Even if these statements are false, P cannot recover for libel unless he can show that the *Times* knew its statements were false or acted with reckless disregard of whether the statements were true or false. [*N.Y. Times v. Sullivan, supra*].

2. **Public figures:** This rule of *Times v. Sullivan* — that P can only recover for defamation if he shows intentional falsity or recklessness about truth — applies not only to public "officials" but also to public *"figures."* Thus a well known college football coach, and a prominent retired Army general, were public figures who had to show that the defendant acted with actual malice. [*Assoc. Press v. Walker*] [570]

   a. **Partial public figure:** Someone who voluntarily *injects himself* into a public controversy will be a public figure for *just that controversy* — thus an anti-abortion activist might be a public figure for any news story concerning abortion, but not for stories about, say, his private life unrelated to abortion.

   b. **Involuntary public figure:** Also, some people may be *"involuntary"* public figures. (*Example:* A *criminal defendant* is an involuntary public figure, so he cannot sue or recover for a news report about his crime or trial unless he shows actual malice.)

3. **Private figure:** If the plaintiff is a *"private"* (rather than "public") figure, he does *not* have to meet the *New York Times v. Sullivan* "actual malice" rule. [*Gertz v. Robert Welch, Inc.*]. On the other hand, the First Amendment requires that he show at least *negligence* by the defendant — the states may not impose strict liability for defamation, even for a private-figure plaintiff. *Id.* [571]

   a. **No punitive damages:** Also, a private-figure plaintiff who shows only negligence cannot recover *punitive* damages — he must show actual malice to get punitive damages. *Id.*

4. **Falsity:** The First Amendment also probably requires that the defamation plaintiff (whether or not she is a public figure) must show that the statement was *false.*

B. Intentional infliction of emotional distress: The *Times v. Sullivan* rule applies to actions for intentional infliction of *emotional distress* as well as ones for defamation. Thus a public-figure plaintiff cannot recover for any intentional infliction of emotional distress unless he shows that the defendant acted with actual malice. [573]

> **Example:** *Hustler Magazine* satirizes religious leader Jerry Falwell as a drunken hypocrite who has sex with his mother. *Held*, Falwell cannot recover for intentional infliction of emotional distress unless he shows that *Hustler* made a false statement with knowledge of falsity or with reckless disregard of falsity. [*Hustler Magazine v. Falwell*] [573]

C. Forbidding other types of false speech: Defamation necessarily involves speech that is false. And as we've seen, in most instances government may ban (or allow damages for) defamatory speech, in part because the falsity of the speech makes it less valuable. This raises the question, can government *categorically forbid factually-false statements*, even ones that are *not* defamatory? Could a state, for instance, *make it a crime to "tell a lie"?*

1. Can't forbid all false speech: The brief answer is *"no."* Except for a few narrow *pre-defined sub-categories* (defamation, fraud, and perjury, for instance), as to which there is a long-standing consensus that the type of false speech in question is especially likely to cause severe harm, government *may not forbid statements merely on the grounds that they are factually false.*

a. Lying about military honors: For instance, the Court has held that Congress' decision to make it a crime for a person to falsely state he has won certain *military medals* violates the First Amendment. [574]

Example: In the federal Stolen Valor Act of 2005, Congress makes it a crime for any person to falsely state, even orally, that he has been awarded any Armed Forces decoration or medal. Alvarez falsely claims, in a public meeting, that he was awarded the Congressional Medal of Honor 20 years before. Alvarez does not appear to be seeking any tangible benefit from the lie; he just wants respect.

Held (by a 6-3 vote), the Act violates the First Amendment. A four-Justice plurality applies *strict scrutiny* to the statute, and concludes that the statute cannot survive that scrutiny. That's because criminalizing such lies is not a "necessary" method of achieving the compelling objective of preventing the debasement of military honors — for instance, an online database could list all medal winners, unmasking those who lie. Two more Justices apply *"intermediate scrutiny"*; but they too agree that the statute cannot survive, because the government has not shown that a "more finely tailored statute" could not adequately address the harms. (For instance, the statute might be rewritten to require that the false statement "caused specific harm" or was "material.") [*U.S. v. Alvarez* (2012)] [574]

VI. OBSCENITY

A. Obscenity: Another of our "unprotected categories" is *obscenity*. Expression that is obscene is simply *unprotected* by the First Amendment, so the states can ban it, punish it, or do whatever else they want without worrying about the First Amendment. [576-582]

B. Three-part test: For a work to be "obscene," all three parts of the following test must be met [578]:

1. Prurient interest: First, the average person, applying today's community standards, must find that the work as a whole appeals to the *"prurient"* interest;

2. Sexual conduct: Second, the work must depict or describe in a "patently offensive way" particular types of *sexual conduct* defined by state law; and

3. Lacks value: Finally, the work taken as a whole, must lack "serious literary, artistic, political or scientific value."

[*Miller v. Calif.*]

C. Significance: So something will not be "obscene" unless it depicts or describes *"hard core sex."* (For instance, mere *nudity*, by itself, is not obscene.) [578]

D. Materials addressed to minors: It will be much easier for the state to keep erotic materials out of the hands of *minors*. Probably even minors have some First Amendment interest in receiving sexually explicit materials, but this is typically *outweighed* by the state's compelling interest in protecting minors against such material. So the distribution of non-obscene but sexually explicit materials may basically be forbidden to minors (provided that the regulations do not substantially impair the access of adults to these materials). [579]

1.   **Adult's rights impaired:** But if a measure aimed at minors *does* substantially impair the access of adults to material that's "indecent" but not obscene, the measure will be struck down. (*Example:* If Congress outright bans all "indecent" material on the Internet (as it has done), out of a fear that the material will be seen by minors, the measure will be found to violate the First Amendment rights of adults. [*Reno v. ACLU*]) [547]

E.   **"Pandering":**   The issue of whether the material appeals primarily to prurient interests may be influenced by the manner in which the material is *advertised* — if the publisher or distributor plays up the prurient nature of the materials in the advertising, this will make it more likely that the materials will be found to appeal mostly to prurient interests and thus to be obscene. The advertisement itself, and expert testimony about the likely effect of the advertising, may be admitted into evidence to aid the determination on obscenity. (The marketing of materials by emphasizing their sexually provocative nature is often called *"pandering."*) [582]

F.   **Private possession by adults:**   The mere *private possession* of obscene material by an adult may *not* be made criminal. [*Stanley v. Georgia*] [579]

> **Example:** While police are lawfully arresting D at his house on a robbery charge, they spot obscene magazines on his shelf. D may not be criminally charged with possession of pornography, because one has both a First Amendment right and a privacy right to see or read what one wants in the privacy of one's own home.

1.   **Child pornography:**   However, the states *may* criminalize even private possession of *child pornography*. [*Osborne v. Ohio*] [580]

2.   **No right to supply to consenting adults:**   Also, the state may punish a person who *supplies* pornography even to consenting adults. In other words, there is a right to *have* pornography for one's own home use, but not a right to supply it to others for their home use. [579]

VII.   COMMERCIAL SPEECH

A.   **Commercial speech generally:**   Speech that is *"commercial"* — that is, speech advertising a product or proposing some commercial transaction — gets First Amendment protection. But this protection is in some ways *more limited* than the protection given to non-commercial (e.g., political) speech. [582]

1.   **Truthful speech:**   *Truthful* commercial speech gets a pretty fair degree of First Amendment protection. The government may restrict truthful commercial speech only if the regulation meets the three following requirements:

[1] it *directly advances* ...

[2] a *substantial governmental interest* ...

[3] in a way that is *"no more extensive than necessary"* to achieve the government's objective.

[*Central Hudson Gas v. Public Serv. Comm.* (1980)]

So basically, the court will apply *mid-level review* to government restrictions based on the content of commercial speech (whereas it applies *strict scrutiny* to content-based restrictions on non-commercial speech). [587]

> **Example:** Virginia forbids a pharmacist from advertising his prices for prescription drugs. Virginia must show that it is pursuing a "substantial" governmental interest, and that materially-less-restrictive alternatives are not available. Here, the state's desire to prevent price-cut-

ting that will lead to shoddy service is not strong enough to qualify as "substantial," so the measure must be struck down on First Amendment grounds. [*Virginia Pharmacy Board v. Virginia Consumer Council*] [582-583]

a. **"Consume less" objective will fail:** The three-part mid-level review described above is often used to strike down advertising regulations that are premised on the government's argument that if advertising of the legal-but-harmful product is limited, people will *consume less* of the item. The limitation will usually flunk requirement [3] above (that the limitations be *"no more extensive than necessary"* to achieve the government's objectives), because government will almost always be free to *increase taxes* on the item, to *regulate how and where it can be sold*, or to conduct an *educational campaign* showing its dangers — and any of these methods would likely be less restrictive than an advertising ban, while still reducing consumption of the harmful product. [589]

Example: Rhode Island prohibits all advertising of liquor prices, except for price tags displayed with the merchandise and not visible from the street. The state defends the prohibition on the grounds that forbidding price advertising will lower liquor consumption, in accordance with the state's goal of "temperance."

Held, the prohibition violates the First Amendment, because it fails the 3-part *Central Hudson Gas* test. For instance, that test requires that a regulation of commercial speech be "no more extensive than necessary." The ban here fails this requirement because the state could have limited alcohol consumption by less restrictive means, such as increased taxation, caps on per capita purchases, or educational campaigns. [*44 Liquormart v. Rhode Island*] [589]

b. **Protect minors:** Similarly, if the government's principal justification for the regulation is to prevent *minors* from gaining access to, or being enticed by, the "vice" product, government will have to *tailor its methods very tightly* so that there is no undue interference with the rights of *adults* to obtain or learn about the product. [589-590]

Example: Massachusetts dramatically restricts the advertising of smokeless tobacco and cigars (e.g., by forbidding billboards). The state defends on the grounds that this limit will protect minors from being attracted to the product.

Held, the regulations violate the free-speech rights of the tobacco industry and its adult customers. "No matter how laudable the state's interest in preventing minors' access to tobacco products, the state may not regulate advertising in a way that interferes materially with the legitimate rights of the tobacco industry, and its *adult customers*, to exchange truthful information." [*Lorillard Tobacco Co. v. Reilly*] [590]

2. **False, deceptive or illegal:** But the principles discussed above assume that the commercial speech — even if it concerns a harmful product — is *truthful*. *False or deceptive* commercial speech may be *forbidden* by the government.

a. **Integral to criminal conduct:** This stems from the more general rule that speech that is *"integral to criminal conduct"* is not protected at all (i.e., that such speech constitutes an "unprotected category"). [586]

i. **Proposing an illegal transaction:** Similarly, commercial speech that *proposes an illegal transaction* (e.g., a help-wanted ad that indicates a preference for white males, in violation of anti-discrimination laws) doesn't receive any First Amendment protection.

ii. **Conspiracy:** And commercially-oriented speech that is part of a *conspiracy* to commit a crime ("We hereby agree to rob the First National Bank") may likewise be punished, because such speech is unprotected.

B. Lawyers: The qualified First Amendment protection given to commercial speech means that *lawyers* have a limited right to advertise. Thus a state may not ban all advertising by lawyers or even ban advertising directed to a particular problem. See, e.g., *Bates v. State Bar of Ariz.* (Thus a lawyer can advertise, "If you've been injured by a Dalkon shield, I may be able to help you.") [584]

    1. In-person solicitation: On the other hand, the states may ban certain types of *in-person solicitation* by lawyers seeking clients (e.g., solicitation of accident victims in person by tort lawyers who want to obtain a contingent-fee agreement. [*Ohralik v. Ohio St. Bar Ass'n.*]) [584]

    2. Direct mail: Similarly, the states may ban lawyers from *direct-mail* solicitation of accident victims, at least for a 30-day period following the accident. [*Florida Bar v. Went For It*]

VIII. REGULATION IN THE CONTEXT OF POLITICAL CAMPAIGNS

A. Campaign spending, generally: The state or federal governments can regulate *campaign spending* to some extent, but other campaign regulations would violate the First Amendment. [592-605]

B. Contributions: *Contributions* made by individuals or groups to candidates, political parties, or Political Action Committees may be *limited*.

    Example 1: Congress may constitutionally prevent anyone from contributing more than $1,000 to a candidate for federal office, in order to curb actual or apparent corruption. [*Buckley v. Valeo*] [593-597]

    Example 2: Congress may prevent national political parties from receiving more than $2,000 from any donor, thus outlawing unregulated "soft money" donations. That's because such donations give the appearance that large donors get special access to office-holders, a type of corruption that Congress may constitutionally combat. [*McConnell v. F.E.C.*] [599]

    1. Lower limit: But contribution limits may not be made *so low* that they substantially interfere with candidates' and parties' ability to *run a competitive election campaign.*

        Example: Vermont prevents any individual or political party from contributing more than $400 to the campaign of any candidate for governor during any two-year period. *Held,* this limit is so low that it violates the free speech and free association rights of individuals and parties (though no majority of the Court can agree on the precise test for "how low is too low"). *Randall v. Sorrell.* [595-597]

C. Expenditures: But a person or entity's *independent* campaign-related *expenditures* (whether he's a candidate or not) may *not* be limited at all.

    Example 1: A candidate may not be prevented from spending as much of his own money on getting elected as he wishes. [*Buckley v. Valeo; Randall v. Sorrell*]

    Example 2: Similarly, private citizen X may spend as much money to try to get Y elected as he wishes, as long as X spends the money in a truly independent manner rather than contributing it to Y or coordinating with Y on how it should be spent. [*Buckley v. Valeo*] [594]

    1. Corporations' expenditures: *Corporations* (and probably *unions*) can spend *limitless sums* from their general treasuries to advocate or advertise for or against particular candidates, as long as the spending is "*independent*," i.e., not coordinated with the candidate.

        a. Rationale: That's because the First Amendment does not permit corporations to be *treated less favorably than individuals,* and individuals are entitled, under *Buckley, supra,* to make unlimited independent expenditures to get others elected. [*Citizens United v. FEC*] [600-602].

Example: Congress forbids any corporation from using its general funds to take out a broadcast advertisement naming a specific candidate for federal office, if the ad runs shortly before a general or primary election. (Individuals are not barred from paying for or running such ads.) The ban applies even if the corporation acts completely independently of the candidate. The consequence of the ban is that if a corporation wants to advertise for or against a named candidate, the corporation has to do so by setting up a highly-regulated Political Action Committee (PAC), which will then be bound by strict contribution and spending limits.

Held, the statute violates the First Amendment rights of corporations. Banning corporations from making independent expenditures to broadcast political messages amounts to censorship. "The Government may not suppress political speech on the basis of the speaker's corporate identity." [*Citizens United v. FEC, supra.*] [600-602]

IX. SOME SPECIAL CONTEXTS

A. **Public school students:** Students in *public schools* have a limited right of free speech. The student's right to speak freely has to be *balanced* against the administration's right to carry out its educational mission and to maintain discipline. [605]

1. **Allowable regulation:** Thus a school may ban profanity. It may also ban the school newspaper from running stories that would disturb the school's *educational mission* (e.g., stories about sex and birth control that the principal reasonably believes are inappropriate for younger students at the school). [*Hazelwood Sch. Dist. v. Kuhlmeier*]

    a. **Advocacy of illegal drug use:** Also, schools may ban the *advocacy of illegal drug use,* even where the advocacy does not pose an immediate threat to discipline or the school's educational mission. [*Morse v. Frederick*]

2. **Non-allowable regulation:** But school officials may *not* suppress students' speech merely because they disagree with that speech on ideological or political grounds. (*Example:* School officials may not ban the wearing of anti-war armbands [*Tinker v. Des Moines Schl Dist.*].)

B. **Group activity:** The rights of a *group* to engage in *joint expressive activity* get special First Amendment protection, generally called the *"freedom of association."* (*Example*: Groups have the right to get together to bring law suits, or to conduct non-violent economic boycotts. Therefore, they cannot be prevented from doing these things by state rules against fomenting litigation or conducting boycotts. [*NAACP v. Button*]) [609]

C. **Government as speaker or as funder of speech:** So far, we've looked only at the role of government as the regulator of speech by non-government actors. But sometimes, *government itself wishes to speak*. And sometimes, government wishes to give *financial support* to certain speech by others. In the former situation, government has a broad right to act in a non-viewpoint-neutral way; in the latter situation, the rules are more complex. [610]

1. **Government as speaker:** When government wishes to *be a speaker itself*, it is pretty clear that government may *say essentially what it wants*, and is not subject to any real rule of viewpoint neutrality. [610]

    Example: Government can pay for ads attacking smoking as a health hazard, without having to pay for opponents' ads saying that the dangers of smoking are overrated.

2. **Government as funder of third-party speech:** If government *funds speech by third parties*, may government be non-viewpoint-neutral, by funding only those viewpoints of which it approves? The answer is heavily dependent on the *details* of the government funding.

a. Use of agents to deliver government's message: Government *may* use content-based criteria when government is selecting third parties who will serve as the ***government's agents*** in ***spreading the government's own message***. [610]

Example: The federal government funds certain family-planning "projects" (essentially, clinics) that are operated by private parties. The program's regulations say that while a person (e.g., a doctor) is working in such a clinic, that person may not discuss the possibility of an abortion with a pregnant clinic patient.

Held, this limitation of private speech does not violate the First Amendment. When the government appropriates public funds to promote a particular policy of its own, it is ***entitled to say what it wishes***. [*Rust v. Sullivan* (as summarized later in *Rosenberger v. Rector & Visitors of the Univ. of Va.*)] [610]

b. No forbidding of some topics or messages for disfavor: On the other hand, if government decides to ***fund*** (or ***allow*** on government property) ***some expressions of private citizens' own views***, government must generally ***behave not only in a content-neutral but also a subject-neutral way***. That is, government cannot (1) decide that it's going to subsidize (or allow on public property) private messages on various topics, but then (2) decline to fund (or decide to exclude from the discussion) a few ***disfavored topics or messages***. [610-611]

　　i. Religion: For example, government cannot decide to fund a broad range of expressive activities and then exclude expressive activities that are ***mainly religious.***

　　Example: The University of Virginia (a public university) funds certain student publications, by paying for their printing costs. The University disqualifies from this funding any primarily-religious publication.

　　Held, this exclusion violates the free speech rights of student religious organizations. If the University were disseminating only its own messages, it would not have to fund opposing viewpoints. But once it chooses to fund some ***third-party viewpoints*** (i.e., some student-run publications), it may not choose which ones to fund based on the viewpoint of the speaker. [*Rosenberger v. Rector & Visitors of the Univ. of Va.*] [611]

c. Unconstitutional conditions: Similarly, where government decides to award public funding for a privately-run program the doctrine of ***"unconstitutional conditions"*** may prevent government from conditioning the funding on the recipient's agreement to (i) give up its right to speak on certain topics, or (ii) deliver certain messages with which recipient doesn't agree. See our discussion of this doctrine *infra*, p. C-89.

3. Blurry line between government speech and government-facilitated private speech: The ***boundary line*** between government speech (where government does not have to be content-netural) and government-facilitated private speech (where government must be content neutral) can sometimes be blurry.

a. Acceptance of privately-donated monument: The issue can arise when government accepts and permanently displays a ***privately-donated monument.*** Here, the court has held that government is probably ***acting as a speaker***, in which case it is free to ***reject other similar donations*** of property bearing messages with which government does not agree. [*Pleasant Grove City v. Summum*]

Example: A city has previously permanently placed in a local park a Ten Commandments monument donated by a private group. The Ps (members of the obscure Summum religion) now ask the city to accept and display in the same park a monument showing the "Seven Aphorisms," which the Ps believe were brought down from Mt. Sinai by Moses before he brought down the Ten Commandments. The Ps argue that when the city accepted and displayed the Ten

Commandments and other privately-donated monuments, the effect was to turn the park into a public forum, thereby requiring the city to accept other kinds of monuments and displays on a content-neutral basis.

   Held: for the city. The monument display was government speech, which therefore does not have to be content-neutral. Although a park is a traditional public forum for *speeches* and other *transitory expressive acts*, the placement of a permanent monument in a public park will be viewed as a form of government speech, which is therefore not subject to strict scrutiny under the Free Speech Clause. [*Pleasant Grove City v. Summum, supra*]

XI. FREEDOM OF ASSOCIATION, DENIAL OF PUBLIC BENEFITS OR JOBS, AND UNCONSTITUTIONAL CONDITIONS

A. Freedom of association generally: First Amendment case law recognizes the concept of *"freedom of association."* In general, the idea is that if an individual has a First Amendment right to engage in a particular expressive activity, then a *group* has a "freedom of association" right to engage in that same activity as a group. [613]

   1. Right not to associate: Individuals and groups also have a well-protected *"right not to associate."* Thus any government attempt to make an individual give *financial support* to a cause she dislikes, or to make a group *take members* whose presence would interfere with the group's expressive activities, will be *strictly scrutinized*. [614-618]

   Example 1: Where public school teachers are required to pay union dues, a teacher has a freedom-of-association right not to have the dues used to support ideological causes the teacher dislikes. [*Abood v. Detroit Bd. of Ed.*]

   Example 2: The Boy Scouts can't be forced (by a state anti-discrimination law) to accept an openly-gay male as a scoutmaster, because this would significantly interfere with the Scouts' First Amendment-protected message that homosexuality is immoral. [*Boy Scouts of America v. Dale*]

B. Illegal membership: The freedom of association means that *mere membership in a group or association may not be made illegal*. Membership in a group may only be made part of an offense if: (1) the group is *actively engaged in unlawful activity*, or *incites others* to *imminent lawless action*; and (2) the individual *knows* of the group's illegal activity, and specifically intends to further the group's illegal goals. (*Example*: Congress cannot make it a crime simply to be a member of the American Communist Party. On the other hand, Congress can make it a crime to be a member of a party that advocates imminent overthrow of the government, if the member knows that the party so advocates and the member intends to help bring about that overthrow.) [618]

C. Denial of public benefit or job: Freedom of expression also prevents the government from *denying a public benefit or job* based on a person's association. [618-622]

   1. Non-illegal activities: If a person's activities with a group could not be made *illegal*, then those activities may generally not be made the basis for denying the person the government job or benefit.

   Example 1: A state may not refuse to hire a person as a teacher merely because he is a member of the American Communist Party, since the state could not make it illegal to be a member of the ACP.

   Example 2: At a time when Republicans are in power, a state may not refuse to hire Democrats for non-policy-making jobs like police officer or clerk. [*Rutan v. Republican Party of Illinois*]

2. **No right/privilege distinction:** There is no constitutional distinction between a *"right"* and a *"privilege."* Even if, say, a particular public benefit or job is defined by the state to be a "privilege," the state may not deny that job or benefit on the basis of the applicant's constitutionally-protected membership in a group or organization. [618]

3. **Loyalty oath:** Government may generally not require an applicant to sign a *loyalty oath*, unless the things that the applicant is promising in the loyalty oath not to do are things which, if he did them, would be grounds for punishing him or denying him the job. (*Example*: You cannot be required to sign a loyalty oath that you are not a member of the Communist Party in order to get a teaching job. But you can be required to sign an oath that you will not advocate the forcible overthrow of our government.) [619]

4. **Compulsory disclosure:** Similarly, the government may not force you to *disclose* your membership activities (or require a group to disclose who its members are), unless it could make that membership illegal. (*Example*: The state cannot require the Communist Party to furnish a list of its members.) [622-623]

5. **Some exceptions:** There are some *exceptions* to the general rule that associational activities that couldn't be outlawed directly also can't be made the basis for public hiring or benefits decisions. In general, these exceptions are for conduct which, although it includes protected expression, directly (and negatively) relates to *performance of the job*.

   a. **Partisan political activities:** For instance, civil servants can constitutionally be forced to choose between their jobs and engaging in *partisan political activities*, since there's a very strong government interest in making sure that civil servants can do their jobs without being coerced into campaigning for or contributing to their elected bosses. [*CSC v. Letter Carriers*]

   b. **Patronage hirings:** Similarly, some public jobs may be awarded as *patronage appointments*, ones the performance of which is *reasonably related to a person's politics*. [618]

   Example: Even though I have a First Amendment right to be a Democrat, the Republican Congressman representing my district doesn't violate my rights when, on the basis of my political beliefs, he declines to hire me as, say, a speech writer, a high advisor, or some other post with a *heavy political content*.

   On the other hand, if I'm a Democrat, and there's a Republican governor in power, he can't block me from getting a government job as a clerk or secretary or police officer — the old fashioned "patronage" system whereby all public jobs could be restricted to supporters of the party in power has been outlawed as a violation of freedom of association, and only jobs with a heavy political content, like speech writer, say, or Chief of Staff, can be based on party membership.

   c. **Speech critical of superiors or otherwise inappropriate:** An employee gets limited protection for speech or associational activities that are *critical of superiors*, or that the employer believes are *inappropriate for the workplace*. Where such speech involves a matter of *"public concern,"* the court will *balance* the speech rights of the employee and the government's interest as employer in promoting efficiency on the job. [*Connick v. Myers*] [620]

   Example: P, a government clerical worker, hears that John Hinckley has tried to shoot Pres. Reagan, and says, "If they go for him again, I hope they get him." P is fired for the remark. *Held*, for P. This remark was intended as political commentary and was thus on a matter of "public concern," so P could not be fired unless the remark heavily affected P's job performance, which it did not. [*Rankin v. McPherson*]

i. **Not a matter of public concern:** But where the speech does *not* involve a matter of public concern, *Connick* and *Rankin*, *supra*, do *not* apply, and the court gives great *deference* to the employer's judgment.

ii. **Must not be part of employee's job function:** Also, even the limited protection given to employee speech on matters of public concern doesn't apply where the speech occurs as *part of the employee's job functions* — here, the employee gets no First Amendment protection at all, no matter how important the issue on which the employee is speaking.

> **Example:** P, a supervising lawyer in a District Attorney's Office (D), is called on to investigate whether an affidavit prepared by a deputy sheriff to obtain a search warrant was properly done. P writes a memo to his supervisor concluding that the affidavit was improperly done. The supervisor retaliates against him for what he says in the memo.
>
> *Held*, for D. "[W]hen public employees make statements *pursuant to their official duties*, the employees are *not speaking as citizens* for First Amendment purposes, and *the Constitution does not insulate their communications from employer discipline.*" Here, because P's investigation and the ensuing memorandum were part of his job responsibilities, D had the right to regulate the content and manner of P's speech. [*Garcetti v. Ceballos*] [621]

D. **Unconstitutional conditions:** Suppose that before government gives a particular *benefit* — such as housing, employment, funding for an activity, or a license — government imposes a *condition*. That is, government says that the recipient must, in exchange for the benefit, agree to *waive her freedom of expression* or other constitutional right. The Court *sometimes* invokes the doctrine of *"unconstitutional conditions"* in order to strike down the condition.

1. **Statement of doctrine:** When the doctrine applies, it holds that government *may not grant a benefit on the condition that the beneficiary surrender a constitutional right*, even if the government may *withhold that benefit altogether*. The idea behind the doctrine is that what the government may not do *directly*, it may not do *indirectly* either. [624]

> **Example:** Suppose that the Republican-controlled legislature of a state passes a statute saying that no one may get or keep a job working for the state — no matter how low-level the position or what the requirements of the position are — unless the person signs a pledge not to criticize any elected Republican official during the employment.
>
> The Supreme Court would undoubtedly invoke the doctrine of unconstitutional conditions to strike down this statute as a violation of state employees' and applicants' freedom of expression. Government obviously couldn't directly forbid citizens from criticizing politicians, and letting the state condition a government benefit (state employment) on the waiver of this right would amount to letting the state do indirectly what it could not to directly.

2. **Guiding principles:** The Court seems to apply the unconstitutional conditions doctrine somewhat inconsistently. But here are three principles (some of which we've already discussed) that seem to explain the outcome in most of the Court's unconstitutional-condition cases. [624-626]

[1] **Government uses agents to deliver government's own speech:** Since government is *permitted* to say pretty much whatever it wants *when the government is itself the speaker,* government is also free to *pay agents* to deliver the government's message, and to *condition that payment* on the agent's willingness to *waive his otherwise-protected right* to engage in speech that would contradict or garble the government message the agent is being paid to deliver. [625]

> **Example:** A state government engages (and pays) P, a celebrity, to make public speeches as part of the government's campaign to have the federal constitution amended so as to

limit the scope of abortion rights under *Roe v. Wade*. Government *may*, as a condition to engaging P, insist that P agree that during the course of the campaign, P will not publicly state that P is in favor of a woman's right to choose an abortion as presently construed by the Supreme Court.

[2] **Limits on use of government's payments:** Government is also free to set up *"subsidy programs,"* under which government funds private groups to help the groups carry out some function. And when government does this, it is free to *refuse* to allow *the subsidy dollars to be used for particular activities opposed by government*, including otherwise-constitutionally-protected activities like *speaking* on certain topics, *performing abortions*, or lobbying legislators. [625]

   Example: Congress provides federal grants to help private groups operate family-planning clinics. When a special-purpose "project" is set up to receive such a grant and operate a clinic, the project's founders are required to prohibit the project's employees (while on the job) from advocating for, or counseling about, abortion.

   Held, the condition is not an unconstitutional condition, and does not violate the First Amendment rights of the group that runs the project. "[T]he Government is not denying a benefit to anyone, but is instead simply insisting that *public funds be spent for the purposes* for which they were authorized." (The way the statute is written, a group that runs the project/clinic and receives the funds for it can continue to engage in abortion advocacy or counseling; the group simply is required to conduct those activities through a program or project that is separate from the project [the clinic] receiving the government funds.) [*Rust v. Sullivan.*] [625]

[3] **No "leveraging" by government:** Although government may (as described in [2] above) put conditions on how the government funds will be used inside a government-subsidized privately-run program, government may not impose conditions that "seek to *leverage funding* to *regulate speech outside the contours* of the [government] *program itself.*" [*Agency for Int'l Dev. v. Alliance for Open Soc'y Int'l, Inc.* (2013)] [626]

Example: Congress gives large money grants to various nongovernmental organizations that are fighting HIV and AIDS. Congress says that no funds may be given to any group "that does not have a policy explicitly opposing prostitution" (the "Policy Requirement"). The Ps are various non-profits that say the Policy Requirement violates their free speech rights.

   Held, for the Ps; the Policy Requirement is an unconstitutional condition. Past cases on unconstitutional conditions have distinguished between conditions on the actual activities that Congress wants to subsidize (these conditions are constitutional) and conditions that "seek to *leverage* funding to *regulate speech outside the contours of the program itself*" (conditions that are unconstitutional). Here, the Policy Requirement falls on the unconstitutional side of the line. "By demanding that funding recipients adopt — as their own — the Government's view on an issue of public concern, the condition ... affects 'protected conduct outside the scope of the federally funded program.'" [*Agency for Int'l Dev., supra*]

XII. SPECIAL PROBLEMS OF THE MEDIA

A. **The media (and its special problems):** Here is a brief review of some special problems related to the *media*: [627-642]

1. **Prior restraint:** In general, the government will not be able to obtain a *prior restraint* against broadcasters or publishers. In other words, only in exceptionally rare circumstances may the government obtain an *injunction* against the printing or airing of a story, and the government will almost never be allowed to require that a publisher or broadcaster obtain a *permit* before it runs a

story. [629-632]

> **Example**: The *New York Times* may not constitutionally be enjoined from publishing part of the Pentagon Papers, even though these government-prepared materials might contain information that is useful to our enemies or that would embarrass the U.S. [*N.Y. Times v. U.S.*]

   a. Gag order: This means that a judge may generally not impose a *gag order* on the media ordering it not to disclose a certain fact about a pending trial. [632-634]

      i. Participants: But the judge may usually order the *participants* not to speak to the press. For instance, a state may prevent a lawyer from making any statement which would have a "substantial likelihood of materially prejudicing" a trial or other court proceeding. [*Gentile v. State Bar of Nevada*] [633]

2. Subpoenas by government: The press does not get any special protection from government demands that the press *furnish information* which other citizens would have to furnish. In particular, if a reporter has information that is of interest to a *grand jury*, the reporter may be required by subpoena to disclose that information to the grand jury even though this would cause him to violate a promise of confidentiality to a source. [*Branzburg v. Hayes*] (But the state is always free to enact a "shield law" making such subpoenas illegal under some or all circumstances.) [634-636]

3. Right of access: The press does not get any general *right of access* to information held by the government. [638-640]

   a. Right to attend trials: However, the media does have a constitutionally protected right to *attend criminal trials*. This right is not absolute — the government can close the media (and the public) out of a trial if it shows that there is an "overriding" government interest being served by a closed trial, and that that interest cannot be served by less restrictive means. [*Richmond Newspapers v. Virginia*] [639]

      i. Showing rarely made: But this showing will rarely be made, so that as a practical matter the press is usually entitled to attend a criminal trial. (*Example:* A state statute automatically bars the press from hearing any trial testimony by a minor who was allegedly the victim of a sex crime. *Held*, the statute unduly interferes with the public's right of access to criminal trials. [*Globe Newspapers v. Sup. Ct.*])

      ii. Other proceedings: Probably the media also has a qualified constitutional right to attend other proceedings, like *civil trials* and *pre-trial proceedings*. [*Gannett Co. v. DePasquale*]. [639]

4. Disclosure of confidential or illegally-obtained information: Government may generally *not* prohibit the media from disclosing information that goverment believes ought to be *secret*. If a media member *lawfully* obtains information about a matter of public significance, government may punish disclosure of the information only if government has "a *need* of the *highest order*," which it will rarely be found to have. [*Smith v. Daily Mail*] [636-638]

> **Example:** A broadcaster may not be held civilly liable for *publishing the name of a rape victim*, if the broadcaster learns the name from reading a publicly-filed indictment. [*Cox Broadcasting v. Cohn*]

   a. Where publisher has acted illegally: If the *publisher itself* has *acted illegally* in obtaining the information, then government *may make it a crime* to punish the information, no matter how newsworthy it is. (*Example:* A newspaper reporter breaks into a private home to steal an audiotape, then publishes a transcript of the tape. The newspaper may constitutionally be punished for the publication.)

b. **Where private party has acted illegally but publisher has not:** On the other hand, the fact that the secret information was originally ***obtained illegally*** by a person ***acting independently*** of the eventual publisher is ***not*** enough to allow publication to be made criminal, at least where the material has significant newsworthiness.

Example: X, a private individual acting alone, intercepts and tapes a cellphone conversation between the Ps (two teachers' union officials) who are discussing their upcoming negotiation with a school board. The interception violates federal wiretapping laws. X anonymously mails the tape to a radio station, which broadcasts it. The Ps sue the station. *Held*, the station may not constitutionally be held liable for damages to the officials, because the station did not participate in the illegality, and the strong First Amendment interest in disseminating this newsworthy material outweighs the admittedly strong interest in safeguarding cellphone conversations. [*Bartnicki v. Vopper*] [637]

CHAPTER 15

FREEDOM OF RELIGION

I. INTRODUCTION

A. **Two clauses:** There are two quite distinct clauses in the First Amendment pertaining to religion.[656]

   1. **Establishment Clause:** First, we have the ***Establishment*** Clause. That clause prohibits any law "respecting an establishment of religion." The main purpose of the Establishment Clause is to prevent government from ***endorsing*** or ***supporting*** religion.

   2. **Free Exercise:** The second clause is the ***Free Exercise*** Clause. That clause bars any law "prohibiting the free exercise of religion." The main purpose of the Free Exercise Clause is to prevent the government from ***outlawing*** or seriously ***burdening*** a person's pursuit of whatever religion (and whatever religious practices) he chooses.

B. **Applicable to states:** Both the Establishment and the Free Exercise Clauses by their terms only restrict legislative action by ***Congress***. However, both clauses have been interpreted to apply also to the ***states***, by means of the Fourteenth Amendment's due process clause. Therefore, you don't have to worry whether the government action in question is federal or state — the same standards apply to each. [657]

C. **Conflict:** Occasionally, the Establishment and Free Exercises Clauses seem to ***conflict*** on particular facts. That is, a religious group may be asking for some government benefit; if the benefit is given, there may be an Establishment Clause problem. Yet if the benefit is not given, this may be a burdening of religion. When the two clauses seem to conflict, the ***Free Exercise*** Clause dominates. In other words, if a particular benefit or accommodation to religion is arguably required by the Free Exercise Clause, then when government grants that accommodation or benefit it is not violating the Establishment Clause.

Example: A public university makes meeting rooms available to all sorts of student groups. If the university allows religious groups to use the room, there might be an Establishment Clause problem. But if it doesn't allow religious groups to use the rooms, while allowing non-religious groups to do so, there might be a Free Exercise Clause problem. Consequently, it will not be an Establishment Clause violation for the university to allow the religious groups to use the rooms. [656]

II. THE ESTABLISHMENT CLAUSE

A. **General rule:** The overall purpose of the Establishment Clause is to put a ***wall between church and state***. In other words, the government must stay out of the business of religion, and religious groups must to some extent stay out of the business of government. [657-658]

1. **Some examples:** Here are some things that would clearly be forbidden by the Establishment clause:

     a. **Official church:** Congress cannot establish an "official religion of the United States." In fact, Congress probably couldn't even declare that "the American people believe in God," because the Establishment Clause means that government may not prefer or endorse religion over non-religion.

     b. **Go to church:** The government cannot force people to worship. In fact, the state can't even intentionally ***encourage*** people to worship — for example, it cannot decide that it wants to promote church attendance, and then give people a special tax deduction that applies to church donations but not to other charitable donations. (But it could, as Congress does, give a *general* tax deduction for charitable contributions, and let contributions to churches be eligible. This would be allowable because the government is treating religion the same as non-religion, not preferring religion over non-religion.)

     c. **Preference of one religion over another:** The government cannot intentionally ***prefer one religion over another religion.*** For instance, a state may not decide that since Christians are in the majority, it will allow tax deductions for contribution to Christian churches but not for contributions made, say, to synagogues.

     d. **Participate:** Government may not actively ***participate*** in religious affairs, or allow religious organizations to have a special participation in government affairs. For instance, Congress probably could not constitutionally use public officials and public polling places to run an election to determine the next head of the American Presbyterian Church — this would be an undue governmental entanglement in religious affairs.

B. **Three-part test:** Government action that has some relationship to religion will violate the Establishment Clause unless it satisfies ***all three parts*** of the following test (known as the "*Lemon*" test, from *Lemon v. Kurtzman*) [658]:

1. **Purpose:** First, the government action must have a ***secular legislative purpose***. In other words, there must be some governmental purpose that has nothing to do with religion. (If there is both a religious and a non-religious purpose, then this prong is probably satisfied.)

     Example: Alabama passes a statute saying, "Every public school student shall have the opportunity to engage in silent prayer or meditation for at least two minutes at the start of every school day." If there is evidence that the legislature was ***motivated*** solely by a desire to help students pray, then the statute will be struck down (and in fact such an Alabama statute was struck down). [*Wallace v. Jaffree*] This is true even if many of the students who take advantage of the statute engage in non-religious meditation — if the sole purpose was to aid religion, that's enough to make the government action void.

2. **Effect:** Second, the governmental action's principal or ***primary effect*** must ***not be to advance*** religion. (But ***incidental effects*** that help religion do not violate this prong.)

3. **Entanglement:** Finally, the governmental action must not foster an ***excessive governmental entanglement*** with religion. (*Example:* Massachusetts lets a church veto the issuance of a liquor license to any premises located within 500 feet of the church. *Held*, this statute violates the Estab-

lishment Clause, because it entangles churches in the exercise of governmental powers. [*Larkin v. Grendel's Den*])

C. Religion and the public schools: If the government tries to introduce religion into the ***public schools***, it is probably violating the Establishment Clause. [658-666]

    1. Instruction: Thus the government may, of course, not conduct religious instruction in the public schools. In fact, it can't even allow privately-employed religious teachers to conduct classes on the public schools' premises during school hours. [658-661]

        a. Accommodation: However, it's probably allowable for the government to allow students to ***leave school early*** to attend religious instruction somewhere else. It's also probably acceptable for government to let religious groups have access to school facilities, as long as non-religious groups are given equal access. Remember our example of the university that lets all kinds of student groups, including religious groups, use meeting rooms — that's permissible.

    2. Prayer reading: The official ***reading of prayers*** in the public schools will virtually always be unconstitutional. See, e.g., *Engel v. Vitale*. That is, it will almost always turn out to be the case that either the sole purpose, or the primary effect, of the prayer reading is to advance religion. [661-663]

        a. Moment of silence: Even the setting aside of a ***"moment of silence"*** at the beginning of the school day will generally violate the Establishment Clause, since a moment-of-silence statute will usually turn out to have been solely motivated by the legislators' intent to advance religion, or will at least have the primary effect of advancing religion. (But this will always turn on the actual purpose and effect of the particular statute — there's no absolute *per se* rule against moments of silence. [*Wallace v. Jaffree*] [661]

        b. Prayer reading at graduation: Similarly, the school may not conduct a prayer as part of a ***graduation ceremony***, at least where school officials can fairly be said to be sponsoring the religious message. [*Lee v. Weisman*] [662-663]

        c. Student-selected speakers don't solve problem: The school can't easily get around prayer-reading problems by having the student body ***elect a student speaker,*** and then having that speaker decide whether to give a prayer. As long as the school's process can be reasonably viewed as supporting school prayer, the fact that a student-body election intervenes is irrelevant. [*Santa Fe Indep. Sch. Dist. v. Doe*] [663]

    3. Curriculum: The state may not design or modify the ***curriculum*** of its schools in order to further religion at the expense of non-religion, or to further one set of religious beliefs over others. (*Example*: A state may not forbid the teaching of evolution. [*Epperson v. Ark.*] Similarly, it probably may not demand that "creationism" be taught in addition to evolution, since "creationism" is mainly a religious doctrine the teaching of which would have the primary effect of advancing religion. [*Edwards v. Aguillard*]) [664-666]

    4. Equal treatment of religion and non-religion: But it's not a violation of the Establishment Clause for government to treat religion and non-religion ***equally*** in the schools (and government may in fact be *required* to do this because of free-speech principles). (*Example*: If a public university funds non-religiously-oriented student publications, it must fund an evangelical Christian publication on the same terms. [*Rosenberger v. Univ. of Virginia.*])

D. Sunday closing laws: Laws requiring ***merchants*** to be ***closed on Sundays*** generally do ***not*** violate the Establishment Clause. The reason is that these "blue laws" have a primarily secular effect and purpose — they permit everyone (Christian, non-Christian and atheist alike) to have a uniform day of rest. [*McGowan v. Md.*] [666-667]

E.   Ceremonies and displays: Any time your exam question involves a governmentally-sponsored *ceremony* or *display*, beware of Establishment Clause problems. [671-678]

   1.   Ceremonies: Thus a *ceremony* put on by the government may not have the sole purpose or primary effect of advancing religion. (For instance, as noted above, the government may not normally conduct a prayer as part of a high school graduation ceremony.) [671-672]

   a.   Long-standing tradition: However, if a particular ceremony has a *long historical tradition* going back to the time when the Constitution was enacted, then it will probably be allowable, especially outside of the public-school context. (*Example*: The practice of opening a session of the legislature with a prayer by the legislative chaplain dates back to colonial days, so presumably the authors of the Bill of Rights thought that it did not violate the Establishment Clause. Therefore, the practice will be upheld. [*Marsh v. Chambers*])

   b.   Incidental references: Similarly, the Establishment Clause probably is not violated when the ceremony has an *incidental reference* to God or to a religious theme. (*Example*: The Pledge of Allegiance, with the phrase "One nation, under God," is probably allowable.)

   2.   Religious displays: Where a *display* with religious themes is either put on by the government, or put on by private groups using government property, there is a potential Establishment Clause problem. The problem usually arises where there is a "Christmas" display, "Easter" display, etc. Ask yourself this question: Would a reasonable observer seeing the display conclude that the government was *endorsing* religion? If so, there is a violation of the Establishment Clause. [672-678]

   a.   Context: *Context* is very important. If there is one religious symbol, but it is surrounded by primarily-secular symbols, then the display would be taken as a whole and probably does not violate the Establishment Clause.

   Example: For instance, if a nativity scene is surrounded by reindeer, Santa Claus, "Season's Greetings" banners, etc., then as a whole the display would seem to be primarily secular, and the nativity scene won't be a violation of the Establishment Clause. [*Lynch v. Donnelly*]. But if the nativity scene or other primarily-religious symbol stands by itself, then that display probably will have a primarily religious effect, and thus violate the Establishment Clause.

   b.   History: The *history* behind the display is also very important. The longer the display has been around without objection or controversy, the less likely it is to be an Establishment Clause violation.

   Example: In Case 1, a display of text of the Ten Commandments has existed for 40 years without objection, before the present suit, and was originally donated as part of an anti-juvenile-delinquincy campaign. *Held*, no Establishment Clause violation. [*Van Orden v. Perry*] In Case 2, a display of the text of the Ten Commandments is recent, and replaced two other recent displays that were from the beginning criticized on Establishment Clause grounds. *Held*, an Establishment Clause violation. [*McCreary County v. ACLU of Kentucky*] [672-675]

F.   Intentional preferences between denominations: The government may not intentionally *prefer one religion over another*, or one sect over another. [678-680] That's true even if government thinks that it's merely trying to "accommodate" a particular religion.

   Example: The New York legislature creates a special school district whose residents consist solely of members of a particular orthodox Jewish sect, the Satmar Hassidim. The purpose and effect of the special district is to let the Satmars get public funding for a public school in their village to educate their handicapped children. *Held*, the district violates the Establishment Clause, because it was created in a way that singled out the Satmars for a special preference not made available to other groups (and also because it amounted to a delegation of state authority to a group chosen according to a religious criterion). [*Bd. of Educ. of Kiryas Joel Vil-*

lage v. Grumet] [678-679]

1. **Unintended effect:** But a regulation that has the incidental unintended *effect* of helping one religion or sect more than another, or hurting one more than another, does not generally violate the Establishment Clause.

2. **Preference of religion over non-religion:** In theory, government can't even "accommodate" *religion generally*, by giving religion in general a preference over non-religion. But in practice, the Court is *less likely to object* to a special accommodation of religion generally than to an accommodation of a particular sect.

    Example: In a federal statute, the Religious Land Use and Institutionalized Persons Act (RLUIPA), the federal government orders prison officials to go out of their way to accommodate the religious needs of all prisoners (e.g., by giving them opportunities for group worship and the right to adhere to the dress mandates of their religion). *Held*, even though comparable accommodations are not given to similar needs/desires that are not mandated by religious belief, RLUIPA (at least on its face) does not violate the Establishment Clause. [*Cutter v. Wilkinson*] [680]

G. **Aid to religious schools:** Whenever your fact patterns shows that the government is giving some sort of *financial aid* to religious schools, you must immediately think "Establishment Clause." And, of course, you must apply the three-part test. [680-688]

1. **General principles:** In general, here are some things to look for when you analyze aid to religious schools:

    a. **Benefit to all students:** A government program that benefits *all students*, at public, private non-parochial and parochial schools alike, is much more likely to pass muster than aid which goes overwhelmingly to parochial-school students;

    b. **Colleges:** Aid to religious *colleges* is easier to justify than aid to high schools or, especially, elementary schools; and

    c. **Aid to parents:** Aid given to *parents* in a way that permits them to choose what school to use the aid at is more likely to be sustained than aid given directly to the *school.*

2. **Transportation:** Programs by which parents may have their children *transported* free to religious schools are probably constitutional, as long as the transport program also covers public and private non-parochial students. [*Everson v. Bd. of Ed.*] [681]

3. **Textbooks and equipment:** Similarly, *textbooks* and *equipment* (e.g., computers) may be loaned to parochial school students as long as loans on the same basis are made to public school and private non-parochial students. But only books and materials that are *strictly secular* may be used (e.g., Bibles can't be lent out). [*Bd. of Ed. v. Allen; Mitchell v. Helms*] [682]

4. **Teachers:** The state *may* send *public school teachers* into parochial schools, even to teach basic academic subjects, as long as what's taught is free of: (1) religious content and (2) influence from the parochial school's administration. [*Agostini v. Felton*] [683]

5. **Tuition vouchers:** The state may give *tuition vouchers* to parents to enable them to pay religious-school tuition, if the vouchers may also be used in non-religious private schools. That's true even if the tuition is used to cover the costs of educating the children in core religious doctrine, and even if the benefits overwhelmingly go to the parents of religious school students. [*Zelman v. Simmons-Harris*] [684-687]

H. **The "excessive entanglement prong":** Don't forget the third prong of the test for Establishment Clause violations: governmental action must not give rise to *excessive entanglement* on the part of government in the affairs of religion, or vice versa.

1. **The "ministerial exception" from government regulation:** For instance, governmental regulation that has the effect of interfering with a religious group's determination of *who is qualified to convey the group's message* and/or *carry out its mission* is likely to violate the Establishment Clause. Thus religious groups are entitled to a *"ministerial exception,"* under which the group's choice of *who may be a minister or leader* will be essentially *immune from regulation*, such as *anti-discrimination* laws. [668]

III. THE FREE EXERCISE CLAUSE

A. **Free Exercise generally:** Let's now turn to the second clause relating to religion, the Free Exercise Clause. Under this clause, the government is barred from making any law "prohibiting the free exercise" of religion. The Free Exercise Clause prevents the government from getting in the way of people's ability to practice their religions. [688-689]

1. **Conduct vs. belief:** The Free Exercise Clause of course prevents the government from unduly burdening a person's abstract "beliefs." (*Example:* Congress cannot ban the religion of voodooism merely because it disapproves of voodooism or thinks that voodooism is irrational.) But the Clause also relates to *conduct*.

   a. **Non-religious objectives:** Free Exercise problems most typically arise when government, acting in pursuit of *non-religious objectives*, either: (1) forbids or burdens conduct which happens to be *required* by someone's religious belief; or conversely, (2) compels or encourages conduct which happens to be *forbidden* by someone's religious beliefs.

B. **Intentional vs. unintentional burdens:** The Free Exercise Clause is much more likely to prevent the government from unduly interfering with religion when the government does so *intentionally* (i.e., with knowledge or intent that a religious practice is being burdened) than when it does so *unintentionally*.

1. **Intentional burden:** If the interference with religion is *intentional* on government's part, then the interference is subjected to the *most strict scrutiny*, and will virtually never survive. [689-690]

2. **Unintentional burden:** If government *unintentionally burdens* religion, it's much harder for a religious person or group to demonstrate a Free Exercise violation. The Free Exercise Clause does not relieve a person of the obligation to comply with a *valid and neutral law* of *general applicability* even though the law forbids (or requires) conduct that his religion requires (or forbids).

We consider the "intentional" and "unintentional" cases in turn.

C. **Intentional interference:** If the government acts with a *purpose* of interfering with a religious practice — in other words, government *singles out* the religious practice, and burdens it *due to anti-religious motives* — then the interference is subjected to the *most strict scrutiny*, and will virtually never survive. (Cases involving such intentional interference with religion are rare — only one has reached the Supreme Court in recent decades, the one in the following Example.) [689]

> **Example:** The Ps practice Santeria, a religion involving animal sacrifice. D (the local city council), motivated by the citizenry's dislike of this religion and of the sacrifices, outlaws all animal sacrifice (but exempts Kosher slaughter).
>
> *Held*, the Ps' Free Exercise rights have been violated. D has acted with the purpose of outlawing a practice precisely because the practice is motivated by religion, so D's act must be most strictly scrutinized. Because there is no compelling governmental objective here, and because any governmental objective that the city is pursuing (e.g., maintenance of public health) could be achieved by less discriminatory means, the law fails this strictest scrutiny. [*Church of the Lukumi Babalu Aye v. Hialeah*] [689]

1. **Perhaps limited to "punishments":** However, this rule of strict scrutiny probably applies only to criminal or civil *"sanctions"* — in essence *punishments* — that are imposed for the purpose of disfavoring religious practices, not to government conduct that merely *withholds some generally-applicable benefit* so the benefit cannot be used in connection with a religiously-motivated activity.

   Example: A state gives merit scholarships to college-bound student with a certain G.P.A., but excludes anyone who wants to use the scholarship to study for the ministry. *Held*, this exclusion doesn't violate the Free Exercise clause, because it doesn't involve a criminal or civil sanction, merely a refusal by government to grant an affirmative benefit to subsidize an "essentially religious endeavor." [*Locke v. Davey*] [691]

D. **Unintentional burdening of religious practices:** Where government *unintentionally burdens* a religious practice by enacting a *generally-applicable* rule, it is very difficult for the affected individual whose religious practice has been burdened to obtain an exemption from the rule on free exercise grounds. In this situation, since 1990 the Court has held that the right of free exercise does not relieve a person of the obligation to comply with a *valid and neutral law* of *general applicability,* even though the law forbids (or requires) conduct that his religion requires (or forbids). [*Employment Division v. Smith*]. [694]

   Example: Oregon makes it a crime to possess the drug peyote, and refuses to give an exemption to Native Americans whose use of the drug is a central part of their religious rites. The Native Americans assert that their rights under the Free Exercise Clause require the state to give them an exemption from the rule, unless the state can show that denial of an exemption is necessary for the achievement of a compelling state objective.

   Held, for the state. Oregon may refuse an exemption. And it may do so without application of strict scrutiny by the court, indeed, without the court's doing any balancing of the strength of the state's interest in its prohibition against the burden on the individual's religious beliefs. "[T]he right of free exercise does not relieve an individual of the obligation to comply with a *valid and neutral law* of *general applicability* on the ground that the law proscribes (or prescribes) conduct that his religion prescribes (or proscribes)." [*Employment Division v. Smith, supra.*] [694]

1. **Other constitutional interests present:** But where the individual's interest in free exercise of religion is *combined* with a *free speech, freedom of association, substantive due process,* or some other *separate constitutional interest,* the individual has a *better chance of prevailing.* [695]

   Example: In *Wisconsin v. Yoder* (1972), the Court held that Wisconsin must exempt 14- and 15-year-old Amish students from the state requirement that students attend school until the age of 16. The decision came before the 1990 decision in *Employment Div. v. Smith, supra,* that free-exercise rights don't require the government to give an exemption from valid and neutral laws of general applicability. But given the special *substantive-due-process interest* of the students and their parents in the subject of education (parents have a fundamental due process interest in deciding how their children are to be educated; see *Pierce v. Society of Sisters* [173]), even the present post-*Smith* Court might give stricter-than-usual review to the state's refusal to give an exemption.

2. **Anti-discrimination laws, and a group's right to pick its "ministers":** *Smith* does *not* apply when the government regulation, even though neutral and generally-applicable on its face, would have the effect of *interfering with the internal decision-making of a religious group* regarding the group's *core faith and mission*. So, for instance, a church will be exempt on free-exercise grounds from a generally-applicable and neutral rule forbidding certain types of *employment discrimination*, if the rule would interfere with the church's right to *select the "ministers"* who will

carry out the church's core religious mission. [695]

> **Example:** Hosanna-Tabor, a combined church and religious school, fires Perich, a minister/teacher. The EEOC claims that this action violated the ADA, a federal anti-discrimination law. The EEOC argues that the case falls within the *Smith* principle that the Free Exercise Clause does not require government to give an exemption from a valid and neutral generally-applicable law.
>
> *Held,* for the church-and-school: *Smith* applies only to government regulation of *"outward physical acts"* (such as ingesting peyote, in *Smith*). Smith does not apply where government is interfering with "an **internal church decision that affects the faith and mission** of the church itself." So the Free Exercise Clause (as well as the Establishment Clause) entitle the church-and-school to a "ministerial exemption," enabling it to fire Perich even if this would otherwise violate the ADA. [*Hosanna-Tabor Evangelical Lutheran Church and School v. EEOC*] [695-696]

E. Conscientious objection: It's not clear whether Congress *must* (as it does) give an exemption for military service for *conscientious objectors* (i.e., those who believe that all war is evil). [696]

    1. Selective c.o.'s: But it's clear that Congress need not give an exemption to "selective" c.o.'s (i.e., those who do not believe that all war is evil, but who believe that the particular war in which they are being asked to fight is evil). [*Gillette v. U.S.*]

F. Public health: Government may have to sacrifice its interest in the *health* of its citizenry, if individuals' religious dictates so require. [696]

    1. Competent adult: Where the case involves a *competent adult*, and only that adult's own health is at stake, government may probably not force treatment on the individual over his religious objection. (*Example:* A state probably can't force a Jehovah's Witness to accept a blood transfusion or other life-saving medical care over that person's religious objections.)

    2. Child: However, where the patient is a *child* whose parents object on religious grounds, the state may probably compel the treatment.

    3. Danger to others: Also, if the case involves not only a health danger to the person asserting a religious belief, but also a health danger to *others*, then government probably does not have to give an exemption. (*Example:* P may be forced to undergo a vaccination over his religious objections. [*Jacobsen v. Mass.*])

G. What constitutes a religious belief: Only *bona fide* "religious beliefs" are protected by the Free Exercise Clause. But "religious beliefs" are defined very *broadly.* [697]

    1. Non-theistic: For instance, *non-theistic* beliefs are protected. That is, the belief need not recognize the existence of a supreme being. (*Example:* Public officials cannot be forced to take an oath in which they say that they believe that God exists. [*Torcaso v. Watkins*])

    2. Unorganized religions: Similarly, *unorganized* or obscure religions get the same protection as the major religions. In fact, even if a person's religious beliefs are followed *only by him*, he's still entitled to free exercise protection.

    3. Sincerity: A court will not sustain a free exercise claim unless it is convinced that the religious belief is *"genuine"* or *"sincere."* (The fact that the belief or practice has been observed by a religious group for a long period of time may be considered in measuring sincerity. But the converse — absence of a long-standing practice — does not mean that the belief is insincere.)

        a. Unreasonableness: The court will *not* consider whether the belief is "true" or *"reasonable."* Even a very "unreasonable" belief (that is, a belief that most people might consider unreasonable) is not deprived of protection, so long as it is *genuine.* [*U.S. v. Ballard*] (*Example:* The practice of voodoo, including sticking pins into dolls representing one's enemies, might be considered by most of us to be "unreasonable." But as long as such a practice is part of a person's genuine set of beliefs and religious practices, it will not be deprived of protection merely because most find it unreasonable.)

CHAPTER 16

JUSTICIABILITY

I. JUSTICIABILITY GENERALLY

A. List: In order for a case to be heard by the federal courts, the plaintiff must get past a series of procedural obstacles which we collectively call requirements for *"justiciability"*: (1) the case must not require the giving of an *advisory opinion*; (2) the plaintiff must have *standing*; (3) the case must not be *moot*; (4) the case must be *ripe* for decision; and (5) the case must not involve a non-justiciable *political question*. [708]

II. ADVISORY OPINIONS

A. Constitutional "case or controversy" requirement: Article III, Section 2 of the Constitution gives the federal courts jurisdiction only over "cases" and "controversies." The federal courts are therefore prevented from issuing opinions on *abstract* or *hypothetical* questions. This means that the federal courts may not give *"advisory opinions."* In other words, the federal courts may not render opinions which answer a legal question when no party is before the court who has suffered or faces specific injury. [708]

> **Example:** Suppose that both houses of Congress approve a bill, but the President has doubts about the bill's constitutionality. The President may *not* go to a federal court and ask the federal court whether the bill is constitutional, so that he may decide whether to veto it. If the federal court were to give its opinion about whether the bill was constitutional, at a time when no party who had been or might soon be injured by the unconstitutionality was before the court, this would be an "advisory opinion" that would violate the constitutional "case or controversy" requirement.

1. Declaratory judgments sometimes allowed: But *declaratory judgments* are sometimes allowed, and are not forbidden by the rule against advisory opinions. A declaratory judgment is a judicial decision in which the court is not requested to award damages or an injunction, but is instead requested to state what the legal effect would be of proposed conduct by one or both of the parties. [709]

    a. Requirements: But the plaintiff is not entitled to get a declaratory judgment on just any question about what the legal consequence of the particular conduct would be. If the declaratory judgment action raises only questions that are very *hypothetical* or *abstract*, the federal court is likely to conclude that what's sought here is an illegal advisory opinion, because no specific, concrete controversy exists.

III. STANDING

A. Function of a standing requirement: Probably the most important rule about when the federal courts may hear a case is that they may do so only when the plaintiff has *"standing"* to assert his claim. By this, we mean that the plaintiff must have a significant *stake* in the controversy. [709-711]

Example: Suppose that during the Vietnam War, P, a federal taxpayer, becomes convinced that, since Congress has never formally declared war, P's tax dollars are being used to support an unconstitutional war. If P were to sue the federal government in federal court to have the war effort enjoined on this ground, the court would not hear his claim — he would be found to lack "standing," since (as we'll see in detail later) a person whose only connection with the controversy is that he is a taxpayer will almost never be deemed to have standing to claim that tax dollars are being used illegally.

B. Requirement of "injury in fact": The key concept behind the law of standing is simple: the litigant must show that he has suffered an *"injury in fact."* At its broadest level, the standing requirement means that the plaintiff must show that *he has himself been injured* in some way by the conduct that he complains of. [710]

C. Who is kept out: The standing rules tend to keep two main types of cases *out* of the federal courts: [711]

    1. Non-individuated harm: First, we have cases in which the harm suffered by the plaintiff is *no different* from that suffered by very large numbers of people not before the court. (*Example:* Suppose P's only connection with the suit is that he is a federal "citizen" or a "taxpayer" who is injured the same as any other citizen or taxpayer by the fact that the government is spending tax dollars illegally or otherwise violating some law. P does not have standing.)

    2. Third parties' rights: Second, we have cases where the rights claimed to be violated are not the rights of the plaintiff, but instead the rights of *third parties* who are not before the court. (But there are some important exceptions to the general rule that the plaintiff can't complain of government actions that violate someone else's rights.)

D. Taxpayer and citizen suits: Here is the single most important context in which standing problems arise: suits that are brought by federal *"citizens"* or *"taxpayers"* arguing that their general rights as citizens or taxpayers are violated by governmental action. [711-713]

    1. Taxpayer suits: Suppose that the plaintiff contends that: (1) he is a federal *taxpayer*; and (2) his tax dollars are being spent by the government in some illegal way. May the plaintiff pursue this suit in federal court? In general, the answer will be, *"no."* The fact that a person's federal taxes are used to fund an unconstitutional or illegal government program is simply not a sufficient connection with the governmental action to confer standing on the plaintiff. [*Frothingham v. Mellon*]. [711]

        a. One exception: There is one very narrow exception: a federal taxpayer has standing to sue to overturn a *congressional tax or spending program* that violates the *Establishment Clause*. [*Flast v. Cohen*] [711]

            i. Tightly limited: But this "*Flast* exception" is extremely *tightly limited:* it applies only to *congressional* spending that violates the Establishment Clause, not even to *Executive-Branch* spending that might violate the Clause. [*Hein v. Freedom from Religion Foundation*] [712]

        b. State taxpayers: A *state* taxpayer, like a federal taxpayer, does *not* have federal-court standing to litigate the legality of the state's expenditures. [*DaimlerChrysler Corp. v. Cuno*] [713]

        c. Municipal taxpayer: But a *municipal* taxpayer definitely *does* have standing to litigate the legality of his city's expenditures. [713]

    2. Citizen suits: Suppose now that plaintiff argues that he is a federal *"citizen,"* and that as such he has the right to have his government act in accordance with the Constitution. Assume that P has no direct connection with the governmental act he's complaining about (he's merely claiming that, like every other citizen, he has the right to have the federal government obey the Constitution). In this "citizen suit" situation, P will *not have standing*. The Court has always held that one federal citizen's interest in lawful government is no different from the interest of any other citizen, and that an individual litigant relying on citizenship has not shown the *"individualized"* injury-in-fact that is required for standing. [713]

E. Cases not based on taxpayer or citizen status: Now suppose that the plaintiff is not arguing that his standing derives from his status as citizen or taxpayer. In other words, we're now talking about the vast bulk of ordinary law suits. [713-718]

   1. Three requirements: Here, there are three standing requirements that the plaintiff must meet: (1) he must show that he has suffered (or is likely to suffer) an *"injury in fact"*; (2) the injury he is suffering must be *concrete* and *"individuated"*; and (3) the action being challenged must be the *"cause in fact"* of the injury. [713]

   2. "Injury in fact": The plaintiff must show that he either *has suffered*, or *will probably suffer*, some concrete *"injury in fact."* [713]

      a. Non-economic harm: This "injury in fact" requirement is pretty loosely applied. For instance, the harm does not have to be *economic* in nature.

      Example: A group of people who use a national forest claim that the construction of a recreation area in the forest will violate federal laws. To get standing, the plaintiffs point to the injury to their "esthetic and environmental well-being" which would result from the construction. *Held*, this esthetic and environmental injury satisfies the "injury in fact" requirement, even though the harm is non-economic and in fact very intangible. [*Sierra Club v. Morton*]) [714]

      b. Imminent harm: If P has not *already* suffered the injury in fact, he must show that the future injury is not only probable but *"concrete"* and *"imminent."* Thus if the threatened harm is too *far in the future*, or its eventual occurrence is too *"speculative,"* the "actual or imminent" element will not be satisfied, and standing will not be found.

      Example: The Ps challenge a federal regulatory action that they say will endanger certain species abroad. The Ps say that they have in the past, and will in the future, travel abroad to visit the habitats of these species. *Held*, the Ps lack standing, because the lack of specific information about their future plans means the harm to them is not sufficiently concrete or imminent. [*Lujan v. Defenders of Wildlife*] [714]

         i. "Certainly impending": In at least one recent case, the Court has said that the threatened harm has to be *"certainly impending."* See *Clapper*, immediately *infra*. The Court's use of this term in *Clapper* seems to mean that if the harm hasn't already occurred, not only does it have to be the case that if the harm occurs, it will occur soon (the requirement of "imminence"), but also that the occurrence of the harm in the near future is *highly probable*.

         ii. Government surveillance in the war on terror: The principle that future harms must not be unduly speculative has made it hard for anyone to challenge certain *federal surveillance programs,* such as those enacted as part of the war on terror.

         Example: A federal statute, §1881a, permits federal intelligence authorities to conduct e-mail and telephone surveillance of non-citizens who are believed to be outside of the country and whom the government suspects of having links to terrorist organizations, where the government's purpose is to obtain "foreign intelligence information" (typically for counter-terrorism purposes). The Ps are various U.S. citizens — including attorneys, reporters, and human-rights workers — who allege that their work requires them to communicate with such non-citizens suspected of having links to terrorist organizations. The

Ps say they reasonably fear that §1881a will be used in the near future to eavesdrop on conversations between themselves and these targeted foreigners.

Held (5-4), the Ps don't have standing. Prior standing cases have required that the threatened injury be "certainly impending." The plaintiffs fail to meet this "certainly impending" requirement. Because the Ps have "no actual knowledge" of what foreign targets the government would choose for surveillance, their fear that their own communications will be captured through surveillance targeting others is "necessarily conjectural" and "highly speculative." [*Clapper v. Amnesty Int'l USA* (2013)] [714]

3. Remedy: In addition to showing an "injury in fact," P must show that the injury would be *remedied* by a favorable court decision. [713]

Example: The various plaintiffs claim to have been injured by the zoning rules of Penfield, New York. They claim that these rules were imposed for the purpose of excluding the building of low- and moderate-income housing in the town. Certain Ps (the only ones we'll discuss here) are low- and moderate-income individuals who have never lived in Penfield, but who allege that they sought housing there and would have moved there had affordable housing been available.

Held, these Ps lack standing for several reasons. One reason is that these Ps fail the *"redressability"* requirement: they can't show that if the court awarded the relief being sought — a striking down of the zoning rules — the desired moderate-income projects will in fact likely be built. Therefore, they can't show that a favorable decision would redress (make better) the harm the Ps complain about. [*Warth v. Seldin*] [717]

4. Individuated harm: The harm that has been or will be suffered by the plaintiff has to be *"individuated."* That is, it can't be the same harm as suffered by every citizen, or every taxpayer.

a. Large number: But the harm may still be found to be "individuated" even though there are a *large number* of people suffering the harm. [715]

i. Same harm: But remember that if the harm complained of by the plaintiff is truly the same harm as suffered by every citizen or every taxpayer in the country, the harm will not be sufficiently "individuated," and the plaintiffs won't have standing.

b. Organizations and associations: What about organizations and associations — does the organization itself have to suffer the harm, or can it merely assert that its *members* will suffer or have suffered the required harm? In general, the answer is that organizations and associations will be able to sue on behalf of their members. However: (1) the members have to be people who would have *standing in their own right* (so that an organization of citizens or taxpayers could not complain of harm that is suffered by all citizens or taxpayers); (2) the interests being asserted by the organization in the lawsuit must be *related to the organization's purpose* (so that an environmental group could probably not try to pursue its members' interests in, say, an effective criminal justice system); and (3) the case cannot be one which requires the *participation of individual members.* [*Hunt v. Wash. Apple Advt'g. Comm.*]. These three requirements are pretty liberally applied. [716]

5. Causation: Finally, the action that the plaintiff is complaining about must be the *"cause in fact"* of his injury. Actually, this causation requirement breaks down into two sub-requirements:

(1) P has to show that the challenged action was a *"but for"* cause of his injury, that is, that the injury would not have occurred unless the challenged action had taken place; and

(2) P must show that a favorable decision in the suit will probably *redress* the injury to him. [716-718]

6. **Perhaps easier test for states:** When the suit is brought by a *state*, the injury-in-fact and causation requirements are probably interpreted a bit *less stringently.*

> **Example:** Massachusetts sues to force the EPA to regulate auto emissions. The state's reasoning is that (1) such regulation will or may slow the speed of global warming "over the next century" (even though non-U.S. sources will concededly grow their own emissions dramatically during this period); and (2) without the slowing, the state's coastal lands will or may be eroded by rising sea levels. *Held*, Mass. has met the injury-in-fact and causation requirements, in part because Mass. is acting as a sovereign state protecting the interests of its citizens. [*Mass. v. EPA*, 2007] [718]

F. **Third-party standing:** One of the key functions of the standing doctrine is that this is how courts apply the general rule that a litigant normally may *not assert the constitutional rights of persons not before the court*. (This principle is sometimes called the rule against use of "constitutional *jus tertii*," — *jus tertii* means "rights of third persons" in Latin.) [719]

> **Example:** Zoning laws enacted by the city of Penfield, N.Y., intentionally exclude the building of low-income housing. The Ps are residents of nearby Rochester, who claim that because Penfield has refused to allow low- and middle-income housing, the taxes of these Rochester residents have risen, since Rochester has to subsidize or build more low-income housing than it would have to build than had Penfield not practiced exclusionary zoning.
>
> *Held*, these Rochester residents lack standing. It is true that their higher taxes are an "injury in fact" to them. But Penfield's zoning laws do not apply to these Rochester residents, and therefore do not violate *their* rights. And the Rochester residents may not claim that the rights of *other people not before the court* have been violated (e.g., people who would have moved to Penfield had exclusionary zoning not been practiced). [*Warth v. Seldin*]) [719]

1. **Not constitutionally required:** This rule against the assertion of third-party rights is *not* mandated by the Article III "case or controversy" requirement. In other words, it is not a rule imposed by the Constitution on the federal courts; instead, it is a rule of *"prudence,"* a policy decision adopted by the Supreme Court. [719]

2. **Exceptions:** Since the rule against asserting third-party rights is not required by the Constitution, the Supreme Court is free to make whatever *exceptions* it wishes to the doctrine.

   a. **Associations:** One exception is that an *association* will normally be allowed to raise the rights of its *members*. For instance, if a group of people would be injured by damage to the air they breathe and the water they drink, an organization of which they are members (e.g., the Sierra Club) would typically be allowed to sue on their behalf. [716]

   b. **Overbreadth:** Another sort of exception to the rule against third-party standing is the First Amendment *overbreadth* doctrine, which we covered earlier in our discussion of freedom of expression. Remember that the basic idea behind overbreadth is that even where a statute could constitutionally be applied to the plaintiff's conduct, if he can show that the statute would unconstitutionally restrict the expression of *some other person not before the court,* the court may hear the lawsuit and strike down the statute. We allow overbreadth in the *First Amendment area* but not elsewhere because statutes that purport to restrict expression in an overbroad manner will have a *"chilling effect"* on citizens' general willingness to exercise their freedom of speech. [719]

G. **"Prudential" standing:** We just saw that the rule against third-party standing is not dictated by the Article III "case or controversy" requirement, and is instead the result of *"prudential"* considerations. More generally, the federal courts retain the right to refuse to hear *any* case on such prudential-standing grounds, even cases falling outside the pure third-party-standing area.

Example: P is the father of a daughter, X, who attends public-school. P claims that the school's policy of reciting the Pledge of Allegiance violates his First Amendment right to have his daughter be instructed in P's atheistic beliefs without government interference. (X's mother, who is divorced from P, opposes the suit.) *Held*, because the suit involves domestic relations questions — typically avoided by the federal courts — and also involves X's rights in a highly controversial matter, the Court's prudential-standing policies dictate that the federal courts not hear the case. [*Elk Grove v. Newdow*] [719]

IV. MOOTNESS

A. **General rule:** A case may not be heard by the federal courts if it is *"moot."* A case is moot if it raised a live controversy at the time the complaint was filed, but *events occurring after the filing* have deprived the litigant of an ongoing stake in the controversy. [720]

> **Example:** P sues D, a state university, claiming that the university's law school admissions program is racially discriminatory. P is permitted to attend the law school while the case is being litigated. By the time the case arrives at the Supreme Court for review, P is in his final year of law school, and the university says that he will be allowed to graduate regardless of how the case is decided. *Held*, the case is moot. Therefore, the appeal will not be decided. [*DeFunis v. Odegaard*]

1. **Constitutional basis for:** Apparently the rule that the federal courts may not decide "moot" cases is *required* by the Constitution. That is, deciding a case when the parties no longer have a live controversy would amount to issuing an advisory opinion, in violation of Article III's "case or controversy" requirement.

B. **Exceptions:** Nonetheless, the courts recognize a few situations where a case that would appear to be "moot" will nonetheless be heard. [720]

1. **"Capable of repetition, yet evading review":** For instance, a case will not be treated as moot if the issue it raises is *"capable of repetition, yet evading review."* This "capable of repetition, yet evading review" doctrine takes care of situations in which, if the case were to be declared moot, a *different person* might be injured in the *same way* by the same defendant, and his claim, too, would be mooted before review could be had. [720]

> **Example:** P, a pregnant woman, attacks the constitutionality of Texas' anti-abortion law. She brings the suit as a class action, in which she is the named plaintiff and other pregnant women who want abortions are unnamed members. By the time the case reaches the Supreme Court, P is no longer pregnant.
>
> *Held*, the case should not be dismissed as moot. A pregnancy will almost always be over before the usual appellate process is complete. Therefore, if the Court insisted that the named plaintiff who starts the suit must still be pregnant by the time the suit gets to the Supreme Court, no plaintiff could ever get to that Court. So the constitutionality of the Texas anti-abortion law is "capable of repetition, yet evading review." [*Roe v. Wade*]

2. **Voluntary cessation by defendant:** The case will generally not be treated as moot if the defendant *voluntarily ceases* the conduct that the plaintiff is complaining about. So if the plaintiff is seeking an injunction, the defendant can't usually get the case dismissed on mootness grounds merely by saying that he has voluntarily stopped the conduct that the plaintiff is trying to get an injunction against — unless the defendant shows that there is no reasonable likelihood that he will return to his old ways, the court will let the action go forward. [721]

3. **Collateral consequences:** Finally, a case will not be moot even if it is mostly decided, if there are still *collateral consequences* that might be adverse to the defendant. For instance, suppose that

a criminal defendant has already served his sentence by the time his attack on the constitutionality of his conviction comes before the federal court. The case will not be moot, because there will probably be future collateral consequences to the defendant from his conviction (e.g., he will lose the right to vote, his reputation or employability will be damaged, etc.). [721]

V. RIPENESS

A. Ripeness problem generally: You can think of the problem of ripeness as being the opposite of mootness. A case is moot, as we've just seen, because it *no longer* involves an actual controversy. By contrast, a case is not yet ripe (and therefore not yet decidable by a federal court) if it has *not yet become sufficiently concrete* to be easily adjudicated. [721]

> **Example:** The Hatch Act prohibits federal executive-branch employees from getting involved in "political management or … political campaigns." The plaintiffs are federal civil servants who want to attack the constitutionality of the Hatch Act. The plaintiffs claim that they want to engage in prohibited political activities. But they concede that they have not yet engaged in such activities.
>
> *Held*, the plaintiffs' claims are not yet ripe. The problem is not that the Ps have not yet violated the statute. Rather, the problem is that the plaintiffs have not been adequately specific about the *precise acts* that they wish to carry out. (If the Ps would specify in detail what they want to do, their suit might not be unripe even though they haven't yet violated the act.) [*United Public Workers v. Mitchell*] [721]

B. Uncertain enforcement of criminal statute: One common ripeness problem arises where the plaintiff attacks the constitutionality of a statute and says that he has violated the statute, but it is clear that the statute is *rarely enforced* and probably will not be enforced in this particular situation. Here, the rules are pretty blurry — suffice it to say that if the court believes that it is *very unlikely* that the statute will be enforced against the plaintiff either for the activity he has already done or similar activity he is likely to do in the future, the court will probably treat the case as being not ripe.

> **Example:** Connecticut forbids the distribution of contraceptives. Two married couples and a physician challenge the law's constitutionality, and allege that they have violated the law. *Held*, the case is not ripe, because the statute has been on the books for 80 years with only one reported prosecution, so there does not exist the required "clear" threat that the plaintiffs will be prosecuted. [*Poe v. Ullman*] [722]

1. Specific threatened harm required: But for a case to be ripe, it is not necessary that the litigant have *already suffered* harm. It will be enough that there is a *reasonable probability* of harm. However, the anticipated harm has to be fairly *specific*. [722]

VI. THE ELEVENTH AMENDMENT AND SUITS AGAINST THE STATES

A. The Eleventh Amendment generally: The *Eleventh Amendment* specifically bars any federal suit "against any one of the *states* by citizens of another state, or by citizens or subjects of any foreign state." [722]

1. Damage suits against states: The Eleventh Amendment has been held to bar most types of *damage suits* against a state.

a. Plaintiff not a citizen of defendant state: By its own terms, the Amendment clearly applies to suits against a state brought by citizens of a *different state* or by foreigners. (*Examples:* A citizen of Missouri may not bring a damage suit against the state of Illinois. Nor may a British subject bring a damage suit against the state of Illinois.)

    b. **Suit by citizen of defendant state:** The Eleventh Amendment has been ***interpreted*** to apply also to bar a damage suit where the plaintiff is a ***citizen of the defendant state***. [*Hans v. Louisiana*] (*Example:* Suppose P is an employee of the Delmarva state legislature. He is then fired, in apparent violation of his employment contract. P brings a suit for contract damages against Delmarva, in federal court. This suit would be a violation of the Eleventh Amendment, as broadly interpreted by the Supreme Court.)

2. **Suits by states or federal government:** The Eleventh Amendment does ***not*** bar federal suits brought by ***one state*** against another state, or by the ***federal government*** against a state.

3. **No counties or cities protected:** Only the ***state itself***, not its ***subdivisions***, such as ***counties*** or ***cities***, is protected by the Eleventh Amendment. (*Example:* P, a county worker, is fired. He brings a federal suit for contract damages against the county. Since the suit is not against the state *per se*, the Eleventh Amendment does not apply, even though the county is in essence a subdivision of the state.)

4. **No bar against injunctions:** The Eleventh Amendment essentially bars only suits for ***damages***. That is, it does not bar most suits for ***injunctions***. For instance, if a private litigant sues a state official to enjoin him from taking acts which would violate the plaintiff's ***constitutional*** or ***federal-law*** rights, the Eleventh Amendment does not apply and the suit may proceed. [*Ex parte Young*]

5. **Congress can't override:** *Congress* generally ***can't change*** the "no federal-court suits against the states" principle behind the Eleventh Amendment, even if it wants to and expressly says it's doing so. [*Seminole Tribe v. Florida*] [724-726]

    Example: Congress passes a statute saying any state *can* be sued in federal court by private citizens for violating, say, federal patent or environmental laws. This statute won't have any effect — a federal court still can't hear a private suit against a state for damages for violating the federal law. [*Florida Prepaid v. Coll. Sav. Bank*] [725]

    a. **Exception for remedial powers:** But there's an ***exception*** — if Congress is acting properly pursuant to its ***remedial powers*** under the Thirteenth, Fourteenth or Fifteenth Amendments, it ***may abrogate*** the states' Eleventh Amendment immunity.

B. **States' sovereign immunity:** The states have a constitutionally-guaranteed ***sovereign immunity*** from certain proceedings brought by private parties.

1. **Suit in states' own courts:** Thus the states have constitutional sovereign immunity from private damage suits brought against the state in the ***state's own courts***. This is true even if the suit is based on a ***congressionally-granted federal right***. [726]

    Example: Congress passes a valid statute saying that state employees must receive premium pay for overtime just as private-sector employees do. Employees of Maine sue the state in Maine courts on this right. *Held*, the Constitution's structure incorporates the doctrine of sovereign immunity, and that doctrine allows Maine to avoid hearing the employees' suit, even if Congress has expressly said that the states must hear such suits. [*Alden v. Maine*] [726]

2. **Proceeding before federal administrative agency:** Similarly, the states have sovereign immunity from being required to respond to a private complaint before a ***federal administrative agency***. [*Federal Maritime Comm. v. So. Car. St. Ports Auth.*] [726]

VII. POLITICAL QUESTIONS

A. The doctrine generally: The final aspect of justiciability is the requirement is that the case not involve the decision of a *"political question."* This rule is even more vague than the other justiciability rules we've talked about already. The doctrine does *not* mean that federal courts will not decide a case that involves politics. It doesn't even mean that courts will refuse to decide cases where political issues are right at the heart of the controversy. Instead, the court will decline to hear a case on political question grounds only if it thinks that the doctrine of *separation of powers* requires this, or if it thinks that deciding the case would be unwise as a policy matter. [727]

    1. Two of the factors used: Two of the factors that seem to be very important in whether a case will be found to involve a non-justiciable political question are:

        a. Commitment to another branch: First, the fact that the case presents an issue which has been committed by the Constitution to *another branch of the federal government*, i.e., to Congress or to the President instead of the courts.

        b. Lack of standards: Second, the fact that there are no manageable *standards* by which a court could resolve the issue.

B. "Commitment to other branches" strand: The courts will refuse to decide a case on political-question grounds if the case raises an issue the determination of which is clearly committed by the Constitution to *another branch of the federal government*. [728-730]

    Example: D, a federal judge, claims that the Senate has used improper procedures in convicting him following his impeachment, because the case was heard before a committee of Senators rather than the full Senate (though the full Senate voted, after receiving a transcript of the committee proceedings). D claims that this violates the Impeachment Clause, which says that "the Senate shall have sole Power to try all Impeachments." *Held*, the case presents a nonjusticiable political question, because the Constitution has given the Senate, not the courts, the power to decide what constitutes a "trial." [*Nixon v. U.S.*]

    1. Other impeachment issues: The same principle probably applies to *all* aspects of the impeachment process. Thus if the House voted to impeach the President and the Senate voted to convict, the Supreme Court would probably refuse to review either of these decisions on "commitment to other branches" political-question grounds (so that if the President tried to get the Supreme Court to hear his argument that the crime for which he was impeached and convicted was not within the constitutionally-defined category of "high crimes and misdemeanors," the Court would probably refuse to consider the merits of this argument).

    2. Rare: It is quite rare for a case to be declined on the grounds that it involves a question committed to some other branch of government.

C. "Lack of judicially manageable standards": The second major factor that may lead the court to decide that there is a non-justiciable political question, is that there are no *manageable standards* by which the courts can resolve the issue. [730]

    Example: Article IV, Section 4 provides that "the United States shall guarantee to every state in this union a republican form of government." Some unhappy Rhode Island citizens stage a rebellion. Ultimately, various Rhode Islanders ask the federal courts to decide which of two competing factions is the lawful government of the state.

    Held, the Court cannot decide this question, because it presents a political question. There are no criteria by which a court could determine whether a particular "government" was "Republican." [*Luther v. Borden*]

D. Reapportionment: Let's now look in some detail at the federal cases on *legislative reapportionment*. [730-734]

1. **One person, one vote rule:** The landmark case of *Baker v. Carr,* and cases following it, establish the so-called *"one person, one vote"* principle: any governmental body, whether it's a federal one (like congressional districts) or a state one (like a state legislature) must be apportioned on a *population* basis, so that *all voters have essentially the same voting power.* If a governmental electoral scheme does not comply with this "one person, one vote" principle, it violates the *equal protection* rights of the under-represented voters. [*Reynolds v. Sims*] [731-732]

   a. **Justiciable:** Such cases raising the "one person, one vote" argument are *justiciable.* The Court has rejected the argument that these cases raise non-justiciable political questions. [*Baker v. Carr*] [731]

   b. **Both houses of state legislature:** One of the consequences of the "one person, one vote" principle is that if a state has a bicameral (two-house) legislature, *both* houses must be elected based on population. Thus, paradoxically, the U.S. Constitution prohibits a state from having one body that awards seats without reference to population (e.g., a house that gives the same number of votes to each county), even though the U.S. Senate is built upon exactly this kind of non-population-based scheme!

2. **How much equality is required:** The rules for *how much equality is required* vary depending on whether we're talking about a congressional districting scheme or, instead, a state or local districting scheme. [733]

   a. **Congressional:** For *congressional districts*, the districts have to be *almost precisely equal.* Even a scheme where one congressional district within a state was only 1% more populous than another has been struck down. States must make a "good-faith effort to achieve *precise mathematical equality*" in the drawing of congressional districts. [*Kirkpatrick v. Preisler*]

   b. **State and local:** *Much greater deviation* from mathematical equality is allowed where what is being apportioned is *state legislatures* or *local governmental bodies.* So for example, a *10%* or smaller deviation between the voting power of a voter in one district versus a voter in another will generally be *upheld.* [*White v. Regester*] Even greater disparities will be allowed if there are good reasons for them. (For instance, suppose a state wants not to have to redraw its county boundaries, and wants to have each county elect its own representative to the state Assembly. This desire to "respect pre-existing political boundaries" will probably justify, say, a 15% or even 20% disparity in per-person voting power.)

3. **Gerrymandering:** Consider *gerrymandering*, that is, the process by which the strength of a particular voting bloc is curtailed by restricting its members to carefully and artificially-constructed districts.

   a. **"Partisan gerrymandering" cases hard to win:** First, consider *"partisan gerrymandering"* cases, i.e., cases arguing that a group is being disadvantaged based on its *political* rather than racial status. These cases are almost impossible for the plaintiffs to win. See C-48 *supra.* (In fact, a near-majority of the Court believes that such cases aren't even *justiciable.* [*Vieth v. Jubelirer*] [734])

   b. **Racial minority:** But if a *racial or ethnic minority* can show that the gerrymandering scheme was intentionally designed to hurt, and did hurt, that minority, the plaintiffs' case *will* be justiciable, and probably winnable. For instance, if the state legislature draws districts for the state senate in a way that intentionally gives African Americans control of 5% of the districts when African Americans constitute 10% of the state population, African American voters have a good chance of winning an equal protection suit. [328]

CHAPTER 1

INTRODUCTION

I. ROADMAP OF CONSTITUTIONAL LAW

A. Roadmap: Here is a very brief "roadmap" of Constitutional Law, giving you the names of the major doctrines/clauses, and the flavor of how each operates:

1. **Federalism:** First, we'll be covering various aspects of *"federalism."* Federalism means that the federal and state governments co-exist. Some of the main principles stemming from federalism are:

   a. **Limited, enumerated powers:** The powers of the federal government are **limited** to those that are **enumerated** in the Constitution. [Chap. 3]

   b. **Separation of powers:** Each of the three branches of the federal government (Congress, the President and the Judiciary) has its own enumerated powers, and one branch may not take actions reserved by the Constitution to one of the other branches. This is the doctrine of *"separation of powers."* [Chap. 8]

   c. **Congress' Commerce power:** The most important power given to Congress is the power to regulate *"commerce."* [Chap. 4]

2. **Dormant Commerce Clause:** Under the *"Dormant* Commerce Clause," the mere existence of the federal commerce power **restricts the states** from **discriminating against**, or unduly **burdening**, **interstate commerce**. [Chap. 6]

3. **Due Process Clause:** The *"Due Process Clause"* of the 14th Amendment has two different types of effects [Chap. 9]:

   a. **Substantive due process:** It limits the *"substantive"* power of the government to regulate certain areas of human life (e.g., child-bearing);

   b. **Procedural due process:** It imposes certain *"procedural"* requirements on government when it takes an individual's *"life, liberty or property."* (*Example:* Before government can take away food stamps you've been receiving, it must give you a hearing.)

4. **Equal Protection Clause:** The *"Equal Protection Clause"* of the 14th Amendment prevents government from making certain types of *"classifications,"* mainly ones that unfairly treat similarly-situated people differently. (*Example:* The Equal Protection Clause is what prohibits governments from running racially segregated schools.) [Chap. 10]

5. **Freedom of Expression:** The First Amendment protects *"speech"* against government interference. This includes the freedom of individuals to engage in **political protest**, the freedom of the **press** to publish, the freedom of individuals to *"associate"* with whomever they wish, and more. As you might expect, this "freedom" is far from absolute — often, government will be able to restrict free expression in some way or another (e.g., by requiring a permit before a large political demonstration takes place, or by prohibiting someone from advocating that a crime be committed). [Chap. 14]

6. **Freedom of Religion:** The First Amendment also protects *"freedom of religion."* There are two distinct clauses in the First Amendment dealing with religion [Chap. 15]:

a. **Establishment Clause:** The *"Establishment"* Clause prevents government from "establishing" an official religion. That is, government may not **endorse** or **support** religion generally, or a particular religion.

b. **Free Exercise Clause:** The *"Free Exercise"* Clause prevents government from **outlawing** or seriously **burdening** a person's pursuit of whatever religion (and whatever religious practices) he chooses.

II. THREE STANDARDS OF REVIEW

A. **Three standards:** There are three key **standards of review** which reappear constantly throughout Constitutional Law. When a court reviews the constitutionality of government action, it is likely to be choosing from among one of these three standards of review: (1) the **mere-rationality** standard; (2) the **strict scrutiny** standard; and (3) the **middle-level review** standard.

1. **Mere-rationality standard:** Of the three standards, the easiest one to satisfy is the *"mere-rationality"* standard. When the court applies this "mere-rationality" standard, the court will **uphold** the governmental action so long as two requirements are met:

    a. **Legitimate state objective:** First, the government must be pursuing a **legitimate governmental objective**. This is a very broad concept — practically any type of health, safety or "general welfare" goal will be found to be "legitimate."

    b. **Rational relation:** Second, there has to be a *"minimally rational relation"* between the means chosen by the government and the state objective. This requirement, too, is extremely easy to satisfy: only if the government has acted in a completely *"arbitrary and irrational"* way will this rational link between means and end not be found.

2. **Strict scrutiny:** At the other end of the spectrum, the standard that is hardest to satisfy is the *"strict scrutiny"* standard of review. This standard will only be satisfied if the governmental act satisfies two very tough requirements:

    a. **Compelling objective:** First, the **objective** being pursued by the government must be *"compelling"* (not just "legitimate," as for the "mere-rationality" standard); and

    b. **Necessary means:** Second, the **means** chosen by the government must be *"necessary"* to achieve that compelling end. In other words, the "fit" between the means and the end must be extremely tight. (It's not enough that there's a "rational relation" between the means and the end, which is enough under the "mere-rationality" standard.)

        i. **No less restrictive alternatives:** In practice, this requirement that the means be "necessary" means that there must not be any **less restrictive** means that would accomplish the government's objective just as well.

3. **Middle-level review:** In between these two review standards is so-called *"middle-level"* review.

    a. **"Important" objective:** Here, the governmental objective has to be *"important"* (half way between "legitimate" and "compelling").

b. "Substantially related" means: And, the means chosen by the government must be *"substantially related"* to the important government objective. (This "substantially related" standard is halfway between "rationally related" and "necessary.")

B. Consequences of choice: The court's choice of one of these standards of review has two important consequences:

1. **Burden of persuasion:** First, the choice will make a big difference as to who has the *burden of persuasion*.

    a. **Mere-rationality standard:** Where the governmental action is subject to the *"mere-rationality"* standard, the *individual* who is attacking the government action will generally bear the burden of persuading the court that the action is unconstitutional.

    b. **Strict scrutiny:** By contrast, if the court applies *"strict scrutiny,"* then the *governmental body* whose act is being attacked has the burden of persuading the court that its action is constitutional.

    c. **Middle-level review:** Where *"middle level"* scrutiny is used, it's not certain how the court will assign the burden of persuasion, but the burden will usually be placed on the government.

2. **Effect on outcome:** Second, the choice of review standard has a very powerful effect on the *actual outcome*. Where the "mere-rationality" standard is applied, the governmental action will *almost always be upheld*. Where "strict scrutiny" is used, the governmental action will *almost always be struck down*. (For instance, the Supreme Court applies strict scrutiny to any classification based on race, and has upheld only one such strictly scrutinized racial classification in the last 50 years.) Where middle-level scrutiny is used, there's roughly a 50-50 chance that the governmental action will be struck down.

C. When used: Here is a quick overview of the entire body of Constitutional Law, to see where each of these review standards gets used:

1. **Mere-rationality standard:** Here are the main places where the "mere-rationality" standard gets applied (and therefore, the places where it's very hard for the person attacking the governmental action to get it struck down on constitutional grounds):

    a. **Dormant Commerce Clause:** First, the "mere-rationality" standard is the main test used to determine whether a state regulation that affects interstate commerce violates the *"Dormant Commerce Clause."* The state regulation has to pursue a legitimate state end, and be rationally related to that end. (But there's a second test which we'll review in greater detail later: the state's interest in enforcing its regulation must also outweigh any *burden* imposed on interstate commerce, and any discrimination against interstate commerce.)

    b. **Substantive due process:** Next comes *substantive due process*. So long as no "fundamental right" is affected, the test for determining whether a governmental act violates substantive due process is, again, "mere rationality." In other words, if the state is pursuing a legitimate objective, and using means that are rationally related to that objective, the state will not be found to have violated the substantive Due Process Clause. So the vast bulk of *economic regulations* (since these don't affect fundamental rights) will be tested by the mere-rationality standard and almost certainly upheld.

c.   **Equal protection:**   Then, we move on to the ***equal protection*** area. Here, "mere-rationality" review is used so long as: (1) ***no suspect*** or ***quasi-suspect classification*** is being used; and (2) ***no fundamental right*** is being impaired. This still leaves us with a large number of classifications which will be judged based on the mere-rationality standard, including: (1) almost all economic regulations; (2) some classifications based on alienage; and (3) rights that are not "fundamental" even though they are very important, such as food, housing, and free public education. In all of these areas, the classification will be reviewed under the "mere-rationality" standard, and will therefore almost certainly be upheld.

d.   **Contracts Clause:**   Lastly, we find "mere-rationality" review in some aspects of the ***"Obligation of Contracts"*** Clause.

2.   **Strict scrutiny:**   Here are the various contexts in which the Court applies ***strict scrutiny***:

    a.   **Substantive due process/fundamental rights:**   First, where a governmental action affects ***fundamental rights***, and the plaintiff claims that his ***substantive due process*** rights are being violated, the Court will use strict scrutiny. So when the state impairs rights falling in the ***"privacy"*** cluster of marriage, child-bearing, and child-rearing, the Court will use strict scrutiny (and will therefore probably invalidate the governmental restriction). For instance, government restrictions that impair the right to use contraceptives receive this kind of strict scrutiny.

    b.   **Equal protection review:**   Next, the Court uses strict scrutiny to review a claim that a classification violates the plaintiff's ***equal protection*** rights, if the classification relates either to a ***suspect classification*** or a ***fundamental right***. "Suspect classifications" include ***race***, ***national origin***, and (sometimes) ***alienage***. "Fundamental rights" for this purpose include the right to ***vote***, to have access to the ***courts***, and to ***travel interstate***. So classifications that either involve any of these suspect classifications or impair any of these fundamental rights will be strictly scrutinized and will probably be struck down.

    c.   **Freedom of expression:**   Next, we move to the area of ***freedom of expression***. If the government is impairing free expression in a ***content-based way***, then the court will use strict scrutiny and will almost certainly strike down the regulation. In other words, if the government is restricting some speech but not others, based on the ***content of the messages***, then this suppression of expression will only be allowed if necessary to achieve a compelling purpose (a standard which is rarely found to be satisfied in the First Amendment area). Similarly, any interference with the right of ***free association*** will be strictly scrutinized.

    d.   **Freedom of religion/Free Exercise Clause:**   Lastly, the court will use strict scrutiny to evaluate any impairment with a person's ***free exercise*** of religion. Even if the government does ***not intend*** to impair a person's free exercise of his religion, if it substantially burdens his exercise of religion, the government will have to give him an ***exemption*** from the otherwise-applicable regulation unless denial of an exemption is necessary to achieve a compelling governmental interest.

3.   **Middle-level review:**   Finally, here are the relatively small number of contexts in which the court uses middle-level review:

a. **Equal protection/semi-suspect:**   First, middle-level review will be used to judge an *equal protection* claim, where the classification being challenged involves a *semi-suspect* trait. The two traits which are considered semi-suspect for this purpose are: (1) *gender*; and (2) *illegitimacy*. So any government classification based on gender or illegitimacy will have to be "substantially related" to the achievement of some "important" governmental interest.

b. **Contracts Clause:**   Second, certain conduct attacked under the Obligation of Contracts Clause will be judged by the middle-level standard of review.

c. **Free expression/non-content-based:**   Finally, in the First Amendment area we use a standard similar (though not identical) to the middle-level review standard to judge government action that impairs expression, but does so in a *non-content-based* manner. This is true, for instance, of any content-neutral *"time, place and manner"* regulation.

CHAPTER 2

THE SUPREME COURT'S AUTHORITY

ChapterScope

This Chapter examines several aspects of the Supreme Court's authority. The most important concepts in this Chapter are:

■ **Supreme Court review:** It is the *Supreme Court, not Congress,* which has the authority and duty to review the *constitutionality* of statutes passed by Congress, and to invalidate the statute if it violates the Constitution.

■ **Review of state court decisions:** The Supreme Court may review state court decisions, but only to the extent that the decision was based on *federal law.*

❑ **"Independent and adequate state grounds":** Even if there *is* a federal question in a state court case, the Supreme Court may not review the case if there was an *"independent and adequate" state ground* for the state court's decision. (That is, if the same result would be reached even if the state court had made a different decision on the federal question, the Supreme Court may not decide the case.)

■ **Federal judicial power:** The federal judicial power is set forth in Art. III, Section 2 of the U.S. Constitution. The federal judicial power includes (a partial listing):

❑ cases arising under the *Constitution* or under *federal statutes*;

❑ cases of *admiralty*;

❑ cases between *two or more states*;

❑ cases between citizens of *different states*; and

❑ cases between a state or its citizens and a *foreign country* or *foreign citizens.*

The federal judicial power does *not* include cases where both parties are citizens (i.e., residents) of the same state, and no federal question is raised.

■ **Congress' control of federal judicial power:** Congress has some meaningful control over the federal judicial power:

❑ **Control of Supreme Court docket:** Congress has the general power to decide *what types* of cases the *Supreme Court* may hear, so long as it doesn't expand the Court's jurisdiction beyond the federal judicial power summarized above.

❑ **Lower courts:** Congress may also decide what lower *federal courts* there should be, and what cases they may hear.

I.   REVIEW OF ACTS OF CONGRESS (*MARBURY v. MADISON*)

A.   **The *Marbury* case itself:**   Which branch of the federal government shall have the *final say in interpreting the Constitution*? That is the principal question resolved by Chief Justice John Marshall's opinion in *Marbury v. Madison*, 1 Cranch 137 (1803), perhaps the cornerstone of American constitutional law.

   1.   **Historical background:**   The background of the case was a political struggle between John Adams and the Federalists, and his successor Thomas Jefferson and the Republicans. Just before leaving office, Adams appointed a number of new judges, including several justices of the peace for the District of Columbia. Commissions for these justices of the peace had been signed by Adams, but not yet delivered by the time he left office. The Jefferson Administration then refused to honor the appointments for which commissions had not actually been delivered prior to the end of Adams' term.

   2.   **Subject of suit:**   Several of the would-be justices of the peace, including William Marbury, brought suit directly in the Supreme Court. They sought a writ of mandamus compelling Jefferson's Secretary of State (James Madison) to deliver their commissions.

   3.   **Marshall's decision:**   Justice Marshall's opinion dealt with a number of issues, of which only the last gives the case its present significance.

      a.   **Right to commission:**   First, Marshall decided that Marbury and the other justices did indeed become entitled to their commissions once these had been signed by the President (and sealed by the Secretary of State, who was none other than Marshall himself!) Marshall could have short-circuited the whole problem by ruling that delivery was required for validity, but he did not take this route.

      b.   **Remedy:**   Secondly, Marshall had to decide whether Madison's failure to deliver the commissions entitled the plaintiffs to some sort of remedy. Marshall distinguished between political acts, which are not reviewable by the courts, and acts specifically required by law, which are reviewable. The refusal to deliver the commissions, Marshall ruled, fell into this latter category.

      c.   **Mandamus not allowed:**   Lastly, Marshall had to decide whether the particular remedy sought by the plaintiffs, an application for a writ of mandamus directly to the Supreme Court, could be granted.

         i.   **Judiciary Act allows:**   The then-effective Judiciary Act provided that the Supreme Court would have jurisdiction "to issue … writs of mandamus … [to] persons holding office under the authority of the United States." Thus the Act itself explicitly authorized the relief being sought by the plaintiffs.

         ii.   **At odds with Constitution:**   However, Marshall concluded, this grant of jurisdiction was in conflict with Article III, §2, of the Constitution, which grants the Supreme Court original jurisdiction only "[i]n all Cases affecting Ambassadors, other public Ministers and Consuls, and those in which a State shall be Party." Since issuance of mandamus is not among the types of cases as to which original jurisdiction is conferred on the Supreme Court, Marshall held, the congressional statute was at odds with the Constitution.

      d.   **Supremacy of Constitution:**   This brought Marshall to the holding for which *Marbury v. Madison* is principally known today. If the Supreme Court identifies a ***conflict*** between a constitutional provision and a congressional statute, *the Court has the authority (and the duty) to declare the statute unconstitutional and to refuse to enforce it*. Therefore, Marshall concluded, the requested writ of mandamus could not be issued. In reaching this conclusion, Marshall made two interlocking arguments:

i. **Constitution is paramount:** The very purpose of a written constitution is to establish a fundamental and paramount law. It follows from this that any act of the legislature repugnant to the Constitution must be void.

ii. **Who interprets:** "It is emphatically the *province and duty of the judicial department to say what the law is*." That is, it is the *court, not the legislature*, which must make the determination whether, in a particular case, an act of Congress is in conflict with the Constitution. To deny the permissibility of judicial review of the constitutionality of a congressional statute would be to say that the courts "must close their eyes on the constitution, and see only the law. This doctrine would subvert the very foundation of all written constitutions."

4. **Criticism of *Marbury*:** Because of its key importance, *Marbury v. Madison* has been subject to a huge amount of analysis and criticism. Only one of these lines of criticism is of interest to us here.

a. **Who determines constitutionality:** Most critics are willing to concede Step One of the two arguments above, i.e., that the Constitution is superior to statutes and that where there is a conflict, the Constitution must be respected. But Step Two is what all the shouting is about: *the critics argue that nowhere in the Constitution is it stated that the courts, not Congress, ought to decide whether a given statute does in fact conflict with the Constitution.*

i. **Congress could decide:** Thus it is possible to imagine a system in which we would still have our written Constitution, acknowledged to be the supreme law of the land, but in which *Congress* (not the courts) would have the final say in interpreting that Constitution. Congress would be seen as having the duty to make sure that no act promulgated by it exceeded the Constitution; but Congress' interpretation of the presence or absence of a conflict, not the courts', would be the method of enforcing constitutional limits. See Tribe, p. 25.

ii. **Assumption, not conclusion:** Many, perhaps most, commentators believe that this criticism is well-taken, at least in the sense that the Constitution nowhere states that courts are to have the last say on whether a conflict between statute and Constitution exists. However, one answer to the critics is to say that Marshall was making an *assumption*, rather than a deduction, when he stated that courts have the ultimate right to interpret constitutionality. That is, the Constitution can be classified as being "indeterminate" as to who has the final say. When viewed in this way (which is Tribe's approach; *id.*), Marshall's assumption is at least as reasonable as the contrary one (that Congress, not the courts, should decide constitutionality) — this contrary assumption is also nowhere to be found in the Constitution.

iii. **Judicial independence:** Furthermore, if one is merely trying to decide which assumption to make, there are some practical reasons why judicial interpretation, rather than legislative interpretation, might be a better means of construing the Constitution. Federal judges are appointed for life, and are thus free of day-to-day political pressures. Since Congress generally responds to the ***majority's*** will, and since one of the key functions of the Constitution is to protect the rights of ***minorities***, the relatively apolitical judiciary will interpret the Constitution in a way more sensitive to this minority-protection goal.

II. REVIEW OF STATE COURT DECISIONS

A. General principles of review: When the Supreme Court reviews the judgment of a state court, it is of course exercising its appellate, rather than its original, jurisdiction. Article III, §2, provides that the Supreme Court's appellate jurisdiction may be regulated and limited as Congress shall provide. (See *infra*, p. 12.) Since the original Judiciary Act was enacted in 1789, the Supreme Court's appellate review of state court judgments has always been limited to the ***federal questions*** decided by the state courts. Tribe, p. 162.

    1. No review of state law issues: Thus the Supreme Court may determine whether a state court has reached a decision that is not in conformity with the Constitution; but it may ***not review state court decisions that merely adjudicate questions of state law.*** How the Court determines whether a state court decision is limited to state law questions is a problem discussed more extensively below; the main point is that the Supreme Court's review of state court judgments is limited to ***questions of federal law.***

B. *Martin v. Hunter's Lessee*: Recall that in *Marbury v. Madison*, the Court held that it had the power to review acts of Congress for constitutionality. In the later case of ***Martin v. Hunter's Lessee***, 1 Wheat. 304 (1816), the Court confronted the similar, and perhaps even more important question, of whether the Supreme Court is constitutionally authorized to review the constitutionality of ***state court decisions.***

    1. Virginia's argument: *Martin* involved the issue of whether a particular Virginia statute conflicted with a federal treaty. The Virginia courts took the position that if litigation commenced in state courts, then it was up to the state court to say whether the state action violated the federal constitution, and the U.S. Supreme Court had no right to review whatever conclusion the state court reached.

    2. Supreme Court's holding: The Supreme Court flatly rejected the Virginia courts' view, and held that the Court could ***review the constitutionality of a decision by a state's highest court***. There were two principal strands to the Court's opinion, which was written by Justice Story:

        a. Sovereignty argument rejected: First, the Virginia court's assertion that it was "sovereign" was rejected, on the grounds that the federal Constitution cut back upon state sovereignty in numerous respects. There was no reason to presume that state judiciaries were immune from this set of limitations.

        b. Uniformity: Secondly, Story wrote, there is a need for ***uniformity*** in decisions throughout the nation interpreting the Constitution. "[I]f there were no revising authority to control these jarring and discordant judgments, and harmonize them into uniformity, the laws, the treaties and the constitution of the United States would be different in different states. ... "

3. ***Cohens v. Virginia:*** *Martin v. Hunter's Lessee* dealt with Supreme Court review of state civil cases. The Supreme Court's right to review state ***criminal cases*** for constitutionality was similarly upheld, in ***Cohens v. Virginia***, 6 Wheat. 264 (1821).

C. **Recent state challenges to Supreme Court authority:** Even though the Supreme Court's right to review the constitutionality of state supreme court decisions has been firmly established since *Martin* and *Cohens*, numerous state challenges to that right have arisen since then.

 1. **Desegregation:** The most recent serious such challenge came in response to the Supreme Court's school desegregation decisions, beginning with *Brown v. Board of Education, infra*, p. 277. For instance, in *Cooper v. Aaron*, 358 U.S. 1 (1958), Arkansas state officials claimed that they were not bound by a lower federal court desegregation order. The Supreme Court went out of its way to state that "the federal judiciary is supreme in the exposition of the law of the Constitution," and that the Supreme Court's interpretation of the Constitution is binding on state legislatures and executive and judicial officers. State challenges such as the one in *Cooper v. Aaron* are generally viewed as not involving any serious issue of constitutional law. See N&R, p. 19.

D. **Independent and adequate state grounds:** The federal judicial power extends, by Article III, §2, to "all Cases, in Law and Equity, arising under this Constitution, the Laws of the United States, and Treaties. ... " On its face, this language seems to allow for Supreme Court review of state court decisions in any case where a federal question was involved, regardless of how the state court disposed of that federal question. Also, nothing in this clause seems to prevent the Supreme Court from reviewing all of the issues raised in any case, so long as a federal question is present.

 1. **Statutory basis:** However, as noted, the Supreme Court's appellate jurisdiction exists only as provided by Congress. The limitations presently in force are discussed *infra*, p. 15. For the moment, it is sufficient to note that the mere fact that a federal question is involved in a case is ***not sufficient*** to entitle the Supreme Court to review it. Furthermore, even if the Supreme Court is entitled to review a case, it will generally adjudicate ***only the federal issues***. (Tribe, at p. 163, suggests that if Congress attempted to give the Supreme Court the right to issue on matters of state law decisions which would be binding under the Supremacy Clause, this would be an interference with state sovereignty violative of the Tenth Amendment.)

 2. **Independent and adequate state ground:** Suppose that a state supreme court upholds a state statute against a federal constitutional attack. This would seem to be by itself enough to bring the case within the Supreme Court's congressionally-granted appellate jurisdiction (see *infra*, p. 12). But another doctrine, that of the "***independent and adequate state ground***," may nonetheless prevent the Supreme Court from reviewing the constitutionality of the state statute.

  a. **How doctrine works:** The federal judiciary may decide only those cases presenting a "justiciable" controversy; one consequence is that the Supreme Court ***may not render an advisory opinion***. (See *infra*, p. 708.) Suppose now that the state supreme court decision rested upon two grounds, each of which would have been sufficient to produce the same result: (1) a determination that the state statute does not violate the federal Constitution; and (2) a determination that, even if the state statute being attacked were invalid, the party attacking it would lose the case anyway. In this situation, a Supreme Court determination that the state statute violated the U.S. Constitution would have *no effect* upon the ultimate outcome of the case (since the party attacking the statute would lose anyway); therefore the Court's opinion would, in effect, be advisory. For this reason, the Supreme Court has repeatedly held that it will not review a state court decision otherwise falling within its appellate jurisdiction if that state decision rests upon an "independent and adequate state ground."

3. **State substantive law:**   Sometimes, the state ground may be *substantive*. For instance, the state court may hold that a state statute *violates both the state and federal constitutions*. However, the holding that the state constitution is violated may be achieved in one of two ways: (1) the state court may have independently interpreted the state constitutional provision, without relying directly on federal cases construing the federal constitutional provision; or (2) the state court may have interpreted the state constitutional provision as being *co-extensive* with the comparable federal constitutional provision, and then attempted to follow the relevant federal case law. In the latter situation, the Supreme Court may find that an independent and adequate state ground really *did not exist*.

4. **State rules of procedure:**   In the "substantive state law" situation discussed immediately above, it is generally clear that the state ground is "adequate," and the real issue is whether it is "independent" of the federal ground. But the state ground may, by contrast, be *"procedural."* That is, because of some state procedural rule, the state court may simply fail to reach a federal issue. In this situation, the state procedural rule is clearly independent of the federal question, but it is not necessarily *"adequate."*

   a. **Meaning of "adequacy":**   The mere fact that the state court itself recites that state procedural grounds bar consideration of the federal claim does not automatically render those grounds "adequate." Instead, the Supreme Court will review the procedural grounds. In several different types of situations, the Supreme Court is likely to hold that the state procedural grounds are *not "adequate,"* and therefore do not foreclose Supreme Court review of the federal issues:

      i. **"Fundamental fairness":**   Most importantly, a state procedural rule must at least meet the requirement of *"fundamental fairness."* This is a requirement imposed on the states by the Fourteenth Amendment Due Process Clause (see *infra*, p. 159).

   b. **Narrow review:**   But modern cases indicate that the present Supreme Court will seek to *respect*, rather than disregard, state procedural rules wherever possible. For instance, the Court has held that in a federal *habeas corpus* proceeding (a collateral attack, brought in federal district court, upon a prior state criminal conviction), state procedural rules will be given serious respect.

III.   CONGRESS' CONTROL OF FEDERAL COURT JURISDICTION

A. **The problem generally:**   To what extent may Congress *curtail the jurisdiction* of the Supreme Court, or of the lower federal courts? If one looks solely at Article III, the only direct grant of jurisdiction to any particular court is that the Supreme Court shall have original jurisdiction in cases involving ambassadors, ministers and consuls, and cases in which a state is a party.

1. **Limits indicated by Article III:**   Article III itself suggests that Congress may place certain limits both on the Supreme Court's appellate jurisdiction and on the jurisdiction of the

lower federal courts. First, Article III, §2 states that in all cases not falling within the Supreme Court's original jurisdiction (but falling within the federal judicial power), the Supreme Court shall have "appellate Jurisdiction both as to Law and Fact, ***with such Exceptions, and under such Regulations as the Congress shall make.***" Similarly, the lower federal courts do not even exist until Congress creates them; Article III, §1, provides that federal judicial power shall vest in the Supreme Court and "in such inferior Courts as the Congress may from time to time ordain and establish."

B. *McCardle* **case:**   The Supreme Court has confirmed that Congress does indeed have at least some power to control the boundaries of the Supreme Court's appellate jurisdiction. The principal case so holding is ***Ex parte McCardle***, 74 U.S. 506 (1869).

1. **Facts of *McCardle*:**   McCardle was imprisoned by a military government imposed by Congress as part of post-Civil War Reconstruction. He brought a *habeas corpus* action in federal circuit court, charging that the Reconstruction Acts under which he was imprisoned were unconstitutional. The circuit court rejected his claim, and he then appealed under an 1867 congressional statute, authorizing the grant of *habeas corpus* by federal circuit courts and also authorizing appeal to the Supreme Court in such cases.

2. **Congress restricts appeal:**   After the Supreme Court heard arguments in the *McCardle* case, but before it handed down its decision, Congress passed a law repealing the portion of the 1867 Act which allowed appeals to the Supreme Court. (Congress did this out of fear that the Court would hold in *McCardle* that the Reconstruction Acts were unconstitutional.) Thus Congress purported to deprive the Supreme Court of its right to decide the *McCardle* case and any other *habeas corpus* case coming to it by appeal from the circuit courts.

3. **Holding:**   The Supreme Court **upheld** Congress' restriction of the Court's jurisdiction. The opinion noted that the appellate jurisdiction of the Supreme Court is conferred "with such exceptions and under such regulations as Congress shall make." The limitation enacted by Congress here was such an exception. Therefore, the Court concluded, it had no jurisdiction to decide the case.

4. **Limited withdrawal:**   Observe that in the statute involved in *McCardle*, Congress was not completely withdrawing the Supreme Court's right to hear *habeas corpus* cases. Rather, it was withdrawing that right only where the Supreme Court got the case by appeal from the lower courts; under the jurisdictional statutes of the time, an ***original petition*** for *habeas corpus* could be commenced in the Supreme Court itself. See Schwartz, p. 21. Furthermore, even if only the lower courts had jurisdiction, this would still not be leaving the litigant without the possibility of federal *habeas corpus* relief; the lower court decision would simply be final.

   a. **Limited significance:**   Thus *McCardle* does not by any means stand for the proposition that Congress may strip the federal courts in their entirety of the right to issue *habeas corpus* relief; such congressional action would probably be a violation of prisoners' Fourteenth Amendment right to due process.

5. **Neutral:**   Also, note that the congressional statute in *McCardle* operated in a ***neutral manner***. That is, appeal to the Supreme Court was not allowed either to the government or to a private party; thus in a future case, it might be the government which suffered because of the statute. The fact that the congressional restriction of jurisdiction would not always

favor the same side makes that curtailment less objectionable constitutionally. See N&R, p. 34.

C. Limits on congressional power: But Congress *does not have unlimited power* to tamper with the Supreme Court's appellate jurisdiction.

1. ***Klein* case:** An important Supreme Court case from the same era as *McCardle* shows that there are some limitations to Congress' power to modify the Supreme Court's appellate jurisdiction. *U.S. v. Klein*, 80 U.S. 128 (1872).

   a. **Facts of *Klein:*** Klein sued in the Court of Claims under a federal statute allowing citizens who had abandoned property to federal troops during the Civil War to recover compensation for it, if they could satisfy a loyalty requirement. Klein won in the Court of Claims, on the strength of earlier cases holding that a general presidential pardon satisfied the statutory requirement that the claimant not have been a supporter of the Confederacy. Before the government's appeal was heard in the Supreme Court, Congress passed a new statute providing that a presidential pardon would show the opposite (that the claimant *had* supported the Confederacy); the statute also provided that the Court of Claims and the Supreme Court were both without jurisdiction to decide cases where a pardon had been granted.

   b. **Statute struck down:** The Supreme Court in *Klein* struck down the statute as ***unconstitutional***, on the grounds that it violated the separation of powers and invaded the judicial function. The Court argued that this was not a valid and *bona fide* denial of appellate jurisdiction in a ***whole class*** of cases; instead, it was merely a "means to an end," i.e., a way "to deny to pardons granted by the President the effect which this Court had adjudged them to have."

   c. **Standard set by *Klein:*** Thus *Klein* seems to stand for the proposition that "[A]ny jurisdictional limitation must be ***neutral***; that is, Congress may not decide the merits of a case under the guise of limiting jurisdiction." N&R, p. 36.

2. **Practical limitation:** Observe that there is also a ***practical*** limitation upon Congress' ability to cut back on the appellate jurisdiction of the Supreme Court. If Congress is motivated by hostility to a particular Court decision, then it might be defeating its own purpose by restricting the Court's subsequent ability to hear similar cases — the adverse precedent will be ***left on the books***. Furthermore, without Supreme Court jurisdiction in an area, the individual courts of appeals will be left to go their own ways, destroying national uniformity of the law in that area. See Sullivan & Gunther, p. 83.

D. Modern congressional controls on federal jurisdiction: In the twentieth century, Congress has acted to cut back on lower federal court and Supreme Court jurisdiction in a number of special situations. None of these curtailments has been found to be unconstitutional.

1. **Forum left open:** When Congress has acted to restrict the jurisdiction of either the Supreme Court or the lower federal courts, it has generally ***not entirely deprived litigants*** of a judicial remedy. For instance, often the ***state courts*** are left with jurisdiction. But if Congress curtailed federal jurisdiction in such a way that a litigant was completely deprived of the right to have his case heard in ***any court***, the congressional scheme would probably be unconstitutional; thus Congress could probably not deprive the federal courts of the right to hear a certain type of case falling within the federal courts' exclusive jurisdiction (e.g., bankruptcy cases).

IV. THE SUPREME COURT'S JURISDICTION TODAY

A. Limited scope of discussion: A full discussion of the jurisdiction of the Supreme Court is beyond the scope of this outline. We will discuss mainly how the Court selects its docket.

B. *Certiorari:* Until recent decades, there were two ways a case could get to the Supreme Court: "appeal" and "*certiorari.*" If a case fell within the Court's appeals jurisdiction, in theory the Court had to hear the case and decide it (though it often did so by means of a "summary disposition," which had almost no precedential value because it did not involve an opinion). But in 1988, Congress virtually eliminated the Court's appeals jurisdiction. Therefore, nearly all cases now come to the Court by ***"writ of certiorari."***

    1. Grounds for grant of *certiorari:* The Court's decision on whether to grant *certiorari* is ***completely discretionary.*** Since *certiorari* is now the sole means by which cases get to the Court, this means that the Court has ***full control*** over what cases it will hear and decide.

        a. Rules: However, the Court's decision whether to grant *certiorari* is not completely unguided. The Court has adopted formal Court Rules, which list several types of reasons which may lead the Court to grant *certiorari*. These include: (1) a ***conflict*** between ***different federal courts of appeal*** (e.g., the Second Circuit disagrees with the Ninth Circuit); (2) a conflict between the ***highest courts of two states***, or between a state's highest court and a federal court of appeals; (3) a state court or federal court of appeals decision on an ***important question*** which has not yet been settled by the Supreme Court. See Supreme Court Rule 17(1). In all of these situations, the issue triggering the decision to grant *certiorari* will of course be one of ***federal*** law.

    2. Four votes needed: The votes of ***four*** of the nine Justices are needed to grant *certiorari*.

        a. Denial not precedent: A ***denial*** of *certiorari* is ***not a decision on the merits***, and is therefore ***not a precedent*** which may be cited in other cases.

Quiz Yourself on

THE SUPREME COURT'S AUTHORITY *(ENTIRE CHAPTER)*

1. The Constitution of the state of Ames contains a due process clause whose language is identical to the Due Process Clause of the U.S. Constitution's Fourteenth Amendment. Tom was a teacher in the Town of Aaron, in Ames. Because Tom's status was that of "probationary teacher," the custom in Aaron was that Tom could be fired at the end of any school year without cause. Tom was fired without cause. He sued Aaron in Ames state court. His suit was premised on the argument that his firing violated the Ames due process clause, in that he was not given a hearing before being fired. The Ames state court agreed, and the highest appeals court in Ames affirmed. Now, the Town of Aaron has appealed the case to the U.S. Supreme Court. May the U.S. Supreme Court hear the case? Give your reasons. _____

2. Same basic fact pattern as prior question. Now, however, assume that Tom in his Ames state court litigation asserted that his firing violated both the Ames constitution's due process clause and the federal Due Process Clause. The state trial court agreed with Tom that both constitutional provisions were violated, and the Ames Supreme Court affirmed the trial court decision in all respects. The trial court's decision on the state-constitution issue was based solely upon the court's reading of prior Ames state court decisions that in turn relied upon the intent of Ames voters in adopting the Ames due process clause. The portion of the decision relating to the federal constitution relied on U.S. Supreme Court cases construing the federal Due Process Clause. May the U.S. Supreme Court review the decision of the Ames Supreme Court?

3. Congress, in an effort to streamline the federal judiciary, passes a statute eliminating diversity jurisdiction (i.e., jurisdiction over cases brought by a citizen of one state against a citizen of another state). The legislation would prevent diversity suits from being brought in federal district court, so that they would have to be brought in state court. (The legislation does not directly change the Supreme Court's appellate jurisdiction, so that the Supreme Court can continue to review the judgments of state courts, including state court suits that turn on a federal question.) Is the congressional legislation constitutional? _____

Answers

1. **No, because the case does not involve a federal question.** The federal judicial power extends, by Article III, Section 2, to cases arising under the U.S. Constitution and federal laws. That power does not extend to cases decided solely on state-law grounds. Here, although the Ames due process clause may have mirrored the language of the U.S. Constitution's Due Process Clause, the state decision was solely based on the Ames courts' interpretation of the Ames constitution. Since no federal issue was involved, the Supreme Court has no jurisdiction (whether by appeal or by certiorari).

2. **No.** In contrast to the prior question, here at least a decision on an issue of federal law (the meaning of the U.S. Constitution) was part of the state court decision. However, the federal judicial power does not extend to Supreme Court review of any state court case for which there is an ***"independent and adequate state ground."*** Because Tom's firing would be unlawful even without any finding that the federal Constitution had been violated (since the state constitution was found to have been violated as well), an independent and adequate state ground exists here. (If the Ames state court decision on the meaning of the Ames constitution's due process provision had derived in part from the court's belief that the clause should mean the same thing as it means in the federal Constitution, the state ground would not be truly "independent." But the facts make it clear that the finding on the meaning of the state constitution here derived solely from Ames state-law sources.)

3. **Yes.** The Constitution gives Congress full control over the jurisdiction of the lower federal courts. In fact, these lower federal courts do not even exist until Congress creates them; Article III, Section 1 grants the federal judicial power to the Supreme Court and to "such inferior courts as Congress may from time to time ordain and establish." This language has been interpreted to mean that Congress may also define the cases that may be heard by the lower federal courts, and that Congress may do this by refusing to let the lower federal courts hear cases that fall within the general federal judicial power (e.g., cases between citizens of different states).

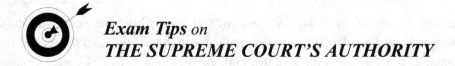

Exam Tips on
THE SUPREME COURT'S AUTHORITY

If the facts describe a lawsuit that takes place in federal court (or a state-court lawsuit that is eventually heard by the U.S. Supreme Court) be alert to *limits* on the *federal judicial power:*

☞ If the facts involve a state-court suit that is heard by the ***Supreme Court*** on ***certiorari***, be sure that the state-court decision was ***based on federal law.***

☞ Be alert to the possible existence of an ***independent and adequate state ground***. That is, if the state court decided some issue of state law in a way that would have been enough to dispose of the case, there is no federal issue that is vital to the case, and the Supreme Court may not decide the federal issue. In particular, be alert for fact patterns where a ***state*** and ***federal constitutional provision*** cover the ***same territory*** — the state court might have decided the state issue as solely a matter of state law, in which case there would be no federal issue necessary to the case.

☛ If a fact pattern involves an attempt by ***Congress*** to ***limit the power*** of either the Supreme Court or the lower federal courts, the main things to remember are:

☞ Congress can within limits ***cut back*** on the kinds of cases the Supreme Court may hear, but cannot ***expand*** the case load beyond the categories set forth as the federal judicial power in the Constitution; and

☞ Congress may cut back, perhaps even completely eliminate, the ***lower federal courts***; as with the Supreme Court, Congress may not ***expand*** the lower courts' dockets beyond the bounds of the constitutional federal judicial power.

CHAPTER 3

FEDERALISM AND
FEDERAL POWER GENERALLY

ChapterScope

In this brief chapter, we examine the following concepts:

■ **Federal system:** The U.S. has a *federal* system. The national government, and the government of each of the states, coexist.

■ **Federal government has limited powers:** The federal government is one of *limited, enumerated,* powers. That is, the three branches of the federal government may only assert those powers *specifically granted* by the U.S. Constitution.

❏ **"Necessary and Proper" Clause:** However, Congress does have the power to make all laws that are *"necessary and proper"* for carrying out its enumerated powers. So if Congress is seeking an *objective* that falls within the specifically enumerated powers, Congress may use *any means* that is *rationally related* to the objective being sought, and that is not specifically forbidden by the Constitution.

I. THE CONCEPT OF FEDERALISM

A. Nature of federalism: The United States has a *federalist* system. That is, the national government, and the government of each of the states, coexist. This chapter, and the several that follow, are devoted to the implications of this fact. Thus we will be examining the limits on federal power imposed in favor of state power, and conversely the limits on state power in favor of federal power.

B. Federal government has limited powers: The fundamental attribute of federal power under the U.S. Constitution is that the federal government is one of *limited, enumerated, powers*. That is, the three branches of the federal government can only assert those powers *specifically granted by the U.S. Constitution.*

   1. Comparison with state power: This limited-power concept should be contrasted with the nature of state power. The power of state governments might be called "inherent" — a state government, at least as far as the federal Constitution is concerned, holds a general "police power", i.e., the power to protect the health, safety or general welfare of state residents. An action by a state government is *valid* under federal law unless it violates some *specific limitation* imposed by the U.S. Constitution. A federal action, by contrast, *must fall within one of the enumerated powers* listed in the Constitution.

      a. No general police power: In other words, there is *no general federal police power*, i.e., no right of the federal government to regulate for the health, safety or general welfare of the citizenry. Instead, each act of federal legislation or regulation must come within one of the very specific, enumerated powers (e.g., the Commerce Clause, the power to tax and spend, etc.).

i. **Tax and spend for general welfare:** Congress *does* have the right to "lay and collect taxes ... to pay the debts and provide for the ... general welfare of the United States. ... " (Article I, Section 8.) But the phrase "provide for the ... general welfare" in this sentence modifies "lay and collect taxes ... to pay the debts. ... " Thus the power to tax and spend is subject to the requirement that the general welfare be served; there is no *independent* federal power to provide for the general welfare.

2. **Review of government action:** Thus for an action by the federal government to be valid, it must meet *two* distinct requirements: (1) it must fall within one of the powers *specifically enumerated* within the Constitution as being given to the federal government; and (2) it must *not violate any particular limitation* on federal power given in the Constitution (e.g., the limitations contained in the Bill of Rights).

> **Example:** Congress, stating that it is acting on behalf of the general welfare of U.S. citizens, passes a law making it a federal crime for any person to read any type of pornographic material in his house. Unless the measure can be shown to fall within the commerce power (*infra*, p. 27), the measure will almost certainly be found by the courts to be invalid, since it is not within any power specifically given to the federal government by the Constitution (and since the power to legislate "on behalf of the general welfare" is not one of the enumerated powers). (Also, the measure will probably be found to violate one or more specific limitations in the Bill of Rights, including the "right of privacy" inferred by modern Supreme Court decisions. See *Stanley v. Georgia*, *infra*, p. 579.)

C. **Specific powers:** The principal grant of specific federal powers is in Article I, §8. That section contains 18 clauses which grant power to *Congress*. (Grants of power to the judicial and executive branches are contained in other parts of the Constitution.)

1. **Congressional powers:** Among the more important powers given to the Congress by Article I, §8, are the power to:

a. lay and collect *taxes*;

b. provide for the *defense* of the country;

c. *borrow money* on the credit of the U.S.;

d. *regulate commerce* with foreign nations, and *among the* several states;

e. regulate *immigration* and *bankruptcy*;

f. establish *post offices*;

g. control the issuance of *patents* and *copyrights*;

h. *declare war*;

i. pass all laws needed to govern the *District of Columbia* and federal *military enclaves* (e.g., military bases); and

j. "make all Laws which shall be *necessary and proper* for *carrying into Execution* the foregoing Powers, and all other Powers vested by this Constitution in the Government of the United States. ... " This is the so-called "*necessary and proper*" clause.

2. **Other sources:** Other parts of the Constitution provide additional grants of power to the various branches of the federal government. Article II defines the powers and duties of the

President. Article III confers the federal judicial power (and also gives Congress power to control Supreme Court jurisdiction). Other grants of power are scattered throughout the document (e.g., Article IV, §3 gives Congress power over U.S. territories and federal property). Finally, many of the *amendments* specifically give Congress the power to enact supporting legislation (e.g., §5 of the Fourteenth Amendment). See N&R, p. 128.

3. **Foreign affairs power:** One exception has been recognized to the general rule that only enumerated powers may be exercised by the federal government. Nothing in the Constitution explicitly gives the federal government the power to regulate *foreign affairs* (though Article I, §8, gives Congress the right to "regulate Commerce with foreign Nations"). The federal government's right to conduct foreign affairs is generally considered to be implied by the nature of the federal union, and by the impracticability of having each of the several states conduct its own foreign policy. N&R, pp. 133-34.

II. *McCULLOCH v. MARYLAND*

A. **Doctrine of implied powers:** Although the federal government may act only where it is affirmatively authorized to do so by the Constitution, the authorization does not have to be *explicit*. That is, by the doctrine of *"implied powers,"* the federal government (especially Congress) may validly exercise power that is *ancillary* to one of the powers explicitly listed in the Constitution, so long as this ancillary power does not conflict with specific constitutional prohibitions (e.g., those of the Bill of Rights). See Tribe, p. 301.

B. *McCulloch* **and the "Necessary and Proper" Clause:** This notion of implied powers is itself explicitly stated in the *"Necessary and Proper"* Clause of Art. I, §8: Congress may "make all Laws which shall be necessary and proper for carrying into Execution" the specific legislative powers granted by Art. I, §8, or by other parts of the Constitution. The first case to make an important interpretation of "Necessary and Proper" was the landmark case of *McCulloch v. Maryland*, 17 U.S. 316 (1819).

1. **Setting of *McCulloch*:** Congress chartered the second Bank of the United States in 1816. The Bank was designed to regulate the currency and help solve national economic problems. However, it soon encountered substantial political opposition, mostly as the result of the Panic of 1818 and corruption within the various branches of the Bank. As a result, a number of states enacted anti-Bank measures.

    a. **The Maryland Act:** One of these anti-Bank statutes, enacted by Maryland, was at the center of the *McCulloch* dispute. Maryland imposed a tax upon all banks operating in the state that were not chartered by the state. The measure was intended to discriminate against the national Bank, and its Maryland branch. The state then brought suit against the Bank and its cashier (McCulloch) to collect the tax. The Supreme Court held the tax constitutionally invalid in *McCulloch*.

2. **Structure of opinion:** The opinion, one of the most significant ever written by Marshall, had two main portions: (1) a determination that the chartering of the Bank was within the constitutionally-vested power of the federal government; and (2) a finding that since the Bank was constitutionally chartered, Maryland's tax upon it was unconstitutional. At this juncture, we examine only the first of these two parts; the second is discussed *infra*, p. 115.

3. **Constitutionality of the Bank:**   In concluding that the Bank was constitutionally chartered, Marshall first disposed of Maryland's argument that the powers of the national government were delegated to it by the states, and that these powers must be exercised in subordination to the states. Marshall concluded that the powers come ***directly from the people***, not from the states *qua* states.

4. **Grant need not be explicit:**   Marshall then turned to the issue of whether the constitutional grant of the particular power (here, the power to charter a bank or a corporation) was required to be made ***explicitly*** in the Constitution. Marshall concluded that particular powers could be ***implied*** from the explicit grant of other powers: "A constitution, to contain an accurate detail of all the subdivisions of which its great powers will admit, and of all the means by which they may be carried into execution, would partake of the prolixity of a legal code, and could scarcely be embraced by the human mind. … *[W]e must never forget that it is a constitution we are expounding*."

   a. **Corporation allowed:**   More specifically, Marshall found that Congress had the power to create a corporation (in this case, the Bank), if this was incidental to the carrying out of one of the constitutionally-enumerated powers, such as the power to ***raise revenue***.

   b. **"Necessary and Proper" Clause:**   Marshall relied upon the "Necessary and Proper" Clause as a justification for Congress' right to create a bank or corporation even though such a power was not specifically granted in the Constitution. In perhaps the most significant part of the opinion, he ***rejected*** the contention that "necessary" meant "absolutely necessary" or "indispensable." Instead, he stated that: "let the end be legitimate, let it be within the scope of the constitution, and all means which are ***appropriate***, which are ***plainly adapted*** to that end, which are not prohibited, [and which are consistent] with the letter and spirit of the constitution, are constitutional."

      i. **Summary:**   Thus so long as the means is ***rationally related*** to a constitutionally-specified object, the means is also constitutional (assuming that it does not violate any specific prohibition, such as those from the Bill of Rights).

   c. **Support for conclusion:**   To support his liberal interpretation of "necessary and proper," Marshall pointed to a number of situations where Congress' power to carry out constitutionally-specified objectives had been liberally interpreted. For instance, the Constitution does not contain any specific grant of the power to ***punish*** the violation of federal laws, yet this power had always been inferred. Similarly, the power "to establish post offices and post roads" had been substantially expanded, to include the federal prohibition on mail theft. Yet these exercises of power could not be termed "indispensable" to a carrying out of the constitutionally-specified ends.

   d. **Separation of powers rationale:**   Marshall also based his opinion upon ***separation-of-powers*** principles: An examination by the judicial branch into the "degree of necessity" justifying a statute would be an invasion of Congress' domain. Thus Marshall felt that the Supreme Court should strike down a law as being beyond the powers of Congress only where it was ***quite clear*** that no constitutionally-specified object was being pursued; in any closer case, the final decision should be left to Congress, not the courts.

5. **Conclusion:**   Marshall thus concluded that the act chartering the national bank was valid, because it bore a reasonable relationship to various constitutionally-enumerated powers of

the government (e.g., the power to collect taxes, to borrow money, to regulate commerce, etc.).

   a. **Maryland tax invalid:**   Marshall then went on to find the Maryland tax invalid, because it interfered with the exercise of a valid federal activity. See *infra*, p. 116, for a discussion of this part of the opinion.

6. **"Rational relation" test still in force:**   The standard set forth in *McCulloch* is ***still in force*** today. Courts interpreting the ***Necessary and Proper Clause*** will uphold a congressional action so long as Congress has employed a means which is not prohibited by the Constitution and which is ***rationally related*** to objectives that are themselves within constitutionally-enumerated powers.

   a. **Motive irrelevant:**   As a corollary, the Court will show great ***deference*** to Congress, and will generally ***not*** inquire into the legislators' ***motives***. Thus as long as the legislation is rationally related to ***one*** constitutionally-enumerated motive which Congress was or might have been pursuing, the fact that other ends not within the enumerated powers of Congress might also be achieved does not invalidate the power. Tribe, pp. 302-03.

   b. **Broad reading given to Clause:**   The ***broad and deferential reading*** that the Court continues to give to the Necessary and Proper Clause is illustrated by 2010 case, *U.S. v. Comstock*, 130 S.Ct. 1949 (2010), set out in the following example.

   Example: Congress passes a statute authorizing the Department of Justice to civilly commit certain federal prisoners at the end of their prison sentences. The statute applies where the prisoner has previously committed or tried to commit sexual violence or child molestation, currently suffers from a serious mental illness, and is as a result sexually dangerous to others. The Department must prove these elements to a federal judge by clear and convincing evidence. Once the Department makes this proof, it must then either persuade a state to take custody of the prisoner or keep the prisoner in a federal treatment facility until he is no longer dangerous. The plaintiffs (prisoners whom the Department is trying to civilly commit after their sentences) argue that the statute is beyond the federal government's powers.

   Held, for the federal government: the commitment statute is justified by the Necessary and Proper Clause. The Clause grants Congress "***broad authority*** to enact federal legislation" (citing *McCulloch*). In deciding whether the Clause grants authority in a particular situation, "we look to see whether the statute constitutes a means that is ***rationally related*** to the implementation of a constitutionally enumerated power." Furthermore, Congress is to be given a "***large discretion***" in choosing the ***particular means*** to carry out a given enumerated power. Here, Congress has a long-recognized power to define federal crimes, and to run a prison system to incarcerate those who commit such crimes. Allowing the Federal Bureau of Prisons to maintain custody of prisoners who would be dangerous to others if released is a rational method of carrying out the federal power to incarcerate those who commit federal crimes. *U.S. v. Comstock*, 130 S.Ct. 1949 (2010).

III. STATE OVERSIGHT OF THE FEDERAL GOVERNMENT — THE "TERM LIMITS" PROBLEM

A. Issue generally: What power do the individual states, as states, have to restrict the federal government? The answer has always been thought to be "essentially none." For instance, if Congress passes an unpopular statute, a vote by all 50 state legislatures purporting to repeal the statute would be irrelevant.

B. The term-limits problem generally: In fact, the kind of question posed in the prior paragraph had long been thought to be of only theoretical interest. But the problem became very practical in 1995, when the Court had to decide the "term limits" problem. In a nutshell, the problem was, may the states *limit the terms of members of Congress*? The Court answered *"no,"* but only after exposing a deep split among the Court's members as to the proper division of authority between the states and the federal government.

C. The term-limits case: The term-limits case was *U.S. Term Limits, Inc. v. Thornton*, 514 U.S. 779 (1995), which was decided by a 5-4 vote.

1. **Facts:** The voters of Arkansas modified the Arkansas State Constitution to prohibit any person from appearing on the ballot for Congress from that state if he or she had previously served three terms in the House or two in the Senate. This provision was similar to term limit provisions that had been adopted — either by statute or state constitutional amendment — in 22 other states.

2. **Federal constitutional provisions:** The case had to be decided against the backdrop of several federal constitutional provisions dealing directly with federal elections.

   a. **Qualifications Clauses:** Most importantly, the *"Qualifications Clauses"* set specific requirements for membership in Congress: Art. I, §2, cl. 2 requires each member of the House to be at least 25 years old, to have been a citizen of the U.S. for at least 7 years, and to be a resident of the state from which she is elected. Similarly, Art. I, §3, cl. 3, governing Senate membership, requires 30 years of age, 9 years of national citizenship, and residence in the state. The key question in *Thornton* became, do these clauses state the *exclusive* requirements for membership in Congress, or are they merely "minimum requirements" that the states may supplement?

3. **Majority strikes down:** A 5-member majority of the Court, in an opinion by Justice Stevens, *struck down* the Arkansas provision as being beyond the states' constitutional authority. A contrary ruling would undermine the whole framework of federalism, Stevens wrote: "Permitting individual States to formulate diverse qualifications for their congressional representatives would result in a patchwork of state qualifications, *undermining the uniformity and the national character* that the Framers envisioned and sought to ensure."

   a. **Congress can't add additional qualifications:** The majority began by reaffirming the holding of *Powell v. McCormack* (see *infra*, p. 729), a 1969 case which established that *Congress* couldn't add qualifications for membership in the House or Senate to those contained in the Qualifications Clauses.

   b. **States can't add qualifications either:** Stevens then went on to say that the states may not add qualifications for membership in Congress any more than Congress may. Here, Stevens rejected Arkansas' two-part argument: (1) the Constitution nowhere explicitly denies the states this power; and (2) therefore, under the Tenth Amendment, the states have this power. (The Tenth Amendment provides: "The powers not delegated to the United States by the Constitution, nor prohibited by it to the States, are reserved to the States respectively, or to the people." See *infra*, p. 53.)

i. **Not an "original power":** There were two problems with this syllogism, according to Stevens. First, the Tenth Amendment only lets the states *retain* powers they already had before enactment of the Constitution, and the power to add qualifications for federal elections was not an "original power" that the states had before enactment, because there was no federal government or electoral system at all.

ii. **Intended as exclusive source of qualifications:** Second, even if there had been such an original power, Stevens wrote, the Framers intended the Constitution to be the *sole source of qualifications* for membership in Congress. Enactment of the Constitution therefore *divested* the states of whatever power to add qualifications they might have had.

iii. **Democratic principles:** Finally, Stevens argued that *"democratic principles"* dictated that the states not be permitted to add qualifications for membership in the national legislature. The right to choose representatives "belongs not to the States, but to the people. ... The Framers ... conceived of a Federal Government directly responsible to the people, possessed of direct power over the people, and *chosen directly, not by States, but by the people.* ... The Congress ... is *not a confederation of nations* in which separate sovereigns are represented by appointed delegates, but is instead a body composed of representatives of the people."

4. **Concurrence by Kennedy:** The swing vote was by Justice Kennedy, who wrote a concurrence agreeing with the majority's core reasoning.

5. **Dissent by Thomas:** Justice Thomas (joined by Rehnquist, O'Connor and Scalia) dissented. His view of the matter stemmed from a view of federal power that was diametrically opposed to the majority's. For Thomas, "the ultimate source of the Constitution's authority is the *consent of the people of each individual State*, not the consent of the undifferentiated people of the nation as a whole."

Quiz Yourself on

FEDERALISM AND FEDERAL POWER *(ENTIRE CHAPTER)*

4. Congress, pursuant to its power to establish and regulate copyrights, has decided that there is far too much counterfeiting of copyrighted musical recordings. Therefore, Congress has passed a statute making it a felony, punishable by up to five years in prison, to give a "bootlegged" (i.e., not authorized by the copyright owner) CD or MP3 recording to any other person, even if it is the donor's neighbor or relative, and even though no compensation is charged. Dennis, charged with a violation of this statute, asserts that it is unconstitutional because it is beyond the scope of Congress' authority. Should the Court agree with Dennis' assertion, and why? _____

Answer

4. **No, because the statute is valid under the "Necessary and Proper" Clause.** *McCulloch v. Maryland*, 17 U.S. 316 (1819), establishes that when Congress is acting in pursuit of a constitutionally-specified objective, the means chosen merely has to be *rationally related* to the objective, not "necessary" to the objective's attainment. Here, Congress is exercising its enumerated power to regulate copyrights. Con-

gress could rationally have believed that even non-profit-motivated transfers of copyright-violating recordings contribute to the general decline of copyright protection, and that felony punishment for such transfers is a reasonable way of combatting the problem. The Court will show great deference to Congress' choice of the means to attain constitutionally-enumerated objectives, so the statute here will certainly be sustained.

Exam Tips *on* ## FEDERALISM AND FEDERAL POWER GENERALLY

Issues covered by this Chapter are often hidden in a fact pattern. Here are some things to watch out for:

☛ Most importantly, any time your fact pattern tells you that Congress (or, for that matter, the Executive or Judicial Branch) is doing something, be sure that the action taken falls within one of the *enumerated* powers.

☛ Remember that there is *no general federal police power*.

  ☞ It's true that Congress has the power to *tax* and *spend* for the "general welfare." But Congress *doesn't* have a general power to *legislate* for the "general welfare."

  ☞ Therefore, if your fact pattern indicates that Congress is *regulating* rather than taxing or spending, it is not enough that Congress is acting for the "general welfare"; it must be regulating pursuant to some other enumerated power, typically the commerce power or the post-Civil War amendments.

☛ Once you identify an enumerated power that might be relied upon by Congress, invoke the "Necessary and Proper" Clause. Under this clause, Congress may use *any means* that is: (1) *rationally related* to the exercise of the enumerated power; and (2) not specifically *forbidden* by the Constitution.

  ☞ Remember that the Clause is *very broadly construed*, to give Congress *lots of authority* to choose the means with which to carry out an enumerated power. So if in your fact pattern Congress seems to be trying to exercise some valid source of power, resolve in favor of Congress any doubts about the validity of the particular method Congress has chosen. Perhaps cite to *U.S. v. Comstock* (holding that Congress can civilly commit dangerous prisoners at the end of their prison terms, as a Necessary and Proper means of enforcing Congress' power to pass and enforce federal criminal statutes).

CHAPTER 4

THE FEDERAL COMMERCE POWER

ChapterScope

This Chapter examines Congress' power to "regulate commerce ... among the several states." This is the "commerce power." The most important concepts in this Chapter are:

- **Test for commerce power:** A particular congressional act comes within Congress' commerce power if both of the following are true:

  - ❑ **Substantially affects commerce:** The activity being regulated *substantially affects commerce*; and

  - ❑ **Reasonable means:** The *means* chosen by Congress is *"reasonably related"* to Congress' objective in regulating.

- **Conclusion:** Where Congress thinks that what it is doing falls within its commerce power, the Court rarely disagrees, especially where the activity being regulated is itself "commercial."

- **The Tenth Amendment as a limit on Congress' power:** The *Tenth Amendment* ("the powers not delegated to the United States by the Constitution, nor prohibited by it to the States, are reserved to the States respectively, or to the People") occasionally limits Congress' ability to use its commerce power to *regulate the states*.

I. THE COMMERCE CLAUSE GENERALLY

A. Introduction: Article I, §8 of the Constitution gives Congress the power "to regulate Commerce with foreign Nations, and among the several States, and with the Indian Tribes."

1. **Foreign and Indian regulation:** Congress' power to regulate foreign trade and trade with Indian tribes is not of great interest to us here. It is sufficient to note that since the adoption of the Constitution, the Supreme Court has always recognized full power on Congress' part to regulate these matters, since there is no countervailing interest in them on the part of the states. See N&R, pp. 133-134.

2. **Commerce among the states:** Congress' power to regulate commerce *among the states*, by contrast, is of paramount importance — it is upon the commerce power that many, perhaps most, congressional activities are based.

B. Limitation on states vs. limitation on Congress: The Commerce Clause serves two distinct functions: (1) it acts as a *source of congressional authority*; and (2) it acts, implicitly, as a *limitation* on *state legislative power*. In this chapter, we examine the commerce power solely as a source of congressional authority; its function as a limitation on state power is treated in a separate chapter beginning *infra*, p. 83.

C. Chronological approach: Our approach to the federal commerce power will be a chronological one, so that development of the power may be clearly seen. Our discussion begins with the landmark commerce-power case of *Gibbons v. Ogden*, proceeds through the late nineteenth and early twentieth century cases, details the broadening scope of the commerce power beginning in 1937, and then covers some post-1995 cases limiting that scope.

II. CASES PRIOR TO 1933

A. The groundwork — *Gibbons v. Ogden*: The first major case construing the Commerce Clause was a Marshall opinion, ***Gibbons v. Ogden***, 9 Wheat. 1 (1824). Although the *Gibbons* opinion contained some discussion of the Commerce Clause as a limitation upon state powers, its principal interest is for its broad-sweeping view of ***congressional power*** under that clause.

    1. Facts of *Gibbons*: Ogden acquired, by grant from the New York legislature, monopoly rights to operate steamboats between New York and New Jersey. Gibbons began operating steamboats between New York and New Jersey, in violation of Ogden's monopoly; Gibbons' boats were licensed, however, under a federal statute. Ogden obtained an injunction in a New York court ordering Gibbons to stop operating his boats in New York waters.

    2. Holding: When the case came to the Supreme Court, Justice Marshall found the injunction against Gibbons invalid, on the ground that it was based upon a monopoly that conflicted with a valid federal statute, and thus violated the Supremacy Clause.

    3. Broad view of commerce power: In reaching this conclusion, Marshall took a broad view of Congress' powers under the Commerce Clause. Under that clause, he said, Congress could legislate with respect to ***all*** "commerce which concerns more States than one." "Commerce," he concluded, included not only buying and selling, but ***all "commercial intercourse."***

        a. May affect intrastate matters: Ogden apparently argued that insofar as his New York-granted monopoly affected his rights in New York waters, this monopoly was superior to any federal rights regarding those New York waters. But Marshall answered that the congressional power to regulate interstate commerce included the ability to ***affect matters occurring within a state***, so long as the activity had some commercial connection with another state. Thus federal law could affect New York waters, if voyages beginning in New York ended in New Jersey. (But Marshall conceded that "[t]he completely internal commerce of a State ... may be considered as reserved for the State itself.")

        b. May be used to "utmost extent": In the most important portion of his opinion, Marshall stated that ***no area of interstate commerce is reserved for state control***. That is, the mere existence of the states does not by itself act as a limit upon Congress' power to govern commercial matters that affect more than one state: "This power, like all others vested in Congress, is complete in itself, may be exercised to its utmost extent, and acknowledges no limitations, other than are prescribed in the constitution."

            i. Tenth Amendment no bar: Thus Marshall implicitly rejected the argument that the Tenth Amendment (which provides that "[t]he powers not delegated to the United States by the Constitution, nor prohibited by it to the States, are reserved to the States respectively ... ") acts as an independent limit on Congress' power to regulate interstate commerce.

    4. Limits on state power: The other portion of Marshall's opinion in *Gibbons* dealt with New York's right to grant a monopoly, and with whether this monopoly was invalid under the Supremacy Clause. This aspect of the opinion is discussed in the treatment of limitations on state power, *infra*, p. 85.

B. Inactive: From *Gibbons* until the late nineteenth century, the Supreme Court had practically no occasion to consider Congress' powers under the Commerce Clause. It was not until enactment of the Interstate Commerce Act (in 1887) and the Sherman Antitrust Act (in 1890) that Congress' powers under the Commerce Clause were again seriously scrutinized by the Court. When this scrutiny did occur, the result was much more hostile to congressional power than it was in the Marshall *Gibbons* approach.

   1. Economic regulation vs. police power: Between about 1880 and 1937, the Supreme Court reviewed (and frequently struck down) two different types of congressional legislation premised upon the commerce power: (1) economic regulatory laws; and (2) "police power" regulations, i.e., those directed at moral or general welfare issues. We consider each of these areas in turn.

C. Economic regulation: The Supreme Court's review of *economic regulatory laws* from about 1880 to 1937 was characterized by what has been called a "*dual federalism*" approach. That is, the Court felt that there were areas of economic life which, under the Tenth Amendment, were to be *left to state regulation*, and other areas of activity which were properly the preserve of the federal government. These two areas were viewed as being essentially *non-overlapping* — either an area was proper for state regulation, or for congressional regulation, but not for both.

   1. "Substantial economic effects": During this period from 1880 to 1937, congressional regulation was found to fall within the Commerce power so long as the activities being regulated had a "*substantial economic effect*" upon interstate commerce.

   a. The Shreveport Rate Case: The best-known example of this "substantial economic effect" approach was the so-called Shreveport Rate Case, *Houston E. & W. Texas Railway Co. v. U.S.*, 234 U.S. 342 (1914). In that case, the Interstate Commerce Commission, after setting rates for transport of goods between Shreveport, Louisiana and various points in Texas, sought to prevent railroads from setting rates for hauls *totally within* Texas which were less per mile than the Texas-to-Shreveport rates. The Commission's theory was that Shreveport competed with certain Texas cities for shipments from other parts of Texas, and that the lower Texas intrastate rates were unfairly discriminating against the Texas-to-Shreveport interstate traffic. The railroads countered that it was beyond Congress' power to control intrastate rates of an interstate carrier.

   i. Commission upheld: The Court rejected the railroads' challenge, and upheld the ICC's right to regulate intrastate charges, at least of interstate carriers. The opinion held that the commerce power necessarily included the right to regulate "all matters having such a *close and substantial relation* to interstate traffic that control is essential or appropriate to the security of that traffic. … ." The fact that the activity being regulated was intrastate did not place it beyond congressional control, since the *ultimate object* was protection of interstate commerce.

   2. "Current of commerce" theory: Apart from the "substantial economic effects" rationale for sustaining congressional action, Justice Holmes developed the "*current of commerce*" rationale. Under this theory, an activity could be regulated under the commerce power not because it had an *effect* on commerce, but rather, because the activity itself could be viewed as being "in" commerce or as being part of the "current" of commerce. *Swift & Co. v. U.S.*, 196 U.S. 375 (1905).

D. **"Police power" regulations and the commerce-prohibiting technique:**   In cases like *Shreveport Rate, supra,* Congress attempted to regulate local activities directly. But Congress also developed a separate technique; instead of regulating intrastate activities directly, Congress used the technique of ***prohibiting interstate transport*** of certain items or persons. This "commerce-prohibiting" technique was used not only for pure economic regulatory matters, but also for "***police power***" or "***moral***" regulation. During the first two decades of the twentieth century, the Court was substantially more sympathetic to this "commerce-prohibiting/ police power" technique than to direct regulation of intrastate affairs.

1. **The Lottery Case:**   For instance, when Congress passed the Federal Lottery Act, which prohibited the interstate shipment of ***lottery tickets***, the Court upheld the statute in *Champion v. Ames* (*"The Lottery Case"*), 188 U.S. 321 (1903). The majority opinion began with the assumption that lotteries were clearly an "evil" which it was desirable for Congress to regulate; since Congress regulated only the interstate shipment of these evil articles, it could not be said to be interfering with intrastate matters reserved for state control. (But a four-Justice dissent contended that only commerce itself could be regulated, and that lottery tickets were not "articles of commerce.")

2. **Regulation of intrastate affairs:**   Once it became apparent that the Court looked favorably upon the commerce-prohibiting technique as a means of asserting national police power, Congress took a significant additional step: it began to regulate ***intrastate*** activities as a ***means of enforcing*** bans on interstate transport. Even this extension was generally favorably viewed by the Supreme Court.

   Example: Congress passed the Pure Food and Drug Act of 1906. Acting under the Act, federal officials seized a shipment of adulterated eggs after they had arrived in the state of their destination. The right to seize adulterated eggs once they had arrived at their destination was "certainly appropriate to the right to bar them from interstate commerce, and completes its purpose, which is not to merely prevent the physical movement of adulterated articles, but the use of them. ... " *Hipolite Egg Co. v. U.S.,* 220 U.S. 45 (1911).

3. **The Child Labor Case:**   But the Supreme Court was more hostile to congressional interference with the ***employer-employee relationship***. The Justices were particularly unwilling to allow congressional legislation which was pro-labor, and which the Justices saw as being an unwarranted interference with the free-market system. This was most dramatically illustrated in ***The Child Labor Case, Hammer v. Dagenhart***, 247 U.S. 251 (1918).

   a. **Holding in case:**   In that case, the Court voted, 5-to-4, to strike down a federal statute which prohibited the interstate transport of articles produced by companies which employed children younger than certain ages or under certain conditions.

   b. **Rationale:**   The majority distinguished this statute from other police power/commerce-prohibiting statutes which the Court had upheld; in those cases, the Court argued, the interstate transportation being prohibited was ***part of the very evil*** sought to be prohibited (e.g., the prohibition on the interstate shipment of lottery tickets, where the tickets themselves were viewed as evil). Here, by contrast, the goods shipped in interstate commerce were themselves harmless; it was only the employment of child labor which was an evil, and this employment was not directly related to interstate commerce.

i. **Powers reserved to states:** The majority reasoned further that if a prohibition on interstate commerce were permitted in this situation, all manufacturing intended for interstate shipment would be brought under federal control, encroaching unconstitutionally on the authority of the states.

c. **Holmes' dissent:** But it was the classic dissent by Justice Holmes that in the long run became the more significant opinion in *Hammer*. Holmes argued that so long as the congressional regulation falls within power specifically given to the Congress (here, the power to regulate interstate commerce), the fact that it has a collateral effect upon local activities otherwise left to state control does not render the statute unconstitutional.

i. **Tenth Amendment of no force:** Thus Holmes' dissent implicitly rejected the Tenth Amendment as a source of limitations on federal authority — so long as congressional action technically comes within a constitutionally-enumerated power, it is valid *no matter how substantially* it impairs the states' ability to regulate what would otherwise be local affairs. This highly restrictive view of the Tenth Amendment became the *majority view* beginning in 1937, and has endured to the present. See *infra*, pp. 53-59.

III. COURT BARRIERS TO THE NEW DEAL

A. **The New Deal threatened:** When Congress and President Roosevelt began implementing the New Deal in 1933, the Supreme Court's view of congressional power under the Commerce Clause stood in an ambiguous state. The "commerce-prohibiting" technique was of doubtful validity, in view of *Hammer v. Dagenhart*. The validity of the "effect upon commerce" rationale was unclear: The *Shreveport Rate Case* (*supra*, p. 29) indicated that intrastate activity having a substantial practical effect on interstate commerce could be regulated; but other cases suggested that there must be a "direct" and "logical" relationship between the intrastate activity being regulated and interstate commerce. Within a few years, it became apparent that the direct-and-logical requirement would carry the Court, and that a majority of the Court would strike down congressional regulation of any area which the majority felt was reserved by the Tenth Amendment to state control.

B. **The *Schechter Poultry* ("Sick Chicken") case:** The decision which caused the greatest public uproar during the New Deal was *Schechter Poultry Corp. v. U.S.*, 295 U.S. 495 (1935), the "Sick Chicken" case. At issue in the case was the validity of the National Industrial Recovery Act (NIRA). The NIRA authorized the President to adopt "codes of fair competition" for various trades or industries; the codes regulated such items as minimum wages and prices, maximum hours, collective bargaining, etc. See Sullivan & Gunther, p. 135.

1. **Facts of *Schechter*:** The *Schechter* case involved the conviction of Schechter Poultry Corp. on charges of violating the wage and hour provisions of the New York Metropolitan Area Live Poultry Industry Fair Competition Code. Although the vast majority of poultry sold in New York came from other states, Schechter itself bought within New York City, and resold its stock *exclusively to local dealers*.

2. **Act held unconstitutional:** The Supreme Court held the NIRA *unconstitutional* as applied to *Schechter*.

a. **Not in "current of commerce":** Schechter's activities were not within the "current" or "stream" of commerce, because the interstate transactions ended when the shipments reached Schechter's New York City slaughter-houses (unlike the cattle in the *Swift* case, which were ultimately reshipped out of state after being slaughtered).

    b. Not "affecting commerce": Nor was the "affecting commerce" rationale applicable; what was required was a ***direct***, not indirect, effect on commerce. Although Schechter's wage and price policies might have forced interstate competitors to lower their own prices, this impact was much too indirect to allow for congressional control.

C. The *Carter Coal* case: The facts of *Schechter* made it a particularly weak case for the government, so the decision was not as damaging as was popularly perceived. A much more significant blow to the New Deal was delivered in ***Carter v. Carter Coal Co.***, 298 U.S. 238 (1936). That case was a challenge to the Bituminous Coal Conservation Act of 1935, which set maximum hours and minimum wages for workers in coal mines.

    1. Held unconstitutional: The Act was found not to be a valid use of the commerce power. The Court returned to the distinction (espoused in *Knight*) between "production" and "commerce." Production, which was what was being regulated here, was a "purely local activity," even though the materials produced would nearly all ultimately be sold in interstate commerce. Nor did the production "directly affect" interstate commerce; the issue was not the ***extent*** of the effect produced on interstate commerce, but the existence or non-existence of a ***direct logical relation*** between the production and the interstate commerce.

        a. Local evil: Furthermore, the Court held, the issue was the link between the employer-employee relationship (the precise matter being regulated) and interstate commerce; it could not be said that this relationship had a sufficiently direct effect upon interstate commerce. Also, the employer-employee relationship was a "local relation," and whatever evils currently characterized that relationship in the coal industries were all "***local evils*** over which the federal government has no legislative control."

    2. Cardozo dissent: The majority opinion did not give separate consideration to the validity of other aspects of the Act, such as the setting of minimum and maximum prices on coal sales. The majority viewed these price rules and the wage-hour rules as being inescapably intertwined, so that the invalidity of the latter made the entire Act invalid. But a dissent by Justice Cardozo contended that at least the price rules were valid, even as applied to intrastate sales. He argued that the prices for intrastate coal sales had such a direct impact on those for interstate sales that regulation of the latter could not be successfully carried out without regulation of the former. Justices Brandeis and Stone joined this dissent, and Chief Justice Hughes agreed in a separate opinion that the price regulations were valid. Thus on the price issue, the decision was a narrow 5-4 one.

D. The Court-packing plan: The *Carter* decision was a body-blow to the New Deal, since it implied that all attempts to deal with what the Court perceived as "local problems," including probably all employer-employee problems, would be struck down. President Roosevelt waited until after the 1937 election to launch a counterattack. When he did so, it was principally in the form of the infamous ***Court-packing plan.***

    1. How the plan was to work: Roosevelt's proposal sought congressional authority for him to appoint an additional federal judge for each judge who was 70 years old and had served on a court for at least 10 years. The plan was to apply to all levels of the federal judiciary, and provided for a maximum of 15 members on the Supreme Court, i.e., an additional six Justices. (Not by coincidence, there were six Supreme Court Justices over the age of 70 in 1937. See Sullivan & Gunther, p. 140.)

2. **Plan defeated:** The plan stirred enormous political controversy. Those opposed to it contended that "its practical operation would be to make the Constitution what the executive or legislative branches of the Government choose to say it is — an interpretation to be changed with each change of administration." (Senate Judiciary Committee Report, June 14, 1937, in Sullivan & Gunther, p. 141.) The plan was ultimately defeated, in mid-1937.

   a. **Practical effect:** However, by that time the Supreme Court had materially "reformed" itself. The retirement of Justice Van Devanter was enough to form a new majority, and the Court decided the important *NLRB v. Jones & Laughlin* case (*infra*, p. 33) in favor of the validity of the NLRA; all this occurred while the debate on the Court-packing plan was still in progress. Thus President Roosevelt made a plausible claim to have lost the battle but won the war.

IV. THE POST-NEW-DEAL TREND

A. **The post-New-Deal trend generally:** Beginning with the Court's 1937 decision in *NLRB v. Jones & Laughlin Steel Corp.* (discussed shortly below), the Court began to show a vastly greater *deference* to Congress' use of its Commerce power. Under these post-1937 cases, the Court will uphold laws based on the Commerce power if the Court is convinced that what is being regulated is economic activity, and that the activity *"substantially affects"* interstate commerce.

   1. **Three theories:** The Court gradually expanded the reach of the Commerce power by recognizing three theories upon which a commerce-based regulation may be premised: (1) an expanded *"substantial economic effect"* theory; (2) a *"cumulative effect"* theory; and (3) an expanded *"commerce-prohibiting" protective* technique. We consider each of these in turn, after which we consider the special case of use of the Commerce power to regulate *civil rights* (*infra*, p. 36).

      a. **Some limits remain:** But there remain some important *limits* on the Commerce power, as the result of several post-1995 Supreme Court decisions, which are discussed beginning *infra*, p. 38.

B. **Expanded "substantial economic effect":** Recall that in pre-1937 cases, the Court had insisted upon a "direct" and "logical" relationship between the intrastate activity being regulated and interstate commerce. But beginning in *NLRB v. Jones & Laughlin Steel Corp.*, 301 U.S. 1 (1937), the Court substantially loosened the nexus required between the intrastate activity being regulated and interstate commerce.

   1. **Facts of *Jones & Laughlin:*** The *Jones & Laughlin* case tested the constitutionality of the National Labor Relations Act of 1935 (NLRA). The case involved the NLRB's attempt to prevent Jones & Laughlin (a large integrated steel producer) from engaging in "unfair labor practices" by the discriminatory firing of employees for union activity.

   2. **NLRA upheld:** In *Jones & Laughlin*, a majority of the Court held that the NLRA, as applied to Jones & Laughlin, lay within the commerce power. The Court noted that while Jones & Laughlin manufactured iron and steel only in Pennsylvania, it owned mines in two other states, operated steamships on the Great Lakes, held warehouses in four states, and sent 75% of its product out of Pennsylvania.

    a.   **Conclusion:**   Because of this multi-state network of operations, the Court concluded, a labor stoppage of the Pennsylvania intrastate manufacturing operations would have a ***substantial effect on interstate commerce***. Therefore, labor relations at the Pennsylvania plants could constitutionally be regulated by Congress.

    b.   **"Current of commerce" rationale not needed:**   The Court expressly declined to rely on the "current of commerce" theory. The Court indicated that "current of commerce" cases (such as *Swift, supra*, p. 29) were merely particular, not exclusive, illustrations of the commerce power.

    c.   **Tenth Amendment rejected as limitation:**   The Court implied, though it did not expressly state, that the Tenth Amendment would no longer act as an independent limitation on federal commerce-clause powers.

3.   **Practical consequence:**   The abandonment of the "current of commerce" rationale, begun in *Jones & Laughlin*, now makes it irrelevant whether the activity being regulated occurs before, during or after the interstate movement. So long as the regulated activity has a ***"substantial economic effect"*** upon interstate commerce, that activity may occur substantially before the interstate movement (e.g., steel production in the *Jones & Laughlin* case, where the steel might not have been shipped out of state for months after its production) or even long ***after*** the interstate commerce. See Tribe, p. 309.

    a.   **Effect must be "substantial:** In fact, for many years after *Jones & Laughin,* observers wondered whether the regulated activity's effect on interstate commerce even had to be "substantial"; the Court's pronouncements on this issue were ambiguous. But in the landmark 1995 case of *U.S. v. Lopez, infra*, p. 38, a majority of the Court decided that a "substantial" effect on interstate commerce *is* indeed required.

C.   **The "cumulative effect" theory:**   The second major expansion of Commerce Clause power might be termed the ***"cumulative effect"*** theory. That theory provides that Congress may regulate not only acts which ***taken alone*** would have a substantial economic effect on interstate commerce, but also an entire ***class*** of acts, if the class has a substantial economic effect (even though one act within it might have virtually no interstate impact at all). As a result of this "cumulative effect" principle, it is not only the type of regulation sustained in *Jones & Laughlin* (regulation of a large steel producer, where that producer's labor problems would ***by themselves*** have a substantial effect on interstate commerce) which may be regulated. See Tribe, pp. 310-11.

1.   ***Wickard v. Filburn:***   The case which established this "cumulative effect" principle was ***Wickard v. Filburn***, 317 U.S. 111 (1942). This case (the facts of which are almost like a law school examination question in their far-fetchedness), is probably the ***furthest*** the Court has ever gone in sustaining Commerce-Clause powers, at least in the economic, as opposed to "police power," area.

    a.   **Facts of *Wickard:***   *Wickard* involved the Agricultural Adjustment Act of 1938, which permitted the Secretary of Agriculture to set quotas for the raising of wheat on every farm in the country. The Act allowed not only the setting of quotas on wheat that would be sold interstate and intrastate, but also quotas on wheat which would be ***consumed on the very farm where it was raised***. Wheat raised in excess of the quota was subject to a per-bushel penalty.

       i. **Home consumption:** Filburn, the plaintiff in *Wickard*, owned a small farm in Ohio. He challenged the government's right to set a quota on the wheat which he raised and consumed on his own farm, on the grounds that this was a purely local activity beyond the scope of federal control.

  b. **Statute upheld:** But a unanimous Court (whose composition had changed radically from the days of the *Carter Coal* case just six years before) ***upheld*** the Act, even as it applied to home-consumed wheat. The Court reasoned as follows:

       i. **Consumption has market effect:** First, the consumption of home-grown wheat is a large and variable factor in the economics of the wheat market. The more wheat that is consumed on the farm where it is grown, the less wheat that is bought in commerce (i.e., from other farmers), whether interstate or not.

      ii. **Cumulative effect:** Plaintiff's own effect on the market, by his decision to consume wheat grown himself, might be trivial. But this decision, "taken together with that of ***many others similarly situated***, is far from trivial. ... " That is, home-grown wheat "supplies a need of the man who grew it which would otherwise be reflected by purchases in the open market," and the home-grown wheat thus "competes with wheat in commerce." Protection of the interstate commercial trade in wheat clearly falls within the commerce power, and the regulation of home-grown wheat is ***reasonably related to protecting that commerce.***

  c. **Still good law:** *Wickard* is ***still good law.*** In a 2005 case, the Court relied extensively on *Wickard* to hold that Congress had the power to forbid cultivation and consumption of home-grown marijuana for medical purposes. In that case, *Gonzales v. Raich*, 545 U.S. 1 (2005), the Court said that "*Wickard* ... establishes that Congress can regulate purely intrastate activity that is not itself 'commercial,' in that it is not produced for sale, if it concludes that failure to regulate that class of activity would undercut the regulation of the interstate market in that commodity." The case is discussed further *infra*, p. 42.

D. **The commerce-prohibiting technique (police power regulations):** Recall that apart from the "affecting commerce" line of cases, another pre-1933 line of cases dealt (ambiguously) with Congress' right to use ***prohibitions*** on the ***interstate transportation*** of items or people in furtherance of "***police power***" or "***general welfare***" regulations. This commerce-prohibiting technique, like the "affecting commerce" principle, was substantially broadened shortly after 1937.

1. ***Darby*** **reverses** ***Hammer:*** Recall that in the *Child Labor Case*, *Hammer v. Dagenhart* (*supra*, p. 30), the Court held that Congress could not prohibit the interstate sale of the products of child labor. *Hammer* was flatly overruled in ***U.S. v. Darby***, 312 U.S. 100 (1941).

  a. **Minimum wage regulations upheld:** In *Darby*, the Court unanimously upheld the Fair Labor Standards Act of 1938, which set minimum wages and maximum hours for employees engaged in the production of goods for interstate commerce. The Act not only prohibited the shipment in interstate commerce of goods made by employees employed for more than the maximum hours or not paid the prevailing rates, but it also made it a federal crime to employ workmen in the production of goods "for interstate commerce" at other than the prescribed rates and hours.

b. Direct ban upheld: The Court first upheld the direct ban on interstate shipments; it disposed of the argument that manufacturing conditions are left for exclusive state control, by stating that "[t]he power of Congress over interstate commerce [can] neither be enlarged nor diminished by the exercise or non-exercise of state power. ... The [Tenth Amendment] states but a truism that all is retained which has not been surrendered."

    i. Tenth Amendment irrelevant: Thus the Tenth Amendment will *no longer act as an independent limitation on congressional authority over interstate commerce.* (See *infra,* pp. 53-59 for a summary of the present status of the Tenth Amendment.) As the result of *Darby,* Congress is completely free to impose whatever conditions it wishes upon the privilege of engaging in an activity that substantially affects interstate commerce, so long as the conditions themselves violate no independent constitutional prohibition (e.g., the Equal Protection Clause of the Fourteenth Amendment). See Tribe, pp. 311-312.

c. Motive irrelevant: The Court also disavowed any interest in Congress' *motive*: "The motive and purpose of a regulation of interstate commerce are matters for the legislative judgment upon the exercise of which the Constitution places no restriction and over which the courts are given no control."

    i. Present rule: The irrelevance of motive remains a feature of Commerce Clause, and most other sorts, of constitutional analysis. (But motive may be relevant where a preferred right, such as the right of free expression or freedom from racial discrimination, is concerned. See, e.g., pp. 266 and 502 *infra.*)

d. Reasonable means to achieve end: Finally, the Court in *Darby* upheld the portion of the Act making it a crime to employ workers engaged in interstate commerce in violation of the wage/hour provisions.

    i. Rationale: Given Congress' right to impose direct prohibitions or conditions on interstate commerce, Congress "may choose the *means reasonably adapted to the attainment of the permitted end,* even though they involve control of intrastate activities." Thus the outright criminalization of employer conduct was a reasonable means of *implementing* the prohibition on interstate shipments.

    ii. Bootstrap: This portion of the *Darby* opinion has been referred to as a "super-bootstrap suggestion"; see Gunther & Sullivan (13th Ed.), pp. 195-96. If it is taken seriously, it means that Congress may attack any problem (even one of overwhelmingly local concern) by prohibiting all interstate activity associated in any way with it; then, the local activity itself could be prohibited as a means of implementing the ban on interstate transactions.

E. Civil rights legislation: A key use of the federal Commerce power has been in *civil rights* legislation. Thus Title II of the 1964 Civil Rights Act bans discrimination in places of public accommodation. This ban applies against all but the very most localized, small hotels or restaurants. It does this by covering any establishment that *serves interstate travelers,* or (in the case of a restaurant) that buys *food,* a substantial portion of which "has *moved in commerce.*"

1. The Court decisions: Any doubts about the constitutionality of the 1964 Act were put to rest by two 1964 Supreme Court decisions upholding it. Both, but especially the second discussed below, involved what might be termed "local" enterprises.

a. ***Heart of Atlanta* case:** In ***Heart of Atlanta Motel v. U.S.***, 379 U.S. 241 (1964), the plaintiff was a motel located in downtown Atlanta, which refused to rent rooms to blacks.

  i. **Contacts with interstate travel:** The motel was near two interstate highways, derived 75% of its occupancy from out-of-state guests, and solicited business in national media.

  ii. **Holding:** The Supreme Court held that the motel could constitutionally be reached by the Civil Rights Act, under the Commerce Clause. The Court took note of Congress' findings that racial discrimination discouraged travel on the part of a substantial portion of the black community, and that such discrimination could therefore be regulated by Congress in the aggregate. Furthermore, the Court held, "[t]he power of Congress to promote interstate commerce also includes the power to regulate the local incidents thereof, including local activities in both the States of origin and destination, which might have a substantial and harmful effect upon that commerce." The Court quoted a prior decision, to the effect that "if it is interstate commerce that feels the pinch, it does not matter how local the operation that applies the squeeze."

  iii. **Police-powers motive acceptable:** Nor was the Court troubled by the fact that Congress' *motive* for this legislation was not purely economic, but rather, principally moral and social.

b. ***Katzenbach v. McClung:*** The other early Civil Rights Act case, ***Katzenbach v. McClung***, 379 U.S. 294 (1964), demonstrates even more clearly the Court's approval of the use of the Commerce Clause to reach what seemed to be overwhelmingly local activities.

  i. **Facts:** *Katzenbach* involved a Birmingham, Alabama restaurant called Ollie's Barbecue. The restaurant was relatively far from any interstate highway or train or bus station, and there was no evidence that an appreciable part of its business was in serving out of state travellers. However, 46% of the food purchased by the restaurant during the previous year had been bought from a supplier who had bought it from out of state. (Recall that the Civil Rights Act applies to any restaurant a substantial portion of whose food has moved in commerce.)

  ii. **Application of Act upheld:** The Court *upheld* the Act as applied to the restaurant. As in the *Heart of Atlanta* case, the Court observed that unavailability of accommodations dissuaded blacks from travelling in interstate commerce. The Court returned to the *Wickard v. Filburn* rationale: even though Ollie's itself was small, and the value of food it purchased from out of state had only an insignificant effect on commerce, the restaurant's discriminatory conduct was representative of a great deal of similar conduct throughout the country, and this conduct in the aggregate clearly had an effect on interstate commerce. Therefore, Congress was entitled to regulate the individual case.

  iii. **Deference to Congress' findings:** Nor did the fact that the bill contained *no congressional findings* about the impact of restaurant discrimination on commerce render the Act unconstitutional. The Court would not scrutinize the facts to make a *de novo* determination of whether restaurant discrimination affected commerce. Rather, "where we find that the legislators, in light of the facts and testimony before them, have a ***rational basis*** for finding a chosen regulatory scheme necessary to the protection of commerce, our investigation is at an end." Such a rational basis was present here.

V.   SOME MODERN LIMITS ON THE COMMERCE POWER

A.   Some limits still exist: But some important ***limits*** still exist on Congress' Commerce powers, as the result of several major decisions since 1995. Here's a brief summary of these key limiting decisions:

    ❏ **"Substantial" effect required:** It is not enough that the activity being regulated merely ***"affects"*** interstate commerce. Instead, the activity must ***"substantially*** affect" interstate commerce. So, for instance, Congress can't prohibit possession of guns near schools, because the effect on Commerce of such possession is not substantial enough. (See *U.S. v. Lopez, infra*, p. 38.)

    ❏ **"Non-economic" activities:** The Court will be more skeptical of Commerce-based regulation if the activity being regulated is essentially ***non-economic***. So, for instance, Congress can't allow women who are the victims of gender-motivated violent crimes to bring federal civil-court suits, because gender-motivated violent crime against women is essentially a non-economic activity. (See *U.S. v. Morrison, infra*, p. 41.)

    ❏ **Forced entry into market:** Congress may not use its Commerce power to compel someone who is ***not already active*** in a commercial market to ***enter that market by purchasing a product***. For instance, Congress can't use its Commerce power to force individuals to ***buy health insurance*** (or pay a penalty if they don't), even though the collective decisions of many people not to buy insurance substantially affect the interstate market for health care. (See *N.F.I.B. v. Sebelius, infra*, p. 44.)

We review these key post-1995 cases below. We also review one post-1995 case that went the other way, in which Congress' use of its Commerce power to regulate some very local transactions (growing marijuana for one's personal purposes) was *sustained*, on the grounds that without such regulation, an entire nationwide scheme for regulating interstate commerce would be jeopardized; see *Gonzales v. Raich, infra*, p. 42.

B.   Can't ban "guns near schools" (*U.S. v. Lopez*):   The case holding that the effect on interstate commerce from the activity being regulated must be ***"substantial"*** was *U.S. v. Lopez*, 514 U.S. 549 (1995). There, the Court for the first time in 60 years ***invalidated a federal statute on the grounds that it was beyond Congress' Commerce power***.

    1.   Gun-Free Schools: The statute was the Gun-Free School Zones Act of 1990, in which Congress made it a federal crime "for any individual knowingly to possess a firearm at a place that the individual knows, or has reasonable cause to believe, is a school zone."

        a.   Little connection to commerce: The statute clearly had less explicit connection to interstate commerce than most federal statutes premised on the Commerce power. For instance:

            i.   No findings: The statute did not include explicit findings by Congress that the activity being regulated (possession of guns in schools) affected commerce.

    ii. **No jurisdictional nexus:** Perhaps more important, the statute did not include a "jurisdictional nexus." For instance, Congress could have made it a crime only to possess a gun that had moved in (or otherwise affected) interstate commerce. (Congress often uses this "jurisdictional" approach to carry out the "commerce-prohibiting" technique; see, for instance, the 1964 Civil Rights Act, discussed *supra*, p. 36, regulating restaurants that buy food a substantial part of which has moved in interstate commerce.) But this isn't what Congress did here — instead it banned even possession of a gun that had never traveled in, or even affected, interstate commerce.

2. **Statute struck down:** By a 5-4 vote, the Court struck down the statute. The majority opinion was by Chief Justice Rehnquist, joined by Justices O'Connor, Scalia, Kennedy and Thomas.

    a. **"Substantial" effect required on Commerce:** The majority opinion first resolved a prior uncertainty, by holding that it is not enough that the activity being regulated merely "affects" interstate commerce. Instead, the activity must "***substantially* affect**" interstate commerce.

    b. **Requisite effect not present:** Then, the majority concluded that the possession of guns in schools had not been demonstrated to "substantially affect" commerce.

        i. **Not commercial:** The majority seemed to think that it was important that the particular activity being regulated — possession of guns in schools — ***was not itself a "commercial" activity***. The majority distinguished *Wickard v. Filburn, supra,* p. 34 (which it called "perhaps the most far reaching example of Commerce Clause authority over intrastate activity. ... ") from the activity at issue here, saying that *Wickard* "involved economic activity in a way that the possession of a gun in a school zone does not." Also, unlike the wheat-growing regulation in *Wickard*, the regulation here was not part of a "larger regulation of economic activity, in which the regulatory scheme could be undercut unless the intrastate activity were regulated."

        ii. **Government's argument:** The federal government, in defending the statute, had argued that gun possession in schools *does* have a "substantial effect" on commerce. The government asserted the following syllogism: (1) possession of a firearm in a school may result in violent crime; and (2) violent crime affects the functioning of the national economy in several ways (e.g., (a) the costs of crime are insured against, and thus spread across state lines because of the interstate nature of the insurance market; (b) violent crime reduces individuals' willingness to travel to areas of the country they believe are unsafe; and (c) violent crime in the schools reduces the schools' ability to educate their students, who thus become less economically-productive).

        iii. **Argument rejected:** But the majority rejected this argument, essentially because it ***proved too much***. For instance, under the "economic productivity" argument, "Congress could regulate any activity that it found was related to the economic productivity of individual citizens: family law (including marriage, divorce, and child custody), for example." In general, under the government's approach, "[I]t is difficult to perceive **any limitation on federal power**, even in areas such as criminal law enforcement or education where States historically have been sovereign.

Thus, if we were to accept the Government's arguments, we are hard-pressed to posit any activity that Congress is without power to regulate."

    iv. Parade of horribles: The majority went on to describe some of the types of federal regulation that would fall within the Commerce power, if the government's approach were accepted: "Congress could mandate a *federal curriculum* for local elementary and secondary schools because what is taught in local schools has a significant 'effect on classroom learning,' and that, in turn, has a substantial effect on interstate commerce." Similarly, "Congress could ... look at *child rearing* as 'fall[ing] on the commercial side of the line', because it provides a 'valuable service — namely, to equip [children] with the skills they need to survive in ... the workplace.' " Such results would make the Commerce power limitless.

    v. Summary: In summary, the majority said, "To uphold the Government's contentions here, we would have to pile inference upon inference in a manner that would bid fair to convert congressional authority under the Commerce Clause to a *general police power* of the sort retained by the States." Prior cases may have extended the Commerce power to great lengths, "but we decline here to proceed any further." To uphold the act here "would require us to conclude ... that there never will be a distinction between what is truly national and what is truly local...."

3. Concurrences: There were two concurrences, one by Justice Kennedy (joined by Justice O'Connor) and the other by Justice Thomas. Kennedy's concurrence suggested that he and O'Connor were less eager than Rehnquist (or, probably, Scalia and Thomas) to cut back the Court's prior Commerce Clause interpretations. He said that he had "some pause" about joining the majority's opinion, and that this was a "necessary though limited holding."

4. Dissent: There were four dissenters (Stevens, Souter, Breyer and Ginsburg), who wrote three separate opinions. The principal one was by Justice Breyer, in which all three of the other dissenters joined.

    a. "Rational basis" test: For Breyer, the test was "whether Congress could have had a *rational basis* for finding a significant (or substantial) connection between gun-related school violence and interstate commerce." (The majority had not mentioned "rational basis" — to the majority, the question was whether there actually *was* a substantial connection, not merely whether Congress could rationally have believed that there was.) With the issue formulated this way, Breyer had no trouble concluding that the answer was yes.

        i. Government's arguments accepted: Breyer accepted the government's arguments on this point. There was ample evidence available to Congress that gun-related violence in the schools interfered with the quality of education. And there was also extensive evidence that education was intimately tied to the economic viability of not only individuals but whole areas (since "many firms base their location decisions upon the presence, or absence, of a work force with a basic education").

    b. Majority's view rejected: Breyer vehemently objected to the majority's approach.

i. Contrary to case law: First, Breyer found that approach contrary to modern cases upholding congressional action regulating activities that (in his opinion) had less connection with interstate commerce than the guns-in-schools at issue here. For instance, he thought that a single instance of racial discrimination at a local restaurant, found regulable in *Katzenbach v. McClung, supra*, p. 37, had no greater connection with interstate commerce than the instance of gun possession being regulated here.

ii. Commercial/non-commercial distinction rejected: Second, Breyer rejected the majority's distinction between "commercial" and "non-commercial" transactions, believing that the line would prove hard to draw. He also thought that the majority drew the line in the wrong place here — if the majority was holding that education as a whole was a non-commercial activity, the majority was mistaken because "Congress ... could rationally conclude that schools fall on the commercial side of the line."

C. Violence against women (*Morrison*): The second major case limiting Congress' Commerce powers was *U.S. v. Morrison,* 529 U.S. 598 (2000). *Morrison* suggests that whenever Congress tries to regulate conduct that is ***essentially non-commercial,*** the Court will be quick to say that the regulation goes beyond the Commerce power. Just as *Lopez* held that Congress can't ban gun possession in schools, *Morrison* says that Congress ***can't broadly regulate violence against women,*** because such violence is essentially non-commercial.

1. Facts: In *Morrison*, Congress was concerned that the states' judicial systems were not taking gender-motivated violence against women sufficiently seriously. Congress therefore passed the Violence Against Women Act of 1994, 42 U.S.C. § 13981. The Act announced that all persons within the U.S. "shall have the right to be free from crimes of violence motivated by gender." To enforce that right, the Act then said that a woman who was a victim of such a gender-motivated violent crime could bring a civil suit against the perpetrator in federal court. A female student at Virginia Tech who said she had been raped by two members of the school's football team sued them under the Act. They defended by arguing that the act was beyond Congress' powers, including its Commerce power.

2. Holding: By the same 5-4 split as in *Lopez*, the Court agreed with the defendants that the Act was beyond Congress' Commerce power. The majority opinion by Chief Justice Rehnquist relied principally on the fact that the activity being regulated was essentially ***non-economic***: "Gender-motivated crimes of violence are not, in any sense of the phrase, economic activity. While we need not adopt a categorical rule against aggregating the effects of any noneconomic activity ... Thus far in our Nation's history our cases have upheld Commerce Clause regulation of intrastate activity only where that activity is economic in nature."

a. Congressional findings not enough: Rehnquist conceded that here, unlike in *Lopez*, there were ***detailed findings*** by Congress detailing the effect of the conduct being regulated on interstate commerce; for instance, Congress had found that gender-motivated violence deterred potential victims from traveling interstate or from being employed in interstate businesses. However, Rehnquist seemed to give virtually no deference to these findings, because they made for too attenuated a causal chain: "If accepted [this] reasoning would ***allow Congress to regulate any crime*** as long as the nationwide, aggregated impact of that crime has substantial effects on employment, production, transit, or consumption. Indeed, if Congress may regulate gender-motivated violence, it would be able to **regulate murder or any other type of violence**. ..."

    b.   Local vs. national distinction: Rehnquist concluded by relying on the **distinction between local and national activities:** "The Constitution requires a distinction between what is truly national and what is truly local ... The regulation and punishment of intrastate violence that is not directed at the instrumentalities, channels, or goods involved in interstate commerce has always been the province of the States."

3.   Dissent: Four Justices dissented, in separate dissents by Justices Souter and Breyer. The dissenters were especially critical of the majority's rejection of Congress' factual findings. They also criticized the majority's view that where an activity is basically non-commercial its aggregate affects on commerce cannot suffice. Justice Breyer pointed out that the economic/noneconomic distinction would be a hard one to implement reliably. (E.g., "Would evidence that desire for economic domination underlies many brutal crimes against women save the present statute?") He also argued that there was no reason for attaching such importance to that distinction in situations where non-commercial local activities have a large *effect* on interstate commerce. (E.g., "If chemical emanations through indirect environmental change cause identical, severe commercial harm outside a State, why should it matter whether local factories or home fireplaces release them?")

D.   Regulation of non-commercial activity as part of broader regulatory scheme: Not every post-1995 Commerce decision has gone against Congress. When Congress is engaged in a **broad regulation of a commercial activity**, even after *Lopez* and *Morrison* the Court has allowed Congress to regulate **purely non-commercial and intrastate instances of that activity,** if it **reasonably believes that failure to regulate these instances would jeopardize the success of the overall regulatory scheme.** Thus in **Gonzales v. Raich**, 545 U.S. 1 (2005), the Court concluded by 6-3 that Congress, as part of its overall ban on the cultivation and sale of marijuana, could forbid even the purely **intrastate and noncommercial cultivation** of **marijuana** for **medical purposes.**

1.   Facts: Congress had since the 1970s classified marijuana as a Schedule 1 drug (drugs with high potential for abuse and lack of any accepted medical use), and had made it a crime to manufacture distribute or possess any Schedule I drug. Congress did so in the Controlled Substances Act (CSA). California then, in 1996, by means of a voter-approved Proposition, established an exemption from criminal prosecution for physicians who recommended marijuana to a patient for medical purposes, as well as for patients and primary caregivers who possessed or cultivated marijuana for medicinal purposes with the recommendation or approval of a physician. (Eight other states also authorized use of marijuana for medicinal purposes.)

    a.   How suit arose: The two plaintiffs in *Raich* were California residents who suffered from very serious medical ailments that they sought to treat with marijuana. (One of them, Monson, grew her own marijuana, which was confiscated by federal Drug Enforcement Administration agents.) The plaintiffs then sued for an injunction barring the enforcement of the CSA against them, on the theory that Congress did not have the power, under the Commerce Clause or any other grant of authority, to regulate the interstate, noncommercial cultivation and possession of marijuana for personal medical purposes. The Ninth Circuit agreed with the plaintiffs, on the basis of *Lopez* and *Morrison*.

2. **Plaintiffs lose by 6-3:** By a 6-3 vote, the Court held against the Ps in *Raich*, concluding that Congress' Commerce clause powers gave it the right to regulate *even the purely intrastate and noncommercial cultivation of marijuana.* The majority opinion was by Justice Stevens.

    a. **Reliance on *Wickard*:** Stevens relied heavily on *Wickard v. Filburn* (*supra*, p. 34), the home-grown wheat case. There, the Court had concluded that when Congress was attempting to regulate the production (and thus pricing) of wheat that moved in interstate commerce, Congress could also regulate farmer Filburn's cultivation of 12 acres of wheat for consumption on his own farm. Stevens asserted that *Wickard* "thus establishes that Congress *can regulate purely intrastate activity that is not itself 'commercial,'* in that it is not produced for sale, if it concludes that *failure to regulate that class of activity would undercut the regulation of the interstate market in that commodity.*"

        i. **Application to facts:** Stevens believed that this *Wickard* principle easily fit the facts of the marijuana cultivation here. "Like the farmer in *Wickard*, [plaintiffs] are cultivating, for home consumption, a fungible commodity for which there is an established, albeit illegal, interstate market." And, just as Congress in *Wickard* rationally feared that "when viewed in the aggregate, leaving home-consumed wheat outside the regulatory scheme would have a substantial influence on price and market conditions," so, here, Congress had "a rational basis for concluding that leaving home-consumed marijuana outside federal control would similarly affect price and market conditions." That is, Congress, in passing the CSA, rationally believed that if cultivation of home-grown marijuana were permitted for medicinal consumption, the high demand in the interstate market would *draw that home-grown marijuana into the interstate market*, frustrating Congress' purpose of banning interstate commerce in marijuana.

        ii. ***Lopez* and *Morrison* distinguished:** Stevens distinguished *Lopez* and *Morrison*. In those two cases, the parties making the "no congressional authority" argument asserted that a particular statute or provision fell outside Congress' commerce power *in its entirety*. For instance, in *Lopez*, the Gun-Free School Zones Act *did not regulate any economic activity at all,* and did not contain any requirement that possession of a gun have any connection to past or future commercial activity. Here, by contrast, Congress' regulation of marijuana grown for home consumption was merely one of many *"essential part[s] of a larger regulation of economic activity,* in which the regulatory scheme could be undercut unless the interstate activity were regulated" (quoting language from *Lopez*).

        iii. **"Economic activity":** Indeed, for Stevens, the activities regulated by the CSA, unlike those regulated in *Lopez* (gun possession near schools) and *Morrison* (violence against women), were *"quintessentially economic."* "Economics," he noted, refers to the "production, distribution and consumption of commodities." Since the CSA regulated the "production, distribution, and consumption of commodities for which there was an established, and lucrative, interstate market[,]" and since the Court had long recognized that prohibiting the *intrastate* manufacture or possession of an article of commerce was a rational means of regulating interstate commerce in that product, the intrastate regulation here easily fell within Congress' commerce powers.

b. Scalia's concurrence: Justice Scalia concurred. Unlike the majority, he relied on the ***necessary and proper clause*** (*supra*, p. 21): he believed that Congress could regulate even noneconomic local activity that did not "substantially affect" interstate commerce, if "that regulation is a ***necessary part of a more general regulation of interstate commerce.***" Since Congress could reasonably conclude that its objective of barring marijuana from the interstate market might be undercut if local growing for medical purposes was allowed, a ban on that local activity was necessary to the success of the overall regulatory scheme.

c. Dissent: Justice O'Connor, joined by Chief Justice Rehnquist and (for the most part) by Justice Thomas, ***dissented*** in *Raich*. She objected that the majority's approach "allows Congress to regulate intrastate activity without check, so long as there is some implication by legislative design that regulating intrastate activity is essential ... to the interstate regulatory scheme." She believed that the majority's method reduced *Lopez* to "nothing more than a ***drafting guide:*** Congress should have described the relevant crime [in *Lopez*] as 'transfer or possession of a firearm anywhere in the nation' — thus including commercial and noncommercial activity ... Had it done so ... we would have sustained its authority to regulate possession of firearms in school zones."

    i. "Separate class of activity" approach: Instead, O'Connor would have treated the possession and use of homegrown marijuana for medical purposes as being a ***separate class of activity*** that had not been shown to have even "a discernible, let alone substantial, impact on the national illicit drug market." Consequently, she would have distinguished that marijuana use from the wheat being consumed in *Wickard*, and would have found it to be beyond Congress' commerce powers.

E. Forcing someone to buy a product (*N.F.I.B. v. Sebelius*): Suppose Congress decides to use its powers under the Commerce Clause to require that a person ***buy some good or service***. It's clear that Congress can regulate individual existing intrastate activities (like a farmer growing wheat for his own consumption in *Wickard*, *supra*, p. 34), if such intrastate activities, taken in the aggregate, have a substantial effect on interstate commerce. But suppose Congress instead says, in effect, "The decisions of many individuals ***not*** to purchase a product, taken in the aggregate, have a substantial ***negative effect*** on the interstate market for that product; therefore, we are going to use our Commerce power to ***require individuals to buy that product,*** even individuals who are not now, and have never been, in the market for that product." Can Congress do this?

In the most significant and controversial Commerce power case since at least the 1930s, the Supreme Court decided by a 5-4 vote in 2012 that the answer is ***"no":*** Congress may ***not*** use its Commerce power to "compe[l] individuals to ***become active in commerce by purchasing a product,***" even if the individuals' combined failure to do so significantly affects interstate commerce. The case was ***N.F.I.B. v. Sebelius,*** 132 S.Ct. 2566 (2012), striking down Congress' use of its Commerce power to force individuals to ***buy health insurance or else pay a penalty***.

1. Adoption of the ACA: Congress passed an elaborate ***health-care reform statute*** in 2010 called the Patient Protection and Affordable Care Act (which we'll call the ***"Affordable Care Act"*** or ***"ACA"***). The ACA was adopted on almost straight party lines, with the vast majority of Democrats (and the Obama administration) in favor, and nearly all Republicans opposed. The Act was a broad-sweeping attempt to dramatically reduce the number of Americans without health insurance.

a. **The "individual mandate" to purchase insurance:** Until the ACA, Congress had never tried to use its Commerce powers to compel an individual to *buy a good or service.* But in one of many provisions of the ACA, Congress set a "minimum coverage provision," by which most healthy individuals were *required to purchase health insurance*, even if they had previously chosen to "self-insure," i.e., to go without health insurance entirely in the hope of being able to get any needed care for free, or pay for it out of their own pockets at the time of need. The Affordable Care Act referred to this requirement that most healthy individuals must buy insurance as the *"individual mandate."* An individual who was subject to the mandate and did not buy the required insurance was required to pay to the Internal Revenue Service (IRS) what the ACA called a *"shared-responsibility payment,"* which was also frequently referred to in the statute as a *"penalty."*

b. **Motivation:** Congress reasoned that under the pre-ACA system, healthy individuals had been permitted to self-insure (and wait to get sick), and thereby *made insurance more expensive for everyone else*. It had never been thought practical to force the uninsured to pay *at the time they got sick and needed care* — many simply wouldn't have the money for treatment, and would be left to die. Therefore, federal and state laws, as well as professional obligations, had long required hospitals and doctors to treat uninsured patients for free in emergencies. The substantial cost of this uncompensated care had then traditionally been *added onto everyone else's health-care bill,* so that employers who bought insurance for their employees, and individuals who bought their own health insurance, had to pay considerably more (an estimated $1,000 per family per year) than if everyone had insurance. The uninsured were thus, in Congress' view, *"free riders"* who received unpaid care at the expense of everyone else.

   i. **The "guaranteed issue" and "community rating" provisions:** The ACA was not just an attempt to deal with the traditional cost of free-riding by the uninsured. The Act was an ambitious attempt to create a system of *near-universal health-care insurance.* Two of the most significant ways by which the ACA attempted to broaden the availability of health insurance were by:

   [1] banning insurance companies from *denying coverage to sick people* (the *"guaranteed issue"* provision); and

   [2] banning insurers from *charging sick people more* than healthy people (the *"community rating"* provision).

   Congress feared that these two new provisions would make the free-rider problem much worse: If Congress did not somehow induce the large numbers of healthy (and cheap-to-insure) people who had been self-insuring to start buying insurance, adding the guaranteed-isue and community-rating provisions would cause rates for everyone else to grow even higher — the insurers would have to start covering lots of much sicker people than before, at the same prices as the non-sick, creating a spiral in which insurers either had to raise prices for everyone, lose money, or drop out of the market.

   ii. **Ban on "free riders":** So the individual mandate was seen by Congress as the only way to fulfill the ACA's overall goal of broadening health-care availability. Those who had previously gone without health insurance would either have to buy insurance, or else make the shared-responsibility payments, which would be pooled and used to cover part of the cost of otherwise-uncompensated care for the remaining uninsured. And the insurers would make money from these new, typically younger and healthier, customers (who would pay the same rates as everyone else), counterbalancing the losses the insurers would incur from the guaranteed-issue and community-rating provisions.[1] Individuals and families below a certain income level would be exempt from the mandate, and would also be given financial assistance to buy insurance.

c. **No desire to tax:** Congress could clearly have accomplished much the same result by using its tax-and-spend power to impose a "tax" on anyone who did not buy insurance.[2] But Congress apparently did not want to be seen to be creating a new tax, so the bill never referred to the shared-responsibility payment scheme as being a tax.

d. **Commerce-regulation rationale:** Therefore, instead of relying explicitly on its power to tax, Congress asserted that the individual mandate and the shared-responsibility payment system together represented a proper exercise of the Commerce power. Congress reasoned that everyone will ultimately need, and consume, health care; even the youngest and healthiest person might well have a health emergency tomorrow, in which case he would receive care without it being practical to charge him at the time of the emergency. Therefore, in Congress' view, the individual mandate and the shared-responsibility payment system were simply a means of regulating *how and when people would pay* (via insurance) for a product (health care) that they would *inevitably consume* even without regulation.

2. **Attacked by states:** Twenty-six states (nearly all with Republican governors), as well as many other plaintiffs including the National Federation of Independent Business (N.F.I.B.), immediately brought suits challenging the ACA's constitutionality. Although these suits focused on various provisions, their principal thrust was against the individual mandate — the plaintiffs contended that forcing people to enter a market to buy a product (health insurance) that they didn't want went beyond the Commerce power.

3. **Majority strikes down Commerce rationale:** Five members of the Court *agreed with the plaintiffs* on this argument: the individual mandate *went beyond Congress' Commerce powers.* The principal opinion on this point was by Chief Justice Roberts. No other justice formally joined his opinion on the Commerce issue, but the four other conservative members (Scalia, Kennedy, Thomas and Alito) agreed with him that the mandate was not authorized by the Commerce power.[3] We concentrate here on Roberts' opinion, in part

---

1. Congress also sweetened the pot for insurers by dramatically increasing the scope of the state-administered *Medicaid* program for poor people, a step that would give the insurers millions of new government-paid customers. But in another part of *N.F.I.B.,* this step was partly struck down by the Court as going beyond the spending power; see *infra,* p. 72.

2. Indeed, by a separate 5-4 vote within *N.F.I.B.,* the Supreme Court saved the bulk of the ACA by holding that what Congress called a "penalty" for those who did not buy the required insurance was in fact a constitutional use of the tax-and-spend power. See *infra,* p. 67.

3. The opinion by Scalia, Kennedy, Thomas and Alito is referred to by some other members of the Court as a *"joint dissent"*; it is signed by all four, with no principal author. It's a "dissent" as to the overall result in the case, because these four Justices rejected the argument that the individual mandate was justified under the tax-and-spend power (see *infra,* p. 69); they would have struck down the entire ACA. But the arguments in the joint dissent about why the mandate doesn't fall within the Commerce power largely parallel Roberts' arguments.

because it is the one to which the dissent by Justice Ginsburg (see *infra*, p. 49) was mostly addressed.

a. Novelty: Roberts began by noting that Congress had never before attempted to rely on the Commerce power "to ***compel individuals not engaged in commerce to purchase an unwanted product.***" He conceded that "Legislative novelty is not necessarily fatal; there is a first time for everything." But, he said, "sometimes 'the most telling indication of [a] severe constitutional problem ... is the lack of historical precedent[.]'"

b. Must regulate "activity": Roberts then got to the gist of his argument: "The power to *regulate* [emphasis in original] commerce ***presupposes the existence of commercial activity to be regulated.***"

    i. "Superfluous powers" argument: If the power to "regulate" something included the power to *create* it, he said, "many of the provisions in the Constitution would be ***superfluous***." For instance, the Constitution gives Congress the power to "coin money," and also the power to "regulate the Value thereof." If the power to regulate the value of money included the power to bring the subject of the regulation (money) into existence, the power to create money would have been superfluous.

    ii. Regulating "activity": Similarly, Roberts argued, the Court's cases describing the Commerce power "uniformly describe the power as reaching *'activity.'*" The individual mandate, by contrast, "does not regulate *existing commercial activity*. It instead compels individuals to *become* active in commerce by purchasing a product, on the ground that their failure to do so affects interstate commerce."

    iii. Unwarranted expansion of Congress' powers: Interpreting the Commerce power to permit Congress to "regulate individuals precisely *because* they are doing nothing" would, he said, ***"open a new and potentially vast domain to congressional authority."*** "Every day individuals ***do not do an infinite number of things."*** Allowing Congress to regulate based on the effect of inaction on commerce "would bring countless decisions an individual could potentially make within the scope of federal regulation[.]"

    iv. *Wickard* example: Roberts pointed to the facts of *Wickard v. Filburn* (the wheat-growing case, *supra*, p. 34) as an example of how the government's theory would expand the scope of permissible regulation. *Wickard* justified regulating the farmer's growing of wheat for home consumption on the ground that his growing allowed him to avoid purchasing wheat in the market, and that this decision to grow his own wheat, when aggregated with the similar decisions of others, would have a substantial effect on the interstate market for wheat. But, Roberts argued, "price can be supported by ***increasing demand*** as well as by decreasing supply. The aggregated decisions of some consumers ***not to purchase wheat*** have a ***substantial effect on the price of wheat,*** just as decisions not to purchase health insurance have on the price of insurance." By the government's theory, "Congress can therefore ***command that those not buying wheat do so,*** just as it argues here that it may command that those not buying health insurance do so."

    v. The "broccoli" argument: During the public debate on the individual mandate, and in the oral argument before the Court, opponents of the mandate's constitutionality had made frequent use of the so-called ***"broccoli"*** hypothetical: if Congress could force people to buy health insurance because lack of widespread health insurance is bad for the nation, Congress could attack the country's dietary and obesity problems, and associated health costs, by forcing everyone to ***"buy broccoli."***

(1) **"Vegetables":** Roberts essentially adopted the broccoli argument, though he made it a touch more generic. "Many Americans do not eat a balanced diet," and therefore become obese. Obese people have higher health costs, which are borne in part by other Americans, "just as the uninsured shift costs to the insured." Under the government's theory, therefore, ***"Congress could address the diet problem by ordering everyone to buy vegetables."***

vi. Fundamental change: But, he said, "That is not the country the framers of our Constitution envisioned." Congress already has vast power to regulate much of what people do. Under the government's theory, Congress would have "the same license to regulate what we do ***not do, fundamentally changing the relation*** between the citizen and the Federal Government."

vii. The "mere financing" argument: The federal government had argued that this was *not* in fact a situation where people were being forced to ***become active*** in a market in which they did not otherwise participate. The government contended that because sickness and injury are unpredictable but unavoidable, "the uninsured as a class are ***active in the market for health care***, which they ***regularly seek and obtain.***" The individual mandate therefore "merely regulates ***how individuals finance and pay*** for that active participation," by requiring them to buy insurance instead of self-insuring.

(1) **Argument rejected:** But Roberts rejected this "mere financing" argument. "An individual who bought a car two years ago and may buy another in the future is not 'active in the car market' in any pertinent sense." The individual mandate primarily affects "healthy, often young adults who are less likely to need significant health-care and have other priorities for spending their money ... If the individual mandate is targeted at a class, it is a class whose commercial ***inactivity rather than activity*** is its defining feature."

(2) **Can't anticipate future activity to regulate it now:** Roberts conceded that prior Commerce Clause cases had allowed Congress to ***anticipate*** the effects of existing local economic activity on interstate commerce. "But we have never permitted Congress to ***anticipate that [economic] activity itself*** in order to regulate individuals not currently engaged in commerce. ... Everyone will likely participate in the markets for food, clothing, transportation, shelter, or energy; that does not authorize Congress to direct them to purchase particular products in those or other markets today. The Commerce Clause is ***not a general license to regulate an individual from cradle to grave***, simply because he will predictably engage in particular transactions."

viii. Necessary and Proper Clause: The government had also argued that even if the Commerce power was not enough, standing alone, to justify the individual mandate, the ***Necessary and Proper Clause*** supplied any additional needed authority. If the guaranteed-issue and community-rating insurance reforms were to be carried out, the individual mandate was a necessary and proper means of doing so, the government contended.

> **(1) Roberts disagreees:** But Roberts again disagreeed, taking a much *narrower* view of the Necessary and Proper clause than the government. Quoting *McCulloch v. Maryland* (*supra*, p. 21), he said that the Necessary and Proper Clause only gives Congress the power to enact provisions "*incidental* to the [enumerated] power," and does not authorize the exercise of any "*great substantive and independent power[s]*" beyond the enumerated ones. What Congress was doing here with the individual mandate, he said, was *not "incidental"* to the exercise of the commerce power, and would "work a *substantial expansion* of federal authority." Therefore, even if the individual mandate was "necessary" to the ACA's insurance reforms, it was *not a "proper" means* of making those reforms effective.

4. **Dissent disagrees on Commerce power:** Four Justices sharply *dissented* from Roberts' conclusion that the individual mandate did not fall within Congress' Commerce powers. The opinion on this point was by Justice Ginsburg, who was joined by Justices Sotomayor, Breyer and Kagan. The Ginsburg opinion was only a partial dissent (since these four joined with Roberts to uphold the individual mandate under the power to *tax*; see *infra*, p. 68). But the opinion was a vigorous dissent to every aspect of Roberts' treatment of the Commerce Clause issue.

   a. **Uninsured are still "active" consumers:** First, Ginsburg rejected Roberts' core assertion that most uninsured were "inactive" in the market for health care. She cited statistics showing that more than 60% of those without insurance visit a hospital or doctor's office each year, and 90% do so within five years. Furthermore, Congress had *no way to distinguish* between uninsured persons who would soon need emergency health care and those who would not. "No one knows when an emergency will occur, yet emergencies involving the uninsured arise daily." Therefore, Congress was entitled to require all persons to have insurance, because (quoting a prior Commerce Clause case) "When it is necessary in order to prevent an evil to make the law embrace *more than the precise thing to be prevented* [Congress] may do so."

   b. **Right to anticipate future conduct:** Ginsburg also disagreed with Roberts' assertion that the Court's precedents did not support the proposition that "Congress may dictate the conduct of an individual today because of prophesied future activity." She pointed to *Wickard* (p. 34) as a counter-example: Congress had said that the farmer in *Wickard* could be prevented from growing too much wheat for home consumption today, because if he did so (and others did likewise), this wheat might *in the future* overhang the market and depress interstate prices.

   c. **Health care market is different:** Roberts had asserted that the fact that a person might some day need health care didn't make him "active" in the health-care market, any more than the fact that he might buy a car some day made him active in the car market. But Ginsburg believed that *health care was a special case.* Roberts' analogy between health care and, say, car sales was inapt, because "The inevitable yet unpredictable need for medical care, and the guarantee that *emergency care will be provided* when required are *conditions nonexistent in other markets."* Although a consumer *might* some day buy a car (or a piece of broccoli), there is no guarantee that she ever will. And if she ever does want a car or broccoli, "she will be obliged to *pay at the counter* before receiving the vehicle or nourishment. She will *get no free ride or food at the expense of another consumer forced to pay an inflated price.*"

    i.   **No worry about later expansion:** Therefore, Ginsburg said, these special features of the health-care market meant that there was no reason to worry that upholding the individual mandate would logically force the Court to later concede to Congress the Commerce-based power to require the purchase of other products and services.

    d.   **Just a payment mechanism:** Ginsburg also rejected Roberts' characterization of the mandate as "compel[ling] individuals ... to *purchase an unwanted product.*" Since virtually everyone would consume health care, Congress was not "mandating purchase of a discrete, unwanted product." All that Congress was doing was merely "*defining the terms on which individuals pay for an interstate good they consume:* Persons subject to the mandate must now pay for medical care *in advance* (instead of at the point of service) and *through insurance* (instead of out-of-pocket)." She concluded that "establishing payment terms for goods in or affecting interstate commerce is *quintessential economic regulation.*"

    e.   **Active/inactive distinction:** Ginsburg also dismissed the significance Roberts attached to the *"active"/"inactive"* distinction. Most actions can be *restated as corresponding inactions* with the same effect. She offered the present case as an example: "An individual who opts not to purchase insurance from a private insurer can be seen as *actively selecting another form of insurance: self-insurance.*" Thus the individual mandate could be described as "regulating activity in the self-insurance market." Similarly, in the *Wickard* wheat-growing case, the statute could be described either as targeting *activity* (the growing of too much wheat) or *inactivity* (the farmer's failure to purchase wheat in the marketplace).

    f.   **Necessary and Proper Clause:** Finally, Ginsburg disagreed with Roberts' assertion that the *Necessary and Proper Clause* did not augment Congress' Commerce powers regarding the individual mandate. She didn't see why requiring individuals to choose between buying health insurance or paying a penalty was any more far-reaching than other implied powers that the Court had found to be justified by the Necessary and Proper Clause. For instance, the Court had used the Clause as the basis for implying a congressional power to enact criminal laws, to impose civil imprisonment, and to create a national bank. She predicted that Roberts' distinction between an "independent power" (not authorized by the N&P Clause) and a "derivative" one (authorized), or between a "substantive" power and an "incidental" one, would prove hard for judges to administer. Roberts was in effect instructing the lower courts, she said, that "You will know it when you see it."

5. **Significance:** So *N.F.I.B.* seems to establish several important limitations on the Commerce power:

❑ Most significantly, "The power to regulate commerce *presupposes the existence of commercial activity* to be regulated." So if the person being regulated is *not already engaged in commercial activity* of the relevant sort (she doesn't have to necessarily be involved in *interstate* commercial activity, but has to be engaged in at least a local version of the commercial activity), Congress cannot require the person to *become* commercially active. And that's true even if the failure of large numbers of people to become commercially active causes, in the aggregate, a *significant (and harmful) effect on interstate commerce*.

❑ As a corollary, Congress cannot force a person who is not already engaged in commerce *"to purchase an unwanted product."*

❑ Even if the person being regulated is likely — or even near-certain — to *become active* in the relevant market *at some time in the future*, that's *not enough* to justify regulating the person now. So even conceding that the vast majority of individuals will at some point use health care (and Roberts did seem to concede this point), that's not grounds for requiring the purchase of health insurance *now*.

a. Practical impact may be small: But the practical impact of these limits may well prove small. After all, Congress had never before used its Commerce power in what the Court characterized as an attempt to force people into a commercial market in which they were not already participating. So it's hard to see how this new "can't force someone to enter a market" doctrine is likely to cramp Congress' style very much going forward.

  i. Tax-and-spend: Furthermore, the individual mandate itself turned out to be sustainable under the *tax-and-spend* power. (See *infra*, p. 67.) So if Congress wants to induce people to take Action X (even if X is the purchase of an unwanted product by someone not already participating in the relevant market), all Congress has to do is to impose a non-punitive "tax" on not taking Action X. To take what Justice Ginsburg refers to as the "broccoli horrible," apparently Congress is still free to impose a tax on anyone who can't prove that she purchased a specified amount of broccoli during the year, as long as the tax is small enough that a rational consumer might elect to pay the tax rather buy the broccoli.

F. Summary of the modern limits on the Commerce power: So the major post-1995 Commerce power cases for the most part — but not always — *limit* Congress' authority:

[1] Where a consumer wants to *"make or grow his own product"* and the product has a somewhat *commercial nature*, Congress can regulate or prohibit his activities, even though the consumer is acting in an entirely *intrastate manner*, and it is only the adding together of many such purely intrastate activities that produces a cumulative effect on interstate commerce. So cases like *Wickard v. Filburn* (Congress can tightly regulate how a farmer may grow his own crops, because if it can't, the whole agricultural regulation system will fall apart) and *Gonzales v. Raich* (Congress can make it a crime for a private citizen to grow her own marijuana, because if she can't be forbidden from growing it, Congress won't be able to effectively regulate interstate marijuana sales either) reflect a broad reading of Congress' Commerce powers.

But ...

[2] Where Congress wants to regulate an activity that is essentially *not a commercial activity*, Congress can quickly go *beyond* its Commerce power, and into the realm of attempting an unconstitutional exercise of power to *"regulate for the general federal welfare."* Cases like *Lopez* (Congress can't forbid the possession of guns near schools) and *Morrison* (Congress can't make it a crime to use violence against

women) reflect a narrow reading of Congress' Commerce powers applicable to those instances where what is being regulated is ***not really economic activity at all.***

and ...

[3] where Congress wants to take an individual who is ***not currently participating in a particular marketplace at all***, and wants to insist that the individual ***purchase a good or service in that marketplace***, Congress may not use its Commerce power to do so. That's the result of *N.F.I.B. v. Sebelius*, where Congress' Commerce powers were held not sufficient to allow Congress to force individuals to ***buy health insurance***, even though the failure of many individuals to buy such insurance might substantially (and negatively) affect the clearly-commercial interstate market for health care.

Here are some additional rules of thumb that come out of these opposing lines of post-1995 cases:

a. **Effect must be "significant":** The activity being regulated must be one that ***"significantly"*** affects commerce — an ***incidental effect*** on commerce is ***not*** enough.

b. **Findings:** The fact that Congress has made particular ***findings*** that an activity substantially affects interstate commerce may make some difference, but is unlikely to be dispositive very often. So legislative findings will at most tip a ***close case*** over the line into the "regulable" category.

c. **Jurisdictional hooks:** Where Congress drafts the statute in a way that requires a ***"jurisdictional hook"*** between the particular activity and commerce, the act is still quite likely to be found within the Commerce power.

   Example: Suppose Congress makes it a crime to possess near a school a gun that ***moved in interstate commerce*** at some point in its career (and Congress doesn't purport to criminalize possession of a gun made and used within a single state up to the point of the arrest). There's a very good chance the statute would be upheld.

G. **Summary of modern view:** In closing, let's summarize the ***four broad categories*** of activities that, even after the post-1995 limiting cases, Congress can still constitutionally regulate:

1. **Channels:** First, Congress can regulate the use of the ***"channels"*** of interstate commerce. Thus Congress can regulate in a way that is reasonably related to highways, waterways, and air traffic. Presumably Congress can do so even though the activity in question in the particular case is quite intrastate.

2. **Instrumentalities:** Second, Congress can regulate the ***"instrumentalities"*** of interstate commerce, "even though the threat may come only from intrastate activities." *Lopez*. This category refers to people, machines, and other "things" used in carrying out commerce. So, for instance, presumably Congress could say that every truck must have a specific safety device, even if the particular truck in question was made and used exclusively within a single state.

3. **Articles moving in interstate commerce:** Third, Congress can regulate ***articles moving*** in interstate commerce. For instance, in *Reno v. Condon*, 528 U.S. 141 (2000), the Court said that computerized information about motorists was an "article of commerce" whose release into the "interstate stream of business" made the information an appropriate subject for congressional regulation. (Apparently this would have been so even if the information did not "substantially affect" commerce, as described in the next paragraph.)

4. **"Substantially affecting" commerce:** Finally, the biggest (and most interesting) category is that Congress may regulate those activities having a *"substantial effect"* on interstate commerce. *Lopez.* As to this category, the following rules now seem to apply:

a. **Real bite:** The requirement of a "substantial" effect has *real bite*.

  i. **Activity is commercial:** If the activity itself is arguably *"commercial,"* then it doesn't seem to matter whether the *particular instance* of the activity directly affects interstate commerce, as long as the instance is part of a general class of activities that, collectively, substantially affect interstate commerce. Thus in the *Gonzales v. Raich* type of situation — P's own marijuana-growing activities are in a sense "commercial," but are entirely intrastate; however, when aggregated with all other local medicinal-marijuana-growing activities P's activities might undermine Congress' interstate-regulatory scheme — Congress can regulate even the solely-intrastate events.

  ii. **Activity is not commercial:** But if the activity itself is *not "commercial,"* then there will apparently have to be a *pretty obvious connection* between the activity and interstate commerce. This is the main legacy of *Lopez* (can't make schools a gun-free zone) and *Morrison* (can't criminalize all violence against women).

  iii. **Must already be an "activity":** Only *pre-existing* commercial *"activity"* may be regulated; Congress may not require persons who are not presently "active" in a commercial market to become active by buying or selling; see Par. (d), "Activity/inactivity distinction" below.

b. **Little deference to Congress:** The Court *won't* give much *deference* to the fact that Congress *believed* that the activity has the requisite "substantial effect" on interstate commerce. The Court will basically decide this issue for itself, from scratch. It certainly will no longer be enough that Congress had a *"rational basis"* for believing that the requisite effect existed — the effect must *in fact* exist to the Court's own independent satisfaction.

c. **Traditional domain of states:** If what's being regulated is an activity the regulation of which has *traditionally* been the *domain of the states*, and as to which the states have expertise, the Court is less likely to find that Congress is acting within its Commerce power. Thus *education*, *family law* and *general criminal law* are areas where the Court is likely to be especially suspicious of congressional "interference."

d. **Activity/inactivity distinction:** Congress may not use its Commerce powers to say to a person who is *not presently active in a market* (i.e., not presently trying to buy, sell or use a product in the relevant market) that the person must *do a transaction in that market or else pay a penalty*. So, for instance, *N.F.I.B. v. Sebelius* (*supra*, p. 44) says that Congress' Commerce powers don't allow it to tell individuals who are presently without health insurance that they must *buy such insurance or else pay a financial penalty to the IRS*. So Congress *can regulate* pre-existing *"activity,"* but not pre-existing *"inactivity."*

VI. THE TENTH AMENDMENT AS A LIMIT ON CONGRESS' POWER

A. **Apparent irrelevance of Tenth Amendment:** For nearly 40 years following the *Carter Coal* decision (*supra*, p. 32), the Supreme Court did not invalidate a single federal statute on the grounds that it violated state or local government sovereignty. This sustained stretch led most observers to conclude that the Tenth Amendment was completely dead as an independent check upon federal power under the Commerce Clause.

B. Once again irrelevant: As of this writing, it does indeed seem to be the case that the Tenth Amendment places relatively few practical limitations upon the exercise of federal power under the Commerce Clause. However, for the period 1976-85, the Supreme Court treated the Tenth Amendment as imposing an important limit on federal power — this Amendment was held to bar the federal government from doing anything that would impair the states' ability to perform their "traditional functions." Then, in 1985, the line of cases establishing this limit was *flatly overruled* by the Supreme Court, in one of the most amazing reversals of doctrine in modern Supreme Court history.[4] Before the 1985 reversal can be understood, some understanding of the prior line of cases is needed.

    1. *National League of Cities:* Like a bolt out of the blue, the Supreme Court in 1976 gave the Tenth Amendment practical significance in *National League of Cities v. Usery*, 426 U.S. 833 (1976). In that case, the Court held that the Tenth Amendment barred Congress from making federal minimum-wage and overtime rules applicable to state and municipal employees. The vote was 5-4.

        a. Rationale: The five-justice majority conceded that the minimum-wage/overtime rules, as applied to state employees, clearly affected commerce. Thus these wage/hour regulations could unquestionably be constitutionally applied to private employers, under the commerce power. But when these wage/hour rules were applied to state employees, they violated the independent requirement, imposed by the Tenth Amendment, that "Congress may not exercise power in a fashion that *impairs the States' integrity* or their *ability to function effectively in the federal system*." The wage/hour rules violated this requirement in two ways.

            i. Cost: First, the wage/hour provisions impaired the states' ability to function effectively purely as a matter of *cost*: compliance would have cost the states and their municipal subdivisions substantial sums.

            ii. Removal of discretion: Secondly, the new rules stripped the states of their discretion to decide how they wished to allocate a fixed pool of funds available for salaries.

        b. Summary: Thus if the wage/hour rules were allowed to stand, the majority reasoned, Congress would have the right to make "fundamental employment decisions" regarding state employees, and "there would be little left of the States' 'separate and independent existence.' "

C. Overruling of *National League of Cities*: *National League of Cities* was on tenuous ground from the day it was decided. The fifth vote came from Justice Blackmun, who stated in his concurrence that he was "not untroubled by certain possible implications of the Court's opinion." All it took to overturn the decision in *National League of Cities* was for Justice Blackmun to abandon his never-passionate attachment to the principle of that case. In *Garcia v. San Antonio Metropolitan Transit Authority*, 469 U.S. 528 (1985), he joined with the four Jus-

---

4. Then, this reversal was partially "re-reversed," in several cases from the 1990s that established that Congress cannot directly command the states to enact or enforce federal policies; see *New York v. U.S.* (p. 56) and *Printz* v. U.S. (p. 58).

tices who had dissented in *National League of Cities* (Brennan, White, Marshall and Stevens) to repudiate that case. By a 5-4 majority, the Court stated that *National League of Cities* "is **overruled**."

1. **Facts:**   In view of the sweeping nature of the holding in *Garcia*, the facts would ordinarily seem to be of little significance. However, they apparently seemed to Justice Blackmun to make the failings of the *National League of Cities* approach especially clear. The issue in *Garcia* was whether the minimum-wage and overtime provisions of the federal Fair Labor Standards Act (the same statute at issue in *National League of Cities*) should apply to employees of a municipally-owned and-operated **mass-transit system**. Under *National League of Cities* and cases later decided under it, this issue translated into the issue: Is municipal ownership and operation of such a transit system a "traditional governmental function?"

2. **Difficulty of line-drawing:**   The majority opinion, by Justice Blackmun, contended that the 8-year period following *National League of Cities* had shown that it was "difficult, if not impossible, to identify an organizing principle" that would distinguish between those functions that are "traditional governmental functions" and those that are not. For instance, federal courts of appeal had held that the licensing of automobile drivers was a "traditional governmental function" (as to which the Tenth Amendment therefore protected state sovereignty from federal control), but that the regulation of traffic on public roads was not.

3. **The problem of subjectivity:**   An additional, but related, problem was that the *National League of Cities* approach inevitably led to judicial subjectivity. "Any rule of state immunity that looks to the 'traditional,' 'integral,' or 'necessary' nature of governmental functions inevitably **invites an unelected federal judiciary to make decisions about which state policies it favors and which ones it dislikes.**"

4. **Procedural safeguards:**   Yet, the *Garcia* majority insisted, its rejection of *National League of Cities* did *not* mean that there are no limitations upon the federal government's right to use its delegated powers to impair state sovereignty. However, state sovereign interests are protected by **"procedural safeguards inherent in the structure of the federal system,"** not by "judicially created limitations on federal power."

   a. **Examples of structural protection:**   For instance, the requirement that each state have two Senators, the fact that the states are given general control over electoral qualifications for federal elections, and the fact that the states have a special role in presidential elections by means of the electoral college, are all indications that the **structure of the federal government** has been constitutionally arranged so as to protect state sovereignty.

5. **Dissent:**   The four dissenters in *Garcia* asserted that the majority approach "effectively reduces the Tenth Amendment to meaningless rhetoric when Congress acts pursuant to the Commerce Clause."

   a. **Powell's dissent:**   Justice Powell, writing the principal dissent, contended that *National League of Cities* was correctly decided and that it articulated a workable standard. The *Garcia* majority's approach, by contrast, established no effective standard at all, in his opinion. Powell was especially troubled by the fact that under the majority approach, "federal political officials, invoking the Commerce Clause, are the **sole judges of the limits of their own power.** ... " He contended that the majority position was inconsistent with the rule, in force since *Marbury v. Madison* (*supra*, p. 8), that it is up to the federal judiciary to "say what the law is" with respect to the constitutionality of congressional actions.

D. Significance of case: *Garcia* appears to mean that once Congress, acting pursuant to its Commerce power, regulates the states, the fact that it is a state being regulated *has virtually no practical significance — if the regulation would be valid if applied to a private party, it is also valid as to the state.*

1. **Political process:**   This is not quite the same as saying that there are no constitutional protections against congressional interference with state sovereignty. Rather, the majority is saying that whatever limits exist inhere in the structure or process of congressional lawmaking.

2. **Later cases cut back:** Several post-*Garcia* cases seem to be *cutting back* the apparently-broad scope of *Garcia*. *New York v. United States* (discussed immediately *infra*) and *Printz v. U.S.* (*infra*, p. 58) both place limits on the extent to which Congress can force state or local governments to *make or enforce laws*. And *Alden v. Maine* (*infra*, p. 726) blocks Congress from forcing the states to *hear damage suits* against themselves in *state courts*, even on federally-created claims. So the principle that there are some limits on the way Congress can regulate a state remains very much alive after *Garcia*.[5]

E. Use of state's lawmaking mechanisms: One aspect of state sovereignty is a state's ability to *make and apply law*, through legislative, judicial, and administrative functions. Even after *Garcia*, there are limits to Congress' right to interfere with these state legislative or executive processes, and Congress will violate the Tenth Amendment if it exceeds those limits. In a pair of cases, the Court has held that the federal government may not: (1) compel a state to *enact* or enforce a particular *law* or type of law; or (2) compel state/local officials to perform federally-specified *administrative* tasks. Holding (1) occurred in *New York v. United States*, 505 U.S. 144 (1992). Holding (2) occurred in *Printz v. U.S.*, 521 U.S. 898 (1997).

1. **Waste disposal case:**   *New York v. United States*, *supra*, dramatically illustrates the principle that Congress may not simply force a state to *enact a certain statute* or to *regulate* in a certain manner.

   a. **Regulatory scheme:**   Congress enacted the Low-Level Radioactive Waste Policy Amendments Act of 1985. The Act attempted to force each state to make its own arrangements for disposing (either in-state or out-of-state) of the low-level radioactive waste generated in that state. The Act tried to do this with several types of incentives. Most significant was the *"take title"* incentive, whereby any state which did not arrange for disposal of its waste would be required to "take title" to the waste (upon request by the waste generator), and would be liable for damages in connection with disposal of this waste.

---

5. In fact, two cases from the late 1990s together strip *Garcia* of most of its practical significance. Under *Seminole Tribe of Florida v. Florida* (*infra*, p. 724), Congress does not have authority to abrogate the 11th Amendment and thus to allow state employees to sue the state in federal court for violating the federal wage-and-hour laws that *Garcia* said apply to the states. And under the just-mentioned *Alden v. Maine* (*infra*, p. 726), Congress can't force the states to waive their sovereign immunity and therefore to hear such employee suits in the state's own courts. So *Garcia* gives state employees a federal right, but the two later cases block individual employees from any state-court or federal-court *remedy* for violation of that right (though the federal government could still be the plaintiff in a federal-court suit to redress a violation).

b. New York attacks statute: New York, unlike most states, made little progress in solving its waste disposal problems, because local residents of each community where the state proposed to put disposal sites fiercely objected. New York then sued the federal government, arguing that the "take title" provision violated the Tenth Amendment, by effectively forcing the state to regulate in a particular area.

c. Tenth Amendment found violated: A majority of the Court agreed that the "take title" provision violated the Tenth Amendment: Congress may not simply *"commandee[r] the legislative processes of the States* by directly *compelling them to enact and enforce* a federal regulatory program."

   i. Explanation: New York was being put to the choice of two "unconstitutionally coercive regulatory techniques": it could either choose to regulate on its own by making arrangements for disposal of waste generated inside the state, or be forced to indemnify waste-generators against tort damages. Because Congress could not employ either of these methods alone, it could not escape the problem by giving the state a choice between the two.

d. Dissent: Three members of the Court (White, joined by Blackmun and Stevens) dissented. White argued that this was not an instance where Congress was forcing its will upon the states. Rather, he said, Congress had responded to a request by many of the states to ratify a compromise worked out among themselves, so that the waste-disposal problem could be solved. "The Court's refusal to force New York to accept responsibility for its own problem inevitably means that some other State's sovereignty will be impinged by it being forced, for public health reasons, to accept New York's low-level radioactive waste. I do not understand the principle of federalism to impede the National Government from acting as referee among the States to prohibit one from bullying another."

e. Alternative methods: Is Congress powerless to make each state deal with its radioactive waste (or any other specific problem)? Probably not. Justice White's dissent suggests several methods that are apparently still open to Congress, notwithstanding *N.Y. v. U.S.*

   i. Spending power: First, Congress clearly may *supply funds* to the states for the purpose of solving the problem, and then *condition* the receipt of these funds on the states' agreeing to Congress' proposed methods for solving the problem.

   ii. Threat of regulation: Second, Congress could *directly regulate* the conduct in question, and could therefore take the less drastic step of telling the states that this direct regulation will follow if the states do not take care of the problems themselves. (For instance, Congress' commerce power would entitle it to say, "No state may ship radioactive waste outside of its own border." Congress could therefore say, as a lesser exercise of this power, "Any state which does not make its own arrangements for disposing of waste, whether in-state or out-of-state, shall be required to keep its waste within its own borders.")

   iii. Summary: In summary, Congress may have to be a little more clever about how it accomplishes its regulatory purposes — and it will not be able to escape the *"political heat"* for unpopular decisions by forcing state officials to make those decisions. But Congress, by careful use of its enumerated powers (including the spending[6] and Commerce powers) can achieve practically any regulatory end it wants without running afoul of the Tenth Amendment.

2. **No commandeering of executive branch:** *N.Y. v. U.S.* limits Congress' power to "commandeer the *legislative* processes of the States. . . ." In a post-*N.Y.* case, the Court has held that Congress may, similarly, not compel a state or local government's *executive* branch to perform functions. And that's true even if the functions are fairly ministerial and easy-to-perform, and even if the compulsion is only temporary. *Printz v. U.S.*, 521 U.S. 898 (1997).

   a. **Brady bill's provision:** In 1993, Congress enacted the "Brady Bill," aimed at controlling the flow of guns. As a temporary 5-year measure, the law *ordered local law enforcement officials* to *conduct background checks* on prospective purchasers, until a national computerized system for doing these checks could be phased in. Printz, a county sheriff in Montana, objected to the background-check requirement and sued. He argued that under *New York v. U.S.*, Congress could not force him to conduct background checks on the federal government's behalf.

   b. **Decision:** By a 5-4 margin, the Court agreed with the plaintiff. Justice Scalia's majority opinion noted that in *N.Y. v. U.S.*, the Court had said that the federal government "may not compel the States to enact or administer a federal regulatory program." Scalia then concluded that the background-check portion of the Brady bill violated this prohibition.

      i. **Rationale:** Scalia *rejected* the dissent's distinction between compelling a state to *make policy* (such as the compelled enactment of a regulatory scheme, like the "take title" scheme at issue in *N.Y. v. U.S.*) and compelling state executive-branch officers to perform *ministerial tasks* (such as the background checks at issue here). Even if no policy-making was involved here, this did not prevent Congress' action from being an intolerable incursion into state sovereignty: "It is an essential attribute of the States' retained sovereignty that they remain *independent and autonomous within their proper sphere of authority.* . . . It is no more compatible with this independence and autonomy that their officers be 'dragooned' . . . into administering federal law, than it would be compatible with the independence and autonomy of the United States that its officers be impressed into service for the execution of state laws."

      ii. **Basis unclear:** It's not clear whether Scalia believed that any *particular* constitutional provision had been violated. He seemed to be relying on a general, non-textual, principle of state sovereignty, rather than on any specific clause (e.g., the

---

6. But even the spending power now appears to be subject to some federalism-based limits. The same federalism-based concerns that led the Court in *New York v. U.S.* to prevent what it saw as Congress' attempt to force the states to regulate in a certain manner later led the Court to hold that Congress' spending power did not allow it to *"coerce" the states into regulating*. In *N.F.I.B. v. Sebelius, infra,* p. 72, the Court held that when Congress made the states choose between participating in a new expanded Medicaid program or forfeiting all the vast federal funding that they had long received under pre-expansion Medicaid, this coercion went beyond Congress' spending powers. While *N.F.I.B.* did not squarely hold that this "coercion" violated the Tenth Amendment, Chief Justice Roberts' opinion on the Medicaid issue quoted *New York v. U.S.*'s Tenth-Amendment-inspired statement that "the Constitution has never been understood to confer upon Congress the ability to require the States to govern according to Congress' instructions."

Tenth Amendment, which he referred to only occasionally and in passing). But two concurring opinions specifically said that the background-check requirement violated the ***Tenth Amendment.***

c. Dissents: Four Justices dissented in *Printz*.

   i. Justice Stevens' dissent: The main dissent was by Justice Stevens. He first pointed out that the federal commerce power gave Congress the authority to regulate handguns. He then concluded that this being so, the ***"necessary and proper" clause*** gave Congress the right to implement its regulation by temporarily requiring local police officers to perform the ministerial step of identifying persons who should not be entrusted with handguns. This was especially true, he said, since Congress could have required *private citizens* to help with such identification: "The [Tenth] Amendment provides no support for a rule that immunizes local officials from obligations that might be imposed on ordinary citizens."

d. Control over purse strings: Again (as in *N.Y. v. U.S.*) presumably Congress could get around the problem by conditioning the state's or local government's ***receipt of federal funds*** on its officials' willingness to do the federal bidding. Only compulsion, not a voluntary *quid pro quo*, seems foreclosed by the majority's analysis.

3. Significance: So *New York v. U.S.* and *Printz* seem to stand for the propositions that Congress may ***not*** (1) ***force a state to legislate or regulate in a certain way;*** or (2) require state ***executive-branch*** personnel to perform even ***ministerial functions.***

a. Distinguished from *Garcia* situation: How does the rationale of these cases fit in with the rationale of *Garcia*? *Garcia* seems to apply mainly to ***generally applicable*** federal lawmaking; that case holds that where Congress passes a generally applicable law (e.g., a minimum wage law that applies to ***all*** or nearly all businesses), the Tenth Amendment does not entitle a state's own operations to an exemption, merely because it is a state that is being regulated along with all the other private entities. But where the federal government tries to force a state or local government to ***enact legislation*** or ***regulation***, or tries to force state or local ***officials*** to perform particular governmental functions, this is not part of a generally-applicable federal scheme, and is instead directed specifically at the state's basic exercise of sovereignty: the state's right to carry out the business of government. The federal government may not use such coercion, *N.Y. v. U.S.* and *Printz* say.

Quiz Yourself on

THE FEDERAL COMMERCE POWER *(ENTIRE CHAPTER)*

5. Congress makes it a federal felony for any individual to place a bet with another individual on a sporting event, or to propose such a bet. The statute is written broadly, so as to cover two friends who bet with each other primarily for purposes of friendship rather than profit. The House and Senate Committee Reports on the bill show that Congress believed that ostensibly "friendly" betting creates a climate that is tolerant of gambling, which in turn increases the interstate gambling profits of organized crime, a multi-million dollar nationwide problem. Devon is charged with violating the statute by placing a bet on the Super Bowl with her best friend, Elaine. They made the bet face to face within a single state.

(a) If Devon challenges the constitutionality of the statute on the grounds that it goes beyond Congress' enumerated powers, what enumerated power should the prosecutors point to in defending the statute's constitutionality? _____

    (b) Is the statute in fact constitutional? State your reasons. _____

6. By 2020, the federal government is paying approximately 50% of total health-care costs for the nation out of general revenues. Congress, concerned that Americans are living increasingly sedentary, unhealthy and medically-costly lifestyles, enacts the Walk to Fitness Act of 2020 ("WFA"). The WFA provides that each American over the age of 16 must purchase a specified government-manufactured pedometer, which when attached to the hip measures how many miles the wearer walks each day. The pedometer is sold to the public at a price of $20 (which provides a small profit to the government, made possible by the huge volumes expected to be sold). The device is custom-fitted so that it can work only on the body of the particular purchaser to whom it is registered. Another provision of the WFA says that after the end of each year, the device-wearer shall print out the total miles registered on the device during the prior year, and enclose the printout with his tax return. Anyone whose age-adjusted total annual mileage walked does not reach a pre-specified threshold (150 miles for a young adult) must pay a "penalty" of $200, payable to the IRS together with the person's taxes. Exemptions are given for those whose doctor certifies that the person is not medically capable of walking the threshold amount. Anyone who does reach the threshold, and sends in the printout, gets a one-time government refund of the $20 cost of the pedometer. Congress defends the constitutionality of the WFA on the grounds that the pedometer program encourages fitness, and that fitter people will cause the nation's ever-increasing health-care bill to decline, leading to a substantial lowering of costs billed in the interstate market for health-care services. Therefore, Congress asserts, the WFA is valid as a regulation of commerce.

    Is the WFA a proper exercise of the Congress' Commerce power? _____

7. After several years of rising unemployment nationally, and falling wage levels, Congress passes a statute prohibiting the employment of any person under the age of 19. Congress' intent is to keep teenagers in high school or college, where they may or may not learn something but will at least not be competing with adults for jobs, thus allowing wage rates to rise. The state of Alahoma employs many 17- and 18-year-olds, for such posts as cleaners in state parks and apprentice state troopers. Alahoma estimates that its total payroll costs will rise by 8% if it is required to obey the new federal statute (which by its terms applies to government as well as private-sector employees).

    (a) Assuming that the federal statute falls within Congress' power to regulate commerce, what is the strongest argument that Alahoma can make as to why the Constitution requires that the state's own hiring be exempted from the statute? _____

    (b) Will this argument succeed? _____

8. Congress has concluded that cigarette smoking raises the nation's annual health-care budget 15% above what it would otherwise be. Congress has therefore enacted a statute that requires each state to: (1) place a tax of at least 10% on the sale of cigarettes (in addition to existing federal cigarette taxes); (2) compile a registry of every premises in the state where cigarettes are sold, and audit those premises quarterly to make sure they're collecting the tax; (3) modify its health-care financing scheme so that the state does not pay any hospital or doctor for the costs of treating any condition found to be caused by cigarette smoking; and (4) modify its tort law so as to treat cigarettes as a "defective product" for which strict liability is allowed under state tort law. Congress does not allocate any funds for the carrying out of these objectives. It provides that if a state is found not to be in compliance one year after enactment of the act, the federal district courts for that state shall have authority to direct the legislature and agencies of the state to comply, and to hold state officials in contempt if they do not comply.

(a) If you are given the job of arguing on behalf of a state that this provision is an unconstitutional infringement of your state's sovereignty, what constitutional provision should you point to? _____

(b) Will your argument succeed? _____

(c) If you are charged with improving the likelihood that the federal scheme will pass muster, what fundamental change will you urge to be made in that scheme? _____

_____

Answers

5. (a) Congress' power to regulate commerce.

(b) Probably, but this is no longer as certain as it once was. Before the 1995 decision in *U.S. v. Lopez*, it was enough that there was a "rational basis" for Congress' belief that a regulated activity "affects" interstate commerce. But *Lopez* establishes that the activity which Congress is regulating must *in fact* have a *"substantial effect"* on interstate commerce.

Where an activity is "commercial," the Court still seems willing to find regulation of it to be within Congress' commerce power even if the particular act is wholly intrastate, as long as the act is part of a *class* of activities which, collectively, substantially affect interstate commerce. See, e.g., *Wickard v. Filburn* (farmer's growing of wheat for family use only can be regulated, because the cumulative effect of all such intrastate wheat-growing decisions significantly affects the interstate price of wheat). The bet here seems to qualify — the bet is probably itself a "commercial" transaction (i.e., one primarily motivated by the desire to make a profit), and private bets taken as a group probably have a substantial effect on interstate commerce (e.g., they are often made over interstate phone lines, they contribute to the use of interstate "handicapping" services and interstate money transfers, etc.). Once the Court finds that the activity substantially affects commerce, the Court requires only that the means selected by Congress be "rationally related" to the objective being sought. Here, prohibition of the damaging activity — friendly sports betting — would certainly seem to be a reasonable means of combatting that activity. The scenario seems a lot like that in *Gonzales v. Raich*, where the Court held that Congress could regulate a purely intrastate but commercially-oriented activity regarding a commodity (personal cultivation of marijuana for one's own medicinal uses) because such regulation was reasonably tied in to Congress' regulation of the interstate commercial aspects of that same commodity.

6. No. *N.F.I.B. v. Sebelius, supra*, p. 44 (the health-insurance case) establishes that five members of the Court believe that Congress' Commerce powers do not allow Congress "to *compel individuals not engaged in commerce to purchase an unwanted product.*" The case also says that "the power to regulate presupposes the existence of commercial activity to be regulated." Since the WFA requires people who are not in the market for a pedometer to buy one, it seems to run afoul of these principles: these individuals are "not engaged in commerce" (at least, commerce of the relevant sort: purchase of walking-measurement devices), and at least some don't want to purchase the pedometer. So it's hard to see how the Commerce power can extend to this compulsory-purchase program. That's true even though Congress is probably correct in reasoning that if everyone either bought and used the device, or paid the penalty, the interstate market for health-care expenditures would be substantially affected.

7. (a) The Tenth Amendment. That Amendment provides that "the powers not delegated to the United States by the Constitution, nor prohibited by it to the States, are reserved to the States respectively, or to the People." Alahoma could make a plausible argument that Congress, by precisely detailing whom the state may hire, has interfered with the sovereignty reserved to the state by the Tenth Amendment.

(b) No, probably. At one time, Alahoma would probably have succeeded with this argument, because of *National League of Cities v. Usery*, which held that the Tenth Amendment prevented Congress from regulating the states in a way that might impair their "ability to function effectively in the federal system"; state employees were exempted from federal wage/hour regulations on this theory. But *National League of Cities* was overruled in *Garcia v. San Antonio Metropolitan Transit Authority. Garcia* seems to mean that when Congress, acting pursuant to its commerce power, regulates the states as part of a generally applicable regulatory scheme, the fact that it is a state being regulated has no practical significance — if the regulation would be valid where applied to a private party, it is also valid as to the state. Consequently, since Congress would almost certainly have the power to set a minimum age for employment in the private sector (on the theory that this directly affects commerce, because of its effect on unemployment and wage limits), the state is not entitled to an exemption.

8. (a) The Tenth Amendment.

(b) Yes. The Tenth Amendment does not have very huge scope in light of *Garcia* (see previous question), but it has some. In particular, Congress may not simply "commandee[r] the legislative processes of the States by directly compelling them to enact and enforce a regulatory program." *New York v. U.S.* Thus in *New York v. U.S., supra,* the Court held that Congress could not force states to regulate nuclear waste. So, here, the Court would almost certainly conclude that Congress may not force a state to enact a specific regulatory framework for dealing with the cigarette/health-care problem. Nor may Congress force state official to carry out administrative tasks (such as the audits of cigarette vendors here); see *Printz* and *Mack.* Congress is always free to regulate health care directly, but it may not thrust onto the states the job of doing this.

(c) Supply federal funds, and make the loss of those funds the only penalty for failure to comply. Congress is always free to use its power to tax and spend for the general welfare in order to carry out a regulatory scheme. Furthermore, it may do this by giving an incentive to the states to get them to do the regulating. See, e.g., *South Dakota v. Dole* (Congress may induce states to prevent underage drinking by withholding 5% of federal highway funds from states that don't prohibit drivers under age 21 from drinking). So long as the only penalty is "mild encouragement" via a loss of funds that are related to the new congressional program, there should not be a constitutional problem. However, Congress cannot cut off major funding for a pre-existing program that has no relation to the regulatory scheme desired by Congress; thus Congress probably couldn't cut off, say, *all educational funding* to states that refuse to enact the cigarette/health-care scheme. That's because when financial inducements are combined with conditions, in a way that is "so coercive as to pass the point at which 'pressure turns into *compulsion*'," and that leaves the states with "no real option but to acquiesce," the scheme goes beyond the spending power. See *N.F.I.B. v. Sebelius, infra,* p. 72. Assuming that federal educational funding is so great a portion of the average state's budget that most states couldn't afford to refuse to enact the cigarette/health-care regulation, the scheme would be found to go beyond the spending power under *N.F.I.B.*

Exam Tips on
THE FEDERAL COMMERCE POWER

Any time your fact pattern involves an action by Congress, you've got to keep the Commerce Clause in mind. In particular:

☛ Whenever you've got to decide whether a congressional statute falls within an enumerated power, **check the Commerce Clause first**. It encompasses a broader variety of congressional action than any other congressional power.

☛ Remember that the Court takes a fairly **deferential** view on the issue of whether a particular action falls within the commerce power. So long as a regulated activity **"substantially affects"** interstate commerce, the regulation will be found to fall within the commerce power.

   ☞ For instance, even if a particular commercial activity being regulated seems to take place solely **intrastate**, the Court will usually find that when all similar activities are considered as a **class**, they have a cumulative effect on interstate commerce. (*Example:* Remember *Gonzales v. Raich*, where the Court upheld Congress' right to ban intrastate cultivation of marijuana for one's own medicinal use because exemption of such cultivation might damage Congress' scheme banning interstate marijuana distribution.)

   ☞ Also, remember that Congress may ban or regulate interstate transport as a way of dealing with local problems.

   ☞ However, look out for congressional regulation of activities that are **not really commercial**. Here, there's a much better chance that the Court will find that the activity does **not** substantially affect interstate commerce. Cite to *U.S. v. Lopez* in this situation.

   Examples of attempts to regulate activities that probably **don't substantially affect interstate commerce**, so that the regulation is probably **invalid**:

      ❏ Congress prescribes the curriculum public schools must use.

      ❏ Congress makes it a federal crime to commit a gender-based violent crime against a woman (see *U.S. v. Morrison*).

      ❏ Congress bans marriage under the age of 18.

      ☞ But if there's a "jurisdictional hook" — like a ban only on those machine guns that passed in interstate commerce — the regulation is probably O.K.

☛ Be alert for fact patterns where Congress purports to tell a person who is not presently in the market for a particular product that they **must purchase that product.** This type of command probably goes beyond Congress' Commerce powers. The result in *N.F.I.B. v. Sebelius* — where Congress was found not to have the Commerce power to require most individuals to **buy health insurance even if they don't want to** — is an example of the kind of fact pattern you may get on an exam. Point out that under *N.F.I.B.*, even the fact that millions of individuals' decision not to buy a product substantially (and negatively) affects the interstate market for that product isn't enough to make Congress' decision to require the purchase a proper exercise of the Commerce power.

☛ Be alert for fact patterns where Congress is regulating **the states**. Such regulation raises a **Tenth Amendment** issue:

   ☞ So long as Congress has merely passed a **generally applicable** law, this law can apply to the states just as it does to private individuals, and there is no Tenth Amendment violation. (*Example:* Minimum wage laws may be applied to state workers just as to private workers.)

☞   But Congress may not directly compel the states to enact or enforce a federal regulatory program. [*New York v. United States; Printz*] When Congress does this, it violates the Tenth Amendment. (But Congress may single out the states for regulation when the states are acting as market participants. [*Reno v. Condon*]

Chapter 5

OTHER NATIONAL POWERS

ChapterScope

The previous chapter covered the Commerce Clause, clearly the most important source of federal power. This chapter considers other sources of federal authority:

■ **Taxing power:** Under the "*taxing* power," Congress is given a far-reaching ability to tax in order to raise revenue.

❏ **Taxation as regulation:** Congress may also *regulate* via taxation.

■ **Spending power:** Under the "*spending* power," Congress may "provide for the common Defense and general Welfare of the United States. ... "

❏ **Conditional spending:** Congress may place *conditions* on its spending power as a kind of regulation. This is true even if Congress could not regulate in an area directly (because the area regulated would be of such completely local concern that the commerce power would not be triggered). Conditions placed upon the doling out of federal funds are usually justified under the "Necessary and Proper" Clause.

❏ **"General Welfare" Clause:** There is *no* independent congressional power to pursue the *"general welfare."* The only relevance of general welfare is that Congress when it taxes and spends must be pursuing the general welfare (a requirement that has very little independent significance today).

■ **War power:** Congress is given the power to *declare war*, and to tax and spend for national defense.

■ **DC:** Congress can regulate the *District of Columbia*.

■ **Federal property:** Congress can regulate and dispose of *federal property* (e.g., federal parks).

■ **Enforcement of Civil War amendments:** Congress can *enforce* the *post-Civil War amendments* (13th, 14th and 15th).

I. THE TAXING POWER

A. **Several provisions on tax:** Several constitutional clauses relate to the power of the federal government to *tax*. The basic power is given in Article I, §8: "The Congress shall have Power To lay and collect Taxes, Duties, Imposts and Excises. ... "

1. **Independent federal power:** This power to tax is an *independent source* of federal authority. That is, Congress may tax activities or property that it might not be authorized to regulate directly under any of the enumerated regulatory powers (e.g., the Commerce Clause). Tribe, p. 318.

Example: Congress could enact a national marriage tax, which would be payable by any couple getting married. Marriage is an area which may be beyond direct federal legislative regulation (unless some tie-in to interstate commerce were devised), but the power to tax stands on its own and does not derive from the commerce power or any other power.

B. Special rules on taxes: In addition to the general enabling provision just discussed, the Constitution imposes several specific limits and rules on the taxing power. These are as follows:

1. **Uniform indirect taxes:** Article I, §8 requires that "all Duties, Imposts and Excises shall be uniform throughout the United States. ... " This requirement merely means that the tax structure may not discriminate among the states; it does not matter that specific individuals are not taxed uniformly. Tribe, p. 318. The requirement applies to "indirect" taxes, that is, ones which tax an activity (e.g., the carrying on of a business) rather than taxing property.

2. **Apportionment of direct taxes:** A more specific, and burdensome, requirement is imposed with respect to so-called "direct" taxes. Article I, §2 provides that "direct Taxes shall be apportioned among the several States which may be included within this Union, according to their respective Numbers. ... " Thus direct taxes must be arranged in such a way that the revenue produced by them comes from each state in proportion to its share of the nation's overall population.

   a. **"Direct" defined:** There has been substantial dispute over the years about what exactly is a "direct" tax. In general, taxes on *real property* are virtually the only kind of tax likely to be imposed today that would be considered "direct." Provisions of the 1894 Income Tax Act were held to be direct (and therefore invalid because not apportioned by population) since they taxed income from real estate and personal property. However, the Sixteenth Amendment, passed in 1913, provides that "Congress shall have power to lay and collect taxes on incomes, from whatever source derived, without apportionment among the several States. ... " This Amendment has essentially put to rest the need to distinguish between "direct" and "indirect" taxes.

3. **No duty on exports:** The final tax-related rule imposed by the Constitution is that no *duty* may be imposed on *exports*. Article I, §9.

C. Regulatory effect: Nearly any measure enacted in the form of a tax will have at least an incidental *regulatory effect*. For instance, if an excise tax on cigarettes is enacted, people may smoke, on average, fewer cigarettes. If the regulatory impact of the tax is one which could be *achieved directly*, by use of one of the other enumerated powers (e.g., the Commerce Clause), the fact that the tax has this regulatory effect is not of constitutional significance.

1. **Disguised regulation:** If, however, the regulatory effect is one which could *not* have been achieved directly (e.g., the subject matter is so purely local that it could not be reached under the Commerce Clause, and there is no other enumerated power which applies), then it is possible that the tax may be stricken as an *invalid disguised regulation.*

   a. **Health Care case:** But in the most famous case on this point, *N.F.I.B. v. Sebelius*, 132 S.Ct. 2566 (2012), the Court did not strike the measure in question as a disguised regulation. Instead, the Court held by 5-4 that the "individual mandate" provision in the 2010 Affordable Care Act — requiring most individuals to buy health insurance or pay a "penalty" — was a valid tax, even though it was essentially regulatory and was found not to fall within Congress' Commerce powers. The tax aspect of the case is discussed *infra*, p. 67.

2. **Modern rules:** The "tax vs. regulation" issue has become somewhat less important in recent years, because almost anything that's even plausibly characterizable as a tax seems to be upheld as one, no matter how great Congress' regulatory motive seems to be. The following rules now seem to apply:

[1] A tax that produces **substantial revenue** will almost certainly be **sustained**, and the Court will not inquire into Congress' principal **motive** (e.g., to regulate) in enacting it;

[2] **Regulatory provisions** that accompany the tax are valid if they bear **some reasonable relation** to the tax's enforcement, an easy-to-satisfy test;

[3] A tax that regulates directly through its **rate structure** is valid. (*Example:* A tax of 1/4 cent per pound on white margarine versus 10 cents per pound on yellow margarine, designed to encourage people to use white margine, is valid.)

[4] Even if Congress calls a measure a *"penalty"* rather than a "tax," if the scheme behaves somewhat like a tax (e.g., it raises material revenue, and doesn't make the activity being taxed flatly "against the law"), it can be sustained as an exercise of the taxing power (see *N.F.I.B. v. Sebelius*, immediately below).

3. **Effect of calling a measure a "penalty" (the Affordable Care case):** The fact that Congress labels a measure as a *"penalty"* does *not* prevent the measure from being upheld as a valid tax, as long as the measure actually functions in a way that resembles a tax. That's the result of probably the most famous case ever on the taxing power, *N.F.I.B. v. Sebelius,* 132 S.Ct. 2566 (2012), involving a federal statute designed to dramatically extend the scope of health insurance (the Affordable Care Act). There, by a 5-4 vote, the Court **upheld** the "individual mandate" portion of the Affordable Care Act as a tax, after finding by a different 5-4 majority that the mandate was not within Congress' Commerce powers (see *supra*, p. 44).

a. **Facts of N.F.I.B.:** In the 2010 Affordable Care Act ("ACA" or "Act"), Congress required most individuals to purchase health insurance, even if they had previously chosen to "self-insure." The Act called this requirement the *"individual mandate."* Covered persons (a group that included nearly all individuals and families having income beyond a certain modest threshold) had to fulfill the individual mandate by **buying health insurance coverage** meeting certain minimum standards. And if a covered person didn't make the purchase, she had to pay to the Internal Revenue Service (IRS) what the Act called a *"shared-responsibility payment,"* a payment that the Act characterized as a *"penalty"* rather than as a tax.

i. **Administered by the IRS:** The ACA said that covered individuals *"shall"* maintain health insurance, a term that made it sound as though the government was **commanding** that people buy insurance. But if a covered person didn't do so, the only consequence was that he had to make an **additional payment to the IRS** when paying his taxes.

(1) **Enforcement mechanism:** In those cases where a covered person did not buy insurance and did not initially make the required shared-responsibility payment, the ACA made the general statement that the payment was to be "assessed and collected [by the IRS] in the same manner" as tax penalties. But the ACA's detailed provisions cut back on the IRS' collection powers consid-

erably: the IRS was barred from using several of its normal enforcement tools, such as **criminal prosecutions**. So the IRS' collection powers were materially weaker than in the case of non-payment of standard taxes.

    ii. Government argument: The federal government would have preferred to see the statute upheld as a valid exercise of Congress' Commerce power. (For this aspect of the case, in which the government was unsuccessful, see p. 44.) But as a fall-back, the Obama administration argued (as the Court characterized the argument) that the individual mandate simply "made going without insurance **just another thing the Government taxes,** like buying gasoline or earning income." Therefore, the government said, the mandate was valid as an exercise of Congress' power to tax and spend for the general welfare.

  b. Found to be a tax: Five members of the Court (Roberts plus the four liberals, Ginsburg, Sotomayor, Breyer and Kagan) **agreed** with this Government position: **the individual mandate was a valid exercise of Congress' taxing power.** The main opinion on this point was by Chief Justice Roberts; the other four members of the majority concurred in the result but didn't formally join Roberts' opinion on this point.

    i. A "fairly possible" interpretation: Roberts conceded that viewing the individual mandate as a tax (rather than as an attempt by Congress to use its Commerce power) was **not the "most natural interpretation"** of the statute — the mandate "reads more naturally as a command to buy insurance than as a tax." But that didn't matter, he said; the only issue was whether interpreting the mandate as a tax was a **"fairly possible"** interpretation. In order to **save a statute from unconstitutionality**, the Court should resort to **"every reasonable construction."** Granting the statute "the full measure of **deference** owed to federal statutes," the mandate could be read as a valid tax, Roberts said.

    ii. "Looks like a tax": Roberts noted that the shared-responsibility payment **"looks like a tax** in many respects." For instance, those required to pay it were to pay it to the Treasury with their tax returns. And, he said, the process "yields the essential feature of any tax: it **produces at least some revenue** for the Government." Indeed, the Congressional Budget Office had projected that the scheme would raise about $4 billion per year by 2017.

    iii. "Penalty" not dispositive: Roberts conceded that the ACA itself repeatedly described the payment as a **"penalty,"** not a "tax." But, he said, Congress' **choice of label was not determinative** on whether the payment could be viewed as an exercise of the taxing power. Rather, the Court had historically used a **"functional approach"** to deciding whether a payment system fell within Congress' power to tax. There were several factors that convinced him that the way the shared-responsibility payment functioned entitled it to be viewed as a tax:

      ❏ The first factor was the **size of the burden** on the "taxpayer." In an important early (1922) case, *Bailey v. Drexel Furniture Co.*, the Court had found that what Congress called a "tax" on employers of child labor was in fact a penalty that went beyond Congress' tax-and-spend (or any other) power. An employer of underage workers was required to pay 10% of the company's net income as a "tax," regardless of the magnitude of the infraction; Roberts characterized this as a "prohibitory" financial punishment.

In the ACA, by contrast, the *size of the payment, relative to the underlying transaction, was much smaller.* For most people who went without health insurance, the payment would be *far less than the price of insurance*, and was guaranteed to never be more. Even someone with an annual income of $100,000 would pay only about $200 per month, compared with an estimated monthly cost for qualifying health insurance of $400.

❏ The second factor was whether *"scienter"* was required. The punitive character of the "tax" in *Drexel Furniture* was demonstrated by the fact that only those who "knowingly" employed underage workers had to make payments. The ACA, by contrast, imposed the shared responsibility payment without regard to the payor's state of knowledge or intent.

❏ Finally, the *mechanisms used to collect* the payments, and the language used in the Act to *describe the group* subjected to the payment requirements, dictated a finding that this was in essence a tax, not a punishment. The IRS was permitted to use only its regular collection efforts, not the "means most suggestive of a punitive sanction, such as *criminal prosecution."* The language of the statute did not classify failure to buy insurance as *"unlawful."* And Congress expected that four million people per year would choose to pay the IRS rather than buy insurance; the fact that Congress seemed to view this as "tolerable" suggested that Congress "did not think it was creating four million *outlaws."*

In summary, despite Congress' decision to call the shared-responsibility payments a "penalty," the actual way the payment system was designed justified a finding that it fell within Congress' power to tax-and-spend, if the alternative was to find the mandate unconstitutional.

c. **Dissent on the tax issue:**   Four members of the Court *dissented* from the conclusion that the shared-responsibility payment was a valid exercise of Congress' taxing power. In a "joint dissent" with no principal author, Justices Scalia, Kennedy, Thomas and Alito argued that while Congress *could* have used its taxing power to enact the payment system, it had *not in fact used* that power. Consequently, the joint dissenters said, Congress had acted unconstitutionally (since the four dissenters joined with Roberts in finding that the scheme was beyond the Commerce power as well; see *supra*, p. 46).

i. **A "penalty" is not a tax:**   For the dissenters, prior cases had established that when a statute "adopts the criteria of *wrongdoing*" and then imposes a monetary penalty as the principal consequence for the wrongdoing, the result is a *"regulatory penalty,"* not a tax.

(1) **Imposed for violation of law:**   The dissenters asserted that by this standard, the shared-responsibility payment scheme was unquestionably a penalty, not a tax. The statute referred repeatedly to the *"requirement"* that individuals maintain specified insurance, and said that individuals *"shall"* maintain the insurance. So failing to buy insurance was defined as a form of *wrongdoing*.

(2) Congress' "penalty" label counts: Most significantly, perhaps, Congress constantly *referred* to the payment system as a *"penalty"* — eighteen times, in fact. "[W]e have never — *never* — treated as a tax an exaction which faces up to the critical difference between a tax and a penalty, and explicitly denominates the exaction a 'penalty.'"

(3) Taxes are unpopular: The majority's decision to call this a tax rather than a penalty amounted to a *"rewriting"* of the statute, the dissenters said. *"Taxes have never been popular,"* and Congress "knew precisely what it was doing when it rejected an earlier version of this legislation that imposed a tax instead of a requirement-with-penalty." The majority's decision *"impos[es] a tax through judicial legislation"*; it thus "inverts the constitutional scheme and places the power to tax in the branch of government least accountable to the citizenry."

    d. Significance: The tax portion of *N.F.I.B.* certainly seems to make it easier for Congress to rely on its taxing power even when, for political purposes, the legislators don't want to admit that what they are doing is passing a tax. Even if Congress labels a required payment as a *"penalty,"* the payment will apparently fall within the tax-and-spend power as long as Congress obeys a few simple and painless formalities, like:

❑ setting the penalty *low enough* relative to the estimated profitability of the underlying conduct that a rational person might *voluntarily choose to pay* the penalty rather than perform (or refrain from) the act that Congress is trying to encourage or discourage;

❑ not calling individual actions that trigger the payment *"unlawful,"* or allowing them to be *prosecuted* as crimes;

❑ *using the IRS* as the means of collecting the payments.

    i. Extended regulatory power: In theory, Congress ought to be able to use the "penalty" technique approved in *N.F.I.B.* to stretch its regulatory powers far beyond what the Commerce power has been held to allow. Take, for instance, the prohibition on possession of guns near schools, struck down in *Lopez* (*supra*, p. 38) as going beyond the Commerce power; Congress could presumably do a pretty good job of discouraging such possession (though not criminalizing it) by imposing a $2,000 "penalty" on possessing a gun near a school, and having the IRS collect the penalty as part of the general tax-collection process.

II. THE SPENDING POWER

    A. The spending power generally: Article I, §8, gives Congress the power "[t]o lay and collect Taxes ... to pay the Debts and provide for the common Defence and general Welfare of the United States. ... " The power to spend is thus linked to the power to tax — money may be raised by taxation, and then spent "for the common Defence and general Welfare of the United States."

    B. Not limited to enumerated powers: Prior to 1937, it was not clear whether Congress could spend for whatever purpose it wished (so long as the "general welfare" was being served), or whether Congress could only spend in order to carry out one of the other enumerated powers listed in Article I, §8. Then, in *U.S. v. Butler*, 297 U.S. 1 (1936), the Court held that *no such limitation exists* — the spending (and taxing) powers are themselves enumerated powers, so Congress may spend (or tax) to achieve the general welfare, even though no other enumerated power is being furthered.

1. **Facts of *Butler*:** *Butler* involved the validity of the Agricultural Adjustment Act of 1933, a New Deal measure which sought to raise farm prices by cutting back agricultural production. The scheme was to be carried out by authorizing the Secretary of Agriculture to contract with farmers to reduce their acreage under cultivation in return for benefit payments; the payments were in turn to be made from a fund generated by the imposition of a "processing tax" on the processing of the commodity.

2. **Separate spending power:** The Court first concluded that the power to "tax and spend for the general welfare" existed as a power *separate and distinct* from the other powers enumerated in Article I, §8. Thus the taxing-and-spending power stood on equal footing with, say, the power to regulate interstate commerce. By this standard, there was no difficulty with the Agricultural Adjustment Act.

3. **Not usable for regulation:** But the Court rejected the contention that Congress had an independent power to "provide for the general welfare" apart from the power to tax and spend. Thus Congress *may not regulate in a particular area merely on the ground that it is thereby providing for the general welfare*; it is only *taxing and spending* which may be done "for the general welfare." Otherwise, the Court noted, the federal government would be one of "general and unlimited powers," rather than enumerated and limited ones.

4. **Can't regulate for general welfare:** The most important principle for which *U.S. v. Butler* stands today is that Congress has *no power* to *regulate* for the purpose of providing for the *"general welfare."* Congress may *spend* for the general welfare, it may *tax* for the general welfare, but it may not regulate for the general welfare. (For this reason, a congressional regulatory scheme has to be justified as a reasonable means of carrying out *some other enumerated power*, typically the commerce power. See *supra*, p. 27.)

5. **Other constitutional provisions as limits:** A federal spending program may still be found invalid because it runs afoul of other, specific, federal constitutional provisions protecting individuals. For instance, Congress could not violate the Due Process Clause of the Fifth Amendment, even as part of an otherwise-valid spending program in furtherance of the "general welfare."

C. **Achievement of otherwise disallowed objectives:** Suppose that Congress could not achieve objective X by direct regulation, since that would lie beyond its enumerated powers. May Congress use its *conditional* spending power to achieve that result *indirectly*, say by depriving the states of money if *they* do not achieve the regulatory result? The answer is, *"yes,"* so long as (1) the action by the state does not violate the constitutional rights of any individual; and (2) Congress has not "coerced" or "unduly influenced" the state into taking the deal (a limit discussed *infra*, p. 72).

1. **Illustration of general rule:** The 1987 case described in the following example is the leading illustration of the general principle that Congress can use its conditional spending power to achieve a result that would be beyond Congress' direct regulatory powers.

Example: Congress, in order to prevent drivers under the age of 21 from drinking, withholds 5% of a state's federal highway funds from any state that doesn't pass a law forbidding individuals younger than 21 from purchasing or possessing in public any alcoholic beverage. South Dakota attacks the statute on the grounds that this condition interferes with its own exclusive powers under both the Tenth and Twenty-First Amendments.

Held, the statute is valid. Even if, *arguendo*, direct congressional setting of the drinking age for the entire country would be unconstitutional, Congress' indirect use of its conditional spending power to achieve the same results is permissible. If, by the use of that conditional spending power, Congress induced the states to pass laws that would *themselves* violate the constitutional rights of individuals, that congressional action would be unconstitutional. But that didn't happen here. Also, if the financial inducement offered by Congress was "so coercive as to pass the point at which *'pressure turns into compulsion,'* " the inducement would so undermine state sovereignty as to go beyond the spending power. But here, Congress has told the states that they will lose only "a relatively small percentage" of their highway funds (5% in South Dakota's case) if they don't comply, and that "relatively mild encouragement" leaves the states free to refuse, "not merely in theory but in fact." Therefore, the inducement was not impermissibly coercive. *South Dakota v. Dole*, 483 U.S. 203 (1987).

D. Spending program can't "coerce" the states (*N.F.I.B.* case): The modern Supreme Court has often worried that the federal government may become *so powerful* that state decision-making power will be diminished and the basic two-government federalist system will be eviscerated. In the *Dole* decision, *supra*, you can see this fear reflected in the Court's statement that a financial inducement so large that it would constitute invalid "compulsion" of the states would undermine state sovereignty and thus be invalid under the Spending Clause. The Court eventually decided in 2012 that such impermissible compulsion had occurred in the form of Congress' decision to make a major change to the *Medicaid* program; the Court concluded that Congress had attached such stringent conditions to large grants it made to states that the set-up unduly *"coerced"* the States, and thus went beyond the spending power.

This result came in the same health-care decision that we've already reviewed in two other contexts (see *supra*, p. 44 and 66), *N.F.I.B. v. Sebelius,* 132 S.Ct. 2566 (2012). The case represents the *first time* the Court has ever overturned an exercise of Congress' spending power as *unconstitutionally coercive*.

1. Facts: As we've seen, in the 2010 Affordable Care Act (ACA), Congress took many coordinated steps to expand the availability of health care. One of the biggest steps was to restructure and broaden the Medicaid program.

a. Nature of Medicaid: Under the Medicaid program as it has long existed, Congress *gives major funding to states to help pay for the medical care of various categories of poor people*, such as pregnant women, families with young children, and the disabled. The program is essentially administered by the states, but a majority of the money spent comes from the federal government. The states have always been free to participate or not participate in Medicaid; but if they choose to participate (as every state has done since 1982), they must obey various federally-mandated rules about whom to cover and what services are to be provided.

b. **The ACA's expansion:** The ACA dramatically broadened the number and types of individuals to whom the states had to give Medicaid. (We'll call this the "Medicaid Expansion.") For instance, the Medicaid Expansion said that states must give Medicaid coverage to *every adult under 65* with income up to 133% of the federal poverty level. Pre-ACA, many states, acting with congressional consent, did not cover childless adults at all, and set a much lower income limit for covering families with children. (For instance, in the case of unemployed parents, pre-ACA the average state covered only the very poorest, those who made less than 37% of the federal poverty level.)

c. **Funding:** For the early years of the Expansion (from 2014 through 2016), Congress committed to paying *100% of the costs* of covering these newly-eligible recipients. After 2016, the federal payment level would gradually decline, but would still cover 90% of the costs.

d. **"All or nothing":** The key feature of the Medicaid Expansion — the feature that led 26 states to bring their constitutional challenge — was that if a state declined to participate in the Expansion, *it would lose all Medicaid funding*, not just the "extra" funding to cover the newly-eligible recipients. Medicaid spending accounts for over 20% of the average state's total budget, and pre-Expansion, federal funds covered 50% to 83% of those costs. So an average state that declined to agree to the Expansion would lose, in addition to the funds to cover the Expansion itself, *more than 10% of its total budget.*[1] And such a state would then be left to find some other, completely non-federally-funded, way to afford health-care coverage for their poorest citizens, or leave them without coverage.

2. **The challenge:** The 26 states that challenged the ACA argued that Congress' "take all or none" approach to the Medicaid Expansion was *so coercive* that it violated the basic principle established in earlier cases under the Tenth Amendment (see, e.g., *New York v. U.S.*, p. 56) holding that "the Federal Government may not *compel the states* to *enact or administer a federal regulatory program.*"

3. **Held unconstitutional:** By a 7-2 vote, the Court *agreed* with the plaintiffs: requiring a state to choose between accepting the Medicaid Expansion and losing all Medicaid funds was *so coercive* that it *exceeded Congress' authority under the Spending Clause.* The main opinion so holding was by Chief Justice Roberts, who was joined, perhaps surprisingly, by Justices Breyer and Kagan. The four-person "joint dissent" (by Justices Scalia, Kennedy, Thomas and Alito) did not officially join this part of Roberts' opinion for reasons that are unclear, but they agreed with Roberts that the scheme was an unconstitutionally coercive violation of the spending power.

a. **"Appropriate conditions":** Roberts agreed that Congress could normally "attach appropriate conditions" to federal taxing and spending programs, in order to preserve its control over the use of federal funds. In the usual case, if a state didn't like the conditions that Congress was attaching, the state as an "independent sovereign" was free to simply decline the funds.

---

1. This was the estimate of Chief Justice Roberts. By the estimate of the "joint dissent," see *infra*, p. 76, the loss would be even greater: states that lost all Medicaid would lose federal payments equal to 22% of all combined state expenditures, not counting the federal Expansion funds.

b. **Threats to terminate "other significant grants":** But, Roberts said, the Court's precedents gave much closer scrutiny to those situations in which Congress, in connection with *one* federally-financed program, imposed conditions that took the form of "threats to *terminate other significant independent grants.*" In that situation, the conditions "are properly viewed as a means of *pressuring the states* to accept policy changes." And if the financial inducements are "so coercive as to pass the point at which *'pressure turns into compulsion'*" (citing a 1937 case, *Steward Machine Co. v. Davis*), Congress will be found to have exceeded its spending powers.

    i. **The *Dole* drinking-age case:** Roberts apparently could not find any case in which the Court had concluded that such impermissible compulsion had actually occurred. But he contrasted the conditions that Congress had imposed in the ADA with the conditions imposed in the only major case since 1937 in which the compulsion issue had arisen, *South Dakota v. Dole*, 483 U.S. 203 (1987) (*supra*, p. 72).

        (1) **The condition in *Dole*:** In *Dole*, Congress had threatened to withhold 5% of federal highway funding (a long pre-existing program) payable to any state, if the state did not raise its drinking age to 21. South Carolina claimed that this was unconstitutional coercion.

        (2) **Court disagrees:** But the *Dole* Court disagreed, on the grounds that Congress was offering only *"relatively mild encouragement* to the States"; for instance, the funds at stake amounted to less than one half of one percent of South Dakota's budget at the time. Therefore, whether to accept the drinking age change remained the prerogative of each state "not merely in theory but in fact."

    ii. **A "gun to the head":** The conditions governing the Medicaid Expansion here, by contrast, were *dramatically more coercive*, Roberts said. In contrast to the "relatively mild encouragement" that Congress had given the states in *Dole*, here Congress' financial "inducement" was in reality *"a gun to the head."* A state that rejected the Medicaid expansion would lose the whole federally-funded portion of its entire Medicaid program, amounting to a loss of over 10% of a typical state's overall budget. This was "economic dragooning that leaves the states with *no real option but to acquiesce* in the Medicaid [E]xpansion."

    iii. **Said to be merely a "modification":** In the *Dole* highway-funds case, Congress was pursuing a new objective (a minimum drinking age) by threatening to withhold funds that had been earmarked for a pre-existing *independent program* (highway building) that had little to do with the new objective. The defenders of the Medicaid Expansion (including Justice Ginsburg; see *infra*, p. 76) argued that the present case was therefore distinguishable: Congress was simply changing the terms of a *single program*, Medicaid, and had a right to do so. And, the defenders said, the states had known, at the moment they first signed on to Medicaid decades ago, that Congress was reserving the right to alter or repeal any provision of Medicaid at any time.

        (1) **Not just a modification:** But Roberts agreed with the state challengers: the Medicaid Expansion was such a huge shift, not just in degree but in kind, that it should be viewed as a *new program*, not a modification of the existing Medicaid program. Whereas the existing Medicaid program had been designed to cover just four "particular categories of the needy" (the disabled, the blind, the elderly, and families with dependent children), the Medicaid Expansion transformed the program into "a program to meet the health-care needs of the ***entire nonelderly population*** with income below 133% of the poverty level," as part of a "comprehensive national plan to provide universal health insurance coverage." Therefore, the situation fell within the *Dole* framework, under which Congress couldn't coerce the states to agree to a set of changes by threatening to terminate a significant grant that was "independent" of the new changes.

(2) **States couldn't have foreseen this:** As for Ginsburg's argument that the states had known all along that Congress reserved the right to alter or repeal Medicaid at any time (so that there was no unfair surprise here), Roberts again disagreed. When the states originally signed on to Medicaid, they could not reasonably have anticipated that Congress' reservation of the right to "alter" or "amend" the program would turn out to include the power to ***transform it so dramatically***. True, Medicaid had been amended on many previous occasions. But none of those amendments had had nearly the scope of the present change, he said.

iv. **Far side of the persuasion/coercion line:** Roberts concluded that Congress had simply ***"conscript[ed] state [agencies] into the national bureaucratic army,"*** something that prior cases (decided under the Tenth Amendment) had said was forbidden under our federalist system.

c. **Severability:** So under Roberts' basic ruling (with which six other Justices agreed), Congress had acted unconstitutionally by threatening to withhold "regular" Medicaid funds from the state as a penalty for refusing to agree to the Medicaid Expansion. But what should be the *consequences* of this finding of unconstitutionality? Could the rest of the ACA (and the Medicaid Expansion itself) be ***"severed"*** from the unconstitutional penalty, and thus survive? Roberts concluded that the answer was ***"yes."***[2]

i. **Congress' presumed intent:** The issue came down to congressional intent: would Congress have wanted the rest of the ACA to stand if it had known that the Court would hold that Congress didn't have the power to withhold all Medicaid funds from any state that declined the Medicaid Expansion? Roberts concluded that the answer was ***"yes."*** It was not even clear to Roberts that any state *would* actually reject the Expansion, given the very high level of federal funding for it. But even if Congress knew that some states would reject the Expansion, Roberts

---

2. On this "severance" issue, Roberts spoke for a bare five-Justice majority: his overall opinion about the Medical Expansion was joined by Justices Breyer and Kagan. And Ginsburg and Sotomayor, though they disagreed with Roberts' conclusion that the loss-of-all-Medicaid-funds penalty was unconstitutional, agreed that the rest of the ACA, including the rest of the Expansion, could be severed so that the remainder survived. (The four members of the "joint dissent," by contrast, believed that severance was improper, and that the entire ACA therefore could not stand; see *infra*, p. 76.)

saw no reason to believe that Congress would have wanted that state-by-state freedom to decline the Expansion to trigger a complete collapse of the ACA.

4. **Two dissenters would allow total withholding:** Justice Ginsburg, joined only by Justice Sotomayor on this point, dissented from Roberts' conclusion that withholding all Medicaid funding from states that declined the Medicaid Expansion was so coercive that it went beyond Congress' spending powers. Ginsburg asserted that Congress' general right to attach conditions to federal funding would have permitted it to **cancel the entire Medicaid program**, and then **replace it with a new Medicaid** that included the Expansion; in that event, it was clear to her that Congress could require the states to choose between taking the entire newly-constituted Medicaid package or none of it. That being so, she said, Roberts' ruling that Congress could not achieve the same objective by an amendment to existing Medicaid, rather than a repeal-and-re-enactment sequence, was a *"ritualistic requirement"* that would not advance any constitutional principle or serve the interests of federalism.

5. **Four "joint dissenters" say entire ACA should fall:** At the other end of the spectrum, the four conservative justices who made up the *"joint dissent"* argued that severance of the Medicaid Expansion should not be allowed: the ACA should instead be found *"invalid in its entirety."* The joint dissenters not only agreed with the majority view that the compulsory Medicaid Expansion was unconstitutional, they believed that the individual mandate, too, was unconstitutional (see *supra*, p. 46). Given the centrality of these two provisions to the overall structure of the ACA, the joint dissenters believed that leaving the numerous other provisions of the ACA[3] in place amounted to "a vast judicial overreaching." The Court was creating, they said, "a debilitated, inoperable version of healthcare regulation that Congress did not enact and the public does not expect."

6. **Consequence of severance for ACA:** As a consequence of the 5-4 lineup on the severance issue, the **entire ACA stays in force as drafted**, with the sole exception of the federal government's right to cut off the full Medicaid funding of any state that declines to participate in the Medicaid Expansion. If a state declines the Medicaid Expansion, that state will **keep its "regular" Medicaid funding**, and will presumably be allowed to continue covering whatever classes of citizens it would have covered had the ACA not been enacted.

    a. **May have small effect:** But it seems likely that most if not all states will "opt in" to the Medicaid Expansion anyway, since opting in looks very attractive economically: opting in will allow states to provide health care to every adult or family with an income less than 133% of the federal poverty level, with 100% of the incremental costs initially being covered by the federal government, and with the federally-funded share diminishing only modestly, to 90%, by 2020.

7. **Macro significance:** On the more macro level, *N.F.I.B.* illustrates a **limit on the spending power:** Congress' freedom to attach conditions to federal spending does not extend to a situation in which the **conditions are so "coercive" that the states are left with "no real option but to acquiesce"** (i.e., situations in which Congress can fairly be described as **holding a "gun to the head"** of the states). The principles of state sovereignty prevent

---

3. These other provisions included, for instance, the community-rating and guaranteed-issue requirements for insurance companies (see *supra*, p. 45), a penalty on larger employers who did not furnish health insurance to their employees, and the establishment of state-administered and federally-subsidized "insurance exchanges" in which people could buy individual health insurance.

Congress from *"conscript[ing] state [agencies] into the national bureaucratic army,"* as the majority concluded had occurred in *N.F.I.B.*

a. **Alteration of pre-existing program:** The Court will apparently be more likely to find such impermissible coercion when Congress dramatically alters a major *pre-existing* federally-funded program, than where Congress creates and funds a new program essentially from scratch, and imposes tough conditions on state participation in such a way that the conditions relate solely to the new program.

E. **"General welfare" still required:** A federal spending program must advance the "general welfare." However, the Court gives great deference to Congress' judgment that a spending program will indeed advance the general welfare. Therefore, this requirement seems to have almost *no bite* at present.

III. THE WAR, TREATY AND FOREIGN AFFAIRS POWERS

A. **War power:** Congress is given the power to *declare war*, and to *tax and spend for national defense*. Also, it is explicitly given the right to "raise and support Armies" and to provide and maintain a navy. All of these powers are given by Article I, §8. The President, by contrast, is made the Commander in Chief of the Armed Forces. (Article II, §2.) Thus Congress and the President in effect split the war powers.

1. **Separation of powers:** This division raises important questions of the separation of powers. (E.g., may the President commit armed forces to battle without express congressional authorization?) However, these questions are deferred until a separate chapter on separation of powers, *infra*, p. 127.

2. **Federalism:** The war powers raise important issues regarding *federalism*.

a. **Economic regulation:** These issues of federalism have principally arisen in a context of *economic regulations* promulgated during wartime. The right to promulgate such regulations as an adjunct to the war powers was broadly construed by the Supreme Court in *Woods v. Miller Co.*, 333 U.S. 138 (1948).

i. *Woods* **case:** *Woods* involved the constitutionality of the Housing and Rent Act of 1947, by which Congress sought to impose rent controls because of the post-war housing shortage. The Court held that even though actual combat had terminated, a state of war still technically existed. Furthermore, the shortage directly resulted from the war; therefore, Congress could act to combat the shortage, under its power to take all "necessary and proper" steps to enforce an enumerated power (the power to declare war).

3. **Impact on private citizens:** The war powers sometimes permit Congress to *regulate private behavior* without the need to rely on broad powers like the commerce or the taxing-and-spending powers. Indeed, when Congress does purport to act under its war powers, the Supreme Court will give the resulting action maximum judicial *deference*, and will be extremely reluctant to hold that the congressional action is unconstitutional.

Example: In a recent case, *Rumsfeld v. FAIR*, 547 U.S. 47 (2006), the Court upheld the constitutionality of the "Solomon Amendment," under which Congress said that any university could receive certain federal funding only if all parts of the university, including its law school, gave the same on-campus access to military recruiters as to other recruiters. A group of law schools argued that the Solomon Amendment infringed their First Amendment rights by forcing the schools to accommodate the anti-gay message of military recruiters. At the outset of its opinion, a unanimous court noted that Congress' war powers "include[] the authority to ***require campus access for military recruiters.***" That is, as an adjunct to its war powers Congress could simply have required every law school and university to host military recruiters, without giving the schools the choice between giving access or foregoing the funding. In the course of finding that the Solomon Amendment was constitutional, the Court noted that ***"judicial deference [to Congress] is at its apogee when Congress legislates under its authority to raise and support armies."***

B. The treaty power: Like the war powers, the ***treaty power*** is divided between two branches of the federal government. The President may make a treaty, but it must be ratified by two-thirds of the Senate. Article II, §2.

1. **Equivalent of federal statute:** A validly-ratified treaty is the rough equivalent of a ***federal statute***. Thus when a conflict arises between a valid treaty and a valid congressional statute, ***whichever was enacted later*** controls, under the rule that "the last expression of the sovereign will must control." See Tribe, p. 226.

2. **Independent source of authority:** The power to ratify treaties is in effect an enumerated legislative power, just like the specific powers listed in Article I, §8. Thus even though a subject area might not otherwise be within congressional control, if it falls within the scope of an otherwise valid treaty, it will be valid as a "necessary and proper means" of exercising the treaty power. It will also be binding on the states, under the Supremacy Clause.

3. **May not violate constitutional guarantees:** A treaty may not violate any distinct constitutional prohibitions or guarantees (e.g., the Bill of Rights). See, e.g., *Reid v. Covert*, 354 U.S. 1 (1957), holding that "no agreement with a foreign nation can confer power on the Congress, or on any other branch of Government, which is free from the restraints of the Constitution."

4. **Executive agreements:** The Constitution's only reference to international agreements is to the treaty power, the exercise of which, as noted, requires ratification by the Senate. However, the Constitution does not explicitly prohibit the President from entering into international agreements without Senate consent, and presidents have traditionally frequently done so. These unratified agreements are usually called ***"executive agreements."***

   a. **Status of executive agreements:** The precise status of such agreements is unclear. It seems settled that they are not *per se* unconstitutional; for instance, if such an agreement is enacted within the scope of an enumerated presidential power, it will surely be upheld. Thus Tribe (pp. 170-71) cites the example of an armistice agreement justified by use of the President's commander-in-chief power.

   b. **Cannot override congressional act:** An executive agreement, unlike a treaty, ***cannot override*** a prior act of Congress. Tribe, p. 171.

   c. **Superior to state law:** But such an agreement, like a treaty, will have ***priority over conflicting state laws***, because the Constitution as a general principle vests all control over international affairs in the federal government. *Id.*

C. Power over foreign affairs: Neither Congress nor any other branch of the federal government is explicitly given power over "*foreign affairs*" as such. However, the Supreme Court has always recognized that Congress and the executive branch have power over foreign affairs, even where no enumerated power is applicable. That is, the Court has recognized a "general constitutional principle" that foreign affairs are the proper province of the federal government. Support for this proposition comes from several constitutionally-imposed limitations on state interference with foreign affairs (e.g., the bans on states' making of treaties, and on their laying of import or export duties, both imposed by Article I, §10).

   1. **State action improper:** Thus "all state action, whether or not consistent with current federal foreign policy, that has significant impact on the conduct of American diplomacy is *void* as an unconstitutional infringement upon an exclusively federal sphere of responsibility." Tribe, p. 230.

IV. OTHER POWERS

A. Other federal powers: It is not profitable to examine in detail all of the constitutionally-enumerated sources of federal authority. However, a brief listing of some of the other sources of federal authority is as follows:

B. Congressional powers: Some of the powers given to *Congress* are:

   1. **Money:** To *coin money*, and to regulate its value (Art. I, §8);

   2. **Bankruptcy:** To establish laws governing *bankruptcy (id.)*;

   3. **Post offices:** To establish *post offices (id.)*;

   4. **Copyrights and patents:** To control the issuance of *copyrights* and *patents (id.)*;

   5. **Federal property:** To govern the District of Columbia, and all other *federal properties (id.)*;

   6. **Immigration and naturalization:** To control *naturalization* (and implicitly, *immigration*) of aliens *(id.)*;

   7. **Civil War Amendments:** To enforce, "by appropriate legislation," the Thirteenth, Fourteenth and Fifteenth Amendments (all arising out of the Civil War). See *infra*, p. 469.

   8. **Constitutional amendments:** To *propose*, by a two-thirds vote, a *constitutional amendment* for ratification by three-fourths of the states (Art. V). (The holding of a constitutional convention is an alternative, but one which has never been used since the Constitution's original ratification.)

C. Powers of the executive: The powers of the *executive branch* will not be reviewed here. However, some of these powers are discussed in the treatment of separation of powers, beginning *infra*, p. 128. See also the discussion of the President's role in the treaty-making process, *supra*, p. 78.

D. Judicial powers: The powers of the federal *judiciary* are spelled out in Article III, §2. These powers, discussion of which is generally reserved for the course in federal courts, include the power to decide:

   1. cases *arising under the Constitution or under federal* laws;

   2. cases involving *ambassadors* and other diplomats;

3. cases involving *admiralty* and *maritime* issues;

4. cases in which the *U.S. is a party*;

5. cases *between two or more states*, between *a state and* citizens of another state, or between *citizens of different states*; and

6. cases between *a state or its citizens and foreign states* or citizens.

> **Note:** Observe that although all of these types of cases fall within the federal courts' constitutionally-vested power, Congress has the right to "regulate" the jurisdiction of the lower federal courts, and to make "exceptions" to that jurisdiction. This has resulted in a substantial curtailment of the theoretically-available powers of the federal judiciary, as a practical matter. This area is more extensively discussed *supra*, pp. 12-14.

Quiz Yourself on

OTHER NATIONAL POWERS *(ENTIRE CHAPTER)*

9. Congress has decided that breast implants, even of the less-dangerous saline variety, are undesirable. Congress has therefore placed a tax of $2,000 on any breast implant, to be paid by the surgeon at the time of implantation. The legislative history of the statute shows that Congress' principal purpose was to discourage the use of such implants, and that Congress did not believe the measure would produce very much revenue. In its first year, the Act produced collections of about $1 million. Doc, a surgeon specializing in implants, sues to have the statute declared unconstitutional on the grounds that it is beyond the powers of Congress. Is Doc's suit likely to succeed? If so, state why. _____

10. Congress, after concluding that the states have lagged behind in educating school children to be tolerant towards homosexuals, enacts a program providing a small subsidy to any public elementary school that conducts a program teaching a better understanding of, and tolerance of, gay people.

    (a) Putting aside the commerce power, what constitutional provision best supplies constitutional authority for this statute? _____

    (b) A parent whose child is about to receive such instruction sues to have the provision found unconstitutional, on the grounds that it encourages homosexuality and thus detracts from the general welfare of the nation. Assuming that the federal court hearing the case concludes that the measure will probably make the nation worse off than it was before, will this constitutional attack on the statute succeed? _____

11. Congress, alarmed about the dramatic rise in teenage pregnancies, passes the Underage Procreation Act of 2012. That Act requires any person under the age of 17 to obtain a federal permit before becoming pregnant. The permit is granted to any woman who shows that she has received one hour of counselling about the dangers of teen pregnancy from a state-licensed social worker. Violators are to be fined. A 16-year-old woman who wishes to become pregnant files suit to attack the statute's constitutionality on the grounds that it is beyond Congress' enumerated powers. The federal government defends the statute on the grounds that it is a proper exercise of Congress' power to regulate for the "general welfare." Will the plaintiff's attack on the statute succeed? (Ignore any issues relating to a woman's constitutional right to privacy or right to become pregnant. Assume that the Court decides that nothing in the activity being regulated affects interstate commerce.) _____

Answers

9. **No.** The fact that the principal purpose of a tax is regulatory rather than revenue-raising does not pose a constitutional problem today. So long as the tax produces at least non-trivial revenue, and does not run afoul of any explicit constitutional limitation on the taxing power (e.g., the prohibition on export duties in Art. I, Section 9), the tax will be found to be within Congress' general power to "lay and collect taxes. ... " Art. I, Section 8.

10. **(a) The spending power.** Art. I, Section 8 gives Congress power to "lay and collect Taxes ... to pay the Debts and provide for the ... general Welfare of the United States. ... " This language includes the "spending" power, although the word "spend" is not used.

(b) No. It is true that the spending power of Art. 1, Section 8 is phrased specifically in terms of providing for the "general welfare" of the nation. However, the requirement that a federal spending program be for the "general welfare" has almost no bite at present — certainly, the Court is not entitled to substitute its own judgment of what would be "best" in lieu of Congress'.

11. **Yes.** There is *no federal "police power."* That is, Congress does not have the right to *regulate "for the general welfare."* Congress' only powers regarding the general welfare are the right to tax and to spend to achieve that welfare. Since nothing in the statute provides for either a tax or an expenditure, the statute is not supported by the taxing and spending power or any other enumerated power. Normally, a federal regulatory scheme could be supported by the commerce power (since the Court takes an extremely expansive view of what activity can be found to "affect commerce"), but the facts tell us to ignore the commerce power here.

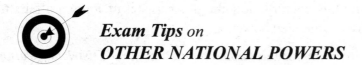

Exam Tips on
OTHER NATIONAL POWERS

Here are some of the ways issues discussed in this chapter can appear on exams:

☛ Professors sometimes test on the blurry line between *taxing* and *regulation*. Your fact pattern might give you a *tax* that is principally for *regulatory purposes*. If so, you can rely on the taxation power as an independent source of congressional power (distinct from the Commerce Clause, for instance) — so long as the tax produces at least a non-trivial amount of revenue, and its regulatory scheme seems *rationally related* to the collection of the tax itself, it's a valid exercise of the tax power.

    ☞ To determine whether a revenue-raising device is a "tax," the Court now does a *"functional"* analysis: if the measure *behaves like a tax* (most importantly, it raises some *material revenue*), it doesn't matter than Congress has labelled it a *"penalty."* Cite *N.F.I.B. v. Sebelius* on this point.

        ☞ But to be a valid "tax," the measure must probably not make the activity being regulated a *"crime"* or *"offense,"* and the money collected must be small enough that a rational person might choose to pay the "tax" rather than committing the act that Congress is trying to encourage (e.g., buying health insurance).

Example: In the Affordable Care Act, Congress said that anyone who didn't buy health insurance (at a typical cost for a high-income person of $400 per month) had to pay the IRS a "penalty" (which for a high-income person would be about $200 per month). Since the ACA didn't make non-purchase a serious offense (e.g., there were no criminal penalties for not buying and not paying the penalty), and since the "penalty" was much smaller than the cost of the actual insurance, the penalty was found valid as an exercise of the Taxing power. *N.F.I.B. v. Sebelius.* (But if failure to buy a $400/month policy had caused a $2,000/month "penalty," and non-penalty-payers could be criminally prosecuted, the scheme probably would *not* have qualified as an exercise of the Taxing power.)

☛ Occasionally, you will be tested on the procedural requirements for a *treaty*. Remember that the President may propose a treaty, but it does not become effective until *ratified* by two-thirds of the Senate.

    ☞   Also, keep in mind that even where the President cannot get a treaty ratified, the President may create an international agreement as an *"Executive Agreement."* (An Executive Agreement is essentially an agreement entered into between the President and some other country but not ratified by the Senate.) An Executive Agreement can't override a prior act of Congress, but is superior to state law.

    ☞   Your fact pattern may involve *foreign affairs* without any war and without any treaty. In this situation, you should pose the question whether the action falls within the enumerated powers. The answer, typically, is that there is no power over foreign affairs expressly given to either the President or the Congress, but the Court has recognized an implicit power of both branches over this domain. For instance, your fact pattern might involve an attempt by Congress to prevent Americans from travelling abroad, to prevent aliens from visiting this country, or some other aspect of foreign affairs not falling within a specifically-enumerated power.

☛ Be on the lookout for questions involving congressional regulation of the *District of Columbia*. Congress has a special enumerated power to govern the District of Columbia, so it may regulate there in purely local matters (which would not fall, say, within the commerce power).

☛ Similarly, remember that Congress can govern all *federal property*. Fact patterns frequently involve national parks, national monuments, military bases, and other types of federal property. In all of these areas, Congress has complete regulatory power, so you do not need to worry about whether the activity being regulated falls within the commerce power or any other general congressional power.

CHAPTER 6

TWO LIMITS ON STATE POWER: THE DORMANT COMMERCE CLAUSE AND CONGRESSIONAL ACTION

ChapterScope

This Chapter examines two federalism-based limits on state and local power: (1) the so-called "dormant" Commerce Clause; and (2) ways in which Congress may block the states from legislating in particular areas. The most important concepts in this Chapter are:

■ **Dormant Commerce Clause:** The *mere existence* of the federal commerce power *restricts the states* from *discriminating against*, or *unduly burdening*, interstate commerce. This restriction is called the "dormant Commerce Clause."

❑ **Three part test:** A state regulation which affects interstate commerce must satisfy *each* of the following three requirements in order to avoid violating the dormant Commerce Clause:

❑ The regulation must pursue a *legitimate state end;*

❑ The regulation must be *rationally related* to that legitimate state end; and

❑ The regulatory *burden* imposed by the state on interstate commerce must be *outweighed* by the state's interest in enforcing its regulation.

❑ **Intentional discrimination:** Courts especially frown on *intentional discrimination* against out-of-staters. If the state is promoting its residents' own economic interests, this will not be a legitimate state objective, so the regulation will almost always be found to violate the Commerce Clause.

❑ **Market participant exception:** There is one key *exception* to the dormant Commerce Clause rules: if the state acts as a *market participant*, it *may* favor local over out-of-state interests.

■ **Preemption:** Congress can *preempt* the states from affecting commerce. There are two ways it can do this:

❑ **Conflict:** First, the congressional statute and the state action may be in *actual conflict*. If so, the state regulation is automatically invalid.

❑ **Federal occupation of field:** Congress may also pre-empt state regulation not because there is an actual conflict between what Congress does and what the states do, but because Congress is found to have made the decision to *occupy the entire field*.

❑ **Consent by Congress:** Conversely, Congress may *consent* to state action that would otherwise violate the Commerce Clause. Congress may even allow a state to discriminate against out-of-staters.

■ **The Supremacy Clause:** Under the *"Supremacy Clause"* of the Constitution, the Constitution and federal laws *take priority* over any conflicting state law.

I.   THE DORMANT COMMERCE CLAUSE — REGULATION

A. **Negative implications of federal power:** Prior chapters of this book have been devoted to limitations on the federal powers. We turn now to limitations on *state power* embodied in the Constitution.

    1. **Express limits:** Some limitations on state action are explicitly set forth in the Constitution; for instance, Article I, §9 flatly prohibits any state from imposing an export duty.

    2. **Implied limits:** With respect to most areas in which the Constitution gives the federal government authority, however, that document does not say anything about whether the states may exercise similar power in the area. For instance, does the Constitution's grant to Congress of the power to issue patents mean that a state cannot give a different kind of protection to inventors?

        a. **No general rule:** The "negative implications" to be drawn from a constitutional grant of power to Congress have generally been resolved by the Supreme Court on an *area-by-area basis*. Thus a finding of no preemption in the patent context would not necessarily mean the same finding in, say, the bankruptcy area.

B. **Negative implications of the Commerce Clause:** There is only one power whose grant in the Constitution has given rise to substantial litigation concerning states' powers: this is the Commerce Clause. The issue which has been posed over and over again in the so-called *"dormant* Commerce Clause" cases is: Does the mere fact that the Constitution gives Congress the power to regulate interstate commerce *prevent a state* from taking a particular action which affects interstate commerce, assuming that Congress has not actually exercised its power in the subject area in question (so that no Supremacy-Clause questions are involved)? In other words, the controversy in the dormant Commerce Clause cases focuses not on what Congress *has* done, but on what it *might* have done.

    1. **No simple test:** As we shall see, no easy answer or test for solving this question has been devised.

C. **Traditional approach:** The early Supreme Court could have adopted either of two extreme views on the significance of the dormant Commerce Clause for state regulation.

    1. **Great freedom to states:** It could have held that where Congress has remained silent as to a particular subject matter, the states are completely free to regulate, no matter what the burden on or discrimination against interstate commerce.

    2. **Exclusive federal terrain:** Alternatively, the Court could have held that Congress' power to regulate interstate commerce is *exclusive*, so that even if Congress has chosen not to act in a certain area affecting interstate commerce, the states are not entitled to act.

    3. **Middle ground:** But rather than adopting either of these two extreme positions, the Court has always chosen something of a *middle ground*, though the precise nature of that middle position has varied through the years. Essentially, the Court's approach has always been to *weigh* the *state interest in regulating its local affairs* against the *national interest* in *uniformity* and in an *integrated national economy.*

    4. **Congress has ultimate say:** Because the limitations on state authority imposed by the dormant Commerce Clause are not explicitly stated in the Constitution, but are rather derived by negative implication, limitations on state commerce-related conduct imposed by the Court *may always be reversed by Congress.*

    a. States given greater freedom: Thus if the Court holds that a particular type of state action unduly burdens interstate commerce, Congress may pass a law explicitly allowing the state to interfere with commerce in this manner.

    b. Stricter standard: Conversely, if the Court holds that a particular type of state action, although it affects interstate commerce, does not burden it unduly, Congress may reverse this ruling either by stating that it intends to *preempt the entire field* to which the state regulation relates, or by passing a statute which *explicitly conflicts* with the state rule.

    c. Summary of Court's role: To put it another way, the Supreme Court's role in this area is limited to *interpreting congressional silence.* See Tribe, p. 404.

D. Early interpretations: From its earliest days, the Supreme Court has given great weight to the purposes behind the Commerce Clause: the creation and nurturing of a *common market* among the states, and the *abolition of trade barriers.*

    1. Failure of Articles of Confederation: The pre-Constitution *Articles of Confederation* had failed largely because the states fought destructive *trade wars* against each other. Tribe, p. 404. These trade wars arose principally from the fact that state governments were too responsive to local economic interests — each state government tended to pursue the interests of its own constituents, at the expense of citizens of other states. *Id.*

    2. Prevention of economic balkanization: Therefore, under the Constitution, the power of the federal judiciary, interpreting the Commerce Clause, had to be used to prevent this *"economic balkanization."*

    3. Congress' silence: Also, the Supreme Court has always well recognized that the fact that Congress has not chosen to speak out in a particular area does not mean that it tacitly approves of state regulation of that area. Congress is simply too busy, with too many pressing matters on its legislative docket, for there to be any assurance that state regulations which burden or discriminate against interstate commerce will be overturned by congressional action. Tribe, p. 402. Therefore, the Supreme Court has always been intensely conscious of its own obligation to *keep the channels of interstate commerce free of state-originated impediments.*

    4. *Gibbons v. Ogden:* The first Supreme Court case interpreting the meaning of congressional silence in a commerce context was *Gibbons v. Ogden*, 22 U.S. (9 Wheat.) 1 (1824). Other aspects of this case, the opinion in which was written by Chief Justice Marshall, are discussed *supra*, p. 28.

        a. Factual summary: To summarize briefly the facts, New York had granted an exclusive steamboat operating license which was ultimately owned by Ogden. Gibbons obtained a federal license to operate his vessel between New York and New Jersey, but was enjoined by the New York courts from sailing it in New York waters because of Ogden's monopoly. Gibbons argued that the New York monopoly violated the federal commerce power.

        b. Holding: After giving a broad definition of "commerce" (see *supra*, p. 28), Marshall went on to hold that the New York monopoly was invalid because it *conflicted with the federal commerce power.* He took two steps to reach this conclusion:

    i.   **Meaning of congressional silence:** Gibbons' counsel had argued that the federal commerce power was *exclusive*; that is, that the states had no right to take any action which affected interstate commerce. Marshall conceded that there was "great force" in this argument, and that he was "not satisfied that it has been refuted." However, he avoided an explicit ruling on the argument, and assumed, without deciding, that the states could regulate commerce in a particular way if there was no actual conflict between the state regulation and an act of Congress.

    ii.   **Actual conflict:** But then, Marshall found that there was indeed an *actual conflict* between New York's action and a law of Congress: the federal licensing law, in Marshall's view, conflicted with the New York monopoly, and the New York monopoly had to fall under the ***Supremacy Clause.***

    iii.   **Effect of silence not adjudicated:** Thus Marshall never made any dispositive holding in *Gibbons* about the effect of congressional silence on the States' regulatory powers.

5. **State "police power" allowed:** But a few years after *Gibbons*, Marshall appeared to concede that a state could sometimes affect interstate commerce as an incidental consequence of its exercise of its "police powers." In *Willson v. The Black Bird Creek Marsh Co.*, 27 U.S. (2 Pet.) 244 (1829), Delaware authorized the construction of a dam on a creek which flowed into the Delaware River. Because the dam blocked navigation of the creek, the owners of a federally-licensed ship broke the dam in order to pass through the creek, and were sued by the dam's owners.

    a. **Holding:** Marshall held in favor of the dam company. First, he found that there was no actual conflict between Delaware's permitting the dam and any act of Congress. (Observe that Marshall seemed to retreat from the view he expressed in *Gibbons*, that congressional licensing of a vessel constituted congressional action which was specifically in conflict with a state's attempt to regulate the use of its waterways.) Then, he found that Delaware's action was not "repugnant to the power to regulate commerce in its dormant state."

        i.   **Rationale:** In so concluding, Marshall apparently reasoned that Delaware was not acting for the *purpose* of regulating interstate commerce, but rather, was attempting to protect the *health* of nearby inhabitants, and to increase the value of property adjoining the creek. Marshall implied, though he did not explicitly state, that a state's attempt to regulate matters of health or local property concerns would normally not be construed as interfering with the dormant federal commerce power.

        ii.   **Non-discriminatory:** Notice that Delaware's action in allowing the dam to be built was *not discriminatory* against interstate commerce; that is, both vessels travelling solely in intrastate traffic, as well as those engaged in interstate voyages, were equally barred from navigating the dammed-up creek. Absence of discrimination against interstate commerce has continued to be an important factor in those cases in which the Court has held that state regulation is permissible even though it affects interstate commerce.

E. **Rise of the "local" vs. "national" distinction:** The *Black Bird Creek* case, and other cases which followed it, turned mainly on the distinction between state regulation which principally governed interstate commerce (which was not allowed, even where Congress was silent) and state regulations which were construed to be "police power" regulations and therefore upheld (e.g., health and safety measures). However, the "regulation of commerce" and "police power" labels were more conclusory than analytical; if the Court wished to uphold the regulation, it termed it a "police power" one. See Tribe, p. 406.

1. **The *Cooley* case:** But in 1851, the Court embarked on a new way of looking at the dormant Commerce Clause problem, a view which continues to have great significance at present. Instead of focusing on whether the state was regulating commerce or using its "police powers," the Court focused on ***whether the subject matter being regulated was "local" or "national."*** In ***Cooley v. Board of Wardens of the Port of Philadelphia***, 53 U.S. (12 How.) 299 (1851), the Court affirmed a Pennsylvania law which required ships entering or leaving the port of Philadelphia to hire a local pilot.

   a. **"Local" vs. "national" problem:** The Court refused to hold either that Congress had an exclusive right to make regulations affecting interstate commerce, or that the states had a complete right to regulate interstate commerce in areas where Congress had remained silent. Instead, ***some but not all*** state regulation affecting interstate commerce was permissible. The states were free, the *Cooley* Court held, to regulate those aspects of interstate commerce that were of ***such a local nature as to require different treatment from state to state***. But the states could not regulate aspects of interstate commerce which, because of their nature, required a ***uniform national treatment*** (which only Congress could provide).

   b. **Application to facts of *Cooley*:** On the facts of *Cooley* itself, the Court found Pennsylvania's regulation was permissible, because pilotage in local harbors was a subject appropriate for local control (at least if that local control did not conflict with an explicit congressional action). In reaching this conclusion, the Court relied on a congressional statute adopted many years previously allowing pilotage to be regulated by the states.

2. **Aftermath of *Cooley*:** There were at least two major shortcomings to the *Cooley* doctrine. First, it was not at all easy to distinguish between those "subjects" that required uniform national regulation, and those that needed diverse local regulation. Secondly, and probably more importantly, the *Cooley* test, since it looked solely to the "subject" being regulated, did not consider how extensively the states' regulation ***impacted*** interstate commerce.

   a. **Significance of impact:** To remedy this second shortcoming, in post-*Cooley* years, the Court looked closely at the actual impact the state regulation had on interstate commerce. "***What the states did***, and ***not what subject they did it to***, came to be seen as the crucial question in deciding whether state action was compatible with the [C]ommerce [C]lause." Tribe, p. 408.

      i. **"Direct" vs. "indirect" impact:** In taking impact into account, the Court distinguished between "***direct***" and "***indirect***" impact on interstate commerce; a state regulation having direct impact on interstate commerce was not acceptable (even though Congress remained silent), but one having only an indirect impact was permissible.

   b. **Legacy of *Cooley*:** But during the time of this "direct" vs. "indirect" test, and up through to the present, the basic policy behind *Cooley* has remained in effect; the dormant Commerce Clause blocks ***some but not all*** state regulations which affect interstate commerce, and the resolution of particular cases turns on, roughly speaking, a balancing between the state interest in regulating local affairs and the national interest in uniformity. Tribe, p. 407.

F. Modern approach: The distinction between "direct" and "indirect" effects upon interstate commerce has proven to be no more satisfactory than the "effect on commerce" vs. "police power" distinction. In recent years, the Supreme Court has shifted to a more complex series of tests. A state regulation which affects interstate commerce must meet *each* of the following requirements in order to be upheld:

1. the regulation must pursue a *legitimate state end;*

2. the regulation must be *rationally related* to that legitimate end; and

3. the regulatory *burden* imposed by the state on interstate commerce, and any *discrimination* against interstate commerce, must be *outweighed* by the state's interest in enforcing its regulation. See Tribe, p. 408.

G. Application of the test: While these three requirements are somewhat vague, and the Court has tended to decide dormant Commerce Clause cases on very much of a case-by-case basis, there are at least some general observations that can be made about how the Court will apply each of the three tests:

1. **Meaning of "legitimate state end":** The Court has sharply distinguished between measures that are designed for promotion of health, safety and welfare objectives, on the one hand, and those that are designed for furtherance of *economic benefits*, on the other.

   a. **Health, safety and welfare:** If the state is acting to further health, safety or "general welfare" objectives, the Court is quite likely to hold that these objectives constitute "legitimate state ends." This is really the "police power" rationale which has been used by the Court ever since the *Black Bird Creek* case (*supra*, p. 86). (However, the Court will not accept at face value a state's contention that it is acting for these purposes, if there is substantial evidence that the state's real purpose is for economic advantage.)

   b. **Economic advantage:** The Court is *much more skeptical* of a state regulatory scheme where the state's objective is to promote the *economic interests* of its *own residents*. Protection of a state's economic interests is generally *not considered to be a legitimate state objective*, where pursuit of that objective materially affects interstate commerce.

2. **Rational means to end:** The second requirement, that the means used have a *rational relation* to the (legitimate) end, usually has *less "bite"* than the first requirement. The Court has been fairly careful not to substitute its judgment for that of the legislature in determining whether the regulation is a good way of attaining the end. A mere "rational relation" between means and end is *all* that is required; it is *not* required that the means used be the *best* way of achieving that end, or the way which least affects interstate commerce.

   a. **Deference to legislative fact finding:** In judging whether there is a requisite "rational relation," the Court will also give *due deference to any "facts" found by the state legislature*; that is, the Court will not conduct its own *de novo* inquiry into the facts.

b. **Similarity to review of Congress' actions:** In general, the Court's role is similar to the one it follows when evaluating whether an act of Congress falls within the commerce power (*supra*, p. 33).

3. **Balancing test:** Once the first two tests (legitimate end, and rationally-related means) have been met, the Court generally performs a rough *"balancing" test*, but one skewed towards a finding of constitutionality. "Where the statute regulates even-handedly to effectuate a legitimate local public interest, and its effects on interstate commerce are only incidental, it will be upheld unless the burden imposed on such commerce is *clearly excessive* in relation to the putative local benefits." *Pike v. Bruce Church, Inc.*, 397 U.S. 137 (1970). Thus in the case of legislation that is non-discriminatory (even if somewhat burdensome to interstate commerce), the state regulation achieves a *presumption of constitutionality*. But this presumption can be overcome by a *clear showing* that the national interest in uniformity or in free commerce outweighs the state benefit.

   a. **Less-restrictive alternatives:** In performing this balancing test, the Court has sometimes considered not only the objectives which the state is pursuing, but also the *necessity of the means* which the state has used to achieve this objective: if the objective could have been achieved by means *less burdensome* (or less discriminatory) to interstate commerce, the Court is more likely to find that the national interest in free commerce outweighs the state's interest. See Tribe, pp. 426-27.

      i. *Dean Milk* **case:** For instance, in *Dean Milk Co. v. City of Madison*, 340 U.S. 349 (1951) (discussed *infra*, p. 93), local regulations preventing importation of milk were struck down. Even though the state's objective (protection of residents against adulterated milk) was permissible, and the regulatory scheme (prohibiting importation so that only regularly-inspected local plants could sell milk) was rationally related to that objective, the safety objective could have been achieved by less burdensome means (e.g., sending of inspectors to out-of-state pasteurization plants to make quality checks, at the out-of-state producers' expense).

   b. **"Local" vs. "national" subject matter:** Recall the "local" vs. "national" distinction made by the *Cooley* case (*supra*, pp. 87-87). Although this distinction is no longer explicitly made in Supreme Court cases, it is implicit in the balancing process: if the matter being regulated is overwhelmingly of local concern, it is much more likely that the state interest in controlling its own affairs will be found to outweigh the national interest in uniformity and free commerce. Tribe. p. 437.

4. **Scope of following discussion:** The remainder of our treatment of state regulation and the dormant Commerce Clause is organized according to the type of regulation being pursued by the state. Five major subject areas are considered: (1) regulation of transportation; (2) regulation of incoming trade; (3) regulation of outgoing trade (including exportation of scarce resources); (4) attempts to compel out-of-staters to perform business activities within the state; and (5) regulation of the environment.

H. **Regulation of transportation:** When states have regulated the *instrumentalities* of interstate commerce (generally, *railroads* and *highways*), they have usually done so in the name of public safety objectives, rather than to benefit local economic interests. Therefore, the existence of a legitimate state objective is generally not in doubt, and the Supreme Court's scrutiny of such measures has usually focused on the second and third of the tests listed above (i.e., rational relation between the means and the safety objective, and balancing benefit to the state against burden on commerce).

1. **Absence of discrimination as factor:**   The Court has been much more likely to find that a transportation regulation does not violate the dormant Commerce Clause where the evidence is that it is *not discriminatory* against interstate commerce, either in *intent* or in *effect*. That is, even though the measure may create burdens on interstate commerce, if *similar burdens are created on intrastate activities*, the Court is likely to take the position that in-state political processes supply a sufficient check against abuse.

    a. *Barnwell* **case:**   For instance, in *South Carolina State Highway Dept. v. Barnwell Bros., Inc.*, 303 U.S. 177 (1938), South Carolina prohibited the use on state highways of trucks wider than 90 inches or weighing more than 20,000 pounds. There was clear evidence that the vast majority of trucks used in interstate commerce exceeded one or both of these limitations, so the regulation clearly burdened interstate commerce.

        i. **Measure upheld in *Barnwell*:**   Yet the Supreme Court, in an opinion by Justice (later Chief Justice) Stone, *upheld the regulation* against Commerce Clause attack. The Court stressed that the regulations were *applicable to interstate and intrastate traffic alike*, and "[t]he fact that they affect alike shippers in interstate and intrastate commerce in large number within as well as without the state is a *safeguard against their abuse*. ... "

2. **Balancing test:**   Even where a transportation regulation pursues a legitimate state objective (e.g., public safety) in a rational manner, the Court will usually apply a *balancing test*, weighing the benefit to the state from the regulation against the burdens it places on interstate commerce. However, the Court has been reluctant to substitute its judgment for that of state legislatures; therefore, it has usually tried to perform this "balancing" in a way that is fairly deferential to state policies.

    a. **Slight safety improvement:**   Thus the balance has generally been struck in favor of interstate commerce interests and against state safety interests only where the regulation's contribution to safety is *so marginal* or *so speculative* that there is little doubt in the Court's mind that the safety interest is outweighed by the burdens on commerce.

3. **Look for discrimination before doing balancing test:**   A plaintiff attacking a transportation regulation on Commerce Clause grounds has a far greater chance of prevailing by showing *discrimination* against out-of-staters than by showing merely that the scheme's burdens outweigh its benefits. It seems probable that a majority of the present Supreme Court is now *unwilling* to use balancing, and will automatically *uphold* a transportation regulation, if the safety interests asserted by the state are more than "slight" or "problematic." Conversely, the Supreme Court remains very quick to strike down any transportation regulation that seems to the Court to be motivated by *discriminatory* or protectionist impulses. See, e.g., *Kassel v. Consolidated Freightways Corp.*, 450 U.S. 662 (1981) (Iowa statute prohibiting 65-foot-long trucks is struck down, but at most four members of the Court seem to use a balancing test, and the remainder decide the case based on whether there is a clear discriminatory purpose).

4. **Cumulative and contradictory burdens:**   A particular regulation, even though it may seem to be non-discriminatory and non-burdensome when viewed in isolation, may be part of a discriminatory or burdensome *mass* of regulations imposed by *many states*. This may occur either because many states impose regulations that *contradict* each other, or

even because many states impose regulations that are not contradictory, but that become burdensome if compliance with all is required. Such a set of multiple regulations is by nature discriminatory in effect against interstate commerce, since only those enterprises that do business in many states will suffer from this problem. The problem is especially likely to occur in the case of regulation of interstate transport.

a. Actual conflict: When an actual *conflict* between the regulations of two or more states is shown, the Court is likely to strike down at least one of the conflicting rules, on the grounds that the need for *national uniformity* outweighs the individual state's interest in regulating its own highways, railroads, etc.

Example: An Illinois statute requires trucks operating in that state to be equipped with contoured rear-fender mudguards. At least 45 other states which have mudguard requirements permit a straight, rather than contoured, mudguard, and one state (Arkansas) explicitly requires a straight mudguard. Thus a particular truck could not be operated in both Arkansas and Illinois (at least without re-welding a new mudguard onto it each time).

Held, the Illinois statute violates the dormant Commerce Clause. "This is one of those cases — few in number — where local safety measures that are nondiscriminatory place an unconstitutional burden on interstate commerce." If the Illinois mudguard were so clearly superior in safety to the straight mudguard, it might be the straight-mudguard regulations which would have to give way; but the safety advantage of the Illinois curved mudguard is far from clear. Therefore, it is Illinois which must conform. *Bibb v. Navajo Freight Lines, Inc.*, 359 U.S. 520 (1959).

b. Cumulative burden: *Bibb* involved, at least in part, an actual conflict between the regulations of two states. But even where no actual conflict exists, it may be the case that the differing regulations of two or more states may place a large *cumulative burden* on interstate commerce. In this situation, the Court is likely to strike down one or more of the measures.

Example: Suppose that many states each impose different limits on the length of trains. The train-length limits are not contradictory; a railroad can simply follow the shortest limit, and thus operate in all states with the same length trains. However, such national compliance with the rule of the most restrictive state would probably be held to be a violation of the Commerce Clause, because it gives the most restrictive state authority beyond its own borders. See *Southern Pacific Co. v. Arizona*, 325 U.S. 761 (1945), so holding.

5. Discriminatory intent or effect: It is vital to remember that, in any regulation of transportation (or other aspect of commerce), the existence of an *intent to discriminate* against interstate commerce, or even an unintended discriminatory effect, will make it dramatically more likely that the Court will strike the measure as violating the dormant Commerce Clause. See, e.g., *Kassel v. Consolidated Freightways Corp., supra* p. 90.

I. State barriers to incoming trade: Many cases have involved state regulations which, either intentionally or otherwise, place *barriers upon the importing of goods into the state*. As a general rule, the test to which these regulations will be subjected depends on the nature of the state interest being served:

1. **Protection of economy:** If the purpose of the regulation is to *protect in-state producers* from competing out-of-state commodities, or otherwise to *strengthen the local economy*, the Court will generally *strike the measure*, without even inquiring whether the benefit to the state outweighs the national interest in free commerce. N&R, pp. 295-296. Protection of local economic interest is thus viewed as an "illegitimate" aim, so that Test One of the three tests described *supra*, p. 88, is failed, and the inquiry goes no further.

   a. **Small size of discrimination irrelevant:** Even if the discrimination against out-of-state commodities is *small*, the Court will strike it down if it is motivated by a desire to protect in-state interests — the *mere fact* of discrimination, not the *magnitude* of it, is what counts.

2. **Health and safety regulations:** If, however, the state is in good faith pursuing *health* or *safety* objectives, then the Court will generally balance the benefit to the state against the burdens to interstate commerce. In conducting this balancing test, the degree to which the regulation has a discriminatory effect (even though an unintended one), and the extent to which less burdensome or less discriminatory alternatives are available, will be considered. *Id.* at 231.

3. ***Baldwin* case:** The classic illustration of an impermissible protection of local economic interests at the expense of interstate commerce is *Baldwin v. G.A.F. Seelig, Inc.*, 294 U.S. 511 (1935).

   a. **Facts of *Baldwin*:** *Baldwin* involved a New York attempt to set minimum prices to be paid by New York milk dealers to New York milk producers. The statute also prohibited retail sales in New York of out-of-state milk, if the milk had been purchased at a lower price than the one set for purchases within New York. The avowed purpose of the statute was to make sure that New York's farmers could earn an adequate income.

   b. **Act stricken:** The act was held unconstitutional by the Supreme Court, in an opinion by Justice Cardozo. The statute "set a barrier to traffic between one state and another as effective as if custom duties, equal to the price differential, had been laid upon the [goods]."

      i. **Danger of interstate rivalries:** Cardozo's opinion observed that "[i]f New York, in order to promote the economic welfare of her farmers, may guard them against competition with the cheaper prices of Vermont, the door has been opened to rivalries and reprisals that were meant to be averted by subjecting commerce between the states to the power of the nation. ... [The Constitution] was framed upon the theory that *the peoples of the several states must sink or swim together. ... "*

   c. **No political check:** Observe that the situation in *Baldwin* was one of those where *only* out-of-staters were burdened (at least directly). Thus the possibility of abuse was heightened by the fact that no strong constituency within New York was likely to fight against the regulation. (It is true that consumers might ultimately have ended up being burdened, by having to pay higher prices, but this was probably an indirect, camouflaged, effect. See N&R, p. 295-296.)

4. **Valid health objective not sufficient:** The New York regulation in *Baldwin, supra,* was clearly designed to foster the purely economic interests of New York residents. The Court is at least somewhat more sympathetic where the state regulation of incoming goods, while it burdens interstate commerce, is in good faith designed to protect the *safety or*

health of residents. But even in the case of such safety or health regulations, the Court will either implicitly or explicitly perform a *"balancing test,"* weighing the state's interest in its regulatory scheme against the national interest in unburdened, free-flowing interstate commerce. A crucial part of this balancing is often whether there are *less burdensome alternatives* which the state might have adopted.

a. **The *Dean Milk* case:** Thus in *Dean Milk Co. v. Madison*, 340 U.S. 349 (1951), the city of Madison, Wisconsin made it unlawful to sell any milk that had not been processed and bottled within five miles of the city. The city claimed (perhaps correctly) that the measure was not intended to discriminate against out-of-state milk producers, but was rather designed to permit inspection of pasteurization quality control so as to guard against adulterated milk. The regulation was attacked by an Illinois corporation which distributed milk in both Illinois and Wisconsin.

b. **Statute stricken:** The Supreme Court agreed that the Madison regulation unduly burdened interstate commerce. The Court conceded that the regulation might have been motivated by *bona fide* safety and health concerns. But the regulation nonetheless discriminated against interstate commerce (in the sense of a discriminatory *effect*). Nor did the fact that companies within Wisconsin, but more than five miles from Madison, were also discriminated against save the regulation from unduly burdening commerce, in the Court's view.

c. **Reasonable non-discriminatory alternatives:** The real crux of the Court's holding in *Dean Milk* was that *reasonable non-discriminatory alternatives*, which would have protected the local interest in unadulterated milk, *could have been implemented*. For instance, Madison could have sent its inspectors to out-of-state plants, and could have passed the cost onto the producers. Alternatively, Madison could have agreed to be bound by the standards of neighboring areas, provided that those standards were at least as high as Madison's own.

d. **Dissent:** Three Justices dissented, principally on the grounds that a good faith effort to promote local safety and health objectives should not be stricken merely because the Court believes that some less-burdensome alternative could produce as good a result.

5. **Intentional discrimination (the *Washington Apple* case):** Although the Court has occasionally stricken barriers to incoming trade that are not enacted for discriminatory purposes (e.g., the *Dean Milk* case), the Court is, as noted, much more likely to strike down a statute whose clear purpose is to *favor local economic interests* by discriminating against out-of-state interests. This is what really happened, for instance, in *Hunt v. Washington Apple Advertising Commission*, 432 U.S. 333 (1977).

a. **Facts of *Hunt*:** North Carolina required that all closed containers of apples shipped into or sold within the state bear the applicable U.S. grade or no grade at all. A group of Washington state apple growers attacked the North Carolina statute, since it prohibited the display in North Carolina of Washington's stringently-policed apple grades. The Washington manufacturers had to either obliterate the printed labels on containers shipped to North Carolina, or repack apples bound for North Carolina in special containers.

b. **Holding:** The Court found that the North Carolina statute unconstitutionally burdened interstate commerce. More significantly, it also *discriminated* against Washington growers, since it raised the costs of doing business for Washington producers but not North Carolina ones; Washington growers had to repack their apples or obliterate their labels, whereas North Carolina growers were unaffected. Furthermore, whereas North Carolina had no grading requirements at all, Washington state had very strict ones; the North Carolina statute hurt Washington by stripping from it the competitive advantages it had earned through its rigorous and well-known inspection and grading system.

    i.   **Intentional:** The Court attached substantial weight to the fact that the North Carolina scheme was apparently ***intentionally*** discriminatory. There was evidence that it was the North Carolina apple growers who were responsible for the passage of the statute. Also, the state's declared purpose for the statute (to safeguard consumers against fraud) was suspect, since: (1) the statute applied only to the labels of closed shipping containers, and retail sales are generally not made while the apples are still in their shipping containers; and (2) the state permitted the sale of apples with no grading at all.

6. **Discrimination by city against out-of-towners:** Suppose a ***city*** or ***county*** tries to protect its own local economic interests by discriminating not only against out-of-***state*** producers, but also out-of-town producers in the ***same state***. Is it open to the city/county to argue, "The fact that we discriminate against other in-state but non-local producers shows we're not discriminating against interstate commerce"? The short answer is ***"no"***: if the locality is protecting its own local interests at the expense of out-of-staters, the protectionism is not saved by the fact that it also comes at the expense of in-staters who are not local.

7. **Facially neutral statutes and the meaning of "discrimination"** (***Exxon v. Maryland***): A statute which is evenhanded on its face may nonetheless turn out to be ***disproportionately burdensome*** to some or all out-of-state businesses. Where this disproportionate impact is truly ***accidental***, and does not directly derive from the fact that the burdened firms are out-of-staters, the Court will normally ***uphold*** the statute. This is what happened in ***Exxon Corp. v. Governor of Maryland***, 437 U.S. 117 (1978).

    a. **Facts of *Exxon* case:** Maryland passed a law prohibiting oil producers or refiners from operating retail gas stations in Maryland. The law was enacted because of evidence that gas stations operated by producers and refiners had received preferential treatment during the 1973 oil shortage. Since no gas is produced or refined in Maryland, the rule against vertically-integrated operations ***affected out-of-state companies exclusively.*** Conversely, the vast majority (but not all) of the non-integrated retailers, who were not harmed and were probably helped by the statute, were in-state business people.

        i.   **Statute attacked:** Exxon and several other out-of-state integrated oil companies sued. They made a three-pronged Commerce Clause argument: (1) that the measure impermissibly discriminated against interstate commerce; (2) that the measure unduly burdened such commerce; and (3) that because of the nationwide nature of oil marketing, only the federal government may regulate retail gas sales.

    b. **Statute upheld:** The Court upheld the statute against each of these attacks.

        i.   **No discrimination:** First, the opinion (by Justice Stevens) held that the statute did not discriminate against interstate commerce. Most significantly, not all out-of-state companies were affected by the statute; Sears Roebuck, for instance, was an out-of-state company which was selling gas at retail within Maryland, yet was not involved in refining it and was therefore not affected by the statute. The mere fact that the entire burden of the statute fell on *some* out-of-state companies was insufficient to establish that "interstate commerce" was discriminated against.

ii. **Not burdened:** Similarly, the Court found that interstate commerce was not impermissibly burdened by the statute. The opinion conceded that the statute might cause sales volume to shift from refiner-operated stations to independent dealers. But, the Court held, the Commerce Clause "protects the interstate market, not particular interstate firms, from prohibitive or burdensome regulation." Furthermore, the Court noted, in all probability the same percentage of gasoline would come from out-of-state suppliers after the statute as before it (i.e., 100%), so that the flow of goods in the interstate market would not be decreased.

iii. **Not preempted:** Finally, the Court quickly dismissed the contention that because the market for gasoline is nationwide, no state may regulate its retail marketing. The dormant Commerce Clause may preempt an entire field from state regulation only when **lack of national uniformity** would impede the flow of interstate goods. What the plaintiffs were complaining of here was not a lack of uniformity, but rather that many or all of the states would pass exactly the sort of divestiture law that Maryland did. Thus the problem was not one of national uniformity.

8. **Personal mobility:** Commerce Clause analysis has also been used to strike down state limits on *individuals'* ability to *migrate* from state to state. Thus in *Edwards v. California*, 314 U.S. 160 (1941), the Court invalidated a law making it a misdemeanor to bring into California an indigent non-resident. (The law was aimed at stemming the flow of "Okies" during the Dust Bowl years.) A majority found that the law was an unconstitutional burden on commerce. (Four Justices concurred, but on the basis of the Privileges or Immunities Clause of the Fourteenth Amendment, discussed *infra*, p. 412.)

J. State barriers to outgoing trade: Another important group of Commerce Clause cases involves attempts by a state to regulate or restrict the *export* to other states of agricultural products, scarce natural resources, or other commodities. The cases in this area are hard to reconcile. However, the following general observations may be made:

1. **"Local" vs. "national" subject:** The *Cooley* distinction (*supra*, pp. 87-87) between subject areas of primarily *"local"* concern and "national" concern continues to be of importance in the export area. If the subject matter being regulated is of *primarily local concern*, and the effect on interstate commerce is *incidental*, the regulation is fairly likely to be sustained, even if it is motivated by local economic concerns rather than public safety and health purposes. However, all of this assumes that the regulation does *not discriminate*, in either purpose or effect, against interstate commerce (although it may burden that commerce).

2. **Discrimination important:** The presence or absence of *discrimination* continues to be an important factor in the outgoing trade cases, as in the other areas we have already examined. If the burden of a particular regulation falls on in-state and out-of-state persons alike, the Court is much more likely to sustain it than if the burden falls more heavily on out-of-staters (whether by design or by accident). This is especially true where the state interest being pursued is an *economic,* rather than public health or safety, one.

Example: New York refuses to give a Massachusetts milk distributor a license to operate an additional milk receiving station in New York (he already has three). The state reasons that such a new receiving station will divert additional New York milk to Massachusetts consumers. The state argues that such a diversion will: (1) dangerously increase the costs, and decrease the volume, of other distributors (who will lose their suppliers to the new plant); and (2) thereby make it likely that there will be a shortage of milk for the local New York market during peak seasons.

Held, the license refusal violates the Commerce Clause. What New York is seeking here is economic advantage, not really the health or safety of the consuming public. This goal of economic security may not be pursued by discriminating against other states. If New York is allowed to withhold its milk from the interstate markets, fatal interstate rivalries will develop. (E.g., Michigan might provide that automobiles cannot be taken out of that state until local dealers' demands are fully met; Ohio might then refuse to export tires to retaliate for Michigan's auto monopoly.) *H.P. Hood & Sons v. DuMond*, 336 U.S. 525 (1949).

3. **Embargo of natural resources:** The most significant, and troublesome, of the barrier-to-outgoing-trade cases are those in which a state attempts to *prevent exportation of scarce natural resources*, either to keep them from being used at all right now, or to restrict their use to in-state residents.

   a. **Strict scrutiny approach:** Courts give relatively *strict scrutiny* to measures which, whether by design or by accident, keep such scarce resources from moving interstate. This strict review is often imposed even where the state's interest is a valid conservation or ecological one, rather than a crude desire to keep economic benefits in-state.

   b. **Less discriminatory alternatives:** A key feature of this stricter scrutiny is that the regulation will generally be upheld only if *less-discriminatory alternatives* for achieving the state's interest are unavailable.

      Example: Oklahoma bars the export for sale of any minnows which are procured from the natural waters of the state. (The statute does not apply to hatchery-bred minnows.)

      Held, the statute violates the Commerce Clause. The statute discriminates on its face against out-of-state commerce. Therefore, the burden falls on Oklahoma to justify it under a balancing test, and the state must show that non-discriminatory alternatives are not adequate to preserve the state interest. Here, regardless of the unquestioned validity of the state's interest in conservation and protection of wild animals, no attempt to use non-discriminatory measures was made. (For instance, the state could have set limits on the number of minnows which could be taken by any dealer, rather than completely prohibiting export of minnows, and placing no restrictions at all on capture of minnows for in-state sale.) *Hughes v. Oklahoma*, 441 U.S. 322 (1979).

K. **Local-processing requirements:** The Supreme Court has been especially suspicious of state regulations which pressure out-of-state businesses to *perform certain operations* within the state. Most often, these regulations require that agricultural products or natural resources produced in the state also be *processed* in the state.

   Example: Arizona requires that all Arizona cantaloupes be packed in Arizona. The regulation is applied to prevent a California company from shipping uncrated cantaloupes from its Arizona ranch to its California packing plant. The purpose of the requirement is to enhance the reputation of (and demand for) Arizona's cantaloupes, which are of high quality.

Held, statute invalid. The state's interest in enhancing the reputation of Arizona cantaloupes is legitimate (though tenuous). However, this interest is clearly outweighed by the national interest in unencumbered commerce. "[T]he Court has viewed with particular suspicion state statutes requiring business operations to be performed in the home State that could more efficiently be performed elsewhere. Even where the State is pursuing a clearly legitimate local interest, this particular burden on commerce has been declared to be virtually *per se* illegal." *Pike v. Bruce Church, Inc.*, 397 U.S. 137 (1970).

1. **Local processing of garbage:** A state or local government may not even require that its own *garbage* be *locally processed*, as a result of *C & A Carbone, Inc. v. Clarkstown*, 511 U.S. 383 (1994). Such a local-processing requirement discriminates against firms that could have done the processing out-of-state.

   a. **Facts:** In *Carbone*, the town of Clarkstown enacted a "flow control" ordinance. The practical effect of the ordinance was to require that any trash generated in the town be taken to a particular "waste transfer station," which charged a tonnage fee for all trash it processed.

      i. **How it came about:** The town had been required by the state to set up the waste transfer station. Instead of building the station itself, the town induced a local entrepreneur to build it, and promised the entrepreneur a certain volume of trash to process. The town then required residents to take their trash there, as a means of delivering the guaranteed volume.

   b. **Holding:** The Court held that the flow control ordinance violated the Commerce Clause. The majority described the ordinance as a "local processing ordinance," whose purpose and effect was to hoard trash processing jobs (and the income from those jobs) within the town. The ordinance thus discriminated against interstate commerce — it deprived out-of-state firms of the opportunity to do the processing. As a discriminatory "protectionist" statute, the ordinance was virtually *per se* invalid.

      i. **Consequence to in-staters irrelevant:** To the majority, it did not matter that lots of *in-state* trash processors were also deprived of the ability to process Clarkstown's trash. A government-authorized monopoly was no less discriminatory against out-of-state commerce than would be a more typical ordinance protecting all local producers against all out-of-state producers, such as the ordinance struck down in *Pike, supra*.

   c. ***Carbone* not applicable where government owns the facility:** But *Carbone* does *not* apply where government awards a monopoly to a *government-owned facility* rather than the type of privately-owned facility at issue in *Carbone*. See *United Haulers Ass'n v. Oneida-Herkimer Solid Waste Management Auth.*, 550 U.S. 330 (2007).

      i. **Facts of *United Haulers*:** *United Haulers* involved a flow-control ordinance virtually indistinguishable from the one in *Carbone*, except that the garbage-transfer station that all residents were required to use was owned by a *public agency* rather than a private company as in *Carbone*. The government monopoly resulted in residents' being required to pay higher fees for trash removal.

   ii. Preference upheld: A majority of the court believed that this distinction between private and public ownership of the transfer station made a critical difference – unlike in *Carbone*, the majority in *United Haulers* concluded that the counties' "all trash must be brought to our facility" ordinance did not discriminate against interstate commerce, and did not violate the dormant commerce clause. The majority thought that the public/private distinction was constitutionally significant for two reasons:

     ❑ First, regulations by which government takes a monopoly on the performance of an activity — especially in an area where the function has been a "traditionally government activity" — raise *fewer fears of protectionism* than where government favors a local privately-owned business. For one thing, any higher costs from the government-owned monopoly are "likely to fall upon the very people who voted for the [monopoly-causing] laws," whereas in the usual discrimination-in-favor-of-local-businesses scenario much of the burden of the regulation falls on out-of-staters who cannot vote.

     ❑ Second, if the traditional strict scrutiny were applied to government regulations that conferred a monopoly on government, the result would be an "unprecedented and unbounded *interference by the courts* with state and local government." Local voters here chose the government to be the exclusive provider of waste management services, and the dormant commerce clause should not be used as a "roving license for federal courts to decide what activities are appropriate for state and local government to undertake, and what activities must be the province of private market competition."

   iii. Significance: So *Carbone* remains in force — and bars government from preferring a local privately-owned business over out-of-staters, at least with respect to trash processing – but under *United Haulers* government is permitted to go into the waste management business itself and then to require that all citizens use the government-owned facility.

L. Environmental regulation: States' attempts to *control their environment* have sometimes been attacked as violative of the Commerce Clause. As the result of a case on garbage disposal, it appears that the Court will now strictly scrutinize any discriminatory or protectionist state action, even if it was enacted in furtherance of environmental or other *non-economic* motives. Only if *no less-discriminatory alternatives* are available will the Court uphold such a statute.

   1. Summary: To put it another way, a state may no longer maintain or improve its environment at the expense of its neighbors' environmental or economic interests, unless no reasonable alternative is available.

   2. The *New Jersey Garbage* Case: The garbage disposal case was *City of Philadelphia v. New Jersey*, 437 U.S. 617 (1978). The case involved a New Jersey statute prohibiting the importing of most solid or liquid waste into the state. The law was enacted in response to the use of New Jersey landfills for disposal of waste from cities in Pennsylvania and New York. Several New Jersey operators and out-of-state users of the landfill sites (including

Philadelphia) sued to have the statute invalidated on the ground that it discriminated against interstate commerce.

a. **Statute stricken:** The Supreme Court (by a 7-2 vote) struck the statute as violative of the Commerce Clause. The majority opinion, by Justice Stewart, concluded that the law was "basically a protectionist measure," rather than a way of resolving legitimate local concerns.

    i. **Purpose unclear:** The opinion declined to decide whether the main purpose of the statute was to protect the state's environment and its inhabitants' health and safety (as New Jersey claimed) or to stabilize the costs of waste disposal for New Jersey residents at the expense of out-of-state interests (as the plaintiffs claimed).

    ii. **Discriminatory means:** It was unnecessary to decide this issue because "the evil of protectionism can reside in *legislative means* as well as legislative ends." Since New Jersey had chosen a discriminatory means of furthering its objectives (whatever those objectives were), it was a protectionist measure. That is, "it imposes on out-of-state commercial interests the full burden of conserving the State's remaining landfill space. … [It is an] attempt by one State to isolate itself from a problem common to many by erecting a barrier against the movement of interstate trade."

b. **Per se rule of invalidity:** In striking the statute, the Court suggested, though it did not explicitly state, that the same "virtually *per se* rule of invalidity" which had previously been applied in cases of protectionism should be extended to non-economic regulations such as the one at hand. See 92 HARV. L. REV. 57.

c. **Quarantine laws distinguished:** The Court's opinion attempted to distinguish *quarantine* laws (i.e., laws preventing the importation of diseased or otherwise dangerous livestock or goods into a state), which had often been upheld by the Court. Such quarantine laws banned the importation of materials which, *at the moment of importation*, were hazardous. Here, by contrast, the solid waste whose importation was prohibited by New Jersey endangered health (if at all) only when buried in landfill sites, by which time there was no valid reason to differentiate between out-of-state and domestic garbage. *Id.* at 54.

d. **Dissent:** A two-Justice dissent, authored by Justice Rehnquist, contended that the quarantine law cases supported the New Jersey law. He saw no reason why New Jersey "may ban the importation of items whose movement risks contagion, but cannot ban the importation of items which, although they may be transported into the State without undue hazard, will then simply pile up in an ever increasing danger to the public's health and safety." The dissent found it reasonable for New Jersey to guard against a worsening of its own waste disposal problem by banning the addition of out-of-state waste.

e. **Criticism of quarantine distinction:** The majority's distinguishing of the quarantine cases does not seem convincing. One commentator has suggested what he contends to be a better way of distinguishing between the quarantine and waste-disposal situations: whereas the typical quarantine case had a limited economic impact (e.g., a few out-of-state cattlemen were prevented from transporting their cattle), waste disposal is "an integral part of modern industrial processes," and raises much more serious problems, so that " '[T]he peoples of the several states must sink or swim together … ' even in their collective garbage." Tribe, pp. 425-26.

3. **Taxation of out-of-state waste:**   Some states have responded to the *Philadelphia* case by trying to *tax* out-of-state waste rather than forbidding it. If the state really taxes out-of-state and in-state waste *equally*, then there is probably no violation of the Commerce Clause. But the Court is extremely vigilant to ensure that any such taxing scheme is *not discriminatory*. For instance, a state may not impose a flat *per-ton* tax on out-of-state waste, and then claim that this tax "compensates" for general income-tax revenues that are collected from in-staters and used to defray the cost of in-state waste. See *Oregon Waste Systems, Inc. v. Dep't of Environmental Quality*, 511 U.S. 93 (1994).

4. **Non-protectionist legislation:**   Although ecological legislation which is purposefully discriminatory appears to be virtually "*per se* invalid" under the *Philadelphia* case, this is not true for environmental acts which merely *burden* (without discriminating against) interstate commerce. For instance, the Supreme Court sustained a state law which banned non-returnable milk containers made of plastic (but permitted non-returnable milk containers made of other substances, principally cardboard cartons), in *Minnesota v. Clover Leaf Creamery Co.*, 449 U.S. 456 (1981).

   a. **Burden on out-of-state firms:**   The Court sustained the statute even though the plastic used for milk cartons was made solely by non-Minnesota firms, whereas pulpwood, used for making the cardboard containers, was a major Minnesota product. The Court concluded that the statute was not simple "protectionist" legislation camouflaged in a recitation of environmental purposes.

M. **State as purchaser or subsidizer:**   All of the cases considered so far involved state action that was purely regulatory. But suppose the state acts as a *market participant*, spending money to run a proprietary enterprise, or to subsidize private businesses. Is the state barred from discriminating against interstate commerce, or unduly burdening it, as it would be if its actions were solely regulatory? Where the state acts as a market participant, dormant Commerce Clause analysis will *not* be applied, and the state may favor local citizens over out-of-state economic interests.

   Example 1: Maryland, in an effort to rid the state of abandoned cars, purchases crushed auto hulks at an above-market price. The state refuses to buy hulks from out-of-state sellers. *Held,* Maryland did not violate the Commerce Clause. The Commerce Clause simply does not apply when a state, in its role as participant in a market, favors its own citizens. *Hughes v. Alexandria Scrap Corp.*, 426 U.S. 794 (1976).

   Example 2: A state-owned cement plant favors in-state customers in times of shortage. *Held,* this preference does not violate the Commerce Clause. When states act as proprietors, they are free of dormant Commerce Clause limitations. *Reeves v. Stake*, 447 U.S. 429 (1980).

1. **Summary of market-participant exception:** So the *"market participant"* exception to the dormant Commerce Clause is pretty *narrow*: it applies only where state or local government, acting as a market participant, *chooses to deal with in-staters rather than out-of-staters in direct transactions.* So a government-owned entity may *prefer in-state buyers* when government sells, *may prefer in-state sellers* when government buys, and the like.

a. Does not affect state's acts as regulator: Importantly, the market-participant exception does *not* permit the state to *regulate* in a way that discriminates against out-of-staters, even if the state is *also* acting as market participant.

   i. Effect on "downstream" participants: For example, the market-participant exception does not apply where the state tries to use its market clout to regulate transactions *involving parties that are not dealing directly* with the state-owned market-participant entity. Thus a state market-participant cannot, for instance, try to regulate *"downstream"* from its own transactions, by saying to its customers, "We'll sell to you [or buy from you] only if you, in turn, discriminate against out-of-staters."

   Example: Alaska sells timber from state-owned lands at below-market prices. The state requires each buyer to promise that it will process the timber inside Alaska before the timber is exported. A non-Alaska firm with no Alaska processing facilities attacks the local-processing rule as violative of the dormant Commerce Clause. The state defends on the grounds that it is a "market participant" that is merely selling a commodity it owns.

   Held, for the plaintiff. The market-participant exception does not apply here, for several reasons. One reason is that the exception will apply only where the effects of the state's terms are *limited to the particular market in which the state is participating*, not to a broader one. Here, the state is trying to engage in "downstream regulation" of the timber-processing market (i.e., trying to affect the conduct of parties with whom the state is not dealing directly), and the market-participant exception does not apply to immunize that downstream regulation from dormant Commerce Clause attack. *South-Central Timber Development, Inc. v. Wunnicke*, 467 U.S. 82 (1984).

b. Lesser scrutiny where state has own market-participating entity: However, even where the market-participant exception does not directly apply, the fact that the state's regulation takes the form of a decision to *conduct the entire activity via its own government-owned entity* seems to make it more likely that the regulation will *pass* commerce clause scrutiny, as the result of a 2007 decision. In *United Haulers Ass'n v. Oneida-Herkimer Solid Waste Management Auth.* (discussed more fully *supra*, p. 97), the Court found no dormant commerce clause violation where a county required that all residents have their trash processed at a county-owned transfer station. The majority did not rely on the market-participation exception. But the fact that the government was electing to perform the entire activity at its own facility rather than preferring a privately-owned one made the critical difference for the majority, mainly because the majority believed that cases in which government takes over a function entirely are less likely to be motivated by protectionism than where government prefers local businesses over out of staters.

   i. Consequence: So even though the market-participant exception does not expressly apply where the government is wearing a "regulator" hat rather than making business-owner-type decisions about with whom it will deal, *United Haulers* suggests that the government's regulations will get gentler review when those regulation are in a domain in which the state has chosen to act as a market participant. That's especially true if the area is one — like waste management — that is a domain in which governments have ***traditionally*** performed the market activity in question.

2. **Privileges and Immunities attack:**   In any case in which out-of-staters are discriminated against by the state acting as a "market participant," the state's actions may be vulnerable to an attack based on the ***Privileges and Immunities Clause*** of Article IV ("The Citizens of each State shall be entitled to all the Privileges and Immunities of Citizens in the several States.") The Supreme Court has held that there is no "market participant" exception to the Privileges and Immunities Clause. See *United Building and Construction Trades Council v. Camden, infra,* p. 119, holding that this Clause might be violated by an ordinance providing that at least 40% of any work force on a city-funded construction project must consist of city residents.

II. STATE TAXATION OF INTERSTATE COMMERCE

A. **Compared with regulation:**   Just as state regulation may violate the dormant Commerce Clause, so may certain types of state *taxation*. This is most likely to happen where a state tries to tax operations of a business that operates in more than one state. Many of the same issues are involved in the two situations; for instance, a tax may be stricken on the grounds that it discriminates against interstate commerce, or on the grounds that an interstate business is being subjected to unfair cumulative taxation.

B. **Limited scope:**   The Supreme Court has decided literally hundreds of state taxation cases involving the Commerce Clause, and most of the decisions are confusing and hard to reconcile. No attempt will be made here to give full treatment to this subject area. Instead, a few of the general principles which the Court has applied will be discussed.

C. **General principles:**   For a multi-state company to succeed in a challenge to a particular state tax, it will generally have to make one of the three following showings: (1) that the company's business activity does not have a ***sufficient connection*** with the taxing state; (2) that the tax ***discriminates against interstate commerce***; or (3) that the tax has led to an unfair ***cumulative burden*** (e.g., it is not fairly apportioned as between the company's in-state and out-of-state activities, or it is unrelated to services rendered by the taxing state).

D. **Minimum contacts:**   Not only because of the Commerce Clause, but also because of the ***Due Process Clause*** of the Fourteenth Amendment, a non-domiciliary company may not be taxed ***at all*** unless there are "***minimum contacts***" between the company and the taxing state. This is a threshold matter, which must be resolved even before examining whether the particular tax involved is equitable.

> **Example:** Iowa has a net income tax, which it applies to corporations. In the case of a corporation doing business in more than one state, the percentage of corporate net income attributable to Iowa (and thus taxed by Iowa) is determined by taking the ratio of Iowa sales to total gross national sales. ABC Corp., a New Jersey corporation, sends one salesman into Iowa for one week during the year; the salesman makes sales in Iowa equal to one-half of one percent of the company's total national gross sales for that year. The Supreme Court would probably hold that ABC's contacts with Iowa are so minimal that Iowa may not tax the company's net income ***at all***. Thus even though the apportion formula (Iowa sales as a percentage of total national sales) may be a fair

way of apportioning net income, no tax could be levied against ABC. This would be true as a matter of both the Commerce and Due Process Clauses.

1. **Not too much bite:** The requirement of "minimum contacts" does not have too much practical "bite" in the context of state taxation of interstate commerce — the dormant Commerce Clause (insofar as it bans both discrimination and undue burdening of commerce) usually is much more likely to lead to invalidation of a tax scheme than is the lack of minimum contacts. Also, any tax that fell on an out-of-stater who did not have minimum contacts would probably also represent a discrimination against or unfair burden on interstate commerce.

E. No discrimination: The state may not tax in a way which ***discriminates*** against interstate commerce, i.e., in a way which unjustifiably benefits local commerce at the expense of out-of-state commerce. Tribe, pp. 453-54.

1. **Facially discriminatory statutes:** Sometimes, the taxing statute can be seen ***on its face*** to be discriminatory. For instance, if the taxing scheme explicitly charges a ***higher tax rate*** (regardless of the type of tax) with respect to goods manufactured outside the state than for those manufactured within it, this will probably be found to be discriminatory against interstate commerce, and therefore *per se* violative of the Commerce Clause.

2. **Burdensome but facially neutral statutes:** Even a *facially neutral* statute, however, may nonetheless place a ***greater burden*** on interstate businesses than on intrastate ones; in such a situation, the tax will be ***stricken*** as discriminatory.

    a. **"Drumming" license fees:** For instance, many states and towns at one time or another have exacted license fees for so-called "drumming," i.e., the ***door-to-door selling*** of items which are to be delivered at some future time (e.g., magazine subscriptions). While such licensing schemes theoretically apply to interstate and intrastate businesses alike, an interstate business is much more likely to make its sales through door-to-door solicitation than is a local business (which can sell out of a store or office). Thus such drummer licensing schemes have generally been stricken.

F. Cumulative burdens: Even a non-discriminatory tax may nonetheless violate the Commerce Clause if the taxpaying company can show that the taxing scheme would expose it to ***unfair cumulative taxation***, and thus unduly ***burden*** interstate commerce.

1. **Administrative complexity:** The main way in which taxation may unduly burden interstate commerce is if it would create undue ***administrative complexity*** for the taxpayer conducting interstate operations. The Supreme Court begins to look at a tax provision by saying to the taxing jurisdiction, in effect, "If we let you do it, we'll have to let every jurisdiction do it." If having all jurisdictions enact the same tax scheme would be administratively unworkable, the tax will be struck down even though the burden imposed by the particular jurisdiction whose tax is being considered at the moment would not be unworkable.

    Example: North Dakota attempts to require all mail order merchants who send mail into North Dakota to collect a North Dakota use tax on sales made to North Dakota buyers, even if the merchant has no employees in the state and conducts no direct business operations there.

    Held, this taxing scheme violates the Commerce Clause, because it unduly burdens interstate commerce. If the scheme here were upheld, "similar obligations might be imposed by the Nation's 6,000-plus taxing jurisdictions ... 'Many variations in rates of tax, in allowable exemptions, and in administrative and record-keeping requirements could entangle [a mail-order house] in a virtual welter of complicated obligations.' " *Quill Corp. v. North Dakota*, 504 U.S. 298 (1992).

   a. **"Substantial nexus" requirement:**   To prevent the problem of thousands of jurisdictions all taxing the same interstate business, the Court has required that there be a *"substantial nexus"* between the taxpayer and the jurisdiction that is imposing the tax. *Quill Corp. v. North Dakota, supra.* (The mere sending of advertising mail into the jurisdiction does not constitute the required "substantial nexus," *Quill* holds.)

III. CONGRESSIONAL ACTION — PREEMPTION AND CONSENT

A. **Federal preemption generally:**   The aspect of the Commerce Clause that we have been examining thus far in this chapter is its "dormant" aspect, i.e., its force as a negative implication where Congress has not acted. A different, but surprisingly similar, set of problems is presented when Congress (or any branch of the federal government) *does exercise its power*: To what extent does this exercise of valid federal power restrict what the states may do?

   1. **Supremacy Clause:**   If there is a conflict between federal law and state law, the resolution is clear: the *state law is simply invalid*. The *Supremacy Clause* of Article VI provides that in case of a conflict, state law must yield to federal law. Federal law is said to have "*preempted*" state law.

   2. **Express vs implied preemption:** Federal preemption of state law is usually described as falling into two main categories: *"express"* preemption and *"implied"* preemption:

   ❑   *Express* preemption occurs when a federal law *specifically* (i.e., "expressly") says that it preempts state or local law. Chemerinsky, p. 434.

   ❑   *Implied* preemption occurs when Congress does *not* expressly state that it intends to preempt state or local law, but *manifests an intent* to do so. *Id.*

   After a brief discussion of express preemption, we'll spend most of our time on implied preemption, which is by far the more complicated of the two categories.

B. **Express preemption:** Congress sometimes, in enacting a statute, takes the trouble to state explicitly that the statute is intended to preempt some area of state or local law. That is, Congress says, "In the area of [X], the only governing law shall be federal law." This is *"express preemption."* As long as the federal statute is validly enacted (e.g., it falls within one of Congress' enumerated powers, such as the commerce power), any state or local law that falls *within the zone* intended by Congress to be *exclusively federal* will be invalid under the Supremacy Clause.

   Example: The federal Employee Retirement Income Security Act (ERISA) says that it "supersede[s] any and all State laws insofar as they ... relate to any employee benefit plan[.]" 29 U.S.C. §1144(a). If a state purports to regulate some aspect of an employee benefit plan, the state regulation will be valid as a violation of the Supremacy Cause. That's true even though the state regulation may be perfectly consistent with ERISA.

C. **Implied preemption:** Most preemption cases involve *"implied preemption,"* i.e., situations in which Congress has not explicitly said that it intends to preempt state or local law, but in which the ***structure or purpose*** of the congressional action suggests that Congress intended to displace non-federal law.

The Supreme Court has identified ***two main types*** of implied preemption:

❑ "***field*** preemption" and

❑ "***conflicts*** preemption"

See *Gade v. National Solid Wastes Management*, 505 U.S. 88 (1992).

We'll look at each type of implied preemption separately.

1. **"Field preemption":** *"**Field preemption**"* occurs "where the scheme of federal regulation is ***so pervasive*** as to make reasonable the inference that Congress ***left no room*** for the states to supplement it." *Gade, supra.* In other words, field preemption occurs where Congress has indicated that it intends to ***"occupy the entire field"*** in question.

   Example: In 1940, Congress passes the Alien Registration Act, which requires aliens 14 and over to register with the federal Immigration and Naturalization Service, be finger-printed, and obey other restrictions. The prior year, Pennsylvania passed a state alien registration act which required all aliens to register with a state agency, and to receive and carry a state-issued alien identification card.

   Held, the state alien registration law is preempted by the federal one. The federal government's special role in immigration and foreign relations, and Congress' decision to enact a "single integrated and all-embracing system" for alien registration, make it clear that Congress intended to displace any state requirements that aliens register. *Hines v. Davidowitz*, 312 U.S. 52 (1941).

   a. **Congressional intent is paramount:** In field-preemption, as with other preemption categories, the issue is always one of ***congressional intent***; Congress could, if it wished, enact one narrow regulation in a broad subject area, yet evince a clear intent to preempt the entire subject area against state regulation. But Congress rarely makes its intent so clear, and the Court must work by inference. Supreme Court decisions indicate that Congress will be deemed to have preempted an area only where either its ***intent*** is ***unmistakable***, or where "the ***nature*** of the regulated subject matter permits no other conclusion. ... " *Florida Lime & Avocado Growers v. Paul*, 373 U.S. 132 (1963).

      i. **Broad federal coverage of area:** Where the existing federal regulatory scheme is ***broad***, and ***covers most of the subject area***, the Court is much more likely to find federal field-preemption than where the federal scheme is less comprehensive. Tribe, p. 497.

      ii. **Field traditionally left to states:** Subject matter areas ***traditionally left to the states*** are ***less likely*** to be found to be the subject of federal field-preemption. This means that if the subject area is usually viewed as ***"local"*** rather than "national," preemption is unlikely to be found. This is especially true in cases involving ***health*** and ***safety*** regulations.

      iii. **National matters:** Conversely, areas ***traditionally left to federal control***, such as foreign relations, bankruptcy, patent and trademark, admiralty, immigration, etc., will normally be found to be federally preempted. Registration of aliens, at issue in *Hines, supra*, is an illustration.

iv. **Federal licensing scheme:** The fact that the federal government has enacted a *licensing scheme* for a particular aspect of interstate commerce usually does *not* automatically mean that state regulation of that aspect of commerce is preempted. The Court will look to the goals of the federal and state policies to see if there is a true conflict.

Example: Congress extensively regulates the nuclear power industry, through power delegated to the Nuclear Regulatory Commission (NRC), which licenses and inspects all nuclear power plants. California passes a law conditioning the construction of any new nuclear plant in the state upon a finding by a state agency that when the plant produces nuclear waste, there will be "adequate storage facilities and means of disposal" for that waste. A utility claims that Congress, by enacting its federal licensing scheme, has shown an intent to preempt the entire field of nuclear regulation.

Held, California's regulation is valid. The federal system of licensing and inspecting nuclear plants was set up solely to deal with *safety* issues, and with the construction and operation of nuclear plants. Since California asserts (and the Court accepts) that its statute was aimed at the *economic* problems of storing and disposing of waste, not safety problems, the California statute does not come within the area preempted by Congress. (But if California placed a moratorium on nuclear construction because of safety concerns, or sought to regulate the way in which nuclear plants are constructed and operated, these actions *would* fall within the area preempted by Congress.) Nor does the California regulation conflict with federal objectives, an aspect of the case discussed *infra*, pp. 106-107. *Pacific Gas & Electric Co. v. State Energy Comm'n*, 461 U.S. 190 (1983).

2. **"Conflicts preemption":** *"Conflicts preemption"* has been described by the Supreme Court as applying to two situations: first, "where compliance with both federal and state regulations is a *physical impossibility*"; and second, "where state law stands as an obstacle to the accomplishment and execution of the *full purposes and objectives* of Congress." *Gade, supra.* Let's talk about each of these two conflicts-preemption scenarios.

a. **Direct physical conflict:** Occasionally, federal and state regulations are drafted in such a way that it is *physically impossible for a person to obey the federal and state regulations simultaneously.* When this happens, the state regulation is of course invalid. *Labelling regulations* sometimes fall into this category.

Example: Wisconsin's syrup-labeling rules are written in such a way that that if out-of-state syrup is labeled so as to comply with the federal Food and Drug Act, the syrup will be mislabeled under Wisconsin law. *Held*, the Wisconsin regulations are invalid under the Supremacy Clause. *McDermott v. Wisconsin*, 228 U.S. 115 (1913).

b. **Conflict in purposes:** Alternatively, a regulatory scheme imposed by a state may be inconsistent with the *purposes* of a federal regulation. Here, too, the issue is always: what was the *intent* of Congress?

Example: Consider the facts of *Pacific Gas, supra*, where California passed a law conditioning the construction of any new nuclear plant in the state upon a finding by a state agency that there would be "adequate storage facilities and means of disposal" for that waste. Does the state scheme conflict with the purposes of the federal nuclear-power regulatory system, in which Congress showed a desire to promote adoption of nuclear power?

Held, "no" — the California waste-disposal requirement does not conflict with federal purposes. While it is true that Congress showed a desire to promote the spread of nuclear power, the history of the legislation demonstrates that Congress only wanted to do this if and where nuclear power could be used safely. Therefore, allowing states to require adequate storage and disposal of hazardous waste does not conflict with the purposes behind the federal regulatory scheme. *Pacific Gas & Electric Co. v. State Energy Comm'n*, 461 U.S. 190 (1983).

D. Easier to win on express than implied preemption: Recent Supreme Court cases show that on average, it is *easier* for a litigant seeking preemption to win on an *express*-preemption theory than on an implied-preemption one.

1. **Regulation of medical devices and drugs:** A pair of recent cases in the area of *medical products,* one on express preemption and the other on implied preemption, demonstrates how a plausible express-preemption argument is more likely to prevail than an implied-preemption one.

   a. **Express preemption (medical-device labelling):** The recent express-preemption case, *Riegel v. Medtronic*, 128 S.Ct. 999 (2008), involved the labeling of *medical devices*. Congress passed a statute (the Medical Devices Amendments of 1976, or "MDA") providing that once a medical device receives "premarket approval" by the federal Food and Drug Administration, no state or local government may impose any "requirement" that either relates to the safety or effectiveness of the device, or that is "different from, or in addition to," any FDA requirement applicable to the device.

      i. **The issue:** In *Riegel*, the issue was whether state *common-law tort recovery* against the maker of a defective device was preempted by the federal regulatory scheme. P was a heart patient into whom a medical device (a balloon catheter) made by D was inserted by a surgeon. The catheter burst, killing P. P's estate claimed that the device was defectively designed and labeled. D claimed that since the device had received premarket approval by the FDA, the MDA statute preempted any state from allowing a tort recovery based on the device's design or labeling.

      ii. **Holding for D:** By an 8-1 vote, the Supreme Court agreed with D's express-preemption argument. State product-liability law in this case imposed a "requirement" on medical devices just as surely as a state administrative-regulatory scheme would have done. "State tort law that requires a manufacturer's catheters to be safer, but hence less effective, than the model the FDA has approved disrupts the federal scheme no less than state regulatory law to the same effect." Therefore, Congress' express-preemption language in the MDA should be read to bar state tort liability premised on the design or labeling of an FDA-approved medical device.

   b. **Implied preemption (drugs):** By contrast, the second medical-related case involved the labeling of a *prescription drug*, and a plaintiff who made an *implied*-preemption argument. Although Congress has given the FDA authority to regulate prescription drugs just as it allowed the agency to regulate medical devices like the one in *Riegel*, Congress has *not expressly dealt with preemption* in the prescription-drug context.

Therefore, the defendant manufacturer in the prescription-drug case, *Wyeth v. Levine*, 129 S.Ct. 1187 (2009), had to win or lose with an implied-preemption argument. The defendant lost, in a stark illustration of how the Supreme Court begins with a presumption against a finding of implied preemption.

    i.   **Facts:** P in *Wyeth* received an anti-nausea drug, Phenergan, made by D. The warnings on the label for Phenergan had been approved by the FDA. There are several ways to administer Phenergan, one of which is by putting it directly into the patient's vein (the "IV-push" method). The IV-push method is the most dangerous, because if the drug is mistakenly put into an artery instead of a vein, it is likely to cause gangrene. That's what happened to P, who ended up having her arm amputated. P claimed that the drug was improperly labeled by D, in that D should have instructed practitioners to avoid the IV-push method. D defended on the grounds that its label had been approved by the FDA, and that the purposes of the FDA regulatory scheme would be impeded by allowing state common-law recovery based on the label. Therefore, D argued, the FDA scheme impliedly preempted state tort-law recovery.

    ii.   **D loses:** But **D lost** with this preemption argument. D argued that the federal scheme showed Congress' "purpose to entrust an expert agency to make drug labeling decisions that strike a balance between competing objectives," and that this purpose would be thwarted by state tort law recovery. But by a 6-3 vote, the Court disagreed.

        (1) **Presumption:** The majority began by noting a ***presumption*** that cuts against implied preemption: "In all preemption cases, and particularly in those in which Congress has 'legislated ... in a field which the states have traditionally occupied,' ... we 'start with the assumption that the historic police powers of the states were not to be superseded by the federal act unless that was the ***clear and manifest purpose*** of Congress.'"

        (2) **Presumption applicable here:** The majority then concluded that nothing in present case suggested a need to disregard the presumption and to find preemption. Congress knew how to forbid state-law suits where such suits posed a danger to congressional objectives, as Congress had long done in the case of medical devices (as in *Riegel, supra*). So the fact that Congress remained silent rather than enacting such a ban in the context of prescription drugs indicated that Congress did not view such suits as being inconsistent with its objectives. Consequently, Congress had not impliedly preempted state-law suits.

    c.   **Summary:** *Riegel* and *Wyeth*, taken together, indicate that on average it will be easier for a litigant to persuade the court that where Congress has expressly preempted some types of state regulation the preemption should be found to extend to the situation at issue, than to persuade the court that although Congress has remained silent on the preemption issue implied preemption should be found.

E. **Federal consent to state laws:**   We turn now to an obverse problem: To what extent may Congress affirmatively ***consent*** to state action which would otherwise be an unconstitutional violation of the Commerce Clause?

1. **Generally allowable:** Early decisions, including *Cooley v. Board of Wardens, supra*, p. 50, suggested that Congress did *not* have the power to consent to what would otherwise be state encroachments on the congressional commerce power. But the more modern view has been that Congress *may affirmatively consent to state interference with interstate commerce*. See Tribe, pp. 524-25; N&R, pp. 286-287.

   a. **Rationale:** One rationale for giving Congress the right to give such consent is that the ban on state interference with interstate commerce stems from the danger that each local part of the national economy will protect its own interests at the expense of the other parts; when Congress acts, by contrast, it is the "whole" rather than any individual part which is consenting to the interference with commerce, so that all affected parties are presumably represented in the political process. See N&R, pp. 281-282.

2. **Discrimination:** Thus the Court has allowed Congress to authorize a state to discriminate overtly against out-of-state corporations.

   Example: Congress passes the McCarran-Ferguson Act, which reserves to the states the power to regulate insurance, and which provides that no federal statute shall be construed to invalidate any state insurance law or tax, unless the federal statute specifically relates to insurance. A New Jersey insurance company sues to overturn a South Carolina tax of 3% on premiums received from all South Carolina insurance underwriting; the tax does not apply to South Carolina insurance firms.

   Held, even though the tax is "discriminatory" and would thus be invalid under ordinary Commerce Clause analysis, the tax is valid under the McCarran Act. Congress itself would have the power to discriminate against interstate commerce and in favor of local trade; there is no reason why such discrimination cannot be conducted by Congress in conjunction with the states. *Prudential Insurance Co. v. Benjamin*, 328 U.S. 408 (1946).

Quiz Yourself on
TWO LIMITS ON STATE POWER *(ENTIRE CHAPTER)*

12. The City of Fairhaven is located in the state of North Texarkansas. The border with the neighboring state of South Texarkansas is three miles south of the Fairhaven city limits. After a serious outbreak of food poisoning, traced to improperly butchered meat, the Fairhaven City Council passed an ordinance forbidding the sale within Fairhaven of any meat not killed at a slaughterhouse inspected by the Fairhaven Department of Sanitation. All evidence suggests that the Fairhaven ordinance was in fact motivated solely by health and safety objectives, not by any desire to favor local producers. Fairhaven Sanitation inspectors survey all slaughterhouses within a 70-mile radius of the city, but do not attempt to cross the boundary to inspect South Texarkansas slaughterhouses. South Texarkansas, at the state level, conducts its own inspections of slaughterhouses for sanitation, using standards that are closely similar to those used by the Fairhaven inspectors.

   Chopem, the owner of a butcher shop in Fairhaven, sells meat purchased from a slaughterhouse in South Texarkansas. Chopem was charged with selling meat that had not been slaughtered in a Fairhaven-inspected slaughterhouse. Chopem would like to get the charges dismissed on the grounds that the statute, as applied here, violates the U.S. Constitution.

(a) What is the strongest argument that Chopem can make for the unconstitutionality of the Fairhaven ordinance? _____

(b) Will this constitutional attack succeed? State your reasons. _____

13. The state of New Wales has a single nuclear power plant. Because the power plant has been in operation for over 20 years, it is now time for the plutonium used in the plant to be disposed of. The safest and cheapest way to do this is to bury it in a lead-enclosed structure 200 feet below the surface. Because residents of the state are worried that their state will become a "toxic dumping ground" if strict measures are not taken, the New Wales state legislature has enacted the following statute: "No plutonium imported into this state after 1994 may be buried anywhere within the confines of this state." The effect of this statute is to permit the state's existing utility to make a one-time disposal of its pre-1994 plutonium by the burial method described above. The owners of a nuclear reactor located in South Brunswick, the state directly east of New Wales, have attacked the new statute on the grounds that it violates the Commerce Clause because it prevents them from shipping their spent plutonium into New Wales and burying it there. Assume that Congress has not spoken on the issue of nuclear-waste disposal at all. Should the court hearing this action agree with the plaintiff? _____

14. The state of Rouge decided to build a new and large state office building. Quarries in Rouge had for years produced fine granite. However, in recent years, the in-state granite industry had begun to suffer because of high costs. In an effort to give a shot in the arm to the local industry, the Rouge legislature provided that all granite used in the new building should be purchased from in-state granite producers, even though the price would inevitably be higher than if the materials were bought from out-of-staters. A granite producer in a neighboring state has sued Rouge in federal District Court, asserting that Rouge's preference for in-staters violates the Commerce Clause. Should the court agree with the plaintiff's argument? _____

15. The state of Sylvan, in order to raise money to repair its existing highways and build new ones, has imposed a flat "axle tax" on any truck travelling more than 100 miles on Sylvan highways during any calendar year. The tax is $200 per axle. (The typical truck has two axles.) If all trucks were required to pay their fair share of maintaining the state's highways, the fairly-allocated cost for a truck driven full time (at least 20,000 miles per year) within the state would be approximately $500 per year. Trucker is a trucking company located in a state adjacent to Sylvan. Trucker's one truck drives about 200 miles a year in Sylvan, carrying goods into and out of the state.

(a) What is Trucker's best argument for attacking the constitutionality of the taxing scheme as applied to it? _____

(b) Will this attack succeed? _____

16. Same facts as Question 13 (on plutonium disposal). Now, assume that Congress has passed the following statute: "Any state may define the circumstances, if any, under which nuclear waste products [defined to include plutonium] may be buried or otherwise disposed of within the confines of that state." If the New Wales statute is attacked on the grounds that it violates the dormant Commerce Clause, should the Court find the statute invalid? _____

Answers

12. (a) That the ordinance unreasonably burdens interstate commerce.

(b) Yes. The dormant Commerce Clause prevents a state or local government from placing **undue burdens** on interstate commerce. Most violations of the dormant Commerce Clause occur when government acts in a "protectionist" manner, i.e., with an intent to favor the economic interests of local residents over out-of-staters. But even a non-protectionist "neutral" regulation will be found to violate the dormant Commerce Clause if it amounts to an **unreasonable burden** on commerce. This can be true, for instance, of regulations that are enacted for the good-faith purpose of protecting the safety or health of local residents. The Court performs a "balancing test," weighing the state or local government's interest in its regulatory scheme against the national interest in unburdened free-flowing interstate commerce. A major part of this balancing is whether there were **less burdensome alternatives** which the government might have adopted.

Here, since South Texarkansas conducts a similar inspection, Fairhaven could simply have accepted the results of South Texarkansas's inspection without materially compromising its own health standards. Therefore, the Fairhaven ordinance will probably be found to have been an "unreasonable" burden on commerce. See *Dean Milk Co. v. Madison*. (The fact that Fairhaven is a municipality rather than a state, and its ordinance might have discriminated against out-of-town but in-state slaughterhouses, i.e., those beyond the 70-mile inspection radius, does not save the ordinance from a dormant Commerce Clause attack.)

13. Yes. Any state or local action that is taken for a **protectionist purpose** — that is, for the purpose of preferring in-state economic interests over out-of-state interests — will be **strictly scrutinized**. This is true even where the measure is taken for what are basically environmental or other non-economic motives. Thus in *City of Philadelphia v. New Jersey* (a garbage disposal case), the Court held that one state could not ban the importation of another's garbage, unless there were no less-discriminatory alternatives. Here, New Wales is clearly preferring local nuclear plant operators to out-of-state operators. New Wales clearly has a less-discriminatory alternative (allow importation, and simply limit the total amount of plutonium that may be buried in the state), so the measure would almost certainly be struck down.

14. No. Ordinarily, if a state prefers the economic interests of in-staters over out-of-staters, we have a classic violation of the Commerce Clause. But there is an important exception: where the state acts as a **market participant**, spending its money to acquire goods or services, dormant Commerce Clause analysis is not applied, and the state may favor local interests over out-of-staters. Here, Rouge is clearly spending its own money, so it is free to limit that money to acquisitions from in-state producers. See, e.g., *Hughes v. Alexandria Scrap Corp.*; *Reeves v. Stake*.

15. (a) That the tax operates as an undue burden on interstate commerce.

(b) Yes, probably. A state may impose a tax that operates "on" interstate commerce. That is, an interstate business may be required to pay to a state the business' fair share of services supplied by that state to the business' operations in the state. So Trucker can be required to pay its fair share of the construction costs of highways it uses. But in determining whether the tax is fair, the Court requires "internal consistency." That is, the Court determines what would happen if all states taxed interstate operators the same way the state in question is doing; if this "all states" approach would produce a tax that is out of all proportion to the fair value of state services supplied to the payor, the tax is likely to be struck down as unreasonable. Here, each trucker who comes into the state for more than a trivial distance is required to pay the same amount as a truck that drives full time on Sylvan's roads, an approach that would make interstate trucking impossibly expensive if applied by all other states. See *American Trucking Assoc. v. Scheiner*, 483 U.S. 260 (1987), striking down such a flat "axle tax."

16. No. Dormant Commerce Clause analysis is only to be performed when Congress has not expressly allowed the type of discrimination against out-of-staters in question. Here, by the federal statute, Congress has in effect allowed a state to prefer its own citizens over out-of-staters.

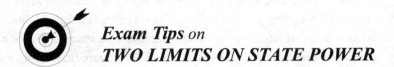

Exam Tips on
TWO LIMITS ON STATE POWER

Issues involving the dormant Commerce Clause and congressional pre-emption can often be well-hidden in a fact pattern; you must be especially vigilant to spot these issues. Here are some particular things to look for:

☛ Remember that one main branch of dormant Commerce Clause analysis is the *"burden"* branch: if a state's regulations would burden interstate commerce, the regulation will be struck down unless the burdens are *outweighed* by the state's interest in enforcing its regulation. Thus you must use a *balancing test* to evaluate "burden" problems. Also:

 ☞ Look for *conflicts* between the laws of two or more states. The existence of conflicting regulations is likely to be an undue burden on commerce, since a business operating in multiple states would find it difficult or impossible to comply with all of the conflicting regulations.

 ☞ Be on the lookout for regulations affecting *transportation*, especially *trucking*. These are classic scenarios where the states have differing regulations and commerce is directly affected because goods have to pass from state to state.

 ☞ Remember that you must do a "burden" analysis even where the state seems totally *even-handed*, and is not showing any protectionism.

  ☞ A common instance of state regulations that are even-handed but nonetheless unduly burdensome are *health* and *safety* regulations. If the state (or local government) insists on performing its own inspection of goods that are imported from elsewhere, this is likely to be an undue burden on commerce even if the state is truly pursuing health and safety rather than protectionism.

☛ Remember that the other main branch of dormant Commerce Clause analysis is the *"protectionist"* branch — if the state is intentionally *discriminating* against out-of-staters, in order to promote its residents' *own economic interests*, this is not a legitimate state objective, so the regulation will almost *automatically* violate the Commerce Clause.

Here are some ways to spot protectionism:

 ☞ Look for rules *restricting* the *export* of *"good stuff"* produced inside the state. This is especially likely where *natural resources* are the "good stuff" (e.g., a rule saying, "No more than x% of coal mined from the state may be exported").

☞   Look for rules barring the *import* of *"bad stuff"* (e.g., "No out-of-state garbage or toxic waste may be buried in our state").

☞   Look for rules whose effect is to *limit imports* of *"good stuff"* because the state is trying to *boost demand* for *in-state-produced* good stuff (e.g., "Coal-fired utilities located in this state must buy at least 10% of their coal from in-state mines").

☛ Remember that the dormant Commerce Clause does not apply at all where the state is a *market participant*. Therefore, be on the lookout for instances where the state is *operating a factory*, *purchasing goods*, or otherwise *directly engaging in commercial transactions* for its own account (as opposed to regulating the commercial transactions done by private parties).

☛ Don't forget that *local ordinances*, not just state rules, can violate the dormant Commerce Clause. This is true even where the ordinance discriminates against out-of-town in-staters as well as out-of-staters.

☛ Remember that *taxes* can be a violation of the dormant Commerce Clause (DCC) just as readily as regulations can be. We have the same two branches of analysis for taxes:

☞   Thus if the state is *discriminating* against interstate commerce by taxing it less favorably than in-staters, this will be a DCC violation.

☞   Alternatively, a tax scheme will violate the DCC if the scheme unfairly *burdens* commerce even though it doesn't discriminate against out-of-staters on its face. One common type of illustration: the state puts a *flat tax* on some activity, regardless of its degree of connection with the state. (*Example:* The state puts a flat annual tax on all trucks entering the state even occasionally, which has the effect of taxing out-of-state trucks much more heavily per mile than in-state trucks.) In considering the burden, consider whatever the fact pattern tells you about the tax policies of *other states* — inconsistencies can make the whole scheme burdensome even though each state's scheme is not burdensome when viewed in isolation.

☛ Separately, be on the lookout for *federal preemption* problems. Remember that this is an aspect of the Supremacy Clause; if Congress (or a federal agency acting under Congress' direction) has acted in a particular respect or occupied a particular domain, the states are often precluded from regulating.

☞   Be on the lookout for a fact pattern telling you that there are federal and state statutes dealing with the *same subject area*. This is a clue to preemption problems.

☞   First, check for *"express"* preemption: if Congress has explicitly said that the states may not regulate in a particular area, then any state regulation in that area is invalid under the Supremacy Clause, even if the state regulation seems to be consistent with the federal regulation.

☞   Next, check for *"implied"* preemption. This can come in either of two flavors: *"conflicts preemption"* and *"field preemption."*

☞   *Conflicts preemption* has two flavors, too, *"direct"* and *"indirect."* First, check for a *direct conflict*. If a person or business *could not simultaneously obey both* the state and federal regulation, then obviously the state regulation must fall. Most fact patterns are *not* of this "direct conflict" type, however.

☞ Next, check for an *indirect conflict*, mainly a conflict due to inconsistencies in the *purposes* of the two regulations. For instance, you may see a fact pattern where there are federal and state statutes dealing with the same activity, and the state statute is *more stringent* than the federal statute. Obviously, a person can obey both (simply by obeying the more stringent state statute). Here, ask yourself whether Congress meant to say, "We're setting a minimum standard, and we'll let the states be more stringent," or meant to say instead, "We're regulating this way, and we don't want states interfering with our scheme by being more stringent." In the latter situation, the state regulation conflicts with the purposes of the federal regulation, so the state regulation is invalid. Remember that it is always a question of *what Congress intended*.

☞ Finally, be on the lookout for *"field preemption."* That is, look for a federal statutory scheme that seems to deal with an *entire broad area*. Where Congress has acted in this way, this may represent Congress' intent to *"occupy the whole field,"* in which case even a state regulation dealing with an aspect of the problem that is not addressed in the federal regulatory scheme may be pre-empted. Commonly, this happens in fact patterns involving *nuclear power* and *immigration* — the existence of a broad federal regulatory scheme in these areas may well prevent the states from enacting even non-conflicting regulations dealing with these subjects.

CHAPTER 7

INTERGOVERNMENTAL IMMUNITIES AND INTERSTATE RELATIONS

ChapterScope

This Chapter, like the ones before it, examines several aspects of federal-state relationships and interstate relationships. As before, the emphasis is on federalism, and the limits it places both on state and federal power. The most important concepts in this Chapter are:

◼ **Several types of immunities:** There are several types of *immunities* produced by our federalist system. The most important are:

❑ **Federal immunity from state taxation:** The *federal* government is immune from being *taxed by the states*.

❑ **State immunity from federal taxation:** The *states* have *partial immunity* from *federal* taxation.

❑ **Federal immunity from state regulation:** The federal government is essentially free from *state regulatory interference.*

❑ **State immunity from federal regulation:** The states generally are *not* immune from federal regulation. However, if a federal regulatory scheme had the effect of preventing the states from exercising their *core functions*, this might be found to be a violation of the Tenth Amendment.

◼ **Interstate privileges and immunities:** The *"Privileges and Immunities"* Clause of Article IV says that "the Citizens of each State shall be entitled to all Privileges and Immunities of Citizens in the several States." This clause means that a state may not *discriminate against non-residents*.

❑ **Rights fundamental to national unity:** But this clause only operates with respect to rights that are *fundamental* to *national unity*. Thus only rights related to *commerce* are covered: the right to *be employed*, the right to *practice one's profession*, and the right to *engage in business* are the prime examples.

I. TAX IMMUNITIES

A. Federal and state immunity: It has long been established that the federal government is *immune* from taxation by any state, unless Congress has consented to such taxation. Likewise, it has always been accepted that a *state*, at least in the performance of its *essential government functions*, is *immune from federal taxation*. However, the scope of this state immunity has been significantly narrowed in recent years. Although the rules in the federal immunity and state immunity situations are similar, there are enough differences to warrant separate treatment of the two.

B. Federal immunity from state taxation: The principle that the federal government is *immune from taxation by any state* derives from *McCulloch v. Maryland*, 4 Wheat. 316

(1819) (discussed *supra*, pp. 21-23).

1. **Holding of *McCulloch*:** Recall that *McCulloch* held that the Bank of the United States was immune from a Maryland tax against it. This conclusion was essentially the result of the following syllogism: (1) the power to tax is the power to destroy; (2) if state taxation were permitted to destroy or harm the Bank, the federal government's exercise of its powers under the Constitution (especially the "Necessary and Proper" and Spending Clauses) would be thwarted; and (3) the federal Constitution must be preserved against such state interference.

2. **Broad rationale:** More generally, the theory behind federal immunity from state taxation is that a government may not tax those it does not represent, so that a state may not tax the entire nation. See Tribe, p. 512.

3. **Modern "legal incidence" test:** Federal immunity from state taxation exists only in those situations where the "*legal incidence*" of the tax is on the United States (or upon one of its instrumentalities, such as a federally-sponsored entity like a VA hospital).

    a. **Meaning of "legal incidence":** "Legal incidence" means "*obligation to pay*," not "economic burden." Thus if a private contractor or other non-government entity is required to pay the state tax, the fact that the burden of this tax might be *passed on* to the government is *not enough* to confer tax immunity. Only where the government entity is *directly required to make the payment* will there be federal immunity from state taxation.

    b. **Employees not immune:** *Employees* of the federal government are *not* immune from state taxation. See *Graves v. New York ex rel. O'Keefe*, 306 U.S. 466 (1939).

4. **Congressional control:** Congress may, whenever it wishes, explicitly *confer additional immunity* from state taxation upon other persons or entities.

5. **Congressional waiver:** Conversely, Congress may *waive* its constitutionally-derived immunity whenever it sees fit.

C. **State immunity from federal taxation:** Similar, though not identical, principles control the *immunity of states* from *federal* taxation. The federal government may not tax in a way which would "interfere unduly with the State's performance of its sovereign functions of government." *New York v. United States*, 326 U.S. 572 (1946) (Stone, C.J., concurring).

1. **Source of limitation:** The Constitution nowhere explicitly provides that the states shall be immune from federal taxation of essential government functions. Rather, the state immunity is implied from the *Tenth Amendment's* preservation of state autonomy.

2. **Essential functions:** Thus the federal government may generally not impose a significant tax on property used in or income received from a state's performance of its *basic governmental functions*. For instance, it is doubtful that the federal government may include a state's *public schools* or *public parks* within a general property tax, or its revenues from state taxes within a general federal income tax. See *New York v. United States*, *supra* (Stone, C.J., concurring).

3. **Non-essential function:** But where a state government engages in a function that is not at the core of traditional governmental functions, the federal government may tax that function as part of a non-discriminatory, generally-applicable tax.

4. **Employees not covered:**   As in the case of state taxation of the federal government, state *employees*, and other persons doing business with the state, will generally ***not be immune*** from federal taxation.

II.   FEDERAL IMMUNITY FROM STATE REGULATION

A. **Federal immunity from regulation:**   The freedom of the federal government from state regulation is governed by principles similar to those in the taxation context. That is, the federal government is essentially ***immune from state regulatory interference***.

> **Example:** Suppose a state attempts to apply its criminal code to actions that take place on a U.S. military base located within the state. Such a state regulation of the federal government would be found unconstitutional, assuming that Congress did not consent to it.

B. **Sources of immunity:**   This federal immunity from state regulation, like federal immunity from state taxation, derives from *McCulloch v. Maryland* (*supra*, p. 21). The theory is that a government may not control those whom it does not represent; thus a state may not control the entire nation. See Tribe, p. 512.

1. **Who is covered:**   Generally, only the United States and its instrumentalities will be free of state regulation. However, sometimes a federal employee will be free of state regulation while acting in the course of his federal duties. See, e.g., *Johnson v. Maryland*, 254 U.S. 51 (1920), reversing the conviction of a post office employee for driving a truck without a state license.

2. **Congress' consent:**   Again, keep in mind that Congress is always free to ***consent*** to state regulation of federal instrumentalities. This is frequently done, for instance, with respect to the law governing ***military posts*** and other federal enclaves. Thus Congress has made the changing body of state criminal law applicable to federal enclaves; the Court found this to be constitutional in *U.S. v. Sharpnack*, 355 U.S. 286 (1958).

III.   STATE IMMUNITY FROM FEDERAL REGULATION

A. **Exits only theoretically:**   The immunity of the *states* from *federal* regulation exists only in a very theoretical way. In general, federal regulation of the states is *valid*.

1. **Interference with core functions:**   However, if a federal regulatory scheme had the effect of preventing the states from exercising their *core functions*, this might be found to be a violation of the ***Tenth Amendment***.

> **Example:** Suppose Congress enacted a statute that said, "No state may have its own criminal code, and the only crimes that may be defined in the United States are those defined in the federal criminal code." The Supreme Court might well hold that this federal regulation so interfered with a traditional state core function — enactment and enforcement of a criminal code — that the Tenth Amendment was violated.

> **Note:** The Tenth Amendment, and the limited extent to which it may prevent the federal government from regulating the states, is discussed *supra*, pp. 53-59. See especially *Garcia v. San Antonio Metropolitan Transit Authority*, *supra*, p. 54.

IV. INTERSTATE RELATIONSHIPS

A. Interstate relationships generally: We now examine two aspects of *interstate* relationships: (1) the Privileges and Immunities Clause; and (2) interstate collaboration, including compacts.

B. The Privileges and Immunities Clause: Article IV, §2, cl. 1 of the Constitution provides: "The Citizens of each State shall be entitled to all Privileges and Immunities of Citizens in the several States."

1. Function: This *interstate* Privileges and Immunities Clause (to be distinguished from the Privileges or Immunities Clause of §1 of the Fourteenth Amendment) *prevents states from discriminating against out-of-state individuals*. As the Supreme Court has put it, the clause "was designed to insure to a citizen of State A who ventures into State B the same privileges which the citizens of State B enjoy." *Toomer v. Witsell*, 334 U.S. 385 (1948). Like the Commerce Clause, the interstate Privileges and Immunities Clause is an attempt to "help fuse into one Nation a collection of independent, sovereign States." *Id.*

2. "Citizenship" vs. "residence":   The Privileges and Immunities Clause speaks of "citizens" of other states. But as a practical matter, discrimination against non-*residents* is what is barred.

   a. Corporations and aliens not protected: The one practical effect of the use of the word "citizens" within the Clause is that *corporations* and *aliens* are not protected by the Clause. (In contrast, observe that both corporations and aliens are protected by the Equal Protection and Due Process Clauses of the Fourteenth Amendment.)

3. Test for P&I violation: Even where a state does discriminate against out-of-staters, it is relatively hard for the out-of-staters to establish a violation of the Privileges and Immunities Clause.

   a. Only "fundamental rights" covered: First, only rights that are *"fundamental to national unity"* are covered. The rights that meet this "fundamental to national unity" standard are all related to *commerce*.

      i. Examples: The right to be *employed*, the right to *practice one's profession*, and the right to *engage in business* are all fundamental, and are therefore protected.

      Example: Alaska requires that Alaskan residents be given an absolute preference over non-residents for all jobs on the Alaska oil pipeline. *Held*, the preference violates the Privileges and Immunities Clause. Access to employment is a right fundamental to national unity. Since the statute cannot survive the two-part standard applicable to discrimination against out-of-staters (described below), the preference is invalid. *Hicklin v. Orbeck* (the "Alaska Hire" case), 437 U.S. 518 (1978).

      ii. Recreational use: Conversely, *non-economic* rights are generally *not* "fundamental to national unity," and thus not protected by the Privileges and Immunities Clause. For example, the right to engage in *recreational* activities is not protected by the clause.

      Example: Montana allows Montana residents to purchase a license for hunting elk and other animals for $30, while non-residents are charged $225. *Held*, this scheme does not violate the Privileges and Immunities Clause, because the right to recreation is not a right that is fundamental to national unity. *Baldwin v. Montana Fish and Game Comm'n*, 436 U.S. 371 (1978).

b. Two-part test: Once the Court concludes that a "fundamental right" *is* at stake, then the Court applies a *two-part test* to determine whether the discrimination against non-residents is acceptable. The plaintiff (who is attacking the discrimination against out-of-staters) will win if *either* of the following is shown:

i. "Peculiar source of evil": First, the discrimination will violate the Privileges and Immunities Clause unless non-residents are a *"peculiar source of the evil"* which the law was enacted to remedy.

Example: In the "Alaska Hire" case, *supra*, Alaska argued that its employment preference for residents was a reasonable response to high unemployment rates. But the Court held that the state did not show that the non-residents were a "peculiar source of the evil" (unemployment), because much of the unemployment came from the fact that too many residents were untrained or lived too far from job opportunities, and the influx of out-of-staters seeking jobs was just a small part of the problem.

ii. "Substantial relationship" test: Second, the plaintiff will win if the discrimination against non-residents *does not bear a "substantial relationship" to the problem* the statute is attempting to solve.

Example: In "Alaska Hire" this prong was not satisfied, either — a blanket and absolute preference for all qualified residents over all non-residents was not *sufficiently "closely tailored"* to the unemployment problem. (In other words, if there is a *less discriminatory alternative* that would solve the problem, the requisite "substantial relationship" between the discrimination against out-of-staters and the problem will not be found to exist.)

Note: Once a "right fundamental to national unity" is shown to be at stake, the Supreme Court uses something close to *strict scrutiny*: the burden is on the state to show both that non-residents are a peculiar source of the evil, and that the discrimination bears a substantial relationship to the problem being solved.

4. Practice of law: The right to *practice law* is a sufficiently important and "fundamental" right that this privilege may not be limited to state residents. Thus in *Supreme Court of New Hampshire v. Piper*, 470 U.S. 274 (1985), the Supreme Court held that New Hampshire could not restrict the right to practice to those who resided within the state.

5. No "market participant" exception for state: Recall that where a state is acting as a *"market participant,"* it is not subject to the Commerce Clause's prohibition on discrimination against interstate commerce. (See *supra*, p. 100.) It can plausibly be argued that a similar "market participant" exception should exist to render the Privileges and Immunities Clause inapplicable where the state discriminates against out-of-state residents for *government jobs*. However, the Court has held that there is *no "market participant" exception to the Privileges and Immunities Clause*. The Court reached this conclusion in ruling that the clause applied to a Camden, New Jersey ordinance which required that at least 40% of the work force on any construction project funded by the city must reside in the city. (The Court did not hold that the ordinance violated the clause; it remanded for a determination on this issue.) *United Building and Construction Trades Council v. Camden*, 465 U.S. 208 (1984).

a. **Grounds for distinction:**   The majority reasoned that the rationale for a "market participant" exemption in the privileges and immunities context was not nearly as strong as in the Commerce Clause context. The Commerce Clause deals only with regulation, and a state acting as "market participant" is simply not regulating. But the Privileges and Immunities Clause bars *any* type of state conduct, regulatory or otherwise, which discriminates against out-of-staters on matters of fundamental concern.

b. **Factor to be considered:**   Nonetheless, the Court indicated, the fact that the discriminatory conduct consists of the state's expenditure of its own funds is *a non-dispositive factor* which militates in favor of upholding the action against a privileges and immunities attack.

c. **Discrimination against municipal residence barred:**   The Supreme Court broke other major new ground in the *Camden* case: it held that the Privileges and Immunities Clause bars discrimination based on *municipal residence*, just as it bars such discrimination based on state residence. The Court conceded that a regulation that discriminates against out-of-towners burdens some in-staters as well as out-of-staters. But it reasoned that in-staters "at least have a chance to remedy at the polls any discrimination against them. Out-of-state citizens have no similar opportunity," so that there is a violation of the Privileges and Immunities Clause as to them.

d. **"Substantial reason" may justify:**   The Court emphasized in *Camden* that the ban on discrimination against out-of-staters is *not absolute*; all that is required is that there be a *tight fit* between the particular discrimination used and a significant evil that the state is combatting. Here, Camden claimed that it was attempting to reverse widespread local unemployment and "middle-class flight." The Court remanded to the trial Court for a consideration of whether this was an appropriate purpose, and whether the particular discriminatory measure chosen was sufficiently closely linked to attainment of that objective. But the Court implied that, especially since the City was spending its own funds, the City would prevail if it could show that emigration was indeed a "peculiar source" of the City's economic decline.

e. **Local residence requirements generally:**   Thus after *Camden*, municipalities may still be able to require that all or a specified portion of their employees live within the city limits. Such provisions will be subjected to privileges and immunities scrutiny, but if the city can show that out-of-towners are a peculiar source of the significant evil at which the discriminatory measure is aimed, the measure will still be upheld. For instance, if a city can show that a particular spending program was created *for the purpose* of reducing local unemployment (e.g., a program giving summer jobs to inner-city youths) a ban on those not living within the city limits, including those living out-of-state, would probably survive privileges and immunities attack.

6. **Distinguished from equal protection:**   Where a nonresident is discriminated against, the case may be actionable under the *Equal Protection Clause* as well as under the Privileges and Immunities Clause. There are two principal differences between these two types of claims:

   a. **Aliens and corporations:**   First, as noted, an *alien* or *corporation* may not take advantage of the Privileges and Immunities Clause, but may take advantage of the Equal Protection Clause.

    b. Not suspect classification: Secondly, nonresidency (unlike alienage) has thus far not been held by the Court to be a "suspect classification" for equal protection purposes. Therefore, a state scheme which discriminates against nonresidents is not subject to *strict* equal protection scrutiny, and must just meet the "mere-rationality" standard. (See *infra*, p. 255.)

        i. Strict scrutiny: Where a privileges and immunities attack is lodged, by contrast (assuming that a right fundamental to national unity is involved), the functional equivalent of *strict scrutiny* is given, since nonresidents must be shown to be a "peculiar source" of the evil, and there must be a relatively close fit between the evil and the state's solution to it.

C. Interstate compacts: No state may enter into any "treaty, alliance, or confederation. ... " Article I, §10, cl. 1. However, by negative implication, Clause 3 of that same section allows certain interstate agreements: "No state shall, *without the consent of Congress* ... enter into any agreement or compact with another state or with a foreign power. ... " Such *"interstate compacts"* are a frequently-used device for insuring cooperation among two or more states.

    1. When congressional consent necessary: Despite the literal wording of Clause 3 (quoted above), *not every agreement between states requires congressional consent*. Rather, congressional consent is required only where the interstate combination "tend[s] to the increase of political power in the States, which may encroach upon the just supremacy of the United States. ... " *Virginia v. Tennessee*, 148 U.S. 503 (1893).

        a. Illustrations: Thus if two states were to agree that one would cede part of its territory to the other, this agreement would probably require congressional consent, since it would increase the power of the latter in the House. But a reciprocal tax agreement (whereby each consenting state would agree not to tax residents of other states) would not affect the national government, and would not require congressional consent.

Quiz Yourself on

INTERGOVERNMENTAL IMMUNITIES & INTERSTATE RELATIONS
(ENTIRE CHAPTER)

17. Arms Co. is a government military contractor. Its sole business is to manufacture M-16 rifles, all of which are then sold by it to the U.S. government. Arms Co.'s contract with the U.S. government is of a "cost plus fixed fee" variety. Okra, the state in which Arms Co. is located, has enacted a generally-applicable sales tax on all wholesale sales of tangible property made within the state. Okra applies this tax to Arms Co., with the result that Arms Co. must pay a tax of 8% on all goods bought by it for use in the manufacture of the M-16 rifle. The net effect of this tax is to increase by 4% the price paid by the U.S. government to Arms Co. for each M-16 rifle.

    (a) If Arms Co. wishes to attack the constitutionality of the Okra sales tax as applied to its purchase of materials for use in the M-16, what is its best argument? _____

    (b) Will this argument succeed? _____

18. The state of River provides that no physician may practice within the state unless that physician resides in the state. The state has enacted this rule because its legislators believed (with at least some rationality) that doctors are frequently called upon to give emergency service after hours, and doctors who live out-of-state will be, on the whole, less able to do this than those who live in-state. Doc, a person who has satisfied all other requirements for a license to practice in River (e.g., passage of the national medical boards), lives in the neighboring state of Lake.

    (a) If Doc wishes to challenge River's residency requirement on constitutional grounds, what is his best argument? _____

    (b) Will this argument probably succeed? _____

Answers

    17. (a) That the tax violates the federal immunity from state taxation.

    (b) No. It is true that the federal government is itself immune from taxation by any state. See *McCulloch v. Maryland*. But this immunity generally does not extend to federal government employees or to contractors who work for the federal government. It does not matter that the "economic incidence" of the tax falls on the federal government — as long as it is not the federal government itself that is being ***directly obliged*** to pay the tax, the fact that the economic burden of the tax may fall on the federal government is irrelevant.

    18. (a) That the requirement violates the Privileges and Immunities Clause of Article IV.

    (b) Yes. Art. IV, Section 2, provides that "the Citizens of each State shall be entitled to all Privileges and Immunities of Citizens in the several States." This Clause prevents states from discriminating against out-of-state individuals. It applies only to rights that are "fundamental to national unity." The right to practice one's profession has been found to be such a right. Once such a "fundamental right" is shown to be at stake, then the defenders of the statute will lose unless they show that non-residents are a "peculiar source of the evil" which the law was enacted to remedy, and that there are no less discriminatory alternatives that would satisfactorily solve the problem.

    Here, the unavailability of physicians after-hours may be an important problem, but it is unlikely the state can show that non-residents are a "peculiar source of the evil" (since resident physicians will also frequently be unavailable after hours). Furthermore, it is highly unlikely that there are no less discriminatory alternatives; for instance, the state could simply require that each physician be reachable after hours and have a method of furnishing service within a certain period of time. Therefore, the statute will almost certainly be found to violate at least one of the two required tests, and will thus be struck down. See *Supreme Court of New Hampshire v. Piper*, holding that a state requirement that lawyers practicing within the state reside within it violated the P&I Clause.

Exam Tips on
INTERGOVERNMENTAL IMMUNITIES AND INTERSTATE RELATIONS

Here are things to watch for in connection with the two main topics from this Chapter, intergovernmental immunities and Art. IV's Privileges and Immunities Clause:

☛ If your fact pattern shows that a ***federal tax*** is being applied directly to an activity conducted by a ***state government***, consider whether the limited state immunity from federal taxation is being violated.

☞ Typical fact patterns raising this issue are: the federal government requires every user, including states, to pay a fee for *federally-sponsored services* (e.g., a tax on airplanes to support the air traffic controller system), or the federal government applies a *general tax* on certain *wages* (e.g., a payroll tax applicable to state as well as private-sector employees).

☞ Remember the general rule: the only real state immunity from federal taxation is that the federal government may not tax in a way which *substantially interferes* with a state's performance of its *basic governmental functions*.

　☞ Thus if the federal government is taxing a state's public parks or schools, you might have a violation of the state immunity.

　☞ But in the vast majority of situations, including virtually all situations where the federal tax is a *generally applicable* tax, there will be *no* interference with basic governmental functions and thus no violation of state immunity. (*Example*: The federal government can tax all airplanes, including state-operated ones.)

☛ Conversely, any time you spot a *state tax* that is applied to an activity somehow connected with the *federal government*, consider whether this violates the *federal immunity from state taxation:*

☞ The federal government is certainly immune from *direct* taxation by any state. For instance, if your fact pattern involves a state or local property tax on, say, a post office, that's a clear violation.

☞ But most exam fact patterns do *not* involve a "direct" tax on a federal instrumentality. Instead, the state taxes a *private party*, in a way that (arguably) increases the federal government's costs. The classic illustration is a tax on the operations of a *contractor* who is performing tasks for the federal government on a cost-plus basis. Here, the rule is that it doesn't matter whether the economic burden is passed onto the federal government; as long as the *"legal incidence"* of the tax is *not* on the federal government, there is *no violation* of the federal immunity. (*Example:* A state may impose a sales tax on materials used by a real estate contractor who is building a post office for the U.S. on a cost-plus basis, since the legal incidence of the tax is not on the federal government.)

☛ Similarly, be on the lookout for state *regulations* that affect the federal government. Such a fact pattern raises the issue of whether the federal immunity from state regulation is being violated.

☞ Typically, federal immunity from state regulation arises where the states are attempting to regulate a *federal enclave*, such as a post office or military post. Even if the state is regulating in a generally-applicable way, federal enclaves are *immune* from this regulation unless Congress has expressly consented to it. (*Example:* A state may not impose its criminal code on a military base, unless Congress consents.)

☛ If your facts show that the *federal government* is *regulating a state*, consider whether the state immunity from federal regulation is being violated.

☞ Here, you should almost always conclude that the state immunity is *not* being violated. State immunity from federal regulation is exceptionally narrow. Only if a federal regulation prevents a state from exercising its *core functions* will there be a violation. (If you do find a violation, it is essentially a violation of the Tenth Amendment.) It is unlikely you will see a fact pattern where the federal regulatory interference with state functioning is so great that this test is satisfied.

☛ Issues involving Article IV's ***Privileges and Immunities Clause*** are easily hidden.

☞ You should be looking for fact patterns where there is *discrimination* against *out-of-staters*. When you see such discrimination, your first instinct will be to see if there is a violation of the dormant Commerce Clause, and you will also want to examine the possibility of an equal protection violation. But don't forget to check for an Article IV P&I violation, since where that clause applies, the standard of review is very tough.

☞ When you do see a state discriminating against out-of-staters, the most important thing to remember about Article IV P&I is that it applies only to rights that are *"fundamental to national unity."* Essentially, the only rights covered are rights related to *commerce*.

☞ In general, for the "fundamental to national unity" standard to be satisfied, your fact pattern will usually involve an individual who is a *U.S. citizen*, *resides out of state*, and is either *totally blocked* from following his *chosen profession or job* in the state, or is subjected to a *higher license fee* than is charged to in-staters. (*Example:* A state law preventing citizens of other states from practicing law or medicine in the state would involve a right "fundamental to national unity," and would in fact violate the Article IV P&I Clause.)

☞ If you conclude that the right in question *is* fundamental to national unity, then be sure to articulate the correct standard for review. Something akin to strict scrutiny is used: the state *loses* unless it can prove *both* that: (1) non-residents are a *"peculiar source of the evil"* which the discrimination against out-of-staters is attempting to remedy; and (2) the discrimination bears a *"substantial relationship"* to the problem the discriminatory statute is attempting to solve. Usually, you should conclude that the state has *failed* to satisfy one or both of these tests (the "peculiar source of evil" test is especially hard for the state to satisfy).

☞ There is one context in which you should always conclude that a right "fundamental to national unity" is *not* involved: where what is involved is the pursuit of *recreation*. Thus your fact pattern will frequently involve an out-of-stater's right to *hunt*, *fish*, use tennis courts, etc.; typically the out-of-stater will either be entirely blocked from doing these things, or charged a much higher fee than in-staters. Even if the ban on out-of-staters is total, you should still conclude that Article IV's P&I is *not* violated, because commerce is not involved and thus there is no right fundamental to national unity. (But if the out-of-stater wants to hunt, fish, etc. as a *professional* who will earn most of his living that way, then this analysis probably will not apply, and the P&I Clause will apply.)

☞ When you spot discrimination against out-of-staters that seems to trigger the Article IV P&I Clause, you typically will want to compare the application of the P&I Clause with the Equal Protection Clause. Keep in mind the important differences between how these two clauses apply to discrimination against out-of-staters:

☞ *Aliens* and *corporations* do *not* get to use the Article IV P&I Clause (since it applies only to "national citizenship," and neither aliens nor corporations are "United States citizens").

☞ On the other hand, once the P&I Clause does apply, something like *strict scrutiny* is applied, and the out-of-stater will almost always win. By contrast, under Equal Protection Clause analysis, non-residency is *not* a suspect classification, so a state can usually discriminate against out-of-staters without violating the Equal Protection Clause as long as the state regulation is rationally related to a legitimate state objective. Often, the state will be able to satisfy this easy standard.

☞ Be sure to specify that it is the *Article IV* P&I Clause, *not* the Fourteenth Amendment "P-or-I" Clause that you're talking about. The Fourteenth Amendment P-or-I Clause is extremely limited, and is virtually never used. Especially on multiple choice questions, be careful not to pick a response stating that the challenged action is a violation of "the Fourteenth Amendment's Privileges and Immunities Clause" — professors love to slip this in as a trick (wrong) answer.

CHAPTER 8

SEPARATION OF POWERS

ChapterScope

A prior Chapter (*supra*, p. 19) summarized the general boundaries of the powers of the three federal branches. Here, we examine closely certain *conflicts* between branches, especially between the Executive and Legislative Branches. Here are the most important concepts in this Chapter:

■ **President/Congress boundary line:** Many separation-of-powers conflicts involve the boundary line between the President (Executive Branch) and Congress (Legislative Branch). Here are some of the more important principles concerning this boundary line:

❑ **President can't make the laws:** The President cannot make the laws. All he can do is to *carry out the laws* made by Congress.

❑ **Declaration of War:** Only *Congress*, not the President, can *declare war*.

❑ **Appointments:** The President, not Congress, has the power to *appoint* federal executive officers.

    ❑ **Removal by Congress:** Just as Congress may not directly appoint federal executive officers, it may not *remove* an executive officer, except by the special process of *impeachment*.

❑ **Removal of federal judges:** Federal *judges* cannot be removed by *either* Congress or the President.

■ **Other issues:** The other main separation-of-powers area involves issues of *immunity* and *executive privilege*:

❑ **"Speech and Debate" Clause:** Members of Congress are given a quite broad immunity by the *"Speech and Debate"* Clause. This clause shields members of Congress from: (1) civil or criminal suits relating to their legislative actions; and (2) grand jury investigations relating to those actions.

❑ **Executive immunity:** Courts recognize an implied *executive* immunity from civil actions.

    ❑ **Absolute for President:** The President has *absolute* immunity from civil liability for his official acts.

    ❑ **Qualified for others:** All other federal officials, including presidential assistants, receive only *qualified* civil immunity.

❑ **Executive privilege:** Presidents have a qualified right to refuse to disclose *confidential information* relating to the performance of their duties. This is called *"executive privilege."*

    ❑ **Outweighed:** Since the privilege is qualified, it may be outweighed by other compelling governmental interests (e.g., the need for the President's evidence in a criminal trial).

I.   DOMESTIC POLICY AND THE SEPARATION OF POWERS

A.   General problem: There are a few powers which are explicitly granted by the Constitution to the President. These are enumerated in Article II, §2, and will not be listed here. They include, for instance, the President's status as Commander-in-Chief of the armed forces and his treaty-making power.

    1.   Implied powers: But unlike the Congress, whose powers are much more closely delineated (by Article I, §8), much of the President's power, in both the domestic and foreign spheres, is *implied*. This process of implication has been derived mostly from Article II, §1, which provides, in relevant part, "The executive Power shall be vested in a President. … " If the Supreme Court concludes that a presidential action is properly regarded as being part of the "executive" (rather than judicial or legislative) sphere, that action will not be rendered unconstitutional merely by the fact that it does not fall within any specific constitutionally-enumerated power. See Tribe, pp. 210-211.

B.   No right to "make laws":   Despite its willingness to infer the existence of broad presidential authority, the Supreme Court has adhered to one over-arching limitation on presidential power: *The President may not make laws*; he may only *carry them out*. The best-known case evidencing this limitation is *Youngstown Sheet & Tube Co. v. Sawyer*, 343 U.S. 579 (1952) (the *Steel Seizure Case*).

    1.   Facts of *Youngstown Sheet:* During the Korean War, President Truman sought to avert a strike in the nation's steel mills. He therefore issued an executive order directing his Secretary of Commerce to seize the mills and operate them under federal direction. Congressional approval of the seizure order was not requested. The steel companies sought an injunction to prevent the seizure.

    2.   Supreme Court strikes down seizure: The Court *struck down the seizure order*, concluding that it was an unconstitutional exercise of the lawmaking authority reserved to Congress. Although the decision was 6-3, four of the six Justices on the majority side wrote separate concurring opinions, making it difficult to summarize the "doctrine" of the case.

        a.   Black's opinion: Justice Black's opinion for the Court flatly stated that the President's seizure order, coming as it did without the consent of Congress, was a clear usurpation of congressional lawmaking power. The order could not be justified under the "Commander-in-Chief" power; the taking of private property in order to keep labor disputes from stopping production of war materiel was too far removed from the actual "theater of war" in which the President had the right to set policy. Nor could the seizure be justified under the President's power to see that the laws are faithfully executed — the very language of the clause shows that the President must merely carry out the laws, not make them.

        b.   Concurring opinions: But the four concurring opinions, unlike Justice Black's opinion for the Court, attached principal importance to the fact that Congress had previously, and repeatedly, *explicitly rejected* plant seizure as a means of handling labor disputes. Justice Jackson's concurrence, probably the best known of the four, contended that the President's powers "are not fixed but *fluctuate*, depending on their disjunction or conjunction with those of Congress." He conceived of three categories:

i. where the President acts pursuant to express or implied *authorization* of Congress, in which case his authority is at its maximum;

ii. where the President acts in the *absence* of either a congressional *grant or denial* of authority, in which case "there is a zone of twilight in which he and Congress may have *concurrent* authority, or in which its distribution is uncertain"; and

iii. where the President acts in *contradiction* to the express or implied will of Congress; in this case, his power is *"at its lowest ebb."* Jackson felt that the steel seizure fell into this third category, and that it could therefore not be constitutionally justified.

c. **Dissent:** Three Justices dissented in *Youngstown Sheet & Tube*. They contended that temporary seizure was justified because of the emergency nature of the situation, and in order to preserve temporarily the *status quo* until Congress could act.

3. **Implied acquiescence by Congress:** Congress may sometimes be found to have *impliedly acquiesced* in the President's exercise of power in a certain area. Where such acquiescence exists, this fact may be enough to tip the balance in favor of a finding that the President acted within the scope of his constitutional authority.

a. *Dames & Moore* **case:** The Court relied on such a theory of implied congressional acquiescence when it upheld President Carter's power to take certain actions for the purpose of obtaining the release of American hostages from Iran, in *Dames & Moore v. Regan*, 453 U.S. 654 (1981).

i. **Facts:** As part of the settlement of the hostage situation, President Carter took a number of actions affecting the claims of American creditors against Iran. The action which posed the most difficult constitutional issue was his *suspension* of all contractual claims against Iran then pending in American courts; such claims were to be later arbitrated by an international tribunal.

ii. **Suspension upheld:** The Court found that the claims suspension was *within* the President's constitutional authority. While Congress had never explicitly delegated to the President the power to suspend such claims, it had *implicitly authorized* that practice by a long history of *acquiescing* in similar presidential conduct. (For instance, Congress had implicitly approved the use of executive agreements between the President and foreign powers to *settle* claims.)

iii. **Limited scope:** The Court carefully stressed the limited scope of its holding. It was not holding that the President has constitutional authority to settle or suspend *all* claims; the Court was simply deciding that where such settlement or suspension is a "necessary incident to the resolution of a major foreign policy dispute," *and* Congress has acquiesced in that type of presidential action, the action will be deemed within the President's constitutional authority.

iv. **Not dispositive:** In any event, the fact that Congress has impliedly consented to Presidential action will almost certainly not *by itself* bring the action within the scope of his constitutional authority; it will merely be a *factor* in the analysis of close cases. In *Dames & Moore*, the President's general executive authority in foreign policy matters (and perhaps his Commander-in-Chief powers) were probably also part of the equation.

b.   Implied acquiescence not found (*Hamdan v. Rumsfeld*):   But the Court will not always be quick to find that Congress has implicitly acquiesced in the President's exercise of power. For instance, in a 2006 decision involving the President's wartime powers, the Court *rejected* President George W. Bush's claim that, in the aftermath of the 9/11 terror attacks, Congress had implicitly granted him power to set up a special category of *"military commissions"* to try Al Qaeda members for war crimes. See *Hamdan v. Rumsfeld*, 548 U.S. 557 (2006).

   i.   Facts of *Hamdan*:   In the Uniform Code of Military Justice (UCMJ), a statute dating from long before the 9/11 attacks, Congress had required that all military commissions must use certain court-martial procedures where these were "practicable." Shortly after 9/11, Congress passed a joint resolution called the Authorization for Use of Military Force (AUMF), which authorized the President to "use all necessary and appropriate force" against any person or organization that the President found to have planned or aided the 9/11 attacks. President Bush then issued an executive order providing that any person thought to be an Al Qaeda member would be tried by a military commission having fewer protections for defendants than the court-martial procedures called for by the UCMJ (e.g., by barring them in some instances from being present at the proceeding, or even from learning what evidence was being presented). Bush claimed that Congress, in passing the AUMF, had intended to repeal the UCMJ's rule barring military commissions that did not use the court-martial procedures where practicable.

   ii.   Hamdan wins: But by a 5-3 vote, the Court disagreed with the President, and sided with Hamdan, the prisoner/plaintiff. The majority believed that Congress had not intended, when it passed the AUMF, to repeal the UCMJ's rule requiring that military commissions use the court-martial procedures where practicable. Since the UCMJ was still in force, its existence made the commissions unconstitutional, because "Whether or not the president has independent power, absent congressional authorization, to convene military commissions, he may not *disregard limitations* that Congress has, in proper exercise of its own war powers, *placed on his powers*."

   iii.   Significance: So *Hamdan* suggests that, especially in the controversial area of the President's wartime powers, the Court will be reluctant to conclude that a vague or ambiguous congressional statute constitutes implicit acquiescence in the President's exercise of the authority in question — if Congress wants to authorize the President to exercise a particular wartime power, it will have to confer that authority relatively *explicitly*.

C.   President's veto power: Article I, §7, gives the President the power to *veto* any bill passed by Congress. If the measure is vetoed, the veto can be overridden (and the measure enacted into law) only by a *two-thirds vote* in each house. There are several major separation-of-powers issues concerning the presidential veto power: (1) To what extent does the President have the ability to make a "pocket veto"? (2) Can the President constitutionally be given a "line-item veto"? and (3) To what extent does the so-called "legislative veto" violate the President's veto power?

1.   The "pocket veto":   Article I, §7 provides that ordinarily, if the President fails within ten days either to sign a bill or to veto it and return it to the house in which it originated (so that a possible override attempt can be made), the bill becomes law. However, that section also provides that if Congress by its *adjournment* has *prevented* return of the vetoed legislation, the statute cannot go into effect unless the President signs it. In this situation, the President is given an *absolute* veto power (i.e., one which cannot be overridden); this is known as a *"pocket veto."*

2. **The "line item" veto:** Nearly every president since Grant has coveted the *"line item veto."* This is the ability to veto a particular part of a bill — typically, a single item of spending — rather than the entire bill. In 1997, President Clinton became the first U.S. President to receive essentially this power from Congress. However, the Supreme Court quickly ruled that the line item veto as implemented by Congress violated the Presentment clause of the Constitution, in *Clinton v. City of New York*, 524 U.S. 417 (1998).

   a. **How the line-item veto worked:** The Line Item Veto Act gave the President the power to *"cancel"* any of several types of provisions contained in new statutes enacted by Congress, including any "item of new direct spending" and any "limited tax benefit." The Act allowed the President to sign an entire bill (containing multiple provisions) into law, and then to "cancel" any individual spending or limited-tax-benefit item he wished, provided that he did so within five days after enactment. At that point, the only way Congress could restore the vetoed item was re-enact it as a separate "disapproval bill," which the President could again veto. The net effect of the Act was to let the President plus one-third of Congress (the percentage necessary to uphold the president's veto of the disapproval bill) veto any individual item of spending or limited tax benefit.

   b. **Majority strikes down:** By a 6-3 vote, the court found that the Line Item Veto Act *violated the Presentment clause,* Art. I, §7, cl. 2. The majority opinion was by Justice Stevens.

      i. **The Presentment clause:** The Presentment clause provides that after a bill has passed both houses of Congress, but before it has become a law, it must be presented to the president; if he approves it, "he shall sign it, but if not he shall return it, with his objections to that house in which it shall have originated, who shall . . . proceed to reconsider it." (The President's "return" of the bill is what is commonly known as a presidential "veto.")

      ii. **Violates Presentment clause:** The majority concluded that the Line Item Veto Act failed to follow the Presentment clause's method of enacting or repealing statutes. The process laid down in that clause was, the majority concluded, the *only* way authorized in the Constitution to enact or repeal a bill. The Act failed to follow this procedure in at least two ways: (1) the President's "return" of the bill (his veto of it) occurred *after* the bill had been signed into law, rather than before, as the Presentment clause requires; and (2) the cancellation could apply to only *part* of the bill, whereas the Presentment clause requires veto of the *entire* bill.

      iii. **Net effect is to let President write new bill:** The net effect of the act was to produce "truncated versions of . . . bills that passed both Houses of Congress," Stevens said. The resulting bills were not the product of the " *'finely wrought' procedure* that the Framers designed." If the act were valid, "it would authorize the President to *create a different law* — one whose text was not voted on by either House of Congress or presented to the president for signature." Stevens noted that he was not expressing any opinion about the wisdom of the procedures reflected in the act; however, if the President was to play a different role in the process of enacting legislation, that change would have to come about through a constitutional amendment.

c. **Kennedy concurrence:** The majority opinion by Justice Stevens concentrated on the narrowly-technical requirements of the Presentment clause, and did not explore the *separation-of-powers* problems that the Line Item Veto Act might pose. But a concurrence by Justice Kennedy did discuss those separation-of-powers problems. Kennedy acknowledged that the act was intended to help restrain congressional spending, something that Congress seemed to have trouble doing on its own. However, he said, "failure of political will does not justify unconstitutional remedies." The act "establishes a new mechanism which gives the President the sole ability to hurt a group that is a visible target, in order to disfavor the group or to extract further concessions from Congress." This "enhances the President's powers beyond what the Framers would have endorsed."

d. **Dissent:** Three Justices — Breyer, O'Connor and Scalia — dissented in *Clinton v. New York*. The dissenters rejected the majority's core assertion that the Line Item Veto Act enabled the President to repeal or amend statutes. The President's use of his power to cancel a spending item was *not a repeal or amendment of a statute*, they said — the statute itself remains fully in force following the President's "cancellation" action. Instead, Congress had merely given the President the *discretion to spend or not spend an appropriated item*, something it had done many times in the past without problems. As Scalia put it, "[T]here is not a dime's worth of difference between Congress' authorizing the President to cancel a spending item, and Congress' authorizing money to be spent on a particular item at the President's discretion. And the latter has been done since the Founding of the Nation." Scalia concluded that the Act did not truly give the President a line item veto; the title of the act ("Line Item Veto Act") "has succeeded in *faking out the Supreme Court*."

e. **Multiple bills as solution:** One way in which Congress might achieve essentially the result it was trying for in the Line Item Veto Act would be to make sure that each item of federal spending is embodied in a *separate bill* — that way, the President could simply veto any item he wished by vetoing the bill that contained that item and only that item. However, this approach would require literally thousands of spending bills per session, each of which would have to be separately produced, and separately voted on by Congress. Nonetheless, some members of Congress have asserted, following the *Clinton* decision, that advances in computer technology make this approach a viable option.

3. **The legislative veto:** The so-called *"legislative veto"* is a device which enables Congress to monitor actions by the executive branch, including federal administrative agencies. Typically, such a legislative veto provision is included as part of a congressional statute delegating certain powers to federal agencies. If, after an agency takes a certain action (usually, issuance of a regulation), Congress disagrees, the veto provision in the original bill allows one or both houses to cancel that administrative action by means of a *resolution*. The resolution is not presented to the President (as a statute must be), and he does not receive the opportunity to veto it.

a. **Veto ruled unconstitutional:**   In one of the most important constitutional law decisions of the 1980's, the Supreme Court held that a typical one-house legislative veto was ***unconstitutional***, because it violated both the President's veto power and the bicameral structure of Congress. ***Immigration and Naturalization Service (INS) v. Chadha***, 462 U.S. 919 (1983).

    i. **Facts:**   Article I, §8 of the Constitution gives Congress the right to establish rules of naturalization and, by implication, immigration. Congress has always possessed, and has frequently exercised, the power to allow an alien who would otherwise be deportable under existing immigration rules to remain in the country; typically, this has been done by means of a "private bill" applicable to one or a few particular aliens. In an effort to relieve itself of the burdens of considering numerous private bills, Congress delegated to the Attorney General, in the Immigration and Nationality Act, the authority to suspend deportation of aliens in certain situations. However, in order to retain some control over this delegated power, Congress reserved to itself a legislative veto over each decision by the Attorney General suspending deportation. The veto could be exercised by a resolution passed by ***either*** house within a certain time after the Attorney General's decision to suspend deportation. Chadha, the plaintiff, was one of several aliens as to whom the House of Representatives used its veto power to reverse the Attorney General's suspension of deportation.

    ii. **Veto provision stricken:**   The Supreme Court ***struck down*** this legislative veto as a violation of two distinct constitutional requirements. First, the veto violated the Presentment Clause (Art. I, §7, cl. 2), which requires that every bill be presented to the President for his signature, so that he may have the opportunity to veto it. Secondly, this particular veto provision, since it could be exercised by a ***single house***, violated the ***bicameral*** requirement of Article I, §§1 and 7, by which both houses must pass a bill before it can become law.

    iii. **Essentially legislative act:**   The real issue in the case was whether the House's issuance of the legislative veto here itself constituted the exercise of ***legislative power***. Not all acts by a house fall into this category, and only the ones that do require presentment and bicameral approval. However, in the Court's view the overruling of the Attorney General's decision on a deportation matter did constitute the exercise of legislative power, since it had the "purpose and effect of altering the legal rights, duties and relations of persons ... outside the legislative branch."

    iv. **Consequence:**   Consequently, Congress could reverse the Attorney General's decision on a deportation matter only by ***passing a law***, in the constitutionally-prescribed manner (passage by both houses, presentment to the President and either signature by him or the overriding of his veto). The fact that the legislative veto mechanism may be a more "efficient" means of controlling administrative action was irrelevant.

b. **Dissent:**   Two Justices, White and Rehnquist, dissented in *Chadha*. The main dissent was by Justice White, who argued that a house's use of the legislative veto was simply not the functional equivalent of passing a law. The legislative veto "no more allows one House of Congress to make law than does the presidential veto confer such power upon the President."

    i. Administrative agencies' lawmaking function: In White's view, executive agencies engage in a sort of "lawmaking" function, and no one contends that every agency decision of a lawmaking nature need be confirmed by subsequent vote of both houses of Congress and by presidential signature. "If Congress may delegate lawmaking powers to independent executive agencies, it is most difficult to understand Article I as forbidding Congress from also reserving a check on legislative power for itself." In White's view, it was "enough that the *initial* statutory authorizations comply with the Article I requirements."

    ii. Change in status quo: Finally, White argued that the legislative veto provision in this case did not violate the separation-of-powers principles behind the bicameral and presidential-veto requirements. White contended that the net result of Congress' delegation of authority to the Attorney General plus its reservation of veto power was that "[a] departure from the status quo occurs only upon the *concurrence of opinion* among the House, Senate, and President." That is, if the determination that an alien is deportable is viewed as a change in the legal status quo, this change can be consummated only with the approval of *each* of the three actors (assuming that the Attorney General is treated as embodying the President's authority). This result preserved the required separation of powers, in White's opinion.

  c. Significance: *Chadha* thus makes the one-house legislative veto completely unusable. If the House or Senate wants to reserve power to undo the action of an administrative agency, both houses will have to pass the same bill and present it to the President for a possible veto.

  d. Two-house veto provisions: In the vast majority of instances, legislative veto clauses allowing a veto only where *both houses* act concurrently are *just as unconstitutional* as a single-house veto provision, since both types of clauses *deprive the President of his veto power.*

    i. Single-house actions approved by Constitution: There are four actions which the Constitution permits a *single house* to take, without possibility of presidential veto. In these four situations, a single-house legislative veto would presumably be *constitutional*. For instance, since the Senate alone is given the power to approve or disapprove presidential appointments (Art. II, §2, Cl. 2), the Senate could presumably pass a resolution that all presidential appointments shall be deemed approved by the Senate if that body does not vote to reject them within a certain period of time. (However, such a provision might be attacked on the theory that it delegates to the Executive Branch powers which must be affirmatively exercised by the Senate itself.)

D. Special prosecutor: Obviously a key element of the President's constitutional power is the power to *enforce the law*, including the power to investigate and prosecute violations of the law. Consequently, it might be thought that any congressional interference with the President's untrammeled right to enforce the laws would be vulnerable to a separation-of-powers argument. But the Supreme Court has recently upheld the Ethics in Government Act, which lets the Judicial rather than Executive Branch appoint a *special prosecutor* to investigate and prosecute crimes by high executive officials, and which restricts the Executive Branch's right to fire such a prosecutor. See *Morrison v. Olson*, discussed further *infra*, p. 142. The *Morrison* case seems to mean that the present Court will allow a fairly significant limitation to be placed by Congress upon the President's previously-untrammeled power to enforce the law.

E. Interference with, or undue delegation to, the Judicial Branch: So far in this section, we have focused mainly on the boundary line between Congress and the Executive Branch, and have looked at how separation-of-powers principles prevent Congress from delegating law-making power to the President (see *Youngstown Sheet*, *supra*, p. 128) or interfering with the President's powers (e.g., his veto power; see *INS v. Chadha*, *supra*, p. 133). Similar separation-of-powers issues can be presented by action that takes place at the boundary line between Congress and the ***Judicial Branch***, or the boundary between the Executive and Judicial Branches.

Basically, the same very general rule applies: the ***Judicial Branch's role cannot be abridged by action of one of the other branches***, and conversely, functions that are the ***appropriate job of the other two branches cannot be given instead to the Judicial Branch***. (Separation issues relating to the Judicial Branch actually don't arise very often.)

1. **Delegation of legislative powers:** However, Congress *does* have considerable flexibility in ***assigning*** to the Judicial Branch tasks that might be considered law-making ones, at least where the subject matter relates to the ***role of the courts***. This principle is illustrated by *Mistretta v. U.S.*, 488 U.S. 361 (1989).

   a. **Sentencing commission:** *Mistretta* involved the U.S. Sentencing Commission, set up by Congress to develop mandatory guidelines that federal judges would have to apply in setting sentences for federal crimes. Congress provided that of the seven voting members (all to be appointed by the President with the advice and consent of the Senate), at least three must be ***federal judges***. The plaintiffs claimed that this was an unconstitutional delegation of law-making power to the Judicial Branch. That is, the plaintiffs argued, Congress was assigning to the judges on the Commission not the job of interpreting the law (the proper judicial role), but the job of making ***sentencing policy***, a classic legislative function.

   b. **Delegation attack rejected:** The Court *rejected* this claim of unconstitutional delegation of law-making authority to the Judicial Branch. It is true, the Court said, that non-judicial duties may generally not be given to the Judicial Branch. But there are some exceptions, and this was one. Because the judiciary plays the major role in sentencing, allowing some judges to participate in the making of guidelines for sentences does not threaten the "fundamental structural protections of the Constitution."

II. FOREIGN AFFAIRS AND THE WAR POWERS

A. Special presidential role in foreign affairs: The Constitution gives the President substantially greater authority with respect to *foreign affairs* than with respect to domestic ones. Article II, §2, explicitly enumerates a number of powers given to him in this area (e.g., the Commander-in-Chief power, the treaty-making power and the right to appoint ambassadors). But even more generally, the need to present a clear and unified face to the world dictates that the President bear a special role in implementing the nation's foreign policy.

1. ***Curtiss-Wright* case:** This special role was emphasized in ***U.S. v. Curtiss-Wright Export Corp.***, 299 U.S. 304 (1936). In *Curtiss-Wright*, a joint resolution of Congress authorized the President to ban the sale of arms to countries engaged in a particular conflict. President Roosevelt proclaimed such an embargo, and Curtiss-Wright was charged with conspiring to sell arms to Bolivia, one of the countries to which the embargo extended. Curtiss-Wright challenged the joint resolution as being an unconstitutionally broad ***delegation*** of legislative power to the President.

   a. **Upheld by Supreme Court:** The Supreme Court ***upheld*** the resolution, and the resulting presidential embargo. The Court stressed the "very delicate, plenary and exclusive power of the President as the sole organ of the federal government in the field of international relations. ... " The need for negotiation, plus the President's special access to sources of information, required "a degree of discretion and freedom from statutory restriction which would not be admissible were domestic affairs alone involved." Here, for instance, the President would be better able than Congress to determine whether Bolivia was in fact engaged in the conflict. Thus the delegation to the President was not unconstitutionally broad, regardless of whether such delegation would be permissible with respect to a domestic issue (a question which the Court did not decide).

   b. **In accord with Congress' intent:** Observe that the presidential embargo in *Curtiss-Wright* was in accord with congressional intent; in fact, the very point of the defendant's argument was that there was excessive ***harmony*** between Congress and the President (i.e., excessive delegation). If, however, the President acted in an area where Congress had been ***silent***, or where Congress had manifested a ***contrary intent***, the President's power to make international policy would presumably be less broad. This is certainly the theory behind Justice Jackson's concurrence in the *Youngstown Sheet & Tube* case (*supra*, pp. 128-129).

   c. **Delegation problems generally:** The *Curtiss-Wright* case was really about the proper limits of delegation of power by Congress to the President. A full discussion of delegation doctrine is more properly made in the course on Administrative Law. However, the following general propositions can be stated:

      i. **International vs. domestic:** Broader delegation of lawmaking power by Congress to the President will be tolerated in the area of international affairs than in the domestic area; this is the explicit holding of *Curtiss-Wright*; and

      ii. **Delegation rules relaxed:** Even in the domestic area, the limits on delegation by Congress to the President or to administrative agencies have been substantially relaxed since the late 1930's. In general, the more precise the ***standards*** laid down by Congress to guide the executive branch or administrative agencies, the less likely it is that excessive delegation will be found.

2. **Executive agreements:** Recall that by Article II, §2, the President may enter into treaties only upon a two-thirds vote of the Senate. Presidents have often used the device of the ***"executive agreement"*** to avoid the need for Senate ratification. This device presents some separation-of-powers difficulties, which are discussed briefly *supra*, p. 78.

B. **The war powers:** The Constitution gives both Congress and the President special powers with respect to *war*:

❏ *Congress* is given the power to *"declare War* ... and make Rules concerning *Captures on Land and Water."* Art. I, § 8, cl. 11. Congress is also given the power to *"raise and support Armies"* (*id.*, cl. 12); to "define and punish ... Offences against the Law of Nations," (*id.*, cl. 10), and to "make Rules for the Government and Regulation of the *land and naval Forces"* (*id.*, cl. 14).

❏ On the other hand, the *President* is made the *"Commander in Chief"* of the *armed forces.* Art. II, § 2, cl. 1. (Also, more generally, "the *executive Power"* is "vested" in the President. Id., § 1.)

So the basic idea is that Congress declares war and maintains the armed forces, but the President, by use of his Commander-in-Chief power executive powers, carries out any war that is so declared.

We consider here two areas in which the division of war powers between Congress and the President has raised important separation-of-powers questions: (1) the President's right to *commit our armed forces abroad* without congressional approval; and (2) the President's right to *detain and try enemy combatants* who have been captured.

1. **Commitment of the armed forces abroad:** The extent to which the President may use his Commander-in-Chief powers to *commit the use of American armed forces abroad*, without a congressional declaration of war, has sparked great controversy during the last two decades.

    a. **Courts silent:** Although the President has committed American armed forces to military action without a declaration of war at numerous times during our history, the courts have rarely passed on the constitutionality of such action. Generally, Congress has tacitly acquiesced in such action, so that no litigation has arisen.

    b. **Sudden attack:** It is settled that the President may commit our armed forces to *repel a sudden attack* upon the United States itself.

    c. **Attack on allies:** It is not clear whether the President may commit forces, without congressional approval, where it is an *ally* of the U.S., rather than the U.S. itself, that is attacked.

    d. **Preemptive strike:** Similarly, the President's right to order a *preemptive strike* in anticipation of an enemy attack is unclear. Since in this situation there would probably not be time for Congress to consider the wisdom of military action, a presidentially-ordered preemptive strike would be likely to be found constitutional.

    e. **Defense treaties:** In many instances, the United States is one of several signatories to a collective *defense treaty*, pledging us to come to the aid of any treaty member who is attacked. Since the treaty has itself been ratified by the Senate, it can be argued that this constitutes sufficient authorization for the President to commit troops when another treaty signatory is in fact attacked.

        i. **Criticism:** But Tribe (p. 233 and n. 14) points out that treaty approval by the *Senate* is not the same thing as a declaration of war by *Congress* (i.e., both houses). He therefore concludes that the treaty may not be relied upon for a prolonged troop commitment, but could be used "in support of a harried ally until Congress has had ample time" to review the matter. *Id.*

f.   Delegation by Congress: Congress sometimes *delegates* to the President in advance the discretion to commit the armed forces. The best known example of this is the Gulf of Tonkin Resolution, enacted by Congress in 1964 during the early stages of the Vietnam War. The Resolution stated that "[t]he United States is ... prepared, *as the President determines*, to take all necessary steps, including the use of armed force, to assist any member or protocol state" of SEATO.

> **i.   Possibly overbroad delegation:**   It may be argued that such a *broad delegation* of Congress' war-making powers is unconstitutional. Tribe (p. 234) suggests that the test for the constitutionality of such a delegation should be the same as in other delegation contexts, i.e., whether there are *"articulated standards"* to guide the President. The Gulf of Tonkin Resolution seemed nearly empty of guidelines.

2.   Habeas corpus, and the rights of enemy combatants to it (*Boumediene*):   The post-9/11 war on terror has caused the Supreme Court to focus on the separation-of-powers implications of the *"writ of habeas corpus."* As we'll see below (p. 139), in a 2008 case, *Boumediene v. Bush*, the Court, relying on separation-of-powers principles, has concluded that non-citizens detained as enemy combatants at Guantanamo Bay, Cuba, have the constitutional right to use the habeas process to challenge in federal district court the lawfulness of their imprisonment.

a.   Nature of the habeas writ: For centuries, Anglo-American law has generally entitled prisoners to use the "writ of habeas corpus." In American law, the right of habeas corpus is basically the right of a state or federal prisoner to go to a federal district court and argue that the prisoner is being held in violation of the federal Constitution or federal law. "Habeas corpus" is Latin for "You have the body," and the idea is that the prisoner can force the "jailer" (i.e., the governmental body that is imprisoning the prisoner) to *justify* to the federal judge hearing the habeas petition *why the imprisonment is proper.*

> **i.   Suspension Clause:** The right to bring a habeas corpus petition is granted by the Constitution. This occurs by means of Art. I, s. 9, cl. 2 (the *"Suspension Clause"*), which says that "The privilege of the Writ of Habeas Corpus shall not be suspended, unless when in Cases of Rebellion or Invasion the public Safety may require it." Under post-Civil War Supreme Court cases, the right applies to *both state and federal prisoners.*

> **ii.   Federal judge can order release:** If a prisoner properly brings a habeas proceeding,[1] the federal judge is authorized to conduct her own factual inquiry into the case. Then, if the judge concludes that the prisoner is indeed being held in violation of the Federal Constitution or federal law, the judge has the power to order the prisoner released.

b.   Applicability to enemy combatants: Prior to 9/11, it had never been clear whether a *non-U.S. citizen* held by U.S. military authorities as an enemy combatant was entitled to bring a federal habeas corpus proceeding, in which the prisoner could have a federal district judge review the legality of his detention.

---

1. Congress has imposed many restrictions on habeas proceedings, especially in connection with state-court convictions. For instance, there is a one-year statute of limitations on such proceedings, and the state-court decision is entitled to a large degree of deference.

i.   **Combatant Status Review Tribunals:**   Beginning soon after 9/11, the U.S. military detained hundreds of non-U.S. citizens (aliens) in combat areas like Afghanistan and Bosnia. U.S. forces designated many of these as *"enemy combatants,"* and brought them to the U.S. base at Guantanamo Bay, Cuba, where they were held, sometimes for years. At Guantanamo, the Defense Department conducts *Combatant Status Review Tribunals (CSRTs)* to determine whether each detainee was properly classified as an enemy combatant. In the CSRTs, detainees have limited rights compared with the rights they would have if subjected to a traditional U.S. criminal trial — for instance, they do not have the right to counsel, they do not have the right to full knowledge of the charges against them, and hearsay evidence is fully admissible against them.

ii. **No habeas, according to administration:**   The Bush administration took the position that once a prisoner at Guantanamo was declared an enemy combatant and the decision was upheld in the CSRT proceeding, the prisoner could be detained indefinitely (for at least so long as the war on terror continued). The administration also contended that such an enemy combatant was not entitled to bring a habeas corpus challenge to his imprisonment.

iii. **Congress agrees:**   In two statutes, Congress agreed with the administration's view that enemy combatants should not have habeas rights. First, in the Detainee Treatment Act of 2005 (DTA), Congress said that no court would have jurisdiction to hear an application for habeas corpus brought by any alien detained by the military at Guantanamo. Instead, the sole jurisdiction to review any decision by a CSRT that a prisoner was indeed an enemy combatant was given to the federal Court of Appeals for the District of Columbia. And the D.C. Court of Appeals was *limited in the facts that it could consider* on the appeal — for instance, it *could not consider newly-discovered evidence* that the prisoner was not in fact an enemy combatant, as the court could presumably have done in a true habeas proceeding.

   (1) MCA: Then, in the Military Commissions Act of 2006 (MCA), Congress said that these jurisdiction-stripping provisions of the DTA were to be applied not just prospectively, but also to cases that were already "in the pipeline" when the DTA was enacted.

c. **The *Boumediene* case:** Several Guantanamo prisoners were able to get to the Supreme Court on two issues regarding the DTA's and MCA's jurisdiction-stripping rules: (1) Did a foreign national held at Guantanamo — which is not officially U.S. territory — have the constitutional right to bring a habeas petition? and (2) if so, did the procedures specified by Congress in the DTA and the MCA violate the prisoners' habeas rights? In *Boumediene v. Bush*, 128 S.Ct. 2229 (2008), by a 5-4 vote, the Court answered *"yes"* to both of these questions. Consequently, all prisoners held as enemy combatants at Guantanamo — and probably held at other foreign military bases that are under the full control of U.S. authorities — *have the right to challenge the legality of their detention in federal district court.*

   i.   **Facts:** The petitioners in *Boumediene* were foreigners taken prisoner by the U.S. in foreign countries such as Bosnia and Afghanistan, as part of the U.S.'s post-9/11 anti-terrorist activities. The petitioners were then brought to Guantanamo and classified as enemy combatants by military CSRT tribunals. They argued that when Congress took away their habeas rights and said they could appeal only by using the special D.C. Court of Appeal process set forth in the DTA, Congress violated their Suspension Clause rights.

ii. **Majority opinion:** Justice Kennedy allied with the four liberal members of the court (Stevens, Souter, Breyer and Ginsburg) to form a majority that found for the petitioners. Kennedy's majority opinion concluded that the MCA's stripping of federal-court jurisdiction over cases brought by foreign nationals detained at Guantánamo *violated the Suspension Clause.* To reach that conclusion, he took several steps:

(1) **"No sovereignty over the territory" argument:** The Bush administration argued that because Guantanamo is not officially U.S. territory (it's leased from Cuba), the constitutional right of habeas does not extend to detentions there. But Kennedy concluded that, since the U.S. has "complete jurisdiction and control over the base," the country *"maintains de facto sovereignty* over this territory." If the detentions occurred at a temporary military base in, say, an occupied foreign country (as happened in a Supreme Court case involving a U.S.-administered prison in allied-occupied Germany in 1950), Kennedy said, the fact that the detention was in foreign territory might prevent habeas rights from attaching. But here, "in every practical sense Guantanamo is *not abroad*; it is within the *constant jurisdiction* of the United States"; therefore, *habeas rights apply as if the prison were on U.S. soil.*

(2) **Not a substitute:** Kennedy then addressed the issue of whether the procedures here violated the Suspension Clause. For there not to be a violation, the federal court review of the results of the CSRT proceeding would have to represent an adequate substitute for habeas corpus. And that, in turn, would mean, Kennedy said, that the federal court must have "the means to correct errors that occur during [the CSRT] proceeding." But under the DTA, the reviewing court (the D.C. Court of Appeals) was *not permitted to consider any evidence outside the CSRT record* — the court's role was limited to determining whether the CSRT had followed appropriate standards and procedures. So the reviewing court could not, for instance, *consider exculpatory evidence that wasn't presented in the CSRT* (e.g., *newly-discovered* evidence). This lack of authority to consider anything beyond the CSRT record meant that the D.C. Circuit review was *not an "adequate substitute"* for habeas corpus, making the review procedures a violation of the Suspension Clause.

(3) **Separation of powers:** Kennedy emphasized *separation-of-powers principles* in rebutting the dissents' suggestion that his opinion unwisely curtailed the president's Commander-in-Chief powers. The exercise of those powers is, he said, "vindicated, not eroded, when confirmed by the Judicial Branch. Within the constitution's separation-of-power structure, few exercises of judicial power are as legitimate or as necessary as the *responsibility to hear challenges to the authority of the executive to imprison a person."*

iii. **Dissents:** Four justices dissented, in two opinions, one by Chief Justice Roberts and the other by Justice Scalia.

(1) Roberts: Roberts' dissent argued that the system devised by Congress here — review by the D.C. Court of Appeals of the CSRT tribunals' conclusions — was an ***adequate substitute*** for habeas corpus, and therefore did not violate the Suspension Clause. Roberts believed that the CSRT proceedings should themselves be viewed as *part* of the habeas-like review process. Since exculpatory evidence could be admitted in front of the CSRT, the combination of the CSRT process and the D.C. Court of Appeals' review was more than adequate to replace habeas. The majority was striking down "greater procedural protections than have ever been afforded alleged enemy detainees — whether citizens or aliens — in our national history." And, Roberts concluded, the majority's decision, while giving detainees few if any significant extra rights, would cause the American people to "lose a bit more control over the conduct of this nation's foreign policy to ***unelected, politically unaccountable judges.***"

(2) Scalia: Scalia's dissent predicted more dire consequences than Roberts' did. For Scalia, the majority opinion "will make the war [on terror] harder on us. It will almost certainly ***cause more Americans to be killed.***" Scalia feared that whatever new rules were implemented to give habeas rights to alien enemy combatants, those new rules would impose a higher standard of proof. And that higher standard would be applied in connection with events that occurred on foreign battlefields, as to which proof would be difficult under the best of circumstances. This higher standard would likely lead to an increase in the number of enemy fighters returned to combat against Americans.

For Scalia, the majority's holding meant that the Supreme Court was ***improperly second-guessing Congress and the President on military matters.*** As a consequence, "[H]ow to handle enemy prisoners in this war will ultimately lie with the branch that ***knows least*** about the national security concerns that the subject entails." The majority opinion "most tragically ... sets our military commanders the impossible task of proving to a civilian court, under whatever standards this Court devises in the future, that evidence supports the confinement of each and every enemy prisoner."

III. APPOINTMENT AND REMOVAL OF EXECUTIVE PERSONNEL (INCLUDING IMPEACHMENT)

A. The President's power of appointment: The President, not Congress, is given the power to ***appoint federal officers***. Article II, §2 (the ***"Appointments" Clause***) provides that the President shall "***nominate***, and by and with the ***Advice and Consent of the Senate***, shall appoint ***Ambassadors ... Judges*** of the Supreme Court, and all other ***Officers of the United States***. ..." That section goes on to provide that "the Congress may by Law vest the Appointment of such ***inferior Officers***, as they think proper, in the President alone, in the Courts of Law, or in the Heads of Departments."

1. Interpretation: This means that ***Congress may not appoint federal officials***.

a. Top-level ("principal") officers: In the case of ***"principal"*** officers of the United States (i.e., top-level officers), the President nominates a candidate, and the Senate must, as a constitutional matter, decide whether to approve the nomination. As to such officers, Congress *may not take away or limit* the President's right of appointment.

  i.   Cabinet members: "Principal" officers are people who have *no boss* except for the President. *Members of the Cabinet* and *ambassadors* are the main examples of principal federal officers.

b. Lower-level ("inferior") officers: In the case of *lower-level* federal officials (the ones that Article II, Section 2 refers to as "*inferior* officers"), Congress *does* have the right to limit the President's right of appointment. This right to limit the President's appointment powers comes from the final portion of the Appointments Clause, quoted above: "Congress may by Law vest the Appointment of such *inferior* Officers, as they think proper, in the *President alone*, in the *Courts of Law*, or in the *Heads of Departments*."

  i.   Three possible appointers: So although Congress cannot itself *make* appointments of inferior officers, it has the right to choose, on a position-by-position basis, to confer the power of appointment on *any* of the following: (1) the *President*; (2) the *federal judiciary*; or (3) the *"heads of departments"* (e.g., Cabinet members).

  Example 1: Congress creates the post of Deputy Secretary of State, and says that the person occupying this post must be appointed by the Secretary of State. There is no constitutional problem with this statute, since (1) the Secretary of State is a cabinet member and is thus automatically a "head of department"; and (2) the Deputy Secretary is an "inferior" federal officer, who Congress may therefore say (by authority of Article II, § 2, final sentence) shall be appointed by the head of the department in which the Deputy will serve.

  Example 2: Congress creates the post of *Assistant* Deputy Secretary of State, and gives the power of appointment for this post to the Deputy Secretary of State. This statute *is* a violation of the final portion of the Appointments Clause, assuming that the post is senior enough that the person who holds it exercises "significant authority" (the standard under *Buckley v. Valeo, infra*, p. 143, for whether a person is an inferior federal officer at all, as opposed to a rank-and-file federal employee who is not even an inferior officer). Although Congress can limit the President's power to make appointment of an inferior federal officer, Congress must give this appointment power either to the President, the judiciary, or a "head of department" (typically, a Cabinet member). The Deputy Secretary of State does not fall into any of these three categories, so Congress can't constitutionally grant her the power to appoint an inferior federal officer.

c. Dividing line: The Supreme Court has established the dividing line between "*principal*" and "*inferior*" officials in a way that leaves *few* if any employees other than Cabinet officials, ambassadors, and federal judges as "principal" officers. As noted, the only principal officers are ones who have *no boss* except for the President.

  i.   Special prosecutor: Thus in *Morrison v. Olson*, 487 U.S. 654 (1988), the Court held that *Special Prosecutors* are "inferior" officers, as to whom the President need not be given appointment power. Therefore, Congress may constitutionally delegate to the *judiciary* the job of appointing such prosecutors, who are named to investigate allegations of wrongdoing against members of the executive branch.

    ii. Consequence: Since such special prosecutors have fairly broad investigatory and litigation powers, and may be removed only for cause, the Court's judgment that they are nonetheless "inferior" probably means that virtually every federal official below Cabinet level will similarly be held to be an "inferior" one whom Congress may require to be appointed by one other than the President. (The *Morrison* case is discussed further *infra*, p. 145.)

2. No appointments by Congress: A key aspect of the Appointments Clause is that Congress itself *may not make any appointments* of federal officials, whether "principal" or "inferior." The most it may do is, in the case of inferior officers, to prescribe the *procedures* by which the President, department heads or the judicial branch shall make appointments. These "procedures" may, however, include fairly detailed qualifications regarding age, experience, etc. N&R, p. 272.

    a. Supporting employees appointable by Congress: Congress may, however, make its own appointments of persons to exercise "powers … essentially of an *investigative and informative* nature." See *Buckley v. Valeo*, discussed *infra*. Thus Congress or one of its committees might appoint a staff to make an investigation into a particular matter, e.g., the investigative staff of a Senate Committee considering reform of the nation's financial system.

B. *Buckley v. Valeo* (the *Election Law* Case): The principal modern case on the Appointments Clause is *Buckley v. Valeo*, 424 U.S. 1 (1976), where the Court invalidated the composition of the Federal Election Commission, established by the Federal Election Campaign Act. The Act provided that a majority of the FEC's members were to be appointed by the President Pro Tem of the Senate and the Speaker of the House.

1. Wide powers: The FEC was given broad powers to enforce the Act, including the right to bring civil actions against violators. The Commission was also given extensive rule-making authority.

2. Holding: The Court held that the tasks performed by the FEC were executive in nature, and could only be exercised by "Officers of the United States." Since Congress had no constitutional right to appoint such federal officers, the Commission as presently constituted was invalid, and could not exercise most of its statutorily-granted powers.

    a. Definition of "Officer of U.S.": The Court defined "Officer of the United States" to include "any appointee exercising *significant authority* pursuant to the laws of the United States. … "

C. The President's right to remove appointees: Apart from setting out the process for impeachment, *infra*, p. 147, the Constitution does not state whether and when the President, Congress, or both, may *remove* federal appointees and employees. (Article III, §1, does provide that federal judges may not be removed except for misconduct.) Accordingly, it has been left to the Supreme Court to determine the extent of the President's right to make such removals.

1. Quasi-legislative and quasi-judicial officers: Where a federal appointee holds a *quasi-judicial* or *quasi-legislative* role, Congress may *limit* or completely *block* the President's right of removal.

a. **"Independent" federal agencies:** This special rule applies to so-called *"indepen-dent"* federal agencies, i.e., agencies that *don't* mainly *carry out the President's poli-cies* (as, say, cabinet members do), but instead make significant rules governing the actions of *persons outside the executive branch,* such as private citizens. It's import-ant that these agencies be *insulated from interference* by the President. Therefore, Congress may under Article I limit the President from removing such agency heads unless he has *just cause* for the firing. Chemerinsky Hnbk, p. 351, § 4.2.

    Example: Congress creates the Federal Trade Commission, an administrative agency whose function is to administer a federal statute designed to guard against certain types of unfair competition. Congress provides that Commissioners will be appointed for fixed terms by the President (with the advice and consent of the Senate), and that the President may remove a Commissioner before the expiration of his fixed term only for cause. The President (Franklin Roosevelt) contends that the statute improperly interferes with what he says is his constitutional right to remove a Commissioner even without cause.

    Held, against the President. The FTC is an independent body designed to act quasi-legislativly and quasi-judicially. It is not part of the executive branch. To perform its functions properly, it must be free from executive-branch inteference. Therefore, Con-gress was constitutionally entitled to maintain the Commission's independence by insisting that the President may remove a Commissioner only for cause. *Humphrey's Executor v. U.S.*, 295 U.S. 602 (1935).

b. **Other agencies:** In addition to the Federal Trade Commission (at issue in *Hum-phrey's*), examples of independent federal agencies include the Securities and Exchange Commission, the Federal Communications Commission, and the Federal Reserve. Cf. Chemerinsky Hnbk, § 4.2, p. 351. So Congress may say that no principal officer in one of these agencies (e.g., a Commissioner of the FCC) may be removed by the President except for good cause.

c. **The two-level-of-protection problem:** The Roberts Court seems to give a quite *broad, pro-presidential-power*, reading to the Appointments Clause. In particular, the Court is now relatively quick to find that Congress has *unduly limited* the President's right to remove inferior officers of independent federal agencies. In a 2010 decision, *Free Enterprise Fund v. Public Company Accounting Oversight Board*, 130 S.Ct. ___ (2010), the conservative wing of the Court held, by a 5-4 vote, that Congress could not set up a *two-level scheme* in which (1) the President was prevented from removing the heads of an independent agency except for cause, and (2) the agency heads were in turn prevented from removing, except for cause, an inferior federal officer that they had appointed. The two levels of good-cause protection together were found to consti-tute a violation of the separation-of-powers principle that the executive power is held by the President only.

    i. **Facts:** After many accounting scandals, Congress set up the Public Company Accounting Oversight Board (PCAOB) to regulate most accounting firms. The members of the PCAOB were to be appointed by vote of the Securities Exchange Commission. The SEC is an independent federal agency, whose members are appointed by the President but can be removed by him only for cause.[2] In setting up the PCAOB, Congress said that Board members, in turn, could only be removed during their terms by a vote of the SEC commissioners, again only for cause.

(1) PCAOB were inferior officers: Members of the PCAOB were (the Supreme Court decided), federal officers, because they had significant authority under federal law. They were "inferior" federal officers, not principal officers, because they were subject to supervision not directly by the President, but by someone appointed by the President (namely, the SEC Commissioners). So the question in the suit was, can the President's ability to remove an inferior officer be limited by *multiple layers* of good-cause protection?

ii. **Violation of separation-of-powers:** Five members of the Court, led by Chief Justice Roberts, answered "*no*": this type of "multilevel protection" from removal *violated Article II's vesting of the executive power in the President.* Roberts reasoned that in the usual case where Congress gives a department head (e.g., a cabinet member) the power to appoint an inferior officer, then even if the inferior officer could only be removed for cause, the President could at least express unhappiness with the inferior officer by removing the department head who appointed her. But here, the two levels of good-cause protection (SEC Commissioners who could not be removed by the President except for cause, and an inferior officer appointed by those Commissioners who, similarly, could only be removed by them for cause) "*subverts the President's ability* to *ensure that the laws are faithfully executed[.]*"

iii. **Significance:** *Free Enterprise Fund* demonstrates that the modern Court takes separation-of-powers problems extremely seriously: the Court will be relatively quick to conclude that Congress has unjustifiably limited the President's executive powers, such as the power to remove lower-level independent-agency officials.

2. **Purely executive officers:** Par. 1 above covered removal only of federal officers whose role is quasi-judicial or quasi-legislative, such as heads of an "independent" federal regulatory agency. What about purely *executive* officers: may Congress limit the President's right to remove such officers?

a. **Inferior officers:** As the result of a 1988 case, the answer seems to be that, at least in the case of "inferior" (lower-level) officers, Congress *may* place similar limits on the President's right to remove even a pure executive-branch officer. Congress may limit the President's right to remove such an officer as long as the removal restrictions are not "of *such a nature that they impede the President's ability to perform his constitutional duty. ...* " *Morrison v. Olson*, 487 U.S. 654 (1988). Typically, Congress' decision to prevent the President from removing the executive officer *without cause* (while letting him remove for cause) *won't* cause a constitutional problem.

i. **Facts:** The statute in *Morrison* required the Attorney General to investigate any allegations of wrongdoing against certain high level members of the Executive Branch (including members of the Cabinet), and to apply to a special federal court (the "Special Division") for the appointment of a *special prosecutor* if he found

---

2. The SEC members were all principal federal officers, but it was permissible, under the principle of *Humphrey's Executor, supra*, p. 144, for Congress to limit the president's power of removal of them to good-cause-shown, because the Commission was an independent quasi-legislative agency.

"reasonable grounds to believe that further investigation or prosecution is warranted." Once the special prosecutor was appointed, she could only be removed by the Attorney General, and only "for good cause, physical disability, mental incapacity, or any other condition that substantially impairs the performance of [her] duties."

    ii. Holding: By a 7-1 vote, the Court held that neither the removal provisions nor the act taken as a whole so restricted the President's powers as to violate the separation-of-powers principle. Because the Attorney General could terminate the special prosecutor for *"good cause,"* the Executive Branch *"retains ample authority* to assure that the counsel is competently performing her statutory responsibilities. …*"*

  b. Top-level officers: Congress' limited right, recognized in *Morrison, supra,* p. 145, to prevent the President from removing federal officers without cause, applies only to "inferior" federal officers (*supra,* p. 142), not to *"principal officers,"* like Cabinet officers. That is, even post-*Morrison,* Congress *may not place any limits at all on the President's right to remove Cabinet officers or other principal officers.* (Recall that the *Morrison* Court determined that the special prosecutor was an "inferior" officer rather than a "principal" officer.) That's because the President's right to make such appointments is *directly and unequivocally guaranteed* by the *Appointments Clause* of Article II.

  Example: Suppose that Congress passes a statute saying, "No Secretary of State may, once appointed by the President and confirmed by the Senate, be removed by the President during the Secretary's first year in office, except either on consent of the Senate or for good cause shown." While such a statute would likely be constitutional if applied to an *inferior* federal officer (like the special prosecutor in *Morrison*), it is clearly **unconstitutional** when applied to a cabinet member like the Secretary of State. That's because the removal restriction would impede the President's ability to perform his constitutional duty of running the executive branch.

D. Removal by Congress: Let's now look quickly at the converse problem: May Congress *reserve to itself* the power to remove an *executive* officer? The brief answer to this question is *"no."* See *Bowsher v. Synar,* 478 U.S. 714 (1986).

  1. Facts: *Bowsher* involved the Gramm-Rudman Act, in which Congress attempted to reduce federal budget deficits by instituting a procedure under which automatic spending cuts would be made in certain circumstances. The Act gave a key role in carrying out these automatic-cut provisions to the Comptroller General of the U.S.

    a. Right to remove Comptroller: By separate, much older, legislation, Congress had reserved to itself the right to remove the Comptroller General from office for five specified reasons.

  2. Statute struck down: By a 7-2 vote, the Court struck down the automatic-reduction provisions of the Act. To reach this result, the Court concluded that (1) the Comptroller, if he did what the Act told him to do, would be exercising executive-branch powers; but (2) Congress' retention of the right to remove the Comptroller for certain specified types of cause *converted him into an agent of Congress, so that he could no longer exercise these executive powers* due to separation-of-powers principles.

3. **Constitutional significance:** So *Bowsher* establishes that ***Congress may not reserve the right to remove an executive officer even for cause***, at least where the definition of "cause" is fairly ***broad*** (e.g., "inefficiency," "neglect of duty," or "malfeasance," three of the causes listed in the Act).

   a. **Narrower grounds:** Apparently the retention of ***narrower grounds*** for removal of an executive officer (e.g., "permanent disability" or "commission of a felony or conduct involving moral turpitude," two other grounds for removal of a Comptroller to which the Court seemed not to object) will *not* be unconstitutional. Furthermore, nothing in the decision seems to have any impact on Congress' right to remove an executive officer by ***impeachment*** (see *infra*, immediately below).

E. **Impeachment:** The standards for ***impeachment*** are set forth in Article II, §4 of the Constitution: "[t]he President, Vice President and all civil Officers of the United States, shall be removed from Office on Impeachment for, and Conviction of, Treason, Bribery, or other ***high Crimes and Misdemeanors***."

   1. **Procedure for impeachment:** The term "impeachment" itself refers to the decision by the ***House of Representatives*** to subject the President, or other federal official, to a trial in the Senate. See Art. I, §2, Cl. 5. A House vote to impeach is thus similar to a grand jury indictment; it is not a conviction, but merely the necessary pre-condition to a trial.

      a. **Trial in Senate:** If the House votes (by a ***majority*** vote) to impeach, the trial itself occurs in the Senate, and a ***two-thirds vote*** of those Senators present is required to convict. Art. I, §3, Cl. 6. In the case of impeachment of a President, the Chief Justice presides over the trial.

   2. **Sparingly used:** The impeachment power has been sparingly used throughout our nation's history. Only three Presidents, Andrew Johnson, Richard Nixon and Bill Clinton, have been the subject of serious impeachment efforts. Presidents Johnson and Clinton were impeached by the House, and escaped conviction in the Senate. President Nixon resigned after three articles of impeachment had been voted against him by the House Judiciary Committee, but before the full House could vote on the impeachment issue.

   3. **Meaning of "high crimes and misdemeanors":** Because the constitutional phrase "high Crimes and Misdemeanors" is inevitably somewhat vague, its meaning has been subject to great dispute.

      a. **Serious crimes:** Some have argued that only "serious indictable crimes" may serve as the basis for impeachment. See Gunther & Sullivan (13th Ed.), p. 411-12.

      b. **Abuse of power:** Others have contended that any serious ***abuse of the powers*** of the presidency may serve as the basis for a President's impeachment, even if the offense would not be a crime.

      c. **Majority view:** Many commentators reject the Nixon view that only crimes may be impeachable. However, they also reject the view that *any* crime is necessarily an impeachable offense.

      Example: Suppose the President deliberately and maliciously decided to weaken our national defenses. This would probably not violate any criminal statute, but it should be considered grounds for impeachment. Tribe, p. 294.

Example: During President Clinton's impeachment, his defenders made a plausible argument that the minor crime of perjury in a civil deposition, at least where it concerned a peripheral matter (whether Pres. Clinton had had sex with someone not a party to the litigation, Monica Lewinsky) should not be treated as an impeachable offense. The Senate, by voting to acquit him despite relatively clear evidence that perjury occurred, seems to have accepted this argument.

4. **Effect of resignation:**   The fact that a federal officer has *resigned* does not bar the use of subsequent impeachment proceedings against him. The same is true of a *pardon*: thus the pardon of President Nixon by his successor, Gerald Ford, would not have prevented the use of impeachment proceedings against Nixon.

5. **Criminal liability:**   The Constitution explicitly provides that an impeachment conviction has no immediate effect other than to remove the officer from office (and to disqualify him from holding any other federal office). Art. I, §3, Cl. 7. But that same Clause provides that "the Party convicted shall nevertheless be liable and subject to Indictment, Trial, Judgment, and Punishment, according to Law." Consequently, following the impeachment conviction a *criminal prosecution* may be brought against the impeached officer, based on the same set of facts as the impeachment. A criminal conviction in this situation does not constitute double jeopardy. Tribe, p. 296.

    a. **No pardon power:**   Furthermore, a criminal conviction following an impeachment cannot be avoided by use of the pardon power. Art. II, §2, Cl. 1 gives the President the power to grant pardons "except in Cases of Impeachment." Thus had President Nixon been convicted by the Senate, Gerald Ford would not have been able to pardon him from criminal liability (at least with respect to offenses of which he was convicted in the Senate).

6. **Reviewability by Court:**   Once the Senate has convicted in an impeachment trial, it is not clear whether the *Supreme Court* may review the conviction. There are no Supreme Court precedents on point.

    a. **Pros and cons:**   The traditional view is that an impeachment conviction presents a *non-justiciable political question*. The contrary view is that the Supreme Court may review an impeachment conviction to determine at least some issues, for instance, whether an adequate definition of "high Crimes and Misdemeanors" was applied. The traditional view is probably the correct one, in light of a recent case, *Nixon v. U.S.*, 506 U.S. 224 (1993) (involving a different Nixon, Walter Nixon, a federal judge) — the Court held there that the question of what procedures validly constitute a "trial" of an impeachment case by the Senate was a non-justiciable political question. See *infra* p. 728.

IV. LEGISLATIVE AND EXECUTIVE IMMUNITY

A. **Scope of discussion:**   We examine now several facets of *immunity* held by the various branches of the federal government. In particular, we examine: (1) Congress' immunity from civil and criminal suits and from grand jury investigations; (2) the civil and criminal immunity of the executive branch; and (3) the doctrine of "executive privilege," and the related issue of protection of state secrets.

B. Congress and the Speech and Debate Clause: Article I, §6, provides that "for any Speech or Debate in either House, [members of Congress] shall not be questioned in any other Place." In general terms, this so-called Speech and Debate Clause shields members of Congress from: (1) *civil or criminal suits* relating to their *legislative actions*; and (2) *grand jury investigations* relating to those actions.

1. Rationale: The Speech and Debate Clause serves important separation-of-powers functions: for instance, it protects members of Congress against executive officials (e.g., Justice Department officials) who might seek unduly to influence congressional conduct by conducting criminal prosecutions or grand jury investigations. More generally, it serves the related function of assuring that members of Congress are not distracted from their duties by being called into court to defend their actions. See Tribe, p. 370.

C. Executive immunity: The Speech and Debate Clause has no counterpart in the Constitution giving any sort of immunity to members of the *Executive* Branch. However, as a common-law matter, the courts have recognized certain types of executive immunity.

1. Judicial process: As the result of *U.S. v. Nixon* (discussed more extensively *infra*, p. 150), there does not seem to be any general doctrine making the President or other members of the Executive Branch immune from *judicial process* (e.g., subpoenas). In the *Nixon* case, the Supreme Court affirmed a federal district court order that the President turn over the Watergate tapes. Although the Supreme Court did not explicitly discuss the issue of presidential (or other executive official) amenability to judicial process, *Nixon* seems to stand for the proposition that there is no general immunity from such process.

2. Civil liability of President for official acts: The President has *absolute immunity* from *civil liability* for his *official acts*, as the result of *Nixon v. Fitzgerald*, 457 U.S. 731 (1982), a 5-4 decision.

   a. Facts: Fitzgerald, the plaintiff, contended that he had been fired from his Defense Department job in retaliation for testimony in which he had criticized military cost overruns. His suit charged Nixon and several Nixon Administration officials with violating his First Amendment and statutory rights.

   b. Holding: In an opinion by Justice Powell, the Court held that the President is entitled to *absolute immunity* from civil damage actions for all acts within the *"outer perimeter"* of his authority. Since the President has authority to prescribe the manner in which the business of the armed forces will be conducted, including the authority to dismiss personnel, Nixon was immune from liability for the firing of Fitzgerald *even if he caused it maliciously or in an illegal manner*.

   c. Dissent: Four members of the Court dissented vigorously. The principal dissent, by Justice White, contended that there was no reason to depart from the usual rule that absolute immunity "attaches to particular functions — not to particular offices." The majority's approach, White argued, *"places the President above the law* [and] is a reversion to the old notion that the King can do no wrong."

3. Civil immunity of presidential assistants: Do presidential *assistants* get a similar absolute immunity from civil suits for their official acts? The brief answer is *"no."* *Harlow v. Fitzgerald*, 457 U.S. 731 (1982), a companion case to *Nixon v. Fitzgerald*.

   a. Qualified immunity granted: But presidential assistants do get fairly broad *"qualified* immunity." Essentially, a presidential assistant has immunity from civil suit for conduct arising out of her performance of her office, except where the official has violated a *"clearly established"* right.

Example: Suppose a cabinet official fires a subordinate, on the grounds that the subordinate is openly gay. Suppose further that at the time of the firing, there is no clearly established law about whether the federal government may fire a person for being gay. Even if, immediately after the firing, the Supreme Court decides that such firings are illegal, the cabinet official will benefit from his qualified immunity. This is because, at the moment of the firing, he was not violating a "clearly established" right.

4. **No presidential immunity for non-official acts:** *Fitzgerald* only established immunity for *official* presidential acts, i.e., those that are within the "outer perimeter" of the President's job. There is *no immunity* — not even qualified immunity — for acts that the President takes that are completely *unrelated to the carrying out of his job*. This was the holding of *Clinton v. Jones*, 520 U.S. 681 (1997).

   a. **Paula Jones case:** *Clinton v. Jones* involved a private damages suit by Paula Jones against President Clinton, filed while Clinton was in office. Jones claimed that while she was employed by the state of Arkansas and Clinton was Governor of Arkansas, Clinton made illegal sexual advances to her. Clinton argued that a President should have "temporary immunity" — to last while he is in office — against virtually all civil litigation arising out of events that occurred before he took office.

   b. **Claim rejected:** But the Court unanimously *rejected* this claim. The Court noted that the rationale for immunity for *official* acts of the President and other officials was that such immunity "serves the public interest in enabling such officials to perform their designated functions effectively *without fear* that a particular decision may give rise to personal liability." This rationale did not apply to the President's unofficial acts, including any acts he took before he became President. Therefore, there was no policy reason for allowing even temporary immunity for unofficial acts.

5. **Criminal prosecution:**   There is *no* executive immunity, either of a common-law or constitutional nature, from *criminal* prosecution. Tribe, p. 268.

   a. **Delay:** However, a strong argument may be made that, at least in the case of the President, the Constitution's provision of impeachment as the means of removing federal officers bars any criminal prosecution of such officials until *after they have been removed from office.* In the case of the President, Tribe states that "[t]he question must be regarded as an open one. ... " Tribe, p. 269.

      i. **People other than the President:** In the case of the Vice-President and other federal officers, criminal prosecution prior to impeachment seems to be permissible. For instance, Vice-President Agnew was indicted by a federal grand jury on bribery and tax evasion charges prior to his resignation, although the Supreme Court did not pass on the "no prosecution prior to impeachment" argument. *Id.* at 268-69.

D. **"Executive privilege":**   Several Presidents have invoked what they described as the doctrine of *"executive privilege"* to justify their refusal to *disclose information* which they claimed to be confidential. The only Supreme Court case to give any definitive scope to the doctrine was *U.S. v. Nixon*, 418 U.S. 683 (1974), the famous "Watergate Tapes" case. In *Nixon*, the Court recognized in general terms a constitutionally-based doctrine of executive privilege, but held that the privilege was only a *qualified* one, which was overcome on the facts of *Nixon* by the needs of a pending criminal investigation.

1. **Facts:** In March of 1974, a federal grand jury indicted seven Nixon aides on charges of conspiracy to obstruct justice and other Watergate-related offenses. The President was named as an unindicted co-conspirator. The Watergate Special Prosecutor then persuaded the federal trial court to issue a subpoena *duces tecum* to the President requiring him to produce various tapes and documents relating to certain meetings involving the President; these documents and tapes were to be used during the trial of the indictments. The President released transcripts of some of the tapes, but refused to produce the tapes themselves, and moved to quash the subpoena. The trial court rejected the President's claim of privilege, and the matter was heard by the Supreme Court on an expedited basis.

2. **Holding:** Although the Supreme Court upheld the general doctrine of executive privilege, the Court held that in this case, *the privilege did not apply,* and ordered the President to comply with the subpoena.

   a. **Court, not President, decides:** First, the Court rejected the President's claim that "the separation of powers doctrine precludes judicial review of a President's claim of privilege." The Court quoted Justice Marshall's statement, in *Marbury v. Madison* (*supra*, p. 9) that it is the duty of the judicial branch to "say what the law is." Thus the *Court*, not the President, must evaluate claims of presidential privilege.

   b. **Privilege exists:** The Court then held that there was indeed a privilege for *"confidentiality of Presidential communications in the exercise of Article II powers*. ... "* The Court noted that confidentiality was required by the fact that "those who expect public dissemination of their remarks may well temper candor with a concern for appearances and for their own interests to the detriment of the decision-making process." Therefore, the Court concluded, the privilege of confidentiality "can be said to derive from the supremacy of each branch within its own assigned area of constitutional duties."

   c. **Privilege only qualified:** However, the Court rejected the President's claim that the executive privilege was an absolute one. At least where the claim of privilege was (as in the present case) a *general* one, and not related to a particular need to protect "military, diplomatic, or sensitive national security secrets," the Court held that the privilege was merely a *qualified* one. As such, it was *outweighed* by the need to *develop all relevant facts in a criminal trial.*

      i. **Rationale:** The Court observed that both the President's claim of privilege, and the criminal justice system's need for access to all relevant evidence, were of constitutional dimension. However, the latter outweighed the former, in part because the Court did not believe that the possibility of infrequent subpoenas like the one here would often have an adverse impact on the candor of discussions to which Presidents are parties.

   d. **Duty of trial court:** The President was therefore ordered to deliver the subpoenaed tapes and documents to the federal district court. However, the district court was ordered to perform a close *in camera* (i.e., non-public) examination of all of the materials. Statements that were both admissible and relevant to the criminal prosecution were to be isolated, and all other statements were to be disregarded and kept secret.

3. **Scope of *Nixon* holding:**   The precise scope of the *Nixon* Court's holding is unclear.

    a. **Status in criminal proceedings:**   Where, as in the *Nixon* case itself, the presumptively privileged material is sought by the ***prosecution*** for use in a criminal case, the Court's opinion seems to mean that the qualified privilege will always be outweighed by the needs of the criminal justice system (at least if military, diplomatic or national security secrets are not involved).

        i. **Possibly more limited scope of holding:**   But the Court may not have meant for the privilege to carry so little weight. Tribe suggests that the Court may have meant that only materials which were "***essential***" to the trial (rather than merely relevant and admissible) will be deemed non-privileged. Tribe, p. 281.

    b. **Criminal defendant:**   Where privileged information is sought by a ***defendant*** in a criminal proceeding (rather than by the prosecution, as in *Nixon*), the reasons for overriding the claim of privilege seem to be even more compelling. Due process demands that a defendant have access to all information relevant to his defense. Also (at least in a federal prosecution) the executive branch, which controls the prosecution, always has the option of dropping the case rather than releasing the privileged information. See Tribe, p. 282.

    c. **Civil suits:**   The *Nixon* case did not touch at all on the fate of presidential privilege in ***civil*** proceedings. Tribe suggests that civil proceedings should be placed on the ***same footing*** as criminal ones, and therefore that "[a] showing that presumptively privileged information is needed in a civil trial should be sufficient to overcome the presumption." Tribe, p. 283.

    d. **State secrets:**   The *Nixon* Court made it clear that "military, diplomatic, or sensitive national security secrets" would be placed upon a different footing from a mere "general" claim of confidentiality (as in *Nixon* itself). It remains to be seen how such "***state secret***" matters will be handled. In cases where external evidence demonstrates to the court's satisfaction that a state secret *is* indeed involved, the Court may well decide, even without an *in camera* inspection, that the presidential privilege outweighs the needs of the judicial system. Where a court is not satisfied, from external evidence, that a state secret is really involved, an *in camera* inspection may be necessary; however, once the Court decides that sensitive matters of state are at issue, it will probably give substantially greater weight to the privilege than in the "general" confidentiality situation. See generally Tribe, pp. 284-85.

    e. **Congressional inquiries:**   Another area carefully left untouched by the *Nixon* Court is the conflict between a presidential claim of privilege and the needs of a ***congressional inquiry***. For instance, had the *Nixon* case involved the Senate Watergate Committee's subpoena for tapes, rather than a subpoena stemming from a grand jury investigation, it is not at all clear whether the result would have been the same. The need to prevent Congress from usurping the President's functions certainly presents an additional separation-of-powers concern not present in the judicial-proceedings situation. The precise weighing of a claim of privilege against congressional needs must be regarded as an open question.

    f. **Assertion by non-incumbents:**   *U.S. v. Nixon*, of course, involved an assertion of executive privilege by the ***incumbent*** President. In a subsequent case, also related to Richard Nixon, the Court held that the qualified privilege could also be asserted by a

non-incumbent. In *Nixon v. Administrator of General Services*, 433 U.S. 425 (1977), the Court held that Nixon could assert executive privilege with respect to his presidential papers, which were to be entrusted to succeeding administrations for archiving under congressionally-prescribed guidelines.

    i.   **Privilege not violated:** However, the Court held that the guidelines, at least insofar as they permitted an Executive Branch employee to screen the materials and return items of a personal nature to the ex-President, did not violate his executive privilege. The Court's decision was influenced in part by the fact that neither of the two succeeding administrations supported Nixon's claim of privilege, thus suggesting that the functioning of the Executive Branch was not threatened by the archiving and screening process.

Quiz Yourself on
SEPARATION OF POWERS *(ENTIRE CHAPTER)*

19. Congress passes the Personal Communications Services Act of 1999. The PCSA authorizes the FCC to award to private applicants, based on competitive bid, various pieces of radio spectrum for use in a new method of providing cellular phone service. The PCSA provides that any spectrum award by the FCC shall become permanently effective 90 days after it is first made, unless Congress has within the 90-day period enacted a Joint Resolution cancelling the particular award. According to the statute, such a Joint Resolution is to take effect immediately, without further action by any government official. The FCC then awards a particular spectrum license to Comm Co. Sixty days after this award, Congress passes a Joint Resolution purporting to cancel the award to Comm Co.

    (a) If Comm Co. wishes to attack the constitutionality of the Joint Resolution stripping it of its license, what is the best argument it can make? _____

    (b) Will this constitutional attack succeed? _____

20. The Caribbean island of Grenoble is a small but strategically important ally of the United States. Grenoble holds a popular election, but the military refuses to allow the democratically elected president to take office. The military then begins to seize the property of American businesses located in Grenoble. The President of the the U.S., concerned that U.S. strategic interests are endangered, and invoking his powers as Commander in Chief, sends 20,000 U.S. troops onto the island. This action is taken after the President confers with congressional leaders, but with no other congressional action. With Congress still inactive, fighting continues for six months, due to the Grenoble military's well-entrenched status. A member of Congress, Senator Piper, then brings suit for a declaratory judgment that the President has acted unlawfully in using U.S. forces in this manner.

    (a) What is the best argument that Senator Piper can make against the constitutionality of the President's actions? _____

    (b) Will Piper's attack succeed? Assume there's no existing relevant federal legislation. _____

21. Congress has established the Federal Truck Safety Board (FTSB). In the statute setting up the FTSB, Congress has provided that the Director of the FTSB shall be appointed by the President, without the need for House or Senate confirmation. The enabling legislation also provides that at any time, without cause, the House and Senate, acting together in the form of a Joint Resolution, may remove the Director. The Director is given certain powers, including the ability to issue an order suspending certain types of truck traffic if the Director concludes that the suspension is needed to protect the safety of interstate commerce.

In the 30 years since the FTSB was set up, Congress has played no role in the appointment or removal of the FTSB's Director. The incumbent, Derrick, was appointed 10 years ago. Recently, there have been a rash of accidents on the highway involving trucks of more than six feet in width. Derrick has decided that such wide trucks are dangerous, and has, therefore, issued an order suspending any truck of that width or greater from moving on the federal highways across a state border. Truck Co., owner of many extra-wide trucks, wishes to challenge the constitutionality of Derrick's action.

(a) What is the best grounds on which Truck Co. can challenge the constitutionality of Derrick's order?

_____

(b) Will this attack succeed? _____

22. Jessica was the White House Press Secretary. After she had served for one year, the President summarily fired her, without giving any reasons. Jessica sued the President for damages in federal court, alleging that he fired her in violation of a federal statute, Title VII. Jessica's claim is that the President made sexual advances to her, and fired her in retaliation for her refusal to entertain those advances. (Title VII does indeed prohibit sexual harassment of the sort charged here.) The President has moved to dismiss the suit on the broad grounds that he has absolute immunity from civil liability for any official act done by him during his term of office, and that the court must dismiss the case without considering whether the allegations are true or false. Should the President's motion be granted? _____

Answers

19. (a) That the Resolution violates the Presentment Clause, by which the President is given the opportunity to veto any bill.

(b) Yes. The scheme described here is a classic two-house *"legislative veto,"* under which Congress attempts to keep oversight over administrative action by reserving the power to cancel that administrative action by means of a Resolution. The scheme here, insofar as it calls for the Joint Resolution to take effect immediately, deprives the President of his opportunity to veto any bill. Therefore, the scheme is invalid. See *INS v. Chadha* (The theory behind the invalidity of the legislative veto is that the Resolution is itself the exercise of legislative power, so it must be carried out by the same procedures as for any other legislative act, i.e., passage by a majority of each house and presentment to the President for his signature.)

20. (a) That it violates Congress' sole power to declare war.

(b) Yes, probably. It is true that Article II, Section 2, explicitly grants the President the power of Commander in Chief of the U.S. Armed Forces. However, the President must use this power subject to oversight by Congress. In particular, the power to "declare war" is given solely to Congress, in Art. I, Section 8. While the President may, without a declaration of war, probably commit our troops to repel an immediate emergency, it is very unlikely that the President may wage a prolonged ground war, without a declaration of war, especially where the United States has not been directly attacked.

Also, the 2006 decision in *Hamdan v. Rumsfeld* indicates that in cases where the President asserts broad power to act in wartime, and it is not clear that Congress has acquiesced to what the President is doing, the Court will favor Congress over the President. So here, probably the Court will say that the President's action violates Congress' sole power to declare war.

21. (a) That by retaining the right to remove Derrick, Congress has improperly vested executive func-

tions in its own agent.

(b) Yes, probably. Congress and its agents can only exercise "legislative power," not "executive power." The FTSB Director's powers are clearly executive — the Director is carrying out the laws (by determining what is required for safety) rather than "formulating" the laws. Congress, by retaining the right to remove the Director without cause, converted the post of Director into an agent of Congress, thus in effect taking executive powers onto itself. Therefore, Derrick is not permitted to exercise his statutory powers, including issuance of the order. See *Bowsher v. Synar*, striking down certain powers of the Comptroller General on the similar analysis that Congress improperly converted him into an agent of Congress by retaining the power to remove him.

22. Yes. The President does indeed have absolute immunity from civil liability for his official acts. See *Nixon v. Fitzgerald*. This immunity applies even if the official act was done illegally or maliciously. If the President did in fact fire Jessica for the reasons she states, the President has clearly violated Title VII, which bans various forms of sexual discrimination, including sexual harassment. However, since the President was clearly acting within the "outer perimeter" of his duties as President (that is, when he fired his Press Secretary he was clearly acting within the bounds of his Presidential authority), the illegality of his actions is irrelevant for civil damage purposes. (Observe that if the conduct charged here had been carried out by any other federal government official, the immunity would have merely been a "qualified" one, since the conduct charged here violated a "clearly established" right. See *Harlow v. Fitzgerald*.)

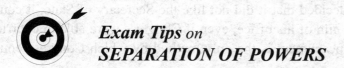

Exam Tips *on*
SEPARATION OF POWERS

Separation-of-powers problems are usually pretty easy to spot. The harder part, usually, is to say something intelligent about how the issue should be resolved, since the law in this area is very hazy. Here are some particular things to watch for:

☛ Whenever your fact pattern indicates that the President is issuing an ***"executive order,"*** consider whether this may amount to the ***making of law*** rather than the mere carrying out of law. If so, the President is probably treading on Congress' domain. (But remember that if Congress acquiesces, even implicitly, to the President's exercise of power, then the problem disappears. See, e.g., *Dames & Moore v. Regan*.)

☛ Always remember that "legislation" cannot go into effect unless the President has been given the opportunity to ***veto*** the bill. Therefore, if your fact pattern has Congress do something by a one-house or concurrent ***resolution***, determine whether what Congress is doing amounts to lawmaking; if so, the action is unlawful. (See, e.g., *INS v. Chadha*, the "legislative veto" case.)

☛ One of the most common separation-of-powers issues involves the President's power as Commander in Chief to ***commit the use of American armed forces abroad***. The general rule, of course, is that only Congress, not the President, may declare war.

   ☞ However, the President may commit our armed forces even without a declaration of war in order to ***repel a sudden attack***, and probably to defend an ally with whom we have a treaty. But if you conclude that one of these exceptions applies, note in your answer that the President probably has the obligation to consult with Congress after the fact, and to bring our troops back if Congress has not passed a declaration of war within, say, a couple of months.

☛ Any time your fact pattern involves the **appointment** or the **firing** of a **federal official**, be alert to possible separation-of-powers problems.

    ☞ The President, not Congress, has the **power to appoint** federal officers. Federal officers include ambassadors, federal judges, Cabinet members, agency heads, etc.

        ❑ When the President appoints a **"principal"** officer of the United States (i.e., a **top-level** officer), the appointment does not take effect until the **Senate "advises and consents,"** i.e., approves. This applies to **members of the Cabinet, ambassadors** and **federal judges.**

        ❑ Congress cannot appoint **"inferior"** (non-top-level) federal officers either. But it can decide **which of three players** (the President, the federal judiciary, and the **"heads of departments,"** i.e., Cabinet members) may appoint any given inferior officer.

    ☞ The most frequently-tested area involving appointment of federal officers involves **removal** of officers once they have been appointed.

        ☞ Congress may **not** itself ever remove a federal officer, **except by impeachment.** (*Example:* If Congress decided that it did not like the Secretary of State, it could not pass a law stripping him of his office, even if Congress were able to override the President's veto. Impeachment is the only method by which Congress could remove this officer.)

        ❑ But Congress **may limit the President's right to remove** a federal official, at least officials working for or heading **"independent"** agencies, and officials who are pure-executive-branch but are **"inferior"** officers.

        Example: Congress can say that no SEC Commissioner may be removed during her fixed term except for cause. (That's so because the SEC is an *independent* agency, i.e., one that's not just in charge of carrying out the President's executive-branch policies.)

        ❑ Congress may **not** limit the President's right to fire **high-level purely-executive-branch officers** (e.g., **Cabinet members**).

        Example: Congress may not pass a law stating, "The Secretary of State shall have a fixed term of at least four years, and may not be sooner removed by the President without cause." That would violate the separation-of-powers, since it would seriously impair the President's power to carry out his own responsibilities as head of the executive branch.

☛ **Impeachment** is occasionally tested.

    ☞ Keep in mind the procedural rules: by majority vote, the House decides whether to "impeach" (which is like an indictment). Then, the Senate conducts a trial, at which a two-thirds vote is necessary for conviction.

☞ Your fact pattern may involve the issue of whether the President or another federal official may only be removed for crimes, or may also be removed for non-criminal "abuses of power." The constitutional phrase is "high crimes and misdemeanors," but it is not clear what this means.

☛ Issues relating to *immunity* of the various branches are sometimes tested:

☞ If a *member of Congress* is sued (either civilly or criminally), or called before a grand jury, be alert to the possibility that the member may be protected by the *"Speech or Debate"* Clause, which is basically a form of immunity.

☞ There is a common-law immunity for the *President* and other members of the *Executive Branch*.

☞ Members of the Executive Branch other than the President get only *qualified* immunity from civil suits. (Focus on whether the right violated by the official was "clearly established" at the time he acted; if it was, he can be liable, if not, he'll be immune.)

☞ Remember that there is *no* Executive-Branch immunity from *criminal* prosecutions.

☛ If your fact pattern involves a President or other Executive-Branch member who wants to *decline to disclose* material, consider the possibility that the doctrine of *"executive privilege"* may apply. If you discuss the doctrine, remember that the privilege is merely a *qualified* one, which can be outweighed by other interests (e.g., the need to develop all facts at a criminal trial). Also, mention that claims of executive privilege are justiciable — that is, the Court will typically decide these claims, rather than avoiding them as non-justiciable political questions.

CHAPTER 9

DUE PROCESS OF LAW

ChapterScope

This Chapter examines principally the Due Process Clause of the *Fourteenth* Amendment, which imposes the obligation of due process on the states. As you read, keep in mind that there is also a *Fifth* Amendment Due Process Clause, which applies only to the federal government; in general, anything that the Fourteenth Amendment Due Process Clause would require the states to do, the Fifth Amendment Due Process Clause requires the federal government to do. Here are the key concepts in this Chapter:

- ■ **Due Process Clause generally:** The Fourteenth Amendment provides (in part) that "no state shall make or enforce any law which shall ... deprive any person of *life*, *liberty*, or *property*, without due process of law. ... " This is the Fourteenth Amendment's Due Process Clause.

- ■ **The Bill of Rights and the states:** One of the major functions of the Fourteenth Amendment's Due Process Clause is to make the *Bill of Rights* — that is, the first ten amendments — applicable to the states.

  - ❑ **Not directly applicable to states:** The Bill of Rights is not *directly* applicable to the states — the Bill of Rights as originally drafted limited only the *federal* government, not state or municipal governments.

  - ❑ **Application of Bill of Rights to states:** But the Fourteenth Amendment, enacted in 1868, essentially changed this rule. That amendment requires that the states not deprive anyone of "life, liberty or property" without due process. Nearly all the guarantees of the Bill of Rights have been interpreted by the Supreme Court as being so important that if a state denies these rights, it has in effect taken away an aspect of "liberty."

  - ❑ **Selective incorporation:** The Supreme Court has never said that due process requires the states to honor the Bill of Rights as a whole. Instead, the Court uses an approach called *"selective incorporation."* Under this approach, each right in the Bill of Rights is examined to see whether it is of "fundamental" importance. If so, that right is "selectively incorporated" into the meaning of "due process" under the Fourteenth Amendment, and is thus made binding on the states.

    - ❑ **Nearly all rights incorporated:** By now, nearly *all rights* contained in the Bill of Rights have been incorporated, one by one, into the meaning of "due process." The only major Bill of Rights guarantees *not* incorporated: (1) the Fifth Amendment's right not to be subject to a criminal trial without a *grand jury indictment* (so a state may begin proceedings by an "information" rather than indictment); and (2) the Seventh Amendment's right to a *jury trial* in *civil cases*.

    - ❑ **"Jot-for-jot" incorporation:** Once a given Bill of Rights guarantee is made applicable to the states, the *scope* of that guarantee is interpreted the *same way* for the states as for the federal government.

- ■ **Substantive due process generally:** One function of the Due Process Clause is to limit the *substantive power* of the states to regulate certain areas of human life. That is, certain types of state limits on human conduct are held to so unreasonably interfere with important human rights that they amount to an unconstitutional denial of "liberty." This use of due process analysis is called "substantive due process" analysis.

❑ **Non-fundamental rights:** In doing substantive due process analysis, courts distinguish between *fundamental* and *non-fundamental* rights. If a right or value is found to be "non-fundamental," then the state action that impairs that right only has to meet the easy "mere-rationality" test. That is, the state must merely be pursuing a *legitimate governmental objective*, and be doing so with a means that is *rationally related* to that objective.

   ❑ **Economic regulation:** Nearly all *economic* regulation (and most *"social welfare"* regulations) implicates only non-fundamental rights, and is thus usually upheld under this easy "mere-rationality" standard.

❑ **Fundamental rights:** But if a state or federal government is impairing a *"fundamental"* right, then the Court uses *strict scrutiny*: only if the governmental action is *"necessary"* to achieve a *"compelling"* governmental objective, will the government avoid violating substantive due process.

❑ **Significance of distinction:** The single most important thing to do when analyzing a substantive due process problem is thus to determine whether the right in question is "fundamental." If the right is not fundamental, there's almost certainly no substantive due process problem. If the right *is* fundamental, then strict scrutiny will almost certainly result in the measure's being invalidated.

■ **Economic and social-welfare regulation:** It is very easy for state *economic* and *social-welfare* regulation to survive substantive due process attack. The state must merely be pursuing a legitimate state objective by rational means. Virtually every state enactment that does not implicate a fundamental right will be upheld under this standard.

■ **Fundamental rights generally:** If a state or federal regulation *does* impair a fundamental right, then the Court *strictly scrutinizes* the regulation.

❑ **Test used:** Here is the test used by courts applying strict scrutiny where a state or federal regulation impairs a fundamental right: (1) the objective being pursued by the state must be *"compelling"*; and (2) the means chosen must be *"necessary"* to achieve that compelling end. In other words, there must not be any *less restrictive means* that would do the job just as well.

   ❑ **Burden of proof:** Strict scrutiny also shifts the *burden of persuasion*. That is, when a fundamental right is involved, it's up to the state to show that it's pursuing a compelling objective and that the means chosen are "necessary" to achieve that objective — it's not up to the plaintiff to show that the state fails to meet these tests.

❑ **Rights governed:** The only rights that are "fundamental" for substantive due process purposes are ones related to the *"right of privacy"* or *"right of autonomy"*:

   ❑ **Birth control:** Individuals' interest in *using birth control* is "fundamental." So the state can't impair that interest without satisfying strict scrutiny.

   ❑ **Abortion:** Similarly, *abortion* is a right protected by substantive due process. (However, the state has a somewhat countervailing interest in protecting "potential life," so that not all restrictions on the right of abortion will be subjected to strict scrutiny.)

❑ **Family relations:** A person's decisions about how to live her *family life* and *raise her children* are also usually "fundamental." Thus the right of relatives to *live together*, a parent's right to direct the *upbringing* and *education* of his children, and the right to *marry* are all fundamental. Therefore, these rights can be impaired only if the state can pass strict scrutiny.

■ **Procedural due process:** The Due Process Clause protects not only "substantive" rights as discussed above, it also requires that the state act with adequate or fair *procedures* when it deprives a person of life, liberty or property.

❑ **Life, liberty or property:** There cannot be a procedural due process problem unless the government is taking a person's *life, liberty or property*. There is *no general interest* in having the government behave with fair procedures.

❑ **Property:** Most procedural due process problems involve the issue of whether the thing being taken constitutes "property."

❑ **Government benefits:** *Government benefits* may or may not constitute "property" rights. Generally, if one is just *applying* for benefits, one does *not* have a property interest in those benefits. But if a person has *already been getting* the benefits, usually he's got a property interest in *continuing* to get them, so the government cannot *terminate* those benefits without giving him procedural due process. The same analysis generally applies to government *jobs*: if you're just applying for the job, you don't have a property interest in it, but if you already have the job, then you may have a property interest, which entitles you to fair procedures before the job can be taken away.

❑ **Process required:** Once you determine that a person's interest in property or liberty is being impaired, you have to determine exactly *what procedures* the person is entitled to get.

❑ **Non-judicial proceedings:** Usually, the issue arises in a non-judicial proceeding (e.g., taking away someone's government job or government benefits). In general, in a non-judicial proceeding, the state does *not* have to give the individual the full range of procedural safeguards needed for a court proceeding. Instead, the court conducts a *balancing* test to determine the required procedures — the strength of the plaintiff's interest in receiving a particular procedural safeguard is weighed against the government's interest in avoiding extra burdens from having to give that safeguard. Thus in a particular situation the government may or may not have to give, say, a hearing, depending on the strength of the plaintiff's interests and the burden to the state in giving the hearing.

I.   THE BILL OF RIGHTS AND THE STATES

A. The Bill of Rights generally: The first ten amendments to the Constitution, all adopted in 1791, are commonly called the *Bill of Rights*. Their principal purpose is to protect the individual against various sorts of interference by the federal government.

1. **Not applicable to the states:** The Supreme Court decided fairly early that the guarantees of the Bill of Rights *were not directly binding upon state governments*. In *Barron v. The Mayor and City Council of Baltimore*, 32 U.S. (7 Pet.) 243 (1833), an opinion by John Marshall, the Court reasoned that "[h]ad the framers of [the Bill of Rights] Amendments intended them to be limitations on the powers of the state governments, they would have … expressed that intention … in plain and intelligible language." This conclusion has generally been accepted as being historically justified. See, e.g., N&R, pp. 339-340.

   a. **Consequence:** As a consequence of the *Barron* holding, however, neither the Supreme Court nor the lower federal courts was able to exercise significant control over the substance of state legislation, or the procedures by which a state law was administered. For instance, in *Barron* itself, the City of Baltimore (a subdivision of the State of Maryland) ended up being able to divert a stream in a way that ruined plaintiff's wharf; the "Taking" Clause of the Fifth Amendment was not applicable to a state government. What little control over state government existed was exercised mainly through the Contract Clause of Article I, §10 (discussed *infra*, p. 395).

B. **Enactment of the Civil War Amendments:** The relative lack of constitutional restrictions on relations between state governments and individuals was drastically changed by the enactment of the three Civil War Amendments, the Thirteenth, Fourteenth and Fifteenth. Each of these three was enacted for the purpose of barring discrimination by states against individuals, especially blacks.

1. **Fourteenth Amendment:** Of greatest interest to us here is the Fourteenth Amendment, especially §1. §1 provides, in full, as follows:

   > "All persons born or naturalized in the United States, and subject to the jurisdiction thereof, are citizens of the United States and of the State wherein they reside. No State shall make or enforce any law which shall abridge the privileges or immunities of citizens of the United States; nor shall any State deprive any person of life, liberty, or property, without due process of law; nor deny to any person within its jurisdiction the equal protection of the laws."

C. **Due process of law and "incorporation":** Shortly after the Fourteenth Amendment was enacted, the Supreme Court seems to have implicitly rejected the notion that that Amendment automatically made applicable to the states all of the Bill of Rights guarantees (which had previously been binding solely on the federal government). See Gunther & Sullivan (13th Ed.), p. 431. But exactly what effect the Fourteenth Amendment had on the states' obligation to honor the Bill of Rights remained quite unsettled until well into this century. Most of the litigation on this issue has involved the *criminal procedure* aspects of the Bill of Rights.

1. **Two contrasting views:** There have been two main contrasting views espoused by members of the Court on this issue: the *"selective incorporation"* or "fundamental rights" approach, and the *"total incorporation"* approach. The former has always held a majority on the Court, but proponents of the latter view have triumphed in practice, although not in doctrine.

2. **"Selective incorporation" or "fundamental rights" view:** The *"selective incorporation"* approach denies that the entire Bill of Rights is made applicable to the states via the Fourteenth Amendment. Instead, the term "liberty" as used in that Amendment is to be interpreted by judges without regard to the Bill of Rights. Only those aspects of liberty that are in some sense *"fundamental"* are protected by the Fourteenth Amendment against

state interference. (That is, those parts of the Bill of Rights which are of fundamental importance are "selectively incorporated" into the Fourteenth Amendment.) For this reason, the selective incorporation approach is sometimes called the "*fundamental rights*" approach.

3. **"Total incorporation" view:** The contrary view, that *all* of the guarantees specified in the Bill of Rights are made applicable to the states by the Fourteenth Amendment's Due Process Clause, is usually referred to as the "*total incorporation*" view.

4. **Modern approach:** As noted, the selective incorporation/fundamental rights approach has always held a majority on the Court. The Court today incorporates into the Fourteenth Amendment any guarantee which is "fundamental in the context of the [judicial] processes *maintained by the American states*." *Duncan v. Louisiana*, 391 U.S. 145 (1968).

   a. **Right to jury trial:** Thus in *Duncan*, the Court held that the Fourteenth Amendment guaranteed the right to a jury trial in state criminal prosecutions for which the potential sentence was two years in jail. A criminal process which was fair and equitable but used no juries was easy to imagine, the Court noted, but in the American scheme, where the jury is extensively used, and very serious punishments are generally imposed only after a right to a jury trial, the jury plays a fundamental role which the Fourteenth Amendment must safeguard.

   b. **Nearly all guarantees incorporated:** Although the Court has continued to adhere, in theory at least, to the selective incorporation/fundamental rights approach, the Warren Court speeded up the process by which individual Bill of Rights guarantees were incorporated into the Fourteenth Amendment. Today, *virtually the entire Bill of Rights* has been incorporated into the Fourteenth Amendment (and thereby made applicable to the states), one guarantee at a time.

      i. **Exceptions:** The only important Bill of Rights guarantees that have *not* been incorporated into the Fourteenth Amendment are the Fifth Amendment's prohibition of criminal trials without a *grand jury indictment*, the Seventh Amendment's right to *jury trial in civil cases,* and the Eighth Amendment's prohibition on *excessive fines*. (Application to the states of the Eighth Amendment's prohibition on *excessive bail* has only been implicit. See N&R, pp. 340-341.)

         (1) **Second Amendment:** The *Second Amendment* right of individuals to *keep weapons* for self-defense is the most recent Bill of Rights guarantee to be selectively incorporated, and thus made applicable to the states. See *McDonald v. City of Chicago*, 130 S.Ct. ___ (2010) (discussed *infra*, p. 437).

   c. **"Jot-for-jot" or "bag and baggage" incorporation:** Once the Court determines that a particular Bill of Rights guarantee is incorporated into the Fourteenth Amendment, is the *scope* of that guarantee the same when applied to the states as when applied to the federal government? Some members of the Court, at various times, have argued that the answer should be "no." But a majority of the Court has always believed that once a particular guarantee is applied to the states, its *contours should be the same* as in its federal application. This majority view has sometimes been characterized (by those not holding it) as the "*jot-for-jot*" or "*bag and baggage*" approach to incorporation. See the dissent in *Crist v. Bretz*, 437 U.S. 28 (1978).

i.   Illustration: An example of the prevailing "jot-for-jot" approach is *Malloy v. Hogan*, 378 U.S. 1 (1964): "[T]he prohibition of unreasonable searches and seizures of the Fourth Amendment ... and the right to counsel guaranteed by the Sixth Amendment are ... to be enforced against the states under the Fourteenth Amendment according to the *same standards* that protect those personal rights against federal encroachment. ... The Court has rejected the notion that the Fourteenth Amendment applies to the states only a *'watered-down' subjective version* of the individual guarantees of the Bill of Rights."

d.   Anomaly on jury trial right: There is one anomalous situation in which a Bill of Rights guarantee is presently interpreted to have a different scope in state proceedings than in federal ones. In *Apodaca v. Oregon*, 406 U.S. 404 (1972), the Court upheld the constitutionality of *non-unanimous jury verdicts* in state criminal cases, even though jury verdicts in federal criminal cases must be unanimous.

D.   The Fifth Amendment's Due Process Clause: Throughout this chapter, we'll be referring almost exclusively to the Due Process Clause of the *Fourteenth* Amendment. But there is another Due Process Clause: the *Fifth* Amendment states that "No person shall be ... deprived of life, liberty, or property, without due process of law..."

1.   Binding on federal government: The Fifth Amendment, since it is part of the Bill of Rights, binds the federal government. Observe that the language of the Fifth Amendment's Due Process Clause is virtually identical to that of the Fourteenth Amendment's Due Process Clause, except as to which government is bound.

2.   Same interpretation: Court decisions have interpreted the two clauses *identically*. That is, if a given type of conduct would be a due process violation when carried out by a state, it's equally forbidden to the federal government. It's important, however, to state which Amendment is triggered: the Fourteenth Amendment governs state action and the Fifth Amendment governs federal action.

II.   SUBSTANTIVE DUE PROCESS — BEFORE 1934

A.   Introduction: The Due Process Clause of the Fourteenth Amendment reads as follows: "Nor shall any State deprive any person of life, liberty, or property, without due process of law[.]"

If this language is analyzed literally, it sounds like a limitation that relates solely to *procedures*. However, the clause came to be interpreted as a limitation upon the *substantive power* of state legislatures to regulate various areas of economic and non-economic life.

1.   Meaning of "liberty":   Courts' willingness to review (and often invalidate) the substance of state legislation has taken place principally through interpretation of the term *"liberty,"* as used in the Due Process Clause. For instance, if a given state regulation is found to be an undue interference with a private person's "freedom of contract," or with his "right to privacy," the regulation is stricken as a taking of "liberty" without due process of law.

2.   Substantive due process: The doctrine relying on the Fourteenth Amendment to invalidate a substantive state regulation is commonly called the *"substantive due process"* doctrine.

3. **Growth, abandonment and rebirth:** The present section of this outline, and the two which follow it, trace: (1) the rise of substantive due process from the late nineteenth century until the 1930s; (2) the doctrine's abandonment (at least with respect to economic regulation) in the late 1930s; and (3) its fairly dramatic rebirth as a means for vindicating a broad range of *non-economic* interests (especially the so-called *"right to privacy"*).

B. **Early history of substantive due process:** When the Fourteenth Amendment was first enacted, it was not clear whether it would be found to limit states' substantive, as opposed to procedural, powers.

1. *Slaughterhouse Cases*: In fact, in a case decided shortly after the Fourteenth Amendment was enacted, the Court seemed reluctant to conclude that that Amendment might limit states' powers. In the *Slaughterhouse Cases*, 83 U.S. (16 Wall.) 36 (1873), the Court had to decide whether Louisiana could give a monopoly on New Orleans-area slaughterhouses to a particular company. The Court held that this monopoly did *not* violate the Due Process Clause. Although one of the dissenters argued that a statute prohibiting a large group of citizens from pursuing a lawful employment deprived them of both liberty and property without due process of law, the majority curtly rejected this contention, apparently on the theory that the Due Process Clause protects only against procedural unfairness.

2. **Rise of substantive due process:** But within just a few years after the 1873 *Slaughterhouse* decision, pressures on the Court to review the *substance* of state economic regulation proved compelling. There were several reasons why this occurred:

   a. **"Natural rights" theory:** First, even before the Civil War, many English and American philosophers espoused the *"natural law"* doctrine. This doctrine held that certain rights (especially the right to own property and the right to contract freely) were "fundamental" or "natural" rights, i.e., rights which derived not from any constitution or legal system but simply from the nature of things. It was only a short step to the view that if a legislature enacted a law which restricted these "natural rights," the statute was a deprivation of "liberty" and/or "property" without due process of law.

   b. **Laissez-faire economic theory:** The nation's rapid post-Civil War economic development coincided with the rise in *"laissez faire"* economic theory, according to which industrial growth and national well-being would be maximized by *minimizing government interference with business.* This "laissez faire" theory was related to so-called *"social Darwinism,"* a doctrine which asserted that, in socio-economic life, as in evolution of species, only the fittest would and should survive.

   c. **Enactment of Fourteenth Amendment:** Finally, enactment of the Fourteenth Amendment, with its explicit guarantee of due process protection of liberty and property against state action, came to be viewed by the Court as a "peg" on which substantive review of state law could be hung. This occurred despite the initial rejection of this view by the majority in the *Slaughterhouse Cases*.

3. **Increasing scrutiny:** In two important post-*Slaughterhouse Cases* decisions, the Supreme Court sustained state regulations, but indicated its willingness to engage in substantive review in some circumstances.

   a. **Regulation of "private" contracts:** In *Munn v. Illinois*, 94 U.S. 113 (1877), the Court deferred to the legislature's judgment as to an issue which the Court found to be "public" rather than "private" (the rates charged by grain elevators); but the Court indicated that in "mere private contracts," the judiciary would determine what regulations were "reasonable."

b. **Violations of "fundamental law":**   And in *Mugler v. Kansas*, 123 U.S. 623 (1887), even though the Court sustained a state ban on alcoholic beverages, the opinion indicated that legislation would be valid under the states' "police powers" only if it truly related to protection of the public health, safety or morals, and only if it did not violate "rights secured by the *fundamental law.*"

4. **Liberty of contract:**   Then, in 1897, the Court finally used substantive due process review to invalidate a state statute. In *Allgeyer v. Louisiana*, 165 U.S. 578 (1897), the Court struck down a Louisiana statute which prohibited anyone from obtaining insurance on Louisiana property from any company not licensed in Louisiana.

a. **Rationale:**   The Court held that the statute violated the Fourteenth Amendment's Due Process Clause because it prevented the defendant (who had bought insurance from an out-of-state firm) from exercising his *freedom of contract*. The guarantee of "liberty" in the Fourteenth Amendment, the Court stated, protected not only physical liberty, but also such intangibles as the right to live and work where one wishes, to earn one's livelihood "by any lawful calling," and to enter any contracts necessary to accomplish any of these goals. While the state's police power might allow it to prohibit certain activities or contracts, that power did not extend to barring contracts, like this one, which were both made and to be performed outside of the state.

C. *Lochner* **and its aftermath:**   The 40 years after *Allgeyer* saw an enormous Supreme Court trend towards striking down state legislation on due process and similar constitutional grounds. Between 1899 and 1937, 159 Supreme Court decisions (not counting civil rights cases) held state statutes unconstitutional under the Due Process and Equal Protection Clauses; another 25 were struck down under the Due Process Clause coupled with some other constitutional provision. L,K&C, p. 439.

1. **The** *Lochner* **case itself:**   The best known, and from today's perspective most infamous, of these cases was *Lochner v. New York,* 198 U.S. 45 (1905). In *Lochner*, the Court struck down as an abridgement of *"liberty of contract,"* and therefore a violation of due process, a New York law which limited the hours which a bakery employee could work to 10 per day and 60 per week.

a. **Two defenses of statute:**   The statute was defended on two grounds: (1) that it was a valid labor law; and (2) that it protected the health and safety of the workers.

b. **Not valid labor law:**   The Court quickly rejected the labor law justification for the statute. The police power extended only to protection of the "public welfare." The readjustment of bargaining power between bakery employees and their employers, the Court implied, was not of sufficiently public (as opposed to private) concern, especially in view of the law's infringement of the "liberty of contract." (The Court suggested that if bakers were not as intelligent as other workers, or for some reason needed unusual protection, the statute might be valid as a labor law; but the Court found no reason to believe that bakers as a class needed such special protection.)

c. **Not safety or health measure:**   Nor did the Court accept the "health and safety" rationale advanced for the statute. The Court did not find bakers to be an especially endangered group (as it had found miners to be in a case a few years previously). And long working hours did not affect the ***public*** health and safety by making the baked goods less fit to eat. In any event, the Court indicated, any interest the state had in guarding the wholesomeness of the baked goods could be satisfied by measures which interfered less with freedom of contract, e.g., inspecting premises, requiring that washrooms be furnished, etc.

d. Legislature's motives suspected: The *Lochner* majority clearly disbelieved that the legislature had in fact acted in part for safety and health reasons. The law's natural effect was to regulate labor conditions, not to protect anyone's health and safety. The Court thus implied that only the legislature's ***actual motive***, not a hypothetical motive, would be looked to in evaluating a statute subjected to substantive due process attack.

e. No deference to legislative fact finding: Another key element of the *Lochner* Court's holding was its ***refusal to defer to legislative findings of fact***. The Court insisted on reaching its own conclusions on the factual issue of whether the health and safety of bakers, or of the bread-eating public, needed special protection. For instance, the Court stated that "[i]n our judgment it is not possible in fact to discover the connection between the number of hours a baker may work in the bakery and the healthful quality of the bread made by the workman."

f. Dissent: Four Justices dissented in *Lochner*.

    i. Harlan's dissent: One dissent, authored by Justice Harlan, argued that there was enough evidence that the statute would promote the health and safety of bakers that the legislature's judgment on this issue should have been accepted.

    ii. Holmes' dissent: The other dissent, a very famous one by Justice Holmes, contended that the Court had no right to impose its own views about correct economic theory on legislatures. He made one of the most famous remarks in constitutional law: "The Fourteenth Amendment does not enact Mr. Herbert Spencer's social statics," a reference to a then popular "social Darwinism"/"laissez faire" theory. Holmes went on to say that "[a] constitution is not intended to embody a particular economic theory, whether of paternalism and the organic relation of the citizens of the state or of laissez faire." "Liberty," as the term is used in the Fourteenth Amendment, should be found to be violated only when "a rational and fair man necessarily would admit that the statute … would infringe fundamental principles as they had been understood by the traditions of our people and our law." By that test, Holmes contended, the statute was valid.

g. Analysis of *Lochner* test: Observe that the *Lochner* majority's test was an extremely stringent one in at least two respects:

    i. Close fit: First, it required a ***very close "fit"*** between the statute and its objectives. In the majority's words, there had to be a "real and substantial" relationship between the statute and the goals which it was to serve. This tight fit was absent in *Lochner* because bakers could have been protected by less restrictive measures, e.g., more frequent inspections, required bathrooms, etc.

    ii. Limited objectives: Second, only certain legislative ***objectives*** were acceptable. Regulation of health and safety was permissible, but ***readjustment of economic power*** or economic resources was ***not***. Thus to the extent that the New York law in *Lochner* was merely a "labor law" which readjusted bargaining power, rather than a true health regulation, it served an impermissible objective. See Tribe, pp. 570-74.

2. **Relation to fundamental interests:** Even today, strict due process scrutiny is used by the Court where a "fundamental interest" is at stake. Perhaps the *Lochner* Court's mistake was in treating "freedom of contract" as a "fundamental interest," so that the counterbalancing state interest had to be subjected to strict-scrutiny rather than minimal-rationality review. Gunther & Sullivan (13th Ed.), pp. 466-67.

3. **Other decisions of the *Lochner* era:** The period from about 1900 to 1937 was characterized, as noted, by widespread invalidation of economic legislation on substantive due process grounds. But not every statute directly affecting economic rights was overturned.

   a. **Maximum hours:** Consider laws setting maximum work hours, for instance. The *Lochner* case, of course, invalidated maximum-hour statutes as they pertained to bakers. But the Court was willing to allow such laws where it found that the benefited class for some reason *needed special protection*, beyond that given to workers in general.

      i. **Women:** Thus in *Muller v. Oregon*, 208 U.S. 412 (1908), the Court sustained a law barring the employment of *women* in a factory or laundry for more than ten hours in a day; the decision viewed women as members of a weaker class "disadvantage[d] in the struggle for subsistence," and therefore needing special protection.

         (1) **"Brandeis brief" technique:** By the way, *Muller* saw the first use of the "Brandeis brief" technique. This type of brief (named after then-lawyer Louis Brandeis, who used it in *Muller*) contained extensive documentation to demonstrate the requisite link between the legislative end and the means used to achieve it (e.g., in *Muller*, the special weaknesses and needs of women, and the extra protection which a ten-hour maximum work day would give them).

   b. **Minimum wages:** On the other hand, the Supreme Court in the *Lochner* era struck down a *minimum wage* law for women. *Adkins v. Children's Hospital*, 261 U.S. 525 (1923). The Court did this even though it had previously accepted maximum-hour laws for women (in *Muller*, *supra*). Again, the rationale was "freedom of contract," and again, Justice Holmes dissented.

      i. **Reconciliation:** One explanation of the apparent inconsistency between *Muller* and *Adkins* is that maximum hour rules could be seen as promoting a legitimate health objective, whereas it was hard to see minimum wage rules as promoting anything other than a lessening of economic inequality. See Gunther & Sullivan (13th Ed.), pp. 472-73, n. 3; Tribe, p. 573, n. 22.

III. SUBSTANTIVE DUE PROCESS — THE MODERN APPROACH TO ECONOMIC AND SOCIAL-WELFARE REGULATION

A. **Initial decline of Lochnerism:** *Lochner*, and the judicial philosophy behind it, were subjected to intense criticism in the three decades which followed that case. In addition to this criticism, the election of Franklin Roosevelt, and his New Deal programs, convinced many people of the need for aggressive legislative programs to ensure the nation's economic survival. Such large-scale government intervention in economic affairs was clearly at odds with the *Lochner* "freedom of contract" philosophy.

1. **Shift in Court personnel:** Turnover in the Court's personnel, together with Roosevelt's threat of Court-packing, contributed to a philosophical shift towards greater deference to legislative intervention in economic affairs. See Tribe, p. 449.

2. ***Nebbia* case:** The decline of Lochnerism was presaged by *Nebbia v. New York*, 291 U.S. 502 (1934), where the Court sustained a New York regulatory scheme for fixing milk prices. The Court did not explicitly reject the *Lochner* philosophy. However, the majority noted that due process required only that "[t]he law shall not be unreasonable, arbitrary or capricious, and that the means selected shall have a real and substantial relation to the object sought to be attained … " A state was free "to adopt whatever economic policy may reasonably be deemed to promote public welfare, and to enforce that policy by legislation adapted to its purpose." (The *Nebbia* majority also explicitly rejected the contention that only businesses involving a special "public interest," such as utilities or monopolies, could be subjected to governmental price regulation.)

    a. **Significance:** *Nebbia's* requirement of a substantial means-end relationship was essentially the test of *Lochner*. But the *Nebbia* Court was clearly determined not to impose upon legislatures its own views about correct economic policy, as the *Lochner* Court had done.

3. ***West Coast Hotel Co. v. Parrish:*** But it was not until several years after *Nebbia* that the Supreme Court explicitly overruled one of the major *Lochner*-era precedents. This occurred in *West Coast Hotel v. Parrish*, 300 U.S. 379 (1937), where the Court upheld a state minimum wage law for women, and thereby explicitly overruled the *Adkins* case (*supra*, 168).

    a. **Rationale:** The Court mentioned the state's interest in protecting the health of women. But it gave substantial weight to the state's interest in redressing women's ***inferior bargaining power*** as well. The Court conceded that the minimum wage law interfered with "freedom of contract," but unlike *Adkins* (or *Lochner*), the decision concluded that a readjustment of economic bargaining power in order to enable workers to obtain a living wage was a legitimate limitation on that freedom of contract.

B. **Judicial abdication in economic cases:** *Nebbia* explicitly (and *West Coast Hotel* implicitly) preserved the requirement of a "real and substantial relation" between an economic regulation and a legitimate state objective. But cases following *West Coast Hotel* virtually abandoned even this degree of scrutiny between means and ends in economic cases.

1. ***Carolene Products:*** The year after *West Coast Hotel*, the Court made it clear that a ***presumption of constitutionality*** would be applied in the case of an economic regulation subjected to due process attack. In *U.S. v. Carolene Products Co.*, 304 U.S. 144 (1938), the Court sustained against a due process attack a federal prohibition on the interstate shipment of "filled" milk, i.e., skimmed milk mixed with non-milk fats.

    a. **Rationale:** The Court noted that Congress had acted upon findings of fact (e.g., committee reports) showing a public health danger from the filled milk. But even in the absence of explicit legislative findings, the Court held, "[t]he existence of facts supporting the legislative judgment is to be ***presumed***, for regulatory legislation affecting ordinary commercial transactions is not to be pronounced unconstitutional unless … it is of such a character as to preclude the assumption that it rests upon some rational basis within the knowledge and experience of the legislators." This test might be characterized as a "*minimum rationality*" standard, coupled with a *presumption of constitutionality.*

2. **Lessening of scrutiny:** But even the relatively mild scrutiny of *Carolene Products* was abandoned by the Supreme Court in subsequent economic regulation cases.

    a. **Hypothetical reasons to support act:** For instance, the court has frequently been willing to *hypothesize* reasons which would support the legislature's action, even though there is *no evidence* whatsoever that these reasons *in fact motivated* the lawmakers.

        i. **Illustration:** Thus in *Williamson v. Lee Optical Co.*, 348 U.S. 483 (1955), the Court upheld an Oklahoma statute which, *inter alia*, prevented opticians from fitting eyeglass lenses into frames (even old lenses into new frames) without a prescription from an ophthalmologist or optometrist. The statute was a rational health measure, the Court found, because the legislature "*might have concluded*" that in some instances prescriptions were necessary to permit accurate fitting, or that "eye examinations were so critical, not only for correction of vision, but also for detection of latent ailments or diseases, that every change in frames and every duplication of a lens should be accompanied by a prescription from a medical expert." Similar hypothetical justifications were given for restrictions on advertising by opticians.

        ii. **Consequence:** A consequence of the Court's tendency to hypothesize reasons in support of economic legislation is that one who attacks such legislation has the burden of rebutting not only reasons given by the legislature, but also all reasons which the legislature "might have" considered. Some of these hypothetical reasons may not even surface until the Court writes its opinion, making the job of attacking such legislation difficult indeed. See N&R, p. 388.

C. **Summary of modern approach:** In summary, the modern Court has *withdrawn almost completely from the business of reviewing state legislative economic regulation for substantive due process violations.* Not since 1937 has the Court struck down an economic regulation for violating substantive due process, and the present members of the Court all seem in agreement with this withdrawal.

    1. **"Minimum rationality" standard:** Assuming that the objective being pursued by the legislature in an economic regulation falls within the state's "police power" (now extremely broadly defined to include virtually any health, safety or "general welfare" goal), all that is required is that there be a *minimally rational relation* between the means chosen and the end being pursued. This easy-to-satisfy standard is frequently called the "*mere-rationality*" standard, and that's the term we'll use here.

        a. **"Arbitrary and irrational":** As the Supreme Court has sometimes phrased the standard, a regulation will be presumed to be constitutional unless government has acted in an "*arbitrary and irrational*" way. *Duke Power v. Carolina Environmental Study Group, Inc.*, 438 U.S. 59 (1978).

    2. **"Social welfare" legislation:** The highly deferential mere-rationality standard applies not only in the case of economic regulation, but also in the case of "*social welfare*" legis-

lation, so long as "fundamental" constitutional rights are not impinged. See, e.g., *Whalen v. Roe*, 429 U.S. 589 (1977), where the Court sustained New York's maintenance of a computerized data base of users of certain prescription drugs; the scheme was held to be an "orderly and rational legislative decision," and therefore not violative of substantive due process.

a. **Distinguished from "fundamental" rights:** But where a law in the economic or "social welfare" area impinges on something the Court has found to be a "*fundamental right*," a substantially higher level of scrutiny is applied. The most important fundamental right, at least in substantive due process cases, has turned out to be the broadly-defined "*right of privacy*." Privacy cases are discussed extensively beginning at p. 172, *infra*.

Quiz Yourself on

SUBSTANTIVE DUE PROCESS — ECONOMIC AND SOCIAL-WELFARE REGULATION

23. The legislature of the state of Utopia was worried about the large number of consumers being abused by the harassing tactics of debt collectors. A committee of the legislature investigated, and discovered that the vast majority of complaints involved debt collection techniques used by non-lawyers. Therefore (and at the urging of the state Bar Association), the Utopia legislature passed a statute providing that no person not admitted to the Bar of the State of Utopia may engage in the business of collecting debts owed by consumers. Kneecap, a non-lawyer debt collector, wishes to challenge the statute's constitutionality.

(a) Putting aside any possible First Amendment issues, what right held by Kneecap is most likely to have been violated by the Utopia statute? _____

(b) With respect to the right you listed in your response to (a), what is the standard for determining whether the right has been violated? _____

(c) Will Kneecap's attack on the statute succeed? _____

Answer

23. **(a) Kneecap's substantive due process rights have been violated.**

(b) Whether the statute bore a rational relation to a legitimate state objective.

(c) No. Where a state statute regulates a purely economic matter, and does not involve any fundamental right, all that is required is that the means chosen be rationally related to a legitimate governmental objective. Here, the objective of reducing the harassment of consumer debtors falls within the state's police power, and is clearly "legitimate." The relation between the means chosen (ban on all non-lawyer collections) and achievement of the objective of reducing harassment is tenuous. But so long as the legislature could rationally have **believed** that non-lawyers were worse offenders on average than lawyers, the requisite "rational relation" between means and end is satisfied. In fact, for over 50 years, no state economic regulation has been overturned for substantive due process purposes, assuming an absence of a fundamental right. (The right to engage in the business of debt collection will almost certainly be held not to be "fundamental," a status limited in substantive due process cases to the "right to privacy," i.e., the areas of sex, marriage, child-bearing and child-rearing.)

IV. SUBSTANTIVE DUE PROCESS — PROTECTION OF NON-ECONOMIC RIGHTS, INCLUDING "FUNDAMENTAL" RIGHTS

A. Overview: We turn now to those cases, mostly modern, in which the Supreme Court has in effect given substantive due process protection for certain *non-economic* rights. In contrast with the economic rights area, where the Supreme Court has virtually abstained from meaningful due process review since the late 1930s (see *supra*, p. 170), the Court has been surprisingly willing, during the last fifteen or so years, to strike down legislation which it finds to violate important non-economic interests.

1. **"Two-tier" scrutiny:** This dichotomy stems from the fact that the Court has applied *two* (or more) different *standards of review* in substantive due process cases. In the case of economic rights, the Court has required merely that there be a *rational relation* between the statute and a legitimate state objective. But where the Court finds that a *"fundamental right"* is impaired by a statute, it has applied a scrutiny that is stricter in two respects:

   a. the state's *objective* must be *"compelling,"* not merely "legitimate"; and

   b. the *relation* between that objective and the means (i.e., the means-end "fit") must be very close, so that the means can be said to be *"necessary"* to achieve the end.

2. **Comparison with equal protection:** This two-tier scrutiny is used in very much the same way in *equal protection* cases; differential treatment of groups will be sustained if it is rationally related to a legitimate state goal, unless either the classification impairs a "fundamental right," or the classification itself is found to be "suspect." See *infra*, p. 234.

3. **Which rights are "fundamental":** In the substantive due process area, the rights which the Supreme Court has found to be *"fundamental"* have tended to be in the related areas of *sex, marriage, child-bearing* and *child-rearing*.

   a. **Right to "privacy":** Generally, the Court has treated most of the interests it has found to be fundamental as falling within the broad category of the *"right to privacy."* However, as will be seen below, the Court's use of the term "privacy" often differs substantially from what we normally consider this term to mean. In many instances (e.g., the child-bearing situation), a more descriptive term might be the right to *"personal autonomy."*

4. **Significance of two tiers:** The significance of the Court's decision to place a particular "right" into the "fundamental" or "non-fundamental" side of the line is even greater than might at first be supposed.

   a. **Non-fundamental right:** Where the right is found not to be fundamental, so that a "legitimate" state objective, and a rational relation between the means chosen and that objective, are all that is required, the Court's deference to the legislative judgment is so extreme that there is *virtually no scrutiny at all*. As noted, for instance, in the economic area no statute has been invalidated on substantive due process grounds in over 50 years.

   b. **Fundamental right:** By contrast, if the right is found to be fundamental, the scrutiny is so strict that few statutes impairing it can meet the double test of showing that the state's objective is "compelling," and that it cannot be achieved in a less burdensome way.

    c. Significance: Thus the Court's decision on "fundamentalness" tends to be ***virtually dispositive*** of whether the statute is sustained or invalidated.

  5. Relevance of "liberty": In some of the cases discussed below, the Supreme Court does not expressly state that it is using the doctrine of substantive due process. Nonetheless, these cases are usually treated as being, at bottom, substantive due process holdings. This is so because these decisions are properly viewed as holding that the right in question (whatever it is) is part of the ***"liberty"*** guaranteed against state action by the Fourteenth Amendment. For instance, Justice Stewart's concurrence in *Roe v. Wade, infra,* p. 176, stated that the prior *Griswold* decision (striking down state barriers to birth control by married couples) "can be rationally understood only as a holding that the Connecticut statute substantively invaded the 'liberty' that is protected by the Due Process Clause of the Fourteenth Amendment."

  6. Scope of following discussion: Most of the discussion which follows is concerned with two principal areas: ***birth control*** and ***abortion*** (*infra,* pp. 174 and 176, respectively). Then, aspects of family relations (*infra,* p. 197) and other privacy/autonomy-related issues (including sexuality, *infra,* p. 200) are treated. We then conclude with a more complete discussion of the process by which the Court deems a particular right to be fundamental or non-fundamental (*infra,* p. 216).

B. The early non-economic cases: Although vindication of non-economic rights by use of the substantive due process doctrine has become of great practical importance only in recent years, several much older cases make similar use of the doctrine. The best known are *Meyer v. Nebraska,* 262 U.S. 390 (1923) and *Pierce v. Society of Sisters,* 268 U.S. 510 (1925).

  1. *Meyer:* In *Meyer,* the Supreme Court struck down a state law which prohibited the ***teaching of foreign languages*** to young children. The Court held that the term "liberty," as used in the Fourteenth Amendment, included many non-economic, but nonetheless important, rights; the right of teachers to teach, and that of students to ***acquire knowledge,*** were among these. The Court applied what appears to have been a "mere-rationality" test (rather than any kind of strict scrutiny), but nonetheless concluded that the statute was "without reasonable relation to any end within the competency of the State."

  2. *Pierce:* In *Pierce,* the Court struck down a state statute requiring children to attend public schools, and thus preventing them from attending private and parochial ones. This decision rested on the "liberty of parents and guardians to direct the upbringing and education of children under their control." The Court denied the power of the state to "standardize its children" by forcing them to accept only public instruction.

  3. *Skinner:* A third case was decided on equal protection grounds, but was motivated by substantive-due-process-like concerns. In *Skinner v. Oklahoma,* 316 U.S. 535 (1942), the Court invalidated an Oklahoma statute which provided for compulsory sterilization of persons convicted three times of felonies showing "moral turpitude," but which did not apply to such "white-collar" crimes as embezzlement. The Court objected to the discrimination between, say, grand larceny and embezzlement, but it emphasized that its reason for strictly scrutinizing the discrimination was that "marriage and procreation are fundamental to the very existence and survival of the race."

a. Probable modern view: If a statute like the one in *Skinner* arose today, it would almost certainly be struck down on substantive due process/"right of privacy" grounds, even without regard to equal protection. Given the Supreme Court's acceptance of the fundamental importance of procreation in *Griswold* (birth control) and *Roe v. Wade* (abortion), it is almost inconceivable that the state would be permitted to sterilize any group (with the possible exception of convicted rapists).

   i. Sterilization of mental defectives: A law allowing involuntary sterilization of institutionalized **mental defectives** would also almost surely be struck down today. Yet such a statute was upheld, in one of the less glorious moments of the Supreme Court, in *Buck v. Bell*, 274 U.S. 200 (1927); Justice Holmes justified the statute with the remark that "three generations of imbeciles are enough."

C. Birth control (the *Griswold* case): The first major modern-era case which used a substantive-due-process-like approach to protect a fundamental right was **Griswold v. Connecticut**, 381 U.S. 479 (1965), the famous **contraceptives** case.

1. **Facts of *Griswold*:** The statute at issue in *Griswold* was a Connecticut law which forbade the use of contraceptives (and made this use a criminal offense); the statute also forbade the aiding or counseling of others in their use. The defendants were the director of the local Planned Parenthood Association and its medical director. They were convicted of counseling **married persons** in the use of contraceptives. No users, married or single, were charged in the case.

2. **Majority strikes statute:** The Court, by a 7-2 vote, **struck down** the statute. The majority opinion, authored by Justice Douglas, declined to make explicit use of the substantive due process doctrine. Instead, the opinion found that several of the Bill of Rights guarantees protect the privacy interest and create a "**penumbra**" or "zone" of privacy. The Court then concluded that the right of married persons to use contraceptives fell within this penumbra.

   a. Examples: Thus the Court claimed that the First Amendment, by its explicit protection of the freedoms of speech and of the press, has "emanations" which create a "penumbra"; it is this penumbra which protects, for instance, the freedom of association, a freedom not explicitly mentioned in the Constitution. Similarly, the Court found, the Fourth Amendment's ban on unreasonable searches has a penumbra which protects privacy interests, as do the Third, Fifth and Ninth Amendments. Collectively, these Amendments establish a zone in which "privacy is protected from governmental intrusion."

   b. Why statute was invalid: Douglas' majority opinion did not specify exactly how the Connecticut ban on contraceptives violated this penumbra of privacy. But a good part of the rationale seemed to have to do with the privacy implications of **proof** in prosecutions. Thus the Court asked: "Would we allow the police to search the sacred precincts of marital bedrooms for telltale signs of the use of contraceptives?" Douglas concluded that "[t]he very idea is repulsive to the notions of privacy surrounding the marriage relationship."

3. **Concurrences:** There were three separate concurring opinions in *Griswold*. All agreed with the Douglas opinion's basic conclusion that the Connecticut statute violated the Fourteenth Amendment interest in liberty, but each reached this conclusion by different means.

a. **Goldberg's Ninth Amendment view:** Justice Goldberg believed that the Fourteenth Amendment Due Process Clause protected all "fundamental" rights, whether or not these were explicitly listed in the Bill of Rights. He contended that the ***Ninth Amendment*** (which provides that "[t]he enumeration in the Constitution, of certain rights, shall not be construed to deny or disparage others retained by the people") supported this view, because it "shows a belief of the Constitution's authors that fundamental rights exist that are not expressly enumerated in the first eight Amendments. ... " Just as the Ninth Amendment showed that certain rights not enumerated in the Bill of Rights were protected as against the ***federal*** government, so (he argued) the Fourteenth Amendment should be found to protect against state action fundamental rights, including some not enumerated in the Bill of Rights. Goldberg found the right of "marital privacy" to be among such fundamental rights, and argued that the statute unconstitutionally violated that right, because it was not necessary for the fulfilling of a "compelling" state objective.

b. **Harlan "ordered liberty" approach:** Justice Harlan's concurrence was essentially in accord with Justice Goldberg's. As he had done several times before, he argued that the Fourteenth Amendment Due Process Clause does not merely incorporate the specific Bill of Rights guarantees, but instead "stands ... on its own bottom," to protect those basic values "implicit in the concept of ordered liberty." He then relied on his prior dissent in *Poe v. Ullman*, 367 U.S. 497 (1961), which had contended that the same Connecticut statute violated the due process interest in marital privacy.

   i. **No protection outside of marriage:** Harlan's *Griswold/Poe* opinions stopped carefully short of finding a general right to privacy for sexual relations. He explicitly rejected the idea that adultery, homosexuality, fornication and incest were protected by the same right to privacy. He distinguished these from the marital relations situation by noting that the state allows (even encourages) the marital relation, and should therefore not be permitted to use the criminal law to regulate the intimate details of that relation. By contrast, the state completely forbids the other types of sexual relations, so that it may permissibly regulate the details of those forbidden relations as well.

c. **White's means-end test:** Justice White's concurrence focused on the means-end relationship. He would apparently have upheld the statute had it been "reasonably necessary for the effectuation of a legitimate and substantial state interest." But the Connecticut statute, which supposedly served the state's policy against promiscuity and illicit sex, was drawn too broadly: there was no need to ban the use of birth control by married couples in order to achieve this objective. Thus White would presumably have upheld the ban as applied to the use of birth control by unmarried couples.

4. **Dissent:** Justices Black and Stewart each wrote a separate dissent. Black reiterated his familiar argument that only those rights explicitly protected by a specific Bill of Rights (or other constitutional) provision were protected by the Fourteenth Amendment; he felt that no "right of privacy," in the broad and general way the majority used that term, was protected by any specific provision. Justice Stewart similarly failed to find a right of privacy in any specific guarantee, and also rejected the Goldberg Ninth Amendment rationale (claiming that it limited only the powers of the federal government).

    a. Stewart reverses view: But Justice Stewart, as noted *infra*, p. 178, ultimately changed his view of *Griswold*, and concluded that the statute was properly invalidated as a substantive invasion of the Fourteenth Amendment Due Process Clause's "liberty" interest.

D. Post-*Griswold* contraceptive law: Developments since *Griswold* make it clear that that case ultimately means much more than that married persons may not be prevented from using birth control — it means that *no person*, single or married, may be prohibited from using contraception, or otherwise be subjected to undue interference with *decisions on procreation*. As the Court said in a post-*Griswold* case, "[r]ead in light of its progeny, the teaching of *Griswold* is that the Constitution protects individual decisions in matters of child-bearing from unjustified intrusion by the state." *Carey v. Population Services Int'l*, discussed *infra*, p. 196.

    1. *Eisenstadt v. Baird*: Much of the expansion of the meaning of *Griswold* came in *Eisenstadt v. Baird*, 405 U.S. 438 (1972), where the Court invalidated a statute which, by permitting contraceptives to be distributed only by registered physicians and pharmacists, and only to married persons, *discriminated against the unmarried*.

        a. Rationale: In striking down the statute, the majority invoked equal protection as well as substantive due process grounds. The Court observed that "[w]hatever the rights of the individual to access to contraceptives may be, the rights must be the same for the unmarried and the married alike. ... If the right of privacy means anything, it is the right of the *individual*, married or single, to be free from unwarranted government intrusion into matters so fundamentally affecting a person as the decision whether to bear or beget a child." (Emphasis in original.)

    2. Private place no longer required: What might be called the right of "*reproductive autonomy*" (see Tribe, p. 1339), protected by both *Griswold* and *Eisenstadt*, now exists *even in non-private situations*. In the post-*Eisenstadt* case of *Carey v. Population Services Int'l* (discussed further *infra*, p. 196), the Court noted that the constitutionally-protected privacy interest in, *inter alia*, procreation and child-rearing "is not just concerned with a particular place, but with a protected intimate relationship. Such protected privacy extends to the doctor's office, the hospital, the hotel room or as otherwise required to safeguard the right to intimacy involved."

    3. Non-marital relationships: Just as *Eisenstadt* broadened at least the contraceptive aspect of privacy to non-married couples, the Supreme Court has begun to recognize *a general right of privacy in sexual or procreational matters* outside the bounds of marriage. This happened in *Lawrence v. Texas*, *infra*, p. 201, in which the Court held that state bans on sodomy violate the substantive due process rights of homosexuals, because there is "an autonomy of self that includes ... certain intimate conduct."

E. Abortion generally: The right of privacy which the Court found to exist in *Griswold* has been extended to the *abortion* context. The case recognizing that the right of privacy limits a legislature's freedom to proscribe or regulate abortion was the landmark case of *Roe v. Wade*, 410 U.S. 113 (1973). That case has since been interpreted in a long line of decisions and, most recently, cut back in important ways in *Planned Parenthood v. Casey* and *Gonzales v. Carhart*, cases decided in 1992 and 2007 respectively. We will first review *Roe v. Wade*, then *Casey*, then various sub-topics relating to abortion including *Gonzales*.

F. *Roe v. Wade*: In *Roe v. Wade*, 410 U.S. 113 (1973), the Court held that a woman's right to privacy is a *"fundamental" right* under the Fourteenth Amendment. Therefore, the legislature has only a limited right to regulate — and may not completely proscribe — abortions. The actual result of the case was to invalidate, on privacy grounds, Texas' nearly-complete ban on abortions.

1. **Precise holding in *Roe*:**   The actual holding of *Roe* was remarkably specific, almost legislative. In an opinion by Justice Blackmun, the Court divided pregnancy into three *trimesters*, and prescribed a different rule for each:

    a. **First trimester:**   During the first trimester, a state *may not ban, or even closely regulate, abortions*. The decision to have an abortion, and the manner in which it is to be carried out, are to be left to the pregnant woman and her physician.

        i. **Rationale:**   The Court's rationale for this approach was that at present, the mortality rate for mothers having abortions during the first trimester is lower than the rate for full-term pregnancies. Therefore, the state has no valid (or at least no compelling) interest in protecting the mother's health by banning or closely regulating abortions during this period. (But the state may require that abortions be performed only by licensed physicians.)

    b. **Second trimester:**   During the second trimester, the state may protect its interest in the *mother's health*, by regulating the abortion procedure in ways that are "reasonably related" to her health. Such regulation might include, for instance, a requirement that the operation take place in a hospital rather than a clinic. (The Court implied that during this second trimester, the risk of maternal death through abortion was higher than that in full-term pregnancies.)

        i. **No protection of fetus:**   But the state may protect only the mother's health, *not the fetus' life*, during this period. Therefore, a flat ban on second trimester abortions is not permitted. Nor may the state regulate in ways that protect the fetus rather than the mother's health.

    c. **Third trimester:**   At the beginning of the third trimester, the Court stated, the fetus typically becomes "*viable*." That is, it has a "capability of meaningful life outside the mother's womb." Therefore, after viability the state has a "*compelling*" interest in protecting the fetus. It may therefore regulate, or *even proscribe*, abortion. However, abortion *must be permitted* where it is necessary to preserve the *life or the health* of the mother.

2. **Rationale of *Roe*:**   The *Roe* decision was premised upon the *right of privacy*. The Court pointed to *Griswold*, as well as to other privacy-derived holdings (e.g., *Pierce v. Society of Sisters* and *Meyer v. Nebraska*, both *supra*, p. 173, recognizing freedom in child-rearing and education). This right of privacy, which the Court found to be part of the "liberty" guaranteed by the Fourteenth Amendment, was "broad enough to encompass a woman's decision whether or not to terminate her pregnancy."

    a. **Standard of review:**   In fact, the Court held, a woman's interest in deciding this issue herself was a "*fundamental*" one, which could only be outweighed if: (1) there was a "*compelling state interest*" in barring or restricting abortion; and (2) the state statute was "*narrowly drawn*" so that it fulfilled only that legitimate state interest.

    b. **Countervailing state interest:**   The Court found that the state had two interests which, in particular circumstances, might be compelling: protecting the health of the mother, and protecting the viability of the fetus. The former would only be compelling after the first trimester (when the abortion-related dangers outweigh the live-birth-related ones); the latter only applied during the last trimester, when the fetus was viable. From these two postulates the Court drew its three-part rule, summarized above.

    i.   **Fetus not person:**   The Court explicitly rejected the argument that the state had a compelling interest, even before viability, in *protecting the fetus as a "person"* as that term is used in the Fourteenth Amendment. The Court reached this conclusion largely on historical grounds.

3.   **Concurrences:**   There were two concurrences in *Roe*, by Justices Stewart and Douglas.

    a.   **Stewart's concurrence:**   The Stewart concurrence reversed that Justice's dissenting position in *Griswold*, and accepted both *Griswold* and *Roe* as substantive due process cases; these and other decisions "make clear that freedom of personal choice in matters of marriage and family life is one of the liberties protected by the Due Process Clause of the Fourteenth Amendment."

    b.   **Douglas' concurrence:**   Justice Douglas wrote that the Fourteenth Amendment protected "freedom of choice in the basic decisions of one's life respecting marriage, divorce, procreation, contraception, and the education and upbringing of children." Douglas conceded that this freedom of choice was subject to regulation where there was a compelling state interest, but found that Texas' nearly-complete proscription of abortion in *Roe* went beyond such state interest.

4.   **Dissent:**   Justices White and Rehnquist wrote separate dissents.

    a.   **White's dissent:**   Justice White objected to what he called the Court's imposition of its own value scheme, preferring the "convenience, whim or caprice of the putative mother [over] the life or potential life of the fetus" prior to viability. He thought that the relative weights which should be assigned to these two interests should be left to "the people and to the political processes."

    b.   **Rehnquist's dissent:**   Justice Rehnquist argued that only a *"mere-rationality"* test, not a strict scrutiny one, should be applied; in his view, at least some of the abortion prohibitions and regulations forbidden by the majority could meet this minimum rationality standard. Also, he criticized the majority's three-part result as being "judicial legislation."

G.   **The modification of *Roe* by *Casey*:**   *Roe* has been *partially overruled*. This occurred in probably the Court's most important[1] post-*Roe* abortion decision, *Planned Parenthood of Southeastern Pennsylvania v. Casey*, 505 U.S. 833 (1992). In *Casey*, a majority of the Court declined to overrule *Roe v. Wade* explicitly. However, important aspects of *Roe* — including abortion's status as a *"fundamental right,"* the state's almost complete inability to *regulate first-trimester abortions*, and in fact the whole *trimester framework* of *Roe* — were all *overturned*. As a result of *Casey*, the states *may restrict abortion* so long as they do not place *"undue burdens"* on the woman's right to choose.

1.   **Pennsylvania statute:**   At issue in *Casey* was a Pennsylvania statute which placed a number of significant restrictions on abortion, such as a requirement that the woman *wait for 24 hours* after receiving from a doctor certain information about abortion, and a

---

1. Another contender for "most important post-*Roe* abortion decision" is *Gonzales v. Carhart*, the partial-birth abortion decision discussed *infra*, p. 190.

requirement that a married woman ***notify her husband*** of her intent to abort. Several of these restrictions were clearly unconstitutional judged by the standards of the Court's post-*Roe* decisions.

2. **Three blocs:** There were three distinct voting blocs in *Casey*. First, two traditionally "liberal" Justices — Stevens and Blackmun (the author of *Roe*) — voted to reaffirm *Roe* completely. Second, a four-Justice "conservative" bloc — Chief Justice Rehnquist, and Justices White, Scalia and Thomas — voted to overturn *Roe* completely. The "swing" votes were supplied by a middle-of-the-road bloc consisting of Justices O'Connor, Souter and Kennedy, who voted to reaffirm the "central principle" of *Roe v. Wade*, but to allow state regulation that did not "unduly burden" the woman's freedom to choose. Thus the Court decided by 5-4 to maintain *Roe v. Wade* as precedent, but by 7-2 to allow states to regulate more strictly than *Roe* and its progeny had allowed.

3. **The joint opinion:** The three "centrist" Justices — O'Connor, Souter and Kennedy — formed a ***plurality*** opinion, which spoke for the Court on all points. This opinion must be closely read, since it is now effectively the law of the land. Interestingly, the plurality opinion was written by all three Justices ***jointly***, rather than by a single Justice with others joining in the opinion. We will refer to this plurality opinion as the "joint opinion."

   a. ***Roe* reaffirmed:** The joint opinion began by stating broadly that it was ***reaffirming*** the ***"essential holding*** of *Roe v. Wade*." The opinion saw this "essential holding" as having three parts: (1) a recognition of "the right of the woman to choose to have an abortion before viability and to obtain it without undue interference from the state"; (2) a confirmation of the State's power to restrict abortions after fetal viability, if the law contains exceptions for pregnancies endangering the woman's life or health; and (3) a recognition of the state's "legitimate interests from the outset of the pregnancy in protecting the health of the woman and the life of the fetus. ... "

      i. **Rationale:** The joint opinion appeared to agree not only with the "essential holding" of *Roe*, but with the constitutional analysis that gave rise to that decision. It remains settled, the three Justices wrote, "that the Constitution places limits on a State's right to interfere with a person's most basic decisions about family and parenthood[.]" Cases upholding the right to use contraception (such as *Griswold, supra*, p. 174) continue to be relevant to the abortion situation as well: both the contraception and the abortion contexts "involve personal decisions concerning not only the meaning of procreation but also human responsibility and respect for it."

      ii. **Decision personal to the woman:** The joint opinion emphasized that the special nature of the abortion decision required that it be left to the woman alone, for it impacts upon her in a ***uniquely personal way***. "The liberty of the woman is at stake in a sense unique to the human condition and so unique to the law. The mother who carries a child to full term is subject to anxieties, to physical constraints, to pain that only she must bear. ... Her suffering is too intimate and personal for the State to insist, without more, upon its own vision of the woman's role, however dominant that vision has been in the course of our history and our culture. The destiny of the woman must be shaped to a large extent on her own conception of her spiritual imperatives and her place in society."

b. ***Stare decisis*:**   However, the joint opinion also suggested that its authors might ***not*** have endorsed the principles of *Roe v. Wade* if the issue were appearing before the Court for the first time. The opinion referred to "the reservations any of us may have in reaffirming the central holding of *Roe*." But, the joint opinion held, what tipped the scales in favor of reaffirming *Roe* was the force of ***stare decisis***, the doctrine that says that courts should not lightly overturn precedent. Where a constitutional decision has not proven "unworkable," and where overturning it would damage reliance interests, *stare decisis* dictated that the decision not be overturned.

  i.   Shouldn't overrule under fire: The ***legitimacy*** of the Court would be undermined if it were to overrule *Roe,* the joint opinion suggested. "Where, in the performance of its judicial duties, the Court decides a case in such a way as to resolve the sort of ***intensely divisive*** controversy reflected in *Roe* … its decision has a dimension that the resolution of the normal case does not carry. It is the dimension present whenever the Court's interpretation of the Constitution calls the contending sides of a national controversy to end their national division by accepting a common mandate rooted in the Constitution." In this respect, the only other comparable case from "our lifetime" was *Brown v. Board of Education*. If the Court overruled *Roe* without a compelling reason to do so, it would be seen as ***surrendering to political pressure***, a result that would "subvert the Court's legitimacy beyond any serious question."

c.   The "undue burden" standard: But what the joint opinion gave, it partly took away. Two aspects of *Roe* and the cases interpreting it should be ***abandoned***, the three Justices held: the ***"trimester framework"*** of *Roe*, and (at least implicitly) the principle that any pre-viability abortion regulation must survive ***strict scrutiny***.

  i.   Trimester approach rejected: The joint opinion noted that *Roe* used a trimester approach to govern abortion regulations: almost no regulation at all was permitted during the first trimester of pregnancy; regulations designed to protect the woman's health (but not to further the state's interest in potential life) were permitted during the second trimester; during the third trimester, because the fetus was now viable, the state could prohibit abortion as long as the life or health of the mother was not at stake. But the joint opinion did not agree that the trimester approach was a necessary method of safeguarding a woman's right to choose. The biggest vice of the trimester approach was that it "undervalues the State's interest in potential life," because it completely ignores that interest during the first two trimesters.

  ii.   The "undue burden" standard: In place of the trimester approach, the joint opinion articulated a new ***"undue burden"*** standard: "Only where state regulation imposes an undue burden on a woman's ability to make [the decision whether to abort] does the power of the State reach into the heart of liberty protected by the Due Process Clause." A state regulation will constitute an "undue burden" if the regulation "has the purpose or effect of placing a ***substantial obstacle*** in the path of a woman seeking an abortion of a nonviable fetus." Under this standard, if state regulations merely "create a ***structural mechanism***" by which the state may "express profound respect for the life of the unborn," and do not place a substantial obstacle in the woman's path, the regulations will be upheld. Similarly, the state may regulate to further the ***health or safety of the woman***, as long as the regulation does not unduly burden the right to abortion. After viability, the state may proscribe all abortions not needed to protect the health or life of the mother (a holding that does not represent any change from *Roe* or later cases).

iii. **Fundamental rights and strict scrutiny:**   The joint opinion implicitly rejected *Roe*'s view that the right to abortion is a "fundamental" right, and *Roe*'s concomitant rule that every pre-viability restriction on this fundamental right must survive *strict scrutiny*. The opinion did not discuss either the "fundamental rights" or "strict scrutiny" issue, but it is clear that the opinion did not in fact apply strict scrutiny to the Pennsylvania statute (and applied the "undue burden" test instead). So we must assume that *abortion is no longer a fundamental right*, and restrictions on it are *no longer to be strictly scrutinized*.

d. **Application to Pennsylvania statute:**   The plurality then applied its new "undue burden" analysis to the Pennsylvania statute. All but one of the Pennsylvania restrictions were *upheld* as not being unduly burdensome:

i. **Informed consent:**   The Pennsylvania statute contained an elaborate *"informed consent"* requirement, which the joint opinion *upheld*. First, at least *24 hours* before performing an abortion, a physician must inform the woman of the nature of the procedure, the health risks of both abortion and childbirth, and the "probable gestational age of the unborn child." (The waiting period was subject to an exception for "medical emergencies," defined as situations where an immediate abortion is required to avert serious risk of death or major bodily impairment to the woman.) Second, either a physician or a qualified non-physician must inform the woman of the availability of state-printed materials describing the fetus and providing information about non-abortion alternatives (e.g., adoption, child support, etc.).

(1) **No undue burden found:** The joint opinion found that these informed consent requirements *did not "unduly burden"* the woman's right to choose to abort. The closest question came as to the 24-hour waiting period; here, the joint opinion relied mainly on the absence of any strong findings by the district court that the increased costs and potential delays which might stem from this waiting period were truly "substantial" obstacles.

ii. **Spousal notification:**   But the joint opinion *struck down* the Pennsylvania statute's *"spousal notification"* provision. Under that provision, a married woman could not receive an abortion without signing a statement that she had notified her spouse that she was about to undergo the procedure. The provision contained several exceptions, including one for the situation where the pregnancy was the result of spousal *sexual assault* (provided that the assault was reported to the police within 90 days), and one applicable if the woman believed that notifying her husband would cause him or someone else to inflict *bodily injury* upon her.

(1) **Struck down as undue burden:** The joint opinion found that this spousal notification requirement was a *substantial obstacle* to abortion for some women: many fear that they will be *psychologically abused* by the husband, or that he will abuse their *children* (neither situation was covered by an exception in the notification requirement); others may fail to be able to use the exception for sexual assaults because they will be terrified to report the epi-

sode to the police, as was required for the use of that exception. The fact that the overwhelming majority of married women *do* notify their husbands was irrelevant; what counted was that as to that small percentage who do not voluntarily notify the spouse, the requirement that they do so was a substantial impediment.

(2) Outmoded view of role of women: The three Justices concluded their ruling on the spousal-notification requirement by asserting that the requirement reflected an outmoded view of the position of women in society: the requirement "embodies a view of marriage consonant with the common-law status of married women but repugnant to our present understanding of marriage and of the nature of the rights secured by the Constitution. Women do not lose their constitutionally protected liberty when they marry."

iii. Parental consent: The joint opinion *upheld* the statute's *parental consent* provision, by which except in medical emergencies, an unemancipated young woman under 18 may not obtain an abortion unless she and one of her parents provides informed consent. The statute allowed for a "judicial bypass," by which a court could authorize performance of the abortion without parental consent, if the judge determined that the young woman had given informed consent and that an abortion would be in her best interest.

(1) Rationale for upholding: The three Justices had little trouble upholding this provision, because it matched other "parental consent with possibility of judicial bypass" provisions that the Court had previously upheld (see the cases summarized *infra*, pp. 184-186). One difference was that here, the parent's consent must be shown to have been *informed* (which under the statute required the parent to listen to the alternatives to abortion and to hear about available state literature, 24 hours before the procedure). But the three Justices believed that the parental informed consent requirement was constitutional just as the requirement that an adult woman give her own informed consent was now constitutional; neither represented an "undue burden" on the right of abortion.

4. The Stevens and Blackmun opinions: Justices Stevens and Blackmun each wrote a separate opinion, concurring in part and dissenting in part. Each agreed that *Roe v. Wade* should be maintained as precedent, but each disagreed with the plurality as to how tightly the states may regulate abortion, and each believed that some of the Pennsylvania regulations upheld by the plurality were unconstitutional.

a. Stevens: Justice Stevens agreed with the joint opinion that the state has a legitimate interest in protecting potential life. But he did not believe that this interest was directly protected by the Constitution, and believed it was therefore a less weighty interest than the woman's constitutional liberty interest in deciding whether to bear a child. Stevens believed that the state could "express a preference for normal childbirth," but that the state could not force the woman to receive the state's obviously pro-life materials just at the moment she was considering her decision.

b. Blackmun: The separate opinion by Justice Blackmun, the author of *Roe*, was notably personal. Blackmun wrote in deeply emotional and metaphorical language not usually seen in Supreme Court decisions: as the result of recent prior court decisions, he said, "All that remained between the promise of *Roe* and … darkness … was a single, flickering flame. … But now, just when so many expected the darkness to fall, the flame has grown bright." Blackmun argued that the standard imposed by *Roe v. Wade* — that any regulation of abortion be subject to **strict scrutiny** — should be maintained, which he believed the "undue burden" standard did not do. Similarly, he believed that *Roe*'s trimester framework should be maintained. For Blackmun, *all* of the challenged regulations were infirm: the pre-abortion counseling requirement, the 24-hour waiting period, the requirement that consent by a minor's parent be "informed" (which the trial court found would require an in-person visit by the parent to the facility), the detailed record-keeping and disclosure provisions — none of these, in Blackmun's view, could survive strict scrutiny.

5. **Dissents:** There were four **dissenters** in *Casey*. Chief Justice Rehnquist wrote one dissent, in which Justices White, Scalia and Thomas joined. Justice Scalia wrote another dissent, in which Rehnquist, White and Thomas joined.

   a. **Rehnquist dissent:** Paradoxically, Rehnquist's dissent read in some ways more like a declaration of victory than a protest against defeat. He argued that the joint opinion "retains the outer shell of *Roe v. Wade* … but beats a wholesale retreat from the substance of that case." By contrast, he said, he and the other dissenters "believe that *Roe* was wrongly decided, and that it can and should be overruled. … " The dissenters would have upheld *all* the challenged provisions of the Pennsylvania statute.

      i. **Not a fundamental right:** To Rehnquist, the right to terminate a pregnancy was not, and should not have ever been declared to be, *"fundamental."* Abortion was quite different from marriage, procreation and contraception (other rights found to be "fundamental"), because it involved the termination of life and was thus a unique situation. Nor was the right to abort rooted in the historical traditions of the American people, which Rehnquist believed was the only way in which a right could become fundamental. Rehnquist believed that a woman's interest in having an abortion is a form of liberty protected by the Due Process Clause, but that since that interest was not a fundamental right, the states could regulate it "in *ways rationally related to a legitimate state interest*."

      ii. **Application to statute:** Given Rehnquist's belief that the regulations merely needed to be "rationally related to a legitimate state interest," it was not surprising that he found them all to be valid. For instance, the spousal notice requirement was a "rational attempt by the State to improve truthful communication between spouses and encourage collaborative decision making, and thereby fosters marital integrity."

   b. **Scalia's dissent:** Justice Scalia's dissent was a scornful, almost personal, attack on the joint opinion. To Scalia, the right to terminate an unwanted pregnancy was simply not a liberty interest protected in any way by the U.S. Constitution. "I reach [this conclusion] for the same reason I reach the conclusion that **bigamy** is not constitutionally protected — because of two simple facts: (1) the constitution says absolutely nothing about it, and (2) the long-standing traditions of American society have permitted it to be legally proscribed." The non-historically-oriented factors relied on by the majority to support abortion's special protected status — for instance, the fact that it is among "a person's most basic decisions" and involves "a most intimate and personal choice" — could be applied equally to homosexual sodomy, polygamy, adult incest and suicide, "all of which can constitutionally be proscribed because it is our own unquestionable constitutional tradition that they are proscribable."

6. **Significance of case:** So what is the significance of *Casey*?

   a. **Abortion as protected interest:** Post-*Casey*, a woman's right to decide whether to terminate her pregnancy remains an interest that receives *special constitutional protection*. For example, it seems completely clear that a state may not simply *forbid* all abortions, or even all abortions occurring in, say, the second trimester. Similarly, it seems clear that a state may not forbid all pre-viability abortions except those necessary to save the life or health of the mother. Any such regulation seems to be an "undue burden" on abortion.

   b. **Regulations easier to sustain:** On the other hand, state provisions that in some way *regulate* the abortion process are much more likely to be sustained than they were prior to *Casey*. The Court's 2007 decision upholding a federal ban on so-called "partial birth abortions" in *Gonzales v. Carhart* (*infra*, p. 190) confirms that both the state and federal governments have far greater scope to regulate the abortion process than they did before *Casey*.

   c. **Future of *Roe*:** Even the preservation of the "central holding" of *Roe v. Wade* seems to hang by a single vote, which since 2007 has belonged to Justice Kennedy.

   d. **Additional discussion:** We discuss the Court's likely future path on abortion in more detail *infra*, p.190.

H. **Post-*Roe* developments, generally:** Post-*Roe* abortion cases have centered around several areas, the most important of which are: (1) requirements that persons other than the pregnant woman *consent* to the operation before it may be performed; (2) limits on *public funding* of abortions; and (3) bans on particular types of *procedures*. In reading the following discussion of these issues, consider that most of these cases were decided before *Planned Parenthood v. Casey* and *Gonzales v. Carhart* (*infra*, p. 190), and might be decided differently today in view of the present Court's "undue burden" approach, which makes state regulations on abortion much more likely to be upheld.

I. **Consent:** A number of states have enacted statutes, usually after the *Roe v. Wade* decision, which impose requirements that third persons *consent* to a woman's decision to get an abortion, or which require *notice* to such third persons. The Supreme Court has decided a number of major cases in this area.

   1. **No absolute veto allowed (*Danforth*):** The first, and most important, of these cases was *Planned Parenthood of Missouri v. Danforth*, 428 U.S. 52 (1976), where the Supreme Court barred the states from giving a pregnant woman's *spouse* or parents, in most instances, an *absolute right to veto* the woman's decision to obtain an abortion.

      a. **Statute invalidated:** The statute struck down in *Danforth* barred abortions unless the operation was consented to by the woman's spouse or (if she was unmarried and under 18) by her parents.

      b. **Husband's consent:** The Court flatly *rejected* the requirement of consent by the husband. Both parents have rights at stake, but since the woman is more directly affected by the pregnancy, the Court concluded, she should have the deciding vote. Also, since the state itself cannot proscribe abortions during the early stages of pregnancy, it cannot delegate this power to the husband by allowing him to veto the procedure.

c. **Effect of *Casey:*** The principal holding in *Danforth* — that the states may not give a pregnant woman's spouse an absolute veto right over the woman's abortion decision — seems still to be good law. In *Planned Parenthood v. Casey, supra,* p. 178, the Court struck down a requirement that the woman's spouse be ***notified*** of the woman's intent to get an abortion. Even this lesser requirement of notice (as distinguished from consent, at issue in *Danforth*) was found to be an "undue burden" upon abortion, and this restriction was, indeed, the only restriction that the Court struck down in *Casey.* So the state may not require spousal consent.

   i. **Effect of *Gonzales:*** Even the 2007 decision in *Gonzales v. Carhart, infra,* p. 190, upholding the federal ban on "partial birth" abortions, doesn't seem to change this result. A majority of the Court that decided *Gonzales* seems likely to uphold procedural limits on the abortion process, but nothing in the *Gonzales* opinion indicates that five Justices are ready to say that a pregnant woman's spouse gets a veto over her right to abort.

2. **Parental consent reexamined:** In numerous cases decided in the last 30 or so years, the Court has reexamined the circumstances under which the state may require ***parental consent*** before allowing a ***minor*** to procure an abortion. See *Bellotti v. Baird,* 443 U.S. 622 (1979); *Akron v. Akron Center For Reproductive Health* (other aspects of which are discussed *infra,* p.189); *Planned Parenthood v. Casey* (*supra,* p. 178). As the result of these cases, the following rules seem to govern consent for minors' abortions:

   a. **No automatic right to abortion:** Where a minor is found to be ***insufficiently mature or emancipated*** to make the abortion decision for herself, the state ***may require parental consent.***

      i. **Informed consent by parents:** When the state requires parental consent, it may insist that that consent be ***"informed."*** More precisely, the state may insist that the parent listen to a presentation by the doctor about the alternatives to abortion, about the probable gestational age of the daughter's fetus, about the availability of state-printed literature, etc. Also, the state may apparently insist that this parental informed consent take place as part of an ***in-person*** visit by the parent to the facility where the abortion will be performed, and may insist that at least 24 hours elapse between the visit and the procedure. See *Planned Parenthood v. Casey, supra,* p. 178.

   b. **Court hearing:** If the state does require parental consent, it must also give the girl an opportunity to ***persuade a court*** that, although she is not sufficiently mature or emancipated to make the decision for herself, an abortion is nonetheless ***in her best interests.*** If she does make such a showing, the court must override the parental veto. This procedure is sometimes called a ***"judicial bypass."***

      i. **Consent of both parents:** If the state supplies the "judicial bypass," it may require the consent of ***both*** parents where the girl does not use the bypass. This is true even if one parent does not live with the girl.

   c. **Emancipation or maturity:** The state must provide for an ***individualized judicial hearing*** in which the girl may persuade the court that she is in fact sufficiently ***mature*** or *emancipated* that she is able to make this decision for herself. If the court concludes that she is mature or emancipated, it must allow the operation whether or not the court feels it is in the girl's best interest.

    d.   Effect of *Gonzales*: But *Gonzales v. Carhart* (*infra*, p. 190) indicates that states can probably go further in requiring parental approval than the above earlier cases suggest. In *Gonzales*, the Court emphasized that government has an interest in protecting women by helping them anticipate that if they have an abortion, they may *later regret* having done so. This rationale seems especially applicable to the area of abortion by minors, and suggests that a majority of the present Roberts Court may well hold that the states may weaken some of the pre-*Gonzales* limits on the parental veto rights over a minor's abortion, such as the requirement that a judicial bypass be available.

3.   Notice and consultation (*H.L. v. Matheson*):   Some states, seeing their ability to require parental consent in minor-abortion cases curtailed by *Danforth* and *Bellotti*, have taken a different route: they require that *notice* be given to the parents before an operation is performed on a minor. Most of these statutes have the express purpose of promoting "consultation" between the minor and her parents (even if the statute does not purport to give the parents veto power over the minor's decision to obtain the abortion). In *H.L. v. Matheson*, 450 U.S. 398 (1981), the Court *upheld* such a notice requirement, when applied to a young woman who is *neither emancipated* (i.e., living on her own) *nor mature enough* to make the abortion decision herself.

    a.   Equivalent to consent: Post-*Matheson* cases suggest, though they do not explicitly hold, that requiring *notice* to parents is constitutionally the equivalent of requiring *consent* by the parents. For instance, the Court has held that a state may not require that notice be given to both parents unless the state supplies a "judicial bypass" as an alternative; this holding (in *Hodgson v. Minnesota*, 497 U.S. 417 (1990)) parallels the Court's holdings in the consent area. Nothing in *Planned Parenthood v. Casey* suggests that the Court there saw the matter any differently — so probably under *Casey* the states may only require parental notice and consultation if they supply a judicial bypass, and if they exempt from the requirement any mature or emancipated woman.

        i.   Weakened by *Gonzales*: But again, *Gonzales v. Carhart* (*infra*, p. 190) seems likely to weaken this principle that the states may only require parental notice and consultation if a judicial bypass is supplied.

J.   Public funding of abortions: While *Roe v. Wade* held that the decision on whether or not to procure an abortion (at least before viability) belongs solely to the woman, not to the legislature, this line of reasoning was not followed by the Court in its decisions on whether *public funding* of abortions is required. In two post-*Roe* decisions, the Court held that the government may pay for the expenses of childbirth, yet refuse to pay the expenses of abortion: (1) where the abortion is non-therapeutic (i.e., not necessary for the health of the mother); and (2) even where the abortion *is* necessary for the health, or even the life, of the mother. In a third post-*Roe* case, the Court held that the state may prohibit the use of any *public facility* or public staff to perform abortions.

1.   Non-therapeutic abortions (the *Maher* case):   In 1977, the Court held that the states may refuse to provide Medicaid funding for *non-therapeutic* abortions, i.e., those where the operation is not necessary to protect the mother's life or health. Although the Court simultaneously decided three cases relating to this issue, the most important is *Maher v.*

Roe, 432 U.S. 464 (1977). In *Maher*, the Court held that Connecticut could constitutionally refuse to give Medicaid financing for non-therapeutic abortions, ***even though it gave Medicaid financing for the expenses of ordinary childbirth***. The decision was 6-3.

    a. Interpretation of *Roe*:   In reaching this conclusion, the majority interpreted *Roe* to mean ***not*** that a woman had a fundamental right to an abortion, but merely that she had a fundamental right to be free of "unduly burdensome interference with her ***freedom to decide*** whether to terminate her pregnancy." The Connecticut statute here placed no obstacles in the pregnant woman's path, but merely failed to alleviate a pre-existing obstacle (her poverty). The fact that Connecticut may have made the alternative to abortion more attractive by subsidizing it was not at all the same thing as placing a direct obstacle in the path to abortion.

2. Funding of medically-necessary abortions (*Harris v. McRae*):   An even more troubling abortion-funding question was posed to the Court in 1980: may the states or federal government refuse to fund ***medically-necessary*** abortions? Here, too, the Court answered "yes," in *Harris v. McRae*, 448 U.S. 297 (1980).

    a. Statute sustained: A bitterly divided Court, by a 5-4 vote, sustained various federal funding limitations, including one that refused to allow Medicaid funding where the mother's health (but not life) was in jeopardy without an abortion, and another that refused to grant an exception even for cases of rape and incest.

        i. Rationale: The majority relied heavily on the *Maher* analysis: funding of other medically-necessary expenses but not ones relating to abortion left an indigent pregnant woman ***no worse off*** than she would have been had there been no funding of any medical expenses. The existence of a constitutionally-protected right did not obligate the government to grant the funds needed to exercise that right.

3. Use of public facilities and staff (*Webster*):   *Maher* and *Harris* both stand for the proposition that the government need not give assistance to women desiring to exercise their constitutional right to an abortion. A more recent case carries this principle even further: in ***Webster v. Reproductive Health Services***, 492 U.S. 490 (1989), the Court held that a state may prohibit all use of ***public facilities*** and ***publicly-employed staff*** in abortions.

    a. Holding: A five-justice majority (Rehnquist, White, O'Connor, Scalia, and Kennedy) believed that this no-public-facilities-or-staff rule was ***constitutional***. To them, the principle was the same as in *Maher* and *Harris*: the state's refusal to allow public employees or public hospitals to participate in abortions "leaves a pregnant woman with the same choices as if the State had chosen not to operate any public hospitals at all."

4. Abortion counseling: *Maher*, *Harris* and *Webster* were all cases holding that the government need not give assistance to women who want to exercise their constitutional right to an abortion. The most recent case in this sequence goes even further: it holds that the government may, as a condition of funding family-planning clinics, insist that the doctor or other professional ***not recommend abortion***, and ***not refer clinic patients to an abortion provider. Rust v. Sullivan***, 500 U.S. 173 (1991).

    a. Facts: Title X of the Public Health Service Act provides federal funding for family-planning clinics. The Act provides that none of the funds appropriated under it "shall be used in programs where abortion is a method of family planning." The Secretary of

Health and Human Services enacted regulations enforcing this prohibition with a vengeance. According to the regulations, a Title X project "may not provide counselling concerning the use of abortion as a method of family planning or provide referral for abortion as a method of family planning." Thus if a woman comes to a Title X clinic looking for birth control information, and tests performed at the clinic disclose that she is pregnant, the clinic doctor may not recommend an abortion, may not list abortion as a possible method of dealing with the woman's situation, and may not refer the woman to an abortion provider.

b. **Holding:** A five-justice majority in *Rust* believed that these tight limits *did not violate* a pregnant woman's right to an abortion. The majority believed that the right-to-abortion argument was completely disposed of by *Maher*, *Harris* and *Webster*. Congress' refusal to "fund abortion counselling and advocacy" merely left a pregnant woman with the same choices as if the government had chosen not to fund family-planning services at all.

c. **Dissent:** On the right-to-abortion claim in *Rust*, there were three dissenters (Blackmun, joined by Marshall and Stevens). The dissenters of course disagreed with the correctness of *Maher*, *Harris* and *Webster* in the first place. But beyond this, they believed that what was being asserted here in *Rust* was "the right of a pregnant woman to be free from affirmative governmental *interference* in her decision," an even more uncontrovertible right than the basic right to abortion. A Title X client would now be receiving physician's advice that was strictly controlled by the government; the client "will reasonably construe [her physician's words] as professional advice to forego her right to obtain an abortion." A woman who listens to this government-controlled advice would thus *not* be left in the same position as she would have been in if there had been no government funding, and thus no clinic and no professional advice, in the first place.

d. **Free expression issue:** The plaintiffs in *Rust* also made a First Amendment claim — Title X doctors argued that the regulations interfered with their own freedom of expression. The majority rejected this claim as well. This aspect of the case is discussed *infra*, p. 613.

K. **Types of abortion allowable:** A state's restrictions on the *types* of abortions which may be used, or the procedures surrounding the performance of abortions, may run afoul of *Roe v. Wade*. However, these restrictions are exactly the sort that are more likely to be upheld today, after *Planned Parenthood v. Casey* (*supra*, p. 178) made it much easier than it had been under *Roe* for a state to regulate abortion. Indeed, in 2007, in *Gonzales v. Carhart*, the Court for the first time **upheld a complete ban on a particular method** of abortion – the so-called "partial birth" method – as we'll see shortly below.

1. *Danforth:* In *Planned Parenthood of Missouri v. Danforth*, 428 U.S. 52 (1976) (other aspects of which are discussed *supra*, p. 184), the Supreme Court struck down a Missouri requirement that the little-utilized prostaglandin method be used rather than the much more common saline amniocentesis method.

a. **Rationale:** The Court reasoned that the prostaglandin method was so largely unavailable in Missouri that the regulation had the effect of blocking most abortions after the first trimester.

b. **Effect of *Casey* and *Gonzales*:** Under *Planned Parenthood v. Casey*, a state may not regulate pre-viability abortions in a way that would impose an "undue burden" on such abortions. If a state forbade a heavily-used method (e.g., D&C or saline), even the post-*Casey* Court might well hold that this constituted an "undue burden" on abortion, and was thus a violation of the constitutionally-protected interest in deciding whether to terminate her pregnancy. On the other hand, the proscription of a little-used method might not be an "undue burden"; *Gonzales v. Carhart,* the 2007 case approving a federal ban on the lightly-used "partial birth" method, suggests that the Missouri ban on the seldom-used prostaglandin method, struck down in *Danforth*, would probably be upheld today.

2. **Hospitalization for second-trimester abortions:** The Court has held that the state *may not impose a blanket rule that all abortions after the first trimester be performed in a hospital*. In *Akron v. Akron Center For Reproductive Health, Inc.*, 462 U.S. 416 (1983), the Court concluded that such a requirement, which had the effect of barring abortions in "outpatients facilities that are not part of an acute-care, full-service hospital" (i.e., licensed clinics) unconstitutionally infringed on the abortion right recognized in *Roe*.

   a. **Effect of *Casey* and *Gonzales*:** But the later cases of *Planned Parenthood v. Casey* (*supra*, p. 178) and *Gonzales v. Carhart* (*infra*, p. 190) suggest that this holding — that the states may not require all abortions after the first trimester to be performed in a hospital — is likely to be overturned eventually.

3. **The health of the mother, and the "partial birth" abortion method:** The most significant holdings about the regulation of particular abortion methods are a pair of rulings on legislative attempts to ban the *"partial birth"* abortion method. In the first of these, *Stenberg v. Carhart*, the Court struck down by 5-4 a Nebraska statute; then, seven years later and after a change in Court personnel, the Court *upheld* a very similar federal statute by 5-4, in *Gonzales v. Carhart*.

   a. ***Stenberg* (the 2000 case):** In the first case of the partial-birth-abortion pair, ***Stenberg v. Carhart***, 530 U.S. 914 (2000), the Court held that if a particular abortion method may be *safer for the mother* in some circumstances, the state may not flatly ban the method, and must instead *allow a maternal-health exception* to the ban.

      i. **Facts of *Stenberg*:** In *Stenberg*, the Nebraska legislature made it a felony to perform a "partial birth abortion" unless the procedure was necessary to save the life of the mother. A "partial birth abortion" was defined as "an abortion procedure in which the person performing the abortion partially delivers vaginally a living unborn child before killing the unborn child and completing the delivery." The principal procedure against which the statute was designed was the so-called "D&X" procedure. In a D&X abortion, the fetus is drawn partly out of the uterus so that the physician can reach the skull, puncture it, vacuum its contents, and thereby bring the now-smaller skull through the birth canal. The D&X procedure is rarely used except after the 16th week.

      ii. **Holding:** By a 5-4 vote, the court *struck down* the Nebraska statute. The majority opinion, by Justice Breyer, found two distinct faults with the statute:

         (1) Lack of health exception: First, the statute did not contain an exception allowing the procedure where it was *necessary to protect the health* (as opposed to the life) of the mother.

(2) Might cover D&E method: Second, the majority concluded, the language of the statute was ambiguous, and might be construed by Nebraska courts and prosecutors to also cover the more-common D&E method. The mere *possibility* that the statute might be so construed was enough to constitute an *"undue burden"* on women's abortion rights, because practitioners might be reluctant to use the clearly-constitutionally-protected D&E method for fear that they would be prosecuted for a felony.

iii. **Dissent:** Significantly, the four dissenters included Justice Kennedy, even though he had been part of the joint opinion in *Casey* that more or less reaffirmed the right to abortion.

    (1) Physicians as healers: Kennedy believed that the state had a significant interest in ensuring that its physicians were *viewed by society as healers*, and that that interest was well served by forbidding a procedure that bore a strong "resemblance to *infanticide*."

    (2) No real safety issue: He also believed that the plaintiffs had not demonstrated that lack of the D&X method would ever deprive a woman of a safe abortion, so forbidding the procedure did not place an undue burden in a woman's path.

    (3) No overbreadth: Finally, Kennedy believed that the majority was twisting the statutory words to reach its conclusion that the ban might also reach the more common and clearly-constitutionally-protected D&E procedure (which would make the statute unconstitutionally "overbroad"). In his view standard rules on statutory construction made it clear that the statute did not reach that procedure.

b. ***Gonzales v. Carhart* (the 2007 case):** By 2007, Justice O'Connor, who had been part of the majority in *Stenberg*, had retired, and had been replaced by Justice Alito. That turned out to make a critical difference, because the Court by a 5-4 vote **upheld**, in ***Gonzales v. Carhart*, 550 U.S. 124 (2007)**, a federal ban on partial-birth abortions that was very similar to the Nebraska ban struck down in *Stenberg*.

i. **Facts:** Congress made it a crime to carry out an abortion by a procedure that the *Gonzales* Court referred to as an "intact D&E."[2] Congress defined the crime of performing a "partial-birth abortion" (the term used in the statute itself) as requiring two intentional steps by the physician:

❑ First, the physician causes a still-living fetus to begin to be *delivered* until either (a) in a head-first delivery, the *entire head* of the fetus is outside the mother's body; or (b) in the case of a breech delivery, any part of the fetus' *body past its naval* is outside the mother's body; and

❑ Second, the physician performs an *"overt act"* on the partially-delivered fetus for the purpose of killing it. (The overt act must be something other than the mere completion of the delivery — typically, the overt act consists of the phy-

---

2. "Intact D&E" seems to be essentially the same procedure as the one at issue in *Stenberg*, which the Court there called the "D&X" procedure. However, as we'll see Congress defined the prohibited procedures somewhat more tightly than Nebraska had in *Stenberg*.

sician's use of scissors to make an opening at the base of the fetus's skull, through which a surgical catheter evacuates the skull contents.)

(1) Distinction from Nebraska statute: Congress enacted the federal ban in response to the *Stenberg* decision, in a clear attempt to overcome some of the *Stenberg* majority's objections to the Nebraska statute. Consequently the federal statute differed from the Nebraska statute in several ways (though the majority and dissent in *Gonzales* sharply disagreed about how significant these differences were):

❑ Unlike the Nebraska Legislature, Congress made various *factual findings* about the procedure it was banning, including that there was a "moral, medical, and ethical consensus" that the partial-birth procedure "is a gruesome and inhumane procedure that is *never medically necessary.*"

❑ Whereas the Nebraska statute seemed to cover any procedure that involved "delivering a living unborn child, or *a substantial portion thereof,*" the federal statute could be triggered only if what was delivered was either the entire head or the lower body from the feet past the navel. This was an arguably important distinction, because the Nebraska statute was relatively vague, and could plausibly have been interpreted to cover (on account of the "substantial portion" clause) a procedure in which only one arm or one leg had been delivered, whereas the federal statute was not susceptible to that interpretation.

❑ Also, the federal statute, by requiring *two steps* before a prohibited abortion would be deemed to have occurred — a partial live birth followed by a *later overt act* of killing — made it pretty clear that the standard *constitutionally-protected* late-term D&E procedure (in which the fetus is killed inside the uterus, and then individual parts are separated and removed one at a time) is *not covered by the statute.* The *Stenberg* majority had concluded that the Nebraska statute was drafted broadly enough to cover the standard D&E procedure, and that even the mere possibility of this interpretation was enough to constitute an undue burden; so Congress, by introducing the two-step / overt-act definition, had pretty clearly overcome this problem.

One respect in which the federal statute did *not* differ from the Nebraska statute, however, was that like the Nebraska act, the federal act *did not contain an exception* allowing the partial-birth procedure where it was necessary to *protection the mother's health* (though there *was* an exception to protect the mother's life).

ii. Attack on statute: The suits in *Gonzales*[3] were *"facial attacks"* rather than "as applied" ones — that is, the plaintiffs were claiming that *all* applications of the statute should be ruled unconstitutional, whether or not application of the statute to

---

3. The case consisted of two separate suits that were consolidated before the Supreme Court.

the plaintiff's own behavior or proposed behavior would be unconstitutional. (See p. 484 for a discussion of the facial / as-applied distinction.)[4]

iii. **Supreme Court upholds the statute:** The Supreme Court concluded by a 5-4 vote that the federal statute was *not invalid on its face.* The majority opinion was by Justice Kennedy, who served as the swing vote as he has so often done in recent years, and who as a dissenter in *Stenberg* would have found the Nebraska statute constitutional too. Kennedy's opinion (which was joined by Roberts, Scalia, Thomas and Alito), *did not overrule Stenberg*, and instead *distinguished* it.

(1) **Not vague:** Kennedy first concluded that the federal act was not void for vagueness. Unlike the Nebraska statute struck down in *Stenberg* — which ambiguously prohibited delivery of a "substantial portion" of the fetus — the federal statute here gave precise "anatomical landmarks" (head and navel, respectively) to establish a clear dividing line between forbidden abortion methods and permitted ones.

(2) **Does not bar standard D&E's:** Next, Kennedy concluded that the statute did not ban standard late-term D&E abortions (i.e., ones in which the fetus was dead and dismembered before being removed from the uterus). So any over-breadth problem was eliminated.

(3) **Not an undue burden:** Finally, Kennedy concluded that the statute *did not impose an undue burden* on a woman's right to control her reproductive destiny. In reaching this conclusion, he seemed to endorse legislative goals and methods that no prior post-*Roe* decision had approved:

❑ Citing *Casey*, Kennedy said that Congress was free to legislate to "show its *profound respect for the life within the woman,"* and to further government's "legitimate interest in *regulating the medical profession* in order to *promote respect for life*, including *life of the unborn*."

❑ He then laid out a chain of reasoning by which, he said, the ban here would *fulfill this legitimate interest* without constituting an *undue burden* on the right of abortion:

(a) "Some women *come to regret their choice* to abort the infant life they once created and sustained ... Severe depression and loss of esteem can follow";

(b) The abortion doctor might not *disclose* to the woman the "precise details" of the means by which an intact D&E might be performed;

(c) A woman who learns *post-operatively* the precise details of the procedure "must *struggle with grief* more anguished and sorrow more profound when she learns, only after the event, what she once did not know: that she allowed a doctor to pierce the skull and vacuum the fast-developing brain of her unborn child, a child assuming the human

---

4. The suit in *Stenberg*, too, had been a facial attack, and had led to a ruling by the Supreme Court that the Nebraska statute could not be enforced against *anyone.*

form";

(d) A "necessary effect" of Congress' ban on the partial-birth procedure "will be to encourage some women to *carry the infant to full term*, thus *reducing the absolute number of late-term abortions*";

(e) "The medical profession ... may *find different and less shocking methods* to abort the fetus in the second trimester," thus avoiding the tendency of the partial-birth method to (in Congress' words) "undermine[] the public's perception of the appropriate role of a physician during the delivery process, and pervert[] a process during which life is brought into the world";

(f) Finally, the federal statute's failure to supply a *mother's-health exception* did *not create an undue burden.* There was "documented medical disagreement whether the act's prohibition would ever impose significant health risks on women." Prior non-abortion decisions by the Court had given state and federal legislatures "wide discretion to pass legislation in areas where there is medical and scientific *uncertainty*." The standard urged by those attacking the statute — that a mother's-health exception was constitutionally required "if substantial medical authority" supported the proposition that the ban might endanger some women's health – was "too exacting a standard to impose on the legislative power ... to regulate the medical profession."

(4) As-applied challenge still available: But Kennedy emphasized that the Court was deciding only this broad *facial* challenge — which he said could succeed only if the plaintiff showed that the act would be unconstitutional in a "large fraction of relevant cases." If in any case involving a particular plaintiff, the lack of a mother's-health exception meant that the mother's health would be placed in jeopardy, an *"as-applied"* challenge could still be brought.

iv. **Concurrence:** In a brief concurrence, Justice Thomas (joined by Scalia), repeated his view that "the Court's abortion jurisprudence, including *Casey* and *Roe v. Wade*, ... has *no basis* in the Constitution."

v. **Dissent:** Justice Ginsburg wrote a long and passionate dissent, in which she was joined by Stevens, Souter and Breyer.

(1) Lack of mother's-health exception: Ginsburg objected especially to the statute's lack of an exception where the *mother's health* was at stake. She noted that this was the first time since *Roe* that the Court had "blessed a prohibition with no exceptions safeguarding a woman's health." She pointed to evidence produced at trial that the banned partial-birth method was *safer* for many women, including those with "uterine scarring, bleeding disorders, heart disease, ... compromised immune systems [or] certain pregnancy-related conditions[.]" Therefore, she thought, the Supreme Court should not blithely defer to Congress' findings that there was a medical consensus that the banned procedure is never necessary to protect a woman's health, a finding that the lower courts had found to be (in her words) "unreasonable and not supported by the evidence."

(2) No fetus saved: Ginsburg noted that the Court was upholding a law that *"saves not a single fetus* from destruction," since another abortion method could always be used. Therefore, the law did not in fact further one of the goals that the Court claimed it furthered, the goal of "preserving and promoting fetal life."

(3) "Regret" rationale criticized: Ginsburg also criticized the Court's *"emotional distress"* rationale, that is, the theory that government was properly acting to spare women the emotional pain of learning the details of the procedure only after it had been carried out. She pointed out that the Court was not permitting government to require that women be *accurately informed* of the risks of the procedure (something that *Casey* had already allowed); instead, the Court was "depriv[ing] women of the *right to make an autonomous choice*, even at the expense of their safety." She concluded that "this way of thinking *reflects ancient notions about women's place* in the family and under the Constitution — ideas that have long since been discredited."

(4) As-applied: Finally, Ginsburg was deeply troubled by the majority's insistence that *as-applied challenges*, rather than the present facial attack, were the proper means to handle those cases where women's health was in fact at stake. Virtually all of the Supreme Court's post-*Roe* abortion cases had been facial attacks. She argued that forcing women to wait for as-applied challenges "jeopardizes women's health and places doctors in an untenable position." For instance, if a woman had a particular medical condition that had not been the subject of a prior as-applied challenge, the treating physician would not have any clarity about whether the woman would have a constitutional right to have the partial-birth procedure, and therefore the physician would *risk prosecution* and imprisonment if she performed the procedure.

(5) "Chip away" at right: Ginsburg closed by saying that the statute, and the Court's defense of it, "cannot be understood as anything other than an effort to *chip away at a right* declared again and again by this Court[.]"

vi. **Significance:** Here are some broad guidelines, in light of *Gonzales*, about whether and how government can regulate particular abortion methods:

❏ Government may sometimes *completely ban* a particular method (e.g., the partial-birth method); all that seems to be required is that the ban not constitute an "undue burden" on women, which it will not apparently constitute if *another reasonably-safe method* is available;

❏ When government decides whether to ban a particular method, it may take into account what it perceives as *risks to the mental health of women* who might elect that method and then *come to regret it;* therefore, government may apparently ban "more regrettable" procedures in favor of "less regrettable" ones;

❑ As long as the legislature has made credible findings that there is medical uncertainty about whether the prohibited procedure is ever necessary to safeguard a woman's health, government need not draft the statute so as to give an *exemption* from its ban for cases where in the physician's opinion the *mother's health would be better served* by allowing use of the method.

L. Future of abortion regulation: The *Gonzales* decision suggests that the Roberts Court will make it *significantly easier* than it has ever been since the decision in *Roe* for governments to *restrict abortion.*

1. **Changes:** Here are some of the respects in which *Gonzales* seems to make it easier for legislatures to regulate abortion:

   ❑ Government's concern for a pregnant woman's *emotional health* is now recognized as an important interest, justifying the state's attempt to prevent types of procedures that the woman is likely later to regret;

   ❑ Government's desire to *reduce the number of abortions* is itself recognized as a *legitimate goal*, justifying measures whose effect will be to reduce the number of abortions;

   ❑ Government's desire to *regulate the medical profession* so as to uphold "the public's perception of the appropriate role of a physician during the delivery process" is a legitimate goal, again justifying restrictions on abortion practices;

   ❑ A statute that forbids certain types of abortions apparently *need not preserve an exception for cases in which the physician believes that the mother's health is at risk*, at least where the legislature makes credible findings of fact that alternative equally-safe methods are available;

   ❑ *Facial attacks* will be *harder to win* than before — after a new regulation is enacted, the Court's preference will apparently be to let the statute go into force, and to wait for an "as applied" attack in which a particular pregnant woman or doctor claims that the plaintiff's own rights have been infringed. This means that newly-enacted restrictive statutes are more likely to "remain on the books" not only before but even after a successful as-applied attack than would have been true before *Gonzales*.

2. **Future of the "undue burden" standard:** It's not clear whether a majority of the present court is still in favor of the *Casey* *"undue burden"* standard, by which any regulation found to be a substantial burden on abortion will be struck down. Kennedy's opinion in *Gonzales* did not say whether he favored maintaining the undue-burden standard; the opinion merely said that the opinion would "assume" *Casey's* validity.[5] Kennedy was part of the 3-justice plurality in *Casey*, which advocated the undue-burden test. It seems likely that he, as the swing vote on this issue, will continue to pay at least lip service to the prohibition on undue burdens, but will be slow to find that any particular restriction constitutes an undue burden.

---

5. As Kennedy's majority opinion in *Gonzales* noted, two members of the Court, Thomas and Scalia, had previously stated their disagreement with *Casey*. It seems likely that the two newest members of the conservative bloc on the Court, Roberts and Alito, have no love for *Casey* and the undue-burden standard either. Therefore, the survival of the undue-burden test pretty clearly depends on Kennedy's vote.

3. **Possible legislative responses:** Here are some of the types of statutes that, if enacted by Congress or a state legislature, would likely be *upheld* by the Roberts court in light of *Gonzales*:

❑ Provisions requiring that the woman be given *extensive warnings*, including detailed descriptions of how the procedure will be performed or what its consequences will be. (*Example:* South Dakota has passed a statute requiring that pregnant women be told that they will be aborting "a whole, separate, unique living human being," and that they be warned in writing of the increased risk of "depression and related psychological distress" and of "suicide ideation and suicide." S.D. Codified Laws § 34-23A-10.1.) Such "informed consent" provisions would presumably be justified by the state's interest, recognized in *Gonzales*, in protecting women's later emotional health and in reducing the number of abortions.

❑ Mandatory *ultrasound examinations* for women who are proposing to have an abortion, with the woman required to look at the fetus in the film. Again, this could be justified on the theory that the state is entitled to guard against the woman's later change of heart and consequent emotional distress.

❑ *Waiting periods* before an abortion can be performed, again on the "prevent later emotional distress" theory.

❑ More-stringent *parental consent* provisions for minor women. For instance, probably the consent of *both* parents may be required. It may also be the case that the state may dispense with the need to furnish an exception for a "mature and emancipated" woman under the age of 18. And states may well be entitled to make the procedure for a "judicial bypass" more burdensome (e.g., by limiting the factors that the court may consider in deciding whether an abortion would be in the young woman's best interests).

❑ Stricter *licensing requirements* for doctors and clinics. For instance, a state might require that all abortions be performed in a hospital, and with the patient staying overnight. So *Akron v. Akron Center, supra,* p. 189, would likely be decided differently post-*Gonzales*.

❑ Bans on particular abortion methods, including *abortion-causing drugs.* For instance, there is nothing in *Gonzales* that suggests that Congress could not ban, say, any physician from prescribing use of a drug whose intended effect would be to kill a fetus that was more than two days old. As long as Congress made findings that there were alternative equally-safe methods of abortion available, and as long as Congress concluded that the ban would help reduce the total number of abortions and thus the incidence of post-abortion maternal regret, this kind of ban would seem to pass the two main requirements under *Casey* and *Gonzales*: (1) be rationally related to the achievement of a legitimate governmental interest, and (2) not cause an undue burden on the right to abortion.

All in all, there seem to be ample opportunities for legislatures to "chip away at [the] right" to abortion, as Ginsburg feared in her *Gonzales* dissent.

M. Post-*Roe* regulation of contraception (*Carey* case): Only one Supreme Court case after *Roe v. Wade* has dealt with the regulation of *contraception*. In that case, ***Carey v. Population Services Int'l***, 431 U.S. 678 (1977), the Court struck down a New York statute which: (1) prohibited anyone but a licensed pharmacist from distributing contraceptives to persons over 16; and (2) entirely prohibited the sale or distribution of contraceptives to minors under the age of 16, except by prescription.

1. **Pharmacists-only rule:** The rule allowing only pharmacists to distribute contraceptives to adults was subjected to *strict scrutiny* (because it bore on the "fundamental" right to decide whether or not to procreate). Since the limitation reduced access to contraceptives, and lessened price competition, that restriction had to be justified by some "compelling" state interest. The interests advanced by the state (e.g., protecting health) were not compelling, so the provision was struck down. Six Justices agreed on this point.

2. **Ban on sale to minors:** As to the complete ban on non-prescription sales of contraceptives to minors, seven Justices agreed that the ban violated the right of privacy, but they were split 4-3 as to the appropriate rationale.

N. **Family relations:** One of the most striking expansions of substantive due process doctrine in recent years has been in the area of *family relations*. In a number of cases, individuals' desires to live together, to marry, or to raise their children in a certain way have come face to face with the state's desire to regulate zoning, marriage, child-rearing or other areas of public concern.

1. **"Fundamental rights" frequently found:** In general, the Supreme Court has in recent years found that a person's decision about how to conduct his family life often rises to the level of a "fundamental right." Consequently, the state may interfere with such a decision only when it shows that the interference is necessary for the fulfillment of a compelling public interest.

2. **Zoning and the "non-nuclear family":** Thus the government may not pass *zoning regulations* which impair the ability of family members to reside together, even if the family is an "extended" rather than "nuclear" one. In *Moore v. East Cleveland*, 431 U.S. 494 (1977), the Court struck down a zoning ordinance which allowed only members of a single "family" to live together.

   a. **"Family" defined:** The ordinance's definition of "family" was a restrictive one, which prevented the plaintiff from living with her two grandsons, who were first cousins. (She would have been permitted to live with two grandsons had they been brothers rather than cousins.)

   b. **Extended family protected:** A four-Justice plurality opinion (authored by Justice Powell) concluded that the right of members of a family, even a non-nuclear one, to live together was a liberty interest, and that state impairment of that interest must be "examine[d] carefully." Although the state interests advanced in support of the ordinance were legitimate ones (e.g., preventing overcrowding, traffic congestion and burdens on the local school system), these interests were only marginally advanced by the ordinance.

   c. **Dissents:** Four Justices dissented in *Moore*. Several of the dissenters contended that the right of members of an extended family to live together was not "fundamental," and that therefore a "mere-rationality" test, rather than heightened scrutiny, should be applied. The dissenters also warned that reference to "traditional values" would lead to widespread and standardless judicial invalidation of state legislative action.

   d. **Stevens' deciding vote:** Only four Justices followed the Powell analysis. The plaintiff won because Justice Stevens concurred on the grounds that the ordinance had no substantial relation to any state interest, and violated the plaintiff's ***property*** rights. Thus it is unclear whether a case involving the rights of extended family members to reside together as lessees rather than landowners would yield the same result.

    e. ***Moore* distinguished from *Belle Terre*:** The *Moore* plurality took pains to distinguish that case from *Belle Terre v. Borass*, 416 U.S. 1 (1974), where a majority of the Court upheld a zoning restriction which excluded most groups of ***unrelated*** people from living together. The *Belle Terre* majority found that unrelated persons had no "fundamental" right to live together. (In particular, no fundamental right of association or privacy was found to be involved.)

        i. **Reconciliation:** Comparing *Moore* and *Belle Terre* illustrates that it is ***family relations, not the right of individuals to choose with whom they live***, that the Court has honored with "fundamental rights" status.

3. **Child-rearing:** Parents clearly have a substantive due process right to direct the ***upbringing and education of their children.***

    a. **Older holdings:** The Court has long recognized this right. See, e.g., *Pierce v. Society of Sisters (supra*, p. 173), holding that parents' substantive due process right to direct their children's education was violated by a rule requiring all children to ***attend public schools*** rather than private schools.

    b. **Right to decide who visits the child:** A recent example of a parent's right to direct the upbringing her child came in ***Troxel v. Granville***, 530 U.S. 57 (2000), where most members of the Court seemed to agree that a parent has a fundamental due process interest in ***determining which people outside the nuclear family will have access to the children.***

        i. **Facts:** In *Troxel*, a state-court judge ordered the mother of two minor girls to give monthly ***visitation privileges*** to the girls' paternal ***grandparents***. The judge did so under a state statute that allowed a court to "order visitation rights for any person when visitation may serve the best interest of the child."

        ii. **Plurality:** There was no majority opinion in *Troxel*. But at least six members of the Court appeared to believe that the compulsory visitation here violated the mother's due process rights. A four-Justice plurality said that "the liberty interest at issue in this case — the interest of parents in the care, custody, and control of their children — is perhaps the ***oldest of the fundamental liberty interests recognized by this Court***" (citing *Meyer v. Nebraska* and *Pierce*). The plurality went on to say that the visitation statute as applied in this case "unconstitutionally infringes on that fundamental parental right." The plurality did not suggest that the custodial parent's decision on visitation issues must always be respected by the state. But the opinion did say that where a parent is fit, a court deciding whether to grant visitation rights "must accord at least ***some special weight*** to the parent's own determination" about whether the proposed visitation would be in the child's best interests.

        iii. **Concurrences:** Two other justices who concurred, Souter and Thomas, agreed with this analysis. In fact, Justice Thomas said that to the extent the Court's precedents recognized a parent's fundamental interest in determining the details of child-rearing, he would apply *strict scrutiny* to infringements of that interest. (The plurality did not say what standard of review it was using.)

    iv. Significance: So at least six present members of the Court seem to be on record as saying that a parent (at least a fit custodial parent) has a *fundamental liberty interest* in controlling the *care and custody of her child*, and that the state's machinery for ordering visitation rights must attach *significant weight* to the *custodial parent's judgment* on visitation matters.

4. Right to marry (*Zablocki v. Redhail*): The *right to marry* is viewed by the Supreme Court as being "fundamental"; substantial interferences with that right will therefore not be sustained merely because they are "rational." *Zablocki v. Redhail*, 434 U.S. 374 (1978).

    a. Facts of *Zablocki*: In *Zablocki*, the plaintiff attacked a Wisconsin law which required that any parent who was under court order to support a minor child not in his custody meet two requirements before being permitted to remarry: (1) payment of all court-ordered support; and (2) a demonstration that the child was not currently, and was not likely to become, a public charge (i.e., supported by welfare). Plaintiff attacked the statute on both equal protection and substantive due process grounds.

    b. Statute stricken: The Court voted 8-1 to strike the statute. Five Justices, in an opinion by Marshall, felt that the right to marry was a sufficiently fundamental one that a "direct and substantial" interference with it should be subjected to strict scrutiny. (The Marshall opinion was, ultimately, an equal protection opinion, but its discussion of "fundamental rights" and strict scrutiny is highly relevant to substantive due process law.)

    c. State interest here not compelling: Applying strict scrutiny to the statute at issue, Justice Marshall concluded that the state's interests were "legitimate and substantial," but that the state's method of furthering these interests *unnecessarily interfered* with the fundamental right to marry.

        i. Less restrictive collection devices: For instance, rather than using the denial of a marriage license as a kind of "collection device" to assure that support payments were made, the state could have used less drastic compliance methods (e.g., wage assignments, civil contempt proceedings, etc.).

    d. Indirect interference is not subject to test: The Marshall opinion was careful to note that where a regulation had some incidental effect upon the ability to marry, but did *not "significantly"* interfere with that ability, only a *"mere-rationality"* test would be used. For instance, the opinion distinguished *Califano v. Jobst*, 434 U.S. 47 (1977), where the Court had applied a mere-rationality test to a Social Security Act provision which cut off benefits to a dependent child upon the parent's marriage to someone not covered by the Act. In the *Jobst* situation, the social security provision did not place a "direct legal obstacle in the path of persons desiring to get married," and did not "significantly discourage" marriage, according to Marshall.

    e. Gay marriage: Although conventional marriage is "fundamental," as *Zablocki* shows, the right of persons of the *same sex* to marry, or to enter some other socially-recognized ceremony of commitment, has so far *not* been classified by the Court as fundamental. However, the Court's 2013 decision in *U.S. v. Windsor* (*infra*, p. 368) probably indicates that the Court's view of the issue is changing. In *Windsor*, the Court struck down Congress' refusal to **recognize same-sex marriages that had been validly performed under state law**. The result and language of *Windsor* suggests that the Court will likely eventually recognize **a general constitutional right of gay people to enter into marriage**.

> **i.** **Language from *Windsor*** In *Windsor*, the majority opinion (written by Justice Kennedy) contains various statements attesting to the deep importance of marriage. For instance, Kennedy says that states that allow same-sex couples to marry confer on those couples **"a dignity and status of immense import,"** and that state-sanctioned same-sex marriage is "a **far-reaching legal acknowledgment** of the **intimate relationship between two people**[.]" It would not be much of a stretch for the Court that decided *Windsor* to conclude that the right of same-sex couples, like that of opposite-sex couples, to marry is "fundamental," and that state laws preventing such marriages cannot survive strict scrutiny under substantive due process (as well as under equal protection).

5. **Right of natural father:** Under the family law of most states, the father of a legitimate child may block that child's adoption. But most states do not give a similar veto right to the natural father of a child born **out of wedlock**, unless the father has "legitimated" his child (by obtaining a court order). In *Quilloin v. Walcott*, 434 U.S. 246 (1978), a Georgia law following this pattern was challenged by an unwed father who had attempted to block the adoption of his eleven-year-old son (whom he had never legitimated or had custody of) by the child's stepfather. The Supreme Court unanimously **rejected** the challenge.

> **a.** **Due process conclusion:** The Court held that the statute did not violate the Due Process Clause. The Court reasoned that the state had a legitimate interest in preserving existing family units; since the plaintiff had never lived with the child, or sought custody of him, the statute as applied here preserved existing families and was therefore arguably in the best interests of the child.

> **b.** **Father lives with child:** The father in *Quilloin* had never **lived with** his child. Where a man has fathered a child out of wedlock but has lived with the child for some substantial period, or has formed a **significant relationship** with the child, it is not so clear that a state can deprive the father of a veto power over the child's adoption. In fact, a majority of the present Court seems to believe that an unwed father who has lived with or has developed a substantial relationship with the child has a substantive due process right to maintain that relationship.

>> **i.** ***Michael H* case:** Thus in *Michael H. v. Gerald D.*, 491 U.S. 110 (1989), five justices seemed to agree with the proposition that "Although an unwed father's biological link to his child does not, in and of itself, guarantee him a constitutional stake in his relationship with that child, such a link combined with a substantial parent-child relationship will do so." (The quoted remark was by a four-Justice plurality; a fifth Justice, Stevens, seemed to agree with this statement, though he believed, unlike the plurality, that the state here had done what was required to protect that interest.)

O. **Sexuality, including homosexuality:** A person's **sexual conduct** — apart from any issues of procreation or family life — receives substantive due process protection, as the result of an important 2003 decision **invalidating** a Texas law **criminalizing homosexual sodomy**. In that case, *Lawrence v. Texas*, 539 U.S. 558 (2003), the majority opened by saying that "liberty presumes an *autonomy of self* that includes freedom of thought, belief, expression, and *certain intimate conduct*. The instant case involves *liberty of the person* both in its spatial and *more transcendent dimensions*." While the case directly holds only that states may not criminalize private homosexual conduct between consulting adults, the expansive language used by the majority suggests that the present Court is willing to recognize a fairly broad autonomy/ liberty interest in *private consensual adult sexual conduct* generally. The case is especially significant because it squarely overruled a fairly fresh precedent, the Court's 1986 decision in *Bowers v. Hardwick*, 478 U.S. 186 (1986).

1. ***Bowers v. Hardwick*:** Before we can understand the significance of *Lawrence*, we must understand what the Court did in *Bowers*, the decision that *Lawrence* overruled. In *Bowers,* the plaintiff, who was openly gay, challenged a Georgia statute making it a crime to perform or submit to "any sexual act involving the sex organs of one person and the mouth or anus of another[.]" The statute did not on its face distinguish between heterosexual and homosexual behavior. Violations were punishable by a prison sentence of up to 20 years!

   a. **Statute upheld:** By a 5-4 vote the Court in *Bowers* **upheld** the statute against the plaintiff's substantive due process attack. The majority, in an opinion by Justice White, phrased the issue as being "whether the Federal Constitution *confers a fundamental right upon homosexuals to engage in sodomy[.]* "

      i. **Not a fundamental right:** The majority asserted that the Court had regarded and should regard as "fundamental" only those liberties that are either "implicit in the concept of ordered liberty" or "deeply rooted in this Nation's history and tradition." Homosexual sodomy was not such a liberty under either of these formulations, the majority found. In view of the fact that, until 1961, all 50 states outlawed sodomy, and 24 still did, any claim that the right to practice sodomy was "implicit in the concept of ordered liberty" or "deeply rooted in this Nation's history and tradition" was "at best, *facetious*."

      ii. **Privacy of home irrelevant:** The plaintiff in *Bowers* asserted that whatever right the state might have to police public sexual practices, conduct occurring in the *privacy of the home* should be protected; he relied on *Stanley v. Georgia (infra*, p. 562), in which the Court had held that a person could not be convicted of possessing and reading obscene material in the privacy of his own home. The majority *rejected* this argument on the grounds that *Stanley* was based on the First Amendment, not the Fourteenth.

         (1) **"Parade of horribles":** The majority believed that plaintiff's *Stanley*-based argument, insofar as it claimed a constitutional protection for all voluntary sexual conduct between consenting adults in the home, would make it logically impossible to protect the claimed right to homosexual conduct "while leaving exposed to prosecution *adultery*, *incest*, and other sexual crimes even though they are committed in the home." The majority was "unwilling to start down that road."

   b. **Blackmun's dissent:** A dissent by Justice Blackmun (in which Brennan, Marshall, and Stevens joined) disagreed not only with the result reached by the majority but with the proper framework for analyzing the Georgia statute.

        i. **What case is about:** The case was not about "a fundamental right to engage in homosexual sodomy" as the majority argued, said the dissenters. Rather, it was about the much broader *"right to be let alone."* The statute was not limited to homosexual sodomy; by its terms, heterosexual conduct was equally covered.

        ii. **Two strands to privacy right:** The dissenters then noted that this "right to be let alone" had two different strands recognized in prior Court decisions: (1) a right to be free of governmental interference in making certain private **decisions** (the "decisional" aspect of the privacy right); and (2) the right to privacy of certain **places** without regard to the activities that go on there (the "spatial" aspect). The dissenters believed that the Georgia statute violated each of these aspects.

2. ***Lawrence* overrules *Bowers*:** That's where constitutional law on homosexual conduct stood for 17 years until 2003, when *Lawrence* came along to overturn *Bowers*.

3. **Facts of *Lawrence*:** *Lawrence* came about when the Houston Police entered the apartment of one of the two Ds through an unlocked door. (The police were responding to a reported disturbance involving a weapon. Although the Supreme Court's opinion doesn't say so, the neighbor who made the report was later convicted of filing a false report.) The police discovered the two Ds, both men, having sex.

    a. **Texas anti-sodomy statute:** The Ds were charged with violating a Texas statute that made it a crime to "engage[] in deviant sexual intercourse with another individual of the same sex." "Deviate sexual intercourse" was defined to include (i) any contact between the genitals of one person and the mouth or anus of another, or (ii) the penetration of the genitals or anus of another by an object. The Ds were not only arrested but held in custody overnight, then tried, convicted, and fined.

4. **Majority opinion:** Justice Kennedy, joined by four other justices (Stevens, Souter, Ginsburg and Breyer), delivered the opinion for the Court in *Lawrence*. That opinion found that the Texas statute violated the Ds' substantive due process rights, and concluded that *Bowers* had been wrongly decided. (Justice O'Connor supplied a sixth vote for striking down the statute, but on equal protection grounds, as described below.)

    a. **Review of older cases:** Kennedy's opinion began by reviewing a number of the Court's older substantive-due-process cases that touched on sexual conduct, and that emphasized some form or another of a right to privacy. Kennedy noted that *Griswold* (*supra*, p. 174), in the course of striking down state restrictions on contraception, had described the protected interest as a right to privacy, and had emphasized the "protected space of the marital bedroom." Similarly, Kennedy observed, *Roe v. Wade* had recognized that "the protection of liberty under the Due Process Clause has a substantive dimension of fundamental significance in defining the rights of the person."

    b. **Review of *Bowers*:** Against this backdrop, Kennedy reviewed the *Bowers* decision. He noted that the majority's decision in *Bowers* phrased the issue as "whether the Federal Constitution confers a fundamental right upon homosexuals to engage in sodomy[.]" But, Kennedy now concluded, that very phrasing of the issue "discloses the Court's own failure to appreciate the extent of liberty at stake. To say that the issue in *Bowers* was simply the right to engage in certain sexual conduct **demeans the claim** the individual put forward, just as it would demean a married couple were it to be said marriage is simply about the right to have sexual intercourse." Laws like the one in *Bowers* and the one here "have more far-reaching consequences, touching upon the *most private human conduct, sexual behavior*, and in the ***most private of places, the home*.**"

i. ***Bowers'* historical analysis wrong:** Kennedy then concluded that *Bowers* was wrong when it concluded that American laws banning homosexual conduct "have ***ancient roots*.**" Kennedy's own historical analysis was that "American laws targeting same-sex couples did not develop until the last third of the 20th-century." At the very least, the historical conclusions in *Bowers* were "overstated."

ii. **Emerging recognition of liberty interest in sex:** Kennedy believed that American "laws and traditions in the ***past half century*"** were the ones that were of "most relevance here." And that recent body of law showed "an ***emerging awareness*** that liberty gives ***substantial protection*** to adult persons in ***deciding how to conduct their private lives in matters pertaining to sex*.**" Kennedy asserted that this "emerging recognition" "should have been apparent when *Bowers* was decided."

iii. **Europe:** Perhaps most startlingly, Kennedy attached great weight to the fact that ***other countries*** had, even before *Bowers*, reached the conclusion that government ought not to bar private homosexual conduct. For instance, he pointed out, the ***European Court of Human Rights*** had, almost five years before *Bowers*, held that a Northern Ireland law forbidding consensual homosexual conduct violated the European Convention on Human Rights.

iv. **Post-*Bowers* developments:** Post-*Bowers* developments, too, had cast doubt on *Bowers'* validity, Kennedy said. For instance, whereas 25 states had laws prohibiting homosexual sodomy at the time of *Bowers*, that number had now been reduced to 13. And even in those states, there was now a "pattern of non enforcement" as to consulting adults acting in private. Furthermore, post-*Bowers* decisions by the Court, in *Planned Parenthood v. Casey* (*supra*, p. 178) and *Romer v. Evans* (*infra*, p. 245) had caused ***"serious erosion"*** of *Bowers*. For instance, *Romer* had concluded that the anti-gay legislation there was "born of animosity towards the class of persons affected" and had no rational relation to any governmental purpose. *Romer* was obviously relevant here, he said, because "when homosexual conduct is made criminal by the laws of the State, that declaration in and of itself is an invitation to ***subject homosexual persons to discrimination both in the public and in the private spheres*.**" Continuing *Bowers* as precedent ***"demeans the lives of homosexual persons."***

c. **Conclusion:** Kennedy concluded that ***"Bowers was not correct when it was decided, and it is not correct today.*** It ought not to remain binding precedent." Therefore, it was now overruled. The Ds "are ***entitled to respect for their private lives.*** The state ***cannot demean their existence or control their destiny*** by ***making their private sexual conduct a crime.*** The right to liberty under the Due Process Clause gives them ***the full right to engage in their conduct without intervention of the government.*** ... The Texas statute ***furthers no legitimate state interest*** which can justify its intrusion into the ***personal and private life of the individual*.**"

i. **What isn't covered:** Kennedy also stressed that there were various types of statutes that were ***not covered*** by the *Lawrence* decision: "The present case does not involve ***minors*.** It does not involve ***persons who might be injured or coerced*** or who are situated in relationship where ***consent might not be easily refused.*** It does not involve *public conduct* or *prostitution*." And, he said, it "does not involve whether the government must give formal recognition to any relationship that homosexual persons seek to enter," an obvious reference to the issue of *gay marriage*.

   d. Rational basis review: Notice that while Kennedy's opinion is filled with broad-reaching language about the importance of the interest being served (e.g., that the right to liberty under the due process clause protects the "full right to engage in [sexual] conduct without intervention of the government"), the opinion does *not* classify the interest in pursuing homosexual conduct as being a *fundamental* interest. Instead, the opinion applies *rational-basis review*, and strikes down the statute on the grounds that it *"furthers no legitimate state interest."*

5. **O'Connor's concurrence:** Justice O'Connor concurred that the Texas statute was invalid. However, she reached this conclusion on *equal protection* rather than due process grounds. The Texas statute here applied only to sodomy between same-sex partners, not to sodomy between opposite-sex partners. Thus Texas was treating the same conduct differently "based solely on the participants." Texas justified its statute as furthering the "promotion of morality." But, O'Connor concluded, *"moral disapproval"* of a group like homosexuals, like a "bare desire to harm" a group, is "an interest that is *insufficient to satisfy rational basis review* under the Equal Protection Clause."

6. **Scalia's dissent:** Justice Scalia, joined by Chief Justice Rehnquist and Justice Thomas, dissented. He criticized the majority for applying "an *unheard-of form of rational-basis review* that will have far-reaching implications beyond this case."

   a. Rational relation: Scalia disagreed with the core of the majority's position, that the law here was not rationally related to the promotion of a legitimate state interest. The Texas statute here "seeks to further the belief of its citizens that certain forms of sexual behavior are '*immoral and unacceptable*'." But this was the same interest, he said, that was furthered by "criminal laws against *fornication, bigamy, adultery, adult incest, bestiality,* and *obscenity.*" Therefore, "if, as the Court asserts, the promotion of majoritarian sexual morality is not even a *legitimate* state interest, *none of the above-mentioned laws can survive rational-basis review.*"

   b. "Homosexual agenda": Scalia closed with an angry invective-filled passage. The majority's opinion was "the product of a law-profession culture, that has largely signed on to the so-called *homosexual agenda*[.]" The Court had, he said, "taken sides in the *culture war*, departing from its role of assuring, as *neutral observer*, that the democratic rules of engagement are observed." He said that he had "nothing against homosexuals, or any other group, promoting their agenda through normal democratic means." But here, the Court was inappropriately allowing gays to *achieve judicially* what they had been *unable to achieve politically* in Texas.

      i. Gay marriage: Scalia was especially fearful that the majority's logic would lead inexorably to a constitutionally-recognized right to *homosexual marriage*. "If moral disapprobation of homosexual conduct is 'no legitimate state interest' [as the majority said] ... what justification could there possibly be for denying the benefits of marriage to homosexual couples exercising [quoting the majority] '[t]he liberty protected by the Constitution'?"

(1) Good prediction: Scalia turned out to be a good predictor of future steps by the Court. Exactly ten years after *Lawrence* was decided, the Court decided in *U.S. v. Windsor* (*infra*, p. 368) that Congress could not constitutionally refuse to *recognize same-sex marriages that had been validly performed under state law*. Indeed, the majority in *Windsor* relied on precisely the reasoning that Scalia had pointed to in his *Lawrence* dissent: that moral disapproval of homosexual conduct cannot be a legitimate state interest. *Windsor* does not recognize a *general* constitutional right to gay marriage (it merely forces the federal government to recognize state-consecrated same-sex marriages), but it seems like a large step in that direction.

Note: For more about the Court's recent treatment of gay rights issues, including gay marriage, see our extensive discussion of this topic beginning *infra*, p. 365, in the chapter on equal protection.

P. The "right to die": Should a *terminally ill* or *comatose* patient have the right to choose to *"die with dignity"*? The so-called *"right to die"* is really a series of sub-issues, on which the law is just starting to develop. The Supreme Court has issued two major decisions, one on the "right to *decline unwanted medical procedures*" (*Cruzan v. Missouri Dept. of Health*, *infra*, p. 205) and the other on the "right to *commit suicide*" (*Washington v. Glucksberg*, *infra*, p. 209).

As the result of these two decisions, there are several major propositions that we can recite at this point:

❑ A competent adult has a Fourteenth Amendment "liberty" interest in *not being forced to undergo unwanted medical procedures*, including artificial life-sustaining measures.

❑ The state has an important countervailing interest in *preserving life.* At the very least, this interest entitles the state to require, before it allows "pulling the plug," *"clear and convincing evidence"* that a now-incompetent patient would have voluntarily declined the life-sustaining measures.

❑ Terminally-ill patients do *not* have a general liberty interest in *"committing suicide."* Nor do they have the right to *recruit a third person* to help them commit suicide (e.g., a physician who would prescribe a fatal does of drugs).

Virtually everything else in this "right to die" area remains unsettled.

1. The *Cruzan* case: The Supreme Court's sole "right to decline artificial life-sustaining measures" case so far was the important 1990 case of *Cruzan v. Missouri Department of Health*, 497 U.S. 261 (1990).

    a. Facts: Nancy Cruzan suffered severe brain damage in an automobile accident. Since 1983, she had lain in a "persistent vegetative state," i.e., a coma in which she had no awareness or cognition but continued to breathe without a respirator. All medical authorities agreed that there was virtually no chance that she would ever become conscious again or be aware of her surroundings. She was kept alive by means of a *feeding and hydration tube* implanted in her stomach. She was cared for in a Missouri state hospital, and the state was paying for her care.

    b. The claim: Nancy's parents asked the hospital to end the artificial nutrition and hydration procedures. Everyone agreed that she would die if these procedures were terminated. But the hospital refused to do this without a court order. Nancy's parents claimed in court that Nancy had a Fourteenth Amendment due process right not to be kept alive by unwanted medical procedures, and that before her accident she had told friends that shae would not want to be kept alive in such a comatose condition. But the Missouri Supreme Court, interpreting the state's "living will" statute, concluded that even if Nancy had such a Fourteenth Amendment right, the right could be exercised under state law only by "clear and convincing" evidence that Nancy would not have wanted the life-sustaining procedures used here. The court concluded that such clear and convincing evidence was not present, and it thus denied Nancy's parents' claim.

c. **Supreme Court affirms:** The U.S. Supreme Court, by a 5-4 vote, agreed that Missouri's continuation of the life-sustaining procedures here did *not violate* Nancy's Fourteenth Amendment rights. The majority opinion, by Chief Justice Rehnquist, turned largely on procedural issues:

   i. **Right exists:** The majority opinion began by holding that "a competent person has a constitutionally protected *liberty interest* in *refusing unwanted medical treatment*. ... " The majority thought that this interest might be outweighed by the state's interest in preserving life in at least some instances, but was willing to assume (without deciding) that a competent person would have a right to refuse lifesaving hydration and nutrition, and that this right would outweigh any countervailing state interest.

   ii. **"Clear and convincing" standard:** But the problem, the majority wrote, was that Nancy was obviously not a competent person who could make a present informed and voluntary choice to discontinue the lifesaving procedures. So the question became, may Missouri require that such procedures be discontinued only when there is *"clear and convincing"* evidence that this is what Nancy would have wanted? The court answered *"yes"* to this question — Missouri's interest in safeguarding human life was strong enough that the state was entitled to "guard against potential abuses" by imposing the "clear and convincing" standard.

   iii. **Standard not satisfied:** The majority then concluded that the Missouri Supreme Court had not committed "constitutional error" when it decided that here there was no clear and convincing evidence that Nancy would have wanted the hydration and the nutritive procedures stopped. The evidence consisted mainly of Nancy's statements to a housemate, about a year before the accident, that she would not want to live as a "vegetable."

   iv. **No "substituted judgment" required:** Finally, the majority held that no constitutional doctrine required Missouri to accept the "substituted judgment" of Nancy's close family members, if there was no proof that the views of these members reflected what Nancy's own views were or would have been.

d. **Dissent:** Four members of the Court dissented in *Cruzan*. The principal dissent was by Justice Brennan (joined by Marshall and Blackmun). Brennan contended that Nancy not only had a constitutionally-protected liberty interest in declining unwanted medical procedures, but that this interest far outweighed any general countervailing state interest in preserving life.

i. Stevens' dissent: Justice Stevens, in a separate dissent, argued that where the patient had made no prior expression of intent, the patient's "best interests," not the state's general policy in favor of preserving life in all instances, must control.

e. Scalia's concurrence: Justice Scalia was the only member of the Court who did not believe that there was a constitutionally-protected interest in refusing unwanted medical treatment. In a concurrence, Scalia argued that the right to refuse unwanted medical procedures, asserted on behalf of Nancy, was equivalent to a *"right to commit suicide,"* and that our nation's law and constitutional tradition gave the states unquestioned power to prohibit suicide.

f. Family wins on remand: By the way, on remand a Missouri judge heard new evidence presented by Nancy's family, which he decided was "clear and convincing evidence" that Nancy would not have wanted to be kept alive under these circumstances. The judge therefore permitted disconnection of the feeding tube, and Nancy died soon thereafter.

g. Significance: So *Cruzan* establishes two major propositions: (1) a competent adult has a constitutionally-protected Fourteenth Amendment liberty interest in declining unwanted medical procedures (though we don't know whether this interest may sometimes be outweighed by the countervailing general state interest in preserving life); and (2) where the patient is incompetent, the state may constitutionally refuse to allow these medical procedures to be terminated except where there is "clear and convincing evidence" that this is what the patient would have wanted. Many other issues remain unsettled, some of which are briefly touched upon below.

2. Incompetent patient, no expression of wishes: Where the patient is *incompetent* to express present wishes (e.g., the patient is in a coma as Nancy Cruzan was), the first question to ask is: has the patient previously expressed *clear wishes* either: (a) that she does not want medical treatment under circumstances like those now existing; or (b) that she wishes some designated other person (e.g., a family member) to make such decisions for her in the event of incapacity? If the answer to this question is "no" (as it was in *Cruzan*), then we know from *Cruzan* that the state may refuse to discontinue the procedures even though all concerned agree that the best interest of the patient would be to discontinue the treatment.

3. Living wills and other clear expressions of intent: Suppose the patient has, prior to becoming incompetent, signed a *"living will,"* or given some other extremely clear expression of desire not to undergo specified medical procedures. (A "living will" is a document in which the signer specifies what treatments are or are not desired in the event of certain medical conditions. Such documents typically state that the signer does not want to be kept alive by artificial feeding or respiration techniques in the event that he is in an irreversible coma.) *Cruzan* suggests, even if it does not expressly hold, that the state is constitutionally *required to honor the patient's wishes* in this situation. Eight members of the Court (all but Justice Scalia) agreed in *Cruzan* that a competent adult has a constitutionally-protected liberty interest in declining unwanted medical procedures. While there is some chance that a majority of the court might conclude that this liberty interest is outweighed by the state's general interest in preserving life, this seems unlikely judging from the tone of the opinions in *Cruzan*. So probably the state is constitutionally required to respect a living will or other *clear expression of intent*.

4. Document delegating decision-making: Another kind of document is likely to become increasingly relevant: the *"health-care proxy."* Whereas in a living will the signer typically attempts to state his own wishes for future situations (e.g., "I don't want artificial feeding if I'm in an irreversible coma"), the health-care proxy attempts to **appoint another person** to make these decisions. Thus a proxy might simply state, "In the event that I should become comatose, I entrust to my spouse Herbert all decisions about what lifesaving or other medical treatments shall be given to me."

   a. Not answered in *Cruzan*: We don't know from *Cruzan* whether the Constitution requires that such a proxy be honored. The majority in *Cruzan* expressly stated that "we are not faced in this case with the question of whether a State might be required to defer to the decision of a surrogate if competent and probative evidence establishes that the patient herself had expressed a desire that the decision to terminate life-sustaining treatment be made for her by that individual."

   b. Legislative response: Many states have responded to *Cruzan* by expressly recognizing such health-care proxies. See, for instance, New York's statute, summarized in *The New York Times*, July 2, 1990, A1.

   c. Prediction: It seems probable that if a competent adult has the constitutional right to decline unwanted medical assistance, that competent adult also has the right to delegate to another the job of exercising this right in the event of incompetence. But even if this is true, the states probably have a great deal of scope in deciding what **evidentiary standards** such a proxy must satisfy. For instance, a state can probably require (as New York does) that any such proxy be signed in the presence of two witnesses, and that the surrogate be allowed to withdraw nutrition and hydration (as opposed to more extraordinary treatments) only if the patient has specifically so requested.

5. Child: Where the patient is a *child*, the issues are even murkier. Since a child can hardly be expected to have left "clear and convincing" evidence of whether she wanted lifesaving medical treatment, *Cruzan* is not directly relevant. It is unclear whether the state may, over the objection of parents, continue to hydrate and feed a child who is in an irreversible coma. The court may conclude, notwithstanding *Cruzan*, that the state must give the parents or a court-appointed guardian the right to make such decisions, so that the child's constitutional rights are not nullified.

6. Right to commit suicide: Suppose that the patient is a competent adult who desires to die. If the adult wishes simply to "pull the plug," i.e., terminate life-preserving medical treatment, *Cruzan* seems to hold or at least strongly suggest that the state may not deny that privilege. A distinct, and tougher, issue is whether the state may forbid a competent adult from taking **active steps** to **commit suicide**.

Thus suppose a patient suffering from terminal cancer desires to commit suicide by taking, say, an overdose of barbiturates. May the state forbid this conduct? And, more interestingly, may the state **forbid others**, including **doctors**, from **assisting** in this conduct? The answer to both questions is now generally **"yes,"** as the result of a landmark 1997 pair of Supreme Court decisions.

   a. Background: In 1996, two federal Courts of Appeal held that there *was* a constitutional right for a terminally ill patient to receive the assistance of a physician in committing suicide. The two courts split on the rationale.

i. **Due process:** The Ninth Circuit held that Washington's ban on physician-assisted suicide violated the ***Due Process Clause***. The court opined that the ban violated the patient's substantive due process "liberty interest in controlling the time and manner of one's death."

ii. **Equal protection:** The Second Circuit struck down New York's assisted-suicide ban on ***equal protection*** grounds. The court noted that New York allowed patients to order their doctor to end artificial life-sustaining measures (i.e., to "pull the plug"), but forbade the doctors to prescribe life-ending medication. According to the court, there was not even a rational basis for making that distinction.

b. **Supreme Court reverses:** But the Supreme Court disagreed, unanimously reversing each of these decisions. We'll focus here on the Court's decision reversing the Ninth Circuit's due process ruling. That decision came in ***Washington v. Glucksberg***, 521 U.S. 702 (1997).

c. **Statutory ban:** *Glucksberg* involved Washington's ban on "promoting a suicide attempt." The state defined this crime as "knowingly caus[ing] or aid[ing] another person to attempt suicide," and made it a felony.

d. **Rehnquist's majority opinion:** Justice Rehnquist wrote the Court's opinion in *Glucksberg*. Four other Justices (O'Connor, Scalia, Kennedy and Thomas) joined his opinion. The remaining four Justices agreed with the result (that the Washington statute was not unconstitutional) but not necessarily with Rehnquist's reasoning.

i. **Broad level of generality:** Rehnquist phrased the issue at a very high level of generality: "whether the 'liberty' specially protected by the Due Process Clause includes a ***right to commit suicide*** which itself includes a right to ***assistance*** in doing so." (Thus Rehnquist rejected the Ninth Circuit's narrower phrasing of the issue: "whether there is a liberty interest in determining the time and manner of one's death.")

ii. **No historical right:** To answer this question, Rehnquist began by canvassing past and present laws on the subject. He noted that "for over 700 years, the Anglo-American common-law tradition has punished or otherwise disapproved of both suicide and assisting suicide." And, today, he noted, in virtually every state — and in almost every western democracy — it was a crime to *assist* in suicide. Although the states had begun to re-examine this prohibition in light of modern medical technology, the prohibition remained on the books practically everywhere, he pointed out.[6]

iii. **Not a fundamental right:** Rehnquist then concluded that any due process liberty interest in ***committing suicide*** was certainly ***not a "fundamental"*** interest.

(1) **Rationale:** He noted that the Court had always been reluctant to expand the list of fundamental due process interests "because guideposts for responsible decisionmaking in this uncharted area are scarce and open-ended." Only rights or interests that were ***"deeply rooted in this Nation's history and tradition"*** could be fundamental. And, in view of the nearly universal past and present

---

6. As of this writing (August 2012), three states have some form of legal assisted suicide: Oregon, Washington and Montana. Cf. www.wikipedia.com, "Assisted Suicide," retrieved August 6, 2012.

prohibition of suicide or assisting suicide, the asserted interest in committing suicide did not come close to meeting this "deeply rooted" test.

(2) *Cruzan* distinguished: Rehnquist then distinguished the interest recognized in *Cruzan, supra,* from the one asserted here. *Cruzan* may have recognized a liberty interest in declining unwanted life-sustaining treatment, but that interest "was not simply deduced from abstract concepts of personal autonomy." Rather, the interest recognized in *Cruzan* derived from "the common-law rule that forced medication was a battery, and the long legal tradition protecting the decision to refuse unwanted medical treatment." So the right recognized in *Cruzan* was "entirely consistent with this Nation's history and constitutional traditions." The interest in committing suicide with another's assistance "may be just as personal and profound as the decision to refuse unwanted medical treatment, but it has never enjoyed similar legal protection."

iv. **State's interest in regulation was "rational":** Having decided that the liberty interest in assisted suicide was not "fundamental," Rehnquist then turned to the issue of whether there were any limitations at all on the state's right to ban such suicides. Rehnquist actually ducked the issue of whether there was a *non-fundamental* liberty interest in assisted suicide. Instead, he seemed to say that even if such a non-fundamental interest existed, the state merely had to show that its ban was "rationally related to legitimate government interests." Rehnquist quickly concluded that the state easily satisfied this test.

(1) Interest in preserving human life: First, Rehnquist said that the state had an ***"unqualified interest in the preservation of human life."*** He noted that many people who desire to commit suicide are clinically depressed (often because of untreated pain), and that of this group many who receive proper treatment withdraw their suicide request. "Thus, legal physician-suicide could make it more difficult for the State to protect depressed or mentally ill persons, or those who are suffering from untreated pain, from suicidal impulses."

(2) Protecting integrity of medical profession: Also, the state had an interest in protecting the ***integrity of the medical profession:*** physician-assisted suicide could "undermine the trust that is essential to the doctor-patient relationship by blurring the time-honored line between healing and harming."

(3) Protecting the vulnerable: Next, Rehnquist wrote, the state had an interest in ***"protecting vulnerable groups*** — including the poor, the elderly, and disabled persons — from abuse, neglect and mistakes." There was a "real risk of ***subtle coercion*** and ***undue influence*** in end-of-life situations." Apart from the state interest in combatting coercion, the state had an interest in protecting these vulnerable groups from societal prejudice: the state's suicide ban "reinforces its policy that the lives of terminally ill, disabled and elderly people must be no less valued than the lives of the young and healthy. . . ."

(4) Slippery slope: Finally, the state could rationally fear that legalizing physician-assisted suicide would set it down a ***slippery slope*** towards "voluntary and perhaps even involuntary ***euthanasia***." For instance, family members would inevitably begin to participate in the suicide, if the patient was unable to self-administer the drugs. And the experience of the Netherlands — the only western nation to allow even voluntary euthanasia — suggested that voluntary euthanasia had led to the *in*voluntary variety for such groups as severely disabled newborns and elderly persons with dementia. Thus recognizing a right to physician-assisted suicide for the competent, terminally-ill patient "is likely, in effect, a much broader license, which could prove extremely difficult to police and maintain."

(5) State interests were rational: These various interests were, Rehnquist wrote, "unquestionably important and legitimate." And Washington's outright ban on assisted suicide was "at least reasonably related" to the promotion of these interests.

v. **The concurrences:** There were several concurrences. Several Justices agreed only with the result reached by Rehnquist, and believed that the issue had been incorrectly phrased by him.

vi. **O'Connor's concurrence:** Justice O'Connor, concurring, supplied the critical fifth vote in support of Rehnquist's opinion. She agreed that there was "no generalized right to 'commit suicide.'" But she seemed to leave open the possibility that a terminally-ill patient suffering great pain might have a ***limited right*** to have a physician prescribe medication to ***alleviate that suffering***, even where this would hasten death. O'Connor thought that there was no need to address that question here, since Washington (and New York, the state whose statute was at issue in the companion case) did not forbid such prescriptions.

vii. **Stevens' concurrence in the result:** Justice Stevens, although he concurred in the result, disagreed with the majority's reasoning. Stevens agreed that statutes like those of Washington and New York were not *always* unconstitutional, so that the plaintiffs' facial attack on the statutes had to fail. However, Stevens believed that "there are situations in which an interest in hastening death is legitimate . . . ***I am also convinced that there are times when it is entitled to constitutional protection.***"

viii. **Souter's concurrence in the result:** Justice Souter, concurring in the result only, would have applied a somewhat different test for determining whether the statute violated plaintiffs' substantive due process rights. He saw the issue as whether the statute sets up "one of those ***'arbitrary impositions'*** or ***'purposeless restraints'*** at odds with the Due Process Clause." In Souter's view, if a statute did this, it would violate due process even if it didn't burden a fundamental interest, and even if it wasn't wholly irrational. In other words, Souter seemed to be advocating a ***"sliding scale"*** approach to due process (though he didn't use that phrase), by which the stronger the individual's interest, the stronger the state's countervailing interest had to be.

(1) Legislature has greater competence: In any event, Souter agreed that for the present, the legislature's judgment recognizing that a right to assisted suicide posed major dangers, should not be disturbed. But he left open the door for some future claim, when the factual realities were better understood.

ix. Breyer's concurrence in result: Justice Breyer, like Stevens and Souter, agreed only with the Court's result, not its analysis. Breyer disagreed with Rehnquist's description of the plaintiffs' claimed liberty interest as a "right to commit suicide with another's assistance." Breyer said that he couldn't be precise about what the plaintiffs' interest truly consisted of, but that his formulation "would use words roughly like a *'right to die with dignity,'*" and that "at its core would lie *personal control over the manner of death*, professional medical assistance, and the *avoidance of unnecessary and severe physical suffering — combined*."

    (1) More direct challenge: So Breyer, like several of the concurring Justices, thought that in a different case, the Court might some day have occasion to find that a state's ban on assisted suicide infringed a constitutional right. He suggested, for instance, that this might be the case if a state prohibited physicians from dispensing drugs needed to avoid pain at the end of life.

e. Significance: So where does *Glucksberg* leave us?

    i. No generalized "right to commit suicide": Clearly, the case establishes that there is no *generalized* right to commit suicide, let alone a right to enlist the assistance of others in doing so. And, in fact, it's pretty clear that even the class of "terminally ill patients in severe pain" do not have such a generalized right.

    ii. Right to be free of pain: But *Glucksberg* was a *facial* challenge, essentially a claim that the statute couldn't constitutionally be applied to *any* terminally-ill competent patient. The Court has carefully left the door open to *"as applied"* claims. Thus a future plaintiff might well succeed with a claim that a particular state ban on suicide or suicide-assistance has infringed *that particular patient's* autonomy-based due process interest. For instance a terminally-ill, competent patient, whose pain can't be reduced by any method that wouldn't bring about death, might well succeed with a constitutional claim if the state prevented him from getting any relief.

    (1) Five Justices leave open possibility: Five members of the Court (O'Connor, Stevens, Souter, Ginsburg and Breyer) seemed to explicitly leave open the possibility that such an "as applied" claim might succeed.

        Example: Suppose that a state passed the following statute: "It shall be a felony for a physician to prescribe a substance for the purpose of alleviating a patient's pain, if the physician knows or should reasonably know that the ingestion of the substance is likely to cause the patient's life to end sooner than it would end without such ingestion." (The Washington statute in *Glucksberg* did *not* contain this sort of prohibition.)

        Suppose further that P is a terminally-ill patient whose severe pain cannot not be dealt with in any way other than by giving him a large dose of painkiller that will hasten his death. It seems probable that a majority of the Court would conclude that the statute, as applied to P, violates his substantive due process rights. This statute would probably, in the words of Justice Breyer, infringe P's liberty interest in "*personal control over the manner of death*, professional medical assistance, and the *avoidance of unnecessary and severe physical suffering — combined*."

iii. States free to permit: Lastly, it is of course the case that the states are ***free to permit assisted suicide***, if they want to. See, e.g., the Oregon voter initiative, *supra,* p. 209, permitting assisted suicide in some circumstances.

Q. Other assorted autonomy issues: The "autonomy" branch of right-to-privacy law has raised a number of other interesting issues, on most of which the Supreme Court has not yet spoken. Some of these are as follows:

1. **Autonomy of mental processes:**   The autonomy branch of the right to privacy probably encompasses an individual's right to what might be called ***"freedom of thought processes."*** That is, the courts have recognized certain limits on what the government may do to ***shape the minds*** of individuals.

   a. **"Mandatory incantation":**   Thus the government does not generally have the right to condition receipt of benefits upon what Tribe (pp. 1315-16) calls ***"mandatory incantation."*** For instance, a state may not require a flag salute and ***recitation of the Pledge of Allegiance*** as a condition of receiving public education. *West Virginia State Bd. of Educ. v. Barnette,* 319 U.S. 624 (1943).

   b. **Freedom of inquiry:**   Similarly, the government may not generally restrict students' ***freedom of inquiry.*** See, e.g., *Meyer v. Nebraska (supra,* p. 173) (state may not ban teaching of foreign languages, at least in private schools); see also *Board of Education v. Pico, (infra,* p. 598) (First Amendment bars school board from removing books from school library for "narrow[ly] partisan or political [reasons].") However, a state is probably substantially free to limit the subject matter that is studied as part of the ***required curriculum*** in the public schools, so long as no other constitutional provision is violated (e.g., the separation of church and state, as violated by public-school prayer sessions, discussed *infra,* p. 658).

   c. **Private use of pornography:**   Similarly, a person has the constitutional right to possess and use ***pornographic*** or other objectionable materials in private. See *Stanley v. Georgia,* 394 U.S. 557 (1964) (discussed more fully *infra,* p. 562). This is true even where the material could be completely banned from ***sale.***

   d. **Drug statutes distinguished:**   But the government does have the right to make possession of specified ***drugs*** illegal, even though what makes the drug objectionable is its effect upon mental processes (e.g., LSD or marijuana).

2. **Rights of committed mentally retarded:**   ***Mentally retarded persons*** who have been ***involuntarily committed*** have been recognized by the Court to have the substantive due process right to be kept in a ***safe environment***, and not subjected to ***undue bodily restraint***. In addition, such persons may have a limited right to ***training***. *Youngberg v. Romeo,* 457 U.S. 307 (1982).

3. **Prohibition of risk-taking:**   Attempts by the state to control the ***amount of risk*** to which an individual may expose himself, may be questioned on autonomy/privacy grounds.

   a. **Motorcycle helmet rules:**   The best-known, and most criticized, example of a government attempt to limit risk-taking is the requirement that ***motorcyclists wear helmets***, a requirement imposed by statute in many states. Helmet requirements have generally been upheld.

   b. **Seat belts:**   Similarly, laws requiring that motorists wear ***seat belts*** have been challenged on autonomy/privacy grounds. These attacks, too, have generally failed.

4. **The right to travel:** The *"right to travel"* from state to state is sometimes viewed as being part of the constitutionally-protected "right to privacy." For instance, Tribe (pp. 1378-80) includes this right within his chapter called "rights of privacy and personhood." However, because the right-to-travel cases (especially *Shapiro v. Thompson*) have often involved equal protection considerations, our discussion of the right is postponed until the chapter on equal protection. See *infra*, p. 367.

5. **Right to occupation:** The right to *engage in one's chosen occupation* could be viewed as one of the elements of privacy/autonomy. Recall that since the demise of *Lochner*, the courts have been reluctant to give more than minimal substantive-due-process weight to "economic" rights. Nonetheless, in at least some kinds of situations, state interference with the right to practice one's chosen occupation is being subjected to more than minimal scrutiny.

    a. **Arbitrary deprivation:** The state may not prevent someone from practicing his chosen occupation for *completely arbitrary reasons*. Thus in *Schware v. Board of Bar Examiners of New Mexico*, 353 U.S. 232 (1957), the Court held that state qualifications to practice law "must have a rational connection with the applicant's fitness or capacity," and that plaintiff's prior membership in the Communist Party did not have such a rational connection with his fitness to practice law.

    b. **Equal protection:** Similarly, rules which deprive members of a *narrow* (and perhaps generally disadvantaged) *group* from practicing a profession are subject to attack, on both substantive due process and equal protection grounds. Thus in *Hampton v. Mow Sun Wong*, 426 U.S. 88 (1976), the Court held that the right to work in the federal Civil Service was important enough to be classed as an "interest in liberty." Consequently, Civil Service Commission rules barring aliens from the civil service could be upheld only if they were "justified by reasons which are properly the concern of [the Civil Service Commission]." Under this test, which appeared to be more than a "mere-rationality" standard, the rules could not be sufficiently justified, and were therefore violative of Fifth Amendment due process.

R. **No right to be protected from privately-imposed harm:** Virtually all of the substantive due process claims we have examined so far are ones in which the plaintiff was asserting the right to be free of *governmentally-imposed restrictions* that impair his life, liberty, or property. Suppose, however, that a person's life, liberty, or property are threatened not by the government itself, but by a *private person*; can one have a substantive due process right to be *protected by the government* from this third-party interference?

In a pair of cases, the Supreme Court has essentially answered *"no"* to this question. As the Court said in the first of those cases, *DeShaney v. Winnebago County Department of Social Services*, 489 U.S. 189 (1989), "[T]he Due Process Clauses generally confer *no affirmative right to governmental aid*, even where such aid may be necessary to secure life, liberty, or property interests of which the government itself may not deprive the individual."

1. *DeShaney*: The tragic facts of *DeShaney, supra,* pose the problem with utmost clarity. P was a boy who was repeatedly beaten by his father, to the point of permanent, severe retardation. The Ds were county social-welfare officials who received repeated complaints that P was being beaten, had reason to believe that this was the case, but did nothing to help P. (In fact, at one point the state took custody of P temporarily, then returned him to his

father.) P's lawsuit argued that the Ds had deprived P of his liberty without due process of law, by failing to intervene to protect him from his father.

a. Claim rejected: By a 6-3 vote, the Court *rejected* P's claim. The purpose of the Due Process Clause, the majority said, is "to protect the people from the State, not to ensure that the State protect[s] them from each other." Thus the Due Process Clause does not impose any duty upon the state to provide substantive services within its borders, whether these services are safety-protection, medical services, adequate housing, or anything else. The state's obligation under the Due Process Clause is simply to avoid affirmatively injuring a citizen's life, liberty or property without due process.

2. ***Castle Rock*:** The later case of *Castle Rock v. Gonzales*, 545 U.S. 748 (2005) posed a related question: may government by its *express pronouncements* in a statute *give a citizen an affirmative right of protection* against third-party harm, such that that right *will* constitute a substantive due process property interest? The Court's answer was that such a result is theoretically possible, but that it will *rarely occur*, and in any event did not occur in the case at hand.

a. Facts: *Castle Rock*, like *DeShaney*, involved tragic facts. P (Mrs. Gonzales) obtained from a Colorado court a *restraining order* compelling her estranged husband to stay away from P and her three daughters. Several weeks after being served with the order, the husband kidnapped the three daughters in violation of the order. Over the next five hours, P repeatedly asked the Town of Castle Rock police to arrest the husband, but the police refused to do so, apparently due to a policy of not normally making arrests for violation of restraining orders. Later that night, the husband came to the police station and was killed in a gunbattle with police; inside his truck, the murdered bodies of his three daughters were found.

b. P's claim: P sued the town on the theory that she had had a due process property interest in having the police enforce the restraining order, and that the police, by their policy of not enforcing restraining orders, had deprived her of this property interest without due process.

i. Colorado statute: In making this claim, P was not relying on the broad assertion (as had been made in *DeShaney, supra*) that government has a generalized duty to protect its citizens by making an arrest where there is probable cause to do so. Instead, P relied on a very specific and recently-passed Colorado statute designed to reduce domestic abuse; the statute provided that a peace officer "shall use every reasonable means to enforce a restraining order," and "shall arrest ... a restrained person when the peace officer has information amounting to probable cause that ... the restrained person has violated or attempted to violate any provision of a restraining order[.]" P asserted that this very specific statutory language demonstrated that Colorado intended to give her a due-process-protected property right.

c. Claim rejected: By a vote of 7-2, the Court concluded that Colorado *had not in fact conferred upon P a due-process-protected property interest* in having the police enforce the restraining order. In an opinion by Justice Scalia, the Court reasoned that P's claim of a property interest failed in three distinct respects:

i. Not mandatory: First, the Colorado statute did not truly make enforcement of restraining orders *mandatory*. "A well established tradition of police *discretion* has long coexisted with apparently mandatory arrest statutes ... [A] true mandate of police action would require some stronger indication [of mandatoryness] from the Colorado Legislature" than was present here.

ii.   **No entitlement to enforcement:** Second, even if the statute should be interpreted to make enforcement of restraining orders "mandatory," this would not necessarily mean that Colorado had intended to give a private person in P's position "an entitlement to enforcement of the mandate." Scalia reasoned that "Making the actions of government employees obligatory can serve various legitimate ends other than the conferral of a benefit on a specific class of people."

iii. **Not a property interest:** Finally, even if Colorado had meant to confer a true entitlement on P, it was not necessarily the case that this entitlement would amount to a "property" interest for due-process purposes. Nearly all the cases in which the Court had recognized a government entitlement as constituting "property" (cases like *Roth, supra*) had involved entitlements that constituted *direct* substantive benefits to the plaintiff (e.g., welfare payments, or a job). Here, the benefit sought by P was an *indirect* one — the right to have government take some action (an arrest) vis a vis a third person, not vis a vis the right-holder. Scalia suggested that any entitlement to an indirect benefit from government's taking an action against a third person was not properly viewed as a due-process "property" interest.

iv.   **Conclusion:** In summary, Scalia said, *Castle Rock* and *DeShaney* taken together mean that "the benefit that a third party may receive from *having someone else arrested* for a crime generally *does not trigger protections under the Due Process Clause*, neither in its procedural nor in its 'substantive' manifestations." He added that this result "reflects our continuing reluctance to treat the 14th Amendment as a '*font of tort law.*' "

S. **Looking back on the "fundamental value" approach:** Let us now briefly recapitulate the Court's current approach to substantive due process. The Court is willing to subject to more than minimal "mere-rationality" review only those legislative acts which materially impair a *"fundamental right."*

1. **Economic rights:** "Economic" rights are rarely found to be "fundamental" (though there are some hints that the right to practice one's chosen vocation may sometimes be viewed as fundamental).

2. **Non-economic rights:** Within the *non-economic* sphere, the Burger and Rehnquist Courts have been most likely to label a right as fundamental if it falls within what Prof. Ely refers to as "the 'area' (at least the Court sees it as an area) of *sex-marriage-child-bearing-childrearing*. ... " 92 HARV. L. REV. 11.

a. **Middle-class values:** Within this "area," the Court has been much more likely to protect what might be seen as *traditional, middle-class* values, than it has the values of more isolated segments.

i.   **Illustrations:** For instance, the Court has given fundamental status to a number of rights exercised within the context of a *traditional marriage* (e.g., the right to use contraceptives — *Griswold v. Connecticut, supra*, pp. 174-176). By contrast, the Court has refused to grant fundamental status to the right of consenting adults to engage in homosexual activity (*Bowers v. Hardwick, supra*, p. 201).[7]

ii. Zoning: Even the Court's substantive due process decisions in the area of ***zoning*** show a willingness to protect the family (e.g., *Moore v. City of East Cleveland supra*, pp. 197-198, protecting the extended family) but not a willingness to protect the right of unrelated individuals to live together (*Village of Belle Terre v. Borass, supra*, p. 198).

Quiz Yourself on

SUBSTANTIVE DUE PROCESS — PROTECTION OF NON-ECONOMIC RIGHTS

24. The state of Aha has enacted a statute that proscribes what the statute refers to as "unnatural sexual acts." The acts described include oral sex. The statute applies to conduct between married persons as well as to conduct between unmarried persons, but contains an exemption for conduct that takes place in a dwelling that is the residence of one or both parties. Joe and Martha Danzig, a married couple, were vacationing at the Happy Times Motel, when a state police officer burst into the room acting on a tip (reasonable-seeming but erroneous) that the couple was using drugs. The officer happened to see Joe and Martha engaging in oral sex at that moment, and arrested them.

(a) If Joe and Martha want to challenge the charges on constitutional grounds, what is their best argument? _____

(b) Will this argument succeed? _____

25. A number of states have enacted regulations bearing on specific aspects of abortion. Consider the following:

(a) The state of Aloha provides that no abortion may be performed within the state if at the moment of the procedure the fetus is more than three months old.

(b) The state of Brie provides that no abortion may be performed on a married woman unless she signs an affidavit that she has notified her spouse. However, the prohibition does not apply if the married woman instead signs an affidavit that she and her husband are not living together, or that her husband is not the father of the child, or that she has not given notice because she fears that he will abuse her if he finds out that she is planning an abortion. The statute is challenged by P, a woman who is two months pregnant, wants an abortion, and does not want to notify her spouse (with whom P lives, whom she believes to be the father of the child, and who is not likely to abuse her if she tells him she wants an abortion).

(c) The state of Caledonia provides that no abortion may be performed on a woman under the age of 18, unless one parent of the woman has received one hour of counselling about alternatives to abortion, and this mandatory counselling has been followed by a 24-hour waiting period. The young woman may avoid the need for parental consent by taking advantage of a procedure under which she is entitled to try to persuade a judge that either: (i) an abortion is in her best interests; (ii) she is living apart from her parents and is effectively emancipated; or (iii) abortion is made necessary by a medical emergency.

State whether each of these provisions is constitutional. (Assume that the suits in (a) and (c) are attacks on the face of the statute, and that the attack in (b) is "as applied.") _____

---

7. However, the 2003 decision in *Lawrence v. Texas* (*supra*, p. 201), overruling the result in *Bowers*, at least gives a more stringent form of rational-relation review to restrictions on homosexual sex, though *Lawrence* did not change *Bowers'* classification of the interest in having same-gender sex as non-fundamental.

26. In recent years, in the state of North Rockland, there has been an increase in the number of marginally-funded, educationally-inadequate private schools, as well as a rise in the number of parents who have been teaching their children at home rather than sending them to the public schools. The North Rockland legislature has, therefore, just passed a statute providing that every child between the age of 6 and 16 must be educated in the state's public schools. Parents who do not comply face criminal punishment. The statute does not allow any exceptions for even educationally-sound private schools or educationally-sound home instruction. Paula, the parent of a seven-year-old son, wishes to educate him at home. Paula was until last year a first-grade teacher in a state public school, and all concerned agree that she is well qualified to teach her child at home provided that she does so full time, which she expects to do. Paula has sued to overturn the statute, as applied to her and her son, on substantive due process grounds.

    (a) What standard of review should the court use in deciding Paula's suit? _____

    (b) Will the statute be found constitutional as applied to Paula and her son? _____

27. The state of Centuria has a criminal statute prohibiting "sodomy," defined to include any instance in which one person's mouth or anus touches another person's genitals. Century Village, a town in Centuria, has a school-board regulation providing that any person who the school board finds to have violated any state statute involving moral turpitude shall be dismissed, and further providing that a violation of the sodomy ban shall be deemed to constitute moral turpitude. Darwin, a non-tenured teacher at Century Village High School, was involved in a sexual relationship with Fred. After Darwin broke up the relationship, Fred sent a video to the Century Village school board, showing Darwin and Fred involved in conduct of the sort proscribed by the Centuria criminal statute. The school board viewed the video, concluded that Darwin had violated the statute, and dismissed Darwin. In recent years, the statute has rarely been enforced, and on those rare occasions has been enforced principally against same-sex sodomy. Darwin has now attacked his firing on the grounds that it violates his substantive due process rights. Assume that issues of procedural due process are ignored.

    (a) What standard should the court use for deciding Darwin's challenge? _____

    (b) Was Darwin's firing constitutional? _____

28. The town of Tinsel originally did not have any written regulation concerning the beard or hair styles of fire fighters. At the time Jordan was hired onto the fire fighting force, he had a beard and hair that was neatly combed but of shoulder length. After Jordan had been on the force two years, Tinsel enacted a regulation providing that no male firefighter could wear a beard or hair extending below his neck. Jordan has challenged this regulation as violating his substantive due process rights. Tinsel has defended the regulation on the grounds that: (i) uniformity of hairstyle is necessary to generate a feeling of esprit de corps among firefighters; and (ii) facial hair and long hair are more likely to catch fire even if the person dons the usual safety equipment.

    (a) What standard should the court use in deciding whether Jordan's substantive due process rights have been violated? _____

    (b) Is the regulation constitutional? _____

29. Two years ago, Pedro signed a "living will," in which he directed that in the event he should ever be in a persistent vegetative state, with no real likelihood of improvement, he should not be artificially respirated or hydrated. Pedro was then in a car accident, and lapsed into a deep coma (a persistent vegetative state) from which, all the doctors who have seen him agree, he is very unlikely to emerge. The hospital where he is being kept is willing to disconnect the respirator and hydration unit, but only if Wanda, Pedro's wife, signs a form agreeing with this step and waiving her right to sue. Wanda refuses to sign this document, arguing that although pulling the plug may well be what Pedro wanted (she does not dispute that he signed the living will while competent) she herself is opposed on moral and religious grounds to pulling the plug. Pedro's brother has been appointed Pedro's guardian *ad litem*, and has brought suit for a court order directing the hospital to discontinue life support even without Wanda's consent.

(a) What is the strongest constitutional argument that Pedro's brother can make as to why the plug should be pulled? _____

(b) Should the court order that the plug be pulled? _____

(c) Now, suppose that Pedro, instead of having had a car accident, is in the last stages of terminal cancer, and is in extreme pain. He is competent, and wishes to have his physician, Doctor, prescribe a fatal dose of morphine so that Pedro can commit suicide. The state makes it a crime to help anyone commit suicide, no matter what the circumstances. Doctor goes to court to seek a declaratory judgment that the ban on assisting suicide is unconstitutional as applied to these facts. Should the court grant Doctor's request? _____

Answers

24. (a) That the charges violate the defendants' substantive due process right to "privacy."

(b) Yes, probably. The Supreme Court has held that every individual has a "zone of privacy," and that government action which invades that zone will be found to violate the individual's substantive due process rights unless the government action is necessary to achieve a compelling governmental objective (strict scrutiny). The Supreme Court has never explicitly held that the sexual acts of a married couple, taken in private, fall within the zone of privacy for all purposes. However, the Court has held (in *Griswold v. Connecticut*) that the right to privacy is violated when the state interferes with a couple's attempts to use birth control. Later cases suggest that state interferences with a married couple's sexual intimacy would similarly violate the right to privacy, assuming that the conduct took place in private (even if it took place in a hotel room or other non-residential but non-public setting). See, e.g., *Lawrence v. Texas*, the homosexual-sodomy case, where the majority opinion refers to "an emerging awareness that liberty gives substantial protection to adult persons in deciding how to conduct their private lives in matters pertaining to sex." In summary, since Joe and Martha are married and were performing the activity in private, their conduct probably fell within the protected zone of privacy. (It is a bit less clear that their "right of privacy" argument would prevail if they had been unmarried, or engaged in an adulterous relationship.)

25. (a) Unconstitutional. *Planned Parenthood v. Casey* and *Gonzales v. Carhart* make it substantially easier than it was formerly for the states to regulate abortion. Nonetheless, even under these cases, the states may not place *"undue burdens"* on the right of abortion. A state regulation will constitute an undue burden if the regulation has the purpose or effect of placing a "substantial obstacle" in the path of a woman seeking an abortion of a *non-viable fetus*. *Casey*. Since a four- or five-month-old fetus is certainly not viable even under present medical advances, the blanket prohibition on abortions during this time frame would likely be found to be a "substantial obstacle" and thus an "undue burden," even given the Roberts Court's more-circumscribed view of abortion rights. (But a state probably could bar all abortions past the moment of viability.)

(b) Unconstitutional, probably. *Casey* struck down a spousal notification provision. The provision here, while it may contain slightly more escape hatches, would likely be found to be a substantial obstacle to the plaintiff (who is not covered by any of the escape hatches). Notice that the attack here is "as applied" rather than "on the face" of the statute. That is, the suit argues that the statute directly violates the rights of the plaintiff, rather than asking the Court to prevent the statute from being enforced against anyone because it violates the rights of persons not before the Court. Even the Roberts Court that decided the *Gonzales* partial-birth-abortion case would likely find that the statute acts as an undue burden *upon P*, even if that Court wouldn't allow a facial attack on the spousal notification provision. (*Gonzales* indicates that the Court will allow facial attacks only if the plaintiffs prove that the statute would be unconstitutional "in a large fraction of relevant cases"; the plaintiffs in a facial attack might not be able to make this "large fraction" showing, given the various escape hatches.)

(c) Constitutional. A provision much like the one here was upheld in *Casey*. In particular, the Court held in *Casey* that states may require the parent to listen to alternatives to abortion, and may establish a 24-hour waiting period following this mandatory counselling. The Court in the post-*Casey* case of *Gonzales v. Carhart* — upholding a federal ban on partial-birth abortions — emphasized the state's strong interest in warning women of the likely emotional regret that they may come to feel after an abortion, so *Gonzales* makes it even more likely that the Court would uphold the provision here than would have been the case before *Gonzales*.

26. **(a) Strict scrutiny, probably.** That is, the statute will probably be struck down unless shown to be ***necessary*** to achieve a ***compelling*** state interest. The question is really whether the right to make core decisions about how one's children shall be educated is a ***"fundamental"*** right. The Supreme Court has not addressed this issue directly in recent years. However, several cases (discussed further in part (b) below) suggest that the Court would hold that the right to direct the education of one's children is indeed "fundamental," in which case strict scrutiny must be applied to any governmental regulation that substantially impairs that right.

(b) No, probably. In *Pierce v. Society of Sisters* (a 1925 case), the Court struck down a state statute requiring children to attend public schools. The decision seems to have been on substantive-due-process-like grounds, and seems to have applied essentially strict scrutiny. Similarly, in more recent years, the Court has held that parents have a fundamental right to decide who may visit the child; *Troxel v. Granville*.

Assuming that the right to choose how one's children are to be educated is in some sense fundamental, it is very unlikely that the statute here could survive strict scrutiny. Ensuring a good education for children is certainly an important state objective, and probably a "compelling" one. However, it is highly unlikely that foreclosing all options other than public schools is a "necessary" means of attaining that objective. For instance, allowing a program of home instruction by one who is clearly a qualified elementary school teacher certainly seems to be an adequate way to assure a good education. And the state could adopt a monitoring program to make sure that home study programs satisfy a minimum quality standard. So the statute will probably flunk strict scrutiny, if strict scrutiny is applied.

27. **(a) The "rational relation," not "strict scrutiny," standard.** The Supreme Court has held that a state may not criminalize sodomy defined in this way. *Lawrence v. Texas* (2003) (p. 201). But in reaching this conclusion, the Court applied the easier-to-satisfy rational-relation standard. However, the Court found that such a ban on sodomy — generally enforced only against homosexual sodomy — could not satisfy even the rational-relation test, because it pursued only the illegitimate aim of expressing moral disapproval of homosexuality. The Court would presumably use the same rational-relation standard in evaluating whether a public body may fire a person for engaging in such sodomy.

(b) No, probably. Although the Court would (as noted in part (a) above) probably apply the rational-relation standard to the school-board regulation here, it is likely that the regulation would be found invalid even under that relatively easy-to-satisfy standard. The essence of the regulation is that one who violates a state statute forbidding a particular act of turpitude may be fired. Since the underlying state statute is no longer valid in light of *Lawrence*, it is hard to believe that the Court would find that it was rational for the school board to fire someone for violating this no-longer-valid statute. This is especially likely given that the governmental objective that the school district seems to be pursuing here — punishing gay people for "moral turpitude" — is the very one that *Lawrence* found to be illegitimate. The conclusion that the state was pursuing an illegitimate objective would be buttressed by the Court's several cases holding that "a ***bare [governmental] desire to harm a politically unpopular group"*** cannot be a legitimate governmental objective. (See, e.g., *U.S. v. Windsor* (2013), using this rationale while striking down Congress' refusal to recognize state-sanctioned same-sex marriages; the Court found that Congress was motivated solely by anti-gay animus.)

28. **(a) The "rational relation" standard, not strict scrutiny.** The choice of standard depends on whether the right of a firefighter to wear a beard, etc., is found to be "fundamental." In a case almost completely on point, *Kelley v. Johnson*, the Supreme Court held that a policeman's right to wear his hair as he wished was not "fundamental," and that the hair-length regulation there should be judged on a rational relation standard.

(b) Yes, probably. Assuming that the rational relation standard is used, the regulation here almost certainly passes muster. The town certainly has a legitimate interest in preserving *esprit de corps* and promoting safety. The contribution of short hair to fulfillment of these objectives may be questionable, but it is certainly "rational." (For instance, the town could reasonably have believed that long-haired male firefighters would not fit in as well.) Certainly the comparable hair-length regulation in *Kelley* was found to be rationally related to a legitimate governmental objective, and was thus upheld, so the same result is likely here.

29. **(a) That Pedro's substantive due process rights would be violated by forcing him to be kept on artificial life support.**

(b) Yes, probably. The Supreme Court has never explicitly faced the issue of whether a person who signs a living will has a substantive due process (or other constitutional) right to have that directive obeyed. But in *Cruzan v. Missouri Dept. of Health*, the Court suggested that a competent adult has a constitutionally-protected liberty interest in declining unwanted medical procedures. The Court might well hold that this interest is a "fundamental" one. If so, the state would have the right to decline to obey the directive only if the refusal was necessary to achieve some compelling governmental interest.

It is highly unlikely that there is any compelling governmental interest here that could only be achieved by keeping Pedro on life support. Certainly Wanda's interest in preserving her own religious or moral objectives would be unlikely to outweigh Pedro's right to control his own destiny. Therefore, the Court will probably order that the plug be pulled even without Wanda's consent (and the Court will probably immunize Hospital from suit by Wanda). (But *Cruzan* does recognize that the states have a significant governmental interest in requiring ***clear evidentiary proof*** about what the patient's wishes really are, so that if Pedro had not signed the living will, the state could probably refuse to accept, say, weak oral testimony from relatives about what Pedro "would have wanted.")

(c) No, probably. The Supreme Court decided in *Washington v. Glucksberg* that state prohibitions on assisted-suicide are not facially invalid, because there is no general right to commit suicide or to enlist another's assistance in doing so. *Glucksberg* seems to apply even where the plaintiff is a competent, terminally-ill person who desires escape from pain. However, it's possible that Pedro or his doctor could convince the Court that his "as applied" challenge (as opposed to the broad "facial" challenge that lost in *Glucksberg*) is narrow enough that he should win: he could argue that where a fatal dose of medication is the *only way* he can escape unbearable pain, it's a violation of his personal autonomy to be denied that relief. (See Justice Breyer's concurrence in *Glucksberg*, recognizing a "right to die with dignity," which he said would encompass "personal control over the manner of death, professional medical assistance, and the avoidance of unnecessary and severe physical suffering — combined." It seems pretty clear that Breyer would give Pedro the relief he seeks on these facts.)

V. PROCEDURAL DUE PROCESS

A. **Introduction:**   We turn now to an element of due process that is quite distinct from that with which the previous part of this chapter was concerned. The requirement that the government act with "***procedural*** due process" derives, like the requirement of substantive due process, from the Due Process Clauses of the Fifth Amendment (in the case of the federal government) and the Fourteenth Amendment (in the case of the states). Recall that both clauses prevent the government from depriving any person of "***life, liberty***, or ***property***, without due process of law."

  1. **State rules:**   In the following discussion, unless otherwise noted, we are talking about the Fourteenth Amendment Due Process Clause, and limits on ***state*** action. However, the same rules generally apply to the federal government via the Fifth Amendment.

  2. **No interest in governmental regularity** *per se:*   It is crucial to understand that the Due Process Clause ***does not bar the government from procedural irregularities per se. Only when "life," "liberty" or "property" are being taken*** is the government required to act with procedural correctness. If none of these interests is implicated by a particular government act, the government may act ***as arbitrarily or unfairly as it wishes*** (at least insofar as the Due Process Clause is concerned). As one commentator has put it, "Procedural due process … is evidently not a free standing human interest." 62 CORNELL L. REV. 452 (quoted in L,K&C, p. 626).

       Example: Suppose a state government announces that it will hire a new secretary for the head of a state agency. P is superbly qualified. The state interviews P, but awards the job to X, who can't type, but who is the daughter of a prominent local politician. Even if P can prove that the state's action was utterly arbitrary or unfair, P has not established any violation of her procedural due process rights. The reason is that P did not have any "property" or "liberty" interest in the job opening (see *infra*, p. 223), so there was simply no protected interest on which any procedural due process rights could hang.

    a. **Significance:**   Thus most of our discussion of procedural due process will focus on the issue of just what types of interests are deemed to be ones in "liberty" or "property," such that they may not be impaired without procedural due process? (Interests in "life" are imperiled by government action only in relatively rare circumstances, principally capital punishment; there, the interest in "life" is so clearly at stake that it is obvious that the government must act with procedural correctness.)

    i.   **Distinguished from substantive due process:**   The need to focus carefully upon exactly what constitutes "liberty" and "property" in the procedural due process area contrasts sharply with the practice in the substantive due process area. In the latter context, it has rarely been an issue in the Supreme Court's decisions whether "liberty" or "property" was implicated; "liberty" has been assumed to include "just about every interest of significance to an individual." Gunther (12th Ed.), p. 583. (Of course, if the interest involved is not deemed "fundamental," only a very small state justification is necessary to support its impairment; but the interest in "liberty" or "property" is nonetheless assumed to exist in virtually every substantive due process situation.)

  b.   **Three-part historical analysis:**   The Supreme Court's definition of "liberty" and "property" has undergone marked variation over the years. Our treatment divides the Court's approach to defining these terms into three major stages: pre-1970, early 1970s and post-1972.

  c.   **What process is due:**   After a comprehensive discussion of the meaning of "liberty" and "property," we turn to a much shorter analysis of a second issue: Once it is determined that a particular government action implicates an interest in "liberty" or "property," *what "process" is due*? That is, must a hearing be given? Must counsel be permitted?, etc.

3.   **Individual adjudications:**   One important difference between procedural due process and substantive due process is that a right to the former will only exist where the government action at issue involves an ***individualized determination.***

  a.   **Illustration of substantive question:**   Thus suppose a state establishes broad, mechanical, requirements (e.g., age, education, residence) which must be met before one may be licensed to practice a certain profession. These requirements will be tested solely by use of a substantive due process analysis (i.e., is a fundamental interest at stake; if not, does the rule have some rational relation to a legitimate state objective?)

  b.   **Illustration of procedural question:**   On the other hand, if a state imposes requirements against which each individual must be carefully, and subjectively, evaluated, the need for procedural due process may also be triggered. Thus if the professional licensing procedure requires an evaluation of "good moral character," the elements of procedural due process (e.g., the right to be heard, the right to an explanation, etc.) must be given. See Tribe, p. 682-83.

  c.   **Simultaneously valid and invalid:**   Thus a regulation may simultaneously be valid from the viewpoint of substantive due process and invalid from the perspective of procedural due process.

B.   **"Liberty" and "property" before 1970:**   The Supreme Court has, historically, taken a broad view of what constitutes "liberty" and "property." As the Court said in *Meyer v. Nebraska (supra*, p. 173), the interest in "liberty" includes "not merely freedom from bodily restraint but also the right of the individual to ***contract***, to engage in any of the common ***occupations*** of life, to acquire useful knowledge, to marry, establish a home and bring up children [and] to worship God according to the dictates of … conscience." Although the Court has never defined "property" explicitly, this term, too, has always been interpreted liberally.

1. Public benefits: But before 1970, there was one notable area in which the Court was reluctant to find that a "liberty" or "property" interest existed. This was the area of *benefits flowing from the public sector*, including *government employment* and monetary benefits (e.g., *welfare*). The Court traditionally took the view that such items were a *"privilege"* not a "right," and that they could therefore be withdrawn without procedural regularity. This view is sometimes referred to as the "right/privilege dichotomy." See Tribe, pp. 680-81.

    a. Constitutionally impermissible reasons: However, even under this traditional view that public-sector benefits were privileges, not rights, it was apparently the case that these privileges could not be withdrawn for *reasons violative of other constitutional protections*. For instance, it was clear prior to 1970 that the government could not fire a worker for exercising his right to free speech off the job.

        i. Right to hearing: A separate issue is whether a worker's mere *claim* that he has been fired or denied government benefits for such unconstitutional reasons entitles him to a due process hearing. The Supreme Court has still not explicitly decided whether such a mere claim of unconstitutional action, without additional evidence, suffices to trigger the need for procedural due process. Tribe, p. 682 and n. 34.

C. Growth in the '70s of "entitlements": During the early 1970s the Supreme Court held that many types of government benefits previously thought to be mere "privileges" rather than "rights" were *in fact interests in liberty or property*, which could therefore not be taken without procedural due process.

1. Welfare benefits (*Goldberg v. Kelly*): The first, and perhaps most important, of these decisions was *Goldberg v. Kelly*, 397 U.S. 254 (1970), in which the Court held that a *welfare recipient* must be given an "evidentiary hearing" before his benefits may be terminated. Welfare payments, for a person statutorily entitled to receive them, were not "mere charity," but were a *right* protected by the Constitution against arbitrary withdrawal.

D. Narrowing of "entitlements" theory: But the expansionary process described above posed a real risk: more and more transactions by state and federal governments might be deemed to impair liberty or property interests, until the entire day-to-day activities of those governments were rendered completely subject to constitutional review (and until the judicial system was drowned by due process claims). Consequently, after the early 1970s the Burger Court began to curtail the types of public benefits which would be deemed to create an interest in liberty or property. This scaled-back view of what constitutes liberty or property remains basically in effect today.

E. The tenure cases (*Roth* and *Perry*): The best-known example of the Court's cutting back is *Board of Regents v. Roth*, 408 U.S. 564 (1972), a *university tenure* case. But a companion case, *Perry v. Sindermann*, 408 U.S. 593 (1972), seemed to put an important brake on the retreat in *Roth*.

1. *Roth*: In *Roth*, plaintiff was given a non-tenured one-year contract to teach at Wisconsin State University. The University declined, without giving reasons, to hire him after the one-year period. Under Wisconsin law, decisions on hiring for non-tenured positions were left totally to the discretion of University officials. The Supreme Court held that plaintiff's interest in being rehired was not an interest in "liberty" or "property," and that he therefore had no right to procedural due process.

a. Rationale: The Court's opinion emphasized that the "weight" (i.e., the importance) of the plaintiff's interest was irrelevant; it was the "nature" of that interest that counted.

b. Not a "liberty" interest: Plaintiff's interest was not one in "liberty," the Court said, because the state's decision not to rehire plaintiff did not include charges which might damage his reputation (e.g., a charge of dishonesty or immorality), nor was he barred from a broader class of employment (e.g., all other jobs in state universities). Had either of these things occurred, the Court indicated, plaintiff's "liberty" would have been affected, and he would have had the right to procedural due process.

    i. Change in law: However, the Court's suggestion that damage to plaintiff's reputation would have been sufficient to invoke a "liberty" interest is probably no longer good law. In the later case of *Paul v. Davis,* (discussed *infra*, p. 226), the Court held that a person's interest in reputation alone is not a constitutionally-protected liberty interest.

c. Not "property" interest: Nor was plaintiff's interest in being rehired a *"property"* interest. Such an interest did not exist merely because the individual had a "need" for a benefit, or even a "unilateral expectation" of it; rather, he must have had a *"legitimate claim of entitlement"* to it.

    i. Scope defined by state law: Whether or not such a "legitimate claim of entitlement" to the benefit existed was, the Court held, to be determined *by reference to state law*. Since Wisconsin law made it clear that rehiring decisions in non-tenured cases were to be completely discretionary, plaintiff had no such entitlement.

d. Present enjoyment required: The *Roth* Court observed that the Fourteenth Amendment due process protection of property applied to interests "that a person has *already acquired* in specific benefits." This remark seems to mean that *unless a person is already enjoying a benefit, he has no procedural due process rights* (at least arising from the "property" as opposed to "liberty" branch) if the benefit is denied to him.

    i. Initial application: Thus where the state turns down an *initial application* for such benefits as welfare, government employment or parole, it may be the case that no procedural due process rights attach, even though the applicable statute or precedents make the applicant eligible for the benefit. But the Supreme Court has never squarely focused on this issue.

e. Marshall's dissent: Justice Marshall, one of three dissenters in *Roth*, advocated the extraordinary view that "every citizen who applies for a government job is entitled to it unless the government can establish some reason for denying the employment," and that this entitlement constituted a Fourteenth Amendment "property" right.

2. ***Perry v. Sindermann's* contrasting view:** Despite *Roth*'s severe approach, the companion case, *Perry v. Sindermann*, indicates that *informal practices or customs* may be sufficient to create a *legitimate claim of entitlement* to a benefit.

a. Facts: The plaintiff in *Perry*, like the one in *Roth*, was untenured. However, he had taught for ten years, and alleged that the college where he worked had a "*de facto*" tenure program, and that the college administration had created an "understanding" that he had tenure under that program.

    b. Holding: The Court held that plaintiff was entitled to a hearing on his *de facto* tenure claim, and that such a claim, if proven, gave plaintiff a property interest. Such an interest will be found to exist if there are "mutually explicit understandings" supporting a claim of entitlement.

F. Breadth of injury is weighed: The ***breadth*** of the public benefit denied is likely to be considered by the Court, especially in public employment cases. For instance, a governmental decision not to hire or rehire a person for one particular government job is much less likely to be held to be violative of a "liberty" or "property" interest than is a decision that the individual may not hold ***any*** government job. See *Board of Regents v. Roth, supra*, p. 224.

G. Freedom from arbitrary procedures: Some commentators have suggested that the courts should recognize, as a ***substantive aspect of liberty***, certain elements of procedural fairness. Professor Van Alstyne, for instance, advocates recognizing ***"freedom from arbitrary adjudicative procedures"*** as an element of "liberty." 62 CORNELL L. REV. 487 (quoted in L,K&C, p. 635). Similarly, Rabin, 44 U. CHI. L. REV. 60 advocates a "right to a ***reasoned explanation*** of government conduct that is contrary to the expectations the government has created by conferring a special status upon an individual." (Quoted in L,K&C, p. 646.)

    1. Significance: These proposals would effectively amount to making procedural due process a "free standing" right which can exist without the presence of any unrelated liberty or property interest. The Supreme Court has never indicated any willingness to do this. See *supra*, p. 222.

H. Narrowing of protected "liberty" interests: In *Bishop*, as noted, the Court appeared to limit constitutionally-protected "property" interests to those which exist under an explicit provision of state law or contract; other sources of substantive property rights (e.g., justifiable expectations, a common-law tradition, etc.) seemed to have been excluded. Very much the same kind of cutting back has also taken place in the definition of ***"liberty,"*** principally as the result of *Paul v. Davis*, 424 U.S. 693 (1976).

    1. Facts of *Paul*: Plaintiff, after being arrested for shoplifting, was listed as an "active shoplifter" in a flyer which the police circulated to hundreds of local merchants. After the shoplifting charges were dismissed, plaintiff sued the police under 42 U.S.C. §1983 (*infra*, p. 440), which allows recovery from public officials for violation of constitutional rights.

    2. Holding: By a 5-3 vote, the Supreme Court held that plaintiff's ***interest in his reputation,*** by itself, was ***not a constitutionally-protected "liberty" or "property" interest.***

    3. Federalism considerations: The majority view in *Paul* seems to have been motivated largely by a desire to ***avoid the federalization of tort law***, and to keep suits alleging wrongdoing by state government officials from deluging the federal court system.

I. Rights of students: The Court has not cut back on the definition of "liberty" and "property" in all contexts. For instance, it has given an expansive reading to these terms in the ***school*** environment. Thus in *Goss v. Lopez*, 419 U.S. 565 (1975), the Court held that a suspension from public school constituted deprivation of a constitutionally-protected property interest. (*Goss'* holding as to the type of procedure required in the suspension situation is discussed *infra*, p. 237.)

J. What process is due: Once a court concludes that a constitutionally-protected "liberty" or "property" interest has been impaired, the issue becomes: ***What process is due?*** While full consideration of this question is generally covered in other courses (particularly *Administrative Law*), a brief outline of the Courts' treatment of the issue is given here.

1. **Traditional adversary model:** The early 1970s saw the Supreme Court require an extremely broad set of procedural protections before the government could take away what the Court found to be a "property" interest. For instance, in *Goldberg v. Kelly*, 397 U.S. 254 (1970) (also discussed *supra*, p. 224), the Court held that an ***evidentiary hearing*** was required before welfare benefits could be terminated. In *Goldberg* and cases following it, the Court seemed to be moving towards a view that in order for the government to take administrative action which might affect a person's "property" or "liberty" interest, the full panoply of procedural safeguards typically imposed in court proceedings was required.

    a. **Wide range of procedures:** This approach, if followed to its logical conclusion, would have guaranteed not only the right to a hearing, but such protections as the right to ***call witnesses***, the right to ***counsel***, the right of ***cross-examination***, the right of ***judicial review***, etc.

2. **Withdrawal towards a "balancing" test:** Provision of such a full set of guarantees any time a "property" or "liberty" interest was at issue would obviously have been extremely expensive, time-consuming, and perhaps administratively impossible. Therefore, in the late 1970s, just as the Court cut back on its notion of what constitutes a "property" or "liberty" interest (see *supra*, p. 224), so it cut back on its interpretation of exactly what procedures are required where a liberty or property interest is at issue.

    a. **Balancing test:** The Court's present view may be summarized as calling for use of a ***"balancing test,"*** in which the costs of requiring a particular set of procedures will be weighed against the benefits from the use of those procedures.

    b. **Illustrated in *Mathews*:** This balancing test was first formulated in ***Mathews v. Eldridge***, 425 U.S. 319 (1976). In holding that disability benefits could be terminated without a prior evidentiary hearing (a sharp contrast with the holding in *Goldberg v. Kelly*, the welfare benefits case), the Court listed the factors to be balanced.

        i. **One side of equation:** On one side of the equation are: (1) the strength of the private interest that would be affected by the official action (so that the bigger the individual's stake in the outcome, the more safeguards would be required), and (2) the "risk of an erroneous deprivation of such interest through the procedures used, and the probable value, if any, of additional or substitute procedural safeguards." These two factors are presumably to be multiplied together in some way.

        ii. **Other side of equation:** On the other side of the equation is "the government's interest, including the function involved and the fiscal and administrative burdens that the additional or substitute procedural requirement would entail."

        iii. **Mathematical form:** Thus the *Mathews* balancing test might be expressed in the following mathematical terms, where "A" is the additional procedural safeguard to which the individual asserts that he is entitled: procedural safeguard, *A*, will be required if and only if

(amount at stake for individual) *x* (likelihood that administrative error will be reduced by using *A*) < cost to the government of granting A

c. **Application in *Mathews*:** The Court applied this equation in *Mathews* as follows:

    i. **Lower stake:** First, unlike the welfare payments at issue in *Goldberg*, the disability payments were less likely to be the individual's sole source of income, so his stake was lower than in *Goldberg*.

    ii. **Value of safeguard:** Second, the value of an evidentiary hearing was less than in *Goldberg*, because the disability issue turned upon a medical assessment of the worker's physical or mental condition, which assessment could probably be evaluated through written documents rather than oral testimony.

    iii. **Burden on government:** Thirdly, the burden of supplying a full administrative hearing was likely to be substantial, and the cost of it "may in the end come out of the pockets of the deserving since resources available for any particular program of social welfare are not unlimited."

    iv. **Conclusion:** Therefore, the Court concluded, no evidentiary hearing was required before termination of disability benefits.

d. **Firing of tenured employee:** Where the protected interest being terminated is a ***public-sector job***, the required procedural safeguards are similarly determined by a balancing test. Thus in *Cleveland Bd. of Ed. v. Loudermill*, 470 U.S. 532 (1985) (discussed more extensively *infra*, p. 236), the Court weighed a tenured employee's interest in retaining his employment against the government's interest in having a quick way to fire unsatisfactory employees; the Court also factored in "the risk of an erroneous termination."

    i. **Conclusion:** The *Loudermill* Court then concluded that although "some kind of a hearing" was required prior to the discharge of the plaintiff, that hearing was required to include only "oral or written notice of the charges against him, an explanation of the employer's evidence, and an opportunity to present his side of the story." It did ***not*** include the right to a ***full evidentiary hearing*** of the sort imposed in the welfare-benefits context in *Goldberg v. Kelly, see supra*, p. 224. Requiring a full adversarial evidentiary hearing would "intrude to an unwarranted extent on the government's interest in quickly removing an unsatisfactory employee."

3. **Traditional civil litigation:** When a person's property is at stake in a traditional ***civil lawsuit***, the range of procedural protections required by the Constitution is broad. Certainly as a matter of practice, and probably as a matter of constitutional due process, the state may not take property as the result of a lawsuit — even if the suit is brought by a private party against another private party — without granting such protections as the right to call witnesses, the right to counsel, the right of cross-examination, and the right of judicial review. A meaningful treatment of what constitutes due process in the civil litigation context is beyond the scope of this outline.

a. **Unlimited discretion:** One aspect of the right to due process in the civil litigation context is that a litigant has the right to be free of excessive ***discretion*** on the part of *juries*. For instance, when a state allows juries to award tort damages against a defendant, the state must give at least some guidance to the jury on when it may allow an award, and in what amount.

b. Punitive damages: In some circumstances the award of *punitive damages* may violate the defendant's due process rights.

i. Ratio of actual to punitive: A punitive damages award will violate due process if it is *"grossly excessive."* BMW of North America v. Gore, 517 U.S. 559 (1996).

(1) Ratio of punitive to compensatory: One of the most important factors in whether an award of punitive damages is grossly excessive is the *ratio* of the *punitive damages* to the *actual damages.* The Court has said that *"few awards* [significantly] exceeding a *single-digit ratio* between punitive and compensatory damages ... will satisfy due process." *State Farm Mut. Automobile Insur. Co. v. Campbell*, 538 U.S. 408 (2003).

Example: In one of the few cases in which the Supreme Court has found that a punitive damages award was so excessive that it violated the defendant's due process right, the court attached a lot of weight to the fact that the punitive award to P was *500 times* the amount of his actual harm as determined by the jury. *BMW of North America, supra.*

ii. Reprehensibility: Another of the key factors in the due process analysis is the *reprehensibility* of the defendant's conduct — the more reprehensible the conduct, the higher the amount of punitive damages that may be awarded without violating due process. *State Farm Mut. Automobile Insur. Co. v. Campbell, supra.*

iii. Conduct vis a vis strangers to the litigation: Only the defendant's conduct *towards the plaintiff*, not its conduct towards *strangers to the litigation,* may be taken into account by the jury in setting the amount of punitive damages. *Philip Morris USA v. Williams*, 549 U.S. 346 (2007).

Example: P (Jesse Williams), a smoker, sues D (a large tobacco manufacturer) for fraud in having knowingly and falsely led P to believe that smoking was safe. P's attorney tells the jury to "think of how many other Jesse Williams in the last 40 years in the state of Oregon there have been. [Cigarettes] are going to kill ten [of every hundred]." The judge refuses D's request that the jury be instructed that in assessing punitive damages, the jury should not punish D for the impact of its alleged misconduct on other persons, who may bring lawsuits of their own. The jury awards P $821,000 in compensatory damages and $79.5 million in punitive ones.

Held, for D, which is entitled to a new trial. "[T]he Constitution's Due Process Clause forbids a State to use a punitive damages award to punish a defendant for injury that it conflicts upon nonparties [who are] strangers to the litigation." That's so because a defendant threatened with punishment for injury to a non-party has no opportunity to respond (e.g., by showing that the other victim is not entitled to damages because she did not rely on the defendant's statements). Furthermore, permitting punishment for injuring a nonparty victim "would add a near standardless dimension to the punitive damages equation." *Philip Morris USA, supra.*

c. **Judicial bias:** A litigant also has a procedural due process right to be free of a *large risk of bias on the part of the judge hearing the case*. That right was first recognized by the Supreme Court in an important recent 5-4 decision, *Caperton v. A.T. Massey Coal Co.*, 129 S.Ct. 2252 (2009). *Caperton* means that in those states (39 at last count) that *elect judges*, *large judicial campaign contributions* by one party in a pending case can give the other party a procedural due process right to have the judge in question *removed from the case*.

   i. **Facts of *Caperton*:** The plaintiffs in *Caperton* were small mining companies and their executives, who claimed that the much larger Massey Coal Company had improperly driven them out of business. The plaintiffs obtained a $50 million damage award from a West Virginia jury. Massey appealed to the West Virginia Supreme Court.

   (1) **Campaign contributions:** While the appeal was pending, the head of Massey, Don Blankenship, spent a total of $3 million in an effort to have sitting Justice McGraw defeated for reelection and replaced by Brent Benjamin. The $3 million was (the majority found) "more than the total amount spent by all other Benjamin supporters and three times the amount spent by Benjamin's own committee."

   (2) **Benjamin wins, votes for Massey's position:** Benjamin won the election (by a 53% margin), repeatedly refused to recuse himself from the appeal, and became part of a 3-2 majority that threw out the $50 million verdict against Massey. The plaintiffs who had been stripped of their jury verdict argued that their constitutional due process rights had been violated by Benjamin's refusal to recuse himself for bias.

   ii. **Majority finds due process violation:** By a 5-4 vote, the Court agreed with the plaintiffs that Benjamin's refusal to recuse himself violated their constitutional due process rights. In an opinion by Justice Kennedy (who joined with the four liberal numbers of the Court), the majority held that due process could be violated not just by proof of "actual bias," but also by a *"serious risk of actual bias ... based on objective and reasonable perceptions*[.]" And such a risk of bias occurs "when a person with a personal stake in a particular case had a *significant and disproportionate influence in placing the judge on the case* by *raising funds or directing the judge's election campaign* when the case was pending or imminent."

   (1) **"Rare instances":** The majority rejected the dissenters' fear of a "flood of recusal motions" and of "unnecessary interference with judicial elections." The facts here were, Kennedy said, "extreme by any measure." Findings of bias that rise to the level of due process violations, Kennedy predicted, would be "confined to rare instances."

   iii. **Dissenters fear flood of challenges:** The four dissenters feared that the majority's new due process right would create more problems than it solved. In the principal dissent, Chief Justice Roberts said that the majority's "probability of bias" standard "cannot be defined in any limited way," and would inevitably lead to an increase in groundless allegations that judges are biased. The result, he said "will do far more to erode public confidence in judicial impartiality than an isolated failure to recuse in a particular case."

    iv. Significance: *Caperton* seems to create an important new constitutional right. It may be, as the majority asserts, that victorious *Caperton* challenges will be rare. But given the nature of litigation — and the incentives for parties, especially defendants, to lengthen the proceedings and make them more expensive for the adversary — it's likely that the making of due process challenges based on alleged judicial bias will become a common litigation tactic.

4. Criminal defendants and prisoners: *Criminal defendants* obviously receive extensive procedural due process protections during the course of their trial. If convicted, the defendant will lose her liberty for a substantial period, and perhaps even her life. So the procedural protections that criminal defendants get during trial are at their broadest: right to counsel, right to present witnesses, right to confront opposing witnesses, etc. The procedural protections given to criminal defendants are typically covered in a criminal procedure course, and are beyond the scope of this outline.

    a. Rights of convicted prisoners: Once a criminal defendant has been *convicted*, the defendant loses many, but not all, procedural due process protections. A large body of case law has arisen concerning both the substantive and procedural due process protections to be given to *prisoners*. Again, full coverage of those cases is beyond the scope of this outline, but here are a few of the key principles:

        i. Limited rights: Prisoners "do not shed all constitutional rights at the prison gate." *Sandin v. Conner,* 515 U.S. 572 (1995). However, the needs of prison administration, and society's right to punish crimes, entitle prison authorities to impose restraints on a prisoner's physical freedom even beyond the mere fact of incarceration, and give the authorities a *broad right* to decide on the *particular restraints* without furnishing a full array of procedural protections during the decision-making.

            (1) The "atypical and significant hardship" test: Prison officials who give extra punishment to a prisoner or change his terms of confinement won't commit a substantive due process violation, and don't need to observe procedural due process protections during their decision-making process, so long as their action doesn't "impose[] *atypical and significant hardship* on the inmate in relation to the *ordinary incidents of prison life.*" *Sandin, supra.*

                ❏ For instance, a prisoner who is charged with disobeying prison regulations is not entitled by due process to *present witnesses* during the disciplinary hearing, even if the hearing leads to his being put in solitary confinement for 30 days. *Sandin, supra.*

                ❏ Similarly, an inmate does not have a constitutionally-protected liberty interest in *not being transferred* from a medium-security prison to a maximum-security prison, because ""[c]onfinement in any of the State's institutions is within the *normal limits or range of custody* which the conviction has authorized the State to impose." *Meachum v. Fano,* 427 U.S. 215 (1976).

                ❏ Unless a statute gives the right, a prisoner does not have a constitutionally protected interest in being **given parole**. So parole boards may, in the absence of a statute imposing particular procedural requirements on them, act arbitrarily. *Greenholtz v. Inmates*, 442 U.S. 1 (1979).

(2) Severe or stigmatizing punishments: On the other hand, some conditions of imprisonment are either **so severe, or so stigmatizing**, that the prisoner's substantive due process rights *will* be abridged if prison authorities do not have adequate reasons for their actions, and do not follow adequate procedures.

❏ Thus a prisoner probably has a substantive due process right not to be **transferred to a mental institution** without cause. Cf. *Vitek v. Jones*, 445 U.S. 480 (1980) (though in *Vitek*, the situation was complicated by the fact that state law allowed the transfer only if the prisoner "suffers from a mental disease or defect" that could not be adequately treated in the prison).

❏ Similarly, some prison **conditions** are so incredibly **punitive** that the prisoner has a constitutionally protected liberty interest in avoiding them. Thus the transfer of a prisoner to a **"Supermax" facility** was found to implicate the prisoner's liberty interest, where the prisoner was kept in **solitary confinement** in a 7 by 14 foot cell for 23 hours a day with a light on at all times, and with just one hour a day outside his cell (to be spent in an indoor recreation cell). *Wilkinson v. Austin*, 545 U.S. 209 (2005). The Court found that this type of confinement imposed an "atypical and significant hardship," the test under *Sandin*, *supra*, p. 231, for whether a liberty interest is at stake. (However, the Court found that the prison's procedures prior to imposing the punishment — which included notice of reasons and a "fair opportunity for rebuttal" — were constitutionally sufficient, even though inmates were not given the right to call witnesses.)

b.   Right to appeal: An issue related to prisoner-rights is whether and when a criminal defendant has a due process right to **appeal his conviction**. The Supreme Court has said in dictum that "a review by an appellate court of the final judgment in a criminal case ... is *not* now a necessary element of due process." *McKane v. Durston*, 153 U.S. 684 (1894). The Court might, nonetheless, today find that there is a due process right to have some sort of criminal appeal. In any event, it is clear that once a state chooses (as all states do) to grant some sort of appeal, the appeals process must **obey certain minimum due process requirements**; thus, for instance, a defendant has a due process right to effective assistance of counsel on a first appeal that is granted of right. *Evitts v. Lucey*, 465 U.S. 387 (1985).

i.   Few rules: But the Supreme Court has largely stayed out of the business of dictating precisely *what* appellate procedures states must supply once they decide to allow criminal appeals at all. Post-conviction remedies given by the state must, in order to satisfy due process, merely "compor[t] with fundamental fairness." *Pennsylvania v. Finley*, 481 U.S. 551 (1987).

ii.   DNA testing: The Court's reluctance to prescribe specific methods by which the states must allow convicted defendants to try to overturn their convictions is illustrated in a 2009 case involving **DNA testing**. In a 5-4 case in which Chief Justice Roberts wrote the majority opinion, the Court held that a prisoner has **no indepen-**

dent liberty interest in being given access to DNA evidence to prove his innocence. District Attorney's Office for the Third Judicial District v. Osborne, 129 S.Ct. 2308 (2009).

(1) **Facts:** Osborne, the prisoner, had been convicted of kidnapping and sexual assault 16 years earlier by an Alaska state court. There was ample evidence of his guilt, including testimony by a co-defendant. Osborne had later admitted guilt in the course of parole hearings (a condition of parole). He now sought to test, at his own expense, the DNA evidence that had been preserved following the crime. The Alaska courts rejected his attempts.

(2) **Procedures were not inadequate:** Roberts agreed that Osborne had a constitutional liberty interest in having access to *some* sort of state-law procedures to demonstrate his innocence via newly-discovered evidence. But the state here had supplied such procedures (which Osborne apparently did not qualify for because the state viewed the evidence as not "newly discovered"). Those procedures, Roberts said, would be unconstitutional "only if they are fundamentally inadequate to vindicate the substantive rights provided." And the procedures here did not flunk that easy-to-satisfy standard.

(3) **No "freestanding right":** Most importantly, Roberts rejected Osborne's argument that he had (as Roberts put it) a *"freestanding right to DNA evidence* untethered from the [prisoner's] liberty interests[.]" Forty-four states had already given criminal defendants a specific statutory right to DNA testing (though Alaska had not). And overall, the states seemed to be handling the DNA issue satisfactorily. Therefore, the Court should be "reluctant to enlist the Federal Judiciary in creating a new constitutional code of rules for handling DNA," for fear that this "would force [the Court] to act as policymakers" on a host of related issues (e.g., to decide whether there is "a constitutional obligation to ***preserve forensic evidence*** that might later be tested").

(4) **Dissent:** The four dissenters in *Osborne* believed that Osborne had some sort of constitutionally-protected liberty interest that the state was abridging by not allowing the DNA testing here, though they did not agree among themselves on the exact nature of that interest. Stevens, joined by two other justices, wrote that Osborne had a substantive liberty interest in being given access to DNA evidence to show his innocence, and that the state's refusal to give him that access while providing no good reason for the refusal "constitutes ***arbitrary action*** that offends basic principles of due process."

5. **Detention of "enemy combatants" who are citizens:** One context in which the Court has made use of the *Mathews* balancing test (*supra*, p. 227) for determining what process is due is the ***detention of "enemy combatants" during war.*** In one of the first cases exploring the President's powers in the post-9/11 war on terrorism, the Court held that if a U.S. citizen is to be held as an enemy combatant, he is entitled to due process, including at a minimum the ***right to counsel***, and the right to ***go before a neutral decisionmaker*** to challenge his designation as enemy combatant. ***Hamdi v. Rumsfeld***, 542 US. 507 (2004).

a. **Facts:** The prisoner in *Hamdi* was Yaser Hamdi, an American citizen who was captured in Afghanistan in 2001 by the Northern Alliance, a coalition fighting alongside

U.S. troops to oust the Taliban. The Alliance turned Hamdi over to the U.S. military, which labeled him an "enemy combatant" based mostly on the fact that he had been associated with the Taliban and had surrendered his rifle to the Alliance. The military transferred him to a naval brig in South Carolina. The Bush administration asserted that by designating Hamdi as an enemy combatant, the executive branch obtained the power to hold him in confinement indefinitely, without formal charges or proceedings, so long as the war in which he had been seized continued.

b.   Ruling against government: Although the Court's rationale was badly splintered, eight members of the Court concluded that the U.S. did not in fact have the power that the government contended it had, i.e., the power to hold Hamdi without counsel, without charges and without opportunity for some sort of trial.

    i.   O'Connor's plurality opinion: Justice O'Connor, writing for herself and three other justices (Rehnquist, Kennedy and Breyer) wrote a plurality opinion concluding that Hamdi had the right to due process, at least with respect to pursuing his claim that he was not in fact an "enemy combatant."[8] In determining to what procedural protections Hamdi was entitled, O'Connor said, the ***balancing test of Mathews v. Eldridge applied.*** That is, the government's interest in the nation's security needed to be balanced against Hamdi's interest in not being deprived of liberty without due process.

        (1)   Government's interest: O'Connor conceded that the government had a strong interest in "ensuring that those who have in fact fought with the enemy during a war do not return to battle against the United States." She also agreed with the Bush administration that the government's interest in being free to wage a war without the distraction of litigation would be impeded by having to follow a system of trial-like procedures — including discovery into the details of military operations and national defense — before someone captured on the battlefield could be declared an enemy combatant.

        (2)   Citizen's interest: But Hamdi had strong countervailing interests: the "fundamental nature of a citizen's right to be free from involuntary confinement by his own government without due process of law."

        (3)   Minimum procedures: O'Connor then spelled out some of the procedural protections to which she believed Hamdi was entitled under the *Mathews* balancing test, if he wished to challenge the correctness of his classification as an enemy combatant:

        ❑   He was entitled to ***"notice of the factual basis*** for his classification" (as an enemy combatant);

        ❑   He was entitled to "a ***fair opportunity*** to ***rebut the government's factual assertions*** before a ***neutral decisionmaker***";

        ❑   He had the right of ***access to counsel*** in connection with the proceedings.

---

8. Hamdi claimed that he never bore arms against the United States, that he arrived in Afghanistan to do relief work less than two months before 9/11, and that he was trapped there when the U.S. military campaign began.

(4) Open questions: But O'Connor also tried not to tie the government's hands unduly. The Court was not being confronted with any particular set of procedures that the government was proposing to use — indeed, the government was contending that it did not have to use *any* procedures at all, and could simply detain Hamdi indefinitely on its own say so. However, O'Connor speculated about certain respects in which procedures *less protective* than the ones guaranteed for a standard criminal trial might nonetheless *suffice* in Hamdi's upcoming challenge to his status as enemy combatant, due to the need to "alleviate [the proceedings'] uncommon potential to burden the Executive at a time of ongoing military conflict." Here are some of O'Connor's speculations:

❑ *Hearsay* "may need to be *accepted* as the most reliable available evidence from the Government."

❑ The Constitution "would not be offended by a *presumption in favor of the government's evidence*," as long as that presumption "remained a *rebuttable* one" and as long as "fair opportunity for rebuttal were provided." Thus once the government put forth "credible evidence" that Hamdi was indeed an enemy combatant, the burden could shift to Hamdi to prove the contrary. (In a criminal case, by contrast, the government would have to prove each element of the crime not just by "credible evidence" but by proof beyond a reasonable doubt.)

❑ Whatever procedures are due, they would *not* be due at the moment a citizen was initially captured on the battlefield; instead, the procedures would be due only when the government decided to *continue to hold* those it had captured. (By the time of the Court's decision in *Hamdi*, for instance, Hamdi had already been held for over two years without any kind of hearing.)

❑ Finally, O'Connor said, it was *not* necessarily the case that a *federal district court* would have to be the one to hear Hamdi's challenge to his confinement. Instead, she said, "there remains the *possibility* that the standards we have articulated could be met by an appropriately authorized and properly constituted *military tribunal.*"

ii. Souter and Ginsburg concur in judgment: Justices Souter and Ginsburg, concurring only in part, disagreed with the plurality's conclusion that Hamdi's detention was authorized at all. But they agreed that if he *was* to be detained, he would certainly have **at least those procedural due process rights that the plurality was willing to give him**. In fact, these two justices indicated that they would give Hamdi even *more* procedural protections than the plurality — for instance, they *disagreed* that the government could be given the benefit of a *presumption* that Hamdi was an enemy combatant, or that litigating the issue before a *military tribunal* might constitutionally substitute for Hamdi's right to bring a habeas corpus petition in federal court.

iii. Scalia and Stevens dissent: Two additional Justices, Scalia and Stevens, dissented from the Court's basic holding that a citizen could be held in wartime by the executive branch without full recourse to the traditional right to challenge his imprisonment by means of a habeas corpus petition. Therefore, they strongly disagreed with the plurality's suggestion that Hamdi was due something less than the full-dress procedural due process protections given to any other imprisoned citizen. They criticized the plurality's "unheard-of system in which the citizen rather than the Government bears the burden of proof, testimony is by hearsay rather than live witnesses, and the presiding officer may well be a 'neutral' military officer rather than judge and jury."

iv. Summary: So eight members of the Court (all but Thomas) believed that the executive branch could not detain a citizen accused of being an enemy combatant unless the citizen was given ***substantial due process protections*** to allow him to challenge the enemy-combatant designation — at a minimum, protections like ***notice of the details*** of the charge, a right to rebut the charge before a n***eutral decisionmaker***, and the ***right to counsel***. Indeed, four members of the court (Souter, Ginsburg, Scalia and Stevens) seemed to believe that the ***full or nearly-full range of protections*** that would be given to any citizen imprisoned while accused of a crime were due to a citizen held on such enemy-combatant charges.

(1) Wartime not that different: *Hamdi* also illustrates that, for the present Court, even the fact that the nation is effectively ***at war*** will not allow the executive branch to dispense with basic due process requirements when it imprisons one of its own citizens. This marks a quite dramatic turnaround from the view of the World War II Court in the 1944 Japanese exclusion case (*Korematsu v. U.S.*, discussed *infra*, p. 261), where the Court held that all citizens of Japanese ancestry on the West Coast could effectively be imprisoned to prevent them from committing espionage and sabotage. As Justice O'Connor put it in her plurality opinion in *Hamdi*, "[A] state of war is ***not a blank check for the President*** when it comes to the rights of the Nation's citizens."

6. Legislature's right to limit procedures: The Court in *Mathews v. Eldridge* (*supra*, p. 227), although it took a limited view of procedural protections, did seem to be applying constitutional criteria in making its decision. But suppose that the ***legislature itself***, in creating a statutory entitlement, ***attempts to define the procedures*** under which the right may be denied or cut off. Do these legislative principles control?

a. No right to limit procedures: The answer is ***"no."*** Even where the legislature creates the property or liberty interest in question, ***it is not free to establish procedures for terminating that right*** — " 'Property' cannot be defined by the procedures provided for its deprivation any more than can life or liberty. The right to due process 'is conferred, not by legislative grace, but by constitutional guarantee.' ... [O]nce it is determined that the Due Process Clause applies, 'the question remains what process is due.' ... The answer to that question is not to be found in the ... statute [creating the property right.]" ***Cleveland Bd. of Ed. v. Loudermill***, 470 U.S. 532 (1985).

i. Application to facts in *Loudermill*: The plaintiff in *Loudermill* was, under state law, a "classified civil servant," who could only be terminated for cause. The statute setting out this tenure provided for administrative review following discharge, but did not allow for any kind of hearing before termination. As the *Loudermill* Court made clear, the procedures to which the *Loudermill* plaintiff was entitled were to be judged by independent constitutional standards, not merely by whether they complied with the state statutory scheme. Since the constitution requires at least **"some kind of a hearing"** prior to the deprivation of any significant property interest, plaintiff here was denied due process. (But only notice of the charges and some kind of opportunity to respond before termination, not a full evidentiary hearing of the sort found necessary in *Goldberg v. Kelly, supra*, p. 224, before welfare payments may be cut off, were required. This aspect of *Loudermill* is discussed *supra*, p. 228.)

7. **Educational cases:** Issues about what process is due have surfaced repeatedly in cases involving public **education**. A brief summary of the Court's major holdings is as follows:

   a. **Disciplinary suspension:** Where a student is **suspended** for disciplinary reasons for more than a trivial period, due process requires that he be given "oral or written notice of the charges against him and, if he denies them, an explanation of the evidence the authorities have and an opportunity to present his side of the story." *Goss v. Lopez*, 419 U.S. 565 (1975). (In *Goss*, a ten-day suspension was held to be clearly more than trivial.)

   b. **Academic dismissal:** By contrast, where a student is dismissed for **academic** (as distinguished from disciplinary) reasons, no hearing is necessary, since this type of decision is more subjective, and less suited to formal judicial or administrative decision making. *Board of Curators v. Horowitz*, 435 U.S. 78 (1978) (involving dismissal of a medical student because of poor clinical performance and personal hygiene).

8. **Rationales for due process:** The Supreme Court's cases on what process is due reflect strongly the notion that the principal reason for procedural safeguards is to **prevent inaccurate decisions**. This notion implies that if the means by which a decision is made does not introduce an unacceptably high risk of error, the procedure is valid, no matter how little chance to participate is given the adversely-affected individual.

   a. **Participation and explanation:** But a number of commentators have argued that a separate, quite distinct, value should be furthered by procedural safeguards: the right of the individual to have his **autonomy respected**, by being permitted to **participate in the decision**, and by receiving a **reasoned explanation** of adverse conduct. See Tribe, p. 713, and Rabin, 44 U. Chi. L. Rev. 74-79 (quoted in L,K&C, pp. 646-47). See also Van Alstyne, 62 Cornell L. Rev. 483 (quoted in Tribe, *loc. cit.*), urging the recognition of "**freedom from arbitrary adjudicative procedures** as a substantive element of one's liberty."

      i. **Significance:** These three commentators all share the view that procedures in which the individual participates are an **end in themselves**, not merely a means to assure correct decisions.

      ii. **Not likely to be accepted:** However, nothing in the Supreme Court's decisions suggest any likelihood that this "procedure as an end in itself" approach is likely to prevail in the near future.

Quiz Yourself on
PROCEDURAL DUE PROCESS

30. The town of Corinth advertised an opening for a position as secretary to the City Clerk. The ad described the job briefly, and said nothing about the criteria that would be used to fill it. Jane Brown applied for the job. She was given a typing test, and then an interview with George Crako, the City Clerk. Crako chose somebody else for the job. Brown asked for a statement of why she didn't get the job, but the Clerk's office refused to respond.

Brown later heard from the grapevine that Crako had told someone else in the department that he thought Brown was probably the best at performing the technical tasks, but that he had declined to hire her because he had heard she was gay. Brown, who was not gay, realized that Crako was probably thinking of another member of the community, Jane Browne, who was widely known to be gay. Brown asked for a hearing at which she could present what she called "information which would cause the Clerk to reverse his decision," but town officials again refused. Brown has now sued, arguing that the procedures used to fill the opening deprived her of her Fourteenth Amendment due process rights. Should the court find in Brown's favor? _____

31. Tennant, a single mother who was receiving Welfare, resided in a public housing project owned by the city of Pretoria. She had lived in the building for over 10 years, pursuant to a series of two-year leases. The rules of the housing project, posted on a bulletin board in the complex, stated that "customarily, residents who are well behaved and current on all of their obligations will be offered the opportunity to renew their leases upon their expiration." There is no statute or other body of state or local law bearing on whether one in Tennant's position is entitled, as a contractual matter, to a renewal. At the end of Tennant's current two-year term, she was not offered the opportunity to renew her lease. Instead, the apartment was given to a woman who turned out to be the niece of Pretoria's Buildings Commissioner, who would not have been given an apartment had the ordinary informal allocation procedures that had previously been followed in the housing project been followed here. Tennant was at no time given an explanation for why she wasn't permitted to renew, or a hearing regarding the decision.

    (a) If Tennant wishes to challenge the city's handling of her tenancy on constitutional grounds, what is the strongest argument she can make? _____

    (b) Will this argument succeed? _____

32. Netsville High School, a public high school, was known for its strong boys' and girls' tennis teams. The administration caused to be published in the school newspaper an invitation for tryouts. This invitation included the following sentence: "All students in good academic standing have the right to compete for the 7 spots on each team. These spots will be awarded to the best players." Priscilla, a high school freshman, had not been on the team previously. However, she had had some strong results in non-school tournaments the summer before her freshman year. During tryouts, the head coach watched Priscilla play only briefly. He very quickly reached the conclusion that her game was not mature enough to make her a varsity player. After one day of practice, he cut her from the team. He did not give her any statement of reasons, or opportunity to present her view of why she should make the team; he merely stated that she was "not good enough." The coach awarded team spots exclusively to those who had been on the team in prior years, including at least one girl whom Priscilla had soundly beaten in a non-school tournament the summer before. Priscilla has sued the school board, arguing that the procedures by which she was dropped from the team violated her due process rights to be awarded a post if she was one of the "best players."

    Assuming that Priscilla can demonstrate that most tennis coaches would have found her to be one of the seven strongest players trying out for the team, should the judge order the coach to reconsider her status? _____

Answers

30. **No.** The Fourteenth Amendment's Due Process Clause only prevents the government from depriving a person of "*life*, *liberty*, or *property* without due process of law." Unless Brown can show that she had a "liberty" or "property" interest that was impaired, she will not even get to the point of being allowed to show that fair procedures were not followed. In other words, the Due Process Clause does not bar the government from procedural irregularities per se, only procedural irregularities in connection with the taking of life, liberty or property. It is very clear that a person applying for an initial government position has no liberty or property interest in the position, so the government may turn the applicant down for totally arbitrary or irrational reasons (so long as the reasons are not themselves violations of independently-guaranteed constitutional rights, such as refusing to hire a person because she is, say, black). So the fact that the Clerk's decision was completely "wrong," in the sense that he had the wrong person in mind, is completely irrelevant. We never get to the question of what type of process (e.g., right to a statement of reasons, or right to a hearing) would have been due.

31. **(a) That it violated her right not to have her "property" taken without due process, and that this right included the right to a hearing.**

    (b) Yes, probably. The core issue is whether Tennant had a *"property" interest* in her apartment. The Court has held that even *informal practices or customs* may be sufficient to create a *legitimate claim of entitlement* to a benefit. See, e.g., *Perry v. Sindermann* (in which a college was found to have created a de facto tenure program that created in P, a college professor, the "understanding" that he would be entitled to tenure). Here, the statement regarding the customary right of renewal was probably enough to create in Tennant such a legitimate claim of entitlement to renew, in view of the lack of any other law bearing on whether Tennant did indeed have such a right. (If there were a statute or body of case law holding that as a matter of state law there is no right to renew despite a seeming indication to the contrary in a housing project's rules and regulations, then this body of state law would be dispositive, and Tennant would not have any "property" interest.)

    If Tennant indeed had a legitimate entitlement to being allowed to renew provided that she was in good standing, then she was presumably entitled to at least a hearing before this property interest could be taken away. (The precise procedures that would have to followed are not clear, but for a right as important as the right to continue to live in subsidized housing, it is likely that some sort of hearing and statement of reasons, however informal, would be required.)

32. **No, probably.** The facts are enough to establish that Priscilla indeed probably had a "property" interest (albeit a weak one) in being awarded a spot if she was in fact one of the best seven players. That is, the notice in the newspaper probably was sufficient to constitute a binding offer on the part of the school to award a place to anyone who tried out and proved that she was indeed among the seven best players, and this contract was enough to give rise to a "property" interest. However, the case really turns on exactly what procedures were "due" to Priscilla when it came time to determine whether she was in fact one of the seven best players. The Supreme Court uses a *balancing test* for deciding whether a particular set of procedures should be required once a property interest (or liberty interest) is at stake. On one side is placed the amount at stake for the individual, multiplied by the likelihood that administrative error will be reduced by using the procedure in question; on the other side is the cost to the government of granting that procedure.

    Here, the amount at stake for Priscilla is relatively weak, compared with, say, the right to continue receiving welfare benefits or the right to keep one's job. The likelihood that "administrative errors" would be reduced by requiring, say, a statement of reasons before anyone is cut, or a right to present one's case, is relatively small — a coach would still have to be the decision-maker, and that decision would still be based principally on what the coach saw, so that a hearing and statement of reasons are unlikely to reduce error by much. Conversely, there is a substantial cost to the government (here, the school board) in having to set up detailed, judicially-challengeable procedures for awarding every spot on an athletic team. Consequently, the court is very likely to decide that such litigation-like procedures as a statement of reasons and an opportunity to present one's case are not worth their cost.

(On the other hand, probably an applicant who has a property interest in being allowed to compete for a spot on the team at least has the right to marginally "fair" procedures, so that, for instance, an applicant who could show that the coach favored the coach's own child or own private-coaching pupils might be able to show that her procedural rights had been violated.)

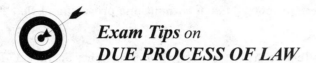

Exam Tips *on* DUE PROCESS OF LAW

In virtually any fact pattern where an individual or company is not permitted to do something, you must be alert to the possibility that there is a *due process* violation. A large portion of all complex-fact-pattern essay questions will raise at least one due process issue. Here are the most important things to keep in mind:

☛ Determine whether it is an issue of *substantive* DP or *procedural* DP that you're faced with.

    ☞ In a *substantive* DP problem, the government is completely taking away a whole group's ability to do something, and there is no issue of whether the particular plaintiff falls into the governmentally-defined group or not. (*Example:* The state says, "No woman may have an abortion after the third month of pregnancy." If the facts make it clear that P is a woman who is four months pregnant, we have a substantive DP problem, not a procedural DP problem.)

    ☞ In a *procedural* DP problem, the overall issue is whether P as an individual does or does not fit into the legislatively-defined group, and the sub-issue is what if any individualized, case-specific, procedures must be followed before the government can determine which group P falls into. (*Example:* A city says, "Public school teachers may only be fired for acts of moral turpitude." If there is an issue about whether P did or did not commit such an act, then we're dealing with procedural due process, i.e., the procedures used to determine whether P did or did not commit such an act.)

☛ If you're dealing with a *substantive* DP problem, decide immediately whether the right at issue is *fundamental* or non-fundamental.

    ☞ Remember that the only rights that are fundamental for substantive DP purposes are those that involve the *"right of privacy"* or *"right of autonomy."* The key examples are:

☞ The right to *marry*. (But there's no evidence so far that the right of a *same-sex* couple to marry is fundamental — only opposite-sex couples have been recognized as having a fundamental right of marriage thus far.)

☞ The right to *bear* (or decide *not* to bear) *children*.

☞ The right to decide how to *rear* one's children.

☞ Perhaps the right to decline *unwanted medical treatment* (and possibly the right to *commit suicide* if competent and terminally ill).

☞ Possibly, the right to control one's *dress* and *personal appearance*.

☞ If you conclude that the right is "fundamental," state that the court must *strictly scrutinize* the regulation. The state *bears the burden* of defending its regulation. The state loses unless *both* the following are true:

☞ The state is pursing a *"compelling"* (not just "legitimate") objective; and

☞ The means chosen by the state are *"necessary"* to achieve that compelling end. (If there are *less restrictive means* that would do the job just as well, or almost as well, then the means chosen aren't "necessary.")

☞ By contrast, if you conclude that the right involved is *non-fundamental*, then state that *"mere-rationality"* review is used. That is, it just has to be the case that the state is:

☞ Pursuing a *legitimate governmental objective*; and

☞ Doing so with a means that is *rationally related* to that objective.

☞ If the government regulation is essentially *economic*, you should almost certainly conclude that the rights involved are non-fundamental, and apply the mere-rationality test. The same is true of most health, safety or other "social welfare" legislation — unless it treads on one of those narrow areas (marriage, child-bearing, child-rearing, "right-to-die"), it's non-fundamental, and you should be using "mere-rationality" review.

☛ Be sure to distinguish between the *Fifth* Amendment's DP Clause and the *Fourteenth* Amendment's DP Clause. If the regulation is imposed by the *federal* government, the relevant clause is the Fifth Amendment. If the regulating is being done by a state or local government, the Fourteenth Amendment is the relevant one.

☛ Here's an overview of some of the most testable issues relating to the substantive due process protection given to *fundamental* rights:

☞ Most regulations restricting access to *contraception* will be strictly scrutinized and will fail. However, it is not clear that *minors* have a substantive DP right to birth control without parental consent — this makes a good testable issue.

☞ A pregnant woman's interest in *abortion*, of course, gets some substantive DP protection. Your professor will expect you to know that this is so, as a general proposition. The particular sub-issues she is likely to test you on are:

☞ Whether the state may require that the woman's *spouse* be given notice prior to the abortion (the answer is *"no"*);

☞ Whether a *minor* may be required to have *parental consent* (the answer is generally *"yes,"* but there must be a "judicial bypass" offered as an alternative); and

☞ Whether *late-term* abortions may be tightly regulated (the answer generally seems to be *"yes"*).

Note: In general, when you're analyzing an abortion problem, remember to say that as a result of *Planned Parenthood v. Casey*, the standard is whether the regulation ***"unduly burdens"*** the woman's interest in deciding whether to have the baby or not. Also, in any case involving regulations on the abortion process (rather than outright bans), mention that under the recent *Gonzales v. Carhart* partial-birth-method decision, the Court has grown more likely to uphold regulations that are justifiable by a desire to spare the woman from later regret about her decision to use a particular method.

☞ If the regulation interferes with *sexual* activities, distinguish between interferences with the rights of *married* couples, and virtually all other types of sex.

☞ Thus if your facts involve a government attempt to make certain practices unlawful when practiced between members of a *married* couple in *private*, you should usually be applying strict scrutiny, and you should conclude that the interference violates substantive DP.

☞ Where the activity consists of *homosexual sex* outside of marriage, you should conclude that (1) the activity is *not* "fundamental," and the regulation is therefore not to be strictly scrutinized; but that (2) the *"mere-rationality"* review that's used should have real *"bite,"* and should be used to *strike down* as "irrational" any regulation that seems motivated solely by the majority's *"moral disapproval."*

Example: If government bans "sodomy" in a way that restricts gay sexual activity, say that even under mere-rationality review the measure must be struck down as an irrational substantive due process violation of the right to sexual expression. Cite to *Lawrence v. Texas*.

☞ If a state chooses to allow *same-sex marriage*, and a couple is validly-married according to the state, you should note that the *federal government may not treat the couple differently* than it treats opposite-sex married couples. (*Example:* Same-sex couples married under state law must receive the same federal income and estate tax treatment as opposite-sex married couples.) Cite to *U.S. v. Windsor* (but note that it's not clear whether *Windsor* is based on equal protection, substantive due process, or both).

☞ If the activity is by unmarried *minors*, it is especially clear that it is not "fundamental," and may be extensively regulated (or probably even forbidden) by the state.

☞ If the state has placed restrictions on a person's right to decline *unwanted medical attention*, say that a fundamental interest is probably at stake.

☞ If the state is declining to honor a properly-prepared *living will* or *health-care proxy* (delegating the health-care decision to another person if the patient is incompetent), conclude that the state is violating substantive DP.

☞ But where there is no living will or health-care proxy, and the patient is incompetent, the state does *not* violate substantive DP by setting very high *evidentiary standards* before concluding that the medical care is really unwanted. Cite to the *Cruzan* case in this kind of situation (where the Court held that the state may require "clear and convincing evidence" that the incompetent really would not have wanted the medical attention).

☞ If the patient is terminally ill (and competent) and the issue is whether a relative or doctor may *assist in the patient's suicide*, indicate that whatever due process interest the patient may have in committing suicide is certainly *not fundamental*, and that the state's countervailing interest in preventing the suicide is stronger. Therefore, the state *may make it a crime* to attempt suicide, or to assist another in committing suicide.

☞ Here are some other contexts where you might find that fundamental interests are being impaired in violation of substantive DP:

☞ The state has impaired opposite-sex couples' right to *get married* to each other (e.g., by disallowing marriage until one party pays some fine or satisfies a back obligation like child support — see *Zablocki v. Redhail*).

❏ Be alert for a question on the constitutionality of a *state's ban on same-sex marriage*. Note that *U.S. v. Windsor* doesn't explicitly address this issue. Note that even if such a ban is given *minimal rational-relation* review, the ban might flunk, on the theory that the ban is motivated simply by moral disapproval of gay people, and that that's not a legitimate state interest.

☞ Relatives are being prevented from *living together* (e.g., by restrictive *zoning* rules such as the no-cousins rule in *Moore v. East Cleveland*).

☞ Parents are being deprived of freedom to choose how their child is to be *educated* (e.g., a state statute banning home-study or private-school education, or unduly restricting these alternatives) or how the child is to be *raised at home* (e.g., a state court order compelling a mother to give lengthy visitation rights to the child's paternal grandparents).

☞ Adults are unfairly restricted in their attempts to *adopt* a child (e.g., by a requirement that the *race* of the parent and child, or the *religion* of the parent and child, *match*).

☛ Whenever you have government denying a person a job, license, benefit, etc., consider whether the individual was entitled to *procedural due process*, and if so, whether the requirements of procedural DP were complied with.

☞ First, make sure that there is *government action* in the denial. (*Example:* If the facts tell you that a private employer is firing someone, you never get to the issue of procedural due process because there is no state action.)

☞ Next, check to make sure that what is being denied is *"life," "liberty"* or *"property."*

☞ You'll never have to worry about "life" being taken unless your fact pattern deals with the death penalty in criminal cases.

☞ Here are some typical situations where "liberty" is at stake:

    ☞ P is deprived of the right to *drive*;

    ☞ P is denied a *license* that she needs in order to practice her profession (e.g., law, medicine, accounting, teaching, or even truck-driving or tour-guiding);

    ☞ P is deprived of the right to *raise his family*, because of charges of child abuse or neglect.

☞ Most commonly, though, you'll see fact patterns suggesting that *"property"* may have been taken.

    ☞ Many situations involve government *benefits*. If you are *already* getting the benefit, the government is probably depriving you of a "property" interest if it tries to *terminate* the benefit. On the other hand, if you are first *applying* for the benefit, then you probably do not yet have a property interest, so the government probably does not have to use procedural DP — it can arbitrarily or irrationally reject your application.

    ☞ Here are some typical kinds of government benefits that pop up on exam questions:

        ❑ receipt of *welfare* payments;

        ❑ right to occupy *public housing*;

        ❑ right to take certain *courses* in public school, or to participate in *extracurricular activities* sponsored by the public school.

    ☞ Remember that a key part of the analysis is whether state law, or perhaps even government custom, gives P a *"legitimate claim of entitlement"* to have the benefit continue. (*Example:* If a statute, regulation or even an informal document like a benefit handbook indicates the circumstances under which a particular benefit will be granted or continued, then a person is likely to have a "property" interest in the benefit on the terms provided in the statute, regulation, etc.)

    ☞ When you're dealing with a state or local government *job*, the same analysis applies: if you've already got the job, you may or may not have a "legitimate claim of entitlement" to it (depending on what state law says about how and when you can be fired). If you do have a legitimate claim of entitlement, then you have a "property" interest that can only be taken away by complying with procedural DP. If you don't have a legitimate claim, then you have no procedural DP rights either.

☞ If P's claim is that government owed P a duty to **protect P from some private third-party's bad deeds**, probably P did **not** have a property or liberty interest in receiving that help from government, even if some statute required government to give that help. (*Example*: A statute says that police "shall arrest" anyone who violates a protective order. P asks the police to protect her by arresting her husband, H, who has just violated such an order. The police refuse, giving H the chance to murder P's children. P has not been deprived of a property or liberty interest. *Castle Rock v. Gonzales*.)

☞ If you've decided that P has a "property" or "liberty" interest that is being taken away, you know that P is entitled to some sort of procedural DP. Now, you must decide exactly **what procedures** are due to P.

    ☞ Here, remember to do a **balancing** test: for each procedural safeguard that may or may not be due, weigh the state's interest in making a prompt disposition against the damage to P in being denied the safeguard. (*Example:* If P is a school teacher who is suspended based on suspicions that he has sexually abused a student, P's interest in being given a formal hearing with counsel *before* the suspension is clearly outweighed by the system's need to get him out of the classroom quickly. By contrast, where the state wants to cut off P's welfare benefits, he's probably entitled to a hearing before any suspension, because the cost to the state of a delay is not very great, and the damage to P from an erroneous determination would be great.)

    ☞ If P has been awarded **punitive damages** against D, consider the possibility that the award is so excessive (or so inappropriately takes account of harm done by D to persons not present in the litigation) that the award violates D's due process rights.

    ☞ If there is evidence that an **elected judge** may be **biased** because one litigant has made unusually large **campaign contributions** to her, consider the possibility that the opposing litigant may have a due process right to have the judge recuse herself. (Cite to *Caperton v. Massey* on this point.)

    ☞ Some of the procedural safeguards that you should consider are (in ascending order of the burden that they typically put on the state):

        ❏ the right to receive a **statement of reasons** why the benefit is being cut off;

        ❏ the right to a **hearing** at which P can plead her case;

        ❏ the right to have **counsel present** at the hearing;

        ❏ the right to **appeal** the adverse decision to a higher body.

    In general, you should conclude that P has the right to counsel and appeal only where the proceedings are criminal or quasi-criminal, but you should be relatively quick to conclude that P has a right to a statement of reasons or a hearing, even in a non-criminal situation such as loss of a job or loss of a financial benefit.

CHAPTER 10

EQUAL PROTECTION

ChapterScope

The Equal Protection Clause is part of the Fourteenth Amendment. It provides that "no state shall make or enforce any law which shall ... deny to any person within its jurisdiction equal protection of the laws." Here are the key concepts concerning equal protection:

■ **Classifications:** The Clause imposes a *general* restraint on the governmental use of *classifications*, not just classifications based on race but also those based on sex, alienage, illegitimacy, wealth, or any other characteristic.

■ **Federal government:** The direct text of the Clause applies only to state governments. But the *federal* government is also bound by the same rules of equal protection — the Fifth Amendment's Due Process Clause is interpreted to bar the federal government from making any classification that would be a violation of the Equal Protection Clause if done by a state.

■ **Government action only:** The Equal Protection Clause (and the Fifth Amendment's Due Process Clause) apply *only to government action*, not to action by private citizens. This is the requirement of *"state action."*

■ **"As applied" vs. "facial":** There are two different types of attacks a plaintiff may make on a classification:

❑ **Facial:** If P attacks a classification that is clearly written into the statute or regulation, he is saying that the statute or regulation violates equal protection *"on its face."*

❑ **"As applied":** If P's claim is that the statute/regulation does not make a classification on its face, but is being *administered* in a purposefully discriminatory way, then he is claiming that the statute/regulation is a violation of equal protection *"as applied."*

■ **What the Clause guarantees:** The Clause in essence guarantees that *people who are similarly situated will be treated similarly.*

■ **Three levels of review:** There are three levels of review that are used in judging whether governmental classifications violate the Equal Protection Clause:

❑ **Strict scrutiny:** At one end of the spectrum, the Court gives *"strict scrutiny"* to any statute that is based on a "suspect classification" or that impairs a "fundamental right." Where strict scrutiny is invoked, the classification will be upheld only if it is *necessary* to promote a *compelling* governmental interest. The three suspect classes are *race*, *national origin* and (for some purposes) *alienage*. The rights that are "fundamental" are principally the right to *vote*, the right to have access to the *courts*, and the right to *migrate interstate*.

❑ **Middle-level review:** In a few situations, the Court uses a *middle level* of review, less demanding than "strict scrutiny." This level is used for *"semi-suspect"* classifications, i.e., those based on *gender* and *illegitimacy*. Under mid-level review, the means chosen by the legislature (i.e., the classification) must be *substantially related* to an *important* governmental objective.

❑ **Ordinary "mere-rationality" review:** At the easiest-to-satisfy end of the spectrum, we have the "mere-rationality" standard. This standard applies to all classifications that are not based on a "suspect" or "semi-suspect" classification (i.e., that do not involve race, national origin, alienage, gender or legitimacy) and do not impair a "fundamental right" (i.e., do not impair the right to vote, access the courts or migrate interstate). Under this standard, the classification will be upheld so long as it is conceivable that the classification bears a *rational relationship* to a *legitimate* governmental objective. Almost every classification survives this easy review.

   ❑ **Economic regulation:** Almost every *economic* and *tax* classification is reviewed under this easy standard.

■ **Suspect classifications:** When a classification involves a *suspect class* (race, national origin and, for some purposes, alienage), here are the key features of how courts do their review:

❑ **Purposeful:** Strict scrutiny will only be applied where the differential treatment of the class is *intentional* on the part of the government. If the government enacts a statute or regulation that merely has the unintended incidental *effect* of burdening, say, blacks worse than whites, the Court will *not* use strict scrutiny.

❑ **Strict equals fatal:** Once the Court decides that a suspect classification is involved and that strict scrutiny must be used, the scrutiny is almost always *fatal* to the classification scheme. For instance, only one purposeful racial or ethnic classification has survived strict scrutiny by the Supreme Court since 1944.

❑ **Segregation:** The clearest example of a classification involving a suspect class and thus requiring strict scrutiny is *segregation*, the maintenance of physical separation between the races. Official, intentional segregation based on race or national origin is a violation of the Equal Protection Clause.

■ **Race-conscious affirmative action:** Government programs that attempt to *assist* racial or ethnic *minorities* (i.e., *affirmative action* programs), and that do so in an explicitly race- or ethnically-conscious way, are strictly scrutinized just the same as those that purposefully *disadvantage* minorities.

■ **Gender:** *Sex-based* classifications get *middle-level review.* If government intentionally classifies on the basis of sex, government must show that it is pursuing an *important* objective, and that the sex-based classification scheme is *substantially related* to that objective.

❑ **Benign as well as invidious:** The same standard of review is used whether the sex-based classification is "invidious" (intended to harm women) or *"benign"* (intended to help women, or even intended to redress past discrimination against them).

■ **Illegitimacy:** Classifications disadvantaging *illegitimate* children are "semi-suspect" and therefore get middle-level review.

■ **Alienage:** Alienage classifications are subjected either to *strict scrutiny* or to *mere-rationality* review, depending on the circumstances.

❑ **General rule:** Usually, discrimination against aliens is subject to *strict scrutiny.*

❑ **"Representative government" exception:** But strict scrutiny does not apply where the discrimination against aliens relates to a *"function at the heart of representative govern-*

ment." This means that government may discriminate against aliens with respect to *jobs* that are closely tied in with politics, justice or public policy, including posts like state trooper, public school teacher or probation officer.

▪ **Fundamental rights:** There will be strict scrutiny not only when a "suspect classification" is used, but also when a *"fundamental right"* is burdened by the classification selected by the government. Whenever a classification burdens a "fundamental right," the classification will be subjected to strict scrutiny *even though the people who are burdened are not members of a suspect class*.

❑ **Voting:** The right to *vote* in state and local elections is "fundamental," so any classification burdening that right will be strictly scrutinized (e.g., a poll tax, or an unduly long residency requirement before voting is allowed).

❑ **Court access:** Access to the *courts* is sometimes a "fundamental right." For instance, if the state imposes a *fee* that the rich can pay but the poor cannot, and the access relates to a *criminal case*, strict scrutiny is used. (*Example:* The state must give an indigent in a criminal case a free trial transcript, and free counsel on appeal.)

❑ **Right to travel:** The *"right to travel"* — which is really the right to *change one's state of residence or employment* — is "fundamental."

   ❑ **Duration of residence:** Thus if the state imposes a substantial *waiting period* on newly-arrived residents, before they can receive some *vital governmental benefit* (e.g., *welfare* payments), the scheme will be strictly scrutinized.

❑ **Necessities:** There is no fundamental right to material *"necessities of life."* Thus *food, shelter and medical care* are not "fundamental," and the state may distribute these things unevenly. Similarly, one does not have a fundamental right to a *public school education*; therefore, the state may impose inequalities in the distribution of that education, without having to pass strict scrutiny.

I. INTRODUCTION

A. **Historical overview:** The Fourteenth Amendment provides that "[n]o State shall make or enforce any law which shall ... deny to any person within its jurisdiction the equal protection of the laws."

   1. **Historical purpose:** This Clause, like all parts of the Thirteenth, Fourteenth and Fifteenth Amendments, was enacted shortly after the Civil War, and its primary goal was to secure free and equal treatment for ex-slaves. But from the beginning, the courts interpreted the Clause to "impose a *general* restraint on the use of classifications, whatever the area regulated, whatever the classification criterion used." Gunther (10th Ed.), p. 676.

   2. **Clause before Warren Court:** Prior to the Warren Court, the Equal Protection Clause played only a very minor role with respect to classifications based on grounds other than race and national origin. So long as the *means* used by the legislature (i.e., the classification) *reasonably related* to the legislature's purpose, the statute was upheld. Very little attention was paid to whether the legislature's purpose was itself valid. Gunther & Sullivan (13th Ed.), p. 629.

a. **Contrast with due process:** Contrast this limited view of the Equal Protection Clause with the broad reading given to the Due Process Clause during the early part of this century (see *supra*, p. 148). The Court was much more likely to strike an economic or social-welfare statute on substantive due process grounds than on the grounds that the classifications made in the statute denied equal protection.

3. **Key clause in Warren Court:** But under the *Warren Court*, the Equal Protection Clause gained new "bite," and became the most important clause for ensuring a broad range of individual rights against legislative encroachment.

   a. **Strict scrutiny:** The principal way in which the Clause gained new vitality in the Warren years was by means of a broadened view of when a statutory classification should be subjected to "*strict scrutiny*," i.e., a scrutiny more demanding than the "mere-rationality" test generally applied in earlier years. Whereas pre-Warren Courts applied strict scrutiny only to statutes classifying on the grounds of race or national origin, the Warren Court was willing to impose strict scrutiny wherever either the classification was a "*suspect*" one (because it discriminated against a politically powerless or unpopular minority) or that classification had an impact on a "*fundamental right*" or interest. Once strict scrutiny was applied to a particular law, the law would be upheld only if it was *necessary to achieve a compelling* governmental interest.

   b. **Suspect classification:** In actual fact, the Warren Court found only race and national origin to be suspect classifications. But there were hints that other classifications might also be subjected to some sort of heightened review (e.g., illegitimacy). Sullivan & Gunther, p. 642.

   c. **"Fundamental rights":** The real change made by the Warren Court was in the development of the "*fundamental rights*" branch of strict scrutiny. If the Court concluded that a statute had a material impact on a fundamental right or interest, it subjected the statute to strict scrutiny, even though the classification itself was not "suspect." The grounds by which the Warren Court determined that an interest was "fundamental" were never quite clear; the actual list of such fundamental rights seemed to be restricted principally to the areas of *voting, criminal appeals* and *interstate travel*. Sullivan & Gunther, p. 642.

4. **Post-Warren Court:** The Court in the post-Warren years has *not* made wholesale cutbacks in the Warren equal protection approach. But the present Court has *declined to expand* the Warren doctrine in the ways that Warren-era opinions suggested might ultimately evolve. For instance, neither the list of classifications deemed "suspect" nor the list of fundamental rights has been materially broadened.

   a. **Middle-level scrutiny:** The most interesting development during the Burger/Rehnquist/Roberts years has been the emergence of what is sometimes called "*middle-level*" or "*intermediate-level*" scrutiny. Most clearly in the area of gender-based classifications, but also probably in the areas of *illegitimacy* and *alienage* classifications, statutes are not subjected to strict scrutiny, but are given a scrutiny more rigorous than the extreme deference with which general economic and social-welfare classifications are treated. See, e.g., *Craig v. Boren,* discussed *infra*, p. 336.

   b. **Lowest level has some "bite":** Also, *occasionally*, even the so-called "mere-rationality" or lowest-level of review has *some bite* under the Burger/Rehnquist/Roberts Court, as it almost never did in previous Courts. Thus a statute will occasionally be found to be so completely lacking in rationality that, even when viewed under a mere-rationality standard, it violates equal protection. See, e.g., *U.S. v. Windsor* (apparently using mere-rationality equal protection review to strike down Congress's refusal to recognize state-sanctioned same-sex marriages), *infra*, p. 368.

B. Operation of the Clause: The following is a broad summary of the present operation of the Equal Protection Clause:

1. **State and federal actions:** The guarantee of equal protection applies to actions by *both* the *state* and *federal* governments. However, the federal guarantee comes from a distinct source.

   a. **State and local governments:** The Equal Protection Clause of the Fourteenth Amendment itself applies only to *state and local governments* ("[n]o state shall deny … "). Local governments are deemed to be subdivisions of the state, and therefore fall within the ban.

   b. **Federal government:** Nothing in the Constitution explicitly requires that the federal government provide equal protection of the laws. But where the federal government makes a classification which, if it were by a state, would violate the Fourteenth Amendment's Equal Protection Clause, the Court has *treated this as a violation of the Fifth Amendment's Due Process Clause* (a clause that is, of course, *directly applicable* to the federal government). See, e.g., *Bolling v. Sharpe*, 347 U.S. 497 (1954). See also N&R, pp. 595-597.

      i. **Special rule for Congress:** The normal rule is that equal protection standards are *identical* for the federal and state governments, so that a federal action which would constitute a violation of equal protection if done by the state will also be a Fifth Amendment Due Process violation. However, the present Court seems willing to grant *acts of Congress* slightly greater deference than acts of state legislatures, in two areas: classifications burdening *aliens* (because of Congress' authority to determine the conditions of immigration) and classifications relating to the *military* (because of the federal government's war power).

2. **Applies only to making of classes:** The Equal Protection Clause prevents governments from making improper classifications. What makes a classification "proper" is, of course, the subject of this Chapter. But it should be noted that if a classification scheme is proper, the issue of *which class a particular individual belongs in* is *not* an equal protection matter. Instead, this will be a matter of statutory interpretation and, possibly, the Due Process Clause. The Equal Protection Clause itself applies only to the *making* of the classifications, not to the adjudication of individual situations. N&R, p. 597.

   a. **Caveat:** But a statute which, on its face, does not draw any classifications may nonetheless be *applied* in a way that indicates that classes *are in fact being drawn* in the *administrative process*. In such a situation, the courts will examine the administratively-derived classifications just as they would review ones which were apparent on the face of the statute.

   Example: Suppose that a state passes a statute instituting a literacy test for voters in statewide elections. Even though the statute does not draw any impermissible classifications on its face, if it is applied by local officials in a way that purposefully discriminates against blacks (i.e., treats blacks as one class and whites as another, and penalizes the former), the Equal Protection Clause is violated. But a court review of the determination that a ***particular voter*** is in fact illiterate would be carried out pursuant to the Due Process Clause, not the Equal Protection Clause.

3. **"As applied" vs. "facial" attacks:** Notice that in the above "Caveat," we referred to how a statute is "applied." This points up the need to make an important distinction between ***"as applied"*** attacks on statutes and ***"facial"*** attacks. (The distinction exists for all sorts of attacks on statutes, but here, we're concentrating on the Equal Protection Clause, so we'll use illustrations involving that Clause.)

If P attacks a classification that is clearly written into the statute or regulation, he is claiming that Equal Protection is violated by the statute or regulation ***"on its face,"*** without the need to examine how it is applied to P. If P's claim is that the statute does not make a classification on its face, but is being ***administered*** in a purposefully discriminatory way, then he is claiming that the statute or regulation is a violation of equal protection ***"as applied."***

> **Example:** A statute that says "you must be a citizen to vote" creates a classification scheme "on its face" — citizens vs. non-citizens. P might therefore attack this statute on its face, arguing that the classification written into the language of the statute is always invalid, i.e., invalid without reference to how it is applied in any particular concrete situation, such as P's own situation.
>
> By contrast, if P claims that in actual administration, blacks are required to prove citizenship but whites are not, then his equal protection claim would be on the statute "as applied."

a. **Same standards for both:** Either kind of attack — facial or "as applied" — may be made. Both follow essentially the same principles. For instance, if no suspect classification or fundamental right is involved, the classification scheme will violate the Equal Protection Clause if it's not rationally related to a legitimate state objective, whether the scheme is on the face of the statute or merely in the way the statute is applied.

b. **Why distinction matters:** However, it is considerably ***harder for P to prevail with a facial attack.*** When P makes an "as applied" attack, P can win if P can show that the statute cannot constitutionally be applied *against P* — the fact that the statute could be constitutionally applied to some other hypothetical person or situation won't save it from being found invalid in P's suit. By contrast, at least in theory, if P makes a facial attack, P can generally win only if P shows that there are ***no circumstances in which the statute is valid.*** See *U.S. v. Salerno*, 481 U.S. 739 (1987) ("A facial challenge to a legislative Act is, of course, the most difficult challenge to mount successfully, since the challenger must establish that no set of circumstances exists under which the Act would be valid.") [1]

4. **What the Clause guarantees:** The Equal Protection Clause, at bottom, guarantees two things: (1) that people who are similarly situated will be treated similarly; and (2) that people who are ***not*** similarly situated will not be treated similarly. Tribe, p. 1438.

---

1. In reality, the Supreme Court doesn't seem to treat facial challenges quite as strictly as this formulation would suggest — often the Court seems to uphold a facial challenge even though there are at least some applications of the statute that would be constitutional. See 46 Stan. L. Rev. 235, 236 (1994). But there's no doubt that facial challenges are harder to win than as-applied challenges.

Examples: As an example of a violation of (1), consider intentional racial segregation in the public schools — this is a failure to treat people who are similarly situated (blacks and whites, at least with respect to public education, though perhaps not with respect to, say, sickle-cell anemia) similarly to each other. As an example of a violation of (2), consider Tribe's (p. 1438) hypothetical statute requiring voters to come to the polls personally regardless of their physical capacity to do so — Tribe suggests that this would be a denial of the equal protection right of the handicapped to be treated differently with respect to voting.

a. **Difficulty of establishing (2):** Most successful equal protection challenges involve a violation of (1), that is, a refusal to treat similarly-situated persons similarly. In any given situation, there may be, but there is not necessarily, a requirement of (2), that is, that the government treat *differently*-situated persons differently. Most claims that wealth/poverty classifications (*infra*, p. 399) violate equal protection are claims of this variety, i.e., claims that the government's demand for payment for goods or services (e.g., poll taxes) or its refusal to pay for benefits (e.g., appellate transcripts for indigent defendants) fail to treat rich and poor differently. However, claims of this (2) type have been hard to raise successfully; in the wealth/poverty area, for instance, such claims have been sustained only where certain narrowly-defined "fundamental rights" are impaired. See Tribe, p. 1439, n. 19.

5. **Must look at statute's objectives:** What does it mean to say that two persons are "similarly situated" or "differently situated"? Obviously, two persons may be similarly situated in some respects and differently in others. For instance, a randomly-selected black person and white person might be similarly situated in many respects (e.g., their right to vote or obtain a job) but differently situated in others (e.g., their statistical susceptibility to sickle-cell anemia). In nearly all instances, the "differentness" or "sameness" of people in the context of equal protection analysis is determined by reference to the *objectives of the statute* being analyzed.

Example: The California "statutory rape" law makes men criminally liable for intercourse with a woman under eighteen but does not make women liable for intercourse under any circumstances. Whether this statute violates equal protection (by treating men and women differently for criminal liability purposes) must be determined by looking at the legislature's *objective* in enacting, or maintaining, the statute.

Here, the principal purpose was to discourage illegitimate teenage pregnancies. The legislature could reasonably have concluded that men are differently situated from women, because the woman already has the deterrent of an unwanted pregnancy. The statute therefore roughly "equalizes" the deterrence on the sexes. Thus it is only by looking at the goal of preventing teenage pregnancy that the "sameness" or "differentness" of men and women who engage in the forbidden intercourse may be evaluated. See *Michael M. v. Superior Court*, 450 U.S. 464 (1981) (discussed in more detail *infra*, p. 288).

a. **Intent and causation:** Common-sense concepts like *"intent"* and *"causation"* may furnish the legislature with a valid basis for treating groups differently. For instance, where two actions produce the same result, the legislature does not violate equal protection where it criminalizes one action and not the other, if one action was taken with intent to produce the result, and the other action was not.

6. **Over- and under-inclusive classifications:**   Consider now the usual equal protection claim that persons who are similarly situated have been treated differently (i.e., a type (1) claim, as organized *supra*, p. 252). The way most classifications work is that they **identify a trait** present in some people, and presume a certain connection between that trait and the legislative goal. This goal may be either the prevention of a harm or the furthering of a good; for our discussion here, we will presume that it is a prevention of a harm. (The analysis would be the same for furthering of a good.)

   a. **Three main mismatches:** There are three major ways there might be a mismatch in the "fit" between the Trait upon which the legislative has based its classification, and the Harm the legislature is trying to prevent: (1) **"under-inclusiveness"**; (2) **"over-inclusiveness"**; and (3) a **combination** of under- and over-inclusiveness.

   Our sample fact-pattern: To illustrate these three main mismatches between Trait and Harm, let's consider the statute construed in *Massachusetts Board of Retirement v. Murgia*, discussed *infra*, p. 262. That statute required all uniformed state police to retire at the age of 50. The purpose of the statute was to help keep the police force free of officers whose physical health would not be sound enough for them to perform their duties.

      i. **"Under-inclusive:"**   It might be the case that all persons who have the Trait contribute to the Harm, but that persons without the Trait **also** contribute to the Harm. Such a classification scheme is called **"under-inclusive."** For instance, if all officers over 50 are in poor health, but some officers under 50 are also in poor health, the scheme is under-inclusive.

      ii. **"Over-inclusive":**   Conversely, all persons who contribute to the Harm might have the Trait, but some people who have the Trait might not contribute to the Harm. In this situation, the classification is said to be **"over-inclusive."** In the retirement example, the classification is over-inclusive if all officers in poor health are over 50, but some officers over 50 are in good health.

      iii. **Over- and under-inclusive:**   The final type of mismatch is one that has attributes of both (i) and (ii), i.e., one that is *both over- and under-inclusive.* Although this sounds impossible, it is in fact probably the most common type of classification. The way this occurs is that the classification is over-inclusive as to some groups of people but under-inclusive as to others. In the retirement example, for instance, it is almost certainly the case that some officers over 50 are healthy (so that the statute is over-inclusive as to these healthy older-than-50 people), and at the same time that some officers who are under 50 are unhealthy (so that the statute is under-inclusive as to these sick younger-than-50 officers).

7. **Significance of under- and over-inclusiveness:**   Although these categories are useful ways of labeling what a given classification is doing, attaching the correct label says very little about whether the Court will find the classification to be violative of equal protection or not. [2]

---

2. Our discussion here of under- and over-inclusiveness assumes that the classification does **not** involve a **"suspect"** or **"semi-suspect"** classification, and does not involve a **"fundamental right."** These terms are discussed beginning at Par. (b) "Strict scrutiny" on p. 255. In other words, we're talking here about the ordinary "mere-rationality" review that's given to the least-problematic tier of economic and social-welfare legislation.

a. **Little review of under-inclusiveness:** The Court *rarely* in practice invalidates an *under-inclusive* law.

    i. **Rationale:** The Court has often justified this reticence by asserting that legislatures are permitted to solve problems *"one step at a time,"* i.e., to regulate certain aspects of a harm without regulating all. Or, as the idea was expressed in *Railway Express Agency v. New York*, 336 U.S. 106 (1949) (discussed *infra*, p. 257), "[i]t is no requirement of equal protection that all evils of the same genus be eradicated or none at all. ... "

b. **Review of over-inclusiveness:** You might think that *over-inclusive* laws would be subjected to greater judicial scrutiny than under-inclusive ones. After all, while the worst that can be said for under-inclusive laws is that they fail to burden some who ought logically to be burdened, an over-inclusive law actually *places a burden on one on whom it should not fall*.

    i. **Little scrutiny:** But in practice, over-inclusive laws *don't* get more scrutiny than under-inclusive ones, assuming that no suspect or semi-suspect classification or fundamental interest is at stake.

8. **Summary of present standards of review:** Traditionally, there has been a "two-tiered" model of equal protection review. Either a statute was subjected to the lower tier (in which case the scrutiny was minimal and the statute almost always upheld) or it was subjected to "strict" scrutiny (and generally invalidated). Since 1970, the Supreme Court has occasionally applied a middle standard, as noted above. A rough summary of the present Court's standards for reviewing statutes under equal protection challenges is as follows:

a. **Ordinary "mere-rationality" review:** The least probing standard of review applies to statutes which are not based upon a "suspect classification," and do not involve the "quasi-suspect" categories implicitly recognized by the Court (principally gender and illegitimacy). The statutes reviewed under this lowest-level scrutiny are generally ones which involve mainly *economic issues*. Just as the Court has, ever since the decline of the *Lochner* philosophy, declined to give more than minimal substantive due process review to economic legislation, so it has declined to impose very searching review of such legislation under the Equal Protection Clause.

    i. **The test:** Therefore, in this least-scrutiny area, the Court "will ask only whether it is *conceivable* that the classification bears a *rational relationship* to an end of government which is *not prohibited* by the Constitution." N&R, p. 601. This test is sometimes called (and we'll call it here) the *"mere-rationality"* standard.

        (1) **Under- or over-inclusiveness:** This easy-to-satisfy mere-rationality standard applies whether the classification is "under-inclusive," "over-inclusive," or simultaneously under- and over-inclusive. (See *supra*, p. 254.)

b. **Strict scrutiny:** At the other end of the spectrum, the Court will give *"strict scrutiny"* to any statute which is based upon a *"suspect classification"* or which impairs a *"fundamental right."* (The meaning of these two terms is discussed extensively beginning *infra*, p. 265.) Classifications based on *race* are a classic example of a "suspect" class; the right to *vote* is an important example of a fundamental right.

    i. **The test:** Where strict scrutiny is invoked, the classification will be upheld only if it is *necessary* to promote a *compelling* governmental interest. Thus not only must the objective be an extremely important one, but the "fit" between the means and the end must be extremely tight.

    c. Middle-level review: In a few situations, the Court has engaged in scrutiny that is more probing than the "mere-rationality" test, but less rigid than classical "strict scrutiny." This has happened principally in cases involving classifications based on *gender* and *illegitimacy*, and in some cases involving access to the judicial process. N&R, pp. 602-603. Classifications based on *alienage* are also sometimes viewed as being based on this middle-level review.

        i. Test: Where the middle level of review is applied, the test is usually stated as follows: the means chosen by the legislature (i.e., the classification) must serve *important governmental objectives* and must be *substantially related* to achievement of those objectives. See, e.g., *Craig v. Boren*, 429 U.S. 190 (1976), a sex-discrimination case discussed *infra*, p. 336. In this middle-level situation, therefore, the legislative objective must be an important one (but not necessarily "compelling") and the fit between means and end must be reasonably tight (not almost perfect, as in a strict scrutiny situation).

II. ECONOMIC AND SOCIAL LAWS — THE "MERE-RATIONALITY" STANDARD

    A. Deferential review: As noted, where neither a suspect class nor a fundamental right is implicated, the Court will review a classification with extreme deference, and with a heavy presumption of constitutionality. Most general *"economic"* and *"social welfare"* legislation falls within this limited review category.

        1. Mere-rationality review: The standard for lowest-level review is generally phrased as the *"mere-rationality"* test. That is, the statute will not be stricken if it's conceivable that there is some *rational relation* between the means selected by the legislature and a *legitimate* legislative objective.

    B. Broad reading of "legitimate public objective": Although the legislature's "purpose" or *"objective"* in enacting a statute must be "legitimate," the courts give *extreme deference* to the legislature's right to define its objectives. Thus of the relatively few cases in which general economic and social policy has been struck down on equal protection grounds in the last fifty years, even fewer have been based upon a finding that the legislature's "objective" was not "legitimate."

        1. Search for objectives: The Court often reviews various "conceivable" objectives which *might have* motivated the legislature, if it is not clear from the legislative history what the precise objectives were. (See *infra*, p. 258.) So long as there is at least one conceivable objective which is legitimate and which is rationally related to the means selected, the possibility that another, illegitimate, objective might have motivated the legislature will be ignored by the Court.

        2. Great deference: Furthermore, any objective that does not strike the Court as being grossly unfair or totally irrational will be upheld. The fact that the Court thinks that the objective behind the legislation is *unwise* will not be sufficient to make it "illegitimate."

3. **Not all objectives legitimate:** Yet not every objective that motivates a legislature will be found by the Supreme Court to be "legitimate."

   a. **Discrimination against out-of-state competitors:** For instance, promoting the success of in-state business over out-of-state competitors has been held not to be legitimate. In *Metropolitan Life Ins. Co. v. Ward*, 470 U.S. 869 (1985), the Court invalidated, on equal protection grounds, an Alabama statute that taxed out-of-state insurance companies at a higher rate than in-state ones. Alabama argued that the statute was a reasonable means of achieving its objective of promoting its domestic insurance industry. But the Court (by a 5-4 vote) concluded that "promotion of domestic business by *discriminating against nonresident competitors* is not a legitimate state purpose."

   b. **Animus towards unpopular groups:** Similarly, legislation that is motivated solely by *"animus"* or *"hostility"* towards a *politically-unpopular group* (e.g., gay people or "hippies") will be held not to be legitimate. See *infra*, p. 260.

C. **"One step at a time" approach:** A key feature of "mere-rationality" review is that legislation will not be invalidated merely because the legislature dealt with only one part of a problem. That is, the legislature may deal with a problem *"one step at a time."* This is really another way of saying that a statute which is "under-inclusive" is not necessarily invalid.

   Example: A New York City traffic regulation bans the placing of advertising on vehicles, except that the owner of a vehicle is permitted to advertise his own products. The purpose of the regulation is to reduce traffic hazards. The act is challenged on the theory that a vehicle carrying advertising for the vehicle's owner is no less distracting than a vehicle carrying advertising for others. Also, the challengers point out that other traffic hazards (e.g., "vivid displays on Times Square") have not been banned.

   Held, the regulation is not a violation of equal protection. "It is no requirement of equal protection that all evils of the same genus be eradicated or none at all[.]" *Railway Express Agency v. New York*, 336 U.S. 106 (1949).

   But a concurrence contended that the majority's rationale was an invitation to arbitrary action, since this kind of under-inclusive act (which the concurrence described as "regulation of the few") would allow legislators to "choose only a few to whom they will apply legislation and thus to escape the political retribution that might be visited upon them if larger numbers were affected." Instead, the concurrence contended, the statute should be upheld because "[t]here is a real difference between doing in self-interest and doing for hire, so that it is one thing to tolerate action from those who act on their own and it is another thing to permit the same action to be promoted for a price."

1. **Support for a "step-by-step" view:** In support of the view that a problem may be attacked "one step at a time," the following arguments have been made: (1) a contrary rule might "preclude a state from undertaking any program of correction until its resources were adequate to deal with the entire problem"; and (2) there might be a legislative majority in favor of attacking one aspect of the problem, but not other aspects, so that an "all or nothing" rule might "restrict the state's opportunities to experiment." 82 HARV. L. REV. 1085 (quoted in L,K&C, p. 1252).

D. Determining a statute's "purpose": Before a court can determine whether the purpose of a statute is "legitimate," and that there is a sufficiently close link between means and end, it must somehow determine what the "purpose" is. The Supreme Court seems always to have agreed that so long as *one* of the purposes of the statute is legitimate, and sufficiently closely linked to the means, the statute will be valid under lowest-level review. But the Court has vacillated over the years about where to look to find the possible purposes.

1. **"Actual" legislative purpose:** Obviously, if the statute itself, either within its text, or in its preamble, contains a statement of purpose, that statement will control. Similarly, if the legislative history of the bill discloses a purpose, that will control. In these two situations, the Court is relying on the legislature's *"actual"* purpose.

   a. **Combination of goals:** The legislature will often have *more than one* objective in mind when it passes a statute. It seems clear that so long as the challenged classification is rationally related to *any one* of these actual objectives, the statute will be sustained, even if it is not rationally related to the others (or the others are not "legitimate" objectives).

2. **"Conceivable basis" standard:** The quest for the legislature's "actual" purpose may be complicated by either of two possibilities: (1) that neither the statute nor its legislative history discloses *any* clear purpose; or (2) that apart from the stated purpose(s) there may have been other objectives which, either solely or in combination with the stated purpose(s), in fact induced the legislature to pass the bill. One way in which the Court has dealt with these possibilities is by being willing to consider *any purpose which the statute's defenders* (i.e., the litigant seeking to have the statute upheld) can assert as having been *the* or even *a*, consideration which *"may"* have motivated the legislature. If the Court agrees that this purpose "may" have motivated the legislature, and that purpose is "legitimate" and rationally related to the means used by the legislature, the statute will be upheld *even if there is no "hard" evidence that that purpose was in fact a motivation* to the legislature.

   a. **Illustration:** For instance, in *U.S. Railroad Retirement Bd. v. Fritz*, 449 U.S. 166 (1980), six members of the Court held that so long as there was a "plausible" reason for Congress to have made the classification scheme it did, lowest-level equal protection review was satisfied; it was *"constitutionally irrelevant whether this reasoning in fact underlay the legislative decision,"* since the Court had "never insisted that a legislative body articulate its reasons for enacting a statute."

      i. **Dissenter's view in *Fritz*:** But two dissenters in *Fritz*, Brennan and Marshall, took a sharply different view on this issue. They believed that "a challenged classification may be sustained only if it is rationally related to the achievement of an *actual* legitimate governmental purpose," and that "any *post hoc* justifications preferred by Government attorneys" should be viewed skeptically. (Justice Stevens concurred with the majority, but believed that a purpose should be considered only if it was either an "actual" one or else a "legitimate purpose that we may reasonably presume to have motivated an impartial legislature.")

   b. **Facts of *Fritz*:** The facts of *Fritz* show that whether or not one insists on an "actual" legislative purpose may sometimes make a difference in the outcome. In *Fritz*, Congress modified a prior scheme, by which persons who worked long enough for both railroad and non-railroad employers could obtain retirement benefits under both the railroad and social security systems. In order to preserve the solvency of the railroad retirement system, Congress eliminated this double-benefit "windfall."

    i. **Order of employment significant:**   To accomplish this, Congress set up four classes; depending on the class into which he fell, a person got either full windfall, reduced windfall, or no windfall benefits at all. At issue in *Fritz* was that portion of the scheme which, within the class of persons who had worked for railroads more than ten years but less than twenty-five, and who had not yet retired when the act took effect, gave different treatment to those who had worked first for a non-railroad employer than to those who had worked first for a railroad. A person in the former situation received at least a reduced windfall; one in the latter received none. Thus the order of jobs was the sole basis for the statutory distinction.

    ii. **Majority view:**   The majority, as noted, was willing to accept any proffered statutory "purpose," whether actually relied upon by the legislature or not. They reasoned that Congress "may" have been attempting to preserve limited windfall benefits only for "career" railroad employees, and that persons still working in railroading (as a second career) when the act went into force were more likely to be "career" railroad workers than those who had left railroading before the act came into force. Since this was a "plausible reason" for Congress' action, it was sufficient to save the statute.

    iii. **Dissent:**   But the dissent, since it required an "actual" legislative purpose, reached an opposite result. By looking to the legislative history, the dissent concluded that Congress' actual intent was *not* to eliminate any "vested" benefit, and that Congress did not intend to deprive members of plaintiff's class of their windfall (which the dissent called an "earned benefit"). Thus, in the dissent's opinion, the classification was not rationally related to any actual government purpose.

  c. **Inconsistent purpose:**   Since, under the *Fritz* majority's view, any "conceivable" purpose advanced by a statute's defender will, if it rationally relates to the classification, be sufficient to validate the statute, a side effect is probably that the Court may consider even those "conceivable" purposes which, the statute's text and history show, *could not have been* the *"actual"* purpose of the statute.

3. **Court imagines "hypothetical" purpose:**   On occasion, the Court has gone even further than in *Fritz*, and has simply used *its own imagination* to *"hypothesize"* a theoretical objective which the legislature "might have" been pursuing when it enacted the statute. Here, too, if this *hypothetical purpose* is adequate, the statute has been upheld. When the Court has been inclined to proceed in this manner, it has stated that it will overturn statutory classifications "only if no grounds can be *conceived* to justify them." *McDonald v. Board of Election*, 394 U.S. 802 (1969).

4. **Pros and cons of "actual" purpose requirement:**   The commentators have disagreed about the wisdom of requiring an "actual" legislative objective, rather than one hypothesized *post hoc* by a defender of the statute or by the Court itself.

  a. **Pros:**   Professor Gunther has argued that no objective should be considered unless it has been articulated by a representative of the state (either by the legislature itself, or at least, say, the attorney general's office). Such a rule would, Gunther contends, "be indirect pressure on the legislature to state its own reasons for selecting the particular means and classifications [and would thus] improve the quality of the political process [by] encouraging a fuller airing in the political arena of the grounds for legislative action." 86 HARV. L. REV. 46 (quoted in L,K&C, p. 1251).

    b. **Cons:** But several difficulties with this view have been articulated.

        i. **Anti-democratic:** The strongest of these is that an "actual purpose" requirement, since it sends the judiciary on a vague quest for the motivations of multiple politicians pursuing differing objectives, "leaves the judiciary free to strike legislation it finds politically objectionable by attributing to the legislature either an illegitimate purpose or a purpose that, though legitimate, is too far removed from the means selected to withstand even minimum scrutiny." 95 HARV. L. REV. 160. The result may well be "anti-democratic," in a manner similar to the striking of economic and social welfare legislation on substantive due process grounds during the *Lochner* era.

        ii. **Different results for same statute.** A second difficulty is that, if the "actual purpose" standard is applied, when two states adopt identically-worded statutes for differing "purposes," *one state's statute might be valid and the other invalid*. Such a result certainly seems anomalous and confusing. Also, if a statute is struck down because it has an inadequate "actual purpose," what happens if the legislature reenacts it accompanied by recitations of an adequate actual purpose? It seems hypocritical of the courts to require legislatures to go through such a charade.

E. **Legal disabilities motivated by "animus" towards unpopular groups:** Occasionally, the Court has examined legislation that it finds to have been motivated by *"animus"* or *"hostility"* towards a *politically-unpopular group*. The Court has been willing to *strike down* such legislation even though only "mere-rationality review" is supposedly being used. In so doing, the Court has said that the *desire to harm an unpopular group* cannot be a *"legitimate governmental objective."* These "animus by government" cases may be said to apply mere-rationality review *"with bite."*

    1. **Discrimination against hippies:** The first case to illustrate this principle that discrimination motivated solely by hostility towards an unpopular group may flunk even mere-rationality was a 1973 case involving what the court found to be congressional animus against "hippies," *U.S. Dep't of Agric. v. Moreno*, 413 U.S. 528 (1973).

        a. **Facts:** Congress changed the Food Stamp program to exclude any household that had two or more unrelated members. As the Supreme Court later characterized the change, it "was intended to *prevent so-called 'hippies' and 'hippie communes' from participating"* in the program.

        b. **Struck down:** The Court found that this change did not even satisfy mere-rationality review. "For if the constitutional conception of 'equal protection of the laws' means anything, it must at the very least mean that *a bare congressional desire to harm a politically unpopular group cannot constitute a legitimate governmental interest."* Therefore, a congressional desire to discriminate against hippies could not meet the requirement of a legitimate governmental interest.

    2. **Ban on protection of gays:** The Court's main use of this "intent to harm unpopular groups" analysis has been in a pair of cases involving the rights of *gays and lesbians.*

a. ***Romer v. Evans* and denial of discrimination protection:**   First, in a 1996 case, the Court struck down an amendment to the Colorado Constitution that would have ***prevented the state or any of its cities from giving various protections*** (e.g., protection against ***"discrimination"***) to gays or lesbians. *Romer v. Evans*, 517 U.S. 620 (1996). The Court found that the amendment's sole purpose was to injure homosexuals. *Romer* is discussed further in our detailed treatment of classifications directed to sexual orientation, *infra*, p. 366.

b. ***Windsor* and the federal definition of marriage:**   Then, in another gay-rights case, the Court relied on *Moreno*'s "desire to harm a politically unpopular group" language to hold that ***Congress could not define marriage*** in such a way as to refuse to recognize, for federal purposes, a same-sex marriage entered into under state law. *U.S. v. Windsor*, 133 S. Ct. 2675 (2013), discussed *infra*, p. 368.

3.   The mentally retarded: Another category that seems to have benefited from a somewhat more rigorous version of mere-rationality review in recent decades is the ***developmentally delayed***. In *City of Cleburne v. Cleburne Living Center*, 473 U.S. 432 (1985), the Court struck down a Texas city's denial of a special use permit for the operation of a group home for the "***mentally retarded***."[3]

a.   Rationale: The Court refused to treat mental retardation as an explicitly "quasi-suspect" classification like gender or illegitimacy (see *infra*, p. 360). Yet while purporting to apply a "mere-rationality" standard, the Court quite clearly gave the challenged classification a more rigorous review than it has given to purely economic regulations. As in the above cases involving gays and "hippies," the Court seems to have been motivated to use a more-rigorous-than-usual variant of "mere-rationality" review because of the widespread prejudice against the retarded — the Court noted that "there have been and there will continue to be instances of discrimination against the retarded that are in fact invidious[.]"

i.   "One step at a time" approach declined: One clue to the fact that more than the ordinary highly-deferential standard of review was being applied in *Cleburne* came from the fact that the Court rejected the defendant city's argument that the proposed home would be unsafe because it was on a "five hundred year flood plain" and because it would have too many people living in it for its size — the Court saw no reason why these arguments justified discriminating between the home for the retarded and, say, a nursing home or a home for convalescents, which could be located in exactly the same place without a special use permit. Yet the Court has historically allowed reform to take place ***"one step at a time"*** (see *supra*, p. 257), so it is hard to see why the city should have been required to protect, say, nursing home patients in order to protect the retarded. (Justice Marshall, dissenting from the majority's refusal to apply intermediate-level scrutiny, made this argument to show that the majority was really applying heightened scrutiny without admitting it.)

---

3. I recognize that the term "mentally retarded" has been replaced by the less-insulting term "developmentally delayed." But since the Court in *Cleburne* repeatedly used the phrase "mentally retarded," I use it here in my description of the case.

F. **Highly deferential standard:** But cases like *Moreno, Romer v. Evans, Windsor,* and *City of Cleburne* — in which "mere-rationality" review nonetheless leads to invalidation under the Equal Protection Clause — are the *exception,* not the rule, even in recent decades. Especially where the case does *not* seem to involve a government purpose to discriminate against a politically-unpopular group (like hippies, gays or the developmentally delayed), the Court continues to give *great deference* to the legislature in cases involving economic and social legislation without the presence of a suspect or semi-suspect class or a fundamental right.

   1. **Means-end link need not be empirical:** One aspect of this deference is in the doctrine that there need not be *in fact* a link between the means selected by the legislature and a legitimate objective. All that is required is that the legislature *"could rationally have believed"* that there was such a link.

   > **Example:** A state statute bans the sale of milk in plastic non-returnable containers, but allows such sale in other types of non-returnable containers, including paperboard cartons. Several justifications are proffered in support of the bill, including: (1) that the elimination of plastic cartons will encourage use of environmentally-superior containers; (2) that banning just plastic containers will cause less economic dislocation within the milk industry than banning both plastic and paperboard simultaneously; and (3) that the law will help to conserve energy. The statute's challengers attempt to show that the statute will not in fact achieve any of these three objectives.
   >
   > *Held,* the statute is not a violation of the Equal Protection Clause. Whether or not the statute will *in fact* achieve any of its objectives is *irrelevant.* The only question is whether the legislature "could rationally have decided" that it would meet these objectives. The burden is on the statute's challengers to show that "the legislative facts on which [a] classification is apparently based could not reasonably be conceived to be true by the governmental decision-maker." Here, whether the classification scheme would meet one or more of these objectives was *at least debatable.* By that fact alone, it cannot be said that the legislature acted irrationally, and the statute must be upheld. *Minnesota v. Clover Leaf Creamery Co.,* 449 U.S. 456 (1981).

   2. **Loose means-end fit suffices:** Since all that is required is that the means-end relationship be close enough that its rationality is *"debatable,"* a *very loose fit between means and ends will be acceptable.*

   a. **Age discrimination case (*Murgia*):** For instance, in *Massachusetts Bd. of Retirement v. Murgia,* 427 U.S. 307 (1976), a Massachusetts statute required state police officers to retire at age 50. All parties conceded that the objective of the statute was to maintain a physically-fit police force. The statute was upheld, even though some (perhaps many) officers over 50 were not in poor physical health, making the statute over-inclusive. In other words, the fact that the "fit" between the *means chosen* (mandatory retirement over 50) and the *end* being pursued (physically-fit officers) was *very loose did not matter*: it was enough that the means-end fit was *not so attenuated as to be irrational*.

   i. **Availability of tighter fits irrelevant:** Furthermore, the fact that a *tighter-fitting, less-discriminatory means* of measuring physical health was *available* (e.g., annual physical examinations) did not make the less-than-best-fitting means selected by the statute impermissible.

ii. Not suspect class: The decision in *Murgia* turned largely on the fact that the Court ***declined*** to treat the classification based on ***age*** as a ***"suspect"*** class, on the theory that old age "marks a stage that each of us will reach if we live out our normal span ... " (Justice Marshall, in dissent, argued that the age classification should be subjected to ***middle-level*** scrutiny, because older workers "constitute a class subject to repeated and arbitrary discrimination in employment." In Marshall's view, the statute certainly could not survive such middle-level scrutiny, because of its over-inclusiveness.)

iii. Still not suspect: By the way, a post-*Murgia* case shows that the Supreme Court still views age as not being a "suspect" class. See *Gregory v. Ashcroft*, 501 U.S. 452 (1991), upholding a scheme by which state judges are required to retire at age 70. The Court held that it was not irrational for the state to distinguish between judges older and younger than 70, nor was it irrational for the state to distinguish between judges and other state employees of the same age, who were not subject to mandatory retirement.

G. Summary of Court's approach: In summary, the Supreme Court takes a generally deferential equal protection approach to economic and social legislation. However, this deference is not complete. The principal features of the present Court's review in these areas may be summarized as follows:

1. **Purpose need not be actual:** The law will be upheld if the means chosen by the legislature bear a ***rational relation*** to ***any conceivable*** legitimate legislative purpose (at least if proffered by any representative of the state, and perhaps even if thought of only by members of the Court); this will be so even though there is no evidence that this was the ***actual*** purpose motivating the legislature.

2. **Means-end link:** It is not necessary that there be an ***actual***, empirical, link between the means selected by the legislature and the (actual or theoretical) legislative objective. All that is necessary is that the legislature could ***"rationally have believed"*** that there was a link between the means and the end. And the legislature will be deemed to have been capable of such a belief so long as it is "debatable" whether such a means-end link exists (even though the Court suspects that it probably does not).

3. **Unpopular trait:** Finally, if the classification involves a politically unpopular trait or group, thereby suggesting bias on the part of the majority, the Court is likely to subject the statute to a somewhat more probing review, even where the Court refuses to apply "strict" or "middle level" scrutiny. Examples are statutes that single out "hippies" (*U.S. Dept of Agric. v. Moreno*), ***gays and lesbians*** (*Romer v. Evans* and *Windsor*), and the ***mentally retarded*** (*City of Cleburne*).

Quiz Yourself on

EQUAL PROTECTION — ECONOMIC & SOCIAL LAWS

33. The state of Chartreuse has delegated to the state bar association the job of determining requirements for the practice of law. Until recently, the bar association imposed no continuing legal education requirements. However, there has been a large rise in the number of malpractice actions against lawyers in the state, some of which appear to derive from the fact that lawyers have not kept pace with changing legal principles. Also, there has been a rise in the disdain with which the public in Chartreuse holds lawyers.

The bar association, therefore, imposed a mandatory continuing legal education requirement of 12 course-hours per year. The state imposes on doctors a continuing education requirement of only 4 hours per year. There is strong evidence that, in general, changes in medicine happen faster than changes in law. Amos, a lawyer in Chartreuse, has challenged the continuing legal education requirement on the grounds that by imposing a much higher requirement on lawyers than on doctors, the state has violated his equal protection rights. Assume that the state bar association's conduct constitutes state action.

(a) What standard should the court use to test whether the legal education requirement satisfies the demands of equal protection? _____

(b) Will Amos' attack succeed? _____

34. The town of Solon established a regulation that all members of the fire department must retire at the age of 50. The Town Council enacted the regulation after reading a news report that in a neighboring town, a 53 year-old firefighter with a bad back was unable to carry a child out of the fourth floor of a burning building, leading to the child's death. The Town Council members reasoned that on average, those over 50 are less able to perform the highly demanding physical functions of firefighting than those under 50. Prentice is the Chief of the Solon Fire Department. His duties are exclusively desk-bound. He has just turned 50, and has challenged the retirement regulation, as applied to him, on the grounds that it violates his right to equal protection. Will Prentice's attack on the regulation succeed? _____

Answers

33. (a) The court should ask whether the classification is rationally related to a legitimate state objective.

(b) No. Unless there is a suspect or semi-suspect class involved, or a fundamental right, the Supreme Court will uphold a state legislative classification against equal protection attack so long as the classification scheme bears a *rational relation* to some *legitimate legislative objective*. The desire to have lawyers be better trained, and to increase public confidence and reduce suits, certainly seem to constitute legitimate governmental objectives. The link between the classification system chosen and the objective being pursued does not have to be a close one. In fact, there does not need to be an actual empirical link between means and end, merely a *rational belief* on the part of the legislature that there is a link between means and end. Here, a bar association (acting as a government body) certainly could rationally have believed that lawyers who take mandatory legal education will be more up to date, and thus less likely to make mistakes through outmoded training. The fact that doctors might need refresher courses even more than lawyers will be ignored by the court, because reform may take place *"one step at a time"* (i.e., the government does not commit an equal protection violation every time it addresses one aspect of a problem without solving all related aspects).

34. No. As in the prior question, the threshold issue is what standard of review the court will give to the challenged classification. Unless a suspect or quasi-suspect class, or a fundament right, is at issue, the court will use the "mere-rationality" standard. The Supreme Court has held repeatedly that age is not a suspect or semi-suspect class. See, e.g., *Mass. Bd. of Retirement v. Murgia* (police officers may be required to retire at age 50). Therefore, the Court applies mere-rationality review to age-based classifications such as the one here. The goal of assuring that each firefighter is fit for the particular duties of the profession is clearly a legitimate one. There is some question about whether the means chosen (outright ban on all over-50 firefighters) is a good way to accomplish that objective, since there are less drastic alternatives (e.g., testing of each applicant, or an exemption for those who perform only desk duties). But all that is required between means and end is a ***rational relation***. Here, the blanket-ban approach was certainly a rational way of assuring physical fitness, even though it was not the best possible approach or even a very well-tailored one. The classification will be upheld unless it is completely irrational, which this one is certainly not.

III. SUSPECT CLASSIFICATIONS, ESPECIALLY RACE

A. Suspect classes generally: We turn now to "suspect" classifications, i.e., statutory classifications which, because they give distinct treatment to a group that has historically been the victim of discrimination, are subjected to "strict scrutiny."

1. **Race and national origin:** The paradigmatic example of a suspect classification is, of course, ***race***. The other principal example is ***national origin***.

2. **Alienage:** Some Court cases appear to make ***alienage*** a suspect classification as well, but more recent cases make such large exceptions to the strict scrutiny of alienage classifications that alienage is probably more properly viewed as involving "middle-level" scrutiny; the subject is therefore discussed along with other middle-level scrutiny classes *infra*, p. 353.

3. **Five subject areas:** In our treatment of suspect classes, five principal subject areas are addressed: (1) What groups have been so frequently the object of discrimination and prejudice that classifications disfavoring them should be labelled as "suspect"? (2) To what extent must discrimination be shown to be "purposeful" before it is outlawed by the Equal Protection Clause? (3) How rigorous must "strict" scrutiny be? (4) How does one demonstrate that public facilities (especially schools) have been ***racially segregated***, and what are the remedies for such segregation? and (5) To what extent may the government make ***"benign"*** use of suspect classifications (i.e., the problem of "affirmative action")?

B. Groups covered: Classification based on ***race*** is, of course, the classic example of a "suspect" classification, because of our nation's long history of both public and private racial discrimination. In addition to blacks (the group Congress of course intended most explicitly to assist by means of the Equal Protection Clause), ***any other racial group*** may, if made the object of a classification intended to disfavor that group, invoke strict scrutiny. See, e.g., *Yick Wo v. Hopkins, infra*, p. 267, treating as suspect administrative discrimination against Asians.

1. **National origin:** Apart from blacks, Asians, and other minorities that are clearly racially distinct, a classification based on ***national origin*** is also suspect. Thus in *Hernandez v. Texas*, 347 U.S. 475 (1954), discrimination against ***Mexican-Americans*** with regard to jury service was treated in the same way that discrimination against blacks would have been.

2. **Extension in *Croson*:** Discrimination against ***any*** racial group will merit strict scrutiny, even if that group has never been the subject of widespread discrimination. A majority of the Supreme Court so concluded in *City of Richmond v. J.A. Croson Co.*, discussed extensively *infra*, p. 313. So if a city discriminates in favor of, say, black contractors at the expense of white contractors, this discrimination must be subjected to strict scrutiny (and probably struck down), as happened in *Croson*.

a. Ethnic groups: Probably the rationale of *Croson* means that any intentional discrimination against a particular *ethnic* group also must be strictly scrutinized, even if the group has not been the victim of widespread prejudice or discrimination. Thus if Whites of Anglo-Saxon Protestant descent were discriminated against in favor of other groups (e.g., Whites of Italian or Mediterranean descent), strict scrutiny would presumably be required even though White Anglo-Saxon Protestants have historically rarely been discriminated against.

3. Other classes: Thus far, the Court has not treated as fully "suspect" classifications based on any grounds other than race and national origin. (But see the discussion of classes treated as "semi-suspect," e.g., sex and illegitimacy, *infra*, pp. 334 and 359.)

a. Wealth: Of special significance has been the Court's refusal to treat classifications based on *wealth* as "suspect." This refusal is discussed *infra*, p. 399.

C. "Purposeful" discrimination: A classification will not be deemed to be "suspect," and therefore subject to strict scrutiny, unless the Court finds that there was a legislative *intent* to discriminate against the disfavored group. That is, the mere fact that a law has a less favorable impact on a minority group than it has on the majority is not sufficient to constitute a violation of equal protection. As is discussed in more detail below, a demonstration of disproportionate *impact* is *a factor* in the equal protection analysis, but it can never by itself suffice; proof of *intentional* discrimination is required.

1. Three ways to show purpose: Purposeful discrimination may appear in any of three ways: (1) the law discriminates *on its face*, i.e., by its explicit terms; (2) the law, although neutral on its face, is *administered* in a discriminatory way; and (3) the law, although it is neutral on its face and is applied in accordance with its terms, was enacted with a purpose of discriminating, as shown by the law's legislative history, statements made by legislators, the law's disparate impact, or other circumstantial evidence of intent.

2. Some examples: Following are some examples of statutes found to have been "purposefully discriminatory," and therefore violative of the Equal Protection Clause:

Example — facially discriminatory: A state statute provides that "all white male persons who are twenty-one years of age who are citizens of this State shall be eligible to serve as jurors." P, a black, is convicted of murder by a jury from which all blacks have been removed pursuant to the statute.

Held, the act on its face discriminates against blacks, and therefore violates the Equal Protection Clause. *Strauder v. West Virginia*, 100 U.S. 303 (1880).

Note: Where a law is found to discriminate "on its face," the Court will *not* require that it be shown to have had an actual discriminatory *impact* in the case at hand. Thus in *Strauder*, P was not required to show that he would not have been convicted by a jury containing blacks, or even to show that some blacks would have been seated on the jury had the statute not been in force. The mere *risk* of discriminatory impact was sufficient, given the facial discrimination.

Example — discrimination in administration: A San Francisco ordinance bars the operation of hand laundries in wooden buildings, except with the consent of the Board of Supervisors. The Board gives permits to all but one of the non-Chinese applicants, but to none of nearly 200 Chinese applicants.

Held, although the ordinance is neutral on its face, there was discrimination in its administration, and this discrimination violates the Equal Protection Clause. *Yick Wo v. Hopkins*, 118 U.S. 356 (1886).

Example — discriminatory purpose shown by circumstantial evidence: Burke County, Georgia elects its five-member Board of Commissioners via an at-large system. Whites are only in a slight majority in the voting-age population, but no black has ever been elected to the Board.

Held, although the at-large system was facially neutral (and although it was not originally adopted, in 1911, for discriminatory purposes), it has been maintained by the state legislature for discriminatory purposes, and has a discriminatory impact on the county's black citizens. In addition to the fact that no black has ever been elected to the Board (which would not by itself be sufficient to show discriminatory purposes), (1) the history of discrimination against blacks with respect to party affairs, primary and general elections; (2) the unresponsiveness of the county's elected officials to the needs of the black community; and (3) the fact that the state legislature's maintenance of the at-large system was basically due to the county's own state representatives (who desired to maintain a system that excluded black participation), all support an *inference* of intentional discrimination. *Rogers v. Lodge*, 458 U.S. 613 (1982).

3. **Proving discriminatory purpose:** If a statute is shown to discriminate on its face, no showing of discriminatory purpose will be necessary. And if those making a discriminatory-administration claim can show that administrators to whom discretion is entrusted have applied the law in a way that is disadvantageous to the suspect class, no additional showing of legislative or administrative motive will be necessary (though the defenders of the law can attempt to rebut the case with an innocent explanation of the disparate administration). In the third situation, however, that of the law which is facially neutral and is applied according to its terms, the difficulties of proving "discriminatory purpose" are much greater.

    a. **No general rule:** There is no general rule that describes exactly how one demonstrates an intent to discriminate on the part of the legislature. Like proof of any other sort of intent, the use of *circumstantial evidence* is required.

    b. **"De jure" vs. "de facto" discrimination:** In any situation where a discriminatory purpose is found to exist, the discrimination is termed *"de jure"* (roughly "by law"). If, on the other hand, a law is found not to result from a discriminatory purpose, then the discrimination will be termed *"de facto"* (even if a discriminatory *effect* has resulted). The most common use of the terms, of course, is to describe the two types of *public school segregation* (with *de jure* segregation being the only judicially redressable one; *infra*, p. 280).

4. **General requirement of purpose (*Washington v. Davis*):** Prior to 1976, it was not completely clear that an intent to discriminate *was* in fact required, if there was a discriminatory *impact* upon a suspect class. But in that year, *Washington v. Davis*, 426 U.S. 229, set forth an explicit requirement that an intent to discriminate be found before an equal protection racial discrimination claim would be upheld.

a. **Facts of *Washington v. Davis*:** *Washington v. Davis* involved a suit brought by unsuccessful black applicants for positions as Washington, D.C. policemen. They had failed a written test of verbal ability and reading comprehension, which blacks failed *four times as frequently* as whites. The plaintiffs claimed that this differential impact made the hiring process violative of equal protection even though those who composed or selected the test had no intent to discriminate against blacks. (The plaintiffs also produced evidence suggesting that performance on the test did not necessarily correlate with job performance.)

b. **Holding:** The Supreme Court held that racial discrimination violative of the Equal Protection Clause exists only where it is a product of a ***discriminatory purpose***. While a showing of disproportionate racial impact is ***a*** factor in ascertaining intent, ***it can never by itself be sufficient to prove discriminatory intent***. Here, other facts, including the D.C. Police Department's affirmative efforts to recruit more black policemen, negated any finding of a discriminatory purpose in the use of the test (which was used throughout the federal Civil Service).

i. **Comparison to Title VII:** The *Washington* Court conceded that under Title VII of the 1964 Civil Rights Act, a hiring practice which disqualifies a substantially disproportionate number of blacks will be stricken, even without a showing of discriminatory intent. But the Court declined to establish a "no-intent" standard where the source of the discrimination claim was simply the Equal Protection Clause, as distinguished from a specifically-worded congressional statute.

ii. **Rationale:** The Court was especially concerned that absence of an intent requirement might invalidate "a whole range of tax, welfare, public service, regulatory, and licensing statutes that may be more burdensome to the poor and to the average black than to the more affluent white." In a footnote, the Court listed numerous statutory schemes that might be open to attack under such a standard, including such items as sales taxes, bridge tolls, minimum wage laws and professional licensing requirements.

5. **Other areas of application:** The principle of *Washington v. Davis* has been extended beyond the public employment context, to include such areas as *jury selection, zoning* and *public housing*, and *voting rights*. It seems apparent that no matter what the subject area, a statute will not be held to establish an impermissible suspect classification merely because of a disproportionately harsh impact on blacks or other minorities.

6. **Need not be sole motive:** Although a discriminatory purpose is required for invocation of strict scrutiny, such a purpose need not be the *sole* purpose of the statute. It is enough that that purpose was a *"motivating factor"* in the legislature's decision to enact the statute. *Arlington Heights v. Metropolitan Housing Corp.*, 429 U.S. 252 (1977).

a. **Two motivations:** Thus if there were two purposes that motivated the legislature to enact a statute, and only one of these was discriminatory against the suspect class, the presence of the second, non-discriminatory motive, will not immunize the statute from strict scrutiny. So long as the legislature would not have passed the statute had the discriminatory motive not been present, the existence of the other motive makes no difference. Cf. *Hunter v. Underwood*, 471 U.S. 222 (1985) (where voting law was enacted to disenfranchise both blacks and poor whites, the fact that disenfranchisement of blacks was a "but-for" motivation for the law was enough to make it a violation of the Fourteenth Amendment).

b. Shifting burden of proof: In fact, the plaintiff only needs to show that an intent to discriminate was a "motivating" or "substantial" factor in the legislature's enactment decision. Once he does this, the burden then shifts to the defendant to show that the statute *would have been passed anyway*, even without that intent. If the defendant succeeds in showing this, the requirement of proof of discriminatory purpose will be deemed not satisfied.

   i. Restatement: To put it another way, the issue is whether a discriminatory motive was a *"but for"* cause of the enactment, but the burden of proof is on the defendant once a *prima facie* showing of "motivating factor" has been made by a plaintiff. Thus in *Hunter v. Underwood, supra*, the requisite discriminatory purpose was shown by the fact that a desire to disenfranchise whites would not have been sufficient to lead to the enactment — the attempt to disenfranchise blacks was the "but for" cause of the enactment.

c. Must be "because of" not "in spite of": It follows from this requirement of "but for" causation that the statute must have been enacted *"because of"* a desire to bring about a discriminatory impact, *not merely "in spite of"* the probability of such an impact. This principle was established in a sex-discrimination case, *Personnel Administrator of Mass. v. Feeney*, 422 U.S. 256 (1979), but it seems clear that this rule will be applied in racial discrimination cases as well.

   i. Facts of *Feeney:* In *Feeney*, P, a woman, challenged a Massachusetts civil service statute which gave an *absolute hiring preference* to any veteran who obtained a passing score on a competitive exam. Since, at the time the suit was brought, over 98% of the veterans in Massachusetts were men, the preference operated overwhelmingly to the benefit of males and to the detriment of females.

   ii. Holding: The Supreme Court held that the statute was not intentionally gender-based, either overtly or covertly. A significant number of *men* were also non-veterans. Therefore, "[t]oo many men are affected by [the law] to permit the inference that the statute is but a pretext for preferring men over women."

   iii. "In spite of" not enough: The Court was willing to accept the plaintiff's contention that the legislature in fact knew that the law would be heavily unfavorable to women. But it rejected her further syllogism that, because a person "intends the natural and foreseeable consequences of his voluntary actions," the inevitable disproportionate impact proved an intent to discriminate. "Awareness of consequences" was *not* sufficient to prove "discriminatory purpose"; only if the legislature chose its course *"because of,"* and *not* merely *"in spite of,"* its adverse effects upon women, could there be said to have been intentional discrimination. And the Court found no evidence that the disparate effect upon women was, in the legislature's mind, anything more than a foreseeable but undesired inevitable byproduct of the basic decision to favor veterans. Therefore, the preference did not violate the Equal Protection Clause.

7. Passage of time: Suppose that a legislature enacts, for discriminatory motives, a provision that disadvantages a suspect class. It is apparently the case that *no matter how long a* *time elapses*, that provision continues to be a violation of equal protection so long as it has a discriminatory impact.

    a.   **Extension of principle:**   Thus in theory even a pre-Civil War statute shown to have been enacted for the purpose of disadvantaging blacks could be struck down today if the law were shown to currently disfavor blacks.

8. **Use of statistics:** Since disproportionate impact will be considered as *a* factor in measuring discriminatory intent (though it can never be the sole factor), the equal protection claimant will often attempt to use *statistical analysis* to show the degree of disproportionate impact. In general, the Court has *allowed* such statistical proof.

    a.   **Heavy weight in subjective discretion cases:**   Statistical evidence will be especially persuasive where the claim is that an *individual selection process* is being discriminatorily performed by administrative officials. See N&R, pp. 622-624. In this situation, it is difficult to gauge the subjective intent of the administrators in any other manner; also, there is less reason for the courts to defer to these officials' subjective decisions than there is to defer to the legislature's own acts.

    Example: When court officials have selected panels of *prospective jurors* by using questionnaires, in-person screening or other factors by which the officials become aware of each prospective juror's race, proof of major statistical deviation from the voting population's racial makeup has generally been enough to establish a *prima facie* case of discrimination. But where the selection process does not involve any discretion by the officials (e.g., random selection from tax lists) the occurrence of statistical underrepresentation of minorities has not been enough to make even a *prima facie* case of discrimination. N&R, p. 623.

    b.   **Prosecutors' peremptory challenges:** Statistics are similarly one of the ways to prove discrimination by *prosecutors* in their use of *peremptory challenges*.

        i.   **Race-based challenges not allowed:** Peremptory challenges enable either side to excuse a certain number of potential jurors "without cause." Prosecutors may not use such challenges based solely on the race of the juror. For instance, a prosecutor may not, in the trial of a black defendant, exclude all black jurors on the theory that such jurors are more likely to side with a black defendant than a white juror would be. *Batson v. Kentucky*, 476 U.S. 79 (1986).

        (1) **Statistical proof:** Statistical proof — i.e., proof that the prosecution has consistently declined to seat black jurors in trials of black defendants — is one way to show that the prosecution has violated this general principle.

        (2) **Other methods:** But other ways of showing impermissible racial bias, not involving statistics, also exist. For instance, *within the defendant's own case*, the prosecutor's questions during voir dire, or even the pattern of his use of challenges, may support an inference of discrimination. Once the inference of discrimination arises, the burden shifts to the prosecution to explain away the racial exclusion. *Batson, supra.*

        (3) **Gender-based challenges:** By the way, a state may no longer allow litigants to make *gender-based* peremptory challenges, either. See *J.E.B. v. Alabama*, discussed further *infra*, p. 345.

 c. **Voting rights:** Statistical evidence can also be important in establishing a discri natory purpose in **voting rights** cases. For instance, in *Rogers v. Lodge*, 458 U.S. 613 (1982), black voters attacked an at-large voting scheme; they argued that use of this arrangement (rather than a series of electoral districts) was intended to dilute the black vote. The Court held that proof of discriminatory purpose, not just effect, was needed. But the Court noted that although blacks composed nearly 54% of the population and 38% of the registered voters in the county, no black had ever been elected to the county Board of Commissioners. The Court affirmed the trial court's finding that the requisite proof of discriminatory purpose had been made — the fact that no black had ever been elected was "important evidence of purposeful exclusion" (though there was other evidence of purposeful discrimination as well).

9. **Consequence of finding of "discrimination":** Suppose that the Court does conclude that the legislature or administration acted in an intentionally discriminatory way in enacting or applying a statute. The state might try to show, in rebuttal, that the same statute *could* have been enacted for perfectly legitimate reasons.

 a. **Probably unsuccessful:** The present Court will not regard this rebuttal as relevant; if a discriminatory purpose was a substantial factor in the enactment, the statute will be *stricken* even though a properly-motivated legislature might also have enacted it.

 b. **Distinction:** This is one of the differences between a statute subjected to strict scrutiny and one which, because it involves only general economic or social welfare considerations, is subjected to a "mere-rationality" analysis — in the latter case, any legitimate objective, whether in fact relied upon by the legislature or not, will probably suffice. (See *supra*, p. 259.)

D. **Other requirements for strict scrutiny:** For discrimination to be subject to strict scrutiny, it is not sufficient that it be "purposeful." It must also be of an especially *"invidious,"* or *prejudicial*, sort. In practice, this has meant that the discrimination must be on the grounds of either *race* or *national origin*.

1. *Carolene Products* **footnote:** The basic theory behind strict scrutiny for these types of discrimination remains that expressed by Justice Stone in his *Carolene Products* footnote: "Prejudice against *discrete and insular minorities* may be a special condition, which tends seriously to curtail the operation of those political processes ordinarily to be relied upon to protect minorities, and which may call for a correspondingly more searching judicial inquiry." *U.S. v. Carolene Products Co.*, 304 U.S. 144 (1938).

 a. **Tribe's formulation:** Or, as Tribe has put the idea, special judicial protection is given to those groups which, because of "widespread, insistent prejudice against them," occupy the position of *"perennial losers in the political struggle."* Tribe, p. 1454.

2. **Immutability:** It is sometimes suggested that a classification is more likely to be treated as suspect if it is based upon an *immutable* trait, which race and natural origin certainly are. (Immutability also goes some of the way towards explaining the middle-level scrutiny given to classifications based on alienage, illegitimacy and gender, all discussed beginning *infra*, p. 334.)

 a. **Criticism:** However, it is not obvious why the fact of immutability should make a difference. As Professor Ely has pointed out, "[c]lassifications based on physical disability and intelligence are typically accepted as legitimate, even by judges and commentators who assert that immutability is relevant." Ely, p. 150.

3. **Stereotypes:** It is also often suggested that the prevalence of *stereotypes* concerning a group makes it more likely that classifications disadvantaging that group will be found to be "suspect." See, e.g., Justice Blackmun's statement in *Bakke* (*infra*, p. 293) that "[r]acial and ethnic distinctions where they are stereotypes are inherently suspect and call for exacting judicial scrutiny."

   a. **Criticism:** However, the term "stereotype" really means little more than an imperfect generalization. Since almost all legislation involves an imperfect generalization (in the sense that nearly all statutes are under- or over-inclusive or both), it would never do to impose strict scrutiny on any legislation based on a stereotype.

   b. **Incidence of falseness:** Perhaps generalizations whose *incidence of falseness is unduly high* are what should be strictly scrutinized. However, determining what is "too high" is difficult. For instance, as Ely suggests, if a generalization were used to determine who should be subject to capital punishment, virtually *any* occurrence of falsity would be intolerably high; by contrast, if the legislature is trying to identify persons susceptible to heart attacks in order to keep them from piloting commercial aircraft, a high rate of false generalization, perhaps well over 50%, would be appropriate. Ely, p. 156.

   c. **Ely's solution:** Ely suggests that "[t]he cases where we ought to be suspicious are not those involving a generalization whose incidence of counterexample is 'too high,' but rather those involving a generalization whose incidence of counterexample is *significantly higher than the legislative authority appears to have thought it was.*" *Id.* at 157.

4. **Modern Court's view:** One Supreme Court case, in discussing why the class of "close relatives" should not be treated as suspect, gave a catalogue of factors the modern Court will view as leading towards strict scrutiny: "As a historical matter, [close relatives] have not been *subjected to discrimination*; they do not exhibit *obvious, immutable*, or *distinguishing characteristics* that define them as a *discrete group*; and they are not a *minority* or *politically powerless.*" *Lyng v. Castillo*, 477 U.S. 635 (1986).

E. **How strict is "strict scrutiny":** Once the decision to apply strict scrutiny has been made, the statute will be upheld only if it is found to be *necessary* (not merely appropriate) to the attainment of some *compelling* (not merely desirable) governmental objective. As Professor Gunther has put it, this scrutiny has generally been "'strict' in theory and 'fatal' in fact." 86 HARV. L. REV. 8.

1. **Rationale for strict scrutiny:** Both the requirement of a "compelling" objective and that of "necessary" means to that objective can be seen as aspects of the same judicial goal: to assure that suspect classifications are used only in those very rare situations where the high cost of sanctioning official invidious discrimination is outweighed by the even higher cost of not doing so.

   a. **Weightiness of objective:** An additional reason for requiring, in strict scrutiny cases, that the state objective be "compelling" is that such a requirement represents *a way of ferreting out discriminatory purposes*. Even if the means-end fit is perfect (i.e., the means is the only way of establishing that particular end), if the end that is advanced as a justification is insubstantial, one can legitimately suspect that this end is merely a *pretext*, and that what really motivated the decision was, say, racial prejudice. See Ely, p. 148.

    i. **Illustration:** For instance, suppose a school principal seats African Americans on one side of the stage at a graduation ceremony, and whites on the other, and justifies the choice by claiming that this arrangement is more esthetically appealing. The objective here is so trivial that one could fairly suspect that it was a pretext to cover racial discrimination. See Brest, *Processes of Constitutional Decision-Making*, p. 489 (1975) (quoted in Ely, p. 148).

    b. **"Necessary" means:** The requirement that the means selected (the suspect classification) be "necessary" to attainment of the goal expresses the view that *less discriminatory alternatives* must *always* be used if they are available to attain the goal. In fact, less discriminatory alternatives may sometimes be required to be used even if they will *not* achieve the compelling goal *quite as well* as the discriminatory means. That is, some degree of sacrifice of the legislative objective may be required in the name of equality of treatment.

2. **Strict scrutiny nearly always fatal:** As an illustration of the strictness with which "strict scrutiny" is applied, consider that only once since 1944 has the Supreme Court upheld a governmental classification based on a racial or national-origin classification to which strict scrutiny was applied.

    a. **May be changing:** However, as the present Supreme Court has expanded the use of strict scrutiny, it may, paradoxically, have become *easier* for a measure to survive that scrutiny. Thus in *Adarand Constructors* (*infra*, p. 320), a case applying strict scrutiny to race-based federal affirmative action programs, the Court went out of its way to "dispel the notion that strict scrutiny is 'strict in theory, but fatal in fact.' "

        i. **Affirmative action in admissions:** The one post-1944 instance in which a race-based governmental classification has actually survived strict scrutiny by the Court illustrates that strict scrutiny may now be less likely to be fatal. That instance involved the use of affirmative action in *university admissions.* See *Grutter v. Bollinger* (*infra*, p. 295), a 2003 case in which the Court upheld the University of Michigan Law School's right to give an admissions preference to black and Hispanic applicants in order to obtain a "diverse" entering class, as long as this preference was granted as part of an individualized evaluation process that treated race as merely one "plus factor" among others.[4]

        ii. **Voting Rights Act:** Another context in which race-conscious governmental action might survive strict scrutiny is the *drawing of race-conscious electoral districts* where the use of race is required by a federal statute called the *Voting Rights Act* (VRA), which strives to prevent the dilution of the racial strength of minority groups in jurisdictions that have previously discriminated against minorities' voting rights. The Court has never actually upheld race-conscious district lines after strict scrutiny in a VRA case, but six members of the Roberts Court have indicated

---

4. But the post-*Grutter* case of *Parents Involved in Community Schools v. Seattle School District No. 1* (*infra*, p. 306), in which the Court struck down the use of race in public-school pupil assignments, suggests that strict scrutiny in the Roberts Court will generally still be very strict indeed.

that the government would have a compelling interest in drawing race-conscious lines where the VRA so required; see *League of United Latin American Citizens v. Perry*, 548 U.S. 399 (2006).

3. ***Korematsu:***   Before 2003's *Grutter* decision, the last case in which a racial or ethnic classification ***survived*** strict scrutiny was ***Korematsu v. U.S.***, 323 U.S. 214 (1944), the infamous ***Japanese Exclusion Case***. (Ironically, *Korematsu* was the first case in which race was explicitly referred to as a "suspect" criterion.)

   a. **Facts:**   *Korematsu* involved a post-Pearl Harbor military order excluding all persons of Japanese ancestry from certain areas of the West Coast, and resulting in their effective imprisonment. The order was applied against citizens as well as non-citizens.

   b. **Holding:**   The Court upheld the order, despite its suspectness. It did so on the theory that there was a ***compelling need*** to prevent espionage and sabotage, and that there was no practical and sufficiently rapid way for the military to distinguish the loyal from the disloyal.

   c. **Dissent:**   Three Justices dissented in *Korematsu*. The strongest dissent was that of Justice Murphy, who argued that the majority's view relied on the "assumption that all persons of Japanese ancestry may have a dangerous tendency to commit sabotage and espionage. ... " He contended that individualized loyalty hearings, at least for those persons who were American citizens, could have been held. Another dissenter, Justice Jackson, pointed out that no attempt was made anywhere in the United States to exclude German or Italian aliens (thus suggesting that the order was based at least in part on racial prejudice, though Justice Jackson did not explicitly so charge).

   d. **Criticism:**   Commentators have almost universally scorned *Korematsu* as one of the worst betrayals of Americans' constitutional rights in the Supreme Court's history. See sources cited in L,K&C, p. 1263, n. c.

      i. **Military necessity:**   Obviously, even the *Korematsu* Court would not have upheld a racial distinction like the one at issue there, if it were not for (what the Court perceived as) extreme emergency. What is most troubling about the decision is not the Court's conclusion that the governmental objective was compelling (since prevention of espionage and sabotage clearly was), but rather, the Court's loose definition of means "necessary" to achieve that objective.

4. **"Separate but equal" treatment:**   Strict scrutiny has traditionally been reserved for those classifications which operate to the ***disadvantage*** of a racial or ethnic minority. But suppose that a classification ***utilizes*** race, but does not explicitly disadvantage either blacks or whites. In this situation, claims that there has been "equal application of the law" have usually failed; the school desegregation cases (including the rejection of the "separate but equal" theory, *infra*, p. 277) are the most notable example.

   Example 1: A Virginia statute prohibits marriage between a white and a non-white. The state rebuts an equal protection attack by contending that the statute applies "equally" to whites and blacks, since members of each race are punished to the same degree.

   Held, the statute violates equal protection. The statute contains a racial classification, and the fact that it has "equal application" does not immunize it from strict scrutiny. Since the legislative history shows that the statute was enacted to "preserve the racial integrity" of citizens (i.e., whites), the statute has only an invidious, discriminatory, purpose, and has no "legitimate overriding" one. ***Loving v. Virginia***, 388 U.S. 1 (1967).

Example 2: Seattle's public-school system, in order to reduce school-by-school racial imbalance, sometimes makes the decision whether to allow a student to transfer into a particular school based solely on whether that student would improve the racial balance in the school.

Held, this race-based scheme, even though it is not intended to systematically disadvantage any race, must be strictly scrutinized (and will be struck down). *Parents Involved in Community Schools v. Seattle School District No. 1*, infra, p. 306.

a. **Special traits:** There may, however, be ***special traits*** applicable to one race or ethnic group which, if they serve as the basis for a classification, do not necessarily lead to invidious discrimination.

    i. **Alcohol susceptibility:** For instance, there is respectable evidence that American Indians and Eskimos are abnormally susceptible to ***alcohol***; a number of states therefore bar the sale of alcohol to these races. While the Supreme Court has never decided the issue, the Court might well hold that such a classification is not invidious, and does not disadvantage the races at which it is directed. If so, such a statute would probably be upheld.

    ii. **Sickle-cell test:** Similarly, a state might require that all African Americans undergo testing for ***sickle-cell anemia***. Again, such a statute would probably be upheld on the theory that it is benign rather than invidious. See L,K&C, p. 1264, n. 2. The same would presumably be true of a requirement that persons of Jewish ancestry undergo testing for Tay Sachs disease.

    iii. **Overbreadth:** However, these statutes could be subject to attack on an ***overbreadth*** theory, i.e., a theory that the government may not use racial groups as a substitute for an individualized determination. Such an argument seems unlikely to succeed where individualized treatment would be impractical (e.g., testing all racial groups for all genetic defects, even though a particular defect could almost never occur in most of the races). But where individualized judgments *are* feasible, the Court may well insist upon them even though the use of race as an initial screening device makes matters simpler.

    iv. **Relation to affirmative action:** This issue of "special traits" is related to the much broader issue of "affirmative action," i.e., the extent to which racial classifications may be used to advantage, rather than disadvantage, the minority race. The affirmative action area is discussed more fully *infra*, p. 285.

5. **Racial classes and the political process:** The Court has not hesitated to strictly scrutinize, and strike down, uses of racial classes as part of the ***political process.***

    a. **Identification of candidates:** For instance, the Court struck down a law requiring each ***candidate's race*** to appear on the ballot, in *Anderson v. Martin*, 375 U.S. 399 (1964). The *Anderson* Court apparently believed that, in light of private attitudes towards African Americans at that time and place, the statute was designed to help white candidates.

b. **More difficult procedures:** Similarly, legislation which, for a racially discriminatory purpose, *modifies the political process* to make certain types of political action more difficult, will be subject to strict scrutiny. Thus in *Hunter v. Erickson*, 393 U.S. 385 (1969), after the Akron City Council adopted a fair housing ordinance, the voters amended the city charter to prohibit any ordinance dealing with racial discrimination in housing, unless it had first been approved by a majority of the voters.

   i. **Holding:** The Supreme Court held that this charter amendment was violative of equal protection, on the theory that it: (1) was an "explicitly racial classification," and (2) clearly made it more difficult to enact antidiscrimination ordinances than other types of ordinances (which automatically passed into law following enactment by the Council).

6. **Other areas:** Some other areas in which the state has used racial classifications are as follows:

   a. **Security:** Prison officials sometimes *separate prisoners by race* in order to quell racial tensions or riots. However, *Johnson v. California*, discussed *infra*, p. 333, holds that a prison system's decision to routinely segregate newly-arrived prisoners by race must be *strictly scrutinized*.

   b. **Official records:** The state may keep official statistics by race, if, but only if, the statistics serve some useful purpose (e.g., a sociological one). Thus the recording of the race of a husband and wife in every divorce has been upheld (*Tancil v. Woolls*, 379 U.S. 19 (1964)), but the keeping of separate lists of blacks and whites in voting and tax records was held to be without useful purpose, and therefore violative of equal protection, in a companion case (*Virginia Board of Elections v. Hamm*, 379 U.S. 19 (1964)).

   c. **Child custody and adoption:** Some states take race into account in decisions on *adoption* and *child custody*. The use of racial considerations for these purposes will certainly be subject to strict scrutiny, and few if any such uses will survive that review.

   i. **Child custody:** The one case decided by the Supreme Court in this area concerned child custody. In *Palmore v. Sidoti*, 466 U.S. 429 (1984), two white parents were divorced, and custody of the child was given to the mother. The mother then married an African American, and the Florida courts transferred custody to the father on the grounds that if the daughter remained with her mother and stepfather, she would become "vulnerable to peer pressures [and] suffer from the social stigmatization that is sure to come." The Supreme Court unanimously reversed, finding that the Florida court's order could not survive strict scrutiny. The Court conceded that the private biases on which the Florida court relied were probably real ones, but held that the law *may not, directly or indirectly, give effect to such private prejudices*. (In strict scrutiny terms, the Court apparently held that the state's goal of awarding custody based on the "best interests of the child" was a sufficiently compelling one, but that bowing to private prejudices was not a necessary means of accomplishing that goal.)

   ii. **Adoption:** If a state were to impose a rule that in *adoption* situations, the adoptive parent and the child must be of the same race, there is little doubt that the rationale of *Palmore* would dictate that the state rule be struck down. It is less clear whether race may be considered as *one factor among many*. The rationale of *Palmore* would appear to mean that the possibility of prejudice and social rejection may not be considered by adoption authorities even as one factor among many. However, the broader interest in ensuring that the adoptive parents and child are culturally compatible, and that the child will feel a sense of unity with the adoptive parents, might well be recognized as a compelling one.

F. Segregation and its remedies: Most of the racial classifications discussed above imposed fairly direct, visible, burdens on racial or ethnic minorities. But some, like the miscegenation statute in *Loving v. Virginia*, purported to treat all races "identically," even though they used a racial classification. The most important example of government action which classifies by race, but which, superficially at least, does not explicitly disadvantage minorities, is ***segregation***, i.e., the maintenance of physical separateness between the races.

1. **Summary of issues:** Since 1954, officially-sanctioned segregation not only in the public schools but in other areas has been treated as a ***clear violation of equal protection***. Therefore, the principal issues related to segregation have been not whether intentional segregation violates the Constitution, but rather: (a) How does one distinguish between "intentional," or *de jure*, segregation (which is unconstitutional) and unintentional, or *de facto*, segregation (which is not)? and (b) What are the ***remedies*** for official segregation? Prior to a discussion of these issues, however, some history is in order.

2. **The "separate but equal" doctrine (*Plessy v. Ferguson*):** Initially, the Supreme Court's view was that ***"separate but equal" treatment did not violate equal protection***. This doctrine was formulated in ***Plessy v. Ferguson***, 163 U.S. 537 (1896), where the Court upheld a Louisiana law calling for separate-but-equal accommodations for white and black railroad passengers.

   a. **Rationale:** The majority reasoned that laws such as this one related only to "social" equality, not to political or civil equality. Social equality was not, the Court held, a goal of the Equal Protection Clause, and could be attained only through ***voluntary action*** by individuals, not by statutes.

      i. **Not badge of inferiority:** Also, the Court reasoned, the law itself did not "stamp ... the colored race with a badge of inferiority." If African Americans felt inferior under the law, "it is not by reason of anything found in the act, but solely because the colored race chooses to put that construction upon it."

   b. **Dissent:** The first Justice Harlan, in a classic dissent, argued that the law did indeed violate equal protection. Although it appeared facially neutral, "[e]very one knows that [it] had its origin in the purpose, not so much to exclude white persons from railroad cars occupied by blacks, as to exclude colored people from coaches occupied by or assigned to white persons." The statute therefore interfered with the personal freedom of African Americans.

      i. **"Color blindness":** Harlan then added, in an oft-cited remark, that "***our Constitution is color-blind***." Some have argued that Harlan meant this remark to include "benign" or "reverse" discrimination based on race.

3. ***Brown v. Bd. of Ed.:*** *Plessy v. Ferguson's* validation of "separate but equal" segregation remained the law until 1954. (However, in a series of pre-1954 cases involving graduate school education, the Court found that facilities available to African Americans were not in fact "equal" to those given to whites.) Then, in ***Brown v. Board of Education***, 347 U.S.

483 (1954), the Court explicitly ***rejected the "separate but equal" doctrine***, at least insofar as public education was concerned.

a. **Rationale:**   The Court reasoned that even where all-black and all-white schools were equal in terms of "tangible" factors, intangible factors necessarily prevented children who were restricted to all-black schools from receiving equal educational opportunities. In particular, racial segregation "generates [in African American students] a feeling of inferiority as to their status in the community that may affect their hearts and minds in a way unlikely ever to be undone. … Separate educational facilities are ***inherently unequal.***"

   i. **Expert opinion:**   In reaching this conclusion, the Court also relied on the findings of psychologists and educators who had concluded from their research that segregation gave African American pupils a sense of inferiority, which in turn impaired their motivation to learn and their success at learning.

   ii. **Fourteenth Amendment's history irrelevant:**   One factor upon which the *Brown* Court did ***not*** particularly rely was the ***legislative history*** of the Fourteenth Amendment itself. The Court noted that, at the time that Amendment was adopted, blacks in the South were not educated at all, and even in the North there was no compulsory public education system for whites, let alone blacks. Therefore, nothing in the legislative history of the Amendment gave the Court any real clue about what Congress intended with respect to school segregation. Instead, the Court decided to focus on public education as it stood in 1954, not as it stood when the Amendment was adopted in 1868.

b. **Also applicable to federal government:**   On the same day as *Brown* was decided, the Court held that the ***federal government*** could not be permitted to operate racially-segregated schools any more than could the states. In *Bolling v. Sharpe*, 347 U.S. 497 (1954), the Court held the racial segregation of the District of Columbia public schools to be in violation of the Fifth Amendment's Due Process Clause. The Court concluded that such segregation was not reasonably related to any proper governmental objective, and thus was an arbitrary deprivation of African American students' liberty. Given that such conduct by the ***states*** was not constitutionally permissible, "[i]t would be unthinkable that the same Constitution would impose a lesser duty on the Federal Government."

4. **Criticism of empirical basis:**   A casual reading of *Brown v. Bd. of Ed.* gives the impression that the Court was relying principally upon ***social science*** and ***empirical evidence***, i.e., factual evidence that segregation indeed harms African American students. But if that is the basis for the Court's decision, it may be criticized. As one commentator has said, "I would not have the constitutional rights of Negroes — or of other Americans — rest on any such flimsy foundation as some of the scientific demonstrations in these records. [Behavioral science findings] have an uncertain expectancy of life." 30 N.Y.U. L. REV. 157-58.

a. **Possibility of new evidence:**   For instance, one could imagine new findings suggesting that, where there are truly equal tangible facilities, African American students do ***better*** in segregated schools than as a minority in a school where they are subject to hostility, and possibly violence, from the white majority. See Wechsler, *Toward Neutral Principles of Constitutional Law*, 73 HARV. L. REV. 33.

b. **Change in African Americans' views:** Furthermore, since such a psychologically-focused theory turns on African Americans' own feelings about segregation, such a theory would presumably no longer be valid if a majority of black students or parents in a given community preferred separation. Constitutional requirements could then theoretically vary from town to town, depending on the views of local African Americans; such a result would not foster the uniformity and predictability usually considered desirable in constitutional (or other) law.

5. **Other public facilities:** Although *Brown* by its terms applied only to schools, the Court extended its rejection of the "separate but equal" doctrine to many ***other public facilities*** during the following ten years.

6. **Implementation of *Brown (Brown II)*:** The Court in *Brown*, by pronouncing official segregation to be a violation of equal protection, did not by that pronouncement alone do much to modify the actual educational patterns of Kansas or any other state. It was only by a long series of "implementation" decisions that a significant reduction in school segregation came about. The first of these implementation decisions was a continuation of *Brown* itself; in *Brown v. Board of Education*, 349 U.S. 294 (1955), the so-called ***Brown II*** decision, the Court did several significant things:

   a. **Lower federal courts:** It gave the ***federal district courts*** primary responsibility for supervising desegregation because of their "proximity to local conditions" and the "possible need for further hearings."

   b. **Equitable principles:** The Court gave no precise guidelines for carrying out desegregation. Instead, it directed the district courts to use "***general equitable principles.***"

   c. **"All deliberate speed":** A plaintiff whose constitutional rights have been violated by state action would normally be entitled to ***immediate*** relief. But, apparently because it feared the chaos and violence that might develop if attempts were made to carry out desegregation instantly, the Court authorized the district courts to take into account the public interest in eliminating desegregation "in a systematic and effective manner." However, the burden of proving any need for delay was placed upon the school boards, and the lower courts were ordered to implement desegregation "with ***all deliberate speed.***"

7. **Aftermath of *Brown*:** For almost a decade after *Brown*, the Supreme Court rarely intervened in the desegregation process, leaving this to the federal district courts and to local politics. However, in *Cooper v. Aaron*, 358 U.S. 1 (1958) (discussed *supra*, p. 11), where the governor of Arkansas had used the National Guard to block desegregation of a Little Rock high school, all nine Justices refused to grant to the Little Rock Board of Education a 2 1/2 year delay in desegregation. The Court refused to allow the constitutional rights of African American children to be compromised by actions of the governor and the legislature, even though the school board itself had made good-faith efforts to desegregate.

8. **Specific rules for desegregating:** Then, beginning in a 1963 case, the Court began to lay down much more specific guidelines concerning what means were acceptable for implementing desegregation. Some of the important principles which emerged from this line of cases are as follows.

   a. **Minority-to-majority transfer invalid:** Some school districts rezoned to create schools that would be initially desegregated, but then permitted any student whose race was in a minority in a particular school to transfer to a school where he would be in the majority. These ***"minority-to-majority" transfer plans*** were invalidated in *Goss v. Board of Education*, 373 U.S. 683 (1963), on the grounds that such schemes "inevitably lead toward segregation of the students by race."

b. Closing of public schools: A county's scheme to ***close its public schools*** rather than comply with a desegregation order, and then to fund white-only private schools through state and local tax credits and grants, was rejected in *Griffin v. County School Board*, 377 U.S. 218 (1964). The Court indicated that a county could under some circumstances close its public schools, but that it could not do so for an ***unconstitutional purpose***, which avoiding desegregation obviously was.

c. "Freedom of choice" plans rejected: Many districts adopted ***"freedom of choice"*** plans, under which any student could attend the school of his choice. In *Green v. County School Board*, 391 U.S. 430 (1968), a small school district had about a 50% African American population, two schools, and little residential segregation. After the "freedom of choice" plan had been in operation for three years, no white child had chosen to go to the formerly black school, and 85% of the black students remained in that school.

   i. Holding: In these circumstances, the Court held, the plan did not adequately desegregate the schools. Once a school system had been officially segregated, the Constitution required that it be converted to a "unitary, non-racial system of public education."

   ii. *Green's* focus on effect, not cost: *Green* is probably most significant not for the fact that it rejected "freedom of choice" plans, but for the fact that it was the first case in which the Supreme Court attached explicit importance to the ***effect*** of desegregation measures, and not merely to the ***intent*** with which those measures were enacted. Once official segregation existed, ***good intentions*** on the part of the school board ***were not sufficient***; whatever affirmative measures were needed to bring about a unitary, non-racial system must be implemented. This doctrine has essentially continued in force to date.

9. *Swann v. Charlotte-Mecklenburg:* Perhaps the most important case giving guidance to the district courts and school boards concerning the techniques of desegregation came in ***Swann v. Charlotte-Mecklenburg Board of Education***, 402 U.S. 1 (1971). In *Swann*, the Court made the following rulings:

a. Must have *de jure* segregation: The federal courts may not order a school board to adjust the racial composition of any of its schools (***no matter how great the racial imbalance as between schools***) unless there has been a finding that there was ***officially-maintained*** (i.e., intentional or *de jure*) segregation. Thus a federal court may not order *de facto* segregation, no matter how severe, to be cured by adjustment of racial balance. (However, the Court noted, the school board itself could constitutionally exercise ***discretion*** to adjust racial balances, "in order to prepare students to live in a pluralistic society. ... ")

b. Racial quotas: Once official segregation is found, the court may, in determining the appropriate remedy, consider what the ***ratio*** is of black students to white students for the district as a whole. While the court may ***not*** require that every school in the district have *precisely that ratio*, the district-wide ratio may be considered as a "useful starting point in shaping a remedy."

c. **Single-race schools:** The fact that one or more schools that are completely or almost completely *single-race remain* in a district does *not* necessarily mean that desegregation has not yet been accomplished. But such schools must be carefully scrutinized by the court, and it is up to the school board to show that the racial concentration in these schools is not due to official segregation but to other causes (e.g., residential patterns).

d. **Rezoning:** *Rezoning*, i.e., the redrawing of attendance zones, is a *permissible* technique for remedying segregation. Furthermore, the new zones do *not* necessarily have to be either "compact" or *contiguous*. Thus the Court approved, in *Swann* itself, a system of *"pairing"* and *"clustering"* schools from non-contiguous parts of the city. The effect of this scheme was to combine predominantly African American schools with predominantly white schools, so as to bring racial balance to each school in the pair or cluster.

   i. **Not usable for *de facto cases*:** Again, the Court emphasized that such an order could never be given to remedy *de facto* segregation; it was only because the school authorities presented the lower court with a "loaded gameboard" that this kind of alteration of attendance zones was permissible.

e. **Busing:** The Court also *approved busing* as a means of bringing about desegregation. "Desegregation plans cannot be limited to the walk-in school." The scheme ordered in *Swann* was valid, because it did not result in excessive amounts of busing, compared with the amount being done voluntarily by the district prior to the desegregation order.

   i. **Danger to health or education:** However, the Court indicated that a busing scheme would not be upheld if "the time or distance of travel is so great as to risk either the health of the children or significantly impinge on the educational process."

f. **Later unintentional imbalances allowed:** *Swann* and later cases establish that once the effects of official segregation have been even *temporarily remedied*, later imbalances caused by *changing residential patterns* or other non-official conduct may not be cured by federal court order. (The school board itself, of course, always remains free to cure such imbalances as a matter of discretion; the board simply cannot be forced by a federal court to do so.)

   i. **Illustration:** A post-*Swann* case illustrates this principle, and demonstrates that court-supervised desegregation will not necessarily ever lead to a desegregated school system. In *Board of Education v. Dowell*, 498 U.S. 237 (1991), the Court held that as long as the school board had complied in good faith with the desegregation decree (which it had apparently done for the six prior years), and as long as the vestiges of past *de jure* discrimination had been eliminated *"to the extent practicable,"* the desegregation decree should be lifted and the school district allowed to revert to a system of neighborhood schools. This was true even though, evidence showed, 33 of the 64 elementary schools would then be either more-than-90% black or more-than-90% white. (If the present residential segregation was due to the prior official school segregation, then obviously the Supreme Court's "vestiges of past discrimination removed" standard would not be satisfied. But if the residential segregation was due primarily to *people's personal choices about where to live*, then, the Supreme Court indicated, the court desegregation order would have to be lifted and the district could revert to neighborhood — and thus *de facto* segregated — schools.) See more about ending federal-court supervision of desegregation, *infra*, p. 285.

10. Desegregation in the North: For the first twenty years following *Brown*, virtually all of the Supreme Court's school desegregation cases involved the South, where segregation was generally *required by law* at the time *Brown* was decided. These cases thus presented the Court with little need to distinguish between *de jure* and *de facto* segregation, or to prescribe methods for determining whether a school board had intended to segregate — all racial imbalance which the Court evaluated could be linked quite directly to statutorily-required segregation. But then, starting in 1974, the Court began to hear cases involving claimed segregation in the *North*, where there was virtually no statutorily-authorized segregation at the time of *Brown v. Bd. of Ed.* In a series of Northern cases, the Court attempted to lay down some rules for dealing with a number of new issues, most of them relating to the *de facto/de jure* distinction.

11. *Keyes* (the Denver case): The first Northern case was *Keyes v. School District #1*, 413 U.S. 189 (1973), involving the Denver system. Segregation in Colorado had never been statutorily required. But the district court found that Denver school authorities had used gerrymandered attendance zones, school construction policies, and other devices to purposely keep one part of the city's school system, the Park Hill area, racially segregated. The Supreme Court then made the following rulings for dealing with this and other cases where there was no statutorily-mandated segregation:

    a. ***De jure* requirement maintained:** The Court repeated that only *de jure* segregation, not *de facto* segregation, could be redressed by court action, and emphasized that *de jure* segregation would be found to exist only where there was a *purpose or intent* to segregate.

    b. Segregation of one part of district: The most important aspect of *Keyes* is in the Court's treatment of the *effects* of a finding that there was intentional segregation as to *one substantial part* of a *larger* metropolitan district. Such a finding could, the Court held, have one or both of the following effects:

        i. Dual system: The finding of intentional segregation of a substantial portion of the district would create a *prima facie case* that there was a "dual" school system, i.e., that the *entire district* was segregated. This *prima facie* demonstration of a dual system could be rebutted only if the school board showed that the segregated part should be viewed as a *separate, unrelated* area, and that segregation in that one part had no effect on the others.

        ii. Probative of segregative intent: Even if the school board succeeded in showing that the district was divided into unrelated areas, the finding of segregative intent as to one area (the Park Hill area) would create a *presumption* that segregated patterns in the other areas were intentional, not coincidental. This presumption, in turn, could only be rebutted if the school board showed either that: (1) segregative intent was not in fact one of the motivating factors in the board's actions as to these other areas (it would not be enough to show that some hypothetical "innocent" motivation "could" have produced those actions by the board); or (2) past segregative acts by the school board did not "create or contribute to the current segregated condition" of the schools. Thus the board would have to prove *either lack of intent*, or *lack of a causal connection* between intent and segregation.

c. **Summary:** Thus, as a practical matter, a plaintiff who is able to show segregative intent as to one portion of a large school district enjoys an enormous tactical advantage over his adversary: the burden of proof is shifted entirely to the school board to explain away segregated conditions in other portions of the district.

d. **African Americans and Hispanics aggregated:** The *Keyes* Court defined as segregated any school having a *combined* predominance of African Americans *and Hispanics*. It did so on the theory that these groups had suffered "identical discrimination in treatment," at least in the Southwest. This conclusion had the effect of identifying more segregated schools than if African American enrollment alone were considered.

12. **Interdistrict remedies:** Many of the country's big-city school districts are now predominantly African American. If a city's school system is shown to be *de jure* segregated, may a federal judge order a remedy which *includes suburban school districts*? In *Milliken v. Bradley*, 418 U.S. 717 (1974), the Court answered this question, for most purposes, in the *negative*. The case was decided by a 5-4 split.

a. **Facts:** The school district for the city of Detroit is predominantly African American. The Detroit suburbs, consisting of numerous towns each having its own school district, are predominantly white. A federal trial judge, after concluding that the city had practiced *de jure* segregation, concluded that a Detroit-only desegregation plan would not be effective, since many schools would remain more than 75% African American. He therefore ordered that 53 surrounding suburban communities participate in the desegregation plan.

b. **Majority holding:** Justice Burger, writing for a majority of the Court, reversed. He cited the general principle of equity that "[t]he scope of the remedy is determined by the nature and extent of the constitutional violation." Thus there could be a cross-district remedy *only if there had been a cross-district wrong*, i.e., segregation in Detroit that *caused an effect in the suburbs*, or vice versa.

   i. **Practical problems:** Burger also pointed to the practical problems that would result from a cross-district desegregation order. Difficult jurisdictional issues would arise regarding the right to levy taxes, the right to establish attendance zones, the authority to locate and construct new schools, etc. And such consolidation would weaken the strong tradition of local control over public education.

   ii. **State's role irrelevant:** The majority also rejected the dissent's argument (an argument also advanced by the district court), that there had been significant participation by the *state of Michigan* in the Detroit segregation. Even assuming that this was so (which the majority denied), the constitutional right of black students in Detroit was merely "to attend a unitary school system *in that district*."

c. **Dissent:** The four dissenters in *Milliken* produced two opinions, the main one by Justice White.

   i. **White's dissent:** White's dissent stressed that the city of Detroit was a *subdivision of the state*, and that it was the state, not the locality, that must "respond to the command of the Fourteenth Amendment." Justice White simply saw no historical support for a rule that desegregation remedies must stop at the district line.

13. **Segregated colleges and universities:** So far, we've spoken only about segregation in the context of elementary schools up through high schools. Where government has intentionally segregated in a **college or university**, the same basic rule applies: this *de jure* segregation violates the Equal Protection Clause and must be dismantled. See *U.S. v. Fordice*, 505 U.S. 717 (1992).

14. **State and congressional efforts to curb busing:** Several states have attempted to **limit** the use of **busing** as a judicially-ordered desegregation tool. The Supreme Court has issued two opinions concerning the states' right to do this.

    a. **Law stricken in Seattle case:** In a case involving a Seattle busing plan, *Washington v. Seattle School Dist. No. 1*, 458 U.S. 457 (1982), the state's effort to nullify the busing plan was ruled **unconstitutional.**

        i. **Facts:** Seattle enacted a plan to undo *de facto* segregation in its schools by, *inter alia*, use of mandatory busing. The State of Washington then enacted, by initiative, a law **preventing local school districts** from enacting busing plans (but not purporting to limit a court's right to order busing as a remedy for *de jure* segregation).

        ii. **Law held violative of equal protection:** By a 5-4 vote, the Court held the state initiative violative of equal protection. The majority opinion, written by Justice Blackmun, relied on *Hunter v. Erickson* (*supra*, p. 276), and held that the **reallocation of governmental decision-making power must be done in a racially-neutral manner.** Since the issue of mandatory busing had strong racial overtones, the state could not strip local school boards of the right to decide busing matters, yet leave these boards with control over other local school matters. The state law was unconstitutional because it made it "more difficult for certain racial and religious minorities … to achieve legislation that is in their interest."

    b. **California case allows limits on remedies:** But in a companion case from California, the Court **upheld** an **amendment to the state constitution** which had the effect of preventing judicially-ordered busing in cases of *de facto* segregation. *Crawford v. Los Angeles Board of Education*, 458 U.S. 527 (1982).

        i. **Facts:** *Crawford* arose from an earlier California Supreme Court opinion which had interpreted the equal protection clause of the **state** constitution to bar *de facto*, not just *de jure*, school segregation. The California Constitution was then amended to prevent state courts from ordering mandatory busing unless a federal court would order such busing to redress a violation of the federal Equal Protection Clause (i.e., unless the segregation were found to be *de jure*).

        ii. **Amendment upheld:** Eight members of the Court found this amendment to be constitutional. The majority's basic rationale was that California, having gone further in enforcing the right to racially-balanced schools than the federal Constitution required, should be **free to return** in part to the federal standard. The majority did not see this as a case in which the *Hunter v. Erickson* principle was applicable, since the political decision-making process with respect to busing had not been modified; this was simply a case in which an anti-discrimination or desegregation law had been modified, **something which a state has always been permitted to do.**

iii. **Absence of discriminatory intent:** Had the amendment clearly been enacted by voters for discriminatory *purposes*, the Court suggested, that fact might have made the amendment unconstitutional. But there was no evidence that such a purpose, rather than, say, a desire to have the benefits of neighborhood schooling, motivated most voters.

c. **Distinction between two cases:** One central theme that emerges from a comparison of the *Washington* and *Crawford* cases is that only the *reallocation of decision-making power*, not the mere elimination of a desegregation or anti-discrimination policy, will be found unconstitutional. Desegregation laws and remedies, like, say, fair housing ordinances, may be repealed at any time. But the power to make decisions about racially-linked issues may not be reallocated in a way that makes it harder for minorities to obtain favorable disposition of such issues (as, for instance, by depriving them of the ability to win at the local level, something they had accomplished in Seattle).

15. **Ending District-Court supervision:** More than 50 years have now passed since *Brown v. Board of Ed.* Some school districts have been under federal-court supervision for desegregation for nearly that entire time. When does that supervision end? It ends when the school district has been "*restored to unitary status.*" That is, supervision (and constitutionally-mandated desegregation efforts) must end as soon as the *effects* of the *official* segregation have been eliminated. Supervision will *not* necessarily last until the system is truly integrated.

a. **Neighborhood re-segregation:** So the fact that *neighborhoods* have become *re-segregated* (after school desegregation began) based *on private housing decisions*, and that this has led to re-segregated local schools, can't be used to justify extending federal-court supervision.

b. **White flight:** Similarly, the fact that busing or other desegregation methods have caused *whites* to *flee* the school district entirely for the surrounding suburbs, leaving the former *de jure* segregated city system heavily minority, can't be used to delay the end of judicial supervision. See *Missouri v. Jenkins*, 515 U.S. 70 (1995).

c. **Use of race for pupil assignments:** Once unitary status has been restored, any use of race in making pupil assignments will be strictly scrutinized, as if the official segregation had never occurred. That's what happened in the Louisville portion of *Parents Involved in Community Schools v. Seattle School District No. 1, infra*, p. 306 — the fact that de facto segregated housing patterns had caused individual schools to become racially isolated once again was not a reason to allow race-conscious pupil assignments to occur, a majority of the Court believed.

IV. AFFIRMATIVE ACTION AND "BENIGN" DISCRIMINATION

A. **"Benign" discrimination generally:** We live in a world in which governments, universities, major corporations, etc., are all trying (or at least claim to be trying) to reverse the effects of past discrimination. Yet, past discrimination often cannot be reversed without treating people differently, based upon explicit consideration of the very criterion on which the past discrimination was based (e.g., race or sex).

1. **Problem:** Not surprisingly, such attempts to remedy past discrimination (sometimes called *"benign"* or *"reverse"* discrimination, and more frequently, *"affirmative action"*)

present major constitutional questions in their own right. Probably the most important is: What standard should be used to review the "benign" use of a "suspect" classification, such as race? Since classifications which disadvantage a racial minority will be strictly scrutinized, and may be justified only where they are "necessary" to fulfill a "compelling" governmental objective (see *supra*, p. 272), is the same strict scrutiny required of "affirmative action" attempts based on race?

    a. Strict scrutiny: The answer is *"yes,"* the same strict scrutiny is required of "affirmative action" attempts based on race as is required of race-based classifications that disadvantage a minority. This is the result of the landmark decision in *City of Richmond v. J.A. Croson Co.*, discussed *infra*, p. 313.

    2. Sex considered before race: Before we begin our discussion of the benign use of racial classifications, however, we will discuss the benign use of *sexual* classes. Although discrimination against women is not viewed with the same extremely high level of suspicion as is discrimination against African Americans (compare *supra*, p. 265 with *infra*, p. 334), the reverse discrimination precedents in the sexual area laid important groundwork for *Croson* and other racial affirmative action cases.

B. Benign use of sex classes: Where a sexual classification *disadvantages* women, it is subjected to "middle-level" scrutiny. That is, the gender-based classification must be "substantially" related to the achievement of "important" governmental objectives. (See *Craig v. Boren, infra*, p. 336.) Perhaps surprisingly, statutes which make sexual classifications which *favor* women, even if enacted solely to remedy past anti-female discrimination, are judged by exactly the same formal standard: the statute will be stricken if the sex-based criterion is not substantially related to an important governmental objective. Thus to put it colloquially, the legislature gets no explicit "brownie points" for attempting to remedy past sexual discrimination.

    1. "Means" aspect most important: However, there is a sense in which a statute that favors women in an attempt to remedy past discrimination may implicitly be subject to gentler review. The Supreme Court has generally acknowledged that the aim of remedying a particular type of past sexual discrimination is itself a worthy and "important" governmental objective. Thus most of the pro-women statutes have passed or failed the Court's middle-level scrutiny principally on whether the *means* part of the test was satisfied, i.e., whether there was a "substantial relationship" between the statute and the discrimination which was to be remedied.

        a. Alimony: Thus an Alabama statute which allowed *alimony* to be awarded only against men was stricken by the Court because of its weakness in the "means," rather than the "end," part of the test. In *Orr v. Orr*, 440 U.S. 268 (1979), the Court recognized that the statute helped serve an important governmental objective, namely, compensating women for discrimination during marriage. But an outright ban on alimony awards against women was *not substantially related* to the worthy objective.

            i. Rationale: The Court observed that the relative financial need of the parties was already required to be considered as part of the divorce process, so that there was no need to use sex as an automatic "proxy for financial dependence." Furthermore, the only women who would be given extra protection by the statute were those who were *not* financially needy; thus the statute's main effect was at odds with its stated purpose.

2. **Difficulty of verifying "benignness":** Observe that it is not always so easy to verify whether discrimination that is claimed to be "benign" really *is*. For instance, a legislature which takes the general view (as Alabama's apparently did, in *Orr, supra*) that women invariably need to be protected may, although claiming that it is helping them by special legislation, in actuality be ***reinforcing a negative and untrue stereotype of them.***

3. **Attempt to remedy past discrimination:** Where a gender classification is used in an attempt to remedy ***specific, objectively-verifiable*** past discrimination against women (rather than to perpetuate stereotypes of women's dependency), the statute is much more likely to be upheld.

   a. **Remedy for job discrimination:** Thus in ***Califano v. Webster***, 430 U.S. 313 (1977), the Court unanimously upheld a Social Security Act provision which in computing a wage earner's "average monthly wage" (upon which benefits are based) allowed women to exclude three more lower-earning years than a man could.

      i. **Rationale:** The Court found that this provision was not the result of "archaic and overbroad generalizations" about women, but was rather the result of prior objectively-verifiable discrimination which had barred most women from all but the lowest-paying jobs. Thus the measure directly, even though only partially, remedied past discrimination.

   b. **Blurry line:** But the line between remedying past discrimination, and merely viewing women stereotypically as incapable of earning a living, may sometimes be quite blurry. For instance, the same year as *Califano v. Webster*, the Court struck down a provision of the Social Security Act which paid benefits to a widow of a covered worker, but paid them to a widower only if he proved dependency on his deceased wife. ***Califano v. Goldfarb***, 430 U.S. 199 (1977). The plurality opinion felt that the provision was not a defensible attempt to help women because they were needier; it was simply an attempt to aid "dependent spouses of deceased wage earners, coupled with a presumption that wives are usually dependent." The plurality found this presumption of dependency impermissible.

      i. **Criticism:** It is hard to see why the presumption in *Webster* (that women have usually received lower wages) is any less objectionable than the presumption in *Goldfarb* that most women are dependents. Each presumption is probably true in most cases though not in all. Perhaps the different result really stems from the fact that one presumption is ***harder to prove or disprove*** in a ***particular case*** than the other. A widow (or a widower) could relatively easily prove dependence on the deceased spouse; therefore, the *Goldfarb* presumption was unnecessary. A woman would find it much more difficult to prove that she had been the victim of lower wages due to employment discrimination, by contrast; therefore, the presumption in *Webster* could not easily have been replaced by a case-by-case determination.

      ii. **Not necessarily benign:** Notice that the discrimination in *Goldfarb* was ***not necessarily "benign,"*** i.e., not necessarily favorable to women. It favored widows over widowers, but a working wife was actually disfavored over a working husband, in that the working wife received for her social security taxes less protection for her spouse than did the working husband. Thus there was not an especially strong reason for the Court to treat this as a statute which favored women and which therefore might be entitled to somewhat less rigorous scrutiny. (However, as stated above, even in true "benign" sex discrimination cases, the formal standard of review seems to be the same as in cases involving anti-women statutes.)

4. **Statutory interpretation or remand:**   The equal protection problem in *Goldfarb* could have been solved *either* by requiring case-by-case determination of dependency for survivors of *both* sexes, or by *not* requiring it for survivors of *either* sex.

   a. **Remove classification:**   Sometimes the Court itself, as a matter of statutory interpretation, may completely remove the sex-based classification (e.g., by completely eliminating the need for case-by-case determination of dependency or, conversely, by making that dependency determination mandatory for both sexes). This will generally happen only where federal legislation is involved.

   b. **Remand:**   Where a state statute is at issue, the Court will typically *remand to the legislature* for the latter to make the decision about which way to modify the statute; this is what happened in *Wengler v. Druggist's Mutual Ins. Co.*, 446 U.S. 142 (1980).

5. **Statutory rape:**   A necessary (though not sufficient) condition for "benign" sex discrimination to be legal is that men and women be *differently situated*, in a way relevant to the statute's purpose. Of all the possible differences between the sexes, the clearest ones are of course *biological*. For instance, the fact that only women may become pregnant led a majority (albeit a bare one) of the Court to declare California's *statutory rape law valid*, even though it applied only to male defendants, in *Michael M. v. Superior Court*, 450 U.S. 464 (1981).

   a. **Nature of statute:**   The statute involved in *Michael M.* made it a crime to have sexual intercourse with a female under the age of eighteen. Thus only men could be liable for "statutory rape" (more precisely, "unlawful sexual intercourse").

   b. **Plurality upholds statute:**   A four-Justice plurality upheld the statute (with Justice Blackmun, concurring in the judgment, supplying the fifth vote). The plurality acknowledged that, since the statute discriminated based on sex, it could be upheld only if the classification bore a "substantial relationship" to "important governmental objectives" (the "middle-level scrutiny" standard of *Craig v. Boren, infra*, p. 336). This test could only be met if men and women were situated differently, in a way that was relevant to the statutory purpose.

      i. **Statutory purpose:**   The plurality found it obvious that the purpose of the statute was to *prevent illegitimate teenage pregnancies*. This purpose was also, the plurality held, an "important governmental objective."

      ii. **Substantial relation:**   The fighting issue in the case, however, was whether there was a *substantial relation* between this important objective and the classification chosen. The plurality felt that there was, for two reasons: (1) Since only women can become pregnant, the male had no direct disincentive from having sex with an unmarried minor. The statute therefore served to "roughly 'equalize' the deterrence on the sexes." (2) Enforcement of the statute was more feasible if the girl was exempted from prosecution, since a successful prosecution would normally require her testimony, which she would generally not give if she might be subjected to prosecution.

   c. **Dissent:**   Four Justices dissented, in opinions written by Justices Brennan and Stevens. The dissenters believed that, even if prevention of illegitimate pregnancy was the statute's goal (something they were not convinced of), the male-only prosecution scheme *did not substantially advance* that objective. They felt that a statute which applied equally to the woman would be a still stronger deterrent (even assuming that *enforcement* might be more difficult). As Justice Stevens put it, "the fact that a class of persons is especially vulnerable to a risk that a statute is designed to avoid is a reason for making the statute applicable to that class."

6. **Draft registration of women:**   The federal government's historical refusal to require the *draft registration* or *conscription* of women might be viewed as "benign" sex discrimination. In *Rostker v. Goldberg*, 453 U.S. 57 (1981), the Court *upheld male-only draft registration*. However, the Court did not view the case as involving affirmative action but rather, military necessity.

   a. **Facts:**   The draft registration process is simply a way of maintaining an inventory of available personnel who may be drafted in the event of a military emergency. An actual draft, in turn, would almost certainly be principally for the purpose of drafting *combat* troops. At least until the Persian Gulf War, the policy of both Congress and the armed services had been that women should not serve in combat. The issue in *Rostker* (at least for the majority) was whether the policy against use of women in combat was sufficient to allow Congress to decline to require registration of women.

   b. **Majority upholds exclusion:**   Six Justices held that the exclusion of women from registration was *not* a violation of equal protection. The majority did not clearly articulate the test to which it was subjecting the regulation. However, it rejected the government's request that a "mere-rationality" standard be used, and implied that it was applying the "heightened scrutiny" (i.e., middle-level scrutiny) standard of *Craig v. Boren*.

   c. **Factors:**   In upholding the exclusion of women despite this middle-level scrutiny, the majority relied upon the following factors:

      i. **Deference to Congress in military affairs:**   In the area of *military affairs*, Congress' authority is extremely broad, and the courts should show even greater-than-usual deference to congressional decisionmaking.

      ii. **Not unthinking stereotype:**   Congress gave careful, and reasoned, consideration whether to register women. In contrast to several other legislative schemes previously reviewed by the Court, the decision not to register women was not the "accidental by-product of a traditional way of thinking about women."

      iii. **Not eligible for combat:**   As noted, women were currently not eligible for combat. (The constitutionality of this restriction was not before the Court.) According to the majority, the purpose of registration is to prepare for the possible drafting of combat troops. Since women would not be drafted for combat posts under the present scheme, the government was justified in not registering them. Because of the combat restrictions, this was a case in which men and women "are *simply not similarly situated* for purposes of a draft or registration for a draft."

7. **New "exceedingly persuasive justification" standard:**   It's not clear whether gender-based schemes that the Court finds to be truly "benign" or compensatory will have to meet the same tough standard that non-benign gender-based enactments now have to meet. In *U.S. v. Virginia, infra*, p. 339, the Court held that gender-based schemes like the one there

(maintenance of all-male status for the Virginia Military Institute) could be sustained only if the state showed an *"exceedingly persuasive justification"* that the Court would look at with "skeptical scrutiny." But the scheme in that case was clearly not a "benign" one, or one that was motivated by a desire to redress past discrimination; it was instead an old scheme that (the Court found) derived from stereotypes about gender roles. It's too soon to tell whether this new, tougher version of mid-level review will be applied to schemes that attempt to reverse prior discrimination against one sex or the other.

C. Race: We turn now to the "benign" use of *racial* classifications. Just as in the sex-based area, the scrutiny is the same "middle level" one for both "benign" and non-benign discrimination, so race-based classification will receive the same *strict* scrutiny whether the classification is supposedly "benign" (i.e., an attempt to help previously disadvantaged racial minorities) or invidious (an attempt by the white majority to hurt African American or other racial minorities). This is the result of *City of Richmond v. J.A. Croson Co.*, discussed *infra*, p. 313.

Croson does not mean that a race-based classification will always be struck down. For instance, a governmental body that had previously discriminated against African-Americans in a very clear way might be able to institute a race-based scheme to eradicate the effects of that discrimination. Similarly, a university that wants to obtain a "diverse" class may give a preference to applicants from underrepresented minorities, as long as this is done as part of an individualized process; see *Grutter v. Bollinger*, *infra*, p. 295. However, any race-based classification will clearly face a *presumption of unconstitutionality*, even if it is motivated by affirmative action concerns.

1. **Significance:** Therefore, a race-conscious affirmative action plan, whether it is in the area of employment, college admissions, voting rights or anywhere else, must be adopted for the purpose of furthering some *"compelling"* governmental interest, and the racial classification must be *necessary* to achieve that compelling governmental interest. The only governmental objectives that have so far been endorsed by the Court as possibly supporting race-conscious affirmative action are (1) the *redressing of clear past discrimination* and (2) the pursuit of *diversity* in a *student body.* The former is the kind of affirmative action on which we will be focusing here.

2. **Past discrimination:** When government institutes an affirmative action plan to accomplish the objective of redressing past racial discrimination, two key questions arise: (1) what kind of *proof* must there be that there's really been past discrimination? and (2) *who is it* who must have discriminated? So far, the Supreme Court hasn't given much guidance on these issues. A reasonable guess would go like this:

    a. **No findings needed:** As to question 1 — what kind of proof of discrimination is needed — there must be *quite strong and specific evidence of past discrimination* against African Americans or other racial minorities whom the plan is helping. It's not enough that the government has a general belief that there's been discrimination. Nor is it enough that African Americans are in some sense *"under-represented"* among the job-holders, students, contractors, or whatever "goody" is in issue.

        Example: The Richmond, Virginia City Council notices that less than 1% of the city's construction contracts have been awarded to minority-owned businesses in the past five years. It therefore infers that general contractors have discriminated against minority-owned firms, and requires that henceforth, 30% of the dollar amount of all City-funded construction projects must go to minority-owned firms.

Held, this racially-based classification must be subjected to strict scrutiny, and will only be upheld if necessary to achieve a compelling governmental purpose. If there were clear evidence of past racial discrimination by general contractors, the City would have a compelling interest in having its tax dollars not used to support such discrimination by private firms. But here, the city did not have "hard" evidence of such past discrimination. The fact that black-owned firms got only a tiny share of contracts, and made up only a tiny portion of the local contractors' association, was not enough to prove such past discrimination — there was no evidence that there really were more black-owned firms than this, and "the relevant statistical pool for purposes of demonstrating discriminatory exclusion must be the number of minorities qualified to undertake the particular task." *City of Richmond v. J.A. Croson Co.*, 488 U.S. 469 (1989), discussed extensively *infra*, p. 313.

    i. **Formal findings probably not necessary:** On the other hand, it's probably not necessary that there be a formal *"finding"* by a court that this discrimination took place. So for instance, if a particular police force had statistically far fewer African Americans than would be expected based on the number of qualified African Americans in the local labor force, this might be enough to demonstrate that there was discrimination; in that case, the police department might be able to voluntarily put in a plan that gave African Americans some preference in the hiring process. Similarly, the department might be able to settle a discrimination suit by agreeing to put in such a plan. But there does have to be quite clear evidence of past discrimination, not mere supposition.

   b. **Discrimination by whom:** Now for Question 2 — *who* must have discriminated? Obviously, a race-conscious affirmative action plan is most likely to be upheld if the past discrimination was by the ***particular government entity in question.*** If the past discrimination was not by the particular governmental entity involved in the present case (e.g., the particular governmental employer), but was in the same ***general domain*** (e.g., the ***same industry***), this probably also justifies a race-conscious remedy. For instance, in *Croson, supra*, the required "compelling" government objective would have been shown by hard evidence that general contractors had discriminated against black-owned contracting firms, even had the City itself not discriminated. On the other hand, ***the mere fact that there has been general "societal" discrimination is not enough to justify race-conscious measures.***

3. **Quotas:** One device that is especially vulnerable to Equal Protection attack is the racially-based *quota*. A racially-based quota is an inflexible number of admissions slots, dollar amounts, or other "goodies" set aside for minorities. (For more about the definition of "quota," see sub-paragraph (a) below.) In the aftermath of the decision in *Richmond v. Croson*, it seems probable that ***virtually all racially-based quotas will be struck down even where the government is trying to eradicate the effects of past discrimination*** — the Court will probably say that a quota is not "necessary" to remedy discrimination, that more flexible "goals" can do the job.

    Example: Recall the facts of *Croson* — Richmond tried to remedy what it saw as past discrimination against black-owned contracting firms by giving them 30% of future city contracts. Even if there had been hard evidence that there really was discrimination in the past (evidence that Richmond didn't have), and thus even had Richmond been acting in pursuit of a compelling objective (getting rid of past discrimination), Richmond would probably still have lost, because the 30% requirement was a hard-and-fast one, i.e., a quota. A majority of the Court would probably have said that a flexible goal would have done the job just as well — the City could have required general contractors to show that they "tried" to assign 30% of the contracts to black-owned firms, without automatically penalizing them if they failed. Since a flexible goal would have done as well, the quota wasn't "necessary," and Richmond would (probably) have lost.

    a. **What is a "quota":**   What, then, will be considered to be a *"quota"*? Apparently the term will now be quite *narrowly-construed* following the affirmative-action-in-admissions decision in *Grutter v. Bollinger, infra*, p. 295. The majority opinion there says that "properly understood, a 'quota' is a program in which a certain *fixed number or proportion of opportunities* are '*reserved exclusively* for certain minority groups.' ... Quotas 'impose a fixed number or percentage which *must be attained*, or which *cannot be exceeded*'." A program that merely contains aspirational *"goals"* does *not* thereby become a quota. Nor does a program become a quota merely because membership in a certain group is made a *"plus factor"* — even a very strong plus factor — as long as the plus factor is administered as part of *individualized evaluations*.

        i. **Point system:**   On the other hand, a system that automatically assigns a certain fixed number of *"points"* for a certain race or ethnicity *will* be treated by the present court as being the equivalent of a quota, even though no particular slots are reserved exclusively for members of the minority group. That's the lesson of the Court's other recent affirmative-action-in-admissions case, *Gratz v. Bollinger, infra*, p. 298.

    4. **Court-ordered vs. voluntary:**   Some affirmative action plans are *ordered by a court* to remedy past discrimination; other plans are *voluntarily adopted* by a public entity to remedy past discrimination. Does it make any difference to the constitutionality of the plan whether it's court-ordered or voluntary? The answer is not yet clear — court-ordered race-conscious remedies may be spared the strict scrutiny given to voluntary plans put in place by legislatures or executive officials, perhaps on the theory that a court-ordered remedy is less likely to constitute disguised political patronage than, say, a legislature's plan.

    5. **Some contexts:**   Let us now turn to some special contexts in which affirmative action has been challenged as being itself a violation of the equal protection rights of the white majority. The contexts which we will examine include: (1) school desegregation; (2) voting rights; (3) preferential admissions; (4) minority set-asides; and (5) employment.

D. **Desegregation:**   The theory that the Constitution requires that all government action be "color-blind" was rejected quite early in one area, that of *school desegregation*. In *Swann v. Charlotte-Mecklenburg Board of Education*, 402 U.S. 1 (1971) (discussed extensively *supra*, p. 280), the Court explicitly upheld the use of race-conscious pupil assignments in order to remedy past intentional segregation.

    1. **Effect of *Croson*:**   But even in the school desegregation area, *Richmond v. Croson*, (*infra*, p. 313) will probably make race-conscious remedies much harder to justify. The Court will presumably apply strict scrutiny to any race-conscious remedy for discrimination, such as pupil assignments or teacher assignments that explicitly take account of race. The Court will have to be satisfied that the race-conscious measure is "necessary" to eradicate the prior segregation, and this may be a hard burden to satisfy.

   a. ***De facto* segregation:** Now suppose that a school district is trying to remedy ***de facto*** segregation. Here, it is even more clear that any race-conscious remedy will be strictly scrutinized, and probably invalidated, in light of *Croson*. First, the Supreme Court might not even agree that maintaining racially-balanced schools (where the racial imbalance is *de facto* rather than *de jure*) is a "compelling" objective. Even if this objective were found to be compelling, the court would be likely to hold that there are race-neutral alternatives that would cure the problem with acceptable speed, so that race-conscious methods (such as a race-based pupil assignment scheme like the one described in the above example) are not "necessary" to fulfill that objective.

E. Preferential admissions to universities: Next, let's turn to the use of race in ***admissions to colleges and universities.*** As the result of three decisions since the turn of the century — two 2003 cases involving the University of Michigan and one 2013 case involving the University of Texas — we now know that:

   [1] public universities and colleges ***may explicitly consider minority racial status*** as a factor that increases the odds of admission, so as to promote the compelling goal of ***"education diversity"***;

   [2] these institutions ***may not award "points" for minority status***, or otherwise pursue ***mechanical quota-like schemes,*** and must instead evaluate each candidate as part of a ***"holistic" review*** that treats race as ***merely one factor among others; and***

   [3] even when an institution uses a non-quota "holistic" race-conscious method, that method may be used ***only*** if the institution carries the burden of showing that ***no workable race-neutral alternatives*** would achieve the educational benefits of diversity ***as well or almost as well*** as the race-conscious method being used.

The three cases are ***Grutter v. Bollinger***, 539 U.S. 306 (2003) (upholding by 5-4 the University of Michigan Law School's "race as one factor among many" approach); ***Gratz v. Bollinger***, 539 U.S. 244 (2003) (striking down as a violation of equal protection, by a 6-3 vote, Michigan's undergraduate scheme, by which members of favored racial and ethnic groups got an automatic 20 points of the 100 points needed for admission); and ***Fisher v. Univ. of Texas***, ___ U.S. ___ (2013) (holding that the University of Texas' race-conscious but non-quota-based system would be valid only if the University showed that no workable race-neutral methods were reasonably available; the case did not decide whether the University could meet that test).

   1. ***Bakke* decision:** Before we analyze these three decisions, we need to review the court's only prior decision on affirmative action in the University context, ***Regents of Univ. of California v. Bakke***, 438 U.S. 265 (1978). The case is now significant principally for Justice Powell's opinion, which provided the swing vote even though no other justice joined its reasoning fully, but which was adopted 25 years later by the pro-affirmative-action majority in *Grutter*.

      a. **Facts:** The admissions procedure at the University of California-Davis Medical School reserved 16 seats in each entering class of 100 for disadvantaged minority students. Only African Americans, Hispanics, and Asian-Americans could compete for these places.

i. Suit against plan: Allan Bakke, a white, sued the University, claiming that the admissions scheme violated the Equal Protection Clause, as well as Title VI of the 1964 Civil Rights Act. Bakke contended that his grade point average and MCAT scores were higher than those of some persons accepted for the minority slots.

b. Supreme Court's holding: No majority opinion emerged from the Supreme Court's consideration of the case. The nine Justices wrote six separate opinions, and no more than four Justices agreed in their reasoning.

i. Justice Powell: It fell to Justice Powell to form a majority. He agreed with four other Justices (Brennan, White, Marshall and Blackmun) that a university should be permitted to *take into account* an applicant's membership in a racial minority as part of the admissions process. But he believed that a racial *"quota"* system, i.e., the explicit reservation of places which could only be filled by minorities, was *unconstitutional*. His holding on this issue, coupled with the belief of the remaining four Justices that the Davis program was invalid for statutory rather than constitutional reasons, led to the striking down of the mechanical Davis approach.

(1) Powell rationale: Justice Powell believed that *any racial or ethnic classification*, regardless of the class against which it is directed or the reason for it, must be subjected to *strict scrutiny*. Powell concluded that (1) the need to obtain "the *educational benefits* that flow from an *ethnically-diverse* student body" was a compelling state interest; but (2) it was *not necessary* (and therefore not permissible) to use a *quota* scheme like Davis', where certain seats were reserved *exclusively* for members of particular races; instead, this goal could be pursued by considering an applicant's minority status as merely *one factor* in the admissions process (the so-called "Harvard plan").

(2) Individual treatment: Powell stressed that a Harvard-type "weigh all factors" scheme, unlike the Davis quota scheme, "treats each applicant *as an individual* in the admissions process." This key distinction by Powell — contrasting individualized assessment of each applicant (constitutionally acceptable) with the reservation of particular "slots" for minorities (unacceptable) — was later adopted by a *majority* of the Court, in *Grutter v. Bollinger, infra*.

2. *Grutter* and *Gratz* together: Twenty-five years later, a majority of the Court, in *Grutter* and *Gratz*, effectively *adopted Powell's approach in Bakke,* by holding that:

[a] Race-conscious admissions measures will *receive strict scrutiny*, and thus must be narrowly-tailored to achieve a compelling objective;

[b] The pursuit of *diversity in the student body* can be a *compelling objective*;

[c] A *one-student-at-a-time evaluation* in which the student's race is merely one factor among various ones considered is *sufficiently narrowly-tailored*; but

[d] Mechanical approaches resembling *quotas*, such as automatically awarding an applicant a fixed number of *points* towards admission based on his race, are *not narrowly-tailored* and therefore violate equal protection.

We consider *Grutter* and *Gratz* in sequence, followed by *Fisher*.

dent; instead, she said, her opinion for the Court *"endorse[s]* Justice Powell's view that *student body diversity is a compelling state interest* that can *justify the use of race* in university admissions."

ii. **Strict scrutiny required:**   Next, O'Connor recited the Court's prior holdings that all racial classifications imposed by government must undergo strict scrutiny, and are constitutional "only if they are narrowly tailored to further compelling governmental interests."

iii. **Diversity as a compelling interest:**   O'Connor then concluded that the Law School had "a *compelling interest* in obtaining a *diverse student body*." She noted that the Law School itself had concluded that such diversity was essential to the school's educational mission. And, she said, the Court had a "tradition of giving a degree of *deference* to a university's academic decisions."

iv. **Narrowly-tailored:**   O'Connor next turned to the even-more-contentious issue of whether the particular race-conscious methods adopted by the Law School were *sufficiently narrowly-tailored* to the achievement of the compellingly-important objective of obtaining diversity in the student body.

(1) **No quotas:**   O'Connor began by adopting Powell's position in *Bakke* that a race-conscious program *cannot use a quota system.* O'Connor defined "quota" somewhat narrowly: a quota was "a program in which a certain *fixed number or proportion of opportunities* are 'reserved exclusively' for certain minority groups'"; quotas "impose a fixed number or percentage which must be attained, which cannot be exceeded," and "insulate the individual from comparison with all other candidates for the available seats."

(2) **Michigan's plan not a quota:**   By this test, the Law School's approach was *not* a forbidden quota, O'Connor said. The Law School's plan was much more like the "Harvard plan" that Powell had approved of in *Bakke* than it was like the plan struck down in *Bakke*. Harvard made, in O'Connor's words, "flexible use of race as a 'plus' factor," as did Michigan Law School.

(3) **"Holistic" review:**   Also, the actual *process* by which the Law School *evaluated* each application was inconsistent with a quota. The Law School, O'Connor said, "engages in a *highly individualized, holistic review* of each applicant's file, giving serious consideration to *all the ways* an applicant might contribute to a diverse educational environment." The school did *not* give any *"mechanical, predetermined diversity 'bonuses'* based on race or ethnicity" (as the Court found that the undergraduate admissions scheme at Michigan did, in the companion case of *Gratz, infra*).

(4) **Race-neutral alternatives:**   Finally, O'Connor considered whether the Law School's approach failed to be narrowly tailored because of the availability of *race-neutral alternatives* for achieving the desired diversity. O'Connor agreed that narrow tailoring "require[s] serious, good faith *consideration* of *workable* race-neutral alternatives that will achieve the diversity the university seeks." But she asserted that "narrow tailoring *does not require exhaustion of every conceivable race-neutral alternative,"* only those alternatives that would *serve the governmental interest "about as well."* She agreed with the Law

School that the various race-neutral alternatives that had been proposed were *not workable ones*. For instance, alternatives like "using a lottery system" or "decreasing the emphasis ... on undergraduate GPA and LSAT scores" were not workable, because they would "require a dramatic sacrifice of diversity, the academic quality of all admitted students, or both."

Similarly, O'Connor said, the type of *"percentage plan"* advocated by the Bush administration — under which all students above a certain class-rank threshold in every school in the state would be guaranteed admission[5] — would not work for graduate and professional schools, and would probably preclude individualized assessments of each student's contribution to other, non-racial, types of diversity.

    v. **"Sunset" after 25 years:** But O'Connor cautioned that race-conscious admissions policies "must be *limited in time*." She noted that it had been 25 years since Justice Powell's opinion in *Bakke*, and she wrote that "We expect that *25 years from now*, the use of racial preferences will *no longer be necessary*[.]"

d. **Dissents:** The four dissenters — Chief Justice Rehnquist and Justices Kennedy, Scalia and Thomas — each produced a separate dissent.

e. **Rehnquist's dissent:** The principal dissent was by Chief Justice Rehnquist, in which the other three dissenters also joined. Rehnquist seemed not to object to the majority's belief that a diverse student body could be a compelling governmental objective. But he very much disputed the majority's conclusion that the Law School's approach was a narrowly-tailored method of achieving that objective. Instead, he believed, the Law School's pursuit of "critical mass" was a *"veil,"* which when stripped revealed "a *naked effort to achieve racial balancing*."

f. **Kennedy's dissent:** Like Chief Justice Rehnquist, Justice Kennedy believed that the majority was not in fact applying strict scrutiny. He accused the majority of giving only a "perfunctory" review of the Law School's policy, which he characterized as using critical mass as a "delusion ... to mask its attempt to *make race an automatic factor* in most instances and to achieve *numerical goals indistinguishable from quotas.*"

g. **Thomas' dissent:** Justice Thomas (joined by Justice Scalia) wrote a long, highly personal, dissent that seemed to stem partly from his own negative personal experience with affirmative action.

    i. **Not a compelling interest:** Unlike Rehnquist and Kennedy, Thomas did *not* even accept the position that the Law School had a *compelling interest* in pursuing diversity in its student body.

    ii. **Affirmative action bad for its beneficiaries:** Thomas then attacked affirmative action, of the sort practiced by the Law School, as being *bad for its beneficiaries.* "The Law School *tantalizes* unprepared [minority] students with the promise of a University of Michigan degree and all of the opportunities that it offers. These

---

5. We'll see that this sort of race-blind percentage plan, when used for undergraduate admissions, got the implicit approval of most members of the Court in the later 2013 decision in *Fisher v. Univ. of Texas, infra,* p. 300.

overmatched students take the bait, only to find that they *cannot succeed* in the cauldron of competition." Furthermore, he wrote, even the "handful" of black students each year who would have been admitted in the absence of racial discrimination are damaged by the policy: "Who can differentiate between those who belong and those who do not? The majority of blacks are admitted to the law school because of discrimination, and because of this policy *all are tarred as undeserving.*"

     h.   **Scalia's dissent:**   Justice Scalia, in a brief dissent (in which Justice Thomas joined) made it clear that he, like Thomas, rejected even the proposition that the Law School's pursuit of a diverse student body was a compelling state interest. He saw Michigan's interest as merely being an "interest in maintaining a 'prestige' law school whose normal admissions standards disproportionately exclude blacks and other minorities." He argued that "if that is a compelling state interest, everything is."

4.   *Gratz*:   The same day as the Court decided *Grutter*, it decided *Gratz*, which involved affirmative-action admissions policies at the University of Michigan's main *undergraduate* College in Ann Arbor.

     a.   **Facts:**   There were several different affirmative-action schemes, used by the College in different years, at issue in *Gratz*. For procedural reasons, most of the Supreme Court's eventual analysis concerned the school's policy after 1998. Under that policy, the school used a "selection index," in which *points were awarded* for various characteristics, up to a maximum of 150 points. A minimum of 100 points was needed for admission. An applicant was entitled to an *automatic 20 points* for membership in an *underrepresented racial or ethnic minority group* (the same three groups — blacks, Hispanics and Native Americans — as in the Law School plan at issue in *Grutter*). The significance of these extra 20 points was great: the University conceded that "the effect of automatically awarding 20 points is that *virtually every qualified underrepresented minority applicant is admitted.*" By contrast, the award given for most other types of non-academic traits was much smaller: a student with "extraordinary *artistic* talent" rivaling that of Monet or Picasso, for instance, or the most outstanding national high school *student leader*, could receive *at most five points.* Students who didn't get enough points but came close could be *manually flagged* for *in-person review* of the file, which might lead to admission.

     b.   **Rehnquist's majority opinion:**   Chief Justice Rehnquist's majority opinion (joined by O'Connor, Scalia, Kennedy and Thomas) concluded that this *point system* was *unconstitutional*, in that it was *not narrowly tailored* to achieve the school's interest in educational diversity.[6] Because Justice Breyer concurred in the result, the vote was 6-3 to strike the point system.

         i.   **Does not conform to Powell's opinion:**   Rehnquist believed that the College's point system did *not* meet the requirements of Justice Powell's *Bakke* opinion. The essence of Powell's approach was that race could be deemed a "plus," but was not to be "decisive"; each applicant was to be evaluated as an *individual*, and each characteristic of that applicant was to be considered. The College's point system was not at all the kind of system that Powell had in mind, Rehnquist said. For

---

6. The majority also rejected a "standing" argument advanced by the dissenters.

instance, the automatic award of 20 points had the effect of making race decisive "for virtually every minimally qualified underrepresented minority applicant."

ii. Flagging not a solution: The fact that an applicant who failed to get the requisite points but came close could have her application *flagged* for special individualized review *did not remedy* these flaws. Flagging would only come into play if the student failed to get enough points to be automatic admitted. Because the 20 points for minority racial status virtually guaranteed admission to minimally-qualified minorities, such minorities would never be near-misses, would therefore never be flagged, and thus never subjected to individualized review.

iii. Large numbers not a defense: Finally, Rehnquist rejected the College's argument that the *large volume of applications* received by the school made a Powell-style individualized review of each file impractical: "[T]he fact that the implementation of a program capable of providing individualized consideration might present *administrative challenges* does *not* render constitutional an otherwise problematic system."

c. O'Connor's concurrence: Justice O'Connor wrote a concurrence, in which Justices Thomas and Breyer joined. Since O'Connor wrote the majority opinion in *Grutter* upholding the Law School's affirmative action plan, her *Gratz* concurrence is important in that it spells out how and why she thought the College's unacceptable plan differed from the Law School's acceptable one.

i. Predetermined points: O'Connor principally objected to the fact that *far fewer points* were available for diversity characteristics other than the race-oriented ones, and to the fact that the point values were completely *hard-wired* at the outset. Thus she pointed out that diversity contributions like "leadership," "personal achievement" and geographic diversity were capped at much lower levels than membership in an underrepresented race (e.g., 5 points maximum for leadership, compared with the 20 automatic points for being black or Hispanic). Furthermore, "by setting up *automatic, predetermined point allocations*" for all of the diversity characteristics, the system "ensures that the diversity contributions of applicants *cannot be individually assessed*." This was in "sharp contrast" to the Law School's plan, under which admissions officers were able to "make *nuanced judgments* with respect to the contributions each applicant is likely to make to diversity of the incoming class."

d. Dissent: Three justices — Stevens, Souter and Ginsburg — dissented in *Gratz*.

i. Ginsburg: One of these dissents was by Justice Ginsburg (joined by Souter and in part by Breyer).

(1) Legacy of discrimination: Ginsburg emphasized that "the effects of centuries-old law-sanctioned inequality remain painfully evident in our communities and schools." Consequently, she thought, "government decision makers may properly distinguish between policies of *exclusion* and *inclusion*. ... Actions designed to burden groups long denied full citizenship stature are not sensibly ranked with measures taken to hasten the day when entrenched discrimination and its after effects have been extirpated."

5. **"No workable race-neutral alternatives"** (*Fisher v. Univ. of Texas*): For 10 years after *Grutter* and *Gratz*, the Supreme Court did not hear any university preferential-admissions cases. Then, in 2013, it decided ***Fisher v. Univ. of Texas at Austin***, ___ U.S. ___ (2013), a 7-1 decision that surprised many for its near-unanimity. *Fisher* did not explicitly make new law, but it emphasized that the Court will take seriously the principle that race-conscious admissions are permissible only if ***no workable race-neutral alternatives are available.***

    a. **Overall significance of case:** The Court indicated that the ***tightness of the link*** between race-conscious admissions and the goal of greater educational diversity must be ***much more closely scrutinized*** than had previously seemed to be the case. As the Court put it in *Fisher*, a court reviewing a challenged race-conscious admissions scheme "must ultimately be satisfied that ***no workable race-neutral alternatives*** would produce the ***educational benefits of diversity***." And on this issue of availability of workable race-neutral alternatives, the Court said that ***no deference*** is to be given to the university's own judgment or expertise.

    b. **The Texas admissions system:** The University of Texas at Austin used an unusual two-tier method for admitting undergraduates. The system evolved from a series of court decisions and actions by the Texas Legislature, which we won't go into here. But the basic structure worked like this:

        [1] **The "Top Ten" component:** Under a ***"Top Ten Percent"*** statute passed by the Texas legislature, any student attending a public high school in Texas who finished in the ***top 10% of her high school class*** was ***guaranteed admission*** to any public Texas university (including U. Texas at Austin), assuming the high school met certain academic standards.[7] The vast majority of admitted freshman were admitted under this Top Ten Percent rule,[8] without any consideration of the student's race (or, indeed, of any other individual attribute of the student). Because of the ***large degree of racial segregation*** from one high school to the next in Texas, use of the Top Ten Percent rule increased the percentage of black and Hispanic students at Texas/Austin beyond what it had previously been.

        [2] **The "holistic" race-conscious method:** Whatever slots remained open after the admission of applicants who qualified under the Top Ten Percent rule were then filled by the best-scoring applicants to emerge from a process of ***"holistic review,"*** in which ***race was expressly considered,*** but was just one factor among many. This "race as one factor" method was designed to comply with *Grutter, supra.* At a point before Ms. Fisher applied, the University added race-consciousness to its pre-existing holistic review method; it did so for the express purpose of increasing

---

7. Some of the details of this plan are not fully disclosed in the Supreme Court's various opinions in *Fisher*; I've taken some details from the Fifth Circuit opinion that approved the University's plan as the plan was applied to the plaintiff, Ms. Fisher.

8. It's not clear from either the Supreme Court or the Fifth Circuit opinions what percentage of the entering class was filled by Top Ten Percent members in the year in which Ms. Fisher applied. But in the years just before the Supreme Court's decision, by order of the legislature 75% of slots were generally reserved for Top Ten Percent applicants, with the remainder reserved for the next-tier "holistic method" described in the following paragraph.

still further the percentages of black and Hispanic students — traditionally under-represented throughout the Texas public university system — beyond what resulted from use of the Top Ten Percent rule.

    (1) Smaller classes and "critical mass": The University decided to add race consideration to the holistic method in large part because the school's analysis of individual classes showed that *smaller classes* — those containing between *five and 24 students* — rarely contained a *"critical mass"* of black and Hispanic students. (Recall that in *Grutter*, the University of Michigan Law School successfully argued that its race-conscious holistic system helped achieve a "critical mass" of minority students. See *supra*, p. 295.)

c. P's application and suit: The plaintiff, Abigail Fisher, who is white, narrowly missed graduating in the top 10% of her high school class, making her ineligible for admission under the Top Ten Percent rule. Her score under the holistic method was also not high enough to give her a seat. She brought a federal suit against the University, claiming that the University's use of race in the holistic method prevented her from gaining admission, and violated her equal protection rights.[9]

d. Lower courts' decision: The District Court granted summary judgment in favor of the University, and the Fifth Circuit affirmed. The Fifth Circuit reasoned that *Grutter* required the court to give *substantial deference* to the University, both as to the University's conclusion that educational diversity was a compelling governmental interest, *and* as to the University's determination that the particular admissions plan chosen by the University was narrowly tailored to achieve this interest.

e. Kennedy's majority opinion, generally: The Supreme Court *reversed* the Fifth Circuit. Justice Kennedy's opinion was joined by six of the seven other members who heard the case — only Justice Ginsburg dissented. (Justice Kagan recused herself, presumably because she had worked on the case while serving as the Obama administration's solicitor general.)

f. Diversity as a compelling interest: Kennedy first dealt with the *"compelling objective"* side of the strict-scrutiny equation. Many observers had thought that in *Fisher*, a majority would overturn *Grutter*'s key holding that the attainment of *"educational diversity"* could at least sometimes be a compelling governmental interest that could justify race-conscious admissions decisions. But Kennedy quoted *approvingly Grutter*'s conclusion (which was in turn based on Powell's original reasoning in *Bakke*; see *supra*, p. 294) that "obtaining the *educational benefits of student body diversity is a compelling state interest* that can *justify the use of race* in university admissions."

    i. Rationale: Why was educational diversity a compelling (not just important) governmental objective? Kennedy's answer emphasized that *racial* diversity was *only part* of the valuable *overall* diversity: "The attainment of a *diverse student body* ... *serves values beyond race alone,* including *enhanced classroom dialogue* and the *lessening of racial isolation and stereotypes.*"

---

9. After being denied admission by Texas, P entered Louisiana State University, from which she had graduated by the time the Supreme Court decided her case.

g.   Narrowly-tailored means-end fit: But the heart of Kennedy's opinion — and his rationale for overturning the courts below — dealt with the other half of the strict-scrutiny equation, the ***tightness of the fit between the means and the end***. "The University must prove," he said, that ***"the means*** chosen by [it] to attain diversity are ***narrowly tailored to that goal.***"

   i.   No deference: As to whether the University had borne its burden of proving the requisite narrow tailoring, he said, "the ***University receives no deference***" from the court. The court, not the University, is to determine whether the particular admissions scheme chosen is ***"specifically and narrowly framed"*** to achieve the sought-after diversity. True, the court "can take ***account of a university's experience and expertise*** in adopting or rejecting certain admissions processes." But the burden of proof on means-end fit must ***remain at all times on the University***, he said.

   ii.   "Necessary" standard: Kennedy then went into more detail about just how tight the means-end fit must be. The University must prove that race-consciousness is ***"necessary"*** for achieving the educational diversity that's being sought. And the court's determination of the "necessity" of race-consciousness "involves a ***careful judicial inquiry*** into whether [the] university ***could achieve sufficient diversity without using racial classifications.***"

   iii.   Exhaustion of race-neutral alternatives: Next, in the part of his opinion that is likely to prove most challenging for universities' future race-conscious admissions policies, Kennedy described how the court is to make the determination of whether race-consciousness is "necessary" for diversity. He conceded that the required narrow tailoring "does ***not require exhaustion of every conceivable race-neutral alternative***." But, he continued, strict scrutiny "does require a court to ***examine with care***, and ***not defer to***, a university's '***serious, good faith consideration of workable race-neutral alternatives***.'"

      (1)   The "about as well" standard: In fact, Kennedy indicated, the University could not carry its burden by showing that race-neutral admissions methods would fall ***slightly short*** in achieving the educational benefits of diversity compared with race-conscious methods. Instead, he said, the University must show that race-blind methods won't even serve the diversity interest ***"about as well"*** as the selected race-conscious method. Citing a case from the race-in-employment area, *Wygant v. Jackson Bd. of Ed.*, 476 U.S. 267 (1986), he said that "*[i]f 'a nonracial approach* . . . could promote the substantial interest ***about as well*** and at ***tolerable administrative expense***' ... ***then the university may not consider race.***"

h.   No "feeble in fact" standard: Kennedy then spoke more broadly about strict scrutiny as a standard. He acknowledged that the Court had previously held that "[s]trict scrutiny must not be 'strict in theory, but fatal in fact[.]' " But, he cautioned, "***the opposite is also true. Strict scrutiny must not be strict in theory but feeble in fact.***"

i.   Kennedy's summary: Finally, Kennedy gave a summary of what universities would have to do to successfully defend their race-conscious admissions plans:

   "In order for judicial review to be meaningful, a university must make a showing that its plan is ***narrowly tailored*** to achieve the ***only interest*** that this Court has approved in this context: the benefits of a ***student body diversity*** that 'encompasses a . . . ***broa[d] array of qualifications and characteristics*** of which ***racial or ethnic origin is but a single though important element*** ' " (citing Powell's *Bakke* opinion).

j. Concurrences by Scalia and Thomas: Justices Scalia and Thomas, although they joined Kennedy's opinion, concurred separately. Each noted that Ms. Fisher had not asked the Court to flatly ***overrule*** *Grutter* — i.e., to say that race could *never* be part of the admissions process. And each said that *had* such a request been before the Court, he would have voted to ***flatly forbid any consideration of race.***

    i. Thomas: Thomas was the only justice who explained in detail why he thought the Constitution categorically prohibited the University from any consideration of race in admissions.

        (1) Injury to the group being helped: Thomas argued, as he had in *Grutter*, that race-based admissions preferences seriously ***injure the very groups that they are supposed to help.*** He contended that among students admitted as part of the race-conscious holistic method (i.e., the non-Top Ten Percent rule), blacks and Hispanics entered with ***inferior average academic credentials*** compared with whites and Asians, and there was no evidence that these gaps narrowed during the students' years at the University. The University's race-based system therefore "stamp[s] [blacks and Hispanics] with a ***badge of inferiority.***" That badge attached not only to the minority students admitted under the race-conscious system, but also to those (more numerous) minority students who were admitted by the *non*-race-conscious method (the Top Ten Percent rule), because "***no one can distinguish*** those students from the ones whose race played a role in their admission."

        (2) The "mismatch" theory: Thomas also embraced the controversial "***mismatch***" theory. As he explained the theory, the University's race-conscious methods ***did not "increase the number*** of blacks and Hispanics who have access to a college education ***generally***. Instead, the University's discrimination has ***a pervasive shifting effect***." That is, "the University admits minorities who otherwise would have attended ***less selective colleges*** where they would have been ***more evenly matched***. But, as a result of the mismatching, many blacks and Hispanics who ***likely would have excelled at less elite schools*** are placed in a position where ***underperformance is all but inevitable*** because they are less academically prepared than the white and Asian students with whom they must compete." This was harmful because of "the damage wreaked upon the self-confidence of these "***overmatched students***"; furthermore, there was "***no evidence that they learn more*** at the University than they would have learned at other schools for which they were ***better prepared***. Indeed, they may learn less."

k. Ginsburg's dissent: The only ***dissenter*** in *Fisher* was Justice Ginsburg. She argued that the lower Texas courts had correctly applied *Grutter*, and had correctly concluded that Texas's holistic race-conscious plan was narrowly tailored to achieve educational diversity, as *Grutter* required.

    i. **"Neutral alternatives" are not unconscious:** Ginsburg rejected the contention that supposedly "race neutral" alternatives were available to Texas, and should be used to the exclusion of any race-conscious method. In particular, she said, the Top Ten Percent rule was in reality not *race neutral at all*; the Texas legislature had adopted this percentage-based plan in explicit reliance on Texas' pattern of *"racially segregated neighborhoods and schools*[.]" She concluded that "[i]t is *race consciousness*, not blindness to race," that *"drives such plans."*

    ii. **Explicit race-consciousness is better:** Since *Grutter* had allowed explicit consideration of race, she said, an admittedly-race-conscious plan like Texas' holistic method was superior to percentage-type systems: approaches to educational diversity "that *candidly disclose* their consideration of race [are] preferable to those that *conceal it*."

l. **Significance of *Fisher*:** Although *Fisher* does not explicitly make any new law, the case is likely to have a significant impact on when and how explicitly race-conscious admissions schemes may be used by public universities.

    i. **Greater scrutiny:** It's clear that as the result of *Fisher*, any court reviewing a university's race-conscious admissions scheme will have to give close scrutiny to whether race-consciousness is *"necessary"* in order to achieve the university's compelling goal of "educational diversity." The *university's expertise* in designing particular methods of bringing about a diverse class will *no longer be entitled to any deference.* That is, if the court believes that some race-neutral method can accomplish the goal of diversity *as well* — maybe even just *"about as well"*[10] — as race-conscious ones, *Fisher* seems to require the court to invalidate the race-conscious method.

    ii. **Program-specific evaluation:** *Fisher* seems to mean that courts' determination of whether the means-end fit is sufficiently tight will be very *context-specific* — the same race-conscious plan might pass muster at one university, program or state and not in another.

        (1) **Top Ten Percent rule:** For instance, a *Top Ten Percent plan* might produce adequate diversity in one state (e.g., one with heavily racially-segregated public high schools, like Texas) but not in another. In that case, it might turn out that only the state for whom a Top Ten Percent approach would *not be workable* would succeed in showing that race-conscious methods are "necessary" for it to achieve diversity.

        (2) **Graduate/professional programs:** Similarly, in *graduate* and *professional* programs — where a Top Ten Percent rule either would be unworkable or would not produce much diversity, because of the lack of racial segregation in the graduating classes from which applicants would be applying — the case for race-consciousness would presumably be *stronger*.

    iii. **Better documentation by universities:** One consequence that's virtually certain is that universities will need to *keep much better documentation* about the process by which they design race-conscious admissions schemes.

---

10. See Kennedy's "about as well" language in Par. g(iii)(1) *supra*, p. 302.

iv. **Scrutiny of what and how much "diversity" is compelling:** Kennedy's opinion in *Fisher* said relatively little about how a court is to apply the *"governmental objective"* (as opposed to the "means") prong of strict scrutiny when race-conscious admission schemes are being reviewed. However, just as *Fisher* clearly signals tougher judicial review of the means-end fit, the case may signal tougher review of *what kind of educational diversity counts* as a *compelling objective*.

    (1) Some deference: Kennedy emphasized that although "educational diversity" is a compelling goal, "A university is not permitted to define diversity as '*some specified percentage* of a particular group merely because of its race or ethnic origin'" — that type of *"racial balancing"* would be a flatly unconstitutional *quota*, under the Court's pre-*Fisher* cases (like *Parents Involved in Community Schools v. Seattle School Dist. No. 1, infra*, p. 306).

    (2) "Critical mass" in small classes: But if "racial balancing" is not permitted, a university's basic rationale for race-conscious admissions may be vulnerable. Recall (*supra*, p. 301) that Texas / Austin added race-consciousness to its holistic method in part because the *smaller* university classes — the "seminar" classes containing between five and 24 students — rarely contained a *"critical mass"* of minority students. Post-*Fisher*, even if a university is entitled to judicial deference towards its conclusion that educational diversity is *in general* a compelling interest, it's not at all clear that a university's conclusion about *just how much and what type of diversity is needed* — e.g., that having a university-defined "critical mass" of minority students in most classes containing between five and 24 students — is entitled to deference.

6. **Significance of the three cases:** So what, then, have we learned from the trio of university affirmative-action cases, *Grutter*, *Gratz* and *Fisher*?

    a. **Core principle of affirmative action preserved:** The core principle of *affirmative action* in higher education to ensure a *racially-diverse class* is *preserved*. As long as admissions officers *individually evaluate* the contribution that each applicant will make towards a diverse class — not just racially diverse, but diverse in other aspects such as life experiences, special talents, etc. — the fact that membership in an underrepresented racial or ethnic minority is given great weight will not constitute a violation of equal protection rights of applicants who are not members of those underrepresented minority groups (assuming the requisite tight means-end fit is shown as discussed in Paragraph (c) below). This is the core result of *Grutter*.

    b. **Can't use points or quotas:** In contrast to the "individualized consideration of race among various factors" system that the Court approved in *Grutter*, a system that the Court perceives as being *"mechanical"* or a *"quota"* rather than *"holistic"* is *vulnerable*. Most obviously, any system in which a certain pre-defined number of *"points"* is automatically given for membership in a particular minority group will pretty clearly be unconstitutional under *Gratz*.

    c. **Tight means-end fit:** But even if the university is pursuing the compelling goal of "educational diversity," race-conscious admissions will be allowed *only* if *no "workable" race-neutral alternatives are available* that would deliver such diversity *as well* (or even *almost as well*) as race-conscious methods. *Fisher*.

i. **i. No deference to university:** And it will be up to the *reviewing court* to *decide* whether workable race neutral alternatives exist — the court must *not give any deference to the university's own belief* that race-neutral alternatives would not suffice, and that the race-conscious methods chosen by the school are thus "necessary" to achieve diversity.

d. **Impact on private universities:** What impact, if any, will *Grutter, Gratz* and *Fisher* have on the admissions practices of *private universities*? You might think that the answer would be "none," since in the absence of state action (see *infra*, p. 417), there can be no equal protection violation. However, various federal *statutes* prohibit racial discrimination in various contexts. Therefore, if a particular practice would constitute an equal protection violation when used by a public university, that same practice would likely violate a federal statute barring "racial discrimination" when used by a private college.

Example: A federal statute known as "Title VI" bars any educational institution receiving federal funds (as virtually all universities do) — public *or private* — from discriminating based on race or ethnicity. Therefore, if the admissions office of a private college were to use an affirmative action plan found to be a race-based "quota" system (outlawed by *Gratz*), or a race-based holistic system in circumstances where non-race-conscious selection methods would have achieved adequate "educational diversity" (a use forbidden by *Fisher*) it is likely that the scheme would be found to be a violation of Title VI.

F. **Admissions to public secondary schools by race-conscious pupil-assignments (the *Parents Involved* case):** To what extent may a *public school system* make *race-conscious pupil-assignment decisions* in order to combat racial imbalances in the district's schools? As a result of a 2007 decision that was the Roberts Court's first consideration of affirmative action, *no individual student's race may be considered in making that student's school assignment.* The case, ***Parents Involved in Community Schools v. Seattle School District No. 1***, 552 U.S. 701 (2007), was a bitter 5-4 split, with Justice Kennedy siding with the four conservative members of the Court in striking down the race-conscious school-assignment plans from Seattle and Louisville, Kentucky at issue there. The case marks an important extension of the Court's recent tendency to strictly scrutinize, and usually invalidate, race-conscious affirmative action decisions by governments.

1. **The assignment plans:** Both Seattle's and Louisville's race-conscious pupil-assignment plans were essentially *voluntary* as opposed to court-ordered. Seattle had never been under court order to desegregate its schools. Louisville had once been under such a court order, but prior to the use of the plan at issue court supervision had ceased because the district had been found to have eradicated the vestiges of official segregation. Both districts enacted plans that *occasionally took account of race,* in an effort to prevent individual schools from becoming *racially isolated.*

a. **Seattle plan:** Under the Seattle plan, *race served as a "tiebreaker"* for the assignment of incoming ninth graders to certain of the city's high schools. Ninth graders were asked to state their preferences; if a school was "oversubscribed" (more students listed it as their first choice than there were slots), a series of tiebreakers was used. The first tiebreaker gave a preference to students with a sibling already enrolled at the school.

The next tiebreaker was what the litigation was about. In the district as a whole, 41% of students were white, and 59% "nonwhite" (a designation that apparently included Asian Americans, African Americans and Latinos). But due to housing patterns, the north end of the city was predominantly white and the south end predominantly non-white. If the school in question was not within 10 points of the district-wide white/nonwhite ratio, the tiebreaker went in favor of *an applicant whose race would bring the school into better balance.* So, for instance, if a school was more than 51% white (i.e., more than 10 percentage points above the 41% district-wide percentage of whites), the tiebreaker would go in favor of a black applicant over a white applicant. Out of a total of about 20,000 high school students in a typical year, about 300 were affected by the race-based tiebreaker (see the dissent of Justice Breyer). The plaintiff was a nonprofit corporation consisting of parents of students who had been or might be denied admission to their first-choice high school on account of the student's race.

b. **The Louisville plan:** In Louisville, a federal court dissolved a prior desegregation order in 2000, finding that the system had been desegregated to the extent feasible. The following year, the school district continued to use the pupil-assignment rules at issue (which had been put into effect during the desegregation-order years), in an attempt to prevent individual schools from becoming racially isolated due to housing patterns. About 34% of the district students were black; most of the remaining 66% were white. The plan allowed students to transfer from their initially-assigned school to another, but a transfer was not allowed if the transferee school had a black enrollment of less than 15% or more than 50% and the *transfer would worsen the imbalance.* The plaintiff was an individual, Crystal Meredith, who sought to transfer her kindergartener son Joshua from an assigned school 10 miles from his house to a school that was only 1 mile from his house; he was denied the transfer on the grounds that the transferee school he selected was outside the 15-50% racial guidelines, and his presence would worsen the imbalance.

2. **Both plans ruled invalid:** The court ruled that both the Seattle plan and the Louisville plan *violated the equal protection clause by considering race.* Four members of the Court, led by Chief Justice Roberts, concluded that *any* use of race in the context of school assignments would be unconstitutional. (I refer to this bloc as the *"plurality."*) Another four-member bloc, led by Justice Breyer's dissent, asserted that both plans were constitutional. The case therefore turned on *Justice Kennedy's concurrence*; he concluded that the taking into account of racial considerations would *not always* be unconstitutional in the school-assignment context, but that the particular plans here — which involved *categorizing each student by race* and then making some students' assignments depend on that race — was an unconstitutional use of race.

3. **The Roberts plurality opinion:** Chief Justice Roberts' plurality opinion was joined in full by Justices Scalia, Thomas and Alito. He concluded that both the Seattle and Louisville plans failed the requisite strict scrutiny on two grounds: first, the districts were *not pursuing a compelling governmental interest*, and second, the race-conscious *means* chosen by the districts were *not narrowly tailored to meet* whatever governmental interests they were designed to pursue.

a. **Strict scrutiny required:** Roberts began by summarizing the standard that the Court's emerging conservative majority had imposed for race-conscious affirmative action plans in cases like *Gratz* (*supra*, p. 298) and *Adarand* (*infra*, p. 320): "When the government distributes burdens or benefits on the basis of individual racial classifications, that action is reviewed under strict scrutiny. ... In order to satisfy this searching standard of review, the school districts must demonstrate that the use of individual racial classifications in the assignment plans here under review is 'narrowly tailored' to achieve a 'compelling' government interest."

b. **No compelling interest being pursued:** Roberts began by examining the issue of what governmental interests being pursued by the two cities could be considered "compelling."   There were only two governmental interests, Roberts said, that the Court had recognized in prior school cases as being "compelling": ***remedying the effects of past intentional discrimination*** and "the interest in ***diversity in higher education***" recognized in *Grutter* (*supra*. p. 295).

   i. **Past intentional discrimination:** Roberts rapidly dismissed the first of these objectives from the present cases: the Seattle school system had never been shown to be segregated by law and had never been under a court-ordered desegregation decree; and the Louisville system had been found to have eradicated all vestiges of official segregation prior to the use of the race conscious plan under analysis here. So neither city could justify its plan based on combating the effects of past intentional discrimination.

   ii. **Educational diversity:** Roberts spent far more time explaining why he believed that neither plan could be found to have been enacted in support of the second objective, the interest in ***diversity***. The objective upheld in *Grutter* was ***not "focused on race alone,"*** he said, but was rather the interest in "***all factors*** that may contribute to student body diversity," including such factors as a student's having lived or traveled abroad, fluency in several languages, overcoming of personal adversity, community service, and the like. Here, by contrast, "When race comes into play, it is decisive by itself. It is ***not simply one factor*** weighed with others in reaching a decision, as in *Grutter*; it is <u>the</u> factor."

      (1) **White / nonwhite distinction:** Even worse, Roberts said, both plans manifested only a ***"limited notion of diversity,"*** viewing race exclusively in white/nonwhite terms (Seattle) or black/other terms (Louisville). For instance, under the Seattle plan, a school with 50% Asian-American students and 50% white would be considered "balanced" but one that was 30% Asian-American, 25% African-American, 25% Latino and 20% white would not. Roberts could not see how this classification scheme could be said to be in pursuit of an enrollment that was "broadly diverse," the objective upheld in *Grutter*.

   iii. **Directed to "racial balance":** Roberts also rejected the school districts' argument that the race conscious plans here pursued a compelling interest in a ***racially integrated learning environment***, in which students would learn more and become better socialized. Roberts declined to decide whether pursuit of educational benefits flowing from racial diversity might ever be a compelling interest because, he said, the plans here pursued ***"only ... racial balance, pure and simple,*** an objective this Court has repeatedly condemned as ***illegitimate***." Accepting racial balancing as a compelling state interest, he said, "would justify the *imposition of racial proportionality throughout American society,"* a tactic that would have *"no logical stopping point."*

c. **Lack of tight means-end fit:** Even if the interests being pursued by the school districts were compelling, Roberts went on to say, the particular race-conscious *means* selected by the districts were not *necessary for achieving those interests.* In both cities, the use of the racial guidelines resulted in the *shifting of only a few students*, suggesting to Roberts that "other means would be effective." Furthermore, he said, cases like *Grutter* had interpreted the requirement of narrow tailoring to require "serious, good faith consideration of workable and race-neutral *alternatives*"; the districts here had flunked that requirement, by failing to show that they had even considered race-neutral methods.

d. **Mantle of *Brown*:** Roberts then argued that the plurality's position, not the dissent's, was true to the legacy of *Brown v. Board of Education.* "It was not the inequality of the facilities but the fact of *legally separating children on the basis of race* on which the Court relied to find a constitutional violation" in *Brown.* Even the plaintiffs in *Brown*, he said, had argued (and he quoted from their 1953 brief) that "the Fourteenth Amendment prevents states from according differential treatment to American children on the basis of their color or race." In sum, he wrote, *"The way to stop discrimination on the basis of race is to stop discriminating on the basis of race."*

4. **The Kennedy concurrence:** Justice Kennedy, in a concurring opinion, supplied the key fifth vote to strike down the Seattle and Louisville plans. But he *disagreed* sharply with the plurality's view that a school system may *never take race into account* as part of a voluntary system of pupil assignments.

a. **Diversity as a compelling educational goal:** Kennedy agreed with the plurality that since both plans "classify individuals by race and allocate benefits and burdens on that basis," the plans were to be subjected to strict scrutiny. But Kennedy rejected the plurality's conclusion that the districts had not identified any compelling interest that they were pursuing. For Kennedy, *"diversity*, depending on its meaning and definition, *is a compelling educational goal* a school district may pursue." (At the end of his opinion, Kennedy was even more specific about what interests should be deemed compelling: a school district had a compelling interest in both *"avoiding racial isolation"* and in "achiev[ing] a *diverse student population."* As to the latter, "race may be one component of that diversity, but other *demographic* factors, plus *special talents and needs*, should also be considered.")

b. **Not narrowly tailored:** But Kennedy voted to strike the plans because, even if they were enacted in pursuit of a compelling objective, they did not manifest the *tightness of means-end fit* required under strict scrutiny. In the case of Seattle, for instance, even accepting as appropriate goals Seattle's desire to reduce racial isolation and promote the educational benefits of diversity, Kennedy could not see how Seattle's use of the *white / non-white distinction as the sole racial classification* furthered those goals. Less than half of Seattle's student body was white, yet the district had used "the *crude racial categories of 'white' and non-white' "* as the basis for its assignment decisions.

Kennedy cited with approval the plurality's criticism that under the Seattle plan, a school with 50% Asian-American students and 50% white students, and with no black, Native-American or Latino students, would qualify as balanced, whereas a school with 30% Asian-American, 25% African-American, 25% Latino and 20% white students would not. "Far from being narrowly tailored to its purposes, this system threatens to defeat its own ends[.]" "Individual racial classifications" like the ones used here, he said later in his opinion, were permissible "only if they are a *last resort* to achieve a compelling interest," and neither district had satisfied this last-resort standard.

c. **Plurality criticized:** But Kennedy also believed that the *plurality* had *gone much too far in its insistence on complete color-blindness.* He criticized Roberts' *"all-too-unyielding insistence that race cannot be a factor* in instances when, in my view, it *may be taken into account."* The plurality opinion, he said, was "too dismissive of the *legitimate interest* government has in ensuring all people have *equal opportunity* regardless of their race."

Kennedy was especially unwilling to accept the plurality's apparent belief that "the Constitution requires school districts to *ignore the problem of de facto resegregation* in schooling." If the plurality was suggesting that the Constitution required that state and local authorities "must *accept the status quo of racial isolation* in the schools," the plurality was *"profoundly mistaken."*

   i. **Right to consider race:** Kennedy believed that school authorities were entitled to use "race-conscious measures" to address the goal of offering "an *equal educational opportunity* to all of their students." But authorities had to "*address the problem in a general way* and *without treating each student in different fashion solely on the basis of a systematic, individual typing by race."*

      (1) **Allowable methods:** Kennedy pointed to several *race-conscious methods* that a school district *might use* without running afoul of his "no individual typing by race" rule:

         ❏ "strategic *site selection* of new schools" based on consciousness of neighborhood demographics;

         ❏ "drawing *attendance zones* with a general recognition of the demographics of neighborhoods";

         ❏ "allocating *resources for special programs*";

         ❏ "*recruiting students and faculty* in a targeted fashion" and

         ❏ "tracking enrollments, performance, and other statistics by race."

      (2) **Rationale:** Kennedy believed that these methods, although they were race conscious, did not need to be strictly scrutinized because they "do not lead to different treatment based on a *classification that tells each student he or she is to be defined by race*[.]"

d. **Summary:** In sum, Kennedy was willing to allow some use of race in the student assignment process, but not the broad use of race, including ***student-by-student classification***, that the dissent would allow. The dissent's approach, he said, had "no principled limit and would result in the ***broad acceptance of governmental racial classifications in areas far afield from schooling***." Kennedy stressed "the dangers presented by individual [racial] classifications," dangers that he said "are not as pressing when the same ends are achieved by ***more indirect means***." He was especially worried about the ***mechanics*** by which any direct-classification process would have to work: "When the government classifies an individual by race, it must first ***define what it means to be of a race.*** Who exactly is white and who is nonwhite? To be forced to live under a ***state-mandated racial label*** is inconsistent with the ***dignity of individuals*** in our society." By contrast, the race-conscious methods he was willing to allow — drawing attendance zones in a race-conscious manner, race-conscious site selection, etc. — did not pose these problems to the same degree because they did not "rely on differential treatment based on ***individual classifications***."

5. **The dissent:** The principal dissent was by Justice ***Breyer***, who was joined by Stevens, Souter and Ginsburg.[11] Breyer disagreed with virtually every step of the plurality's analysis, saying that the plurality's views "threaten a ***surge of race-based litigation***," violated long-established precedent, and were likely to jeopardize *Brown*'s promise of progress towards racial equality.

a. **De jure / de facto distinction rejected:** At the outset, Breyer rejected the importance the plurality gave to the distinction between de jure and de facto segregation. Both Seattle and Louisville had had racially segregated schools, and had long struggled to reduce that racial isolation. For Breyer, the fact that Seattle had never been under a formal court finding of official segregation, and that Louisville's official segregation had been declared eradicated, should not have deprived either district of the power to make voluntary use of race-conscious factors in pupil assignments.

b. **Gentler form of strict scrutiny:** Breyer also believed that the plurality was misinterpreting the legal standard set by then-recent cases on raced-based affirmative action, like *Adarand* and *Grutter*. He conceded that those cases seemed to require that strict scrutiny be applied to all race-based classifications. But he thought that in practice, these cases applied a far more forgiving form of strict scrutiny to "racial classifications that seek to ***include***" than to "racial classifications that harmfully ***exclude***." And he believed that the plans here were entitled to the more forgiving version of scrutiny, because what was at issue here was "not a context that involves the use of race to decide ***who will receive goods or services*** that are normally distributed on the basis of merit and which are in short supply" but instead, a context of "racial limits that seek, not to keep the races apart, but to ***bring them together***." Therefore, Breyer said, he thought that the plan should be given merely a ***"careful review,"*** not a review that was " 'strict' in the traditional sense of that word[.]"

---

11. Justice Stevens wrote his own, briefer, dissent. He found Roberts' reliance on *Brown* to be a "cruel irony," and noted that "history books do not tell stories of white children struggling to attend black schools." For Stevens, the racial classifications here should be viewed differently than the ones struck down in *Brown*, because the ones here "do not impose burdens on one race alone and do not stigmatize or exclude." Stevens closed by lamenting that "It is my firm conviction that no Member of the Court that I joined in 1975 would have agreed with today's decision."

c. Meets even true strict review: But even if full-fledged strict scrutiny were applied, Breyer said, the plans here passed muster: they were ***narrowly tailored*** to the achievement of a ***compelling objective***.

i. Compelling objective: Breyer characterized the interest being pursued by the school boards as the interest in ***"promoting or preserving greater racial 'integration' of public schools."*** He thought that this interest was in turn motivated by several sub-interests: (1) a ***historical*** interest in "setting right the consequences of prior conditions of segregation"; (2) an ***educational*** interest in "overcoming the adverse educational effects produced by and associated with ***highly segregated schools***" and (3) a ***democratic*** interest in "helping our children learn to ***work and play together*** with children of different racial backgrounds." He then asked rhetorically, "If an educational interest that combines these three elements is not 'compelling', what is?"

ii. Narrow tailoring: Kennedy next turned to whether the race conscious means chosen by the school boards here were ***"narrowly tailored"*** towards achievement of this compelling objective in preserving integration. He thought that the answer was yes, even under "the strictest 'tailoring' test." He listed several factors in support of this conclusion:

(1) First, the use of race-conscious criteria here was only a small part of the decision-making process in school assignments, a process that depended mainly on other, non-racial, elements. The plans depended mainly on the non-racial factor of ***student choice***, and race was used only to set "the ***outer bounds*** of ***broad ranges***." This made the plans less like a quota and more like the kinds of "useful starting points" that the Court had previously approved.

(2) Second, he thought that the use of race here was more narrowly tailored than the use of race approved in *Grutter*: here, "race becomes a factor only in a ***fraction*** of students' ***non-merit-based*** assignments," whereas in *Grutter*, race affected "***large numbers*** of students' ***merit-based*** applications."

(3) Finally, the history behind each plan showed that it was the product of the district's long efforts to "enhance student choice, while diminishing the need for mandatory busing"; each plan thus made ***less use of race*** than the plans it replaced, demonstrating how hard the districts had tried to use race in the most narrowly-tailored way that would still accomplish the objective of integration.

6. Significance: So what is the significance of the *Parents Involved v. Seattle* case?

a. Direct impact: The direct impact on the operation of the nation' public schools will probably ***not be great***.

i. Use of non-racial grounds: Most importantly, nothing in the *Parents Involved* decision seems to prevent school districts from promoting school-by-school diversity so long as only ***non-racial grounds*** are used for measuring diversity. Most promising is the use of ***socioeconomic status*** ("SES"), a factor already used by many districts. For instance, the fact that a student qualifies for the free or reduced-cost federally-financed ***school lunch program*** gives districts a way to promote socio-economic integration: assignment and transfer policies can be implemented so as to place the same ratio of school-lunch and non-school-lunch (i.e., poor and non-poor) students in each of a district's schools. Because minority students tend to be on average from poorer families, such an SES-based program will also tend to reduce school-by-school racial isolation while being beyond reproach from an equal protection standpoint.

Note: Notice that the use of race-neutral *socioeconomic status* as an allowable proxy for race in the K-12 context is quite analogous to the use of race-neutral *class-rank-percentage systems* like those lauded by the Court in the university-admissions context (see *Fisher*, *supra*, p. 300).

    b. Indirect impact: But the case is more significant for what it shows about the right-ward drift of the Court from the Rehnquist era to the Roberts era. *Parents Involved* was the Court's first affirmative action decision since Justice O'Connor was replaced by Alito, and that seems to have made a key difference — Justice O'Connor voted with the majority to allow consideration of race in law school admissions in *Grutter*, whereas Justice Alito voted with the plurality in *Parents Involved* (and would almost certainly have voted with the dissent in *Grutter*).

G. Minority set-asides by states and cities: Congress and many states and cities have enacted so-called minority *"set-aside"* programs, by which some fixed percentage of publicly-funded *construction projects* must be set aside for minority-owned businesses. Where such a program is enacted by a city or state (as opposed to the federal government), such set-aside programs will be subjected to *strict scrutiny*, and will often be found unconstitutional. This is exactly what happened in the landmark case of ***Richmond v. J.A. Croson Co.***, 488 U.S. 469 (1989), the first case in which a majority of the Court finally agreed on what level of review should be applied to race-conscious affirmative action programs. Because of the significance of *Croson*, it is worth going into the facts and holding in some detail.

    1. Facts: The city of Richmond, Virginia, enacted a Minority Business Utilization Plan. The plan required prime contractors on construction contracts funded by the city to sub-contract at least 30% of the dollar amount of the contract to one or more Minority Business Enterprises, or MBEs. To be an MBE, a business had to be at least 51% owned by minority group members. "Minority group members" were defined to include African Americans, Hispanics, Asians, Indians, Eskimos and Aleuts. An MBE need not be based in the Richmond area: it could be anywhere in America, and still qualify under the set-aside program.

        a. Rationale: The City Council declared that its plan was designed to overcome the effects of past discrimination against African Americans in the Richmond-area construction industry, and was thus "remedial" in nature. The Council said it wanted to "promot[e] wider participation by minority business enterprises in the construction of public projects."

        b. Waiver: A prime contractor could obtain a waiver from the MBE requirement, but only if he showed that there were no qualified MBEs available and willing to participate in the contract.

    2. Evidence before the Council: The Council had before it some evidence that there had been extensive racial discrimination in the construction industry:

        a. None by city: There was no evidence that the *city itself* had ever discriminated with respect to construction.

    b. **No contracts:** However, there was evidence before the Council that even though Richmond was 50% black, only .67% of the city's prime construction contracts had been awarded to minority businesses in the prior five years.

    c. **Associations:** Also, most of the contractors' associations active in the area had virtually no minority businesses within their membership.

    d. **Congressional plan:** Lastly, the Council had before it reports issued by Congress, at the time Congress enacted a similar minority set-aside program for federal public works projects. Those congressional findings contained strong evidence that there had been extensive discrimination against African American construction concerns nationwide.

3. **Nature of the claim:** The plaintiff in *Croson* was a white-owned prime contractor seeking a contract to install toilets in the city jail. P claimed that he was unable to find an MBE who could supply 30% of the work at acceptable cost. P sued the city, claiming that the set-aside violated its right to equal protection of the law.

4. **Holding:** The opinion for the Court was written by Justice O'Connor. On some points, she spoke for only a plurality. But on the key point, she spoke for a majority: ***any governmental action that is explicitly race-based must be "necessary" to achieve a "compelling" governmental interest***. In other words, the majority held, race-based affirmative action plans must be subjected to the same ***strict scrutiny*** as are governmental actions that intentionally discriminate ***against*** racial minorities.

    a. **Rationale:** Justice O'Connor seemed to assert three distinct reasons why race-conscious affirmative action plans must be subjected to strict scrutiny:

        i. **No way to tell:** First of all, there is no easy way to tell which racial classifications are truly "benign" or "remedial" and which ones are ostensibly benign, but in reality motivated by "illegitimate notions of racial inferiority or simple racial politics." (For instance, since the measure here was enacted by a City Council that had a black majority, it might well have been merely a successful political attempt to get more of the economic pie.) Use of strict scrutiny, Justice O'Connor said, would help "smoke out" the illegitimate use of race by insisting on a compelling governmental objective and a very tight fit between the means chosen and that objective. (See *supra*, p. 272, for a discussion of how strict scrutiny helps to "smoke out" illegitimate objectives.)

        ii. **Stigmatic harm:** Second, O'Connor asserted, classifications based on race "carry a danger of ***stigmatic harm***." That is, the group "benefitted" by an affirmative action program (e.g., African American contractors in Richmond) might in the long run be harmed, because society will believe that the favored group is less competent and cannot succeed without special protection.

        iii. **Can't get beyond race:** Finally, she argued, unless race-conscious affirmative action plans are strictly scrutinized, as a society we will never achieve our goal of becoming truly ***race-neutral***. Justice O'Connor accused Justice Marshall's dissent (discussed below) of advocating a "watered-down version of equal protection review [that] effectively assures that race will always be relevant in American life. …"

b. As applied to Richmond plan: Strict scrutiny clearly required that the Richmond plan be struck down, Justice O'Connor thought.

   i. Objective: Although Richmond claimed to be pursuing the objective of overcoming past racial discrimination in construction, there was not nearly adequate proof that this discrimination had in fact occurred. For instance: (1) there was no direct evidence of discrimination by ***anyone*** in the Richmond construction industry (merely "an amorphous claim that there has been past discrimination"); (2) there was no evidence that there would be more minority contracting firms had there not been past societal discrimination; and (3) there was no showing of how many MBEs in the local labor market could have done the work (a relevant factor, since "where special qualifications are necessary, the relevant statistical pool for purposes of demonstrating discriminatory exclusion must be the number of minorities ***qualified to undertake the particular task***").

   ii. Inadequacy of evidence: The evidence pointed to by the city and by the dissenters was inadequate to make the requisite showing of clear past discrimination, O'Connor thought. For instance: (1) the fact that only .67% of publicly-funded prime construction contracts in prior years had been given to African American contractors was irrelevant, because there was no showing that ***qualified MBEs*** represented more than this tiny fraction of overall qualified construction firms in the Richmond area; (2) the fact that MBE membership in local contractors' associations was extremely low did not prove discrimination, because "[B]lacks may be disproportionately attracted to industries other than construction"; and (3) the fact that Congress had previously (in adopting a federal minority set-aside program upheld in a prior Court decision) made legislative findings that there was a lot of discrimination against African Americans in the construction industry ***nationwide***, was almost irrelevant, since the degree of discrimination would vary from market to market, and what was relevant was how much discrimination there was in the ***Richmond market***.

   iii. Conclusion: In conclusion, Richmond, like any other public entity that wants to use race-conscious affirmative action measures, "must identify [the] discrimination, public or private, with some specificity before [it] may use race-conscious relief."

c. Tailoring: Not only did Richmond not show that it had a compelling need to redress past discrimination, it also was unable to show that its plan was ***narrowly tailored*** to this remedial objective. For instance, there was no showing that ***race-neutral*** means (e.g., city financing for small firms without regard to the race of their owners) would not increase minority participation adequately. Similarly, the 30% quota was not narrowly tailored to any goal. (True, Richmond was 50% black; but there was no showing that qualified African American firms could or would get 30% of the work in the absence of discrimination, so the 30% quota was not a narrowly tailored way of redressing past discrimination even if that discrimination had been adequately shown.)

d. Sometimes might survive: Justice O'Connor did not believe that ***all*** race-conscious remedial plans would necessarily fail this strict scrutiny test. If there was clear evidence of discrimination either by the government or perhaps even by private parties, eradication of this discrimination might be a sufficiently compelling objective. For

3. **Grutter**: In *Grutter*, the Court **upheld** by a 5-4 vote the University of Michigan Law School's admission process, in which the school pursued the objective of diversity by subjectively adding race into the mix when a student's entire application was considered. Justice O'Connor wrote the Court's opinion, in which she was joined by Justices Stevens, Souter, Ginsburg and Breyer.

a. **Facts:** The Law School was (and is) an elite, highly-selective one, which at the time in question received more than 3500 applications each year for a class of around 350 students. The Law School's admissions policy required admissions officials to **read each applicant's entire file.** Admission was based upon undergraduate grades, LSAT scores, and a number of "soft" variables (e.g., enthusiasm of recommenders, quality of the undergraduate institution, difficulty of undergraduate courses taken, etc.). One of the soft variables was the extent to which the applicant's presence would **contribute to "diversity"** at the school. There were (according to the official admissions policy cited by O'Connor) "many possible bases" for an applicant's contribution to student-body diversity. But one type of diversity was singled out in the official policy: "**racial** and **ethnic** diversity with special reference to the inclusion of students from groups which have been **historically discriminated against**, like **African-Americans**, **Hispanics** and **Native Americans**, who without this commitment **might not be represented in our student body in meaningful numbers.**"

   i. **"Critical mass":** The Law School defended its race-conscious admissions policy principally on the grounds that the school was seeking to enroll a " **'critical mass'** of [underrepresented] minority students." The school's officials testified that "critical mass" meant **"meaningful representation,"** which in turn meant "a number that encourages underrepresented minority students to **participate** in the classroom and **not feel isolated.**"

   ii. **Numbers:** The school **denied** that there was **any particular number**, percentage or range of numbers or percentages that constituted critical mass. During the years in question, the percentage of students in each class that were members of the three favored groups (black, Hispanic and Native American) varied from 13.5% to 20.1%. The Law School denied that this was a quota, but did acknowledge that consideration of race significantly increased the numbers of minorities who attended.

b. **Plaintiff's argument:** P was a white Michigan resident who unsuccessfully applied to the Law School. Her undergraduate GPA and her LSAT scores were, she claimed, higher than those of many minority applicants who were accepted. Consequently, she alleged, the Law School's use of race as what P termed a "predominant" factor constituted a denial of equal protection to her.

c. **O'Connor's majority opinion:** Justice O'Connor's opinion **applied strict scrutiny** to the Law School's consideration of race as an admissions factor, but concluded that the school's method was **sufficiently narrowly tailored** to achieve the compelling interest in maintaining diversity.

   i. **Adoption of Powell *Bakke* opinion:** O'Connor began by summarizing Justice Powell's opinion in *Bakke*, which she said "approved the university's use of race to further only one interest: 'the attainment of a diverse student body'." She declined to decide whether Powell's opinion was binding on the Court as prece-

instance, had there been clear evidence of discrimination by specific general contractors in the Richmond area, eliminating the effects of this discrimination might have been a "compelling" objective, and some sort of race-conscious plan might have been a sufficiently-narrowly-tailored means of correcting that discrimination.

    i.   **Statistical inference:**   Furthermore, Justice O'Connor noted, if there was a "significant *statistical disparity* between the number of qualified minority contractors willing and able to perform a particular service and the number of such contractors actually engaged by the locality or the locality's prime contractors," then an *inference* of discrimination might arise, even in the absence of direct proof of discrimination by a particular contractor against a particular sub-contractor on a particular project.

5. **Array of judges:** Five members of the Court in *Croson* agreed with the key proposition that all race-conscious measures, even supposedly "remedial" ones, must be subjected to strict scrutiny. Three justices (Rehnquist, White, and Kennedy) joined O'Connor's opinion on this point; a fifth, Scalia, said in a concurrence that he agreed with this proposition (though he would go even further than O'Connor, and would not allow race-conscious measures *ever* as a means of remedying past discrimination committed by anyone other than the government itself).

6. **Stevens' concurrence:** Justice Stevens, in a concurrence, seemed to agree with the basic holding that where the government institutes a race-conscious measure for remedial purposes, that measure must be subjected to strict scrutiny. But he saw the majority opinion as having an underlying premise that "a governmental decision that rests on a racial classification is never permissible except as a remedy for a past wrong," and he disagreed with that premise. That is, he thought that there might be some legitimate public purposes, other than relief of past discrimination, that might be served by race-conscious measures (e.g., "In a city with a recent history of racial unrest, the superintendent of police might reasonably conclude that an integrated police force could develop a better relationship with the community and thereby do a more effective job of maintaining law and order than a force composed only of white officers"). He agreed with the majority that Richmond's plan should be held invalid in part because the class of persons benefitted by the ordinance was not limited to victims of discrimination — for instance, it included persons who had never been in business in Richmond.

7. **Dissent:** Three justices bitterly dissented. The principal dissent was by Justice Marshall, joined by Justices Brennan and Blackmun.

    a.   **Standard:** The dissenters sharply disagreed with the majority's assertion that strict scrutiny was the appropriate standard for measuring race-conscious remedial plans. They believed that *intermediate level* scrutiny was the appropriate one: "[R]ace-conscious classifications designed to further remedial goals 'must serve important governmental objectives and must be substantially related to achievement of those objectives. ... ' "

    b.   **Rationale:** Marshall asserted that "[a] profound difference separates governmental actions that themselves are racist, and governmental actions that seek to remedy the effects of prior racism or to prevent neutral governmental activity from perpetuating the effects of such racism." By adopting the strict scrutiny standard, the majority "signals that it regards racial discrimination as largely a phenomenon of the past." Marshall, by contrast, did not believe that the country was "anywhere close to eradicating racial discrimination or its vestiges."

c. Minority control of Richmond: Marshall conceded that the fact that Richmond now had a population and a City Council that were both mostly African American was a factor to be considered in determining the appropriate level of scrutiny. But he disagreed that this should be dispositive. A city that had recently come under minority control was likely to be the very kind of city that would have the most prior discrimination to rectify; certainly that was true of Richmond. Furthermore, the affirmative action plan here was voted for not only by the black city council majority, but also by one of the four white council members, with a second one abstaining.

d. Important objective: Under Marshall's intermediate-level standard of review, the Richmond plan was clearly constitutional. Unlike the majority, he thought that the fact that less than 1% of public construction contracts had gone to minority-owned prime contractors strongly suggested (though it didn't directly prove) discrimination. Also, Marshall would have given substantial weight to the descriptive testimony of Richmond's leaders that the small presence of minorities in construction stemmed from past exclusionary practices. He would have given substantial weight to the fact that there were practically no minority members of area trade associations. And perhaps most importantly, he would have given great weight to the congressional findings of past nationwide discrimination in the construction industry. All of this evidence taken together made a strong showing that past discrimination had caused the present lack of minority participation in the Richmond construction industry, and therefore made the goal of promoting minority participation in that industry an "important" one.

e. "Substantially related": Also, Marshall thought, the particular 30% set-aside was "substantially related" to achieving this objective. The set-aside applied only to public contracting dollars, and amounted to merely 3% of overall Richmond-area contracting. Also, the Richmond plan did not interfere with any vested right of a contractor to a particular contract; instead, it operated almost entirely prospectively, and was therefore less damaging than a plan which took away a contract already awarded to a white contractor. Finally, while the 30% set-aside was in a sense a quota, it was merely a "half-way" measure — it set a percentage about half-way between the present percentage of Richmond-based minority contractors (nearly zero) and the percentage of minorities in Richmond (50%).

8. Significance: What does *Croson* signify about the constitutionality of the many hundreds of minority set-aside programs enacted by states and cities across the country? The Richmond plan was probably unusually vulnerable, because of the relative weakness of the findings of past discrimination, the relatively high (30%) set-aside, and the relatively narrow procedures for obtaining a waiver. But the case will undoubtedly make it dramatically harder for other set-aside programs to pass constitutional muster as well.

a. Findings: Governmental bodies that want to pursue set-asides (or other race-conscious remedial plans) will have to make ***very precise*** legislative findings that there has been past discrimination.

i. Discrimination by governmental body: If there are specific findings that the ***governmental body itself*** has practiced intentional racial discrimination, eradication of the effects of this discrimination will presumably constitute a "compelling" governmental objective. However, governmental bodies will rarely voluntarily make such findings about their own conduct, because of the public relations and legal liability problems this would entail.

ii. **Discrimination by others:** If the government entity comes up with clear evidence that *others* (even private parties) have practiced discrimination in the past, and shows a danger that non-remedial government activity would compound the effects of that discrimination, apparently avoiding this will also suffice as a "compelling" governmental objective. For instance, if Richmond had had clear evidence of past discrimination by prime contractors, Richmond would apparently have been entitled to reason, "If we award city construction funds without making an affirmative attempt to eradicate the effects of this prior private discrimination, we will be ourselves compounding the effects of this past discrimination, and we have a compelling interest in not doing so."

iii. **Societal discrimination:** Clearly, it is not enough for the governmental body to come up with findings of past *societal discrimination*. For instance, no matter how clear the evidence was that there had been widespread racial discrimination by society as a whole in the Richmond area, this would have been irrelevant — what counted was discrimination *in the construction industry*.

iv. **Inference:** It will also be possible to prove past discrimination by *inference*. Generally, this can be done by statistics. But the statistics will have to be much more carefully worked out than they were in the Richmond case. For instance, it will not be enough to show that only a tiny percentage of, say, construction contracts go to African American firms. Instead, the government will apparently have to show fairly precisely how many *qualified* minority firms there are, and will have to demonstrate that these firms are getting a much smaller percentage of the work than their numbers would indicate — only then can a statistical inference of discrimination be made. Of course, since widespread discrimination will tend to prevent minority firms from existing in the first place, it will be a rare instance where there will be qualified minority firms in existence, who are nonetheless receiving very disproportionately little work.

b. **Other objectives:** The curing of past intentional discrimination is almost the *only* objective that will be found "compelling" and thus justify a race-conscious set-aside plan. For instance, a governmental body's desire to improve the general economic status of its poorer citizens will virtually never justify a race-conscious plan.

i. **Pursuit of educational diversity:** The only other objective that the Court has ever found to be a "compelling" one that may justify race-conscious measures is the pursuit of *diversity* in an *educational setting*. Recall that in *Grutter v. Bollinger, supra*, p. 295, a bare five-justice majority found that a public law school had a compelling interest in seeking broad diversity — including but not limited to racial and ethnic diversity — in its entering class. (We will have to wait and see whether the pursuit of racial/ethnic diversity can be compelling in other contexts, such as in university faculty hirings, or non-education-related hirings by such organizations as the armed forces and police departments. See *supra*, p. 306.)

c. Narrowly tailored: The requirement that the means chosen be very ***"narrowly tailored"*** to meet the compelling governmental objective will also make it very hard for minority set-asides to pass muster.

i. Quota: Probably a rigid *quota* will almost always be invalid. Thus even had Richmond set aside only 10% of its contracts for minorities (the figure used by Congress, as opposed to the 30% figure actually used by Richmond), it is hard to imagine that the case would have turned out differently. The Court would almost always conclude that a less rigid plan would have been adequate.

ii. Race-neutral plans: Probably the requirement of narrow tailoring means that the government must first either try out, or at least consciously eliminate, ***race-neutral*** means before using race-conscious means. Thus the Richmond City Council would presumably have to have either tried race-neutral methods (like giving a preference for small or new construction firms, regardless of the race of their owners), or at least come up with specific findings as to why such race-neutral means would not succeed, before it could be allowed to use race-conscious methods.

(1) Race-neutral means of achieving educational diversity: On the other hand, the requirement of narrow tailoring seems to have been somewhat ***weakened*** in the main affirmative-actions-in-admissions case, *Grutter v. Bollinger, supra,* p. 295. There, the majority certainly examined whether workable race-neutral means of attaining diversity were available, such as a race-blind lottery system open to all minimally-qualified candidates. But the Court did not insist that the University ***try out*** these race-neutral methods first, or even that the university conduct some sort of formal ***fact-finding*** to determine whether these alternative methods might be workable. Instead, the Court seemed to give broad ***deference*** to the university's assertion in the litigation itself that these methods would prove unworkable. However, there is not yet any indication that outside of the diversity-in-admissions context, there will be any weakening of the requirement that race-neutral methods be carefully evaluated by the defendant before race-conscious means are used.

iii. Goals: Probably set-asides will at least have to be replaced by less rigid, ***"soft"*** racial preferences, if racial preferences are to be allowed at all. For instance, Richmond would have had a better chance if it had expressed a ***"goal"*** or ***"preference"*** for minorities that would remain in force until 30% of contracts were awarded to minority-owned firms, instead of the hard and fast "quota" which it used. Similarly, a city might fare better if it allowed consideration of race as ***one factor*** among many to be considered when the city decides who should get a contract. But even a "goal" or "one factor among many" plan will probably be struck down if there is no clear evidence of past discrimination, and no showing that race-neutral means would be inadequate. [12]

---

12. Again, ***university admissions*** present a slight exception. The use of goals for minority enrollment to achieve diversity in the student body (rather than to remedy past discrimination) was officially endorsed by the court in *Grutter, supra,* p. 295. But *Grutter* also demonstrates that, as the main text suggests, soft "goals," as opposed to rigid quotas, are far more likely to be found to be an acceptably narrowly-tailored means of achieving whatever compelling interest justifies the use of race-conscious decision making.

H. Set-asides by Congress: The rules are the same for minority set-asides imposed by *Congress*, though this has been true only since mid-1995. In *Adarand Constructors, Inc. v. Pena*, 515 U.S. 200 (1995), the Court overturned prior law and announced that *strict scrutiny must be applied to race-based affirmative action schemes imposed by Congress*, just as it is applied to those imposed by state and local governments.

1. **Pre-*Adarand* law (*Metro Broadcasting*):** *Adarand* overruled a prior case, *Metro Broadcasting, Inc. v. FCC*, 497 U.S. 547 (1990), which had applied intermediate level review, not strict scrutiny, in judging whether "benign" race-conscious action by Congress violated the equal protection rights of non-minorities.

2. **Facts of *Adarand*:** The minority preference at issue in *Adarand* was subtle but nonetheless real. Plaintiff (Adarand) was a white-owned construction firm that had bid for a sub-contract to supply guardrails to a federal highway project in Colorado. P's bid was the lowest. But the general contractor took a bid from a minority-owned firm that qualified under federal regulations as a Disadvantaged Business Enterprise (DBE). The prime contractor was not *required* to award the sub-contract to a minority-owned DBE, but it received a financial incentive (10% of the amount of the sub-contract, or 1.5% of the amount of the prime contract, whichever was less) for doing so.

   a. **Whites can be DBE's:** Small white-owned firms could also be DBE's. But a firm owned by an African American, Hispanic or certain other ethnic minority (as well as a firm owned by a woman) was automatically, though rebuttably, *"presumed"* to be disadvantaged. A firm owned by a white male, by contrast, had to prove disadvantage by "clear and convincing evidence." In any event, P in *Adarand* could not or did not gain DBE status, and the winning bidder for the sub-contract did.

3. **Strict scrutiny applied:** The Court in *Adarand* overruled *Metro Broadcasting*, and held that *congressionally-authorized race-conscious affirmative action programs must be subject to strict scrutiny*. In other words, the rule of *Richmond v. Croson, supra* — that race-conscious "reverse discrimination" may be upheld only if "necessary" to achieve a "compelling" governmental interest — applies to congressional statutes the same as it applies to the actions of state and local governments. On this issue, the vote was 5-4; the Court's opinion was by Justice O'Connor (joined by Rehnquist, Kennedy, Thomas and Scalia).

   a. **Rationale:** O'Connor believed that *Metro Broadcasting* should be overruled because it departed from what she said was one of the core principles of the Court's pre-*Metro* cases on affirmative action: the principle of *"congruence,"* that "equal protection analysis in the Fifth Amendment area [applicable to the federal government] is the same as that under the Fourteenth Amendment [applicable to state and local government]." No matter what level of government is involved, "[W]henever the government treats any person unequally because of his or her race, that person has suffered an injury that falls squarely within the language and spirit of the Constitution's guarantee of equal protection."

      i. **Other principles undermined:** O'Connor also believed that *Metro*'s application of the more lenient "mid-level review" to congressional actions undermined two other core principles: *skepticism* of all racial classifications, and *consistency* of treatment irrespective of the race of the burdened or benefited group. The three core principles of congruence, skepticism and consistency "derive from the basic principle that ***the Fifth and Fourteenth Amendments ... protect persons, not groups.***"

b. Strict scrutiny not necessarily fatal: But O'Connor went out of her way to assure that the use of strict scrutiny did ***not*** necessary mean that the governmental action being reviewed would be struck down: "we wish to ***dispel*** the notion that strict scrutiny is '***strict in theory, but fatal in fact.***' " She suggested that if government is responding to "the ***lingering effects of racial discrimination*** against minority groups," and does so in a ***"narrowly tailored way,"*** even race-conscious methods may survive.

c. Particular regulation not addressed: The Court's opinion did not decide whether the particular set-aside regulations at issue could survive strict scrutiny. Instead, the Court remanded the issue to the lower courts. O'Connor suggested that on remand, the lower courts should consider whether the governmental interest being served was ***"compelling,"*** whether ***race-neutral*** means might have been effective to achieve that interest, and whether the remedy was appropriately ***short-lived*** so as not to "last longer than the discriminatory effects it is designed to eliminate."

4. Concurrences: Two members of the majority would have gone even further than O'Connor. Both Scalia and Thomas indicated in concurrences that they would have ruled that race-conscious affirmative action can ***never*** be justified. As Thomas put it, "government-sponsored racial discrimination based on benign prejudice is just as noxious as discrimination inspired by malicious prejudice. In each instance, it is racial discrimination, plain and simple."

5. Dissents: The four Justices in the minority wrote three dissents. Perhaps the most interesting dissent was the one by Justice Stevens, since he had voted with the majority in *Croson* to apply strict scrutiny to state and local affirmative action programs.

a. Good motives less suspect: Stevens rejected the majority's "consistency" principle: "There is no moral or constitutional equivalence between a policy that is designed to perpetuate a caste system and one that seeks to eradicate racial subordination. ... The consistency that the Court espouses would ***disregard the difference between a 'No Trespassing' sign and a welcome mat.*** It would treat a Dixiecrat Senator's decision to vote against Thurgood Marshall's confirmation in order to keep African Americans off the Supreme Court as on a par with President Johnson's evaluation of his nominee's race as a positive factor."

b. "Congruence" derided: Stevens also believed that there were at least two strong reasons for rejecting the majority's "congruence" principle, and for giving ***more deference*** to race-based affirmative action efforts by Congress than to state and local programs.

i. Special enforcement powers: First, Congress' powers concerning matters of race were ***"explicitly enhanced"*** by §5 of the 14th Amendment (which gives Congress the power to "enforce, by appropriate legislation, the provisions of the 14th Amendment"). By contrast, the states' use of race-conscious measures was what the Amendment was specifically directed *against*.

ii. Entire nation's representatives: Second, "federal affirmative-action programs represent the will of our ***entire Nation's elected representatives***, whereas a state or local program may have an impact on ***nonresident entities*** who played no part in the decision to enact it." Just as Congress may burden interstate commerce even though the individual states may not (see *supra*, p. 68), so Congress should have greater leeway to use race to combat the effects of past discrimination, Stevens argued.

6. **Significance of *Adarand***: Here is a summary of what *Adarand* seems to establish, and what it leaves unresolved:

   a. **Federalizes *Croson***: Most importantly, *Adarand **"federalizes"** Croson*: the federal government must satisfy the same "strict scrutiny" standard for race-based affirmative actions as must state and local governments. That is, government may use race only in a way that is "narrowly tailored" to achieve some "compelling" governmental objective.

   b. **"Compelling" interest and "narrowly-tailored means"**: *Adarand* doesn't tell us much new about what governmental objectives are "compelling," or about how to tell whether the means chosen are sufficiently "narrowly tailored." Clearly the prevention of ***ongoing discrimination*** in the particular area being regulated (e.g., the awarding of highway construction sub-contracts in a particular city) will qualify, but it's not clear what other objectives would suffice.

   c. **Applies to non-set-aside contexts**: *Adarand* does not just apply to minority set-asides or to contracting. It applies equally to ***educational admissions***, ***employment***, and any other domain. For instance, a congressionally-funded scholarship fund that gave a preference to African American and Hispanic students would presumably be subjected to strict scrutiny.

   d. **Possible greater deference to Congress**: Even though *Adarand* makes the "same" test (strict scrutiny) applicable across all levels of government, the Court may be willing to grant Congress ***greater deference*** than it would to a state or local government body. For instance, the Court might be quicker to accept a congressional finding that there had been discrimination in a particular domain — or a finding that the discrimination could only be redressed through race-conscious means — than it would be to accept such a finding from a state or local legislature.

      i. **Nationwide findings**: Similarly, Congress may be entitled to make findings on a ***national*** rather than local basis. If so, it could be relatively easy for Congress to protect some widesweeping programs.

      ii. **Degree of congressional involvement needed**: If Congress does get greater deference compared with state and local governments, the action probably has to be one taken fairly directly by ***Congress itself***, not one taken by a federal ***administrative agency*** acting under broad congressional guidelines.

   e. **Degree of outcome-determinativeness**: The degree to which the minority preference ***determines the outcome*** will presumably be part of the equation when the Court decides whether the program is sufficiently narrowly-tailored. A modest preference like that in *Adarand* (in essence, an at-most-10% advantage given to minority subcontractors, with the final decision left to the prime contractor) is likely to be easier to justify than a flat quota or set-aside (e.g., a commandment to prime contractors, "You may not receive this contract unless x% of the sub-contracts go to minority firms.").

    i. Presumptions: Similarly, *rebuttable* presumptions are more likely to pass muster than *irrebuttable* rules. Thus the scheme in *Adarand* (where a minority-owned firm is presumed to be economically and socially disadvantaged, and a firm owned by a white male is presumed not, but either presumption can be overturned by particularized evidence) is more likely to survive than a flat rule stating "All black-owned firms shall be conclusively deemed to be disadvantaged, and no white-male-owned firm shall be deemed disadvantaged."

    f. "Diversity" as an objective: It remains unclear whether the pursuit of racial *diversity* can ever by itself be a "compelling objective." The best guess is that a majority of the present Court will ultimately conclude that pursuit of racial diversity, without more, is *not* a compelling objective. (However, where diversity is tied to a more specific objective — like assuring that a police force has some common bonds with, and understanding of, the minority neighborhoods it polices — a compelling interest might be found.)

I. Hiring, lay-offs, and promotions: Are race-conscious affirmative action programs constitutional when they relate to *hiring*, *lay-offs*, *promotions*, and other *job-related* decisions? Voluntary arrangements by a private company do not raise any constitutional issue, since no state action is present. Constitutional issues do, however, arise when a race-conscious employment policy is either:

❑ voluntarily entered into by a *public employer*; or

❑ *imposed* upon either a public or private employer *by a court* as a remedy for a judicial finding of prior discrimination.

No case raising these issues has been decided by the Supreme Court since the decision in *Croson*, requiring strict scrutiny for all race-conscious affirmative action measures. Here is what can be said at present about affirmative action plans in the employment area:

1. Standard: A race-conscious plan in the employment area, like a race-conscious plan adopted by government in any context, must be *strictly scrutinized,* as the result of *Croson*. That is, the government objective must be a "compelling" one, and the means chosen must be very "narrowly tailored" to that objective — "narrowly tailored" seems to mean that there must be no feasible less-restrictive alternative. Thus the employer must either have tried race-neutral methods, or at least come up with a convincing argument as to why such race-neutral methods would not suffice.

2. Governmental objective: The Court has now either adjudicated or alluded in dictum to five possible governmental objectives in the employment area, only some of which are sufficiently important to survive scrutiny:

    a. Redress of past discrimination: The redress of *past discrimination* by the *particular employer* enacting the affirmative action program is sufficiently compelling to pass muster with all or nearly all members of the Court.

        i. Broader discrimination: Furthermore, it will sometimes suffice that there is evidence of past discrimination in a particular *industry*, rather than on the part of a particular employer.

b. **"Societal" discrimination:** On the other hand, the remedying of *"societal"* discrimination, i.e., discrimination by society as a whole, does ***not*** constitute an objective that is important enough to justify use of race-conscious measures.

c. **Encouragement of "diversity":** It is possible that the goal of promoting *"racial diversity"* in a workforce may sometimes be a sufficiently weighty goal.

> **i.** **Admissions context as precedent:** We now know, of course, of that the goal of promoting racial diversity in a ***university student body*** can be a compelling governmental interest; that's the core holding of *Grutter v. Bollinger, supra,* p. 295. We will have to see whether promoting racial diversity in a ***workforce*** as opposed to student body can sometimes similarly be compelling. Perhaps where the ***constituency served*** by a workforce is highly ***integrated***, attaining racial diversity among the work force itself will be deemed especially weighty, as in the case of an inner-city police force or a corrections staff serving a highly integrated prison population. Similarly, where a public workforce itself is highly integrated, having an integrated ***leadership*** at the top of that workforce may be deemed to be compelling, as in the case of the officer corps of our nation's very-integrated armed forces; see Justice O'Connor's opinion for the court in *Grutter*, relying heavily on an amicus brief by various retired military leaders that argued for the need to use affirmative action to ensure an integrated officer corps.

d. **Balanced workforce:** The goal of assuring a *"balanced workforce,"* by itself, clearly will ***not*** justify use of race-conscious employment policies. Thus even where, say, a public employer has a smaller percentage of minorities in its workforce than are present in the relevant local labor force, the goal of bringing minority participation up to the labor-pool average will not suffice, in the absence of evidence of discrimination by that particular employer, or at least discrimination by the industry or union covering the labor market in question.

e. **Furnishing of "role models":** The goal of supplying "role models" to minority students is probably ***not*** a goal adequate to support race-conscious measures. That is, although it may be appropriate to seek some degree of diversity on a high school faculty, it is almost certainly not permissible to give preferences to minorities for the purpose of increasing minority representation on the faculty to match the percentage of minority students.

3. **Narrowly tailored means:** On the "means" side of the equation, employment cases have focused on three broad classes of methods for achieving the various objectives discussed above: (1) goals and "quotas" in hiring; (2) protections against lay-offs; and (3) preferences in promotions.

a. **Hiring goals:** Explicitly race-conscious *"hiring goals"* are generally permissible when they are an attempt to redress ***clear past discrimination*** by the employer who is using them.

Example: Employer, who has been found by a court to have discriminated against African Americans in the past, is ordered by the court to make best efforts to ensure that 18% of all new employees it hires are African American. African Americans make up 18% of the local labor force for the type of worker commonly employed by Employer. This type of "hiring goal" will probably be found to be constitutional.

i. **Non-victims as beneficiaries:** It does not matter that **non-victims** benefit from the hiring goals. Thus on the facts of the above example, even if it were shown that few or none of the African Americans who obtained jobs from Employer had ever been discriminated against on racial grounds (either by Employer or by other companies), the scheme would remain valid.

ii. **Quotas:** However, "hiring goals" are not the same thing as "**quotas**." Quotas are probably **not constitutional** even where used by an employer who has discriminated in the past. While the difference between a "hiring goal" and a "quota" is fuzzy, the difference mainly relates to **flexibility**. A hiring goal is flexible in the sense that the employer does not adopt a hard-and-fast rule that a particular percentage of new hires **must** belong to the minority, no matter what their relative qualifications. Similarly, if the program is under the supervision of a court, in order to avoid a presumptively unconstitutional quota the court must grant a temporary waiver to the employer if there is a plausible reason why the employer was not able to meet the goals.

iii. **Absolute bar to majority advancement:** The goals cannot act as an **absolute bar to majority advancement**. Thus a goal calling, even briefly, for 100% of new hires to belong to the minority would presumably be unconstitutional, no matter how egregiously the employer had discriminated in the past, and no matter how far the percentage of minorities in the employer's workforce fell below the percentage in the overall local workforce.

iv. **Temporary:** The goals must be **temporary**. That is, they must expire as soon as the percentage of minorities in the employer's workforce equals the percentage in the relevant labor force, since at that point the result of past discrimination has presumably been eliminated. Thereafter, it does not matter if the minority participation in the employer's workforce drops **below** the percentage in the local labor pool, so long as there is no evidence of actual discrimination. (Remember that race-conscious affirmative action programs cannot be used to achieve the objective of a racially balanced workforce; see *supra*, p. 324.)

v. **Percentage of places reserved:** It may be unconstitutional for the goals to call for reservation, even temporarily, of a **higher** percentage of places in the employer's workforce than minorities occupy in the local labor force. This is an issue on which the Court has not yet taken an explicit position.

vi. **Tested against race-neutral means:** Race-conscious hiring goals will probably always be tested against possible **race-neutral** methods. Thus if the employer cannot show that it has considered and rejected for good reason race-neutral means, the race-conscious hiring goal will probably be struck down. For instance, the employer will normally have to show that it has considered **more aggressive recruiting** of minority workers, special training programs for new workers regardless of race, or other methods apart from race-based selection procedures, before the employer may use race-conscious hiring goals.

b. **Lay-offs:** Preferential protections against **lay-offs** are far harder to justify, as a constitutional matter, than are hiring preferences. Since lay-offs affect a worker's present job, rather than merely one of several possibilities for future employment, the harm suffered by "innocent" members of the majority is far greater than in the hiring-preference case. See, e.g., *Wygant v. Jackson Bd. of Educ.*, 476 U.S. 267 (1986) (plurality opinion). Therefore, it seems unlikely that there is any scheme for giving minorities preferential protection against lay-offs that would be supported by a majority of the Court.

   c. Promotion preferences: Preferences in *promotions* of existing employees fall somewhere between hiring preferences and lay-off preferences in terms of the disruption to the lives of existing employees. Therefore, they are somewhat harder to justify than hiring goals but easier than lay-off preferences. A preferential promotions plan is most likely to survive constitutional scrutiny where it is a closely calibrated attempt to *restore* minority workers to the senior positions they *would have had* in the employer's workforce had the past discrimination never occurred.

4. Significance of context: The *context* in which the employment preference occurs is also significant:

   a. Judicial finding: Where the employer, whether public or private, is found by a court to have discriminated in the past, and the preference scheme is one ordered by the court, the above analysis controls. That analysis would probably also control if the employer settled a serious discrimination suit by agreeing to the preference scheme, but this has not been definitively established.

   b. Voluntary arrangement by private party: Where the preference scheme is a *voluntary* one enacted by a *private* employer which has *discriminated* in the past, there is no constitutional problem at all because there is no state action.

   c. No past discrimination: Where the scheme is enacted by a private employer for some purpose other than the remedying of past discrimination by that employer (e.g., to maintain a balanced workforce, or to remedy "societal" discrimination), there is similarly no constitutional problem. (However, there may be problems with Title VII, the main federal anti-discrimination *statute*.)

   d. Voluntary arrangement by public employer: Where a *public* employer *voluntarily* enacts preferences without evidence that it has discriminated in the past, the Court will presumably *strictly scrutinize* the preference. While this strict scrutiny will make it hard for the voluntary plan to survive, it has a respectable chance of surviving if: (1) there is strong statistical evidence of an imbalance that could not have happened by chance; (2) there is some evidence of discrimination by the industry or unions in the relevant market (even if not evidence of discrimination by the particular employer); and (3) race or sex is merely made "one factor" in the hiring or promotion decision.

J. Drawing of election districts: The process by which the boundaries of *election districts* are drawn has often led *groups of voters* to claim unconstitutional reverse racial discrimination. When election districts are drawn by state legislatures or other government bodies, those drawing the lines almost always take race into account, just as they take account of party affiliation, ethnic breakdown, and other demographics. In light of *Richmond v. Croson, supra,* p. 313, at first glance it would seem that once the plaintiff could show that she had been disfavored by the racially-conscious drawing of election district boundaries, the Court would strictly scrutinize the boundaries. But this is generally not in fact the case. A plaintiff will succeed with a reverse discrimination claim regarding electoral districting only by showing either: (1) that the lines were drawn with the *purpose* and *effect* of *disadvantaging the group* of which the plaintiff is a part; or (2) that *race* was the *"predominant factor"* in how the district lines were drawn. We consider each of these types of attacks in turn.

1. **"Partisan gerrymander" claims:**   Traditionally, the type of claim most frequently brought by groups believing themselves to have been disadvantaged by the district-drawing process has been an equal protection claim based upon *"dilution of voting strength."* In this type of claim, the plaintiffs argue that their group's ability to elect representatives of their choice has been weakened by the drawing of boundary lines that advantage some other group.

   These claims are typically directed at *"partisan gerrymanders,"* i.e. the drawing of districts in a highly artificial way for the principal purpose of disadvantaging a particular political group.[13]

   > **Example:** In most states, the boundary lines for congressional districts are drawn by the state legislature. Let's assume that the legislature in State X is controlled by Democrats, and that the state has 14 congressional districts. Let's further assume that 51% of the state's registered voters are Democrats and 49% are Republicans (and let's pretend that there are no independents). If the congressional districts were drawn in a non-partisan and essentially random way, most of the time the state would elect seven Democrats to Congress and seven Republicans. Now, however, let's assume that through some quirk of local politics the State X legislature is so completely controlled by Democratic legislators that the Democrats have the ability to enact any districting plan they want, so long as it meets the requirement of mathematical equality (i.e., that each district have the same population, in accordance with the Supreme Court's "one-person, one-vote" rule, described *infra*, p. 733).
   >
   > When it next comes time to redraw congressional district boundaries,[14] the Democrats spring into action. They propose a redistricting plan that packs most Republican voters into four districts in each of which at least 75% of the voters are Republican. Conversely, Democratic voters are spread out so that they have a narrow but clear majority in the other 10 districts. Let's also assume that this map drawing is done in such a way as to create very oddly shaped districts, to disrespect political subdivisions (e.g., by splitting cities), and to ignore natural geographical features (e.g., by putting both sides of a river in the same district while splitting a neighborhood). Then, the Democrats use their control of the state legislature to enact the redistricting plan, over the fierce objection of the Republicans. If the Democrats have drawn their lines well, and if voters vote on party lines, the Democrats will have 10 of the 14 members of the state's congressional delegation, verses the seven seats that would be produced by a neutral plan. This is a classic "partisan gerrymander."

   a. **Nearly impossible to win:** Claims attacking such partisan-gerrymandered districts are *virtually impossible to win.* In the final years of the Rehnquist Court, four Justices believed that such claims were *non-justiciable*, and should thus not be heard at all. Of

---

13. Here, we're assuming that the claim is that the gerrymander was principally based on some factor *other than race,* such as *membership in a particular political party.* As to racially-motivated gerrymanders, which are easier to attack, see *infra*, p. 328. In our present discussion, we are talking about garden-variety political-party-based gerrymanders in which, say, Republicans try to disadvantage Democrats, or vice versa.

14. This normally happens every 10 years, shortly after the 1990, 2000, etc. Census.

the five members of that Court who were theoretically willing to hear such claims, all agreed that the standards for winning such a claim should be very demanding, but the five could not even agree among themselves on just what the standards should be. See *Vieth v. Jubelirer*, immediately *infra* and p. 736. In any event, no plaintiff in recent generations has succeeded in winning a partisan-gerrymandering Equal Protection claim at the Supreme Court level.[15]

   b. No agreement on standards (*Vieth v. Jubelirer*): In ***Vieth v. Jubelirer***, 541 U.S. 267 (2004), apart from the four members of the Rehnquist Court who said that partisan-gerrymandering claims were not even justiciable all, the remaining five members could not agree among themselves on what the standards for a gerrymandering claim should be. Here is a very brief summary of the views of several of those five Justices on what the plaintiff in a partisan gerrymandering case should have to show:

   i.   **Stevens:** Justice Stevens would let the plaintiff win if she could show that "the legislature *allowed partisan considerations* to *dominate and control* the lines drawn, *forsaking all neutral principles."* So if "the only possible explanation for a district's bizarre shape is a naked desire to increase partisan strength," Stevens would find the district a violation of Equal Protection. (Stevens thought that under this test, there would be "only a few meritorious claims," but that "extreme abuses" would be prevented.)

   ii. **Souter:** Justice Souter proposed a complex five-element standard for a prime facie case. Space prevents us from summarizing all the elements. But, for instance, Souter would require the plaintiff to show that the district in which she resided "paid little or no heed to those *traditional districting principles [like] contiguity, compactness, respect for political subdivisions,* and *conformity with geographic features like rivers and mountains."* The plaintiff would also have to "establish *specific correlations* between the district's deviations from traditional districting principles and the distribution of the population of his group." For instance, if P was complaining that the lines were drawn in a way that split particular towns and communities, P would have to show that "Democrats tended to fall on one side and Republicans on the other."

   iii. **Kennedy:** Justice Kennedy couldn't say what the precise standard ought to be, but thought that a standard based on the *First Amendment* might work better than one based on the Equal Protection clause. That is, Kennedy thought that the Court should try to use First Amendment *free-association* principles to protect the disfavored voters' right not to be discriminated against on account of their association with the disfavored political party.

   iv. **Conclusion:** So following *Vieth*, it's hard to see how plaintiffs in a partisan-gerrymandering case can ever convince a majority of the Court that a particular partisan gerrymander would violate the plaintiffs' Equal Protection rights.

2. "Racial gerrymanders" violate Equal Protection: Until the mid-1990s, "partisan gerrymandering" claims (described above) seemed to be the only way in which voters could

---

15. Nothing from the Roberts Court has changed the difficulty of winning a partisan gerrymander claim. See, e.g., *League of United Latin Amer. Citizens v. Perry*, 126 S.Ct. 2594 (2006), where the plaintiffs failed with a partisan-gerrymander claim.

bring an equal protection attack against the race-conscious drawing of election districts. But the Supreme Court has since held that there is a second type of equal protection claim under which voters may attack the drawing of electoral districts: if the plaintiffs can show that the use of *race* was the *"predominant factor"* in drawing the district lines, the districting scheme will be subjected to **strict scrutiny**. The Court has referred to such schemes as *"racial gerrymanders."* This second type of equal protection claim was recognized in a pair of cases, one in 1993 and the other in 1995. And, in contrast to partisan-gerrymander cases, racial-gerrymander cases have often proved to be winnable by the plaintiffs.

a. **The "facially irrational" theory (*Shaw v. Reno*):** The first racial-gerrymandering decision by the Court was ***Shaw v. Reno***, 509 U.S. 630 (1993). By a 5-4 vote, the Court held that if the plaintiffs could show that the districting scheme was "so ***irrational*** on its face that it can only be understood as an effort to segregate voters into separate voting districts because of their race," strict scrutiny would be triggered, and the districting struck down unless it was shown to be "narrowly tailored to further a compelling governmental interest."

    i. **Bizarre shape:** The majority in *Shaw* seemed to concentrate on the **shape** of the district. The district at issue in *Shaw* was in fact strangely-shaped and non-compact. Because North Carolina's African American population is relatively dispersed, a long, narrow, irregularly-shaped district was the only way to create two districts that would be majority-black in the state, a goal the state legislature was willing to achieve and the Voting Rights Act may have required. The district as drawn was 160 miles long, and in some places was only as wide as the interstate highway.

        (1) **Remanded:** The Court remanded for a determination of whether this district was so bizarre as to violate the Court's new standard. Later, in *Shaw v. Hunt*, 517 U.S. 899 (1996) (also discussed *infra*, p. 330), the Court held that the district *did* violate the standard.

    ii. **Significance of shape unclear:** The *Shaw* decision left it unclear whether a bizarre shape was a requirement for showing an illegal "racial gerrymander," or whether instead *any* racially-motivated districting scheme would be strictly scrutinized, with bizarre shape merely being one possible indicator of racial motive.

    iii. **Rationale:** In any event, the majority in *Shaw* made it clear that 5 members of the Court thought that "racial gerrymanders" were bad, and constitutionally suspect, policy. There were two reasons. First, the drawing of district lines based mainly on race would have a **socially-divisive impact** on **voters**, resembling "**political apartheid**" and "**balkaniz[ing]** us into competing racial factions." Second, racially-motivated districting sends a bad message to the **officials** elected from the gerrymandered districts, that their primary obligation is to **represent only the members of the racially-dominant group** rather than the whole constituency.

b. **"Predominant factor" test (*Miller v. Johnson*):** The next racial-gerrymandering case, ***Miller v. Johnson***, 515 U.S. 900 (1995), then made it clear that a bizarre shape is *not* a requirement for such a claim, and that all the plaintiffs must prove is that race was a *"predominant factor"* in the drawing of the district lines. Once the plaintiffs make this showing, the Court will use strict scrutiny. *Miller*, like *Shaw*, was a 5-4 vote.

i. **Kennedy's opinion:** The majority opinion in *Miller*, by Justice Kennedy, spoke in broad terms: "Just as the state may not, absent extraordinary justification, segregate citizens on the basis of race in its public parks, buses, golf courses, beaches, and schools," so it may not "separate its citizens into different voting districts on the basis of race."

ii. **Facts:** The facts in *Miller* illustrate at least one scenario in which an illegal racial gerrymander will be found. Because Georgia had previously been found to have discriminated against African Americans in voting, it was subject to the "pre-clearance" provisions of the federal Voting Rights Act. Under these provisions, any redistricting plan had to be pre-approved by the Justice Department. The Justice Department (the majority found) took the position that any redistricting plan must create at least three majority-black districts. After initially resisting, the Georgia legislature eventually came up with a plan that included three such districts, including the district at issue here (the 11th). In the litigation, the state essentially conceded that the drawing of the lines for the 11th was done mostly for racial reasons, because of the need to produce three majority-black districts to satisfy the Justice Department. The fact that the district was relatively **compact**, and no more "irregular" or "bizarre" in its shape than many districts, was not enough to save it, given the race-conscious motives with which it was drawn.

iii. **Flunks strict scrutiny:** Because the districting had been done primarily for racial reasons, the Court applied strict scrutiny. The majority found that the lines for the 11th district flunked because the state was not pursuing any "compelling" interest. If the drawing of three majority-black districts had really been necessary to redress past discrimination, the Court suggested, the requisite compelling interest might have been found. But here, the only interest the majority found was the interest in satisfying the Justice Department's rules. And these rules, the majority concluded, were not necessary for eliminating past anti-black discrimination in the state.

iv. **O'Connor's concurrence:** Justice O'Connor, who in a concurrence supplied the vital fifth vote to strike the districting plan, suggested that she might make it harder than the other four members of the majority would for plaintiffs to win such challenges. She characterized the standard for those challenging race-conscious districts as being a "demanding one" — plaintiffs must show that the State has "relied on race in *substantial disregard of customary and traditional districting practices*." Only "*extreme instances* of gerrymandering" would be subjected to strict scrutiny, she said.

v. **Dissent:** As in *Shaw*, four Justices dissented. The principal dissent, by Justice Ginsburg, argued that the majority was unduly expanding *Shaw*. Ginsburg objected to the use of strict scrutiny whenever race was a "predominant factor" — she believed that this would open the door to federal litigation over the legitimacy of any districting plan that even took account of race.

c. **Additional districts struck down:** A pair of 1996 cases shows that majority-minority districts will in fact frequently be struck down under *Shaw* and *Miller*. See *Bush v. Vera*, 517 U.S. 952 (1996) and *Shaw v. Hunt*, 517 U.S. 899 (1996). In this pair of cases, the Court struck down *all four* of the districts whose constitutionality it considered, on the grounds that in each, race was the predominant factor.

d. Significance: So what do *Shaw* and *Miller*, taken together, mean for the future of voting rights? Here are some thoughts:

   i. Race-consciousness still allowed: States are not prevented from being "race conscious" when they draw lines, as long as race does not become the ***"predominant factor."*** If, as seems likely, the Court goes only as far as Justice O'Connor is willing to go, plaintiffs will have to show that the state "relied on race in substantial disregard of customary and traditional districting practices." So if race is heavily considered, but so are such (traditional) objectives as protecting incumbents, keeping "communities of interest" (e.g., large urban neighborhoods) together, using county and precinct lines, and not diluting the voting strength of other ethnic groups (e.g., Irish Americans), the plan may survive.

   (1) Race as predominant factor: But the fact that the people drawing the district lines consider other factors in addition to race certainly ***won't immunize*** the districting scheme from being invalidated for making race the "predominant factor." The Supreme Court will take a very detailed look at exactly *how* the line-drawers went about their business, and won't hesitate to find that race was the most important factor. For instance, in *Bush v. Vera*, *supra*, p. 330, a plurality of the Court attached great weight to the fact that the legislature used maps and computer programs that ***provided racial data at the block-by-block level***, but other data (e.g., incumbency and political affiliation) only on a broader basis; this fact helped convince these Justices that race was more important to the line-drawers than all other factors taken together, including incumbency.

   ii. Minority districts vulnerable: "Majority-minority" districts are clearly more vulnerable than they were before *Shaw* and *Miller*. Any plan that seems to have been motivated principally by a desire to create the maximum possible number of such districts will be open to attack.

   (1) Compliance with Voting Rights Act: But a majority of the Court now believes that ***compliance with the Voting Rights Act can*** supply the requisite "compelling" state objective to support intentional creation of majority-minority districts. This is demonstrated by a post-*Shaw/Miller* 2006 case, *League of United Latin American Citizens v. Perry*, 548 U.S. 399 (2006), in which six members of the Court agreed that compliance with the VRA can be a compelling state objective that justifies drawing race-conscious district lines. So if the creation of one or more majority-minority districts were in fact necessary to comply with the VRA's requirement that the political processes be ***"equally open to minorities,"*** a solid six-justice majority of the Roberts Court would apparently uphold the districts even though race was in some sense the predominant factor.

   iii. Dispersed racial majority: Districting authorities will find it toughest to avoid a violation where African Americans or other racial minorities are ***widely dispersed***. For instance, the plan struck down in *Miller* was weakened by the fact that it reached from the outskirts of Atlanta in the middle of the state to Savannah, on the coast 260 miles away. By contrast, districts that are relatively ***compact***, and that consist completely of neighborhoods within a single large city, are more likely to survive.

K. Harm to members of minority: Thus far, we have implicitly assumed that race-conscious affirmative action programs disadvantage only the majority, if they disadvantage anyone. But suppose that such a program, while it perhaps benefits *most* members of the previously-disadvantaged minority, *harms certain members of the minority class*. Does the existence of this harm render the plan a violation of equal protection? So far, the Supreme Court has not had to face this issue.

1. **Housing:** One area in which the question may arise involves attempts to prevent *"tipping"* in residential areas. Such attempts have generally taken one of two forms: (1) the expenditure of public funds to create a program of *"benign steering"* in which prospective purchasers are shown homes solely in areas where they will contribute to integration rather than segregation (e.g., African Americans would not be shown homes in areas already containing more than, say, 40% blacks); (2) actual racial *quotas* in *public housing projects.*

    a. **No clear rule for "benign steering":** With respect to the *"benign steering"* programs, there have been very few decisions. But it seems probable that such plans would be *upheld*, since the plans do not prevent members of the minority from living wherever they wish — the plans simply use public funds in a way that encourages integration.

    b. **Absolute quotas:** Absolute racial quotas for public housing projects, on the other hand, seem more difficult to justify, since such quotas will lead to a person's being absolutely deprived of a particular good (an apartment in a particular project) solely on the ground of his race. Probably the majority's opinion in *Richmond v. Croson* (see *supra*, p. 313), casting doubt on whether a racial preference is ever truly "benign," means that an absolute racial quota for public housing projects will be strictly scrutinized and in fact struck down.

2. **Racial balance in schools:** Similarly, suppose that a school board, in an attempt to maintain integration in an area that seems to be suffering from "white flight," decrees that only a limited percentage of African Americans living in a particular school district may attend the neighborhood school, but that all whites may.

    a. **Effect of *Croson:*** Recall that *Richmond v. Croson* (*supra*, p. 313) apparently requires strict scrutiny of *any* race-conscious government decision. Although preventing "white flight" might be found to be a compelling governmental objective, it is doubtful that a majority of the Court would conclude that an explicitly race-conscious plan that permits all white students in a neighborhood to attend their local school, but deprives African Americans of this right, is a "necessary" means of solving the white flight problem. (Instead, a majority of the Court would probably conclude that magnet schools, anti-racist public relations programs, and other race-neutral means could and must be used to deal with the problem.)

    b. **Voluntary one-race schools:** As a twist on the usual integration problems, suppose that African American (or Hispanic or other minority) students decide that *they* wish to have a segregated school, dormitory or facility limited to their own race. May the majority accede?

        i. **Possible justification:** Such voluntary segregation could be justified on the grounds that it promotes racial pride and cohesiveness on the part of groups which have been the victims of long discrimination and consequent poor self-image.

    ii. Criticism: Yet making a school or dormitory off-limits to whites certainly deprives them of a good solely on the grounds of race. *Richmond v. Croson* (*supra*, p. 313) certainly seems to require that such single-race facilities must be subjected to *strict scrutiny*. If strict scrutiny were applied, it seems unlikely that the Court would find that one-race facilities were a *necessary* means of promoting racial pride or cohesiveness among minorities. Special courses in black culture, a representative proportion of minority instructors, etc., certainly seem like adequate and less-intrusive ways of achieving the same result.

L. Law enforcement, prison administration and military operations: Governments sometimes make race-conscious decisions not in order to redress past discrimination, but in order to further *operational* needs, especially in the *law-enforcement, prison administration* and *military* contexts. The Supreme Court's only modern-era decision in these areas — which applied strict scrutiny to a state's policy of racial segregation in the *cell assignments of recently-arrived prisoners* — suggests that race-conscious policies will be *strictly scrutinized* despite governments' operational needs in these contexts. That ruling came in *Johnson v. California*, 543 U.S. 499 (2005).

    1. Facts of *Johnson*: *Johnson* involved California's unwritten policy under which, when prisoners entered a new correctional facility, they were racially segregated in double cells for up to 60 days. (After the initial up-to-60-day period, prisoners were allowed to choose their own cellmates.) The state defended this segregative practice as being "necessary to prevent violence caused by racial gangs."

    2. Subjected to strict scrutiny: Of the eight members of the Court who expressed an opinion (Chief Justice Rehnquist did not participate), six agreed that the state's policy *must be strictly scrutinized.* In an opinion by Justice O'Connor, the Court remanded the case to the lower courts for a determination whether the segregative policy could survive the strict scrutiny standard.

        a. Applies to all classifications: O'Connor noted that the Court had held that " '*all* racial classifications [imposed by government] ... must be analyzed by a reviewing court under strict scrutiny' " (quoting *Adarand*, supra).

        b. "Benign" use irrelevant: California defended its segregation policy on the grounds that it was a "neutral" one that "neither benefits nor burdens one group or individual more than any other group or individual." But O'Connor quickly dismissed this rationale: the Court had "rejected the notion that separate can ever be equal – or 'neutral' – 50 years ago in *Brown v. Board of Education*," and there was no reason to resurrect that notion now.

        c. Might increase racial hostility: Indeed, O'Connor said, the use of racial classifications in prison housing assignments might well ***breed further hostility*** among prisoners and reinforce racial and ethnic divisions. By perpetuating the notion that race matters most, racial segregation of inmates 'may exacerbate the very patterns of [violence that it is] said to counteract.' " She noted that virtually all other states and the federal government "manage their prison systems without reliance on racial segregation." And she rejected the argument that the operational needs of prison administration dictated a different result: "[C]ompliance with the 14th Amendment's ban on racial discrimination is not only consistent with proper prison administration, but also bolsters the legitimacy of the entire criminal justice system."

    i.   **Might still survive:** O'Connor emphasized that the Court was not deciding whether California's policy here could *survive* the required strict scrutiny — that would be left to the courts below. But she noted that "prisons are dangerous places, and the special circumstances they present may justify racial classifications in some contexts."

3. **Dissent:** Justice Thomas, joined by Justice Scalia, dissented in *Johnson*. Thomas thought that "The Constitution has always demanded less within the prison walls," and believed that the Court should adopt a *"deferential standard* for reviewing prisoners' constitutional claims."

4. **Other contexts:** *Johnson* suggests that the present Court will **apply strict scrutiny** to any race-conscious government policy, even in the demanding operational areas of law enforcement, prison administration and the military. However, it is probably the case that in these areas, race-conscious schemes have a better chance of surviving the requisite strict scrutiny than in many other areas. Here are some domains in which the issue might arise:

    a.   **Police:** *Police departments* have sometimes preferred black applicants to white ones not in order to remedy past discrimination, but in order to have more African American policemen available for duty in predominantly-black neighborhoods, where it is felt that African American officers will have better rapport. Such a plan might even survive the strict scrutiny presumably required by *Croson* and *Johnson*.

    b.   **Prison guards:** Similarly, there have been attempts to hire more minorities as **prison guards**, in order to match more closely the racial composition of the prison population. Such a plan might well be sustained, on the grounds that the state's interest in reducing racial strife in the prison system is a compelling state interest.

    c.   **Officer corps in military:** The U.S. armed forces, too, have adopted explicitly-race-conscious means to develop more minority officers (e.g., by relaxing admissions criteria for the military academies). Given the heavily integrated rank-and-file in the military (e.g., 32% of rank-and-file were black or hispanic in 2002), and the much lower percentage of minority officers, it seems likely that the present Court would approve limited race-conscious methods. See Justice O'Connor's opinion for the court in *Grutter, supra*, p. 295, commenting favorably (albeit in dictum) on the armed services' use of affirmative action to ensure an integrated officer corps.

V. CLASSIFICATIONS BASED ON SEX

A. **Introduction:** When examining a racially-conscious statute, it is generally not too difficult to ascertain whether the statute was intended as "benign" affirmative-action legislation designed to benefit a disadvantaged minority, or was, rather, garden-variety discrimination *against* a racial minority. But when one examines a statute which classifies by *gender*, it will usually be much more difficult to decide whether the statute is "benign" (i.e., beneficial to women) or not.

    1. **Prior cases:** Many of the cases arguably involving benign sex-based classifications were discussed *supra*, p. 286, in conjunction with the general discussion of affirmative action. We turn now to the remainder of the sex-classification cases. The statutes in many of these cases may seem neither more nor less "benign" than those considered previously, so that the prior materials should be reviewed together with the ones which follow.

2. **Rarely outright hostility:** The reason for the difficulty of determining "benignness" is that legislatures have almost never acted out of *hostility* or *ill-will* towards women. Nearly all gender-based legislative classifications have evolved out of some kind of desire to *"protect"* women.

    a. **Early laws:** Early statutes typically did so on the theory that a woman's place was *at home raising children*, and that women therefore needed to be protected from a whole list of dangers lurking in the male-dominated world outside the home: alcohol, physical labor, jury duty, etc.

    b. **Later laws:** A second group of laws, generally enacted after 1960, were protective in another way: they attempted to *undo the effects* of past paternalistic attitudes which had curtailed opportunities for women.

    c. **Intermediate standard throughout:** Perhaps surprisingly, the Court today ostensibly applies a *single* standard to all gender-based classifications, whether these are found to be truly compensatory or merely paternalistic and stereotypical: *any gender-based classification must be "substantially related" to "important" governmental objectives*. This is, of course, the *intermediate level* of scrutiny, also applicable to illegitimacy and, perhaps, alienage. (See *supra*, p. 256.)

        i. **"Exceedingly persuasive justification":** But the Court will now, as the result of a 1996 case, apparently apply intermediate scrutiny in a quite *rigorous* way, which makes it *closer to strict scrutiny* than to "mere-rationality" review. As the result of *U.S. v. Virginia, infra*, p. 339, the defenders of a gender-based scheme must show an *"exceedingly persuasive justification"* for the scheme, and the Court will apply *"skeptical scrutiny."* The Court still officially applies the intermediate-level test ("substantially related to an important governmental objective"), but apparently the government won't often pass this test.

        ii. **Stereotypical thinking vs. attempt to reverse discrimination:** A gender-based scheme is especially likely to be invalidated where it is an older one that arguably stems from a *traditional, stereotypical* way of thinking about gender roles, rather than a newer one that is intended to *combat past discrimination* against women. See *U.S. v. Virginia, infra*, p. 339 (all-male status of Virginia Military Institute struck down, based in part on the state's stereotypical views of the skills and interests of men vs. women).

B. **Traditional deference by Court:** Until 1971, the Supreme Court treated classifications based on gender as not meriting any special scrutiny, so that the highly deferential "mere-rationality" test was applicable. Thus a statute was upheld if the Court could find it to be *rationally related* to some *legitimate state objective*, usually the preservation of women's "proper role."

> **Example:** A Michigan law provides that no woman may obtain a license to tend bar unless she is the wife or daughter of the male owner of a licensed tavern. The state argues that bartending by women may cause "moral and social problems" but that oversight of the barmaid by her husband or father will minimize these problems.

Held, statute upheld. The state could forbid *all* women from working in bars. This is so despite the possibility that public attitudes have changed, since "[the] Constitution does not require legislatures to reflect sociological insight, or shifting social standards. ... " Furthermore, it was not irrational for the legislature to conclude that the social and moral problems posed by having women tend bar would be less grave where the barmaid's husband or father was available to supervise. Therefore, the statute is not invalid. *Goesaert v. Cleary*, 335 U.S. 464 (1948). (*Goesaert* was later explicitly disapproved by the Supreme Court, in *Craig v. Boren*, *infra*, p. 336.)

C. Stricter review: But in the early 1970's, the Court began to give more than trivial review to gender-based classifications.

1. *Reed:* This occurred first in *Reed v. Reed*, 404 U.S. 71 (1971), where a statute preferring men over women as administrators of estates was struck down. The Court purported to apply the traditional "mere-rationality" standard. But in rejecting the state's contention that the preference reduced the workload of probate courts by eliminating hearings on the merits, the Court was clearly putting more bite into the traditional standard than it had done previously.

2. Explicit strict scrutiny: The "mere-rationality" standard for gender-based classifications was then explicitly *rejected* by the Court in *Frontiero v. Richardson*, 411 U.S. 677 (1973). In fact, that case went virtually to the other extreme, with a plurality holding that classifications based on sex, "like classifications based upon race, alienage, or national origin," are "inherently suspect and must therefore be subjected to strict judicial scrutiny."

3. Retreat to "intermediate scrutiny": The Court then settled (permanently, it now appears) on an ***"intermediate"*** level of scrutiny for gender-based classifications, whether "benign" or not. This standard was formulated in ***Craig v. Boren***, 429 U.S. 190 (1976).

a. Facts of *Craig:* *Craig v. Boren* was a successful challenge to an Oklahoma statute which forbade the sale of "3.2% beer" (supposedly non-intoxicating) to males under the age of 21, and to females under the age of 18. The constitutional claim was that the statute denied equal protection to males aged 18 to 20.

b. Standard articulated: The Court articulated the applicable standard as being that "classifications by gender must serve ***important*** governmental objectives and must be ***substantially*** related to achievement of those objectives."

i. New standard not explicit: The majority did not explicitly announce that it was applying a new standard different from either the traditional "mere-rationality" test or the "strict scrutiny" reserved for suspect classifications and fundamental rights. In fact, the Court purported merely to be applying standards established in previous cases, including *Reed* and *Frontiero*. But the concurring and dissenting opinions clearly viewed the majority as having formulated a third, ***middle***, level of scrutiny.

c. Defense of statute: Oklahoma defended the statute on the grounds that it promoted traffic safety, since, statistically, 18- to 20-year-old males were arrested for drunken driving much more frequently than females in the same age group. (2% of males and .18% of females in that age group were arrested for drunk driving.)

d. Insufficient correlation: The majority found this statistically-based defense ***insufficient.***

i. Maleness not "proxy": First, since such a small portion even of *males* in the relevant age group were convicted of drunken driving, maleness could not serve as a "proxy" for drinking and driving.

ii. Non-intoxicating beverage: Secondly, even if 18- to 20-year-old males did drive while drunk with a sufficiently greater frequency than similarly-aged females, this did not establish that the state's regulation of *3.2%* beer was reasonable, since that beverage was supposedly non-intoxicating.

iii. Only sale prohibited: Lastly, the statute only prohibited the *selling* of the beer to males, not their *drinking* it once they acquired it (perhaps via a purchase by an 18- to 20-year-old female companion).

iv. Poor overall fit: Thus, overall, the *"fit"* between the *means* of regulation selected (ban on sale of 3.2% beer to 18- to 20-year-olds) and the *end* sought to be achieved (promotion of traffic safety) was simply *too tenuous* to constitute the required *"substantial relation"* between means and end.

e. Dissent: Justice Rehnquist, dissenting, argued that the case should be judged according to a "mere-rationality" standard. He apparently would not have objected to intermediate-level scrutiny for discrimination *against women*, but saw no reason why discrimination against *males* should be given any greater scrutiny than that given to the great majority of other statutes attacked on equal protection grounds.

i. Means-end "fit": Rehnquist also objected to the majority's conclusion that the statute was invalid because the *fit* between being an 18- to 20-year-old male and driving while drunk was unduly tenuous. In his opinion, what counted was not the relative size of the percentage of young males who drank, but *whether this percentage was higher than for females*. Since there was evidence that, however few young males were arrested for drunken driving, it was far more proportionately than the number of females, he found the connection between regulation of 3.2% beer and promotion of traffic safety "rational," meriting upholding of the statute.

f. "Exceedingly persuasive justification": But the "intermediate" level of review is today *quite difficult to meet*. A 1996 case holds that the state must show an *"exceedingly persuasive justification"* for a gender-based scheme, and that the courts must give "skeptical scrutiny" to such a scheme. See *U.S. v. Virginia, infra,* p. 339. So even though intermediate-review remains the official standard, it's a standard that's closer to strict scrutiny than to mere rationality.

D. Middle-level review not always fatal: However, the intermediate-level scrutiny now given to gender-based classifications, although substantially more probing that the traditional "mere-rationality" standard, has by no means proven to be universally fatal to the statutes examined.

1. Most interests "important": Almost every governmental interest urged in support of a gender-based statute has been found *"important"* and therefore sufficient to meet the first prong of the test. The sole exceptions have been: (1) *"administrative convenience"* (see, e.g., *Frontiero, supra,* p. 336; *Wengler v. Druggists' Mutual Ins. Co., supra,* p. 288); and (2) providing women, but not men, with "a choice of educational environments" (rejected as a rationale for a single-sex admissions policy in *Mississippi University for Women v. Hogan, infra,* p. 342).

a. **Must be "actual" objective:** But to qualify as an important governmental objective, the objective must be one that *"actually"* motivated the legislature, as opposed to one that is articulated after the gender-based scheme was adopted. See *U.S. v. Virginia* (the VMI case), *infra*, p. 339 ("a tenable justification must describe actual state purposes, not rationalizations for actions in fact differently grounded").

2. **"Substantially related":** The requirement that the means chosen be *"substantially related"* to the end has had considerably more bite. But it, too, has frequently been satisfied.

>   **Example 1:** In *Michael M. v. Superior Court*, 450 U.S. 464 (1981) (discussed more fully *supra*, p. 288), the Court held that California could constitutionally make men but not women liable for sexual intercourse with a partner under the age of 18. The state's asserted purpose of protecting against teenage pregnancy was deemed important, and punishing the man but not the woman was held to be "substantially" related to achievement of that end — only women could become pregnant, so that a criminal sanction against men "equalized" the deterrence on the sexes. Also, women would be less likely to report statutory violations if they themselves could be punished, so that a gender-neutral statute might be unenforceable.

>   **Example 2:** Congress was permitted to require that only men register for the draft, in *Rostker v. Goldberg*, 453 U.S. 57 (1981) (discussed more extensively *supra*, p. 289). Since the purpose of draft registration was to facilitate eventual drafting of combat troops, and since only men were eligible for combat, the male-only registration scheme was "closely related" to the purpose of the statute.

>   **Note:** One can disagree about whether the means chosen in *Michael M.* and *Rostker* are indeed substantially related to the ends sought to be achieved by those two statutes. But if one accepts the majority's characterization of the aims of those two statutes, it does seem that *neither* was enacted as "the accidental by-product of a *traditional way of thinking about females*" (*Califano v. Webster, supra*, p. 287). It is the latter sort of statute, typically enacted more than 60 years ago, that is the sort most likely to fail to withstand intermediate-level scrutiny. See, e.g., *U.S. v. Virginia*, discussed immediately below.

a. **Some imprecision allowed:** Even if the fit between the means chosen by the legislature and the governmental objective is *far from perfect*, the Court may nonetheless conclude that there *is* the required "substantial relation" between means and end. A good illustration of the imprecision that the Court will tolerate came in *Nguyen v. INS*, 533 U.S. 53 (2001), where the Court held that Congress could make it easier for the out-of-wedlock child of an American mother to achieve citizenship than for such a child of an American father.

>   i. **The statutory scheme:** Congress has set up some detailed rules for determining the citizenship of a child who is born abroad, and out of wedlock, to parents one of whom is an American citizen and the other of whom is not. These rules make it easier for the child to become an American citizen if the American parent is the mother. When the American parent is the mother, the child is *automatically* deemed an American citizen at birth. But when the American parent is the father, the child will become a citizen only if, before the child turns 18, the father's pater-

nity is legally established by one of several specified means (e.g., the father acknowledges paternity in writing under oath, or a court finds paternity).

    ii. Holding: By a 5-4 vote, the Court *upheld* this scheme against an equal protection claim by the son of an American father who never took any of the legitimating steps before the son turned 18. The majority reasoned that by imposing the requirement of one of three legitimizing steps before the child was 18, Congress was promoting parent-child bonding by requiring "that an *opportunity for a parent-child relationship occur* during the *formative years* of the child's minority." And the fact that none of the legitimizing steps would *necessarily* indicate that a parent-child bond had developed did not mean that the requisite substantial relation between means and end was absent, for "*none* of our gender-based classification equal protection cases have required that the statute under consideration must be *capable of achieving its ultimate objective in every instance.*"

    iii. Dissent: Justice O'Connor, dissenting in *Nguyen*, argued that there was not even close to a substantial relation between the means chosen by Congress and Congress' supposed objectives. For instance, with respect to the supposed congressional interest in making sure that there was an "opportunity" for father-child bonds, she contended that the way to promote that objective would have been to require that there actually *be* a real father-child relationship, not to require that *proof* of that relationship be obtained by the time the child was 18. Instead, O'Connor believed, Congress' scheme was based on an "overbroad sex-based generalization," and reflected "a *stereotype* … 'that mothers are significantly more likely than fathers … to develop caring relationships with their children.'"

E. Stereotypical thinking rejected: The Court is especially likely to strike down a gender-based classification system that seems to be based on *faulty generalizations* or *stereotypes* about the *differing abilities and interests of the two sexes*. Such generalizations were at the heart of the Court's conclusion in *U.S. v. Virginia*, 518 U.S. 515 (1996), that Virginia's publicly-operated men-only military academy, Virginia Military Institute (VMI), violated equal protection.

    1. Facts: Virginia had operated VMI as a men-only institution since its founding in 1839; the school's purpose was and is to develop "citizen-soldiers." VMI was the only single-sex school among Virginia's 15 public universities. Virginia's principal defense of its single-sex policy was that three aspects of VMI's approach — its extremely rigorous physical training, its technique of depriving students of privacy, and its "adversative" approach (under which entering students are extensively hazed, in a manner comparable to Marine Corps boot camp) — would have to be materially changed if the school were made co-ed. Instead, the state sought to create a less rigorous program for women — but still one in theory devoted to developing citizen-soldiers — at a pre-existing all-women private liberal arts college, Mary Baldwin College.

    2. Holding: By a surprisingly broad 7-1 majority, the Court held that: (1) Virginia's policy of excluding women from VMI was a violation of women's equal protection rights; and (2) the program at Mary Baldwin College was not sufficiently comparable to the VMI program to redress the injury. The majority opinion by Justice Ginsburg was a sweeping one:

        a. No "overbroad generalizations": Ginsburg began by noting that gender-based classifications "must not rely on *overbroad generalizations* about the different talents, capacities or preferences of males and females. … [Gender-based] classifications may not be used, as they once were . . . to create or perpetuate the legal, social, and economic inferiority of women."

    i. **Suitable for some women:** Ginsburg rejected Virginia's claim that the VMI program would have to be materially changed if women were admitted. It may be true that, as Virginia asserted, *most* women wouldn't like the rigorous, adversative martial VMI program, and would prefer a more cooperative program. But the experience of women in the U.S. military academies, and in the U.S. military, suggested that these fears were overblown. In any event, there were clearly *some* women for whom the existing VMI program was an attractive and suitable program, and Virginia could not deprive these unusual women of the opportunity to attend VMI. "*[G]eneralizations about 'the way women are,'* estimates of what is appropriate for *most women*, no longer justify denying opportunity to women whose talent and capacity place them *outside the average description*."

    ii. **Diversity policy:** Virginia had also defended its men-only rule as being in furtherance of a state policy of "diversity in educational approaches." But the majority rejected this objective as well, concluding that this was not an "*actual* state purpose," given that Virginia had no women-only public universities, and that the no-women policy at VMI dated from a time when Virginia did not offer any sort of public higher education for women.

  b. **Mary Baldwin program insufficient:** The majority then concluded that the proposed women-only program at Mary Baldwin would *not constitute an adequate remedy* for the equal protection violation caused by VMI's men-only status. To remedy an equal protection violation, the solution would have to "place [victims] in the *position they would have occupied in the absence of discrimination*," and "to eliminate [so far as possible] the discriminatory effects of the past." The Mary Baldwin program would not be in any way the equivalent of VMI: it would not give its students the same intense military and leadership training (for instance, it would not use the adversative method); it would not have a student body or faculty of the same quality; it would not benefit from the same strong alumni ties, etc. It would, in sum, be a *"pale shadow"* of VMI.

  c. **"Exceedingly persuasive justification" needed:** The majority opinion was also notable for the *stricter tone* with which it applied mid-level scrutiny. The Clinton Administration had asked the Court to change course, and apply strict scrutiny, instead of traditional mid-level review, in gender cases. The majority did not do this. But it said that sex-based classifications would have to undergo *"skeptical scrutiny,"* and would be upheld only if the state demonstrated an *"exceedingly persuasive justification"* for any gender-based governmental action.

    i. **Objective must be one that really motivated state:** Perhaps the most important aspect of the new "skeptical scrutiny" is that when the government articulates a justification for the gender-based classification, this justification "must describe *actual state purposes*, not rationalizations for actions in fact differently grounded." Thus when Virginia asserted that its policy fulfilled the objective of diversity-in-education, the Court's response was not that this wasn't an important objective (or that the men-only program wasn't closely related to achieving that objective), but that this wasn't the state's *real* objective, merely a pretext.

3. Dissent: The lone dissenter was Justice Scalia. (Even Chief Justice Rehnquist concurred in the result, though not in the majority's full reasoning; Justice Thomas recused himself because his son was attending VMI.)

   a. Objection to majority's standard: Scalia objected first to the majority's choice of standard. He claimed that while the majority admitted to having changed the traditional intermediate level of review, it was in fact substituting a new and improper "exceedingly persuasive justification" standard that contradicted the reasoning of the Court's prior gender cases. In Scalia's view, this standard was an "*unacknowledged adoption* of what amounts to (at least) *strict scrutiny.*"

   b. Satisfies mid-level review: Scalia believed that operation of VMI as an all-male school *satisfied mid-level review* when that standard was properly applied. The state had an important interest in achieving the educational diversity provided by single-sex colleges. And when Virginia elected to have an all-male school that used the adversative model (VMI) and an all-female school that used the cooperative model (the new Mary Baldwin program), it had selected a strategy that was "substantially related" to the achievement of that interest in diversity.

   c. End of single-sex public education: Scalia said that the majority's approach "ensures that *single-sex public education is functionally dead.*" In fact, he said, this approach even endangered *private* single-sex colleges, since the government's furnishing of all-important financial assistance (e.g., tax deductions for private donations) might be held to be state action in support of discrimination, as it had been in cases involving private racially-discriminatory colleges.

4. Significance: The *VMI* decision is highly significant:

   a. New standard: Justice Scalia seems to be correct in observing that the "exceedingly persuasive justification" standard is tougher than the traditional mid-level review. However, it does not seem as though the Court will apply full-bore strict scrutiny to gender-based classifications. Instead, the Court will apparently still require only that the means chosen be substantially related to achievement of an important governmental objective (the traditional mid-level test), but will apply that test in a way that is at least marginally more demanding than before.

   i. Real objective: For instance, the Court will apparently now insist that the objective being advanced be one that *actually motivated the government* when it devised the system, a requirement that the Court has traditionally applied in strict scrutiny cases but not necessarily in mid-level cases.

   ii. Suspicion of stereotypes: Furthermore, the Court seems to be exceptionally intolerant of anything that strikes it as being *stereotypical thinking* about the differences between the sexes. Even if there is respectable scientific evidence that *most* women *are* different from most men in a particular way, this will apparently not support a gender-based classification. Thus the majority did not really dispute evidence advanced by Virginia that far fewer women than men would like the adversative method — but this didn't matter: as long as there were *some* women who didn't fall within that (arguably correct) generalization, it was a violation of these women's equal protection rights to not have the same opportunity as was given to men.

b. **Single-sex public education:** It's not clear whether the VMI case means that practically all single-sex public education is dead. It may well be that if a single-sex program is designed for the purpose of *remedying past discrimination* against women (or curing the particular problems faced by women), it will be easier to sustain, even though the Court has not expressly said that it will treat remedial classifications less stringently.

c. **Tax and loan breaks for private schools:** It's also not clear whether even *private* same-sex schools are doomed if they *get substantial government support*. The Court's prior race-discrimination cases suggest that the furnishing of indirect government assistance to private schools that racially discriminate amounts to government support of racial discrimination in violation of the 14th Amendment. But the majority may well decline to apply the same standard to sex discrimination, perhaps somehow relying on the theory that mid-level review means that greater ties between government action and private discrimination must be shown before the government action is treated as itself discriminatory.

d. **"Separate but equal":** It also remains to be seen whether a state can maintain a pair of single-sex schools, one for men and one for women, on the theory that the two are *"separate but equal."* The Court in the VMI case held that an all-women's military training course that Virginia proposed to set up at Mary Baldwin College was not sufficiently comparable to the all-male Virginia Military Institute to satisfy the requirements of equal protection. The VMI case seems to mean that: (1) a pair of single-sex schools (one for each sex) can *theoretically* pass equal protection scrutiny, if the two schools are truly equal; but that (2) it will be very hard, as a *practical* matter, for the state to show that the two are so substantially equal that the new "exceedingly persuasive justification" standard will be satisfied.

F. **Remedial statutes:** If the Court finds that a gender-conscious statute represents an attempt to *remedy past discrimination* against women, both prongs of the intermediate-level test will almost certainly be found to be satisfied.

1. **Redress for lower earnings:** For instance, in *Califano v. Webster*, 430 U.S. 313 (1977) (*supra*, p. 287), the Court upheld a Social Security provision by which a female worker's "average monthly wage" (against which social security benefits are calculated) could exclude three more lower-earning years than a male worker's. The Court found this provision to be a strictly remedial one, whose purpose was one of "redressing our society's longstanding disparate treatment of women," not one of "role-typing" women by casually assuming that they are "the weaker sex" or are "more likely to be child-rearers or dependents."

2. **Remedy must be specific:** But it is not enough that the statute is intended to improve the position of women. It must also be the case that this improvement comes *in a particular narrowly-defined sphere*, in which women have *previously been disadvantaged*. An especially vivid illustration of this rule came in *Mississippi University for Women v. Hogan*, 458 U.S. 718 (1982), in which the Court struck down Mississippi's policy of barring men from the University's School of Nursing.

a. **Facts of *MUW v. Hogan*:** The Mississippi University for Women (MUW) is a state university that has enrolled only women since its establishment in 1884. The School of Nursing was not established until 1971. The nursing school, like the other university departments, allowed men to audit courses but not to take them for credit. The plaintiff, Hogan, was denied admission to the degree program at the nursing school, which was located in the town where he lived and worked. There were co-ed degree programs at other Mississippi-supported nursing schools, but he would have had to commute a substantial distance to attend any of them.

b. Holding: A five-Justice majority (in one of the first opinions authored by Justice O'Connor) ***struck down*** the women-only policy of the nursing school. The majority opinion applied the intermediate level of scrutiny prescribed by *Craig v. Boren*; Justice O'Connor then added her own gloss on that standard, arguing that an "exceedingly persuasive justification" must be shown for any sex-based classification. The statute was unable to survive this scrutiny.

c. Not affirmative action: Most significantly, Justice O'Connor rejected the state's assertion that the single-sex admissions policy ***compensated for discrimination*** against women and was therefore "educational affirmative action." Such a "compensatory purpose" justification would be valid, the Justice stated, only if members of the sex benefitted by the classification "actually suffer a ***disadvantage related to the classification***." In the present case, this would have required a showing that women were disadvantaged ***in the field of nursing***, not merely in the general sphere of education or employment.

    i. Nursing as woman's field: The state made no such showing regarding nursing. In fact, Justice O'Connor noted, the evidence was just the contrary: nursing in Mississippi (as well as in the rest of the country) was widely viewed as exclusively a woman's job. Thus the single-sex policy of the nursing school in fact merely ***perpetuated a stereotype about proper roles for women***, and had nothing to do with compensation for past discrimination.

G. Discriminatory purpose required: In the sex-discrimination cases which we have examined so far, there was usually little dispute about whether the statute was intended to classify on the basis of sex. Most of the statutes explicitly mentioned sex, and the main issue was whether the classification was justifiable. But it is important to remember that, in sex-discrimination cases as in race-discrimination ones, the plaintiff is nonetheless required to show a ***discriminatory purpose***, not merely a discriminatory ***effect***.

1. *Feeney*: One illustration of this requirement is *Personnel Administrator of Massachusetts v. Feeney*, 442 U.S. 256 (1979) (discussed more fully *supra*, p. 269). In *Feeney*, the Court held that Massachusetts' absolute veterans' preference for civil service jobs did not violate equal protection, even though over 98% of the veterans in Massachusetts were men. Only "purposeful discrimination" against women could give rise to an equal protection violation — "[T]he Fourteenth Amendment guarantees equal laws, not equal results." (The fact that Massachusetts legislators may have ***foreseen*** that the statute would operate to women's extreme detriment was not enough; an equal protection claim could be valid only upon proof that the legislature acted in part "because of," not merely "in spite of" adverse effects on women.)

2. Use of biological factors: A legislature's use of ***biological factors*** may similarly cause a disparate effect upon the two sexes. Again, only if there is proof that the disparate effect was ***intended*** by the lawmakers will the statute be struck down on equal protection grounds. ***Geduldig v. Aiello***, 417 U.S. 484 (1974), purports to be an illustration of this principle.

    a. Facts: *Geduldig* involved a provision of California's disability insurance system which excluded coverage for "disability that accompanies normal pregnancy and childbirth."

    b. Holding: The Court held that the statute did not violate the Equal Protection Clause, because it did not use an intentionally ***sex-based classification***. There was no evidence that the distinction based on pregnancy was a pretext designed to effect invidious discrimination against women. "The program divides potential recipients into two groups: pregnant women and nonpregnant persons. While the first group is exclusively female, the second includes members of both sexes. The fiscal and actuarial benefits of the program thus accrue to members of both sexes."[16]

        i. Mere-rationality standard: Therefore, the legislature's choice of conditions to be covered or not covered, being "gender neutral," needed simply to satisfy the "mere-rationality" test. The state's legitimate interests in keeping the insurance system solvent and in making benefits adequate for those conditions covered, were rationally related to the means chosen (exclusion of pregnancy-related conditions).

3. Explicit differentiation by sex: But where the statute itself ***explicitly differentiates*** based on sex, the Court will give heightened scrutiny to a justification based on biological considerations.

    a. Parents of illegitimate children: For instance, a New York statute giving the mother of an illegitimate child, but not the father, the right to ***veto the child's adoption***, was invalidated by the Court (5-4) in *Caban v. Mohammed*, 441 U.S. 380 (1979). The father, mother and child in *Caban* had lived together for several years as a family. The majority concluded that New York could not deny the father the right to block an adoption by withholding consent, if it gave this right automatically to the mother; there was no "universal difference," at every stage of a child's development, between the closeness of the father-child relationship and that of the mother- child one.

        i. Other adoptions: But the majority emphasized that the state was free to differentiate between mothers and fathers as to adoptions taking place while the child was ***still an infant***, or where the child was past infancy but the father had ***not participated*** in its rearing.

    b. Wrongful death action: But not all schemes which treat the father of an illegitimate child less favorably than the mother will be struck down. For instance, in *Nguyen v. INS* (*supra*, p. 338), a 2001 case, the Court upheld a federal statute that allowed a mother who is a U.S. citizen to automatically confer U.S. citizenship on her illegitimate child, while a father who is a citizen must take one of several affirmative steps before the child turns 18 in order to confer citizenship. The majority relied heavily on the theory that the mother automatically establishes ties to the child merely by giving

---

16. But four members of the Court in 2012 called for *Geduldig* to be overruled. In a dissent in *Coleman v. Court of Appeals of Maryland*, 132 S.Ct. 1327 (2012), Justice Ginsburg (joined by Justices Breyer, Sotomayor and Kagan), said that "it is simply false that a classification based on pregnancy is gender-neutral. ... Rather, discriminating on the basis of pregnancy [b]y definition . . . discriminates on account of sex; for it is the capacity to become pregnant which primarily differentiates the female from the male."

birth and being present at the birth, whereas the father does not have such automatic ties.

4. **Co-ed bathrooms and lockerrooms:** Public bathrooms, lockerrooms, sleeping quarters and other facilities related to *intimate bodily functions* of course generally remain sex-segregated. The Court has not explicitly dealt with this sort of segregation, but there is little reason to believe that such facilities-separation would be struck down as violative of equal protection.

     a. **Privacy argument:** Perhaps the best argument against a finding of an equal protection violation in this context is that sex-segregated facilities such as these are not expressions of invidious discrimination, but rather, expressions of the recognized desire for *sexual privacy*. Recall that the Court has recognized a substantive, constitutionally-protected, "right of privacy" (*supra*, p. 156), which seems to be applicable in this situation.

H. **"As applied" challenges:** So far, nearly all of the challenges to gender-based classifications we have considered have been "facial" ones, i.e., ones directed to gender-based classifications that are present in the text of the statute or regulation itself. But remember that the Equal Protection Clause also allows for *"as applied"* challenges — if the plaintiff can show that government has *enforced* a neutral-sounding provision in a way that discriminates against one or the other gender, this discrimination, too, will have to satisfy mid-level review.

1. **Peremptory challenges:** Consider, for instance, statutes that allow for civil or criminal litigants to use *peremptory challenges*, by which potential jurors may be dismissed without any showing of cause. The Court has held that the use of peremptory challenges to *exclude all women* from a jury cannot survive mid-level review, and thus violates equal protection. *J.E.B. v. Alabama*, 511 U.S. 127 (1994).

     a. **Rationale:** The Court phrased the issue as being "whether discrimination on the basis of gender in jury selection substantially furthers the State's legitimate interest in achieving a fair and impartial trial." It then answered "no," concluding that the assumption that women jurors will have certain types of attitudes in certain cases (such as the paternity case that was at issue in *J.E.B.*) reinforced stereotypical assumptions about women. So, just as a state may not permit litigants to strike jurors peremptorily on the grounds of race (see *Batson v. Kentucky*, discussed *supra*, p. 270), so the state may not allow gender-based strikes.

Quiz Yourself on

EQUAL PROTECTION — SUSPECT CLASSES, AFFIRMATIVE ACTION AND CLASSIFICATIONS BASED ON SEX

35. The state of Minnetonka has enacted an adoption statute that specifies the criteria to be used when public agencies make adoption placements. (No private adoptions are permitted in the state.) According to the statute, the "racial compatibility" between the child and the adoptive parents is the most important factor to be considered, though many other factors are also to be considered. Peter and Jill, a white couple in their 40's, wished to adopt a child. They learned that a large number of African American children were being raised in state-sponsored orphanages, because no homes could be found for them. The couple applied to a state adoption agency, requesting to adopt any African American child under the age of four, who was currently living in an orphanage. The adoption agency replied, "Because applicable statutes require us to give racial matching heaviest weight in making adoption placements, and because you are seeking a relatively young child who may well be placeable with a racially-compatible, i.e., African American family in the future, we cannot grant your request." Peter and Jill have sued in federal court for a ruling that the statute providing for race-matching violates their equal protection rights. They have presented evidence that African American children are staying longer in orphanages than white children who are otherwise similar, and that this lengthier stay is due in part to the heavy statutory weight placed on race-matching.

(a) By what standard should the court test the constitutionality of the race-matching statute as it applies to Peter and Jill? _____

(b) Should the court agree with Peter and Jill's contention that their equal protection rights have been violated? _____

36. Carolene High School, a public high school, has for years maintained special remedial reading classes. Students can take these classes in lieu of the regular English class, if they are shown to have learning disabilities or otherwise shown to be behind on their reading skills. Students of African American ancestry make up 12% of the student body of the high school. Forty-five percent of the students in the remedial reading program are African American. Because of reduced federal aid to education and a local recession, the school board has reluctantly concluded that it must reduce expenditures. Therefore, it has cancelled the remedial reading program, which is about 15% more expensive per student than the regular English program. The school board has not cut funding for the honors English program, which similarly costs about 15% more per student than regular English. About 9% of the students in the honors English program are African American. All of the evidence is that the school board made the decision it did on the honest belief that the honors program accomplishes more per dollar and strengthens the school system more, than does the remedial reading program. Carl, an African American student enrolled in the remedial reading program, has now challenged the termination on the grounds that it violates his right to equal protection.

(a) What standard should the court use in deciding Carl's challenge? _____

(b) Will Carl's challenge succeed? _____

37. Smithville is a small town located near the Canadian border. A significant minority of the children attending Smithville High School are American citizens of French-Canadian descent. The school board has just canceled the honors French program. The decision was made by the school principal, an American of Anglo-Saxon descent, who told school board members, "If we keep running an extensive French program, we'll just attract more Americans of French-Canadian ancestry to the town, and soon they'll be a majority." Since the school board was completely dominated by Anglo-Saxon Americans, they concurred with the decision. Jacques, an American student at the school of French-Canadian descent, has sued the school district, arguing that the cancellation has violated his constitutional rights.

(a) What standard of review should the court use to judge the school district's cancellation decision? _____

(b) Will Jacques' challenge succeed? _____

38. Same facts as prior question. Now, however, assume that the town of Smithville, and its school board, both contain a majority of Americans of French-Canadian descent. The board has now voted to dramatically expand the French program, and to cancel the honors English program. Strong evidence suggests

that the board was motivated by a desire to attract more French-Canadian Americans into town, and to solidify this group's majority over Anglo-Americans. Does either of your answers to question 41 change here, and if so, how? _____

39. The city of Monroe enacted an ordinance providing that 10% of all procurements of office supplies in the city for the coming year must be purchased from office supply companies majority-owned by either African Americans or Hispanics, the two largest ethnic groups in the city. African Americans and Hispanics together make up a substantial minority (approximately 40%) of the city's population. The City Council did not conduct legislative hearings or investigations prior to enacting the bill. However, minutes of the Council's deliberations show that Council members enacted the bill primarily because they felt that minority business people, especially in the office supply industry, had had less general economic opportunity than white-owned firms, and that the 10% set-aside was the best way to increase the opportunities for minority owned companies. At the moment the bill was enacted, firms owned by African Americans or Hispanics amounted to approximately 10% of the total office supply companies in the city, but these companies did only about 4% of the total office supply business in the city, since the average minority-owned firm was much smaller than the average white-owned firm.

   Anglo Office Supply, a white-owned office supply firm, has challenged the Monroe set-aside on equal protection grounds.

   (a) What standard should the court use in evaluating the constitutional sufficiency of the set-aside?

   _____

   (b) Will Anglo's attack succeed? _____

40. The Oneanta state legislature mandated that any employer with five or more employees grant a paid six-month maternity leave to any woman who gave birth while on the company's payroll. The legislature imposed no requirements regarding paid or unpaid family leave for men who had just had a child. In deciding to enact the measure, the legislators relied principally on evidence that various rising social problems, such as drugs and crime, were caused in part by the rise in working women and a consequent failure of mothers to bond with their infants. Frank, the father of a newborn infant who wished to have a paid paternity leave, has challenged the statute on the grounds that it violates his equal protection rights.

   (a) What standard should the court apply in evaluating Frank's challenge to the maternity-leave statute?

   _____

   (b) Will Frank's attack succeed? _____

41. Congress was dismayed by statistics indicating that although African Americans and Hispanics now compose approximately 15% of America's university-age population, these two groups comprise only 7% of enrollees at colleges and universities nationally. Most members of Congress believed that the shortfall was due to the residual effects of past official discrimination by state and local governments, including public university systems. Therefore, Congress enacted a statute providing that any college or university receiving federal funds was required to treat an applicant's African American or Hispanic status into account as a "positive factor," and to "make best efforts" to enroll as high a percentage of African American and Hispanic students as are present in the school-age population for the geographical area being served by that college or university. The statute further provided that statistics regarding actual enrollments would be treated as follows: a university would be rebuttably presumed to have failed to comply with the statute if the number of African American and Hispanic students actually enrolled was less than 80% of what would be predicted from the pool of recent high school graduates in the region from which the university draws the bulk of its enrollees. The statute's preamble recited Congress' belief that enroll-

ment disparities stemmed in major part from past governmental discrimination, but neither the statutory text nor the statute's legislative history either (1) described the particulars of this discrimination (e.g., whether it was national, whether it was by universities or other governmental actors, etc.) or (2) considered whether race-neutral methods might suffice to cure the lingering effects of the discrimination. Penny, a white female with good grades and test scores, was denied admission to Statesville University, a large and prestigious public university. She sued the University, pointing out that her grades and test scores were above the average for those accepted at the University, and arguing (correctly, as a factual matter) that but for the federally-required racial preference, she would probably have been admitted. She therefore contends that the federal statute violates her equal protection rights.

(a) What standard should the court use in deciding whether the federal statute violates Penny's equal protection rights? _____

(b) Will Penny's attack succeed? _____

42. In the state of Delta, 12% of recent high school graduates are African-American. The state's premier public university, Delta State, has historically made its decisions about whom to admit on a "holistic basis." Under the holistic system, admissions officials look at the student's entire academic and extracurricular profile, without ever explicitly treating (or even knowing) the student's race as a factor. Two years ago, the university's administration observed that its entering freshman class during the prior four years had been, on average, 6% black. A survey done by the university administration then determined that 75% of seminar classes at the university — "seminar" meaning classes having between 5 and 16 students — contained either zero or one African-American student. The administration decided that it would be vital to admit — and hopefully enroll — a substantially greater number of African-American students, so as to increase the critical mass of such students in seminar classes and thereby increase the overall educational diversity of the undergraduate experience. To that end, the admissions department considered two different plans. Under Plan A, half the entering class's seats would no longer be allocated on the holistic method, and would instead be subjected to a "Top Seven Percent" arrangement, under which any applicant who had been in the top 7% of his in-state public high school graduating class would automatically be offered admission. A statistician consulted by the university predicted that because of the highly segregated nature of Delta's public high schools, the adoption of Plan A would result in many more offers to (and acceptances by) black students, so that the percentage of seminar classes without at least two black students would likely drop from 75% to about 45%. Under Plan B, the university would amend its existing holistic plan so that race could be explicitly considered as one factor among many; under this plan, all seats would be allocated under the newly-revised race-conscious plan. Admissions officials determined, after some modeling, that Plan B would result in an increase in black students (and a decrease in seminars with fewer than two black students) comparable to that anticipated from Plan A.

Admission officials decided to use Plan B instead of A. They made this choice mainly because they reasonably concluded that Plan B would result in the admission of a slightly-more-highly-credentialed group of black students than Plan A, because Plan B would enable the school to attract a significant number of black students graduating in the top 15% (but not top 7%) of their class at relatively affluent and high-achieving majority-white public high schools in the state. Paula, a white non-Hispanic student who graduated 5th in her class of 100 at a high-achieving in-state suburban high school, was denied admission to Delta State. She has sued the university in federal district court, alleging that its use of Plan B violated her federal equal protection rights by discriminating against her because she was white. The university has defended on the grounds that its use of Plan B, although admittedly race-conscious, conforms with applicable Supreme Court precedents. Assume that (1) pursuit of a "critical mass" of two or more black students in a larger percentage of seminar classes constitutes a compelling governmental interest in "educational diversity"; and (2) had Plan A been in force instead of Plan B, Paula would have automatically been offered admission.

(a) Which party, Paula or Delta State, bears the burden of proof on the issue of whether Paula's equal protection rights have been violated by Delta State's use of Plan B? _____

(b) What standard of review should the trial court use in deciding whether the party who bears the burden of proof (as identified in your answer in (a)) has carried that burden? _____

(c) When the court applies the review standard you specified in (b), which party is likely to win? _____

Answers

35. **(a) The court should apply strict scrutiny, and ask whether the statute is necessary to achieve a compelling governmental objective.**

(b) Yes, probably. The Supreme Court has generally given strict scrutiny to any race-based classification scheme, even if it does not appear to be enacted for the purpose of disadvantaging African Americans. In a somewhat analogous situation involving child custody, the Court held that child custody decisions could not be made by taking into account race-matching or social prejudices; see *Palmore v. Sidoti*. So unless the mandatory consideration of race here is shown to be a necessary method of achieving a compelling state objective, it will be struck down. The state undoubtedly has a compelling interest in guaranteeing that a child be raised by a family that will be compatible. All other factors being equal, a racial match probably will make it easier for the child to develop a strong sense of identity. However, it is hard to see where the mandatory first-preference for a racial match is a "necessary" means of achieving state objectives, especially in light of evidence that it may keep children in institutional care longer. Therefore, the odds are that the court will find that the "necessary means" part of the equation has not been satisfied, and will strike down the mandatory first preference. (But a scheme merely requiring that race be considered as one factor among many, without making it the most important factor, probably would survive even strict scrutiny.)

36. **(a) The court should use the mere-rationality standard, not the strict scrutiny standard.**

(b) No, probably. Race is a "suspect category," and classifications based on race are therefore ordinarily subject to strict scrutiny. However, strict scrutiny will only be applied where the court finds that there was a governmental *intent* to discriminate against the disfavored group. The mere fact that a law has a less favorable *effect* on a racial minority than it has on the majority is *not* sufficient to trigger strict scrutiny. Disparate effect can be used as circumstantial evidence of an intent to discriminate, but such evidence is not dispositive. Here, the facts tell us that an intent to disfavor African American students was not present on the part of the school board. Therefore, strict scrutiny will not be applied, and instead the "rational relation" standard will be used. Under this standard, the classification will be upheld so long as it is rationally related to the achievement of a legitimate state objective. Here, cutting an expensive program is certainly rationally related to saving money for the school system, and saving money is certainly a legitimate state of objective in a time of economic hardship.

37. **(a) Strict scrutiny.** Classifications based on *national origin* are suspect. Similarly, classifications based on ethnic ancestry are suspect. So whether the French-Canadians are being discriminated against because they or their ancestors came from another country, or because they are part of a different ethnic group that

speaks a different language, they are clearly a suspect class. Since all the evidence indicates that the decision was made for the purpose of disadvantaging members of this group (i.e., the disadvantage was not merely an inadvertent effect of action taken for some other reason), the requisites for strict scrutiny have been satisfied.

(b) Yes. Once strict scrutiny is applied, the challenged classification will only be upheld if it is necessary to achieve a compelling governmental objective. Preventing a particular group of citizens from becoming a majority in a town or school system is certainly not a compelling state objective (and probably not even a "legitimate" objective). Therefore, even if the challenged classification is a "necessary" means of achieving that objective, the classification must fall.

38. No. Discrimination against *any* racial, ethnic or national-origin group will be strictly scrutinized, even if that group has traditionally not been the victim of widespread prejudice or discrimination. Thus even discrimination against whites of Anglo-Saxon Protestant descent will be strictly scrutinized. This is the result of *City of Richmond v. J.A. Croson Co.*, striking down a minority set-aside program that disadvantaged whites. So the analysis, and outcome, should be exactly the same as in the prior question.

39. (a) Strict scrutiny.

(b) Yes. The facts here are fairly similar to those of *Richmond v. Croson*. That case makes it clear that any race-based affirmative action scheme will be strictly scrutinized, and will thus be struck down unless it is necessary to achieve a compelling governmental objective. Here, the scheme has at least two shortcomings, each of which is probably separately fatal. First, the city is not trying to remedy past official discrimination, or even explicitly trying to remedy past unofficial discrimination — the facts tell us merely that there has been an inequality of "economic opportunity," which is not the same as racial discrimination. In the absence of a legislative finding of discrimination in the office supply industry in the city of Monroe itself, any attempt to give a racial preference would probably be struck down regardless of how that preference was carried out. Secondly, the plan here is essentially a *quota* — it allocates a particular fixed percentage of city contracts for minority-owned firms. Rarely if ever will quotas be found to be a "necessary" means of redressing even clear past discrimination — certainly a city needs to consider, and probably try, less restrictive measures first, such as voluntary goals, an outreach program to solicit more bids from minority-owned firms, or some other means that is less hard-and-fast than an absolute set-aside.

40. (a) Mid-level scrutiny, i.e., whether the statute is "substantially related" to the achievement of an "important" governmental objective. (*U.S. v. Virginia* says that gender-based classifications will now need an "exceedingly persuasive justification," and will be "skeptically scrutinized," but the case seems not to officially reject mid-level scrutiny, merely to indicate that mid-level scrutiny will now be applied in a rigorous way.)

(b) Yes, probably. Government classifications involving suspect or semi-suspect claims are evaluated by the same standard regardless of whether the purpose is to discriminate against the traditionally disfavored class or to redress past discrimination. In other words, there is no easier standard for "affirmative action." Thus the Supreme Court applies the same mid-level review to all gender-based classes, whether the classification is old-fashioned discrimination against women or affirmative action designed to improve the lot of women. In both cases, the gender-based classification will be upheld only if it is substantially related to the achievement of important governmental objectives.

Here, encouragement of bonding between parent and newborn child is probably an "important" governmental objective. However, a court would probably conclude that there is no "substantial relation" between a mother-only parental-leave program and achievement of this objective. It is highly likely that whatever social problems are caused by not having either parent at home during a child's infancy, those problems can be redressed as well or almost as well by having the father be at home. Therefore, a scheme that entitled either parent, but not both parents, to take a paid maternity leave would accomplish the legislative purposes as well or almost as well as the mother-only scheme. Consequently, the court will probably, thought not certainly, strike down the statute.

In general, courts are likely to strike down any statute that reflects **stereotypes** about the "proper place of women." See, e.g., *U.S. v. Virginia*, finding Virginia's belief that VMI's intense military training program is unsuitable for women to be an unconstitutional generalization about "the way women are." The scheme here — which implies that a mother's place, but not a father's place, is to be home with the newborn infant — reflects similar stereotypical thinking.

41. **(a) Strict scrutiny — the statute must be necessary to achieve a compelling governmental objective.**

(b) Yes, probably. There are three key issues here: (1) whether the fact that the preference was enacted by **Congress** rather than by a state or local government should change the standard for judicial review; (2) whether Congress' attempt to **wipe out past discrimination** renders the measure constitutionally acceptable; and (3) whether the Court's decision in *Grutter v. Bollinger*, allowing race-conscious university admissions, affects the answer.

As to the first issue — whether the fact that the preference was enacted by **Congress** rather than by a state or local government should change the standard for judicial review — the answer is **"no."** Because of the decision in *Adarand Constructors v. Pena*, strict scrutiny will be given to race-conscious congressionally-enacted affirmative action plans. Since the statute clearly classifies on the basis of race, it falls within this rule.

As to the second issue — whether Congress' desire to wipe out past governmental discrimination renders the measure acceptable — the answer is again **"no."** The eradication of past governmental discrimination is indeed probably a "compelling" goal. However, the preference probably would **not** be found to be **"necessary"** for the rooting out of the effects of past governmental discrimination. Congress did not make detailed **findings** about which geographical regions this discrimination exists in, or about which governmental units (e.g., universities versus other governmental actors) caused it. Also, there is no indication that Congress considered **race-neutral means** (e.g., use of "socio-economic" criteria rather than racial ones) as a possible way to solve the problem. As the Court said in another race-conscious university-admissions case, *Fisher v. Univ. of Texas* (2013), strict scrutiny "require[s] a court to examine with care, and not defer to, a university's '**serious, good faith consideration of workable race-neutral alternatives**.'" If there was a **"workable race-neutral alternative available"** to the university, then the race-conscious means can't be deemed to have been "necessary." *Id.* There's no evidence here that Congress ever gave "serious, good faith consideration" of race-neutral alternatives to see whether they might be workable.

The "rebuttable presumption" used here is better than an outright quota, but *Adarand, supra*, which involved a similar presumption-based scheme, suggests that racially-based presumptions will nonetheless be hard to justify (though the *Adarand* Court didn't actually decide whether the preference there survived strict scrutiny). Also, the Court might give slightly greater deference to Congress than it would to a state or local body. Nonetheless, the best guess is that the statute here would be struck down.

As to the final issue — whether the Court's decision in *Grutter v. Bollinger*, allowing race-conscious university admissions, changes the outcome — the answer once again is **"no."** Race-conscious affirmative action was allowed in *Grutter* because the majority was satisfied that the University there was pursuing the compelling goal of achieving diversity in the student body, and doing so in a narrowly-tailored way by use of individualized evaluations of each applicant. Here, there is no indication that Congress was seeking true diversity in each student body — Congress seems to have been nakedly pursuing ***"racial balancing"*** (i.e., making the portion of minority students at each university mirror the local student-age population), and the *Grutter* majority opinion makes it clear that this is not a legitimate objective. The numerically-based presumption of illegality just makes things worse, since such a presumption is more like the point system struck down by the Court in *Gratz v. Bollinger* than it is like the individualized evaluations upheld by the Court in *Grutter*. The Court's post-*Gratz* decision in *Parents Involved in Community Schools v. Seattle School District*, where a majority struck down pupil-assignment plans that gave a preference to students whose presence would lessen the racial imbalance in the target public school, further buttresses the conclusion that the racial preference here would be found to be in essence an illegitimate quota or "racial balancing" plan. The same is true of the even-more-recent decision in *Fisher, supra*, repeating *Grutter*'s holding that strict scrutiny will be applied to any race-conscious admissions method, and quoting approvingly *Parents Involved*'s statement that "Racial balancing is not transformed from 'patently unconstitutional' to a compelling state interest simply by relabeling it 'racial diversity.'"

42. **(a) Delta State.** Plan B, by amending the holistic method to explicitly take account of a student's race, makes use of a suspect classification (race). When government uses a suspect classification and is challenged on equal protection grounds, the burden of proof as to whether the classification is constitutional is imposed on the government. So it will be up to Delta State to show, by a preponderance of the evidence, that its use of a race-conscious admissions method was constitutional.

(b) Strict scrutiny. That is, Delta State will have to show that Plan B was a ***"necessary" means*** of accomplishing the university's admittedly-compelling interest in educational diversity. To decide whether Plan B was a "necessary" means, the court will have to make "a careful judicial inquiry into whether [the] university could achieve sufficient diversity ***without*** using racial classifications." *Fisher v. Univ. of Texas* (2013). If there *was* a ***"workable race-neutral alternative available"*** to the university, then the race-conscious means can't be deemed to have been "necessary." *Id.* And a race-neutral plan will be deemed to be a workable alternative if it would "promote ... the [governmental] interest ***about as well*** [as the selected race-conscious method] and at ***tolerable administrative expense.***" *Id.* Furthermore, the court ***may not defer*** to the university's conclusion about what workable race-neutral alternatives might have existed — the court must make its *own* determination on that issue. *Id.* These aspects of *Fisher* will all combine to make it difficult for the university to make the required showing that the race-conscious means it chose were "necessary" for achieving diversity.

(c) Paula. It's pretty clear that Plan A was a "workable race-neutral alternative." Why? Since the University has defined its compelling goal of achieving educational diversity largely in terms of getting a critical mass of two or more students into more than the previous 25% of seminar classes, and since you're told that Plan A would likely do this essentially as well as Plan B, it's hard to see how the court can conclude that Plan A *wasn't* a workable race-neutral alternative. And where a workable race-neutral alternative existed, that alternative ***must be used*** in preference to a race-conscious method. *Fisher*. The university's best hope is to argue that Plan A was not "workable" because it had the drawback of resulting in admission of a *somewhat-less-academically-qualified* group of black students (because that plan will do worse than Plan B in bringing about the admission of academically-talented black students ranking between the 8th and 15th percentile in stronger mostly-white school districts). But the court is likely to conclude that even if this assertion is true, Plan A was still "workable" — nothing says that a plan that fails to enroll the absolutely most-academically-talented class consistent with educational diversity cannot be "workable." (Indeed, in *Fisher* itself, about 75% of the University of Texas' students were admitted under a "Top Ten Percent" plan very similar to Plan A's Top Seven Percent component; both the University and the Court implicitly concluded that this method was workable and race-neutral, and no one seems to have made a serious argument that students admitted under this feature were on average seriously academically-underqualified.)

VI. CLASSIFICATIONS BASED ON ALIENAGE

A. Alienage generally: Recall that in deciding whether or not to treat a particular type of classification as "suspect," the Court has given substantial weight to whether the class which is disadvantaged is a "discrete and insular minority," i.e., a minority which is politically powerless and which has historically been discriminated against. (See *supra*, p. 271.) We have already seen that race, and its close relative national origin, have been treated by the Court as suspect classifications (*supra*, p. 265). In general, the Court has also purported to apply strict scrutiny to classifications disadvantaging **aliens**. However, the status of alienage classifications is much less clear than those of race and national origin.

    1. Definition: "Alienage," as the term is used by the Court, means *"not having U.S. citizenship."* Thus the term is not co-extensive with "national origin," since (1) discrimination against a person because he is of a particular national origin might occur even if he is a citizen (e.g., discrimination against a Mexican-American); and (2) discrimination against aliens often takes the form of discrimination against *all* aliens, without regard to their country of origin.

    2. Powerless and discriminated against: Aliens as a class do seem to bear the two principal traits which make a minority "discrete and insular." It seems clear that aliens as a class are *"politically powerless,"* since they are not permitted to vote. And it is at least arguable that there has been traditional discrimination against aliens (though much of this is probably more easily explained as either discrimination against persons of particular national origins, or discrimination against undocumented, i.e., "illegal," aliens).

      a. Not "immutable": But one factor often relied upon by the Court in establishing that a given classification is "suspect" is lacking in the case of aliens: *"immutability."* Thus in the case of race and national origin (and also in the cases of sex and illegitimacy, both subject to intermediate-level scrutiny), the trait is *beyond the power of the individual to change it.* But in the case of an alien, at least one who is legally in this country, there will normally come a time when he becomes *eligible for citizenship*; at that moment, of course, his alienage is no longer immutable.

        i. Significance: The "mutability" of the alienage trait may explain, at least in part, the wavering quality of the Court's commitment to strict-scrutiny treatment for the trait. This seems, for instance, to have been a sub-theme in the majority's handling of *Ambach v. Norwick, infra*, p. 355, involving two aliens who were already entitled to citizenship but who declined to claim it.

    3. Federal preemption: Unlike nearly all the other classifications typically reviewed under equal protection analysis, those based on alienage raise significant questions of *federal* *supremacy* and *preemption*. This is because the Constitution vests in the federal government full authority to deal with issues of immigration.

    a. **Consequence:** Therefore, when a state classifies in a way that disadvantages aliens, a relevant question is: Is this disadvantaging consistent with the fact that the federal government has permitted the aliens in question to reside in this country (or, in the case of "illegal" aliens, with the fact that the federal government has *not* so permitted them).

    b. **Increasing importance:** While issues of federal supremacy have not usually been dispositive in cases involving state treatment of aliens, the supremacy aspect seems to be becoming increasingly important. For instance, both the majority and the minority in *Plyler v. Doe* (a case deciding that illegal aliens may not be barred from free state education) relied in part on their views about whether such a ban comported with congressional immigration policy. See *infra*, p. 356.

B. **General rule of "strict scrutiny":** In the early 1970's, the Court began to treat discrimination against aliens as calling for *strict scrutiny*. There were three main cases in which such scrutiny was applied, and the statute under review invalidated:

    1. **Welfare benefits:** First, the Court held that states *cannot deny welfare benefits* to aliens. *Graham v. Richardson*, 403 U.S. 365 (1971). The opinion deemed aliens to be a "discrete and insular minority," and held that the state's fiscal interest in preserving limited resources for its citizens was not a sufficiently strong countervailing governmental interest.

        a. **Rationale:** The opinion noted that *aliens pay taxes* (from which the funds to pay welfare benefits come), just as citizens do.

    2. **Bar admissions:** Then, the Court held that states may not prevent resident aliens from *practicing law. In re Griffiths*, 413 U.S. 717 (1973). None of the state interests supposedly served by the ban (e.g., maintaining "high professional standards" and having lawyers serve as "officers of the court") was sufficiently closely linked to exclusion of aliens to overcome strict scrutiny.

    3. **Civil service:** Lastly, the Court held that a state may not bar aliens from holding positions in the state *civil service. Sugarman v. Dougall*, 413 U.S. 634 (1973).

C. *Sugarman* **exception:** But in what was to become an extremely important dictum, the Court in *Sugarman* stated that a state *could* prevent aliens from holding state *elective* executive, legislative and judicial positions, and even important *nonelective* positions in any of the branches of state government.

    1. **Rationale:** The Court reasoned that such persons "perform *functions that go to the heart of representative government*." Therefore, just as a state could exclude aliens from voting, it could exclude them from "participation in its democratic political institutions."

    2. **Consequence:** This "exception" to the principal doctrine of *Sugarman* has *virtually swallowed the rule*. See, e.g., *Cabell v. Chavez-Salido, infra*, p. 355, placing "Spanish-speaking Deputy Probation Officers" within the *Sugarman* exception. See generally Sullivan & Gunther, pp. 812-13.

    3. *Sugarman* **exception interpreted broadly:** The trend towards interpreting the *Sugarman* exception extremely broadly, so as to bar aliens from a wide range of state employment, began with *Foley v. Connelie*, 435 U.S. 291 (1978), where the Court held that New York could prevent aliens from becoming **state troopers**. Since state troopers were engaged in "execution of broad public policy," and since they held a large degree of **discretion** in doing so, they fell within the *Sugarman* exception.

4. **Public school teachers:** The *Sugarman* exception was broadened again, when the Court permitted New York to bar aliens from becoming **public school teachers. Ambach v. Norwick**, 441 U.S. 68 (1979), a 5-4 decision.

   a. **Facts:** The bar in *Ambach* applied to all aliens except those who had "manifested an intention to apply for citizenship." Plaintiffs refused to apply for citizenship even though they were eligible for it.

   b. **Standard:** The majority in *Ambach* expressed the test as being whether the employment was a *"governmental function,"* i.e., a function which was *"bound up with the operation of the state as a governmental entity. ... " Public school teaching, in the majority's opinion, qualified under this standard.*

   c. **Application of test:** Since public school teaching fell within the exception rather than the rule of *Sugarman*, only a mere-rationality review was appropriate, and the classification passed muster under that review.

5. **Probation officers:** *Deputy probation officers* were added to the list of jobs from which aliens may be barred, in *Cabell v. Chavez-Salido*, 454 U.S. 432 (1982) (another 5-4 decision).

6. **Notaries public:** In the only post-*Sugarman* case in which the Court found *Sugarman* not applicable, the Court held that **notaries public** do **not** perform "functions that go to the heart of representative government." *Bernal v. Fainter*, 467 U.S. 216 (1984). Since the duties of a notary public are "essentially **clerical** and **ministerial**," aliens may be barred only if the state can establish a justification that survives strict scrutiny (which the state was not able to do in *Bernal*).

7. **Summary of present position:** It seems clear, then, that the present majority of the Court will allow states to ban aliens from any post involving a *"political"* rather than "economic" function, and that any post **related to education or law enforcement** is likely to be found "political." In fact, it is not even at all clear that *Griffiths* (the attorney case) would be decided the same way under the present Court, though *Bernal* (the notary case) may indicate that it would.

D. **The federal government:** Suppose a classification disadvantaging aliens is made by the **federal government**, rather than by a state. As noted, the Equal Protection Clause would not directly apply to the government's action; instead, the Fifth Amendment Due Process Clause would be interpreted to impose requirements similar to those which the Equal Protection Clause places upon the states. But because of the federal government's **exclusive responsibility for supervising immigration**, a given instance of discrimination against aliens, if made by the federal government, will be reviewed with **greater deference** than would the same type of discrimination when carried out by a state.

1. **Balancing test:** Roughly speaking, the Court has *"balanced"* the federal government's interest in controlling the terms of immigration against the alien's right to fair treatment.

2. **Administrative agency action:** The Court has granted this greater deference more readily to actions taken directly by Congress and the President than to action taken by **admin-**

istrative agencies. See, e.g., *Hampton v. Mow Sun Wong*, 426 U.S. 88 (1976) (regulation issued by the Civil Service Commission barring resident aliens from jobs in the federal Civil Service is struck down, though ban would not necessarily have been invalid if promulgated directly by the President or Congress).

3. **Medical benefits:** In the Court's only case where *Congress itself* discriminated against certain aliens, the Court *upheld* congressional power to do so. In *Matthews v. Diaz*, 426 U.S. 67 (1976), the Court held that Congress could impose the double requirement that aliens be both admitted for permanent residence and have resided continuously in the U.S. for five years, in order to receive Medicare. The Court (a unanimous one) stressed Congress' *full power over immigration*, a power which justified some discriminations against aliens which might not be permitted to the states.

E. **Education of illegal aliens:** In all the cases considered in this section thus far, the aliens who claimed to be discriminated against were *legally present* in this country. But what are the rights of aliens who have not been legally admitted, i.e., so-called *"illegal"* or *"undocumented"* aliens? The Supreme Court has not yet dealt with the rights of *adult* illegal aliens. But it has established that illegal aliens of *school age* may *not*, consistent with the Equal Protection Clause, be charged a *fee for public school education. Plyler v. Doe*, 457 U.S. 202 (1982).

1. **Facts of *Plyler*:** *Plyler* involved a Texas statute which: (1) denied local school districts funds for education of illegal-alien children; and (2) allowed school districts to deny free public education to such children.

2. **Majority strikes statute:** By a 5-4 vote, the Court *struck down* the statute as violative of equal protection. The majority opinion required several steps to reach this result:

   a. **Protected by Fourteenth Amendment:** First, the Court rejected Texas' argument that the Equal Protection Clause applies only to state action against "any person within [the state's] jurisdiction," and that illegal aliens are not "within Texas' jurisdiction" at all. The Court concluded, as a matter of legislative history, that the Clause was intended to cover *any person physically within a state's borders*, regardless of the *legality* of his presence.

   b. **Intermediate scrutiny applied:** The Court then devoted much of its opinion to determining the proper level of scrutiny. It concluded that *intermediate-level scrutiny* was appropriate here, since both the powerless nature of the group and the importance of education were factors.

      i. **"Not suspect class":** The Court explicitly *rejected* the suggestion that illegal aliens should be treated as a *"suspect class."* Entry into the class was a *voluntary* act (since entry into the nation was voluntary), in contrast to the involuntary nature of membership in other suspect classes. Also, illegal immigrant status was clearly not a constitutional irrelevancy, since Congress possessed, and had exercised, the power to exclude certain aliens, and the states could "follow the federal direction."

      ii. **Not mere "rational relation":** But "mere-rationality" review was not sufficient, either. Although the action by adult aliens in illegally entering this country was voluntary, the action of their *children* was *not*. Also, public education, while not a "right" guaranteed by the Constitution, was certainly more important than other social welfare "benefits." Denying these children an education would render them illiterate, and would thus prevent them from advancing based on their individual merit and from becoming useful members of society.

c. **Congressional policy:** Texas argued that Congress' failure to admit these children, and indeed its "apparent disapproval" of their presence, gave the state authority to treat them less favorably than citizens and resident aliens. The majority agreed that if Texas' denial of public education to these children was indeed in accord with an "identifiable congressional policy," Texas' action might well be valid. But, the majority believed, this denial *was not in accord with any identifiable congressional policy.* For instance, there was no evidence that Congress had ever even considered conservation of state educational resources as a reason for restricting immigration.

d. **State interest supporting action:** Texas also asserted three interests of its own which, it believed, justified the denial of free public education. But the Court did not find any of these interests sufficiently weighty to overcome the intermediate-level scrutiny.

　　i. **Prevent influx:** First, the state contended that its statute might help *stem the flood* of illegal immigrants. But the Court found this a "ludicrously ineffectual" way of stemming this tide, especially in view of an alternative measure: prohibiting the *employment* of illegal aliens.

　　ii. **Preserving high quality of education:** Texas also contended that illegal alien children imposed an especially heavy burden on the state's ability to provide *high quality public education*. But, the majority responded, even if excluding the children would improve the overall quality of education (an assertion as to which the Court found no evidence), Texas still bore the burden of showing why *this particular group of aliens*, as distinguished from documented aliens, was the appropriate one to exclude. Texas was unable to discharge this burden, since documented and undocumented alien children were "basically indistinguishable" in terms of their educational needs.

　　iii. **Less likely to remain resident:** Finally, Texas claimed that illegal alien children were less likely than other children to remain within the state and therefore less likely to put their education to use there. The Court also rejected this claim, essentially because it found nothing in the record to suggest that this was true as a factual matter.

e. **General "conservation of resources" argument:** The majority also rejected Texas' more general claim, that it had an interest in *preserving the state's limited educational resources* so that it could spend these on the education of its lawful residents. The majority found it easy to dismiss this argument, by resort to precedent. Preservation of scarce resources was simply *never a sufficient reason* for denying those resources to one particular group; this had already been established in the case of welfare benefits (*Graham v. Richardson, supra*, p. 354).

　　i. **Comparison:** The Court's response to this "scarce resources" argument is similar to its rejection of "administrative convenience" as a grounds for discrimination against a particular group (e.g., married servicemen in *Frontiero v. Richardson, supra*, p. 336). In the most general sense, the fact that the state saves money, time, effort, etc. is *never by itself enough to justify the selection of a particular group*

to bear the brunt of the state's conservation efforts (at least where the group is one which receives the benefit of intermediate-level or strict scrutiny).

3. **Dissent:** Justice Burger dissented in *Plyler*, joined by three other members of the Court (White, Rehnquist and O'Connor).

    a. **Unduly result-oriented:** First, Burger objected to the general way in which the majority arrived at the decision to use intermediate-level scrutiny. Since the majority was not treating illegal aliens as a suspect class nor education as a fundamental right, the Court was "[p]atching together bits and pieces of what might be termed quasi-suspect-class and quasi-fundamental-rights analysis [making the Court] guilty of an unabashedly result-oriented approach. ... " In the dissent's view the majority's theory had so little generality that it established "little more than that the level of scrutiny employed ... applies only when illegal alien children are deprived of a public education."

    b. **Voluntariness irrelevant:** Burger also objected to the fact that the majority took into account the "involuntariness" of the children's presence in this country. For Burger, it was simply irrelevant that the trait upon which the discrimination was based (illegal presence) was involuntary. For instance, the state could distinguish between mentally-ill persons and mentally-healthy ones, even though the condition of the former might be beyond their control. Nor was it relevant that the Court had previously given intermediate-level scrutiny to classifications based on illegitimacy; here, the discrimination was not based merely on "status of birth" but on a congressionally-unsanctioned illegal presence.

    c. **Education:** Burger also objected to the extra weight that the majority gave to the interest in education, as distinguished from other governmental benefits. He contended that *Rodriguez (infra*, p. 380) had definitively established that education was not a "fundamental right," and that therefore, the fact that it was education which was being denied (as opposed to, say, welfare, medical care or housing) could not make any difference to the level of scrutiny applied.

    d. **Rational relations:** Since neither the plaintiff's illegal alien status nor the nature of education should, in Burger's opinion, trigger any special scrutiny, he believed that the ***"mere-rationality" test was the appropriate one.***

        i. **Application of test:** Not surprisingly, Burger found that denial of free public education to these children was rationally related to legitimate interests held by Texas. The state had an interest in preserving its fiscal resources, and could reasonably conclude that it had no obligation to spend those resources on education for persons illegally in the country. Also, the state had a legitimate interest in attempting to curb the influx of illegal immigrants; denial of public education might not be the most effective way of accomplishing this end, but that means was not completely irrational.

        ii. **Congressional policy:** The dissent also argued that the ***federal*** government's exclusion of illegal aliens from various social welfare programs (e.g., the food stamp and AFDC programs) supported the rationality of a state's excluding such aliens from state programs.

4. **Scope of case unknown:** Because the majority, in deciding to apply intermediate-level scrutiny in *Plyler*, relied upon the **combination** of a disadvantaged group (illegal aliens) and an unusually important interest (education), the Court avoided the need for deciding whether *either* of these factors *by itself* might justify intermediate scrutiny.

    a. **Intermediate review for illegal aliens:** Thus it remains a possibility that *other types of discrimination against illegal aliens* (even if not involving something as basic as the complete denial of education) *might nonetheless trigger intermediate-level scrutiny.*

    b. **Complete denial of education:** Similarly, it is possible that the **complete denial of education** to any group (even one without the special powerlessness that marks illegal aliens) might be given intermediate-level or even strict scrutiny, despite the fact that lesser variations in the furnishing of education are subjected only to "mere-rationality" review (under *Rodriguez, infra*, p. 380).

VII. ILLEGITIMACY

A. Discrimination against illegitimates: Many states have statutes which disadvantage illegitimate children. The discrimination may take the form of ineligibility to take by intestate succession, inability to sue for the parent's wrongful death, disentitlement to claim a presumption of dependency (relevant for receipt of certain government benefits, such as social security survivors' benefits), etc.

B. Present state of the law: The Supreme Court has vacillated considerably over the years on how classifications based on legitimacy should be treated. Here is a summary of the present state of the law:

1. **Mid-level review:** *Mid-level review* is used. That is, the classification disadvantaging illegitimates must be substantially related to an important governmental objective. *Clark v. Jeter*, 486 U.S. 456 (1988).

2. **Claims can't be flatly barred:** Consequently, the state cannot simply bar unacknowledged illegitimate children from bringing wrongful death actions, from having any chance to inherit, etc. Such children must be given at least *some reasonable opportunity* (typically, via a proceeding brought by their mother) to obtain a *judicial declaration of paternity.* Once they obtain such a declaration, they must be *treated equivalently to children born legitimate.*

    a. **No short statutes of limitation:** Furthermore, the statute of limitations on paternity claims must be no longer than is reasonably needed to fulfill the state's interest in, say, weeding out stale or fraudulent claims.

        Example: Pennsylvania passes a statute of limitations saying that no action for child support may be brought on behalf of an out-of-wedlock child unless the action is brought before the child turns 6. *Held*, the statute violates the child's equal protection rights. Since the classification is based on out-of-wedlock status, it will be upheld only if it is substantially related to an important governmental objective. Concededly, Pennsylvania has an interest in avoiding the litigation of stale or fraudulent claims. But the 6-year statute of limitations is not "substantially related" to the achievement of that interest. *Clark v. Jeter, supra.*

VIII. MENTAL RETARDATION AND MENTAL ILLNESS

A. Mental retardation: The Supreme Court has refused to treat *mental retardation* as a quasi-suspect classification. *City of Cleburne v. Cleburne Living Center*, 473 U.S. 432 (1985).

1. **Rationale:** The Court in *Cleburne* advanced four reasons why it would not be appropriate to accord heightened scrutiny to classifications based on mental retardation:

   a. **Judicial second-guessing undesirable:** First, the states have a legitimate interest in giving special treatment to the mentally retarded, because of their "reduced ability to cope with and function in the everyday world." The treatment to be given to the mentally retarded is "a difficult and often a technical matter, very much a task for legislators guided by qualified professionals and not by the perhaps ill-informed opinions of the judiciary." If heightened scrutiny were given to classifications based on mental retardation, the judiciary would be more likely to be required to make "substantive judgments" about the legislative handling of the retarded, judgments which it is ill-equipped to make.

   b. **No antipathy by lawmakers:** Secondly, the array of national and state legislative responses to the plight of the mentally retarded (responses which, in general, *benefit* the retarded) show that there is no "continuing antipathy or prejudice" on the part of lawmakers.

   c. **Not politically powerless:** Thirdly, the very fact that these legislative responses have occurred "negates any claim that the mentally retarded are politically powerless in the sense that they have no ability to attract the attention of the lawmakers."

   d. **Other groups:** Finally, if quasi-suspect status were given to the "large and amorphous class" of the mentally retarded, there would be no "principled way" to deny quasi-suspect status to a number of other groups, including the aging, the disabled, the mentally ill, and the infirm. And this kind of expansion is something the courts should be "reluctant" to embark upon (though the Court did not say why).

2. **D flunks mere-rationality review:** As it happened, the fact the retarded were not given quasi-suspect status in *Cleburne* did *not* mean that the retarded plaintiffs lost the case. Although the Court purported to apply only the "mere-rationality" standard (by which the classification would be upheld so long as it was rationally related to some legitimate governmental objective), the particular governmental classification at issue in *Cleburne* was *struck down*. The defendant municipality's refusal to grant a "special use permit," required by the municipal zoning ordinance before a group home for the mentally retarded could be operated, was found not to be even rationally related to any legitimate state purpose. Rather, the denial of the permit seemed to "rest on an *irrational prejudice* against the mentally retarded."

   a. **Rigorous application of test:** The Court appeared to be applying the "mere-rationality" test with considerably *more rigor — and less deference to the government —* than it has done in most recent cases involving that test (as to which, see *supra*, p. 262). So the standard might fairly be called mere-rationality review *"with bite."*

3. **Dissent:** Three members of the Court (Marshall, Brennan, and Blackmun) disagreed with the Court's refusal to give the mentally retarded quasi-suspect status. They contended that the mentally retarded have been subject to a " 'lengthy and tragic history' … of segregation and discrimination that can only be called grotesque." They argued that at least where

what is at issue is the right of the retarded to establish a group home (the right to "establish a home" being clearly a "fundamental liberty"), heightened scrutiny should be given to any regulation that burdens their right to do so.

a. Majority's rationale rejected: The three Justices dissenting on this point also contended that the majority's reasoning was illogical:

i. Legislation irrelevant: For instance, the fact that extensive legislation had recently been enacted to protect the retarded did not mean that there was no ongoing discrimination against the retarded, or that this group was necessarily less needful of the benefits of heightened scrutiny. The dissenters pointed out that "race-based classifications [did not become] any less suspect once extensive legislation had been enacted on the subject."

ii. Relevance of trait: The dissenters also could not see why the fact that retardation was relevant to *some* types of regulation should mean that it was relevant to the kind of regulation here. "That a characteristic may be relevant under some or even many circumstances does not suggest any reason to presume it relevant under other circumstances where there is reason to suspect it is not. A sign that says 'men only' looks very different on a bathroom door than a courthouse door." For the dissenters, the fact that retardation is irrelevant in some circumstances, when coupled with a history of discrimination against the retarded, was enough to require heightened scrutiny.

4. Significance: Beyond establishing that mental retardation will not be treated as a quasi-suspect classification, *Cleburne* appears significant for at least two other reasons:

a. Hostility to heightened scrutiny: The case probably indicates that a majority of the present Court is *reluctant* to establish **additional "quasi-suspect" classes.** The majority went out of its way to indicate that it thought quasi-suspect status should not be given to certain other classifications that arguably merit it, such as "the aging, the disabled, the mentally ill, and the infirm." Therefore, few if any new entries into the catalogue of quasi-suspect classes can be expected from the present Court.

b. Burdens vs. benefits: The case also seems to confirm the Burger/Rehnquist Court's reluctance to treat a classification as more suspicious when it is used to *burden* the historically-disadvantaged group than where it is used to *benefit* that group. Recall that in the case of gender-based classifications, the Court gives the same level of review (intermediate scrutiny) to such classifications whether they purport to benefit women or not. Similarly, in the case of mental retardation, the Court will apparently apply the same level (rigorous "mere-rationality" review, but not intermediate-level scrutiny) to the classification, regardless of whether the particular classification in question appears to have been motivated by a desire to benefit or to burden the retarded.

B. Mental illness: The Court has never explicitly decided whether classifications based on *mental illness* should be treated as quasi-suspect.

1. Unlikely to be quasi-suspect class: However, in light of *Cleburne*, it seems very unlikely that the Court would give the mentally-ill quasi-suspect status.

2. "Mere-rationality with bite": However, the mentally ill, like the mentally retarded, have often been discriminated against, and do bear some of the traits of a "discreet and insular minority." (See *U.S. v. Carolene Products Co., supra*, p. 271.) Therefore, although the Court would probably give to classifications based on mental illness only low-level "mere-rationality" review, it may apply that level of review in the same fairly stringent way (mere-rationality *"with bite"*) that it did to the mental-retardation classification in *Cleburne*.

IX. GENERAL PRINCIPLES OF MIDDLE-LEVEL SCRUTINY

A. General principles: Once a court decides that traditional deferential, "mere-rationality" review is appropriate, it is almost a foregone conclusion that the statute will be upheld. Conversely, if the court decides to apply strict scrutiny, the statute will almost invariably be struck down. Thus in these two situations, it is not usually important to focus on exactly how the review takes place; the important thing is how the choice of standards gets made. By contrast, the decision to apply "middle-level" or "intermediate" review does not by any means dispose of the matter; the precise way in which the court applies the middle-ground scrutiny thus becomes extremely important. This section reviews briefly some of the principles that seem to be guiding the courts in applying intermediate-level review.

B. Importance of objective: The *objective* sought to be achieved by the statute must be *"important,"* even if it need not be "compelling" (as required in strict scrutiny situations).

     1. Little "bite": However, this requirement has not proven to have a lot of bite, since most asserted state objectives have been found to be "important." However, there are some exceptions, such as "administrative convenience" and "conservation of scarce resources" (see *supra*, p. 357).

C. Close means-end fit: The *means* chosen by the state must be *"substantially related"* to achieving the important objective. That is, the *means-end fit* must be a *reasonably tight one*.

     1. Less-restrictive alternatives: Looking at this requirement another way, the demands of intermediate scrutiny are more likely to be satisfied if there are *no available alternatives* that would carry out the asserted objectives as well or better, without causing needless disadvantage to anyone.

     2. Smoking out bad motivation: One reason for requiring a close means-end fit is that it furnishes a way of *"flushing out" unconstitutional motivation*. See Ely, p. 146 (regarding strict scrutiny); see also *supra*, pp. 272-273. That is, if the state claims that a particular objective was the motivation behind the statute, yet the means is not closely related to the ends, the court will be justified in suspecting that the asserted motivation was not the real one (which may have been an unconstitutional one).

D. Refusal to hypothesize state purpose: Recall that in the area of general social and economic welfare legislation, where "mere-rationality" review is all that is applied, the Court seems to be willing to consider possible objectives to which the means chosen by the legislature are rationally related, even though there is no evidence that this objective *in fact* motivated the legislature. (*Supra*, p. 258.) In the intermediate-review area, however, the Court *will not hypothesize a state objective*; only those objectives which are shown (by the terms of the statute, legislative history, or otherwise) to have *actually motivated the legislature* will be considered. If none of these actual objectives is sufficiently "important," or sufficiently tightly related to the means chosen, the statute will be struck down.

> **Example:** In *Trimble v. Gordon*, 430 U.S. 762 (1977), the state argued that one purpose of its ban on intestate succession by illegitimates was to enforce the "presumed intention" of intestate decedents. The Court rejected this asserted objective, stating "[we] do not think [the law] was enacted for this purpose [and] we will not hypothesize an additional state purpose. ... "

Quiz Yourself on
EQUAL PROTECTION — ALIENAGE AND ILLEGITIMACY

43. The state of Pacifica enacted a statute providing that no person who is not a U.S. citizen could hold title to beach-front land located in the state. Pacifica's west coast consists entirely of ocean-front property. The statute was enacted in part because state residents were annoyed that Japanese nationals and citizens of other Pacific rim countries were paying high prices for Pacifica beach-front property, making it harder for U.S. citizens living in Pacifica to compete for ownership of that property. Yukio, a Japanese citizen who resides permanently in the United States, and who wishes to buy ocean-front property in Pacifica, has sued to have the statute overturned on the grounds that it violates her equal protection rights.

     (a) What standard of review should the court give to the Pacifica statute? _____

     (b) Will Yukio's attack succeed? _____

44. The city of Xenon was concerned that many applicants for posts as public school teachers in the town, and some hires, were foreigners who spoke with a hard-to-understand accent. Therefore, the Xenon school board enacted a regulation that henceforth, all new hires for the post of school teacher in the local school system must at the time of their application be United States citizens. Ted, an Englishman married to an American citizen, was a permanent resident of the U.S. but had no desire to become a U.S. citizen (even though his marital status entitled him to become one). Ted sued Xenon to have its citizens-only rule overturned, on the grounds that it violated his equal protection rights.

     (a) What standard should the court use in reviewing the Xenon citizens-only provision? _____

     (b) Will Ted's attack on the provision succeed? _____

45. The village of Tesla had a fine school system, generally believed to be better than that of surrounding towns. Tesla is located less than 100 miles from the border with Mexico, and has a large number of both Mexican Americans as well as undocumented aliens from Mexico. In order to discourage enrollment by students who in fact reside in other towns, the village enacted a set of strict regulations providing that only students who satisfied two conditions could attend the village's schools: (1) they had a bona fide residence within the village limits; and (2) they were either U.S. citizens or resident aliens. One effect of this regulation, as intended by the town elders, was to make undocumented aliens unable to attend the village schools even if they resided in the village. The principal motive for the no-illegal-aliens rule was to conserve tax dollars, because undocumented aliens on average pay lower property taxes, and education in the state is financed principally through property taxes. The village allowed an exception to its enrollment restrictions for anyone willing to pay a tuition fee of $4,000 per year.

     Pedro, a resident of Tesla who was undocumented, sued the village, arguing that as applied to him the enrollment restrictions violated the Equal Protection Clause.

     (a) When the court reviews Pedro's challenge to the enrollment restrictions, what standard of review should it use? _____

(b) Will Pedro's attack succeed? _____

46. The state of Rigor provides that no illegitimate child may receive any part of his or her father's estate if the father dies intestate. This statutory exclusion applies even if there has been a judicial finding of paternity prior to the father's death. When Stuart was 11, he was found (in a proceeding brought on his behalf by his mother) to be the illegitimate son of David. Two years after this finding, David died intestate. Stuart has sued for a declaratory judgment that the state's exclusion of him from an intestate share of David's estate violates his, Stuart's, equal protection rights.

    (a) What standard of review should the court use in examining the exclusion of illegitimate children from the intestacy scheme? _____

    (b) Will Stuart's attack succeed? _____

―――――――――――――

Answers

43. **(a) Strict scrutiny.**

    (b) Yes, probably. Discrimination against aliens (at least aliens who are legally in this country) is to be strictly scrutinized, because aliens as a class are politically powerless and frequently discriminated against. Therefore, any statute that discriminates against aliens on its face, or whose purpose is to disadvantage aliens, will be struck down unless it is necessary to achieve a compelling governmental interest. Here, the state's interest in keeping land prices low for American citizens is almost certainly not "compelling." In any event, discrimination against aliens is not a "necessary" way to achieve that objective, since there are other less-discriminatory options available (e.g., price controls that apply to everybody).

44. **(a) The mere-rationality standard.**

    (b) No. As noted in the answer to the prior question, discrimination against aliens is generally subjected to strict scrutiny. However, under the so-called "*Sugarman* exception," this strict scrutiny does not apply to discrimination against aliens who apply for jobs that ***"go to the heart of representative government."*** The Court has held that the post of public school teacher falls within this "heart of representative government" exception, because of a teacher's opportunity to "influence the attitudes of students towards government, the political process, and a citizen's social responsibilities." *Ambach v. Norwick.* Therefore, only a mere-rationality review is used, and the regulation will be upheld if it is rationally related to the achievement of a legitimate state objective. Here, the regulation almost certainly satisfies this standard. Hiring teachers who can be easily understood is surely a legitimate state objective, and there is at least a rational relation between citizenship and ease of understanding (since non-citizens on average probably have harder-to-understand accents than citizens).

45. **(a) Intermediate-level review, under which the measure will be invalidated unless it is "substantially related" to the achievement of an "important" governmental objective.**

    (b) Yes, probably. The Court held in *Plyler v. Doe* that intermediate-level review should be given to any state law denying free public-school education to illegal aliens of school age. In *Plyler*, the Court held that the various state interests advanced there (e.g., preventing an influx of illegal immigrants, conserving tax dollars, etc.) were not sufficiently weighty to overcome this mid-level review. The enrollment restriction here is essentially identical to that struck down in *Plyler*. The fact that non-residents of the village are also excluded is irrelevant — the key fact is that among residents of the village, those who are illegal aliens are excluded, whereas those who are citizens or resident aliens are allowed. Even if the village shows that it has to spend tax dollars on educating these additional students, and even if it is able to show that it does not get state aid to compensate it for these incremental burdens, the interest in conservation of resources is likely to be found insufficient to overcome the mid-level review (and similar fiscal interests were found insufficient in *Plyler* itself).

46. (a) Mid-level review.

(b) Yes, probably. After waffling a lot about what the appropriate level of review is for classifications that disadvantage illegitimates, the Supreme Court has finally held that intermediate scrutiny should be used. That is, the statutory classification that disadvantages illegitimates must be "*substantially* related to an *important* governmental objective." Here, the state's total exclusion of illegitimates from intestate succession, even those who have been found by a reliable court proceeding to be the decedent's child, is very unlikely to be found to be substantially related to the achievement of an important state objective. (For instance, while the state may have an important objective of repelling false claims of paternity, this objective is not advanced at all by excluding one who has, during the decedent's lifetime, been found to be truly his child.) See *Trimble v. Gordon*, 430 U.S. 762 (1977), roughly matching the facts of this case, and striking down the total exclusion.

X. UNEQUAL TREATMENT OF GAYS, AND THE BANNING OF SAME-SEX MARRIAGE — ENHANCED "MERE-RATIONALITY" REVIEW

A. Issues generally: Perhaps the most important and controversial issue in equal protection today is the status of *gays and lesbians*: to what extent may government classify people on the basis of their sexual orientation, or otherwise intentionally disfavor homosexuals? The principal modern manifestation of the issue is whether government may *ban same-sex marriage*. The answers remain uncertain, but there is a strong tendency towards recognizing *greater protections for gays*. Based on the three major gay-rights cases decided by the Supreme Court since 1996, we can say the following:

❏ **No "semi-suspect" status:** The Court has been *unwilling* to treat classifications based on sexual orientation as having official *"semi-suspect"* or *"suspect"* status. So when the Court hears a challenge to a classification based on sexual orientation, the Court purports to use easy-to-satisfy *"mere-rationality"* review, not mid-level review (which is given to semi-suspect classifications, like gender) or strict scrutiny (given to suspect classifications, like race and ethnicity).

❏ **Mere rationality "with bite":** However, the gay *plaintiffs* have *prevailed* in their constitutional challenge in *all three* of these cases. That has occurred, in major part, because although the Court has purported to apply mere-rationality review, it has in fact given *much less deference* to the legislature's sexual-orientation-based classification system than is typically applied in mere-rationality cases. The level of review used can fairly be described as "mere rationality *with bite*."

❏ **Animus towards unpopular minority:** A persistent theme in these decisions has been the majority's conclusion that legislative classifications based on sexual orientation have historically been *based solely on animus towards a disfavored minority*, and that such animus ***cannot be a "legitimate governmental interest."*** Therefore, the Court concludes, the classification system fails mere-rationality review because of the lack of a legitimate interest. (See *supra*, p. 260, for a more general discussion of the Court's decisions turning on a finding of legislative animus towards disfavored minorities.)

1. **Three major cases:** The majority opinion in each of these three major gay-rights cases was written by Justice Kennedy. The three cases, listed in the order in which they were decided, are:

   ❏ *Romer v. Evans*, a 1996 case in which the Court struck down a state constitutional amendment that would have prohibited any local government from ***giving various anti-discrimination protections*** to gays and lesbians.

   ❏ *Lawrence v. Texas*, a 2003 decision in which the Court struck down a ***state's criminalizing of same-sex "sodomy"*** between consenting adults. The case was decided based on substantive due process rather than equal protection grounds, which is why we discuss it in the chapter on due process (see *supra*, p. 201). But because the Court used a quite stringent form of mere-rationality review, *Lawrence*, like the two cases apparently decided on equal protection grounds that we're considering here, exemplifies the modern Court's trend of giving unusually close review to laws that single out gays.

   ❏ *U.S. v. Windsor*, a 2013 decision in which the Court struck down a key definition in the federal Defense of Marriage Act (DOMA), under which only opposite-sex couples could be deemed married for federal purposes. The effect of the decision is that ***if a same-sex couple is married under the law of a state***, the federal government ***may not treat the couple any differently*** than it would treat a ***heterosexual couple*** married under that same state's law.

   We discuss *Romer* and *Windsor* here, since these two cases were decided mainly on equal protection grounds.[17]

B. **Singling out of gays because of animus (*Romer v. Evans*):** The first case in the trio described above was ***Romer v. Evans***, 517 U.S. 620 (1996). There, the Court ***struck down*** a Colorado constitutional amendment that would have ***prevented the state or any of its cities from giving certain protections to gays or lesbians***. The Court found that the measure flunked "mere-rationality" review on two separate grounds: there was no legitimate state interest in fact being served, and the means chosen by the state were not rationally related to the (possibly legitimate) interest that the state asserted.

1. **Facts:** The Colorado provision, known as "Amendment 2," modified the Colorado constitution to provide that neither the state nor any subdivision (including state agency, city or school district) shall "enact, adopt or enforce any statute, regulation, ordinance or policy whereby ***homosexual, lesbian or bisexual orientation, conduct***, practices or relationships shall constitute or otherwise be the basis of or entitle any person or class of persons to have or claim any ***minority status***, quota preferences, ***protected status*** or ***claim of discrimination***."

---

17. Actually, there's some uncertainty about whether the majority opinion in *Windsor* is premised on equal protection, or rather on substantive due process. But most of the prior cases cited in *Windsor*, and the thrust of the argument, appear to based on equal protection analysis. See *infra*, p. 371.

a. **Bans anti-discrimination laws:** The main practical impact of Amendment 2 was that it prevented both the state legislature and any city from passing statutes or ordinances that would *protect gays and lesbians from discrimination*. For instance, the cities of Aspen, Boulder and Denver had all passed (prior to the enactment of Amendment 2) ordinances barring discrimination against gays in housing, employment, education, public accommodations, and the like; each of these ordinances would apparently have been wiped out by Amendment 2. Only by re-amending the state constitution — something requiring a state-wide referendum — could gays obtain any protection against discrimination on the basis of sexual orientation.

2. **Holding:** By a 6-3 vote, the Court struck down Amendment 2, even though the majority used only "mere-rationality" review. The opinion by Justice Kennedy relied on several grounds:

a. **Gays not put in "same position" as others:** Colorado defended the amendment on the grounds that it merely (in Kennedy's words) "puts gays and lesbians in the *same position* as all other persons" and "does no more than deny homosexuals *special rights*." But Kennedy found this interpretation "implausible." The amendment in fact singled gays out for *worse* treatment than other groups: "Homosexuals, by state decree, are *put in a solitary class* with respect to transactions and relations in both the private and governmental spheres. The amendment *withdraws from homosexuals, but no others, specific legal protection* from the injuries caused by discrimination[.]"

   i. **Wide protection of other groups:** Kennedy noted that existing state and municipal laws in Colorado protected many groups, not just the racial, ethnic or gender groups to which the U.S. Supreme Court has given heightened Equal Protection review. For instance, various ordinances protected persons from discrimination based on "age, military status, marital status, pregnancy, parenthood, custody of a minor child, political affiliation, [or] physical or mental disability of an individual or of his or her associates. . . ." So Amendment 2 was not simply withdrawing special rights from gays, it was *"forbidd[ing them] the safeguards that others enjoy or may seek without constraint*."

b. **Desire to harm is not a legitimate interest:** Kennedy then asserted that Amendment 2 "seems inexplicable by anything but *animus toward the class that it affects*." He quoted approvingly the statement in *U.S. Dep't of Agric. v. Moreno*, 413 U.S. 528 (1973) (discussed *supra*, p. 260), that "If the constitutional conception of 'equal protection of the laws' means anything, it must at the very least mean that a *bare* . . . *desire to harm a politically unpopular group cannot constitute a legitimate governmental interest*."

c. **"Protection of liberties of landlords or employers" rationale rejected:** Colorado argued that Amendment 2 was rationally related to the protection of *other citizens' freedom of association*, in particular the freedom of landlords or employers who have personal or religious objections to homosexuality. Kennedy did not reject this as a legitimate state interest. But he found the *means-end fit* to be so loose that it was not credible that this free-association interest was even part of what had motivated the state: "The breadth of the Amendment is so far removed from these particular justifications that we find it impossible to credit them."

    d. **Conclusion:** Kennedy concluded by saying that "Amendment 2 classifies homosexuals not to further a proper legislative end but to make them *unequal to everyone else*. This Colorado cannot do. A State *cannot so deem a class of persons a stranger to its laws*."

3. **Dissent:** The dissent, by Justice Scalia (joined by Rehnquist and Thomas) was unusually vitriolic. Scalia accused the majority of *"tak[ing] sides in the culture wars,"* and said that its striking down of the Amendment was "an act, not of judicial judgment, but of political will."

    a. **No singling out:** Scalia rejected the majority's view that Amendment 2 singled out homosexuals for unfavorable treatment. All the Amendment did was to say to gays that "they may not obtain preferential treatment without amending the state constitution." If it was a violation of equal protection to force gays to resort to the state-constitutional-amendment level when others don't have to, then it would also violate equal protection, Scalia wrote, to force any group to "have recourse to a more general and hence more difficult level of political decisionmaking than others." He posed the example of a state law prohibiting the award of municipal contracts to relatives of mayors or city councilmen: "Once such a law is passed, the group composed of such relatives must, in order to get the benefit of city contracts, persuade the state legislature — unlike all other citizens, who need only persuade the municipality. It is ridiculous to consider this a denial of equal protection[.]"

    b. **Not politically unpopular:** Scalia noted in passing that it was "nothing short of preposterous to call 'politically unpopular' a group which *enjoys enormous influence in American media and politics*." And he accused the majority of siding with the "views and values of the lawyer class," whose tolerant views of homosexuality are reflected by the fact that law schools require interviewers to pledge their willingness to hire homosexuals.

    c. **Rationally related:** Lastly, Scalia believed that the Amendment was in fact reasonably related to a legitimate governmental interest. That interest was the prevention of *"piecemeal deterioration of the sexual morality* favored by a majority of Coloradans." And a measure that merely denied homosexuals "preferential treatment" was surely an appropriate means of achieving that end.

C. **The federal Defense of Marriage Act struck down (*Windsor*):** The biggest debate in the area of gay rights currently is whether and when gay and lesbian couples have a constitutional right to *enter into same-sex marriages*. So far, the Supreme Court has decided only one case in this domain, but it is a major one: in *U.S. v. Windsor*, 133 S. Ct. 2675 (2013), the Court decided that *when a same-sex couple has been married under the law of a state*, the federal government *may not treat the couple any differently*, for federal-law purposes, than it would treat a *heterosexual couple* married under that same state's law.

The *Windsor* decision invalidated, on essentially equal protection grounds, a major part of a 1996 federal statute called the *Defense of Marriage Act*. The effect of *Windsor* is that any same-sex couple who has been married under the law of a state that permits same-sex marriage is entitled to the *same federal benefits* as any opposite-sex married couple.

1. **The 1996 Defense of Marriage Act (DOMA):** In the mid-1990s, it became apparent to many members of Congress that some states might soon give gay people the right to marry. A majority of Congress wanted to make sure that the same-sex-marriage idea would not be extended to unwilling states or to the federal government. Congress tried to accomplish this by passing, in 1996, the ***Defense of Marriage Act (DOMA),*** 1 U.S.C. § 7 and 28 U.S.C. §1738C.

a. **Two sections:** DOMA, as enacted by Congress, had two independent provisions.

   i. **State recognition of other states' marriages:** One section of DOMA said that no state was required to ***recognize the validity of a same-sex marriage*** contracted in ***another state.*** 28 U.S.C. §1738C.[18] This section is known as "§2" of DOMA. (This section remains in force, because it's not directly affected by *Windsor.*)

   Example: *A* and *B*, both men, residing in New York, get married there, as New York allows. The two then move to New Jersey, which does not allow same-sex marriage. DOMA says that New Jersey is free to (but doesn't have to) treat *A* and *B* as unmarried.

   ii. **Federal recognition of state's same-sex marriage:** The other section of DOMA said that the ***federal*** government ***doesn't have to recognize a same-sex couple as being married*** — even if they are married under state law — for purposes of any *federal* ***benefits*** or federal ***regulations.*** (This is the section that *Windsor* struck down.)

   (1) **How it worked:** The section of DOMA that refused federal recognition of state-approved same-sex marriages was 1 U.S.C. §7 (known as ***"§3"*** of DOMA. This was a definitional section, which said that in interpreting federal law:

   "The word 'marriage' means only a legal union between ***one man and one woman*** as husband and wife, and the word 'spouse' refers only to a ***person of the opposite sex who is a husband or wife.***"

   So under this federal statute, ***no same-sex couple could ever be deemed "married"*** for federal-law purposes.

b. **States allow same-sex marriage:** By the time of the Supreme Court's 2013 decision in *Windsor*, 12 states and the District of Columbia had granted same-sex couples the right to marry.[19]

   i. **DOMA's consequence:** Section 3 of DOMA meant that no federal statute or regulation — dealing with ***income tax, estate tax, immigration, health insurance***, etc. — was ***permitted*** to treat a same-sex couple that had been legally married in any of these states as being married for federal purposes.

2. **Facts and procedural setting of *Windsor*:** *Windsor*'s challenge to DOMA's ban on federal recognition of state-sanctioned marriages was based on an especially sympathetic

---

18. §1738C says that "No State ... shall be ***required to give effect*** to any ... record ... of any other State ... respecting a relationship ***between persons of the same sex*** that is ***treated as a marriage*** under the laws of such other State[.]"

19. As the practical result of a case the Court dismissed on standing grounds the same day as *Windsor*, *Hollingsworth v. Perry*, ___ U.S. ___ (2013), California seems to have become the 13th state to allow same-sex marriage. These 14 jurisdictions together account for 30% of the American population. *NY Times*, June 27, 2013, p. A1.

set of facts. Edith Windsor and Thea Spyer had begun a long-term relationship in 1963, and had lived together in New York City ever since. Then, in 2007, at a time when New York State did not yet allow same-sex marriage, the couple traveled to Canada and got married there. Spyer died in 2009, at a moment when New York had not yet itself given same-sex couples the right to marry,[20] but a moment at which the New York courts would have *recognized* the couple's Canadian marriage.[21]

 a. **Estate tax issue:** When Spyer died, she left her entire estate to Windsor. Under the federal estate tax's "marital exemption," when one married spouse dies, any property left to the other passes free of estate tax. But section 3 of DOMA, by preventing the federal government from recognizing any same-sex couple as being married, deprived Spyer's estate of the deduction. Consequently, Windsor had to pay $363,000 in federal estate taxes out of the money Spyer left her.

 b. **Theory of suit:** Windsor paid the estate tax and then sued the IRS for a refund. She contended that DOMA §3 deprived her of the guarantee of equal protection, as applied to the federal government through the Fifth Amendment's due process clause. (See *supra*, p. 251 for how the guarantee of equal protection is made applicable to the federal government via Fifth Amendment due process.)

 c. **Obama administration refuses to defend:** While the suit was pending in federal district court, the Obama administration decided that it would not defend DOMA's constitutionality. But a group of members of the House of Representatives, acting under the name Bipartisan Legal Advisory Group (BLAG), intervened as an "interested party," and defended DOMA against Windsor's attack.[22]

3. **Kennedy's opinion strikes down DOMA:** By a 5-4 vote, the Court held that section 3 of DOMA was an ***unconstitutional infringement*** of the ***rights of same-sex couples whom state law regarded as properly married***. The majority opinion was by Justice Kennedy, who had also authored the majority opinion in the Court's two other major gay-rights cases, *Romer v. Evans* (*supra*, p. 366) and *Lawrence v. Texas*, (*supra*, p. 201). Kennedy was joined by the four members of the Court's liberal wing, Justices Ginsburg, Breyer, Sotomayor and Kagan.

 a. **Basis for Kennedy's opinion:** It's not so easy to state which constitutional provision(s) Kennedy found DOMA to have violated, or what standard of review he used.

   i. **Mere-rationality review under equal protection:** Kennedy's opinion relied upon concepts sounding in equal protection, substantive due process, as well as federalism; however, the core guarantee that Kennedy seems to have found to be violated is the guarantee of ***equal protection***. And as to the standard of review, Kennedy seems to have reached his equal protection conclusion not by use of any official heightened scrutiny, but by a ***relatively demanding version of mere-rationality review***.

---

20. New York later enacted this right by legislation, in 2011.

21. The majority opinion in *Windsor* deferred to the Second Circuit's conclusion that at the time of Spyer's death, New York would have recognized the Canadian marriage as making the couple married under New York law.

22. The majority in *Windsor* decided that BLAG's participation as an intervening party was enough to satisfy the Article III "case or controversy" requirement.

b. State regulation of marriage: Kennedy began by talking at length about the tradition that *marriage would be primarily regulated by the states*, not the federal government. He said that DOMA massively interfered with this tradition that the states get to decide who should be recognized as married; DOMA did this by denying federal equality "to a class of persons that the laws of New York, and of 11 other States, have *sought to protect.*"

    i. Uniformity within each sate: In particular, Kennedy said, DOMA rejected the "long-established precept" that the *incidents of marriage* within any given state should be "*uniform for all married couples within each State*, though they may vary ... from one State to the next."

    ii. Apparent federalist basis: This discussion sounded as though Kennedy was about to say that in §3, DOMA had exceeded Congress' powers under our system of *federalism*.

    iii. Federalism unnecessary for decision: But then, Kennedy's opinion seemed to turn sharply in a new direction. After his extensive discussion of what seemed to be federalism-based concerns, Kennedy said that it was "*unnecessary to decide* whether this federal intrusion on state power is a violation of the Constitution because it *disrupts the federal balance.*" The states' power to define marriage was "of central relevance in this case *quite apart from principles of federalism.*"

c. Equal protection as basis: From this point, Kennedy's opinion seemed to rely *mainly on equal protection*, secondarily on *substantive due process*, and virtually not at all on federalism. He asserted that DOMA should be subjected to *more than casual review*, to determine whether it was a constitutionally "obnoxious" discrimination; he then decided that DOMA could not survive this review. In getting to this conclusion, Kennedy proceeded through several steps:

    i. "Dignity" interest: First, he said, when New York (or any other state) decided to allow the class of same-sex couples to marry, the state was conferring on the class "*a dignity and status of immense import.*" Then, a bit later,[23] he described state-sanctioned same-sex marriage as "a *far-reaching legal acknowledgment* of the *intimate relationship between two people*, a relationship deemed by the State worthy of *dignity* in the community *equal with all other marriages.*"

    ii. Departure from tradition of reliance on states: But DOMA, he said, "*departs from [the] history and tradition of reliance on state law* to define marriage."

    iii. Congressional purpose to injure: In fact, Kennedy said, DOMA was using the New-York-defined class of married persons for a *purpose opposite the state's own purpose*. Congress was "impos[ing] restrictions and disabilities" on some married couples; "[w]hat the State of New York treats as *alike* the federal law deems *unlike* by a law *designed to injure the same class the State seeks to protect.*" This raised the question "whether the resulting injury and indignity is a *deprivation of an essential part of the liberty protected by the Fifth Amendment.*"

---

23. I discuss some of Kennedy's statements in a different order than they occur in his opinion; I do so in an attempt to make clearer the doctrinal basis for his conclusion that DOMA violated equal protection and due process.

iv. Due process and equal protection: Kennedy's answer was *"yes,"* DOMA deprives same-sex married couples of "essential Fifth Amendment liberty." As he summarized his conclusion: "DOMA seeks to injure the very class New York seeks to protect. By doing so it *violates basic due process and equal protection principles applicable to the Federal Government.*" He then supported his conclusion with several propositions:

(1) **"Bare desire to harm" not a legitimate objective:** He noted that the Court's equal protection precedents foreclosed one particular type of governmental objective from supporting a classification scheme: the guarantee of equal protection " 'must at the very least mean that a *bare congressional desire to harm a politically unpopular group* cannot' justify disparate treatment of that group" (quoting *U.S. Dept. of Agriculture v. Moreno, supra,* p. 260).

(2) **"Careful consideration" of "unusual" discriminations:** He then asserted that in determining whether a law is motived by such an *improper animus,* if the discrimination is of an *"unusual character,"* the discrimination especially calls for *"careful consideration"* (quoting *Romer v. Evans, supra,* p. 366).

(3) **DOMA stigmatizes:** DOMA was an *"unusual deviation"* from the "usual tradition of recognizing and accepting state definitions of marriage," in a way that deprived same-sex couples of the "benefits and responsibilities" that ordinarily come with federal recognition of a state-sanctioned marriage. This unusual deviation was *"strong evidence* of a law having the *purpose and effect of disapproval"* of the class of same-sex married couples; the law placed "a *stigma"* on every married same-sex couple.

(4) **Intentional discrimination:** And, Kennedy said, DOMA's interference with the "equal dignity" of same-sex marriages was *not just an incidental effect*; it was the *"essence"* of the statute. He quoted the House Report on the bill, which said that the statute expresses "both *moral disapproval* of homosexuality, and a moral conviction that heterosexuality better comports with *traditional (especially Judeo-Christian) morality.*"

(5) **Ill effects:** This intentional discrimination by Congress "places same-sex couples in an unstable position of being in a *second-tier marriage"* and *"demeans the couple,* whose *moral and sexual choices* the Constitution protects." (At this point, Kennedy cited *Lawrence v. Texas, supra,* p. 201, where the Court had held that government cannot criminalize gay sexual activity between consenting adults.) And, he said, Congress's discrimination *"humiliates tens of thousands of children* now being raised by same-sex couples."

(6) **Unclear standard of review:** Kennedy's opinion never precisely articulated *which standard of review* he was applying to Congress' decision to treat same-sex married couples differently from opposite-sex ones. The language he quoted from *Romer v. Evans* (see Par. iv(2) *supra*), that discriminations of an *"unusual character"* call for *"careful consideration,"* is as close as he came to specifying a standard. But as I discuss below (p. 378), his review seems to

be *less deferential — more rigorous and hard-to-survive* — than is usual in cases purporting to apply mere-rationality review.

    v. **Summary:** In summary, Kennedy said, "*no legitimate purpose* overcomes [DOMA's] purpose and effect to *disparage* and to *injure* those whom the State, by its marriage laws, sought to *protect in personhood and dignity.*" By treating married same-sex couples as "living in marriages *less respected* than others," Congress had violated the Fifth Amendment.

        (1) **Limited to married couples:** But Kennedy noted that the Court's holding was *"confined"* to couples who are *married under state law*; thus, he implied, the opinion does not say anything about the rights of same-sex couples who have *not* gotten married because they live in a state that forbids same-sex marriage.

4. **Dissents:** The Court's four most conservative members — Roberts, Scalia, Alito and Thomas — wrote three *dissents* among them. The dissents varied both in rationale and as to predictions about how the Court would decide subsequent issues, but all the dissents agreed that DOMA section 3 was constitutional.

    a. **Scalia's dissent:** The most extensive dissent was by Justice Scalia, who delivered a stinging criticism of the majority's handling of the merits.

        i. **Basis for ruling:** He began by calling it "remarkable" how *"rootless and shifting"* the majority's justifications were. Later, he summarized what he saw as the *vagueness* of the majority's holding: "The sum of all the Court's nonspecific hand-waving is that this law is invalid (*maybe on equal-protection grounds, maybe on substantive-due-process grounds, and perhaps with some amorphous federalism component playing a role*) because it is motivated by a 'bare . . . desire to harm' couples in same-sex marriages."

        ii. **Lack of equal protection standard:** Scalia was especially critical of Kennedy's failure to even *mention* "what had been the *central question* in this litigation: whether, under the Equal Protection Clause, laws restricting marriage to a man and a woman are reviewed for *more than mere rationality.*"

            (1) **Court uses more severe version of mere-rationality review:** Scalia then tried to discern what standard of review Kennedy was in fact using. He concluded that Kennedy's opinion *"does not apply strict scrutiny,* and its *central propositions* are *taken from rational-basis* cases like *Moreno*" (*supra*, p. 260). But, he indicated, Kennedy was *not in fact* applying traditional mere-rationality review: "the Court certainly does not apply anything that resembles that *deferential framework*."

            (2) **"Mere rationality:"** Scalia gave his own answer to the standard-of-review issue that Kennedy had avoided: that DOMA's classification between same-sex and opposite-sex state-consecrated marriages should be reviewed *"only for its rationality."* Judged by this mere-rationality standard, for Scalia this was an easy case, because §3 of DOMA was rationally related to the achievement of several legitimate objectives (e.g., having a *"uniform federal definition of marriage,"* to deal with issues such as a same-sex couple that marries in a state where same-sex marriage is legal and then moves to one where it is not).

(3) Congress' intent disputed: Scalia also sharply disagreed with Kennedy's assertion that, in passing DOMA, Congress had acted with a purpose to "disparage," "injure," "degrade" and "humiliate" same-sex couples and their children. DOMA ***"did no more than codify an aspect of marriage that had been unquestioned in our society for most of its existence — indeed, had been unquestioned in virtually all societies for virtually all of human history."***

(4) Right to same-sex marriage in the states: Finally, Scalia disbelieved what he called Kennedy's "bald ... disclaimer" that the *Windsor* opinion was "confined" to couples married under state law. A ruling that a ***state*** that ***refuses to allow gays to marry violates their constitutional rights*** is ***not far off***, he was sure, if the Court's composition doesn't change. He predicted that the present majority, "which finds it so horrific that Congress irrationally and hatefully robbed same-sex couples of the 'personhood and dignity' which state legislatures conferred upon them," will "of a certitude be ***similarly appalled by state legislatures'*** irrational and hateful failure to acknowledge that 'personhood and dignity' in the first place." "[N]o one should be fooled; it is just a matter of listening and ***waiting for the other shoe***."

b. Alito's dissent: In another lengthy dissent, Justice Alito said he believed that the DOMA provision did not violate either substantive due process or equal protection.

i. Substantive due process: Alito interpreted a sentence in Kennedy's opinion as "suggest[ing] that ***substantive due process*** may partially underlie the Court's decision[.]" But Alito argued that substantive due process protects only "those ***fundamental rights and liberties*** which are, objectively, *'deeply rooted in this Nation's history and tradition'*." Noting that no state had permitted same-sex marriage until 2003, he said it was "beyond dispute" that ***"the right to same-sex marriage is not deeply rooted in this Nation's history and tradition."*** He concluded that the Constitution "simply does not speak to the issue of same-sex marriage," and that "[a]ny change on a question so fundamental should be made by the people ***through their elected officials***."

ii. Equal protection: As to ***equal protection***, Alito asserted that ***mere-rationality review*** was the appropriate standard (and he implied that this was the test that Kennedy, too, was employing).

(1) Two views of marriage: In explaining how he would decide the equal protection issue, Alito commented that there are today two quite different views of the ***nature of marriage***. What he called the ***"traditional"*** view "sees marriage as an ***intrinsically opposite-sex institution***[.]*" The ***"newer"*** view, which he called the ***"consent-based*** vision of marriage," defines marriage primarily as "the ***solemnization of mutual commitment*** — marked by strong emotional attachment and sexual attraction — ***between two persons***." Proponents of same-sex marriage, he said, hold this newer consent-based view, and then argue that "because gender differentiation is not relevant to this vision, the exclusion of same-sex couples from the institution of marriage is rank discrimination."

(2) Either view is constitutional: However, Alito said, "The Constitution *does not codify either of these views* of marriage." Since neither view of marriage is countermanded by the Constitution, "both Congress and the States are entitled to enact laws recognizing *either* of the two understandings of marriage."

(3) Reliance on state sovereignty: Alito then turned to Kennedy's reliance on concepts of *state sovereignty* as bearing on the equal-protection issue. Alito said he "wholeheartedly agree[d]" with Kennedy's view that the question of same-sex marriage should be *primarily resolved at the state level.* But he disagreed with Kennedy's conclusion that §3 of DOMA encroached on state prerogatives — all the section did was to *"define a class of persons to whom federal law extends certain special benefits*[.]" And, he believed, Congress had the power to construct its own definition of that class, and to base that definition on its own concept of "marriage."

(4) State bans on same-sex marriage: Anticipating the issue of *state bans* on same-sex marriage, Alito said, "I hope that the Court will ultimately *permit the people of each State to decide* this question for themselves."

5. **Significance:** What's the significance of *Windsor*? On its face, the case establishes a fairly narrow proposition: if a same-sex couple is recognized as being married for purposes of the law of the *appropriate state*,[24] then the *federal* government must for all purposes treat that couple *exactly the same way it treats married opposite-sex couples*.

> **Example:** About two weeks after the *Windsor* decision, the House of Representatives notified all of its employees that if an employee is part of a same-sex couple that is married under state law, the federal government will now provide the couple with the same health-care options that it provides to married opposite-sex couples. See *NY Times*, July 10, 2013, p. A14.

   a. **Detriments imposed:** Apart from the estate-tax discrimination at issue in *Windsor* itself, DOMA section 3 caused a number of other federal-law provisions to apply differently to same-sex married couples than to opposite-sex ones. Presumably all of these differential treatments are now abolished by the *Windsor* decision. Here is a partial list, mostly taken from Kennedy's opinion:

   ❑ The same-sex spouse of an federal employee will now receive *government health care benefits* (as in the above example of the House of Representatives).

   ❑ A same-sex married couple will be able to file a joint federal income-tax return (and will also no longer have to use a complicated procedure if they want to *file their state and federal taxes jointly*).

   ❑ If a *private employer* provides *health care benefits* to a worker's same-sex spouse, those benefits will no longer be *subjected to federal income tax*, just as

---

24. What state is the "appropriate" one for any given couple and marriage is one of the many things left unresolved by *Windsor*. See Par. 6(b) on pp. 376-377, *infra*.

the health care benefits of an employee's opposite-sex spouse are not taxed.

❏ If a ***U.S. citizen*** is married to a non-citizen, the non-citizen receives certain ***immigration preferences*** by virtue of the marriage. Non-citizens who have entered a same-sex marriage with a citizen will now receive those same preferences.

    b. Limited ruling: But the *Windsor* opinion is as notable for what it does ***not*** resolve as for what it does decide. Most importantly, the opinion says nothing — explicitly, at least — about whether a ***state*** violates equal protection or any other constitutional provision when it allows opposite-sex couples to marry but ***refuses to allow same-sex couples to do so***. Thirty-four states have such a ***"mini-DOMA"*** statutory or constitutional provision,[25] limiting marriage to one man and one woman. It seems virtually certain that the Supreme Court will find itself deciding the constitutionality of such mini-DOMA provisions relatively soon.

        i. Challenge in Pennsylvania: For instance, less than three weeks after *Windsor* was decided, the ACLU brought a federal suit challenging Pennsylvania's mini-DOMA statute on equal protection and due process grounds. The complaint prominently relies on *Windsor*. See *NY Times*, July 10, 2013, p. A11.

6. Open questions: Here are some of the major questions left open by *Windsor*:

    a. State's right to ban same-sex marriage: Foremost, as I've noted, is whether a ***state*** violates equal protection (or for that matter substantive due process) if it ***refuses to allow same-sex marriage***.

        i. Prediction: My prediction is that if the issue comes before the Court as presently constituted, the five-member *Windsor* majority will decide that ***yes***, a state's refusal to permit same-sex marriage is a ***denial of equal protection*** (and perhaps substantive due process as well).

            (1) Rationale: I agree with Justice Scalia's prediction, quoted *supra* p. 374, that any justice who subscribed to Kennedy's *Windsor* rationale that Congress "robbed same-sex couples of the 'personhood and dignity'" given them by state law will "be similarly appalled by state legislatures' irrational and hateful failure to acknowledge that 'personhood and dignity' in the first place." So the five members of the *Windsor* majority will likely conclude that state prohibitions on same-sex marriage violate either equal protection substantive due process, or both.

    b. Which state counts for federal recognition: Another question of great immediate importance is, ***which state's marriage law counts*** for purposes of determining whether a same-sex couple is entitled to "married" status under *Windsor*? The issue matters mainly when a couple gets married in State *A*, then moves to State *B*, and State *B* has a different rule on same-sex marriages.

        i. Out-of-state marriage recognized by state of couple's residence: First, let's consider what turns out to be the ***easiest*** of the multi-state scenarios: The couple

---

25. In 29 states, the ban on same-sex marriages is written into the state constitution, making a simple legislative repeal impossible. See *NY Times*, July 10, 2013, p. A11. In addition, five states have statutes containing such a ban, and in two states (New Jersey and New Mexico), same-sex marriage is neither banned nor expressly permitted. See http://features.pewforum.org/same-sex-marriage-state-by-state, accessed July 10, 2013.

resides in and gets properly married in State *A*; the couple then moves to State *B*, which does not allow same-sex marriage but which *recognizes* such marriages if valid under the law of the state where contracted. Some event (a triggering of estate tax, a filing of a joint federal tax return, or whatever) then occurs while the couple resides in State *B*. These are essentially (though not precisely) the facts of *Windsor*, so we know from the holding in *Windsor* that the couple's marriage must be recognized by the federal government in the same way as if the couple had been married in State B.[26]

ii. **Out-of-state marriage not recognized by state of couple's residence:** Now, a harder question: the same-sex couple gets properly married in state *A*, then moves to state *B*, which not only does not permit same-sex marriage, but explicitly *refuses to recognize out-of-state* same-sex marriages that were proper in the state where performed (i.e., the State *A* marriage). Must the federal government treat the couple as married?

(1) **Prediction of "yes" answer:** We just don't know the answer yet. My guess — and it's only a guess — is that the present Supreme Court would answer *"yes,"* that the couple has an equal protection right to be treated the same way by the federal government as they were treated in State *A* (the place in which they properly got married). As in virtually all scenarios involving same-sex marriage right now, the question, how will the Supreme Court vote? is identical to the question, how will Justice Kennedy vote? The core of Kennedy's rationale seems to be that where the federal government "identif[ies] a subset of *state-sanctioned marriages* and *ma[kes] them unequal*," the federal government has violated equal protection. This rationale ought to mean also that when one state (State *B* in our hypo) "identifies a subset of state-sanctioned marriages [in this case, marriages sanctioned by State *A*, the state where the marriage occurred] and makes them unequal," State *B* has violated equal protection. If so, then the federal government would have violated equal protection by deferring to the equal-protection-violative approach of State *B*, rather than to State *A*'s original grant of "personhood and dignity."

c. **DOMA Section 2:** Another key issue is the constitutionality of §*2* of DOMA (as opposed to §3, which *Windsor* struck down).

i. **What §2 provides:** Recall (see *supra*, p. 369) that §2 says that even if one state (call it State *A*) allows a particular same-sex couple to marry within that state, no other state (call it State *B*) — even a state to which the now-married couple moves — is required to recognize that marriage.

---

26. We know this because that was essentially the situation in *Windsor* itself. The couple in *Windsor*, Edith and Thea, although they resided in New York, got married in Canada (at a time when New York did not yet allow same-sex marriage); at Thea's death they still lived in New York at a time when New York recognized out-of-state same-sex marriages that were valid where performed. Since *Windsor* found that DOMA unconstitutionally discriminated against the couple with respect to estate tax, we can deduce that it was sufficient for the *Windsor* majority that the couple's state of residence at the relevant time (Thea's death) *recognized an out-of-state marriage* that could not have been performed in New York; in other words, in this situation an actual New York marriage, or even an affirmative right to marry in New York, was not essential to giving the couple the protection of *Windsor's* holding.

ii. **My prediction:** This problem is ***practically identical*** to the problem of whether *Windsor* applies to protect a couple that gets married in State *A* and then moves to the same-sex-marriage-forbidding State *B*. If (as I predict in Par b(ii)(1) above) the Supreme Court finds that equal protection requires that the *federal* government recognize the couple's State *A* marriage even after the couple moves to state *B*, there's a good chance that the Court will also find that letting State *B* refuse to recognize the marriage — which is what §2 purports to do — is itself a violation of equal protection.

   (1) **My rationale:** Such a holding could easily be premised on the common-law idea of ***"detrimental reliance."*** Once a couple voluntarily subjects themselves to the obligations that accompany a marriage (e.g., effectively agreeing that neither can get married to someone else without first ***dissolving*** the original marriage), that detrimental reliance dictates that the destination state be required to uphold this reliance interest by recognizing the marriage. Such a holding is also consistent with the strong federal interest in allowing people to ***migrate easily from state to state.***

d. **Heightened scrutiny:** Another open question is ***what standard of review*** is to be used from now on in evaluating equal protection attacks on governmental barriers to same-sex marriage.

   i. **"Careful consideration":** Recall (*supra*, p. 372) that Kennedy's *Windsor* opinion is ***silent*** on this standard-of-review issue. The closest he comes to touching on the topic is to say that where a law is motivated by an "improper animus" towards the disadvantaged class, and the discrimination is of an "unusual character," then the court is to make ***"careful consideration"*** (quoting *Romer v. Evans*) of whether the discrimination violates equal protection principles. So "careful consideration" is apparently the new standard for judging at least those government rules that (1) are motivated by moral disapproval of gay lifestyles; *and* (2) fail to recognize a same-sex marriage consecrated by a state that has jurisdiction.

   (1) **Meaning of "careful consideration"** How does this apparent "careful consideration" standard compare with the various standards of review traditionally used by the Court in equal protection and other cases?

   (2) **Contrast with usual mere-rationality review:** Before we try to answer, recall a couple of features of the usual mere-rationality scenario:

   [1] Even a ***hypothetical*** governmental objective (one that "could have been" legitimately considered by government, but wasn't in fact considered) can suffice (see *supra*, p. 259); and

   [2] A ***very loose means-end fit will suffice*** — it's enough that government "could rationally have believed" that the means it chose ***might help slightly advance*** any legitimate governmental interest. (See *supra*, p. 262.)

   (3) **Kennedy's approach (review with "mere bite"):** It seems pretty clear that Kennedy's *Windsor* opinion does ***not*** apply these two features, especially [1]. As Scalia points out in his dissent, Kennedy's *Windsor* opinion gives extremely short shrift to the ***possible policy reasons*** actually or potentially offered by the Congress that enacted DOMA, like the administrative-simplicity interest in having a single uniform definition of marriage. From this dismissive treatment of Congress' reasoning, we can infer that the "careful consideration" test seems to be **considerably more stringent than ordinary mere-rationality review**. Thus it seems fair to refer to the test as mere-rationality review *"with bite."* For other illustrations of the use of this standard, see *supra*, p. 260.

XI. FUNDAMENTAL RIGHTS

A. Introduction: In the equal protection cases which we have discussed so far, the decision to apply more than extremely deferential "mere-rationality" review was made because of the peculiar nature of the **group** burdened by the statutory classification. But there is another way in which more-than-deferential equal protection review may be triggered: If the classification burdens a *"fundamental right"* or "fundamental interest," the classification will be subjected to strict scrutiny, **regardless of the characteristics of the people who are burdened**.

1. **Meaning of "fundamental":** There are two general classes of rights which are deemed "fundamental," so that any interference with them will give rise to strict equal protection scrutiny. The first consists of rights which are **independently and explicitly guaranteed by some other constitutional provision** (distinct from the Equal Protection Clause). The second consists of rights which are not independently and explicitly given by other constitutional provisions, but which are felt to be both important and implicitly granted by the Constitution, so that large deviations in equality as to them are viewed as suspect.

   a. **Example of first class:** A primary example of the first type of "fundamental right," one independently guaranteed by constitutional provisions apart from the Equal Protection Clause, is the right of **interstate migration** (see *infra*, p. 396). While there is some dispute as to exactly which part of the Constitution guarantees this right, it is clear that the right exists apart from the Equal Protection Clause. Nonetheless, the Equal Protection Clause will be used to strictly scrutinize a classification which restricts the migration rights of some but not all citizens. See *Shapiro v. Thompson, infra*, p. 397.

   b. **Example of second class:** As an example of the second type of fundamental right, one which does not exist outside the Equal Protection Clause and therefore relies entirely on that clause for its vindication, consider substantial interferences with the **right to vote** in state elections (see *infra*, p. 384). Thus a law imposing a $1.50 poll tax on anyone who wished to vote was strictly scrutinized and invalidated under the Equal Protection Clause, in *Harper v. Virginia Board of Elections, infra*, p. 384.

2. **Developed by Warren Court:** Strict scrutiny of classifications impairing fundamental rights began in the Warren Court. The three principal areas in which that Court found fundamental rights to be at stake were: (1) the **right to vote** (and the related right to participate as a candidate); (2) the right to **use the courts**; and (3) the right of **interstate migration**. (Each of these is considered in its own section below).

   a. **Proposals for extensions:** Proponents of a broad reading of the fundamental rights doctrine argued that that doctrine should also be applied in a number of other contexts; most interestingly, they contended that this treatment should be used to strictly scrutinize legislation impairing equal access to **"necessities"** (e.g., welfare, housing, and education). The Warren Court never dealt with the fundamental rights doctrine's applicability to such necessities.

3. **The post-Warren Court:** The post-Warren Court has resolutely refused to expand the list of fundamental rights beyond the broad areas recognized by the Warren Court. For instance, **"necessities"** like **welfare** and **education**, despite their conceded societal importance, are **not fundamental**, the Burger Court has held.

4. **Education:** The prime example of the post-Warren Court's refusal to treat "necessities" as fundamental rights was **San Antonio Ind. School Dist. v. Rodriguez**, 411 U.S. 1 (1973), in which the Court held (by a 5-4 vote) that there was no fundamental right to equality in **public-school education**.

   a. **Facts:** In *Rodriguez*, the plaintiffs claimed that Texas' system of financing public education violated equal protection, because it relied principally on local property taxes. Although there were other state and federal funds which remained available to each school district, districts with a high property tax base per pupil consistently spent more on education than those with a low base were able to do.

   b. **Majority's holding:** The majority rejected the plaintiffs' two main arguments: (1) that residents of property-base-poor districts formed a "suspect class," especially since (the plaintiffs contended) poorer families tended to live in districts with smaller property tax bases; and (2) that education was a fundamental right, inequalities in the distribution of which must be strictly scrutinized.

   c. **Not suspect class:** The "suspect class" theory was rejected in large part because the majority simply disagreed that the poorest families lived in the districts with the smallest tax bases. The Court conceded the validity of the plaintiff's contention that districts with smaller property tax bases spent less money per pupil on education; but this fact did not make residents of those districts a suspect class.

      i. **Rationale:** These residents had "none of the traditional indicia of suspectness." The class was "large, diverse, and amorphous ... unified only by the common factor of residence in districts that happen to have less taxable wealth. ... " Members of the class had not been subjected to a history of "purposeful unequal treatment," or relegated to a position of political powerlessness so as to require "extraordinary protection from the majoritarian political process."

      ii. **Wealth:** The Court implied, though did not state, that even a class composed entirely of poor people would not by that fact alone be "suspect." See *infra*, p. 399, for additional discussion of the Court's refusal to treat wealth as a suspect classification.

   d. **Not fundamental interest:** Most of the majority's opinion, however, was devoted to explaining why the deviations in per pupil expenditures did not constitute interference with a fundamental right. Most critically, the majority stated that the **"importance"** of a service performed by a state does not determine whether it is "fundamental" for equal protection purposes. "Relative societal significance" of an interest is irrelevant. Rather, the issue is whether **the right is "explicitly or implicitly guaranteed by the Constitution."**

i. Education not guaranteed: By this standard, education was not "fundamental." It was certainly not explicitly guaranteed by the Constitution. The plaintiffs argued that a right to education was implicitly guaranteed by the Constitution, because education was essential to effective exercise of First Amendment freedoms and the right to vote. The majority responded that *absolute equality* in education was certainly not guaranteed, even implicitly, by the Constitution.

e. Absolute deprivation issue not addressed: But the Court in *Rodriguez* seemed to acknowledge the possibility that an *absolute deprivation* of education, if imposed on some group, might nonetheless be found to be an impairment of a fundamental right: "Even if it were conceded that some identifiable quantum of education is a constitutionally protected prerequisite to the meaningful exercise of either [the First Amendment or the right to vote], we have no indication that the present [Texas] system fails to provide each child with an opportunity to acquire the *basic minimal skills* necessary." Only the less-than-absolute *differences* among districts were at issue in *Rodriguez*.

i. *Plyler* leaves door open: That a complete denial of education may constitute an interference with a fundamental right appears to remain a possibility even following the post-*Rodriguez* case of *Plyler v. Doe (supra*, p. 356). In *Plyler*, the majority paid lip service to the *Rodriguez* conclusion that public education was not a "right" granted to individuals by the Constitution. But it stressed that education was not merely "some governmental 'benefit' indistinguishable from other forms of social welfare legislation," and that it was vital to achievement of "one of the goals of the Equal Protection Clause: the abolition of governmental barriers presenting unreasonable obstacles to advancement on the basis of individual merit." While denial of public education to illegal aliens was held not to be an infringement of a fundamental right, the Court may well hold that denial of such education to a *U.S. citizen does* constitute such an infringement. For instance, Justice Blackmun, concurring in *Plyler*, seemed to believe this to be true. (Similarly, charging *tuition* for public elementary or high school education might be held to violate a fundamental right.)

f. Rational relation test: Since neither a suspect class nor a fundamental right was at issue, the majority held in *Rodriguez*, the traditional "mere-rationality" test applied. The Texas system passed this test. The scheme had been enacted (the majority appeared to find) for the purpose of giving each *local district* a large *measure of control* over the education given to its residents, a goal which the majority found legitimate.

i. Imperfect means-end fit not fatal: The Court conceded that some districts (the ones with a lower property tax base) had less control over spending than others. But this was merely a slight imperfection in the means-end fit, an imperfection which did not negate the existence of a "rational relationship" between the means chosen (use of local property taxes) and the ends sought (local control). It was not mandatory that the "least restrictive alternative" be selected.

g. Dissents: Four Justices dissented; the two longest opinions were by White and Marshall.

h. White's dissent: Justice White's dissent stressed that the property-tax-based scheme offered the low-tax-base districts virtually no ability to increase their per-pupil expenditures, and did give such a choice to the districts that were richer in property. Therefore, he argued, the scheme was not even rationally related to Texas' asserted goal of giving local districts control over the size of per-pupil education expenditures.

i. Marshall's dissent: Justice Marshall's dissent swept much more broadly. Most importantly, he disagreed with the majority's view that only those rights that are "explicitly or implicitly guaranteed by the Constitution" should be treated as "fundamental" for equal protection analysis. He claimed that at least three of the rights previously found "fundamental" (the right to procreate, recognized in *Skinner v. Oklahoma, supra*, p. 157, the right to vote in state elections, discussed *infra*, p. 383, and the right to appeal from a criminal conviction, discussed *infra*, p. 395) were not guaranteed in other constitutional provisions, but that discriminatory state treatment in these areas nonetheless received strict scrutiny.

    i. Marshall's proposed test: Marshall then proposed his own test for "fundamentality." The issue should be "the extent to which constitutionally guaranteed rights are ***dependent on interests not mentioned in the Constitution***. As the nexus between the specific constitutional guarantee and the non-constitutional interest draws closer, the non-constitutional interest becomes more fundamental. ... " For instance, the right to appeal from a criminal conviction was "fundamental" because of its close interrelationship with the Fourteenth Amendment's specific guarantee of due process of law.

    ii. Education as "fundamental": By this test, education was a fundamental right, since it "directly affects the ability of a child to exercise his First Amendment interests. ... " Similarly, educated persons exercise the right to vote more frequently than those who are not educated.

    iii. Wealth as suspect classification: Marshall also contended that the Texas statute in *Rodriguez* classified by ***wealth***, and did so in a manner that merited "careful judicial scrutiny." That the classification was based on "group wealth" (i.e., each district's taxable property) rather than the wealth of the individual did not make the classification less objectionable to Marshall. In one respect it was *worse*: since the individual had no control over the wealth of his district, the classification ran afoul of what Marshall described as the Court's precedent of "treat[ing] discrimination on a basis which the individual cannot control as constitutionally disfavored." (citing, e.g., *Levy v. Louisiana*, 391 U.S. 68 (1968)). Furthermore, here the ***government***, by its zoning and other land-use policies, had helped allocate particular areas for residential or commercial use, and had therefore ***contributed significantly*** to the fact that districts differed in their property wealth. Thus unlike the usual wealth classification, which is based upon inequality not created by the government, here the government had actually helped create the inequality, and had then discriminated based upon that inequality.

    iv. Sliding scale: Throughout his dissent, Justice Marshall was apparently not suggesting that full-fledged "strict scrutiny" should be given to the Texas statute. Rather, he was apparently arguing in favor of a ***"sliding scale"*** of review (a concept he had pioneered in his dissent in *Dandridge v. Williams, infra*, p. 399), whereby the degree of scrutiny in equal protection cases, rather than being a rigid two-pole scheme, would vary along a continuum depending on the importance of the interest and the suspectness of the classification. Since education was highly important, and since the wealth classification was at least somewhat suspect, this combination required substantially more than "mere-rationality" review, even if traditional strict scrutiny was not merited (a point he did not address explicitly).

    j. Significance of *Rodriguez*: We will discuss *Rodriguez* again in the treatment of wealth classifications *infra*, p. 399. For now, several significant principles may be deduced from the case: (1) whether a right or interest is "fundamental" is determined by whether it is ***expressly or impliedly guaranteed by the Constitution, not*** by its ***"societal importance"***; (2) by this standard, the right to public education (or, at least, the right to ***equality in the expenditures made for one's public education***) is ***not fundamental***; and (3) for a classification related to wealth to be "suspect," it must probably both be against a discrete, insular, historically-discriminated-against and powerless class, and involve an almost total deprivation of the good in question, not mere inequality in the amount of that good given.

B. Adult sexual relations: An interesting question is whether the Court will come to recognize certain forms of ***adult sexual relations*** as being fundamental rights for equal protection purposes. The Court has not yet done so. Indeed, in the now-overruled case of *Bowers v. Hardwick* (*supra*, p. 185), the Court held that there was ***no*** "fundamental right [of] ***homosexuals*** to engage in sodomy" (a due-process decision that seemed to have implications for equal protection analysis as well). Even when *Bowers* was overruled by *Lawrence v. Texas* (*supra*, p. 185), the Court still did not recognize the interest in adult ***same-sex sexual relations*** as being "fundamental."

    1. Unusually-rigorous review: But *Lawrence*'s use of ***unusually-rigorous*** rational-relation review, and that case's striking down of statutes ***criminalizing gay sodomy***, suggest that a majority of the present Court may well view adult sexual expression — whether same-sex or different-sex — as effectively being of more-than-usual importance (perhaps ***"quasi-fundamental"***) for both substantive-due process and equal-protection purposes.

    2. Same-sex marriage: The Court may also eventually come to view the interest of gay couples in being ***allowed to marry*** as being quasi-fundamental for equal protection purposes. Recall that in *U.S. v. Windsor*, *supra*, p. 368, the Court struck down §3 of the federal ***Defense of Marriage Act*** ("DOMA"), a provision that barred the federal government from recognizing state-sanctioned same-sex marriages for any purpose. The majority on its face seems to have applied mere-rationality review — not a stricter standard — in conducting its equal-protection analysis. But the Court's disregard of possible legitimate objectives that Congress might have been pursuing (e.g., the interest in a single uniform definition of "marriage"), when taken together with the outcome in the case (the statute flunked whatever standard the Court was using), suggest that the Court was applying mere-rationality review ***"with bite."*** So perhaps the right to enter into a same-sex marriage will ultimately be held to be "quasi-fundamental," even when the regulation prohibiting it exists solely at the state level. (For more about this issue, see Par. 6(a), *supra*, p. 376.)

C. Voting rights: The Constitution does not place any explicit limits on the power of states to control state and local elections. Relying in part on this constitutional silence, the Court has held over the years that the states may exercise substantial control over the ***right to vote.***

1. **State right to regulate voter qualifications:** For instance, the states have the right to determine *voter qualifications* for state elections, so long as they do not exercise that right in a way which violates any specific constitutional prohibitions (or any statute which Congress has enacted pursuant to a constitutional provision). Thus states may require that voters be of *reasonable age*, and that they be *citizens and residents* of the state.

    a. **State regulation of federal voter qualifications:** Interestingly, the Constitution indirectly gives the *states* the right to set voter qualifications not just for state elections but for *federal* ones. Article I, §2 provides that voters in House of Representatives elections shall have the same qualifications as such voters need for voting in elections for the state legislature, and the Seventeenth Amendment, §1, provides the same for election of U.S. Senators. (Article I, §4 gives Congress the right to *override* these state-created voter qualifications for federal elections. But Congress has no such right of override of qualifications for state elections, so that state power there is exclusive.)

2. **Voting as fundamental right:** Yet voting is integrally related to the First Amendment right to free speech, including political expression. Furthermore, maintenance of other constitutionally-guaranteed civil rights and liberties depends on public officials' accountability to the electorate. Therefore, the Court has labelled the *right to vote* in state and local (as well as federal) elections as *"fundamental."*

    a. **Strict scrutiny:** Because the right to vote is "fundamental," the Supreme Court has — but only in some circumstances — subjected laws that impair some group's right to vote to *strict scrutiny*. The Court's cases are quite jumbled in this area, and it's hard to articulate a single standard for when the Court will use strict scrutiny. It's also hard to predict whether a particular measure will *survive* that strict scrutiny, an outcome that happens more often in voting-rights cases than in other areas.

    b. **The "unrelated to voter qualifications" test:** In deciding whether to use strict scrutiny, the Court seems to place great weight on whether the voting regulation is reasonably *"related to voter qualifications."*

        i. **Not reasonably related (strict scrutiny):** If the Court decides that the regulation is *not* "reasonably related to voter qualifications," then the Court *uses strict scrutiny*, and will probably strike down the regulation. As we'll see below, poll taxes, property-ownership requirements and duration-of-residence requirements fall into this strictly-scrutinized-and-generally-struck-down category.

        ii. **Reasonably related (intermediate review):** If, on the other hand, the Court decides that the regulation *is* reasonably related to voter qualifications, then the Court generally does *not* use strict scrutiny. Instead, it uses some less stringent review method (typically, an intermediate-level *balancing test*), and is likely to *uphold* the measure. Basic residency requirements, voter ID requirements, and regulations disenfranchising felons all fall into this category; see *infra*, p. 386.

3. **Not reasonably related to voter qualifications:** Let's first look at various types of regulations that the Court has found to be *not reasonably related to voter qualifications*, and as to which it has therefore *applied strict scrutiny.*

    a. **Poll tax:** The seminal area in which regulations have been found not to be reasonably related to voter qualifications is the imposition of a *poll taxes*. A poll tax, no matter how minor, creates an inequality in the right to vote that must be strictly scrutinized, and struck down as an Equal Protection violation. Thus in ***Harper v. Virginia Board of Elections***, 383 U.S. 663 (1966), the Court struck down an annual poll tax of only $1.50, imposed as a prerequisite for voting.

i. **Rationale:** The Court began by holding that the right to vote was fundamental, because it was "preservative of all rights." Therefore, inequality in its distribution was to be "closely scrutinized" (i.e., strictly scrutinized).

(1) Application of strict review: The tax in *Harper* could not survive such scrutiny, even though the state clearly had a right to charge standardized fees for the exercise of other types of rights (e.g., a fee for a driver's license). The means-end link there did not have the requisite tightness, because "wealth, like race, creed, or color, is not germane to one's ability to participate intelligently in the electoral process."

ii. **Dissent:** Three dissenters in *Harper* contended that a "mere-rationality" rather than "strict scrutiny" standard should be applied. If this were done, they argued, the statute should be upheld, since it was rationally related to several legitimate state objectives, including promotion of civic responsibility (on the theory that "people with some property have a deeper stake in community affairs … ").

b. Ballot restricted to "interested voters": Another type of inequality which has often (but not always) been strictly scrutinized and invalidated is the requirement that voters ***own property*** or otherwise have some ***"special interest"*** entitling them to vote. Such requirements tend to exist not in general elections, but in elections on ***special issues*** (e.g., bond issues) or for ***special boards*** (e.g., water districts).

i. **Summary:** The law in this area is somewhat confused. In general, the Court has been suspicious of state claims that only a certain group is "interested" in the results of an election. If, however, the state proves that only members of that group do indeed have a major objective interest or "stake" in the issue (as opposed to a subjective curiosity about it), the limitation may be upheld. But if the state doesn't succeed in making that proof, then the Court will strictly scrutinize, and probably invalidate, the limitation.

ii. **School board elections:** Thus in *Kramer v. Union Free School District No. 15*, 395 U.S. 621 (1969), the Court **struck down** a New York statute which limited ***school district*** elections to persons who either: (1) owned or leased property within the district; or (2) were parents of children in the district's public schools. The Court said that any requirement which had the effect of giving the franchise to some residents but not others (apart from reasonable requirements of age and citizenship) must be ***"carefully scrutinized"*** to determine whether the scheme was ***"necessary*** to ***promote*** a compelling state interest."

(1) Means not sufficiently tailored: By this standard, the statute here was inadequate. The state's asserted interest in limiting elections to persons "primarily interested" in, or "primarily affected" by, the elections might be a legitimate objective (the Court did not decide). However, the ***means chosen*** (property ownership or rental) was an inadequate way of reaching that goal, since some people who had a substantial interest in the outcome of the elections were excluded (e.g., plaintiff, who was a 31-year-old bachelor stockbroker living with his parents), while other people without a real interest could vote (e.g., "an uninterested unemployed young man who pays no state or federal taxes, but who rents an apartment in the district[.]") The means was "not sufficiently tailored" to the goal of limiting the vote to people "primarily interested" in school affairs.

(2) Dissent: The three dissenters in *Kramer* argued that some linedrawing was essential to lawmaking, and that discrepancies like the one here were the inevitable results of such linedrawing.

iii. Exception for "special purpose" body: However, if the Court finds that the governmental unit for which elections are being held has a *limited purpose* which *disproportionately affects* only one group, the franchise may be limited to that group. Thus *"special purpose bodies"* may restrict the vote to persons who are directly affected by the body's activities.

(1) Water district: For instance, votes for a special-purpose *"water storage district"* can be *limited to landowners*, and can be on a "one acre, one vote" basis. See, e.g., *Ball v. James*, 451 U.S. 355 (1981) (even though water district finances its operations by selling electricity to hundreds of thousands of residents, the vote can be limited to landowners because the district can't enact laws, and doesn't perform "normal functions of government").

c. Duration-of-residence requirements: Requirements that voters have *resided within the state* for *more than a certain time* prior to Election Day are strictly scrutinized.

i. *Dunn v. Blumstein:*   Thus in *Dunn v. Blumstein*, 405 U.S. 330 (1972), Tennessee's duration-of-residency requirements (one year in the state and three months in the county) were struck down, both on the ground that they interfered with the fundamental right to vote and on the ground that they impaired the right to travel. (The "right to travel" aspects of the case are discussed briefly *infra*, p. 399.)

(1) Fifty-day statutes: But *shorter* residency requirements have been *upheld*, on the theory that these are merely methods of ensuring that the person *really is a resident.* Thus the Court has twice *upheld fifty-day* residency requirements, on the grounds that such a period is needed to allow the state to maintain accurate voting lists. See, e.g., *Marston v. Lewis*, 410 U.S. 679 (1973).

4. Reasonably related to voter qualifications: Let's look now at some types of regulations that the Court has found to be *reasonably related to voter qualifications*, and thus to be reviewed by a *less-than-strict-scrutiny* standard. Typically, the standard the Court uses is some form of *intermediate-level* review. As the Court said in the leading case in this area, "When a state election law provision imposes only *'reasonable, nondiscriminatory restrictions'* upon the First and Fourteenth Amendment rights of voters, the state's important regulatory interests are generally sufficient to justify" the restrictions. *Burdick v. Takushi*, 504 U.S. 428 (1992).

a. Voter identification requirements: For example, a state requirement that every voter *present a photo ID* was *upheld* under this non-strict-scrutiny standard, in *Crawford v. Marion County Election Board*, 128 S.Ct. 1610 (2008).

i. **Facts:** In *Crawford*, Indiana required any voter casting a physical (as opposed to absentee) ballot to ***present a government-issued photo ID at that time.*** The state offered a free qualifying photo ID to anyone who could prove residence and identity.

ii. **Challenge:** The plaintiffs brought a "facial" Equal Protection challenge to the statute. That is, they argued that the statute should be struck down for *all* voters, not just for particular voters to whom they posed especially great burdens. The plaintiffs argued that the photo ID requirement was analogous to a poll tax, and should thus be subjected to strict scrutiny and invalidated as the poll tax was in *Harper v. Virginia Bd. of Elections* (*supra*, p. 384).

iii. **Challenge rejected:** A 6-member majority *rejected* the facial challenge, and the argument that the statute should be strictly scrutinized. There was no majority opinion, because the six Justices split on the proper rationale. But all six Justices who voted to uphold the statute agreed that ***strict scrutiny was not appropriate.***

   (1) **Plurality:** An opinion signed by three of these six Justices (Stevens, joined by Roberts and Kennedy) asserted that prior cases had held that ***"evenhanded restrictions* that *protect the integrity and reliability of the electoral process itself"*** are not "invidious" and therefore should not be strictly scrutinized. Instead, these three said, a ***"balancing approach"*** should be used, under which the interests being pursued by the state in making the regulation must be balanced against the burdens imposed. (We'll call this the plurality opinion.) At least for this facial attack, the plaintiffs had not carried their burden of showing that ***enough voters were significantly burdened*** by the photo-ID requirement, or that the burdens on those voters were sufficiently great and unfair, as to outweigh the state's interest in combatting in-person voter fraud. (But the plurality seemed to leave open the possibility that in a later ***"as applied"*** suit, particular voters without photo IDs might show that *as to them*, the ID requirement *did* constitute an unconstitutionally great burden.)

   (2) **Concurrences:** In a separate concurrence in the judgment, three more justices (Scalia, joined by Thomas and Alito) agreed with the plurality opinion that strict scrutiny should not be given to any voter regulation that imposes what the concurrence called "nonsevere, nondiscriminatory restrictions." And, the concurrence said, a regulation that places "ordinary and widespread burdens, such as those requiring 'nominal effort' of everyone, are not severe" (and therefore should not trigger strict scrutiny). The photo ID requirement here was the sort of "non-severe" widespread burden that should be judged even more deferentially than the plurality opinion would have judged it. The state's burden of justification should be ***"minimal,"*** Scalia said, so that the state's interests ***merely needed to be "reasonable,"*** a standard which Scalia thought was easily met here.

iv. **Dissent:** There were three dissenters (Souter, joined by Ginsburg, in one dissent, and Breyer in another).

   (1) **Souter:** Souter contended that even if the plurality opinion's balancing test was used, the photo ID requirement here should be struck down, because a sig-

nificant number of voters lacked the requisite photo ID and would therefore be seriously burdened. By contrast, the state's main interest — its need to combat in-person voter fraud — had not been demonstrated to be a significant one. (Souter pointed out that Indiana had ***"not come across a single instance*** of in-person voter impersonation fraud in all of [the state's] history.")

    (2) Breyer: Breyer's dissent asserted that the photo ID requirement had the effect of imposing on a significant number of voters — those without a driver's license or other valid form of photo ID, a group largely made up of the poor, elderly or disabled — a disproportionate burden, perhaps more severe than the $1.50 poll tax struck down in *Harper*. And, he believed, a statute that placed a "disproportionate burden" on a class of voters (here, the class without photo IDs) should be struck down.

    v.   **Summary:** So as the result of *Crawford*, at least six members of the Roberts court are on record as believing that as long as a restriction on voting rights is an ***"even-handed*** [one] that ***protect[s] the integrity and reliability*** of the electoral process itself," ***strict scrutiny should not be used.*** And these six further agree that the requirement of a photo ID for all persons casting physical ballots is an evenhanded restriction that should not be strictly scrutinized. But these six are evenly split about whether the standard of review that should be used is (1) a moderately-severe balancing test (the plurality's view) or (2) a very deferential standard under which, when the impact of the restriction is "not severe," the state's burden of justification should be ***"minimal"*** so that the state's interests merely need to be ***"reasonable"*** (the Scalia concurrence's view).

  b. **Denial of vote to felons:** Many states deny the vote to ***felons***, even ones who have served their sentence and finished any parole. It's clear that such measures won't receive strict scrutiny, and will at least as a general matter be upheld. Such disenfranchisement was ***upheld*** by the Court in *Richardson v. Ramirez*, 418 U.S. 24 (1974). The Court relied on the rarely-invoked §2 of the Fourteenth Amendment, which calls for reduced representation for states which deny the vote to residents, but which makes this sanction inapplicable in cases of "participation in rebellion, or ***other crime***." The majority in *Richardson* felt that §2 demonstrated Congress' intent to permit disenfranchisement as a sanction for crime.

  c. **Burden on right to vote by limiting voter's choices:** The restrictions we have examined so far typically had the effect, where they applied at all, of ***preventing the voter from voting at all***. But suppose the state regulation of voting merely has the effect of ***"burdening"*** the right to vote, by ***limiting the voter's choices***. Here, as in the voter-ID and disenfranchisement-of-felons scenarios just discussed, the Court does ***not*** use strict scrutiny; instead, the Court balances the degree of burden against the magnitude of the state's interest, and the Court is slow to strike down the regulation. It was in such a case involving a voter-choice-limiting regulation that the Court first articulated the rule relied on by the plurality in *Crawford*, supra, that "When a state election law provision imposes only ***'reasonable, nondiscriminatory restrictions'*** upon the First and Fourteenth Amendment rights of voters, the state's important regulatory interests are ***generally sufficient*** to justify" the restrictions. *Burdick v. Takushi*, 504 U.S. 428 (1992).

  i. Ban on write-in votes: For example, in *Burdick*, the Court held that Hawaii could **completely ban** all **write-in votes.** So long as the state gave candidates reasonable access to the ballot (thus preserving each voter's interest in having a reasonable choice of candidates), the state was not required to protect each voter's interest in being able to vote for **any** candidate of his choosing.

5. Inequality in ballot-counting procedures: As the result of the Court's decision that effectively handed the 2000 presidential election to George W. Bush over Al Gore, voters now seem to have some sort of equal protection right to have their votes **counted according to uniform standards.** **Bush v. Gore**, 531 U.S. 98 (2000).

 a. Facts: The election came down to the vote in Florida. The Florida Supreme Court ordered that a statewide recount of all "undervotes" be conducted. ("Undervotes" are ballots on which, according to the machine tabulation, no candidate was selected.) The U.S. Supreme Court issued a stay blocking the continuation of this recount, then decided that no constitutionally-acceptable recount could be completed within the time available.

  i. Chads: Most Florida counties had a punch-card system which required a voter to perforate the ballet by a stylus. The ballots in dispute were mainly ones in which the voter did not completely perforate the ballot, making the vote uncountable by machine. Many of these ballots left a piece of the card hanging by one, two, or three corners (a "hanging chad") or contained mere indentations indicating perhaps that the voter had tried but failed to punch the card (an "indented chad").

  ii. No uniform standards: The Florida Supreme Court ordered a hasty manual statewide recount of all of these undervotes, without specifying uniform standards for determining when a vote should count. For example, it was left to each county's election commissioners to decide whether an indented chad should count.

  iii. Partial counts accepted: The Florida Supreme Court also ordered that in those instances where counties had reported partial counts from recounts that had not been finished by the prior state-law deadline, those partial recount totals be accepted as legal votes.

 b. Holding: By a 5-4 vote, the U.S. Supreme Court ruled that the entire recount procedure violated voters' equal protection rights. The Court's conservative bloc (Rehnquist, Scalia, Thomas, O'Connor and Kennedy) voted together to form a majority, and the liberal bloc (Stevens, Souter, Breyer and Ginsburg) dissented.

  i. Rationale: The unsigned per curiam opinion for the Court said that "The right to vote is protected in more than the initial allocation of the franchise ... Having once granted the right to vote on equal terms, the state may not, by later arbitrary and disparate treatment, value one person's vote over that of another." To the majority, the recount mechanisms "do not satisfy the **minimum requirement** for **non-arbitrary treatment of voters** necessary to secure the fundamental right [to vote]. ... The formulation of uniform rules to determine intent ... is practicable and, we conclude, necessary." The majority pointed out that "the standards for accepting or rejecting contested ballots might vary not only from county to county but indeed within a single county from one recount team to other."

    ii. Not enough time: Normally, the equal protection problem would have been taking care of by ordering the Florida Supreme Court to issue uniform standards for the recount. But the high court was ruling on Dec. 12th, and the 12th was already the last day on which the state could certify its vote and still be certain that that vote would not be challenged in Congress. That is, Dec. 12 was the last day to use the "safe harbor" built into the federal system. The five members of the majority believed that holding a fresh constitutionally-adequate recount, and requiring Florida to miss the safe harbor, would have violated Florida's own election code, made binding upon the presidential election by the Constitution. Therefore, there could be no recount, and the original Florida certification of Bush as the winner stood.

   c. Dissent: Of the four dissenters in *Bush v. Gore*, two (Souter and Breyer) believed that the lack of uniform standards indeed raised serious equal protection problems. But those two believed that the way to handle the problem was to remand to the Florida Supreme Court with instructions that the state could try to get the recount done, with uniform standards, by the Dec. 18 final deadline. The other two dissenters (Stevens and Ginsburg) believed that the equal protection problem was not substantial.

   d. Significance: *Bush v. Gore* probably does not have much significance for future elections. The majority took pains to observe that "[o]ur consideration is ***limited to the present circumstances***, for the problem of equal protection in election processes generally presents many complexities." However, the case probably does stand for at least the vague proposition that there are some equal-protection limits to how much variation is tolerable in the standards for determining whether a ballot is a legal vote.

  6. Dilution of votes: The Court has also recognized a voter's ***fundamental right*** not to have his vote ***diluted*** by use of electoral districts that are not constructed strictly on the basis of ***population***. The "reapportionment" cases (especially *Reynolds v. Sims*, the case establishing "one man, one vote" as a constitutional principle) are discussed as part of the treatment of political questions, *infra*, p. 733.

  7. Fifteenth Amendment: When you analyze a governmental action that arguably restricts of the right to vote, do not overlook the ***Fifteenth Amendment***, which in §1 says that "The right of citizens of the United States to ***vote*** shall not be denied or abridged by the United States or by any State on account of ***race, color, or previous condition of servitude***." (§2, a provision analogous to §5 of the Fourteenth Amendment, see *infra*, p. 441, gives Congress the power to "enforce this article by appropriate legislation.") As we have already seen, most restrictions on the right to vote are given Fourteenth Amendment due process/fundamental rights analysis. But occasionally, a direct limit on the right to vote on racial grounds will be found to violate the Fifteenth Amendment.

      Example: The Hawaiian Constitution provides that the trustees of the Office of Hawaiian Affairs (OHA) may be elected solely by persons who are descendants of the original Native Hawaiians who inhabited the island prior to Captain Cook's arrival in 1778. *Held*, this provision constitutes racial discrimination in voting, and therefore violates the Fifteenth Amendment. *Rice v. Cayetano*, 528 U.S. 495 (2000).

D. Access to the ballot: Related to the "right to vote" is the right of a person to ***be a candidate***, and of members of a ***political party*** to ***place their candidate on the ballot***.

  1. State interest in regulating elections: Before we look at whether these "rights" to ballot access really exist in a constitutional sense, consider the state's interest in ***limiting*** the presence of candidates and parties on a given ballot. There are two main interests which a state may be pursuing when it attempts to control the number of candidates or parties listed: (1) the interest in *reducing voter confusion*; and (2) the interest in maximizing the probability that the winning candidate will have received a *majority* of the *popular vote*. See N&R, p. 877. If these goals are not met, there is a danger that the result will be "only the cacophony of an atomized body politic, not the orchestrated voice of an electorate." Tribe, p. 1097.

2. **Interest of candidates, parties and voters:** However, there are a number of counter-vailing interests in easy ballot access, on the part of: (1) individuals who wish to be candidates; (2) members of minor or newly-formed parties; and (3) the voters themselves. These interests may be summarized as follows:

   a. **Interest in being a candidate:** Individuals clearly have an *interest in being a candidate*. While the Supreme Court has never recognized this interest as being a "fundamental right" (and has probably implicitly decided that it is not), the interest clearly has some constitutional weight. It is related to the First Amendment right of free speech, and to the general right to participate in the political process.

   b. **Party's right of association:** A group of individuals has a strong interest in being able to *band together to form a political party*. In fact, *freedom of association*, guaranteed by the First Amendment (see *infra*, p. 608) clearly requires that they be permitted to do so. It is less clear, however, that freedom of association requires that they be permitted to be an *effective* party, in the sense of being able to place their candidates on the ballot. In general, the Supreme Court has held that this right of association does mean that parties with *significant popular support* must be given *reasonable opportunities to appear on the ballot.*

   c. **Voters' interest in suitable candidate:** The *voters* have an interest in being offered a variety of candidates representing a *range of political views*. While there is certainly no constitutional requirement that every voter be offered a candidate matching the voter's own views, a system which consistently prevented participation by candidates representing particular controversial views (at least if shared by a significant part of the electorate) would probably be constitutionally suspect. See Tribe, p. 1100, n. 13.

3. **Candidate eligibility rules:** Some requirements concern the *eligibility* of the *individual candidate*. Since there is no general "right to be a candidate" which the Supreme Court has been willing to recognize as fundamental, these restrictions are generally reviewed under the highly deferential "mere-rationality" standard. Thus *minimum age* requirements, and requirements that the candidate have *resided for a certain period of time* in the state or district where he is seeking office, have generally been *upheld*, on the grounds that they are rationally related to a legitimate state interest (e.g., the interest in having elected officials who have reasonable experience and maturity, and who have an interest in matters concerning their constituency). See Tribe, pp. 1100-01.

   a. **Violation of other constitutional right:** Candidate eligibility requirements may not, of course, violate any other *independent* constitutional right. For instance, if a state imposed an unusually long *state residency* requirement for candidacy (e.g., four years), a strong argument could be made that such a requirement violates the individual's *right to interstate migration* (*infra*, p. 396), or at least that the requirement should be given scrutiny. See Tribe, p. 1101.

4. Party organization and popular support: Many states require candidates to be *affiliated with a political party* in order to obtain a place on the ballot. (Special rules, usually fairly burdensome, govern independent candidacies.) Yet only those parties that have demonstrated a certain amount of *popular support* are generally entitled to place their candidates on the ballot. In some states, the popular support requirements (perhaps coupled with requirements of an elaborate party structure, and use of nominating conventions) are quite burdensome; in such states, candidates from the two major parties have an even greater than usual advantage.

    a. Overall Supreme Court view: The Supreme Court has decided several major cases concerning the extent to which such popular-support and organizational requirements may be placed upon newly-formed or minor parties. These cases do not yield an easily-stated unified principle. However, the cases taken together do seem to hold that: (1) states may, in order to keep ballots from becoming confusingly large, require parties (or independent candidacies) to show a *significant amount of community support*; but (2) the restrictions may not be so great that minority parties or independent candidates have *no realistic chance* of getting on the ballot. See Tribe, p. 1110-01.

    b. *Williams* case: The first of the cases, *Williams v. Rhodes*, 393 U.S. 23 (1968), was quite easy to decide, since the ballot access restrictions there were so severe that even a party with significant popular support stood almost no chance of getting on the ballot.

       i. Facts: The Ohio law struck down in *Williams* required a minor party (defined as one which had not received 10% of the votes in the previous gubernatorial election) to meet, as a condition to getting on the presidential ballot, three stringent requirements: (1) the filing, earlier in the election year, of petitions signed by *15%* of the number of votes cast in the prior gubernatorial election; (2) the creation of an *elaborate party structure*; and (3) the conducting of *primaries*. The statute also *forbade independent* and *write-in* candidacies. The law was challenged by the American Independent Party, whose candidate, George Wallace, was blocked from the 1968 presidential ballot.

    c. Statute struck down: A majority of the Court found that the scheme violated the equal protection rights of minority parties, since it made it *"virtually impossible"* for a new party, even one with hundreds of thousands of members, to get a place on the ballot, and therefore gave a large advantage to the two existing major parties.

       i. Interests implicated: The majority found that two specific constitutional interests were impaired by the statute: (1) the right of individuals to *associate* for advancement of their political beliefs; and (2) the right of voters to *"cast their votes effectively."* These interests were sufficiently important that *strict scrutiny* should be applied to the state law.

       ii. State interests inadequate: None of the state's asserted interests was sufficiently compelling, when measured under this strict test. For instance, the state's desire to promote the two-party system might be legitimate (the Court did not decide), but giving a permanent monopoly to two *particular* parties, Republicans and Democrats, was clearly not.

d. ***Jenness:*** The next case, *Jenness v. Fortson*, 403 U.S. 431 (1971), marks the other end of the spectrum, i.e., a set of restrictions so lenient that they were clearly constitutional.

    i. **Facts:** *Jenness* was a challenge to a Georgia rule which permitted independent candidates (i.e., ones with no party affiliation) to appear on the ballot, but only if they filed petitions with the signatures of at least 5% of the number of votes in the previous election. Petitions could be filed later in the election year than they could in *Williams*.

    ii. **Holding:** The Court found this situation vastly different from that in *Williams*, and quickly upheld the scheme. A key distinction was that Georgia, unlike Ohio, "in no way freezes the status quo, but implicitly recognizes the potential fluidity of American political life."

e. **Middle-ground cases:** If *Williams* and *Jenness* represent two ends of the spectrum of ballot-access restrictions, later cases discuss restrictions that are somewhere in the middle. In these later cases, the Court has seemed to apply a kind of mid-level review: The Court upholds the ballot-access measure as long as it is a ***"reasonable and non-discriminatory"*** way of achieving an ***"important"*** state interest, such as the maintenance of "ballot integrity" or "political stability."

    i. **Organization requirement:** For instance, a Texas requirement that minor parties hold precinct, county and state ***nominating conventions*** was ***upheld***, in *American Party of Texas v. White*, 415 U.S. 767 (1974). The key factor was the lack of discrimination against minor parties; since *major* parties in Texas were required to hold these three types of conventions in order to promulgate party platforms, the minority parties were not placed at a relative disadvantage. (But in a state where the major parties do *not* hold such conventions, presumably the requirement that minority parties do so would be a violation of their right to equal protection.)

    ii. **Ban on fusion candidates:** Similarly, the Court has held that a state may prohibit a party from putting a ***"fusion"*** candidate on the ballot, i.e., a candidate who has ***already been nominated by another party***. *Timmons v. Twin Cities Area New Party*, 520 U.S. 351 (1997). The minor party in *Timmons* argued that the rule against fusion candidates abridged its freedom of association (mostly by giving popular candidates a large disincentive to accept the minor party's early nomination). But the Court upheld the rule, on the grounds that it was a "reasonable [and] nondiscriminatory" way of achieving the state's "important regulatory interests" in "ballot integrity" and "political stability."

f. **Empirical test:** In gauging the effect of signature requirements, organizational requirements, etc., the Court generally takes into account the ***actual historical success or failure*** that minor parties have had in getting on the ballot. Obviously, the more often minor parties or independent candidates have in fact succeeded in getting on the ballot, the less likely the Court will be to find a violation of equal protection. See Tribe, p. 1111.

5. **Filing fees:** ***Filing fee*** requirements imposed on candidates will be struck by the Court, if they prevent ***indigent*** candidates from appearing on the ballot. In *Lubin v. Panish*, 415 U.S. 709 (1974), the Court unanimously invalidated a California filing fee set at a percentage of the salary for the position being sought (a $700 fee in plaintiff's situation). The

Court reasoned that a state may not charge a candidate filing fees which he is incapable of paying, unless it gives him alternative means of getting on the ballot (e.g., by filing a petition demonstrating popular support).

6. **Right to be a candidate:** *Lubin* spoke in terms of the right of an indigent candidate to get on the ballot, not the right of *voters* to choose an indigent candidate. This seems to be the closest the Court has come to suggesting that there may be *an independent constitutional right to be a candidate.* See Tribe, p. 1111. However, the existence of such a right is not at all clear, in light of the Court's failure to find such a right in other cases.

E. **Access to courts:** Existence of a classification based on *wealth* has never, by itself, been enough to trigger strict scrutiny. But where the state *imposes fees* which have the effect of preventing the poor from gaining access to a significant constitutionally-protected right, the Court has sometimes been willing to apply strict scrutiny. This was the case, for instance, with respect to the poll tax and with respect to candidate filing fees (*supra*, pp. 384 and 393). The Court has at times made the *litigation process* another such area; state-imposed fees or other economic barriers which prevent the poor from *gaining access to the courts* may be subjected to strict scrutiny, if the particular type of judicial access being sought is found to be sufficiently important.

1. **No general principle:** The Court's course in the area of judicial access has been confused and changing, so that it is difficult to state a general principle. Generally, the Court has shown a greater likelihood of striking down barriers to the pursuit of judicial remedies in *criminal cases* than it has in most *civil* contexts.

2. **Equal protection vs. due process:** Nor is it clear whether equal protection or due process is the relevant doctrine in these cases. Sometimes, the Court has seemed to hold that *due process* is what matters: if fundamental procedural fairness requires that all persons, rich or poor, be given a particular type of judicial access, the Court will order this to be done, without focusing on the distinction between rich and poor. In other cases, however, the issue has been one of equal protection: if the type of access sought is judged to be highly important, the Court has decided that what the rich are permitted to pay for, the poor must be given, in order to avoid what the Court sees as the unfairness which would inhere in making the access in question available only to those who can pay for it.

   a. **Equal protection dominant:** The *equal protection* aspect appears to have *dominated* the Burger/Rehnquist Court's decisions. However, the due process aspect crops up from time to time (e.g., in *Little v. Streater, infra,* p. 396, involving an indigent paternity defendant's right to blood-grouping tests).

3. **Not "fundamental" rights:** The Court has generally *not* labeled the rights at issue in these judicial-access cases as *"fundamental"* ones. But it has conceded that the rights at issue are highly important, and that they merit at least some extra measure of constitutional protection. Unlike the right-to-vote cases, where the right itself was "fundamental," and therefore was sufficient to trigger strict scrutiny, the judicial-access cases have generally involved strict scrutiny only where there was a *combination* of a *"quasi-suspect" wealth classification* (usually in the form of a state-imposed *fee*) *and* an *important interest.*

4. **Cutting back by Burger/Rehnquist Court:** The most important cases giving special protection to judicial access by the poor came during the Warren era. In both the criminal

and civil areas (probably more so in the latter), post-Warren Courts have curtailed, though not completely overturned, the Warren-era results.

5. **Transcripts:** The first Warren-era case involved the right of indigents to a ***trial transcript*** in ***criminal appeals***. In ***Griffin v. Illinois***, 351 U.S. 12 (1956), the Court held that the state ***must provide indigent criminal defendants with a trial transcript***, if such a transcript is ***necessary for effective appellate review***.

   a. **Rationale:** *Griffin* was decided on both equal protection and due process grounds. In ringing rhetoric (which was never taken to its logical conclusion in subsequent, harder cases), the Court observed that "[t]here can be no equal justice where the kind of trial a man gets depends on the amount of money he has."

   b. **Harlan dissent:** But Justice Harlan, in dissent, made a point which has had continued relevance in cases involving wealth criteria. He observed that in the usual equal protection case, the state ***makes a classification***, and places disabilities upon persons falling on one side of the classifying line. Here, by contrast, by charging a fee for transcripts the Court was ***not making any classification at all***; it was simply failing to "alleviate the consequences of differences in economic circumstances that exist wholly apart from any state action."

      i. **Consequence:** Consequently, Harlan argued, the majority was imposing on states "an affirmative duty to lift the handicaps flowing from differences in economic circumstances" and was interpreting equal protection to require that "Illinois must give to some what it requires others to pay for." This was not the meaning of the Equal Protection Clause, Harlan contended.

   c. **No "right" to an appeal:** Even the majority agreed with Harlan that there was ***no "right" to an appeal***; the state could, for instance, provide that a criminal trial was simply the final judicial event. But what the states could not do, in the majority's view, was to grant an appeal to some (those who could pay for a transcript) and not to others.

6. **Counsel during appeal:** Then, the Warren Court held that indigent criminal defendants had the right to the ***assistance of counsel*** on appeal, at least if: (1) this was the first appeal taken in the case; and (2) the appeal was granted as a matter of right (not judicial discretion) to all persons. *Douglas v. California*, 372 U.S. 353 (1963). The decision was, like *Griffin*, based on both equal protection and due process grounds.

7. **Discretionary appeals:** *Douglas* did not deal with the right to appointed counsel in ***discretionary*** appeals. But in the later case of *Ross v. Moffitt*, 147 U.S. 600 (1974), the Court explicitly ***refused*** to find such a right in discretionary appeals.

   a. **Rationale:** Most of the majority's opinion was addressed to the equal protection argument. The majority distinguished *Douglas*, on the grounds that the interest in equal access to appellate review was "one of degrees," and that denial of counsel's assistance in discretionary appeals (e.g., appeals to the highest state court or petitions for *certiorari* to the U.S. Supreme Court) was only a "relative handicap," much less severe than lack of counsel during the initial appeal of right.

   b. **Dissent:** Three dissenters, Douglas, Brennan and Marshall, contended that the *Douglas* rationale should be applied even with respect to discretionary appeals.

8. **Civil litigation:** Indigents have also argued that filing fees and other payments to the state should be waived for them in ***civil litigation***. But such arguments have generally

been *unsuccessful*; in only one category of action, loosely *"family law,"* has the Court agreed that indigents are entitled to access to the civil courts.

a. **Boddie:**   The main family-law decision involved *divorce*. That case was **Boddie v. Connecticut**, 401 U.S. 371 (1971). The parties seeking divorce were welfare recipients who could not pay the $60 filing fee. The Supreme Court agreed that *denial of access to divorce was a violation of the plaintiffs' due process rights.*

   i. **State monopolization as factor:**   Two factors were found by the Court to be basic to this due process conclusion: (1) marriage occupies a *fundamental place* in our society's scheme of values; and (2) the *state* has a *monopoly* on the means for dissolving this relationship. Thus access to divorce is quite different from use of the civil courts for the *resolution of private disputes*; in the latter situation, other, nonjudicial, means of resolution are generally available.

b. **Not applicable to bankruptcy:**   Post-Warren Courts have taken an extremely narrow view of what other situations, apart from family law, entitle indigents to civil court access. For instance, indigents do *not* have a right to a waiver of the $50 filing fee for *bankruptcy*, the Court held in **U.S. v. Kras**, 409 U.S. 434 (1973).

c. **Review of welfare terminations:**   Similarly, the Court has held that indigents could be forced to pay a $25 filing fee in order to gain judicial review of *welfare-benefit terminations*. *Ortwein v. Schwab*, 410 U.S. 656 (1973). By the same 5-4 majority as in *Kras*, the Court held that welfare payments were in the area of "economics and social welfare," and thus had "far less constitutional significance" than the interest in divorce.

d. **Other family-law contexts:**   But the Court *has* granted fee relief to indigents in two contexts that are theoretically civil, but that have a *family-law* dimension:

   i. **Paternity suits:** First, in *Little v. Streater*, 452 U.S. 1 (1981), the defendant was an indigent against whom a *paternity action* had been brought. The Court held that he was entitled to *state-subsidized blood grouping tests* to determine whether he could have been the child's father.

   ii. **Termination of parental rights:** Then, the Rehnquist Court held that where a child's father successfully sued to have the child's mother's *parental rights terminated* so that the child could be adopted by the father's wife, the state had to pay for a *trial transcript* to be used by the mother on *appeal*. *M.L.B. v. S.L.J.*, 519 U.S. 102 (1996). In that case, the decision seemed to turn more on the "quasi-criminal" nature of the proceeding than on the fact that it involved family-law matters. But the Court characterized "the interest of parents in their relationship with their children" as being "fundamental."

e. **Summary:**   So where the proceeding is nominally *"civil,"* an indigent has *no general right to fee relief.* Thus actions for *bankruptcy* and for review of *welfare terminations* fall into this general "no equal protection right to fee relief" category. But an indigent *does* have an equal protection right to fee relief in three situations falling within the family-law area: actions for *divorce*, for *determinations of paternity*, and for *termination of parental rights*.

F. **The right to travel:**   We live in a federal system, one of the basic principles of which is that *any American is free to travel from state to state*, and to *change his state of residence* or employment whenever he desires. This *"right to travel"* (or, a better way of putting what is usually being litigated, this *"freedom of interstate migration"*) is not explicitly given by any one constitutional provision. But the Court has nonetheless treated the right as *"fundamental."* Consequently, when a state treats *newly-arrived residents* significantly *less favorably* than those who have lived in the state longer, strict equal protection scrutiny may be triggered.

1. ***Shapiro v. Thompson:*** The classic case applying strict equal protection scrutiny to classifications penalizing the "right to travel" (or to migrate interstate) is ***Shapiro v. Thompson***, 394 U.S. 618 (1969). In that case, the Court invalidated the denial by two states and the District of Columbia of *welfare benefits* to residents who had *not resided in the jurisdiction for at least a year.*

    a. **"Right to travel" rationale:** By requiring the one-year waiting period, the states were impairing the "fundamental right of interstate movement," the Court held. The Court declined to locate this right in any particular constitutional clause. Rather, the right derived from the fact that "the nature of our federal union and our constitutional concept of personal liberty unite to require that all citizens be free to travel throughout the length and breadth of our land. ... "

    b. **Severe impact:** Furthermore, what was being denied to newly-arrived residents was something of *extreme importance* — welfare aid "upon which may depend the ability of the families to obtain the *very means to subsist* — food, shelter, and other *necessities of life."*

    c. **Strict scrutiny:** Because of this major interference with freedom to travel, the Court applied *strict scrutiny*, requiring that the one-year waiting period be *necessary* to achievement of a *compelling governmental interest*. None of the interests asserted by the state was sufficient.

        i. **Unconstitutional objectives:** In fact, several of the asserted state interests were flatly unconstitutional. For instance, the state's argument that it wished to preserve the financial integrity of the state welfare program by preventing an influx of indigent newcomers was itself flatly inconsistent with the newcomers' right to travel interstate.

        ii. **Other interests:** Other interests asserted (e.g., providing an "objective test of residency," discouraging fraudulent collection of payments from more than one state, etc.) were legitimate. But these interests were not "compelling," and could in any event have been served by less drastic means.

    d. **Dissent:** There were three dissenters in *Shapiro*. The most important of the dissents was by Justice Harlan, who was especially concerned about the importance the majority attached to the fact that the newcomers might be deprived of "food, shelter, and other necessities of life" — Harlan feared that the Court might ultimately apply strict scrutiny to any classification bearing on the availability of such "necessities," an exception which he said would "swallow the standard equal protection rule" and make the Court a "super-legislature."

        i. **Fifth Amendment:** Harlan also thought that the right of interstate movement, which he conceded was an independently-valid constitutional right, could be and should be protected by resort to the *Fifth Amendment's Due Process Clause* rather than by the Equal Protection Clause.

e. **Aftermath of *Shapiro:*** Justice Harlan's fear that the Court would find a generalized fundamental right to the ***"necessities of life,"*** triggering strict equal protection scrutiny whenever the state failed to guarantee those necessities to all citizens, never materialized. The Court's subsequent treatment of "necessities" is discussed in the section on wealth classifications, *infra*, pp. 399-400. But the Court's recognition in *Shapiro* of a fundamental right to interstate travel, and its application of strict equal protection scrutiny of any classification impairing that right, have remained good law.

2. **Deterrent or penalty:** The *Shapiro* Court did not make clear exactly what sort of effect on the right to interstate travel must occur before that right would be impaired sufficiently so as to trigger strict scrutiny. The Court might have meant that the right was impaired only where the residency requirement was so obviously burdensome that it had a ***deterrent effect*** on interstate migration. But later cases have construed *Shapiro* to mean that the right to travel is impaired wherever it is ***"penalized,"*** even if there is no actual deterrence. Thus since the one-year residency requirement for welfare payments caused substantial hardship to those who moved to the state (as the *Shapiro* Court found), this would be sufficient to trigger strict scrutiny, ***even if there was no showing that anyone actually declined to migrate*** because of the requirement.

   a. **Medical benefits:** The principle that merely a "penalty," not an actual deterrent effect, is required to trigger strict scrutiny, was illustrated in the post-*Shapiro* case of ***Memorial Hospital v. Maricopa County***, 415 U.S. 250 (1974). That case struck down an Arizona requirement of one year's residence as a condition for indigents to receive free non-emergency ***medical care***. The ability to receive such care was clearly not a significant deterrent to interstate migration, since it was unlikely that people would change or decline to change their state of residence to receive such care. Nonetheless, denial of the medical care was a "penalty" on the right to migrate, the Court held. As such, it was to be subjected to strict scrutiny, which it did not survive.

      i. **Definition of "penalty":** But, the Court in *Memorial Hospital* held, not all differences in treatment between residents and non-residents are "penalties"; only inequalities in distribution of ***"vital government benefits and privileges"*** are sufficiently severe to be considered penalties. The right to medical care was as much a "basic necessity of life" as were the welfare payments in *Shapiro*, so inequality in their distribution was a penalty.

   b. **Divorce:** Other government-supplied benefits have been found to be less important, so that their denial to newcomers does ***not*** trigger strict scrutiny. For instance, Iowa's requirement that a person reside in that state for one year before suing a non-resident there for ***divorce***, was ***upheld***, in *Sosna v. Iowa*, 419 U.S. 393 (1975).

      i. **Rationale:** The majority did not speak in terms of "penalties." But it held that a requirement that a person wait one year for a divorce was a ***less severe hardship*** than waiting one year for medical benefits or welfare assistance — in the latter situation, some part of what was being sought would never be obtained (benefits applicable to the one year wait). In the divorce situation, by contrast, the plaintiff would ultimately end up with the very thing sought, i.e., an adjudication of divorce.

      ii. **Stronger state interest:** Furthermore, the countervailing state interest was much stronger in the divorce situation. In the welfare benefits and medical care cases, the state's interests were largely those of budget concerns and administrative convenience. Here, by contrast, the state had a strong interest in ***not becoming a "divorce mill"*** whose divorce decrees might be susceptible to collateral attack.

3. ***Bona fide* residence requirements:** Nothing in the Constitution, however, prevents the state from requiring that persons show that they are ***bona fide residents*** before receiving public services or benefits.

4. **Voting rights:** Some cases previously discussed in the ***voting rights*** area involve a right-to-travel component. For instance, in *Dunn v. Blumstein*, 405 U.S. 330 (1972) (*supra*, p. 386) Tennessee's duration-of-residency requirements for voting were strictly scrutinized not only because they burdened the fundamental interest in voting, but also because they impaired the interest in interstate travel.

5. **Privileges or Immunities Clause as alternate rationale:** Recall that there has been some confusion about just where in the Constitution the "right to travel" is granted. For instance, *Shapiro v. Thompson* (*supra*, p. 397) failed to specify where in the document the right was provided. But a 1999 case suggests that the "right to travel" should be founded upon the ***Fourteenth Amendment's Privileges or Immunities Clause,*** which prohibits any state from abridging "the privileges or immunities of citizens of the United States." That case, *Saenz v. Roe*, 526 U.S. 489 (1999), is discussed *infra*, p. 383.

G. **Wealth classifications:** During the Warren Court, there were some indications that a broad range of government programs which arguably failed to take account of the special needs of the ***poor*** might be subjected to strict scrutiny.

1. **Possibility of suspect class:** Some observers expected this to happen by the placing of "wealth" on the list of ***suspect classifications***.

2. **Possible "fundamental interest" in "necessities":** Alternatively, there were hints that the Warren Court might find a fundamental right or interest in the ***"necessities of life,"*** like food, shelter or clothing.

3. **Post-Warren Court declines to expand view:** But the Warren Court never explicitly held either that wealth without more was a suspect classification or that statutes impairing the right to "necessities" of life, without more, impaired a fundamental interest. The post-Warren Court has explicitly ***refused to support either of these propositions***.

4. **Not suspect classification:** For instance, in *James v. Valtierra*, 402 U.S. 137 (1971), the majority held that ***wealth classifications***, unlike, say, racial ones, ***simply do not trigger any heightened scrutiny.*** The Court therefore upheld a California constitutional amendment providing that no low-income housing projects could be built in any community without achieving majority support in a popular referendum. The non-suspect nature of wealth classifications seems to have been reiterated (though this is not completely clear) in the school financing case, *San Antonio Ind. School Dist. v. Rodriguez, supra*, p. 380.

5. **No fundamental interest in "necessities":** Similarly, in a series of cases the Court also rejected claims that various ***"necessities of life"*** were fundamental interests whose impairment should trigger strict scrutiny.

a. **Welfare benefits:** The first such area was that of ***welfare benefits***. In ***Dandridge v. Williams***, 397 U.S. 471 (1970), the Court upheld a Maryland welfare scheme which set a maximum monthly payment of $250, regardless of family size or need.

i. **Rationale:** The majority reasoned that the statute, like all welfare schemes, lay in the area of "economics and social welfare" and therefore called only for "mere-rationality" review. The scheme satisfied this deferential standard, since it bore a rational relation to several legitimate state objectives (e.g., encouraging employment by prohibiting payments that might compare favorably with what a job would provide).

ii. **Marshall's "sliding scale" dissent:** Justice Marshall dissented in *Dandridge*. He conceded that strict scrutiny was not appropriate. But he also disagreed with the majority's finding that the traditional, deferential, "mere-rationality" test was the correct one. Instead, he gave the first major exposition of his *"sliding scale"* theory: Rather than a rigid "two-tier" standard, by which all statutes are given either extreme deference or strict scrutiny, the degree of review should be adjusted along a *spectrum*, depending on: (1) the type of classification; (2) the *"relative importance* to individuals in the class discriminated against of the governmental benefits that they do not receive;" and (3) the strength of the interests *asserted by the state* in support of the classification. When this analysis was applied to the facts of *Dandridge*, Marshall concluded that a significant degree of scrutiny should be given, since the welfare recipients' interest in the benefits was large, and (Marshall believed) the state's asserted interest in its scheme relatively weak. The scheme was not sufficient to withstand this significant scrutiny, he contended.

b. **Housing:** Similarly, the right to *housing* is *not* a constitutionally fundamental one. See *Lindsey v. Normet*, 405 U.S. 56 (1972), where the Court applied deferential "mere-rationality" review to a state statute making it relatively easy for landlords to evict tenants if the landlord claimed that the rent had not been paid.

c. **Difficulties with contrary approach:** A contrary approach, holding that there *is* a fundamental interest in necessities, would pose large problems.

i. **Extension of state's role:** It is true that the Court has required states to pay for certain goods rather than charging indigents for them (e.g., trial transcripts in *Griffin* and appellate counsel in *Douglas*). But the goods there, as well as in the "right to vote" cases, were used in *areas in which the state is already dominant*. An extension of the fundamental rights doctrine to include necessities like food and shelter would expand the state's obligations into huge new areas, which until now have been left *principally to the private sector*.

ii. **Other difficulties:** Furthermore, there would be major difficulties in having courts determine issues like: (1) What level of food, shelter, clothing, etc. is so essential that one has a fundamental right to it? and (2) Does the claimant already have the resources to be able to purchase these goods? (and if he has part of the resources needed, what part?) Nor would it be appropriate for the court to be deferential to the legislature's statutes or regulations governing these matters, since the very idea of a fundamental right is that it is one as to which claims of impairment must be strictly scrutinized by the judiciary.

6. **Procedural safeguards:** Keep in mind that in the welfare context and in cases involving other governmental benefits, *procedural safeguards* may accomplish part of the protection of the poor that the post-Warren Court has been unwilling to impose in the name of equal protection. See, e.g., *Goldberg v. Kelly*, 397 U.S. 254 (1970) (*supra*, p. 213), holding

that a person's welfare benefits may not be terminated without an administrative hearing at which certain procedural standards are adhered to.

Quiz Yourself on

EQUAL PROTECTION — UNEQUAL TREATMENT OF GAYS; FUNDAMENTAL RIGHTS

47. Many members of Congress observed that as more and more states allowed same-sex marriages, there was in these states a corresponding increase in same-sex marriages between a U.S. citizen and a non-citizen. The House Committee on Immigration and Naturalization conducted hearings on the issue, and then reported out to the full House a bill called "The Defense of Heterosexual Naturalization Act of 2014" (DHNA). The bill directed the federal Citizenship and Immigration Service (CIS) to deny a green card (conferring permanent-resident status) to the non-citizen member of any same-sex marriage, even though existing federal immigration law automatically granted a green card to the non-citizen spouse in any *opposite*-sex marriage between a citizen and non-citizen. The Committee's report on the DHNA bill said that "A majority of the Committee disapproves of same-sex marriages on moral grounds, and wishes to discourage the creation of additional same-sex marriages in the U.S. by denying a path to naturalization for non-citizens who enter into such marriages when permitted by state law." There was no other legislative history on the bill. The DHNA passed both houses without significant debate, and was signed into law by the president. After the bill became law, two men, Bill and Li, entered into a marriage in California, where both live and where same-sex marriages are legal. Bill is a U.S. citizen; Li is not. After the marriage, Li applied for green-card; the application was denied by the CIS under authority of the DHNA. Li has sued the CIS in federal district court; he contends that the agency's denial of a green card violated his federal constitutional right to equal protection as applied to the federal government under the Fifth Amendment. The CIS has defended the statute's constitutionality on all available grounds. Will Li's claim succeed? _____

48. The state of Booth has enacted a statute governing the issuance of absentee ballots in state elections. Under the statute, any male under the age of 65 will be issued an absentee ballot only upon written proof that the applicant will be unable to be present at the voting place on the scheduled day for the election. If the applicant is a female, however, no written proof is required, and the applicant's statement that she cannot be present at the polling place is accepted at face value. The motivation for the statute was the legislature's belief that many women voters are the mothers of infants, who cannot easily get to the polling place to vote. Marvin, a male resident of Booth, has attacked the requirement of written proof on the grounds that it violates his Fourteenth Amendment equal protection rights.

    (a) What standard should the court use in reviewing the requirement of written proof? _____

    (b) Will Marvin's attack succeed? _____

49. The county of Gardenia has established a Forest Conservation District. The purpose of this district is to levy a special tax on owners of forested property, and to use these funds to buy certain parcels of forested property in the county from willing sellers so that the property can remain forested. The ultimate purpose of the District is to ensure that there is enough forested land that erosion will not get a foothold locally, something that would happen if many forested parcels become denuded by logging. The district is to be administered by a Board of Directors having five members. The five members are to be elected annually. Only owners of forested property in the county are permitted to vote in the election for directors. Bruce,

the owner of non-forested real estate, has sued for a declaration that the "one person, one vote" principle has been violated by this arrangement.

    (a) What standard of review should the court use in deciding Bruce's challenge? _____

    (b) Will Bruce's attack succeed? _____

50. The state of Illowa provided that in order for a "minor" party to have its presidential candidate appear on the ballot, the party must file petitions containing the signatures of 15% of all eligible voters in the state. (A party was defined as "minor" if it had not received at least 10% of the votes cast in the state in the previous presidential election.) The petition had to be filed nine months before the general election. Also, a minor party did not qualify for the ballot unless it conducted a primary election. Other Illowa electoral provisions prevented anyone from running for president as an independent, and did not allow for write-in candidacies for president. The Anti Washington Party, a newly-formed party dedicated to "throwing the rascals out of Washington," wished to have its candidate appear on the Illowa presidential-election ballot. The AWP sued on the grounds that these restrictions violated the equal protection rights of minority parties, as well as the freedom-of-association rights of party members.

    (a) What standard should the court use in hearing this challenge? _____

    (b) Will the AWP's attack on the restrictions succeed? _____

51. The state of Amazonia has a program called MedAmaz, which provides emergency medical assistance for indigent citizens. Under the rules for the program, a person who has moved to Amazonia is not eligible to receive emergency medical care until he or she has resided in the state for at least one year. Penelope, who moved to Amazonia three months ago from Ohio, needed an emergency appendectomy. The hospital refused to perform it because she did not meet the residency requirement, and Penelope almost died. Now, she has sued the state for damages, arguing that the residency requirement violated her right to equal protection of the laws.

    (a) What standard of review should the court use? _____

    (b) Will Penelope's attack succeed? _____

52. The state of New Canada has set its maximum welfare payment at $1,250 per month. For families of one child through three children, extra sums are paid for each additional child (with the $1,250 figure being paid for a family with three children). The net effect of the scheme is that a family does not receive any extra money for children after the first three. A further effect is that for a family of five children, the maximum paid by the state is 25% less than the federal poverty level. Hilda, a single mother of five children, whose only income comes from New Canada welfare payments, has sued the state, arguing that her family's equal protection rights have been violated, in that the state has discriminated against large families such as hers.

    (a) What standard of review should the court use in evaluating the statute? _____

    (b) Will Hilda's attack succeed? _____

———————————————

Answers

47. Yes. The facts of this question are fairly closely modeled on the facts of *U.S. v. Windsor* (2013), where the Court invalidated a section of the Defense of Marriage Act that forbade the entire federal government from recognizing, for any federal purpose, any state-consecrated same-sex marriage. Although the majority's reasoning in *Windsor* is somewhat opaque, the opinion seems to mean that (1) if Congress acts solely for the purpose of expressing moral disapproval of or **animus towards gays**, this is **not a legitimate governmental objective**; and (2) therefore, if Congress, acting with such a purpose, decides to treat same-sex couples validly married under state law significantly differently from similarly-situated married opposite-sex couples, Congress has violated the same-sex couples' right to equal protection (as imposed on the federal government by operation of the Fifth Amendment's due process clause). The Court's opinion in *Windsor* does not make it clear what standard of review is to be used in cases (like *Windsor* itself) attacking a federal classification system based solely on animus towards gays, but the case seems to mean that such a classification system cannot survive **even mere-rationality review**, given the absence of a legitimate state objective.

Here, the only legislative history indicates that the Committee with jurisdiction over the bill was acting solely out of hostility towards gay people, the same motive as (the Court found) motivated the passage of DOMA. Therefore, a lower federal court interpreting *Windsor* should find that DHNA was, similarly, not supported by any legitimate governmental objective, and therefore fails even mere-rationality equal protection review. (When the plaintiff contends that the federal government has failed to comply with equal protection principles, the claim is properly brought — as Li's was — under the *Fifth* Amendment, whose grant of the right to "due process" has been interpreted by the Court as obligating the federal government to follow equal-protection principles.) Therefore, regardless of what standard of review the trial court believes the Supreme Court to have chosen in *Windsor*, the trial court should conclude that *Windsor* means that the CIS' denial of a green card violated Li's Fifth Amendment rights.

48. (a) Strict scrutiny — the differential treatment must be necessary to achieve a compelling governmental interest.

(b) Yes. Normally, a statutory scheme that distinguishes on the basis of gender must undergo merely mid-level review, i.e., it must be "substantially related" to the achievement of an "important" governmental interest. However, because the right to vote is **"fundamental,"** classifications disadvantaging this right are subjected to strict scrutiny. Therefore, unless the state can show that distinguishing between men and women in issuance of absentee ballots is necessary to achieve a compelling governmental interest, the restriction must fall. Here, even if the state is pursuing some kind of compelling interest (perhaps the need to avoid the fraudulent use of absentee ballots), it is highly unlikely that the gender-based discrimination chosen here is a "necessary" means to achieve that interest. For example, a provision that *each* person who wants to use an absentee ballot must furnish a written excuse would appear to be a satisfactory way to handle the fraud problem.

49. (a) "mere-rationality" review.

(b) No, probably. Normally, any deviation from the "one person, one vote" principle, will be strictly scrutinized, and will probably be found to violate the Equal Protection Clause. But the Supreme Court has made a limited exception for **"special purpose"** bodies, that is, governmental units having a strictly limited purpose which disproportionately affects only one group. In that situation, the right to vote may be limited to the disproportionately-affected group. Here, since all funds disbursed by the district come from taxes on the owners of forested lands, and only such owners can receive the disbursed funds, this standard is probably satisfied. If so, the court will only give mere-rationality review to the arrangement. Since limiting votes for a body to those who have some interest in the body's actions is a rational way to achieve the body's purposes, the mere-rationality standard is probably satisfied. See *Ball v. James*.

50. (a) Strict scrutiny.

(b) Yes, probably. States are certainly entitled to impose ballot restrictions to ensure that only parties with a certain degree of popular support appear on the ballot. However, where ballot restrictions are so severe that they prevent virtually any but the two established parties from getting candidates on the ballot, these restrictions will be strictly scrutinized and probably struck down. The restrictions here seem to be so severe that they would be almost impossible to meet, so the court will probably invalidate the restrictions. See *Williams v. Rhodes*, one of the few ballot-access cases containing a restriction so severe that the statute was struck down; the restrictions here are virtually identical to those in *Williams*.

51. (a) Strict scrutiny.

(b) Yes, probably. Normally, when the state furnishes free goods or services, and does not discriminate against a suspect class, only a "mere-rationality" level of review is used. But when the state is dispensing a *"vital government benefit or privilege," and* the state treats *newly-arrived resident*s significantly less favorably than those who have lived in the state longer, strict scrutiny is used. The Supreme Court has held that even non-emergency medical care is a "vital government benefit or privilege" (*Memorial Hospital v. Maricopa County*), so emergency care certainly would be. The one-year residency requirement has the effect of treating recently-arrived people less favorably, so the conditions for strict scrutiny are met. It is doubtful that there is any state interest here that is "compelling" (the state's fiscal interest probably is not), and even more doubtful that a flat ban on any assistance to those who have not yet lived in the state for a year is a "necessary" method of achieving the state's objectives.

52. (a) The "mere-rationality" standard.

(b) No. First, large families (or any particular family size) have has never been found to constitute a "suspect" or "semi-suspect" class. Nor are poor people members of such a class. Hilda's only hope would be to establish that one has a "fundamental interest" in the "necessities of life." However, the Supreme Court has explicitly held that welfare benefits and other "economic necessities" are *not* fundamental interests. See, e.g., *Dandridge v. Williams* (no fundamental interest in welfare benefits). Therefore, any classification system used by the state in allocating such economic necessities is judged by the easy-to-satisfy "mere-rationality" standard. Here, the state's scheme bears a rational relation to several legitimate state objectives (e.g., encouraging employment by prohibiting payments that might compare favorably with what a job would provide).

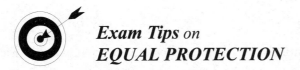

Exam Tips on
EQUAL PROTECTION

Equal protection issues, like due process ones, are often hidden, and are likely to be part of almost any complex fact pattern. It is not uncommon for 20-25% of a total Con. Law exam to consist of equal protection issues, scattered throughout multiple fact patterns. Here's what to look for:

☛ Above all else, anytime you see a legislative *classification* — a placement of people or businesses into *two or more groups* — think about the possibility that the classification might violate equal protection.

    ☞   For there to be an equal protection problem, the issue must be whether the government has behaved reasonably in *setting up* the classes in the first place. If the issue is whether the government has correctly placed an *individual* into the "right" group or class, you have a problem of procedural due process, not equal protection. (*Example:* If the government says, "All firefighters must retire at age 55," there is an EP problem because the issue is whether the government can set up the classes in this way. But if the government says, "Any firefighter too weak to do the work will be discharged," and the government then says, "Norman, you are too weak," the issue of whether Norman has been treated fairly is a procedural DP issue, not an EP issue, because the issue is whether the government has given Norman procedural regularity in deciding which class he falls into.)

☞ For there to be an EP problem, there must be *"discrimination"* against members of one of the classes, i.e., one class must be treated intentionally less favorably than the other. Use the adjective *"invidious"* to describe the required discrimination.

☛ If you state that P can make an EP attack on the classification at issue, state whether the attack would be "on the statute's *face*" or "*as applied*." Remember that a "facial" attack is used where the statute itself in its text discriminates against a class; an "as applied" attack is used where discrimination against one class stems from how the statute or regulation is *carried out*. (*Examples:* If government imposes a literacy test, or allows public prosecutors to use peremptory challenges, you're likely to be dealing with an "as applied" test.)

☛ Examine whether the discrimination is being practiced by a *state/local* government, or by the *federal* government. If it's the state or local government, then you're using the Fourteenth Amendment's EP Clause. If it's the federal government, you're using the Fifth Amendment's Due Process Clause, which by the process of "reverse incorporation" includes the principle of equal protection. (Especially in multiple choice tests, Profs like to give you an instance of federal discrimination and then try to tempt you to make a choice that involves "the Fourteenth Amendment's Due Process Clause," which is the wrong answer for the reason just stated.)

☛ Once you have identified an EP problem, devote extreme efforts to choosing the correct *level of review*. Remember that there are three levels used in evaluating EP situations:

☞ *Strict scrutiny* is used where either a classification is based upon a *suspect class* (race, national origin or alienage) or where the classification impairs the exercise of a *fundamental right* (e.g., the right to vote or the right to change your state of residence).

☞ *Mid-level* review is used for two "semi-suspect" classifications, those based on *gender* and *illegitimacy*.

☞ The *"mere-rationality"* standard is used for all other types of classifications.

Suggestion: After you identify the issue, immediately state what the likely standard of review is, including details of that test. (*Example:* "Since the classification here is on the basis of gender, the Court will use a mid-level standard of review. That is, the Court will strike down the statute unless it is shown to be important to the achievement of a substantial governmental objective.")

☛ Here are the main things to remember about the *"mere-rationality"* standard, and the places where it is used:

☞ If the classification relates to *economic* regulation, you will almost certainly be using the "mere-rationality" standard. (*Examples:* The state says no one can put a sign on a rooftop, but gives an exception for a sign advertising goods produced by the owner of the building. Or, the state taxes one group more heavily than another (e.g., there's a sales tax on "refined petroleum," but not on "unrefined petroleum").)

☞ Most types of *"social welfare"* classifications will also be judged by the "mere-rationality" standard. (*Examples:* Discrimination based on *age*; discrimination against *aliens* where the function relates to the heart of representative government (see further discussion of aliens below); discrimination in the issuance of *licenses* or *permits*; discrimination against *out-of-staters*; discrimination against the *poor* (in the sense that government fails to pay for things the poor need that the rich can pay for themselves).)

☞ If there's no suspect or semi-suspect class or fundamental right, and the government is trying to *combat an evil*, you'll probably note that the government has only attacked *part* of that evil. The question becomes whether the government has violated EP by not attacking the other evil. Here, you should say something like: "The regulation is valid, because the government is entitled to combat evils *one step at a time*." You might then want to cite to *Williamson v. Lee Optical Co.* (*Example:* The government requires lawyers, but not doctors, to take mandatory continuing education — this is OK, because the government may combat the evil of non-up-to-date professionals one step at a time.)

☞ If the government is trying to *single out an unpopular group* (but one that doesn't get suspect or semi-suspect status) for unfavorable treatment, indicate that although only "mere-rationality" review is used, that review will be applied "with bite," and the scheme may well be struck down.

    ❏ Unequal treatment of *gays* and the *mentally retarded* seems to fall into this category. So, for instance, Congress' decision in the Defense of Marriage Act not to recognize state-sanctioned same-sex marriages apparently flunked even mere-rationality review. (Cite to *U.S. v. Windsor*, where the Court doesn't expressly say it's applying the mere-rationality standard, but seems to be applying that standard "with bite.")

☛ If the classification has to do with *race*, here are the key things to remember:

☞ Race is a *"suspect class."* Therefore, any intentional discrimination based on race — either in the face of the statute/regulation, or in the way it is applied — must be *strictly scrutinized*. That is, the classification must be struck down unless it is *necessary* to achieve a *compelling governmental interest*. You should almost always conclude that this standard is *not* satisfied. Typically, your reason will be because there is some alternative non-race-conscious method of handling the problem, so the race-conscious means are not "necessary."

☞ Remember that race as a suspect classification will not be deemed to be involved unless government is acting with the *purpose*, *not just the effect*, of classifying based on race. (*Example:* If government takes an action which happens to disadvantage more blacks than whites, there's no suspect class, and thus no strict scrutiny, unless there's evidence that government acted with the purpose of disadvantaging blacks.) *This is*

the single most commonly tested aspect of strict scrutiny.

☞ Your fact pattern will usually ***not*** contain a racial classification "on its face." Yet, the facts will indicate to you that some racial group is affected more than other groups. This should be your tip-off that you have an " 'effect' vs. 'purpose' " problem.

☞ Keep in mind, however, that ***circumstantial evidence*** can always be used to show that government has the ***intent*** to discriminate against the unfavored group, and that the effect is not merely an unintended by-product. (*Example:* If government chooses grand jurors from the rolls of registered voters, the fact that this produces far fewer black grand jurors than other methods would is admissible as circumstantial evidence that the government really intended to discriminate against black grand jurors.)

☞ Remember that the discrimination must be ***"invidious."*** That is, there must be an attempt to treat some racial group in a ***less favorable***, stigmatizing, way. You will want to examine whether this element of "invidiousness" is present whenever the governmental scheme tends to merely ***record*** racial differences, or to impose some kind of racial ***"matching."*** (*Examples:* If the government publishes the race of each political candidate, or the government requires that the race of an adoptive parent match the child's race, or the government imposes a sickle-cell test applicable only to African Americans, you'll want to examine whether there is a "stigmatizing" or "invidious" discrimination. Often, but not always, you will conclude that the answer is "yes.")

☞ Be on the lookout for ***segregation*** — any government program that intentionally ***separates*** the races, or intentionally encourages the races to separate themselves, is likely to be invidious and thus needs to be strictly scrutinized. (*Example:* If a state university allows dormitories to classify themselves, by vote of the existing residents, as "primarily black" or "primarily white," this probably represents intentional governmental support of segregation, and probably requires strict scrutiny.)

☛ Special rules apply to race-conscious ***affirmative action***:

☞ ***Strict scrutiny*** is applied to the affirmative action situation just as much as to the "invidious" situation. Cite to *Richmond v. Croson* when you have a race-conscious affirmative action program.

☞ Typically, the only governmental objectives that are strong enough to overcome strict scrutiny in the affirmative action context are: (1) the eradication of ***past discrimination*** by government (and only if the discrimination is shown by ***clear evidence***) and (2) the pursuit of ***diversity*** in a ***student body***.

☞ The fact that it's ***Congress***, rather than state or local government, that's doing the affirmative action now makes ***no*** formal difference — strict scrutiny is still applied. (Cite to *Adarand* if a congressional act is at issue.) However, you may want to allude to the possibility that even though the Court applies strict scrutiny, it may end up giving ***slightly greater deference*** to Congress' conclusion that race-conscious measures are needed, than it would to a similar conclusion by a state or local body.

☞ Be on the lookout for race-conscious affirmative action in ***university admissions***.

Here, say that this is OK (because student-body diversity can be a compelling objective) *if* the school (1) evaluates each applicant as an ***individual***; (2) treats minority-race as merely ***one "plus factor" among others***; (3) ***doesn't use mechanical means*** (like ***quotas*** or a fixed number of "points") to obtain the desired number of minority-group admittees; and (4) proves that there were no ***"workable race-neutral alternatives"*** available to achieve the desired "educational diversity."

☞ Cite to the three cases of *Grutter v. Bollinger* (race as an individualized "plus factor" is OK), *Gratz v. Bollinger* (mechanical point systems are not OK) and *Fisher v. Univ. of Texas* (workable race-neutral methods for achieving student-body diversity must be shown to be unavailable).

☞ Also, be on the lookout for race-conscious ***pupil-assignment plans*** for ***public elementary or high schools.*** Here, any plan that classifies each student's race, and makes any pupil assignment based on whether the student's presence would improve or worsen the target school's racial imbalance, will almost certainly flunk the requisite strict scrutiny. Cite to *Parents Involved v. Seattle School District* on this point.

☞ Here are some contexts in which race-conscious affirmative action programs may pop up on exams:

☞ preferential ***admissions*** to universities and public schools (see above);

☞ minority set-asides in the award of public ***construction*** and other ***contracts***;

☞ allocation of public-sector ***jobs*** (including layoffs and promotions as well as original hiring);

☞ the drawing of ***election districts***.

☛ The drawing of classifications based on ***national origin*** is also to be strictly scrutinized. However, exams rarely pose a national-origin problem.

☛ Here's what to look for when there is a classification based on ***gender***:

☞ Remember that ***mid-level*** review is used for gender-based classifications. That is, the governmental objective must be ***"important,"*** and the means must be ***"substantially related"*** to that objective. (But note that this mid-level review is now a pretty tough standard, with the court requiring an "exceedingly persuasive justification," and giving "skeptical scrutiny." Cite to *U.S. v. Virginia*, the VMI case, as the source for these new descriptions of how the mid-level review is to be conducted.)

☞ Remember that the same review standard is in theory used whether the sex-based classification is "invidious" (intended to harm women) or "benign" (intended to help women). Any classification that derives in part from "stereotypical" views about women (e.g., that women's place is in the home, or that women are physically weak) is especially likely to be struck down.

☞ Where the classification disadvantages ***men***, the same rules apply: mid-level review is used.

☞ As with race-conscious discrimination, only governmental action whose ***purpose***, not mere effect, is to discriminate against one gender, will be considered. (*Example:* A strength requirement for paramedics would not be subjected to mid-level review, if the requirement's purpose was not to discriminate against women, and it was merely an unintended effect that fewer women than men could qualify.)

☞ Here are some areas where gender-based classifications have popped up on exams:

  ☞ (1) The government provides that pregnant women in the work force are to be treated differently than all others, e.g., with respect to exposure to toxic substances. (This is not necessarily true gender discrimination, since women who are not pregnant are not impacted, so probably you don't apply mid-level review, just "mere-rationality" review.)

  ☞ (2) Women are given different school activities than men. (*Example:* Women are not allowed to play football. Probably it's appropriate to use mid-level review, but the classification system will probably survive that review in light of the different average size and strength of women.)

☛ Classifications based on *illegitimacy* are also "semi-suspect" and thus get mid-level review. Most commonly, you would be tested on a state statute that discriminates against illegitimates with respect to the right to *inherit*.

☛ Discrimination against *aliens* is very frequently tested.

  ☞ As a *general* rule, remember that discrimination against aliens is subjected to *strict scrutiny*. (*Examples:* A state's refusal of welfare benefits to aliens, or its refusal to let an alien practice a profession, will be strictly scrutinized.)

    ☞ Note that discrimination against "aliens" typically refers to discrimination against *legal* aliens. Probably strict scrutiny is *not* used for discrimination against *illegal* or "undocumented" aliens.

  ☞ Remember that there is a key *exception* to the general rule of strict scrutiny: where the alien has applied for a *job* that goes to the *"heart of representative government,"* only mere-rationality review is used. Most government jobs that have a *policy*, *law enforcement* or *education* component fall within this "representative government" exception. (*Examples:* Jobs as a public school teacher, police officer, or probation officer are all within the exception, so the state merely has to be rational in its decision to close these positions off from foreigners.)

    ☞ But there are some jobs that are sufficiently ministerial that they do not fall within the "representative government" exception. (*Examples:* Secretary in a governmental agency; meter reader for a publicly owned electric utility.)

☛ Classifications impairing a *"fundamental right"* are tested less frequently than those involving a suspect or semi-suspect class. Nonetheless, these classifications sometimes pop up on exams.

  ☞ Any impairment of the right to *vote* is an impairment of a fundamental right, and thus strictly scrutinized, if it is *not reasonably related to determining the voter's qualifications.*

    Examples: (1) Poll taxes; (2) a requirement that the voter have resided in the jurisdiction for one year before the election; and (3) a requirement that the voter be a land-owner or tenant, are generally not reasonably related to determining the voter's qualifications. Therefore, they'll be strictly scrutinized and struck down.

☞ But if the measure *is* reasonably related to determining the voter's qualifications, then it will be subjected only to *mid-level review*, and probably upheld.

Examples: (1) A requirement that a voter present a government-issued photo ID; and (2) A requirement that a voter prove that he's a bona fide resident (e.g., by having lived in the jurisdiction for 50 days) won't be strictly scrutinized, and will probably be upheld.

☞ A person's right to be a *candidate* seems to be "semi-fundamental," and thus gets more-than-mere-rationality review. (*Example:* A high candidate filing fee that is imposed even on indigent candidates violates EP.) Similarly, restrictions that unfairly keep *new, not-yet-established, political parties* off the ballot get this semi-fundamental review.

☞ Access to the *courts* is sometimes a "fundamental interest." Look for situations where the state imposes a *fee* that it refuses to waive for indigents. The two contexts that count are *criminal* cases (so that the state may not charge an indigent for a trial transcript or for counsel) and *family law* cases (so that the state may not charge a filing fee to indigents who want a *divorce*). But other types of civil access (e.g., small claims court or bankruptcy court) are not deemed "fundamental," so the state's refusal to subsidize indigents gets only mere-rationality review.

☞ The *"right to travel"* (really the right to *change* one's state of *residence* or *employment*) is "fundamental."

☞ Therefore, look for patterns where the state imposes a substantial *waiting period* on newly-arrived residents: if they have to do this wait before they get some *vital governmental benefit* (e.g., *welfare*), a fundamental right has been impaired. But non-vital benefits are not "fundamental" (so that there's only mere-rationality review where the state makes newcomers wait for, say, low in-state university tuition rates).

☞ The right to *"necessities"* is *not* fundamental. So if your fact pattern involves the state's refusal to equalize the right of indigents to such items as *public school education, food, shelter or medical care*, you probably need to apply only "mere-rationality" review, not strict scrutiny fundamental interest review.

MISCELLANEOUS CLAUSES: 14TH AM. PRIVILEGES OR IMMUNITIES; TAKING; CONTRACT; RIGHT TO BEAR ARMS; EX POST FACTO; BILLS OF ATTAINDER

ChapterScope

This chapter considers several clauses that have little in common except that they protect individuals against specific types of government conduct. The most important concepts in this chapter are:

- **Privileges or Immunities:** The 14th Amendment has a "Privileges or Immunities" Clause. But this clause is very narrowly interpreted: it only protects the individual from state interference with his rights of *"national"* citizenship (principally the right to *travel from state to state* and the right to *vote in national elections*).

- **"Taking" Clause:** The Fifth Amendment's "Taking" Clause provides, essentially, that the government may take private property under its power of "eminent domain," but if it does take private property, it *must pay a fair price*.

  - ❏ **Land-use regulations:** What the government calls mere "regulation" may occasionally amount to a "taking" for which compensation must be paid. This happens mostly in cases of *land-use regulation*. For a land-use regulation to avoid being a taking, it must satisfy two requirements: (1) it must *"substantially advance legitimate state interests"*; and (2) it must *not "deny an owner economically viable use of his land."*

- **"Contract" Clause:** The "Contract" Clause provides that "no state shall... pass any... law impairing the obligation of contracts." The meaning of this Clause depends on whether the government is impairing its own contracts or contracts between private parties:

  - ❏ **Public contracts:** If the state is trying to escape from its *own financial obligations*, then the Court will *closely scrutinize* this attempt: the state's attempt to "weasel" will be struck down unless the modification is *"reasonable* and *necessary* to support an *important* public purpose."

  - ❏ **Private contracts:** But when the state is re-writing contracts made by *private parties*, the state merely has to be acting *"reasonably,"* a much easier-to-satisfy standard. (And if the state's action is a *generally applicable* rule that has only the incidental effect of impairing contracts, the Contract Clause does not apply at all.)

- **Right to Bear Arms:** The Second Amendment has been held to guarantee private individuals the right to keep firearms at home for purposes of self-defense.

- **Ex Post Facto Laws:** Both the state and federal governments are prohibited from passing any "ex post facto" law. An ex post facto law is a law which has a *retroactive punitive effect*. So government may not impose a punishment for conduct which, at the time it occurred, was *not punishable*. Nor may government *increase* the punishment for an offense over what was on the books at the time of the act.

- ▓ **Bills of Attainder:** Both state and federal governments are prohibited from passing any "bill of attainder." A bill of attainder is a legislative act which "applies either to *named individuals* or to *easily ascertainable* members of a group in such a way as to *punish* them without a *judicial trial*."

I. THE 14TH AMENDMENT'S PRIVILEGES OR IMMUNITIES CLAUSE

A. **"Privileges or Immunities" Clause:** The *"Privileges or Immunities"* Clause of the Fourteenth Amendment comes at the beginning of the second sentence of Section I: "No State shall make or enforce any law which shall *abridge* the privileges or immunities of citizens of the United States. ... " At least some of the members of Congress who participated in the drafting of the Fourteenth Amendment expected and hoped that this Clause would constitute a substantial restraint on state government action against individuals. See Tribe, p. 550.

1. *Slaughterhouse* **Cases:**   But the Supreme Court did not take this view. In the *Slaughterhouse Cases*, 83 U.S. (16 Wall.) 36 (1873), the Court held (5-4) that the Fourteenth Amendment's Privileges or Immunities Clause merely forbade state infringement of the rights of *national* citizenship, not the rights of state citizenship.

   a. **Facts of *Slaughterhouse* Cases:**   The *Slaughterhouse Cases* arose when Louisiana passed a law giving a monopoly on New Orleans-area slaughterhouses to a particular company. Butchers not included in the monopoly claimed that the statute deprived them of the opportunity to practice their trade, and thereby violated the Thirteenth and Fourteenth Amendments. The plaintiffs' most serious argument was that the statute was a denial of the privileges or immunities of Louisiana citizenship, including the right to practice one's calling.

   b. **Argument rejected:**   But the Supreme Court rejected all of the plaintiffs' contentions, including the privileges or immunities argument. The Court observed that the first sentence of the Fourteenth Amendment distinguishes between U.S. citizenship (for which one need merely be born or naturalized in the United States) and state citizenship (for which residence is required). "Fundamental" civil rights, including the right to practice one's calling, were the domain of the states, not the federal government. Therefore, the plaintiffs should look to Louisiana law for protection; if there was no protection under Louisiana law (as apparently there was not), the plaintiffs were out of luck, since the Privileges or Immunities Clause added nothing to their rights in this area.

      i. **Rights of national citizenship:**   The *Slaughterhouse* majority attempted to rebut the suggestion that under its interpretation, the Privileges or Immunities Clause accomplished nothing. The majority observed that there were several rights of "national" (as opposed to state) citizenship. The majority's short catalogue of "national" citizenship rights included "free access to ... seaports," federal protection "when on the high seas or within the jurisdiction of a foreign government," and a few other limited rights. These rights, the majority acknowledged, could not be infringed by any state, by virtue of the Fourteenth Amendment Privileges or Immunities Clause.

c. **Minority view:** The four-Justice minority in the *Slaughterhouse Cases* flatly rejected the majority's limited reading of the Fourteenth Amendment Privileges or Immunities Clause. Even without the Fourteenth Amendment, the dissent argued, the privileges and immunities of national citizenship were already protected against state action (by virtue of the Supremacy Clause). Thus the majority view made the P-or-I Clause utterly useless. The correct view, the dissent contended, was that the Clause guaranteed to every U.S. citizen that his "fundamental rights," rights which "belong to the citizens of all free governments," would not be infringed by any state. These fundamental rights included the right to "pursue a lawful employment in a lawful manner."

2. **View of clause until 1999:** Until 1999, the *Slaughterhouse* majority's view of the Fourteenth Amendment Privileges or Immunities Clause prevailed. For 125 years after that decision, only one state law was ever invalidated under the clause, and that decision was soon overruled. Only a few rights of "national" (as opposed to "state") citizenship were deemed protected, such as the right to *travel physically from state to state*, to petition Congress for redress of grievances, to *vote in national elections*, to enter federally-owned lands, and to be protected while in the custody of U.S. marshall (see *Twining v. New Jersey*, 211 U.S. 78 (1908)), and these were rarely even claimed to be abridged by state laws.

3. **View expanded in *Saenz*:** But then, a surprising 7-2 decision in 1999 breathed dramatic new life into the Fourteenth Amendment Privileges or Immunities Clause. In *Saenz v. Roe*, 526 U.S. 489 (1999), the Court held that the clause protects a particular and important aspect of the so-called "right to travel," namely the right of a person who has *recently become a citizen* of a state to the same privileges enjoyed by *longer-standing citizens* of that state. *Saenz* became only the second case in 125 years to strike down a state law on Fourteenth Amendment P-or-I grounds.

a. **Welfare rights:** *Saenz* involved the right of a newly-arrived resident in California to receive the same state *welfare benefits* as a person who had been in the state longer. California, acting under express congressional authority, said that anyone who had resided in the state for less than one year would receive welfare benefits no greater than the level of benefits the person had received in her prior state of residence. (45 of the 49 other states had lower benefit levels than California.) Although California denied that the purpose of its provision was to deter the migration of poor people into California, the lower federal courts in *Saenz* found that this was indeed the statute's purpose.

b. **Struck down:** The Court found that California's rule setting welfare benefits based on the recipient's state of prior residence violated the Fourteenth Amendment P-or-I Clause: *"[T]he Clause does not tolerate a hierarchy of 45 subclasses of similarly situated citizens based on the location of their prior residence."* Even if California was acting for the purpose of reducing expenditures (rather than in order to deter in-migration of poor people), using a means predicated on length of state citizenship was not acceptable, since a family's financial needs were not dependent on how long it had been in the state or where it had previously resided.

    i. Strict scrutiny: The Court in *Saenz* seems to have applied ***strict scrutiny*** to California's rule disfavoring recent newcomers: the Court said that "[n]either mere rationality nor some intermediate standard of review should be used to judge the constitutionality of a state rule that discriminates against some of its citizens because they have been domiciled in the State for less than a year." California's fiscal justification did not come even close to satisfying this strict standard of review.

  c. Significance: So *Saenz* probably means that the Fourteenth Amendment Privileges or Immunities Clause requires the states to ***satisfy strict scrutiny*** before they may ***treat newly-arrived residents less favorably than those of longer standing.***

    i. Bona fide residence requirements: One last note: *Saenz* probably does not change the rule that a state is entitled to impose a ***requirement of bona fide residency as a pre-condition to receiving state benefits.***

4. Distinguished from Article IV Clause: It is important to distinguish the Fourteenth Amendment Privileges or Immunities Clause from the Privileges and Immunities Clause of Article IV, §2 (described *supra*, p. 100). To summarize the distinction: The Fourteenth Amendment Clause bars a state from abridging any U.S. citizen's rights of "national" citizenship (of which the most important now seems to be the right to travel, and relocate, from one state to another). The Article IV Clause protects rights of "state" citizenship, but only when a non-resident of the state is not treated the same as a resident with respect to an important state right, essentially a right involving commerce.

II. THE "TAKING" CLAUSE

    Introductory Note: We turn now to two other specific constitutional protections of private (usually economic) interests: (1) the ban on the taking of private property for public use, without just compensation; and (2) the prohibition on the impairment of contracts. These two protections are related to the same concern which gave rise to the substantive due process doctrine, the danger that public action will interfere with private property rights. But the "taking" and "contract" clauses also protect an additional interest: the interest in "settled expectations," or as they are sometimes called, "vested rights." See Tribe, p. 587. The rationale behind the two clauses is that pre-existing interests in physical property and in contracts should not be disturbed by the government except under certain limited conditions.

A. The Taking Clause generally: Governments, both state and federal, have the right to take private property for public use, provided that "just compensation" is paid. This power is known as the right of ***"eminent domain."*** Nothing in the Constitution explicitly confers this eminent domain power upon either the federal or state governments. But the Fifth Amendment, originally intended to apply solely to the federal government, provides that "private property *[shall not] be taken for public use, without just compensation."* This so-called Taking Clause is at least a "tacit recognition that the power to take private property exists." N&R, pp. 438-440.

1. **Two major issues:** A full discussion of the eminent domain power, and the accompanying obligation to pay just compensation, is beyond the scope of this outline. (The subject is treated more extensively in *Emanuel on Property.*) For present purposes, we are interested in the general aspects of two issues: (1) what is the borderline between a "taking" (for which compensation must be paid) and a mere "regulation" (for which no compensation is due)? and (2) when is a taking made for "private" rather than "public" use, so that there is no right of eminent domain, even if compensation is paid? The first of these issues is the more important.

2. **States subject to rules:** The federal government, as noted, is explicitly bound by the Fifth Amendment's ban on the taking of private property for public use without just compensation. The Supreme Court has repeatedly held that *state governments* are similarly prohibited, by the Fourteenth Amendment's Due Process Clause, from taking private property without paying for it. But since the Fourteenth Amendment Due Process Clause does not refer explicitly either to takings or to compensation, the theory by which the just compensation requirement is imposed on the states is not clear.

    a. **Competing views:** One view is that the Fifth Amendment just compensation requirement is directly incorporated into the Fourteenth Amendment Due Process Clause. An alternate view (which produces essentially the same result) is that the Fourteenth Amendment Due Process Clause, although more general, implicitly contains the same ban on takings of private property without just compensation as does the more explicit Fifth. See N&R, p. 440. In any event, essentially the same standards for determining when there has been a taking, and what constitutes just compensation, are applied to the states as to the federal government.

B. **The taking/regulation distinction:** If the court finds that private property has been "taken" by the government, compensation must be paid. But if the state merely *regulates* property use in a manner consistent with the state's "police power," then no compensation needs to be paid, even though the owner's use of his property, or even its value, has been substantially diminished. It thus becomes crucial to distinguish between a compensable "taking" and a non-compensable "regulation." Most of the cases requiring a distinction between taking and regulation have involved *land-use regulations*; these include zoning regulations, environmental-protection rules, landmark preservation schemes, and other schemes by which the government does not attempt to take title to a landowner's property but does regulate his use of that property.

Here are some of the principles governing when a land-use regulation will become a taking for which compensation must be paid.

1. **Physical use:** If the government makes or authorizes a *permanent physical occupation* of the property, this will *automatically* be found to constitute a taking, no matter how minor the interference with the owner's use and no matter how important the countervailing governmental interests. In *Loretto v. Teleprompter Manhattan CATV Corp.*, 458 U.S. 419 (1982), the Court formulated this *"per se"* rule, and applied it to invalidate a statute which required landlords to permit cable television companies to install their cable facilities on the landlord's rental property. (The scheme permitted landlords to charge the cable companies what was in most instances a maximum one-time fee of $1.)

    a.　Easement is physical occupation:　A post-*Loretto* case shows that the Court will take an expansive view of what kind of regulation constitutes a "physical occupation" of the owner's property. In that case the Court held that a state's refusal to grant a building permit except upon the transfer to the public of a permanent *easement* for the public to pass along a strip of the owners' property constituted a "permanent physical occupation" of that property. See *Nollan v. California Coastal Commission*, discussed more extensively *infra*, p. 421. The easement in *Nollan* would simply have permitted members of the public to walk along the owner's sandy strip parallel to the ocean on their way from one public beach to another. Even though this easement would not have permitted any given individual to remain on the owner's land, a physical occupation was found to exist, so that there was a taking of the owners' property.

2.　Diminution in value:　The more drastic the *reduction in value* of the owner's property, the more likely a taking is to be found. For instance, in ***Pennsylvania Coal Co. v. Mahon***, 260 U.S. 393 (1922), a landowner had bought the surface rights to land, and the house on it, under a chain of title which reserved to a coal company the right to mine coal from under the property. Thereafter, Pennsylvania enacted a statute preventing subsurface mining where a house might be caused to sink. The effect of the statute was to bar the coal company completely from mining under the owner's land.

    a.　Holding:　The Supreme Court held that the regulation so utterly impaired the right to mine coal that it was nearly the equivalent of an appropriation or destruction of the coal. Therefore, the regulation was a taking, which could not be carried out without compensation to the coal company. The Court, in a majority opinion by Justice Holmes, noted that "while property may be regulated to a certain extent, if regulation goes too far it will be recognized as a taking."

    b.　Dissent:　But a dissent, by Justice Brandeis, argued that the regulation was merely "the prohibition of a noxious use," and therefore did not require compensation. (The "noxious use" factor is discussed immediately below.)

    c.　Result may no longer be valid:　The result in *Pennsylvania Coal* may no longer be valid. In *Keystone Bituminous Coal Ass'n v. DeBenedictis*, 480 U.S. 470 (1987), the Court by a 5-4 vote upheld a modern (1966) Pennsylvania version of the statute struck down in *Pennsylvania Coal*. The 1966 statute required that 50% of the coal beneath existing public buildings and dwellings be left in place to provide surface support. The majority made some efforts to distinguish *Pennsylvania Coal*, but there is so little difference between the two statutes that it seems likely that *Pennsylvania Coal* would turn out the other way if decided today. However, the general principle for which the case is cited — that the more drastic the reduction in value of the owner's property, the more likely a taking is to be found — remains valid. (*Keystone* also illustrates that where the state is acting to prevent *harm to the public*, the courts will be very reluctant to invalidate the regulation as a "taking." See the discussion of the "prevention of harm" rationale, *infra*.)

3.　Denial of all economically viable use of land:　Since (as just noted) the more drastic the reduction in value of the owner's property, the more likely a taking is to be found, it's not surprising that the Court has imposed a flat rule that a taking occurs where an owner has been deprived of **all economically viable use** of his land. See *Agins v. Tiburon*, 447 U.S. 255 (1980).

a. **Particular use eliminated:** Cases in which such an extreme taking by deprivation of economically viable use is found are very rare. The fact that the *particular* use made by the plaintiff has been completely foreclosed will not be enough. For instance, suppose a parcel contains an aluminum smelter worth $100 million, and the city where the smelter is located then bans all smelting. The fact that P's *particular* land use — operation of the smelter — has been totally foreclosed will not be enough to make the regulation a "taking"; P is still free to convert the smelter to other uses, or even to raze it and put up some other structure (or sell it to someone who will).

b. **Total ban:** On the other hand, a **total and permanent ban** on the building of **any structure** on property *is* likely to be enough to deny the owner "all economically viable use" of his land, and thus to constitute a taking automatically. See, e.g., *First English Evangelical Lutheran Church v. Los Angeles County*, 482 U.S. 304 (1987) (*held*, a permanent ban on building any dwelling on the property constitutes denial of all economically viable use, and is thus a taking).

Example: South Carolina, in order to protect its coastline from continued erosion, enacts the Beachfront Management Act, which defines certain "critical areas" of erosion danger, and bars any owner of a lot in a critical area from building any permanent habitable structure on the parcel. P is the owner of two parcels which, at the time he bought them for nearly $1 million, were allowed to have houses built upon them; passage of the Act has the effect of preventing P from building any permanent structure on either lot. P contends that this "regulation" deprives him of all economic use of his property, and thus constitutes a taking. A lower state court agrees that P has been deprived of all economically viable use, but the South Carolina Supreme Court reverses on the grounds that even if this is true, the state may regulate to preserve its citizens' health and safety, and that such regulation is not a taking.

Held (by the U.S. Supreme Court), if P has truly been deprived of all economically viable use of his property, a "taking" has occurred. It is up to the South Carolina courts to decide whether P has really been deprived of all economically viable use. If he has been, a taking exists even though the state is trying to protect the health and safety of residents (unless the state already had, under the "background principles of the state's law of property and nuisance" the right to prevent the particular use by P, an issue to be decided by the state courts on remand; this aspect of the case is described *infra*, p. 419, Par. 6). ***Lucas v. South Carolina Coastal Council***, 505 U.S. 1003 (1992).

c. **Temporary moratorium on development:** In *Lucas*, the ban on all economically viable use of P's property purported to be permanent. What happens if the government merely imposes a *temporary* delay on all economically viable use of property, as where a planning board institutes a *"moratorium"* on development of certain property — is the government automatically required to pay just compensation for this delay? As a result of a post-*Lucas* case decided in 2002, the answer is *"not necessarily"* — the court will instead consider **all the surrounding circumstances** to determine whether the delay of all economically viable use was so severe as to require that compensation be paid. ***Tahoe-Sierra Preservation Council, Inc. v. Tahoe Regional Planning Agency***, 535 U.S. 302 (2002).

    i. **Categorical ruling rejected:** The Supreme Court, by a 6-3 vote, ***refused*** to find a categorical right to compensation for such a temporary delay in the right to make any economically-viable use of one's property. In an opinion by Justice Stevens, the court said that "the answer to the abstract question whether a temporary [development] moratorium effects a taking is neither 'yes, always' nor 'no, never'; the answer depends upon the ***particular circumstances*** of the case."

        (1) **Distinction:** The Court distinguished sharply between physical takings and regulatory takings. Even a temporary physical occupation of P's property entitles him to compensation. But a similar rule for temporary regulatory takings would wreak havoc: "Land-use regulations are ubiquitous and most of them impact property values in some tangential way — often in completely unanticipated ways. Treating them all as *per se* takings would transform government regulation into a ***luxury few governments could afford.*** By contrast, physical appropriations are relatively rare, easily identified, and usually represent a greater affront to individual property rights."

        (2) ***Lucas*** **marginalized:** So as the result of *Tahoe-Sierra*, the *Lucas* decision is ***marginalized***. As Justice Stevens put it in *Tahoe-Sierra*, "the categorical rule in *Lucas* was carved out for the 'extraordinary case' in which a regulation ***permanently*** deprives property of all value; the ***default rule*** remains that, in the regulatory taking context, we require a more ***fact specific*** inquiry."

    ii. **Significance:** *Tahoe-Sierra* does *not* mean that a ban on all economically-viable use of one's property need not be compensated merely because it turns out to be temporary. The case merely means that there is no *automatic* right to compensation — instead, the surrounding circumstances must be considered in deciding whether there has been a taking. For example, if the property actually ***increased in value*** during the moratorium, that would probably strongly cut against a finding that there had been a taking.

4. **"Prevention of harm" or "noxious use" rationale:** A regulation rather than a taking is likely to be found where the property use being prevented is one that is ***harmful*** or "***noxious***" to others. For instance, a zoning ordinance may properly prevent the operation of a steel mill in the middle of a residential neighborhood; in general, anything which the common law would recognize as a public or private ***nuisance*** may be barred by regulation, without the need for compensation.

    a. **Favoring one private interest over another:** Occasionally, a zoning or other public decision that a land use is "noxious" will be the product of a clear decision to ***favor one private interest over another***. Nonetheless, the fact that a private interest, rather than the "public interest" as a whole, is being benefitted, will not render the regulation a compensable taking.

    Example: Many red cedar trees in the state of Virginia are infected with cedar rust, a disease that is highly dangerous to apple orchards. Virginia passes a law requiring the destruction, as a public nuisance, of all red cedar trees within a prescribed distance from an apple orchard. Cedar owners are paid only the cost of removing their trees, not the value of the trees.

Held, the ordinance, and the consequent uncompensated destruction of the cedars, were not a compensable taking. The state had the right to conclude that apple orchards were more important to the state economy than cedars, and its decision to sacrifice the latter to save the former did not violate due process. *Miller v. Schoene*, 276 U.S. 272 (1928).

b.   Bar must fall within common-law nuisance principles: However, the mere fact that the legislature has labeled a certain use as being "harmful" or "noxious" is ***not enough*** to ensure that the land-use restriction will be found to be a regulation rather than a taking. If a land-use regulation is so severe that it deprives the owner of "all economically beneficial use of his land," then the restrictions must "do no more than duplicate the result that could have been achieved in the courts — by adjacent land owners ... under the State's law of ***private nuisance***, or by the State under its complementary power to abate nuisances that affect the public generally. ... " In other words, the legislature cannot suddenly decide that a particular use is so harmful that it should be immediately banned, if the ban will deprive an owner of all economically viable use of his land, and if the common law principles of nuisance would not allow the state to get the use forbidden by a court.

Example: Recall the *Lucas* case, *supra*, p. 417: South Carolina bans P and similarly-situated coastal land owners from building any permanent habitable structure on their property. *Held* (by the Supreme Court), given that the state courts have decided that this ban deprives P of all economically viable use of his land, then P has suffered a "taking" unless, under South Carolina law, the state could have achieved the same total ban on dwellings by use of the common law of nuisance. Furthermore, "it seems unlikely that common-law principles would have prevented the erection of any habitable or productive improvements on [P's] land; they rarely support prohibition of the 'essential use' of land." However, resolution of this issue is up to the South Carolina courts. *Lucas v. South Carolina Coastal Council*, *supra*, p. 417.

5.   **Zoning regulation:**   In cases where ***zoning regulations*** impair an owner's use of his property, the Court has been especially reluctant to find a compensable taking. A zoning ordinance will not be stricken as violative of due process unless it is ***"clearly arbitrary and unreasonable***, having no substantial relation to the public health, safety, morals or general welfare." *Moore v. East Cleveland*, 431 U.S. 494 (1977).

a.   *Moore:*   *Moore* itself was an extremely rare invalidation of a zoning ordinance. The ordinance there allowed only members of a "family" to live together, and defined "family" so narrowly that a grandmother was barred from living with her two grandchildren, one by each of two different children.

6.   **Other environmental regulation:**   Regulations designed to protect the ***environment*** are usually similarly subjected to only mild review, even if the property owner's ability to use his land is substantially circumscribed. See, e.g., *Goldblatt v. Hempstead*, 369 U.S. 590 (1962), upholding a town "safety regulation" preventing a property owner from continuing to mine a sand and gravel pit as he had done for 30 years; the ban was justified as a

"reasonable" exercise of the "police power," and the Court contended that the diminution in the value of the property, although relevant, was not conclusive. (But again, remember that if the regulation completely deprives an owner of economically viable use of his land, and that regulation could not be justified under common-law nuisance principles, a "taking" will occur even if the government's objective is to protect the environment. See *Lucas v. South Carolina Coastal Council, supra*, p. 417.)

7. **Landmark preservation:** *Landmark preservation* schemes, like zoning and environmental regulations, will *seldom* constitute a taking. In *Penn Central Transportation Co. v. New York City*, 438 U.S. 104 (1978), the Court found that the New York City Landmarks Preservation Law did not effect a taking of plaintiff's property.

   a. **Facts:** Plaintiff was the owner of Grand Central Terminal, which was designated as a "landmark" under the Law. As a consequence, the building's exterior was required to be kept "in good repair," and administrative approval was necessary for any alteration. Plaintiff sought such approval to construct a 55-story office building above the Terminal, but this request was denied on the grounds that the new structure would clash with the Terminal's beaux arts facade.

   b. **Holding and rationale:** A six-Justice majority held that so long as landmark preservation is carried out as part of a *comprehensive* preservation scheme, development of individual landmarks may be curtailed without effecting a taking. The New York City statute met the requirement of comprehensiveness. The opinion found landmark preservation schemes to be akin to zoning laws (although the Court conceded that the effect of a preservation scheme typically falls heavily upon a few, in contrast to the widespread impact of a zoning scheme).

      i. **Use of "transferable development rights":** In determining that there was no taking, the Court took into account the fact that New York City gave the owners of landmark buildings so-called "transferable development rights" (TDRs), which could be used to increase the permissible size of other, non-landmark, buildings owned by the same owner. Because, in the Court's opinion, these TDRs had value, the economic impact on the owner of a landmark building fell short of what would be required before a taking could be found.

   c. **Dissent:** Justice Rehnquist, joined by two other members of the Court, dissented from the *Penn Central* holding. The regulation here was a taking, the dissent contended, because it was a serious destruction of property, and was not justified either under the "nuisance" rationale (see *supra*, p. 418) or the rationale of zoning-type laws. The latter are not takings, the dissenters argued, only because they apply to a broad cross-section of land, and thereby materially benefit as well as restrict the affected landowners. In the case of a landmark preservation scheme, by contrast, an extreme sacrifice is made by a small number of landowners, who receive only a negligible benefit.

8. **Tight means-end fit required:** The Supreme Court has for the last several decades required, in at least some kinds of cases, a *very close fit* between the *means* chosen by the state (i.e., the particular land-use regulation selected) and the governmental *objective* being pursued. In this category of cases, even a compelling state interest will be to no avail

if the means chosen by the government are not quite closely tailored to advance that interest.

a. Applies only to "dedications": This approach requiring a tighter means-end fit applies, so far, only in the special case in which the government attempts to require property owners to *"dedicate"* (i.e., *give away*) to the public some piece of land, cash or other property in return for approval of a land-use permit.

b. Summary of rule: As the Court has summarize this approach to dedications, "a unit of government *may not condition the approval of a land-use permit* on the owner's *relinquishment of a portion of his property* unless there is a *'nexus'* and *'rough proportionality'* between the government's demand and the effects of the proposed land use." *Koontz v. St. Johns River Water Mgmt. Dist.*, 133 S. Ct. 2586 (2013).

  i. Contrast with other areas of regulation: This requirement of a tight means-end fit in land-use cases involving dedications contrasts quite sharply with the Court's easy-to-satisfy standard in other economic regulation contexts, where all that is required is that the relation between the means chosen and the end being pursued be *"merely rational"* (see *supra*, pp. 170 and 256).

  We'll look at the three main cases in which the Court has imposed its tough approach to dedications. In these cases, the Court in sequence decided that:

  [1] When government makes a permit conditional on a dedication, the means chosen by government (the particular dedication required) must *"substantially advance"* the land-use objective that the government is pursuing. (See *Nollan*, immediately below);

  [2] There must be a *"rough proportionality"* between the *burdens* that issuance of the land-use permit would cause to the public, and the *benefits* that would accrue to the public from the dedication. (See *Dolan*, *infra*, p. 422.)

  [3] The above two requirements apply not only where the government *grants* the permit *on condition* that a dedication be made, but also where the government *denies the permit outright*, while *"suggesting"* that the outcome would be different — i.e., that the permit would be issued — if the landowner voluntarily makes the dedication. (See *Koontz*, *infra*, p. 423.)

c. The "substantially advance" requirement: The first case announcing tougher standard for dedications was *Nollan v. California Coastal Commission*, 483 U.S. 825 (1987). There, the Court required that the *means chosen* by the government (the dedication required as a condition to the permit) *"substantially advance"* the governmental *objective* being pursued. Or, as the Court also put it, there must be an *"essential nexus"* between the dedication exacted as a condition to issuance of the permit, and the "legitimate state interest" being pursued by government in demanding the dedication.

  i. Facts: The land-use regulation at issue in *Nollan* said that the Ps could rebuild their house on their beach front property only on condition that they first *gave the public an easement* across a sandy strip of the property adjacent to the ocean. The government body that issued the regulation was mainly concerned that the Ps would replace their small bungalow with a much bigger house, thus blocking the public's view of the beach.

ii.   Holding: By a 5-4 vote, the Court held that the Commission's conditioning the issuance of the building permit upon transfer of the easement *amounted to a taking*, for which compensation must be paid. In arriving at this conclusion, the majority opinion (written by Justice Scalia), reasoned as follows:

[1] If the government had simply *required the Ps to give the public an easement* over their property, this would clearly have been a taking, since it would be a "permanent physical occupation" (even though no particular individual would be permitted to station himself permanently on the property);

[2] On the other hand, an outright *refusal* by the government to grant the permit would *not* constitute a taking, so long as the refusal "substantially advanced a legitimate state interest" and did not "deny an owner economically viable use of his land"; and

[3] The granting of the permit *subject to conditions* must be evaluated by the same standard as an outright refusal would have been. Therefore, *only if the conditions* attached to the grant of the permit *"substantially advance"* — or have an *"essential nexus"* with — *the legitimate state interests being pursued* will the conditions be valid.

iii.   Loose means-end fit: Requirement (3) was *not satisfied* on the facts of *Nollan*, in the majority's view, because the *harms feared* by the government would *not be cured or even materially lessened* by the means chosen (the easement). For instance, there was no reason to believe that the easement would reduce obstacles to viewing the beach created by the new house, since the easement would only help people already on public beaches north or south of the Ps' property. In the majority's view, the building restriction was "not a valid regulation of land use but 'an out-and-out *plan of extortion*.' "

d.   The "rough proportionality" requirement: After *Nollan*, in an even more striking use of rigorous review, the Court held that when a city conditions a building permit on some *"give back"* ("dedication") by the owner, there must be a *"rough proportionality"* between the *burdens on the public* that the permitted development would bring about, and the *benefit* to the public from the give back on which the permit was conditioned. This "rough proportionality" standard was announced in *Dolan v. City of Tigard*, 512 U.S. 374 (1994).

i.   Facts: In *Dolan*, P was a property owner who wanted to enlarge the plumbing and electric supply store she ran on the property. D, the city of Tigard, issued her a permit to do this, but conditioned the permit on P's willingness to (among other things) convey a 15-foot strip of land on her property to the city, to be used as a bicycle pathway. (She would have been required to convey approximately 10% of the property.) The city, at the time it asked for the trade-off, asserted two reasons for it: (1) P would be paving over a larger part of her property, thus expanding the "impervious surface" and *worsening the danger of flooding* from a nearby creek; the unpaved pathway would help soak up some of the flood waters; and (2) P's bigger store would *increase automobile traffic* to her site; the bike path, by increasing the attractiveness of biking, might result in a *countervailing decrease in car traffic.*

ii. P's attack: P attacked the requirement that she convey the 15-foot strip as an unconstitutional taking of her property without compensation.

iii. Court agrees: The Court, by a 5-4 vote, *agreed* with P that the trade-off requirement was an unconstitutional taking of P's property. The Court first repeated *Nollan*'s statement that there had to be an "essential nexus" between the permit condition exacted by the city, and the "legitimate state interest" being pursued.

(1) Satisfied: The Court found this requirement *satisfied* here. There was a nexus between preventing flooding from the creek and limiting development on P's property. Similarly, there was a nexus between reducing traffic congestion and providing for an alternative means of transport, biking.

iv. "Rough proportionality": But the novel part of the Court's holding came in the imposition of a *second* requirement that any permit condition must now meet: there must be a *"rough proportionality"* between the size of the give-back demanded by the city and the burden to the public caused by P's proposed development (for which the give-back was supposed to compensate).

(1) Not satisfied: The Court found that the city here had *not* satisfied this "rough proportionality" requirement. For example, although the city had calculated somewhat precisely the number of additional car trips per day that would be caused by P's expansion, the city had not tried to show how much of this traffic *would be reduced by the proposed bikeway* — it was not enough for the city to conclude, as it had, that the proposed bikeway *"could"* offset some of the traffic demand (though a finding that the bikeway "would" or "was likely to" offset some of the demand would apparently have sufficed).

e. Denial of permit plus suggestions for a cure: *Nollan* and *Dolan* were both cases in which the government *granted* a permit, but *conditioned the grant* on the owner's compliance with what the Court later found to be inappropriate conditions (the exaction). Suppose, instead, that government *denies* the permit outright, but then *suggests* that if the land owner were to make some specified dedication, or pay some specified sum of money to be used on another parcel, the permit denial might be reversed. Does government's use of this structure — *"denial with suggestions for a cure"* — change the analysis? The court answered this question in the *negative* in *Koontz v. St. Johns River Water Mgmt. Dist.,* 133 S. Ct. 2586 (2013).

i. Facts: P, the owner of wetlands property, was required to get a permit for a state-run Water Management District in order to that develop the property. Under state law, the District could issue the needed permit only if it was satisfied that P was mitigating the environmental damage the development would cause. P proposed particular mitigation measures to the District, but the District rejected them as insufficient, and indicated it would not issue the permit. However, the District indicated that if P was willing to pay for certain improvements to wetlands property owned by the District, the District would issue the permit. P refused this suggestion, the District refused to issue the permit, and P sued the District on a *Nollan/Dolan* taking theory.

ii. Issue: The issue was whether *Nollan* and *Dolan* applied to situations like this, in which the government never issues a conditional permit, but instead denies the permit outright while indicating that the owner could change the results by making a particular dedication or paying for some improvement on other land.

iii. State loses: The Court answered, by a 5-4 vote, that *Nollan* and *Dolan* **apply even to this "suggestion" scenario.** The majority opinion, by Justice Alito, said that the principles behind *Nollan* and *Dolan* "do not change depending on whether the government **approves a permit on the condition** that the applicant turn over property or **denies a permit because the applicant refuses** to do so."

   (1) Unconstitutional condition: Alito conceded that the government would have been entitled to simply **deny the permit outright**, with no possibility for P to make a dedication that would reverse the denial. But, he said, under the doctrine of *"unconstitutional conditions"* (see *infra*, p. 624), "we have repeatedly rejected the argument that if the government need not confer a benefit at all, it can withhold the benefit because someone refuses to give up constitutional rights."

   (2) Rationale: Alito also reasoned that a contrary rule would enable governments to **evade *Nollan* and *Dolan*.** "[A] government order stating that a permit is *'approved if'* the owner turns over property would be subject to *Nollan* and *Dolan*, but an identical order that uses the words *'denied until'* would not." The form of words used should not make a constitutional difference, he said.

iv. Ginsburg's dissent: Justice Ginsburg dissented on various grounds. Most importantly, she believed that the government commits a taking "only when it **appropriates a specific property interest**, not when it **requires a person to pay or spend money**." Here, the District never took or tried to take an interest in P's property; it merely tried to extract from him a commitment to **spend money** to repair public wetlands.

   (1) Government will never give suggestions: Ginsburg also thought that the majority's approach would lead governments to go out of their way to avoid helping applicants. Suppose, she said, that the lawyer advising a government body concludes that a permit application does not meet legal requirements. The lawyer can advise the government in two different ways: that it simply issue a flat denial of the permit without explanation; or, that it **suggest ways** for the landowner to **bring his application into compliance**. "If every suggestion could become the subject of a lawsuit under *Nollan* and *Dolan*," the lawyer will advise the government to "[d]eny the permits, without giving [the applicant] any advice — **even if he asks for guidance**." She concluded that "nothing in the Takings Clause requires that folly."

f. Significance: *Nollan, Dolan* and *Koontz* demonstrate a much harsher review by the Court of land-use regulations. We now have a scheme whereby, when government conditions some land-use permission on the owner's "give-back" of a significant property right — or even suggests that permission won't be granted until the owner makes such a give-back — two conditions must be met:

❏ the means chosen by the local government unit must **"substantially advance"** a legitimate aim; and

❏ the benefit to the public from the give-back must be **"roughly proportional"** to the harm caused by the new land use.

9. **Subsequent owner who takes with notice of restriction:** Suppose the case is one of those relatively uncommon ones in which the land-use restriction is so great that a taking will be deemed to have occurred. What happens if the person who owns the property at the time the regulation is put into effect does not sue, but a **subsequent buyer** — who buys the property **with knowledge** of the restriction — then sues on a takings theory?

   a. **New buyer may sue:** The Supreme Court has held that the subsequent buyer **may proceed** with the suit just as the original owner could have. A contrary rule, the Court held, would enable the state in effect "to put an expiration date on the Takings Clause." This ought not to be the rule, the Court continued, because "[f]uture generations, too, have a right to challenge unreasonable limitations on the use and value of land." *Palazzolo v. Rhode Island*, 533 U.S. 606 (2001).

C. **Requirement of "public" use:** Recall that the Taking Clause says that private property shall not be taken **"for public use"** unless just compensation is paid. This language has been interpreted by the Supreme Court as prohibiting the taking of private property for **private use, even if just compensation is made.** Thus the federal government (and, under an analogous interpretation of the Fourteenth Amendment, a state government) cannot simply take private property from one person, and give it to another, without any public purpose.

1. **"Public use" construed broadly:** However, the Supreme Court has construed the requirement of a "public use" quite **broadly.** Here are two principles illustrating just how broadly the Court stretches the phrase:

   ❏ So long as the state's use of its eminent domain power is **"rationally related** to a **conceivable public purpose,"** the public use requirement is satisfied. *Hawaii Housing Authority v. Midkiff*, 467 U.S. 229 (1984).

   ❏ The property **need not be open to the general public after the taking.** As the first rule above suggests, all that "public use" means is that the property be used for a "public purpose." *Kelo v. New London*, 545 U.S. 469 (2005). Therefore, the fact that the property is **turned over to some private user** does not prevent the use from being a public one as long as the public can be expected to derive some benefit (e.g., economic development) from the use. *Midkiff, supra.*

2. **Transfer to private owner:** The principle that there can be a public use even though the property is **turned over to a private user** is illustrated by **Hawaii Housing Authority v. Midkiff**, *supra*. There, the Court upheld a scheme whereby Hawaii used its eminent domain power to acquire lots owned by large landowners, and transferred them to the tenants living on them, or to other non-landowners. Since there was tremendous inequality in land ownership (on Oahu, the most urbanized island, 22 landowners owned 75.5% of the privately-owned land), and since thousands of homeowners had been forced to lease rather

than to buy the land under their homes, the state's scheme was a rational attempt to remedy a social and economic evil. As with any other state conduct sought to be justified as an exercise of the police power, all that was required was that the legislature "rationally could have believed" that the act would promote a legitimate objective; the scheme here easily passed this test.

3. **Urban renewal and economic development:** Similarly, the public use requirement can be met even though the government is pursuing the diffuse goal of *"economic development,"* and even if it is doing so by condemning parcels in *non-blighted* areas. This was the controversial result in a 5-4 decision in the 2005 case of *Kelo v. New London, supra.*

   a. **Facts:** In *Kelo*, the long-struggling city of New London, Connecticut wanted to revitalize itself economically by carrying out a redevelopment plan that included building a $300 million research facility for the Pfizer pharmaceutical company, plus an adjacent conference hotel, residences and pedestrian "riverwalk" along the Thames River. The city believed that the development plan would create jobs, generate tax revenue, and revitalize the downtown. The plaintiffs were the owners of about 15 properties condemned by the city. These properties were mostly owner-occupied houses; none was in poor condition, but all were in the development area.

   b. **Ps' claim:** The plaintiffs claimed that a city's decision to take non-blighted property for the purpose of economic development was not a "public use."

   c. **Majority upholds taking:** By a 5-4 vote, the Supreme Court disagreed with the plaintiffs and upheld the condemnation. Justice Stevens wrote for the majority.

      i. **Only a "public purpose" is required:** Stevens began by saying that the requirement of public use did *not mean that the property had to be made open to, or used by, the public at large.* All that was required was that there be a *"public purpose"* behind the taking. Furthermore, the concept of "public purpose" was to be broadly defined, reflecting the court's "longstanding policy of *deference to legislative judgments* in this field."

      ii. **Application:** Stevens then quickly concluded that New London's plan here met the requirement of public purpose. The city's economic development plan was "carefully formulated," and "comprehensive in character." The city believed that the plan would create new jobs and increased tax revenue. Therefore, Stevens concluded, it easily met the requirement that it serve a public purpose.

   d. **Dissent:** Justice O'Connor *dissented*, joined by Chief Justice Rehnquist and Justices Scalia and Thomas. She would have held that takings for the purpose of economic development are simply not constitutional, because they are not for public use. "Under the banner of economic development, all private property is now vulnerable to being taken and transferred to another private owner, so long as it might be upgraded — i.e., given to an owner who will use it in a way that the legislature deems more beneficial to the public[.]" Indeed, O'Connor could not see *any logical limit* on government's power under the majority's approach: "For who among us can say she already makes the most productive or attractive possible use of her property? *The specter of condemnation hangs over all property.* Nothing is to prevent the State from replacing any

Motel 6 with a Ritz-Carlton, any home with a shopping mall, or any farm with a factory."

    i. Justice Thomas' dissent: Justice Thomas dissented separately. He would have gone even farther than O'Connor, allowing a taking "only if the government or the public *actually uses* the taken property." Thomas also warned that the majority's rule allowing economic-development takings "guarantees that [the] losses will fall disproportionately on *poor communities*."

e. Raw transfer to the politically favored: After *Kelo*, does the "public use" requirement have any bite at all? The answer seems to be "very little." One sliver of continuing significance is hinted at by a concurrence by Justice Kennedy, in supplying the fifth vote to uphold New London's plan. Kennedy asserted that if a taking were clearly shown to have been ***"intended to favor a particular private party***, with only *incidental or pretextural public benefits,"* it would be invalid. (That obviously hadn't happened in *Kelo*, since New London's plan was a comprehensive one, and since the identity of most of the private beneficiaries was unknown at the time the plan was formulated.)

    i. Conclusion: Since four members of the Court would not allow economic-development takings at all, Kennedy's opinion makes it clear that a transfer whose only real purpose is shown to be to take *A*'s property for the purpose of advantaging the politically powerful *B* would be invalid for failing to serve a public purpose. However, it will be a rare case indeed when the government acts so crudely (and with such poor legal advice) that such a conclusion of no-public-purpose will be reached. For all practical purposes, the public use provision *no longer meaningfully binds government.*

III. THE "CONTRACT" CLAUSE

A. The "Contract" Clause generally: One of the few protections against state action given to individuals in the body of the Constitution (as distinguished from the Bill of Rights or other amendments) comes in Article I, §10: "No State shall ... pass any ... Law impairing the Obligation of Contracts. ... " This so-called Contract Clause by its terms applies only to the states. But a similar or identical rule has been held applicable to the federal government, by virtue of the Fifth Amendment's Due Process Clause. See *Lynch v. U.S.*, 292 U.S. 571 (1934); see also Tribe, p. 613.

1. Purpose: The Contract Clause was enacted principally for the purpose of protecting creditors against *debtor relief laws*, by which the obligations of debtors were often postponed or even completely lifted. Such protection of creditors' rights was thought to be necessary for the economic development of the country. See N&R, p. 406.

2. Extension to public grants: But the Clause was quickly extended to include the prevention of the impairment of "public" contracts, i.e., contracts between the government and private parties.

3. Two-part discussion: Our discussion below is divided into two aspects: (1) the use of the Contract Clause to protect *public* agreements, i.e., those to which government is a party; and (2) the use of the Clause to protect agreements between private parties. There is reason to believe that the Supreme Court today favors stricter review of cases falling within (1) than of those coming within (2).

B. Protection of public agreements: Until 1977, it appeared that the Supreme Court had virtually abandoned the Contract Clause as a limitation on states' rights to modify "public" contracts.

1. **Some elements remain (*U.S. Trust* case):**   But the Clause has turned out to have some real bite left in it, due in large part to *U.S. Trust Co. v. New Jersey*, 431 U.S. 1 (1977). That case marked the first time in almost four decades that the Supreme Court invalidated a state law on Contract Clause grounds. The case indicates that the Court will scrutinize somewhat closely a state's attempt to *escape* from its *financial obligations*, and will only permit such an escape where a *significant public need* exists that cannot be reasonably handled in any other way.

   a. **Facts of *U.S. Trust*:**   In a 1962 bond issue, the Port Authority of New York and New Jersey promised bondholders that certain revenues pledged as security for the bonds would not be used to finance unprofitable passenger railroad systems in the future. In 1974, New York and New Jersey retroactively repealed this covenant, so that the pledged revenues (including bridge and tunnel tolls) could be used to improve rail service. U.S. Trust Co., one of the bondholders, sued on the grounds that the repeal violated the Contract Clause.

   b. **Contract Clause found violated:**   The Supreme Court found, by a 4-3 majority, that the repeal violated the Contract Clause. The majority opinion, by Justice Blackmun, stated the following test: an impairment of contractual obligations will be constitutional only if it is "*reasonable* and *necessary* to support an *important public purpose*."

      i. **"Necessity" defined:**   A contractual impairment was "necessary" only when the state's public interest objectives could not be met by *less drastic* modification of the contract. Here, alternative means existed for improving mass transit (and also of discouraging automobile use, a second major state goal).

      ii. **"Reasonable" defined:**   An impairment was "reasonable," as the Court used the term, only if the modification was induced by *unforeseen developments* occurring after the original contract was made. In contrast to the situation in *El Paso v. Simmons*, 379 U.S. 497 (1965), where the dramatic increase in land values stemming from the discovery of oil and gas was unforeseeable, the public need for mass transit improvements was quite foreseeable at the time the covenant to bondholders was made in 1962. Indeed, it was precisely to forestall use of pledged revenues to cope with concerns like those motivating the Port Authority here, that had led to the making of the covenant.

C. Protection of private contracts: The principal purpose of the Contract Clause was to curtail populist *debtor-relief* laws. The Framers' fears of such laws seem to have been justified; most of the private-agreement cases under the Contract Clause have indeed involved debtor relief. The development of Contract Clause doctrine in private-agreement cases has been roughly similar to that in the public-agreement situations discussed above: originally a fairly broad use of the Clause to strike down legislation, a near abandonment of the Clause during the 20th century, and a resuscitation by the Burger/Rehnquist Court.

1. **Debtor relief laws:** The Court has steadily cut back on the use of the Contract Clause as a limitation on debtor relief laws. It remains the case that a state legislature may not completely absolve debtors of obligations incurred prior to the legislature's action. But whereas the Contract Clause was once a barrier to any impairment of creditors' rights, the impact of the Clause has been curtailed in a number of ways.

2. **Prospective only:** Insolvency laws may relieve debtors from obligations contracted *after* the law is enacted. That is, only *retroactive* laws are barred by the Contract Clause. *Ogden v. Saunders*, 25 U.S. (12 Wheat.) 213 (1827).

3. **Remedies:** Although a creditor's basic rights may not be impaired, his "*remedies*," i.e., the means by which he enforces those rights, may be modified. For instance, extensions of time can be given. This distinction between rights and remedies is an obscure and difficult one; but the basic idea is that the underlying obligation may not be impaired, although the creditor's right to strict compliance with all aspects of the contract may be modified.

4. **Protection of public interest:** An even broader exception to the Contract Clause is that debtors' obligations may be modified where a *vital public interest*, especially an economic emergency, so demands.

   a. ***Blaisdell* case:** One of the best known modern Contract Clause cases, ***Home Building & Loan Ass'n v. Blaisdell***, 290 U.S. 398 (1934), involved such an emergency modification of debtors' obligations. That case involved a Minnesota statute, enacted at the height of the Depression, which allowed local courts to give relief from mortgage foreclosure sales. The courts were permitted to give extensions from such sales, provided that the mortgagor paid "all or a reasonable part" of the property's fair income or rental value. The measure was intended to apply to mortgages issued prior to the date of the law; i.e., the statute was retroactive.

      i. **Right to protect public interest:** The Supreme Court *upheld* the statute, on the theory that the state had at least the right to temporarily delay enforcement of a mortgage's literal terms, where "vital public interests" would otherwise suffer. In view of the enormous economic emergency which gave rise to the statute, the modification was a limited and reasonable one. The Court stressed that principal remained due, interest continued to run, the right of foreclosure would ultimately be restored, and the statute would (the Court assumed) be rescinded once the economic emergency was over.

      ii. **Implied power to modify:** In justifying this limited right to modify contracts in order to protect the public interest, the *Blaisdell* Court noted that "[t]he reservation of *essential attributes of sovereign power* is … read into contracts as a postulate of the legal order." As Tribe (p. 616) interprets this statement, it means that "[o]ne of the 'rules' that may be read into every contract at its inception is the rule that all *other* rules are subject to change if and when the legislature reasonably concludes that such change is needed."

5. Renaissance of the Clause (The *Allied Structural Steel* case): The Contract Clause has been saved from extinction in private-agreement cases, just as *U.S. Trust Case* (*supra*, p. 428) did this in public-contract cases. In *Allied Structural Steel Co. v. Spannaus*, 438 U.S. 234 (1978), the Supreme Court invalidated an attempt by Minnesota to expand the pension obligations of certain Minnesota employers who closed a plant in the state. Perhaps even more than the *U.S. Trust* decision, the *Allied Structural* holding seems to indicate that the Contract Clause may now be used as a significant weapon against state police power regulations which affect contracts.

a. **Facts:** The Minnesota statute provided that when certain Minnesota employers closed down their operations in the state, or terminated a pension plan, any employee who had worked for the firm for more than ten years became "vested" in (i.e., entitled to benefits under) any pension plan the company might have. Allied's pension plan did not provide, in most cases, for vesting until long after ten years; the plan also provided that it could be terminated at any time, with no obligation to those employees who had not yet vested. When Allied closed its plant (which it had planned to do even before the statute was enacted, and which it did shortly thereafter), it was therefore required to pay pensions to workers who would not have been covered by the plan absent the statute.

b. **Holding:** By a 5-3 majority, the Supreme Court found that the Minnesota statute violated the Contract Clause. The majority opinion, by Justice Stewart, conceded that the police power allowed the states to make minor, and in a few circumstances substantial, modifications to contracts.

  i. **Strict requirements:** But the Court held that the modification here was a substantial one, and that it could therefore be sustained only if a series of factors like those existing in *Blaisdell* (*supra*, p. 429) also existed. The Court read these to include: (1) that there be an *emergency*; (2) that the measure be enacted to protect a "*basic societal interest, not a favored group*"; (3) that the relief be "appropriately *tailored*" to the emergency; (4) that the modifications be "*reasonable*" in scope; and (5) that the statute be limited to the duration of the emergency. The Court found that factors (1) and (2) were not present, since the legislative history did not disclose any major emergency to which the statute was a response, and since, in the Court's view, only a very limited number of employers and employees would be affected. The Court also implied that the effect on a company like Allied was also so drastic and permanent that conditions (3), (4) and (5) were not met either.

  ii. **Violation of reasonable expectations:** The majority also objected to the fact that the statute imposed a "sudden, totally unanticipated, and substantial *retroactive* obligation." This, coupled with the fact that Minnesota had never regulated the area of pensions previously, seemed to the majority to violate Allied's *reasonable expectations* about what it was getting into when it started a pension plan.

c. **Dissent:** Justice Brennan dissented (joined by Justices White and Marshall). Brennan argued that the Minnesota statute simply created an "additional, supplemental duty of the employer," and that the Contract Clause, in its prohibition on the "impairment" of contractual duties, did not prohibit the creation of new duties.

D. More deferential standard: The *U.S. Trust* and *Allied Steel* cases represent significant revitalizations of the Contract Clause, in the case of public and private agreements, respectively. However, developments following these two decisions indicate that the Court will probably not embark on a course of wholesale invalidation of state legislation on Contract Clause grounds. The Court articulated a new standard of review for Contract Clause challenges, a standard which is apparently applicable to both public and private agreements. Although the Court claimed to be relying principally on *U.S. Trust* and *Allied Steel*, this newly-formulated standard of review seems to be **significantly more deferential** to state legislative judgments. **Energy Reserves Group, Inc. v. Kansas Power and Light Co.**, 459 U.S. 400 (1983).

1. **Three-part test:** In *Energy Reserves*, the Court articulated the following three-step test for evaluating Contract Clause challenges:

   a. **Threshold inquiry:** First, the court must make a "threshold inquiry" as to "whether the state law has, in fact, operated as a **substantial impairment** of a contractual relationship."

   b. **Legitimate public purpose:** If this threshold inquiry yields an affirmative result (i.e., the court finds that there has been a "substantial impairment"), the state must demonstrate that it has a **"significant and legitimate public purpose"** which the regulation is intended to serve.

   c. **"Reasonable and appropriate":** If the state does show such a "legitimate public purpose," the court must then take the final step of determining "whether the adjustment of 'the rights and responsibilities of contracting parties [is based] upon **reasonable conditions** and [is] of a character **appropriate to the public purpose**'" asserted in support of the regulation.

2. **Distinction between public and private contracts:** The three-part *Energy Reserves* test is, as noted, apparently now applicable both to contracts in which the state is a party and to purely private contracts. However, the Court will undoubtedly apply that test with **significantly greater strictness** where the state is attempting to make **its own contractual obligations less burdensome**. In a footnote, the *Energy Reserves* Court cited approvingly the statement in *U.S. Trust* that when the state is a party to the contract, "complete deference to a legislative assessment of reasonableness and necessity is not appropriate because the State's self-interest is at stake."

E. Incidental effect on contracts: Even the relatively deferential standard now in force as the result of *Energy Reserves* is applicable only where the state takes an action that is **specifically directed** at contractual obligations. If the state applies a **"generally applicable rule of conduct"** which has the **incidental by-product** of impairing contractual obligations, the Contract Clause **does not apply at all**. This rule was stated and applied in *Exxon Corp. v. Eagerton*, 462 U.S. 176 (1983).

1. **Facts:** In *Exxon*, Alabama increased its severance taxes on oil and gas, and prohibited oil and gas producers from passing on the increase directly or indirectly to consumers. This prohibition had the effect of blocking Exxon from taking advantage of clauses in its existing contracts permitting it to pass on tax increases to its customers.

2. **Regulation upheld:** The Court unanimously upheld the Alabama pass-through prohibition. The Alabama law "did not prescribe a rule limited in effect to contractual obligations or remedies, but instead imposed a generally applicable rule of conduct." Therefore, the law did not trigger Contract Clause analysis at all.

F. **Other retroactivity issues:** The notion of retroactivity has been a strong theme in the Contract Clause cases discussed above — one could argue that the very idea behind the Contract Clause is that contractual obligations, once fixed, will not be retroactively upset by legislative action. Retroactivity is similarly a key theme of the *Ex Post Facto* and Bill of Attainder Clauses (discussed *infra*, p. 440 and p. 441 respectively).

1. **Use of Due Process Clauses:** Still other possible sources of protection against retroactive legislative action are the *Due Process* Clauses of the Fifth and Fourteenth Amendments. Because these clauses are less specific than the Contract, Bill of Attainder and *Ex Post Facto* Clauses, it is a rare retroactive act which will be invalidated by use of due process analysis.

   a. **Rational relation test:** In most situations, the Supreme Court now seems to require merely that there be a *rational relation* between the retroactive legislation and a legitimate government objective.

   b. **Modification of government's own obligation:** But where the government *modifies its own contractual obligations*, the standard for judicial review is likely to be somewhat more stringent than that of the "mere-rationality" test.

IV. THE SECOND AMENDMENT "RIGHT TO BEAR ARMS"

A. **Text of the Amendment:** The Second Amendment provides: "A well regulated Militia, being necessary to the security of a free State, the right of the people to *keep and bear Arms*, shall *not be infringed*."

B. **Applicable to private individuals (the *Heller* case):** Until recently, the Amendment had never been recognized by the Supreme Court as giving *private citizens* the right to keep firearms. But in a stunning 2008 case, decided by a 5-4 vote, *District of Columbia v. Heller*, 128 S.Ct. 2783 (2008), the Court struck down the District of Columbia's strict gun-control laws on Second Amendment grounds. The majority asserted that "the inherent right of self-defense has been central to the Second Amendment right," and concluded that the *Amendment confers on private individuals a right to keep basic firearms, including handguns, at home for self-defense.*

1. **Significance of *Heller*:** The only significant prior Supreme Court decision on the meaning of the Second Amendment, a 1939 case, had been widely interpreted as saying that the Second Amendment gave no rights to private individuals, and merely protected the right of "well regulated militias" (now known as state National Guard units) to keep their members armed while on duty. But *Heller* concluded that this was not the correct reading of the 1939 case, and that the Amendment confers on private citizens, not just militias, the right to keep at least some kinds of weapons for self-defense and recreational purposes.

2. **D.C. statute:** The D.C. gun-control statute at issue in *Heller* was among the two or three strictest such statutes in America. The statute contained two distinct prohibitions that were challenged:

❏ First, the statute effectively ***banned the possession of handguns in the home*** — only registered firearms could be kept, and handguns could not be registered.

❏ Second, the statute required that firearms other than handguns (e.g., ***rifles*** and shotguns) could only be kept in the home if they were kept ***unloaded*** and either ***disassembled or disabled*** by a trigger lock.

3. **Challenge by P:** The plaintiff, Dick Heller, was a police officer who wanted to keep a handgun in his house. He asserted that each of the above two prohibitions violated his Second Amendment right to bear arms.

4. **Majority upholds:** By a 5-4 Vote, the court ***agreed*** that ***both provisions*** of the D.C. statute violated P's Second Amendment rights. The majority opinion was by Justice Scalia, and may well be his most important majority opinion since he joined the Court in 1986. Four members of the majority were those generally considered the conservative bloc of the court — in addition to Scalia they included Chief Justice Roberts and Justices Thomas and Alito. The critical fifth vote was supplied by Justice Kennedy, as has so often been the case in the Rehnquist and Roberts courts.

    a. **Language and history:** Scalia's opinion began by considering the history and language of the Second Amendment. He separately analyzed the "prefatory" clause ("A well regulated Militia, being necessary to the security of a free State...") and the "operative" clause ("the right of the people to keep and bear Arms shall not be infringed").

       i. **Operative clause:** As to the meaning of the *operative* clause, Scalia pointed to several elements that he said demonstrated that the clause was intended to give rights to ***individuals***, not just to members of state militias. First, the operative clause codified a ***"right of the people,"*** and the use of this phrase by other constitutional provisions (e.g., the First Amendment's assembly-and-petition clause) demonstrated that the phrase customarily referred to individual rights, not collective ones, he said. Second, historical and linguistic analysis showed that the phrase "keep and bear arms" was "unambiguously used to refer to the carrying of weapons outside of an organized militia." In summary, he said, the text and history of the operative clause "conferred an individual right to keep and bear arms."

       ii. **Prefatory clause:** Next, Scalia analyzed the ***prefatory*** clause, that is, the reference to "a well regulated militia, being necessary to the security of a free State..." As to the meaning of a "well regulated militia," Scalia rejected the dissent's reading of this term as being limited to officially-organized state-militias. For Scalia, the term "the militia" referred to ***"all males physically capable of acting in concert for the common defense,"*** and the adjective "well-regulated" implied merely "the imposition of proper discipline and training." The reference to "security of a free State" referred merely to a "free country" or "free polity," not to states as the operators of state militias. So the prefatory clause was not inconsistent with Scalia's "individual rights" interpretation, he argued.

iii. Historical purpose: Scalia then analyzed the ***historical purpose*** of the Amendment. The history behind the enactment of the Second Amendment, he said, was that English tyrants had eliminated the ability of "the militia" (i.e., able-bodied men) to resist tyranny "not by banning the militia but simply by taking away the people's arms," enabling a standing army supporting the tyrant to "suppress political opponents." Consequently, Scalia asserted, "[t]he threat that the new Federal Government would destroy the citizens' militia by taking away their arms was the reason that right ... was codified in a written constitution."

iv. Summary of history and language: In sum, the history leading to the enactment of the Second Amendment, and the common 18th-century meaning of the phrases used in it, convinced Scalia that the framers intended to grant individual citizens the right to bear arms for self-defense, not merely to confer such a right upon official state militias.

b. Later interpretations: Scalia then argued that ***post-enactment interpretations*** of the Second Amendment had reached this same conclusion, that the Amendment conferred an individual right to bear arms for self-defense.

i. Distinguishing *Miller*: Scalia paid special attention to *U.S. v. Miller*, 307 U.S. 174 (1939), the Supreme Court's principal prior case on the meaning of the Second Amendment. *Miller* involved criminal charges of transporting an unregistered short-barreled shotgun; the Court rejected the defendants' argument that their conduct was protected by the Second Amendment.

(1) Dissent's view rejected: The dissent in *Heller* contended that in *Miller*, the Court had held that ***only military uses of guns were protected by the Amendment.*** But Scalia disagreed about what *Miller* said: *Miller* said "only that the Second Amendment does not protect those weapons not typically possessed by law-abiding citizens for lawful purposes, such as short-barreled shotguns." So for Scalia, *Miller* was not inconsistent with the *Heller* majority's conclusion that the Amendment protects the rights of law-abiding citizens to possess guns for self-defense.

c. What the amendment protects: Having concluded that the Amendment protects at least some rights of non-military individuals to bear arms, Scalia now turned to the ***scope*** of the right. On this score, he conceded that the right was ***not absolute or unlimited.*** The majority was not, he said, "cast[ing] doubt on long-standing prohibitions on the possession of firearms by ***felons*** and the ***mentally ill***, or laws forbidding the carrying of firearms in ***sensitive places such as schools and government buildings***, or laws imposing ***conditions and qualifications*** on the ***commercial sale*** of arms."

i. "Dangerous and unusual weapons": Furthermore, Scalia said, the Amendment protects only the carrying of weapons that were ***"in common use at the time"*** the Amendment was enacted, so that ***"dangerous and unusual weapons"*** (quoting an 18th century commentator) would ***not*** be protected. In an ambiguous sentence, Scalia seemed to be saying that what he called "weapons that are most useful in military service — M-16 rifles and the like," may be banned because they were not in common use at the time the Amendment was enacted.

d. Application to D.C. statute: Scalia then applied his reading of the Second Amendment to the D.C. statute before the Court. He addressed both of the District's bans: the complete ban on handgun possession, and the requirement that any non-handguns kept at home be kept in unloaded and inoperable form.

i. Ban on handguns: As to the absolute handgun ban, Scalia asserted that "the *inherent right of self-defense* has been *central* to the Second Amendment right." And, he said, D.C.'s complete ban on handgun possession in homes "amounts to a prohibition of an *entire class of 'arms'* that is *overwhelmingly chosen by American society* for that lawful purpose." Since handguns were the favored method of self defense in the home, a complete ban on them violated the Amendment. But Scalia did not specify what precise standard should be used, reserving that issue for future cases. The choie of standard was unnecessary to make here, he said, because the handgun ban was unconstitutional "under *any of the standards of scrutiny* that we have applied to *enumerated constitutional rights*." (In a footnote, Scalia explained that he was not asserting that the handgun ban would violate *rational-basis* review. But he seemed to be saying that under any of the more stringent standards used by the Supreme Court, such as intermediate-level review and strict scrutiny,[1] the complete handgun ban would be invalid.)

ii. Requirement that guns be unloaded and trigger-protected: Scalia then turned to the requirement that any gun the possession of which is not completely forbidden (e.g., rifles and shotguns) be kept *unloaded and inoperable* in the home. This requirement, he said, "makes it impossible for its citizens to use [such guns] for the core lawful purpose of self-defense and is hence unconstitutional." Therefore, this requirement, too, violated the Second Amendment.

e. Rejects "interest-balancing" approach: As noted, Scalia did not specify exactly *what standard of review* should be used in evaluating government actions that impact Second Amendment rights. But Scalia did reject the standard proposed by Justice Breyer in his dissent (see *infra*, p. 436). Breyer proposed an *"interest-balancing inquiry"*; for any regulation that significantly implicated competing constitutionally-protected interests, Breyer would ask merely whether the statute burdens a protected interest in a way or to an extent that is *"out of proportion"* to the statute's beneficial effects on some other protected interest. But Scalia dismissed this approach, saying that "a constitutional guarantee subject to future judges' assessments of its usefulness is no constitutional guarantee at all." In any event, he said, the Second Amendment "surely elevates above all other interests the *right of law-abiding, responsible citizens to use arms in defense of hearth and home."*

f. Application to *Heller*: Scalia then wrapped things up by saying that so long as the plaintiff (Heller) was not "disqualified from the exercise of Second Amendment rights,"[2] the District of Columbia *"must permit him to register his handgun* and must *issue him a license* to *carry it* in the home."

---

1. However, Scalia did not mention either of these standards by name.

2. Scalia seemed to be referring to classes of people whose right to possess arms may be nullified, such as felons and the mentally ill.

i. Handgun violence: Scalia conceded that *handgun violence* was a serious problem in America, and that "some measures *regulating* handguns" would be constitutionally acceptable methods of dealing with the violence problem. But, he said, "the enshrinement of constitutional rights necessarily *takes certain policy choices off the table.* These include the *absolute prohibition of handguns held and used for self-defense in the home.*"

5. Dissents: Four Justices *dissented,* in two separate opinions.

a. Stevens' dissent: The principal dissent was by Justice Stevens (joined by Justices Souter, Ginsburg and Breyer). Stevens reached a completely opposite conclusion from Scalia's as to the purpose and intent of the Second Amendment. The Amendment, he said, "was adopted to protect the right of the people of each of the several States to *maintain a well-regulated militia.* It was a response to concerns ... that the power of Congress to disarm the state militias and create a national standing army posed an intolerable threat to the sovereignty of the several states." The framers had not evidenced "the slightest interest in limiting any legislature's authority to regulate *private civilian uses* of firearms."

i. Burden on the Judiciary: Stevens then issued the kind of warning that in recent decades has usually been made by conservatives: that the majority's approach would *encourage judicial activism.* That approach "will surely give rise to a far more active judicial role in making vitally important national policy decisions than was envisioned at any time in the 18th, 19th and 20th centuries."

b. Breyer's dissent: Justice Breyer wrote a separate dissent, in which Stevens, Ginsburg and Souter joined. Breyer fully agreed with Stevens' argument that the Second Amendment only protects militia-related, not self-defense-related, interests. But, he said, even if the Amendment *were* read to protect self-defense-related interests, the D.C. statute should be found not to violate the Amendment.

i. Interest-balancing: Whenever a governmental regulation "significantly implicates *competing constitutionally protected interests* in complex ways," Breyer said, the Court does and should use an explicit *"interest-balancing inquiry."* That is, the Court asks "whether the statute burdens a protected interest in a way or to an extent that is *out of proportion to the statute's salutary effects upon other important governmental interests."*[3]

For instance, Breyer said, a proportionality approach is often used by the Court in free-speech and due process cases. Since gun control statutes, by reducing violence, have beneficial effects on citizens' constitutionally-protected interest in their lives and physical safety, the interest-balancing approach should be used here.

ii. Deference to legislature's empirical judgment: A key feature of the interest-balancing approach advocated by Breyer is, he said, that the Court *"defers to a legislature's empirical judgment* in matters where a legislature is likely to have *greater expertise and greater institutional fact-finding capacity."* Thus here, the

---

3. This is essentially a form of intermediate scrutiny, as Breyer correctly characterizes it.

legislature (of D.C.) concluded that a handgun ban would meaningfully reduce crime, and did so after a careful consideration by the relevant committee of extensive evidence about the link between handguns and urban violence. The only role of the courts should be to "assure that, in formulating its judgments, the legislature has *drawn reasonable inferences based on substantial evidence.*" And D.C. had easily met this standard here, Breyer said.

    iii. Summary: In sum, Breyer believed the District's gun-control law was "a *proportionate*, not a disproportionate, response to the compelling concerns that led the District to adopt it." Therefore, even if the Second Amendment were read to apply to keeping arms for self-defense purposes, the measure would be valid.

6. Applies to states and cities: *Heller* applied only to the federal government, since the District of Colombia is part of that government. But in a post-*Heller* case, **McDonald v. City of Chicago**, 130 S.Ct. ___ (2010), a 5-4 majority of the Court decided that the Second Amendment *applies the same way to state and local governments as it applies to the federal government.*

    a. Facts of *McDonald*: *McDonald* involved the very strict gun-control laws of two cities, Chicago and Oak Park, Ill. The ordinances effectively banned possession of handguns by almost all private citizens residing there. As in *Heller*, the plaintiffs were private citizens who wanted to keep guns in their homes for self-defense.

    b. Majority says incorporation applies: Five members of the Court agreed that the Second Amendment applies to state and local governments, not just to the federal government. However, no majority agreed with on *why* this should be. Justice Alito wrote for a four-justice plurality, and Justice Thomas, in a concurrence, added the fifth vote but on a different theory.

        i. Alito's plurality opinion: Justice Alito (joined by Roberts, Kennedy and Scalia), said that the Second Amendment was *incorporated* into the 14th Amendment's *Due Process Clause*, and thereby made applicable to the states.

            (1) Fundamental: Under the Court's precedents, for any Bill of Rights guarantee to be incorporated into due process, the guarantee had to be *"fundamental to our scheme of ordered liberty."* (See *supra*, p. 162.) For Alito, it was clear that the right to keep and bear arms satisfied this test: the right is "deeply rooted in this nation's *history and tradition*." For instance, he said, at the time the Fourteenth Amendment was ratified, 22 of the 37 states in the union had state constitutional provisions protecting the right.

            (2) Remanded: The Court did not decide whether the two city ordinances violated the Second Amendment; the Court remanded the cases to the lower courts to decide this question.

        ii. Thomas and the P-or-I Clause: Justice Thomas supplied the needed fifth vote, but he disagreed on the appropriate rationale. Thomas believed that the appropriate means to make the Second Amendment applicable to state and local governments was by use of the 14th amendment *"Privileges or Immunities" Clause* (*supra*, p. 412). Thomas thought that the Due Process Clause should be interpreted only to guarantee "***processes***," and that a Bill of Rights guarantee that was essentially ***substantive*** rather than procedural should be made applicable to the states if and only if the drafters of the 14th Amendment would have regarded it as a privilege or immunity (i.e., right) associated with national citizenship.[4]

    iii. Dissent: Justices Stevens, Ginsburg, Breyer and Sotomayor ***dissented***, in separate opinions by Stevens and Breyer. The dissenters believed that *Heller* had been incorrectly decided. But even if it had been correct, the dissenters would not have applied it to state and local governments, because they believed that the right to keep arms in the home for self-defense was ***not "intrinsic to ordered liberty,"*** as rights must be in order to be selectively incorporated into the Fourteenth Amendment Due Process Clause.

        (1) Stevens: Stevens, for instance, argued that there was no evidence that the right to keep a gun for self-defense was "critical to leading a life of ***autonomy, dignity, or political equality.***" He said that the fact that ***other advanced democracies***, including those sharing our British heritage, generally ***regulate firearms extensively*** "tends to weaken [the argument] that the right to possess a gun of one's choosing is fundamental to a life of liberty."

7. Standard to be used: It is unclear what ***standard*** the court will use for reviewing governmental restrictions that impair Second Amendment rights. Justice Scalia avoiding answering this question in *Heller*, saying merely that "under any of the standards of scrutiny that we have applied to enumerated Constitutional rights," the District's complete ban on handguns in the home would "fail constitutional muster." And the Court didn't address this issue of standard-of-review in *McDonald*, either.

    a. Intermediate-level review: The most likely outcome is that the Court will end up judging gun-control regulations by use of some variant of ***mid-level review***.

        i. Interest-balancing rejected: Justice Scalia's majority opinion in *Heller* explicitly ***rejected*** at least one version of intermediate-level scrutiny, namely the ***"interest balancing"*** approach advocated by Justice Breyer, under which the Court should ask "whether the statute burdens a protected interest in a way or to an extent that is out of proportion to the statute's salutary effects upon other important governmental interests."

        ii. Substantial-relation-to-important-interest: However, Scalia did not comment on the more ***traditional*** form of mid-level review, under which the question is whether the means chosen by government is ***"substantially related"*** to the achievement of an ***"important"*** governmental interest (a standard used in several free-speech areas such as regulation of commercial speech; see *infra*, p. 587).

---

4. Justice Thomas was unable to persuade any other member of the Court that the Privileges or Immunities Clause, rather than the Due Process Clause, was the correct basis on which to evaluate whether the Second Amendment should apply to the states. Justice Alito's plurality opinion rejected the P-or-I approach on grounds of *stare decisis*: for many decades, the issue of whether any particular Bill of Rights guarantee should be made applicable to the states via the 14th Amendment had been analyzed under Due Process Clause, and Alito saw no good reason to change that settled approach.

There is a good chance that this version of mid-level review will prove to be the ultimate standard.

b. Effect on gun laws: Even though we now now from *McDonald* that the Second Amendment applies to state and local gun laws, it's not clear that governments will lose very much of their practical power to regulate gun use.

i. Handgun bans: *Heller* and *McDonald* together pretty clearly mean that a ***total ban on handgun possession*** in the home would be unconstitutional, as would a requirement that non-handguns be stored in an interoperable and unloaded manner. So, for instance, Chicago's virtually complete ban on handguns — at issue in *McDonald*, but as to which the Supreme Court remanded to the lower courts — is vulnerable. But few cities, and no states, regulate handguns nearly as extensively as D.C. and Chicago do, so their restrictions may well survive.

ii. Licensing: It seems likely that ***licensing requirements*** will ***not*** be found to violate the Second Amendment as long as the procedures for obtaining a license are ***not unreasonably burdensome***, and are directed towards keeping guns out of the hands of people who do not have a Second Amendment right to possess them. So, for instance, since *Heller* makes it clear that government may ban ***felons*** and the ***mentally ill*** from possessing guns, a licensing requirement that would deny permits to such people — and that would give government a reasonable amount of time to check whether the applicant fell into these categories — would presumably be ***valid*** even if some form of strict scrutiny were used.

iii. Concealed-carry permits: Similarly, it seems likely that the Amendment will be found not to prohibit governments from banning the ***carrying of concealed weapons in public places.*** The majority opinion in *Heller* commented, seemingly approvingly, that "the majority of the 19th century courts to consider the question held that prohibitions on carrying concealed weapons were lawful under the Second Amendment or state analogues." Furthermore, if as the *Heller* majority asserts the thrust of the Second Amendment is to protect citizens' right of self-defense at home, it's hard to see how the Amendment is violated by prohibiting the carrying of concealed weapons outside the home.

iv. Barring certain types of weapons: One last open question is the ***types of weapons*** the possession of which is guaranteed by the Second Amendment. Scalia's opinion in *Heller* seems to agree that the 1939 *Miller* opinion was correct in holding that only those weapons that were ***"in common use at the time"*** the Amendment was adopted are protected, and that (in the words of an 18th Century commentator) ***"dangerous and unusual weapons" may be prohibited***. So presumably governments may ban the possession of modern weapons that are much more advanced and dangerous than those existing in 1791, such as ***machine guns, assault rifles*** and the ***sawed-off shotguns*** at issue in *Miller*.

v. Summary: So although the Second Amendment now recognizes some sort of individual right to bear arms, that right is likely to be found to be subject to ***heavy governmental regulation***. At the end of the day, it may well be the case that of gun regulations actually adopted by states or cities somewhere, only the very most extreme measures — like the virtually-total ban on handguns, and the requirement of trigger-locking of guns stored at home, both of which were invalidated in *Heller* — will be struck down.

V. *EX POST FACTO* LAWS

A. **Constitutional prohibition of *ex post facto laws:*** The Constitution prevents both the federal and state governments from enacting *ex post facto* laws. See Article I, §§ 9 and 10, respectively. An *ex post facto* law is one which has a *retroactive punitive effect*. This can happen in any of four ways:

1. **Definition altered:** The law retroactively *alters the definition* of a crime, so that an act that wasn't a crime at all at the time it was committed is now defined as a crime; or

2. **Aggravation:** The law retroactively *aggravates a crime*, re-defining it so as to make it a greater offense than it was when it was committed (e.g., by transforming what would have been manslaughter into murder);

3. **Increased punishment:** The law *increases the punishment* for an act that was a crime when it was committed; or

4. **Rules of evidence:** The law *alters the rules of evidence*, by allowing a conviction based on lesser evidence than was required at the time the act was committed.

Calder v. Bull, 3 U.S. 386 (1798) .

B. **Criminal conduct only:** The ban on *ex post facto* laws applies only to measures which are *criminal* or *penal*.

1. **Ambiguity:** However, the dividing line between criminal and civil penalties is not always clear. The following are major illustrations of what measures have and have not been considered criminal (and therefore barred or not barred by the *ex post facto* clause when applied to conduct occurring before enactment of the measure).

    a. **Criminal:** The following have been found to be criminal measures:

        i. **Imprisonment:** Any measure calling for *imprisonment;*

        ii. **Criminal fine:** Any other punitive measure which the government identifies as being part of its system of criminal punishment. For instance, if the statute defining a particular crime states that violators will be *fined* upon conviction, the fine will be treated as a criminal measure falling within the *ex post facto* clause.

    b. **Not criminal:** Conversely, other types of measures, even though they may be "punitive" in the broad sense, are deemed civil rather than criminal, and therefore *not* subject to the ban on *ex post facto* laws.

        i. **Professional disqualification:** Thus laws disqualifying convicted felons from certain *professions* (e.g., the practice of medicine) are not deemed penal, usually on the theory that such measures are a reasonable way of ensuring that the professions are practiced only by those who are fit for them.

    ii. Deportation: Similarly, laws providing for the ***deportation*** of persons based on certain acts committed before the enactment of the deportation measure are not penal, and therefore not subject to the *ex post facto* ban.

C. Increase in punishment: Any ***increase*** in the ***severity*** of a criminal punishment, compared with that authorized at the time the act was committed, violates the *ex post facto* clause. (But a retroactive ***reduction*** of a penalty does not.)

    1. "Prior offense" measures: But ***"prior offense"*** measures (i.e., measures providing for ***more severe criminal penalties*** for a given crime if the offender has been previously convicted of ***other offenses***) are ***not*** subject to *ex post facto* laws merely because the prior convictions occurred before the measure was enacted.

        Example: D is convicted of burglary in 2000, and again in 2001. In 2005, the legislature enacts a statute providing that robbery shall carry a prison term of one to five years, but that where the defendant has been previously convicted of two other felonies, the term shall be one to fifteen years. D is convicted of robbery in 2007 for a robbery he committed in 2006. He may be sentenced to fifteen years, even though the only grounds for the harsher-than-ordinarily-permitted sentence is criminal activity (the first two burglaries) committed before the increased-penalty statute was enacted. Cf. Tribe, p. 637.

D. Rationale for ban: The usual rationale for the *ex post facto* ban relates to the concept of ***"fair notice"*** — it is felt to be unfair to punish a person for an act which, at the time he committed it, he could not have known was subject to such a penalty.

    1. Knowledge of who will be affected: But another possible rationale is that the legislature should not be permitted to act "with knowledge of whom [the new measures] would adversely affect and how." Tribe, p. 640, n. 26. This rationale is similar to that behind the ban on bills of attainder, discussed immediately *infra*.

VI. BILLS OF ATTAINDER

A. Constitutional provision: The Constitution prohibits both the federal government and the states from passing any ***"bill of attainder."*** Article I, §§ 9 and 10, respectively. The term "bill of attainder" has been interpreted to include not only the English bill by that name (which condemned named individuals to death and prohibited inheritance of their property) but also the English "bill of pains and penalties," which included lesser penalties. See Tribe, pp. 641-42

    1. Coverage: Thus the prohibition covers any legislative act which "appl[ies] either to ***named individuals*** or to ***easily ascertainable members of a group*** in such a way as to ***inflict punishment*** on them without a judicial trial ... " *U.S. v. Lovett*, 328 U.S. 303 (1946).

        Example: In response to charges made by the House Un-American Activities Committee, Congress passes a measure which prohibits the payment of salaries to three named federal agency employees, on the grounds that they are engaged in "subversive activities."

Held, the act is invalid as a bill of attainder, since it applies to named or easily-identified individuals, and punishes them without a judicial trial. *U.S. v. Lovett, supra.*

B. Rationale for clause: The rationale for the ban on bills of attainder rests in the concept of *separation of powers*. The process of deciding which individuals should be subject to punishment is inherently a judicial process, and must be performed by the judicial branch, not by the legislature. Because of the political non-independence of the legislature, and its extreme responsiveness to popular will, it must act by rules of *general applicability*, not ones directed at specific individuals (at least where matters of punishment are concerned).

C. Definition of "punishment": The Bill of Attainder Clause applies only to legislative *"punishment"* of specific individuals or narrowly-defined groups. But recent cases have defined "punishment" somewhat broadly, to include measures having not only a "retributive" function, but also measures whose purpose is "rehabilitative," "deterrent" or "preventative." Thus a ban on union participation by Communist Party members was deemed "punishment" (and was thus a bill of attainder) even though the ban's purpose was to prevent strikes. See *U.S. v. Brown*, 381 U.S. 437 (1965).

    1. Pure regulation not covered: However, measures which are taken solely for the purpose of *regulation*, and which have no substantial stigmatizing element, are not prohibited by the Bill of Attainder Clause, even though they may contain aspects that are unfavorable to certain individuals. For instance, in *Hawker v. New York*, 170 U.S. 189 (1898), a ban on the practice of medicine by convicted felons was justified on the grounds that it was solely a regulatory measure.

Quiz Yourself on
MISCELLANEOUS CLAUSES (ENTIRE CHAPTER)

53. The state of Okansas has a state-paid health plan, whereby the state pays the medical bills of indigent families after a $1,000-per-family annual deductible. Because of the generosity of this plan, the state has become concerned that some impoverished residents of other states offering less-generous (or no) medical coverage have been moving to Okansas to take advantage of the plan. Therefore, the Okansas legislature has provided that a family moving to Okansas from another state shall, for its first year of genuine residence in Okansas, be entitled only to those medical-bill payments that the family would have received in the state in which it previously resided.

    (a) You represent a poor family that has just moved to Okansas from Nebraska, which has no indigent medical coverage at all. What is the best constitutional argument you can make that Okansas' provision violates your client's rights? _____

    (b) Will the claim you make in (a) succeed? _____

54. Mill Co. has operated a steel mill in the Township of Fuschia for many years. Mill Co. owns both the factory and the land on which it is located. The mill has always obeyed all state and federal pollution control requirements. However, operation of a steel mill is inevitably a somewhat messy enterprise, with a fair amount of noise, smoke, etc. As the township has become more affluent and residential in character, the inhabitants have become increasingly unhappy with having a steel mill in their midst. Now, the township has amended its zoning ordinance so as to provide that no "heavy industry" (defined in a way that includes Mill Co.'s steel mill and a variety of other manufacturing operations) shall be permitted to operate anywhere in the town after four years from the ordinance's adoption. The effect of the ordinance is that Mill Co. or the next owner of its property may build houses, stores or warehouses on the site, but not operate a heavy manufacturing plant. Although the end of the four-year period is still two years away, Mill Co. wishes to challenge the ordinance.

(a) Assuming that the ordinance was enacted in a procedurally satisfactory manner, what is the strongest argument that Mill Co. can make attacking the constitutionality of the ordinance as applied to it?

_____

(b) Will this argument succeed? _____

55. The village of Green Valley wished to incinerate its trash and garbage in an ecologically sound way, rather than using up scarce landfill. It also wished to raise revenue as part of the process. Therefore, it entered into an arrangement with Waste Co., a trash management company. The arrangement provided for Waste Co. to build an incinerator in Green Valley, and for Waste Co. to pay Green Valley a 50¢ per ton "franchise fee" for every ton of trash or garbage processed by the plant over a 15-year period. (Waste Co. would make money by charging the public a fee for each load processed.) In return, Green Valley agreed to require by law, for the 15 years, that all trash and garbage produced in the town be sent to the Waste Co. facility. The arrangement operated as expected for the first five years, during which time Waste Co.'s fees to the town averaged about $2 million per year.

Then, New Co., another waste company that competed with Waste Co., proposed a new deal to Green Valley. New Co. asked Green Valley to require that trash (i.e., dry refuse) but not garbage (wet refuse, such as food remains) be sent to *its* facility. In return, New Co. would pay Green Valley a minimum of $1.5 million per year. Green Valley agreed, and changed its laws so that now, the Waste Co. plant would only get garbage, and the New Co. plant would get the trash. The net effect was that Green Valley's receipts went from $2 million a year to $3 million per year. (Green Valley, like most municipalities, could certainly benefit from the extra $1 million per year, but the town is not faced with extreme financial hardship.) The effect on Waste Co. was to reduce its profits by $500,000 per year.

(a) If Waste Co. wishes to challenge Green Valley's conduct on constitutional grounds, what is its best argument? _____

(b) Will this attack succeed? _____

56. Last year, Byer purchased a small shopping center in the town of Happy Farms. There were several other similar shopping centers in town, as well as various other types of retail stores. At the time of the purchase, Happy Farms allowed retail stores to operate seven days a week, 24 hours a day, if they wished. At the time of the purchase, the shopping center had so called "percentage leases" with its tenants, whereby the rent paid was a percentage of the retail sales generated by the stores. Each percentage lease required the store owner to maintain hours on Sunday from noon to 6:00 p.m. Byer computed the amount that it was appropriate for him to pay for the center based on this flow of percentage rent. Six months after Byer made the purchase, Happy Farms changed its zoning ordinance to prohibit any retail store from opening on Sunday. This action (taken at the request of certain small store owners who wanted to be able to take Sundays off without losing sales to their competitors), caused Byer's tenants to suffer a 10% drop in revenues, which translated into a substantial loss of rent for Byer.

Byer now asserts that the Sunday closing law constitutes an impairment of his contractual rights, in violation of the Obligation of Contracts Clause. Is Byer's assertion correct? State your reasons.

_____

57. In 2008, Dennis had sex with a 14-year-old girl, who purported to give consent. However, the state's criminal statutes regarded sex with a female under the age of 15 as statutory rape, regardless of ostensible consent. The penalty for rape was a prison sentence of up to five years. In 2009, the state legislature changed the penalty for statutory rape from a maximum of five years to a maximum of 10 years. Dennis was tried and convicted in 2010, and was sentenced to a prison term of seven years.

(a) If Dennis wishes to attack his conviction and/or sentence on constitutional grounds, what is his strongest argument? _____

(b) Will this argument succeed? State your reasons. _____

58. The Phrenic Brotherhood is a small, dedicated group of religious fundamentalists, located throughout the United States, whose stated mission is to dissuade the U.S. from opposing the rise of the religion of Phrenology throughout the world. Certain acts of terrorism have been traced to the Brotherhood, though it is not known who in particular committed these acts. The state of New Righteous, in response to a recent act of terrorism in the state thought to be associated with the Brotherhood, passed the following statute: "No member of the group known as the Phrenic Brotherhood shall be hired or retained on the payroll of any branch of the government of this state." Oren, who was employed as a file clerk at the New Righteous Department of Social Security, was known to his superior to be a member of the Brotherhood. The superior, citing the newly enacted statute, fired Oren.

(a) If Oren wishes to attack the statute on constitutional grounds, what argument (putting aside any argument based directly upon the First Amendment) has the best chance of success for him?

_____

(b) Will this attack succeed? _____

_____

Answers

53. (a) That it violates the "right to travel," a right protected by the 14th Amendment's Privileges or Immunities Clause.

(b) Yes, probably. The Court held in *Saenz v. Roe* that a state may not provide that when a family moves into the state, for one year after arrival the family's welfare payments shall be limited to the amount that the family would have received in their prior state of residence. The Court reasoned that this violates the "right to travel" — one of the rights of "national citizenship" guaranteed by the 14th Amendment's P-or-I clause — because the state's action was irrational except as an attempt to carry out the forbidden objective of discouraging poor people from moving into the state. There is no reason why the same principle shouldn't apply here, since we're told the state's action is based upon this same unlawful motive.

54. (a) That the ordinance constitutes a "taking" in violation of the Fifth Amendment.

(b) No, probably. The Fifth Amendment provides that "nor shall private property be taken for public use, without just compensation." This clause, though by its terms applies only to the federal government, also applies to states and municipalities via the Fourteenth Amendment's Due Process Clause. An enactment that is labelled a "land-use regulation" will generally not constitute a "taking," unless it "den[ies] an owner economically viable use of his land." Here Mill Co. is not being deprived of *all* economically viable use of its land — it is free to build houses, stores or warehouses on the site. The fact that the *particular* use being made of the property at this moment is now being foreclosed is not enough to meet this "no economically viable use" standard. See, e.g., *Goldblatt v. Hempstead* (town does not commit a "taking" where it bans the continued operation of a sand and gravel pit). If the ordinance had *immediately* taken effect, without any "amortization" period (here, four years), this might have tipped the balance in favor of a finding that a taking had occurred. But the amortization period, together with the fact that the mill owners had already had many years to derive value from the plant, remove this difficulty.

55. (a) That it violated the Obligation of Contracts Clause.

(b) Yes, probably. Art. I, Section 10, provides that "no State shall … pass any … Law impairing the Obligation of Contracts. … " This provision applies both to states and to municipalities. The Clause has been interpreted by the Supreme Court to mean that a state's attempt to *escape from its financial obligations* will be sustained only where a *significant public need* exists that cannot be *reasonably handled* in any other way. Here, Green Valley has in effect modified the terms of its agreement with Waste Co., by changing the law so that Waste Co. no longer gets the town's trash. The fact that Green Valley is somewhat better off financially as a result of this decision, and even the fact that the gain to Green Valley is greater than the loss to Waste Co., will not be enough to meet the requirement that there be a significant public need that cannot be reasonably handled in any other way. Court decisions show that an impairment will be "reasonable" only if it was induced by *unforeseen developments* occurring after the original contract was made; here, it was certainly foreseeable that some other waste management company might come along with a more financially attractive deal. Also, the Court has refused to merely balance the benefit to the public against the damage to the other party to the contract. See *U.S. Trust Co. v. New Jersey.* If Green Valley had been on the verge of insolvency, with this modification able to make the difference, then the impairment might stand; however, the facts do not indicate this level of hardship. Therefore, the Court would probably find that the Obligations of Contracts Clause was violated.

56. No. The Obligation of Contracts Clause applies only where the state takes an action that is *specifically directed* at contractual obligations. If the state applies a *"generally applicable rule of conduct"* which has the *incidental by-product* of impairing contractual obligations, the Contract Clause does not apply at all. See *Exxon Corp. v. Eagerton.* Here, Happy Farms has enacted a generally applicable rule, one requiring Sunday closings. The fact that certain contractual obligations (the store owners' contractual duty to remain open on Sundays) happen to be impaired is irrelevant. Therefore, we never get to the point of even determining whether the impairment here was justified by pressing needs of public policy (as we would have to do in a situation where the state specifically directed its new law at contractual obligations).

57. (a) That it is an *ex post facto* law.

(b) Yes. The Constitution prevents a state government from enacting an *ex post facto* law; see Art. I, Section 10. An *ex post facto* law is one which has a retroactive punitive effect. Some *ex post facto* laws are ones which outlaw conduct that was not criminal at the time it was committed. But there is a second kind of *ex post facto* law: one which *increases* the *severity* of a criminal punishment, compared with that authorized at the time the act was committed. Here, Dennis could not have been sentenced to more than five years in prison at the moment he committed the offense, so his sentence now constitutes a violation of the *ex post facto* ban.

58. (a) That the statute violates the prohibition on bills of attainder.

(b) Yes, probably. The Constitution prohibits both the federal government and the states from passing any "bill of attainder." (See Art. I, Section 10, for the provision as it applies to states.) The term covers any legislative act which "applies either to *named individuals* or to *easily ascertainable members of a group* in such a way as to *inflict punishment* on them without a judicial trial. … " Here, since the Phrenic Brotherhood is a relatively small group, and its members are fairly easily ascertained, the requirements seem met. Assuming that dismissal from the state payroll is found to be "punishment," the law seems to be a bill of attainder. Measures taken solely for the purpose of *regulation*, and which have no substantial stigmatizing element, are not prohibited by the Bill of Attainder Clause. Here, however, since the law applies to all state government jobs, and applies without respect to whether the individual has a specific intent to espouse the terrorist beliefs of some Brotherhood leaders, the law seems more like punishment than regulation. Especially since there is a risk that freedom of association values will be infringed, the Court will probably conclude that the law is a bill of attainder. See, e.g., *U.S. v. Brown* (law making it a crime for a Communist Party member to serve as an officer of a labor union is struck down as a bill of attainder).

Exam Tips *on* MISCELLANEOUS CLAUSES

The Clauses covered in this chapter are easy to miss on an exam, because each applies to fairly specialized facts and is likely to be buried within a much larger fact pattern. Most of your work will therefore consist of spotting the issue; once you do so, analyzing it correctly shouldn't be too hard. Here are some things to look for:

☛ If your fact pattern happens to involve a person who is prevented from *travelling* from state to state, or blocked from *voting* in a national election, consider whether the *14th Amendment's Privileges or Immunities Clause* has been violated. A 1999 decision (*Saenz v. Roe*) makes questions on this Clause more likely — if the state is discriminating against people who recently moved into the state, the clause is probably violated. (But if your fact pattern involves a target state that discriminates against out-of-staters who have not moved into the target state, probably it's the *Article IV* P&I Clause, *not* the 14th Amendment P&I Clause, that's been violated.)

☛ If you have a fact pattern that involves *land-use regulation* by the state or federal government, be alert to a *Takings* Clause issue.

   ☞ The main kinds of regulations that should put you on notice to look for a Takings problem are: (1) *zoning* regs; (2) *environmental-protection* regs; and (3) *landmark-protection* regs. In general, if government is telling the owner, "You can't do such-and-such with your property" or "If you want to do such-and-such with your property, you'll have to submit to the following conditions … ," there is likely to be a Takings issue.

   ☞ Remember that for a land-use regulation to avoid being a taking it must *not deprive an owner of all economically viable use* of his land.

      ☞ The typical zoning regulation, which is generally-applicable and leaves the owner with at least some reasonable alternative uses of the property, will *not* normally be a "taking."

      ☞ But a *permanent ban* on constructing any building on a lot *would* be a "taking," if there was no economically attractive use of the property (e.g., recreational) that did not involve construction.

☞   Also, if you have a fact pattern in which the government has clearly exercised its *eminent domain powers*, don't forget to say that the taking must be for a *"public use."* But "public use" is a very watered-down standard — there must merely be some "public benefit," and almost anything qualifies (e.g., economic development such as more jobs or tax revenues). It can still be a public benefit even though the condemned property is turned over to private developers. Cite to *Kelo v. New London* on this point.

☛ If your fact pattern has the government *"rewriting the rules"* in a way that seems to *change previously-executed contracts*, consider whether the *"Contract"* Clause has been violated. It's important for you to distinguish between government's attempt to re-write contracts to which it's a party, and government's attempt to re-write contracts between private parties:

    ☞   Where government is trying to escape from *its own "bad deals,"* you should be quick to find a Contract Clause violation. Remember that the Court scrutinizes this type of government action closely, and will allow it only if a *"significant public need"* exists that cannot be reasonably handled in any other way. (*Example:* If a state government faces bankruptcy unless it re-writes the payment schedule on some bonds, and the problem can't be handled by borrowing fresh funds, this might be sufficient.)

    ☞   Where government is re-writing contracts made by *private parties*, remember that the judicial review is not so tough. So long as the government is dealing with an emergency, and protecting broad social interests (rather than a narrow, favored group), the Court will tend to uphold any contract-rewriting that is *"reasonable"* in the circumstances.

    ☞   If the state applies a *"generally applicable* rule of conduct" that merely has the *incidental by-product* of impairing contractual obligations, the Contract Clause *doesn't come into effect at all*. This element is perhaps the most frequently tested aspect of the Contract Clause — fact patterns typically involve some general environmental or other regulatory change that happens to make one party's promised performance under a private contract no longer legal. Here, you should conclude that the Contracts Clause never comes into play, because the government action wasn't "directed at" (enacted for the purpose of affecting) the contractual obligation.

☛ *Ex post facto* laws are fairly easy to spot — whenever you see government *making something a crime* that wasn't a crime when it was done, or *increasing the penalty* for something beyond what was on the books when it was done, you may have an *ex post facto* violation.

    ☞   Remember that only *"criminal"* penalties, not "civil" or "regulatory" ones, are covered. Often this distinction is what's being tested.

☛ *Bill of attainder* issues are rare. Only when you see the legislature trying to punish a group that is so *narrowly-defined* that it's possible to name all the affected people in advance, should you even think about bill of attainder. Typical example: The legislature holds that members of a particular named *organization* may not hold a certain post or receive a certain benefit.

CHAPTER 12

STATE ACTION

ChapterScope

Nearly all of the rights guaranteed by the Constitution to individuals are protected only against interference *by government*. This is sometimes called the requirement of *"state action."* However, sometimes even a private individual's actions are found to be "state action," and thus subject to the Constitution. Here are the main concepts in this Chapter:

- **"Public function" doctrine:** Under the *"public function"* doctrine, if a private individual or group is entrusted by the state to perform functions that are traditionally viewed as *governmental in nature*, the private individual becomes an agent of the state, and he constitute "state action." Therefore, his acts must obey the Constitution.

- **"State involvement" doctrine:** Alternatively, a private individual's conduct may be transformed into "state action" if the state is *heavily involved* in those activities. This is the *"state involvement"* branch of state-action doctrine. Examples are where:

  ❏ the state *"commands"* or *"requires"* the private person's action;

  ❏ the state *"encourages"* the private party's actions;

  ❏ the state and the private actor have a *"symbiotic"* or *"mutually beneficial"* relationship;

  ❏ the state is *"entangled"* with the private actor (e.g., they act together to carry out the action being challenged).

I. INTRODUCTION

A. Only state conduct covered: Nearly all of the rights and liberties which the Constitution guarantees to individuals are protected only against interference *by governmental entities*. For instance, the guarantees of due process and equal protection, given by §1 of the Fourteenth Amendment, are introduced by the words "No State shall. ... "

1. **Self-executing rights:** In fact, of the constitutional rights which are "self-executing" (i.e., capable of enforcement by courts even without specific congressional legislation enacted to enforce the right), *only* the Thirteenth Amendment's prohibition on slavery (discussed *infra*, p. 444) includes private as well as governmental conduct. See Tribe, p. 1688, n. 1.

2. **Need for "state action" doctrine:** Therefore, in virtually every litigation in which an individual argues that his constitutional rights have been violated, the court can grant relief only if it finds that there has been *state action*, i.e., some sort of *participation by a governmental entity* sufficient to make the particular constitutional provision applicable. This chapter examines the various ways in which the Supreme Court has gone about determining whether state action exists.

3. **Sometimes apparent:** In many instances, the existence of state action will be so apparent that this will not be a real issue. For instance, whenever the constitutional claim is that

a *statute or regulation itself* violates the Constitution (e.g., by being racially discrimina-tory), the existence of state action is apparent. Similarly, the existence of state action is clear in the case of a claim that a state official, while engaged in performance of his duties, has violated the plaintiff's constitutional rights. The issue arises only where the specific action alleged to interfere with a constitutional right is taken by a *private individual*, i.e., one not acting on behalf of the government.

    a. Two sides: In this situation, the defendant typically argues that there cannot have been a constitutional violation because there has been no state action. The plaintiff, in contrast, typically contends that the state has in some way encouraged, benefitted from, or at least acquiesced in the private individual's conduct, thereby furnishing the requisite state involvement.

4. Governmental units: Putting aside the *degree* of governmental action required, the term "government" is broadly defined for purposes of determining the existence of "state action." Not only actions taken by the state, but those taken by any of its *subdivisions*, will count as state action. Thus actions by a *city, county, municipally-owned utility*, etc., will all qualify. Furthermore, in the case of those constitutional rights which are protected against interference at the hands of the federal government, *any federal instrumentality* (e.g., any federal agency or commission) will be included.

    a. Government-run corporation: In fact, even a *corporation* will be treated as a gov-ernmental entity, if it's set up by the government, remains under governmental control, and furthers governmental objectives. Thus *Amtrak* was found to be part of the federal government, for First Amendment purposes, because it was created by the U.S., the President appoints a majority of its board of directors, and it carries out the federal mission of avoiding the extinction of private passenger-train service. *Lebron v. National Railroad Passenger Corp.*, 513 U.S. 374 (1995).

5. Confusing doctrines: The Supreme Court has been largely unable to formulate rules about when the degree of state involvement is sufficiently great to convert a private per-son's conduct into "state action." Instead, the Court has said, in essence, that each case must be judged on its own facts. The result is a series of cases that are difficult or impossi-ble to reconcile, and a consequent inability of observers to predict how the next case will be decided.

B. Early interpretations of "state action": The greatest importance of the state-action requirement is in connection with the Fourteenth Amendment's equal protection and due pro-cess guarantees.

1. *The Civil Rights Cases:* The first significant articulation by the Supreme Court that these Fourteenth Amendment rights are applicable only where state action is present was in the *Civil Rights Cases*, 109 U.S. 3 (1883).

    a. Facts: The *Civil Rights Cases* involved the Civil Rights Act of 1875, in which Con-gress prohibited all persons from denying, on the basis of race, any individual's equal access to inns, public transportation, theaters and other places of public accommoda-tion. The statute was clearly applicable to private conduct. The question before the Court was whether Congress had the *power* to enact such a statute.

    b. Holding: In deciding the case, the Court made three main holdings, which have varying degrees of acceptance today.

c. **Applicable solely to state action:** First, the Court held that the guarantees of equal protection and due process, given by §1 of the Fourteenth Amendment, apply by their own terms *solely to state action*. This holding remains valid today, at least in the sense that, in the *absence* of congressional legislation, the courts *will not find conduct that* *is exclusively private to be violative of these Fourteenth Amendment guarantees.*

d. **Congress without power:** Secondly, the Court held that the grant to Congress in §5 of the Fourteenth Amendment of the power to enforce these guarantees did *not authorize Congress to regulate solely private conduct*. §5 "does not authorize Congress to create a code of municipal law for the regulation of private rights. ... " The only law-making power given to Congress under §5 of the Amendment, the Court held, was the ability to pass laws to prevent the *states, by their own action*, from interfering with these rights.

   i. **Probably no longer the law:** It is not clear whether this aspect of the *Civil Rights Cases* remains good law, but it probably does not. There is no case in which a majority of the Court has held, in a single opinion, that §5 of the Fourteenth Amendment allows Congress to reach purely private conduct. But six Justices in *U.S. v. Guest*, 383 U.S. 745 (1966), in two separate opinions, argued that Congress has such power. See the fuller discussion of this issue *infra*, p. 442.

e. **Thirteenth Amendment inapplicable:** Lastly, the Court held that the statute could not be justified as an exercise of the *Thirteenth* Amendment. The Court conceded that that Amendment is *applicable to private as well as state conduct*, since it prevents private individuals from holding others in slavery. But the Amendment by its terms bars only "slavery [and] involuntary servitude," and the Court took a narrow view of this phrase. Refusal to allow blacks to use public accommodations was simply not a "badge of slavery."

   i. **Overruled:** This narrow view of what constitutes a "badge of slavery" prohibited under the Thirteenth Amendment has clearly been overruled, at least with respect to Congress' power to enact *legislation* to enforce that Amendment (an enforcement power given in §2 of the Amendment.) See, e.g., *Jones v. Alfred H. Mayer Co.*, 392 U.S. 409 (1968), discussed *infra*, p. 444. But the Court has continued to take a narrow view of the definition of slavery when analyzing state or private conduct directly, where there is no relevant congressional statute. Only conduct involving *actual peonage* (e.g., state laws imprisoning workers who violate labor contracts) has so far been held directly violative of the Amendment itself. See Tribe, p. 1688, n. 1.

f. **Statute invalidated:** Since there was, in the majority's view, no satisfactory constitutional basis for the 1875 Civil Rights Act, the Act was *invalidated.*

g. **Dissent:** Justice Harlan, in dissent, objected to the majority's view of both the Thirteenth and the Fourteenth Amendments.

   i. **Broad view of Thirteenth:** As to the Thirteenth, he believed that freedom from slavery necessarily entailed not only the liberation from physical bondage, but also the eradication of all *"burdens and disabilities"* suffered by black people because of their race. Therefore, he believed that Congress could prevent black people from being denied, on grounds of race, those *"civil rights"* which white people have. In his opinion, these civil rights included the right to use inns, public transport, and other public facilities.

    ii. Harlan's Fourteenth Amendment view: With respect to the Fourteenth Amendment, Harlan pointed to a part of §1 that the majority ignored, the provision that "[a]ll persons born or naturalized in the United States and subject to the jurisdiction thereof, are citizens of the United States and of the State wherein they reside." He believed that this section gave blacks *state citizenship*, and that this grant of state citizenship in turn entitled them to "exemption from race discrimination in respect of *any civil right belonging to citizens of the white race* in the same State." As in the case of the Thirteenth Amendment, he believed that these civil rights included access to public accommodations. (Apart from this argument, Harlan also contended that railroad companies, innkeepers, etc., since they serve the public and are subject to state regulation, should be viewed as *agents of the state*, so that their conduct constitutes state action for equal protection and due process purposes.)

2. Consequence of case: The *Civil Rights Cases*, and other cases decided shortly thereafter which took an equally narrow view of congressional power, had a devastating effect on Congress' ability to prevent the emergence of virtual apartheid in the South. It was not until the 1940s that some meaningful limits on unofficial racial discrimination were imposed; this happened principally through a broadening of the concept of "state action," a process described below.

C. Modern approach to state action: The narrow view of what constitutes "state action," implicit in the *Civil Rights Cases*, remained in force until the 1940s. Then, the Court began to broaden the concept of state action, with the result that various acts that were carried out by private persons, not state officials, were nonetheless attributed to the state. The Court has used a number of theories (or, perhaps "descriptions" is a better term) to explain why particular private conduct is so closely linked to official conduct that it should be considered state action. The cases generally seem to fall into two main groups: (1) those in which the private activity is attributable to the government because the private actor is fulfilling a *"public function"*; and (2) those in which the various connections (the *"nexus"*) between the state and the private actor are sufficiently great that the state can be said to be *involved in*, or even to have *"encouraged,"* the private activity which is being complained of. We will consider each of these lines of cases in turn.

1. Limitations by post-Warren Court: In both of these areas, the broadening of the state action concept culminated during the Warren era. The Burger/Rehnquist/Roberts Court has clearly stopped the state action concept from further expansion, and in numerous respects appears to have in fact narrowed it.

2. Relation between two doctrines: The relation between the "public function" doctrine and the "nexus" doctrine remains somewhat obscure. Apparently, the party who is attempting to show that his adversary's conduct constitutes state action will prevail if he can show *either* that that adversary performed a "public function" *or* that there was a sufficient "nexus" of contacts between the state and the adversary to justify subjecting the latter to constitutional prohibitions.

II. THE "PUBLIC FUNCTION" APPROACH

A. The "public function" approach generally: The *"public function"* doctrine holds that when a private individual (or group) is entrusted by the state with the performance of functions that are *governmental in nature*, he becomes an agent of the state and his acts constitute state action. This public function analysis at one time appeared to be potentially extremely broad-sweeping. But the Burger/Rehnquist Court has cut back the doctrine substantially, principally by insisting that the function be one that is normally "exclusively" reserved to the state. See *infra*, p. 455.

B. The *White Primary Cases*: The "public function" analysis seems to have had its start in the so-called *White Primary Cases*. In a series of decisions, the Court held that despite state attempts to delegate more and more of the nominating process to private political parties, the *entire electoral process is a public function* and the political parties are acting as agents of the state. Therefore, they may not practice racial discrimination.

   1. Discrimination by political parties: For instance, where a state convention of Democrats established a rule that only whites could vote in the Texas Democratic Primary, the racial restriction was held to be violative of the Fifteenth Amendment, in *Smith v. Allwright*, 321 U.S. 649 (1944).

   2. Extended to pre-primary: This rationale was carried even further in *Terry v. Adams*, 345 U.S. 461 (1953), where state action was found even in the racially-restrictive "*pre-primary*" elections held by the Jaybird Democratic Association, a group whose candidate almost always won the ensuing Democratic Primary (usually unopposed).

      a. Rationale: There was no majority opinion, but the prevailing rationale appeared to be that the state, by inaction, had permitted this unofficial pre-election to *usurp the role of the official primary* (which, under *Smith*, was itself an integral part of the election process). Several of the Justices seemed to rely on the fact that the state's tolerance of private discrimination reflected a *purposeful* decision to maintain a racially discriminatory system of elections. See Tribe, p. 1708.

   3. Scope of rationale: It is not clear how broadly applicable the rationale of the *White Primary Cases* is. It does not seem likely that all or most other conduct by political parties will be deemed to be state action; for instance, the selection of party chairmen would probably not be held to be the performance of a public function. Nor is it clear that discrimination based on grounds other than race, even in the primary process, would necessarily be held to be state action; the *White Primary Cases* were founded on the Fifteenth Amendment, which applies only to racial discrimination. Thus a party which limited its membership solely to men, or solely to Protestants, might well be found not to be engaged in state action. See Tribe, p. 1119, n. 11.

C. Company towns and shopping centers: A second major area in which "public function" analysis developed concerned actions taken by the owners of *company towns* and *shopping centers.*

   1. Issue: The issue in these cases was whether the owner of the property had the right to use *state trespass laws* to keep out people who wished to *speak* or *distribute literature* on the property. Where operation of the property was held to be a public function, First Amendment guarantees became applicable, barring the use of state trespass laws. By contrast, where there was no public function, there were no First Amendment rights and the owner therefore had the ability to keep the outsiders off his property.

2. **Company town:** The first of this line of cases involved a company town. In *Marsh v. Alabama*, 326 U.S. 501 (1946), a Jehovah's Witness was charged with criminal trespass for distributing religious literature in the town of Chickasaw, Alabama, a town *wholly owned* by the Gulf Shipbuilding Corporation. The Court held that, since the town was just like any other town (except for the fact that title to the real estate was vested in a private company), *operation of the town was a public function*. Prior cases had held that ordinary non-private towns could not bar distribution of religious literature, under First Amendment principles; these principles were therefore applicable to Chickasaw as well.

   a. **Public access:** The *Marsh* Court attached some importance to the fact that the town was not limited to housing, but also included a downtown shopping district, which was accessible to and freely used by outsiders. The Court's stress on this fact may mean that privately-owned communities that are *purely residential*, as well as *camps for migrant workers*, are *not* fulfilling public functions, since these are typically not used by outsiders. Later cases, discussed *infra*, holding that shopping centers are not by themselves engaged in public functions, seem to buttress this more limited view of what types of property will be found to be used for public functions.

   b. **Balancing:** Strict logic would indicate that, since Chickasaw fulfilled a "public function," *any activity* taken in connection with its administration would be subjected to constitutional scrutiny. For instance, by this analysis, any person hired as a *sanitation worker* under a contract would presumably have the right to procedural due process before being discharged. Yet the *Marsh* Court's analysis leaves open the possibility that the operation of a town may be a public function only for *some, but not all*, purposes. The opinion seems to call for a *balancing test*, whereby "the constitutional rights of owners of property" are balanced against the right of the people to "enjoy freedom of the press and religion."

      i. **Application:** Under such a balancing test, the right of a town worker not to be discharged without a fair hearing might be found to weigh less heavily on the scale than did the right to distribute literature, and might lead to a decision that such firings are not part of the town's public function. A similar holding might be made in response to charges that the town refused to hire, say, women for sanitation positions.

3. **Shopping centers:** For a while, it appeared that *shopping centers* would also be treated as engaged in a public function, so that First Amendment guarantees, at least, would be applicable to activities there. But cases so indicating were overruled in 1976 by *Hudgens v. NLRB*, 424 U.S. 507 (1976).

   a. **Facts and holding:** In *Hudgens*, union members who were engaged in a labor dispute with one of the stores in a shopping mall attempted to picket in the open area and the parking lot of the mall. A majority of the Court held that, prior cases to the contrary notwithstanding, a large self-contained *shopping center* was *simply not the equivalent of the company town* in *Marsh*, and that *no First Amendment guarantees were applicable to activities in it.*

   b. **State of company-town cases:** *Marsh* itself presumably remains good law. But the effect of *Hudgens* is to limit *Marsh* to its own facts; thus operation of a company-owned town will be deemed a public function, but operation of property that supplies less than a full range of municipal services will not be.

D. Parks and recreation: Operation of a *park* has been considered the exercise of a "public function."

1. ***Evans case:***   Thus in *Evans v. Newton*, 382 U.S. 296 (1966), a park in Macon, Georgia had been left in trust by Senator Bacon, with the proviso that it be used only for whites. At first, the City of Macon acted as trustee and enforced the proviso; then, it was replaced by private trustees who did the same.

   a. **Holding:**   The Supreme Court held that operation of the park in a racially discriminatory manner violated the Fourteenth Amendment. One reason for this conclusion was that the services rendered even by a private park were *"municipal in nature"*; like fire and police departments, a park *"traditionally serves the community."*

   b. **Aftermath of case:**   The Supreme Court was subsequently required to decide whether the reverter in Senator Bacon's will, which was to be triggered if the park was no longer racially restricted, could constitutionally be enforced by the state. It concluded that it could, in *Evans v. Abney*, discussed *infra*, p. 459.

2. **Present status:**   It is unlikely that the "public function" analysis of *Evans v. Newton* will be extended to include other types of recreational facilities, such as country clubs or amusement parks. The post-Warren Court has held that only those functions which are traditionally *"exclusively"* performed by the state will be deemed public functions. A footnote to Justice Rehnquist's majority opinion in *Flagg Bros., infra*, below, suggests that "parks for recreational purposes" do not fit into this category, and that the real explanation for *Evans* lay in the city's day-to-day involvement in the park's maintenance. Thus if the issue were to arise again, purely private operation of even an ordinary park might no longer be held to be a public function.

E. The requirement of state "exclusivity":   In the post-Warren years, the Court has dramatically narrowed the situations in which "public function" analysis will apply, by requiring that the function be one which has traditionally been *exclusively* the domain of the government. The Court has used this exclusivity requirement on at least four occasions to reject the application of the public function doctrine.

1. **Utilities:**   Operation of a *privately-owned utility* licensed and regulated by the state was held *not* to be performance of a public function, in *Jackson v. Metropolitan Edison Co.*, 419 U.S. 345 (1974).

   a. **Rationale:**   Public function analysis is applicable, the Court said, only where a private entity exercises "powers traditionally *exclusively reserved* to the State." This exclusivity requirement was not met by operation of the utility in *Jackson*, the Court concluded; this was demonstrated by the fact that state law did not *obligate* the state to furnish power.

      i. **"Public interest" rationale rejected:**   The *Jackson* Court explicitly rejected the argument that all heavily regulated businesses "affected with a public interest" should be treated as exercising public functions.

   b. **Dissent:**   Justice Marshall, in dissent, would have treated as state action the provision of any service *"uniquely public in nature,"* which in his view included operation of a utility. The mere existence of governmental regulation of an enterprise was not sufficient, he conceded; but in the case of a utility, the state invariably either provided the service itself, or so heavily regulated it that the private enterprise in effect had "surrender[ed] many of the prerogatives normally associated with private enterprise and behave[s] in many ways like a government body."

2. **Warehouseman's lien:** The impact of the exclusivity requirement was still more evident in a case in which the Court held that sale by a *warehouseman* of goods stored with him in which he had a *warehouseman's lien* for unpaid storage charges was not a public function. *Flagg Bros., Inc. v. Brooks*, 436 U.S. 149 (1978).

   a. **Rationale:** The majority, in an opinion by Justice Rehnquist, rejected the contention that resolution of private disputes was traditionally an exclusive government function. Here, for instance, Rehnquist argued, the dispute need not have been settled by the warehouseman's sale: the owner of the goods could have brought a replevin action, or could have sued for damages based on her claim that she had not authorized the storage.

      i. **Application to other areas:** Yet the majority seemed to be slightly uncomfortable with its rigid holding that only functions traditionally reserved exclusively to the state would be deemed "public" ones. In certain areas, the majority opinion said, there was a "greater" degree of exclusivity than that involved in the dispute-resolution situation; these areas included "education, fire and police protection, and tax collection." The majority expressly declined to say whether performance of these functions would be deemed "public"; yet it was also unwilling to characterize them as manifesting complete (as opposed to "greater") exclusivity. Thus the public function doctrine's application in these areas remains uncertain.

   b. **Dissent:** Three dissenters, in an opinion written by Justice Stevens, objected to the majority's imposition of an exclusivity requirement. The dissenters believed that such a requirement was not imposed by prior cases; they pointed to *Evans v. Newton (supra*, p. 455), for instance, and insisted that that was a case in which the activity (operation of a park) was found to be a public function even though it was *not* "exclusive." (The majority claimed that the case had really been decided in reliance on the city's day-to-day involvement in maintaining the park.)

      i. **Exclusivity satisfied:** The dissenters also objected to the majority's conclusion that the debt-resolution mechanism at issue was not an exclusively public one; the fact that the owner of the goods could sue the warehouse for damages for wrongfully disposing of them did not make the lien foreclosure itself any less an exclusively public function (any more than allowing a citizen to sue a policeman for false arrest transformed the arrest into a private rather than a public act).

   c. **Encouragement theory:** In *Flagg Bros.*, the owner of the goods also claimed that there was state action because the state, by statutorily authorizing the warehouseman to impose a lien and foreclose on it in these circumstances, was "encouraging" the warehouseman's conduct. This aspect of the case is discussed in the treatment of the "encouragement" or "involvement" cases *infra*, p. 464.

3. **Nursing homes:** Operation of *nursing homes*, including the making of decisions about patient care, was found *not* to be a public function, in *Blum v. Yaretsky*, 457 U.S. 991 (1982). The majority seemed to be imposing still another requirement for application of the public function doctrine: that the activity be one which the state is *required* to provide

by statute or by the state constitution. Since the state was not required to supply nursing home, or other medical, care, no public function was involved. (Other aspects of the case are discussed *infra*, p. 459.)

4. Private school: One of the issues expressly left open in *Flagg Bros.* was resolved when the Court held that operation of a *private school*, even one whose income comes primarily from public grants, is *not* a public function. *Rendell-Baker v. Kohn*, 457 U.S. 830 (1981). Provision of education was not the "exclusive" prerogative of the state, even though it was a function normally provided by the state out of public funds.

F. Future of "public function" doctrine: In summary, the "public function" doctrine has been *substantially narrowed* by the post-Warren Court. It will probably only be applied where two quite stringent conditions are met: (1) the function is one which is *traditionally the exclusive prerogative* of the state; and (2) some statute or state constitutional provision *in fact requires the state* to perform the function.

1. Where satisfied: The present Court seems to regard only two groups of prior cases as meeting these requirements: the maintenance of *streets* (in *Marsh v. Alabama*, the company-town case) and the maintenance of an *electoral system* (in the *White Primary Cases*).

III. "NEXUS" — THE SIGNIFICANCE OF STATE INVOLVEMENT

A. The "nexus" theory generally: The second broad branch of the state action doctrine relates not to the type of activity carried out by the private actor, but to the *conduct of the government*. If the government is sufficiently *"involved"* in the private actor's conduct or *"encourages"* that conduct, or *benefits from* it, the private party's acts will be deemed state action, and subjected to constitutional review. A common catch-all way of referring to this branch of state-action analysis is to call it the *"nexus"* approach; that is, the issue is the nexus, or *points of contact*, between the state and the private actor.

B. "Commandment": One way in which the state can become responsible for a private party's conduct is by *commanding* that conduct. Some examples of commandment are so obvious that no one would dispute the presence of state action; for instance, if the state ordered private restaurant owners to serve only white customers, both the order, and the private owners' execution of it, would be state action.

1. Facially neutral law: Much more interesting are those situations where the state, by *applying facially neutral laws, enforces private agreements* with the result that one person is judicially ordered to discriminate against another. Even the application of such neutral laws may be construed as a commandment to discriminate, and therefore state action.

2. *Shelley v. Kraemer*: The classic illustration of this principle is *Shelley v. Kraemer*, 334 U.S. 1 (1948).

a. Facts of *Shelley*: *Shelley* involved the enforceability of *racially restrictive covenants*. Most homeowners in an area had entered into a covenant that their property would not be owned by anyone but Caucasians for 50 years. When blacks bought homes from willing white owners despite the covenants, other whites, who were owners of properties also subject to the covenants, sued to block the blacks from taking possession. The issue before the Supreme Court was whether the state courts could award the white plaintiffs the relief they sought, without violating the Fourteenth Amendment.

    b. Holding: The Supreme Court held that ***judicial enforcement*** of the restrictive covenant ***would constitute state action***, and would therefore violate the Fourteenth Amendment. "[B]ut for the active intervention of the state courts, supported by the full panoply of state power, [defendants] would have been free to occupy the properties in question. ... " Nor was it relevant that enforcement by the state occurred because of a longstanding ***common-law***, rather than ***statutory***, policy of granting such enforcement.

        i. Not inaction: The Court also noted that this was not a case in which the state was simply remaining ***inactive***, while one private person discriminated against another. The *Shelley* Court stressed that the case involved ***willing sellers*** as well as buyers, so that it was only the state's coercive judicial machinery which would cause the discrimination to occur.

    3. Damage actions: Suppose the white plaintiffs in *Shelley* had sought not an injunction against the black purchasers, but ***money damages*** against the ***white sellers***. Granting this relief, too, would be state action and a violation of the Fourteenth Amendment, the Court held in ***Barrows v. Jackson***, 346 U.S. 249 (1953).

        a. Rationale: The Court's rationale was that awarding such relief would impede an agreement between an otherwise willing seller and buyer just as the injunction sought in *Shelley* would have, since the seller would be either completely dissuaded from selling to a black by the possibility of a damage action, or at least motivated to charge black buyers a higher price to cover a possible damage award.

    4. Scope of *Shelley* uncertain: The scope of *Shelley* (and *Barrows*) is highly unclear.

        a. Broad reading: A broad reading of *Shelley* would be that anytime a person's decision to discriminate, or an agreement between two or more people to discriminate, is enforced or left undisturbed by the state's legal system (even pursuant to a facially neutral legal rule), state action exists.

            i. Refusal to sell: By this reading, if a white homeowner who had signed a racially restrictive covenant like the one in *Shelley* simply ***refused to sell*** to a black in reliance on the covenant, the judiciary's refusal to ***prevent*** the white from relying on the agreement would be state action and thus unconstitutional.

            ii. Refusal to serve: Similarly, by this reading of *Shelley*, a restaurant owner's decision not to allow black civil rights workers to conduct a sit-in on his premises could not constitutionally be backed up by use of the state's trespass laws, even though this law was a facially neutral provision that entitled any property owner to decide who may come on his property.

        b. Narrower reading: But a strong case can be made that the proper reading of *Shelley* is much ***narrower***. For instance, there is reason to believe that the rationale of *Shelley* was meant to apply ***only*** to those situations where there are a ***willing seller and buyer***, and the state is asked to use its power affirmatively to prevent them from consummating their sale. (This reading is suggested by the *Shelley* Court's statement that this was not a case "in which the states have merely abstained from action, leaving private individuals free to impose such discriminations as they see fit.")

    i. **Narrower view probably accurate:** Subsequent Supreme Court cases certainly have not disproved the narrower view of *Shelley*. For instance, the great lengths to which the Court has gone to develop other theories for finding state action (such as the "symbiosis" rationale of *Burton v. Wilmington Parking Authority, infra,* p. 460) suggest that mere invocation of neutral state laws to preserve individuals' "right" to discriminate probably does not constitute state action. The Court's refusal to rely on the broader reading of *Shelley* in sit-in cases decided in the 1960s also lends some support to this narrower view of *Shelley.*

5. **Reverter in deed:** In any event, if a private agreement calls for discrimination, it is not unconstitutional state action for a court to enforce a provision in the agreement dealing with the contingency that the discrimination is held unenforceable. This was demonstrated by ***Evans v. Abney,*** 396 U.S. 435 (1970), a further development in the litigation of which *Evans v. Newton (supra,* p. 455) was a part.

    a. **Facts:** After *Evans v. Newton* established that Baconsfield Park could not be operated in a racially discriminatory way, the state trial court determined that, since fulfillment of Senator Bacon's intent was no longer possible, the trust should ***terminate*** (presumably causing the property to close as a park), and the property should revert to the Senator's heirs. This reversion was called for by operation of Georgia law in the event of a trust's termination.

    b. **Ruling upheld:** The Supreme Court held that this state ruling did ***not violate*** the Fourteenth Amendment. The only discrimination was by Senator Bacon, not by the state's laws calling for reversion. This situation was distinguishable from *Shelley,* the majority held, because in *Shelley,* the state court was called upon to ***enforce*** a private scheme of discrimination; here, the state ruling, rather than enforcing discrimination, in fact nullified discrimination by preventing the park from being used by either blacks or whites.

6. **Delegation:** The Court since the '80s has taken a quite narrow view of the circumstances in which the state will be deemed to have "***commanded***" particular actions by private persons. If any real degree of ***discretion*** is delegated to the private party, this will probably be enough to relieve the state of responsibility for those private actions, even though they take place within a fairly rigid framework of state-created rules. For instance, in *Blum v. Yaretsky,* 457 U.S. 991 (1982), a class of Medicaid patients in private nursing homes unsuccessfully claimed that decisions by the homes to discharge them or send them to facilities giving less extensive (and less costly) service constituted state action.

    a. **Facts:** The patients contended that the decisions on level-of-care, although made in individual cases by the nursing home's staff, were tightly circumscribed by the state rules, and that the state therefore bore responsibility for these decisions.

    b. **Claim rejected:** But a majority of the Court, in an opinion by Justice Rehnquist, disagreed. The actual discharge or transfer decisions were based on "medical judgments," which were made by independent nursing home professionals who were not controlled by the state. Therefore, these decisions were not state action.

C. **"Encouragement" by the state:** If *Shelley v. Kraemer* may be seen as a case where the state "commanded" the discrimination (by attempting to enjoin the willing white sellers from selling to the black purchasers), other cases have found that the state has "***encouraged***" discrimination. Such encouragement, too, will constitute state action, and may thus trigger a constitutional violation.

1. **Repeal of civil rights laws as "encouragement":** Such an "encouragement" theory was used in **Reitman v. Mulkey**, 387 U.S. 369 (1967). In *Reitman*, the Court found state action where California voters amended their constitution to prohibit the government from interfering with any private individual's right to discriminate in the sale or lease of residential real estate. An immediate effect (and purpose) of the constitutional amendment was to overturn two statutes which barred some sorts of private residential housing discrimination. The California Supreme Court, in striking the constitutional amendment, found that its purpose and effect would inevitably be to encourage private discrimination. The U.S. Supreme Court, in affirming, agreed that this was *encouragement* by the state, *not even-handedness*.

    a. **Deference to state court finding:** The U.S. Supreme Court, in agreeing that the constitutional amendment would have the effect of encouraging private discrimination, gave deference to the California court's finding that, "in the California environment," the amendment would have this effect.

    b. **Scope of *Reitman*:** Even giving *Reitman* a broad reading, it seems extremely *unlikely* that the *mere failure by a state to forbid private discrimination constitutes state action*. Thus had California simply never enacted any legislation or regulation dealing with private housing discrimination, its inaction would almost certainly not be deemed state conduct. Even had it enacted legislation, the *mere repeal* of the statute(s) by the legislature would probably not have been state action, since a strong argument could be made that such a repeal merely restored the status quo. It was probably only the fact that the change was made to the state's *constitution*, and thus acted as a bar to enactment of fair housing legislation in the future, that state "encouragement" was found.

D. **"Symbiosis" between state and private actor:** Another way in which the state can become so involved with private discrimination that the latter will be subjected to constitutional scrutiny is if there is a "symbiotic," i.e., *mutually beneficial*, relation between the state and the private discriminator. That is, if there are *extensive contacts* between the state and the private party, in such a way that each benefits from the other's conduct, the requisite state involvement may be found.

1. **The *Burton* case:** The classic example of such a symbiotic relationship is *Burton v. Wilmington Parking Authority*, 365 U.S. 715 (1961).

    a. **Facts:** *Burton* involved the relationship between a parking building owned and run by the Wilmington Parking Authority (a state agency) and a restaurant run by a private company within the building, under a 20-year lease between the Authority and the company. The restaurant refused to serve blacks. (No provision in Delaware or federal law at the time required private companies to do so.) A black who was refused service contended that the Authority's involvement with the restaurant was sufficiently great as to make the private discrimination "state action" violative of the Fourteenth Amendment.

    b. **State action found:** The Supreme Court agreed that *state action was present*. The Court relied heavily on various indications that the restaurant was essential to successful operation of the overtly public facility (the parking portion). For instance, the project could not have been financed without rents from commercial tenants like the restaurant. Furthermore, since the restaurant claimed that its business would be hurt if it were forced to serve blacks, the "profits earned by discrimination" were indispensable elements in the project's financial success.

c. No relevant lease provision: Unlike the constitutional amendment in *Reitman*, nothing the state did in *Burton* expressly conferred on the restaurant the right to discriminate. The lease was completely silent on the issue of discrimination. But the Supreme Court held that, in view of the symbiotic relation between the parties, the state had an *affirmative obligation* to insert a non-discrimination requirement in the lease (which, under state law regarding leases of public property, it had the power to do). This obligation could not be avoided even upon a showing by the state of perfect good faith, and of a complete absence of desire to encourage discrimination.

d. Scope of *Burton*: As with many of the other state action decisions, it is difficult to gauge the scope of *Burton*. The case probably does *not* stand for the proposition that any time the state has the power to prevent discriminatory use of public property, it must exercise that power. For instance, if the Authority had *sold* the entire building as surplus, it seems unlikely that an anti-discrimination clause in the deed would be constitutionally required. A key aspect of *Burton* is undoubtedly that the state *benefited* heavily from the lease, and may in fact have benefited from the discrimination itself (since the absence of an anti-discrimination clause probably made the restaurant willing to pay higher rents). In fact, *Burton* may be seen as a case in which there was *circumstantial evidence* that the *government itself had racially discriminatory motives* in failing to prohibit the private discrimination. See Tribe, p. 1701, n. 13.

E. Involvement or "entanglement" by state: There are some situations in which the state is so heavily *involved* in or "entangled with" private action that, even though the state does not *benefit* from or encourage the private conduct (thus ruling out the "symbiosis" approach, *supra*, p. 460) the court will nonetheless attribute to the state the private conduct.

1. Licensing by the state: Where the state *licenses* a private entity to perform a particular function, it is often claimed that the act of licensing is sufficient state involvement to make the private conduct state action. But in general, the Supreme Court has *rejected* such claims.

a. Liquor license: The best-known case on state action through licensing is *Moose Lodge No. 107 v. Irvis*, 407 U.S. 163 (1972), involving a liquor license.

i. Facts: In *Moose Lodge*, the Lodge, a private club, refused service to the black guest of a member. The guest contended that, since the state had given the club one of a limited number of liquor licenses, this act of licensing was sufficient to render the club's discrimination state action.

ii. Claim rejected: The Supreme Court disagreed, holding that the mere fact that a state grants a license to an entity does not transform the latter's conduct into state action, *even where the number of licenses is limited*. (But the majority hinted that the result might have been different if the licenses were limited in such a way that clubs holding them had a "*monopoly*" in the dispensing of liquor.")

iii. "Significant involvement" standard: The majority phrased the issue as being whether the state was "*significantly involved*" with invidious discrimination. The mere fact of licensing did not constitute such significant involvement. The Court distinguished this situation from that in *Burton*, where there was a "symbiotic relationship" between a public restaurant and a public building; here, by contrast, there was a *private* club in a private building.

    iv. Dissent: Three Justices dissented. One of the dissents, written by Justice Douglas, conceded that as a general rule, the activities of a private club were beyond the reach of the Constitution, even if the club operated pursuant to some sort of license. But this case was different, he contended, because there was a "state-enforced *scarcity of licenses*" that restricted the ability of blacks to obtain liquor. If individuals wanted to form a club that would serve blacks, they would have to buy an existing club license, and would have to pay a *monopoly price*; the creation of this monopoly scheme was directly attributable to the state. Therefore, Douglas contended, the Lodge's discrimination was state action.

  2. Grant of monopoly: Related to the problem of licensed businesses is that of "natural monopolies," i.e., areas of commerce where, usually because of high capital requirements, only one business can profitably exist. Such natural monopolies are usually *highly regulated*, since there is no competition to keep their charges reasonable. Yet despite this intense regulation, actions by these monopolies will *not* generally be deemed state action. The classic example is conduct of a public *utility*.

    a. *Jackson v. Metropolitan Edison:* The Court refused to find that the conduct of an electric utility, which had a monopoly in its area, constituted state action, in *Jackson v. Metropolitan Edison Co.*, 419 U.S. 345 (1974). Consequently, plaintiff's claim that her electric service should not have been turned off for nonpayment without notice and fair hearing was unsuccessful. The Court was not convinced that the state had really "granted" the utility a monopoly (since the monopoly was a "natural" one). But even if it had, this was not sufficient to transform the utility's activities into state action, because there was an "insufficient relationship between the challenged actions of the [utility] and [its] monopoly status."

    b. Dissent: Three Justices dissented in separate opinions. Two of them believed that the state *had* conferred a monopoly on the utility, and appeared to believe that this fact justified subjecting the utility's actions to constitutional review. One of the dissenters, Justice Marshall, pointed out that an important part of the state's regulatory program was its decision not to have the state itself *compete* with private utilities, and to regulate the latter "in a multitude of ways to ensure that the [utilities'] service will be the functional equivalent of service provided by the State." (See the discussion of the majority and dissent's viewpoints on this "public function" issue *supra*, p. 455.)

  3. State funding: The fact that a private entity *receives substantial state funding* will not by itself convert its activities into state action. Thus in *Rendell-Baker v. Kohn*, 457 U.S. 830 (1982), the Court held that a *private school*, whose income came primarily from public funding, and which was regulated by public authorities, was not committing state action when it fired employees.

  4. "Joint participation": The necessary state involvement with a private party *will* be found where the private party and a state official have *jointly participated* in the activity being challenged. This "joint participation" theory was used to find state action in *Lugar v. Edmondson Oil Co.*, 457 U.S. 922 (1982).

a. Facts: *Lugar*, like *Flagg Bros. (supra*, p. 456), involved a creditor's right to summarily seize or dispose of his debtor's property. In *Lugar*, the creditor (Edmondson) sued to collect a debt, and obtained a pre-judgment attachment against the property of the debtor, Lugar, which had the the effect of preventing Lugar from being able to sell it (though he remained in possession). To obtain the attachment, Edmondson was required only to file an *ex parte* petition stating a belief that Lugar might dispose of the property in order to defeat his creditors; a clerk of the court then issued a writ of attachment, which was executed by the sheriff.

b. Holding: The Court held that because the clerk and sheriff acted **together with** Edmondson, Edmondson's conduct in obtaining the attachment was state action. Therefore, Edmondson could be held liable for violating Lugar's constitutional rights if (as Lugar alleged) the attachment statute failed to comply with the requirements of due process.

c. Limited scope: But only Lugar's allegation that the **statutory procedure itself** was unconstitutional, **not** Edmonson's alleged **misuse** of the statute, was held to involve state action. Misuse of a properly-drafted statute was not "conduct that can be attributed to the state," because such misuse did not give rise to a "[constitutional] deprivation ... caused by the exercise of some right or privilege created by the state or by a rule of conduct imposed by the state. ... "

d. Peremptory challenges as joint participation: For another illustration of the principle that joint participation between the state and a private party can be enough to transform the private party's action into state action, consider the use of **peremptory juror challenges** in trials. The Court has held that when a **private litigant** — either a civil litigant or a defendant in a criminal case — uses peremptory challenges to exclude jurors on racial grounds, this conduct constitutes state action and therefore violates the Equal Protection Clause. See *Edmonson v. Leesville Concrete Co.*, 500 U.S. 614 (1991) (in a civil case, private litigants cannot exercise their peremptory challenges in a racially discriminatory manner); *Georgia v. McCollum*, 505 U.S. 42 (1992) (same rule for criminal defendants).

e. Regulation of interscholastic athletics: For yet one more illustration of how joint participation between the state and a private party can constitute state action, consider the regulation of **interscholastic athletics** within a state. In a 2001 decision, the Court held that although high school interscholastic athletics within a state were regulated by a nominally private association, the association was a state actor due to the extensive participation of state entities in the association's affairs. The fact that 84% of the association's members were public high schools, and the fact that educators from those public schools were fulfilling their own job responsibilities when they worked with the association, contributed to the Court's conclusion that the association was a state actor. See *Brentwood Academy v. Tenn. Secondary School Athletic Assoc.*, 531 U.S. 288 (2001), discussed more extensively *infra*, both immediately below and on p. 465.

5. "Entwinement": A 2001 decision suggests that where the links between a state entity and a private group are so extensive that the two can fairly be said to be **"entwined,"** this entwinement will itself be strong evidence that the private group should be deemed to be a state actor. In *Brentwood Academy v. Tenn. Secondary School Athletic Assoc.*, 531 U.S. 288 (2001) (also discussed immediately *supra*, and *infra* at p. 465), the majority said that

"Entwinement will support a conclusion that an ostensibly private organization ought to be charged with a public character and judged by constitutional standards; entwinement to the degree shown here requires it."

a. Facts: *Brentwood* involved the question whether an Association regulating secondary-school athletics within a state should be treated as a state actor. The Court found two types of public-private entwinement in *Brentwood.* First, the State Board of Education was intertwined with the Association in numerous ways (e.g., the Board appointed non-voting members to the Association's committees). Second, most of the public secondary schools within the state not only belonged to the Association but performed some of their official functions (e.g., the running of interscholastic sports programs) in close conjunction with the Association. These two forms of entwinement justified the conclusion that the Association's conduct constituted state action.

6. Acquiescence by the state not enough: Mere *acquiescence* by the state in the private individual's conduct is not enough to make the latter "state action." The government must *actively encourage* or *facilitate* the private conduct, not merely *tolerate* it. This is true even where the state has the clear power to *prevent* the challenged private conduct, but chooses not to exercise that power.

> **Example 1:** A utility files with the State Public Utilities Commission a tariff, which among its terms states a right to terminate a customer's service for nonpayment. The Commission does not object to this provision.
>
> *Held,* the utility's practice of terminating service for nonpayment, without giving notice or an opportunity for a hearing, is not transformed into state action merely because the Commission (a state agency) allowed it. (A prior case in which a utility's conduct was carefully scrutinized by a utilities commission, and in which the commission ultimately praised the practice as improving service, was distinguishable, since there, the state placed its "imprimatur" on the practice). *Jackson v. Metropolitan Edison Co.,* 419 U.S. 345 (1974), also discussed *supra,* p. 455.

> **Example 2:** The state, by enacting the Uniform Commercial Code, grants a warehouseman a lien for unpaid storage charges against goods deposited with him, and permits him to sell these goods to satisfy the lien. Plaintiff, whose goods are about to be sold in this manner, argues that the sale constitutes state action, and that its terms must therefore satisfy procedural due process.
>
> *Held,* the carrying out of the sale does *not* constitute state action. The state has merely *permitted, not encouraged,* such sales by warehousemen. Plaintiff's claim is merely that the state has refused to act (i.e., that it has refused to bar the sale), and mere inaction by the state cannot transform private acts into state acts. *Flagg Bros., Inc. v. Brooks,* 436 U.S. 149 (1978) (also discussed *supra,* p. 456).

> **Note:** A dissent by Justice Stevens in *Flagg Bros.* argued that the majority's distinction between "permission" and "compulsion" cannot be the determining factor in state-action analysis. Under the majority's rationale, the state could also pass a statute providing that "any person with sufficient physical power [may] acquire and sell the property of his weaker neighbor"; such sales would then not be state action. Justice Stevens instead believed that state action was present, because the state had delegated to a private party what was essentially a state function, the non-consensual transfer of

property to satisfy debts. (See the discussion of this part of his dissent *supra*, p. 456.)

7. **Recognition by state:** If a state *formally recognizes* the role played by a private association in a particular type of state-organized activity, that recognition will itself make it more likely that the association will be deemed to be a state actor. Thus in a 2001 case in which the Court found that a state association regulating interscholastic secondary-school athletics was a state actor, the Court relied heavily on the state's recognition of the association's special role as regulator of the athletic activities of public junior-high and high schools. *Brentwood Academy v. Tenn. Secondary School Athletic Assoc.*, 531 U.S. 288 (2001).

Quiz Yourself on
STATE ACTION (ENTIRE CHAPTER)

59. Pablo, an American of Hispanic origin, attempted to receive treatment at Green Valley Hospital. He believes that he was denied admission solely because he was Hispanic. Green Valley Hospital is owned by the Little Sisters of Green Valley, a private religious order. Pablo has brought suit against the Little Sisters, arguing that they have violated his right to equal protection under the Fourteenth Amendment. Assuming that the facts are as asserted by Pablo, will his suit succeed? _____

60. A statute enacted by the state of Albatross makes it a felony for any individual to "interfere with any right guaranteed by the Equal Protection Clause of the Fourteenth Amendment of the U.S. Constitution." Delbert was the manager of a housing project funded and operated by a federal housing agency. Delbert refused to rent to a family solely because they were black. If Delbert is charged with violating the Albatross statute, should he be convicted? _____

61. Ninety percent of the kindergarten-through-twelfth-grade students who attend school in the state of Mongoose attend public schools. The other 10% attend private schools, some of which are parochial and some of which are not. Beaver Academy is a non-sectarian private school, 40% of whose operating funds are supplied by the state as part of an innovative program to encourage excellence in education. The state does not prescribe any aspect of the Beaver curriculum, beyond checking to make sure that students achieve a minimum level of competency in core subjects like reading. Pamela, a sixth-grade student, has brought suit against Beaver Academy, asserting that she was denied admission to Beaver solely on the grounds that she is black. Because Mongoose has extremely limited civil rights statutes, Pamela's suit consists solely of the assertion that the school's failure to admit her violated her Fourteenth Amendment equal protection rights. Assume that Pamela's factual assertions are true.

   (a) When Pamela attempts to prove the presence of state action, what doctrine offers her the best chance of success? _____

   (b) Will Pamela's suit succeed? _____

62. State U is a large public university located in the fairly small town of Arborville. Students at the university represent a substantial share of the local demand for housing. Much of the housing stock in Arborville consists of two-family homes, in one part of which the owner lives and the other part of which is rented to students. State U's housing department maintains a list of local homeowners who have such housing to offer to students. State U allows a homeowner to indicate his or her racial or ethnic preferences on the listing; thus one who prefers whites may request that a "W" designation be affixed, one who prefers blacks that a "B" be affixed, etc. The university does not charge for these listings. Because State U does not have enough dormitory space to house all students, the availability of private housing like that contained in the list is an important resource for the university. There is evidence that some homeowners who have partic-

ipated in the list would not do so if they were not able to indicate their racial preferences and thus reduce the possibility of an embarrassing face-to-face refusal to rent to minorities.

Bernard, a black student at State U, has been unable to find what he considers suitable housing. He believes that there are substantially fewer housing units available to black students than to white students, and that on average the ones that are available to blacks are either more costly or less attractive. Assume that no federal or state statute bars discrimination by an owner/occupier of a two-family house in the selection of a tenant. Bernard has sued State U for an injunction against continued use of the racially-coded housing list, on the grounds that the U's maintenance of that list violates his equal protection rights.

(a) What is the best argument Bernard can make as to why maintenance of the list violates his equal protection rights? _____

(b) Assuming that many private landowners on the list are in fact discriminating against black students, and that black students on average have to pay more for less attractive accommodations than whites when they rent from the list, should Bernard's request for an injunction be granted? _____

Answers

59. No. The Fourteenth Amendment, like all aspects of the Constitution (except the Thirteenth Amendment) only restricts **government** action. Here, the facts tell us that Green Valley Hospital is operated by a private religious order. Since there is no government involvement, there cannot be an equal protection violation.

60. No. This is essentially a "trick question." The Fourteenth Amendment applies only to conduct by **state** and **local** governments. Therefore, any conduct by or on behalf of the housing agency here could not have violated the Equal Protection Clause, because it was conduct of the federal government, not the state government. Delbert therefore did not cause any interference with equal protection rights. (Equal protection **principles** are binding on the federal government via the Fifth Amendment's Due Process Clause, and these equal protection principles are interpreted the same way as are the Fourteenth Amendment's equal protection principles. But the question here has been carefully worded to refer only to conduct that violates the Fourteenth, not the Fifth, Amendment.)

61. (a) The "public function" doctrine.

(b) No. The "public function" doctrine holds that when a private actor (or group) is entrusted by the state with the performance of functions that are governmental in nature, that actor or group becomes an **agent of the state** and his/their acts constitute state action. However, for the "public function" doctrine to apply, the function must be one which has traditionally been **exclusively** the domain of the government. The Court has held that the providing of education is **not** the exclusive prerogative of the state, even though it is a function normally provided by the state out of public funds. Therefore, the "public function" doctrine will not apply to Beaver. See *Rendell-Baker v. Kohn*, refusing to treat a private school as involving a public function, even where the school's income came primarily from public grants. (It is also conceivable that the state might be found to have been so heavily "involved" or "entangled" in the private school here that state action should be found, but the Court has held that mere government funding of a private actor's operations does not convert those private operations into state action, so this argument, too, would almost certainly fail.)

62. (a) That there is a symbiotic relationship between State U and the private landowners, sufficient to turn the private acts of discrimination into state action.

(b) Yes, probably. If the state is deeply involved with private discrimination, that private discrimination can sometimes be viewed as itself being state action. One of the ways this can happen is if there is a *"symbiotic,"* i.e., mutually beneficial, relation between the state and the private discriminator. Here, a strong argument can be made that the university is benefitting greatly from private acts (the rental of housing to State U students), and that the private discriminators are receiving important benefits from the state (free listings and a free flow of potential tenants).

To the extent that the pool of homeowners willing to list their properties has been increased by the coding option, it can be argued that State U has actually achieved a benefit not just from the overall listing program, but from the very acts of discrimination being complained of; if so, this makes it even more likely that state action would be found. All in all, there is a better than even chance that State U would be found to be so heavily involved with the private acts of discrimination that state action should be found in the maintenance of the list. The symbiosis here is reminiscent of that in *Burton v. Wilmington Parking Authority* (where restaurant paid rent for space in publicly-owned building, discrimination by restaurant was state action).

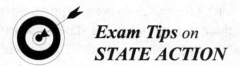

Exam Tips *on* STATE ACTION

You need to be on the lookout for State Action problems in any question that involves the rights of individuals (i.e., due process, equal protection, freedom of expression, freedom of religion, etc.). Remember that these constitutional guarantees only come into play when government is acting. Here are some specific things to watch for:

☛ Before you start to write about how the due process, equal protection, or other guarantee has been violated, make sure that there is "state action," i.e., that the challenged action is really *action by the government*, or at least that the challenged action can somehow be *ascribed* to the government.

☛ If a private individual is doing something that would clearly pose constitutional problems were it done by government, that's a tip off to a state action problem. Examples:

A private apartment owner refuses to rent to a black;

A private employer refuses to hire a person because of her gender;

A private shopping center refuses to allow P to distribute political campaign literature.

☞ In all of these situations, there will be no state action (and thus no constitutional violation), unless additional facts are presented that somehow tie the state in to the private actor's conduct.

☛ Be alert to situations where the only action is by a private individual, but the activity in question is one that is a *"public function,"* i.e., a function *"traditionally" done by the states.* Thus you may have at least an issue of whether a "public function" is being performed if your facts involve any of the following:

a private (but partly state-funded) *school*;

a privately-operated *park*;

a *political party* conducting a primary or other party business;

a *"company town;"*

a person taking some action typically done by the *judicial system* (e.g., a seller or lender foreclosing on collateral).

☞   Remember that today, the "public function" doctrine applies only where the function has traditionally been done *"exclusively"* by the states. This requirement knocks out a large percentage of the cases (including at least the private-school situation above).

☛ Also, be on the lookout for situations where the state is somehow heavily *"involved"* in the private actor's actions. The common scenarios for this are:

☞   The state has *"commanded"* or *"required"* the private action. (*Example: Shelley v. Kraemer,* where the state, by enforcing restrictive covenants, in effect commanded private individuals not to sell their homes to blacks.)

☞   *Testable issue:* May the state enforce some *neutral state law* where this has the effect of facilitating private discrimination? (*Example:* Where a private store owner refuses to serve blacks and wants them evicted, does the state's use of its trespass laws turn the property owner's action into "state action?" The answer is probably "no," as long as the state is evenhanded in how it uses the trespass law.)

☞   The state has *"encouraged"* the private action.

☞   The state has a *"symbiotic relationship"* with the private action, i.e., the state and the private actor *benefit from each other's conduct.* Classic illustration: *Burton v. Wilmington Parking Authority* — the state builds a state-operated building, and rents space in it to a restaurateur who discriminates; because the state is getting major benefits from the restaurateur's operations, his conduct is transformed into "state action."

☞   The state is heavily *"involved," "entangled"* or *"entwined"* in the activity.

☞   Where the state merely *licenses* the private activity, that's not enough involvement or entanglement to produce state action. (*Example:* Where government gives a liquor license to a private club, that's not enough to turn the club's discriminatory actions into state action. *Moose Lodge v. Irvis.*)

☞   But where state entities *participate* heavily in the private activity, and the state *recognizes* that activity as being closely related to important state concerns, this will probably be enough entanglement to make the activity state action.

Example: A state statute provides that a private association of high schools, all of which are located within a single state, has the role of regulating interscholastic sports in the state. Most association members are public high schools, and nearly all public high schools are members. The association's activities will probably found to be so entwined with state concerns as to make the association a state actor. (*Brentwood Academy*)

CHAPTER 13

CONGRESSIONAL ENFORCEMENT OF CIVIL RIGHTS

ChapterScope

This Chapter involves several aspects of Congress' power to enforce the Amendments enacted immediately after the Civil War. The main concepts are:

- Congress has special powers to enforce the Civil War Amendments, i.e., the 13th, 14th, and 15th Amendments.

- Congress probably can't prohibit *purely private discrimination* under the 14th and 15th Amendments.

  ❏ But Congress *can* prohibit purely private discrimination under the *13th* Amendment, if it finds that the discrimination is a *"badge or incident of slavery."*

- Congress does not have power to *define the scope* of the Civil War Amendments. Only the federal courts may do this.

  ❏ So Congress may not *"expand"* the meaning of these Amendments, i.e., define them in a way that causes more government action to run afoul of these Amendments.

  ❏ Nor may Congress *"reduce"* the scope of these Amendments. Thus once the Supreme Court says for instance, that the Equal Protection Clause prohibits a certain kind of government action, Congress can't use its enforcement powers to say, in effect, "The conduct shall no longer be deemed to be a violation of the Equal Protection Clause."

I. INTRODUCTION

A. Issues presented: This chapter examines Congress' power to *enforce* the Amendments enacted immediately after the Civil War, i.e., the Thirteenth, Fourteenth and Fifteenth Amendments. There are two main issues regarding this power:

1. **Reaching private actors:** To what extent may Congress enact legislation pursuant to these Amendments so as to reach *purely private conduct*, given that these Amendments (at least the Fourteenth and Fifteenth) only refer to conduct *by the states?*

2. **Interpreting the Amendments:** What power does Congress have to *interpret* these Amendments *differently from the Supreme Court*, with respect to: (i) *remedies* to impose for what the Court and Congress both would agree constitutes violations of these Amendments; and (ii) the *substantive content* of these rights?

B. Applicable statutes: Our focus will be upon the constitutional boundaries of Congress' power to enforce the amendments, not upon the precise interpretation of the statutes which Congress has in fact enacted. Nonetheless, a brief overview of the existing statutory framework is helpful. Our summary of this framework is done from the perspective of statutes now on the books.

1. **Civil provisions:**   A number of statutes *grant civil rights* as distinguished from those imposing criminal penalties:

   a. **General equal rights:**   The most general grant of civil rights is made under what is today 42 U.S.C. §1981. That section gives all persons within the United States the same right "as is enjoyed by white citizens" to *make and enforce contracts*, to sue, and to be subject to identical punishments, taxes, and other treatment by the government. This statute was originally enacted as part of the Civil Rights Act of 1866, which was premised on the Thirteenth Amendment (since the Fourteenth did not yet exist).

   b. **Property rights:**   What is now 42 U.S.C. §1982 gives all United States citizens the *same property rights* as whites have, including rights of inheritance, purchase and sale and lease. This provision, too, was part of the 1866 Civil Rights Act, and was given a broad reading by the Court in *Jones v. Alfred H. Mayer Co., infra*, p. 474.

   c. **Deprivations "under color of law":**   42 U.S.C. §1983 allows a private suit for damages to be brought against any person who, *"under color of any statute"* or other law, deprives the plaintiff of *"any rights, privileges or immunities secured by the Constitution and laws."* §1983, one of the best-known of all federal statutory provisions, has often been used to bring suit against *state and local government officials who violate individuals' civil rights*. It derives from the 1871 Civil Rights Act, and relies on at least the Fourteenth Amendment, and perhaps the Thirteenth, for constitutional authority.

   d. **Private conspiracies:**   Two or more persons who *conspire* to deprive anyone of *equal protection* or *equal privileges and immunities under the law*, may be subjected to civil suit under 48 U.S.C. §1985(c). This provision, which derives from the 1871 Civil Rights Act, appears to be applicable *even where there is no state action*, so long as access to a federally-guaranteed right is infringed or sought to be infringed. The constitutionality of this statute's application to conduct involving only private persons is suggested, but not made explicit, in *U.S. v. Guest, infra*, p. 472.

2. **Criminal statutes:**   Two statutory provisions, deriving (like the ones above) from the post-Civil War period, provide *criminal penalties* for roughly the same types of conduct for which private civil actions are permitted by those provisions summarized in (c) and (d), respectively, above.

   a. **Color of law:**   Thus the criminal analog to §1983's civil "color of law" provision is 18 U.S.C. §242, which imposes a fine or imprisonment upon any person who *"under color of any law*, statute, ordinance, regulation or custom," willfully deprives another of any rights protected by the Constitution or federal statutes, on account of *color, race or alienage*. If death results from the deprivation, life imprisonment is authorized.

   b. **Private conspiracies:**   The criminal analog to §1985(c)'s civil conspiracies provision is 18 U.S.C. §241, setting criminal penalties for *conspiring* to "injure, oppress, threaten, or intimidate any citizen in the free exercise or enjoyment of any right or privilege secured to him by the Constitution or the laws of the United States."

3. **Modern statutory additions:**   Major civil rights laws enacted in the 1960's have added some important new provisions. Among these are the following:

a. Public accommodations: Discrimination in the furnishing of *public accommodations* is banned, and made subject to private and governmental civil suits in the Public Accommodations Title of the Civil Rights Act of 1964, 42 U.S.C. §2000a *et seq*. This title was based on Congress' power to regulate interstate commerce, not its power to enforce the Civil War Amendments. See *supra*, p. 46.

b. Voting: Various provisions to ensure *the right to vote* were contained in the 1965 Voting Rights Act, 42 U.S.C. §1973, including measures to restrict the discriminatory use of literacy tests and other voter registration requirements. The Act is discussed in the treatment of *South Carolina v. Katzenbach, infra*, p. 486.

c. Fair housing: Important restrictions on the ability of private entities and individuals to discriminate in the sale or rental of *housing* were contained in Title VIII of the 1968 Civil Rights Act, the Fair Housing Title.

d. Violence: *Violent interference* with a person's enjoyment of his civil rights, even if it is not part of a conspiracy (as is required for application of 18 U.S.C. §241) and even if it involves no state action (as is required for 18 U.S.C. §242) is prohibited by 18 U.S.C. §245, part of the 1968 Civil Rights Act.

II. CONGRESS' POWER TO REACH PRIVATE CONDUCT

A. Purely private conduct: The Fourteenth and Fifteenth Amendment, by their terms, apply only to *state* interferences. As we saw in the previous chapter, the Court has (especially in recent years) read this state action requirement to impose substantial "bite." But §5 of the Fourteenth Amendment, and §2 of the Fifteenth Amendment, explicitly grant Congress the power to *enforce* each of those amendments *"by appropriate legislation."* Thus the issue arises, to what extent may Congress "appropriately" enforce the Fourteenth and Fifteenth Amendments by *proscribing conduct which the Court would not construe to be "state action?"*

    1. Some latitude: While the precise answer to this question has never been decided, it seems clear that Congress has at least some latitude, and that certain types of private conduct unaccompanied by state involvement may nonetheless be prohibited.

       a. Link to state conduct: For instance, private conduct which *prevents state officials* from giving equal protection or due process to others may clearly be prohibited by Congress. Similarly, private conduct which intentionally interferes with rights guaranteed to an individual by federal constitutional provisions *other than* the Fourteenth Amendment (e.g., the *right to travel interstate*) may be barred by Congress.

       b. Gray area: The principal gray area is the extent to which Congress may prevent *purely private discrimination* by one individual against another, where no state facilities, programs or rights are directly involved. For instance, may Congress prohibit discrimination by small private social clubs that hold no state licenses?

B. Early decision: The first time Congress' power to regulate private discrimination was considered, that power received an extremely narrow reading by the Court. Recall that in the *Civil Rights Cases*, 109 U.S. 3 (1883), discussed *supra*, p. 418, a majority of the Court held that, since only state action could violate the Fourteenth Amendment, Congress' enforcement power *only permitted it to restrict state action*, and not private conduct.

1. **Consequence:** Under the logic of the *Civil Rights Cases* (though this was not made explicit in the opinion), Congress did not even have the power to prevent one private individual from forcibly blocking another's exercise of the right to vote in state elections, the right to attend public schools, or other exercises of state rights. Such private conduct would presumably be in violation of state law, but it would not itself be a violation of "equal protection of the [state] laws;" only action *by* the state could be that. And Congress' enforcement power was limited to enactment of those statutes which were needed to ***prevent the state*** from abdicating its equal-protection obligations.

C. **The *Guest* case:** This extremely narrow view of congressional power under the Fourteenth Amendment was not re-examined until the 1960's. Then, in ***U.S. v. Guest***, 383 U.S. 745 (1966), six members of the Court stated that Congress could, under §5 of the Fourteenth Amendment, reach a substantial range of ***private racially discriminatory conduct***. But since three Judges did so in one concurring opinion and the other three in another, *Guest* did not produce a single majority articulation of the scope of Congress' right to reach private conduct.

1. **Facts of *Guest*:** *Guest* concerned a prosecution for criminal conspiracy under 18 U.S.C. §241 (see *supra*, p. 470). The defendants were private individuals. The first count of the indictment charged them with conspiring to interfere violently with the rights of several blacks to use state-owned facilities.

2. **Court's opinion:** The opinion for the Court, written by Justice Stewart, avoided deciding whether §241 could constitutionally be applied to racially discriminatory, but entirely private, interference with the use of public facilities, as charged in the first count. It did so by pointing to the possibility that the indictment might be claiming, although ambiguously, that ***state officials participated*** in the interference.

3. **Concurrences:** Six Justices, in two concurrences, were willing to go further. They thought that the first count of the indictment was constitutional even if it charged only purely-private conduct, with no participation by state officials.

    a. **Clark's concurrence:** One concurrence, by Justice Clark, reasoned that "[t]he specific language of §5 [of the Fourteenth Amendment] empowers the Congress to enact laws punishing all conspiracies — ***with or without state action*** — that interfere with Fourteenth Amendment rights." But he gave no explanation of *why* §5 should be read so as to dispense with any requirement of state action.

    b. **Brennan's concurrence:** Justice Brennan's separate concurrence, however, *did* deal with the question Justice Clark ducked. Brennan believed that §5 gave Congress the power to make any law which it concluded was ***"reasonably necessary*** to protect a right created by and arising under" the Fourteenth Amendment. Thus he would apply the same standard as applied by Chief Justice Marshall in *McCulloch v. Maryland*, in interpreting "the Necessary and Proper" Clause.

        i. **Application of test:** In Brennan's view, Congress could reasonably have concluded that prevention of ***private*** interference with access to state-owned facilities was a reasonably necessary means toward preventing ***governmental*** interference with that access. In fact, he believed that Congress could punish ***all*** conspiracies that interfered with Fourteenth Amendment rights, even if no state officers were involved.

D. ***Morrison* wipes out the expansive interpretation of *Guest*:** For 34 years after *Guest*, no one knew whether the views of the six concurring justices in *Guest* — that Congress could use its §5 remedial powers to reach purely private conduct that interfered with Fourteenth Amendment rights — represented good law. But in a case decided in 2000, ***U.S. v. Morrison***, 529 U.S. 598 (2000) (also discussed *supra* p. 39), the Court decided by a 5-4 vote that the concurrences in *Guest* did *not* represent a holding of the Court, and should be disregarded. Consequently, it is now clear that ***it is not within Congress' §5 powers to reach purely private conduct,*** even if that conduct interferes with rights protected by the Fourteenth Amendment.

1. **Context:** *Morrison* involved a federal statute, the Violence Against Women Act, which allowed women who had been the victims of gender-motivated violent crimes to sue the perpetrator in federal court. When the defendant attacked the statute as beyond Congress' powers, the plaintiff argued (among other things) that even if the statute reached purely private conduct, that private conduct consisted of attempts to violate women's equal protection rights, and was therefore reachable on the theory of the six concurring justices in *Guest*.

2. **Claim rejected:** But the five-justice majority in *Morrison* squarely **rejected** this argument. The Court conceded that the three-Justice concurrence authored by Justice Brennan in *Guest* represented a real view on the merits that Congress could use its §5 powers to reach purely private conduct that interfered with Fourteenth Amendment rights. But the *Morrison* majority pointed out that the other three concurring justices in *Guest*, led by Justice Clark, had given no explanation at all for their similar views. Consequently, Clark's statement that Congress could reach purely private conduct was ***"naked dicta"*** that could not be added to the opinions of the Brennan group for pruposes of deriving a constitutional holding.

   a. **Conclusion:** Therefore, the *Morrison* majority concluded, *Guest* said nothing authoritative about whether Congress could reach purely private conduct, and the *Civil Rights Cases* still represented prevailing law. Under the *Civil Rights Cases*, purely private action that interferes with rights protected by the Fourteenth Amendment is simply beyond Congress' §5 remedial powers.

E. Current state of the law: So here's what the present law seems to be regarded Congress' use of its Fourteenth Amendment §5 powers to reach conduct by private individuals:

1. **Conduct not relating to public officials:** Where Congress tries to reach purely private conduct that has ***nothing to do with state officials***, it's now clear as the result of *Morrison* that Congress cannot do this under its §5 enforcement powers.

   Example: In *Morrison* itself, we saw that Congress could not use its §5 remedial powers to give private citizen *A* a federal cause of action against private citizen *B* merely because *B* practiced gender discrimination against *A* of a sort that would have been a Fourteenth Amendment violation had *B* been acting under color of state law. The same would clearly be true if *B* was a private individual who practiced *racial* discrimination against *A* (e.g., *B* refused to rent an apartment to *A* on racial grounds, and Congress tried to use its §5 powers to give *A* a federal cause of action against *B*).[1]

2. **Interference with state officials:** On the other hand, suppose that Congress merely prohibits private individuals from ***interfering with state officials' attempts*** to furnish equal protection or due process. Here, it seems clear that Congress' action *does* fall within its §5 remedial powers, notwithstanding *Morrison*.

Example: Suppose that Congress makes it a federal crime for a private individual to prevent or attempt to prevent a public School Board official from complying with a federal court's school-desegregation order. Since the private action being regulated is closely tied to state action (the school board desegregation efforts), it seems clear that Congress has acted validly under its Fourteenth Amendment §5 remedial powers.

3. **Private-state interaction:** Finally, where a private party acts in ***conjunction with a state official***, it is quite clear that Congress may punish the private conduct. In fact, 18 U.S.C. § 242 (the statute preventing discriminatory action committed "under color of law") is applicable even to the private actors in this situation.

   a. ***Price* case:** For instance, in *U.S. v. Price*, 383 U.S. 787 (1966), the Court held that private individuals who acted together with local law enforcement officials in the infamous 1964 murder of three civil rights workers near Philadelphia, Mississippi, acted "under color of law" (and could therefore be charged under § 242) even though they themselves were not law enforcement officers.

F. **The Thirteenth Amendment and private conduct:** §1 of the ***Thirteenth*** Amendment provides that "[n]either slavery nor involuntary servitude, except as a punishment for crime … shall exist within the United States. … " §2 gives Congress the power to "enforce this [amendment] by appropriate legislation." Because the Thirteenth Amendment, unlike the Fourteenth and Fifteenth, is ***not explicitly limited to governmental action***, the Amendment has proved to be a useful source of congressional power to reach certain private conduct.

1. **Originally narrowly construed:** The Court has always conceded that Congress could reach purely private conduct under the Thirteenth Amendment; this was one of the holdings of the *Civil Rights Cases*, discussed *supra*, p. 418. However, the Court, beginning with those cases, took a very narrow view of the ***type*** of conduct which the Thirteenth Amendment forbade. The Amendment, and any congressional statutes enforcing it, could only deal with slavery and its ***"badges and incidents"***; private ***discrimination***, even in the furnishing of transportation, hotels and other accommodations, did not constitute a badge of slavery prohibited by the Thirteenth Amendment.

2. **Broadened in *Jones v. Mayer*:** This narrow view of the Thirteenth Amendment's scope was dramatically broadened in a startling case, ***Jones v. Alfred H. Mayer Co.***, 392 U.S. 409 (1968). That case held that Congress had the power, under the Thirteenth Amendment, ***"rationally to determine what are the badges and incidents of slavery."*** Furthermore, it held, Congress' definition of those badges and incidents could rationally be a very ***broad*** one, broad enough to encompass private racial discrimination in ***real estate transactions***.

   a. **Facts:** In *Jones*, plaintiffs complained that defendant (a private developer) refused to sell them a house solely because they were black. Plaintiffs claimed that this was a violation of 42 U.S.C. §1982, which provides that "[a]ll citizens of the United States

---

1. Remember, we're talking here only about whether Congress' *Fourteenth Amendment* enforcement powers can be used. In the rental situation, other congressional powers, such as the Commerce power and the *Thirteenth* Amendment's enforcement power (see *infra*, p. 474), could clearly be used. That's why, for instance, 42 U.S.C. §1982's grant of equal rights to "inherit, purchase, lease, sell, hold, and convey real and personal property" without racial discrimination is clearly still valid notwithstanding *Morrison* — it's almost certainly valid under the Commerce power, and certainly valid under the 13th Amendment (see *Jones v. Alfred H. Mayer Co.*, *infra*, p. 474).

shall have the same right, in every State and Territory, as is enjoyed by white citizens thereof to inherit, purchase, lease, sell, hold, and convey real and personal property." §1982 derives from the 1866 Civil Rights Act, which was enacted solely in reliance on the Thirteenth Amendment, since the Fourteenth had not yet been enacted. Defendant argued that even if §1982 was not intended to apply to private conduct (which Defendant claimed it was not), such conduct could not constitutionally be reached under the Thirteenth Amendment.

b. Holding: The Supreme Court disagreed, finding that the statute was ***within Congress' power under the Thirteenth Amendment***. §2 of the Amendment, giving Congress enforcement powers, allowed Congress to pass "all laws necessary and proper for abolishing all badges and incidents of slavery in the United States" (quoting the *Civil Rights Cases*). And this section gave Congress the right rationally to determine ***what the badges and incidents of slavery are***. This "rationality" test was satisfied here, since it was not irrational of Congress to conclude that barriers to enjoyment of real property were badges of slavery; "when racial discrimination herds men into ghettos and makes their ability to buy property turn on the color of their skin, then it too is a relic of slavery."

c. Potentially broad impact: *Jones* seems to acknowledge Congress' power to define the "badges and incidents of slavery" in almost any way it wishes, so long as the definition is rational.

d. Possible limitations: However, this view of *Jones* seems unduly broad. For instance, while Congress' power to define "slavery and its incidents" may indeed be broad, it is not clear whether Congress may treat anything other than ***racially motivated*** (or ***ethnically*** motivated) discrimination as coming within the Amendment.

    i. Protection of whites: It does seem clear that Congress may use its Thirteenth Amendment enforcement powers to protect ***groups other than blacks*** against racial discrimination.

    ii. Non-racial discrimination: Apart from discrimination based on race, Congress may probably use the Thirteenth Amendment to prohibit private discrimination on grounds of ***ancestry***, or ***ethnic characteristics***. However, the Court has never squarely addressed the issue of whether the Thirteenth Amendment can support legislation banning these types of discrimination.

    iii. Other types of discrimination: The Court has never explicitly indicated that Congress may use the Thirteenth Amendment to prohibit invidious discrimination on ***grounds other than race, ancestry, or ethnic background***. So, for instance, it is highly questionable whether Congress could, say, ban purely private discrimination against ***gays***, lawyers, or other unpopular groups under authority of the Thirteenth Amendment.

    iv. Purposeful discrimination: In any event, whatever discrimination is banned under authority of the Thirteenth Amendment must probably be ***purposeful*** and ***invidious***.

3. Self-executing scope of amendment: Keep in mind that this broad view of the "badges and incidents of slavery" applies only where Congress has enacted a ***statute*** under its powers to enforce the Thirteenth Amendment. Where the ***direct***, self-executing meaning of the

Amendment itself, absent any statute, is concerned, the Court gives a very narrow reading to "badges and incidents of slavery" — perhaps only peonage is included.

> **Example 1:** Suppose that a state passes a law stating that "any owner of residential real estate may discriminate on the basis of race in the sale or lease of that property." Assume that Congress has not passed any statute which would conflict with this state statute. A court probably could ***not*** strike down the state statute on the grounds that it violated the Thirteenth Amendment — that Amendment has practically no self-executing scope.

> **Example 2:** Suppose that a state passed a statute providing that where one person owes a debt to another and cannot pay, the former may be required to work at minimum wage for the latter until the debt is paid off, and that a person who refuses to do such mandatory labor shall be sent to prison. Even in the absence of a federal statute prohibiting this kind of compulsory work, a court probably would hold that the state statute violates the Thirteenth Amendment — the self-executing scope of the Thirteenth Amendment, while very narrow, probably does cover true "peonage," and this state statute would probably be held to involve peonage.

G. Violation of other constitutional rights: So far, we have considered only private conduct which may be barred by congressional statutes relying on the Civil War Amendments. But there are also some rights which are secured by ***other constitutional provisions*** (that is, apart from the Thirteenth, Fourteenth and Fifteenth Amendments) which are applicable against private, not just state, interference.

1. **Right to travel:** Perhaps the most important of these is the ***right to travel from state to state***. See, e.g., *U.S. v. Guest*, 383 U.S. 745 (1966) (other aspects of which are discussed *supra*, pp. 396-98), in which the Court held that Congress was authorized to punish purely private conspiracies to interfere with the exercise of this right (although the Court did not point to any specific constitutional provision as being the source of this right).

2. **Other examples:** Other constitutional rights that are applicable against private interference include: the right to ***vote*** in ***federal primary*** and ***general elections***, the right to ***inform federal officials of violations of federal law***, and the right to ***assemble to petition Congress*** for a redress of grievances. See Justice Harlan's concurrence in *U.S. v. Guest*, 383 U.S. 745 (1966), for his catalogue of such rights.

   a. **Tie-in with civil rights statutes:** These rights are ***not*** necessarily ***self-executing***. That is, it is not clear that one private citizen may recover damages against another, or obtain an injunction against him, for violation of any of these rights, unless a congressional statute so provides. But the post-Civil War civil rights statutes, especially the criminal and civil conspiracy provisions, 18 U.S.C. §§241 and 1985(c) respectively, authorize the federal courts to give civil and criminal relief for certain types of violations of ***any*** constitutional provision, not merely the provisions of the Thirteenth, Fourteenth and Fifteenth Amendments.

III. CONGRESS' POWER TO REMEDY VIOLATIONS OF THE CIVIL WAR AMENDMENTS

A. General problem: We turn now to several questions about the extent of Congress' powers under the Civil War amendments extends:

[1] What kinds of explicitly "remedial" actions may Congress take? (We consider this question generally in Paragraph (B) below, and specifically in the case of voting rights in Paragraph (C), *infra*, p. 478.)

[2] If Congress disagrees with the Supreme Court about the ***proper scope*** of the rights guaranteed by the Thirteenth, Fourteenth or Fifteenth Amendment, may Congress use its remedial powers to ***change the meaning and scope*** of these guarantees? (We discuss this in its own section, section IV, *infra*, p. 486.)

[3] Under what circumstances may Congress ***abrogate*** the states' ***Eleventh Amendment immunity***, so as to let ***private citizens recover money damages*** from a state that violates a federal statute enacted under authority of the Civil War Amendments? (On this question, see section V, *infra*, p. 489).

As to (1), the brief answer is, "a very broad, but not unlimited, range of measures." As to (2), the brief answer is "no." As to (3), the brief answer is, "only if Congress' response is proportional to the state's threatened constitutional violations."

B. Congress' broad "remedial" powers: It is clear that congressional power to adopt ***"remedial"*** legislation concerning the Thirteenth, Fourteenth and Fifteenth Amendments is ***extremely broad,*** though not unlimited.

1. **Reference to "Necessary and Proper" clause:** Congress' power to enforce these Amendments is to be judged generally by reference to the ***"Necessary and Proper"*** clause (*supra*, p. 23). That is, as long as the ***means*** chosen by Congress are ***"rationally related"*** to achieving an objective that one of these Amendments is designed to fulfill, Congress has not exceeded its enforcement authority.[2]

2. **Can act based on state law's effect rather than purpose:** For instance, if Congress reasonably fears that the ***effect*** of a state law will be interferences with a right guaranteed by one of these three Amendments, Congress can prohibit the state law from being enforced. That's true even if it's clear that the members of the state legislature did not, when they enacted the law, have a ***purpose*** of promoting violations of any of the Amendments.

> **Example:** Congress enacts the Voting Rights Act (discussed extensively below) pursuant to its powers to enforce the Fifteenth Amendment, which prohibits racial discrimination in voting. One section of the V.R.A. says that certain states and local governments with a history of intentional discrimination in voting must get federal pre-approval before making any change to the state's voting regulations, if the "effect" of the change may be to abridge voting rights on the basis of race. Rome, Georgia, a city that is required to get pre-approval for various voting-related changes, argues that since §1 of the Fifteenth Amendment prohibits only intentional discrimination, Congress has exceeded its §2 enforcement powers by prohibiting practices based solely on the practices' possible discriminatory effect.
>
> *Held*, Rome loses. The Court will assume, without deciding, that the city is correct in its contention that §1 of the Fifteenth Amendment itself bars only state action that is

---

2. As we'll see below, there is one important limitation on this principle, the "congruent and proportional" standard for judging Congress's exercise of its Fourteenth Amendment enforcement powers; see *City of Boerne v. Flores, infra*, p. 487.

intended to discriminate in voting based on race. But even if that's true, Congress has **broad discretion** in choosing what enforcement methods to use, at least where the defendant has previously violated one of the Civil War Amendments — Congress must merely act rationally in making that choice. Here, "Congress could rationally have concluded that, because electoral changes by jurisdictions with a demonstrable history of intentional racial discrimination in voting create the risk of purposeful discrimination, it was proper to prohibit changes that have a discriminatory impact." *City of Rome v. U.S.*, 446 U.S. 156 (1980).

C. The Voting Rights Act: Most cases about how far Congress' "remedial" powers extend under the Civil War amendments have concerned the constitutionality of *voting-rights* measures adopted by Congress beginning in the 1960's. The most important such measure is the *Voting Rights Act*, the first version of which was enacted by Congress in 1965.

   1. Historical background of the V.R.A.: Reconstruction-era efforts by Congress to eradicate racial discrimination in voting in the South were only marginally successful, and most of the federal statutory provisions were repealed in 1894. Meanwhile, many of the southern states enacted *literacy tests* and other tests that were often used to deny blacks the franchise. The Fifteenth Amendment was of course theoretically available for relief in these situations, but litigation under it was generally time-consuming and difficult. Even when states or counties *were* ordered by the courts to eliminate one discriminatory practice or another, they were often able to devise some new scheme by which to perpetuate racial discrimination in voting. Initial statutory efforts by Congress in 1957, 1960, and 1964 proved largely ineffective.

   2. Voting Rights Act of 1965: Therefore, Congress enacted the *Voting Rights Act of 1965* (the *V.R.A.*), designed to eradicate racial discrimination in voting in part by *preventing it from occurring*, as opposed to detecting and punishing it after the fact.

      a. Suspension of any "test or device": The most important aspect of the Act, from the perspective of Congress' power to enforce the Fifteenth Amendment, was its treatment of *literacy tests* and other *voter eligibility standards*. The Act *suspended*, for an initial period of five years, literacy and similar voter-eligibility tests in any state or political subdivision, if the U.S. Justice Department made an administrative finding that the jurisdiction *had used such tests* as of the last election, and had had an unusually *low voter turnout* in that election.

         i. No intent required: Thus the V.R.A. applied special anti-discrimination administrative rules to certain states and local governments, regardless of whether the jurisdiction had ever been found to have had an *intent* to discriminate on racial grounds.

   3. Upheld in *South Carolina v. Katzenbach*: The V.R.A.'s scheme of suspending all literacy and other voting tests in pre-identified states was *upheld* by the Supreme Court in *South Carolina v. Katzenbach*, 383 U.S. 301 (1966).

      a. "Rationality" standard: The Court in *Katzenbach* construed Congress' power to enforce the Fifteenth Amendment *broadly*. It held Congress could use *"any rational means"* to enforce that Amendment's ban on racial discrimination in voting.

      b. Ban on tests rational: The particular congressional scheme at issue in *Katzenbach* — banning tests or devices in any jurisdiction where they coincided with less-than-

50% registration — *satisfied the rationality standard.* This was so because there was evidence presented to Congress that all of the areas known to have practiced racial discrimination in voting shared these two characteristics. Also, the use of tests or devices clearly furnished a means of carrying out racial discrimination, and low registration figures were an obvious symptom of such discrimination.

   c. **Court's own view of literacy tests:** *South Carolina v. Katzenbach* demonstrates that Congress' remedial powers under §2 of the Fifteenth Amendment permit Congress to *outlaw practices which the Court would not on its own find to violate §1 of that Amendment,* as long as these practices are *reasonably closely related* to practices that *would* violate §1. (But, as we'll see from the 2013 *Shelby County* case, if Congress wants to outlaw practices that don't necessarily manifest a discriminatory intent, Congress must be acting based on "current conditions.")

   d. **Discriminatory effect:** A post-*Katzenbach* case on the Voting Rights Act confirms that Congress's §2 remedial powers give it the power to ban even practices that are discriminatory *only in their effect*, not their purpose. See *Rome v. U.S.*, 446 U.S. 156 (1980), discussed *supra*, p. 478. In other words, if Congress reasonably fears that a state will commit intentional discrimination, Congress can "remedy" that discrimination *in advance*, by banning a given practice that would have the *effect* of hurting minority voters, whether or not there's proof that the jurisdiction proposing to use that practice did so for discriminatory *purposes*.

4. **Obligation to rely on current data (*Shelby County v. Holder*):** Nearly everyone would agree that the massive, purposeful racial discrimination by the southern states that gave rise to the original 1965 version of the V.R.A. has dramatically *decreased* in recent years. Does the passage of long periods — and the consequent large *reduction in purposeful discrimination* — mean that a specific remedy that once fell within Congress's Fifteenth Amendment enforcement powers might now *exceed those powers*?

A major 2013 decision shows that the answer in some instances is *"yes."* That is, if in the present era Congress wants to use its Fifteenth Amendment enforcement powers to prevent future violations of the Amendment — rather than punish past violations — Congress must *adjust the measures it uses* to reflect *current rather than historical voting circumstances*. The decision is *Shelby County v. Holder*, ___ S.Ct. ___ (2013), a 5-4 decision, which because of its overruling of a major and long-standing part of the V.R.A. is worthy of detailed discussion.

   a. **Summary of holding:** The Court held in *Shelby County* that because Congress relied only on *40-year-old data* when it identified certain state and local governments and required them to get federal "preclearance" for many voting-related changes, Congress exceeded the scope of its Fifteenth Amendment enforcement powers. So these preclearance requirements of the V.R.A. — which in many ways are the heart of the V.R.A. — are as of this writing (August 2013) *unenforceable*, and will remain so unless and until Congress passes a new law using much more up-to-date voter information as the basis for identifying covered jurisdictions.

   b. **The preclearance procedures:** You can't understand *Shelby County* without a fairly detailed understanding of the V.R.A.'s *"preclearance"* scheme. Under that scheme, mainly specified in §5 of the Act, any state or subdivision of a state that has been determined to have a certain *history* of voter discrimination based on race or color cannot make any change to its registration or other electoral processes without getting advance approval (i.e., "preclearance") from the U.S. Justice Department.

i. **"Coverage formula":** An integral part of the preclearance scheme is the idea of a ***"coverage formula,"*** which the V.R.A. uses to determine *which jurisdictions* are to be required to preclear their voting-related changes. When the V.R.A. was first passed in 1965, §4 of the Act specified a formula to be applied by the U.S. Justice Department for ***identifying*** those states or subdivisions of states likely to have previously practiced large-scale racial discrimination. In the 1965 version of §4, the formula covered any state or subdivision that met two conditions:

   [1] At the time of the November 1964 elections, the jurisdiction had used a ***literacy test***, ***character test*** or similar device as a ***prerequisite to voter registration***; *and*

   [2] In that 1964 election, the jurisdiction had either a ***voter registration*** percentage or a ***voter turnout*** percentage that was significantly ***below the national average***.

ii. **Consequence of being on list:** Under the original V.R.A. (as well as its subsequent versions), if a state or local government appeared on the Justice Department's coverage list, the government ***could not change any of its voting procedures*** — ranging from minor changes like moving a polling place or changing the hours for voting, all the way to major changes like redistricting — without getting ***preclearance*** either from the Justice Department or from a federal court in Washington DC.

iii. **Initial list:** The initial coverage list compiled by the Justice Department soon after the V.R.A.'s 1965 passage included six entire states, all in the deep South — ***Alabama, Georgia, Louisiana, Mississippi, South Carolina and Virginia*** — as well as several counties in other states. (Although the coverage list has changed slightly in the ensuing decades, all of these six states remained covered as of the 2013 *Shelby County* decision, and a couple of new ones, such as Texas, have been added.)

iv. **Original "sunset" provision:** In the initial 1965 V.R.A., these preclearance procedures were set to ***expire automatically after five years***, on the theory that the voting discrimination to which they were addressed would likely have been remedied by then.

   (1) **Reauthorized:** But in the ensuing decades, Congress repeatedly ***reauthorized*** the preclearance and coverage-formula provisions, for increasingly long periods: another five years in 1970, seven years in 1975, 25 years in 1982, and 25 years in 2006. The reauthorization at issue in *Shelby County* was the one that occurred in 2006, which by its terms was to keep the preclearance formulas in place until 2031.

   (2) **Hearings:** As part of the 2006 reauthorization, Congress conducted ***extensive hearings*** into minority voting patterns. As the result of these hearings, Congress concluded that while significant progress had been made in reducing racial barriers to voting, ***newer types of barriers*** to minority representation were still sufficiently prevalent that preclearance should be maintained. Both

parties in both Houses of Congress overwhelmingly voted in favor of the reauthorization,[3] which was then signed by a Republican president, George W. Bush.

(3) Coverage formula unchanged: In what became the critical aspect of the *Shelby County* litigation, Congress in the 2006 reauthorization *maintained the coverage formula as it had stood in 1975*. This meant that the sole factors used to determine what jurisdictions would be subject to preclearance were whether the jurisdiction had *used a voting test in 1972* and whether the jurisdiction had had less than 50% voter registration or turnout in *that year*. So no post-1972 developments could count at all, either to include or exclude a jurisdiction.[4]

c. **More acts covered:** Over the years following the initial 1965 V.R.A., as Congress reauthorized the Act, it also expanded the *types of changes* that would be subject to preclearance in covered jurisdictions. By the 2006 version of the Act, the statute had been broadened to require preclearance for any change that would diminish the ability of racial minorities to *"elect their preferred candidates of choice."* So, for instance, if a covered jurisdiction made *redistricting changes* — even ones that would not make it harder for a racial minority group to register or vote, but that would lessen that group's *voting clout*[5] — the changes would be subject to preclearance.

i. **Effect vs. purpose:** Post-1965 changes to the V.R.A. also made it clear that if a voting-related change had one of these bad voting-related racial *effects,* it would be subject to preclearance even if the government's *purpose* in enacting the change did not appear to be discriminatory. See 42 U.S.C. ss. 1973c(b)-(d). (That's the provision that was upheld in *City of Rome v. U.S., supra*, p. 478.)

d. **Shelby County's suit:** Now, on to the *Shelby County* case. Shelby County, in Alabama, brought a challenge to the constitutionality of both §4's coverage formula (which included all local governments in Alabama) and §5's preclearance procedures. The county claimed that each of these sections went beyond Congress' powers. The lower federal courts rejected the challenge, concluding that both of the sections were proper exercises of Congress' Fifteenth Amendment enforcement powers.

e. **Majority strikes down §4:** The Supreme Court, by a 5-4 vote, *struck down* §4's *coverage formula.* The majority opinion was by Chief Justice Roberts. He was joined by

---

3. The votes in Congress were lopsided: 98 to 0 in the Senate and 390 to 33 in the House.

4. However, the V.R.A. included so-called "bail-in" and "bail-out" provisions, discussed briefly in the treatment of Justice Ginsburg's *Shelby County* dissent, *infra*, p. 484. These allowed for the federal government to get a court order requiring that a jurisdiction not captured by the coverage formula nonetheless be required to get preclearance ("bail-in") or, conversely, allowed a jurisdiction captured by the coverage formula to get a court order that the jurisdiction be exempted from preclearance ("bail-out"). These bail-in and bail-out provisions remain in force after *Shelby County*.

5. For instance, Congress feared various types of *"racial gerrymanders."* One type that many members of Congress feared was where voting-district boundaries would be redrawn so as to *concentrate minority voters* into a small number of heavily-minority districts, thus diluting the voting power of the reduced number of minority voters left in the redrawn non-heavily-minority districts.

the three other conservatives (Scalia, Thomas and Alito), and got the decisive fifth vote from the frequent swing justice, Kennedy.

i. **Nature of decision:** Roberts did not decide whether the basic §5 *preclearance* procedure was constitutional. But he held that the *particular coverage formula* used in §4 was beyond Congress' Fifteenth Amendment enforcement powers, because that formula was *based on 40-year-old data* and thus *did not adequately reflect current conditions.*

ii. **Originally a valid approach:** Roberts agreed that when the original coverage-formula approach to preclearance was enacted in 1965, it was a *proper exercise* of Congress' powers: requiring certain states to obtain federal permission before enacting any change to their voting laws was *"strong medicine,"* but Congress had properly determined that this step was needed to combat *"entrenched racial discrimination"* in voting. And the coverage formula — "the means of linking the exercise of the unprecedented authority with the problem that warranted it" — *"made sense."*

iii. **Change to country:** But, Roberts said, *"our country has changed"* since 1965.

(1) **Change in voter turnout patterns:** He pointed out that Census Bureau data from the most recent (2012) elections showed that African-American voter turnout *exceeded* white voter turnout in five of the six states originally (and still) covered by the preclearance requirement, and was only one half of one percent behind the white turnout in the sixth state. *"No one can fairly say,"* he continued, that the record in these covered states "shows anything approaching the *'pervasive,' 'flagrant,' 'widespread,' and 'rampant'* discrimination that faced Congress in 1965, and that clearly distinguished the covered jurisdictions from the rest of the Nation at that time."

(2) **Due to V.R.A.:** Roberts conceded that "[t]here is no doubt that these improvements are in large part *because* of the Voting Rights Act."

iv. **Equal sovereignty principle:** Roberts then questioned whether Congress' continued singling out of certain states by use of the coverage formula violated what he called the *"fundamental principle of equal sovereignty"* among the states. True, he said, Congress is given the power to enforce the Fifteenth Amendment; but this power must be used "not ... to *punish* for the past [but rather] to *ensure a better future.*" Therefore, if Congress is to "divide the States," the equal-sovereignty principle requires Congress to "identify those jurisdictions to be singled out on a *basis that makes sense in light of current conditions.* It cannot rely simply on the past."

v. **Current data not used:** Then came the nub of Roberts' analysis: Congress, in the recent 2006 reauthorization of the V.R.A., *had not taken into account "current conditions"* when it reenacted the previously-used coverage formula. It was true that Congress had conducted extensive *hearings* prior to the reauthorization. But Congress had not *used this record* to design a new formula based on current conditions. Instead, Congress had "reenacted *a formula based on 40-year-old facts having no logical relation to the present day."*[6] The "extraordinary and unprecedented features" of the V.R.A. had been reauthorized *"as if nothing had changed."*

(1) Conclusion: This failure by Congress to use data reflecting current conditions made the coverage formula unconstitutional, he said. Roberts noted that in a 2009 case on the V.R.A. (*Northwest Austin Municipal Util. Dist. v. Holder*, 557 U. S. 193 (2009)), the majority had "expressed serious doubts about the Act's continued constitutionality" because of this obsolete-data issue. Congress could have taken the Court's hint in *Northwest Austin* and re-worked the coverage formula, but it didn't do so. Congress' "failure to act," he said, "leaves us today with *no choice* but to declare [the coverage formula] unconstitutional."

vi. **No standard stated:** Roberts' opinion nowhere specified exactly *what standard* he was using for determining whether Congress has acted beyond the scope of its Fifteenth Amendment enforcement powers. The opinion did not, for example, specify whether the Court was using mere-rationality review, or instead the tougher "congruent and proportional" standard that the Court has used in recent years to evaluate Congress's use of its *Fourteenth* Amendment enforcement powers (see *City of Boerne v. Flores, infra*, p. 487).

(1) "Rationality" reference: However the language used by Roberts early in his opinion indicates that he was in fact applying mere-rationality review. At the start of Roberts' opinion, he mentioned that when the Court had upheld the constitutionality of the *original* coverage formula in the 1966 decision in *South Carolina v. Katzenbach* (*supra*, p. 478), the Court did so based on the conclusion that the formula "was *'rational in both practice and theory.'* " And, he said, the initial coverage formula "made sense." These references to "rationality" and "making sense" — coupled with the absence of any indication of a change in standard — suggest that Roberts thought that mere-rationality review was and should be the standard, and that Roberts was concluding that Congress' use of 40-year-old data could not meet even this extremely easy-to-satisfy standard.

vii. **Preclearance itself left untouched:** Roberts expressly declined to rule on whether §5 of the V.R.A. — the section that lays out the preclearance requirements — is constitutional: "We issue no holding on §5 itself, *only on the coverage formula.*" Therefore, "Congress may *draft another formula* based on current conditions." (But as we discuss below, p. 485, it's unlikely that Congress will be able to agree on a new formula anytime soon.)

f. **Thomas concurrence:** In a concurrence, Justice Thomas said that he would have gone *further* than Roberts, by finding that §5's preclearance procedures — not just §4's coverage formula — were unconstitutional. No other member of the Court stated an agreement with Thomas on this point.

---

6. This statement is factually correct: no event occurring after the 1972 elections had any effect on what jurisdictions would be covered by the formula. See *supra*, p. 481.

g. **Ginsburg's dissent:** Justice Ginsburg *dissented*, in an opinion joined by the Court's three other liberals, Breyer, Sotomayor and Kagan. Ginsburg's two major themes were that (1) the majority had failed to give the *requisite deference* to Congress's judgment about what means were required to combat discrimination in voting; and (2) the V.R.A. as reauthorized was far better calibrated to current conditions than the majority gave it credit for being.

   i. **Highest level of congressional power:** Ginsberg began by arguing that Congress' powers to enforce the Fifteenth Amendment should be construed especially *broadly*. The Fifteenth Amendment — and the V.R.A. as a method of enforcing that Amendment — deals with not one but *two* issues of major constitutional concern — *racial discrimination* and the *right to vote*. And in this "combination" situation, *"Congress' power to act is at its height."* The majority's decision that Congress had acted beyond its enforcement powers amounted to *"hubris,"* she said.

   ii. **No standard of review:** Ginsburg criticized the majority for not even articulating the *standard of review* it was using. She believed that this was clearly a case in which the appropriate standard was the easy-to-satisfy *mere-rationality* review, as the Court had used when it upheld the original V.R.A. in *Katzenbach* (*supra*, p. 478).

      (1) **Significance of reauthorization:** Furthermore, she contended, the fact that the coverage formula here was part of a *reauthorization* of a previously-enacted statute, rather than a new statute, should make the rational-basis standard even *easier* to satisfy than usual, for several reasons. For instance, Congress had already established a "legislative record" when it first enacted the V.R.A. in 1965, and it was entitled to *consider that pre-existing record* as well as the new findings it had made just prior to the reauthorization.

   iii. **"Throwing out an umbrella":** Ginsberg rejected the accuracy of the majority's conclusion that the coverage formula failed to take account of "current conditions." One such "current condition" was *the very existence of the preclearance remedy* in the covered jurisdictions, a remedy that Congress had designed in part to "guard against [a] return to old ways." She said that *"[t]hrowing out preclearance when it has worked and is continuing to work to stop discriminatory changes is like throwing away your umbrella in a rainstorm because you are not getting wet."*

   iv. **Bail-out and bail-in provisions:** Ginsburg also thought that the existence of *"bail-out"* and *"bail-in"* provisions in the V.R.A. made the Act more responsive to current conditions than the majority claimed. The "bail-out" provision, for instance, permitted a covered jurisdiction to *leave the preclearance regime* by convincing a court that it had complied with the V.R.A. for 10 years and had tried to eliminate voter harassment and intimidation; nearly 200 jurisdictions had successfully bailed out of the coverage formula. So the V.R.A. was not, as the majority claimed, "static"; it was on the contrary "a *dynamic statute, capable of adjusting to changing conditions."*

   v. **Second-generation devices** Ginsberg rejected, too, the majority's heavy reliance on the uncontested fact that there had been dramatic improvements in minority registration and turnout in covered jurisdictions. Direct barriers to minority voter registration and turnout were *"first-generation"* barriers that existed in the 1960s, and had indeed been dramatically reduced by the V.R.A. But Congress had reasonably concluded that these barriers had been **replaced** by efforts to "**reduce the impact of minority votes**," efforts aptly described as *"second-generation barriers."* These vote-dilution efforts, typically pursued by white incumbents, included strategies like **racial gerrymandering** (see *supra*, p. 481, n. 5) and **at-large** municipal voting. During the reauthorization, Congress had concluded that preclearance and the coverage formula were important methods of combating these growing second-generation barriers, and that conclusion was entitled to deference.

vi. Summary: In summary, Ginsburg said, Congress' own judgment about what means fell within its power to enforce the Civil War amendments "by appropriate legislation" merited the Court's "***utmost respect***." The Court "errs egregiously" by overriding Congress' decision.

h. Significance: It's too soon to know how much of a practical difference *Shelby County* will make either in the conduct of American elections or in general constitutional analysis.

i. No preclearance may be required: Unless and until Congress is able to **agree on a new coverage formula**, the preclearance regime of §5 might as well not exist, since **no jurisdiction can be subject to it.**

ii. Conduct of elections: Most observers think that it's very unlikely that Congress will be able to **agree on a new coverage formula** anytime soon. (That's the reason, politically speaking, why the existing formula was left unchanged in the 2006 reauthorization, even though huge majorities in both houses voted for reauthorization.)

(1) Tougher Voter ID rules: The unenforceability of pre-clearance means that all states and subdivisions are now free to **make whatever changes they wish to their election procedures** without seeking advanced federal approval. In the immediate aftermath of *Shelby County*, the most dramatic impact of the decision has been that several states that had previously been subject to preclearance have enacted or announced more rigorous **voter identification** requirements. These include measures such as requiring a **government-issued photo ID** as a prerequisite for registration and prohibiting same-day voter registration. Some of these states have also moved to **limit early voting.** See generally, *NY Times*, August 13, 2013 (p. A11) and August 8, 2013 (p. A1).

(2) "Bail-in": But the U.S. Justice Department remains free to use the V.R.A.'s §3 *"bail-in"* provision to attack these and other voting changes, since the bail in provision is not affected by *Shelby County*. So if a jurisdiction — whether one previously subjected to the now-invalid coverage formula or not — makes a voting rule change that Justice believes constitutes intentional discrimination, the Justice Department can, under §3 of the V.R.A., **ask a federal court** to **treat that jurisdiction as being subject to the preclearance rules**. If the court agrees, the jurisdiction may then not make any change to its voting rules unless either the court or the Justice Department preapproves the change. This

§3 approach requires the Justice Department to sue one jurisdiction at a time, but it gives the federal government the potential power to put a jurisdiction under preclearance.

(3) **Suit against Texas:** In fact, just weeks after *Shelby County*, the Justice Department began to take this bail-in approach with respect to one jurisdiction, Texas. Prior to *Shelby County*, Texas enacted both a voter ID law and a revised districting plan; each was blocked by a federal court on the grounds that Texas was one of the states subject to preclearance under the V.R.A.,[7] and the Justice Department hadn't issued that preclearance for either change. Two hours after the *Shelby County* decision was released, Texas announced that it was putting both changes into effect. Within a week, the Justice Department announced that it would be suing Texas in federal court to have the state placed back into a preclearance mode via the bail-in procedure. See *NY Times*, July 26, 2013, p. A1.

iii. **Constitutional doctrine:** With respect to *Shelby County*'s effect on **constitutional doctrine generally**, the case does not seem to make much difference. Although the Roberts opinion does not recite what standard of review is being used, the Court seemed to use traditional mere-rationality review on the issue of whether Congress exceeded its Fifteenth Amendment enforcement powers. True, this review seemed a bit more stringent than the usual mere-rationality process, but there has been no official change in doctrine.

(1) **No "congruent and proportional" review:** Most significantly, the Court seems to have intentionally *ignored* the chance to use the more stringent test that it has begun using in cases involving Congress' *Fourteenth* Amendment enforcement powers. In *Boerne v. Flores, infra*, p. 487, the Court said that any means chosen by Congress to enforce the Fourteenth Amendment must be *"congruent and proportional"* to the harm being addressed. But *Shelby County* does not use — or even discuss — the congruent-and-proportional standard in the context of Congress' powers to enforce the *Fifteenth* Amendment. So the ostensibly easier-to-satisfy mere-rationality standard seems to remain in place for Fifteenth Amendment cases.

IV. CONGRESS' POWER TO REDEFINE THE MEANING AND SCOPE OF CONSTITUTIONAL GUARANTEES

A. **Substantive modifications:** Most of the time, when Congress claims to be using its power to enforce the Civil War amendments, Congress is clearly acting for *"remedial"* purposes — that is, the statute is designed to combat what, by the Court's own opinions, constitute past or prospective violations of these Amendments. Even in *Shelby County*, although the Court found

---

7. As the result of a 1975 change to the coverage formula, three states, Texas, Arizona and Alaska, were added to the preclearance regime on account of their having, in 1972, provided electoral materials and ballots only in English while members of a single non-English-speaking *"language minority"* constituted more than five percent of the state's voting-age citizens. Portions of six other states, including California, New York and Florida, were also subjected to preclearance as part of this language-minority provision.

that Congress went beyond its powers, there was no doubt that Congress was seeking mainly to prevent what the Court agreed would have been violations of the Fifteenth Amendment.

But other legislation enacted by Congress from time to time under its Civil War Amendment enforcement powers is harder to justify on a "remedial" theory. This latter type of legislation seems to constitute an attempt by Congress to *redefine the meaning and scope of constitutional guarantees themselves.* Can Congress do this?

1. **Congress may not redefine scope of guarantees:** After decades of uncertainty, the Court in 1997 finally decided that Congress may *not* do this — *it's up to the Court alone, not Congress, to define the scope of constitutional rights,* even rights (such as those given by the Fourteenth Amendment) as to which Congress has an explicit remedial power.

2. *Boerne v. Flores*: The landmark case in which the Court found that Congress has *no right to specify the substantive contours of constitutional rights* was *City of Boerne v. Flores*, 521 U.S. 507 (1997). In that case, the Court held that Congress could not use its Fourteenth Amendment remedial powers to prevent local governments from unintentionally burdening individuals' religious freedom in certain ways. The decision's effect was to prevent Congress from effectively overruling a prior Supreme Court decision about the meaning of the Free Exercise clause.

   a. **Statutory and caselaw background:** Before we can understand *Boerne*, we have to understand a bit about that prior Court decision, and Congress' response to it.

      i. **Prior Court decision:** In 1990, the Supreme Court decided *Employment Division v. Smith* (*infra*, p. 696), a case about the meaning of the First Amendment's guarantee of the free exercise of religion. The Court reversed its prior doctrine, and held that where a state enacts a criminal ban that is generally applicable, the state may automatically enforce that ban — without any balancing of the government's interest against the individual's interest — even where the ban has the effect of substantially interfering with an individual's exercise of his religion. (The ban at issue in *Smith* prevented Native Americans from making their traditional religious use of the drug peyote.)

      ii. **Congress' response:** The *Smith* decision was very unpopular. Congress responded in 1993 by overwhelmingly passing the "Religious Freedom Restoration Act" (RFRA). The RFRA forced federal, state and local governments to apply pre-*Smith* law, by which no government action that had the effect of "substantially burdening" a person's exercise of religion could be taken unless that action was the least restrictive means of accomplishing a "compelling governmental interest." (In other words, Congress was effectively saying that any governmental action that substantially burdened the exercise of religion had to survive strict scrutiny.)

      iii. **Based on Congress' Fourteenth Amendment remedial power:** In applying its new rule to state and local governments, Congress relied on its Fourteenth Amendment remedial powers: since the First Amendment (including the guarantee of free exercise of religion) is made applicable to the states through the Fourteenth Amendment's guarantee of due process (see *supra*, p. 143), Congress reasoned that it could tell the states how to enforce that free-exercise guarantee as a means of "enforcing" due process.

b. Result: In *Boerne v. Flores*, the Supreme Court held that the RFRA was ***unconstitutional***. Writing for a 6-3 majority, Justice Kennedy said that "[Congress] has been given the power 'to enforce,' ***not the power to determine what constitutes a constitutional violation.***" (In fact, even the three dissenters agreed that Congress did not have the power to define substantive aspects of the Fourteenth Amendment.)

   i. Rejection of *Katzenbach v. Morgan*: Justice Kennedy admitted that there was language in a prior Court opinion, *Katzenbach v. Morgan*, 384 U.S. 641 (1966), which he said "could be interpreted as acknowledging a power in Congress to enact legislation that expands the rights contained in §1 of the Fourteenth Amendment." But he said that this was not the best interpretation of what *Katzenbach* was saying.

   ii. Effects would be unbounded: Kennedy then argued that allowing Congress to expand or contract the scope of constitutional guarantees would produce an unstable, easily-changed Constitution: "If Congress could define its own powers by altering the Fourteenth Amendment's meaning, no longer would the Constitution be 'superior paramount law, unchangeable by ordinary means.' It would be 'on a level with ordinary legislative acts, and, like other acts, . . . alterable when the legislature shall please to alter it' [citing *Marbury v. Madison*]. Under this approach, it is difficult to conceive of a principle that would limit congressional power. . . . Shifting legislative majorities could change the Constitution and effectively circumvent the difficult and detailed amendment process contained in Article V."

   iii. RFRA struck down: Justice Kennedy then concluded that the RFRA in fact modified the scope of the free exercise clause, rather than merely enforcing that clause.

      (1) Congress can sometimes prohibit state statutes: Kennedy acknowledged that Congress could sometimes prevent states from enacting certain types of statutes that were not facially unconstitutional, as a method of preventing likely constitutional violations. For instance, in the Voting Rights Act provision upheld in *Katzenbach v. Morgan*, Congress could, and did, prohibit states with a history of voting-rights violations from applying literacy tests.

      (2) The "congruence and proportionality" test: Kennedy then set forth a new test for when Congress has gone beyond its Fourteenth Amendment §5 remedial powers: He conceded that Congress must have "wide latitude" in determining where the line is between an appropriate remedial provision and an improper substantive re-definition of a Fourteenth Amendment right. But, he said, "there must be a ***congruence and proportionality*** between the injury to be prevented or remedied and the means adopted to that end."

      (3) RFRA out of proportion: But the RFRA, Kennedy said, flunked this "congruence and proportionality" test. It was "so ***out of proportion*** to [any] supposed remedial or preventive object that it cannot be understood as responsive to, or designed to prevent, unconstitutional behavior. It appears, instead, to attempt a substantive change in constitutional protections." Therefore, it was invalid.

   iv. Dissent: Three Justices dissented in *Boerne*. But even the three dissenters agreed that Congress can't expand or contract the scope of constitutional guarantees, even the scope of the Fourteenth Amendment guarantees as to which Congress has an explicit remedial power. (These Justices dissented only because they disagreed with the *Smith* decision, and therefore didn't believe that Congress was in fact modifying the scope of the Free-Exercise clause from what these dissenters believed that scope should be.)

   c. Significance: The main significance of *Boerne*, taken together with Eleventh Amendment cases decided in its aftermath (like *Kimel v. Florida Bd. of Regents, infra*, p. 490), is to establish two related propositions, both captured in the above-noted phrase that Congress' use of its enforcement powers under § 5 of the 14th Amendment must be *"congruent and proportional"* to the harm that's being remedied:

   [1] Congress has power under § 5 of the 14th Amendment to allow private plaintiffs to sue the state *only if Congress properly found widespread unconstitutional state conduct in the area in question,* and ...

   [2] Even if Congress properly found such widespread unconstitutional conduct by the state, Congress must choose *narrowly-tailored methods* for combating the state conduct.

V. CONGRESS' POWER TO ABROGATE THE ELEVENTH AMENDMENT, AND THUS AUTHORIZE PRIVATE DAMAGE SUITS AGAINST THE STATES FOR DISCRIMINATION

A. Private money-damage suits against states for discrimination: Congress often prohibits a certain type of *discrimination*, and then attempts to make *state and local governments*, not just private individuals, obey the prohibition. Sometimes, Congress goes even further, and attempts to *give private individuals the right to bring private actions* for *money damages* against a *state or local government* that commits the prohibited discrimination.

   1. Significance of Eleventh Amendment: But because of the existence of the *Eleventh Amendment* (described below), it will often turn out that Congress *has overstepped its boundaries* by such an attempt to let private individuals sue state and local governments for discrimination.

   2. Must use Civil War Amendment remedial powers: As we'll see in a minute, if Congress wants to subject the states to private money-damage suits for violating federal anti-discrimination laws, Congress *must act under its Civil War Amendment enforcement powers*, not under its other powers such as the Commerce Clause. That means that a special restriction the Court has placed on Congress' powers to enforce the Civil War amendments significantly limits Congress' ability to let private citizens sue state governments for discrimination.

B. The Eleventh Amendment: The Eleventh Amendment says, in brief, that the *states are immune* from being sued for *money damages by private citizens in federal court*. We discuss the Amendment in much greater detail later in this outline (see p. 725).

   1. Congress' power to abrogate the immunity: It's always been clear, however, that Congress has in some circumstances the power to *abrogate* the states' Eleventh Amendment immunity from private suits. But the Supreme Court's view of how and when Congress can do so has changed over the years.

a. **Cannot use Commerce powers:** Originally, nearly everyone thought that Congress could use its extremely broad *Commerce Clause* powers to abrogate the states' Eleventh Amendment immunity. That is, it was thought that Congress could ban a particular type of discrimination by use of its Commerce powers, and under those same powers (i) require the states to comply with the ban, and (ii) strip their Eleventh Amendment immunity so that private citizens could sue the state for violation of the federal ban. But in the 1996 case of *Seminole Tribe v. Florida* (discussed further *infra*, p. 727), the Court surprised the world by holding that the Commerce powers *cannot* serve as the basis for a congressional abrogation of the Eleventh Amendment.

b. **Can use Civil War Amendment powers:** On the other hand, it's always been clear that Congress *may* rely on its *Civil War Amendment remedial powers* as the source of authority for a general anti-discrimination statute. And under those powers (unlike the Commerce power), Congress can not only ban discrimination that would violate the Civil War amendments, but can subject state governments to the ban, and *abrogate the states' Eleventh Amendment immunity*, so as to let private victims sue a discriminating state for damages.

2. **"Congruent and proportional" rule:** But when Congress wants to regulate the states and subject them to private damage suits, there's an important rub. Remember that when Congress purports to use its Civil War Amendment enforcement powers (at least its Fourteenth Amendment powers), there must be a *"congruence and proportionality"* between the constitutional injury that Congress is trying to prevent or redress, and the means that Congress has chosen. (That's the key holding of *Boerne v. Flores, supra*, p. 487.)

   a. **Consequence:** This "congruence and proportionality" rule can easily get in Congress' way. Suppose Congress prohibits a certain form of discrimination (e.g., age discrimination in employment), includes state governments within the ban, and then purports to strip the states of their Eleventh Amendment immunity so that state employees can sue the state for damages if the state discriminates against them. If the Supreme Court then decides that Congress used a remedy so broad that it was not "congruent and proportional to" the problem, then Congress's attempt to abrogate the Eleventh Amendment immunity will be *invalid*, and employees won't in fact be able to sue the states for damages even though that was Congress' intent.

C. **Age and disability discrimination:** This scenario — Congress fails in its attempt to make the states liable in private money-damage suits alleging discrimination — has in fact unfolded on several occasions. For instance, in a pair of decisions the Court held that when Congress tried to make the states (acting as employers) liable in federal court for *age and disability discrimination*, Congress *exceeded* its Fourteenth Amendment §5 remedial powers. *Kimel v. Florida Bd. of Regents*, 528 U.S. 62 (2000) and *Bd. of Trustees of Univ. of Alabama v. Garrett*, 531 U.S. 356 (2001). We'll discuss *Kimel* first.

1. **The ADEA statute (*Kimel*):** Back in the 1960s, Congress passed the Age Discrimination In Employment Act (ADEA), which prohibits various forms of age discrimination in employment. Congress expressly subjected the states to the ADEA's requirements when they act as employers. And for quite awhile, state employees often successfully sued the states in federal court for damages for age-discrimination based on ADEA violations.

a. State arguments after *Seminole Tribe* and *Boerne*: But after the 1996 decision in *Seminole Tribe* and the 1997 decision in *Boerne v. Flores*, states started defending these private ADEA suits with the following pair of arguments:

> [1] the states can be liable for ADEA violations only if Congress was acting properly under its power to enforce the equal protection clause of the Fourteenth Amendment (since that's the only clause of the Thirteenth, Fourteenth and Fifteenth Amendments that even arguably has anything to do with age discrimination); and

> [2] Congress didn't find that the states were ***significant violators of equal protection*** when they discriminated on the basis of age, so making the states obey the ADEA as a means of combating equal protection violations was not a "congruent and proportional" response to an equal protection problem, as required by *Boerne v. Flores*.

b. States win: In *Kimel*, the state of Florida ***prevailed*** with this 2-pronged argument. The only real question was whether argument [2] would convince the Court. Five members of the Court concluded that the argument had merit.

i. Lack of discriminatory history by state: The majority noted that prior to passage of the ADEA, older persons were ***not commonly the victims of equal protection violations at the hands of state or local governments.*** Older workers had not been subjected to a "history of purposeful unequal treatment," and were not a "discrete and insular minority." Therefore, as the Court had previously decided in *Mass. Ret. Bd. v. Murgia* (*supra*, p. 249), state discrimination on the basis of age need only survive mere-rationality review, not some form of a ban scrutiny.

ii. No congruence or proportionality: Consequently, any attempt by Congress to subject the states to extensive age-discrimination rules ***could not possibly have been a "congruent and proportional" response*** to equal protection violations, as required by *Boerne*. This meant that individual employees could not constitutionally be permitted to recover damages for ADEA violations against state or local employers.

2. Same result for disability discrimination under ADA (*Garrett*): Then, a year after *Kimel*, the Court reached a similar conclusion about Title I of the ***Americans with Disabilities Act (ADA).*** Just as *Kimel* found that Congress did not have §5 remedial power to subject the states as employers to ***age*** discrimination rules, the Court held in a 5-4 ruling in *Bd. of Trustees of Univ. of Alabama v. Garrett*, 531 U.S. 356 (2001) that Congress did not have §5 power to bar the states from discriminating against ***employees with disabilities***, as it tried to do in Title I.

a. Lack of adequate proof: The ADA was a more modern statute than the ADEA (at issue in *Kimel*), and Congress tried hard to document, through extensive hearings, that the states as employers often discriminated unconstitutionally against the disabled. But this showing, too, failed to satisfy a majority of the Court. The majority conceded that the states may often have discriminated against disabled employees. But since the disabled were not a suspect or semi-suspect class, the only discrimination against them that would be a violation of the Fourteenth Amendment was ***"irrational"*** discrimination. And, the majority found, Congress despite its efforts failed to identify *"**a pattern of irrational state discrimination in employment** against the disabled."*

b. **Lack of congruence:** Furthermore, the majority concluded in *Garrett*, the **remedy** chosen by Congress in the ADA **lacked *"congruence and proportionality"*** to any equal protection violations that the states may have been guilty of, just as had been the case in *Kimel*. For the ADA required states to spend hard dollars to modify existing facilities to make them readily accessible to disabled employees; that duty of accommodation went far beyond what could possibly have been required to address whenever small equal protection violations the states may have been guilty of.

c. **Significance:** So the Eleventh Amendment means that a state, when it acts as an employer, is not liable for money damages if it discriminates against a disabled employee or applicant in a way that would violate the ADA.

D. **Significance of standard of review:** The cases we've examined so far involving the "congruence and proportionality" requirement — that is, the cases discussing when Congress may abrogate the Eleventh Amendment and make the states defend private damage suits in federal court — have involved Congress' efforts to legislate in areas where the states' actions, if challenged on constitutional grounds, would receive ***only mere-rationality review.*** For instance, when a state is alleged to have discriminated in employment on the basis of age or disability — the types of discrimination at issue in *Kimel* and *Garrett* — equal protection review of the states' conduct would involve just the easy-to-satisfy mere-rationality level of review, since neither age nor disability has ever been found to be a suspect or semi-suspect category, and employment is not a fundamental right.

1. **Class or right triggering heightened scrutiny:** But now, suppose that Congress is trying to combat state discrimination either based on a ***suspect or semi-suspect category***, or involving a ***right that is "fundamental"*** for due process or equal protection purposes. Does the fact that a ***heightened level of review*** gets used in these contexts[8] entitle Congress to act ***more aggressively*** when it tries to include states in a private-damages remedy for the discrimination in question?

The answer seems to be ***"yes."*** That is, if the discrimination involves a suspect or semi-suspect category (or a fundamental interest), the courts will apparently be ***quicker to conclude*** that when Congress gave individuals a right to sue the states in federal court for this type of discrimination, Congress acted in a way that *was* "congruent and proportional," and thus proper under §5, than where the area requires only mere-rationality review.

2. **Court access for disabled:** For instance, in *Tennessee v. Lane*, 541 U.S. 509 (2004), a 5-Justice majority concluded that Congress had power to permit federal court suits against the states for money damages under Title II of the Americans with Disabilities Act (ADA), at least for activities relating to ***access to courts.***

a. **Court access:** Title II provides that no disabled person can be excluded from participating or getting the benefits of any "***services***, programs or activities of a ***public***

---

8. Remember that for suspect categories like race and alienage, the Court uses strict scrutiny (see *supra*, pp. 252-253), and for a semi-suspect category like gender the Court uses mid-level review (*supra*, p. 322). Similarly, when an equal protection or due process violation is alleged regarding a right that the court deems to be "fundamental," the Court uses strict scrutiny here as well. See, e.g., equal protection challenges involving voting rights (*supra*, p. 355) or access to courts (*supra*, p. 364).

entity," or be discriminated against by such an entity. The plaintiffs in *Lane* were paraplegics who sought damages because they did not have adequate access to court services. One plaintiff, for instance, was required to crawl up stairs to answer criminal charges, because the county courthouse had no elevator.

    b. Compared with Title I of ADA: Recall that in *Garrett* (*supra*, p. 491), a narrow majority of the court held that Congress could not authorize damage suits against states for violations of Title I of the ADA, which covers employment discrimination. But Justice O'Connor changed sides from *Garrett* to *Lane*, forming a majority for the proposition that Congress had power to allow damages for Title II violations, at least in the court-access area.

        i. Rationale: The majority reasoned that the **right of access to courts** is subject to **"more searching judicial review"** than the rational-relation review used in disability-discrimination-in-employment cases like *Garrett*. Furthermore, there was much clearer evidence before Congress that the states had failed to ensure equal treatment for the disabled in the provision of state services (Title II) than there was that the states as employers had discriminated against disabled employees (Title I).

E. Right to allow damages for actual constitutional violations: Congress is always free to give private individuals a right to sue the states in federal court for damages for *actually violating the individual's constitutional rights*, and when Congress does so it doesn't have to worry about the "congruent and proportional" rule. It's only when Congress acts *"prophylactically"* — when it forbids the states from taking some action that wouldn't necessarily violate anyone's constitutional rights, but which action is somehow *related* to possible constitutional violations that Congress is trying to prevent — that Congress' response must be "congruent and proportional" to the constitutional violations that Congress is trying to avoid.

    Example: The federal ADA statute requires states (as well as private citizens) to accommodate disabled persons' access to certain public facilities. The statute lets state prisoners sue the state for violating these rights. P, a disabled prisoner, sues the state for actual damages caused to him when his disability is not accommodated (his cell isn't big enough for him to turn his wheelchair around in it).

    Held, it was within Congress' power to let P sue the state on these facts. Because P's suit is premised on an actual violation of his 14th Amendment liberty interest (not merely based on a federal statute enacted out of a general fear that states or private citizens would discriminate), the Court will not consider whether this ADA disabilities-access provision is "congruent and proportional" to the constitutional violations feared by Congress. *U.S. v. Georgia*, 126 S.Ct. 877 (2006)

F. 3-step analysis: So to summarize this welter of cases regarding Congress' power under § 5 of the Fourteenth Amendment to authorize federal-court damage suits against states, you should follow a three-level analysis:

❑ First, ask whether the state conduct that the plaintiff is complaining of was an *actual violation* by the state of the plaintiff's *constitutional rights*. If the answer is yes, then Congress can clearly grant the plaintiff the right to recover damages against the state in federal court, without worrying about whether its response is congruent-or-proportional to the violation. Cf. *U.S. v. Georgia*, *supra*.

❑ Now, assuming that the state conduct complained of by the plaintiff was not an actual constitutional violation, ask whether the federal statute that creates the private right of action (i.e., the right of the plaintiff to sue for damages) deals with an area that involves *either a suspect or semi-suspect class or a fundamental right.* If the answer is yes, then, since the Court applies some form of *heightened scrutiny* to this area, the Court will be quite likely to find that Congress' decision to allow a damages suit *meets the "congruent and proportional" requirement* and is thus constitutional. (See *Tennessee v. Lane supra,* p. 492.)

❏ Finally, assume that the answer to both of the above questions is "no." Now, Congress has power under §5 of the Fourteenth Amendment to allow the plaintiff to sue the state *only if Congress found widespread unconstitutional state conduct in the area in question.* And even if such widespread conduct was found, Congress must choose *narrowly-tailored methods* for combating the state conduct. This is all captured in the slogan that Congress' response must be *"congruent and proportional"* to the pattern of unconstitutional state actions relied on by Congress. (See *Bd. of Trustees of Univ. of Alabama v. Garrett, supra,* p. 491).

Quiz Yourself on

CONGRESSIONAL ENFORCEMENT OF CIVIL RIGHTS *(ENTIRE CHAPTER)*

63. The U.S. Congress has decided that it would now be desirable to extend the reach of federal anti-discrimination laws to the rental of units in 1-4 family homes, which have previously been exempt from such laws. Therefore, Congress proposes to make it a crime for any homeowner, regardless of the size of his dwelling or the number of units in it, and regardless of whether the owner resides in it, to decline to rent to another person on the grounds of the latter's race, ethnic group or national origin. Do Congress' remedial powers under the Fourteenth Amendment furnish adequate constitutional support for this statute?

———————————

64. Same facts as prior question. Now, however, assume that you are asked to find a constitutional basis for the proposed statute other than the Fourteenth Amendment and other than the Commerce Clause. What provision would you point to? ———————————

65. After a sharp right-ward shift in the politics of the nation, Republicans and conservative Democrats gained a majority in both houses of Congress. They passed, and the President signed into law, a statute providing as follows: "It shall be a federal felony for any person to perform an abortion on a woman who is more than three months pregnant, unless the pregnancy was caused by rape or incest or the abortion is necessary to save the woman's life." Assume for purposes of this question that if a state passed a comparable statute, Supreme Court precedents already on the books would compel the conclusion that the state statute was an unconstitutional violation of women's right of privacy. A woman and her doctor have challenged the federal statute on the grounds that it is a violation of the right to privacy, as embodied in the Fifth Amendment's Due Process Clause. Will this attack on the statute succeed? ———————————

Answers

63. No, probably. The Fourteenth Amendment is generally triggered only where there is "state action." Thus the clause dealing with equal protection provides that "[n]o State shall make or enforce any law which shall … deny to any person within its jurisdiction the equal protection of the laws." On the other hand, §5 of the Fourteenth Amendment grants Congress the power to enforce that amendment "by appropriate legislation." The issue is whether Congress may "appropriately" enforce the Equal Protection Clause by proscribing private, as opposed to governmental, conduct.

Certainly some types of private conduct may be reached under Congress' remedial powers. For instance, Congress may prevent a private person from interfering with a state official's attempts to furnish equal protection (e.g., Congress may punish private individuals to who prevent local school board officials from carrying out desegregation). But where the conduct being proscribed is *purely* private, involving the interaction of one private individual with another, it is clear that Congress' power to enforce the Equal Protection Clause does not extend that far; see *U.S. v. Morrison*.

64. **The Thirteenth Amendment.** The Thirteenth Amendment provides that "[n]either slavery nor involuntary servitude, except as a punishment for crime ... shall exist within the United States. ... " The Thirteenth Amendment, unlike the Fourteenth and Fifteenth, is thus not explicitly limited to governmental action. Section 2 of the Thirteenth Amendment gives Congress the power to "enforce this [amendment] by appropriate legislation." This §2 remedial power has been construed to mean that Congress has the right to decide what the ***"badges and incidents of slavery"*** are. If Congress makes a finding that one of the badges and incidents of slavery is the refusal of private homeowners to rent to others on the basis of race, the Court would uphold the proposed statute here as a valid exercise of this remedial power. All that is required is that Congress act "rationally" in determining that a particular aspect of private conduct is indeed a badge or incident of slavery, and Congress' conclusion here would certainly be found to be "rational." See *Jones v. Alfred H. Mayer Co.* (Thirteenth Amendment is broad enough to let Congress conclude that private racial discrimination in real estate transactions is a badge or incident of slavery).

65. **Yes, probably.** The question boils down to, "May Congress reduce the substantive content of individuals' constitutional rights?" The answer to this question is "no." The Court held in *Boerne v. Flores* that Congress' power to enforce the Civil War Amendments does not include the power to redefine the substantive boundaries of the rights given by those Amendments. Here, Congress has tried to reduce the substantive contours of a woman's substantive due process right to abortion, and under *Boerne* (and other Court cases), Congress may not do this.

Exam Tips on
CONGRESSIONAL ENFORCEMENT OF CIVIL RIGHTS

Exam questions on the subjects covered in this Chapter are relatively rare. Here are the few things to keep in mind:

☛ Probably most important, the 14th and 15th Amendments cannot be used to reach ***purely private conduct***, i.e., conduct not involving the state in any way. (This is another way of stating that "state action" is required.) But where government action and private action ***combine***, then Congress can reach this activity. (*Example:* Congress can make it a crime for a private citizen to interfere with government desegregation efforts.)

☛ Sometimes tested: The ***13th*** Amendment is the only Amendment that can reach ***purely private conduct***. That is, Congress gets to say what is a "badge or incident of slavery," and to then forbid it. *Example:* Congress can ban purely private discrimination in housing, under authority of the 13th Amendment. *Jones v. Alfred H. Mayer Co.*

☞ This means that the 13th Amendment can be the basis for federal anti-discrimination legislation that would otherwise have to be based on the Commerce Clause.

☞ The 13th Amendment can be used to ban racial discrimination against *non-blacks* (e.g., whites, Asians, etc.).

☞ Testable issue: Can Congress ban, under the 13th Amendment, discrimination on *other than racial grounds*? Probably Congress can attack discrimination based on *national origin* and *ethnicity*, but not on other characteristics (e.g., gender or sexual orientation). Also, probably only *purposeful* discrimination can be reached.

☛ Where Congress is trying to combat a clear problem of *discrimination by a state*, its *remedial* powers are *relatively broad*. So as long as Congress is behaving rationally in combatting discrimination, you should conclude that it is acting constitutionally under its power to enforce the 13th, 14th and 15th Amendments.

    ☞ But where Congress wants to use its remedial power to *prevent* state discrimination that has not yet occurred, Congress must act on *reasonably up-to-date information* about where discrimination is likely to be occurring.

    Example: Congress uses its 15th Amendment remedial powers to single out certain states, and to require only those states to get federal preapproval of any changes to state voting laws. Congress can't rely solely on 40-year-old voter data as the basis for picking which states must get the federal preapproval. (*Shelby County v. Holder.*)

    ☞ Also, even where Congress is using its 14th Amendment powers to combat state discrimination, Congress' response must be *"congruent and proportional"* to the discrimination — Congress can't choose methods that are much *broader* than the discrimination being cured. (*Boerne v. Flores*.) So Congress can't ban certain state discriminatory conduct, and then make the states liable in damages to private plaintiffs for that conduct, unless Congress had evidence that the states frequently violated people's constitutional rights in that area.

    Example: Suppose Congress rationally concludes that states, acting as employers, occasionally (but not frequently) violate the 14th Amendment equal protection rights of disabled employees. Congress still can't give state employees the right to sue the state for damages for violating the statute — the states have 11th Amendment immunity from private damage suits, and that immunity can be overcome only by proof that Congress' response was congruent and proportional to widespread state discrimination of the type being addressed, something not present here. (*Bd. of Trustees of Ala. v. Garrett*.)

    ☞ But where the area of discrimination that Congress is trying to prevent is one that gets *heightened scrutiny* (i.e., involves a *suspect or semi-suspect class*, or a *fundamental right*), then Congress can allow private damages based on a *lesser showing* that the states have discriminated.

    Example: Congress orders state and private employers to give employees various rights to take unpaid leave to care for sick family members. In doing so, Congress is acting to combat gender discrimination. Even if the states have practiced only occasional leave-related gender discrimination against their employees, Congress can still let state employees sue for violations of the state, because gender-discrimination gets heightened (mid-level) review. (*Nevada Dept. of Hum. Res. v. Hibbs*)

☛ Occasionally, you'll notice buried in a fact pattern that Congress is arguably ***expanding*** or ***contracting*** the ***scope*** of a right guaranteed under one of the Civil War Amendments. Say that under *Boerne v. Flores*, Congress may ***neither*** expand nor contract the boundaries of any constitutional right, even under Congress' power to "enforce" the Civil War Amendments.

CHAPTER 14

FREEDOM OF EXPRESSION

ChapterScope

The First Amendment provides, in part, that "Congress shall make no law ... abridging the freedom of speech, or of the press. ... " These rights (plus the accompanying "freedom of association") are often grouped together as "freedom of expression." Here are the key concepts relating to freedom of expression:

- **Content-based vs. content-neutral:** Courts distinguish between *"content-based"* and *"content-neutral"* regulations on expression.

  - ❑ **Content-based:** If the government action is *"content-based,"* the action will be generally subjected to *strict scrutiny*, and the action will usually be struck down.

  - ❑ **Content-neutral:** On the other hand, if the government action is *"content-neutral,"* the government's action is subjected to a much easier-to-satisfy test, and will usually be upheld.

  - ❑ **Classifying:** A governmental action that burdens expression is "content-based" if the government is *aiming* at the *"communicative impact"* of the expression. By contrast, if the government is aiming at something other than the communicative impact, the action is "content-neutral," even if it has the *effect* of burdening expression.

- **Analysis of content-based government action:** Where a government action impairing expression is "content-based," here's how courts analyze it:

  - ❑ **Unprotected category:** If the speech falls into certain pre-defined *unprotected* categories, then the government can more or less completely ban the expression.

    - ❑ **Listing:** The main "unprotected" categories are: (1) obscenity; (2) fraudulent misrepresentation; (3) defamation; (4) advocacy of imminent lawless behavior; and (5) "fighting words."

  - ❑ **Protected category:** All expression not falling into one of these five categories is "protected." If expression is protected, then any government ban or restriction on it based on its content is *presumed to be unconstitutional*. The Court subjects any such regulation to *strict scrutiny* — the regulation will be sustained only if it (1) serves a *compelling governmental objective*; and (2) and is *"necessary,"* i.e., drawn as *narrowly as possible* to achieve that objective.

- **Analyzing content-neutral regulations:** If the government restriction is *content-neutral*, then here is how the Court analyzes it:

  - ❑ **Three-part test:** The government must satisfy a *three-part test* before the regulation will be sustained, if the regulation substantially impairs expression:

    - ❑ **Significant governmental interest:** First, the regulation must serve a *significant governmental interest*;

    - ❑ **Narrowly tailored:** Second, the regulation must be *narrowly tailored* to serve that governmental interest; and

❏ **Alternative channels:** Finally, the state must *"leave open alternative channels"* for communicating the information.

■ **Overbreadth:** A person whose expression is impaired by the government may make use of the doctrine of *"overbreadth."* A statute is "overbroad" if it bans speech which could constitutionally be forbidden but *also* bans speech which is protected by the First Amendment. Overbreadth doctrine lets a litigant prevail if he can show that the statute, applied according to its terms, would violate the First Amendment rights of *persons not now before the court*.

■ **Vagueness:** A second important First Amendment doctrine is that of *vagueness*. A statute is unconstitutionally vague if the conduct forbidden by it is so *unclearly defined* that a reasonable person would have to *guess at its meaning*.

■ **Advocacy of illegal conduct:** The government may ban speech that *advocates imminent illegal conduct*. To be banable, the speech must satisfy two requirements: (1) the advocacy must be *intended* to incite or produce *"imminent lawless action"*; and (2) the advocacy must in fact be *likely* to incite or produce that imminent lawless action.

■ **"Time, place and manner" regulations:** The government frequently tries to regulate the *"time, place and manner"* of expression.

❏ **Three-part test:** A "time, place and manner" regulation of speech or expressive conduct has to pass the *three-part test* summarized above, i.e., (1) it has to be *content-neutral*; (2) it has to be *narrowly tailored* to serve a *significant governmental interest*; and (3) it must "leave open *alternative channels*" for communicating the information.

❏ **Licensing:** There are special limits on the government's right to require a *license* or *permit* before expressive conduct takes place.

  ❏ **No excess discretion:** Most importantly, the licensing scheme must set forth the grounds for denying the permit *narrowly* and *specifically*, so that the *discretion* of local officials is curtailed.

❏ **Fighting words:** Expression that constitutes *"fighting words"* can be flatly banned or punished by the state. "Fighting words" are words which are likely to make the person to whom they are addressed commit an *act of violence*, probably against the speaker.

  ❏ **Limits:** But the "fighting words" doctrine is tightly limited. For instance, the police must *control* the angry crowd instead of arresting the speaker, if they've got the physical ability to do so.

❏ **Offensive language:** Language that is *"offensive"* is nonetheless protected by the First Amendment. (Thus language that is *profane*, or language that preaches *racial or religious hatred*, is protected.)

■ **The public forum:** Speech that takes place in a *"public forum"* is harder to regulate.

❏ **Content-based:** If a regulation is *content-based*, it makes no difference whether the expression is in a public forum: strict scrutiny will be given in any event.

❏ **Neutral "time, place and manner":** If a regulation is content-neutral, then the fact that the speech does or does not take place in a public forum makes a difference. Usually, we're talking about "time, place and manner" restrictions here.

- ❑ **Non-public forum:** When expression takes place in a ***non-public forum***, the regulation merely has to be ***rationally related*** to some ***legitimate*** governmental objective, as long as equally effective alternative channels are available.

- ❑ **Public forum:** But where the expression takes place in a ***public forum***, the regulation has to be ***narrowly drawn*** to achieve a ***significant*** governmental interest (roughly ***intermediate-level*** review). It is still necessary (but not sufficient) that the government leaves alternative channels available.

❑ **What are public forums:** "True" public forums are: (1) streets; (2) sidewalks; and (3) parks. Also, places in which a public government ***meeting*** takes place are probably true public forums.

- ❑ **Designated-public:** There are also ***"designated-public"*** forums. These are locations where the government has decided to open the place to particular open-expression purposes. The rules are essentially those for true public forums, except that government may at any time decide to close the forum.

- ❑ **Non-public forums:** Other public places are "non-public forums." Here, government regulation merely has to be rationally related to some legitimate governmental objective, as long as alternative channels are left open. (*Examples:* Airport terminals, jails, military bases, courthouses, schools used after hours, and governmental office buildings.)

■ **Access to private property:** In general, a speaker does not have any First Amendment right of access to another person's private property to deliver his message. Thus there is no First Amendment right to speak in a private ***shopping center***.

■ **Defamation:** The First Amendment places limits on the extent to which a plaintiff may recover tort damages for ***defamation***.

- ❑ **Plaintiff as public official or public figure:** Where P is a ***public official*** or ***public figure***, he may only win a defamation suit against D for a statement relating to P's official conduct if P can prove that D's statement was made with either ***"knowledge*** that it was false" or ***"reckless disregard"*** of whether it was true or false.

■ **Obscenity:** Expression that is ***"obscene"*** is simply ***unprotected*** by the First Amendment. For a work to be "obscene," all three parts of the following test must be met:

- ❑ **Prurient interest:** First, the average person, applying today's community standards, must find that the work as a whole appeals to the ***"prurient"*** (i.e., sexual) interest;

- ❑ **Sexual conduct:** Second, the work must describe or depict in a "patently offensive way" particular types of ***sexual conduct*** defined by state law; and

- ❑ **Lacks value:** Finally, the work taken as a whole must lack "serious literary, artistic, political or scientific value."

Note: But the mere ***private possession*** of obscene material by an adult may ***not*** be made criminal.

■ **Commercial speech:** Speech that is ***"commercial"*** gets First Amendment protection. But this protection is more limited than protection given to non-commercial speech:

- ❑ **Truthful speech:** Content-based restrictions on truthful commercial speech get only mid-level review: the government must be: (1) *directly advancing* (2) a *substantial* governmental interest (3) in a way that is *reasonably tailored* to achieve the government's objective. (This compares with strict scrutiny of content-based restrictions on non-commercial speech.)

- ❑ **False, deceptive or illegal:** False or deceptive commercial speech, or speech proposing an *illegal transaction*, may be forbidden by the government.

■ **Freedom of association:** First Amendment case law recognizes the concept of *"freedom of association."* If an individual has a First Amendment right to engage in a particular expressive activity, then a *group* has a "freedom of association" right to engage in that same activity as a group.

- ❑ **Illegal membership:** The freedom of association means that *mere membership in a group or association may not be made illegal*. Membership may only be made part of an offense if: (1) the group is *actively engaged* in unlawful activity, or incites others to imminent lawless actions; and (2) the individual *knows* of the group's illegal activity, and specifically *intends* to *further* the group's illegal goals.

- ❑ **Denial of public benefit or job:** The government may not deny a *public benefit or job* based on a person's protected associations. If a person's activities with a group could not be made *illegal*, then those activities may generally not be made the basis for denying the person the government job or benefit.

- ❑ **Loyalty oath:** Similarly, the government may generally not require a job applicant to sign a *loyalty oath*, unless the things the applicant is promising not to do are things which, if he did them, would be grounds for punishing or denying him the job.

I. GENERAL THEMES

A. Text of First Amendment: The First Amendment provides that "Congress shall make no law … abridging the *freedom of speech*, or of *the press*; or the right of the people peaceably to assemble, and to petition the Government for a redress of grievances."

  1. Related rights: There are thus several distinct rights which may be grouped under the category "freedom of expression": freedom of *speech*, of the *press*, of *assembly*, and of *petition*. Additionally, there is a well-recognized "freedom of association" which, although it is not specifically mentioned, is derived from individuals' rights of speech and assembly.

B. Two broad classes: When government "abridges" freedom of speech, its reasons for doing so can be placed into two broad classes. The first is that the government is restricting the speech *because of its content*, that is, because of the *ideas or information contained in it*, or because of its general subject matter. The second reason for abridgment has nothing to do with the content of the speech; rather, the government seeks to avoid *some evil unconnected with the speech's content*, but the government's regulation has the *incidental by-product* of interfering with particular communications.

1. **Two tracks:** The Supreme Court has implicitly recognized that the dangers posed by governmental action taken for the first reason are different (and generally more severe) than those posed by regulation carried out for the second reason. Therefore, the Supreme Court's rules for determining whether the government has violated the First Amendment differ depending on whether the governmental control falls within the first class or the second.

   a. **Track one (communicative impact):** Where the government's conduct falls within the first class, which Tribe summarizes as governmental actions "aimed at ***communicative impact***," he has labeled the appropriate analysis ***"track one"*** analysis. (Tribe, p. 791).

   b. **Track two (noncommunicative impact):** Where the government's conduct falls within the second class (which Tribe describes as government actions "aimed at ***noncommunicative impact*** but nonetheless having ***adverse effects on communicative opportunity***"), he calls the relevant analysis ***"track two."*** Tribe, p. 792.

   c. **We adopt terms:** For ease of labeling, we will follow the same "track one" and "track two" terminology.

2. **Some examples:** Following are some examples of governmental actions punishing or restricting speech, and the track into which each falls:

   Example 1: The state forbids pharmacists to advertise the prices of prescription drugs, because it is afraid that the public will buy drugs at the lowest available price and will therefore receive low-quality goods and service. This case falls within "track ***one***," since the speech is being regulated because of the government's fears about consumers' reaction to the speech's ***content***. See *Virginia Pharmacy Board v. Virginia Consumer Council*, 425 U.S. 748 (1976) (invalidating the restriction, as discussed *infra*, p. 582).

   Example 2: The state forbids "maliciously and willfully disturb[ing] the peace or quiet of any neighborhood or person [by] offensive conduct." D is convicted under the statute for wearing a jacket bearing the words "Fuck The Draft" in a corridor of the county courthouse. The case should be analyzed under "track ***one***," since the asserted offensiveness caused by D results ***solely from the content*** of his communication. (To see this, observe that bystanders who ***could not read English*** would ***not*** have been offended.) See *Cohen v. California*, 403 U.S. 15 (1971) (reversing D's conviction, as discussed *infra*, p. 536).

   Example 3: Under Maryland tort law, if a speaker (D) intentionally makes outrageous statements attacking another person (P), P may be able to recover against D for intentional infliction of emotional distress (IIED). In a federal-court diversity case based on Maryland tort law, a jury grants P (the father of a Marine killed in Iraq) a civil judgment for IIED against the Ds, who are members of a church that thinks God punishes the U.S. military for tolerating homosexuality. The IIED consists of the Ds having carried, during and nearby the Marine's funeral, picket signs attributing the Marine's death to God's desire to punish the military for not rooting out homosexuality.

   Maryland's constitutional authority to allow such a recovery under its substantive tort law, notwithstanding the Ds' First Amendment right to speak out on matters of public interest, is to be analyzed under "track ***one***." That's because the "outrageousness" of the Ds' messages on the picket signs results solely from the content of those messages. (If the Ds' statements on the picket signs addressed to P constituted pleasant rather than nasty messages, the statements wouldn't be "outrageous" — so giving the jury power to impose liability for IIED is a content-based rather than content-neutral regulation.) See *Snyder v. Phelps*, 131 S.Ct. 1207 (2011), *infra*, p. 538 (reversing the verdict against the picketers as a violation of their First Amendmen right not to have their statements on public affairs be regulated on content-based grounds).

Example 4: A city prohibits the use of sound trucks which emit "loud and raucous noises" while operating on the streets. The ordinance should be analyzed under "track ***two***," since the harm which the government seeks to prevent is ***independent of the content*** of the messages being amplified — even a listener who ***could not understand English*** would be a victim of the harm. See *Kovacs v. Cooper*, 336 U.S. 77 (1949) (upholding such a ban, as discussed *infra*, p. 531).

Example 5: A city forbids distribution of leaflets, because it wishes to prevent littering. The case should be analyzed under "track ***two***," since the harm sought to be avoided exists regardless of what information is contained on the leaflets. (In fact, even ***blank*** leaflets could end up being litter.) See *Schneider v. State*, 308 U.S. 147 (1939), striking the ban (on the grounds that the First Amendment requires a less restrictive alternative, such as only punishing actual littering; the case is discussed *infra*, p. 527).

C. **Analysis of "track one" cases:** If a case falls within "track ***one***," that is, if the government objects to the ***communicative impact*** of the expression, a very rigid analysis must be followed. The most important general rule is the following (as phrased by Tribe, pp. 833-34): ***"whenever the harm feared could be averted by a further exchange of ideas, governmental suppression is conclusively deemed unnecessary."***

1. **Marketplace of ideas:** This rule reflects the view, implicit in the First Amendment, that it is not the government's place to suppress ideas because they are "wrong"; rather, as Justice Holmes put it in his dissent in *Abrams v. U.S.*, 250 U.S. 616 (1919) (discussed more extensively *infra*, p. 511), there is to be ***"free trade in ideas,"*** and truth will become accepted through "the ***competition of the market.***" Only where the circumstances are such that there is ***no time to expose evil ideas*** (and to prevent their harmful effect) through ***more speech*** may the government bar expression.

2. **Unprotected categories:** Furthermore, in "track one" cases, it is generally not open to the government to argue that ***in the particular case at hand***, the feared harm cannot be avoided by more speech. Instead, the Court has defined certain ***pre-defined categories*** of speech, which are deemed essentially ***unprotected*** by the First Amendment.[1] The creation of a given category amounts, in effect, to a finding by the Court that that ***type*** of speech is harmful, not valuable under the First Amendment, and not "nullifiable" by more speech. These ***"unprotected categories"*** have traditionally included ***obscenity, fraudulent misrep-***

---

1. Speech falling into these "unprotected" categories gets one small degree of First Amendment protection: government must nonetheless regulate even this speech on a ***viewpoint-neutral basis***. So, for instance, although a state can ban all obscene photographs, it can't choose to ban just those obscene photographs that carry, say, an anti-government message. For more about the requirement of content-neutrality even as to "unprotected categories," see *R.A.V. v. City of St. Paul*, discussed *infra*, p. 541.

resentation, advocacy of imminent lawless behavior, defamation, "fighting words," and a few others.

a. Consequence to speech not in unprotected category: *Unless speech falls within one of these pre-defined "unprotected" categories*, it is simply *not open to the government to argue that the speech is harmful* because of its content, and that it should be suppressed or punished.

Example: Consider Example 1, *supra*, p. 503, in which the state prohibited pharmacists from advertising their prices for prescription drugs. The state contended that barring this information would be in the public interest, since a contrary policy would lead people to be interested only in price, and therefore to receive low-quality goods or services. The Court conceded the plausibility of the state's claim. But it held that the weighing of the state's interest in protecting its citizens versus the value of free-flowing information was *not the Court's or the Virginia legislature's to make.* "It is precisely this kind of choice between the dangers of suppressing information, and the dangers of its misuse if it is freely available, *that the First Amendment makes for us.*" *Virginia Pharmacy Board v. Virginia Consumer Council*, 425 U.S. 748 (1976) (discussed more extensively *infra*, p. 582).

b. Significance of categories: By generally allowing government to suppress for "track one" reasons only if the speech falls in a previously-defined unprotected category, the Court has made it less likely that governments, or popular majorities, will be able *intentionally to stifle dissent*.

   i. Alternative is unsatisfactory: To see this, consider the alternative, a system in which government could prohibit a particular message on the ground that the dangers posed *by that particular message* are greater than the benefits (both to the speaker and to his listeners) of allowing the idea to be expressed. In such an *ad hoc* balancing system, unpopular ideas would be quite likely to be suppressed, by legislatures in the first instance (who directly represent the majority), and by judges in the second instance (who, although presumably somewhat more independent, are nonetheless not immune to the sentiments of the majority). In times of national crisis, the tolerance for dissent would be even less.

   ii. Categories approach: An "unprotected categories" approach, by contrast, at least means that "consideration of likely harm takes place at *wholesale, in advance*, outside the context of specific cases." Ely, p. 110.

3. Cases outside of unprotected categories: If content-based regulations are imposed in a situation that does *not* fall within one of these pre-existing "unprotected categories," there is a *strong presumption* that the regulation is *unconstitutional*. In this situation, the Court will *strictly scrutinize* the regulation: the government bears the burden of showing "that its regulation is necessary to *serve a compelling state interest* and that it is *narrowly drawn* to achieve that end." *Widmar v. Vincent*, 454 U.S. 263 (1981). The techniques of strict scrutiny here are therefore comparable to those in the due process (*supra*, p. 172) and equal protection (*supra*, p. 272) contexts.

a. Consequences: Use of strict scrutiny to cover content-based restrictions not involving an unprotected category entails the following consequences:

  i.   Effect of more speech: Any time *more speech* could eliminate the evil feared by the state, the Court will conclude that the regulation is *not "necessary"* to prevent that evil (no matter how serious the evil is). This is simply an application of the general principle, previously noted, that whenever possible, "harmful" speech must be fought by more expression, not by government-imposed silence.

  ii. Other speakers' opportunities irrelevant: The government may not claim that the content of the expression has been adequately articulated by *other speakers*, and that proponents of *different viewpoints* on the issue should be given a chance to speak instead.

  iii. Other times and places irrelevant: The government may not claim that the speaker can make his point just as well in *some other place*, at *some other time*, or in *some other manner*. Once the government is seen to be objecting to a message based on its content, *not even a "trifling" or "minor" interference with expression will be tolerated by the courts*.

b. Illustration: For an example of strict (and fatal) scrutiny applied to a content-based statute, see *Boos v. Barry,* 485 U.S. 312 (1988). The statute prohibited the display of any sign within 500 feet of a foreign embassy if that sign tends to bring that foreign government into *"public odium"* or *"public disrepute."*

  i.   Facts: The statute, applicable to the District of Columbia, prohibited such signs in order to serve the governmental interest in protecting the dignity of foreign diplomatic personnel. Since only signs bearing certain messages were prohibited (those bringing the foreign government into "public odium" or "public disrepute"), the regulation was clearly not content neutral. Therefore, it had to be subject to strict scrutiny, and could be upheld only if it was necessary to serve a compelling state interest and narrowly drawn to achieve that interest.

  ii. Result: The statute failed that test, according to the Court. Even if the interest in preserving the dignity of foreign diplomats was "compelling" — which the Court did not decide — more narrowly-drawn measures (e.g., a ban on harassing foreign officials) would have protected that interest adequately.

4. Content-based regulation of unprotected categories: Until relatively recently, by contrast, if speech fell *within* one of the pre-defined "unprotected categories," even a non-content-neutral regulation abridging that speech was generally subjected only to *"mere-rationality"* review, not "strict scrutiny." But a majority of the Court now seems to have *abandoned* this distinction between the protected-categories situation and the unprotected-categories situation: in *either* case, *viewpoint-based restrictions will now be strictly scrutinized.* See *R.A.V. v. St. Paul,* 505 U.S. 377 (1992) (discussed further *infra,* p. 540).

a. Significance of categories: If that's so, what significance remains to the fact that particular speech does or does not fall within an "unprotected category"? The main consequences of the unprotected/protected distinction now are probably that:

[1] Government may *completely proscribe* materials falling in an unprotected category (so long as government acts in a content-neutral manner within the category); by contrast, government obviously may not enact such a total ban on materials not falling within an unprotected category; and

[2] *Time/place/manner* restrictions on speech in public forums will be ***presumptively valid*** when applied to unprotected categories, but will be subjected to careful review (see *infra*, p. 527) in the case of protected categories.

5. **Distinction between subjects or between types of speech:** The normal requirement of content-neutrality clearly means that the government may not show favoritism as between differing points of view on a particular subject. But it also means that the state ***may not place a particular issue off-limits while allowing other subjects to be discussed.***

    a. ***Con Edison* case:** For instance, in *Consolidated Edison v. Public Serv. Commission*, 447 U.S. 530 (1980), the Court prevented the New York Public Service Commission from ordering utilities not to discuss, as part of their monthly billing materials, the desirability of nuclear power. The Court reasoned that "[t]he First Amendment's hostility to content-based regulation extends not only to restrictions on particular viewpoints, but also to prohibition of public discussion of an ***entire topic***."

    b. **Significance of public forum:** Government's possible right to discriminate between broad classes of speech exists only where ***no public forum is involved***. Where expression takes place in a ***public forum***, not even content-***neutral*** restrictions will be tolerated unless they are ***closely-tailored*** to serve significant governmental interests. (See *infra*, p. 527.)

    c. **Taxation:** A *tax*, like a regulation, may be found to be directed at the communicative impact of speech, and therefore presumptively invalid. Thus in *Minneapolis Star & Tribune Co. v. Minnesota Comm'r of Revenue* (discussed further *infra*, p. 627), the Court concluded that a special Minnesota "use tax" applicable only to the cost of ***paper and ink*** consumed in the production of ***publications***, violated the First Amendment.

    d. **Religious speech gets equal protection:** The requirement of content-neutrality is so strong that it takes precedence over the ***Establishment Clause*** (designed to protect separation of church and state; see *infra*, p. 657). That is, if the government allows private speech in a particular forum, government may not treat religiously-oriented speech less favorably than non-religiously-oriented speech.

    Example: If a public university gives funding for student publications on various topics, the requirement of content-neutrality means that the university must give the same funding to a student publication whose mission is to proselytize for Christianity. See *Rosenberger v. University of Virginia*, 515 U.S. 819 (1995), discussed further *infra*, p. 660.

D. **Analysis of "track two" cases:** Let us turn now to the analysis of a case which belongs on "track *two*," that is, one in which the government's interest in regulation ***does not relate to the communicative impact of the expression.*** Regulations of the ***"time, place and manner"*** of speech (assuming that they do not mask discrimination based on the communicative content of the speech) fall within "track two."

1. **General principles:** Analysis on "track two" depends on whether or not the expression takes place in a ***"public forum."*** (This term includes traditional public places like streets and parks, and is further defined *infra*, p. 549.)

    a. **Public forum:** Where the expression takes place in a public forum, the regulation must not only be ***content-neutral*** (which it must be no matter what the forum, unless the expression falls within an "unprotected category" as discussed above), but it must also *not close adequate alternative channels* for communications, and it must be *narrowly-tailored* to serve a *significant governmental interest.* Tribe, p. 992. Regulations that impair the use for expressive purposes of such public forums may *not* be justified merely by the government's *convenience* (e.g., a ban on handbills to prevent littering).

b. **Private places:** Where the expression takes place in a location that is *not* a public forum, it's much easier for the government to regulate the expression:

i. **Insubstantial restraint:** If the impairment of expression caused by the regulation is *not substantial*, the state must merely show that its regulation is *rational* (assuming, as always, that the restraint is content-neutral).

ii. **Substantial:** If the impairment of expression *is* "substantial," the state must show that its own interest is even more substantial. But in contrast to the public-forum situation, the state can prove that a restraint on expression in a non-public-forum is not substantial by showing that there are *alternate channels* by which the speaker can reach the same audience with the same message. Tribe, p. 982.

E. **Regulation of "pure conduct":** So far, we have assumed that "expression" is somehow being regulated by the government. But how do we decide whether what is being regulated *is in fact "expression"*? The fact that what is being regulated is "conduct" rather than "pure speech" is not dispositive — a long line of Supreme Court cases holds that "expressive conduct" receives First Amendment protection just as "pure speech" does. (For instance, marching down the street in a protest is in a sense "conduct," but it is also clearly "expression." See the discussion of this conduct/speech distinction *infra*, p. 528.) But some conduct may contain such a *small* component of expression that it is found to be *not protected by the First Amendment at all*.

1. **Supreme Court's test:** The Supreme Court has articulated a two-part test for determining whether conduct possesses sufficient *"communicative elements"* to trigger the First Amendment protection: it must be the case that *both*: (1) an "intent to convey a *particularized message* was present"; and (2) "the likelihood was great that the message would be *understood* by those who viewed it." *Spence v. Washington*, 418 U.S. 405 (1974).

Example: A court might hold that panhandling on the street has so little expressive content that it gets no First Amendment protection at all. The court might reason that the express or implied statement "Please give me money" (or even "Please give me money because I'm poor") does not really convey any communicative element that would be so understood by the people to whom it is addressed. (The Supreme Court has never decided whether panhandling gets any First Amendment protection.)

F. **Unprotected categories:** As noted above (*supra*, p. 504), there are a number of *"unprotected categories,"* categories that essentially receive *no First Amendment protection at all,* assuming that the government is *not singling out particular viewpoints* within the category.

1. **List of categories:** Here is a list of these unprotected categories, as the Supreme Court has recognized them:

[1] *"Incitement."* This category includes advocacy of *imminent lawless behavior* (p. 515), as well as the utterance of *"fighting words,"* i.e., words that are likely to precipitate an immediate physical conflict (p. 533);

[2] *Obscenity* (p. 576);

[3] *Misleading or deceptive speech (i.e., fraud)* (p. 586);

[4] Speech *integral to criminal conduct* (p. 586), such as speech that is part of a *conspiracy* to commit a crime or speech *proposing an illegal transaction*; and

[5] *Defamation* (p. 569).

2. **Few if any new additions:** The unprotected status of the five above categories has existed for decades, though the precise contours of some of the categories have varied a bit. But over the last few decades, the Supreme Court *has refused to add any new entries* to this unprotected-categories list.

    a. **Animal-crush videos:** For example, the Court recently refused to add to the list of unprotected-categories the class of *"depictions of animal cruelty."* See *U.S. v. Stevens*, 130 S.Ct. 1577 (2010). In *Stevens*, the majority rejected the federal government's assertion that in deciding whether a given category of speech should get First Amendment protection, the Court should make a "categorical *balancing* of the value of the speech against societal costs." The Court said that it did not have "a freewheeling authority to declare new categories of speech outside the scope of the First Amendment," and called the government's proposed balancing test a "highly manipulable" one that was "startling and dangerous."

    b. **No "false statements" category:** Similarly, the Court has declined to establish an unprotected category consisting of *"factually-false statements."* See *U.S. v. Alvarez*, 132 S.Ct. 2537 (2012), *infra*, p. 574.

    c. **Consequence:** Therefore, outside of the five well-defined categories listed above, *all speech is presumed worthy of First Amendment protection.* The Court may decide in a particular instance that a given *form* of regulation of the speech is constitutionally permissible, but the starting point is that as long as the speech does not fall within one of these five categories, it gets at least some degree of First Amendment protection.

II. ADVOCACY OF ILLEGAL CONDUCT

A. **Introduction:** If any kind of speech can lay claim to special constitutional protection, it is probably speech of a *political* nature. Our entire system of representative government operates on the assumption that political and social change will come about peacefully, through public discussion, rather than through violence.

1. **Dangerous speech:** Yet, certain types of political speech may seem to most of us to pose a threat to the very system of representative democracy which freedom of speech is supposed to ensure. For instance, speech calling for immediate assassination of the President, or the institution of a military coup, seems dangerous to tolerate. However, once the government is permitted to prevent or punish some types of political speech, there arises the threat that those in power may also *stifle legitimate dissent.*

2. **Advocacy of illegal conduct:** Since early 20th century, when the Supreme Court first began its serious grappling with the limits of valid political speech, the Court has generally tried to distinguish between, on the one hand, general *political dissent* and advocacy of *abstract theories* (which may not be punished), and on the other hand, *incitement* of

particular illegal acts (which constitutes an "unprotected category," and may therefore be punished). But the Court has vacillated dramatically during this period in drawing the line between these two types of speech. Most commentators agree that the current standard, articulated in 1969 in *Brandenburg v. Ohio*, 395 U.S. 444 (1969) (discussed *infra*, p. 515) gives substantially greater protection to political speech than the various tests in force before it.

B. The "clear and present danger" test: For most of the 20th century prior to *Brandenburg*, the dividing line between legal advocacy and illegal incitement of criminal acts was drawn by use of the *"clear and present danger"* test. Under this test, speech could be punished as an attempt to commit an illegal act if the speech created a "clear and present danger" that the illegal act *would come about* (even if it never in fact occurred).

1. ***Schenck:*** The test was first articulated by Justice Holmes (speaking for a unanimous Court) in ***Schenck v. U.S.,*** 249 U.S. 47 (1919). The case arose in a wartime context, and involved the degree to which citizens had a constitutional right to oppose the First World War.

   a. **Facts:** In the 1917 Espionage Act, Congress made it a crime, *inter alia*, to "willfully cause or attempt to cause insubordination, disloyalty, mutiny, or refusal of duty, in the military or naval forces of the United States," or to "willfully obstruct the recruiting or enlistment service" of the U.S. The defendants were not charged with violating the Act, but rather, with *conspiring* to violate it. The defendants had sent two draftees a document opposing the draft, calling it "despotism," and urging the draftees, "[d]o not submit to intimidation." But the document *did not explicitly advocate illegal resistance* to the draft; it merely advocated *peaceful measures,* such as petitioning for repeal of the Conscription Act.

   b. **Holding:** Nonetheless, the Court unanimously found that the defendants *could constitutionally be convicted* of conspiracy to violate the statute. Whether or not a given utterance is protected by the First Amendment depends, Holmes wrote, on the circumstances; the defendants' document might have been constitutionally protected, for instance, in time of peace. The issue was "whether the words used are used in such circumstances and are of such a nature as to create a *clear and present danger* that they will *bring about the substantive evils* that Congress has a right to prevent." Whether the defendants' conduct in fact posed a "clear and present danger" was a factual issue, the jury's disposition of which the Court refused to disturb.

   c. **Crying "fire" in theater:** In his *Schenck* opinion, Holmes illustrated his assertion that not all speech was constitutionally privileged by posing the now-famous example of *falsely crying "fire!" in a crowded theater.*

      i. **Criticism:** However, the nature of crying "fire!" in a crowded theater seems dramatically different from the speech in *Schenck*; for one thing, the false cry of "fire" is clearly understood by its listeners to be a statement of *fact,* not an exhortation or expression of opinion as the *Schenck* document obviously was. Also, if one believes that the best way to combat false speech is by combatting it in the "marketplace of ideas" (a view espoused by Holmes himself in *Abrams v. U.S., infra,* p. 511), the two situations are clearly different: there is not time to argue with the cry of "fire!", but probably ample time to argue about the merits of conscription.

2. *Frohwerk* **and** *Debs:* Very shortly after *Schenck*, Justice Holmes wrote two more opinions, for a unanimous Court, upholding Espionage Act convictions against First Amendment arguments.

   a. *Frohwerk:* One of these, *Frohwerk v. U.S.*, 249 U.S. 204 (1919), involved writers of editorials criticizing the draft in a German-language newspaper. Holmes' opinion seemed to **shift the burden of proof to the defendants** — because of the lack of clarity of the record on appeal, it was "impossible to say that it might not have been found" that the publication might have been enough to "kindle a flame" of draft resistance.

   b. *Debs:* The other case, *Debs v. U.S.*, 249 U.S. 211 (1919) is perhaps even more disturbing to those who believe that general opposition to government policies, unaccompanied by explicit advocacy of illegal acts, ought to be protected by the First Amendment. The defendant in *Debs* was the well-known socialist and presidential candidate Eugene V. Debs, who made a speech opposing the First World War. Debs' conviction of obstructing military recruitment was upheld by the Court.

   i. **Weak standard:** Although Holmes purported to be applying the "clear and present danger" standard, he phrased it as merely requiring that the words have as their **"natural tendency and reasonably probable effect"** the obstruction of recruitment. As in *Schenck*, the Court refused to reject the jury's finding that Debs' speech met this test.

   ii. **Criticism of** *Debs:* The "clear and present danger" standard which the *Debs* opinion purported to apply gave very little protection to Debs. There was, for instance, no evidence that any obstruction of recruitment actually occurred as a result of the speech. Holmes did not acknowledge that there was a difference between mailing anti-draft leaflets *directly* to draftees (as in *Schenck*) and addressing a general audience. Debs' conviction was "somewhat as though George McGovern had been sent to prison for his criticism of the war [in Vietnam]." 40 U. CHI. L. REV. 237 (quoted in L,K&C, p. 653, n.a.).

3. **Holmes' dissent in** *Abrams:* It was not until *Abrams v. U.S.*, 250 U.S. 616 (1919) that application of the "clear and present danger" standard was sufficient to produce even so much as a dissent against a conviction for anti-war speech. In that case, Justice Holmes' dissent (joined by Justice Brandeis) finally placed some First Amendment "bite" into the standard; *Abrams* is one of his best-known dissents.

   a. **Facts:** The defendants in *Abrams*, American socialists of Russian-Jewish birth, were convicted of violating a newly-added section of the Espionage Act, which prohibited the urging of any curtailment of war production with intent to hinder the United States' prosecution of the War. The defendants had published two pro-Bolshevik leaflets, which attacked the United States' production and supplying of arms that might be used against Russia (against whom the U.S. had not declared war); neither leaflet was pro-German, and in fact one was violently against German militarism. The leaflets urged workers not to make bullets which would be used not only against Germans but Russians as well.

   b. **Majority view:** The key factual issue in the case was whether the defendants had the requisite intent to interfere with the war effort **against Germany**. The majority conceded that the defendants' *primary* purpose may have been only to aid the Russian Revolution. But "[m]en must be held to have intended ... the effects which their acts were *likely to produce*." Curtailment of production to protect Russians could not have been accomplished except by also impairing the war effort against Germany, the majority believed, so that the intent requirement was satisfied. (The majority also went out of its way to emphasize, repeatedly, that the defendants were self-proclaimed "anarchists.")

c. **Holmes' dissent:** Much of Holmes' dissent was on the fairly pedestrian issue of intent. Unlike the majority, he believed that an actor does not "intend" a consequence "unless that consequence is the aim of the deed." By this standard, the defendants simply had no intent to interfere with the war effort against Germany, however likely that possible outcome may have seemed to them.

   i. **Value of free speech:** But Holmes' dissent is best known for its more general words about the value of free speech. He articulated what could be called the "marketplace of ideas" theory: he urged *"free trade in ideas,"* and argued that "[t]he best test of truth is the power of the thought to get itself accepted in the competition of the market. ... " The importance of allowing ideas to compete with each other, he argued, was so great that even opinions which we "loathe and believe to be fraught with death" should not be suppressed, "unless they so imminently threaten immediate interference with the lawful and pressing purposes of the law that an immediate check is required to save the country."

4. **Criticism of "clear and present danger" doctrine:** Holmes' "clear and present danger" doctrine has been criticized on a number of grounds.

   a. **Not very protective:** First, at least as it was applied in early cases, the doctrine obviously did not give very much protection to freedom of speech, since the defendants in *Schenck, Frohwerk, Debs*, and *Abrams* were all convicted, without a showing that the words of any of them actually brought about a substantive evil.

   b. **Opinion about threat:** Second, the test, since it relies upon the fact-finder's opinion about the immediacy of a specific threat (e.g., obstruction of military recruitment), makes political speech particularly vulnerable to the mass hysteria which tends to strike in times of national crisis. For instance, the test gave the least protection to speech during the First World War and during the McCarthy anti-Communist scare, as discussed below.

   c. **Ineffectiveness rewarded:** Finally, the test seems to say that any kind of speech is permissible *as long as it is ineffective*, making the test a very peculiar way of carrying out the First Amendment notion of political change through peaceful speech rather than through violent action.

C. **The Learned Hand test:** Because of these weaknesses in the "clear and present danger" test, Judge Learned Hand, one of the greatest federal district and appeals court judges in our history, articulated a different test, one focusing *solely on the words spoken, not on the surrounding circumstances*. Hand's test was put forth in *Masses Publishing Co. v. Patten*, 244 F. 535 (S.D.N.Y. 1917), a pre-*Schenck* decision.

1. **Terms of test:** Hand believed that words could be punished if they "counsel or advise others to *violate* the law as it stands," but not if they are merely *critical* of the law.

   a. **Application:** The speech at issue in *Masses* consisted of anti-war cartoons and text which criticized the War and the draft, and which expressed great sympathy for draft resisters. Yet for Hand, this was still only *abstract advocacy* of the anti-war position, not a direct call to violate the law. Consequently, he found the materials beyond Congress' power to prohibit or punish.

2. **Significance:** The main significance of Hand's test is that it makes the *likely effects* of the speech *completely irrelevant*. Even if it were shown that the materials in fact caused many readers to resist the draft illegally, the publication would still be beyond Congress' reach. By the same token, if the publication *did* constitute a *direct call* to violate the law, it would be punishable *even if it was utterly ineffectual*.

3. **Fate of Hand test:** Hand's test was immediately rejected; not even the federal court of appeals in *Masses* itself was willing to affirm it. Instead, the "clear and present danger" test prevailed for the next 50 years. But the Hand approach has ultimately had its day; *Brandenburg v. Ohio (infra*, p. 515) incorporates the main aspects of that test, though it adds aspects of "clear and present danger" as well.

D. **Statutes directly proscribing speech:** In the cases considered thus far, the legislature proscribed *acts*, not speech; speech became relevant only because the prosecution claimed that the speech constituted an attempt, or conspiracy, to bring about the forbidden act. Later, however, legislatures began enacting statutes which *directly forbade* certain types of speech. A major debate erupted on the Court about whether the "clear and present danger" test applies to prosecutions under such statutes as well.

1. **Test not applied:** The argument was won, at least temporarily, by those who claimed that the "clear and present danger" test had *no application* in this instance, and that the legislature's *own conclusion* that certain types of speech were *intrinsically dangerous* was to be respected.

2. *Gitlow:* Thus in *Gitlow v. New York*, 268 U.S. 652 (1925), the Court construed the New York "criminal anarchy" statute, which banned advocating (orally or in writing) the overthrow of a government by assassination or other violent means. The defendant, a socialist, was involved in the publication of a "Left-wing Manifesto," which advocated establishment of a dictatorship of the proletariat through mass strikes and other "revolutionary mass action."

   a. **Majority view:** There was no showing at trial that the publication had posed any present danger of governmental overthrow or other substantive evil. Nonetheless, the majority *upheld* the defendant's conviction.

      i. **Rationale:** The "clear and present danger" test of *Schenck* was only to be applied "in those cases where the statute merely prohibits certain *acts* involving the danger of substantive evil, *without any reference to language* itself. … " Here, by contrast, the legislature had *already* determined that *certain types of language* (advocacy of violent overthrow of the government) posed a risk that substantive evils would result. It was not open to the Court to dispute the legislature's judgment and to conclude that, in a particular case, utterances coming within the statute were not dangerous.

      ii. **No immediacy requirement:** Furthermore, there was no requirement that the legislature proscribe only speech advocating *definite* or *immediate* action. Thus the defense that the Manifesto called only for action at some indefinite time in the future was unavailing.

b. **Dissent:** A dissent by Justice Holmes (joined by Justice Brandeis) argued that the "clear and present danger" test ***should*** be applied on these facts. Under this test, he argued there should be no conviction because the Manifesto "had ***no chance*** of starting a ***present conflagration.***" But Holmes did not respond directly to the majority's argument that the test should not be applied where the legislature has directly forbidden certain types of speech.

3. ***Whitney:*** The legislature's right to ban a certain type of speech, regardless of the substantive dangers posed by it, was presented again in ***Whitney v. California***, 274 U.S. 357 (1927).

    a. **Facts:** The California Criminal Syndicalism Act forbade the knowing membership in any organization advocating the use of force or violence to effect political change. Miss Whitney, who did not deny being a member of the Communist Labor Party, was convicted even though she did not agree with the Party's advocacy of violent means of change, and had in fact voted for a more temperate plank.

    b. **Holding:** But a majority of the Court upheld the conviction, believing that the legislature's conclusion that mere knowing membership in an organization advocating criminal syndicalism was substantively dangerous, "must be given great weight."

    c. **Brandeis' dissent:** Justice Brandeis' concurrence in *Whitney* (joined by Holmes) is one of his most eloquent on free speech.

        i. **The value of free speech:** Brandeis' concurrence is most remembered for its general discussion of the value of free speech. An orderly society ***cannot be maintained merely through fear and enforced silence***, for "fear breeds repression … repression breeds hate … [and] hate menaces stable government." On the contrary, "the path of safety lies in the opportunity to discuss freely supposed grievances and proposed remedies. … ***[T]he fitting remedy for evil counsels is good ones.***" This might be thought of as the ***"safety valve"*** theory of free speech (in contrast to the view that human expression is an end in itself, not merely a means to maintenance of order).

        ii. **Emergency:** For Brandeis, it followed that anytime bad ideas could be combated by good ones, this combat, rather than suppression of the bad ideas, must be allowed to take place. Only where "the incidence of the evil apprehended is so ***imminent*** that it may befall ***before there is opportunity for full discussion***" may speech be prohibited or punished. Furthermore, even if the danger is imminent, it may not be suppressed unless it is ***"relatively serious"***; for instance, advocacy of the right of pedestrians to cross unfenced vacant lands could not be prohibited, even if there were imminent danger that such advocacy would lead to trespass.

        iii. **Concurrence:** However, Brandeis' opinion was cast as a concurrence, not a dissent, because in Brandeis' opinion the defendant had not raised the appropriate constitutional claims at the trial level.

    d. **Overruled:** *Whitney* was explicitly overruled in *Brandenburg v. Ohio*, 395 U.S. 444 (1969), discussed extensively *infra*, p. 515.

E. **Threat of communism and the Smith Act:** During and immediately following the Second World War, fears of an international communist threat became even more pronounced. One response was the passage by Congress in 1940 of the Smith Act, which was similar to the New

York Criminal Anarchy Statute upheld in *Gitlow (supra,* p. 513).

1. **The *Dennis* case:**   The most important Smith Act case was ***Dennis v. U.S.***, 341 U.S. 494 (1951), in which the Court purported to apply the "clear and present danger" standard, but did so in a manner that gave dramatically ***less First Amendment protection*** to political speech than Holmes or Brandeis would presumably have wanted.

    a. **Facts:**   The defendants were convicted under the Smith Act of conspiring to advocate the overthrow of the United States Government, and of conspiring to reorganize the U.S. Communist Party, which the prosecution claimed was a group that advocated such overthrow.

    b. **Majority upholds:**   A majority of the Court ***upheld*** the conviction. The opinion, by Justice Vinson, purported to be applying the "clear and present danger" test. However, the majority refused to interpret the test as requiring that there have been a clear and present danger of an ***actual attempt*** to overthrow the government; the Holmes test "cannot mean that before the Government may act, it must wait until the putsch is about to be executed, the plans have been laid and the signal is awaited."

        i. **Adoption of Hand balancing test:**   Instead, the majority applied a test which had been formulated by Learned Hand, writing for the appeals court below: the test was "whether the ***gravity*** of the 'evil', ***discounted by its improbability,*** justifies such invasion of free speech as is necessary to avoid the danger." (Hand thus abandoned his *Masses* test, and instead tried to reshape the Holmes test.) Here, the evil (violent overthrow of the government) was so great that even a ***small, non-imminent***, chance of success justified curtailing the speech.

    c. **Significance of *Dennis*:**   *Dennis* represents "the temporary eclipse of the Holmes-Brandeis formulation of the clear and present danger test." Tribe, p. 846. Once the evil's ***seriousness*** became a ***substitute*** for its ***immediacy,*** speech could be restricted ***no matter how remote its anticipated consequences***.

F. **The modern standard:**   Today, the Supreme Court generally gives ***greater protection to free speech***, at least in the political area, than it has given in previous eras.

1. ***Brandenburg:***   The present status of freedom of political speech is best expressed in ***Brandenburg v. Ohio***, 395 U.S. 444 (1969), a case in which the Court combined the most speech-protective aspects of ***both*** the ***"clear and present danger"*** test and the ***"advocacy/ incitement"*** distinction.

    a. **Facts:**   Defendant was a leader of an Ohio Ku Klux Klan group. He was charged with violating Ohio's Criminal Syndicalism Statute, which (like that of California, sustained in *Whitney v. California, supra,* p. 514) forbade the advocacy of crime or violence as a means of accomplishing industrial or political reform.

    b. **Holding:**   The Court (in a unanimous *per curiam* opinion) ***struck down*** the Ohio statute, without considering whether the defendant's actual speech could have been properly proscribed.

        i. **New test:**   In so doing, the Court articulated new requirements which a statute proscribing speech must meet. Speech advocating the use of force or crime can be proscribed only where two conditions are satisfied:

        [1] the advocacy is ***"directed to inciting or producing imminent lawless action"***;

and

[2] the advocacy is also *"likely to incite or produce such action."*

2. **Significance of new test:**   The two-part *Brandenburg* standard is usually viewed as combining aspects of both the Holmes and Hand tests, in a way that gives "double protection" to speech.

   a. **Holmes aspect:**   The Holmes "clear and present danger" legacy is reflected in the requirement that the speech be *"likely* to incite or produce" *imminent* unlawful action. Thus the concern with immediate, likely, consequences remains.

   b. **Hand aspect:**   But *Brandenburg* also reflects Hand's insistence that what should be restricted is only direct advocacy of *action*, not mere advocacy of *abstract doctrine*. This distinction is imposed by the requirement that the speech be *"directed"* (i.e., *intended*) to *"inciting* or *producing"* an unlawful response.

   c. **Consequence:**   Apparently, therefore, no speech that would have been protected by *either* the Holmes or Hand tests may be prohibited under *Brandenburg*.

   d. **Application to Ohio statute:**   The significance of the *Brandenburg* test is illustrated by the way the Court applied it to the Ohio statute at issue there. The Ohio act punished all advocacy of the "duty, necessity or propriety of crime [or] violence … as a means of accomplishing industrial or political reform. … " This language was sufficiently broad that it forbade advocacy of the *abstract doctrine* of violent political change, as well as incitement to imminent unlawful action. Therefore, it was held unconstitutional, even though some applications of it might have been constitutional (an illustration of the "overbreadth" doctrine, discussed below).

3. **Severity of harm:**   The *Brandenburg* test does not explicitly take into account the *severity* of the harm which is threatened. Reading *Brandenburg* literally, a speaker who advocated use of nuclear weapons for terrorist purposes, but only after a one-year moratorium, could not be punished (since the harm would not be "imminent"). Conversely, one who incited his listeners to jaywalk immediately could be punished. Tribe (p. 849, n. 59) advocates taking into account seriousness, at least on the less-serious side of the spectrum.

4. ***Whitney* overruled:**   *Brandenburg* explicitly overruled *Whitney v. California, see supra,* p. 514, which had upheld a Criminal Syndicalism statute nearly identical to that struck down in *Brandenburg*.

5. **Other modern cases:**   Other cases decided in the late 60's or later present additional illustrations of the twin modern requirements of: (1) *incitement* (as distinguished from abstract advocacy); and (2) harm that is *imminent* (as distinguished from remote).

   a. ***Bond:***   The Court held that the Georgia House of Representatives' exclusion of Julian Bond from membership violated his First Amendment rights, in *Bond v. Floyd*, 385 U.S. 116 (1966). Bond, an opponent of the war in Vietnam, had joined a statement of "sympathy with, and support [of] the men in this country who are unwilling to respond to a military draft." The Georgia House reasoned that Bond could not truthfully swear to "support the Constitution of this State and of the United States." But the Court held that Bond could not be penalized for his statement, since it did not constitute a call for unlawful draft resistance, but was merely a *general, abstract*, declaration of opposition to the war.

b. *Watts:* A black anti-war activist, in a speech, said "[i]f they ever make me carry a rifle, the first man I want to get in my sights is L.B.J. They are not going to make me kill my black brothers." He was convicted under a law making it a crime intentionally to threaten to kill the President. In *Watts v. U.S.*, 394 U.S. 705 (1969), the Court reversed the conviction, on the grounds that the circumstances showed that the speaker did not intend to make a ***"true threat"*** but rather, to state his ***political opposition*** to the President (albeit in a "very crude, offensive" way). The Court relied especially on the fact that the "threat" was conditional, and that the audience responded by laughter.

c. *Hess:* *Bond, Watts* and *Brandenburg* were all decided during the Warren era. But the post-Warren Court has also applied the *Brandenburg* standard. One instance is *Hess v. Indiana*, 414 U.S. 105 (1973), growing out of a campus anti-war demonstration in which demonstrators blocked a street until they were moved off it by the police. Defendant then said "We'll take the fucking street later [or again]." (The record was ambiguous as to the precise word used.) The Court found this to be protected speech, rather than an unprotected incitement to illegal action. Construed least favorably to the defendant, the statement was "nothing more than advocacy of illegal action at ***some indefinite future time***"; only words intended to produce (and also likely to produce) ***imminent*** disorder could be punished.

6. Mere membership not enough (*Scales*): Are there some organizations that are so subversive that ***mere knowing membership*** in them can be forbidden? The answer so far has been ***"no"*** — membership in a group can be punished only if the member is an ***active*** (not passive) member who ***specifically intends to further the organization's illegal ends.*** *Scales v. U.S.*, 367 U.S. 203 (1961).

a. "Active support" is enough: On the other hand, a post-9/11 decision shows that although government may not be entitled to make "mere membership" in an organization illegal, the state *can* constitutionally prohibit virtually any kind of ***active support*** of an illegal organization, even support that is intended to further the organization's ***legal*** aims. See ***Holder v. Humanitarian Law Project***, 130 S.Ct. 2705 (2010), in which the Court upheld a federal statute making it a crime to provide ***"material support"*** to a designated foreign terrorist organization, and defining "material support" in an exceptionally broad way.

i. What the statute forbids: The statute in question in *Holder* let the U.S. Secretary of State designate an entity as a ***"foreign terrorist organization."*** Once an organization had been designated in that way, it was then a federal crime to give the organization "material support or resources." "Material support" was defined to include not just financial support, but also a number of intangible services such as ***"training"*** and the giving of ***"expert advice or assistance."***

ii. The plaintiffs: Two of the organizations put on the terrorist list were the Kurdistan Workers' Party (which had the aim of establishing an independent Kurdish state in southeast Turkey) and the Liberation Tigers of Tamil Eelam (which aimed to created an independent Tamil state in Sri Lanka). The plaintiffs were various American citizens and organizations that wanted to train members of these groups in how to use international law to resolve their disputes peacefully, and also wanted to engage in political advocacy on their behalf. The plaintiffs claimed that the statute was inconsistent with *Scales* — they argued that it effectively made mere membership in the organization illegal, even if the member wanted to pursue only the organization's lawful aims.

iii. Statute upheld:
By a 6-3 vote, the Court **upheld** the statute against First Amendment attack. In an opinion by Chief Justice Roberts, the Court said that *Scales* was irrelevant, because that case did not deal with the issue of whether the giving of material support to an organization could constitutionally be forbidden. The statute here did not criminalize "mere membership" (as the one in *Scales* had done), but instead criminalized the giving of "material support" to the organization. There was no constitutional difficulty, Roberts said, with prohibiting material support of an illegal organization (at least a foreign one), even if the supporter did not have a specific intent to further the organization's illegal aims.

(1) Freeing up of resources: Roberts argued that even support of a terrorist organization's *legitimate* aims could be *harmful*. For instance, such support *"frees up other resources within the organization* that may be put to violent ends." And that support "helps *lend legitimacy* to foreign terrorist groups — legitimacy that makes it easier for those groups to persist, to recruit members, and to raise funds — all of which facilitate more terrorist attacks."

(2) Statute is limited: But, Roberts asserted, the statute applied only to material support that was *"coordinated with or under the direction of"* the designated terrorist organization, not *"independent* advocacy that might be viewed as promoting the group's legitimacy." So *Holder* does not answer the question of whether Congress could make it a crime to engage in truly independent advocacy on behalf of a terrorist organization.

iv. Dissent:
Three justices (Breyer, joined by Ginsburg and Sotomayor) dissented in *Holder*. They argued that the statute should be strictly scrutinized, because it authorized the criminal prosecution of those who engage in the communication and advocacy of political ideas. The dissenters were especially troubled by the majority's argument that the forbidden support "helps lend legitimacy" to terrorist groups; the dissenters believed that there was "no natural stopping place" once this argument was accepted — "speech, association and related activities on behalf of a group will often, perhaps always, help to legitimate that group."

b. "Incitement" law today:
Holder suggests that today, as we are actively waging the war on terror, the Supreme Court will be *quicker to uphold government restrictions on subversive or terrorist organizations* than it was in the relatively liberal 1960s era in which *Brandenburg* and *Scales* were decided. True, *Brandenburg* and *Scales* technically remain the law: mere advocacy of even violent political change cannot be forbidden unless the speaker is calling for imminent lawless action, and mere membership in even the most dangerous organization cannot be flatly prohibited. But *Holder* means that any support beyond pure advocacy or membership — even *"training"* of an organization's personnel, or *"advocacy"* that is coordinated with the organization — *may be criminalized*, and that's true even if the support is intended to further only the organization's *legal* objectives.

i. Less free-speech protective:
That's a less free-speech-protective approach than pre-9/11 cases seemed to allow. See Bollinger (quoted at SST&K, p. 1066, n. 5), presciently saying in 2002 that "the fact that the last 30 years since *Brandenburg*

have been remarkably peaceful and prosperous means that the understandings we now have about the meaning of free speech have not really been tested ... [J]ust about every time the country has felt *seriously threatened* the First Amendment has *retreated*."

III. OVERBREADTH AND VAGUENESS

A. Overbreadth: Because of the especially great importance of freedom of expression in our constitutional scheme, the Supreme Court has developed several techniques of statutory analysis to make sure that that freedom gets the extra protection it requires. One of these techniques is the use of the doctrine of *"overbreadth."*

1. **Definition:** A statute is overbroad if, in addition to proscribing activities which may constitutionally be forbidden, it *also* sweeps within its coverage speech or conduct which is *protected by the guarantees of free speech or free association*. See *Thornhill v. Alabama,* 310 U.S. 88 (1940).

2. **Significance:** There are two respects in which the doctrine of statutory overbreadth changes the usual rules of constitutional litigation:

   a. **Standing:** First, a litigant who is attempting to have a statute ruled unconstitutional must normally show that it is unconstitutional *in its application to him.* For instance, in a First Amendment case that does not involve overbreadth, the challenger to a statute must show that his own speech or conduct was protected by the First Amendment. But the overbreadth doctrine permits the challenger to prevail if he can show that the statute, applied according to its terms, would violate the First Amendment rights of persons not now before the Court. Thus overbreadth can be viewed as an *exception to the usual requirements of "standing"* (see *infra,* p. 709), by which a person is not normally permitted to assert the constitutional rights of others, only his own. Or to put it in terms of the usually-employed set of labels, most constitutional attacks are required to be *"as applied"* attacks (the plaintiff is saying that the statute is unconstitution "as applied" to her, i.e., the statute violates *her own rights*), whereas an overbreadth attack is a *"facial"* attack, i.e., an attack *"on the face"* of the statute, saying that it's invalid *no matter to whom it's applied*.

      i. **Statute's application to challenger:** In fact, where overbreadth analysis is applied, the Court simply *assumes* that a more narrowly-drawn statute *could* constitutionally proscribe the challenger's own conduct. Ordinarily, the Court never even decides this question explicitly; by deciding to apply overbreadth analysis, it is able to decide instead the usually *easier* question of whether the statute by its terms covers hypothetical constitutionally-protected conduct by third parties.

   b. **Statute found void on its face:** Secondly, in the usual situation, where a court finds a statute to be unconstitutional it will simply *excise* the statute's unconstitutional applications, *leaving the statute in force* as to those situations where its application would be constitutional. But where overbreadth is applied, the statute is *completely struck down*. That is, the statute is found to be void *"on its face."* Until a different statute is enacted (a more limited one, applying only where it may constitutionally do so), or until another court with authority construes the statute more narrowly (in a way that forbids only constitutionally-proscribable speech or conduct), the statute is simply unenforceable against **anyone.**

3. **Rationales:**   There are two main rationales for using the overbreadth doctrine in First Amendment cases:

a. **"Chilling effect" on speech:**   First, the mere existence of an overly broad statute (that is, a statute which by its terms forbids some protected speech) is likely to have a **"chilling effect"** on free speech. Some people whose speech the statute could **not** constitutionally reach (and who thus would presumably prevail in court if they spoke and then litigated the statute's application to them) might simply be **intimidated** into **not exercising their right to speak.**

   i. **Explanation:**   As Justice Marshall put it in a dissent to *Arnett v. Kennedy*, 416 U.S. 134 (1974), an overbroad statute "hangs over [people's] heads like a Sword of Damocles. … That this Court will ultimately vindicate [a person] if his speech is constitutionally protected is of little consequence — for the value of a sword of Damocles is that it hangs — not that it drops." He added that the focus of the overbreadth doctrine "is not on the individual actor before the court but on others who may forego protected activity rather than run afoul of the statute's proscriptions."

b. **Selective enforcement:**   Secondly, an overly-broad statute is highly vulnerable to **selective enforcement** by the authorities, i.e., enforcement that discriminates against certain classes of people or certain points of view. The problem of selective enforcement exists in any statute. But the risk is greater in the case of an overbroad one, since the statute gives officials, by hypothesis, not only the opportunity to treat people differently (a problem with any statute, since it is always possible to prosecute only one of two people who may constitutionally be prosecuted), but also the chance to **violate the constitutional rights** of one person without violating those of another.

   Example: Assume that a town ordinance proscribes "all demonstrations, involving 100 or more persons, held in public streets." This ordinance by its terms applies both to activity which may constitutionally be proscribed (e.g., demonstrations that include violence or a substantial breach of the peace) as well as to those which may **not** be constitutionally prohibited (peaceful demonstrations, conducted at an appropriate time, without causing major interference with traffic).

   Within the class of activities to which the statute may **not** constitutionally be applied, there is an open invitation to the police to allow their own views about acceptable content to color their decision. For instance, they may "look charitably at a post game victory celebration in the streets of a college town [but] not feel the same way about an antiwar demonstration." See 43 CHI. L. REV. 38 (quoted in L,K&C, p. 733). Therefore, the statute will be found to be overbroad, and thus void "on its face"; that is, it may not be applied even to activity which **could** constitutionally be proscribed by a more narrowly-drawn statute (e.g., demonstrations that include violence to bystanders).

4. **Doctrine cut back — "substantial" overbreadth now required:**   However, the modern Court has significantly **curtailed** the use of overbreadth analysis in First Amendment cases. It has done so principally by requiring that the overbreadth be **"substantial,"** compared with the legitimate applications of the statute. This requirement was first set forth in

Broadrick v. Oklahoma, 413 U.S. 601 (1973), a case which remains the best statement of the modern Court's view on overbreadth.

a. **Facts:** §818 of Oklahoma's Merit System Act prohibited civil servants from engaging in certain political activities, including taking part in the management or affairs of any political party or campaign, and soliciting for campaign contributions. Broadrick, who had campaigned for a superior and had solicited money for him, challenged §818 on overbreadth (as well as vagueness) grounds. He pointed out that §818 had been construed as applying to such political expression as the wearing of political buttons and the displaying of bumper stickers, which (he asserted) were constitutionally-protected free speech activities. Therefore, he contended, the section must be struck down, regardless of whether his own activity could have been constitutionally proscribed by a more narrowly-drawn statute.

b. **Holding:** By a 5-4 vote, the Court *rejected* Broadrick's claims, spending most of its time on the overbreadth one.

c. **Speech vs. conduct:** The opinion distinguished between statutes primarily regulating conduct and those directly governing speech. In situations involving the latter, the Court did not modify the overbreadth rule. But in the case of statutes *governing conduct*, where the conduct happens to have an expressive content, the "strong medicine" of complete invalidation of the statute should not invariably be applied. Instead, the majority believed, for facial invalidation to be appropriate, "the overbreadth of a statute must not only be real, but *substantial* as well, judged in relation to the statute's plainly legitimate sweep." Where the overbreadth is not substantial, unconstitutional applications should be rooted out one at a time, by analysis of the particular fact situations in which successive litigants find themselves.

d. **Application:** The Oklahoma statue, under this analysis, *did not call for overbreadth treatment*. The statute was primarily directed at *conduct* (taking part in a political campaign), not at pure speech. The statute was *not "substantially overbroad,"* since in the majority's judgment, it applied to a "substantial spectrum of conduct" that could constitutionally be subjected to state regulation.

   i. **Some protected applications:** The Court conceded that the statute by its terms could be applied to the wearing of political buttons or the use of bumper stickers, and that these might be constitutionally-protected expressions. But such potential unconstitutional applications of the statute were *not numerous enough compared with the body of permissible applications*, so there was no "substantial overbreadth."

   ii. **Applied to litigant:** Since Broadrick's own conduct was clearly regulable rather than protected, the statute was upheld as applied to him.

e. **Makes hard cases easy:** The overbreadth doctrine, even with its requirement of "substantial" overbreadth, often has the effect of *making "hard" cases into "easy" ones*. That is, a case that would be a difficult one if it had to be decided on its own facts often becomes easy once the statute can be taken literally and applied to a substantial number of other hypothetical situations, as to which it would clearly be unconstitutional. See Sullivan & Gunther, p. 1346.

B. Vagueness: The doctrine of *"vagueness"* is similar, but not identical, to that of overbreadth. A statute will be held void for vagueness if the conduct forbidden by it is so **unclearly defined** that persons "of common intelligence must necessarily **guess at its meaning** and differ as to its application." *Connally v. General Construction Co.*, 269 U.S. 385 (1926).

1. **Constitutional basis:** Theoretically, the proscription against vagueness stems from the Due Process Clause's requirement that people be given **fair notice** of what conduct is prohibited. But many void-for-vagueness holdings stem more from violations of other constitutional provisions, particularly the First Amendment. In the First Amendment area, an unduly vague statute has the same *"chilling"* effect on speech or association as does an overbroad one: a person does not know whether or not his conduct will ultimately be held to be constitutionally protected, so he declines to exercise his right of speech or association.

2. **Curbing discretion:** The other main function of the vagueness doctrine is to **curb the discretion** afforded to law enforcement officers or administrative officials. Observe that this danger, too, is also a danger posed by an overbroad statute (*supra*, p. 520).

3. **Distinguished from overbreadth:** Yet vagueness and overbreadth are quite distinguishable doctrines. Their differences can be illustrated by the following example:

   Example: Statute I prohibits anyone from "publicly display[ing] a red flag [as] a sign, symbol or emblem of opposition to organized government." Statute II prohibits anyone from "publicly displaying a red flag for any purpose whatsoever."

   Statute I is unconstitutionally **vague**, because there is no way to tell whether it is meant to apply to peaceful displays of opposition to the political party currently in office, or to other constitutionally-protected expressions of political opposition. (See *Stromberg v. California*, 238 U.S. 359 (1931), so holding.)

   Statute II is unconstitutionally overbroad. It is obviously not "vague," since its meaning is perfectly clear. But since by its terms it appears to apply to constitutionally-protected conduct, and since there is no "bright line" rule to separate out the constitutional from unconstitutional applications, neither a member of the public nor a court has an easy way to articulate what the statute may constitutionally cover.

   Note: These two statutes show that vagueness and overbreadth are both, in part, attempts to deal with the same problem. Both statutes leave the user uncertain about which applications of the statute may **constitutionally** be imposed. The main difference is that in the overbreadth situation, the vagueness is "latent"; for this reason, overbreadth has been called "really a special case of the problem of vagueness." See Freund, *The Supreme Court of the United States* (quoted in L,K&C, p. 732).

Quiz Yourself on

FREEDOM OF EXPRESSION — GENERAL THEMES; ADVOCACY OF ILLEGAL CONDUCT; OVERBREADTH AND VAGUENESS

66. Darwin and 10 others were all members of the basketball team of State U, a public university. The Chancellor of State U had recently suspended Xavier, one of the members of the team, from both the team and the school for alleged cheating in an exam. At 10:00 a.m. on a Tuesday morning, Darwin and his 10 teammates stood in front of the University administration building, which contained the Chancellor's office.

They carried signs saying, "Reinstate Xavier"; they also chanted and sang. The Chancellor happened to be away from the office that day (unbeknownst to Darwin and his friends), and nobody in the building was considering Xavier's case at the time.

A statute of the state in which State U is located provides as follows:

> "No group of 10 or more persons shall demonstrate on the sidewalk or other public way in front of a state or local government office building during business hours, unless the demonstration is related to matters currently under consideration by government officials working in the building. Violation of this provision shall be punishable as a misdemeanor."

Darwin has been charged with violating this section. He wishes to defend on the grounds that the section violates his First Amendment freedom of expression.

(a) What is the best argument he can make as to why his First Amendment rights would be violated by a conviction? _____

(b) May Darwin constitutionally be convicted of violating the provision? _____

67. The city of Munford has enacted the following ordinance: "No person shall attempt to give to passersby on any sidewalk or public thoroughfare any handbill during a Restricted Time Period. 'Restricted Time Period' shall mean the hours between 8:00 and 9:30 a.m. and the hours between 4:30 and 6:00 p.m., Monday through Friday. 'Handbill' is defined to include any piece of printed literature, four pages or less, dealing with a single topic." The purpose of the definition is to cover advertising circulars and brochures, but not to cover newspapers and magazines. The ordinance was enacted in response to two fears: (1) that during the busy rush hour, people were handing out so many handbills that the flow of pedestrian traffic was frequently impaired; and (2) that an extraordinary amount of litter was being generated when people who had handbills thrust into their hands dropped them on the sidewalk. Kermit, a political candidate who was giving out brochures in support of his own candidacy, was charged with violating the statute. Kermit now argues that a conviction would violate his First Amendment rights. Should the Court agree?

_____

68. Picketers picket on the public street adjacent to the house of CEO, the head of a company that makes drones used in an unpopular foreign war. The signs they carry contain intentionally hurtful messages (e.g., "CEO is a cowardly murderer"). The state common law of intentional infliction of emotional distress (IIED) allows recovery for any "outrageous and intentionally offensive" language carried on a picket sign near the plaintiff's house. In a suit brought by CEO against the picketers, a jury imposes a $100,000 civil judgment in favor of CEO. May the judgment be constitutionally imposed? _____

69. Leonard, a resident of a state that bordered Mexico, believed that the federal government should vastly increase the physical barriers to illegal immigration from Mexico. One day he went to a park that was frequented by people on both sides of the immigration issue. Before a moderately interested audience of about 20 people, all of whom had come to the park for other purposes, Leonard began to make a speech. He said, "If the federal government doesn't start doing a whole lot more to keep out illegal immigrants, we'll have to make 'em do it. Let's start by building up an arsenal of automatics and machine guns. Eventually, we'll have guerilla cells throughout the Southwest to make the federal government's life such a hell they'll build the kind of huge border fence we need." A few of the listeners applauded, one asked a question, but no one took any other action in apparent response to Leonard's speech. Immediately after his speech, Leonard was arrested by the police for violating §123 of a state statute. That statute provided that it is a felony to "advocate insurrection against the state or federal government or any local subdivision

thereof." Leonard now defends on the grounds that a conviction would violate his First Amendment rights. May Leonard constitutionally be convicted of violating the statute? _____

70. Robert was a tenured teacher in a public high school, in the state of Cartesia. He was also a member of NAMBLA, the National Association of Man Boy Love Affairs. NAMBLA's charter says that it is dedicated to the furtherance of social and sexual interaction between men and boys. Cartesia makes it a crime for an adult male to have sexual relations with a boy under the age of 17. Robert knows the aims of NAMBLA, and supports those aims; in fact, he himself has in the recent past had sexual relations with a boy. School officials, worried about recent publicity concerning teachers who belong to NAMBLA, asked Robert and all other teachers at the school to sign an affidavit stating that "I am not now nor have I ever been a member of NAMBLA." (The affidavit said nothing else.) School officials announced that if a teacher did not sign the affidavit, they would consider that refusal to sign presumptive evidence of unfitness to be a teacher. Robert has so far refused to sign the affidavit. He wishes to challenge the constitutionality of the school's insistence that he sign.

(a) What is the strongest argument Robert can make as to why the affidavit requirement is unconstitutional? _____

(b) Will Robert's attack on the requirement's constitutionality succeed? _____

71. Becky, a young woman, walked topless on the boardwalk of Straitsville. She was arrested for violating a town ordinance that banned "lewd or lascivious public conduct." The statute contains no other relevant language, and there is no legislative history. For purposes of this question, assume that it would be possible to draft a statute in such a way that it could constitutionally proscribe appearing topless in public. Instead, concern yourself only with whether Becky may be convicted for violating *this* statute.

(a) What is Becky's strongest argument as to why she cannot constitutionally be convicted of violating the statute? _____

(b) Will Becky's argument succeed? _____

Answers

66. (a) That the section is a content-based regulation on speech, and is thus invalid unless necessary to achieve a compelling state interest.

(b) No. Government may impose reasonable regulations on the "time, place and manner" of speech that takes place on public forums. However, government's right to do this is contingent on its behaving in a ***content-neutral*** way. If government chooses to allow some messages and not allow others based on the content of the speech, then the restriction will be strictly scrutinized, and will be struck down unless it is: (1) necessary to achieve a compelling objective; and (2) narrowly drawn to achieve that objective. See, e.g., *Widmar v. Vincent.*

Here, government allows messages that pertain to matters under discussion inside the office building, but not messages pertaining to other matters. The government might defend on the grounds that it has not objected to the content of the messages, but has merely allowed some whole "categories" of speech while not allowing other whole categories. However, even distinctions between topics or categories is likely to be found to be content-based. See, e.g., *Consolidated Edison v. Public Serv. Comm.* (state may not prevent utilities from discussing the issue of nuclear power's desirability, because "[t]he First Amendment's hostility to content-based regulation extends not only to restrictions on particular viewpoints, but also to prohibition of public discussion of an entire topic.") In any event, the speech here is taking place in a public forum, so the court will be especially reluctant to allow such a broad interference with it.

67. **Yes.** First, we need to analyze whether the restriction is content-neutral. In contrast to the restriction in the prior question, the one here probably *is* content-neutral; that is, the government truly does not seem to be interested in what topics are described in the materials being given out, so long as the materials are essentially single-topic short pieces, rather than newspapers and magazines. Although it could be argued that distinguishing between newspapers/magazines on one hand and all other communications on the other is not content-neutral, the court would probably conclude that the distinction here is at such a high level of generality that there is no attempt to suppress a particular message or group of messages.

Assuming content-neutrality, the regulation here must be evaluated by the standards for testing "time, place and manner" restrictions. In general, such restrictions must be ***"narrowly tailored"*** to serve a ***"significant governmental interest,"*** and must ***"leave open alternative channels"*** for communicating the information. The restriction here probably *fails* to satisfy the "narrowly tailored" requirement. That is, the city could probably find methods that are less intrusive of freedom of expression than the total ban on handbills for large parts of the day. For instance the city could strictly enforce its ordinary anti-littering laws, or could prohibit anyone from blocking other pedestrians' right of easy passage on the street or sidewalk. It is important to note that the communication here is occurring in a ***public forum*** (the street or sidewalk), and the availability of different public forums or the present public forum at a different time, usually will not be enough to constitute an "alternative channel." (This is especially true here, where large segments of the population, i.e., commuters, will be on the street *only* during rush hours, and will thus never get to hear Kermit's message if the regulation is enforced.)

68. **(a) No.** It would be a violation of the picketers' First Amendment rights for them to be held liable under this statute, because such liability would effectively allow for content-based regulation of the picketers' speech, and cannot survive strict scrutiny. The case is comparable to *Snyder v. Phelps*, where picketers located on a public street who carried signs that intentionally offended the family of a soldier killed in Iraq were found to be shielded on First Amendment grounds from state-court liability for IIED.

69. **No.** The government may forbid a person from advocating illegal conduct, such as insurrection or overthrow of the government. However, under *Brandenburg v. Ohio*, speech advocating such illegality may only be proscribed if two conditions are satisfied: (1) the advocacy is directed to inciting or producing *imminent* lawless action; and (2) the advocacy is *likely* to incite or produce such action. Here, neither of these requirements seems to be met. Leonard is not calling for *imminent* illegality — he says "let's start … ," but he does not indicate that action should take place immediately. Furthermore, although his statement about having guerilla cells could probably be interpreted as a call for illegality, his statement about "building up an arsenal" is not necessarily a call for illegality, since there are many legal ways to buy guns, even automatics and machine guns. Even if the court decides that Leonard was attempting to incite imminent lawless action, it is pretty clear that there was very little risk that his speech was *likely* to produce that effect, since he had only a small crowd in front of him, they were in the park for other reasons, and they did not in fact respond with immediate illegal actions.

70. **(a) That it is overbroad.** A statute or regulation is overbroad if, in addition to proscribing activities which may constitutionally be forbidden, it also sweeps within its coverage future conduct which is protected by the guarantees of free speech or free association.

(b) Yes, probably. The government is clearly entitled to insist that Robert not commit crimes, and that he not advocate that others imminently commit crimes. However, the government may *not* make mere membership in an organization, without more, a crime, and it may not deprive a person of a government job or benefit for being merely a member or for refusing to say that he is not a member. Here, the affidavit merely requires Robert to say that he has not been a member; since Robert would be entitled to be a mere member of NAMBLA, so long as he did not agree with its aim of advocating imminent commission of the crime of man-boy love, the affidavit requirement would punish some membership that is constitutional. Robert's own membership here is ***not*** constitutionally protected, since he in fact knows of NAMBLA's stated aims and supports those (illegal) aims. But under the overbreadth doctrine, Robert is permitted to say, in effect, "The affidavit requirement would be unconstitutional if applied to (hypothetical) other people who merely belong to NAMBLA without supporting its criminal aims, so it should be struck down as facially invalid."

Under the requirement of ***"substantial*** overbreadth," the overbreadth doctrine would not be applied unless the invalid applications of the requirement are substantial compared to the legitimate applications. Here, however, this requirement of substantial overbreadth is probably satisfied, since quite a number of people are likely to belong to NAMBLA just to get information about the law and politics surrounding this question rather than to advocate or practice illegal man-boy sex. Therefore, Robert's overbreadth attack will probably succeed.

71. (a) That the statute is unconstitutionally vague.

(b) Yes, probably. A statute will be held void for vagueness if the conduct forbidden by it is so unclearly defined that a person of ordinary intelligence would not know what is forbidden.

Here, the statute uses the words "lewd or lascivious," but furnishes no further information about what type of conduct is being forbidden. A reasonable observer would probably be in doubt as to whether it is necessarily lewd for a woman to appear topless. Because of the ordinance's lack of specificity, undue discretion is given to local law enforcement officials, who depending on how they felt about Becky or toplessness generally could decide to look the other way rather than making an arrest. Therefore, while the city might be entitled to ban women from appearing topless in public if the ordinance specifically applied to toplessness, the formulation here is probably unconstitutionally vague.

IV. REGULATION OF CONTEXT — "TIME, PLACE AND MANNER"

A. **Context regulations generally:** Recall that the state is somewhat more free to regulate expression when it does so for reasons independent of the speech's communicative content (a "track two" situation) than where the regulation is motivated by the expression's content (the "track one" case). Or, to put it another way, the state is substantially freer when it acts in a ***content-neutral*** manner. This section discusses various factual settings in which the state has claimed (not always successfully) that it is merely regulating the ***"time, place and manner"*** of speech and is therefore entitled to "track two" analysis.

1. **Rules for "track two" cases:** In general, the Court has applied a ***balancing test*** to determine whether the government's interest in content-neutral regulation of speech-related conduct outweighs the speaker's (or his listeners') interest in a particular form of communicative activity. But in performing this balancing test, the Court in effect places a "thumb on the scale" on the side of free expression, to reflect the exceptional importance of such expression.

2. **Disproportionate impact:** In performing the balancing test, the court will take into account the extent to which the regulation "falls *unevenly upon various groups* in ... society." Tribe, p. 980. For instance, the poor cannot generally afford television spots or full-page newspaper announcements; they must use cheaper means such as demonstrations, leafletting and door-to-door canvassing. Therefore, regulations which inhibit these economical forms of expression will be especially closely scrutinized because of their unequal impact.

3. **Public forum:** Speech in a *"public forum"* (defined *infra*, p. 549) may not be restricted, even in a content-neutral way, unless the restriction is a *narrow one* which is *necessary* to serve a *significant governmental interest*. Tribe, p. 982. Thus citizens have in essence a *"guaranteed access"* to streets, parks and other public forums. See *Hague v. CIO*, 307 U.S. 496 (1939): "The privilege [to] use the streets and parks for communication of views on national questions may be regulated in the interest of all; [but] it must not, in the guise of regulation, be abridged or denied."

   a. **Mere inconvenience:** This "guaranteed access" to public forums is implemented by several rules not applicable to non-public-forum situations. In a public forum context, *mere inconvenience* to the government will *not suffice* to outweigh the interest in public expression. Also, the government must use the *least restrictive means* of achieving its legitimate content-neutral objectives.

      Example: Ordinances in several cities completely forbid distribution of leaflets. The cities claim that the bans are necessary to prevent littering.

      Held, the flat bans violate the First Amendment. The objective of keeping the streets clean is insufficiently substantial to justify preventing a person with a right to be on a public street from giving literature to one who wants to receive it. Also, the state's objective can be met by means which place less of a burden on the freedom of expression (e.g., punishing only those who actually litter). *Schneider v. State*, 308 U.S. 147 (1939).

   b. **Alternative places or times:** Similarly, where a public forum is involved, the fact that the same message may be expressed by the speaker at a *different place* or time, or in a different manner, will not by itself suffice to validate a content-neutral restriction on the expression.

4. **Non-public forum:** By contrast, where the expression does *not* take place in a "public forum," the analysis depends on whether the regulation constitutes a *substantial interference* with communication. Here, the existence of alternatives is relevant — the availability of a different time, place, or manner for expressing the same message is likely to mean that the regulation's interference with speech is not substantial. If there is no substantial interference with expression, the state must merely show a *rational justification* for the regulation (assuming that it is content-neutral). Tribe, p. 982.

5. **General rule for "time, place and manner" rules:** Where a regulation is claimed to be a valid *"time, place and manner"* regulation, the Court now applies the following *three-part test*. The regulation will not be valid unless it satisfies *all* of these these three requirements:

   ❏ It must be "justified without reference to the content of the regulated speech"; that is, it must be *content-neutral* (thus avoiding "track one" analysis);

❏ It must be *"narrowly tailored"* to serve a *"significant* governmental interest." (The requirement that the regulation be "narrowly tailored" to serve the interest means that it must be the case that the interest cannot be equally well-served by a means that is substantively less intrusive of First Amendment interests. See *Clark v. Community For Creative Non-Violence*, 468 U.S. 288 (1984));

❏ It must *"leave open alternative channels* for communication of the information." *Metromedia, Inc. v. San Diego*, 453 U.S. 490 (1981).

Note: The above test does not explicitly distinguish between speech which takes place in public forums and that which does not. However, the *second* and *third* of the above requirements are *interpreted more stringently in the public forum situation*. As noted, "mere governmental convenience" (e.g., prevention of littering) is not treated as a "significant governmental interest" where a public forum is involved, and the availability of other public forums or other times for using the one at issue is not deemed to constitute "alternative channels."

a. **Mid-level standard:** This 3-part standard essentially amounts to a *middle level of review:* it will *not* almost-inevitably lead to an *invalidation* of the regulation (as *strict scrutiny* does), but at the same time it's a *meaningful obstacle* for the regulation (unlike "mere-rationality" review, used for things like reviewing most social-welfare and economic regulation). The mid-level standard also *shifts the burden of proof to the government* to defend the regulation, instead of placing it on the speaker to show why the regulation violates the speaker's First Amendment rights.

B. **Meaning of "narrowly tailored":** As we noted above (*supra*, p. 527), the regulation of "time, place and manner" must not only be serving a significant government interest, but must be *"narrowly tailored"* to serve that interest. However, this "narrowly tailored" requirement does *not* mean that the state must choose the *least-restrictive* or least-intrusive means of achieving its objective. Instead, the state must merely avoid choosing means that are *"substantially broader* than necessary to achieve the government's interest." *Ward v. Rock Against Racism*, 491 U.S. 781 (1989). In other words, the fact that an alternative method would have interfered somewhat less with expression while still fulfilling the government's objectives, is irrelevant — all that is required is that the means-end fit be *fairly close*, not perfect.

1. **Illustration:** The facts of *Ward, supra*, illustrate this principle. To cut down on complaints by citizens that rock concerts in the city's parks were too loud, New York City imposed a requirement that rock performers use only city-provided sound equipment and sound technicians. The Court upheld this requirement as a valid "time, place and manner" restriction. The Court conceded that the city might have found a less-restrictive means of solving the loudness problem. (For instance, it could have monitored the performances, and punished the performers who exceeded pre-defined sound limits.) But the availability of less-restrictive means of regulating volume was irrelevant — since the means chosen by the city were not *"substantially* broader than necessary" to keep sound low, the requirement that the means be "narrowly tailored" to serve the government's interest was satisfied.

a. **Dissent:** Three justices dissented in *Ward*. They argued that the majority was eviscerating the "narrowly tailored" requirement. For instance, if the city did not have to choose the least-restrictive means of regulating loudness here, the dissenters argued, a city could also ban all handbill distribution as a way of controlling litter (rather than using the less-restrictive method of punishing litterers directly, a method that prior decisions had required cities to use; see *supra*, p. 527).

C. "Leave open alternative channels" requirement: The third and final requirement for a "time, place and manner" regulation is that it *"leave open alternative channels* for communication of the information." See *supra*, p. 528. Usually, a regulation that satisfies the other requirements (content-neutral, and narrowly tailored to serve a significant governmental interest) will also satisfy this final requirement. But occasionally, the requirement does turn out to make a difference. It is especially likely to do so where the government tries to foreclose an *entire medium* or *method* of communication, and the method is so easy-to-use or inexpensive that other channels simply are not substitutes.

1. Use by individuals: In general, the more a particular method is likely to be used by *individuals* who are trying to disseminate core political messages without spending a lot of money, the more likely the method is to be found so vital that its prohibition fails to leave open "alternative channels." Thus complete bans on *handbills* (see *supra*, p. 527) or on the display of *homemade signs* are likely to be struck down as not leaving open alternative channels.

> **Example:** The City of Ladue, Missouri generally prohibits "signs," and defines that term broadly. All residential signs are prohibited except for "identification signs" and "for sale" signs. P places an 8.5 x 11 inch sign in the second story window of her home, stating "For Peace in the Gulf." The city asserts that P's sign must come down, and defends its ordinance on the grounds that it is merely a "time, place and manner" regulation whose purpose is to minimize the visual clutter associated with signs.
>
> *Held*, for P. By forbidding residents from displaying virtually any "sign" on their property, the city "has almost completely foreclosed a venerable means of communication that is both unique and important." The city has not "[left] open ample alternative channels for communication. … Residential signs are an unusually cheap and convenient form of communication. Especially for persons of modest means or limited mobility, a yard or window sign may have no practical substitute." Therefore, even though the city's ordinance may be content-neutral, and even assuming that the ordinance is narrowly tailored to serve a significant governmental interest, it unconstitutionally infringes P's free speech. *City of Ladue v. Gilleo*, 512 U.S. 43 (1994).

D. Licensing: One way in which governments often attempt to regulate speech or expressive conduct is through *licensing* or *permit* requirements, by which official permission is required *in advance* of a public address, march, solicitation campaign, or other expressive activity.

1. Multiple techniques: The Court has used a number of techniques to ensure that such requirements will not stifle the freedom of expression:

a. Content-neutrality: The government must apply the permit requirement in a *content-neutral* manner. If, for instance, a permit is required before any parade, the officials charged with granting or denying permit requests *may not take into account the ideas or politics being espoused* by the paraders. (Only if the content of the expression places it within an "unprotected category," such as "advocacy of imminent illegal activity," may this content be taken into account.)

i. Consequence: Thus if the government wishes to have its advance-permit requirement sustained in a particular fact situation, it will almost certainly have to show either that the case belongs on "track two" rather than "track one," or that the speech's content falls into an unprotected category.

ii. **Fee based on content of speech:**   For example, the government almost certainly cannot charge a ***different fee*** for the license or permit, based on the content of the speech. In fact, the government may not vary the fee according to the ***costs of security*** that the government will bear in connection with the expression, because such costs will inevitably depend on the content of the speaker's message, and the hostility generated by that message. Cf. *Forsyth County v. The Nationalist Movement*, 505 U.S. 123 (1992).

b. **Excessive administrative discretion:**   The grounds upon which a permit may be denied must be set forth ***specifically***, and ***narrowly***, in the ordinance. If the official charged with granting or denying permit applications is given ***too much discretion***, the ordinance will be voided for overbreadth, vagueness, or both (see *supra*, p. 519).

Example: A municipal ordinance forbids the distribution anywhere within the town of "literature of any kind," unless a permit has first been obtained from the City Manager. D is convicted of violating the ordinance for distributing religious literature published by the Jehovah's Witnesses.

Held, the ordinance is an unconstitutional violation of freedom of speech. It gives a censor's power to the City Manager, since his right to deny a permit is not tied to the avoidance of littering or disorderly conduct, or to regulation of time and place. Because the ordinance is void on its face (for what would today be called overbreadth), D was not required to seek the permit and then challenge its denial in court; she was free to disregard the permit requirement and to challenge the ordinance after her arrest. *Lovell v. Griffin*, 303 U.S. 444 (1938).

2. **Prior restraint:**   One of the reasons the courts look with particular disfavor on permit requirements is that these amount to ***prior restraint*** on the freedom of speech. That is, in contrast to statutes which merely ***punish*** certain types of expressive conduct ***after*** they have occurred, the permit requirement, if enforced, prevents the expression from ever taking place at all.

a. **Restraint of press:**   The Court's hostility to prior restraints on free expression is even more noteworthy in the case of the ***press***. See, e.g., *Near v. Minnesota*, discussed *infra*, p. 629.

3. **General right of regulation:**   However, if the statute or ordinance *does* adequately constrain administrative discretion, does require content-neutrality, and does have an adequate means-end fit, it will be upheld if it is a ***reasonable means of ensuring that public order is maintained.***

Example: The Ds (Jehovah's Witnesses) are charged with holding a parade on public streets, in violation of a state statute that requires a permit before any "parade or procession" is held on a public street. The statute sets forth elaborate procedural requirements for the hearing of such permit requests. The Ds claim that the advance-permit requirement abridged their First Amendment rights.

Held, ordinance sustained (and the Ds' conviction affirmed), because: (1) the statute required ***content-neutrality*** in the issuance of permits; and (2) the Ds would, if they had applied for a permit, have had an unqualified right to a permit so long as their proposed parade was to be at a time and place where it would not unduly disturb public use of the streets. The government's interest in not having overlapping parades, and in having advance notice so as to be able to ensure proper policing, furnished adequate justification for the permit requirement. *Cox v. New Hampshire*, 312 U.S. 569 (1941).

E. Intrusive speakers vs. right to be left alone: One way in which the state has sometimes justified content-neutral regulations on expressive activity is by claiming that the would-be audience has an interest in *not being forced to listen* to the speaker's message. The Court has not been completely unsympathetic to this "right to be left alone." But it has generally held that it is *up to the unwilling listener* (or viewer) to *avoid the undesired expression*, and that the state may not issue a blanket proclamation shielding both the willing and unwilling from the expression.

1. **Loudspeakers:**   Thus the Court has carefully scrutinized restrictions on *loudspeakers* and *soundtrucks*. Where such restrictions give *uncontrolled discretion* to local officials, they will be struck down (just like other types of overbroad or vague permit schemes, discussed above).

   a. **"Loud and raucous noises" prohibitable:**   But if administrative discretion is sufficiently restricted, and the statute is not overbroad or vague, regulation of amplification devices will be permitted, as a valid regulation of the "time, place and manner" of expression.

      i. **Loudspeakers:**   For instance, in *Kovacs v. Cooper*, 336 U.S. 77 (1949), the Court *upheld* a ban on all amplification devices operated in public places which emit *"loud and raucous noises."* The municipality's interest in avoiding distractions to traffic, and in protecting the "quiet and tranquility" of its inhabitants, was sufficient to justify the regulation, despite the "preferred position of freedom of speech." (It is not clear whether the logic of the majority opinion in *Kovacs* would allow a city to ban *all* public amplification devices, since it is not clear whether all such devices make "loud and raucous noises." A concurring Justice, and three dissenters, all believed that the majority's opinion would allow a complete ban on such devices.)

      ii. **Regulating sound equipment:**   Similarly, the Court held that New York City could require that any musician performing in a public forum (the bandshell in Central Park) use city-provided sound-amplification equipment and sound technicians. The city had a significant governmental interest in protecting citizens from unduly loud sounds, and the regulation was not substantially broader than necessary to achieve that interest. *Ward v. Rock Against Racism* (other aspects of which are discussed *supra*, p. 528).

2. **The captive audience:**   Whenever speech is directed towards a *captive audience*, that is, one which *cannot easily avoid exposure* to the speech, this is a factor which the Court will weigh in favor of *allowing restriction* on that form of expression. A number of cases show how the presence of a captive audience is a factor making the Court more willing than usual to allow restrictions on expression:

   a. **Print advertising on city buses:**   For instance, in *Lehman v. Shaker Heights*, 418 U.S. 298 (1974), the Court upheld restrictions on some but not all types of print advertising on city-owned buses. The Court held that the fact that commercial advertising was accepted did not give political candidates a right to have *their* advertising accepted; the majority relied in part upon the city's interest in limiting access so as to reduce "the risk of imposing upon the captive audience."

b. Picketing in front of residence: Similarly, the Court has held that a municipality may ban all *picketing* in front of a *particular residence*, in order to protect the inhabitants of that house from hearing or seeing unwanted messages. *Frisby v. Schultz*, 487 U.S. 474 (1988), also discussed *infra*, p. 550.

c. Women visiting abortion clinics: Finally, *women* who are *visiting abortion clinics* or other health-care offices can get significant protection from unwanted expression. The Court held in a 6-3 decision, *Hill v. Colorado*, 530 U.S. 703 (2000), that a state may create a 100-foot *"buffer zone"* around the entrance to any health-care facility, in which no one may make an unwanted approach to within eight feet of another person in order to counsel that person, pass out a leaflet, or picket.

   i. No general rule: But don't let *Hill* lead you to think that the Court has adopted a broad rule that the public has an absolute *"right to be left alone."* The interest in avoiding unwanted intrusion is merely *one factor* to be placed into the balance. Even in the abortion context, it is clear that citizens in public places must tolerate some unwanted messages — the listener's remedy is generally to avert his eyes and ears, not to have government forbid or restrict the delivery of the message.

F. Canvassing and soliciting: The interest in being left alone also plays a role in the case law on *canvassers and solicitors*. Here, too, however, this interest has been merely one factor in the balancing of society's interest in regulating the form of expression against the speaker's interest in unrestrained communication.

   1. Significance of place: The *place* in which the canvassing or solicitation occurs is important; the Court has granted greater weight to the rights of canvassers and solicitors in *public places* than at *private residences* (though even as to the latter, access may not be completely cut off by a blanket ban).

   2. Mailboxes: The Court's concern with the sanctity of the home has led it to be sympathetic to legislative acts which restrict access to *home mailboxes.*

   a. Homeowner's right to block receipt: Thus a congressional provision allowing a homeowner who has received what he (in his sole judgment) believes to be "erotically arousing or sexually provocative" material to obtain a post office order requiring the mailer to remove the homeowner's name from its mailing lists, was upheld in *Rowan v. Post Office Dept.*, 397 U.S. 728 (1970). The Court found that "[t]he right of every person 'to be let alone' must be placed in the scales with the right of others to communicate." Whatever rules might apply outside the home, "[a] mailer's right to communicate *must stop at the mailbox* of an unreceptive addressee."

   b. Not public forum: The mailer's "right of access" to home mailboxes was further undermined when the Court upheld a federal statute which prohibited depositing *unstamped materials in home mailboxes,* in *U.S. Postal Service v. Greenburgh Civic Assns.*, 453 U.S. 114 (1981). There, several civic groups argued that they had a constitutional right to deliver messages to local residents by placing unstamped pamphlets and notices in such mailboxes. But the Court held that *home mailboxes do not constitute a "public forum,"* even though they are in effect controlled by the government; therefore, any reasonable, content-neutral, regulation of their use was permissible.

3. **Personal visits at home:** Those who wish to solicit or canvass by making ***personal visits*** to homes have received substantial First Amendment protection from the Court, notwithstanding the homeowner's interest in being left alone. In general, the Court has taken the view that ***it is up to homeowner himself to indicate his desire to be left alone*** (in which event the state may enforce that desire); the state may not simply ***assume*** that all homeowners wish to be undisturbed.

> **Example:** An ordinance prohibits anyone from distributing handbills to residents by either ringing their doorbell or otherwise calling them to the door. (Nor is there any way to get a permit that would allow this.) The town defends this prohibition on privacy grounds. *Held*, this flat ban on canvassing is unconstitutional, because less restrictive alternatives are available (e.g., letting a homeowner post a no-soliciting sign, and then making it an offense for anyone to ring the bell of such a person). *Martin v. Struthers*, 319 U.S. 141 (1943).

4. **Heightened scrutiny:** Even where an ordinance regulating canvassing is written in a way that does not give officials undue discretion, it will not pass constitutional muster if it: (1) directly and substantially impairs protected First Amendment expression; and (2) is not substantially related to achievement of a ***"strong, subordinating interest."*** This two-part test was applied to invalidate an ordinance barring door-to-door or in-the-street solicitation by charitable organizations that do not use at least 75% of their receipts for "charitable purposes" (defined to exclude overhead and solicitation expenses). *Schaumburg v. Citizens For Better Environment*, 444 U.S. 620 (1980).

5. **Solicitation in public places:** Where canvassing or solicitation occurs in ***public places***, essentially the same constitutional standards apply as in the door-to-door situation. That is, the regulation must be content-neutral, and authorities may not be given excessive discretion in determining who may solicit, or in what manner. Reasonable "time, place and manner" regulations which satisfy both of these requirements will be upheld, so long as they serve a ***significant governmental interest*** and ***leave open ample alternative channels*** for communicating the same information.

   a. **Less judicial tolerance:** But since the "governmental interest" and "alternative channel" factors inevitably involve a kind of balancing, the Court has been ***less tolerant*** of regulations on solicitation done in public forums than in the door-to-door situation (where the governmental interest in having citizens be left alone is stronger).

G. The hostile audience and "fighting words": One of the "unprotected categories" of speech consists of so-called ***"fighting words,"*** that is, words which are likely to make the person to whom they are addressed ***commit an act of violence*** (probably against the speaker). "Fighting words" receive no First Amendment protection, because, like other unprotected categories (e.g., defamation, obscenity, etc.) they are not normally part of any "dialogue" or "exposition of ideas." But the Supreme Court today keeps this exclusion within tightly circumscribed bounds.

1. *Chaplinsky:* The "fighting words" doctrine originated in ***Chaplinsky v. New Hampshire***, 315 U.S. 568 (1942).

   a. **Facts:** The defendant in *Chaplinsky* was a Jehovah's Witness who called the city marshall a "goddamned racketeer" and "a damned fascist," and then got into a fight with him on the sidewalk. He was convicted under a broadly-worded statute, which provided that "no person shall address any offensive, derisive or annoying word to any other person who is lawfully in any street or other public place ... " But the New Hampshire Supreme Court had interpreted the statute to bar only "words *likely to cause an average addressee to fight.*"

    b. Conviction upheld: The conviction was *upheld.* The Supreme Court believed that the defendant's words were indeed ones which would *likely provoke the average person to retaliate.* It then held that among the classes of speech which are not protected by the First Amendment are "fighting words," which the Court defined as "those which by their very utterance *inflict injury* or *tend to incite an immediate breach of the peace.*" Such words are "*no essential part of any exposition of ideas,* and are of such *slight social value as a step to truth* that any benefit that may be derived from them is clearly outweighed by the social interest in order and morality."

    c. Two branches: Observe that this *Chaplinsky* formulation defines "fighting words" quite broadly — in addition to words which are likely to incite an immediate fight, words are also included which "inflict injury." Here, we are concerned only with words likely to provoke a fight or other breach of the peace.

2. Limitations on doctrine: The Court realized, soon after *Chaplinsky,* that giving a broad scope to the "fighting words" doctrine would lead to the swallowing up of important First Amendment protections. Therefore, the Court has *limited* the "fighting words" doctrine in a number of ways.

    a. "Stirring to anger" not enough: To constitute "fighting words," it is not enough that the speaker's words *make the listeners angry; incitement to violence* (whether or not the violence actually ensues) is required. For instance, in *Terminiello v. Chicago,* 337 U.S. 1 (1949), D made a race-baiting speech, which attracted an angry crowd; the speaker then denounced the crowd as "snakes" and "slimy scum." The Supreme Court reversed D's conviction under a breach-of-the-peace statute which the trial court had interpreted to include speech which "stirs the public to *anger* [or] *invites dispute,*" as well as speech which creates a disturbance.

        i. Rationale: The Supreme Court reasoned that speech which "stirs the audience to anger" or "invites dispute" is *protected* under the First Amendment and that, in fact, *the most valuable expression may well be that which, because it is provocative and challenging, produces these emotions.* Therefore, the statute (as interpreted by the trial judge) was *overbroad* on its face; D's conviction had to be reversed, regardless of whether *his actual words* could have been made criminal under a more narrowly-drawn statute covering only words likely to incite violence.

    b. Crowd-control required: Wherever the police have the physical ability to *control the angry crowd* as a means of preventing threatened violence, they *must do so* in preference to arresting the speaker for using "fighting words." For instance, in *Cox v. Louisiana,* 379 U.S. 536 (1965), 2,000 civil rights demonstrators picketed a courthouse; about 75 policemen separated the demonstrators from 100-300 whites gathered on the other side of the street. The Court, in reversing the breach of peace conviction of the demonstration's leader, rejected the state's claim that the conviction was justified because "violence was about to erupt" — the Court relied in part on the fact that the police could have "handled the crowd."

> **i.** **"Heckler's veto":** Observe that a contrary rule, allowing the police to silence a speaker whenever the audience threatens violence, would legitimate what has been called the *"heckler's veto."* That is, members of the audience would gain the right to silence any speaker with whose ideas they did not agree.

c. **Mere dislike of speaker's identity not sufficient:** If it is the *mere identity* or lawful acts of the speaker or demonstrator, *not his threatening words or actions*, which lead the police to believe that violence is imminent, the "fighting words" doctrine may *not* be applied.

> **i.** **Civil rights sit-ins:** For instance, in several breach-of-peace cases involving civil rights sit-ins of segregated facilities, the state was able to justify its fear of imminent violence only by asserting that the *mere fact that blacks were using segregated facilities* made whites likely to attack them. Even if this anticipation of whites' response was accurate, it was constitutionally irrelevant, since the blacks' use of these facilities was not evidence of any crime. See *Garner v. Louisiana*, 368 U.S. 157 (1961). See also Tribe, p. 854.

3. **Doctrine sometimes applicable:** But these *are* occasional situations in which none of these exceptions or limitations applies, and the "fighting words" doctrine is applicable. These will be those situations in which "imminent spectator violence cannot be satisfactorily prevented or curbed by means of crowd control techniques, and ... the speech itself is the apparent cause of the impending disorder." Tribe p. 855.

a. *Feiner:* The last true "fighting words" conviction sustained by the Court was in *Feiner v. New York*, 340 U.S. 315 (1951).

> **i.** **Facts:** D, a left-wing college student, made a street-corner speech in which he called President Truman a "bum" and the American Legion a "Nazi Gestapo," and said that blacks should "rise up in arms and fight for [legal rights]." One member of the racially-mixed crowd said that if the police did not get that "son of a bitch" off the stand he would do it himself. D refused to heed requests from the police to stop speaking, and was then arrested for disorderly conduct.

> **ii.** **Conviction upheld:** A majority of the Court believed that D's conduct constituted *incitement to riot*, and that his arrest was motivated by the police's legitimate desire to prevent a fight, not by disagreement with the content of D's message. The Court conceded that "the ordinary murmurings and objections of a hostile audience cannot be allowed to silence a speaker," but implied that the crowd response here went beyond that. Therefore, the Court *upheld* D's conviction.

> **iii.** **Black's dissent:** But Justice Black dissented, disagreeing with the majority's view of both the facts and the law. As a factual matter, he did not agree that violence was imminent; he believed that D had in reality been arrested and convicted for the unpopularity of his views, not the tendency of his speech to induce violence. He also believed, as a legal principle, that the police must, before interfering with a lawful speaker, make *"all reasonable efforts to protect him ... even to the extent of arresting the man who threatened to interfere."* (Black believed that the majority's opinion implied that there was no such requirement.)

    iv. *Feiner* **to be read narrowly:**   However, the present Court would probably construe *Feiner* quite **narrowly**, and it is not at all clear that the case would be decided the same way if it arose today. In particular, the Court is probably less inclined to accept the police's self-justifying rationales for their action ("We didn't think we could control the crowd.") See Tribe, p. 855.

4. **Relation to "clear and present danger":**   The problem of "fighting words" is similar to, and in some ways a subset of, the problem of advocacy of illegal conduct (*supra*, p. 509). Just as under *Brandenburg, supra*, p. 515, only speech which is intended to advocate **imminent** lawless action, and which is in fact **likely** to result in such action, may be punished, so only those words which are likely to result in violence that cannot be prevented in any other way (e.g., by controlling the crowd) will be preventable or punishable under the "fighting words" doctrine.

    a. **Perhaps no longer valid:**   This requirement of imminent unpreventable violence is so strict that many commentators doubt that the fighting words doctrine has much real practical value today. For instance, it is probably the case that there are no words which by themselves are "automatically" fighting words — each utterance has to be evaluated *in context* to determine whether there were actual listeners who were likely to resort to violence. This, coupled with the fact that no regulation has been upheld under the fighting words exception since *Feiner* in 1951, may render the doctrine largely irrelevant.

H. **Offensive words and the sensitive audience:**   A related issue is whether the government may prevent or punish words which listeners will find *offensive*, even though these words are not likely to lead to actual violence. In general, the Court has *not* allowed government to suppress speech or expressive conduct on the grounds that others would find it "offensive," at least where matters of *public interest* rather than purely private interests are at stake.

1. **Foul language:**   Most of the cases involving "offensive language" have focused upon *profanity*. Generally, the Court has held that statements *may not be punished merely because they are profane* and are therefore offensive to their listeners. These cases, even though they involve "four-letter-words" with a sexual connotation, must be sharply distinguished from speech that is "obscene"; here, we deal with statements whose tone is *not erotic*, so that the law of obscenity is irrelevant.

    a. *Cohen v. California:*   The most important case involving the state's right to ban offensive language of the profane sort is *Cohen v. California*, 403 U.S. 15 (1971). The case stands basically for the proposition that *profane, offensive language is nonetheless First Amendment speech*, and may not be suppressed under the guise of regulating the "manner" of speech.

        i. **Facts:**   Cohen wore a jacket bearing the legend "Fuck the Draft" in a corridor of the Los Angeles County Courthouse, where women and children were present. He was convicted of violating a statute prohibiting the intentional "disturb[ing] the peace or quiet of any … person [by] offensive conduct."

        ii. **Conviction reversed:**   The Court, in a classic opinion by Justice Harlan, *reversed the conviction* on First Amendment grounds. In so doing, Harlan rejected a number of arguments advanced by the state.

iii. Not obscene: Harlan found that the legend on the jacket was ***not obscene***. An expression is obscene only if it is "in some significant way, erotic." No erotic "psychic stimulation" could reasonably have been expected to result when anybody read the jacket.

iv. Not "captive audience": The state claimed that *Cohen's* message had been "thrust upon unwilling or unsuspecting viewers," and that the state had the power to protect such ***"captive audiences"*** from offensive language. But Harlan's opinion took a narrow view of what constitutes a true "captive audience." Those in the courthouse could have "avoid[ed] further bombardment of their senses simply by ***averting their eyes***."

v. Right to purge offensive language: Lastly, Harlan rejected the state's most general claim, that it had the right to ban certain expletives in order to "maintain what [officials] regard as a ***suitable level of discourse*** within the body politic." He stressed that the First Amendment's general function is to ***"remove governmental restraints for the arena of public discussion."*** Only where speech falls within relatively narrow pre-established categories may government regulate its form or content; none of these exceptions was applicable here. But Harlan also found more specific reasons for finding that the state could not ban expressions like Cohen's from public discourse:

(1) No stopping point: First, there was no principled way to distinguish "fuck" from other words. Yet the state clearly did not have the right to "cleanse public debate to the point where it is grammatically palatable to the most squeamish among us." The preferable constitutional result was simply to ***leave matters of "taste and style" to the individual***, especially since "[o]ne man's vulgarity is another's lyric."

(2) Emotional content: Secondly, this was not simply a situation in which Cohen chose vulgar words to express an idea that could have been equally well expressed by more polite language. The language chosen by Cohen, like much expression, conveyed not only an intellectual idea, but also ***"otherwise inexpressible emotions."*** The Constitution protects this ***"emotive function"*** of speech just as much as the cognitive content of expression.

(3) Smokescreen for censorship: Finally, governments might often ban particular words as a ***smokescreen*** for banning the ***expression of unpopular views***. "One [cannot] forbid particular words without also running a substantial risk of suppressing ideas in the process."

2. Emotionally hurtful speech: A second important category of speech that is entitled to full First Amendment protection even though offensive is speech that is ***emotionally hurtful*** to the listener. No matter how much psychic pain the speech inflicts — indeed, is *intended* to inflict — on the listener, the speech gets ***full First Amendment protection***, as long as

[1] The speech is on a matter of ***public*** (not purely private) ***interest***; and

[2] The pain comes from the ***content*** of the message (i.e., the attempted state regulation is "content-based" as discussed *supra*, p. 503).

A 2011 case striking down a state's right to allow recovery for speech that under state law constituted ***intentional infliction of emotional distress*** (IIED) is the leading illustration of this principle. That case, which upheld the First Amendment right of picketers to use hateful speech to attack the character of a dead soldier at his funeral, is ***Snyder v. Phelps***, 131 S.Ct. 1207 (2011).

a.   Facts: The speakers in *Snyder* were members of a small church, the Westboro Baptist Church of Topeka, Kansas, founded in 1955 by Fred Phelps and still run by him and his family in the 2000s, when the events in the suit took place. The church members' core belief was that God hates homosexuality and hates (and punishes) the U.S. military for tolerating homosexuality.

   i.   Protest strategy: The church members' main First Amendment activity has long been to picket military funerals. *Snyder* grew out of one such picketing session, in which the church members carried hateful signs on public land adjacent to the Maryland funeral of a Marine Lance Colonel killed in Iraq, Matthew Snyder. Matthew's father, Albert Snyder, saw the signs on a TV broadcast after the funeral and became severely distressed at their content. He brought a federal-court diversity action based on substantive Maryland law for the tort of IIED. He ultimately obtained a civil judgment for $4 million in combined compensatory and punitive damages against the church members. The issue was whether that — or indeed any — civil judgment could be enforced without violating the church members' First Amendment rights. (The Supreme Court's answer turned out to be a very clear "no," as we'll see.)

   (1)   Hateful signs: The picketers at the Snyder funeral carried signs with messages like "God Hates the USA/Thank God for 9/11," "God hates fags," and "Thank God for Dead Soldiers." The picketers' message was apparently that Matthew and other soldiers had been killed in combat because God wanted to punish the United States for tolerating homosexuality. Some viewers seem to have assumed that the picketers were saying that Matthew was himself gay; in any event, Matthew was not in fact gay.

   (2)   On public property: A key aspect of the case was that the protest took place entirely on a small plot of ***public land adjacent*** to a public street. Picketing took place 1,000 feet from the church where the funeral was held; none of the church members ever entered the church or the cemetary, or in any way interfered with the funeral.

b.   The Ds win: In an opinion by Chief Justice Roberts that seven members of the Court (all but Alito) joined, the Court held that allowing Matthew's father Albert to recover any damages at all would be a ***violation*** of the Ds' First Amendment right to ***speak freely on a matter of public interest.***

   i.   The test: Roberts began by saying that whether the First Amendment prohibited holding the church members liable for their speech "turns largely on whether the speech is of ***public*** or ***private*** concern." Speech on matters of "***public*** concern" is "at the ***heart*** of the First Amendment's protection" and "occupies the ***highest rung*** of the hierarchy of First Amendment values [making it] entitled to special protection." By contrast, if the speech involved solely a "***purely private*** matter," it would *"not implicate the same constitutional concerns"* because there would be "no potential *interference with a meaningful dialogue of ideas."* [2]

    ii. Public concern: Roberts then quickly concluded that the speech here was indeed on a matter of *public* concern. Speech involves a matter of public concern when it either (1) "can be fairly considered as relating to *any matter of political, social, or other concerns to the community,*" or (2) "is a subject of *legitimate news interest.*" The fact that the statement is "inappropriate or controversial" is *irrelevant* to the question of whether it involves a matter of public concern. The messages on the picket signs here "may fall short of refined social or political commentary" but those messages were clearly designed to *speak on a broad public issue,* and indeed, to reach as broad a public audience as possible.

    iii. Content-based rather than content-neutral: Roberts was also in no doubt about whether the governmental regulation here (namely, the availability of a *tort recovery* under state law) was of the forbidden *content-based* variety rather than an easier-to-justify *content-neutral* "time, place and manner" regulation. Maryland *could* indeed have imposed some content-neutral time, place and manner regulation, such as prohibiting picketing within a specified short distance of a funeral service or procession (something that Maryland and many other states have eventually done — for instance, under a Maryland statute enacted post-*Snyder*, picketing is prohibited within 100 feet of a funeral service or procession).

        (1) Content-based jury deliberations: But that isn't what happened here: the substantive tort law of Maryland gave the jury the right to allow recovery for *"outrageousness,"* a concept that has an *"inherent subjectiveness about it"* that would make the jury *"unlikely to be neutral with respect to the content of the speech."*

  c. Alito dissent: The sole member of the Court to believe that the First Amendment did not bar Albert Snyder from recovering was Justice Alito, who dissented. He believed that notwithstanding the First Amendment, any speaker *may not "intentionally inflict[] severe emotional injury on private persons* at a time of intense emotional sensitivity by launching *vicious verbal attacks* that make no contribution to public debate."

  d. Nazi-Skokie dispute: Before *Snyder,* the leading case showing that speech may not be banned merely because it is emotionally hurtful was a federal Court of Appeals case involving plans by an American Nazi group to demonstrate in front of the Skokie, Illinois Village Hall. Skokie is a predominantly-Jewish community, and about 5,000 of its residents were survivors of the concentration camps. When the village learned of the Nazis' demonstration plans, it passed an ordinance to ban the demonstration.

---

2. Roberts did not say how he thought the case would turn out if the speech had involved only a purely private matter, though he clearly seems to have thought that some sort of damage award against the church members would have been far easier to justify constitutionally. He did give two illustrations of fact patterns where the Court had determined that *only a private matter* was involved: an individual's *credit report* sent to five members of a credit reporting service, and the video of a government employee *engaging in sexually explicit acts* having nothing to do with the employee's public job.

i. **March could not be banned** But the Seventh Circuit explicitly *rejected* the argument that the village had the right to prevent a substantive evil, the "infliction of psychic trauma on resident Holocaust survivors." *Collins v. Smith*, 578 F.2d 1197 (7th Cir. 1978).

(1) Rationale: The court in *Collins* agreed that the demonstration might be shocking to the village's residents. But any shock effect would be due to the ***content of the ideas expressed***, and "public expression of ideas may not be prohibited merely because the ideas are themselves offensive to some of their hearers."

3. **Strict scrutiny to be used:** If the state *does* want to regulate speech on the grounds of its offensive content, the courts will use *strict scrutiny* to review the regulation, and the regulation will *virtually never survive that strict scrutiny.*

a. ***Snyder v. Phelps:*** *Snyder v. Phelps, supra*, illustrates this — once the Supreme Court determined there that allowing a recovery for intentional infliction of emotional distress constituted a form of content-based regulation of speech related to a public issue, the reversal was virtually automatic.

I. **Regulation of "hate speech":** As we just saw, government may generally not prevent or punish words on the grounds that listeners will find them hurtful or otherwise offensive. Groups interested in eliminating discrimination against *minorities* have argued that an exception should be made for *"hate speech"* directed against racial minorities, women, homosexuals, and other traditionally disfavored groups. State legislatures have generally agreed — all but four states have some form of "hate crime" law criminalizing bias-motivated speech or acts.

However, if government *singles out bias-motivated speech*, criminalizing it while not criminalizing other types of angry speech, the government can properly be accused of acting in a forbidden *content-based* rather than content-neutral way. In a series of three cases since 1992, the Supreme Court has tried to lay out some rules for when government may single out hate speech and punish it specially. Two of the three cases have involved *cross burning*, a particular form of hate speech that has a long history of expressing racial hatred (and, often, of preceding racial violence).

1. **Three rules:** These three cases stand for the following main propositions, which represent a general rule about what the state may not ban, and three exceptions to that major rule:

❑ **General ban:** A ban on speech or conduct intended or likely to incite anger or violence based solely on *particular listed topics or motives* — such as race, color, religion or gender hatred — is *impermissibly content-based.* That's true even if all the speech/conduct banned falls within an *"unprotected"* category such as, here, *"fighting words."* (See *R.A.V., infra.*)

❑ **Worst examples:** However, a state *may* impose a content-based ban on *particular instances* of unprotected speech if the ban forbids *only the very worst examples* illustrating *the very reason the particular class of speech is unprotected.* (Thus the state may choose to criminalize just the very most dangerous "fighting words," the very most obscene obscene images, etc.) (*R.A.V.*)

❑ **Penalty-enhancement statutes:** Also, a state may identify particular generally-applicable criminal proscriptions, and may then choose to punish *more severely* those criminal acts that happen to be motivated by hate than those not motivated by hate. This is called the *"penalty enhancement"* approach. For instance, from within the overall class of acts that constitute criminal vandalism or arson, the state may punish vandalism or arson more seriously if it's motivated by bias against particular groups. (*Wisconsin v. Mitchell, infra*, p. 543.)

❏ **All intimidating acts:** Finally, a state may select a particular type of expressive act (e.g., cross-burning), and punish *all instances* where that act is done with a purpose of *intimidating or threatening* someone, even though the state doesn't punish other types of intimidating or threatening acts. (*Virginia v. Black, infra*, p. 544.)

2. **The general principle of *R.A.V. v. St. Paul*:** The first of this trio of Supreme Court cases on hate-speech was *R.A.V. v. City of St. Paul*, 505 U.S. 377 (1992). The case involved a *cross-burning*, but seems applicable to anti-hate-speech laws in general.

   a. **Facts:** In *R.A.V.*, D and several other teenagers allegedly burned a homemade cross inside the fenced yard of a black family that lived across the street from D; the incident took place in the middle of the night. D was prosecuted under the St. Paul "Bias-Motivated Crime Ordinance," which provided that "whoever places on public or private property a symbol, object, appellation, characterization or graffiti, including, but not limited to, a burning cross or Nazi swastika, which one knows or has reasonable grounds to know arouses anger, alarm or resentment in others on the basis of *race, color, creed, religion or gender* commits disorderly conduct and shall be guilty of a misdemeanor." D contended that the ordinance violated the First Amendment in two respects: (1) it was substantially overbroad; and (2) it was impermissibly content-based.

   b. **Court agrees:** The Court unanimously agreed that the ordinance, on its face, violated the First Amendment. However, the Court was bitterly split, 5-4, on the proper rationale.

   c. **Opinion of the Court:** Justice Scalia, joined by four other Justices (Rehnquist, Kennedy, Souter and Thomas), wrote the opinion for the Court. Scalia concluded that the law was *impermissibly content-based*, because "it prohibits otherwise permitted speech solely on the basis of the subjects the speech addresses."

      i. **Only applicable to "fighting words":** The Minnesota Supreme Court, in construing the ordinance, had concluded that it was intended to apply only to *"fighting words"* (see *supra*, p. 533), not to bias speech that would not threaten an immediate breach of the peace. Scalia believed that he had no choice but to accept the Minnesota court's construction of the statute.

      ii. **No content-based regulation of unprotected categories:** The Supreme Court had previously held, as noted (see *supra*, p. 533) that fighting words are an "unprotected category" under the First Amendment. But Scalia's opinion asserted that *even when government is regulating a supposedly "unprotected" category, it may not do so in a content-based manner.*

         (1) **Examples:** Scalia gave two examples of what he considered to be impermissibly content-based regulations of "unprotected" categories: The government may proscribe libel, but it may not make the further content discrimination of proscribing *only* libel critical of the government. Similarly, a city council may

not enact an ordinance prohibiting only those legally obscene works that contain criticism of the city government.

iii. Ordinance unconstitutional: By Scalia's standard, the St. Paul ordinance was clearly **unconstitutional**, even though applicable only to generally-unprotected "fighting words." The ordinance was certainly content-based, because it applied only to fighting words that insult or provoke violence "on the basis of *race, color, creed, religion or gender*" — abusive language, no matter how vicious or severe, was permitted under the ordinance unless it was addressed to one of the *"specified disfavored topics"*; fighting words used to express hostility based on political affiliation, union membership or homosexuality, for instance, were not covered by the ordinance.

(1) Viewpoint based: In fact, Scalia said, the ordinance was not only content-based but "*viewpoint* based." That is, where two opposing sides had a confrontation concerning a matter of race or religion, one side could use fighting words while the other could not. "One could hold up a sign saying, for example, that all 'anti-catholic bigots' are misbegotten; but not that all 'papists' are, for that would insult and provoke violence 'on the basis of religion.' " St. Paul has no authority, Scalia asserted, "to license one side of a debate to fight free-style, while requiring the other to follow Marquis of Queensbury Rules."

iv. Remedy: Proponents of the ordinance argued that even if it was content-based, it could survive the strict scrutiny given to content-based regulations because it was necessary to serve a compelling state interest. Scalia conceded that the state had a compelling interest in safeguarding the rights of traditionally-disfavored groups, including their right to live in peace where they wish. But he argued that the ordinance was not *"necessary"* to achieve this state interest, because there were *"adequate content-neutral alternatives."* In particular, St. Paul could enact an ordinance prohibiting *all* fighting words, not merely fighting words motivated by racial, religious or other specifically-enumerated biases. To Scalia, burning a cross in someone's front yard is "reprehensible," but St. Paul had "sufficient means at its disposal to prevent such behaviour without adding the First Amendment to the fire."

d. Concurrence: The main concurrence in *R.A.V.* (by Justice White, joined by Blackmun, O'Connor and, in most respects, Stevens) read more like a dissent.

i. Unprotected categories: Justice White believed that where a category is "unprotected," the states are *not* prevented from regulating it on the basis of content. "It is inconsistent to hold that the government may proscribe an *entire category* of speech because the content of that speech is evil ... but that the government may not treat a *subset of that category differently* without violating the First Amendment; the content of the subset is by definition worthless and undeserving of constitutional protection."

(1) Overbreadth: But White nonetheless agreed with the result in the case. White believed that the case should instead have been decided on *overbreadth* grounds. He interpreted the Minnesota court to have ruled that the ordinance prohibited expression that "by its very utterance" causes "anger, alarm or resentment." By this interpretation, the ordinance reached not only words tending to incite an immediate breach of the peace (words which may constitutionally be proscribed), but also words and expressive conduct that cause *only* hurt feelings, offense, or resentment (words and conduct which may not be constitutionally proscribed). Since the ordinance reached both protected and unprotected speech, it was *overbroad*, and thus invalid.

3. **Enhancement-of-penalty statutes:** The Court's approach in *R.A.V.* invalidates many anti-hate crime statutes that, like St. Paul's, define certain activities as a ***new, separate, crime***.

   a. **Enhancement-of-penalty statutes may be valid:** But *R.A.V.* does ***not invalidate*** statutes that approach the hate-speech problem in a quite different way: these statutes punish ***existing crimes*** like vandalism and arson ***more seriously*** if the prosecution shows that the crime was motivated in part by one of the listed types of bias. The Court found such a ***"penalty enhancement"*** statute to be ***valid***, in ***Wisconsin v. Mitchell***, 508 U.S. 476 (1993). This unanimous decision seems to validate all of the dozens of state and local hate-crime laws of the "penalty enhancement" variety throughout the country.

   b. **Facts:** In *Wisconsin v. Mitchell*, D, a black teenager, was convicted of aggravated battery, a crime that in Wisconsin ordinarily carries a maximum sentence of two years in prison. However, there was strong evidence that D had selected his victim, V, based on race; for instance, he pointed to V, told his friends, "There goes a white boy; go get him," then led them in a severe beating of V. Under Wisconsin's statute, the ***maximum sentence*** for aggravated battery was ***increased*** to seven years because of D's race-based selection of a victim.

   c. **Statute upheld:** The Court unanimously held that this penalty-enhancement scheme did not violate D's First Amendment rights, and thus ***upheld*** the statute.

      i. **Defendant's argument:** D argued in *Mitchell* that since the only reason for the enhanced sentence was his discriminatory motive for selecting his victim, the statute punished his beliefs. Therefore, he argued, the penalty-enhancement statute was no more constitutionally acceptable than the ban on certain "fighting words" struck down in *R.A.V.*

      ii. **Speech/ conduct distinction:** But the Court rejected this argument. In doing so, the Court relied heavily on the distinction between speech and conduct. The ordinance struck down in *R.A.V.* was explicitly directed at expression, whereas the penalty-enhancement statute here was aimed at ***conduct***, and this conduct was completely unprotected by the First Amendment. (That is, there is no constitutional protection for the act of battery, whatever the actor's motive.)

      iii. **Analogy to anti-discrimination laws:** The Court also observed that many other statutes punish a defendant based on his motive for acting. For instance, federal Title VII makes it unlawful for an employer to discriminate against an employee "because of such individual's race, color, religion, sex, ... ," yet that statute has always been found to conform with the First Amendment.

4. **Ban on all acts intended to intimidate:** Finally, in the most recent cutting back on the general rule of *R.A.V.*, the Court has held that ***all instances*** of a certain type of expressive act — such as cross-burning — may be prohibited if done for the purpose of ***intimidation***

or threat, even if other intimidating acts with expressive content are not prohibited. *Virginia v. Black*, 538 U.S. 343 (2003).

   a.   Statute: The statute at issue in *Black* made a crime to burn a cross in a public place or on the property of another, if done "with the intent of *intimidating any person or group of persons.*" The statute also added a clause (we'll refer to it here as the "prima facie" clause) saying that "Any such burning of a cross shall be *prima facie evidence* of an intent to intimidate[.]"

   b.   Main provision upheld: The Court's opinion in *Black* was fragmented — there was no opinion that spoke for a majority on all points. But there were separate majorities for two propositions: (1) that government may *single out cross burning* as a particularly virulent form of intimidation, and may thus *ban all cross burnings done with intent to intimidate* even while not banning other expressive acts intended to intimidate; and (2) that the statute here was *unconstitutional* (though no majority agreed about why).

   i.   Government may single out cross-burning: As to proposition (1), a majority of the Court in *Black* agreed that "[i]nstead of prohibiting all intimidating messages, Virginia may choose to *regulate this subset of intimidating messages* in light of cross burning's long and pernicious history as a *signal of impending violence.*"

   c.   Significance: *Black* is significant mainly for the proposition that a properly-constructed statute may *ban a particular type of intimidating expression* — such as cross burning — while *declining to ban other types of intimidating expressions.*

J.   All speech not necessarily created equal (the disfavoring of indecent speech):   Implicit in *Cohen v. California*, supra, p. 536, is the principle that all constitutionally-protected expression is *created equal* in the eyes of the First Amendment, so that the government *may not prefer certain ideas or subject matter to others.* But a number of cases suggest that certain types of expression, while not directly suppressible on the grounds of their content, are viewed as inherently *less valuable* and may therefore be *regulated more extensively* than speech closer to the "core" of First Amendment values, such as political speech. This less-favored of speech seems to include mainly speech that is "*indecent.*"[3] This is sometimes referred to as the *"two-tier"* theory of First Amendment protection.[4]

   Example: New York criminalizes the distribution of non-obscene materials showing *children engaged in sexual conduct.* The ban covers such sexually-explicit materials even if they are not obscene (e.g., materials that have serious literary value, a factor that automatically prevents them from meeting the formal definition of "obscene"; see *infra*, p. 578).

   Held, the ban does not violate the First Amendment. Materials showing children engaged in sexual conduct, even if the materials are not "obscene," have an "exceed-

---

3. *Commercial* speech also seems to be somewhat less-favored. See *infra*, p. 582.

4. Don't confuse this "two-tier" theory with the "two track" analysis on p. 503 *supra*. "Two-tier" refers to the Court's distinction based on the "value" of the speech. "Two track" refers to two ways of analyzing restrictions on speech, one track for content-based regulations and the other for content-neutral "time, place and manner" regulations.

ingly modest, if not *de minimis,"* First Amendment value. The state has a countervailing, compellingly strong interest in stopping sexual exploitation of child actors. Therefore, the First Amendment does not demand that the state allow distribution of such materials. *New York v. Ferber*, 458 U.S. 747 (1982) (discussed further *infra*, p. 580.)

1. **Consequences of being "lesser-valued" speech:** So in what way may lesser-valued speech such as indecent speech be more extensively regulated than high-value speech? Sometimes, the low-value speech may be completely banned; more commonly, its "secondary effects" can be regulated.

2. **Complete ban:** Occasionally, as in the indecent-speech-involving-minors area at issue in *Ferber, supra*, the Court has allowed government to ***completely ban*** the speech despite its slight First Amendment value.

3. **The "secondary effects" doctrine:** But a more important practical difference between high-value and low-valued speech is that the ***"secondary effects"*** doctrine seems to apply to this lesser-valued speech.

   a. **Nature of doctrine:** Under the secondary effects doctrine, if the court is satisfied that the government was merely trying to eliminate the undesirable ***non-content-related consequences*** of an expressive activity — things like increased crime or declining property values — the regulation will be found to be ***content-neutral*** and will be given only relatively un-strict "track two" review.

      i. **Regulation passes review:** Furthermore, in cases qualifying for the secondary effects doctrine, the Court seems very willing to find that the measure ***passes*** that track two review. That is, the Court typically accepts that the government is indeed pursuing an important interest, and that the regulatory means being chosen appropriately further that interest while leaving open adequate alternative channels for communication.

   b. ***Erie v. Pap's*** **expands the doctrine to allow a complete ban:** For instance, a 2000 case holds that the secondary effects of lower-valued speech may entitle government to ***completely ban*** the disfavored expressive conduct (not merely limit the speech to a certain geographical area). The case is ***Erie v. Pap's A.M.***, 529 U.S. 277 (2000).

      i. **Facts:** *Pap's* was a ***"nude dancing"*** case. The city of Erie, Pa. passed an ordinance that required live dancers to wear at least "pasties" and a "G-string." (Neither the city nor anyone else claimed that nude dancing was obscene and therefore constitutionally unprotected.) The city said that it was attacking not the expressive content of nude live entertainment, but rather its secondary effects, such as violence, sexual harassment, public intoxication, prostitution, and the spread of sexually transmitted diseases. The ban applied throughout the city, not just in a delimited area (as a prior Supreme Court case had approved). A nightclub that presented live nude dancers attacked the ordinance.

      ii. **Plurality:** The Court ***upheld*** the ordinance. However, there was no majority opinion on the underlying constitutional issues. A four-Justice plurality (opinion by O'Connor, joined by Rehnquist, Kennedy and Breyer) found that the secondary effects doctrine applied, so that the ordinance should be judged by the more-forgiving track two analysis for ***content-neutral*** time, place and manner regulations.

(1) Bad motivation irrelevant: In fact, to the plurality it didn't even matter that the city may have been *motivated in part* by a desire to *suppress particular expression.* According to the plurality, as long as *one* of the purposes of the regulation was to combat secondary effects, it didn't matter that government also had the motive of suppressing speech.

(2) Passes track two analysis: The plurality then found it easy to conclude that the ordinance satisfied the track two "time, place and manner" standard.

    iii. Additional votes: Justices Scalia and Thomas concurred. They believed that because the ordinance was a "general law regulating conduct and not specifically directed at expression," the ordinance was *not subject to First Amendment scrutiny at all.* Therefore, they agreed that the ordinance easily passed constitutional muster.

    iv. 6 votes for using secondary effects analysis: So there now seem to be at least six votes on the Court for holding that even an *absolute government ban* on a particular form of expressive conduct motivated by a desire to combat the conduct's secondary effects is to be viewed as *content-neutral,* and may be upheld if the ban is a reasonably effective means of combating those effects.

    v. Limited to indecency or other less-favored speech: So far, the secondary effects doctrine has not been applied outside of the *indecency* context. Thus as far as we know, government can't attack what it says are the bad secondary effects of protected speech other than indecency (e.g., *core political speech*) except by surviving strict scrutiny.

K. Regulation of indecency in media: A number of cases have dealt with *indecency in the media.* A brief summary of the Court's holdings is that the government has substantial latitude in regulating indecent expression on the *public airwaves,* but much less latitude when it tries to carry out such regulation in media that are more one-on-one, such as *phone systems,* modern individually-addressable *cable TV systems,* and *computer networks* such as the *Internet.*

1. Public airwaves: The government has the power to regulate non-obscene "indecent" material broadcast over the *public airwaves* (standard broadcast *radio and TV*).

2. Regulation of indecency on phone, cable and computer systems: But when government tries to limit indecency in *other media* that are not as intrusive and widely-disseminated, the limits will be *strictly scrutinized.* These cases have involved *phone networks* ("dial-a-porn"), *cable TV* systems, and the *Internet.*

    a. Cable programming: For instance, if government tries to perform content-based regulation of indecent speech on *cable TV systems,* the court will use *strict scrutiny.*

        i. Less restriction permissible: Therefore, much less regulation of indecency will be tolerated in the cable TV area than in the over-the-air broadcast area, because of cable's technological ability to *block access on a household-by-household basis.* Since content-based restrictions will be strictly scrutinized, any reasonably-effective less-restrictive alternative must be used. Therefore, government, instead of curtailing transmission of indecent material to *all* households, must instead give cable operators the right to offer blocking to *just those households that want it.*

b. Indecency on the Internet: What about *"cyberspace,"* and in particular the *Internet*? Is the Internet more like over-the-air broadcasting (as to which the Court has traditionally allowed substantial government regulation), or is it more like books and newspapers (which receive the greatest First Amendment freedom)? The Supreme Court has answered this question by saying that the Internet *more closely resembles books and newspapers,* and is therefore deserving of the *utmost freedom from content regulation*. The Court did so in two major opinions concerning Congress' efforts to restrict the access of *minors* to *indecent content* over the Internet.

    i.   *Reno v. ACLU*:   The first of the two cases was *Reno v. American Civil Liberties Union*, 521 U.S. 844 (1997). The plaintiffs attacked two provisions of the federal Communications Decency Act (CDA). The first provision made it a crime to use a "telecommunications device" to transmit any communication which is "obscene or *indecent*," while *"knowing that the recipient* of the communication is under 18 years of age." The second made it a crime to "use any interactive computer service" to "display in a manner *available to a person under 18*," any communication that uses *"patently offensive"* language or images. (For easy reference, we'll call the first provision the "knowing transmission" provision and the second the "make available" provision.) Both provisions were directed mainly at the Internet.

       (1) Unanimously struck down: All nine Justices agreed that at least parts of the CDA were *unconstitutional*. The Court's opinion was by Justice Stevens, who found the CDA to be both overly vague and overbroad.

       (2) Less risk of intrusion: Stevens concluded that the burden on government to justify content regulation of the Internet was much greater than for such regulation of over-the-air broadcasting. Over-the-air broadcasting merited regulation in part because there was no way to adequately *protect the listener from unexpected messages*. By contrast, the risk that a computer user would *stumble upon* indecent material by accident was *"remote,"* because "a series of affirmative steps is required to access specific material." So cases allowing tight regulation of indecency in the over-the-air context (like *FCC v. Pacifica, infra*, p. 640) furnished no support for a finding that the CDA was constitutional.

       (3) Statute found overbroad: Stevens concluded that the statute was *overbroad*, because it restricted the free-speech rights of *adults*. "In order to deny minors access to potentially harmful speech, the CDA effectively suppresses a large amount of speech that *adults have a constitutional right to receive* and to address to one another." For instance, if one member of a 100-person chat group was a minor, the entire group would be foreclosed from discussing an "indecent" topic, even though the 99 adults clearly had a right to discuss that topic.

       (4) Fails strict scrutiny: This suppression of protected adult speech had to survive *strict scrutiny*, Stevens said. Therefore, the government had to show that there was *no less restrictive alternative* that would accomplish the same ends. The government had failed to carry this burden, he concluded. For instance, the government might have just imposed the less-restrictive alternative that indecent material be "tagged" so that user-installed filters could block it.

ii. Replacement statute is also found invalid: After *Reno*, Congress tried to fix the CDA's constitutional problems by enacting a replacement statute, the ***Child Online Protection Act (COPA)***. But in ***Ashcroft v. American Civil Liberties Union***, 542 U.S. 656 (2004), the Court found that COPA, too, was very likely a violation of the First Amendment. (Because of the preliminary-injunction posture of the case, the Court did not definitively decide the statute's constitutionality.)

(1) Terms of statute: COPA made it a crime to put on to the Web content that was "harmful to minors." Material was deemed "harmful to minors" if it was either obscene or was designed to appeal to minors' prurient interests in a "patently offensive" way that lacked serious literary or other value to such minors. (Minors were defined as persons under 17.) Web operators were given an affirmative defense if they screened minors from access by some ***age-verification mechanism***, such as by requiring a credit card or by "any other reasonable measures that are feasible under available technology." So basically, COPA said that anyone who wanted to operate a commercial Web site containing material that might be harmful to minors had to impose a mechanism for checking that only adults used the site.

(2) Lower court issues injunction: A federal district court issued a preliminary injunction against COPA, on the grounds that it, like the CDA before it, violated the First Amendment rights of adults.

(3) Supreme Court agrees with injunction: By a 5-4 vote, the Supreme Court held that the lower-court had ***not abused its discretion in entering the injunction***. Justice Kennedy's opinion for the majority began by repeating *Reno*'s holding that if a statute suppresses a large amount of speech that adults have a constitutional right to receive, the government must bear the burden of showing that there are ***no less-restrictive alternatives*** that would be at least as effective.

(4) Filtering not shown to be less effective: Kennedy concluded that the government had not born this burden of proof here. In particular, he focused on ***"blocking and filtering software"*** that could voluntarily be installed by users on their own computers. Such filtering software would clearly be less restrictive than the age-verification scheme required by COPA; for instance, an adult with children could simply turn off the filter when the adult wanted to use the computer. And, Kennedy asserted, user-installed filters might well prove more effective than COPA — for instance, filters could block ***foreign-hosted material*** (which COPA could not effectively reach). Therefore, the injunction should be permitted to stand while the case was tried on the merits, and the statute would be found valid only if the government could show (as seemed very unlikely) that the statute was in fact the ***least-restrictive available means of effectively blocking minors*** from accessing indecent Internet material.

(5) Dissent: The four dissenters, led by Justice Breyer, believed that COPA did indeed satisfy the least-restrictive-alternative requirement. They believed that COPA blocked very little content that was not in fact obscene (and thus forbiddable even to adults).

iii. **Significance:** Here are some of the things that *Reno v. ACLU* and *Ashcroft v. ACLU* seem to establish:

(1) Broad protection for Internet: The Internet, and publicly-available computer networks in general, deserve the same *very broad First Amendment protection as books and newspapers,* not the lesser protection given to scarce over-the-air broadcast media. (*Reno.*) This means that any "time, place and manner" restriction on the Internet will have to be very closely linked to the achievement of an important governmental interest.

(2) Protection of rights of adults: When government tries to protect minors from non-obscene material, government must make great efforts to see to it that the *rights of adults* to access material that they have a constitutional right to access are not inadvertently hampered. *Reno.* (So a ban on putting non-obscene "indecent" material in any place where minors might see it infringes the rights of adults, since adults have a right to see the material and the ban will dissuade people from making the material broadly available.)

(3) No-restrictive available alternatives: Indeed, if government *is* going to make it harder for adults to access material that they have a First Amendment right to see — even if "harder" means imposing a hurdle as relatively small as requiring the user to prove that she is in fact an adult — government must bear the burden of proving that there are *no less-restrictive available alternatives.* For example, if Congress wants to impose an age-verification requirement, Congress would have to prove that this device is less restrictive, or more effective, than filtering software voluntarily installed by private (adult) users, clearly a hard-to-make showing. (*Ashcroft.*)

L. The public forum: We turn now to a detailed discussion of the *public forum* as a factor in determining whether governmental regulation that purports to be merely of the "time, place and manner" of expression nonetheless violates the First Amendment.

1. **Recap of rules:** To recapitulate briefly how the status of a place as a public or non-public forum fits into the constitutional analysis, here is a summary of the relevant rules:

   a. **Content-neutrality:** If the regulation occurs because the government objects to the *communicative impact* of the expression (i.e., the government is not being content-neutral), it *does not make a difference* whether the expression takes place in a public forum or not; in either event, the governmental regulation is presumptively invalid, unless the expression falls in a pre-defined "unprotected category" (or, apparently now, if it falls within a class of speech that has "lesser social value," such as the "offensive" or "indecent" speech in *American Mini Theatres* and *Pacifica* or the child pornography in *Ferber).*

   b. **Public forum:** Assuming content-neutrality, if the speech occurs in a *public forum,* it (and conduct related to it) can only be regulated in *narrow ways* which the government shows to be *necessary* to serve *significant governmental interests*. Tribe, p. 982. The availability of *alternative channels* for the communication will *not* by itself be enough to make the regulation valid.

c. **Designated public forum:** Some government-owned property is viewed as a *"designated public forum."* This happens where government makes the decision to open non-public-forum property to broad expressive uses. (*Example:* Government decides to let any student group use its classrooms for any expressive activity.) The same rules (given in (b) above) apply to designated public forums as to true public forums, but government can at any time *change its mind* and remove the designation, making the site or use a non-public forum. (For more about designed public forums, including how they are defined, see p. 552 *infra*.)

d. **Non-public forum:** Where the speech does *not* occur in a public (or designated public) forum, the state's right to regulate it in a content-neutral manner depends on whether the regulation's interference with expression is *"substantial"* or not.

   i. **Substantial interference:** If the interference *is* substantial, the same rule applies as in the public-forum situation: the regulation must be narrowly drawn, and necessary to serve some significant government interest.

   ii. **Insubstantial interference:** But if the interference is *not substantial*, the government must only show a *rational justification* for its regulatory scheme. Tribe, p. 982. The government's scheme may allow access to some speakers and some subject matters while excluding others, "so long as the distinctions drawn are reasonable in light of the purpose served by the forum and are *viewpoint neutral*." *Cornelius v. NAACP Legal Defense and Educational Fund*, 473 U.S. 788 (1985).

   iii. **Alternative channels:** One significant difference between expression occurring in a public (including designated public) forum and that occurring in a non-public forum is that in the latter situation, the *availability of equally effective alternative channels* is *sufficient to make the interference "insubstantial"* (so that the "rational relation" test is all that has to be met). Tribe, p. 982.

2. **Necessary for significant state interest:** In applying the requirement that public-forum regulations must be narrow ones that are necessary to serve significant governmental interests, the Court has held that *mere administrative convenience does not suffice* as a governmental interest. Recall, for instance, that a city's interest in keeping its streets clean was held not to constitute a sufficient justification for a ban on distribution of handbills, in *Schneider v. State*, 308 U.S. 147 (1939) (*supra*, p. 527).

   a. **Safety:** But a need to *control crowds* to prevent *physical danger* from say, demonstrators or their audience, *will* suffice, provided that the Court is convinced that the crowd-control justification is not really a smokescreen for censorship (non-content-neutrality), and provided that there is no problem of vagueness or overbreadth (so that administrative discretion is held within acceptable limits).

   b. **Protection of unwilling listener:** Similarly, the need to protect an *unwilling listener* against being forced to hear or see a message is a sufficiently strong governmental interest. For instance, a municipality may ban all picketing in front of a single residence, in order to protect the inhabitants' right to be free of unwanted messages while at home. See *Frisby v. Schultz*, 487 U.S. 474 (1988), so holding. (In *Frisby*, the Court upheld such an ordinance, whose effect was to prevent anti-abortion activists from picketing the residence of a doctor who performed abortions.)

c. Access to public and private places: The need to allow *access* to public and private buildings will clearly justify some regulation of demonstrators. For instance, at least where less-intrusive measures have not worked, a judge may enjoin protesters or picketers from blocking access to the place that they are picketing.

d. Traffic flow: Even the need to keep streets *free for ordinary traffic* may justify *limited* regulation of marchers or demonstrators (e.g., a requirement that they use a street that is not a main thoroughfare).

3. Private places: Even where expression takes place in a *private* place, content-neutral regulations may be found to so impair the freedom of expression that the First Amendment has been violated. This will be true where the channel of communication being impaired *has no adequate substitutes.*

> **Example:** The City of San Diego bans all billboards containing non-commercial messages, apart from a few narrowly-defined exceptions. The City raises the defense (among others) that the ordinance is a reasonable "time, place and manner" restriction.
>
> *Held*, the ban is not a valid "time, place and manner" restriction; such restrictions, to be valid, must not only be content-neutral, but must also serve a significant governmental interest and *"leave open ample alternative channels for communication of the information."* Here, the parties stipulated that many advertisers rely on outdoor advertising because other forms of advertising are "insufficient, inappropriate and prohibitively expensive." Thus these other forms of advertising do not represent adequate alternative channels. *Metromedia, Inc. v. San Diego*, 453 U.S. 490 (1981).

a. Other locations: In private-forum situations, there is no general rule to predict when alternative channels will be found to be "adequate." One rule of thumb that seems to have emerged, however, is that a different *location* (as distinguished from a different medium) is much more likely to be an adequate substitute when it is in the *same city* as the location which has been placed under restriction, than where this alternative location is in a neighboring city.

4. "True" or "traditional" public forums: Let us now consider in more detail the various types of forums. First, and easiest to analyze are *"true" public forums,* sometimes referred to as *"traditional"* public forums. These are forums that by custom, rather than by any explicit government decision or designation, are completely public.

The clearest examples of a completely public forum, recognized as such since the 1930's, are *streets, sidewalks and parks*. See *Hague v. C.I.O.*, 307 U.S. 496 (1939) ("Use of the streets in public places [for assembly and debate of public questions] has, from ancient times, been a part of the privileges, immunities, rights and liberties of citizens.") Even a *quiet street* in a *residential neighborhood* is a true public forum. See *Frisby v. Schultz*, *supra*, p. 550, so holding (but concluding that the state nonetheless was entitled to ban all picketing on a residential street in front of a particular house).

a. Rules: Remember the *rules* applicable to true public forums:

❏ any *content-based* regulation will be *strictly scrutinized* (regulation must be necessary to achieve a compelling governmental interest) and rarely sustained; and

❑   any *content-neutral* "time, place and manner" regulation must be *narrowly drawn* to serve *significant governmental interests*, while leaving open adequate *alternative channels* for the communication.

5. **Designated public forums:** An additional class consists of what are called *"designated public forums."* These are public facilities as to which the government *has made the decision to open the place up to a broad range of expressive activities.* (As we explain below, these are treated essentially the *same way as true public forums*.)

   a.   **Municipal theater:** For instance, a *municipal theater* held open as a place where *any group* may put on productions becomes a designated public forum, and certain groups or productions may not be excluded merely because a different theater is available. See *Southeastern Promotions, Ltd. v. Conrad*, 420 U.S. 546 (1975) (city theater may not exclude production of "Hair," even though some other, privately-owned theater in the city was available).

   b.   **School classrooms:** The same would be likely to be true of *school classrooms*, if the school district has decided to let practically *any* community group or school group use the premises *after hours.* Such a decision makes the classrooms (at least after hours) a designated public forum, at which point the government can't allow or disallow particular groups to use the rooms based on agreement/disagreement with the group's message.

   c.   **Rules:** Once a place becomes a designated public forum, the *same rules apply as apply to true public forums:* (1) content-based regulation will be strictly scrutinized; and (2) content-neutral "time, place and manner" regulation must be narrowly drawn to serve significant governmental interests, while leaving open adequate alternative channels for the communication.

      i.   **Government may change its mind:** The only difference between a true public forum and a designated public forum is that with a designated forum, government may at any time *change its mind*, and *remove the designation* — at that point the forum becomes a non-public forum (see immediately below), which may be subjected to much greater "time, place and manner" regulation.

6. **Non-public forums:** A final category consists of those public facilities which are used for purposes *not particularly linked to expression*. Such a facility is usually referred to as a *"non-public forum"* (or sometimes, a *"limited public forum"*). Of the three categories of public areas, this group offers the *least* constitutionally-protected access for First Amendment expression. The government regulation of expression in a non-public forum must merely be:

[1] *reasonable* in light of the *purpose served* by the forum; and

[2] *viewpoint neutral*.

See, e.g., *Int'l Soc. for Krishna Consciousness, Inc. v. Lee*, 505 U.S. 672 (1992).

   a.   **Reasonableness:** The requirement of *"reasonableness"* has relatively little bite here, as in the due process and equal protection areas. Government may limit speech in the non-public forum even if *less restrictive alternatives are readily available*, and even if the restriction chosen is not the *"most reasonable."*

Example: The public authority that operates the three major New York City airports bans all repetitive solicitation of money within the terminals, and all distribution of literature.

Held, because airport terminals are not public forums, the regulation of expression within them must merely be reasonable. The ban on face-to-face solicitation of money is reasonable, because "passengers who wish to avoid the solicitor may have to alter their path, slowing both themselves and those around them [with the result that] the normal flow of traffic is impeded." Also, face-to-face solicitation presents risks of duress and fraud. (But, a different majority of the Court holds, the sale and distribution of literature may *not* be banned; at least one member of the Court believes that such regulation is not even "reasonable.") *Int'l Soc. for Krishna Consciousness, Inc. v. Lee, supra.*

b. **Viewpoint neutrality:** But the requirement of *viewpoint neutrality* has a real impact in these non-public-forum cases. The government can restrict speech across the board in these forums, but it can't restrict speech by *preferring some messages or perspectives over others.*

  i. **Can't bar religious viewpoint, even if it involves worship:** The most dramatic example of the requirement of viewpoint-neutrality for non-public forums is that when a government allows use of *public facilities* by various (even though not all) community groups, *religious groups* must be given *equal access.*

  (1) Funding of student activities: For instance, where a public university funds a broad range of *student publications*, it may not exclude publications on the grounds that they are religiously-oriented. See *Rosenberger v. Univ. of Virginia*, discussed *infra*, p. 554.

  ii. **Candidate forums on government-owned TV:** Similarly, government must be viewpoint-neutral when it organizes a debate or forum for *competing political candidates*. See *Arkansas Educational Television Comm'n v. Forbes*, 523 S. Ct. 666 (1998), holding that a state-owned TV station which held a candidates' forum was not entitled to choose which candidates to invite based upon the candidate's political views (but also holding that the station did not violate this principle).

  iii. **Even spending must be viewpoint-neutral:** The requirement of viewpoint-neutrality is so strict that it applies even to activities that are *funded by the government*. Thus government may *not* choose to *fund some third-party activities and not others, based on the viewpoints expressed*.

  Example: The University of Virginia (a public university) funds certain student publications, by paying for their printing costs. The University disqualifies from this funding any publication that "primarily promotes or manifests a particular belie[f] in or about a deity or an ultimate reality." P is the publisher of *Wide Awake*, a student newspaper that gives a "Christian perspective" on the University. P argues that the University's refusal to fund *Wide Awake* violates his free-speech rights. The University concedes that its policy puts a whole subject — religion discussed from a proselytizing perspective — off limits, but claims that its policy is viewpoint-neutral. (For instance, the university points out that those opposing the practice of religion are equally excluded.)

Held, for P (by a 5-4 vote). The regulation here was *not* viewpoint-neutral. "The University does not exclude religion as a subject matter but selects for disfavored treatment those student journalistic efforts with religious editorial viewpoints." Nor does the fact that the University is spending money make any difference: If the University were disseminating only its own messages, it would not have to fund opposing viewpoints. But once it chooses to fund some ***third-party viewpoints*** (i.e., some student-run publications), it may not choose which ones to fund based on the viewpoint of the speaker. (Also, requiring the University to fund publications like P's does not violate the Establishment Clause. See *infra*, p. 660.) *Rosenberger v. University of Virginia*, 515 U.S. 819 (1995).

(1) Can ban discrimination by others: But when government gives a subsidy to certain organizations, it *may* require as a condition of the subsidy that the organizations themselves ***not discriminate against certain viewpoints.*** When government pursues such an ***"all-comers"*** policy, the Court has held, government is not engaging in forbidden viewpoint-based discrimination. See *Christian Legal Society Chapter v. Martinez*, 130 S.Ct. 2971 (2010), a 5-4 decision set out in the following Example.

Example: The University of California's Hastings College of Law gives official recognition and some funding only to those organizations ("Registered Student Organizations," or RSOs) that comply with the school's nondiscrimination rules (the "all-comers" policy). The all-comers policy requires any RSO to accept all students who apply, and also forbids RSOs from discriminating on the basis of various specified criteria, one of which is sexual orientation. P (the Christian Legal Society) refuses to accept any student who engages in "unrepentant homosexual conduct," or who holds religious convictions different from those contained in a "Statement of Faith" the Society has adopted. Hastings refuses to grant P the RSO status because of these limits on who may join. P claims that the all-comers policy violates the First Amendment requirement that when government restricts access to limited public forums (i.e., nonpublic forums) the restriction must be both reasonable and viewpoint neutral.

Held, for Hastings: the all-comers policy is constitutional. The policy is viewpoint neutral: "[It is] hard to imagine a more viewpoint-neutral policy than one requiring all student groups to accept all comers." The requirement that student groups accept all applicants is " 'justified without reference to the content [or viewpoint] of the regulated speech.' " (Also, the all-comers requirement is *reasonable* for several reasons, including that Hastings could reasonably conclude that (1) an equal-access policy promotes the educational experience, and (2) in light of the fact that RSOs get school funding, no Hastings student should be forced to fund a group that would reject her as a member.)

(The four dissenters argue that the policy is not in fact viewpoint neutral because it "single[s] out one category of expressive associations for disfavored treatment: groups formed to express a religious message. Only religious groups [are] required to admit students who [do] not share their views.") *Christian Legal Society Chapter v. Martinez, supra.*

c. **"Subject neutrality" not required:** The requirement of neutrality in non-public forum cases is merely one of *"viewpoint* neutrality," *not "subject neutrality."* Thus "[a] speaker may be excluded from a non-public forum if he wishes to address a *topic* not encompassed within the purpose of the forum ... or if he is not a member of the class of speakers for whose special benefit the forum was created. ... [But] the government violates the First Amendment when it denies access to a speaker solely to suppress the *point of view* he espouses on an otherwise includable subject." *Cornelius v. NAACP Legal Defense and Educational Fund, Inc.*, 473 U.S. 788 (1985).

Example: The federal government says that non-profits may solicit from federal employees in the workforce by using a particular fundraising mechanism administered by the federal government. However, no agency that seeks to influence the outcome of elections or the determination of public policy through politics, lobbying or litigation, may participate. *Held*, the government may exclude litigation and advocacy organizations, assuming that it is acting in a viewpoint-neutral way. *Cornelius, supra.*

d. **Particular types of places that are non-public forums:** The Court is increasingly quick to find that particular publicly-owned places are *non-public forums*. The test is whether the government has intended to create *"general access for a class of speakers"* (in which case the forum is true public or designated public) or, instead, *"selected access for individual speakers"* (in which case the forum is probably non-public). *Arkansas Educational Television Comm'n v. Forbes*, 523 U.S. 666 (1998). In most cases where the issue has been discussed by the Court, a non-public forum has been found.

   i. **Airport terminals:** An *airport terminal* is a non-public forum. ***Int'l Soc. for Krishna Consciousness v. Lee***, 505 U.S. 672 (1992).

      (1) **Rationale:** Six members of the Court in *Krishna* believed that an airport terminal was a non-public forum. The majority opinion, by Chief Justice Rehnquist, asserted that public forums have two principal characteristics: they have *traditionally* been used for purposes of assembly and expression, and they have as a *"principal purpose ... the free exchange of ideas."* Airports do not satisfy either of these tests: only recently have they been made available for speech activity, and their principal purpose is to facilitate travel and make a regulated profit, not to facilitate free expression.

   ii. **Other transportation hubs:** What about *subways, bus stations, railroad stations,* and other publicly-owned and operated parts of transportation systems? The rationale of the majority's opinion in the *Krishna* case suggests that these, too, will be found to be non-public forums — they have not traditionally been used for purposes of free expression (with the possible exception of big-city subways), and their principal purpose is transportation, not expression.

   iii. **Jails:** Another good example of a non-public forum is the *jailhouse*. Jailhouses serve the limited function of housing prisoners, and nearly any type of expressive conduct, whether by prisoners or members of the public, is likely to be seen as incompatible with this basic purpose.

   iv. **Military bases:** Similarly, *military bases* may be placed off-limits to political speakers. In *Greer v. Spock*, 424 U.S. 828 (1976), a majority of the Court so held, reasoning that the purpose of a military base is to "train soldiers, not to provide a public forum." The policy against political campaign appearances was also justified by the "American constitutional tradition of a politically neutral military under civilian control."

v. **Use of school facilities by student groups:** Where facilities and funding are made available by a public school system to ***student groups*** (not to all members of the public generally), this usage will be classified as falling within the non-public-forum category. See *Christian Legal Society Chapter v. Martinez*, 130 S.Ct. 2971 (2010), *supra*, p. 554 (Court uses the phrase "limited public forum," but it's clear the Court means the same thing as "non-public forum.")

vi. **School mail system:** A ***school system's*** internal ***mail*** system, including teachers' mailboxes, has been held to fall into this non-public-forum category. *Perry Education Ass'n v. Perry Local Educators' Ass'n*, 460 U.S. 37 (1983). The fact that the official teachers' union, as well as a number of other outside organizations (e.g., YMCA and Cub Scouts) were permitted to use the mail system was not enough to convert the system into a public forum. Therefore, the school district's rule that no "school employee organization" except the official union could use the system was valid.

vii. **Governmental workplace:** A ***governmental workplace*** will apparently be treated as a non-public forum. In *Cornelius v. NAACP Legal Defense and Educational Fund*, *supra*, p. 555, the Court held that a charitable campaign held at federal workplaces fell into the non-public forum category.

viii. **Candidates' debates or fora:** When government organizes a ***forum or debate for political candidates,*** this will often be a non-public forum. For instance, in a case in which a state-owned TV station organized a televised debate to which the two leading candidates for a congressional seat were invited, the court found that the forum was a nonpublic one, because the debate "did not have an open-microphone format," i.e., the station did not make its debate "generally available to candidates" for that seat. Therefore, the station was within its rights not to invite plaintiff, a minor candidate (so long as the station made its decision based upon an objective determination of the plaintiff's lack of strength rather than upon lack of enthusiasm for his views). *Arkansas Educational Television Comm'n v. Forbes*, 523 U.S. 666 (1998).

ix. **Internet connections in libraries:** *Internet connections at public libraries* appear not to constitute public forums. Therefore, the government may require libraries receiving federal funding to install anti-pornography filters on any computer connected to the Internet. See *U.S. v. Amer. Library Ass'n.*, 539 U.S. 194 (2003) (4-justice plurality holds that "a public library does not acquire Internet terminals in order to create a public forum for Web publishers to express themselves, any more than it collects books in order to provide a public forum for the authors of books to speak." A fifth Justice, Breyer, in concurring, says he agrees with this determination.)

x. **Buses:** *Buses* that are part of a municipally-owned transit system also appear to fall within the category of non-public-forum facilities. See *Lehman v. Shaker Heights*, 418 U.S. 298 (1974), where a plurality reached this conclusion.

      xi. Utility poles: *Utility poles* owned by the government are not a public forum, so that a city may prevent the posting of signs on them, in order to reduce "visual blight." See *Los Angeles v. Taxpayers For Vincent*, 466 U.S. 789 (1984).

M. Right of access to private places: In most of the First Amendment cases which we have examined so far, the speaker sought to use *public property* to deliver his message. In a few of the other cases above, he sought to use his own property, or that of a willing owner (e.g., billboard advertisers in *Metromedia v. San Diego, supra,* p. 551). We turn now to the rights of a speaker to use *private property, against the owner's will,* for expressive purposes. In this group of cases, speakers have in effect argued that there should be recognized certain *"private forums,"* to which the government should guarantee speakers access, just as it guarantees access to public forums like streets and parks.

    1. Rationale: The main argument in support of recognizing a guaranteed right of access to certain private forums is that a contrary view would *close off many important channels of communication.* The mere fact that government itself has not closed down these channels is of small consolation, "[f]or if no one will rent an unpopular speaker a hall or print the speaker's views, it may be of little use that the government has not gone out of its way to muzzle the speech." Tribe, p. 998.

    2. Shopping centers: The main type of "private forums" to which speakers have asserted a guaranteed right of access is *shopping centers.*

        a. Initial success by claimants: Speakers asserting a right to access to privately-owned shopping centers were, initially, partly *successful* — the Court held that a center's owner could not constitutionally be permitted to use state trespass law to bar peaceful union picketing of a store in the center.

        b. Change of law: But the Court eventually changed its mind, and concluded that the First Amendment does *not* guarantee any speaker a right of access to a privately-owned shopping center, even if the speech relates to the center's (or its tenants') operations. *Hudgens v. NLRB*, 424 U.S. 507 (1976).

        c. Present rule: So neither labor picketers, anti-war activists *nor any other citizens have a First Amendment right to express themselves in shopping centers over the property owner's objection.*

        d. Access guaranteed by state constitution: Although there is no right of access to a shopping center under the First Amendment to the federal constitution, at least one state, California, has interpreted *its own constitution* as guaranteeing such a right. In *Pruneyard Shopping Center v. Robins*, 447 U.S. 74 (1980), the Court held that this interpretation of the California State Constitution did not violate a shopping center owner's federal right of free speech, nor his right not to have his property taken without just compensation.

V. SYMBOLIC EXPRESSION

A. Problem generally: Just as expression may consist of speech accompanied by conduct (e.g., a protest march), so expression may sometimes consist solely of *non-verbal actions.* The Supreme Court has for a long time been willing to recognize that certain non-verbal conduct is protected by the First Amendment (e.g., *Stromberg v. California*, 283 U.S. 359 (1931), striking a statute prohibiting display of a red flag as a symbol of opposition to organized government). Yet the Court has been wary of giving generalized First Amendment protection to any act which is an attempt to convey a message; this reluctance stems principally from the fear that granting such protection would legitimatize actions like political assassinations, Patty Hearst-type bank robberies, pouring blood on draft records, and other violent actions. See Tribe, p. 601.

1. **Two-track analysis:** The Court's recent cases on symbolic expression seem to have implicitly followed the "two-track" method of analysis (*supra*, p. 503). That is, where the Court believes that certain symbolic expression is prohibited because the government objects to the ***communicative content*** of the expression (what we're calling "track one"), the Court applies ***strict scrutiny***. Conversely, where the Court believes that the government's interest in regulating the conduct has nothing to do with the conduct's expressive content ("track two"), a more-easily-satisfied balancing test is applied, in which the interest being pursued by the state may well be found to outweigh the individual's interest in using that particular mode of expression.

2. **Draft card burning:** The Court's choice of "track two" rather than "track one" analysis seems to have been dispositive in the well-known case involving a conviction for ***draft card burning, U.S. v. O'Brien***, 391 U.S. 367 (1968).

    a. **Facts:** O'Brien and several others burned their draft cards in public, as part of a protest against the war in Vietnam. They were convicted of violating an amendment to the draft laws making it a crime to "knowingly destroy [or] mutilate" a draft card.

    b. **Court finds right to regulate:** O'Brien contended that the burning was "symbolic speech" protected by the First Amendment. But the Court held that even if this were true, conduct combining "speech" and "non-speech" elements could be regulated if four requirements were met:

       [1] the regulation was within the constitutional power of the government;

       [2] it furthered an ***"important or substantial governmental interest"***;

       [3] that interest was ***"unrelated to the suppression*** of free expression"; and

       [4] the ***"incidental restriction"*** on First Amendment freedoms was ***"no greater than is essential*** to the furtherance" of the governmental interest.

    The *O'Brien* Court found that all of these requirements were satisfied.

    Note: This four-part test continues to be the one used by the Court for analyzing "time, place and manner" regulations. Therefore, it's worth memorizing.

       i. **"Track two" analysis:** The four-part test turns out to be indistinguishable from what we've been calling "track two" analysis (see *supra*, p. 507). The requirement that the governmental interest be "unrelated to the suppression of free expression" is a somewhat clumsy and conclusory way of saying that the harm which the regulation seeks to avoid must not stem from the ***communicative content*** of the conduct; this is the key finding of "content neutrality" that places a case on "track two" rather than "track one." Requirement (4) is equivalent to the "track two" requirement that content-neutral regulations of conduct in public forums must not close alternative channels for communication.

c. **Content neutrality:** The Court in *O'Brien* identified several governmental interests served by the prohibition on draft-card destruction, interests the Court said were all ***"limited to the non-communicative aspect* of O'Brien's conduct."** For instance, the government had an interest in making sure that all draft-age males had in their possession a document indicating their availability for induction in an emergency. This and the other governmental interests were "important and substantial," and could not have been achieved with any less impact on O'Brien's freedom of expression. Therefore, his conviction did not violate the First Amendment, the Court concluded.

d. **Relevance of motive:** O'Brien argued that Congress' ***"purpose"*** or ***"motive"*** in enacting the statute was the improper one of suppressing dissent. But the Court rejected this argument, concluding that ***congressional "purpose" was simply irrelevant to a statute's constitutionality, so long as there was a legitimate governmental interest which could support the statute*** (whether or not Congress actually relied on it).

i. **Still a rule:** It apparently remains the case that in First Amendment cases, the existence of a legitimate non-content-based government interest can save a statute that burdens expressive conduct, even if one of the government's motives is to suppress or oppose the message being communicated.[5]

3. **Protest in schools:** The Court's initial judgment about whether or not the government's regulation of symbolic expression is targeted at the expression's communicative impact will usually be dispositive. This was true in *Cohen*, and also true in another Vietnam-War-protest case, ***Tinker v. Des Moines School District***, 393 U.S. 503 (1969). In *Tinker*, several high school and junior high school students were suspended for wearing black armbands as a symbol of opposition to the War; a rule forbidding the wearing of such armbands had been adopted by school officials two days before, in anticipation of the protest.

a. **Free expression right upheld:** The Court held that the prohibition on armbands ***violated*** the students' First Amendment rights. What was being suppressed was not "actually or potentially disruptive conduct," but rather, something that was nearly "pure speech."

i. **Wish to avoid controversy:** The authorities seem to have acted out of a wish to ***avoid controversy*** which might stem from the students' silent expression of opinion about the War. But this fear was not a valid reason for banning the expression: "Undifferentiated fear or apprehension of disturbance is not enough to overcome the right to freedom of expression."

ii. **Other symbols not barred:** The lack of content-neutrality in the school officials' conduct was also shown by the fact that they did not prohibit the wearing of ***all*** political or other controversial symbols; buttons for national political campaigns, and even the Nazi iron cross symbol, were permitted.

---

5. Notice, though, that the same "motive irrelevant" rule doesn't apply to at least some constitutional rules *outside* the First Amendment area. For instance, the legislature's motivation is often relevant in *equal protection* cases; see, e.g., *Washington v. Davis*, 426 U.S. 229 (1976), *supra*, p. 267, holding that the absence or presence of government intent to commit racial discrimination is relevant in equal protection cases.

    b. **"Track one" analysis:** Thus the *Tinker* Court seems to have applied conventional "track one" analysis, under which any regulation of expression which is done because of the communicative impact of the expression will be strictly scrutinized, and allowed only if necessary to serve a compelling governmental interest.

        i. **Possibility of "track two":** But, the Court indicated, had the students' act "materially and substantially interfere[d] with the requirements of *appropriate discipline* in the operation of the school," the officials would have been justified in preventing it. If the officials had been able to show that they acted for this reason, this presumably would have been the equivalent of showing that they were content-neutral, and would thus have entitled them to the less stringent review of "track two."

    c. **Regulation of hair and clothing:** The Court in *Tinker* explicitly declined to deal with the constitutionality of school regulations dealing with *hair length, clothing type*, and other aspects of *personal appearance* which arguably have an expressive content. Nor has the Court ever been willing to confront this issue after *Tinker.*

        i. **Lower courts:** Most lower courts have held that such aspects of personal appearance are not sufficiently communicative as to be entitled to full First Amendment protection. However, particular regulations have sometimes been struck down on the grounds that they infringe the personal liberty protected by the *Fourteenth* Amendment. See Tribe, p. 1386. .

4. **Sleeping in park:** The low level of scrutiny given to content-neutral regulations that affect symbolic expression was again demonstrated in *Clark v. Community For Creative Non-Violence*, 468 U.S. 288 (1984). There, the Court held that a National Parks Service *ban on sleeping in public parks* did *not* violate the First Amendment rights of demonstrators who wished to sleep in tents in two Washington D.C. national parks in order to dramatize the plight of the homeless. (The Court assumed, without deciding, that sleeping in connection with the demonstration constituted symbolic expression.)

    a. **Application of test:** The Court found that the regulation was valid under the four tests of *U.S. v. O'Brien, supra*, p. 558. Most significantly, the Court found a substantial governmental interest in "maintaining the parks in the heart of our capital in an attractive and intact condition," and concluded that the ban on sleeping furthered this interest by limiting the extent and duration of demonstrations like the one involved here.

B. **Flag desecration:** One context in which the right of symbolic speech is important is the area of *flag desecration*: nearly all states (as well as the federal government) make it a crime to mutilate or otherwise desecrate an American flag. Most such statutes seem to have been enacted for the purpose of preserving the flag as a symbol of *national unity*, or some similar rationale. If such a statute, either on its face or as applied, applies to some flag-related conduct but not others based on the actor's *message*, the Court will presumably apply strict scrutiny, and will therefore probably strike the statute.

1. **Texas v. Johnson:** This is what happened in *Texas v. Johnson*, 491 U.S. 397 (1989), the first of the Court's two highly controversial decisions on flag burning.

    a. **Statute:** The Texas statute at issue in *Johnson* made it a crime to "intentionally or knowingly desecrate … a state or national flag." "Desecrate" was defined to mean "deface, damage, or otherwise physically mistreat in a way that the actor knows will *seriously offend* one or more persons *likely to observe* or discover his action."

b. Facts: Johnson, the defendant, participated in a political demonstration outside the 1984 Republican National Convention in Dallas. At the end of the demonstration, he unfurled an American flag, doused it with kerosene, and set it on fire. While the flag burned, the protestors chanted, "America, the red, white, and blue, we spit on you." Johnson was charged with violating the desecration statute; at his trial, several witnesses testified that they had been seriously offended by the flag burning, and he was convicted.

c. Holding: By a 5-4 vote, the Court held that the Texas statute violated the First Amendment as applied to Johnson's acts. The majority opinion was written by Justice Brennan.

    i. "Track one" analysis: The key to the result reached by the majority was that the Court applied what we have called "track one" analysis. That is, the majority determined that the prosecution of Johnson was *"directly related to expression."* In reaching this conclusion, the Court reviewed the two objectives that Texas asserted it was pursuing: (1) preventing breaches of the peace; and (2) preserving the flag as a symbol of nationhood and national unity. As to objective (1), the majority simply disbelieved that preventing breaches of the peace was what had motivated Texas on these facts (since no disturbance of the peace either actually occurred or was threatened by this particular flag burning). As to objective (2), the need to protect the flag as a symbol of national unity would only be implicated if the defendant's conduct had a contrary message associated with it, so this objective was "directly related to expression" and thus called for track one scrutiny. The content-based nature of the statute was illustrated by the fact that particular conduct was covered only if an observer's likely reaction would be to be "seriously offended" — the offense could only flow from the message accompanying the act. (For instance, if D had burned the flag as a means of respectfully disposing of it because it was dirty or torn, he would not have offended anyone, and he would not have been convicted under the statute.)

    ii. Strict scrutiny applied: Since Johnson was prosecuted only because of the content of the particular message he was conveying, the Court applied strict scrutiny to the statute. "If there is a bedrock principle underlying the First Amendment, it is that the Government may not prohibit the expression of an idea simply because society finds the idea itself offensive or disagreeable." Here, Texas's objective — preserving the flag as a symbol of national unity — may have been worthy, even "compelling." But the means chosen by Texas to serve that objective were not necessary ones. First, the majority didn't believe that the nation's belief in the cherished significance of the flag would be undermined by acts of mutilation; indeed, these acts might produce the opposite result. Second, the government could combat such acts by acts of its own, such as giving the remains of the flag a respectful burial (as one witness to Johnson's burning did).

d. Dissent: Four members of the Court bitterly dissented. The principal dissent was by Justice Rehnquist (joined by White and O'Connor). The dissenters thought that a state could prohibit the burning of a flag without violating the First Amendment prohibition on suppression of ideas. "The flag is not simply another 'idea' or 'point of view' competing for recognition in the market place of ideas." Also, the dissenters thought that flag burning is so inherently inflammatory that it inevitably threatens a breach of the peace, and thus could be analogized to "fighting words" and deprived of First Amendment protection entirely. In a separate dissent, Justice Stevens thought that the flag, even though it is in a sense an intangible asset, could be protected from desecration just as, say, the Lincoln Memorial could be protected from having a political message spray-painted upon it.

2. **The federal statute:** The problem with the Texas statute in *Texas v. Johnson* seemed to be the statute's proscription of flag burning that would "seriously offend" observers — this reference to "offensiveness" made it clear that only flag burning intended to convey a particular message (disrespect) was proscribed by the statute. Therefore, immediately after the *Johnson* decision, the U.S. Congress tried to enact a *federal* flag burning statute that would ban all or most flag burning without being content-based and thus unconstitutional. This federal statute, the Flag Protection Act of 1989, punished anyone who "knowingly mutilates, defaces, physically defiles, burns, maintains on the floor or ground, or tramples upon any flag of the United States. ... " However, even though the statute avoided any reference to conduct that would "offend" an observer, the Supreme Court, by a 5-4 vote, found that this statute, too, was a violation of the First Amendment. *U.S. v. Eichman*, 496 U.S. 310 (1990).

    a. **Rationale:** The five-justice majority in *Eichman* found that despite the more careful wording, this statute, like the one in *Johnson*, was content-based. "Although the [Act] contains no explicit content-based limitation on the scope of prohibited conduct, it is nevertheless clear that the government's asserted *interest* is 'related to the suppression of free expression' ... and concerned with the content of such expression." The majority noted that the government was asserting its interest in preserving the flag as a *symbol for certain national ideals*; this goal was intimately related to the content of the burner's message (so that, for instance, a person's secret burning of the flag in his basement would not threaten this symbolic meaning of the flag). Since Congress was attempting to "suppress ... expression out of concern for its likely communicative impact," the statute had to be strictly scrutinized. It failed that scrutiny. (Interestingly, Justice Scalia was part of the five-member majority voting to strike down the statute, a surprise given his generally conservative views.)

3. **Significance:** As a result of *Johnson* and *Eichman*, there is probably no way for government (whether state or federal) to "wipe out flag burning." Even if the statute uses the most content-neutral language (e.g., "No one may burn a flag under any circumstances"), the statute will presumably be struck down so long as the Court believes that it was *motivated* by a desire to preserve the symbolic value of the flag. Therefore, a constitutional amendment is probably the only way to prevent such acts.

Quiz Yourself on

"TIME, PLACE AND MANNER" RESTRICTIONS; SYMBOLIC EXPRESSION

72. Centerville is a small town. Its two biggest streets are Broadway and Main. After several recent parades and demonstrations that badly snarled traffic, Centerville's City Council enacted an ordinance that forbade all parades from taking place on either Broadway or Main. The ordinance did not forbid parades on

the other, smaller streets in town. There is no evidence that the ordinance was motivated by hostility to particular types of parades, and the ban has been enforced even-handedly as to all parades. Citizens Against Corruption, a group wishing to protest what it believed was corruption in the mayor's office, paraded in an organized way down Broadway, and its leaders were arrested. The city has asserted that its ban on parades is a valid "time, place and manner" regulation.

(a) What standard should the court use in evaluating the ordinance as applied here? _____

(b) Should the court uphold the ordinance, and convict the marchers, under the test you specified in (a)? _____

73. An ordinance in the town of Harmony provides that "no demonstration or parade involving more than 20 persons shall take place on the town's streets, parks or other city-owned property without the prior issuance of a permit." The permit is free, and is to be granted by the mayor's office, "if the mayor concludes, acting in a reasonable manner, that the proposed activity would not be detrimental to the overall community, taking into account the "time, place and manner" of the activity." Firebrand, the head of a local group of anarchists, wished to conduct a demonstration in the park, at which he planned to urge his followers to immediately attempt a "sit in" of the mayor's office. The mayor, without knowing the precise purpose of the demonstration and knowing only that it was to be a demonstration against the local government, refused to issue the permit. In announcing the refusal, the mayor stated that "there has been too much demonstration, and not enough cooperation, around here recently." Firebrand then brought suit for an injunction against continued application of the permit requirement, and for a declaratory judgment that the permit requirement as drafted was unconstitutional. Should the court find the ordinance unconstitutional on its face? _____

74. Same facts as prior question. Now, however, assume that Firebrand ignored the ordinance, did not ask for a permit, and held a demonstration involving 30 people in a city park. He was arrested and charged with violating the ordinance. He now wishes to defend on the grounds that the ordinance is overbroad and thus facially invalid. Assuming that the ordinance is indeed overbroad, should the court acquit Firebrand? _____

75. The town of Lawton had a very carefully worded permit requirement. For any demonstration or parade involving more than 30 people, a permit was required, application for which must be made at least one hour prior to the close of business on the day before the proposed activity. Under the terms of the ordinance, the police commissioner was required to issue the permit, subject only to the rule that if in the commissioner's reasonable judgment, a breach of peace would be likely to occur which could not be controlled with the manpower available to the Lawton Police Department, the permit could be denied until such later date as proper police protection could be arranged (by borrowing from other police departments, if necessary).

Rouser, a radical, applied late on Friday afternoon to make a speech on Saturday. Because past speeches by Rouser had led to skirmishes, and because the commissioner believed that under weekend police schedules only three officers would be available (a number which the Commissioner believed would not be sufficient if problems should occur), the Commissioner turned down the request for a permit, and suggested that Rouser wait until the following Saturday. A local Justice of the Peace Court was open Friday night, and the Justice would have had jurisdiction to issue an injunction against the permit requirement. However, Rouser did not seek an injunction. Instead, Rouser gave his speech anyway, and no violence occurred. Rouser was charged with violating the permit requirement. He is now defending on the grounds that he was wrongfully denied the permit, because there was not in fact a serious threat of a breach of the peace, and that even if there was one, the presence of three officers would have been sufficient.

Assuming that the court agrees with Rouser's factual contentions about the danger of breach of the peace, should Rouser be acquitted? _____

76. The city of Blue Bell has enacted an ordinance providing as follows: no "canvasser or solicitor" may ring the doorbell of a private home, or knock on the door of a private home, where her purpose is to distribute handbills or to solicit an order for goods, services or charitable contributions. The ban does not prevent a person from simply sticking advertising material under the door or into the mail slot, so long as there is no bell-ringing or door-knocking. The purpose of the ordinance is to avoid disturbing residents (including those who work nights and sleep days), and also to prevent crime (e.g., people who want to see into the residence to "case the joint" for a later burglary).

Delrina, a Jehovah's Witness, was charged with violating the statute in that she rang doorbells so that she could personally hand inhabitants the literature requesting donations to the Jehovah's Witness organization. She has defended on the grounds that the ordinance represents an unconstitutional infringement of her right to free expression. May Delrina be convicted? _____

77. The city of Crooklyn had two substantial ethnic populations that were frequently at odds with each other, Middle-eastern Moslems and Orthodox Jews. After complying with a city requirement calling for a permit before the making of a public address, Mohammed, a self-proclaimed Islamic Fundamentalist, gave a speech in a park in Crooklyn. There were approximately 100 Islamic followers in the audience, as well as a group of about 30 Orthodox Jews. The Jews carried signs opposing Mohammed. Mohammed then made various anti-Semetic inflammatory statements, such as "Jews are corrupt" and "Jews control the U.S. government." He also addressed the Jews in the audience, saying, "You Jews in the audience today, you're not fit to kiss the dung-stained shoes of my poorest follower." At no time did Mohammed urge his audience to attack any of the Jewish onlookers or to otherwise commit immediate illegal acts.

Some of the Jews in the audience began to shake their fists and yell back at Mohammed; five of them then began to move towards the podium with upraised fists. There were 15 police officers at the scene to prevent disturbances, most of them ringed around the podium. They immediately arrested Mohammed and charged him with violating an ordinance prohibiting anyone from inciting a riot or causing a breach of the peace. Mohammed has defended on the grounds that his arrest violated his freedom of expression.

(a) What doctrine can the prosecution point to as justifying the arrest? _____

(b) Do First Amendment principles prevent Mohammed's conviction? _____

78. The Women's Health Alliance is a clinic that principally performs abortions. Abortion protesters decided to demonstrate outside the clinic. The protesters waved signs containing messages such as "Abortion Equals Murder." Whenever the protesters saw a woman leaving the clinic, they shouted, "Baby Killer," at her. The protesters remained at least 20 feet away from the front door of the clinic, and they did not block anyone's access to or from the clinic. All protesting took place on public property. A local ordinance forbids "the making of any public statement or the showing of any sign where the speaker knows the statement or sign is likely to be offensive to the person to whom it is addressed." May a protester who has waved the sign and shouted the epithet described above be convicted of violating the statute?

79. State U, a public university, recently added the following provision to its Student Code: "No student or faculty member shall address to any other student or faculty member any verbal slur, invective, insult or epithet based on the addressee's race, ethnicity, gender, handicap or sexual orientation." The penalty for a first offense is suspension, and for the second offense is expulsion. Desmond, a white student at the university, addressed the following remark to Vera, a black student, "You nigger, go back to Africa where you belong." State U has commenced disciplinary proceedings against Desmond. You are the university's general counsel. The president has asked you the following question: "May the university constitutionally suspend Desmond for making this remark?" If your answer is "no," please describe the types of changes that might be made in the Code to alleviate the problem. _____

80. The state of Morality makes it a crime to post any "indecent" photo on a computer system located in the state, if the computer is connected by means of a physical wire or a telephone line to any other computer. "Indecent" is defined to include "any photo of a naked man or woman that would be offensive when measured by local community standards." The legislature means for its prohibition to apply even to pictures that would not be "obscene," including photos having significant artistic value. The legislature's purpose is to prevent minors from seeing indecent material. *Playpen* magazine puts a photo of a naked woman (which is not obscene under U.S. Supreme Court rulings) on its dial-in computer, located in Morality. Peter, a 16-year-old, dials in and retrieves the photo. A local prosecutor in Morality prosecutes the owner of *Playpen*, Hugh, and shows that Hugh had ordered that the photo be placed on the system. May Hugh constitutionally be convicted? _____

81. The Grand Union Station is a large train station owned and run by a public agency, the Tri-State Transit Authority. The Authority has enacted a "policy statement," prominently posted on the walls of the Station, which says, in part, that "no person or organization shall solicit for funds within this Station." Hussan, a member of the Hari Krishna religious sect, approached numerous passengers in the Station one day, asking each one, "Would you like to contribute to my religious organization?" Authority police stopped him and politely but forcibly removed him from the station for violating the no-solicitation policy. The police appear to enforce the no-solicitation rule uniformly, i.e., they stop everyone from soliciting, regardless of whether the solicitation is religiously-oriented, regardless of whether it appears to be "begging" or on behalf of an organized charity, etc.

(a) Is the Station a "public forum" for purposes of First Amendment analysis? _____

(b) Was the police's treatment of Hussan constitutional? _____

82. For many years, Acadia High School, a public high school, has had a School Dress and Appearance Code. The Code provides that, among other things, no student may go barefoot, hair must be worn in a way that will not interfere with school functions (including getting caught in machinery in shop and home economics classes), and that girls may not wear skirts more than one inch above the knee. One of the purposes behind the Code (including specifically the skirt-length provision) was to avoid dress or appearance that might distract other students or cause discipline problems. Alicia is a member of an informal group of girls who call themselves the "Sexed Up Girls." The members of this group, all of whom attend Acadia High School, wish to dress in a way that expresses their notion of themselves as sexually active women who are aware of that fact and wish other students to know it. Alicia came to school wearing an extremely short and tight mini skirt, four inches above the knee. She was suspended for violating the Code. She has defended on the grounds that the Code, as applied to her, violates her First Amendment rights.

(a) Does the application of the Code to Alicia's skirt impair any expression on her part (putting aside the issue of whether any interference is justified)? _____

(b) Assuming, for purposes of this part only, that some expression by Alicia has been interfered with, is the application of the Code to Alicia's skirt constitutionally permissible? _____

Answers

72. **(a) The ban must be: (1) content-neutral; (2) narrowly tailored to serve a significant governmental interest; and (3) leave open alternative channels for communication of the information.**

    (b) No, probably. The facts indicate to us that the ban is content-neutral both in terms of the purposes for which it was enacted and the way in which it is applied. However, it seems not to be "*narrowly tailored* to serve a *significant* governmental interest." Since the proposed speech would take place in the most traditional of all public forums — the streets — mere convenience, such as avoiding traffic obstructions, probably does not qualify as a "significant governmental interest." Also, there are more narrowly-tailored restrictions that could be used, such as an advance permit requirement which would give the police time to detour traffic and thereby reduce disruption. Finally, the requirement that alternative channels be left open is strictly construed in a public-forum context; the fact that there may be other public places (e.g., smaller streets) where the same expression is allowed will not generally be enough to qualify as an adequate alternative channel.

73. **Yes.** An advance permit requirement will be upheld if it is content-neutral, adequately constrains administrative discretion, and is a reasonable means of insuring that public order is maintained. However, in order to avoid giving the official charged with granting or denying permit applications too much *discretion*, the grounds upon which a permit may be denied must be set forth *specifically* and *narrowly* in the ordinance. Here, the standard given for granting or denying a permit — that the proposed activities "not be detrimental to the overall community" — gives the mayor virtually uncontrolled discretion, and acts as an invitation to him to behave in a content-based way. This excessive discretion makes the statute overbroad and vague. Therefore, even though Firebrand's own proposed conduct might be capable of being prohibited by an appropriately-drawn ordinance, the ordinance here must be struck down as invalid on its face.

74. **Yes.** If a permit that is required prior to the exercise of First Amendment rights is unconstitutional *on its face*, the speaker is *not required* to apply for a permit. He may decline to apply, then speak, and avoid conviction on the grounds of the permit requirement's unconstitutionality. See, e.g., *Lovell v. Griffin*. Because a statute that is overbroad is facially invalid, this rule applies to overbreadth claims. Therefore, Firebrand may assert overbreadth even though he failed to ever apply for a permit.

75. **No.** Where a permit requirement is not facially invalid (e.g., not unduly vague or overbroad), and the speaker's claim is merely that he has been wrongfully denied a permit, the speaker *must seek judicial relief* before speaking. That is, for an "as applied" as opposed to "facial" challenge to a permit requirement, one who ignores the denial of the permit loses the right to object to the permit scheme's unconstitutionality. There is an exception where the applicant shows that he could not have obtained prompt judicial review of the administrative denial of the permit; however, the facts here tell us that Rouser could have obtained judicial review prior to the time for the speech, if he had wanted to do so.

76. **No.** As with any "time, place and manner" restriction, the ordinance will be valid only if it is content-neutral, is narrowly tailored to serve a significant governmental interest, and leaves open alternative channels for communicating the information. Here, probably the requirement of content-neutrality is satisfied (unless there is evidence that, say, Jehovah's Witnesses were a special target of the ordinance). The government probably has a significant government interest in preventing homeowners from being disturbed

at home when they do not want to be. However, it is doubtful that the ordinance is "narrowly tailored," since there are less restrictive alternatives (e.g., permitting a homeowner to indicate on his door that he does not wish to be disturbed by solicitors) — when the city makes a blanket assumption that *no* home-owner wishes to receive a solicitor, this is probably not a sufficiently narrowly tailored approach. Further-more, it is doubtful whether alternative channels have been left open, since for many types of organizations, door-to-door and face-to-face is the only affordable means, given the large expense associ-ated with, say, newspaper and TV advertising. Upon facts similar to these, the Court struck down a blan-ket ban. See *Watchtower Bible and Tract Soc. v. Stratton* (ban on solicitation without prior permit is unconstitutional).

77. **(a) The "fighting words" doctrine.**

(b) Yes, probably. Among the classes of speech which are not protected by the First Amendment are "fighting words," which the Court has defined as "those which by their very utterance … tend to incite an immediate breach of the peace." *Chaplinsky v. New Hampshire*. However, there are several exceptions and clarifications to the "fighting words" doctrine, which make it seldom applicable. One of those excep-tions is that if the police have the physical ability to **control the angry crowd** as a means of preventing threatened violence, they **must do so** in preference to arresting the speaker for using "fighting words." *Cox v. Louisiana*. Here, it seems probable that the 15 police officers could have either arrested or at least restrained those Jews who were moving forward towards the podium, and probably any other hostile Jew in the audience. At the very least, the police needed to make some effort to do this, rather than immedi-ately arrest the speaker.

78. **No.** In general, government may not forbid speech merely because it would be *"offensive"* to the listener. For example, language cannot be forbidden merely because it is profane. *Cohen v. California* (D cannot be punished for wearing a jacket bearing the legend "Fuck the Draft"). Here, the statute is phrased specif-ically to reach only "offensive" conduct, so it runs afoul of this principle. Furthermore, the statute is prob-ably unconstitutionally vague, since a reasonable reader of it would not know exactly what types of language would be forbidden.

79. **No.** The problem is that the ban here is *content-based*. That is, it proscribes only certain types of speech, based on the content or message of that speech. Thus insults based on race, ethnicity and three other attri-butes are banned, but insults based on other attributes are not (e.g., the addressee's politics, intelligence, short or tall stature, etc.). Even if the university interprets the ban so as to bar only "fighting words," this will not be enough to save the statute, because *R.A.V. v. City of St. Paul* (striking down an anti-cross-burn-ing statute) establishes that government may not ban some fighting words but not others, based on the words' precise message. The best way for State U to solve the problem is to amend its code so as to ban "all slurs, invectives, insults or epithets that would have the likely effect of either inducing the listener to respond with violence, or which would be likely to create in the listener an apprehension of imminent physical harm." Such a formulation would essentially ban all fighting words, plus all words that would constitute an assault; these two categories may clearly be constitutionally proscribed, as long as the pro-scription occurs in a content-neutral way. (Of course, this re-write would fail to prohibit a lot of hate speech, so it would not be a perfect solution, but at least it would be content-neutral.)

80. **No.** The Supreme Court has held that computer networks are more like newspapers than like broadcast TV, and that content-based restrictions on what is placed on such networks must therefore be strictly scru-tinized. See *Reno v. ACLU*. Applying strict scrutiny, the measure is clearly unconstitutional, since it's con-tent-based (only materials with an "indecent" message are proscribed), and it's not narrowly tailored towards the (admittedly "compelling") objective of keeping indecent materials away from minors — for

instance, the state could give parents free filtering software that would block access to these materials by minors. See *Ashcroft v. ACLU*. Furthermore, the statute is overbroad: it applies to viewing by adults (who have a right to see the photo), as well as to viewing by minors (who probably don't have a First Amendment right to see such a photo, though this is not completely clear). Since the rights of adults are being curtailed in a content-based way, the statute will surely fail strict scrutiny. *Reno v. ACLU.*

81. **(a) No.** The Supreme Court has held that airport terminals are not "public forums," even though they are public places. *Int'l Soc. for Krishna Consciousness, Inc. v. Lee.* Assuming that train stations are analyzed the same way as are airport terminals — which seems virtually certain — the terminal here falls into the category of "non-public forum." Non-public forums are public facilities that are used for purposes that are not especially linked to expression; thus the terminal here is primarily linked to transportation, and has never historically been viewed as a center for expression.

(b) Yes. A non-public forum offers the *least* constitutionally-protected access for First Amendment expression. Government regulation of expression in a non-public forum must merely be: (1) *reasonable* in light of the *purpose* served by the forum; and (2) *viewpoint neutral*. See *Krishna v. Lee, supra*. The Court in *Krishna* held that these tests were met by a ban on funds solicitation in airport terminals; presumably the same analysis would apply to the fund solicitation in the train station here. The ban on face-to-face solicitation of money was found to be reasonable in *Krishna* because such solicitation might slow pedestrian traffic within the terminal, interfering with its transportation-related function. (But a *total ban* on *literature distribution* was found not to be even "reasonable" in *Krishna*.)

82. **(a) Yes, probably.** The Supreme Court has never spoken on whether a public school student's choice of clothing or other aspects of appearance is sufficiently "communicative" that the choice receives First Amendment protection. (The only relevant case is *Tinker v. Des Moines School District*, holding that the wearing of a black armband as a protest was expressive conduct.) However, a majority of the Court believes that "nude dancing" contains enough expressive content to be protected by the First Amendment. See *Barnes v. Glen Theatre*. Regardless of whether a typical student's selection of clothing would be found to be sufficiently communicative to be covered by the First Amendment, Alicia's selection here has a clear expressive component, in that she is trying to make a statement about her sexuality. Therefore, Alicia probably would receive some First Amendment protection for her choice of skirt (though, as described in the answer to the next part, the fact that she receives some protection does not mean that the Code is invalid as applied to her).

(b) Yes, probably. The first question is whether the restriction is "content neutral." If there were evidence that the skirt-length provision was enacted principally for the purpose of suppressing statements about the wearer's sexuality or sexual availability, then we would have a content-based regulation, which would have to survive strict scrutiny (which it probably could not). However, on the facts here, all aspects of the Code seem to be directed at the maintenance of discipline and order, and not at the suppression of any particular type of message. Therefore, the Code is probably content-neutral. If so, we apply the standard "track 2" analysis: the regulation must be *narrowly tailored* to serve a *significant governmental interest*, and must leave open *"alternative channels"* for communicating the information. Probably all parts of this test are satisfied. The school district certainly has a significant interest in maintaining discipline and avoiding distraction. Assuming that there is at least some evidence that short mini skirts would lead other students to gawk, make sexual propositions to the wearer, or otherwise be distracted, the requisite "narrow tailoring" is probably present. And there probably are adequate alternative channels for women such as Alicia to communicate their sexual availability (e.g., by making verbal statements of availability, by wearing tight-fitting sweaters, etc.).

VI. DEFAMATION, INTENTIONAL INFLICTION OF EMOTIONAL DISTRESS, AND THE BANNING OF "FALSE SPEECH"

A. Regulation of defamatory and other false speech: Recall that there are certain pre-defined categories of speech that receive no, or virtually no, First Amendment protection. (See *supra*, p. 508). These include such categories as obscenity, "fighting words," and commercial fraud. We concentrate here on one of those unprotected categories, ***"defamation,"*** i.e., the making of ***false statements*** that are ***damaging to reputation***. We also consider ***intentional infliction of emotional distress*** (*infra*, p. 573) as well as the more general problem of whether government may forbid speech on the grounds that it is ***factually false*** (see *infra*, p. 574).

B. Initially no protection: Initially, the Supreme Court took the view that any language treated as ***defamatory*** under state law was not entitled to First Amendment protection. For instance, in *Chaplinsky (supra*, p. 533), the Court included libelous statements in the list of categories which are "no essential part of any exposition of ideas," and as to which there is therefore no First Amendment protection.

C. *New York Times v. Sullivan:* But the Court eventually concluded that the First Amendment protections for speech and the press place at least ***some limits on the rules states may establish for defamation actions***. This limiting process occurred initially in ***New York Times Co. v. Sullivan***, 376 U.S. 254 (1964), where the Court concluded that the First Amendment requires that a defense for ***"honest error"*** be allowed in the case of false statements made about ***public officials*** relating to their ***official conduct***.

    1. Facts: Plaintiff in *New York Times* was a public official one of whose duties was supervising the Montgomery, Alabama Police Department. He alleged that the *Times* had libeled him by printing an advertisement that stated that the Montgomery police had attempted to terrorize Martin Luther King and his followers. (Plaintiff was not even named in the advertisement; but under Alabama libel law, criticism of the department of which he was in charge was deemed to reflect on his reputation.)

        a. Truth as affirmative defense: The libel law of Alabama, like that of most states at the time, provided for ***strict liability***. That is, a publisher could not avoid liability by showing that he reasonably believed his statement to be true, if it was in fact false. Furthermore, although "truth" was an available defense under Alabama law, it was an ***affirmative defense*** as to which the defendant bore the burden of proof. Therefore, although the factual errors in the *Times* ad were minor (e.g., that Dr. King had been arrested seven times, rather than the actual four times), and even though there was no showing that the *Times* ought to have known that the ad prepared by others contained falsehoods, the paper was nonetheless subjected to a $500,000 libel judgment. The net result was that familiar rules of libel gave Alabama's "white establishment" a formidable weapon with which to punish the *Times*, and any other proponents of civil rights. See Tribe, p. 863.

    2. Libel judgment reversed: A unanimous Supreme Court ***reversed*** the damage award. In so doing, the Court for the first time established that ***state defamation rules are limited by First Amendment principles***.

a. Robust debate: The Court viewed this case as one involving *criticism of government policy*, not merely factual statements about an individual. Debate on public issues must be "uninhibited, robust, and wide open," and may often include "vehement, caustic, and sometimes unpleasantly sharp attacks on government and public officials." Requiring critics of official conduct to guarantee the truth of all their factual assertions would lead to *self-censorship*, rather than free debate.

i. Sedition Act: The Court found that the effect of Alabama's libel rules was similar to that of the original federal Sedition Act of 1798. The Sedition Act made it a crime to publish any "false scandalous and malicious writings" against the federal government with intent to bring it into "contempt or disrepute." Although the Act expired before the Supreme Court determined its constitutionality, the view that the Act violated the First Amendment had "carried the day in the court of history," according to the *New York Times* Court. So, here, criticism of government public officials could not be curtailed, without violating the First Amendment.

3. Formal rule: The Court was not content merely to strike the libel judgment as a disguised ban on criticizing the government. Instead, it articulated a formal rule, so that future speakers would not have to worry about liability for libel in similar circumstances: the First Amendment prohibits a *public official* from recovering damages for a defamatory falsehood *relating to his official conduct* unless he proves that the statement was made with *"actual malice"* — that is, *"with knowledge that it was false* or with *reckless disregard of whether it was false or not."* The case thus establishes a *"constitutional privilege for good faith critics of government officials."* Tribe, pp. 864-65.

a. Knowing or reckless falsity: *New York Times* requires the public official to prove that the defendant *knew* his statement was false, or *recklessly disregarded* whether it was true or not. It is *not* enough for the official to show that a *"reasonably prudent man"* would not have published the statement, or would have investigated further before publishing. Rather, there must be evidence to permit the conclusion that "the defendant *in fact entertained serious doubts* as to the truth of his publication." *St. Amant v. Thompson*, 390 U.S. 727 (1968). Thus at least with respect to statements published about public officials relating to their duties (and also statements about "public figures," see *infra*), *"ignorance is bliss."* Tribe, pp. 870-71.

D. Extension to "public figures": The *New York Times* "actual knowledge or reckless disregard of the truth" test was extended to include *"public figures"* in *Curtis Pub. Co. v. Butts* and *Associated Press v. Walker*, both reported at 388 U.S. 130 (1967). In these cases both the University of Georgia football coach and a prominent retired Army General were held to be public figures.

1. "Public figure" narrowly defined: However, the Court has read the "public figure" category *narrowly* in cases since *Butts* and *Walker.* The Court has recognized three classes of public figures: (1) those who have *"general fame* and notoriety in the community," who are public figures for *all* purposes; (2) those who have "voluntarily *injected themselves* into a *public controversy* in order to influence the resolution of the issues involved," who are public figures *only* with respect to *that controversy*; and (3) *"involuntary* public figures," who are directly *affected* by the actions of public officials, such as a *defendant in a criminal case* (who would be an involuntary public figure with respect to news items concerning that case). See *Gertz v. Robert Welch, Inc.,* 418 U.S. 323 (1974) (discussed extensively *infra*).

2. **Meaning of "voluntarily injected":** The Court will not be quick to conclude that a person has "voluntarily injected" himself into a controversy (required for category (2) above). For instance, in *Time, Inc. v. Firestone*, 424 U.S. 448 (1976), *Time* incorrectly reported that one of the grounds for Ms. Firestone's divorce was adultery. The Court found that she was not a "public figure," even though she had held some press conferences during the divorce trial, and even though the trial itself had been widely reported in the Miami newspapers. (Nor did Ms. Firestone's extensive activities before the trial as a prominent member of Palm Beach society make her a public figure.)

3. **"Involuntary" class narrow:** Similarly, category (3), that of "involuntary public figures," has also been narrowly construed by the Court; such involuntary figures will be relatively rare.

E. **Private figures:** The *New York Times* standard does *not* apply to suits by *private figures*. That is, where the plaintiff is neither a public official nor a public figure, there is *no constitutional requirement* that he prove that the defendant *knew his statement to be false or recklessly disregarded the truth. Gertz v. Robert Welch, Inc.,* 418 U.S. 323 (1974).

1. **Facts:** The plaintiff, Gertz, was a locally well-known lawyer who represented the family of a youth who was killed by a policeman. Defendant, publisher of a John Birch Society magazine, falsely attacked Gertz as having helped "frame" the policeman and as being a communist.

2. **Negligence standard permitted:** The Supreme Court held, 5-4, that in libel actions brought by *private figures*, the First Amendment *does not forbid use of a simple negligence standard*. The states are free to decide whether they wish to establish negligence, recklessness or knowing falsity as the standard (but they *may not impose strict liability*).

   a. **Reasoning:** The majority reasoned that private individuals are both more vulnerable, as well as more deserving of recovery for defamation, than public figures. They are more *vulnerable* because public figures generally have "significantly greater access" to the media, and can use that access to counteract false statements. They are *deserving* of extensive protection against defamation, because public figures have generally "voluntarily exposed themselves to increased risk of injury from defamatory falsehoods," unlike private persons.

3. **Punitive damages not allowed:** The majority also held that, if a private figure shows only negligence on the part of the defendant, rather than recklessness or knowing falsity, he *may not recover presumed or punitive damages*. ("Presumed" damages are ones awarded where there is no proof of actual harm, but the jury believes that damage would ordinarily result from a defamatory communication like the one in issue.) The Court imposed this limitation because the state's interest in giving broader protection to private figures only justified awarding "compensation for *actual* injury."

4. **Who is private figure:** In holding that Gertz himself was a private figure, the Court implicitly took a narrow view of the term "public figure." Gertz was a well-known lawyer locally, and had agreed to take a case which he knew would attract substantial publicity. Nonetheless, Gertz had not achieved "general fame or notoriety in the community" (so

that he was not public figure for all purposes); similarly, he was not a public figure for the limited purposes of this case, because he had played only a "minimal role" in it.

5. **Dissents:** The four dissenters differed significantly among themselves in reasoning. For instance, Justice Brennan continued to believe (as he had in *Rosenbloom v. Metromedia, Inc.*, 403 U.S. 29) that the *New York Times* standard should be applied to private-person libel actions arising out of events of "public or general interest." But Justice White argued the quite opposite position that the *Gertz* majority should not even have stripped the states of their right to apply ***strict liability*** in suits brought by private persons.

6. **Proof of falsity:** As noted, one aspect of *Gertz* is that the states may not impose strict liability, even in cases brought by private figures. This aspect of *Gertz* was broadened in the later case of *Philadelphia Newspapers, Inc. v. Hepps,* 475 U.S. 767 (1986), where the Court held that the private figure suing a media defendant must bear the burden of proving not only "fault," but also the ***falsity*** of the defendant's statement. That is, *Gertz* has been held to replace the common-law rule ***presuming*** falsity. (This holding applies only where the suit involves a matter of "public interest"; the presumption of falsity is probably constitutional where there is no matter of public concern, in light of *Dun & Bradstreet, Inc. v. Greenmoss Builders, Inc., infra*, p. 572.)

F. **Non-media defendants:** Both *New York Times* and *Gertz* involved ***media*** defendants, and in those cases the Court relied heavily on freedom-of-the-press considerations, especially the need to prevent media self-censorship. It is not clear whether the public-figure standard of *New York Times* and the private-figure standard of *Gertz* also apply where the ***defendant*** is a ***private person*** or other ***non-media defendant.***

1. **Possibility of different standard:** Thus it is possible that such defendants might be liable ***without*** a showing of reckless disregard or knowledge of falsity when they defame a public official or public figure. Similarly, they might even be ***strictly liable*** where they defame a ***private*** figure.

   a. **Unlikely:** However, no Supreme Court case after *Gertz* has made a constitutional distinction between media and non-media defendants, and it's ***unlikely*** the Court will do so in the future. That's especially true now that the rise of the Internet has dramatically blurred the distinction between media and non-media speakers. (For instance, if the Court were to hold non-media defendants to a stricter standard in defamation cases, should an amateur blogger who blogs once a week be deemed a "media" speaker or a "non-media" one?)

G. **Statements of no "public interest":** If the communication does ***not involve any matter of "public interest,"*** special constitutional rules apply. These were laid down in ***Dun & Bradstreet, Inc. v. Greenmoss Builders, Inc.,*** 472 U.S. 749 (1985).

1. **Facts:** D was a credit reporting agency which falsely reported to several subscribers that P, a small corporation, was insolvent. The issue in the case was whether presumed and punitive damages could be awarded without a showing of reckless disregard for the truth or actual knowledge of falsity.

2. **Result:** Although no opinion commanded a majority of the Court, the divided Court affirmed an award of both types of damages. Three Justices thought that presumed and punitive damages could be awarded even without a showing of reckless disregard for the truth or knowledge of falsity if the statements did not involve any issue of "public inter-

est"; two more Justices thought that *Gertz* was entirely wrongly decided (and thus that presumed and punitive damages should be allowed to all private plaintiffs, regardless of whether an issue of public interest was involved).

3. **Consequences:** Thus *Dun & Bradstreet* seems to put a majority of the Court behind two constitutional principles:

    a. Presumed and punitive damages: First, where a private plaintiff sues concerning statements that involve no issue of public interest, he can recover ***presumed and punitive damages without*** a showing that the defendant recklessly disregarded the truth or knew of the falsity of his statement. This is the actual result of *Dun & Bradstreet.*

    b. Strict liability: Secondly, *Dun & Bradstreet* probably means that where a private figure sues on a statement relating only to matters of private concern, ***he is not constitutionally required to show even ordinary negligence*** in order to recover. (At least one member of the Court that decided *Dun & Bradstreet*, Justice White, concurring, stated that he believed this result to follow from *Dun & Bradstreet*.)

H. Statements of opinion: The Supreme Court has refused to give special First Amendment protection for statements of ***"opinion."*** So some statements, even though they express opinions, may be the subject of defamation actions. But only when a statement contains or implies a statement of ***provably false fact*** may the suit proceed. *Milkovich v. Lorain Journal Co.*, 497 U.S. 1 (1990).

1. **Holding:** In *Milkovich*, the Supreme Court held that statements of opinion ***get no special First Amendment protection***. However, the majority opinion in *Milkovich* makes it clear that the Court's prior First Amendment rulings will ensure that statements of ***pure*** opinion are not found to be defamatory. The Court observed that these prior cases require any libel plaintiff to prove: (1) that the statement is ***"false"***; and (2) that the statement can be reasonably interpreted as stating ***"actual facts"*** about an individual. A pure statement of opinion (e.g., "In my opinion Mayor Jones shows his abysmal ignorance by accepting the teachings of Marx and Lenin.") would not be actionable, because it: (1) is not provably false; and (2) cannot reasonably be interpreted as stating actual facts about the plaintiff.

I. Intentional infliction of emotional distress: The *New York Times* standard also applies to actions for ***intentional infliction of emotional distress (IIED).*** That is, a public figure or public official may recover against the publisher who causes such distress only if he can prove that the publication contained a false statement of fact published either with knowledge that the statement was false or with reckless disregard as to whether it was true or not. The Supreme Court so held in *Hustler Magazine v. Falwell*, 485 U.S. 46 (1988).

1. **Facts:** The facts of *Hustler* vividly illustrate this extension of *New York Times* to suits for emotional distress. Hustler Magazine published a parody of an advertisement for Campari Liqueur, which portrayed P (the Reverend Jerry Falwell) as a drunken hypocrite who had sex with his mother. The ad contained a legend at the bottom, "Ad parody, not to be taken seriously." A jury found that the parody could not reasonably be understood as describing actual facts about Falwell; the jury therefore rejected his libel claim, but gave him an award for intentional infliction of emotional distress.

2. **Holding:** All eight members of the Court who heard the case agreed that Falwell could ***not*** receive such an award consistent with the First Amendment. The Court observed that "even when a speaker or writer is motivated by hatred or ill-will, his expression [is] pro-

tected by the First Amendment." The Court noted that political parody and satire is an important element of political speech, and believed that there is no way to distinguish such "core" political speech from the kind of satire involved here. The "outrageousness" of the speech here did not furnish an acceptable distinction, because that term is inevitably highly subjective.

3. **Remains good law:** *Hustler* remains good law in a general sense, as we know from a 2011 case: actions for IIED can violate the First Amendment if they make it too easy for the plaintiff to establish liability. *Snyder v. Phelps*, 131 S.Ct. 1207 (2011), *supra*, p. 538, involved a suit against a private-figure defendant, but on a matter of public interest. So it raised a somewhat different issue than *Hustler* (where the defendant was a public figure, requiring the plaintiff to show actual malice). But *Snyder*, like *Hustler* before it, establishes that as a general principle suits for IIED will violate a civil defendant's First Amendment right to content-neutrality unless the plaintiff can show that the state law of IIED, when it allows the content of the defendant's message to trigger liability, can survive strict scrutiny (a standard that a state's common law of IIED will rarely meet).

J. False statements of fact outside the defamation context: Successful actions for defamation necessarily involve a factually-false statement. And as we've just seen, despite cases like *New York Times v. Sullivan*, the First Amendment does not generally prevent governments from forbidding defamatory (and thus factually false) speech. The treatment of defamation raises a more general question: can government ***categorically forbid factually-false statements***, even ones that are *not* defamatory? Could a state, for instance, ***make it a crime to "tell a lie"?***

1. **Content-based regulation:** Keep in mind that a ban on making false statements would be a form of ***content-based regulation***: if there are two statements made in exactly the same context, punishing the "false" one and not the "true" one would require government to regulate based on the message being delivered.

2. **Can't generally forbid false statements:** Given the extreme scrutiny given to content-based regulation of speech, it's not surprising that the brief answer to the question, "Can government generally forbid lying?" is ***"no."*** Except for a few narrow ***pre-defined sub-categories*** (defamation, fraud, and perjury, for instance), as to which there is a long-standing consensus that the type of false speech in question is especially likely to cause severe harm, government ***may not forbid statements merely on the grounds that they are factually false.***

3. **Can't criminalize lying about military medals (*U.S. v. Alvarez*):** The principle that government may not ban factually-false speech not falling into the few pre-defined specially-harmful categories was demonstrated in ***U.S. v. Alvarez,*** 132 S.Ct. 2537 (2012). The Court held by a 6-3 vote that Congress' decision to make it a crime for a person to falsely state that he had won certain ***military medals*** violated the First Amendment.

   a. **The Stolen Valor Act:** In the federal ***"Stolen Valor Act"*** of 2005, Congress made it a crime for any person to falsely state, even orally, that he had been "awarded any decoration or medal authorized by Congress for the Armed Forces of the United States." Alvarez falsely claimed, in a public meeting, that he had been awarded the Congressional Medal of Honor 20 years before. Alvarez did not appear to be seeking any tangible benefit from the lie; as the plurality Supreme Court opinion in his case eventually put it, his statement was "but a pathetic attempt to ***gain respect*** that eluded him." But Alvarez was indicted for violating the Act, pled guilty, and was allowed to challenge the Act as an unconstitutional content-based restriction on his speech.

b. 6 votes against the Act: Six members of the Court *agreed with Alvarez* that the Act violated the First Amendment. No opinion commanded a majority, because the six justices were not in agreement about how stringent a test should be used to evaluate the law.

c. Plurality: A four-Justice plurality (written by Justice Kennedy, and joined by Roberts, Ginsburg and Sotomayor) applied "exacting scrutiny" — essentially, *strict scrutiny* — to the statute, and concluded that the statute could not survive that scrutiny.

   i. "No First Amendment value" argument rejected: The government argued that false statements "have *no First Amendment value* in themselves," and are therefore not entitled to constitutional protection. But the plurality *rejected* this "categorical" assertion. True, certain categories of false statement could be restricted — categories like defamatory statements, perjury, and fraudulent statements intended to extract some material benefit from another (e.g., fraudulent commercial speech). But outside of these few pre-defined categories where there was inevitably some special harm caused by the falsehood, the Court had *never held that false statements are without constitutional protection*, and the plurality wasn't willing to do so now.

   ii. Would give government power to censor: The plurality noted that the Stolen Valor Act made no attempt to take account of the *circumstances* in which the lie was told. The Act applied to "a false statement made at any time, in any place, to any person ... [It] would apply ... to *personal, whispered conversations within a home.*" Permitting government to declare false speech to be a criminal offense without regard to the surrounding circumstances "would endorse government authority to *compile a list of subjects about which false statements are punishable.*" And that government power "has *no clear limiting principle* ... It would give government a *broad censorial power* unprecedented in [our] constitutional tradition."

   iii. Strict scrutiny applied: Therefore, the plurality held, the statute needed to be subjected to "the *most exacting scrutiny.*" The plurality conceded that the government's interest in ensuring that the public's general perception of military awards not be diluted by false claims was a compelling interest. But no matter how compelling the government's interest, the statute could survive only if the particular restriction imposed was "actually necessary" to achieve that interest.

      (1) Alternatives available: The plurality concluded that the government had not made this showing of "actual necessity." In particular, the government had not shown why *"counterspeech"* would not suffice. For instance, in the case of false claims concerning the Congressional Medal of Honor (the most-heavily-punished type of violation under the Act, and the one with which Alvarez had been charged), the government could combat the lying problem by creating an *online database* that would list Medal of Honor winners, making it "easy to verify and expose false claims."

d. Two additional votes: Justice Breyer (joined by Kagan) agreed with the plurality that the Act was unconstitutional, making 6 votes for that proposition. But Breyer applied *"intermediate scrutiny"* rather than the plurality's strict scrutiny. Even under this easier-to-satisfy standard, however, the statute could not survive, because the government had not shown that a "more finely tailored statute" could not adequately address the harms. For instance, the statute might be rewritten to require that the false statement "caused specific harm" or was "material."

e. Dissent: Three Justices dissented, contending that the statute was constitutional. Justice Alito (joined by Scalia and Thomas) pointed out that the statute was narrowly drafted, and reached only "knowingly false statements about *hard facts directly within a speaker's personal knowledge."* Also, he said, the statute was "strictly *viewpoint neutral"* — it reached *all* false statements about medals, whether the statements disparaged or commended the military or the system of military honors.

  i. Harmful: On the other hand, Alito said, the lies forbidden by the statute "inflict substantial harm," because they *"debase the distinctive honor"* of military awards, by making them *seem more common* than they really are. This debasement harms military morale.

  ii. No First Amendment protection: The dissent asserted that "false statements of fact *merit no First Amendment protection in their own right."* Alito conceded that in many areas (e.g., defamation suits brought by public figures), government needs to "extend a measure of strategic protection" even to false statements, in order to ensure sufficient *"breathing space"* for protected speech, so that protected (and truthful) speech is not *"chilled."*

    (1) Act is narrow: But, Alito said, the Stolen Valor Act was not one of those situations requiring that some false statements be tolerated in order to avoid a chilling of protected speech. The Act presented *"no risk at all that valuable speech will be suppressed,"* leading Alito to conclude that the Act was fully constitutional.

VII. OBSCENITY

A. Generally unprotected: Obscenity, like defamation and "fighting words," was listed in *Chaplinsky (supra*, p. 533) as being a type of speech *unprotected by the First Amendment*. But again, as with defamation, the states are no longer completely free to define obscenity however they wish, and to then punish the distribution or sale of the material so defined.

1. Attempt to define: Instead, the Supreme Court has attempted to lay down specific guidelines for what materials may, compatibly with the First Amendment, be punished as "obscene." However, none of these attempts to define "obscenity" has turned out to be specific enough to give legislatures and lower courts reliable guidance about what materials are covered. Therefore, the Supreme Court has remained very much in the business of deciding, case by case, whether given materials meet the Court's definition.

2. *Roth:* The first case which required the Court to face directly the issue of whether obscene materials are protected by the First Amendment was *Roth v. U.S.*, 354 U.S. 476 (1957). In *Roth* (in an opinion by Justice Brennan), the Court confirmed what its dictum in

Chaplinsky had suggested — that "obscenity is not within the area of constitutionally protected speech or press." But the Court also held that First Amendment concerns *limit the acceptable definition of "obscenity."*

a. Definition of "obscene": The Court formulated its own definition of "obscenity": *"whether to the average person, applying contemporary community standards, the dominant theme of the material taken as a whole appeals to prurient interest."* The Court purported to be repeating the definition of obscenity laid down in certain prior lower-court cases. However, the definition seems to have been intended as a *minimal constitutional standard*; that is, the state could not, consistent with the First Amendment, ban a given item as obscene unless it satisfied this *Roth* definition.

b. Meaning of "prurient": The Court defined "prurient" as "material having a tendency to excite lustful thoughts." (But in a much later case, the Court interpreted this definition of "prurient" to *exclude* materials which, although they "excite lustful thoughts," provoke "only normal, healthy sexual desires." *Brockett v. Spokane Arcades, Inc.*, 472 U.S. 491 (1985). However, the *Brockett* Court did not define its phrase "normal, healthy sexual desires.")

c. Redeeming social value: Of primary importance to the *Roth* Court was distinguishing between obscenity and "the portrayal of sex ... in *art, literature and scientific works*." The latter must be given full constitutional protection. It is not clear from the Court's opinion whether, apart from the definition cited above, there is an *additional* requirement for obscenity that the work not constitute art, literature, or other category having social value. But the Court did say that "all ideas having even the *slightest redeeming social importance*" are to be protected (and, implicitly, are to be judged not obscene).

    i. Ambiguity: If a work had some serious social value (e.g., of a literary nature), but its dominant theme was nonetheless one which "excites lustful thoughts" and is therefore "prurient," it is simply not clear whether the material could be obscene under *Roth*. (In any event, the presence of a small amount of "redeeming social importance" is *no longer sufficient* to prevent a work from being obscene, under *Miller v. California*, the presently-applicable test, discussed *infra*, p. 578.)

3. Post-*Roth* cases: In a long string of post-*Roth* cases, the Court was forced to decide whether particular materials were obscene under the *Roth* definition. In many instances, no majority of the Court could agree on a single rationale, though of course there was always either a majority of the Court believing that the materials were obscene or a majority believing that they were not. From *Roth* until 1973, in fact, no majority of the Court ever agreed on a definition of obscenity.

a. Stewart's remark: Perhaps the most candid, and certainly the most famous, comment made during the post-*Roth* period on the difficulties of defining "obscenity," was that of Justice Stewart. Concurring in *Jacobellis v. Ohio*, 378 U.S. 184 (1964), he conceded that he might never be able intelligibly to describe "hard core pornography," which he believed to be the only type of material bannable under *Roth*. However, he observed, *"I know it when I see it*, and the motion picture involved in this case is not that."

B. *Miller:* Finally, in ***Miller v. California***, 413 U.S. 15 (1973), five Justices agreed on a ***new definition*** of "obscenity," one which was built upon the *Roth* definition but which also resolved some additional issues.

1. ***Miller's* definition:** *Miller* laid out the following three-part test (all parts of which must be met) for identifying material which may be banned as obscene:

   a. the ***"average person***, applying ***contemporary community standards"*** would find that "the work, ***taken as a whole***, appeals to the ***prurient*** interest" (citing *Roth*);

   b. the work "depicts or describes, in a ***patently offensive way, sexual*** conduct specifically defined by the applicable state law" and

   c. the work, taken as a whole, lacks ***"serious literary, artistic, political, or scientific value."***

2. **Changes:** This definition changes or clarifies prior law in two major respects:

   a. **"Community" standards:** The *Miller* majority explicitly ***rejected*** the argument that what appeals to the "prurient interest" or is "patently offensive" should be determined by reference to a ***national standard***. What counts are the standards of the ***local community*** where the prosecution is taking place. Thus "the people of Maine or Mississippi [need not] accept the public depiction of conduct found tolerable in Las Vegas, or in New York City."

   b. **Limited to "hard core" sex:** *Miller* also establishes that the states may ban as obscene only depictions or descriptions of ***"hard core"*** sexual conduct. Since the states must ***be specific*** about what sexual conduct is being banned (in order to satisfy the First Amendment need for "fair notice" of what is forbidden, and in order to avoid a chilling effect on expression), the Court provided several examples of materials which could be banned:

      i. **Ultimate sexual acts:** "Patently offensive representations or descriptions of ***ultimate sex acts***, normal or perverted, actual or ***simulated"***;

      ii. **Other:** "Patently offensive representations or descriptions of ***masturbation, excretory functions***, and ***lewd exhibition*** of the ***genitals***."

      Note: Later Court cases show that mere *nudity*, by itself, is *not obscene*, and indeed gets some First Amendment protection. See, e.g., *Erie v. Pap's A.M., supra*, p 545.[6]

3. **Dissents:** Four Justices dissented in *Miller*. The reasoning of three of them was more fully expressed in their dissent to a companion case decided the same day, *Paris Adult Theatre I v. Slaton*, discussed *infra*.

4. **Some limits on right to define terms:** Notwithstanding *Miller's* "community standards" approach, the Court will impose some limits on the right of the local community to apply its own interpretation of the meaning of terms like "patently offensive" or "prurient interest." For instance, the Court has made it clear that the definition of "prurient interest" (part of the definition of obscenity in *Miller*, and in *Roth, supra*, p. 576) ***may not include*** a concept of lust that encompasses "only normal, healthy sexual desires." *Brockett v. Spokane*

---

6. However, 7 members of the Court held in *Pap's* that totally nude dancing, though not obscene, could nonetheless be prohibited as part of a content-neutral attempt to combat nude dancing's "secondary effects." See *supra*, p. 545.

Arcades, Inc., 472 U.S. 491 (1985). That is, the community is not free to say, in effect, that material that excites "normal, healthy sexual desires," and that does not incite sexual responses above and beyond these normal ones, is "prurient" or "offensive."

C. Private possession by adults: The mere *private possession* of obscene material by an adult *may not be made criminal. Stanley v. Georgia*, 394 U.S. 557 (1969).

1.   **Rationale:**   In reaching this conclusion, the Supreme Court relied both on the weakness of the state's interest in controlling private possession of obscenity, and on the strength of the individual's interest in not being forbidden such private usage. The state's interest was only the weak one of "protect[ing] the individual's mind from the effects of obscenity." The individual's interest was directly contrary, and much stronger: that of *not having his thoughts controlled*. "If the First Amendment means anything, it means that a State has *no business telling a man, sitting alone in his own house, what books he may read or what films he may watch.*"

   a.   **Two interests:**   Thus the *Stanley* rule relied on two distinct interests held by individuals: the First Amendment interest in having free access to ideas, and a distinct *privacy* interest in not having what one does in one's own home made the subject of government scrutiny.

2.   **Possession of child pornography:**   There is one important exception to *Stanley's* rule that private possession of obscene material by an adult may not be made criminal: the states may criminalize even private possession of *child pornography*. See *Osborne v. Ohio*, discussed *infra*, p. 580.

3.   **No right to supply consenting adults:**   Since *Stanley* recognized a right held by consenting adults to possess and use obscenity in their homes, it would not have been illogical for the Court also to conclude that there was a right to *supply* obscene materials to such adults. But the Court has refused to extend the rationale of *Stanley* in this manner.

   a.   **Mailing of obscene material:**   For instance, government may make it a crime to *mail* obscene materials to consenting adults. *U.S. v. Reidel*, 402 U.S. 351 (1971). *Reidel* concluded that the focus on *Stanley* had been on "freedom of mind and thought and on the privacy of one's home" (the privacy strand of *Stanley*), and that *Stanley* did not recognize any First Amendment right to acquire obscene materials from commercial suppliers.

   b.   **Adult movie theaters:**   Similarly, the holding of *Paris Adult Theatre I v. Slaton*, 413 U.S. 49 (1973), that there is no right to *show obscene movies to consenting adults*, represents an unwillingness to carry the rationale of *Stanley* beyond its immediate facts.

D. Protection of children: The Court has developed special doctrines to give the states additional authority to protect *children* from pornography. Two sorts of dangers are involved: (1) that children may *read, view or listen* to pornography; and (2) that children may be induced to *take part in sexual conduct* in order to be *filmed* for pornographic pictures and movies.

1.   **Protection of children as audience:**   A state may prohibit the distribution of sexually explicit materials to children, even though those materials would not be obscene if distributed to an adult.

   a.   **Can't impair access of adults:**   But if the state wants to keep materials that are sexually explicit (but not obscene) out of the hands of minors, it must do so in a way that does ***not substantially impair*** the access of ***adults*** to those materials. That is, the state must ***narrowly tailor*** its regulations so that the materials are forbidden ***only*** to minors.

2. **Children as photographic subjects:** A state may also ban the distribution of materials ***showing children engaged in sexual conduct, even though the material is not legally obscene***. In reaching this conclusion, the Court in ***New York v. Ferber***, 458 U.S. 747 (1982) relied on the state's "compelling," surpassingly important, interest in ***preventing the sexual exploitation and abuse of children*** who are photographed for production of such materials.

    a. **Private possession may also be banned:** The state's interest in preventing the sexual exploitation and abuse of children is so strong that even the ***private possession*** of sexually explicit nude pictures of children may be prohibited. In the post-*Ferber* case of *Osborne v. Ohio*, 495 U.S. 103 (1990), the Court upheld a statute criminalizing most private possession of nude pictures of children. Even though *Stanley v. Georgia* (*supra*, p. 579) had held that adults have a First Amendment right to privately possess pornography, the *Osborne* Court held that materials showing children are different: the state's interest in preventing the pornographic exploitation of children is much stronger than the interest in protecting the minds of adults, so any First Amendment interest in possessing nude pictures of children is outweighed by this anti-child-exploitation interest. And this is true even if the materials are ***not "obscene,"*** merely ***"indecent."***

3. **Virtual child pornography:** On the other hand, government may ***not*** ban non-obscene ***"virtual child pornography,"*** by forbidding either ***computer-generated images*** that appear to be of children having sex, or explicit images of ***young-looking adults posing as minors***. In *Ashcroft v. Free Speech Coalition*, 535 U.S. 564 (2002), the Court rejected the federal government's argument that barring such virtual images was necessary to restrain the market for actual child pornography, and therefore necessary to protect children.

4. **Protection against non-obscene violence:** Government's extensive power to protect children by banning them from access to non-obscene materials applies only where the materials involve ***sexual content***, not where the materials involve ***violent conduct*** without any direct sexual connection.

    a. **Violent video games:** Thus in a 2011 case, *Brown v. Entertainment Merchants Ass'n*, 131 S.Ct. 2729 (2011), the Court struck down a California law that prohibited the sale or rental of ***"violent video games"*** to minors. The Court reasoned that ***"video games qualify for First Amendment protection,"*** in the same way as ***books, plays and movies*** do, and the obscenity exception to the First Amendment does not apply to violent games any more than it does to violent books, if there is no direct depiction of sexual conduct.

E. **Protection of animals, and the "animal crush video" issue:** Just as the state has an interest in avoiding the harm to children that inevitably occurs during the filming of child pornography (as in *N.Y. v. Ferber*, *supra*, p. 580), animal-rights activists have claimed that government ought to be able to prevent the harm to ***animals*** that inevitably occurs during the making of videos depicting animal cruelty. But a 2010 case, *U.S. v. Stevens*, 130 S.Ct. 1577 (2010), demonstrates that any attempt by government to prevent such harm will have to be ***narrowly constructed*** to avoid First Amendment problems.

1. **Facts of *Stevens*:** *Stevens* involved a federal statute that made it a crime to create, sell or possess any depiction of "animal cruelty," if done for "commercial gain" and in violation

of any federal or state law existing in the place where the video was created, sold or possessed. The statute gave an exemption for a depiction that has "serious religious, political, scientific, educational, journalistic, historical or artistic value." The legislative history of the statute showed that it was designed to eliminate the market for ***"crush videos,"*** videos depicting the intentional torture and killing of small animals, often by showing women slowly crushing the animals to death with their bare feet or high-heeled shoes.

    a. The defendant: But in *Stevens*, D was convicted not for selling a crush video, but for selling videos of ***dogfights*** involving pitbulls. D argued that the statute was an unconstitutional infringement of his First Amendment rights.

2. D wins: By an 8-1 vote, the Supreme Court ***agreed*** with D, on overbreadth grounds. There might well be portrayals of animal cruelty that government *could* constitutionally ban in order to avoid harm to animals. But the statute here criminalized a far ***greater range of content*** than could be prohibited consistently with the First Amendment. For instance, the statute covered depictions in which a living animal was "wounded or killed," even if no cruelty was involved. It was true that the statute applied only where the conduct depicted was against the law of the state where the video was made, possessed, or sold. But the statute by its terms would apply to, say, the depiction of hunting done by a particular method that was legal in the place where it happened, but illegal in the place where the resulting video was possessed or sold. Therefore, ***a substantial number of the possible applications of the statute*** were unconstitutional. That made the statute ***void on its face*** under the doctrine of ***substantial overbreadth*** (*supra*, pp. 520-521).

F. Other issues: Here are a few other substantive rules regarding obscenity laws:

1. Book without pictures: A book without pictures, in which sexual acts are ***verbally described***, may nonetheless be obscene under the *Miller* test.

2. Community standards: In *Miller*, the Court held that the "community standards" by reference to which terms like "patently offensive" should be defined did not have to be national. In *Jenkins v. Georgia*, and its companion case, *Hamling v. United States*, both reported at 418 U.S. 87 (1974), the Court ***rejected*** the argument that the standards should have to be at least ***statewide***. Thus an obscenity case can be tried in a small, conservative rural town, and the ***standards of that town*** may be made the relevant ones (though the judge is not ***precluded*** from allowing evidence of standards in other communities).

    a. Venue for federal suits: Permitting local community standards to control becomes especially significant in view of state and federal prosecutors' ability to pick as the venue for trial ***any town through which the allegedly obscene materials have passed***. The federal statute prohibiting the mailing of obscene matter, for instance, has been held to allow venue ***anywhere along the route that the mailed material travels***, not just the point of mailing or receipt.

        i. Consequence: Thus a publisher or distributor who wishes to sell his materials nationally must face the possibility that any small town anywhere in the country through which a mail train or truck carrying one copy of the materials passes may be selected by federal prosecutors as the venue for a criminal trial. That place's local standards for determining what is "patently offensive," "prurient," etc. will then control.

3. **Scienter:**   The seller of an obscene work may not be convicted unless the prosecution proves *scienter*, that is, knowledge by the defendant of the **contents** of the materials. *Smith v. California*, 361 U.S. 147 (1959). (But there is no requirement that the prosecution prove that the defendant knew, as a conclusion of law, that the materials were obscene. Thus "ignorance of the law is no excuse" in obscenity prosecutions, any more than it is in most other contexts. See *Hamling v. U.S.*, 418 U.S. 87 (1974).)

VIII. COMMERCIAL SPEECH

A. **Overview:**   Like libel, obscenity and a few other types of speech, most kinds of *"commercial speech"* were traditionally viewed as being an "unprotected category" totally outside the scope of the First Amendment. But just as the Court in recent decades has held that the states do not have an unlimited right to ban or regulate speech merely by labeling it "libelous" or "obscene," so the Court has now given substantial First Amendment protection to speech which can be described as "commercial."

1. **Extensive change:**   In fact, in some senses this change towards more extensive First Amendment protection has been even greater in the commercial-speech area than in the areas of defamation and obscenity: in the latter two areas, the Court has simply limited governments' ability to define these areas as broadly as they wish. Once speech falls within the allowable definition of "libel" or "obscenity," it is completely without First Amendment protection. But most types of commercial speech, by contrast (all types except those that are misleading or that propose illegal transactions), are now *entitled to some First Amendment protection*. However, this protection is generally not as extensive as that reserved for speech nearer the "core" of First Amendment values, especially "political" speech.

B. **The *Virginia Pharmacy* revolution:**   Since a 1976 case, the Court has held that *even "purely commercial" speech is entitled to First Amendment protection. Virginia Pharmacy Bd. v. Virginia Consumer Council*, 425 U.S. 748 (1976).

1. **Facts:**   *Virginia Pharmacy* involved a state statute making it "unprofessional conduct" for a pharmacist to *advertise prescription drug prices.*

2. **Statute stricken:**   This ban was held by the Court to violate the First Amendment. The Court conceded that this case involved speech that was *purely* commercial, and that the only "idea" expressed was "I will sell you the *X* prescription drug at the *Y* price." Nonetheless, the Court held, such wholly commercial speech was protected by the First Amendment.

   a. **Informational value:**   In reaching this conclusion, the Court relied on society's strong interest in "the *free flow of commercial information*." Here, for instance, consumers, especially poor ones, had a compelling interest in who was charging how much for what drug.

   b. **Weak state interest:**   The countervailing state interest in suppressing price advertising was that of maintaining "a high degree of professionalism on the part of licensed pharmacists," an interest implicated by the possibility that advertising might lead to aggressive price competition, which might in turn lead to shoddy services. But this interest amounted to saying that consumers would be best protected *if kept in igno-*

rance. And, the Court concluded, the First Amendment *flatly forbids the state from deciding that ignorance is preferable to the free flow of truthful information*.

3. **Exceptions:** However, the Court hinted that although purely commercial speech is entitled to First Amendment protection, that protection might be *less extensive* than for other types of speech. *False or misleading* advertising could clearly be prohibited (whereas such statements when made about public figures cannot be, unless there is actual malice — see *New York Times v. Sullivan, supra*, p. 569). Similarly, *broader regulation of "time, place and manner"* might be justified, and the strong *presumption against prior restraints* might not apply.

4. **Audience's right to information:** Apart from the fact that it recognizes purely commercial speech as being entitled to First Amendment protection, *Virginia Pharmacy* is of interest because it demonstrates the Court's recognition of a First Amendment right to *receive* information. Prior First Amendment cases had almost all involved the right to *express* oneself, that is, to be a *disseminator* rather than a recipient of information.

   a. **Third-party rights:** By contrast, the successful plaintiffs in *Virginia Pharmacy* were in fact consumers (the recipients of the information), not pharmacists (the disseminators of the information). It is not yet completely clear whether disseminators of information may assert the third-party rights of their audiences in First Amendment cases, though it seems probable that they may. This would be an exception to the usual rules of standing (discussed *infra*, p. 709), which normally permit a litigant to assert only that his *own* rights have been violated.

5. **No right to ban "For Sale" signs:** The rationale of *Virginia Pharmacy*, especially the principle that dissemination of even purely commercial information may not be barred because that information would be "harmful," was later applied in *Linmark Associates, Inc., v. Willingboro*, 431 U.S. 85 (1977). There, the Court unanimously held that a racially-integrated town's prohibition on *real estate "For Sale" and "Sold" signs* violated the First Amendment, despite the town's interest in stemming "white flight."

   a. **Suppression of truthful information:** The fatal flaw of the *Linmark* ordinance was that it, like the ban in *Virginia Pharmacy*, was an attempt to protect the public (residents of the town) by *keeping them in ignorance*. The town's claim that the information about sales might cause residents to act "irrationally" would, if accepted, permit "every locality in the country [to] suppress any facts that reflect poorly on the locality."

6. **"Track one":** *Virginia Pharmacy* and *Linmark* can be viewed as classic "track one" cases (see *supra*, p. 503). That is, in those cases the government tried to suppress information based on the chance that the *communicative impact* of the message might cause harm. Such "track one" abridgements will be allowed only where they either fall into pre-defined "unprotected categories" or survive strict scrutiny; the point of *Virginia Pharmacy*, of course, is that "commercial speech" is no longer such an unprotected category.

   a. **Later case:** But the later case of *Central Hudson Gas, infra*, p. 585, indicates that such content-based restrictions may be upheld if they are a *narrow and direct means* of pursuing *substantial governmental interests*, essentially a type of *"intermediate"* scrutiny.

C. Regulation of lawyers: First Amendment protection for commercial speech has also been conferred by the Court in several cases involving regulation of the way in which *lawyers* acquire clients.

1. **Newspaper advertising in general:** The first of these cases established that states *may not ban all newspaper advertising of legal services*. In *Bates v. State Bar of Arizona*, 433 U.S. 350 (1977), the Court upheld by a 5-4 vote the right of a "legal clinic" to offer in newspaper advertisements certain routine services at "very reasonable fees."

2. **In-person solicitation:** The majority in *Bates* explicitly excluded considerations of whether lawyers could be barred from *in-person solicitation* of clients. But in a pair of 1978 cases, the Court held that some (though not all) types of in-person solicitation of clients may be banned. The two cases were at absolute opposite ends of the spectrum in terms of the acceptability of the lawyer's conduct. Therefore, it is hard to know where the line will be drawn between solicitation that may constitutionally be prohibited and that which may not.

   a. **Pecuniary gain:** *Ohralik v. Ohio State Bar Ass'n*, 436 U.S. 447 (1978) represented the most prohibitable kind of solicitation, classic *"ambulance chasing."* There, the Court held that a state may forbid *in-person solicitation* for *pecuniary gain*. So a state may forbid the kind of conduct at issue in *Ohralik*, in which the lawyer solicited accident victims in person, to induce them to let him represent them for a contingent fee.

   b. **Right of association:** The other case, *In re Primus*, 436 U.S. 412 (1978), represented the kind of solicitation that is least objectionable and most worthy of protection.

      i. **Facts:** Primus, a South Carolina lawyer who did occasional work without pay for the ACLU, wrote a letter to a woman who had allegedly been illegally sterilized as a condition to her further receipt of Medicaid benefits; the letter offered the ACLU's free services in filing a lawsuit on her behalf. Primus, like Ohralik, was disciplined for violating anti-solicitation rules.

      ii. **Punishment reversed:** But the Supreme Court held that Primus *could not constitutionally be punished* for what she did. Her letter, and the ACLU litigation itself, were attempts to further her *political and ideological goals*. Therefore, her conduct implicated her interest in *free "political expression"* as well as *freedom of association*, both core First Amendment values. (This was the same sort of associational activity that the Court had earlier protected in *NAACP v. Button*, *infra*, p. 609.) These First Amendment interests were sufficiently strong that the state could *not* use *prophylactic measures* because of the mere potential for overreaching, fraud or other abuse; instead, Primus could only be disciplined if there was a showing that her solicitation had *in fact* led to one of these harms.

   c. **Some in-person solicitation allowed:** A much more recent case suggests that some types of *in-person solicitation* by professionals will be *allowed*, and that it was the unusually *vulnerable and susceptible condition* of the prospective clients in *Ohralik* that made the difference there. See *Edenfield v. Fane*, 507 U.S. 761 (1993), striking down Florida's ban on direct, in-person uninvited solicitation of business owners by Certified Public Accountants.

D. Commercial speech doctrine curtailed: *Virginia Pharmacy* seemed to hold that the states may not suppress even "purely commercial" speech, so long as the speech was not false or misleading and did not propose an illegal transaction. But later cases show that *Virginia Pharmacy* cannot be read this broadly. While purely commercial speech is entitled to First Amendment protection, it ***does not receive the full range*** of that Amendment's protection.

1. **The *Central Hudson* case:** In ***Central Hudson Gas v. Public Service Commission***, 447 U.S. 557 (1980), the Court laid down a formal ***four-part test*** to determine whether a given regulation of commercial speech violates the First Amendment. This test indicates that, even apart from the states' right to prevent misleading speech or speech that proposes illegal transactions, the government has ***significantly more power to regulate commercial speech*** than might have been supposed from a simple reading of *Virginia Pharmacy*.

   a. **Facts:** In *Central Hudson Gas*, the New York State Public Service Commission (PSC) banned all "promotional advertising" by electric utilities. The stated purpose of the ban was to conserve energy; "promotional advertising" was defined as advertising intended to stimulate the purchase of utility services (so that all other types of advertising by utilities, including "institutional" ads, were permitted).

   b. **Four-part test:** Before analyzing the ban, the Court reviewed prior commercial speech cases, and derived for the first time a ***four-part test*** for determining whether a given regulation abridges the First Amendment.

   [1] **Protected speech:** First, courts must determine whether the commercial speech is protected ***at all*** by the First Amendment. All commercial speech receives at least partial protection except for: (1) speech that is ***misleading*** or ***fraudulent***; and (2) speech that ***concerns unlawful activity.*** (The contours of these two exceptions are discussed further, *infra*, p. 586.) Speech that falls into one of these exceptions raises no First Amendment issues at all, and may thus be fully regulated by the government.

   [2] **Substantial government interest:** Second, the court must ask whether the ***governmental interest*** asserted in support of the regulation is ***"substantial."*** If not, the regulation will be struck down without further inquiry. If the interest is substantial, the government must still meet the final two parts of the test.

   [3] **Interest "directly advanced":** Third, the court will decide whether the regulation ***"directly advances"*** the governmental interest evaluated in part (ii) of the test. If it does not, the regulation will be struck down. If it does, it will still have to meet the fourth part of the test.

   [4] **Means-end fit:** Finally, the court will ask whether the regulation is ***"not more extensive than is necessary"*** to serve the government interest. If it *is* more extensive than necessary, the regulation will be struck down. (But a post-*Central Hudson Gas* case has watered down this "not more extensive than is necessary" test. Today, all that is required of the fit between the means and the end is that the means be ***"reasonably tailored"*** to serve the governmental objective, so that some looseness in the means-end fit will be tolerated where what is regulated is commercial speech. See *Edenfield v. Fane*, discussed further, *infra*, p. 587.)

   c. **Application to facts:** The Court then applied its test to the facts of *Central Hudson Gas*.

    i. Protected speech: Utilities' promotional advertising was clearly speech *protected* by the First Amendment, satisfying part (i). The Court rejected the argument that advertising by a monopolist has no value; for one thing, even a monopolistic electric utility faces competition from alternative energy sources.

    ii. State interests: The state asserted two interests in support of its ban: conservation of energy and maintenance of a fair and efficient rate structure (which, the state contended, would have been impaired by an increase in usage, because of the peculiarities of the rate structure). The Court agreed that each of these interests was *substantial*.

    iii. Direct link: The Court found that there was a *direct link* between the ban and one (but not the other) of the asserted state interests, that of energy conservation. (The link between promotional advertising and inequitable rates was, by contrast, too speculative to satisfy the "direct link" requirement.)

    iv. Least-restrictive alternative: With respect to the ban as a way of promoting energy conservation, part (iv) was *not satisfied*; the ban was *more extensive than needed* to further that interest. For instance, it prevented a utility from promoting the use of electricity even for those applications where it was a more efficient power source than that currently being used.

  d. Rehnquist dissent: Justice Rehnquist was the sole dissenter in *Central Hudson*. He thought that the majority's four-part test did not give the government enough power to regulate commercial speech, and that the test gave commercial speech falling within the First Amendment protection that was "virtually indistinguishable" from that given to non-commercial speech. Rehnquist believed that the regulation here was more an economic regulation than a restraint on "free speech." Therefore, he would have given it "virtually complete deference," in contrast to what he viewed as the majority's resurrection of the discredited doctrine of *Lochner v. New York* (see *supra*, p. 166).

E. Current status: The *current status* of the protection given to "commercial speech" may be summarized as follows:

  1. Misleading or deceptive statements: Commercial speech that is *misleading* or *deceptive*, or that *proposes an illegal transaction*, is *not* entitled to *any* First Amendment protection at all.

    a. Potential to mislead: Even speech which merely has a *potential* to mislead may be regulated. But if information may be presented in *either* a misleading or a non-misleading way, the state must attempt to prohibit *only* the misleading method (i.e., it must use the *least-restrictive alternative*). *In re R.M.J.*, 455 U.S. 191 (1982).

    b. Integral to criminal conduct: Speech that is *integral to criminal conduct* is not protected.

      i. Proposing an illegal transaction: So, for instance, speech that *proposes an illegal transaction* doesn't receive any First Amendment protection. See, e.g., *Pittsburgh Press Co. v. Human Relations Commission*, 413 U.S. 376 (1973), upholding an order forbidding newspapers from publishing sex-designated help-wanted columns. The Court reasoned that such columns act as an aid to illegal sex discrimination in employment.

ii. Conspiracy: Similarly, speech that is part of a ***conspiracy*** to commit a crime ("We hereby agree to rob the First National Bank") may be punished, because such speech is unprotected.

2. **Three-part test:** If the commercial speech is covered by the First Amendment, then it may be regulated only if the state shows that the regulation:

[1] ***directly advances*** ...

[2] a ***substantial governmental interest*** ...

[3] in a way that is ***reasonably tailored*** to achieve that objective.

(These are essentially the last three prongs of *Central Hudson Gas*.) This is basically ***"mid-level"*** review.

3. **"Reasonably tailored means":** Part (3) of the *Central Hudson Gas* test requires that the regulation of commercial speech be "no more restrictive than necessary" to achieve the government's objective. But several post-*Central Hudson Gas* cases show that the Court is ***not*** taking the phrase "no more restrictive than necessary" ***literally***, as if it meant "least restrictive possible alternative." Instead, all that is required of the means-end fit is that the means be ***"tailored in a reasonable manner"*** to serve the government objective, i.e., that the means advance the objective in a ***"direct and material way."*** *Edenfield v. Fane*, 507 U.S. 761 (1993).

   a. **Looseness of means-end fit:** The fact that there may be ***some other means*** that would serve the government interest as well, while restricting the commercial speech less, will ***not be fatal***. In other words, some degree of ***looseness in the means-end fit*** will be ***tolerated*** when what is being regulated is commercial speech. See *Board of Trustees of SUNY v. Fox*, 492 U.S. 469 (1989).

   b. **Can still have "bite":** But the not-so-demanding means-end test still has considerable ***"bite"*** — If the Court is convinced that there is some alternative method of achieving the same end as well or almost as well, with ***significantly less interference*** with protected speech, the Court will not hesitate to ***strike down*** the restriction. Indeed, the Court will generally place upon the government the burden of ***showing*** that ***proposed less-restrictive alternatives would not adequately fulfill*** the governmental objective being sought. See *Thompson v. Western States Medical Center*, 535 U.S. 357 (2002).

   c. **Internal consistency required:** An important factor in whether the means will be found not to be uncessarily restrictive is whether the means selected by the government are ***internally consistent*** — where the means are not self-consistent, the Court is likely to find that the scheme is too irrational to advance the stated objective sufficiently.

   Example: A federal statute prohibits beer manufacturers from listing their beverage's alcohol content on the label. The federal government defends the ban on the grounds that it's needed to prevent brewers from engaging in "strength wars," in which each maker increases its beer's alcohol content and then tries to lure drinkers by advertising the high content.

Held, the statute violates the brewers' free speech rights. The federal government does not prohibit alcohol strength listings in advertising, only on labels. Similarly, the government doesn't ban such listings for the labels of wines and spirits, only beer. These inconsistencies make the scheme so irrational that it does not "directly and materially advance" the objective of preventing strength wars. *Rubin v. Coors Brewing Co.*, 514 U.S. 476 (1995).

d. **Some chance of success:** A second factor in determining whether the means are reasonably tailored to the government objective is whether the means have a ***reasonable probability of achieving the objective*** at least some of the time. The means-end fit will be too loose if it "provides only ***ineffective or remote support*** for the government's purpose" (*Edenfield, supra*), or if there is ***"little chance"*** that the restriction will advance the state's goal (*Greater New Orleans Broadcasting Assoc.*, 527 U.S. 173 (1999).

Example: Massachusetts regulates indoor advertising for smokeless tobacco and cigars in a number of ways. One restriction is that advertising for such products cannot be placed lower than five feet above the floor of any retail establishment located within 1,000 feet of any school or playground. The purpose of the regulation is to make tobacco products less appealing to minors, by limiting minors' exposure to advertising about the products.

Held, the restriction is unconstitutional. The five-foot rule "does not seem to advance" the state's goal. "Not all children are less than five feet tall, and those who are certainly have the ability to look up and take in their surroundings." Therefore, the height restriction "does not constitute a reasonable fit" with the state's goal. *Lorillard Tobacco Co. v. Reilly*, 533 U.S. 525 (2001) (also discussed *infra*, p. 590).

e. **Fear of bad public decisions not sufficient:** Government's fear that if the commercial information is divulged to the public, the public will make ***"bad decisions"*** is not a legitimate state objective. "Fear that people would make bad decisions if given truthful information cannot justify content-based burdens on speech." *Sorrell v. IMS Health Inc.*, 131 S.Ct. 2653 (2011).

4. **Advertising of lawful but harmful products:** Advertising of unlawful products may clearly be prohibited under *Central Hudson Gas*. But what about the advertising of products or services that are ***lawful***, but believed by the legislature to be ***harmful***? Examples include ***cigarettes***, ***liquor***, and ***gambling***.

a. **Regular commercial-speech rules apply:** The Court's relatively pro-free-speech approach towards regulation of commercial speech generally — applying fairly-tough ***mid-level review*** to such regulations (see *supra*, p. 587) — seems to ***apply the same way to "vice" products*** as to products or services not generally considered harmful. This tough attitude towards speech regulation in this area is shown by the Court's ***rejection*** of several arguments commonly made in favor of regulation of arguably harmful products:

i. **Right to ban product irrelevant:** The fact that the state could have ***banned the sale of the product completely*** probably does ***not*** confer on the state the right to ban or tightly regulate ***commercial speech about the product***. That's so because the Court seems to agree that banning speech about certain conduct may often be *more intrusive* than banning the conduct itself.

(1) Rationale: Thus in *44 Liquormart v. Rhode Island*, 517 U.S. 484 (1996) (also discussed immediately *infra*), the Court unanimously held that a state statute forbidding the *advertising of liquor prices* violated the First Amendment, even though the state would have had the freedom to *ban all liquor sales.* Justice Stevens, speaking for a plurality in *44 Liquormart*, said, "We think it quite clear that *banning speech* may sometimes prove *far more intrusive* than banning conduct. ... [A] local ordinance banning bicycle lessons may curtail freedom far more than one that prohibits bicycle riding within city limits. ... The text of the First Amendment ... presumes that *attempts to regulate speech* are *more dangerous than attempts to regulate conduct.*" Based on recent cases, it's likely that a majority of the present Court would agree that a legislature's right to ban the sale of a product does not confer a right to issue content-based regulations seeking to sell the product.

ii. "Consume less" objective will fail: If the government's sole justification for limiting advertising of the legal-but-assertedly-harmful product is that the limitation will cause people to *consume less* of the item, it will be extremely *difficult* for the limitation to pass muster. First, the government will have to show that the limit *"significantly"* reduces consumption, and this will generally be quite hard to do. Second, the government will have to show that no means are available that are significantly *less intrusive*; since the government will almost always be free to *increase taxes* on the item, or to *regulate how and where it can be sold*, or to conduct an educational campaign showing its dangers, it's again unlikely that the government will succeed in making the required showing that materially less restrictive alternatives don't exist.

Example: Rhode Island prohibits all advertising of liquor prices, except for price tags displayed with the merchandise and not visible from the street. The state defends the prohibition on the grounds that price advertising will lead to lower prices, and lower prices will lead to increased consumption, a result at odds with the state's interest in "temperance."

Held, the prohibition violates the First Amendment. First, the three-part test of *Central Hudson Gas supra*, p. 587) requires that any regulation of commercial speech *"directly advance"* the state's interest. This "directly advance" requirement means that the regulation must "significantly," not just slightly, advance the state's goal. Here, there is no evidence that prohibiting price advertising *significantly* curtails alcohol consumption. Second, *Central Hudson Gas* also requires that a regulation of commercial speech be *"no more extensive than necessary."* The ban fails this requirement, too, since the state could have limited alcohol consumption by less restrictive means, such as increased taxation, limits on per capita purchases, or educational campaigns.[7] *44 Liquormart v. Rhode Island*, 517 U.S. 484 (1996).

iii. Protect minors: Finally, if the government's principal justification is to prevent *minors* from gaining access to, or being enticed by, the "vice" product, government will have to **tailor its methods very tightly** so that there is no undue interference with the rights of **adults** to obtain or learn about the product.

   (1) Tobacco regulation: As the Court said in a case striking down Massachusetts' restrictions on the advertising of smokeless tobacco and cigars, "no matter how laudable the state's interest in preventing minors' access to tobacco products, the state may not regulate advertising in a way that interferes materially with the legitimate rights of the tobacco industry, and its **adult customers**, to exchange truthful information." *Lorillard Tobacco Co. v. Reilly*, 533 U.S. 525 (2001).

5. **Constitutionally-protected products:** The use of some products is so tightly tied in with the **exercise of constitutional rights** that sale of the product could **not** constitutionally be banned; therefore, advertising of these products may also not be banned or heavily regulated. For instance, since there is a constitutional right to use **contraceptives**, a ban on the advertising of contraceptives would not be any more constitutional than would a ban on the sale of them. Indeed, the Court held this to be the case, in *Bolger v. Youngs Drug Products Corp.*, 463 U.S. 60 (1983).

Quiz Yourself on

DEFAMATION, OBSCENITY AND COMMERCIAL SPEECH

83. Joe was the owner of "Joe's Jewelry," a jewelry store that was the only such store in the town of Liberty. Since Liberty was a small town, most people knew who Joe was, but they didn't know much about his personal life, and he had never been involved in politics. One day, the local newspaper, the *Liberty Post*, reported that Joe had shot Tim, a shopper in the store, based on Joe's mistaken belief that Tim was attempting to rob the store. In fact, Tim was shot in Joe's store, but by Pete, Joe's employee, who Joe then immediately fired. (Tim was not in fact trying to shoplift, and Pete simply made a bad mistake.) Joe has brought a libel action against the *Post*. The state's policy is to allow a libel recovery whenever such a recovery would be allowed at common law and would not be forbidden by the U.S. Constitution. At the end of the case, the judge charged the jury that Joe could recover against the *Post* if the jury found that the *Post* had been negligent, but not if it found that the *Post* had made a non-negligent error as to the underlying facts. Does this charge correctly reflect the relevant constitutional principles? _____

84. After Emilio failed to pay numerous traffic tickets, the police came to his house to arrest him on a bench warrant. While they were standing inside the foyer of his house making the arrest, they saw copies of two unusual publications. One was *Kiddie World*, which contained pictures of nude adolescents; the adolescents were suggestively posed, but were not engaged in real or simulated sexual activities. The second publication was *Barnyard Illustrated*, which consisted exclusively of pictures of men and women having real or simulated sex with a variety of barnyard animals, including sheep and goats. A state ordinance forbids the sale or possession of "any pictorial material containing sexually explicit photographs that are obscene under prevailing constitutional standards." Assume that Emilio can be shown to have known the contents of both of these magazines.

---

7. The two arguments discussed here — that the measure failed because there was no evidence that it significantly diminished alcoholic consumption, and because less restrictive means would have sufficed — were joined only by a plurality of the Court. But all 9 members of the Court agreed with the result, that Rhode Island's ban violated the First Amendment.

(a) Can Emilio be convicted for violating the ordinance as to *Kiddie World*? _____

(b) Can Emilio be convicted for violating the ordinance as to *Barnyard Illustrated*? _____

85. Congress has concluded that the nicotine used in cigarettes is "highly addictive." Congress has also concluded that cigarette advertising causes many minors (who under federal and state laws can't legally buy the product) to take up smoking. Therefore, Congress has now banned all print advertising for cigarettes. Together with a prior ban on broadcast advertising for cigarettes, this means that billboards and handbills are now the only allowable means of advertising cigarettes. The cigarette industry asserts that this near total ban violates its right of free expression.

(a) What is the test that the Court will use in evaluating the constitutionality of the ban? _____

(b) Is the statute constitutional? _____

_____

Answers

83. **Yes, probably.** The first question is whether Joe is a *"public figure."* If he is a public figure, he may not be permitted to recover unless he shows "actual malice" on the part of the *Post*, i.e., that either the *Post* had knowledge that its statement about who did the shooting was false, or that the *Post* acted with "reckless disregard" of whether the statement was false or not. So if Joe is a public figure, then the judge's instruction is wrong. Joe might be held to be an "involuntary public figure" because of his involvement in this matter of obvious public interest; however, since he is not a criminal defendant, and since the Court has construed the "involuntary public figure" category narrowly, probably Joe does not fall into this category. Joe is certainly not a generally famous person (even locally), nor one who has voluntarily injected himself into a public controversy, so he probably doesn't fit into either of the other public figure categories recognized by the Court.

If Joe is in fact a "private figure," then the judge's charge is correct. Under *Gertz v. Robert Welch*, where P is neither a public official nor a public figure, there is no constitutional requirement that he prove that the defendant knew his statement to be false or recklessly disregarded the truth. (On the other hand, the state would not be permitted to grant Joe a recovery based on strict liability; the First Amendment requires that the *Post* be proven to be at least negligent, even in a suit brought by a private figure.)

84. **(a) Yes.** On these facts, Kiddie World is probably not, strictly speaking, "obscene" under Supreme Court definitions. The reason is that mere nudity, without any attempt to portray sexual activity, is not considered "obscene." However, the state's interest in preventing the sexual exploitation and abuse of children is so strong that states may prohibit the sale, and even the private possession, of sexually explicit nude pictures of children, even though these are not strictly speaking "obscene." *Osborne v. Ohio.*

(b) No. The material here is almost certainly "obscene." Under *Miller v. California*, material is obscene if it depicts "patently offensive representations or descriptions of ultimate sex acts, normal or perverted. ... " It must be the case that the average person, applying contemporary community standards, would find that the work taken as a whole appeals to the prurient interest, and that the work taken as a whole lacks serious literary, artistic, political or scientific value. These tests all seem to be satisfied by the material here. However, the mere ***private possession*** of obscene material by an adult may not be made criminal. *Stanley v. Georgia.* Therefore, even though the state might be able to punish the person who sold the magazine to Emilio, it may not punish Emilio for knowingly possessing the material in his house. (As noted in part (a), possession of material showing sexually explicit photos of children does not come within the purview of *Stanley*.)

85. **(a) In theory, the four-part test of *Central Hudson Gas v. Public Service Comm.*,** as modified by later cases. First, the Court will determine whether the commercial speech is protected at all by the First Amendment; commercial speech receives at least partial protection so long as it is not "misleading" and does not propose unlawful activity. Next, the Court asks whether the governmental interest in support of the regulation is ***"substantial."*** Third, the Court decides whether the regulation ***"directly advances"*** the governmental interest being sought. Finally, the Court asks whether the restriction is ***"not more extensive than is necessary"*** to serve the governmental objective. (But some post-*Central Hudson* cases suggest that when a ban on advertising is premised on the idea that less advertising of a harmful product will lead to less consumption, the Court may apply **strict scrutiny**, not the mid-level standard of *Central Hudson Gas*. So the *Central Hudson Gas* test might not be applied here.)

(b) Unclear, but the statute would probably be struck down. Even if the not-so-hard-to-satisfy *Central Hudson Gas* test were applied, the restriction would probably not survive. General cigarette advertising is not "misleading" and does not propose unlawful activity (since Congress has not outlawed the sale of cigarettes), so the speech gets some First Amendment protection. It's true that the government's interest in preventing additional people (especially minors) from becoming "addicted" certainly seems to be "substantial." It's also true that a ban on all print advertising certainly seems to "directly advance" the objective of preventing the creation of new smokers, given the power of advertising. However, *44 Liquormart* says that the anti-consumption impact of the regulation must be "significant," and it's not clear that the impact here would qualify. Furthermore, it's not clear whether the ban is "not more extensive than is necessary" to serve this interest, since there are some less-restrictive methods (e.g., a broader anti-smoking campaign, or higher taxes) that haven't been tried yet.

It may be that the fact that the users that Congress is principally targeting are **minors**, who under state and federal law can't be legal purchasers of the product, may lead the Court to give more deference to the restriction here than it did to the no-liquor-price-ads restriction struck down in *44 Liquormart*. But in *Lorillard Tobacco Co. v. Reilly*, the Court struck down several state regulations against smokeless tobacco advertising where the regulations were designed to protect minors (e.g., a ban on outdoor advertising, and a rule that advertising within a retail store had to be at least five feet above the floor). In *Lorillard*, the Court said that regardless of the importance of protecting minors, "the state may not regulate advertising in a way that interferes materially with the legitimate rights of the tobacco industry, and its **adult customers**, to exchange truthful information." So protection of minors probably won't be enough to save the statute here from being found to flunk the *Central Hudson Gas* requirements that the government regulation (1) *significantly* reduce the use of the harmful substance; and (2) be *"not more extensive than necessary"* to serve the state interest.

IX. REGULATION IN THE CONTEXT OF POLITICAL CAMPAIGNS

A. **Money in political campaigns, generally:** In the modern political campaign, speech and the expenditure of money seem inevitably to go hand in hand. Whether money is spent by a private citizen who is contributing to a candidate, by a political action committee which runs advertisements backing or opposing certain candidates, or by a candidate himself, campaign spending has a strong expression component. Yet if corruption and the appearance of corruption are to be curbed, and if the cynical view that the richest candidate generally wins is to be proved wrong, some sorts of limits on campaign spending are probably necessary.

1. **General principles:** In a series of cases beginning in 1976, the Supreme Court has attempted to work out a line dividing those types of election spending which the states or the federal government may prohibit from those which are constitutionally-protected. While this line is a somewhat blurry one, several basic principles have emerged:

   ❏ *Contributions* made by individuals or groups to individual candidates, to Political Action Committees (PAC's) or to political parties, may be *limited in dollar amount,* so long as the limits are not so low as to substantially interfere with candidates' and parties' ability to *run a competitive election campaign.*

   ❏ On the other hand, *independent expenditures by individuals,* as well as by *corporations and unions,* may *not* be limited at all.

   ❏ Similarly, expenditures by *candidates from their own funds* may *not* be limited at all.

   ❏ Congress may not treat *corporations* and unions *less favorably than individuals* (e.g., by preventing corporations from paying for independent election-time ads out of their own treasuries).

B. *Buckley v Valeo:* The seminal case on the First Amendment implications of campaign-finance regulation is *Buckley v. Valeo,* 424 U.S. 1 (1976), in which the Supreme Court upheld some but not all provisions of the Federal Election Campaign Act of 1971 (FECA), as amended in 1974 (shortly after Watergate).

1. **Statutory provisions:** Of the several provisions of the Act whose constitutionality the Court reviewed in *Buckley,* two are of concern to us here: (1) the Act's limitation on *individual political contributions* to $1,000 to any single candidate per election (with a corollary $25,000 limit on *aggregate* contributions by any one individual in any year); and (2) its limitations on *expenditures,* including a $1,000-per-year limit on *independent* expenditures by individuals and groups on behalf of a "clearly identified" candidate, various limits on expenditures *by a candidate* from personal or family funds, and various limits on *total* campaign spending.

2. **Result:** In brief, the Court's *per curiam* decision *sustained* the contribution limits, but found *unconstitutional* the limits on independent expenditures by individuals, on expenditures by a candidate from personal or family funds, and on aggregate campaign spending.

3. **Contribution limits upheld:** The Court applied what it called its "closest scrutiny" to the *contribution* limits. But despite the close scrutiny, the Court *upheld* the limits, on the following analysis:

   a. **Marginal restriction:** Although these limits placed some quantity restriction on political expression, the restriction was only *"marginal."* Since a dollar contribution does not communicate the "underlying basis" for the contributor's support of the candidate, the amount of "communication" being done by the contributor *does not increase* as the size of the contribution increases — whatever expression takes place when a contribution is made derives from the "undifferentiated, symbolic act of contributing," whose symbolism is largely independent of dollar amount.

b. **Strong governmental interest:** On the other side of the scale, the governmental interest supporting the limits was a powerful one, that of limiting the ***actuality and appearance of corruption*** resulting from large individual contributions, which are sometimes made to secure a political *quid pro quo* from the candidate. ***No less restrictive alternative*** would have been adequate; for instance, anti-bribery and disclosure laws could not deal fully with the need to root out all apparent as well as actual opportunity for corruption.

4. **Expenditures by individuals:** By contrast, the Court struck down the limitations on ***expenditures*** by ***individuals acting independently*** from candidates. The Court concluded these independent-expenditure limits imposed "***direct and substantial restraints*** on the quantity of political speech," and unconstitutionally limited political expression "at the core … of First Amendment freedoms." For instance, the restrictions would have made it impossible for an individual or association legally to take out a single quarter-page advertisement backing a particular candidate in a big-city newspaper.

    a. **State interest insufficient:** When viewed with the requisite "exacting scrutiny," the governmental interest in combating corruption, asserted in support of the limits on expenditures by individuals, was ***inadequate***.

        i. **Wouldn't eliminate *quid pro quos*:** First, not all apparent or actual *quid pro quo* deals would be eliminated, since the limits applied only to expenditures "advocating the election or defeat" of a "clearly identified candidate," so that ads could still be run supporting the candidate's ***views*** (as part of a *quid pro quo*), without expressly advocating his election.

        ii. **Complete independence reduces danger:** Secondly, the expenditure limits only applied where the expenditures were made ***totally independently*** of the candidate and his campaign; spending which was controlled by or coordinated with the campaign was treated as a contribution. Where such complete independence existed, a carefully-orchestrated *quid pro quo* was less likely, the Court concluded, making the need for the contribution limits less pressing.

5. **Spending of candidate's own money:** The Court in *Buckley* also struck down limits on the amount that a ***candidate*** may spend from his ***own personal or family funds***. The interest in preventing actual or apparent corruption did not apply to this situation, since obviously a candidate would not bribe himself. And the interest in ***equalizing the resources*** of competing candidates was not well served by the spending limit, since a candidate who spent less of his own money than his opponent could nonetheless outspend the latter by raising more money from outside sources. Therefore, no state interest was sufficient to outweigh the candidate's own "First Amendment right to engage in the discussion of public issues and vigorously and tirelessly advocate his own election. …"

    a. **Still valid:** This principle that the amount a candidate may spend from his own resources may not be capped remains intact — and indeed has been expanded — in the Roberts court. See the discussion on p. 600 of *Citizens United*, where the Court held that even ***corporations and unions***, not just individuals, must be permitted to ***spend uncapped amounts*** of their own funds to buy advertising for or against a candidate, as long as the corporation or union acts independently of the candidate.

6. **Limits on total campaign spending:** Finally, the Court struck down limits on what a candidate could ***spend from all sources combined***. Candidates have a First Amendment right to spend as much as they wish to promote their own political views, and the governmental interest in curbing the skyrocketing costs of political campaigns is not sufficient to outweigh that right, the Court held. (But Congress may create a scheme for ***publicly funding*** elections, in which case the candidate *may* be required to choose between respecting an aggregate spending limit and losing the public subsidy.)

7. **Other opinions:** Only three Justices joined the Court's *Buckley* opinion in its entirety. Five others concurred only in part, and one did not participate.

   a. **Burger's concurrence:** Justice Burger dissented from the plurality's upholding of the contribution limits. In his view, contributions, no less than expenditures, were ways of communicating. Contributions were simply a way of "pooling" money, and were thus associational activities comparable to, say, volunteer work; therefore, freedom of ***association*** as well as freedom of speech required that these not be restricted unless there was no less-restrictive satisfactory alternative. In Burger's view, anti-bribery laws and disclosure requirements could solve the corruption problems inherent in large contributions just as they could in the expenditure context.

   b. **White's concurrence:** Justice White, like Justice Burger, saw no principled distinction between expenditures and contributions. But in sharp contrast to Justice Burger's view, White believed that ***both*** the contribution and expenditure limits were ***valid***. He disagreed with the plurality's equation of money with speech. Also, he would have deferred much more completely to Congress' superior knowledge of what motivates politicians, and to its conclusion that expenditure limits on both private citizens and candidates are needed to accomplish the goals of preventing bribery and corruption and equalizing "access to the political area."

8. ***Buckley* remains valid (*Randall v. Sorrell*):** A 2006 decision involving Vermont's campaign-finance reform statute shows that ***Buckley's general approach remains valid*** in the Roberts Court. That case, *Randall v. Sorrell*, 548 U.S. 230 (2006), held that:

   ❏ limits on ***candidate expenditures*** remain flatly ***unconstitutional***, as *Buckley* had held them to be; and

   ❏ limits on ***contributions*** will often be constitutional (as the ones in *Buckley* had been held to be), but the particular Vermont limitations at issue were so low (e.g., $400 per election cycle for gubernatorial candidates) that they ***interfered with candidates' ability run a competitive election***, and thus ***violated*** the First Amendment.

9. **Attempts to level the candidate playing field:** In the decades after *Buckley*'s ruling that limits on a candidate's expenditure of her own personal funds violated her First Amendment rights, both Congress and many states have sought to find other ways to ***reduce the advantages held by wealthy candidates willing to spend their own funds***. Essentially, legislatures have devised arrangements under which, if a wealthy candidate spends a large amount of his own or well-heeled contributors' funds, the opposing non-wealthy candidate gets to ***"level the playing field"*** by either ***qualifying for public financing***, or being able to ***receive larger private donations*** than would otherwise be allowed.

But in a pair of decisions, one from 2008 and the other from 2011, the Court by a 5-4 vote has ***struck down two of these "level the playing field" structures,*** one created by Congress and the other by Arizona. In both cases, the majority's theory was that the ***wealthy candidate's*** right to ***spend on her campaign*** was being ***substantially and unconstitution-***

ally burdened by having that spending trigger extra campaign money for the non-wealthy opponent.

a. **Millionaire's Amendment:** The first of the cases involved a federal statute, the so-called *"Millionaire's Amendment,"* passed by Congress in 2002. This amendment said that when a candidate for the House of Representatives spent more than $350,000 of his own funds, the candidate's *adversary* could receive individual contributions at *three times the usual rate* (i.e., subject to a per-donor limit of $6,900 rather than the usual $2,300). The idea was to "even the playing field," so that the millionaire candidate wouldn't have an unfair advantage from his ability to self-fund without limit. But in *Davis v. F.E.C.*, 128 S.Ct. 2759 (2008), the Court by a 5-4 vote found that the Millionaire's Amendment *violated the First Amendment rights of wealthy candidates.*

    i. **Burden on speech:** The majority agreed with the plaintiff (a wealthy candidate) that the amendment required candidates to "choose between the First Amendment right to engage in unfettered political speech and subjection to discriminatory fund-raising limitations." Therefore, the amendment imposed a *"substantial burden"* on the exercise of the First Amendment right to use personal funds for campaign speech, triggering strict scrutiny.

        (1) **Flunks strict scrutiny:** The measure could not survive that strict scrutiny, the majority held. The measure did not further the governmental interest in eliminating corruption, because a candidate's use of his own funds *reduces* the threat of corruption rather than increasing it. And as for the asserted interest in *"level[ing] electoral opportunities* for candidates of different personal wealth," this was *not a legitimate governmental objective* because it would "permit Congress to arrogate the voters' authority to evaluate the strengths of candidates competing for office."

b. **Right to public funding:** The second case involved an Arizona statute that created a *voluntary public financing system* to fund the primary and general campaigns of candidates for state office. Candidates could agree to limit their own spending to $500, and thereby receive public funds. The key innovation was that during the course of the campaign, if a candidate who did not take the public option then spent more than a certain amount of her own money (or raised more than a certain amount from contributors), the publicly-funded candidate would *get additional equalizing or matching funds.* In *Arizona Free Enterprise Club's Freedom Club PAC v. Bennett*, 131 S.Ct. 2806 (2011), a five-Justice majority found that this violated the First Amendment rights of the privately financed candidate, because it *"substantially burdens protected political speech without serving a compelling state interest."*

    i. **Rationale:** The majority relied on the rationale of the decision in the "Millionaire's Amendment" case (*Davis v. FEC, supra*). Since "each personal dollar spent by the privately financed candidate results in an award of almost one additional dollar to his opponent," the structure "forces the privately financed candidate to *'shoulder a special and potentially significant burden'* when choosing to exercise his First Amendment right to spend funds on behalf of his candidacy."

        (1) **Not permitted to level the field:** The majority believed that "leveling the playing field," as Arizona was trying to do, did not justify these burdens. "It is *not legitimate* for the government to attempt to equalize electoral opportuni-

ties in this manner. ... Campaigning for office is *not a game."* Some public funding schemes are constitutionally acceptable. But the one here *"inhibit[s] robust and wide-open political debate* without sufficient justification[.]"

    ii. Dissent: The four dissenters, in an opinion by Justice Kagan, believed that the matching-funds mechanism here was perfectly proper. Far from substantially burdening speech, the program *"creates more speech* and thereby *broadens public debate."*

C. Contributions to Political Action Committees: The original election statute reviewed in *Buckley* also prohibited individuals and associations from contributing more than $5,000 per year to any "multi-candidate political committee" (commonly called a *Political Action Committee* or *PAC*). This limitation was *upheld* in *California Medical Assn. v. FEC,* 453 U.S. 182 (1981).

    1. Contributions by Political Action Committees: But a $1,000 limitation on the amount that may be contributed *by* a PAC to a Presidential candidate was *struck down,* in *FEC v. National Conservative Political Action Committee,* 470 U.S. 480 (1985).

D. "Soft money" and pre-election "issue ads" (*McConnell, Wisconsin Right to Life* and *Citizens United*): The federal campaign finance reform measures approved by the Court in *Buckley* turned out not to be tremendously effective over the several decades that followed. Sophisticated and wealthy donors and advocacy organizations — and the national political parties — bypassed these measures by various devices, most notably the institutions of *"soft money"* and *"issue ads."* Finally, Congress responded by enacting the Bipartisan Campaign Reform Act of 2002 ("BCRA"), popularly known as the *McCain-Feingold Act* after its chief Senate sponsors. In an important trio of decisions, the Court first approved the key measures of the BCRA, but then (after a switch in Court personnel) reversed itself by striking one of the two key measures.

The three cases are: *McConnell v. Federal Election Comm.,* 540 U.S. 93 (2003) (approving both key measures, mostly by a 5-4 vote); *Federal Election Commission v. Wisconsin Right to Life,* 127 S.ct. 449 (2007) (dramatically narrowing the scope of the ban on election-time issue ads, also by a 5-4 vote); and *Citizens United v. Federal Election Commission,* 130 S.Ct. 876 (2010) (stripping nearly all the rest of the BCRA's regulation of such issue ads, by holding, again by a 5-4 vote, that *corporations and unions can't be treated worse than individuals*). *Citizens United,* in particular, is the most important campaign-finance decisions by the Court since *Buckley.*

    1. Twin targets of the BCRA: The BCRA addressed the two practices that Congress believed were the most egregious ways in which wealthy donors and special-interest groups were corrupting and distorting the federal election process:

        a. Soft money: First was the giving of *"soft money"* donations. Political contributions whose amounts were regulated by the FECA (the act upheld in *Buckley*) were and are known as *"hard money"* donations. But the FECA as interpreted by the Federal Election Commission treated certain donations and expenditures as not falling within this regulated, hard-money classification; these unregulated sums are what is known as soft money. For instance, donors could contribute *unlimited soft-money sums to the Democratic and Republican national parties* (or special committees run by those parties), and the parties could then *re-spend the money* however they wanted as long as the funds were not used to expressly advocate the election or defeat of a particular candidate. Such large soft-money donations could be given by wealthy individuals, corporations, labor unions, and anyone else, as long as the funds were used in this no-advocacy-of-election-or-defeat-of-a-specific-candidate manner.

   i.   Get-out-the-vote and other uses of soft money: So, for instance, the national political parties could raise large sums from wealthy donors, then spend those sums on activities like *get-out-the-vote drives* (directed at voters expected to vote for the party putting on the drive), and *generic party advertising* (e.g., "Vote for the Democratic ticket this November 2nd.")

b. Issue ads: The second practice that was upsetting Congress was the use of *special-issue broadcast ads* by groups like *corporations* and *labor unions*. If a corporation or union wanted to buy an ad expressly advocating the election or defeat of a particular candidate, that ad had to be paid for with hard (and thus tightly-regulated) dollars, and lots of information about the sponsor of the ad had to be disclosed. But if the sponsor avoided the "magic words" — i.e., words expressly advocating a particular candidate's election or defeat — then the ad could be funded by *unlimited sums furnished by the corporation or union*, and with no disclosure of the sponsors' identity. These ads are generically known as *"issue ads"* (and ones attacking rather than supporting a particular candidate are known as *"attack ads"*).Thus a Republican-leaning advocacy group might purchase ads attacking Democratic Congressman Joe Smith's voting record on Social Security, and then conclude, "Call Joe Smith and tell him to stop weakening Social Security." These attack ads were in fact often *more effective* than direct "vote for [or against] Jane Doe" ads.

2. Congress attacks the twin evils: So by enacting the BCRA, Congress tried to curb the abuses associated with both unregulated soft money and with issue ads purchased by that unregulated money. In doing so, Congress believed that it was acting to reduce not only corruption but the *appearance* of corruption, stemming from wealthy donors' apparent attempt to purchase access to office holders. The heart of the BCRA consisted of Titles I and II.

a. Title I on soft money: Title I of the BCRA was Congress' attempt to plug the soft-money loophole. The main provision in Title I *prohibited the national political parties and their committees from soliciting, receiving or spending any soft money.* As the *McConnell* majority later summarized this provision, Title I "takes national parties out of the soft-money business."

b. Title II on issue ads: Title II mainly *prohibited corporations* and *labor unions* from using their general funds for *broadcast advertisements naming specific candidates for federal office near election time.*

   i.   Electioneering Communications: Title II defined a new category called *"Electioneering Communications,"* which consisted of *TV and radio ads,* broadcast within 60 days before a general election or 30 days before a primary, and referring to an *identified candidate* for federal office.

   ii. Ban on ads: Title II then said that *corporations and labor unions may not use their general funds to pay for Electioneering Communications,* and must instead pay for these with money from their Political Action Committees (see *supra,* p. 597).

iii. **Significance:** Since PACs are *subject to contribution limits* and other types of regulation (e.g., the requirement that the names of individual donors be *publicly disclosed*), Title II significantly restricted the ways in which *corporations* (including *non-profit advocacy corporations* like the ACLU and the NRA) could pay for and carry out their own election-time broadcast advertising.

3. **The twin evils meet different fates:** Both Title I on soft money and Title II on issue ads were promptly attacked in multiple litigations. As we'll see below, as of mid-2010, Title I's *soft-money* restrictions have *survived* constitutional scrutiny, but Title II's restrictions on *corporations' and unions' right to pay for issue ads* have been completely *overruled* as First Amendment violations. We consider the attacks on each title independently, first Title I (in Paragraph 4) and then Title II (in Paragraph 5).

4. **Title I (soft-money ban) survives:** The ban on *soft-money donations* imposed by Title I of the BCRA has, at least for now, survived First Amendment attack. That happened in *McConnell, supra,* the 2003 case that was the first, and least successful, of the trio of First Amendment attacks on the BCRA.

   a. **Attacked by odd grouping:** In *McConnell,* a consortium of non-profit groups attacked the constitutionality of the BCRA, including such unlikely allies as the American Civil Liberties Union and the National Rifle Association. (They attacked both Title I and Title II; here, we cover the Title I attack, with the Title II attack postponed to p. 600 below).

   b. **Court upholds Title I in *McConnell*:** The *McConnell* Court *upheld the constitutionality of Title I,* as part of a decision *upholding nearly all of the BCRA.*[8] The majority opinion on Title I was jointly authored by Justices Stevens and O'Connor (joined by Souter, Ginsburg and Breyer). Most of the case was decided on a 5-4 vote.

      i. **Rationale:** The majority wrote that soft money had enabled candidates and parties to *circumvent* FECA's limits. The majority agreed with the congressional drafters of Title I that there was ample evidence to support the conclusion that large soft-money contributions to the national political parties had had a *corrupting influence,* or at the very least had given rise to the *appearance* of corruption. There was "no meaningful distinction between the national party committees and the public officials who control them." There was evidence that "candidates and donors alike [have] exploited the soft-money loophole, the former to increase their prospects of election and the latter to *create debt on the part of officeholders,* with the national parties serving as *willing intermediaries*[.]" Therefore, it was not a violation of donors' First Amendment rights for Congress to regulate donations so as to curb the reality or appearance of that corruption.

   c. **Dissents in *McConnell*:** Four justices — Kennedy, Scalia, Thomas and Rehnquist — *dissented* from the majority's wholesale upholding of Title I in *McConnell.*

      i. **Scalia's dissent:** Justice Scalia's dissent said that the majority had "smiled with favor upon a law that cuts to the heart of what the First Amendment is meant to protect: the right to *criticize the government.*" In particular, he thought the law

---

8. The one part of the Act that was struck down was a ban on contributions by *minors* — Congress was worried that rich parents would funnel, through their minor children, contributions in excess of the hard-money limits. But the Court said that there was no evidence that such evasions were occurring.

improperly allowed Congress to *insulate its own incumbent members against criticism* by political parties and corporations. The BCRA might be "evenhanded" in the sense that it similarly prohibited criticism of those running *against* incumbents. But "this is an area in which *evenhandedness is not fairness*. [If] incumbents and challengers are limited to the same quantity of electioneering, *incumbents are favored.*"

d.   **Present status:** Title I's ban on soft-money donations *remains in force*. Nothing in the revolutionary case of *Citizens United* (*infra*, pp. 600-602), giving corporations and unions the same independent-campaign-spending rights as individuals, directly invalidates the soft-money ban upheld in *McConnell*.

   i.   **Vulnerable:**   However, notice that Title I treats the *national political parties less favorably* than all other non-candidate election players, since outside groups (e.g., Political Action Committees) may receive unlimited donations to use for electioneering, whereas the national political parties may not. The same logic that led the Court in *Citizens United* to say that Congress couldn't radically disfavor one type of player (corporations) as to issue ads, arguably applies the same way to prevent Congress from disfavoring one type of player (national political parties) as to political fund-raising. Therefore, Title I may not survive in a post-*Citizens United* world.

5.   **Title II (issue-ad ban) struck down:** Recall (p. 598 *supra*) that Title II of the BCRA banned *issue ads*, i.e., pre-election ads mentioning a candidate, paid for by corporations or unions. That ban, unlike Title I's ban on soft-money, has *not survived* in the Supreme Court.

   a.   **Title II initially upheld :** In *McConnell*, *supra*, a majority of the Court thought that Title II, like Title I, was *constitutional*. Those attacking Title II argued that under *Buckley*, speakers had an absolute First Amendment right to engage in "issue advocacy" (as opposed to express advocacy of the election or defeat of a particular candidate). But the majority disagreed: corporate-paid broadcast ads near the time of an election, mentioning specific candidates, were just as clearly intended to influence the election as were the type of express-advocacy ads regulated under *Buckley*. Therefore, it did not violate the First Amendment for these issue ads to be regulated in the same way.

   b.   **Reversal of Court's view on Title II:** But beginning four years after *McConnell*, and following a change in the Court's membership, the Court *reversed itself* as to Title II's ban on issue ads near election time. In a pair of cases, *FEC v. Wisconsin Right to Life* (2007) and *Citizens United v. FEC* (2010), Justice O'Connor's replacement by Justice Alito produced a *switch* to 5-4 the other way, with the ultimate result that *even corporations and labor unions may run whatever issue ads they want during political campaigns*, as long as they *operate independently* of the candidate.

   c.   **Narrowed in *Wisconsin Right to Life*:** First, in *FEC v. Wisconsin Right to Life*, 551 U.S. 449 (2007), the Court dramatically narrowed the scope of the ban on issue ads.

   d.   **Ban overturned (*Citizens United*):** Then, in the much more important *Citizens United v. FEC*, 130 S.Ct. 876 (2010), by the same 5-4 alignment as in *Wisconsin Right to Life*, the Court explicitly *overruled* the part of *McConnell* that had upheld Title II. *Citizens United* establishes that *corporations have a full measure of First Amend-*

ment protection in the area of politics, and that Congress may not prohibit them from using their *general funds to run campaign advertising*, as long as the corporation *acts independently* of the candidate.

i. **Facts:** Citizens United, a non-profit organization that was the plaintiff, made a documentary presenting an unflattering portrait of then-presidential candidate Hillary Clinton. Citizens United wanted to pay for a cable TV video-on-demand presentation of the movie shortly before the 2008 Democratic presidential primary. Regulations of the Federal Election Commission prohibited Citizens from paying for this broadcast with its unrestricted funds, on the theory that this would be a forbidden corporate-paid "electioneering communication." Citizen United sued the FEC for a ruling that its free speech rights had been violated.

ii. **Plaintiff wins:** By a 5-4 vote, Citizens United *prevailed*. In a very broad opinion by Justice Kennedy, the majority held that Title II's ban on corporate issue ads violated corporations' free speech rights.

    (1) *Austin* **and** *McConnell* **overruled:** In reaching this conclusion, Kennedy's opinion squarely overruled the Title II holding of *McConnell* (*supra*, p. 600). The opinion rejected the rationale that corporate campaign speech could be limited because of its distorting effects. To Kennedy, this rationale would *reach too far*: "If the *anti-distortion rationale* were to be accepted ... it would permit government to *ban political speech* simply because the speaker is an association that has taken on the corporate form." Nor did Kennedy believe that independent corporate campaign expenditures could be banned in order to *prevent corruption* or the appearance of corruption; an anti-corruption rationale justified limits on contributions to *candidates*, he said, but there was no evidence that independent corporate expenditures that were *not coordinated* with a candidate fostered corruption or the appearance of corruption.

    (2) **Censorship:** Kennedy concluded that banning corporations from making independent expenditures to broadcast political messages *amounted to censorship*: "When government seeks to use its full power, including the criminal law, to *command where a person may get his or her information* or *what trusted source he or she may not hear*, it *uses censorship to control thought.* ... The Government *may not suppress political speech* on the basis of the *speaker's corporate identity.*"

    (3) **Disclaimer and disclosure provisions upheld:** But Kennedy's opinion *upheld* provisions in the BCRA requiring "*disclaimers*" and "*disclosures*." Therefore, Congress continues to have the right to insist that (1) any televised electioneering communication — whether paid for by a corporation or not — must *state who was responsible for it*, and that it was *not authorized by the candidate* (the *disclaimer* requirement) and (2) anyone who spends more than $10,000 a year on such communications must *file a statement* with the FEC listing various information, including the *names of certain contributors* (the *disclosure* requirement).

iii. Dissent: Justice Stevens (joined by Justices Ginsburg, Breyer and Sotomayor) *dissented* from the key holding in *Citizens United*, that Title II's ban on corporate-funded issue ads violated corporations' free speech rights.

(1) Rationale: Stevens believed that Congress was entitled to *distinguish between corporate and human speakers.* Lawmakers have a "compelling constitutional basis" to guard against the *potentially-damaging effects of corporate spending* in local and national elections, he said, a basis reflected in the the special limitations that Congress had imposed on corporate campaign spending ever since a 1907 law. The majority's rule "threatens to *undermine the integrity of elected institutions* across the Nation."

(2) Regulation, not ban: Stevens rejected the majority's assertion that BCRA Title II was a "ban" on corporate political spending. Corporations were free under the BCRA to fund issue ads through a PAC (see *supra*, p. 597). It was true that running a PAC involves some administrative bookkeeping. But requiring that corporate-funded issue ads be administered through a regulated PAC was far from turning the FEC into a "censor," as the majority was claiming.

(3) Antidistortion and anticorruption: Stevens argued that regulation of corporate electioneering expenditures was a necessary means of avoiding corporations' *unfair influence in the electoral process.* Unregulated corporate expenditures would be likely to *drown out non-corporate voices*, and to "generate the impression that corporations dominate our democracy." The majority's approach was premised on the idea that "there is no such thing as too much speech." This might be true "if individuals ... had *infinite free time* to listen to and contemplate every last bit of speech uttered by anyone, anywhere[.]" But, he continued, "[i]n the real world, we have seen, corporate domination of the airwaves prior to an election may *decrease the average listener's exposure to relevant viewpoints*[.]"

(4) Protection of shareholders: Furthermore, Stevens argued, when corporations use general treasury funds to praise or attack a particular candidate, "it is the *shareholders* [who] are effectively *footing the bill*"; Congress' decision to require corporations to use the PAC mechanism ensures that shareholders are *not forced to pay to support candidates against their will*, and that "managers do not use general treasuries to *advance personal agendas*."

iv. Unions: *Citizens United* dealt directly only with speech by corporations, not by other types of entities such as *labor unions* (who were also forbidden by Title II to run issue ads). But the rationale of the case is broad — the majority says that for First Amendment purposes, the particular form of legal organization doesn't matter. Therefore, *Citizens United* strongly implies that independent campaign spending by labor unions *cannot be barred or heavily regulated — or treated much differently* — than such spending by individuals.

v. Significance: *Citizens United* will likely lead to a significant *increase in corporations' and labor unions' direct campaign spending.* As long as the corporation or union acts "*independently*" of the candidate that it is supporting, and discloses to the world that that is what it is doing, there seems to be *no limit to how much the entity can spend* to advocate the election or defeat of a particular candidate, right up until election day.

6. **Prognosis:** So here is where federal regulation of *soft money* and *issue ads* seems to stand after *McConnell* and *Citizens United*:

❑ Title I's ban on *soft money contributions to the national political parties* remains *constitutional*, at least for now. There is no indication that a majority of the present Court, even after *Citizens United*, disagrees with *McConnell*'s conclusion that Congress can constitutionally fight the appearance of corruption by tightly regulating the making of cash contributions to candidates or parties. (However, the logic of *Citizens* may be extended to prohibit Congress from treating the national political parties less favorably than independent advocacy groups, in which case Title I might end up being struck down, too.)

❑ Title II's ban on *"electioneering communications"* is *defunct* — all types of speakers, including *corporations and unions*, can spend *apparently-limitless sums* from their general treasuries to advocate for or against particular candidates, as long as the spending is *"independent,"* i.e., not coordinated with the candidate.

❑ Consequently, corporations, unions and *non-party special-interest groups* will all likely have *more influence* on elections than they used to have, because of their ability to spend limitless sums on political ads. Conversely, the *national political parties* may *lose influence* relative to these other kinds of groups, since the political parties' fundraising abilities have been restricted and the independent entities' fundraising and fund-spending abilities have not.

❑ The core distinction dating back to *Buckley* — between *contributions* to candidates, and *independent spending* to help elect a candidate — *remains in effect*. Contributions can be heavily regulated (because they give the appearance of corruption), whereas independent expenditures cannot (because they're less likely to feed corruption or the appearance of it). This distinction continues to be much criticized, but there's no sign the present Court is ready to abandon it.

E. **Campaign spending by political parties:** Campaign spending by *political parties* on behalf of congressional candidates *may not be limited*, as long as the party is working *"independently"* of the candidate rather than in "coordination" with her. This was the result of the pre-*McConnell* case of *Colorado Republican Federal Campaign Committee v. Federal Election Commission*, 518 U.S. 604 (1996) ("*Colorado Republican I*").

1. **Limited by BCRA:** But the BCRA (*supra*, p. 597) means that such spending by political parties will be limited, because the parties are now restricted to *raising only tightly-regulated hard-money donations* from which to make even such candidate-independent expenditures.

2. **Limits on coordinated spending are constitutional:** Furthermore, it is *constitutional* for Congress to limit campaign spending by parties that *is coordinated* with the candidate. The court so concluded in *Federal Election Commission v. Colorado Republican Federal Campaign Committee*, 533 U.S. 431 (2001) ("*Colorado Republican II*").

3. **Effect of *Citizens United***: *Citizens United* does not seem to change these twin rules that the national political parties may raise only highly regulated hard-money donations, and that the parties' spending may be limited when it is coordinated with the candidate. However, the core philosophy articulated by the majority in *Citizens United* — that one class of speakers may not be systematically disfavored — may eventually lead to a striking down of the BCRA's ban on soft-money donations to the national parties.

F. **How low can limits be set:** We know from *Buckley* that government can set a dollar limit on campaign contributions, and we also know from that case that a $1,000 limit (in 1976 dollars) per-contributor/per-candidate is valid. But may the limits constitutionally be *set even lower*? As the result of a 2000 case, *Nixon v. Shrink Missouri Government PAC*, 523 U.S. 666 (2000), we know that the answer is *yes*: as long as the limitation is not so radical as to *"render contributions pointless,"* it will be *sustained* even though it buys far less campaign speech than $1,000 did in 1976. (So, for instance, a limit of $1,075 in donations for statewide offices was upheld in *Shrink Missouri*.)

   1. **Applies to states:** *Shrink Missouri* means that the **states** may limit campaign contributions for state elections, just as *Buckley* and *McConnell* said that Congress may do for federal elections.

   2. **Some limits are too low:** In only one case has the Court concluded that contribution limits were **unconstitutionally low.** In *Randall v. Sorrell, supra*, p. 595, the Court concluded that Vermont's limits — for instance, a $400 limit on what an individual or party could contribute to a candidate for governor during a two-year election cycle — were so low as to "disproportionately burden" the First Amendment rights of candidates, parties and volunteers. Only in a truly extraordinary case — where the limits are so low that they prevent challengers from making an effective campaign against incumbents, for instance — will the Court find that the limits are unconstitutionally low. (No majority of the Roberts Court has been able to agree on a standard for determining when contribution limits are "too low.")

G. **Corporate and judicial expression during campaigns:** So far, our discussion of free speech and campaigns has focused mostly on money. We turn now to two other issues involving regulation of campaign speech: (1) to what extent may political expression be regulated on account of the fact that the speaker is a **business** or **corporation**?; and (2) in places where **judges** must run for office, what restrictions may be placed upon the candidates' campaign speech? The Supreme Court has issued one decision on each of these questions; in each case, the Court has ruled in favor of the First Amendment claim by the speaker or candidate.

   1. **Corporate political expression:** On the issue of campaign-related speech by **businesses** and **corporations**, the Court has held that political expression may not be denied Fourteenth Amendment protection merely because its source is a **corporation** rather than an individual. In *First National Bank of Boston v. Bellotti*, 435 U.S. 765 (1978) the Court, by a 5-4 vote, struck down a Massachusetts ban on **corporate political advocacy**. The decision relied on the **public's right to know**, rather than on the corporation's right to speak.

       a. **Reaffirmed in *Citizens United***: *Citizens United* (*supra*, p. 600) makes it clear that *Bellotti* is still good law. The majority in *Citizens* cited *Bellotti* for the proposition that "First Amendment protection extends to corporations." After *Citizens United*, it appears that independent political expression by a business or corporation cannot be treated any less favorably than such expression by an individual.

2. Campaign speech in judicial elections: The Court has similarly protected campaign speech by those seeking election to *judgeships*. The Court struck down a Minnesota rule that a candidate for judicial office shall not "announce his or her views on disputed legal or political issues." *Republican Party of Minn. v. White*, 536 U.S. 765 (2002).

    a. Purpose of the rule: Drafters of the rule reasoned that when a candidate publicly makes known her views on issues that may come before her court, the *due process rights* of later litigants are likely to be abridged.

    b. Struck down: By a 5-4 vote, the Court struck down Minnesota's rule, on the theory that it violated the *First Amendment rights of judicial candidates.* The opinion, by Justice Scalia, conceded that opposition to judicial elections "may be well taken." But, he said, "the First Amendment does not permit [opponents of judicial elections] to achieve [their] goal by leaving the principle of elections in place while preventing candidates from discussing what the elections are about."

    c. Dissent: The four dissenters contended that the Minnesota rule was a reasonable way for Minnesota to pursue its legitimate goal of maintaining judicial impartiality.

X. SOME SPECIAL CONTEXTS

A. Scope: We now examine several particular contexts in which special First Amendment problems have arisen. Generally, these special problems arise because the First Amendment comes into conflict with unusually strong "public policy" interests, for instance, the interest in running an effective public-school system, or in the smooth administration of justice.

B. Schools: The conflict between First Amendment values and society's substantial interest in pursuing other important values can be seen clearly in the *public school* context. On the one hand, the public school system is the community's principal means for transmitting knowledge and values from one generation to the next; this process unavoidably involves teaching students how, and sometimes what, to think. See 96 HARV. L. REV. 151. Yet students and teachers have First Amendment rights, which they do not completely surrender when they enter the school.

1. Reluctance to intervene: The Supreme Court has generally been reluctant to intervene in school authorities' handling of school operations. The Court will not intervene in those operations unless "basic constitutional values" are "directly and sharply implicate[d]." *Epperson v. Arkansas*, 393 U.S. 97 (1968).

2. Illustrations of interference: But the Court has, nonetheless, occasionally held that school authorities have violated the First Amendment or other constitutional rights of students or teachers. For instance, the Court has held that the state *may not forbid* the *teaching of foreign languages*; see *Meyer v. Nebraska*, 262 U.S. 390 (1923) (decided on substantive due process grounds; see *supra*, p. 173). Similarly, the Court has held that school children *cannot be required to salute the flag; West Virginia Bd. of Ed. v. Barnette*, 319 U.S. 624 (1943). And recall that a student's right to wear an armband and to protest symbolically against the Vietnam War was not permitted to be suppressed by school authorities, at least where this was done to suppress a particular point of view; *Tinker v. Des Moines School District*, 393 U.S. 503 (1969) (*supra*, p. 559).

a. Permissible purposes: However, school authorities may act to preserve *discipline*, the *rights of other students*, and the *educational function of the school*. For instance, the Court in *Tinker* indicated that the armband display could have been prohibited if there had been a showing that it did or would substantially interfere with school work or discipline.

3. **Choice of materials to be taught:** Perhaps the most difficult First Amendment issue in the school context is the extent to which that Amendment restricts educators' choices of *curriculum* and *teaching materials*. Educators must of course be given the right to determine what is to be taught in the public schools. Yet there is a potential conflict between this right and the First Amendment principle that "no official, high or petty, can prescribe what shall be orthodox in politics, nationalism, religion, or other matters of opinion. ... " *West Virginia Bd. of Ed. v. Barnette, supra.*

     a. School libraries: The only Supreme Court case to deal directly with this conflict did so in a limited context, the right of school authorities to *remove books from a school library.* In *Board of Education v. Pico*, 457 U.S. 853 (1982), a plurality of the Court held that such a removal must not be carried out in a *"narrowly partisan or political manner,"* or for the purpose of denying students access to *ideas with which the authorities disagree.*

       i. Facts: The school board in *Pico* ordered nine books to be removed from its high school and junior high school libraries, including Richard Wright's *Black Boy* and Eldridge Cleaver's *Soul on Ice*. The books were all on a list published by a conservative parents' group and were labelled by the board as "anti-American, anti-Christian, anti-Semitic, and just plain filthy."

       ii. Holding: Because of the procedural posture, the Supreme Court did not directly decide whether the school board had violated the Constitution in ordering the removal of the books. The plurality did, however, articulate what it saw as the appropriate constitutional standard: a school board has wide authority in determining what books to remove from a library, but it may not remove books for the purpose of *denying access to ideas for political or partisan reasons*. As an extreme example, the plurality noted that a Democratic school board could not, motivated by party affiliation, order the removal of all books written by Republicans.

     b. Curriculum and textbooks: It is hard to know what standard the Court will apply to the issue of school authorities' discretion to select the *curriculum* and *required textbooks*. Although, as noted, the Court will probably recognize greater discretion here than in the library-book-removal situation of *Pico*, it is not clear that this discretion will be much broader. Something like *Pico*'s ban on "narrow partisan or political motives" will probably be applied in this situation as well. For instance, it is doubtful that a majority of the Court would uphold a school board's rule that no teacher may express in class the opinion that the war in Vietnam was morally and legally wrong.

       i. Teacher's own expression of views: At the same time, *individual teachers* may probably take actions which a school board would not be permitted to take on a system-wide basis. For instance, a teacher may certainly constitutionally express to his students a view about the morality or legality of the Vietnam War, whether or not the school system may formulate an "official" view on the same subject; this distinction is appropriate because an individual teacher's views do not represent an "official" or "orthodox" position in the same way that a system-wide position does.

4. **Speech by students:** What about *speech by students?* Students do not "shed their constitutional rights to freedom of speech or expression at the schoolhouse gate." *Tinker v. Des Moines School District*, 393 U.S. 503 (1969), discussed more extensively, *supra*, p. 559. Thus in *Tinker*, the Court held that the First Amendment rights of several high school and junior high school students were abridged when they were suspended for wearing black armbands in school as a symbol of opposition to the Vietnam War.

However, the Supreme Court has recognized some important *limits* on *Tinker*. Two of the more important are that school authorities are free to limit student speech when:

[1] this is needed to *maintain school discipline* and fulfill the school's *educational mission*; or

[2] the speech *advocates illegality*, at least in the special case of *drug use*.

Let's examine each of these exceptions in more detail.

a. **Maintenance of discipline and the school's mission:** Notwithstanding *Tinker*, school authorities have a strong and valid interest in *maintaining school discipline and in carrying out their educational mission.* Pursuit of these goals will sometimes entitle the authorities to regulate speech in a way that would not be permissible outside the school context. The cases of *Bethel School District No. 403 v. Fraser* and *Hazelwood School District v. Kuhlmeier* illustrate this principle.

   i. **Speech at a school assembly (*Bethel*):** In *Bethel School District No. 403 v. Fraser,* 478 U.S. 675 (1986), a high school student addressing a high school assembly gave a speech that school authorities found to be lewd. The speech, made in support of a candidate for a student government office, contained an elaborate sexual metaphor (e.g., "Jeff Kuhlman is a man who takes his point and pounds it in. ... He doesn't attack things in spurts — he drives hard, pushing and pushing until finally — he succeeds."). School authorities suspended the speaker and removed him from the list of candidates for commencement speaker.

      (1) **Disciplinary action upheld:** The Court *upheld* the disciplinary actions over the student's claim that they violated his freedom of expression. "The undoubted freedom to advocate unpopular and controversial issues in schools and classrooms must be balanced against society's countervailing interest in *teaching students the boundaries of socially appropriate behavior."* When balanced in this way, the school's interest in prohibiting "vulgar and lewd speech" outweighed whatever First Amendment interests the student might have had, especially since the penalties were *"unrelated to any political viewpoint," i.e., they were content-neutral.*

   ii. **Student newspaper (*Hazelwood*):** Similarly, school officials may exercise editorial control over the contents of *student newspapers* if they do so in a way that is *reasonably related to legitimate pedagogical concerns. Hazelwood School District v. Kuhlmeier*, 484 U.S. 260 (1988).

      (1) **Facts:** Thus in *Hazelwood*, the Court upheld a school principal's decision to remove two articles from the student newspaper: (1) a story describing three

students' experience with pregnancy; and (2) a story discussing the impact of divorce on students at the school. The principal believed that the first story might indirectly identify the students (even though their names weren't used), and that its references to sexual activity and birth control were inappropriate for some of the younger students at the school. He believed that the second article, which in the draft the principal saw identified a student who blamed her father for her parents' divorce, unfairly denied the father the chance to respond.

(2) Holding: A majority of the Court held that where a school a *sponsors an activity*, in such a way that students and others may reasonably perceive the activity as *bearing the school's imprimatur*, the school's right to restrict student speech is much greater than in the *Tinker* situation (*supra*, p. 559). In *Tinker*, the students who wore armbands were not in any school-sponsored activity; they merely happened to be on school property, but did not forfeit their right of free speech. But expression that occurs during the course of a school-sponsored publication, theatrical production, or other school-sponsored activity may be subject to school authorities' control "so long as [the authorities'] actions are *reasonably related to legitimate pedagogical concerns.*"

(3) Application: Applying this "reasonable relation" test, a majority found that the school principal acted reasonably: based on the facts as the principal then knew them, suppression of the articles was reasonably related to the school objectives of protecting privacy, shielding younger students from inappropriate subject matter, and teaching journalistic fairness.

b. **Advocacy of illegal drug use:** Both of the above cases (*Bethel* and *Hazelwood*) were ones in which either school discipline or the school's pedagogic mission was at stake, so it seemed realtively painless for the Supreme Court to carve out an exception from *Tinker* to justify the regulation of student speech. Where the student speech does *not* place discipline or the school's pedagogic mission in danger, the Court has been less likely to approve regulation. Thus in the core scenario typified by *Tinker* — student engages in political or social expression in a way that cannot plausibly be thought to pose discipline or pedagogic problems – *Tinker* remains the law, and restraints on student expression will be strictly scrutinized. But the Court has recently carved out one special *exception* to this general rule: speech *advocating the use of illegal drugs* may be restricted. That was the holding of *Morse v. Frederick*, 551 U.S. 393 (2007).

   i. **Facts:** In *Morse*, students at a public high school were permitted to leave school to observe the carrying of the Olympic Torch; the excursion was treated as a school trip. One of the students, Frederick, while watching the Torch procession, unfurled a banner that said "BONG HiTS 4 JESUS." (No one seems confident of what the banner was supposed to mean, though it seemed to express the owner's view that marijuana use was a good thing.) The principal demanded that Frederick take down the banner, because she thought it encouraged illegal drug use in violation of school policy; she also suspended him from school.

   ii. **Action upheld:** The Court held that the confiscation of the banner and suspension of Frederick *did not violate* his First Amendment rights. The Court concluded that "a principal may, consistent with the First Amendment, restrict student speech at a school event, when that speech is reasonably viewed *as promoting illegal drug use.*" That was true even though the speech here could not reasonably be viewed as a threat to the school's discipline or mission. The Court reasoned that schools have "an important, perhaps compelling" interest in deterring drug use by schoolchildren.

C. **Furnishing of legal services by lay groups:** As part of their interest in regulating the *legal profession*, states have a strong interest in preventing any conduct which interferes with the relationship between a client and his attorney. One concern which many states have had is that people or organizations might *stir up litigation* in which they have no direct pecuniary interest, and might then exercise control over the handling of the law suit, control which should normally be solely in the hands of the lawyer and client. Most states would, for instance, prohibit the creation of a for-profit corporation whose purpose is to advertise to personal-injury victims the availability of contingent-fee representation, and to receive a commission, or "forwarding fee" from the lawyer to whom the corporation assigns a case; even under the modern Court's relaxed view of lawyer advertising, such prohibitions would almost certainly be upheld.

1. **Rights and political expression:** However, these valid state interests may sometimes conflict with the interests of an organization in *furthering political goals* or obtaining economic benefits for its members, by notifying individuals of their legal rights, referring them to lawyers, or paying their legal bills. In general, where a *lay organization* (i.e., one not composed solely of lawyers) is able to make a respectable claim that it is engaged in *associational activities* when it gives such advice, referrals or funding, these freedom-of-association rights will *prevail* over the state interest in regulating the attorney-client relationship.

2. *NAACP v. Button:* The classic case demonstrating the strength of such associational interests is *NAACP v. Button*, 371 U.S. 415 (1963), in which the Supreme Court upheld the NAACP's right to refer to lawyers individuals who were willing to become plaintiffs in public school desegregation cases, and to pay these plaintiffs' litigation expenses.

   a. **Facts:** In *Button*, Virginia made it a crime for any organization to employ or compensate any attorney "in connection with any judicial proceeding in which [the organization] has no pecuniary right or liability." The state also forbade any organization to "control" or "exploit" the lawyer-client relationship, or to "intervene between client and lawyer." The Virginia NAACP brought about school desegregation cases by encouraging parents to become plaintiffs, by referring them to non-NAACP-staff lawyers, and by paying all litigation expenses. The Virginia courts held that these activities violated both the anti-control and anti-compensation rules.

   b. **Activities held protected:** But the Supreme Court held that the NAACP's activities were "modes of *expression* and *association* protected by the First and Fourteenth Amendments," and *could not be prohibited* under the state's power to regulate the legal profession. The Court reasoned that the litigation promoted by the NAACP was not a "technique of resolving private differences," but was rather a means for achieving equal treatment for blacks, and was thus a *"form of political expression."*

3. *Primus: Button* has been extended, to allow an *individual lawyer* to solicit clients as part of her *pro bono* work on behalf of the ACLU. See *In re Primus*, 436 U.S. 412 (1978) (discussed more extensively *supra*, p. 584).

D. Government as speaker or as funder of speech: So far, nearly everything we have said in this chapter concerns the role of government as the regulator of speech by non-government actors. But sometimes, *government itself wishes to speak*. And sometimes, government wishes to give *financial support* to certain speech by others. In these two contexts — government as speaker, and government as funder of speech — government seems to have at least somewhat greater ability to prefer one viewpoint over another than it does when it merely regulates. However, the law governing these two special contexts is far from settled.

 1. Government as speaker: When government wishes to *be a speaker itself*, it is pretty clear that government may *say essentially what it wants*, and is not subject to any real rule of viewpoint neutrality. As the Court noted in *Pleasant Grove City v. Summum*, 555 U.S. 460 (2009) (discussed more fully *infra*, p. 612), "The Free Speech Clause restricts government regulation of private speech; *it does not regulate government speech.*"

  a. No obligation to fund opposing viewpoints: Furthermore, when government — acting as a speaker — uses its own funds to deliver a particular message, government is *not thereby obligated to also fund other points of view* on the same topic.

  Example: "When Congress established a National Endowment for Democracy to encourage other countries to adopt democratic principles, it was not constitutionally required to fund a program to *encourage competing lines of political philosophy* such as communism and fascism." *Rust v. Sullivan*, 500 U.S. 173 (1991) (also discussed *infra*, pp. 625-626).

 2. Government as funder of third-party speech: But a much tougher question arises when government *funds speech by third parties*, who are essentially expressing their own beliefs rather than the government's. Here, may government be non-viewpoint-neutral, by funding only those viewpoints of which it approves? The answer is heavily dependent on the details of the government funding.

  a. Use of agents to deliver government's message: Government *may* use content-based criteria when government is selecting third parties who will serve as the *government's agents* in *spreading the government's own message*. As the Court said in *Rosenberger v. University of Virginia*, 515 U.S. 819 (1995), "we have permitted the government to *regulate the content of what is or is not expressed* when it is the speaker or when it *enlists private entities to convey its own message*."

  Example: The federal government funds certain family-planning "projects" (essentially, clinics) that are operated by private parties. The program's regulations say that while a person (e.g., a doctor) is working in such a clinic, that person may not discuss the possibility of an abortion with a pregnant clinic patient.

  Held, this limitation of private speech does not violate the First Amendment. *Rust v. Sullivan*, 500 U.S. 173 (1991). As the Court later summarized this aspect of *Rust* (in *Rosenburger, supra*), "the government did not create a program to encourage private speech but instead *used private speakers* to *transmit specific information pertaining to its own program*. We recognized that when the government appropriates public funds to *promote a particular policy* of its own it is *entitled to say what it wishes*."

  b. No forbidding of some topics or messages for disfavor: On the other hand, if government decides to *fund* (or allow on public property) *some expressions of private cit-*

izens' own views, government must generally *behave not only in a content-neutral but also a subject-neutral way.* That is, government cannot (1) decide that it's going to subsidize or facilitate private messages on various topics, but then (2) decline to fund (or exclude from the discussion) a few *disfavored topics or messages.*[9]

    i.   **Religion:** For example, government cannot decide to fund a broad range of expressive activities and then exclude expressive activities that are *mainly religious.*

> **Example:** Recall the facts of *Rosenberger* (*supra,* p. 554): The University of Virginia (a public university) funds certain student publications, by paying for their printing costs. The University disqualifies from this funding any primarily-religious publication.
>
> *Held*, this exclusion violates the free speech rights of student religious organizations. If the University were disseminating only its own messages, it would not have to fund opposing viewpoints. But once it chooses to fund some *third-party viewpoints* (i.e., some student-run publications), it may not choose which ones to fund based on the viewpoint of the speaker. *Rosenberger v. University of Virginia*, 515 U.S. 819 (1995).

    c. **Unconstitutional conditions:** Similarly, if government decides to award public funding for a privately-run program, the doctrine of *"unconstitutional conditions"* may prevent government from conditioning the funding on the recipient's agreement to give up its right to speak on certain topics, or requiring the recipient to deliver certain messages. The doctrine of unconstitutional conditions, especially as applied to free speech, is a quite confused area of the law, which we discuss in its own section *infra*, p. 624.

    d. **Government as patron of excellence:** Suppose that government acts a *"patron"* by giving subsidies to a *select number* of speakers. In this context, it appears that the Court will *not* require government to remain rigidly viewpoint-neutral. In this type of "reward for excellence" situation, the government cannot be expected to fund every speaker, so it is entitled to some degree of discretion in what speakers, and messages, it wishes to fund.

> **Example:** The National Endowment for the Arts gives various grants to artists of unusual merit. Congress requires the NEA, in deciding which artists should receive grants, to "tak[e] into consideration general standards of decency and respect for the diverse beliefs and values of the American public." The Ps (various artists) bring a facial challenge to this requirement that the standards be taken into account, arguing that it's inconsistent with *Rosenberger*'s holding that when a public university funds student publications, it cannot exclude those with religious content.
>
> *Held*, the artists lose. *Rosenberger* is *inapplicable*, and that NEA statute is *constitutional* on its face: "[Any] content-based considerations that may be taken into

---

9. Note that here, we're not talking about the situation in which government selects agents to disseminate what the public will realize is government's *own* message (a topic we discussed *supra*); we're talking about the situation in which government gives funding to private speakers (or gives them access to public property, even non-public-forum public property, see Par. 6(b) *supra*, p. 553), and in effect decrees, "Say whatever you want, but you can't use this funding to deliver Message X or to speak on Subject X."

account in the grant-making process are a consequence of the *nature of arts funding*. ... The 'very assumption' of the NEA is that grants will be awarded according to the 'artistic worth of competing applications,' and *absolute neutrality is simply 'inconceivable.'*" (But the "decency" requirement here is very general, and the Ps aren't claiming that it's being used to discriminate against the Ps' particular viewpoints. "If the NEA were to leverage its power to award subsidies on the basis of subjective criteria into a penalty on disfavored viewpoints, then we would confront a different case.") *National Endowment for the Arts v. Finley*, 524 U.S. 569 (1998).

3. **The boundary between government-as-speaker and government-as-facilitator-or-funder-of-private-speech:** As we've just seen, government can behave in a non-content-neutral way when it is the *speaker*, but generally *not* when it is the *funder or facilitator of private citizens' speech*. But the boundary line between government speech and government-facilitated private speech can sometimes be blurry.

   a. **Monuments and plaques:** Thus it can be hard to determine whether the speech in question is or isn't by government when a message is *inscribed* on a piece of tangible property — a *monument or a plaque*, for example — by a private citizen who then *donates* the property to government and asks that it be permanently *displayed*. If government takes and permanently displays the item, is government a speaker (making it free to reject other messages) or a facilitator of private-party speech (making it obliged to accept similar property expressing other views)?

   b. ***Pleasant Grove v. Summum* case:** As the result of a 2009 case, it seems that where government accepts and permanently displays the monument or plaque, government is likely to be found to be *acting as a speaker*, and thus is free to *reject other similar donations* of tangible items bearing messages that government does not agree with. The case is ***Pleasant Grove City v. Summum***, 555 U.S. 460 (2009).

      i. **Facts:** Prior to the litigation, Pleasant Grove, Utah had permanently placed in a local park 11 displays and monuments donated by private groups. One of these was a Ten Commandments monument donated in 1971. Members of the Summum religion then asked the city to accept and display in the same park a monument showing the "Seven Aphorisms," which Summum adherents believe were brought down from Mt. Sinai by Moses before he brought down the Ten Commandments. The proposed Summum monument was similar in size and nature to the Ten Commandments one.

         (1) **The Ps' argument:** The Summum members argued that when Pleasant Grove accepted and displayed the Ten Commandments and other monuments, the effect was to turn the park into a public forum, thereby requiring the city to accept other kinds of monuments and displays on a content-neutral basis. To the surprise of many observers, the Tenth Circuit agreed with the group, holding that because parks have traditionally been public forums, the city could not reject the Summum monument unless it had a compelling justification that could not be served by more narrowly-tailored means (the strict scrutiny standard for content-based regulation of public forums; see *supra*, p. 505).

      ii. **Held to be government speech:** But the Supreme Court unanimously reversed. In an opinion by Justice Alito, the Court held that the monument display was *gov-*

ernment speech, which therefore did not have to be content-neutral: "Although a park is a traditional public forum for *speeches and other transitory expressive acts*, display of a *permanent monument in a public park* is not a form of expression to which forum analysis applies. Instead, the placement of a permanent monument in a public park is best viewed as a *form of government speech* and is therefore *not subject to scrutiny under the Free Speech Clause*."

(1) No other choice: Alito pointed out that using public-forum analysis would be impractical in monument cases. The public-forum doctrine is properly used in situations in which government-owned property is "capable of accommodating a *large number of speakers* without defeating the essential function of the land or the program." By contrast, "public parks can accommodate only a *limited number* of permanent monuments." If public parks were treated as traditional public forums with respect to privately-donated monuments, "most parks would have little choice but to refuse all such donations." The obvious solution, Alito said, was not to use public-form analysis for permanent displays like monuments.

XI. FREEDOM OF ASSOCIATION, DENIAL OF PUBLIC JOBS OR BENEFITS, AND UNCONSTITUTIONAL CONDITIONS

A. **Freedom of association generally:** The First Amendment does not explicitly mention the freedom of *association*. But in numerous cases, the Supreme Court has held that that freedom derives by *implication* from the explicitly-stated right of speech, press, assembly and petition.

1. **Limited scope:** However, the freedom of association has not been broadly construed by the Court. For instance, the Court has never held that any activity which an individual may lawfully do by himself, he is constitutionally entitled to do in concert with others. Rather, all that has been recognized is "a right to join with others to pursue goals *independently protected* by the First Amendment." Tribe, p. 1013. These goals include *political advocacy*, *literary expression* and *religious worship*, among others.

   a. **Litigation:** The pursuit of *litigation* has also been regarded by the Court as an activity which generally receives First Amendment protection where carried out by an individual, and which therefore may be carried out jointly as well. Recall, for instance, the Court's recognition of the NAACP's right to group legal action in *NAACP v. Button*, *supra*, p. 609. Cases following *Button*, principally ones involving unions, have established that the freedom of association protects group pursuit even of litigation on non-political topics (e.g., workmen's compensation or personal injury claims). See *supra*, p. 610.

   b. **No general right of "social association":** Since there is a special freedom of association only where the goals being pursued are independently protected by the First Amendment, there is no special freedom to engage in *"social association."* That is, a group of people do not have any specially-protected First Amendment right to gather together for social purposes such as dancing, partying, watching a sporting event, etc. These events are not primarily expressive events, so there is no special First Amendment right to *gather* for purposes of engaging in these events.

2. **Strict scrutiny:** Government is not absolutely forbidden to impair the freedom of association, just as it is not absolutely forbidden to interfere with freedom of speech. However,

before the government may significantly interfere with protected associational activity, two showings must be made: (1) that the governmental interest being pursued is a *compelling* one; and (2) that that interest cannot be achieved by means *less restrictive* of the freedom of association. In other words, *strict scrutiny* is normally applied. See *NAACP v. Alabama*, 357 U.S. 449 (1958) (discussed further *infra*, p. 623), holding that "[s]tate action which may have the effect of curtailing the freedom to associate is subject to the closest scrutiny."

    a. Anti-discrimination measures: One governmental interest that is almost always found to be compelling, and that often cannot be achieved without restrictions on First Amendment freedoms, is the interest in *preventing discrimination* based on race, sex, or other suspect criterion. For instance, the Supreme Court has held that Minnesota could constitutionally require the Jaycees to admit women members, even though there might be some impairment of existing members' freedom of association or freedom of speech. *Roberts v. United States Jaycees*, 468 U.S. 609 (1984).

        i. Rationale: Minnesota's desire to eliminate discrimination in "places of *public accommodation*" (found as a factual matter to include quasi-commercial organizations like the Jaycees) was a compelling interest which the state was achieving through the least restrictive available means.

        ii. California Rotary case: Similarly, the Court has held that California was constitutionally empowered to force Rotary Clubs in that state to admit women, because "the relationship between Rotary Club members is not the kind of intimate or private relation that warrants constitutional protection." *Board of Directors of Rotary International v. Rotary Club of Duarte*, 481 U.S. 537 (1987).

B. Right not to associate: The Court has also recognized, in effect, a right *not* to associate. That is, individuals have a constitutional right *not to be compelled to support*, either financially or otherwise, most types of expressional activities by organizations of which they do not approve. Additionally, an association or other *group* has a right not to be *compelled to accept unwanted members* whose presence would significantly interfere with the group's message.

1. Right to avoid compulsory financial support: An important aspect of the "right not to associate" is the right not to be compelled to give *financial support* to organizations or activities where the money will be used to disseminate messages with which one disagrees.

    a. Union service fee: For instance, *union members* have a first amendment right not to have their *compulsory union dues used to support causes or ideas of which the member disapproves*. The main case so holding is *Abood v. Detroit Board of Education*, 431 U.S. 209 (1977). There, public-school employees (teachers) were not required to join the union, but anyone who did not join was required to pay a "service fee" equal in amount to union dues. The Court held that non-union employees had a constitutional right not to have their service fees used for *support of ideological causes* of which they disapproved. (But they had no right to refuse to have their service fees used for the costs of maintaining a collective bargaining system, as discussed in the Example in Par. (b) below.)

    b. Protection is not absolute: However, a person's right to not be required to give financial support to the expression of ideas with which she disagrees is *not an absolute right*. An important distinction is between expressive activities that are highly *ger-*

mane to the group's purposes, and those that are not — the members may be required to fund the former but not required to fund the latter.

> **Example:** It's true that public-school teachers who are required to be union members have the right not to have their union dues used for the support of ideological causes, since these are not germane to the union's function. *Abood, supra.* But the teachers have no right to refuse to have their dues used for the costs of *maintaining a collective bargaining system*, since these uses are germane to the union's function. *Id.*

i. **Where germane/non-germane distinction won't work:** But where government requires private citizens to fund a group's expressive activities that are so *diffuse* that it's hard to distinguish between the activities that are highly germane to the group's purpose and those that are not, the Court will *not* use the germane/non-germane distinction, and will instead merely insist that financial support be given to groups on a *viewpoint-neutral* basis.

> **Example:** A public university requires all students to pay a "student activity fee," which is then used to fund various student groups that engage in expressive activities. The plaintiff students object to having their fees used to support those student organizations that espouse ideas with which the plaintiffs disagree.
>
> *Held*, against the plaintiffs — they do not have the right to prevent use of their activity fees to support messages they oppose. The Court declines to use the germane/non-germane distinction, because it would be too difficult to apply in the university student-activity context (how would the Court decide which student activities are germane to the university's function, and which are not?) All that's required is *viewpoint-neutrality* in the allocation of student dollars. That is, instead of each student's having a First Amendment right to withhold her dollars from causes she disapproves of, all the student is constitutionally entitled to is that the dollars be allocated in a viewpoint-neutral way, i.e., in a way that will not differentiate based on the messages spread by the various funded activities. *Board of Regents of the University of Wisconsin System v. Southworth*, 529 U.S. 217 (2000).

2. **Veto on unwanted participants:** The "right not to associate" extends well beyond the right not to have to give financial support to groups or causes of which one disapproves. An other important aspect of the right is that a group has a First Amendment right *not to be forced to accept participants whose presence would interfere with the group's expressive activities.*

a. **Parade:** For instance, private parties who conduct a *parade* may exclude unwanted members — or at least unwanted messages — from the parade. Thus in *Hurley v. Irish-American Gay, Lesbian, and Bisexual Group of Boston*, 515 U.S. 557 (1995), the Court held unanimously that Massachusetts could not require a private group that conducts a St. Patrick's Day parade in Boston to include gay and lesbian marchers marching under their own banner.

i. **Expressive conduct:** The "right not to associate" is closely related to the **"right not to speak,"** which the Court has also long recognized. Thus in *Hurley*, the parade organizers were in fact willing to have gays and lesbians in the parade — the fight was about whether the gays should be allowed to march in their own unit *under their own banner*. The Court found that a parade inevitably has expressive content, and that gays marching under a banner would be sending a message (presumably a message supporting gay rights and gay lifestyles) that the parade organizers had a right to refuse to endorse. "It boils down to the choice of a speaker not to propound a particular point of view, and that choice is presumed to lie beyond the government's power to control," the Court said in *Hurley*.

b. **Must be perceived as group's own speech:** But the right of a group not to be forced to accept co-participants of whose message the group disapproves applies *only* where the *group's own "message" will be affected by the unwanted participation.* This principle is demonstrated by *Rumsfeld v. FAIR*, 547 U.S. 47 (2006), where the Court upheld the constitutionality of the "Solomon Amendment," under which Congress said that any university could receive certain federal funding only if all parts of the university, including its law school, gave the same on-campus access to military recruiters as to recruiters from other employers.

  i. **The claim:** A group of law schools argued in *FAIR* that since the military discriminates against gays, the Amendment unconstitutionally forced the schools to *support a message they abhorred*; the plaintiffs contended that by forcing the schools to serve as host for on-campus military recruiting, the Solomon Amendment infringed the schools' freedom not to associate with the military just as directly as the forced participation of gays in *Hurley* infringed the rights of the St. Patrick's Day parade organizers.

  ii. **Argument rejected:** But the Court in *FAIR* *disagreed* with the plaintiffs' assertion that the two cases were the same. The compelled-speech cases like *Hurley* turned on the fact that "the *complaining speaker's own message was affected* by the speech it was forced to accommodate." Thus in *Hurley* itself, the parade was expressive, and a law forcing the inclusion of an unwanted group altered the expressive content of the parade. In *FAIR*, by contrast, "[A]ccommodating the military's message *does not affect the law schools' speech,* because *the schools are not speaking when they host interviews and recruiting receptions.* Unlike a parade organizer's choice of parade contingents, a law school's decision to allow recruiters on campus *is not inherently expressive* ... Nothing about recruiting suggests that law schools agree with any speech by recruiters, and nothing in the Solomon Amendment restricts what the law schools may say about the military's policies."

3. **Right to exclude from membership in group:** Perhaps most significantly, the "right not to associate" also means that an association has a First Amendment interest in *not being forced to accept unwanted members*. For instance, the rights of a Democratic club would probably be impaired if the government forced the club to admit registered Republicans as members, and the rights of NAACP members would be impaired if the organization were forced to admit, say, Nazi supremacists or Ku Klux Klanners.

a. **Gays in the Boy Scouts:** The most dramatic example of this "right not to associate" came in *Boy Scouts of America v. Dale*, 530 U.S. 640 (2000), where the Court held that because opposition to homosexuality was part of the Scouts' "expressive message," the Scouts' freedom of association was violated by a state anti-discrimination law that barred the group from excluding gays as members.

i. Ouster upheld: By a 5-4 vote, the Court found for the Scouts. The majority, in an opinion by Justice Rehnquist, concluded that the Scouts had an "official position" that avowed homosexuals should not be Scout leaders, and that homosexual conduct was in the Scouts' view incompatible with the requirement that a Scout be "morally straight." Given this viewpoint, Rehnquist wrote, requiring that the Scouts keep Dale as a member would "at the very least, force the organization to **send a message**, both to the youth members and the world, that the Boy Scouts **accept homosexual conduct** as a legitimate form of behavior." It didn't matter that the Scouts were not formed "for the purpose" of opposing homosexuality — as long as being forced to admit a practicing homosexual would **impair the organization's message**, this was enough to trigger a strong First Amendment interest, one which the state's anti-discrimination interest could not overcome.

(1) Strict scrutiny: Chief Justice Rehnquist didn't expressly say that he was using strict scrutiny. But he rejected the *O'Brien* content-neutral standard, which he characterized as an "intermediate standard of review," and he appears to have in fact used a variant of strict scrutiny.

ii. Dissent: The four dissenters did not disagree with the general proposition that an organization cannot be forced to accept members whose presence would materially impair the group's message. But they disagreed about the application of this test here. As Justice Stevens' principal dissent put it, the Scouts had never — at least outside of various litigations — made a **"clear, unequivocal statement"** of opposition to homosexuality. And such a clear statement, in his view, was necessary before an organization could claim an infringement of its associational rights. All the Scouts had done was to "adopt[] an exclusionary membership policy" without any "shared goal of disapproving of homosexuality."

b. Compulsory membership won't necessarily interfere with expression: As *Boy Scouts* implies, the more **central and unequivocal** the organization's views on a particular matter, the **greater the interference** with associational rights will be if the organization is forced to accept a member with opposing views. Therefore, if a particular point of view is **not clearly articulated by the organization**, or **not especially central** to the organization's mission, compulsory membership by one with opposing views or conduct may **cause so little harm** that a countervailing governmental objective may outweigh the associational interest. And where that governmental interest is the possibly-compelling interest of reducing discrimination, the government is especially likely to prevail.

i. Illustration: This is what happened, for instance, in *Roberts v. United States Jaycees, supra*, p. 614: the originally all-male membership of the Jaycees had a First Amendment interest in not being required to accept women as members, but the organization's no-women stance was (the Court found) **not very central** to the organization's purposes. Consequently, this relatively weak interest was outweighed by the state's compelling interest in banning discrimination in places of public accommodation, an interest which could not be fully achieved by narrower measures.

C. Ways of interfering with right: The right of association may be interfered with in a number of different ways. Forcing a person or group to support (or accept as a member) an unwanted message or individual is one way, which we've already discussed above. We now consider several other types of interference:

❑   government makes it ***illegal to be a member*** of a group (see *infra*, this page);

❑   government ***withholds public jobs and benefits*** from members of particular groups or associations (see *infra*, p. 618); and

❑   government requires that an individual ***disclose*** his organizational affiliations (or, conversely, that a group disclose its members) (see *infra*, p. 622).

D. Illegal membership: Mere membership in an association or group may not be made ***illegal***. Membership in a group may only serve as an element of a criminal offense if the following additional requirements are satisfied:

[1]   the group is ***actively engaged in unlawful activity***, or ***incites*** others to ***imminent lawless action*** (in such a way that the incitement is punishable as a "clear and present danger" under the modern *Brandenburg* test, *supra*, p. 515); and

[2]   the individual member ***knows*** of the group's illegal activities, and has the ***specific intent*** of furthering the group's illegal goals.

This series of requirements evolved through the case law on subversive advocacy and the "clear and present danger" text, a subject treated in detail *supra*, p. 510.

E. Denial of public job or benefit: The freedom of association may be unconstitutionally abridged if a ***job in the public sector***, or a license or benefit issued by the government, is denied because of the applicant's associational activities. This possibility arises most commonly where a job or license is denied on the grounds of the applicant's membership in the ***Communist Party*** or other subversive group.

   1. No ban based solely on membership: A public job or other public benefit ***may not be denied merely on the basis of the applicant's constitutionally-protected membership in a group or organization***.

   2. Subversive group: Therefore, unless an individual's group activities could be made ***illegal***, those group activities cannot be grounds for denying him a job, license to practice law, or other public benefit.

      a. Same test as for outright ban: Thus the test applied in the public-job-or-benefits context is the same as the two-part test used connection with the ***outright outlawing*** of subversive group activity (see *supra*, Par. (D)).

      Example: A state statute provides for the discharge of any public employee who knowingly becomes a member of the Communist Party or of any party whose purposes include overthrow of the state government, if the employee has knowledge of this unlawful purpose. *Held*, the statute violates the First Amendment, because it does not also require that the employee have the "specific intent" to further the organization's illegal aims. *Elfbrandt v. Russell*, 384 U.S. 11 (1966).

   3. Patronage hirings and dismissals: The use of ***political patronage*** presents special free association problems: when a person or party who controls public-sector jobs gives those jobs out as a means of rewarding faithful party workers, applicants without political connections can plausibly claim that they have been discriminated against based on their political affiliation (or lack of one).

   a. Rule for ordinary jobs: In general, the Supreme Court has *agreed* with such claims, at least in the usual case where effective performance of the job does not depend on political affiliation. The rule is that in making *hiring, promotion and dismissal* decisions concerning such ordinary jobs, party affiliation may *not* be a factor. *Rutan v. Republican Party of Illinois*, 497 U.S. 62 (1990).

   i. Massive patronage rejected: The facts of *Rutan, supra*, show the kind of patronage scheme that will *not* be allowed. Plaintiffs alleged that the Republican governor of Illinois prohibited any hiring, firing or promotions for any state office except on his "express permission," and that only those who had voted for or supported the Republican party in past years were favored. The Court held that these employment practices, if proven, violated the First Amendment free association rights of those not given special treatment.

   b. Inherently political posts: On the other hand, some government posts are by their nature so bound up with party affiliation — so *inherently "political"* — that the "wrong" party affiliation can get in the way of effective job performance. In that scenario, party affiliation *may* be considered in hiring and firing. For instance, "Democrats have no right to consideration on equal terms with Republicans when the newly elected Republican government of a state is choosing a speech writer or a high-level special assistant." Tribe, p. 1018.

   i. "Effective performance" test: The test is "whether the hiring authority can demonstrate that party affiliation is an *appropriate requirement* for the *effective performance* of the public office involved." *Branti v. Finkel*, 445 U.S. 507 (1980).

   (1) Assistant public defender: The one Supreme Court case deciding whether party affiliation was appropriately required for effective job performance is *Branti, supra*. There, the Court held that two Republican *assistant public defenders* could *not* be discharged on party-affiliation grounds when a Democrat was named to head the public defender's office. The majority reasoned that a rank-and-file public defender's *effectiveness* depends on how he handles his client's needs, not on any partisan political interests.

4. Loyalty oaths: Normally, denial of a job or license based on associational activities does not occur as the result of extensive investigation by the government. Rather, such denials have generally occurred where the applicant or employee is required to take an *oath* that he has not belonged to certain types of organizations, or engaged in other activities, and he is unwilling or unable to take such an oath.

   a. Rule: In general, the rule regarding such *"loyalty oaths"* is that one may not be required to state that one has not performed a certain act, or that one will not perform it in the future, unless actual *performance* of that act would be grounds for discharge. That is, the permissible scope of such oaths is co-extensive with the scope of grounds for *non-hiring or discharge*. See *Cole v. Richardson*, 405 U.S. 676 (1972).

   i. Illustration: For instance, recall that a person may not be discharged for membership in an organization advocating overthrow of the government, unless she had *knowledge* of the organization's purpose and *specific intent* to further that purpose. Consequently, a person may also not be required to swear a blanket oath that she has never been a member of an organization advocating such overthrow — language referring to the affiant's knowledge of the illegal purposes, and to her specific intent to further them, must be inserted into the oath itself.

5. **Speech critical of superiors:**   Thus far, we have examined the denial of public jobs and benefits for *associational* activities. Similar issues arise when the government attempts to deny a public job or benefit because of a person's *speech*-related activities. For instance, under what circumstances may a government employee be fired for *criticizing his superiors?*

    a. **"Public concern" as key factor:**   The key issue is whether the speech involves a matter of *"public concern."* Governmental attempts to fire or otherwise penalize its employees for speech on matters of "public concern" will be *strictly scrutinized*, but speech on matters that are *not* within this category will receive substantially less protection. *Connick v. Myers*, 461 U.S. 138 (1983).

        i. **Public concern:**   Where speech involves a matter of *"public concern,"* the Court held in *Connick*, the judiciary must carefully examine the justification given by the state for penalizing the speech, and must strike a *balance* between the free speech rights of the employee and the "interest of the State, as an employer, in promoting the efficiency of the public services it performs[.]"[10]

        ii. **Matters not of "public concern":**   By contrast, where the matters discussed by the employee are *not* ones of public concern, the court should give "a wide degree of *deference* to the *employer's judgment."* The employer's interest in, for instance, avoiding "the *disruption of the office* and the *destruction of working relationships*" should be *weighed heavily.*

            Example: P is an assistant D.A. After learning that she has received an unwanted transfer to a new post within the D.A.'s office, she gives her co-workers a questionnaire soliciting their views on a number of matters concerning the office, including whether they have "confidence in" particular superiors, and whether they ever "feel pressured to work in political campaigns on behalf of office supported candidates." The D.A., upon learning of the questionnaire, views it as an act of insubordination, and fires P for both the questionnaire and for refusing to accept the transfer.

            Held (5-4), P's firing is sustained. The D.A. reasonably believed that P's actions would "disrupt the office, undermine his authority and destroy close working relationships." Since the questionnaire as a whole touched only slightly on matters of "public concern," the D.A.'s judgment is entitled to great deference. (But if matters of public interest been been more plainly implicated in the questionnaire, less deference would be due the D.A.'s judgment, and a much stronger showing of danger to the efficiency of the office would be required to sustain the firing.) *Connick, supra.*

---

10. But there's a major exception to this rule of *Connick*: under *Garcetti v. Ceballos*, discussed *infra*, p. 621, if the speech occurs "pursuant to the employee's *official duties*," it *doesn't* get this significant protection, even if it involves a matter of public concern.

iii. Expansive reading to "public concern": The Court has sometimes given a surprisingly broad reading to the definition of "public concern," the key definition used by *Connick* for determining whether a public employer can fire an employee for speech-related reasons.

> **Example:** P is a 19-year-old black clerical employee in the office of D (the County Constable). When P hears of John Hinckley's attempted assassination of President Reagan, P says (in the office) to a co-worker who happens to be her boyfriend, "If they go for him again, I hope they get him." The remark is overheard by another co-worker, who informs D about it; D fires P.
>
> *Held* (by 5-4 vote), P's dismissal violated her First Amendment rights. P's comment was on a matter of "public concern," thus satisfying the first prong of the *Connick* test. Taken in the context in which it was made, the remark was essentially a commentary on the President's policies and the attempted assassination, both of which were matters of public concern. Since the statement touched on a matter of public concern, the dismissal could only be upheld if the State bore the burden of justifying the discharge on legitimate grounds. Any justification had to take into account the context in which the statement was made, including "time, place and manner." Here, P had no policy-making or law-enforcement responsibilities and her statement had no discernible impact on the functioning of the Constable's office, so the State failed to justify the dismissal. *Rankin v. McPherson*, 483 U.S. 378 (1987).

b. Need not have "property" interest: Observe that in the "speech critical of superiors" cases (*Connick*, for instance), the employee has a qualified right not to be fired for First Amendment activity even if she has no *"property"* interest in the job. This is very different from the rule in cases brought under the Due Process Clause (see *supra*, p. 225), under which the employee has no right to due process before being fired unless she is found to have had a property interest in the job.

c. Speech must not occur as part of job responsibilities: There's a very important exception to the *Connick* rule. In order for speech on matters of public concern to get the protection of *Connick*, the speech *must not be made "pursuant to the employee's official duties."* So speech on matters of public concern made in furtherance of the public employee's *job functions* receives *less First Amendment protection* than speech the employee makes as a "citizen" acting outside of his job. The Court announced this principle in *Garcetti v. Ceballos*, 547 U.S. 410 (2006).

i. Facts: The plaintiff in *Garcetti* was a supervising lawyer in the L.A. County District Attorney's Office. P was called on to investigate whether an affidavit prepared by a deputy sheriff to obtain a search warrant was properly done. After his investigation, P wrote a memo to his supervisor concluding that the affidavit had been improperly done, and recommending dismissal of the criminal case premised upon it. This memo precipitated a chain of events at the end of which, P claimed, his superior retaliated against him for writing the memo. The D.A.'s office retorted that P's act of writing the memo was not entitled to First Amendment protection because the memo was created as part of P's job responsibilities.

ii. Court agrees: By a 5-4 vote, the Court agreed with the D.A.'s position: "[W]hen public employees make statements *pursuant to their official duties,* the employees are *not speaking as citizens* for First Amendment purposes, and *the Constitution does not insulate their communications from employer discipline."* Here, because P's investigation and the ensuing memorandum were part of his job responsibilities, the employer had the right to regulate the content and manner of P's speech.

(1) Rationale: The majority reasoned that "employers have heightened interests in *controlling speech made by an employee in his or her professional capacity* ... Supervisors must ensure that their employees' official communications are accurate, demonstrate sound judgment, and *promote the employer's mission."*

iii. Dissent: The four dissenters conceded that the majority was correct to recognize a government employer's important interest in ensuring that employees who speak for it while doing their work have competence, honesty and good judgment. But the dissenters, led by Justice Souter, would nonetheless apply a *Connick*-style *balancing* when on-the-job speech implicates matters of public concern — they thought that the government's interest in job performance could sometimes be *outweighed* by the employee's interest in speaking (and the public's interest in hearing the speech) on matters of public concern. For Souter, such a balancing was appropriate, for instance, "when a public auditor speaks on his discovery of embezzlement of public funds, when a building inspector makes an obligatory report of an attempt to bribe him, or when a law enforcement officer expressly balks at his superior's order to violate constitutional rights he is sworn to protect."

6. Imposition of burdens: So far, we have talked about the award by the government of *benefits* (e.g., public-sector jobs). But a similar rule applies where the government metes out *burdens*. That is, the government may not use as a basis for selecting which individuals are to be burdened the individuals' exercise of constitutionally-protected rights (or any other constitutionally-illicit criterion, e.g., race). This is true even if the government would otherwise have the right to place that burden upon the individuals in question. For instance, "there are First Amendment problems if only Democrats, or only critics of government, or only Socialists, are selected for *income tax audit*." Gunther, 1985 Supp., p. 66. The same is true of any other government prosecution or penalty.

F. Compulsory disclosure: Frequently, interference with associational freedoms will be alleged where the government does not deny a job or benefit based on organizational membership, but rather *inquires* of an employee or applicant about the organizations to which he belongs (or, conversely, asks an organization who its members are). Typically, this is done by requiring the filling out of a questionnaire or affidavit detailing all of one's associational memberships. (Use of a "loyalty oath" sometimes fulfills the same function; see the discussion of such oaths *supra*, p. 619.) Ordinarily, refusal to submit the required document is made grounds for non-hiring or discharge.

1. Evolution of law: The principles governing such compelled disclosure have changed dramatically in the last thirty years. Whereas in the early 1950's broad inquiry was permitted, today inquiry must be restricted to little more than matters that would constitute substantive grounds for non-hiring or firing.

2. Modern "strict scrutiny": The test now applied is essentially that of *strict scrutiny*: if the governmental interest sought through mandatory disclosure is not a *compelling* or "subordinating" one, or if that interest could be attained by means *less restrictive* of associational or expressional freedoms, the mandatory disclosure will not be upheld.

a. **NAACP membership lists:** The classic illustration of this new heightened means-end scrutiny is a case involving compulsory disclosure of NAACP membership lists, *NAACP v. Alabama*, 357 U.S. 449 (1958).

    i. **Facts:** Alabama demanded the names and addresses of all the NAACP's Alabama members. The demand was part of a request made by the state for an injunction against the organization, to stop it from conducting activities in Alabama on the grounds that it had not satisfied a requirement that foreign corporations qualify before doing business there.

    ii. **Holding:** In holding that compulsory disclosure of the membership lists would *violate members' associational rights*, the Court emphasized that "privacy in group association may in many circumstances be indispensable to preservation of freedom of association, particularly where a group espouses *dissident beliefs*." Here, the NAACP showed that on past occasions, members whose names were publicly released had been subjected to loss of jobs, physical threats, economic loss and other public hostility. Therefore, this was clearly one of those situations where disclosure would impair the freedom of association.

    iii. **Balancing:** Only a compelling, *"subordinating"* state interest could outweigh the harm to freedom of association that compulsory disclosure would bring about. The names of the NAACP's rank and file members, the Court concluded, did not have the requisite "substantial bearing" on the state's interest in preventing unregistered foreign corporations from conducting intrastate business.

b. **Disclosure of campaign contributions:** Compulsory disclosure of *campaign contributions* has been upheld over the objection that such disclosure violates the freedom of association. *Buckley v. Valeo*, 424 U.S. 1 (1976) (other aspects of which are discussed *supra*, p. 623).

    i. **Disclosure requirements:** The federal statute construed in *Buckley* required candidates to disclose the source of any contribution over $10, and also required individuals who made political contributions or independent expenditures of more than $100 per year to itemize their spending. The *Buckley* plaintiffs claimed that these disclosure rules violated the associational freedoms of *minor parties* and of *small contributors.*

    ii. **Strict scrutiny standard:** The Court concluded that the compulsory disclosure provisions did indeed encroach significantly on First Amendment rights, and therefore must be subjected to *strict scrutiny.*

    iii. **Scrutiny survived:** But the Court then concluded that the disclosure provisions *survived* this strict scrutiny.

G. **The bar membership cases:** Cases on qualifications for *admission to the bar* are a kind of hybrid, raising problems both as to the grounds for denial of publicly-conferred benefits (the license to practice) as well as issues of the scope of required disclosure. Most of the bar cases have involved state qualification procedures designed to deal with *subversive* activities. Here's what seems to be the present state of affairs about bar-admission inquiries:

1. **No disqualification:** The state cannot ask the candidate a question whose ***sole function*** is to determine whether the candidate has been a knowing member of an organization which advocates forcible overthrow of the government. Thus ***knowing membership*** in such an organization, without more, ***can't be the basis*** for denying admission. *Baird v. State Bar of Arizona,* 401 U.S. 1 (1971).

2. **Screening device:** However, the state *can* use a ***two-part question***, where the first part acts merely as a ***screening device.*** Thus the state can ask the initial question, "Have you ever been a member of an organization which advocates forcible overthrow of the government, while knowing that that was the organization's aim?" Then, if the answer is "yes," the state can ask the follow-up question, "Do you ***support*** this aim?" An affirmative answer to this second question (or a refusal to answer it) can apparently then be grounds for denying bar admission. *Law Students Research Council v. Wadmond,* 401 U.S. 154 (1971).

H. Unconstitutional conditions: Government actions sometimes raise the problem of ***"unconstitutional conditions."*** The problem arises "when government attaches ***constitutionally troublesome 'strings'*** to ***government benefits,*** such as housing, employment money, or licenses." S,S,S,T&K pp. 1608-09. Most often — but not always — the "string" is that the recipient of the government benefit must, in order to get the benefit, agree to ***waive her freedom of expression***.

1. **Statement of doctrine:**   To deal with this problem, the Court sometimes invokes the doctrine of unconstitutional conditions in order to strike down the condition. When the doctrine applies, it holds that "government ***may not grant a benefit on the condition that the beneficiary surrender a constitutional right,*** even if the government may ***withhold that benefit altogether***." 102 HARV. L. REV. 1415. The idea behind the doctrine is that what the government may not do ***directly***, it may not do ***indirectly*** either. *Id.*

    > **Example:** Suppose that the Republican-controlled legislature of a state passes a statute saying that no one may get or keep a job working for the state — no matter how low-level the position or what the requirements of the position are — unless the person signs a pledge not to criticize any elected Republican official during the employment.
    >
    > The Supreme Court would undoubtedly invoke the doctrine of unconstitutional conditions to strike down this statute as a violation of state employees' freedom of expression. Every citizen has the right to criticize politicians, and letting the state condition all state employment on the waiver of this right amounts to letting the state do indirectly what it could not to directly.[11]

2. **Guiding principles:**   The Court seems to apply the doctrine somewhat inconsistently. But following are three principles that seem to explain the outcome in most of the Court's unconstitutional-condition cases. (See S,S,S,T&K p. 1615.) We have already covered

---

11. Notice that I've designed this hypothetical statute so that it applies even where the state has no legitimate interest in curbing the criticism. If such a law instead only applied, say, to high-ranking policy-making employees to prevent them from publicly criticizing their own superiors while performing the functions of the job, the unconstitutional-conditions doctrine wouldn't apply. In this situation, the Court would almost certainly hold that the government has an overriding interest in assuring that high-level employees don't impair their own performance or that of their superiors by on-the-job criticisms of superiors. See *Garcetti v. Ceballos, supra,* p. 621.

most of these principles in earlier parts of this chapter, especially in the discussion of government's rights as funder of speech, *supra*, p. 610.

[1] **Government uses agents to deliver government's own speech:** Government is *permitted* to say pretty much whatever it wants *when the government is itself the speaker.* (See *supra*, p. 610.) Furthermore, government is permitted to *select agents* to deliver the government's own message. (*Supra*, p. 610.) Therefore, government is free to *pay agents* to deliver the government's message, and to *condition that payment* on the agent's willingness to *waive his otherwise-protected right* to engage in speech that would contradict or garble the government message the agent is being paid to deliver.

Example: Congress provides funding for a public-education campaign called "Smoking Kills." The funding pays for lecturers to travel the country giving anti-smoking speeches. It's clear that Congress may insert into its contract with any lecturer a provision saying, "In any public lecture you are giving as part of the 'Smoking Kills' program, you shall make no statement inconsistent with the view that smoking is inherently hazardous."

By doing so, Congress has not attached an unconstitutional condition to its lecture contract; the nature and advertising of the program make it clear that any lecturer who is speaking under the auspices of the program is delivering the government's own message, so it is not unconstitutional for the government to insist on speakers who will faithfully deliver the message that the government has selected.

[2] **Limits on use of government's payments:** Government is also free to set up *"subsidy programs,"* under which government funds private groups to help them carry out some function. And when government does this, it is free to *refuse* to allow *the subsidy dollars to be used for particular activities opposed by government*, including otherwise-constitutionally-protected activities like *speaking* on certain topics, *performing abortions*, or lobbying legislators. (But this exception applies only when the restriction limits just the use of the actual *dollars paid by the government*, not when the program restricts the grantee's freedom to engage in other activities being privately funded. As to this latter situation, see [3] below.)

Example: Recall the facts of *Rust v. Sullivan* (*supra*, p. 187): Congress has long provided federal grants to help private citizens operate family-planning clinics. Any program using these grants is known as a "Title X project." The Secretary of Health and Human Services then makes a new interpretation of the grant program, under which every Title X project is prohibited from "counselling [patients] concerning the use of abortion" or from "encourag[ing] or promot[ing] abortion." Grantees who have been receiving funds argue that this new condition violates their and their patients' freedom of speech, by stripping the grantees of the right to counsel a patient that she has a constitutionally-protected right to have an abortion in certain circumstances.

Held, the new interpretation is not an unconstitutional condition, and does not violate the First Amendment. "[T]he Government is not denying a benefit to anyone, but is instead simply insisting that *public funds be spent* for the purposes for which they were authorized." A critical distinction is between the "project" (the particular activity paid for by the grant funds, namely operating a family-planning clinic), and the "grantee" (the individuals or group that are running the project). The way the statute and interpretation are written, a Title X *grantee* can continue to engage in abortion advocacy or counselling; the grantee simply is required to conduct those activities "through programs that are *separate and independent from the project* that receives Title X funds."[12] *Rust v. Sullivan,* 500 U.S. 173 (1991).

[3] **No "leveraging" by government:** But although government may (as described in [2] above) put conditions on how the government funds will be used inside a government-subsidized privately-run program, government may not impose conditions that "seek to *leverage funding* to *regulate speech outside the contours* of the [government] *program itself.*"

Example 1: Congress gives funding to noncommercial TV and radio stations, but only on condition that they do not do any editorializing, even with private funds.

Held, the no-editorializing rule is an unconstitutional condition. Congress had the power to limit how subsidy dollars are spent. But here, Congress went beyond that power, by preventing all editorializing by even stations that didn't use federal funding for this purpose. For the no-editorializing condition to have been constitutional, Congress would have had to give a station a way to use private funds for editorializing as long as the station made sure not to use the federal grants for these editorializing purposes. *FCC v. League of Women Voters,* 468 U.S. 364 (1983).

Example 2: Congress gives large money grants to various nongovernmental organizations that are fighting HIV and AIDS. Congress says that no funds may be given to any group "that does not have a *policy explicitly opposing prostitution[.]*" (This is the "Policy Requirement.") The Ps are various non-profits that fear that if they obey the Policy Requirement and adopt an explicitly anti-prostitution message, their mission will be adversely affected (e.g., they may find it harder to persuade prostitutes to promote condom usage).

Held (6-2),[13] for the Ps; the Policy Requirement is an unconstitutional condition. The Court's cases on unconstitutional conditions have distinguished between "conditions that define the limits of the government spending program, [i.e., that] specify the activities Congress wants to subsidize" (which are constitutional) and "conditions that seek to leverage funding to regulate speech outside the contours of the program itself" (which are unconstitutional). It may sometimes be hard to tell on which side of the line a particular condition falls. But here, the Policy Requirement falls on the unconstitutional side of the line. "By demanding that funding recipients adopt — as their own — the Government's view on an issue of public concern, the condition by its very nature affects 'protected conduct outside the scope of the federally funded program.'" *Agency for Int'l Dev. v. Alliance for Open Soc'y Int'l, Inc.,* 133 S. Ct. 2321 (2013).

---

12. Indeed, that's the way Planned Parenthood and other recipients of Title X funding operated after *Rust* — they set up federally-funded clinics to do non-abortion-related family planning such as distribution of contraceptives, and separately set up non-federally-funded abortion clinics.

13. Justice Kagan recused herself.

XII. SPECIAL PROBLEMS CONCERNING THE MEDIA

A. Summary of issues: Certain First Amendment problems arise only where the First Amendment right is being asserted by a member of the *media*, i.e., professional *publishers* and *broadcasters*. The four issues which we address that pertain specially to the media are:

1. Does the press have a special role to play under the First Amendment, so that it has *rights* which an *ordinary member of the public would not?*

2. Under what circumstances, if any, may the media be *restrained* from publishing or broadcasting material (as distinguished from being punished after such dissemination has already occurred)?

3. Does a journalist have any greater rights to *resist governmental demands for information* known to the journalist, than does an ordinary member of the public? and

4. Do the media have any First Amendment *right of access* to information *within the government's possession* or control?

B. Special role for the press: The First Amendment explicitly prohibits abridgment of the freedom "of the press," in addition to protecting the freedom "of speech." On its face, this language suggests that the organized press is entitled to somewhat greater First Amendment protection than are ordinary members of the public; otherwise, the explicit reference to the press would seem to be redundant.

1. Not yet recognized: However, in no case has a majority of the Court ever recognized the Press Clause of the First Amendment as having independent constitutional significance. Yet, neither has the Court ever squarely held that the Clause is redundant.

2. Laws of general applicability: The Court has heard a number of cases in which the press argued that it should receive an *exemption* from rules of general applicability. The Court has virtually always *denied* any special exemption for the press. For instance, if a state's generally applicable procedural rules allow a person to be forced to give *testimony* to a grand jury or petit jury, then the press must obey those rules like anyone else. See *Branzburg v. Hayes*, *infra*, p. 634. Similarly, the same rules apply to the issuance of *search warrants* to search a publisher's premises as apply to searches of a non-publisher. *Zurcher v. Stanford Daily*, *infra*, p. 636. And newspapers may be made to pay damages for violating contractual promises of *confidentiality*, the same as any private citizen may be. See *Cohen v. Cowles Media Co.*, *infra*, p. 638.

a. Access right: There is one situation in which the press may have rights superior to those of the public at large. The press may have a right of *access* to newsworthy information within the government's control — such a right of access for the press, based on general free-expression principles, may have been recognized by the Court in the *Richmond Newspapers* case, *infra*, p. 639.

3. Government can't single out press: Regardless of whether the press has special rights, what is clear is that government may not *single out* the press for *unfavorable* treatment.

a. Taxation: This has been clearest in cases involving *taxation*. The government may not impose a tax that applies to newspapers (or all media) but that is not generally applicable. Thus in *Minneapolis Star & Tribune Co. v. Minnesota Comm'r of Revenue*, 460 U.S. 525 (1983), the Court held that a special Minnesota "use tax" applicable only to the cost of ***paper and ink*** consumed in the production of ***publications***, violated the First Amendment.

i. **Rationale:** The Court did not find any evidence that the Minnesota legislature had tried to censor or chill the press. But the tax was a special one, not part of the state's generally-applicable use tax. Therefore, the Court concluded, the state had "singled out the press for special treatment." Consequently, the tax had to be strictly scrutinized — it would be invalid unless "necessary to achieve an overriding governmental interest."

ii. **"Chilling" effect:** There was evidence that the particular tax here was not especially burdensome to the press (since it was at the same percentage rate as the general state sales and use taxes, and applied only to paper and ink, not to the total price of the newspaper). Nonetheless, because the state had singled out the press, the "***political constraints*** that prevent a legislature from passing crippling taxes of general applicability are weakened, and the threat of burdensome taxes becomes acute." The ***mere threat*** of crippling taxes might well have a censorial effect, the Court argued.

iii. **Strict scrutiny test failed:** The statute was not able to withstand the strict scrutiny to which the Court subjected it. The state's interest in raising revenue might be a compelling one (the Court did not say); but the singling out of the press for a special tax was ***not a necessary means*** of achieving that objective. The state could, for instance, simply have made newspaper sales part of the ***general state sales tax*** already in force.

iv. **Dissent:** Justice Rehnquist, in dissent, argued that not all "differential treatment," but only that differential treatment which ***burdens*** the press, should be strictly scrutinized. Here, he calculated, the use tax was ***more favorable*** to the press than, say, a sales tax set at the same percentage, but applicable to the newspaper's gross revenues. Therefore, there was a "benefit" to the press, not a "burden."

b. **Taxation based on content:** Where a tax operates differently upon different members of the press depending on the ***content*** of a publication, it is even more likely to be found invalid. In the post-*Minneapolis Star* case of *Arkansas Writer's Project, Inc. v. Ragland*, 481 U.S. 221 (1987), an Arkansas statute that taxed general interest magazines, but exempted newspapers and other special-interest publications, was invalidated by the Court. The fact that the tax did not discriminate among particular *views*, merely among subject areas, was not sufficient to save the statute.

i. **Exemption that is denied to large category:** On the other hand, where a generally-applicable tax is applied to most media as well as to non-media, and an exemption is given to a certain media segment, denial of the exemption to the rest of the media seems ***not*** to be unconstitutional. Thus if a state has a generally-applicable sales tax on goods and services, it may decide to cover cable TV services while continuing to exempt newspapers, magazines, and satellite broadcast services. *Leathers v. Medlock*, 499 U.S. 439 (1991). The idea seems to be that as long as it is not the case that a small segment of the media is singled out for negative treatment, the fact that some segment of the media *is* given an exemption is irrelevant.

C. Prior restraints: A key aim of the drafters of the First Amendment was to forbid any system of *prior restraints*, similar to the English licensing scheme, by which nothing could be published without government or church approval. This aim remains a vital part of modern First Amendment doctrine, so that any governmental action which prevents expression from occurring (as distinguished from punishing it once it has occurred) is *presumed to be constitutionally invalid*. This is all the more true where the prior restraint is directed against the organized press. See Tribe, p. 1041.

1. **Procedural obstacles:** The dangers of prior restraints also stem from the fact that procedural rules applied in American courts make such restraints more likely to *"chill"* the exercise of First Amendment rights than would a subsequent punishment. Where a person is sought to be punished *after* his speech-related conduct, he is completely free to raise the claim that the statute at issue is unconstitutional, either on its face or as applied to him. But where a person is enjoined *prior* to his expressive act, and yet goes ahead and does that act anyway, he will not be permitted to argue that either the underlying statute or the injunction was unconstitutional as applied to him (though he may argue that the statute was void on its face). See, e.g., *Walker v. City of Birmingham*, 388 U.S. 307 (1967). Thus an unconstitutionally-imposed prior restraint is likely to cow the defendant into foregoing his First Amendment rights, at least during the length of time it takes to conduct an appeal. See Tribe, pp. 1042-45.

2. **Examples of prior restraints:** There are two basic types of pre-publication restraints. One consists of governmental orders and court injunctions telling a particular person that he cannot engage in a certain type of communication. The other consists of a scheme requiring a *license or permit* before a particular type of expression may be engaged in. Movie-censorship schemes are illustrations of the latter category. All of the cases involving the organized press, with which we are concerned here, are of the governmental-order or court-injunction type.

3. *Near v. Minnesota:* The classic case articulating the heavy presumption against prior restraints is *Near v. Minnesota*, 283 U.S. 697 (1931).

    a. **Facts:** In *Near*, a state procedure for closing down as a public nuisance any "malicious, scandalous and defamatory newspaper" was used to permanently enjoin the publication of a newspaper which criticized local officials.

    b. **Holding:** In striking the injunction as an unconstitutional infringement of free speech, the Court held that the primary aim of the First Amendment was to prevent pre-publication restraints. The proper remedy for false accusations against public officials was by a post-publication libel action, not by a pre-publication procedure which the Court found to be tantamount to censorship.

        i. **Exceptional cases:** The prohibition on prior restraints, in the *Near* Court's view, was almost, but not quite, complete. There could be a few "exceptional cases" in which prior restraint would be permissible; the Court gave as illustrations actual obstruction of recruitment for the armed forces, and publication of "the sailing dates of transports or the number and location of troops."

        ii. **Burden of proof:** One aspect of the Minnesota statute to which the Court took particular exception was that the *burden of proof* was placed *upon the publisher* to show his truthfulness or good faith, rather than on the party seeking the injunction to show falsity or malice. However, nothing in the *Near* opinion (or in subsequent case law) suggests that placing the burden of proof in these issues on the party seeking the injunction would validate such a generalized prior restraint scheme.

4. Pentagon Papers case: The only other case to reach the Court on the issue of prior restraint of political speech is the famous ***Pentagon Papers*** case, ***New York Times Co. v. U.S.***, 403 U.S. 713 (1971). This case establishes that the press has ***almost absolute immunity*** from pre-publication restraints. See Tribe, p. 1039.

    a. Facts: *The New York Times* and *The Washington Post* began publishing portions of a secret Defense Department study (popularly known as the "Pentagon Papers") of U.S. policy in Vietnam. The government sought an injunction against the two papers to prevent further publication. The government conceded that the Papers discussed only historical events which transpired prior to 1968, but argued that publication would prolong the War by giving the enemy information useful to it and would embarrass our diplomatic efforts.

    b. *Per curiam* opinion: The opinion of the Court was a brief *per curiam* one, which recited prior case law that there is a heavy presumption against the constitutionality of prior restraints, but which contained no other reasoning. By a 6-3 vote, the Court determined that the government was ***not entitled*** to the injunctions.

    c. Nine separate opinions: *Every member* of the Court wrote a separate opinion, and no majority of the Court agreed on a precise rationale for the decision. The opinions fell into three broad categories: Justices Black and Douglas argued that there could ***never*** be a prior restraint on the press; Justices Brennan, White, Stewart and Marshall contended that there could be prior restraint in extraordinary circumstances, but that the present case did not qualify; and Justices Burger, Harlan, and Blackmun believed that prior restraint was appropriate here.

    d. Absolutist view: Justices Black and Douglas appeared to be saying that *ever* to permit the publication of news to be enjoined would "make a shambles of the First Amendment."

        i. Criticism: But as Professor Cox has pointed out, in 94 HARV. L. REV. 6, "Surely [Black and Douglas] would not have ruled during World War II that a newspaper had a constitutional right to publish for Nazi eyes the knowledge that, because of … cryptographic work … British authorities were reading the orders of the Nazi High Command."

    e. Possible restraints: The four other Justices in the six-man majority believed that prior restraint of news publication could sometimes occur, but not in this case. This group, consisting of Brennan, Stewart, White and Marshall, argued that there must be a ***virtual certainty*** that grave damage to the country would result if publication were not enjoined; as Justice Stewart, joined by White, expressed the test, there must be a showing that disclosure "will ***surely result*** in ***direct, immediate, and irreparable damage*** to our Nation or its people."

        i. Danger not substantially certain: Most or all of these Justices seemed to believe that publication would ***probably*** damage the nation. It was only because there was not a ***substantial certainty*** of such damage that they voted to strike the injunction.

ii. Absence of statutory authorization: To all of these four Justices except Brennan, an important weakness of the government's position was that *no statute* provided for an injunction against news publication in circumstances like these. Separation of powers principles made it impermissible for the Court to issue an injunction where Congress had declined to act. (But Justices Stewart and White seemed to say that even in the *absence* of statutory authorization, a certainty of direct, immediate and irreparable damage to the country might permit issuance of an injunction. This view would probably command a majority of the Court today. See 94 HARV. L. REV. 7.)

f. Dissent: Three Justices, Harlan, Burger and Blackmun, dissented. They criticized the haste with which the Court heard and decided the case. (Less than one week elapsed between filing of the case and announcement of the decision.) Only one Justice, Harlan, formulated a test for evaluating the constitutionality of such injunctions.

i. Harlan's test: In Harlan's view, the Court's role should be limited to determining: (1) whether the subject matter of the dispute lies within the *proper scope* of the *President's foreign relations power*; and if the answer is "yes," (2) whether the determination that disclosure would irreparably impair the national security was personally made by the head of the relevant executive department, here, the Secretary of State or Secretary of Defense. If the answer to this question, too, was "yes," the injunction should be upheld.

ii. Rationale: Harlan argued that it was a violation of separation of powers principles for the judiciary to go beyond these two inquiries and to "redetermine for itself the probable impact of disclosure on the national security."

g. Receipt of stolen goods: As is well known, the newspapers' source for the Pentagon Papers was Daniel Ellsberg, who was given them in confidence while he did work for the government. Had the government been able to show that the newspapers were *receivers of stolen goods*, by showing that the newspapers were aware that Ellsberg's making and distributing copies was a violation of his obligation of confidentiality, it is possible that the Court might have found this to be grounds for an injunction. No subsequent case to reach the Court has faced this question squarely.

i. Difficulty: One difficulty with allowing an injunction based on such a receivership-of-stolen-goods theory is that "requiring a newspaper to decide at its peril whether information that it has received about an official proceeding is confidential would have a chilling effect upon the publication of legitimate news." 94 HARV. L. REV. 12.

5. The *Progressive* H-bomb case: At least one court has interpreted the *Pentagon Papers* case to *permit* an injunction against publication of newsworthy information if a statute so authorizes, and if the danger is sufficiently compelling. In *U.S. v. The Progressive, Inc.*, 467 F. Supp. 990 (W.D. Wis. 1979), the district court enjoined a magazine from publishing an article containing *technical information about the H-bomb*. At least some of the materials had previously been declassified. But the U.S. convinced the court that these materials, taken together with other classified information (also sought to be released by the magazine), could pose a direct threat to national security by possibly "allow[ing] a medium size nation to move faster in developing a hydrogen weapon."

a. **Rationale:**   The judge reasoned that two main considerations made this case distinguishable from the *Pentagon Papers* case: (1) here, a statute, the Atomic Energy Act, authorized an injunction against publication of certain information relating to the use or manufacture of nuclear weapons (including some of the information in the proposed article); and (2) publication might well lead to nuclear proliferation, which in turn might lead to "thermonuclear annihilation for us all."

b. **Balancing test:**   The court then balanced the dangers to the paper's First Amendment rights against the danger to the nation. As to the former, although the injunction might interfere with the magazine's broadly-defined First Amendment rights, it would not interfere with its "laudable crusade to stimulate public knowledge of nuclear armament and bring about enlightened debate on national policy questions." The balance was struck in favor of the injunction; the "disparity of risk" between the danger to the nation and the damage to the paper's First Amendment rights justified what the court conceded was "the first instance of prior restraint against a publication in this fashion in the history of this country."

c. **Outcome:**   Before the paper's appeal could be heard, the government's attempt to get a permanent injunction against it was dropped, because the information was published elsewhere.

6. **"Gag orders" and preservation of fair trials:**   The media's exercise of its First Amendment rights may sometimes come into conflict with a *criminal defendant's right to a fair trial*. Extensive pre-trial publicity, including disclosure of confessions (possibly inadmissible) by the defendant, may make it much more difficult to find jurors who can be impartial. Nonetheless, the United States has never gone even a single step towards the English rule, which makes illegal the pre-trial publication of information that might cause prejudice.

a. **Standard for biased jury:**   If the defendant can show that the jury was biased against him, he is entitled to a *reversal* of his conviction. But it is *not* sufficient for him to show that the jurors had *knowledge before they were sworn in about the facts and issues involved in the case* — requiring complete ignorance would be virtually impossible in important trials, given today's mass communications. Rather, the defendant must show that the jury was *prejudiced* against him as the result of pre-trial publicity.

b. **Publicity during trial:**   Similarly, publicity *during* the trial may be so great that, if the jury is exposed to it, the defendant's right to a fair trial will be found to have been violated. See, e.g., *Sheppard v. Maxwell*, 384 U.S. 333 (1966), the famous Sam Sheppard murder case, where massive prejudicial publicity during the trial, to which the jury was exposed, was held to be grounds for reversal; the Court observed that the problem could have been avoided by *sequestering* the jury for the length of the trial.

c. **Gag orders:**   Because of these dangers of publicity, especially before the trial begins, trial judges have sought ways of assuring that they will be able to find an unbiased jury. One appealing method that some seized upon is the *"gag order,"* a pre-trial order *prohibiting the press from publishing certain types of information* about the case. But as the result of the one case involving a gag order to reach the Court, such orders will *almost never be constitutionally permissible*. That case is *Nebraska Press Ass'n v. Stuart*, 427 U.S. 539 (1976).

i. Facts of *Nebraska Press:* In *Nebraska Press*, a man was about to be tried for a heinous mass murder, which had attracted widespread media attention. The trial judge, in order to assure his ability to select an unprejudiced jury, issued an order prohibiting the press from reporting any confessions or admissions by the defendant, or any other fact "strongly implicative" of him, until after impaneling of the jury.

ii. Holding: The Supreme Court held unanimously that the gag order ***violated*** the press' First Amendment rights.

iii. Majority opinion: The majority opinion was written by Chief Justice Burger, with whom four other Justices joined. Burger declined to hold that a ban on pretrial publicity could ***never*** be constitutional. Instead, he applied a test long ago advocated by Learned Hand for subversive-advocacy cases: the restraint should be allowed only if the "gravity of the 'evil,' discounted by its improbability" is greater than the damage from impairment of First Amendment rights.

(1) Standard not met: Here, Burger said, this test was not satisfied. The trial judge's conclusion that pretrial publicity would impair the defendant's rights "was of necessity ***speculative***," rather than certain. Furthermore, the trial judge should have considered ***other alternatives*** for reducing the harmful effect of such publicity (e.g., change of venue, postponement of trial, careful *voir dire*, restricting statements by the lawyers, police and witnesses, etc.). Finally, the trial judge should have considered whether his gag order would even be effective, in view of the rumors which usually circulate in a sensational case. On balance, then, it was not sufficiently established that the benefits of the gag order outweighed its First Amendment dangers.

d. Significance: *Nebraska Press* probably presents about the strongest case imaginable for a gag order furthering the right of fair trial. Therefore, the result of that decision is that such orders will virtually never be constitutional, at least as long as the press acquires its information without violating the law.

e. Distinguished from subsequent punishment: What made the order in *Nebraska Press* a "prior restraint" was not simply that it forbade publishing a certain type of material; it was that the restriction took the form of an order applicable to one particular, specifically-identified factual setting (this particular trial). Had the ***legislature*** made it a ***crime*** to publish prejudicial information in advance of *any* criminal trial, such a statute could ***not properly be termed a prior restraint***, and would ***not*** necessarily be unconstitutional.

i. Analysis: General First Amendment principles might be interpreted to make such a statute violative of freedom of expression, but the heavy presumption against prior restraints would have nothing to do with the decision.

f. Silencing the lawyer: The "gag order" in *Nebraska Press* was directed at the media; the case establishes that such press-directed orders will rarely be constitutional. But courts have a far greater ability to issue a constitutional gag order against the ***lawyers*** in the case, as the result of a post-*Nebraska Press* case decision. In *Gentile v. State Bar of Nevada*, 501 U.S. 1030 (1991), the Court held that states may prevent a lawyer from making any statement that would have a ***"substantial likelihood of materially preju-***

dicing" an adjudicative proceeding. The Court upheld a Nevada rule patterned on the American Bar Association's Model Rule (prohibiting statements posing a substantial likelihood of material prejudice) over the lawyer's claim that a "clear and present danger" standard should be used.

g. **Closure orders:** Since trial judges will almost never be permitted to use a pre-trial gag order directed at the press, an obvious alternative is for them simply to *close pre-trial proceedings to the public (and press)*. The use of such closure orders, at least where they are limited to pretrial proceedings and are not opposed by either the prosecution or the defense, was upheld by the Supreme Court, in *Gannett Co. v. DePasquale*, discussed *infra*, p. 639.

D. **Governmental demands for information held by press:** First Amendment issues may arise when the government seeks *disclosure* of information *obtained by the press* during its news-gathering activities, but not yet published. Typically, the government seeks such disclosure as part of its *law enforcement* efforts. The two Supreme Court cases on point, one involving a grand jury investigation and the other the use of an *ex parte* search warrant, indicate that the press is *not entitled to any special First Amendment protection* against what would otherwise be proper compulsory disclosure of information obtained during news-gathering.

1. **Indirect impact on First Amendment rights:** Observe that the nature of the interference with First Amendment expression is quite different in this compulsory-disclosure setting than in the prior restraint area. In the latter setting, restraint is almost always sought *because of the communicative impact* which publication would have; thus prior restraints almost always call for "track one" analysis (to use Tribe's term), and strict scrutiny is obviously appropriate. But in the compulsory disclosure area, any interference with First Amendment expression (e.g., the drying up of information from informants, because they are afraid their confidentiality will not be preserved) is *incidental to,* not the purpose of, the disclosure. Therefore, these cases call for "track two" analysis, which as noted (*supra*, p. 507) is handled by a much less stringent balancing of harms and benefits. Therefore, it is not surprising that the Supreme Court has been much less quick to accept the press' arguments in the compulsory-disclosure area than in the context of prior restraints. See 94 HARV. L. REV. 55.

2. ***Branzburg* and grand jury investigations:** In *Branzburg v. Hayes*, 408 U.S. 665 (1972), the Court held by a 5-4 vote that requiring newsmen to testify before *grand juries* concerning *information obtained from confidential sources* during news-gathering does *not* violate the First Amendment. In so deciding, the Court *rejected* journalists' requests for at least a *qualified privilege* to refuse to disclose the *identities of confidential sources* or the *information* received from them.

a. **Journalists' argument:** The argument raised by Branzburg and two other journalists was that news-gathering often requires confidential sources, who agree to supply the journalist with otherwise unavailable information only if non-disclosure of the informant's name and/or some of the information is promised. If a grand jury could compel disclosure, the journalists argued, not only the source of the particular information sought, but other confidential sources in the future, would be dissuaded from talking to journalists.

b. **Holding:** In rejecting the claim for a privilege, the Court held that such a privilege had never been found to exist, and that journalists had always been viewed as having the *same duty as any other citizen* to disclose to grand juries information about crime. The majority was not convinced that a significant portion of information supplied by confidential sources would dry up, especially since such information was widely available to newsmen even though no privilege had ever been recognized.

    i. **Balancing:** Even if significant impairment of confidential sources did occur, the majority saw no reason why "[t]he public interest in possible future news about crime from undisclosed, unverified sources" should take precedence over the governmental interest in prosecuting crimes about which journalists possess evidence.

    ii. **Definitional problem:** Also, the majority saw a *definitional* problem: recognition of a privilege would require the courts either to decide that only the "organized press" should be protected (and to define that term), or to make the privilege dangerously broad by protecting "lectures, political pollsters, novelists, academic researchers, dramatists" and anyone else claiming to be informing the public and to be relying on confidential sources.

c. **Qualified privilege rejected:** The majority also rejected even a *qualified* privilege, by which disclosure of confidential information could not be compelled unless the state showed that a crime had been committed and that the journalist possessed relevant information not available from other sources.

d. **Protection against harassment:** But the majority preserved the right of a journalist to obtain relief against *harassment*, e.g., a subpoena issued not to pursue law enforcement ends but for the purpose of disrupting the reporter's relationship with his news sources (perhaps because of official displeasure with the newsman's work). However, so long as the questions were relevant and material, and were part of a good faith grand jury investigation, the newsman could not decline to answer.

e. **Powell's concurrence:** The crucial fifth vote was supplied by Justice Powell, who although he joined the Court's opinion submitted a separate concurrence as well; this concurrence made the result of the case somewhat ambiguous. Whereas the other four members of the majority rejected a qualified privilege, and left room only for a defense of harassment, Justice Powell's concurrence stated that claims of privilege should be decided on a *case-by-case basis*, by balancing freedom of the press against the obligation of all citizens to give relevant testimony. Powell suggested, for instance, that a newsman may obtain relief if he can show that he has been asked for information bearing "only a remote and tenuous relationship to the subject of the investigation," or that his confidential sources would be compromised "without a legitimate need of law enforcement."

f. **Dissent:** Three of the four dissenters in *Branzburg* did not argue for an absolute privilege against grand jury disclosure of confidential sources. But they did support a type of *strict scrutiny* of such compulsory disclosure, by which the government would have to make three showings before a reporter could be required to reveal confidences: (1) that there is "probable cause to believe that the newsman has information which is *clearly relevant* to a *specific probable violation of law*;" (2) that the information cannot be obtained by "*alternative means* less destructive of First Amendment rights"; and (3) that the government has a "compelling and overriding interest" in the information.

i. **Relation to Powell's view:** As the dissenters pointed out, this type of qualified privilege may not be so different from the position taken by Justice Powell. The absolute position taken by the other four members of the majority, by contrast, would "annex the journalistic profession as an investigative arm of government," the dissenters argued.

3. **Limited scope of ruling:** In addition to grand jury proceedings, the rationale of *Branzburg* obviously applies to **criminal trials** as well. But it is not clear that the theory of *Branzburg* also deprives newsmen of a constitutional privilege regarding testimony in **civil suits.** Some lower courts have granted a **qualified privilege** in this situation, which may be overcome only by a showing that the confidentially-obtained information is not available from other sources. See N&R, p. 1051.

4. **Shield laws:** The majority in *Branzburg* noted that Congress and state legislatures are free to enact **statutes** granting to newsmen a privilege against disclosure of confidential sources or information in grand jury or other proceedings. More than half of the states have, either before or after *Branzburg*, conferred such a privilege by means of so-called *"shield laws."*

   a. **No Court decisions:** The Supreme Court has not yet had occasion to determine whether some applications of such a shield law unconstitutionally interfere with other constitutional rights, most notably a criminal defendant's Sixth Amendment **right to a fair trial.**

   b. *Farber* **case:** One well-known state court case, involving a trial judge's order to a reporter to produce interview notes in connection with a murder case, concluded that such a shield law **must yield to the defendant's Sixth Amendment rights.** *In re Farber*, 394 A.2d 330 (N.J. 1978).

5. *Ex parte* **search warrants:** Another press claim for special protection against compelled disclosure for law enforcement purposes failed in *Zurcher v. Stanford Daily*, 436 U.S. 547 (1978). There, the Court upheld an **ex parte warrant** for the search of a student newspaper's offices, based on probable cause to believe that photographs of a riotous demonstration might be found there.

   a. **Usual rules applied:** The majority opinion spent most of its time talking about the Fourth Amendment, not the First, and saw no reason to depart from usual principles allowing the issuance on probable cause of *ex parte* warrants (that is, warrants issued without notice to the person whose property is to be searched).

   b. **Qualified privilege rejected:** As in *Branzburg*, the Court **rejected** the press' request for at least a **qualified** privilege, under which an *ex parte* warrant would be issued only where there was reason to believe that a **subpoena** might lead to the destruction of the evidence.

E. **Disclosure of confidential or illegally-obtained information:** To what extent may government prohibit the media from **disclosing information** that government believes ought to be **secret**? The interests that government may be trying to protect can include the **privacy of individuals**, the **rehabilitation of juvenile offenders**, or the maintenance of **national security**, among others. A good summary of the Court's decisions in this area is that "[i]f a newspaper **lawfully obtains truthful information** about a matter of **public significance** then [government] officials may not constitutionally punish publication of the information, absent a ***need ... of the highest order.***" *Smith v. Daily Mail Publishing Co.*, 443 U.S. 97 (1979).

1. **Information about legal proceedings:** A number of the Court's decisions concerning publication of "secret" material have involved information about ***legal proceedings*** or ***law enforcement***. Here, government has almost always been ***unsuccessful*** in ***making it a crime to publish*** legally-obtained truthful information. Here are some examples:

   ❑ A broadcaster may not be held civilly liable for ***publishing the name of a rape victim***, if the name is learned from the reading of a publicly-filed indictment. *Cox Broadcasting Corp. v. Cohn*, 420 U.S. 469 (1975).

   ❑ A state may not make it a crime for a newspaper to report (accurately) that a state judicial commission is contemplating an ***investigation of a particular sitting judge***. *Landmark Communications, Inc. v. Virginia*, 435 U.S. 829 (1978).

   ❑ A newspaper cannot be punished for publishing the ***name and photo of a juvenile offender***, where the newspaper obtained the name from witnesses to the crime and from law-enforcement officers who investigated it. *Smith v. Daily Mail Publishing Co.*, 443 U.S. 97 (1979).

2. **Information obtained by means of a crime:** An important sub-question is whether this rule — that publication of newsworthy confidential information may not be criminalized absent an extremely strong state interest — applies even to ***illegally-obtained*** information.

   a. **Where publisher has acted illegally:** If the ***publisher itself*** has ***acted illegally*** in obtaining the information, then it is quite clear that government ***may make it a crime*** to punish the information, no matter how newsworthy it is.

      Example: Suppose that, in 1974, a reporter for the *Washington Post* broke into the White House and found a tape that recorded White House officials conspiring to burglarize the Democratic National Committee's offices. If the *Post* published a transcript of that tape, it's quite clear that a state could constitutionally punish the paper for the publication (apart from the break-in), because the newspaper obtained the information as a result of a crime by its own employee.

   b. **Where private party has acted illegally but publisher has not:** On the other hand, the fact that the secret information was originally obtained illegally by a person ***acting independently*** of the eventual publisher is ***not*** enough to allow publication to be made criminal, at least where the material has significant newsworthiness.

      i. **Illegal interception of cellphone calls:** A vivid illustration of this principle occurred in a 2001 case in which a radio station played a tape of a cellphone conversation that had been intercepted in violation of a federal wiretapping law. Because the interception occurred without the participation of the station, and because the conversation involved important public events, the station could not be prosecuted for the broadcast. *Bartnicki v. Vopper*, 532 U.S. 514 (2001).

         (1) **Facts:** In *Bartnicki*, the conversation was a cellphone conversation between two officials of a teachers union, who were discussing a bitter contract negotiation that they were having with the local school board. During the conversation, one of the officials said that if the board remained intransigent, it might be necessary for the union to go to board members' homes and "blow off their

front porches." An unknown person intercepted the conversation in violation of federal law and sent it anonymously to a radio station, which broadcast it. The two officials sued the station for damages, as allowed by federal and state wiretap statutes prohibiting the disclosure of intercepted telephone conversations.

(2) Holding: By a 6-3 vote, the Court held that the station could not constitutionally be held liable for damages — the extreme newsworthiness of the conversation outweighed the strong governmental interest in protecting the privacy of electronic communications. The majority conceded that the government had a strong interest in deterring illegal interceptions, but believed that barring publication by a third person who did not participate in the interception would not significantly deter the illegal conduct.

(3) Newsworthiness: It seems clear that the extremely strong **newsworthiness** of the conversation in *Bartnicki* — which contained not only news about the bitter negotiation but a possible threat to people's physical safety — played a key role in the Court's decision.

(4) Significance: So what we know from *Bartnicki* is merely that where a publisher innocently comes into possession of illegally-intercepted conversations, and those conversations involve matters of unusually great public interest, the publisher may not be punished for disseminating them. There is a good chance that where the conversation involves matters that are ***not*** of major public interest (e.g., trade secrets or personal gossip), publication *can* be criminalized. And, of course, the person who does the illegal intercepting may be punished for publishing, no matter how great the public interest in the intercepted conversation.

3. Enforcement of confidentiality promises: Now consider one last aspect of government's power to enforce the confidentiality of information: if a journalist promises confidentiality to a source and then breaches that promise by publishing the confidential information, may the state allow the source to recover damages? The brief answer is "yes" — the Supreme Court has held that the states may ***enforce such confidentiality promises*** as they would any other contract, without thereby running afoul of the First Amendment. *Cohen v. Cowles Media Co.*, 501 U.S. 663 (1991).

F. Right of access to government-held information: Much newsworthy information is ***within the government's possession*** or control. Until recently, nothing in any Supreme Court decision supported any First Amendment right on the part of the press to have ***access*** to this newsworthy information. Thus although the press has long been recognized to have a broad First Amendment right to publish information which it obtains, the press has ***not*** been constitutionally entitled to ***assistance in obtaining information.*** Such a right of access has still not been explicitly recognized by the Court, but the decision in *Richmond Newspapers, Inc. v. Virginia*, discussed *infra*, p. 639, upholding a right of access to criminal trials, may presage some form of right of access to government-controlled newsworthy material.

1. Access to jails: Several cases have established that the press has little or no special right of access to information about ***prison conditions.***

a. ***Pell*** and ***Saxbe:*** In the companion cases of *Pell v. Procunier*, 417 U.S. 817 (1974) and *Saxbe v. Washington Post Co.*, 417 U.S. 843 (1974), the Court ***upheld*** state and federal regulations ***prohibiting press interviews*** with any specific prisoner. The Court rejected First Amendment claims raised by both the media and by prisoners. The majority opinion in both cases, by Justice Stewart, relied mainly on the fact that the regulations ***treated the press no worse than they did members of the general public***. While the First Amendment prevents the government from interfering with the media's attempt to gather news, it does ***not*** "require government to accord the press special access to information not shared by members of the public generally."

2. **Access to pretrial proceedings:** Trial judges are ***not*** permitted to issue pretrial ***"gag orders"*** in order to preserve the defendant's right to an unbiased jury, except where the danger to the defendant's right to a fair trial is unusually great. See *Nebraska Press Ass'n v. Stuart,* 427 U.S. 539 (1976). Therefore, some courts have instead ***closed pretrial proceedings to the public***. In *Gannett Co. v. DePasquale*, 443 U.S. 368 (1979), the Court held that such pretrial closure orders are at least ***sometimes constitutional***; the Court's opinion may even mean that the press and public ***never*** have a First Amendment right to attend such pretrial proceedings.

3. **Closure of criminal trials:** One key question left unresolved by *Gannett* was whether a criminal defendant's interest in a fair trial could be preserved by ***closing the entire trial*** to the public. In ***Richmond Newspapers, Inc. v. Virginia***, 448 U.S. 555 (1980), the Court answered this question largely in the ***negative***, holding that "absent an ***overriding interest*** articulated in findings," the First Amendment requires that "[t]he ***trial of a criminal case must be open to the public***." Although the vote was 7-1, there was no majority opinion, and the precise scope of the decision remains unclear.

a. **Significance of case:** At a minimum, *Richmond Newspapers* establishes that the public and press have a First Amendment right to attend criminal trials, and that entire trials can be closed only if that right is outweighed by ***overriding*** interests which ***cannot be satisfied by less restrictive means***. Whether the decision means more than that is not clear.

i. **Civil trials:** It seems probable that the decision is also applicable to ***civil trials***, since such trials, like criminal ones, have traditionally been open to the public, and since there is a strong public interest in observing the administration of civil justice. Several of the Justices in *Richmond Newspapers* specifically stated that they believed the decision to be applicable to such civil proceedings.

ii. **Pretrial context:** The First Amendment right of access to criminal trials recognized in *Richmond Newspapers* has been extended to certain ***pretrial proceedings***. For instance, the public has a right to attend the *voir dire* of the jury; see *Press Enterprise Co. v. Superior Court*, 467 U.S. 501 (1984).

iii. **Closure of portions of trial:** Trial judges presumably retain their traditional power to close ***certain portions*** of a criminal trial in order to protect the integrity of the proceedings. For instance, testimony of a particular witness might be held outside of the presence of the public, in order to prevent other witnesses from hearing his testimony and adjusting their own to match it (though sequestration of subsequent witnesses is a preferable technique for solving this problem). Also, any trial proceedings *not held in the presence of the jury* (e.g., discussions of the admissibility of evidence) probably may be closed to the public.

    iv. Limited seats: Also, the right of access to public trials does not mean that *every* person who desires to see a particular trial has a right to do so. Obviously, courtrooms have limited seating, and a trial judge may use a reasonable scheme of allocating seats. However, the First Amendment right recognized by *Richmond Newspapers* probably does require that *at least some seats be given to media representatives*.

4. Less-restrictive alternative required: Although *Richmond Newspapers* established that there is a First Amendment right to access to criminal trials, *no* Justice suggested that that right is an *absolute* one. The test for determining when that right is outweighed by other countervailing interests has been developed in later cases.

    a. *Globe Newspapers:* In *Globe Newspapers v. Superior Court*, 457 U.S. 596 (1982), the Court applied what amounted to a traditional *strict scrutiny* standard: access to criminal trials may be denied only if the denial is "necessitated by a *compelling governmental interest*, and is *narrowly tailored to serve that interest*." Under this test, a Massachusetts statute was unconstitutional in *requiring* the exclusion of the press and public from the courtroom during the testimony of any minor who is allegedly the victim of a sex offense.

G. Regulation of broadcast media: The Supreme Court has always recognized that the *broadcast* media may be subject to *closer regulation* than newspapers and other non-broadcasters. The closer regulation of broadcasters derives from the fact that broadcast frequencies are a *naturally scarce* commodity — whereas there can in theory be an unlimited number of newspapers serving any particular market, the technology of broadcasting is such that there could only be a strictly limited number of television and radio stations serving any particular market. (This distinction is, in practical terms, much less convincing in today's world of UHF and cable television, massive FM as well as AM radio, Internet video, etc., than it was when broadcasting was largely limited to VHF television and AM radio. But the Court has not fundamentally altered its willingness to tolerate closer regulation of the broadcast media.)

1. Means of regulation: This regulation has generally been carried on through the Federal Communications Commission (FCC). The Court has several times sustained the FCC's power to ensure various types of *public access* to the broadcast media. See, e.g., *Red Lion Broadcasting Co. v. FCC*, 395 U.S. 367 (1969), in which the Court upheld the FCC's "fairness" doctrine, by which broadcasters are compelled to grant individuals the right to reply on the air to political editorials or personal attacks. Similarly, the Court is probably more willing to tolerate closer regulation of *context* where the source of speech is a broadcaster; see, e.g., *FCC v. Pacifica Foundation*, 438 U.S. 726 (1978), in which the Court permitted the FCC to ban language that was "indecent" (but not "obscene") from the airwaves during afternoon hours when children were likely to be in the audience.

2. "Mere-rationality" review for content-neutral regulations: Where regulations against broadcasters are *content-neutral*, these regulations are judged very deferentially, essentially according to the "mere-rationality" standard. For instance, *Red Lion, supra,* seems to have applied "mere-rationality" review to the FCC's fairness doctrine, on the theory that that doctrine is essentially content-neutral.

3. **Middle-level scrutiny for content-based restrictions:** However, where the regulation against broadcasters is **content-based**, the Court seems to apply a **middle-level scrutiny**, more stringent than "mere-rationality" review. But even here the standard of review reflects the Court's view that broadcasters should be subjected to tighter regulation because of their access to scarce airwaves: the mid-level review given to content-based broadcasting regulations is clearly less stringent than the "strict" (and almost always fatal) review given to content-based regulations against newspapers and other non-broadcasters. (See *supra*, p. 505.) This middle-level scrutiny was demonstrated in ***FCC v. League of Women Voters***, 468 U.S. 364 (1984), a 5-4 decision.

   a. **Ban on editorializing struck down:** In *League of Women Voters*, the Court struck down (by a 5-4 vote), a congressional prohibition on *editorializing* by public broadcasters who receive federal funding. The majority viewed the ban as being non-content-neutral. The test set forth by the Court was that such restrictions impinging on broadcasters' First Amendment rights will be upheld only if they are *"narrowly tailored* to further a *substantial governmental interest*, such as ensuring adequate and balanced coverage of public issues. ... "

   b. **Test not satisfied:** The Court concluded that the ban on editorializing could not survive this middle-level review. For instance, Congress may have had a substantial governmental interest in making sure that public broadcasters did not become "vehicles for governmental propagandizing" as the result of federal funding, but there were other, more narrowly-tailored, ways of making sure that government did not interfere with the broadcasting judgment of station officials.

4. **Cable gets greater free speech:** The Court has held that *cable* television is, in effect, *somewhere between broadcast TV and newspapers* in terms of the amount of government regulation of speech that operators must tolerate.

   a. **Content-neutral regulation:** Thus where the regulation of cable TV is *content-neutral*, *mid-level review* is to be used. In *Turner Broadcasting System, Inc. v. FCC*, 512 U.S. 622 (1994) (*"Turner I"*), the Court held that where cable TV operators are subjected to content-neutral regulations, mid-level review, not the easy-to-satisfy "mere-rationality" standard used in the over-the-air broadcast cases, should be used.

      i. **Regulations upheld:** But content-neutral governmental regulation of cable TV certainly can sometimes *pass* constitutional muster, even though mid-level rather than rational-relation review is used. For instance, Congress has enacted "must carry" provisions, which require cable TV systems to devote some of their channels, free of charge, to the retransmission of local broadcast TV stations. In a successor to *Turner I, supra*, the Court upheld these must-carry rules after mid-level review. The Court gave special deference to Congress' legislative findings on the need for must-carry, because Congress was better equipped than the judiciary to "amass and evaluate the *vast amounts of data*" bearing on legislative questions, especially ones concerning "regulatory schemes of the *inherent complexity*" and "assessments about the likely interaction of *industries undergoing rapid economic and technological change*." *Turner Broadcasting System Inc. v. FCC*, 520 U.S. 180 (1997) (*"Turner II"*).

b. Content-based regulation: Where cable TV operators and programmers are regulated in a ***content-based*** way, ***strict scrutiny*** must be used. See *U.S. v. Playboy Entertainment Group, Inc.*, 529 U.S. 803 (2000).

Quiz Yourself on

FREEDOM OF ASSOCIATION; DENIAL OF PUBLIC JOBS OR BENEFITS; SPECIAL PROBLEMS OF THE MEDIA

86. There have been several bombings of government office buildings on the island of Puerto Rico recently. After each bombing, an anonymous caller has told the local newspaper that the bomb was planted by "People for a Free Puerto Rico" (PFPR), an organization dedicated to using any means necessary to end Puerto Rico's status as a United States territory and establishing it as a sovereign nation. There is evidence that the PFPR was able to plant the bombs so successfully inside the buildings because its members or sympathizers have jobs in government agencies located in those buildings, who could furnish information and access for placement of the bombs. To deal with the threat, the territorial government of Puerto Rico has now imposed a requirement that any new applicant for any government position must before being hired sign a loyalty oath stating, among other things, that "I am not a member of the People for a Free Puerto Rico or of any group advocating the use of force to alter the territorial status of Puerto Rico." Ramona, an applicant for a position as a clerical worker in the Puerto Rican government, has declined to sign the oath, without specifying her reasons. Can the government constitutionally decline to hire her on the grounds that she has refused to sign? _____

87. Sheryl was a low-level clerk in her state's Department of Motor Vehicles. News reports were published stating that Horace, the Commissioner of the Department of Motor Vehicles (and thus, ultimately, Sheryl's boss) may have taken payments from Computer Systems Inc. in return for helping Computer Systems get a contract to install a large new computer system at the Department. Horace protested his innocence, and the District Attorney eventually decided that no charges should be brought. Shortly thereafter, Sheryl said to a co-worker, while on the job, "I still think Horace took the money, and I think he's a crook." Another employee who overheard the remark reported it to Horace, who immediately fired Sheryl for insubordination and fomenting discord in the Department. Under the relevant Civil Service rules, Sheryl was an at-will employee who had no reason to expect continued employment. Sheryl now seeks a court order restoring her position, on the grounds that she was fired in violation of her First Amendment rights. Should the court grant reinstatement to Sheryl? _____

88. The state of Calizona, which shares a border with Mexico, was in the middle of a divisive in-state political battle about whether the nation's immigration rules should be reformed so as to make it easier for immigrants, especially ones from Mexico, to become U.S. citizens. The party with a majority in the state legislature opposed this type of immigration reform, but supported efforts to register more voters. That party caused the legislature to enact the Get Out The Vote Subsidy Act (GOTVSA), under which Calizona would provide a $100,000 subsidy to any private non-profit group whose principal function was to organize voter-registration and voter-turnout drives. As a condition to any group's eligibility for the funds, the Act required the group to promise that the group would not expend any sums — regardless of whether or not the funds came from the subsidy — to advocate or lobby for "national immigration reform." Hispanic Voters Unite (HVU) is a non-profit group devoted principally to increasing the voter registration and turnout percentage of Calizona citizens of Hispanic ethnicity, but secondarily to advocating and lobbying for national immigration reform. HVU would have been eligible for the subsidy except for its refusal to make the immigration-reform promise. HVU brought a federal suit against the state, claiming that the Act's ban

on immigration-reform-related activities violated the group's First Amendment freedom of expression. Should the court find in favor of HVU, and why/why not? _____

89. P.J. Summers, a former football player turned sports announcer, was charged with the brutal murder of his wife. While in police custody, Summers gave a confession. In pretrial hearings, the trial judge determined that the *Miranda* rules had not been complied with, and decided that the confession would not be admissible at the trial. The press learned of the confession through pretrial proceedings in open court, and did not act improperly in obtaining this information. Prosecutors decided to try Summers as a principal in the murder, and also decided to charge B.C. Scowling, a long-time friend of Summers, as an accomplice. Both trials were to be held simultaneously (but in front of separate juries) in proceedings conducted by Judge Jones.

Judge Jones was very worried that disclosures about the confession might make it difficult or impossible to impanel a jury that would be fair to Summers. Therefore, several days before jury selection was to start, Jones issued two orders from the bench: (1) he ordered that no newspaper, magazine or broadcaster report the existence or details of the inadmissible confession until after the jury had been picked (once the jury was picked, it could be sequestered, so that prejudicial disclosures would not matter anymore); (2) he also ordered that no lawyer on the case, including the lawyer for Scowling, disclose to the press or to anyone else the existence of Summers' confession. (There was reason to believe that Scowlings' lawyer planned to say in a public press conference, "My client is innocent; P.J. confessed, and in his confession he said that he acted alone").

   (a) Is the judge's order in part (1) constitutional? _____

   (b) Is the judge's order in part (2) constitutional? _____

90. Roger is a reporter for the Hillsdale Star, a local newspaper. In the most celebrated crime to hit Hillsdale in many years, Joshua, an eight-year-old boy, was found strangled in front of his house. The police have not found any suspects. One week after the killing, Roger published an article saying, "A source that I cannot identify saw the crime from a distance, and believes that the perpetrator was a young white male about 22 years old, six feet tall, weighing about 175 pounds." In the ensuing months, the police have never been able to find this or any other witness to the crime. The prosecutor called Roger in front of a grand jury, and demanded that he identify the witness who served as his source. Roger stated under oath that the witness was fearful that the killer would kill her to silence her. Roger further stated that he had signed a written pledge to the witness that he would never reveal her name; only in response to this pledge did the witness agree to speak to him. Roger did say, however, that the witness lived in the neighborhood and that in his opinion, she could be identified by good police work. The judge then ordered Roger to disclose the witness' identity, or be found in contempt of court. Roger refused. There is no state law relevant to the issue. Can Roger constitutionally be found in contempt and imprisoned until he divulges the name of the witness? _____

Answers

86. **No.** One may not be required to state in a loyalty oath that one has not performed a certain act (or that one will not perform it in the future) unless *actual performance* of that act would be grounds for discharge. One may not be discharged for membership in an organization advocating overthrow of the government or other illegality, unless one has ***knowledge*** of the organization's purpose and ***specific intent*** to further that purpose. Consequently, one may not be required to swear a blanket oath that one has not been a member of such an organization — language referring to the swearer's knowledge of the illegal purposes, and

to her specific intent to further them, must be inserted into the oath. Since the oath here does not refer to Ramona's specific intent to use force to alter the Puerto Rican government, she cannot be penalized for refusing to sign it. See *Cole v. Richardson*.

87. **Yes, probably.** When government attempts to deny a public job or benefit because of a person's speech-related activities, the level of judicial review depends on whether the speech related to matters of ***"public concern."*** If the speech did relate to matters of "public concern," then the Court gives something like strict scrutiny to the situation, striking a balance between the free speech rights of the employee and the state's interest as an employer in conducting its activities efficiently. *Connick v. Myers.* Here, the speech is clearly relating to a matter of public concern, i.e., whether the head of the department took a bribe. Since Sheryl was engaging in core political speech, her interest in being allowed to do so was a strong one. On the other side of the equation, Sheryl was a low-level clerk, not a policy-making official; therefore, her speech was unlikely to have created a severe additional threat to the department's efficiency, especially since other people inside and outside the department were undoubtedly discussing the same much-publicized issue anyway. *Rankin v. McPherson.* Consequently, a court would probably conclude that Sheryl's free speech interest outweighed the department's interest in maintaining smooth operations; if so, the court should order Sheryl reinstated.

By the way, it makes a difference that here, Sheryl's statement was ***not required as part of her job duties.*** *Garcetti v. Ceballos* establishes that where an employee speaks as part of her official duties, what she says ***gets no First Amendment protection at all.*** So if, say, Sheryl's official duties had included the obligation to make a report about any conflicts-of-interest she observed on the job, her statement, "Horace took money from Computer Systems in violation of our Department's conflict-of-interest rules," made in her officially-required report, would not get First Amendment protection, and Sheryl would now not be entitled to reinstatement. So it's only because Sheryl was speaking "as a citizen" (not as an employee) to her co-worker that she gets protection under *Connick v. Myers.*

Lastly, observe that because Sheryl was an at-will employee, she could be fired at any time for "no reason"; even so, under *Connick* she had a First Amendment right not to be fired for the ***particular*** reason that she was exercising her free speech rights.

88. **Yes, because the immigration condition is an unconstitutional condition.** Government is free to set up a program subsidizing a particular private activity, and when government does so, it is free to prohibit the ***subsidy dollars themselves*** from being used for particular expressive activities opposed by government. *Rust v. Sullivan.* This right includes even the right to place viewpoint-based restrictions on the recipient's expressive activities conducted with the subsidy dollars. *Id.* So here, Calizona *would* have been free to say, for instance, "Receipt of the subsidy is conditioned on the recipient's promise that it will not use any of the grant monies to advocate for immigration reform." But this power of government to put conditions on how the subsidy funds will be used does *not* include the right to impose conditions that "seek to ***leverage funding*** to ***regulate speech outside the contours*** of the [government-subsidized] ***program itself.***" *Agency for Int'l Dev. v. Alliance for Open Soc'y Int'l, Inc.*, 133 S. Ct. 2321 (2013). When government tries to do such a "leveraging of funding" — by restricting recipients' expressive activities not carried out through use of the subsidy dollars — it violates the potential recipient's freedom of expression. *Id.*

This forbidden "leveraging" is what Calizona is trying to do here. The state is *not* saying, "The $100,000 can't be used for advocacy of immigration reform"; it's saying, "If you take the $100,000, then you must give up your right to use *even privately-raised funds* to advocate for immigration reform." Speech urging immigration reform is clearly "outside the contours" of the GOTVSA program, since the program's purpose is solely to increase in-state voter registration and turnout, not to influence national immigration policies. The case is therefore like *FCC v. League of Women Voters* (where the Court held that Congress couldn't condition funding to public broadcast stations on the stations' promise not to do editorializing even with private funds) and *A.I.D., supra* (where the Court held that Congress couldn't condition funding to combat HIV/AIDS on the recipient's promise to officially oppose prostitution).

89. **(a) No.** "Gag orders" — that is, pretrial orders prohibiting the press from publishing certain types of information about the case — are virtually never constitutionally permissible. See *Nebraska Press Ass'n v. Stuart*. A gag order is a species of prior restraint, so it can be allowed only if its benefits substantially outweigh its First Amendment dangers, something that will virtually never happen. Here, there are other methods available to the judge to help assure a fair trial (e.g., careful *voir dire* to make sure that each juror has either not heard about the confession or understands that it is to be absolutely disregarded). (A gag order might be allowed if the press had ***illegally*** gotten the information, e.g., by bribing a member of the police department to release sealed information; but where the press comes by the information legally, a gag order preventing it from disseminating the material will almost never be upheld.)

(b) Yes, probably. States may prevent a lawyer from making any statement that would have a ***"substantial likelihood of materially prejudicing"*** an adjudicative proceeding. *Gentile v. State Bar of Nevada*. The state must give guidelines that are reasonably specific about what kinds of disclosures are and are not allowed. The ban here, which refers specifically to the facts of the confession, seems to have adequate specificity. While some sorts of gag orders might unconstitutionally restrict a defense lawyer's right to defend his client in the public eye (e.g., the states probably can't prevent a lawyer from asserting that his client is innocent, or from generally describing the client's proposed defense), references to a co-defendant's inadmissible confession are probably the sort of unduly prejudicial remarks that a lawyer falling within the court's jurisdiction may be barred from making.

90. **Yes.** The First Amendment is not violated when a reporter is required to testify before a grand jury concerning information obtained from confidential sources during newsgathering. In fact, reporters are not even entitled to a ***qualified privilege*** to refuse to identify their sources or information received from those sources — thus a reporter, like any other citizen, may be required to divulge information that could be obtained by police or prosecutors from other sources. *Branzburg v. Hayes.* (Over half of the states have enacted ***statutes*** that grant reporters a privilege against disclosure of confidential sources or information. If such a "shield law" existed here, it would prevent Roger from being held in contempt on these facts.)

Exam Tips on *FREEDOM OF EXPRESSION*

Freedom of expression typically makes up a larger portion of a full-year Con. Law exam than does any other single topic. Almost any regulation of an individual's conduct may pose a free expression issue, so think very broadly. Here are some particular things to keep in mind:

☛ Remember that free expression issues are posed not just where government is regulating "speech" but also where government is regulating ***"conduct"*** that includes an ***expressive component***. So for each activity that's being restricted, first deal with the issue: "Is there an expressive component to the activity?" If you answer "yes," you've got a free expression issue. (*Example:* Panhandling on the subway has been held to be expressive — and thus protected — conduct.)

☛ Always keep in mind the five *"unprotected categories,"* the categories thought to be of *so little value* that they get *no First Amendment protection at all* (as long as government is not singling out particular disfavored *viewpoints,* something that will trigger strict scrutiny even for an unprotected category). If your facts fall into an unprotected category, you don't have to worry about whether the government is unreasonably restraining expression, as long as government is being content-neutral.

☞ Here is a list of the five unprotected categories:

[1] *"Incitement."* This category includes advocacy of *imminent lawless behavior,* as well as the utterance of *"fighting words,"* i.e., words that are likely to precipitate an immediate physical conflict.

[2] *Obscenity.*

[3] *Misleading or deceptive speech (i.e., fraud).*

[4] Speech *integral to criminal conduct,* such as speech that is part of a *conspiracy* to commit a crime or speech *proposing an illegal transaction.*

[5] *Defamation.*

Example: A state can flatly *forbid all obscenity,* without even trying to make its ban narrowly tailored to achieve a significant governmental interest (something government would have to do for a content-neutral regulation outside an unprotected category).

☛ Once you've identified a situation where government is "substantially impairing" protected speech or expressive conduct, decide whether the regulation is *"content-neutral"* or not.

☞ A tip to help you decide: Ask whether the harm the government is trying to prevent would exist to the same degree if the listener/reader didn't understand English. If the answer is "no," the government's action is probably content-based.

☞ Always consider the government's *motive* in regulating the speech — the issue is what the government wished to do: did it want to suppress/control ideas, or did it really want to regulate "secondary" concerns not related to the expressive content?

☛ If you decide that the regulation is "content-based," apply *strict scrutiny.* That is, write that the regulation must be struck down unless the government shows that the restriction is *necessary* to achieve a *compelling* governmental purpose. You should almost always then conclude that the government restriction can't survive. (Usually, the key reason will be that there is some less restrictive way to deal with the problem, even if that less restrictive way is not an absolutely perfect way of handling the problem.)

☞ One commonly-tested scenario: A public school district allows community groups to use the school for their own purposes after hours. A particular group is denied access because of the type of activity, or because of the group's controversial views. (Typically, you should conclude that the restriction here is content-based, and therefore apply strict scrutiny.)

☞   Keep in mind that strict scrutiny for content-based regulations limits a state's right to ***impose civil liability for hurtful speech.*** So, for instance, be ready to say that there is a First Amendment violation if the state lets a person against whom ***intentionally-offensive speech is directed*** recover under state law for ***intentional infliction of emotional distress (IIED).*** (Cite to *Snyder v. Phelps*, where funeral picketers were shielded from IIED liability.)

☞   For a regulation to be "content-neutral," the regulation must be more than just ***"viewpoint"*** neutral. "Content neutral" means "without reference to the content." For instance, restrictions that put ***whole topics*** off limits usually are not content-neutral. (*Example:* If a city requires a permit for political demonstrations, but does not require one for sports victory celebrations, then the distinction is not content-neutral, because the general type of speech or emotion being expressed serves as the basis for imposing or not imposing the permit requirement.)

☛   If you conclude that the regulation is truly "content-neutral," use a three-part test. For instance, any regulation of the ***"time, place and manner"*** of demonstrations or other expressive conduct will be analyzed by this test if you find that it is content-neutral. Here are the three parts (***all*** of which must be satisfied):

☞   The regulation must serve a "***significant*** governmental interest";

☞   The regulation must be ***narrowly tailored*** to achieve that objective; and

☞   The regulation must leave open adequate ***alternative channels*** for communication.

Note: Of these three, the "narrowly tailored" requirement is the one most commonly violated — if there is some ***less restrictive means*** available for dealing with the problem, that means must usually be selected. (However, the less restrictive means probably counts only if it is truly ***"as effective,"*** not just "almost as effective," as the means chosen by government. This makes it hard for the plaintiff challenging the restriction to establish that the "narrowly tailored" requirement has been violated. Cf. *Rumsfeld v. FAIR*.)

Note: In assessing a "time, place and manner" restriction, consider whether a ***public forum*** is involved. The "narrowly tailored" and "alternative channels left open" requirements are ***more strictly construed when a public forum is involved.*** (The public forum is discussed further below.)

☛   Always consider whether either of two key First Amendment doctrines applies:

☞   First, ***overbreadth***. Remember that most litigants in Con. Law are not permitted to assert the rights of others. But under First Amendment overbreadth, P is allowed to assert that the government regulation violates the rights of a person who is not now before the court. (*Example:* A city bans the sale of "sexually explicit" materials. P is charged with violating the statute. The materials sold by him are clearly obscene. Yet, he can defeat the prosecution by showing that the ban also applies to non-obscene sexually explicit materials, which cannot be constitutionally prohibited.)

☞   Second, ***vagueness***. Remember, a statute or regulation is unconstitutionally vague if a person of normal intelligence wouldn't know whether the action in question was forbidden or not. (*Examples:* Statutes forbidding conduct that is "demeaning," "offensive," or "disruptive to public order" might all be found to be unconstitutionally vague, because it is not clear where the line is between what they do and do not proscribe.)

☛ Many exam questions involve a speaker who tries to rouse the crowd to take *subversive* or *illegal action*. Be on the lookout for persons charged with "inciting to riot," "urging the overthrow of the government," "advocating illegal conduct," or the like. When you have such a fact pattern, check for three things:

☞ Was the riot or illegality *imminent*, as opposed to something that would take place at a later date? Only speech urging imminent illegality may be punished. (*Example:* If the speaker says, "Start thinking about forming guerrilla units … ," the required imminence is not present.)

☞ Was the advocacy *intended* to produce illegality? (If illegality was the *unintended by-product* of the speaker's speech, he can't be punished for it.)

☞ Was the advocacy *likely* to produce the illegality? Ineffectual efforts don't count. (*Example:* If people are in a park for other purposes, happen to listen to the speaker, and then go about their business, the "likely to produce illegality" requirement probably is not met.)

☛ When government attempts to require a *license* or *permit* before expressive activity (typically a speech or demonstration) may occur, here are the things to check for:

☞ Make sure that the license/permit requirement is truly *content-neutral*, both as written (i.e., "on the face" of the statute) and as applied (i.e., as the permits are actually handed out by officials). A permit/license requirement cannot be used as a smokescreen for suppressing unpopular views or unpopular topics.

☞ Make sure that the scheme does not give *excessive discretion* to the official charged with issuing the permit. (*Example:* If the fact pattern tells you that the permit is to be issued "based on the Police Commissioner's overall assessment of the good of the community," that's excessive discretion.) This is a commonly tested aspect.

☞ Profs frequently test on whether a speaker has a right to *ignore* a permit requirement.

☞ If the permit requirement is unconstitutional *on its face* (e.g., it's content-based, in that it requires a permit for certain topics but not others), the speaker is *not* required to apply for a permit. He may decline to apply, speak, and then defend on the grounds of the permit requirement's unconstitutionality.

☞ But if the permit is not facially invalid, only unconstitutional *as applied* to the speaker, then the speaker generally does *not* have the right to ignore the requirement. He must apply for the permit, then seek prompt judicial review rather than just going ahead and speaking. (But an exception exists where the applicant shows that *sufficiently prompt judicial review* of the denial was not available.)

☞ When the speaker is judicially *enjoined* from speaking, marching, etc., he generally may *not* ignore the injunction and then raise the constitution as a defense in a subsequent contempt proceeding. Instead, he must seek prior judicial review.

☞ If the above requirements are satisfied, then the permit requirement is valid. (*Example:* A permit will not be invalid merely because it is issued upon conditions that the marchers or demonstrators not block the public's access to a particular place, e.g., an abortion clinic or government building.)

☛ Be on the lookout for expression that may constitute *"fighting words."* These are words that are likely to induce the addressee to **commit an act of violence**, typically against the speaker. Government may forbid fighting words, or punish them after they are spoken.

☞ But be skeptical of claims by the government that the speech in question really constituted "fighting words." Most importantly, remember that the police must **control the crowd** if they have the ability to do so — they can't stand back, then punish the speaker for rousing the crowd to violence.

☞ Also, distinguish fighting words from mere *"offensive speech."* Speech may not be forbidden merely because the listeners are likely to find it offensive. (*Examples:* Nazis demonstrating in front of Holocaust survivors, or black students calling white students "honkey" at a public university, are probably not using "fighting words," merely "offensive speech" — unless the circumstances made violence very likely, the speech cannot be forbidden.)

☞ Look out for attempts to restrict *"hate speech."* A **broad ban** on **all fighting words** is OK. So is a broad ban on all words or acts intended to **harass** or **intimidate** others. Government can even single outs certain intimidating acts and forbid them (e.g., **cross burnings**, when done as a threat or intimidation), while declining to forbid other intimidating acts (e.g., burnings in effigy). But government **can't forbid just those fighting words or threats that are motivated by particular kinds of hatred** (e.g., racial or gender hatred). (Cite to *R.A.V. v. St. Paul* on this point.)

Example: University, a public university, passes a speech code that says "All students are forbidden to harass or threaten other students on the basis of race, gender, or sexual orientation. Violations are punishable by suspension." Since the code bans just certain types of harassment or threats (those based on race, gender and sexual orientation) and not others (e.g., those based on political affiliation), the code is a content-based regulation, and must be strictly scrutinized. It will probably fail that scrutiny, since there are content-neutral alternatives that are less restrictive of speech and will do the job almost as well (e.g., a code banning *all* harassments and threats, regardless of the speaker's motive).

☞ Speech cannot be banned on the mere grounds that it is **profane**. This merely makes it "offensive," not "obscene" or "fighting words." (*Example:* D can wear a jacket saying, "Fuck the Draft." Cite to *Cohen v. California*.)

☞ Whenever you're dealing with a ban on "offensive" conduct or "harassment," consider the possibility that there may be a **vagueness** problem with the regulation.

☛ Whenever your fact pattern involves a restriction on speech that takes place in a *public forum*, note this fact, and try to explain what difference it makes.

☞ The fact that the expressive conduct is taking place in a public forum only makes a difference if the regulation is content-neutral. Assuming that it is content-neutral, the principal difference is that we use ***mid-level review*** (the restriction must be narrowly drawn to serve a significant governmental interest, while leaving open adequate alternative channels for the communication) as opposed to "mere-rationality" review for non-public-forum speech.

☞ The classic *"traditional"* public forums are: ***streets, sidewalks, parks***. There are also ***"designated"*** public forums, where government has decided to open the place to a broad range of expressive activity (e.g., an open City Council meeting or a school whose classrooms are made available after hours to any community group); the same rules apply to designated forums as to true forums, except that government can change its mind and make the place a non-public forum.

　☞ The mere fact that something is public property does not mean it is a public or designated-public forum. There are public spaces that are ***"non-public forums,"*** as to which "mere-rationality" review is all that is used. (*Examples:* Airport terminals, jails, military bases, courthouses, government office buildings.)

　☞ But even in a non-public forum, regulation must still be ***rational*** and ***viewpoint-neutral***. Be especially alert for a violation of viewpoint-neutrality when government ***excludes religious groups*** from benefits that it gives to a wide range of non-religious groups.

　Example: A school district allows a variety of local community groups to use elementary school classrooms after hours to run programs promoting the "general welfare." However, the district excludes from this program any activity or group that is "primarily of a religious nature." This will be unconstitutional viewpoint-based discrimination, even though school classrooms used this way are probably a non-public forum.

　☞ Even if a private group is somehow involved in speech, check to see whether ***government*** is the ***real speaker.*** If the real speaker is government, ***don't use public-forum analysis.*** Instead, say that government-as-speaker can behave in a content-based way, delivering just the message it wants.

　Example: A private group donates a message-bearing monument that a city government decides to take and display in a park. Government will be deemed to be the speaker by virtue of its decision to accept and display the monument. Therefore, the city can discriminate based on the message: the city doesn't have to accept other donated monuments with messages that the city doesn't approve of. [Cite to *Pleasant Grove v. Summum.*]

☛ Fact patterns often involve speech that takes place on ***private property***. Here are the two aspects that are most frequently tested:

☞ The ***public*** has no First Amendment right of access to private property. (*Example:* A person does not have a First Amendment right to distribute literature in a privately-owned shopping center.)

☞ Government may limit an owner's right to use, or to rent his property to others, for expressive purposes. Here, use standard "time, place and manner" analysis, except that no public forum is involved. Therefore, the regulation will usually be upheld if it is content-neutral and other avenues are left for the message. (*Example:* Government may prevent owners from putting signage on their property advertising their wares, as long as the ban applies to all types of signage, and there are other advertising channels available.)

☛ The same rules apply to regulation of *"symbolic expression"* as apply to speech and speech-mixed-with-conduct. "Symbolic expression" refers to **non-verbal acts**.

    ☞ For instance, if government wants to ban destruction of the flag, it must do so in a content-neutral way (e.g., it cannot ban flag burning that is intended as a means of political dissent while allowing flag burning that is intended as a means of destroying worn-out flags).

☛ Remember that when the government regulates **defamation**, there are First Amendment limitations:

    ☞ Most important, under *New York Times v. Sullivan*, if P is a **public official** or **public figure**, he may only win a defamation suit against D for a statement relating to P's official conduct if P can prove that D's statement was made either "with **knowledge** that it was false" or "with **reckless disregard**" of whether it was true or false. Use the phrase "actual malice" to describe this requirement.

    ☞ Be sure to examine whether the plaintiff is truly a public or, rather, private figure. If P is a private figure, he merely has to prove negligence rather than "actual malice."

    ☞ Remember that in an action for "intentional infliction of emotional distress," P must, similarly, follow *New York Times v. Sullivan* and prove "actual malice," if P is a public figure.

☛ Remember that government **can't generally make it a crime to "tell a lie."** Government can forbid making factually-false statements within certain long-established **pre-defined categories** (e.g., defamation, perjury, fraud). But outside those categories, government can't pass a law making it a crime to lie, even if the lie would be likely to cause harm.

    Example: Congress can't make it a crime to falsely state that the speaker has received the Congressional Medal of Honor. Cite to *U.S. v. Alvarez* on this point.

☛ **Obscenity** is frequently tested. Here are some of the most commonly-tested sub-issues:

    ☞ The relevant standard is the *"community"* standard — if the relevant sale and trial take place in a small town in Kansas, what counts is whether the average member of that town would find that the work as a whole appeals to the "prurient" interest.

    ☞ The fact that the work shows **nakedness** is not enough — there must be real or simulated sex that is described or portrayed.

    ☞ The fact that D, the seller of the obscene material, has engaged in *"pandering"* is relevant on the issue of whether the material appeals primarily to "prurient interests." D has "pandered" if he has marketed the goods by emphasizing their sexually provocative nature (e.g., by using sexually explicit advertising, packaging materials, etc.).

☞ Remember that no matter how obscene the work is, its ***private possession*** by an adult in the privacy of his own home cannot be punished. (But the ***seller*** can still be punished.)

☞ Be sure to distinguish between material that is truly "obscene," and material that's merely ***"indecent."*** Mere nakedness, for instance, doesn't make something obscene (e.g., because of the possibility that the material may have artistic or social value, or because the material may not be "patently offensive.")

☞ So if government tries to regulate "indecency," indicate that the material gets First Amendment protection and that government has to satisfy strict scrutiny.

Example: Congress prohibits the furnishing of "indecent" material on the Internet, hoping to keep this stuff away from minors. You should apply strict scrutiny, and strike down the restriction, because the total ban is overbroad — the ban covers material that could be proscribed because it's obscene, but also material that's not obscene and thus protected as to adults. Cite to *Reno v. ACLU.*

Same analysis if Congress, trying to avoid having minors access indecent material, says that a Web site can show such material only if the user is required to provide proof that he is an adult; this will flunk strict scrutiny if a less-restrictive and equally-effective alternative — say, user-installed filtering — is available. Cite to *Ashcroft v. ACLU.*

☞ But government has a relatively free hand to regulate the ***"secondary effects"*** of indecent speech. (*Example:* A town can ban live nude dancing if it reasonably believes that nude dancing establishments contribute to increased drug use, prostitution, etc.)

☛ Ascertain whether the regulated speech is ***"commercial"*** (as opposed to core political) speech. Commercial speech is speech proposing a sale or other commercial transaction. Here are the things to remember about regulation of commercial speech:

☞ If the commercial speech is truthful and proposes a ***legal*** transaction, the Court uses mid-level review. The restriction survives only if it: (1) ***directly advances*** (2) a ***substantial*** governmental interest (3) in a way that is ***"not more extensive than is necessary"*** to achieve the government's objective. This is true even if the regulation is ***content-based***. (So it's somewhat easier for government to do content-based regulation of commercial speech than of non-commercial speech, as to which strict scrutiny has to be used.)

☞ If the speech is ***false, deceptive*** or proposes an ***illegal transaction***, government can ***flatly ban*** it.

☞ Profs frequently test on whether the government may prohibit or regulate truthful advertising about products that are ***harmful*** but ***lawful***. Generally, this regulation gets mid-level review, which it will often ***flunk*** because ***substantially less-restrictive means are available***. (*Examples:* If government tries to prohibit or tightly regulate truthful advertising for ***cigarettes, liquor*** or ***gambling***, the Court is likely to say that less-restrictive means like educational campaigns, or higher taxes, must first be tried.

Cite to *Lorillard*, the Mass. case that banned outdoor tobacco advertising, on this point.)

☞ Restrictions on *lawyer advertising* are often tested. Except for some *in-person solicitation* by profit-motivated lawyers seeking clients, states generally can't block truthful advertising. (*Example:* States can't block a public interest lawyer or advocacy group from soliciting clients, even through direct mail or in-person contacts.)

☛ If the regulation is of *public school students*, state that the courts apply a "balancing" test: the student has a limited right of free speech, to be balanced against the administration's right to carry out its educational mission and to maintain discipline. (So officials may not suppress students' speech merely because they disagree with it on ideological or political grounds, but they may ban profanity, or ban school-newspaper stories that would disturb the school's educational mission, such as stories about sex.)

☛ If you have a fact pattern that involves *group activity* of an expressive nature, refer to the protected *"freedom of association."* (*Example:* If a group gets together and pursues class action litigation, their right to do so is protected by the associational freedom.)

☞ Remember that there's also a "right *not* to associate"; for instance, a group can't be required to take unwanted members whose presence will detract from the group's expressive activities. (*Example:* The NAACP can't be forced to accept white supremacists as members.)

☛ Many fact patterns involve the denial of *public jobs or benefits* to persons based upon their expressive conduct. This is a very commonly tested area. Here are some key aspects to keep in mind:

☞ In general, the standard for whether government may refuse to hire, or may fire, based on expressive conduct is the same as for when government may *prosecute*. (*Example:* Since a person may not be prosecuted for belonging to an organization unless there is a showing that he had the specific intent to further the organization's illegal aims, so a person may not be fired for belonging to the organization without such a showing of specific intent.)

☞ A person may be required to sign a *loyalty oath* as a condition for getting or keeping a public job, but he may not be forced to promise to refrain from doing anything that he would be constitutionally permitted to do. (*Example:* You may be forced to sign a loyalty oath that you have not belonged to the Communist Party while specifically intending to further the overthrow of the government, but you may not be required to sign a loyalty oath stating simply that you do not belong to the Communist Party — since you can't be prosecuted for mere membership without specific intent to further illegal aims, you can't be forced to sign a loyalty oath that you won't be a mere member.)

☞ There is an *exception* to these limits: you can be deprived of expressive freedom where the expression would truly interfere with your *job performance*. (*Example:* Civil servants can be forced to choose between their jobs and engaging in partisan political activities, since there's a strong governmental interest in making sure that civil servants don't get coerced into campaigning for their elected bosses.)

☞ Where a public *benefit* as opposed to a job is at stake, there is no "performance" exception, and it's hard for government to restrict free speech. (*Example:* A person's right to continue as a tenant in public housing, or to receive welfare payments, generally can't be made contingent upon their forfeiting their freedom of expression, because they generally don't have a "performance" obligation that would be impaired by pursuit of expressive conduct or speech.)

☛ Look out for *"unconstitutional conditions,"* where government *unfairly conditions* the award of funding or other benefits on the recipient's *waiver of constitutional rights.*

☞ Government *can* sometimes require as a condition to giving you a financial benefit (e.g., a subsidy) that you waive your right to free expression. But that condition can generally apply only to *how you use the particular government-supplied funds*, not how you spend *non-subsidy dollars*.

Example: Congress gives subsidies to private groups fighting AIDS. Congress can require that each grantee promise not to spend subsidy dollars on activities that will likely promote prostitution (e.g., use of subsidy money to buy condoms that are then distributed to prostitutes). But Congress may *not* require that recipients promise that they won't even use *private (non-subsidy) funds* on speech or activities that will promote prostitution — that's an "unconstitutional condition," because it tries to "leverage" the government dollars to restrict speech *outside of the activities receiving the government funding*. Cite to *Agency for Int'l Dev. v. Alliance for Open Soc'y Int'l, Inc.*

☛ If your question involves restrictions placed on the *media* (publishers or broadcasters), there are some special considerations:

☞ If the governmental action consists of a *prior restraint*, you should almost certainly conclude that the restraint is not valid. For instance, if the government is trying to get an injunction against a newspaper that will publish a story, it's almost impossible for the government to succeed.

☞ The media must obey a *subpoena* (e.g., to give information to a grand jury) pretty much the same as a private citizen must.

☞ The press does not get any special *right of access* to government-held information, beyond what the public as a whole has.

☞ Some issues turn on the *type of media*:

☞ *Over-the-air broadcast radio and tv* may be subjected to somewhat greater *"time, place and manner" regulation* than print media, because these are scarce resources, and they are potentially intrusive (someone may stumble upon unwanted content while dial-turning).

☞ *Print publications*, and the *Internet*, by contrast, are neither scarce nor intrusive. So these media get *very great freedom* from "time, place and manner" regulation.

CHAPTER 15

FREEDOM OF RELIGION

ChapterScope

Here are the key concepts involving "freedom of religion":

- **Two clauses:** There are two distinct clauses in the First Amendment pertaining to religion:

  - ❑ **Establishment Clause:** First, there is the ***Establishment Clause***. That clause prohibits any law "respecting an establishment of religion." The main purpose of the Establishment Clause is to prevent government from ***endorsing*** or ***supporting*** religion.

  - ❑ **Free Exercise Clause:** The second clause is the ***Free Exercise*** Clause. That clause bars any law "prohibiting the free exercise of religion." The main purpose of the Free Exercise Clause is to prevent government from ***outlawing*** or seriously ***burdening*** a person's pursuit of whatever religion (and whatever religious practices) she chooses.

- **Applicable to states:** Both religious clauses, by their terms, apply only to action taken by ***Congress***. However, both clauses are interpreted to apply also to the ***states***, by means of the Fourteenth Amendment's Due Process Clause.

- **Establishment Clause:** The purpose of the Establishment Clause is to put a ***wall between church and state***. Mainly, this means that government must stay out of the business of religion. (*Example:* Government can't intentionally prefer one religion over another religion.)

  - ❑ **Three-part test:** Government action that has some relationship to religion will violate the Establishment Clause unless it satisfies ***all three parts*** of the following test:

    - ❑ **Purpose:** First, the government action must have a ***secular legislative purpose***.

    - ❑ **Effect:** Second, the government action's principal or ***primary effect*** must ***not be to advance*** religion. (But ***incidental effects*** helpful to religion do not violate this prong.)

    - ❑ **Entanglement:** Finally, the governmental action must not foster an ***excessive government entanglement*** with religion.

- **The Free Exercise Clause generally:** Under the Free Exercise Clause, the government is barred from making any law "prohibiting the free exercise" of religion. The Free Exercise Clause prevents the government from getting in the way of people's ability to practice their religions.

  - ❑ **Includes conduct:** The Free Exercise Clause prevents the government from unduly burdening both a person's abstract "beliefs" as well as a person's religiously-oriented ***conduct***. Most real-world problems relate to regulation affecting conduct.

    - ❑ **Non-religious objectives:** Free exercise problems most typically arise when government, acting in pursuit of ***non-religious objectives***, either: (1) forbids or burdens conduct which happens to be ***required*** by someone's religious beliefs; or (2) conversely, compels or encourages conduct which happens to be ***forbidden*** by someone's religious beliefs.

    - ❑ **Intentional vs. unintentional burdens:** The Free Exercise Clause prevents the government from unduly interfering with religion whether the government does so ***intentionally*** or ***unintentionally***.

❏ **Intent:** If the interference is ***intentional*** on government's part, then the interference is subjected to the ***most strict scrutiny***, and will virtually never survive.

❏ **Unintentional burden:** If the government ***unintentionally burdens*** religion, the Free Exercise Clause is still applied. Here, however, the Court uses a somewhat less stringent form of strict scrutiny. (In fact, if the government makes certain conduct a ***crime***, and this unintentionally burdens the exercise of religion, the Court does not use strict scrutiny at all, and instead uses "mere-rationality" review.)

❏ **Coercion required:** The Free Exercise Clause only gets triggered where government in some sense ***"coerces"*** an individual to do something (or not to do something) against the dictates of his religion. If the government takes an action that unintentionally happens to make it harder for a person to practice his religion — but without coercing him into taking or not taking some action as an individual — the Free Exercise Clause does not apply.

❏ **Exemptions required:** Because strict scrutiny is traditionally given even to unintentional impairments of religion, government ***must give an exemption*** to avoid such an unintentional interference with religion, if this could be done ***without seriously impairing some compelling governmental interest***. (*Example:* The state may not deny unemployment benefits to a person who refuses to work on his religion's holy day.)

❏ **Criminal prohibition:** But a generally applicable ***criminal law*** is ***automatically enforceable***, regardless of how much burden it causes to an individual's religious beliefs (assuming that the government did not ***intend*** to disadvantage a particular religion or religious practice when it enacted its law).

I. INTRODUCTION

A. **Two clauses:** The First Amendment contains two distinct clauses designed to protect religious freedom. One is the ***Establishment*** Clause, which prohibits any law "respecting an establishment of religion." The other is the ***Free Exercise*** Clause, which bans laws "prohibiting the free exercise" of religion.

B. **General function of clauses:** These two clauses are designed to protect the same basic value, the freedom of every individual to worship (or not worship) as he wishes, without governmental interference. The two clauses have been summarized as requiring "that government neither engage in nor compel religious practices, that it effect no favoritism among sects or between religion and nonreligion, and that it work deterrence of no religious belief." *Abington School District v. Schempp*, 374 U.S. 203 (1963) (Goldberg, J. concurring).

C. **Conflict between clauses:** However, in some contexts the two clauses ***conflict***.

1. **Illustration:** Consider, for instance, state financial assistance to private schools, including parochial schools. If such aid is given, a strong argument can be made that the Establishment Clause is violated, since government is assisting parochial schools in an activity that has a strong religious component. Yet if such aid is not given, while public schools are given large amounts of assistance, a claim can be made that students' free exercise of reli-

gion is infringed, because economic burdens force them to abandon parochial schools for public ones.

2. **No solution:**   The Supreme Court has not yet found a precise way of harmonizing the two clauses. The Court has asserted that government rules must be *"neutral"* towards religion. But the Court has used the concept of neutrality in such a vague way that the term does not aid in the solution of any of the difficult cases of conflict between the clauses.

3. **Zone of permissible accommodation:**   Tribe suggests that the Court's cases recognize a *"zone of permissible accommodation,"* a zone which "the Free Exercise Clause carves out of the Establishment Clause for permissible accommodation of religious interests." Tribe, p. 1169. Under this view, if any governmental action is *"arguably compelled"* by the Free Exercise Clause, then that action is *not forbidden by the Establishment Clause.* Tribe, p. 1168. Thus wherever one action might violate the Free Exercise Clause and a contrary action might violate the Establishment Clause, *it will always be safe for the government to elect the course whose threat is to the Establishment Clause.* To put it another way, "[t]he free exercise principle should be dominant in any conflict with the anti-establishment principle." Tribe, p. 1201.

D. **Application of clauses to states:**   Although the First Amendment by its terms only restricts legislative action by *Congress*, the two religion clauses, like most of the other guarantees of the Bill of Rights, have been incorporated into the Fourteenth Amendment's due process guarantee, and thereby made *applicable to the states*. See, e.g., *Everson v. Board of Education*, 330 U.S. 1 (1947) (application of Establishment Clause to states).

II. THE ESTABLISHMENT CLAUSE

A. **Background:**   The basic purpose of the Establishment Clause is, in the words of Thomas Jefferson, to erect "a *wall of separation* between church and state." However, the image of a "wall" does not help very much in determining what types of state actions violate the Clause.

1. **Specific prohibitions:**   There are some types of governmental actions which clearly violate the Establishment Clause. The majority catalogued some of these in *Everson v. Board of Education, supra*:

   a. **No official church:**   Neither a state nor the federal government may *set up an official church.*

   b. **No coercion:**   Government may not *"force* [or] *influence* a person *to go to* or to *remain away* from church against his will or force him to *profess a belief* or *disbelief* in any religion."

   c. **Punishment for beliefs:**   No one may be *"punished* for entertaining or professing *religious beliefs or disbeliefs*, for church *attendance* or *non-attendance."*

   d. **No preference:**   Government may not *prefer* one religion over another. Also, government may not prefer religion to non-religion.

   e. **Participation:**   Government may not *participate in the affairs* of religious organizations, and such organizations may not *participate* in the affairs of government.

   Note: Some of these prohibitions (e.g., the right not to be punished for one's religious beliefs) are also protected by the Free Exercise Clause, perhaps even more directly than by the Establishment Clause. Nonetheless, the *Everson* Court purported to be listing solely those prohibitions stemming from the Establishment Clause.

2. **Three-part test:** The modern Court applies a ***three-fold test*** to determine whether governmental action violates the Establishment Clause. See ***Lemon v. Kurtzman***, 403 U.S. 602 (1970). Only if the action satisfies ***each*** of the following conditions will it be valid:

    a. **Purpose:** It must have a ***secular legislative purpose***;

    b. **Effect:** Its principal or ***primary effect*** must neither ***advance*** nor ***inhibit*** religion; and

    c. **Entanglement:** It must not foster an ***excessive government entanglement*** with religion.

    d. **Political division:** Also, the law must not create an ***excessive degree of political division*** along religious lines. (However, this seems to be simply an aspect of the requirement of no "excessive entanglement"). See N&R, p. 1262.

3. **Possible single "endorsement of religion" standard:** There are some hints that the present Court may be unhappy with this *Lemon* three-part test, and that the Court may be moving to a single test: Does the state's conduct amount to an ***"endorsement of religion"***? See, e.g., *Texas Monthly, Inc. v. Bullock*, 489 U.S. 1 (1989), where the majority stated the main test as being whether the legislation "constitutes an endorsement of one or another set of religious beliefs or of religion generally."

    a. **May fall into disuse:** The Court may well overrule *Lemon* at some point. Alternatively, the Court may simply stop using it, without overruling it. This is in effect what happened in a recent major Establishment Clause case, *Board of Education of Kiryas Joel v. Grumet*, discussed *infra*, p. 678. The majority found that the challenged practice there (the establishment of a school district consisting solely of members of a particular Jewish sect) violated the Establishment Clause, but the majority opinion referred only briefly to *Lemon* and did not purport to apply the *Lemon* test.

B. **Religion and the public schools:** The extent to which the government may accommodate religion in operating the ***public schools*** has provoked much controversy and several important cases. The primary areas of concern are the extent to which the state may: (1) accommodate students' desire to ***receive religious instruction*** during school hours, or on school property; (2) allow the ***reading*** of state-composed ***prayers*** or the Bible, as part of a daily ritual; and (3) ***modify the curriculum*** in order to accommodate the religious views of some. In general, the Court has permitted the public schools ***very little leeway*** in pursuing these objectives.

1. **Religious instruction:** In two cases, the Court has analyzed the extent to which public schools may accommodate religion by ***releasing students*** for ***optional religious instruction.***

    a. **Instruction on public school premises:** In the first of these, *McCollum v. Board of Education*, 333 U.S. 203 (1948), the public school allowed privately-employed religious teachers to conduct classes ***on the public school's premises, during school hours***. While attendance was voluntary, students who did not attend the religious classes studied secular subjects elsewhere in the building. The Court ***struck down*** this scheme as a violation of the Establishment Clause, on the theory that the program helped religious groups obtain pupils "through the use of the state's compulsory public school machinery."

b. Release for classes held elsewhere: But the Court then, in *Zorach v. Clauson*, 343 U.S. 306 (1952), upheld a program which was quite similar to the one struck down in *McCollum*, except that the students who elected to participate were released to receive religious instruction *away from the public school's physical facility.*

c. Use of college facilities by student groups: Notwithstanding *McCollum*, a state-supported school's policy of allowing religious groups to use its physical facilities does not violate the Establishment Clause if the policy is *truly neutral* as between religious and non-religious groups. Thus in *Widmar v. Vincent*, 454 U.S. 263 (1981) (also discussed *supra*, p. 468), a state university banned the use of its facilities for purposes of worship by student-run religious groups, but allowed all non-religious student groups to use them. In holding that this policy was unconstitutional on free speech grounds, the Court rejected the university's claim that an equal-access policy would have violated the Establishment Clause.

i. *McCollum* **distinguished:** It was precisely the fact that the facilities were also available to *non-religious* groups that made the situation in *Widmar* distinguishable from the use of school facilities for religious purposes in *McCollum*. Here, equal access would not "confer any imprimatur of state approval on religious sects or practices," and the advancement of religion would not be the "primary effect" of such a policy.

ii. Possibility of dominance by religion: However, the majority in *Widmar* put aside the issue of whether a different result would be required if there were evidence that religious groups would *dominate* the use of facilities under an open-access scheme. Arguably, such dominance would cause the scheme to run afoul of the requirement that the state not pursue policies whose *"primary effect"* is to advance religion.

d. Use of school facilities by student groups: Congress has made the result of *Widmar* applicable to *high schools* receiving federal financial assistance. The *Equal Access Act*, 20 U.S.C. §§4071 et seq., enacted in 1984, requires public high schools receiving federal financial assistance to allow *student religious groups* to *hold meetings* before and after school hours, if other extra-curricular groups are given similar rights. The bill applies only to meetings that are *student-initiated, voluntary*, and carried out *without sponsorship by the school* or its employees (who may be present only as non-participants).

i. Constitutional: The Equal Access Act was found *constitutional*, in *Board of Education v. Mergens*, 496 U.S. 226 (1990). A majority of the Court agreed that where a public high school allows student religious groups to meet outside of school hours on the same basis that non-religious extracurricular groups are allowed to meet, this does not violate the Establishment Clause any more than does a similar policy at the university level.

ii. Religious groups in elementary schools: Even if it is a public *elementary* school that allows religious groups to meet on the same after-school basis as non-religious groups, there is no Establishment Clause problem, the Court has held. *Good News Club v. Milford Central School*, 533 U.S. 98 (2001) (also discussed *supra*, p. 531). And this is true even if the attendees will be *elementary school students*. The five-justice majority that decided *Good News* was not worried that young children might think that the school was endorsing a religious message, because "we cannot say the danger that children would misperceive the endorsement of religion is any greater than the danger that they would perceive a ***hostility*** toward the religious viewpoint if the [religious group] were ***excluded*** from the public forum."

iii. Prayer no problem: The equal access principle of *Widmar* is now so powerful that even if the religious group wants to conduct activity that is essentially a ***prayer service***, there is apparently no Establishment Clause problem with allowing the group to do so, as long as the facilities are equally opened to non-religious groups. Thus in *Good News, supra*, the majority was not troubled by the fact that the program in question "chooses to teach moral lessons from a Christian perspective through live storytelling and prayer" (the majority's characterization). Nor did the majority seem to disagree with the dissent's characterization of the program as "an evangelical service of worship calling children to commit themselves in an act of Christian conversion" — however the speech was labeled, it could be permitted without Establishment Clause problems as long as non-religious speech was allowed on the same basis.

  (1) Worship services: So apparently, after *Good News*, if government opens a particular public facility to wide community use, the fact that one of those uses is the conducting of ***traditional religious worship services*** will not pose an Establishment Clause problem, as long as the religious group is given no favoritism or endorsement by the government.

iv. School-initiated: But if attendance at a religious meeting at a public school is ***not truly voluntary***, or if ***school officials actively participate***, this would almost certainly be sufficient governmental "sponsorship" to make the meeting a violation of the Establishment Clause. Similarly, if meetings are held ***during school hours***, even the lack of participation by school officials, and the theoretical "voluntariness" of the meetings (in the sense that students could pursue alternate activities) would probably not be enough to save the meeting's constitutionality; this situation would seem to fall within *McCollum v. Board of Education's (supra*, p. 658) ban on programs which help religious groups obtain pupils "through the use of the state's compulsory public school machinery."

v. Rights for non-religious groups: Similarly, if a school allowed religious groups to conduct voluntary meetings outside of school hours, but ***did not grant this right to non-religious groups***, there would probably be an Establishment Clause violation, on the theory that this type of conduct had the purpose and effect of primarily aiding religion; such a policy would also arguably offend the free speech rights of the non-religious groups. (Paradoxically, the surest way for a school system to stay clear of both Establishment Clause and free speech problems, as well as problems under the Equal Access Act, may be to ban ***all*** extracurricular activities!)

e. Funding of student activities: The "equal access" principle of *Widmar* — that a school must treat religious and non-religious activities equally — now applies even where what the school is supplying is ***funding*** for activities, rather than merely access to pre-existing facilities. In ***Rosenberger v. University of Virginia***, 515 U.S. 819 (1995), the Court held by a 5-4 vote that it would not be an Establishment Clause violation for the University of Virginia to fund an evangelical Christian student publication on the same basis it funded other student publications, so long as the funds were paid to third parties (e.g., the printer) rather than to the students running the publication. (The Court also said that the University's failure to treat the Christian publication equally was a *free speech* violation; see *supra*, p. 532).

    i.   **Dissent:** A four-member dissent in *Rosenberger* vehemently objected, arguing that the Court "for the first time, approves direct funding of core religious activities by an arm of the State. ... Using public funds for the direct subsidization of preaching the word is categorically forbidden under the Establishment Clause, and if the Clause was meant to accomplish nothing else, it was meant to bar this use of public money." In the dissenters' opinion, the fact that the government was neutral as between religious and non-religious publications could not overcome this problem — the requirement of evenhandedness should be in *addition* to the requirement that religion not be directly advanced by the expenditure of public funds.

2.   **Prayer reading:** The official *reading of prayers* in the public schools has several times been held by the Court to *violate* the Establishment Clause.

    a.   **State-composed prayer:** First, the in-classroom reading of a *state-composed* "non-denominational" prayer was held to violate the Establishment Clause, in *Engel v. Vitale*, 370 U.S. 421 (1962). The Court reached this determination even though *no child was compelled to recite the prayer*. Neither this non-compulsory aspect, nor the non-denominationality, saved the scheme, because it was clearly part of a "religious program carried on by government."

    b.   **Reading from Bible:** Similarly, a daily classroom ritual of *reading from the Bible* was struck down in *Abington School Dist. v. Schempp*, 374 U.S. 203 (1963). As in *Engel*, it made no difference that no child was compelled to participate.

        i.   **Rationale:** The Court for the first time articulated in *Schempp* two prongs of the present three-prong test for determining whether governmental action violates the Establishment Clause: (1) the *purpose* of the action must be secular, rather than advancing or inhibiting religion; and (2) the *primary effect* of the action must also not be to advance or inhibit religion.

        ii.   **Application:** The Bible readings were clearly "religious exercises," and thus failed at least the "primary effect" prong. Because of this primarily religious effect, it was no defense for the state to argue (even if accurately) that its *purposes* were the secular ones of promoting morality, anti-materialism, tradition and great literature.

        iii.   **Dissent:** The sole dissenter in *Schempp*, Justice Stewart, contended that a completely non-compulsory scheme of Bible reading, which provided alternative activities for non-participating students, was not violative of the Establishment Clause, and might even be compelled by the Free Exercise Clause.

    c.   **Voluntary silent prayer:** A state statute that explicitly authorizes *"voluntary" silent prayer* in the public schools will not be saved from constitutional problems merely because the prayer is silent and non-compulsory. Any such statute is to be analyzed according to the three-prong *Lemon* test (*supra*, p. 658) — if the provision has no secular purpose, or has the primary effect of aiding religion, or results in excessive government entanglement with religion, it will be struck down even though each student is given the freedom not to participate in the prayer. Thus the Supreme Court has struck down an Alabama statute which authorized a ***one-minute silent period*** at the start of each school day which was to be used "for meditation or voluntary prayer." ***Wallace v. Jaffree***, 472 U.S. 38 (1985). The vote was 6-3.

    i.   **Rationale of majority:**   The *Wallace* majority concluded from various pieces of evidence that the legislature's ***sole purpose*** in enacting the statute was to endorse religion, a violation of the first prong of *Lemon*. (For instance, the bill's chief sponsor testified that the bill's purpose was to return voluntary prayer to the schools.) Since the first prong of *Lemon* was not satisfied, the Court did not need to reach the issue of the statute's conformance with the second and third *Lemon* prongs (primary effect and state entanglement).

d.   **Academic study:**   The school prayer decisions do not prohibit the ***study*** of the Bible in public schools, as long as this study takes place in a purely ***academic manner***. The issue is whether the school, by including Bible study in the curriculum, intends to (or does in fact materially) advance religious beliefs.

e.   **Ceremonies:**   So far, we have considered only prayers that take place in ***classrooms***. Suppose that a school conducts an official ***ceremony*** or ritual outside the classroom, and prayer is part of that ceremony. At least where school officials can fairly be said to be ***sponsoring*** the religious message, a prayer will be found to be a ***violation*** of the Establishment Clause. The Court so held in ***Lee v. Weisman***, 505 U.S. 577 (1992). *Lee* also establishes that even a completely ***non-denominational*** school prayer will violate the Establishment Clause if it is state-sponsored.

    i.   **Facts:**   *Lee* involved prayers at public middle-school and high-school graduation ceremonies. In one instance, a middle-school principal invited a rabbi to deliver a prayer, told him the prayer should be non-sectarian, and gave him a pamphlet (prepared by the National Conference of Christians and Jews) detailing the kinds of prayers that would be appropriate at a public civic occasion. The prayers delivered by the rabbi were indeed non-denominational, and consisted mainly of thanks to God (e.g., "Oh, God, we are grateful to You for having endowed us with the capacity for learning which we have celebrated on this joyous commencement. ... Send Your blessings upon the teachers and administrators who helped prepare [the students]"). P was a graduating student who argued that she shouldn't be required to listen to a prayer as part of her graduation ceremony.

    ii.   **Practice struck down:**   By a 5-4 vote, the Court ruled that the delivery of the prayer in this context violated the Establishment Clause. The five-Justice majority, in an opinion by Justice Kennedy, held that the state here effectively ***coerced*** students into participating in, or at least supporting, the prayers. The school district had argued that attendance at the commencement ceremony was voluntary, in the sense that P could have received her diploma even without attending. But this argument ignored reality, Kennedy said; "To say each student has a real choice not to attend her high school graduation is formalistic in the extreme. ... Everyone knows that in our society and in our culture high school graduation is one of life's most significant occasions. ... The Constitution forbids the State to exact religious conformity from a student as the price of attending her own high school graduation." Nor was it a defense that P was not required to specifically *participate* in the prayer — the combination of school supervision and peer pressure effectively required her to stand or at least maintain respectful silence, and this was tantamount to requiring her to participate in the religious exercise. Finally, the fact that the prayer was non-sectarian was irrelevant; there is no such thing as an "official" or "civic" religion which, because it is non-sectarian, is exempt from the Establishment Clause.

iii. Dissent: Four Justices (Scalia, joined by Rehnquist, White and Thomas) dissented. The dissenters principally argued that there was *no official compulsion* here — P was not required to attend the graduation ceremony at all (thus distinguishing the case from the in-classroom prayer cases), and certainly was not required to join in the prayers in any way, merely to accommodate others who wished to pray. Also, the dissenters contended, invocations and benedictions at public ceremonies, such as the prayers here, were part of an old *tradition* dating back to Jefferson's inauguration; "The long-standing American tradition of prayer at official ceremonies displays with unmistakable clarity that the Establishment Clause does not forbid the government to accommodate it." Finally, the dissenters believed that there was an important national objective to be served by group prayer in public settings, the objective of *unifying* participants of different backgrounds. "To deprive our society of that important unifying mechanism, in order to spare the nonbeliever of what seems to me the minimal inconvenience of standing or even sitting in respectful nonparticipation, is as senseless in policy as it is unsupported in law," Scalia concluded.

iv. Incidental references to religion: Suppose that an official ceremony or ritual contains mere *occasional* references to God, which are *incidental* to the ceremony. In this situation, it seems likely that the majority of the Court would *allow* the reference, despite its religious content. For instance, a majority of the Court has indicated in dictum that the use in public schools of the *Pledge of Allegiance*, with its reference to God, does not violate the Establishment Clause, because this is merely a "reference to our religious heritage," rather than an endorsement of religion. *Lynch v. Donnelly*, discussed *infra*, p. 675(the Nativity Scene case). (But see our further discussion of the Pledge issue *infra*, p. 671.)

f. "Student-sponsored" speeches: A key aspect of the Establishment Clause problem in *Lee v. Weisman* was that the school clearly endorsed the prayer — the principal invited a rabbi to give the prayer, and gave him instructions about what type of prior to use, making the prayer effectively school-sponsored. In part to get around *Lee*, a number of school districts after *Lee* put in place procedures whereby a *student* can be *elected by the student body* to be a speaker at a school-sponsored event. If the speaker then chooses on her own to give a prayer, the school can plausibly claim that the speech is private speech — posing no Establishment Clause problem — rather than school-sponsored speech. But a post-*Lee* case, in which the Court struck down a pre-football-game prayer delivered by an elected student speaker, suggests that this technique will rarely be successful. *Santa Fe Independent School Dist. v. Doe*, 530 U.S. 290 (2000).

i. Facts: Prior to the litigation, the Sante Fe, Tex., school district elected a *"Chaplain"* of the high school student council each year, whose function was to deliver a prayer over the public address system before each varsity football game. After this practice was challenged on Establishment Clause grounds, the school instead instituted a formal written "policy" for dealing with the issue.

  (1) Two-election procedure: The policy provided for two elections. First, the class would vote by secret ballot whether a "statement or invocation" should be delivered before each game, to "solemnize the event." If the vote was yes, a second election would be held to choose the spokesperson to deliver the invocation/statement.

  (2) Prayers delivered: The student body in fact voted to have the invocations, and those invocations turned out to be, the lower court later found, prayers that appealed to "distinctively Christian beliefs."

ii. Struck down: By a 6-3-vote, the Court found that the school policy *violated* the Establishment Clause.

  (1) Not private speech: The majority rejected the school district's claim that the pregame invocations should be regarded as *"private speech."* The school policy itself encouraged religious messages (e.g., by providing that the purpose of the message must be to "solemnize the event"). And the fact that the invocation was delivered at a school-sponsored event, over a school-owned public address system, added to the impression that this was school-sponsored, not private, prayer.

  (2) Sham: An important aspect of the majority's reasoning in *Santa Fe* was that the *real* governmental purpose, not the stated one, should prevail. Thus the majority found it highly significant that the current policy had evolved from the prior practice of having a "Student Chaplain," and that prior versions of the policy had candidly included the title "Prayer at Football Games." In sum, the ostensibly religious-neutral policy was a *sham*, an unsuccessful attempt to disguise a government desire to promote prayer.

iii. Dissent: The three dissenters in *Santa Fe*, led by Chief Justice Rehnquist, agreed with the district's argument that the prayers should be viewed as private speech, because it was up to the elected students to decide what to say in the pre-game speech.

3. Modification of curriculum: The state may not design or modify the *curriculum* of its schools in order to further religion at the expense of non-religion, or one set of religious beliefs over others.

  a. Anti-evolution laws: This principle is most vividly demonstrated by the Court's invalidation of an Arkansas *"anti-evolution" statute*, which forbade public school teachers from teaching "the theory or doctrine that mankind ascended or descended from a lower order of animals." *Epperson v. Arkansas*, 393 U.S. 97 (1968). (This statute was an offshoot of a comparable Tennessee statute, which was the subject of the famous 1927 Scopes trial.)

  i. Rationale: The *Epperson* Court concluded that the statute violated the Establishment Clause because its *sole purpose* was a religious one: to bar the teaching of a theory that was at odds with the "fundamentalist sectarian conviction" that man was created in the manner described in the Bible. Even if the statute was intended only to prohibit teaching Darwinian theory as "true" (rather than barring even any *explanation* of what the theory says), the law's solely religious motivation was sufficient to make it unconstitutional.

b. **Requirement that Bible be taught:** May the state require that the biblical theory of creation be taught *in addition to* the theory of evolution? Such a requirement could, of course, be defended on the grounds that it preserves neutrality as between religion and non-religion, and presents all viewpoints. However, if such a requirement were imposed solely or primarily for the same religious *purpose* as the *Epperson* statute, it would violate the Establishment Clause. Thus in one case, the Supreme Court held that a Louisiana statute, the "Balanced Treatment for Creation-Science and Evolution-Science in Public School Instruction" Act, was motivated solely by religious purposes, and therefore violated the Establishment Clause. *Edwards v. Aguillard,* 482 U.S. 578 (1987).

i. **Facts:** The Louisiana Act forbade the teaching of evolution in public schools unless that teaching was *accompanied by instruction in "creation science."* No school was required to teach evolution or creation science, but if either was taught the other must also be taught.

ii. **Statute stricken:** The outcome of the case essentially turned on the extent to which one believed that the Louisiana legislature could have had a valid secular purpose in enacting the statute. Seven members of the Court, represented in a majority opinion by Justice Brennan, concluded that there *could not have been such a secular purpose*. Brennan concluded that "[t]he preeminent purpose of the Louisiana legislature was clearly to advance the religious viewpoint that a supernatural being created humankind." In reaching this conclusion, Brennan relied heavily upon the *legislative history* of the statute, including statements made by the bill's sponsor and testimony at the legislative hearings by the leading expert on creation science; both of these sources indicated that the theory of creation science includes a belief in the existence of a "supernatural creator," and is thus a religious doctrine.

iii. **Dissent:** Justice Scalia, joined by Chief Justice Rehnquist, issued a forceful dissent that challenged the majority's analysis on both factual and legal grounds. Factually, Scalia disagreed that the record was adequate to allow the Court to conclude that the principal or sole motivation for the statute was to advance religious beliefs. Scalia noted that the act recited a secular purpose ("protecting academic freedom") and that the act was endorsed by a vast majority of legislators, only a small minority of whom were members of fundamentalist religious denominations. Furthermore, he stressed, the issue was not whether the statute would actually achieve the purpose of enhancing academic freedom, but merely whether the legislators were *sincere* in believing that it would have this outcome.

(1) **Disagreement on standard:** The dissenters also disagreed about what the proper standard should be in determining whether a statute violates the Establishment Clause. They contended that the first prong of *Lemon* (*supra*, p. 658) — that the act have a secular legislative purpose — should be abandoned. "[D]iscerning the subjective motivation of those enacting the statute is, to be honest, almost always an impossible task." So long as the statute satisfied the second and third *Lemon* prongs — that it not have the primary effect of either advancing or inhibiting religion, and that it not foster an excessive government entanglement with religion — the dissenters would uphold it.

    iv. Significance: Observe that the majority approach in *Edwards* — that a religious motivation will invalidate the statute — can mean that when two states adopt an identically-worded statute, the statute may be *valid in one state and invalid in the other*, since the two legislatures may have been differently motivated. It is, therefore, at least possible (though in practice unlikely) that the same statute invalidated in *Edwards* might be upheld in some other state, if the Court were convinced that *those* legislators, unlike the ones in Louisiana, were really motivated by a non-religious intent.

    c. No secular purpose: *Epperson* and *Edwards* are two of the few cases in which the religious purpose of a law was dispositive. The "purpose" prong of the three-prong Establishment Clause test is that there must be *a* "secular purpose," not that there may not be a religious purpose. Thus if there is *both a religious and secular purpose*, the prong is *not violated*. The statutes in *Epperson* and *Edwards* are two of the few legislative enactments as to which members of the Court could find no conceivable secular purpose. (For another such statute, see the Alabama "voluntary prayer" statute struck down in *Wallace v. Jaffree, supra,* p. 661.)

C. Sunday closing laws: Laws requiring merchants to be *closed on Sunday* do *not* violate the Establishment Clause. *McGowan v. Maryland*, 366 U.S. 420 (1961).

    1. Rationale: The Court reasoned in *McGowan* that, as these statutes are administered today, they have a *secular purpose and effect:* providing a *uniform day of rest for all citizens*. (The Court believed it irrelevant that the laws were originally enacted for purely religious reasons.)

    2. Overlapping of secular and religious purposes: Of course, the fact remains that the day chosen for this uniform day of rest is Sunday, the day of religious observance for most Americans. The case therefore illustrates the rule that a statute does not violate the Establishment Clause if it has *both a religious and secular purpose*. See Tribe, p. 1205-06.

    a. Effect: Similarly, the fact that the law had both a secular and religious *effect* did not cause a violation of the Establishment Clause, since the religious effect was not the primary, or even major, one. The Court seems correct in viewing the Sunday closing laws as having merely an *incidental* unofficial effect of advancing religion.

    3. Employees' right not to work on Sabbath: But if a statute relating to Sabbath observance *does* have the primary effect of advancing religion, it will be found to violate the Establishment Clause. For instance, a Connecticut statute requiring all employers (including private employers) to give any employee the day off on that employee's Sabbath, was struck down as violative of the Establishment Clause, in *Thornton v. Caldor, Inc.*, 472 U.S. 703 (1985).

    a. Rationale: The statute in *Thornton* went beyond the government's right to "accommodate" the needs of religious observers. There, the preference given to Sabbath observers was an *absolute* one. For instance, suppose that an employer is faced with having to choose which of two employees should have Sunday off: one employee points to Sunday as his Sabbath; the other, who has more seniority, has a pressing and legitimate, but non-religious need for Sundays off (e.g., to have the same day off as his working spouse and school-aged children). The Connecticut statute mandated an absolute preference for the former. The statute thus had the primary effect of "impermissibly advanc[ing] a particular religious practice" (namely, Sabbath observance).

b. Non-absolute preference: But a statute that merely required an employer to make "reasonable attempts" to accommodate the religious interest of workers probably would *not* violate the Establishment Clause.

Note: There is sometimes a tension between Establishment Clause and Free Exercise principles — government can occasionally find itself in a position where, if it accommodates a religious practice, it risks violating the Establishment Clause, but if it denies an accommodation, it risks violating the Free Exercise Clause. Accommodating Sabbath observance is one of those areas of tension. Contrast *Thornton* (accommodation was so great that it violated the Establishment Clause) with *Sherbert v. Verner*, *infra*, p. 691 (government's refusal to adjust its rules on unemployment benefits to accommodate the needs of individuals to observe the Sabbath held to violate the Free Exercise Clause).

D. Property-tax exemptions for churches: The granting of *property tax exemptions* to churches generally does *not* violate the Establishment Clause. *Walz v. Tax Commission*, 397 U.S. 664 (1970).

1. Sales tax exemption violates clause: On the other hand, some kinds of tax exemptions given to religious groups *will* be held to violate the Establishment Clause. For instance, Texas exempted from *sales tax* all (and only) periodicals "published or distributed by a religious faith and [consisting] wholly of writings promulgating the teaching of the faith and books that consist wholly of writings sacred to a religious faith." This exemption was struck down by the Court in *Texas Monthly, Inc. v. Bullock*, 489 U.S. 1 (1989).

2. Distinction: How was the property tax exemption in *Walz* different from the sales tax exemption in *Texas Monthly*? The main difference seems to be that the exemption in *Walz* was part of a *broader scheme* that did not prefer religion over non-religion — property owned by most types of non-profit organizations (including hospitals, libraries, patriotic groups, etc.) was also exempted. In *Texas Monthly*, by contrast, *only* religious writings published by religious groups were exempted, so the exemption's sole purpose (and apparently its principal effect) was to advance religion.

E. Military and prison chaplains: Recall that government has some ability to *accommodate* the religious needs of citizens, so long as government is not "sponsoring" official religious practices. The right of public schools to release their students so that they can receive religious instruction outside of the school is one illustration of this principle. The "accommodation" principle is also applicable when government supplies *military chaplains* or *prison chaplains* to soldiers or prisoners who wish to use them, or otherwise accommodates the religious needs of solders or prisoners.

1. Religious accommodation to prisoners: For instance, the Court has upheld the Religious Land Use and Institutionalized Persons Act (RLUIPA), which essentially requires all prison systems to accommodate the religious needs of prisoners unless refusing to do so would further a compelling governmental interest by the least restrictive means. See *Cutter v. Wilkinson*, 544 U.S. 709 (2005), discussed *infra*, p. 680. Even though RLUIPA clearly prefers religion over non-religion (e.g., by effectively requiring that prisoners be given the right to attend organized group prayer meetings and the right to wear religiously-dictated non-standard apparel while prisoners who wish to engage in these activities for non-religious reasons are not given the right to do so), the Court found no Establishment Clause violation.

F. Helping religious groups spread their message: Recall that one of the prongs of the *Lemon v. Kurtzman* test (*supra*, p. 658) is that the governmental action's principal effect must not be to *advance* religion. Thus government actions whose primary effect is to help religious organizations *spread a religious message* or *obtain converts* would presumably fail this prong and thus violate the Establishment Clause.

> **Example:** Suppose that Congress passed a law providing grants to religious (and only religious) organizations, for the express purpose of giving them the financial resources to run expanded membership drives and to explain their beliefs to the general population. This statute would almost certainly violate the "primary effect" prong of *Lemon*.

1. Incidental effect: But if grants are made to a wide variety of institutions, only some of which are religiously-affiliated, the fact that some of the recipients happen to be religious organizations who use the funds to spread the organization's religious message will not lead to a striking down of the entire statute (though it may cause grants to the particular organizations who use the funds in this way to be struck down). Only if a *significant portion* of the government funding flows to institutions that are *"pervasively sectarian"* will the entire funding scheme be a violation of the Establishment Clause.

> **Example:** Congress enacts the Adolescent Family Life Act (AFLA), which is mainly a scheme for giving grants to public or non-profit private organizations so that the organizations can give adolescents counseling about sex and pregnancy. In order to receive a grant, an organization may (but need not) be religiously-affiliated; every grant recipient must, even if not itself religious, describe how it will "involve religious … organizations in its activities."
>
> *Held* (by a 5-4 vote), the AFLA is not unconstitutional on its face. It does not have the primary effect of advancing religion because: (1) a wide variety of organizations is eligible to receive funding under the Act, only some of which are religious; and (2) there is no reason to believe that any significant proportion of the funds will flow to "pervasively sectarian" institutions. *Bowen v. Kendrick*, 483 U.S. 1304 (1988).

G. The "excessive entanglement prong": Recall that the third prong of the test for Establishment Clause violations is that the governmental action must not give rise to *excessive entanglement* on the part of government in the affairs of religion, or vice versa.

1. The "ministerial exception" from government regulation: One consequence of the "no excessive entanglement" rule is that governmental regulation that has the effect of interfering with a religious group's determination of *who is qualified to convey the group's message* and/or *carry out its mission* is likely violate the Establishment Clause. Religious groups are entitled to a *"ministerial exception,"* under which the group's choice of *who may be a minister or leader* will be *immune from regulation*, at least regulation that takes the form of *anti-discrimination* laws.

a. Anti-discrimination laws (the *Hosanna-Tabor* case): The only Supreme Court case discussing the ministerial exemption is *Hosanna-Tabor Evangelical Lutheran Church and School v. EEOC*, 132 S.Ct. 694 (2012).

i. **Facts:** Hosanna-Tabor was a Lutheran church that also operated a school. Cheryl Perich was a *"called" teacher* at the school. "Called" teachers are regarded by the church as having been called to their vocation by God, acting through the congregation. Perich had to undergo special training, including extensive theological study, in order to be "called." She then had to be "elected" to the post of minister by the congregation.

(1) **Dispute over ADA:** After Perich took a disability leave for narcolepsy, the school asked that she resign. She refused, and threatened to sue the school for violating the Americans with Disability Act (ADA). The ADA forbids an employer from discriminating against a qualified individual on the basis of disability; it also prohibits an employer from *retaliating* against an employee for making a charge that the employer has violated the ADA.

(2) **Lawsuit:** The school then fired Perich, and the congregation revoked her calling. The school's notice of firing cited, among other reasons, the damage Perich had done to her "working relationship" with the school by her threat of litigation. Perich then complained to the Equal Employment Opportunity Commission (EEOC). The EEOC investigated, then sued the school for violating the ADA's anti-retaliation provision by firing Perich for having threatened legal action.

(3) **Defense:** The school, in seeking to dismiss the suit, claimed that it was entitled to a ministerial exception. Some anti-discrimination statutes (but not the ADA) contain an explicit ministerial exception, by which religious institutions can avoid liability for discrimination in connection with their employment of "ministers." The school argued that although the ADA did not contain a ministerial exception, the two religion clauses required that the school be given such an exception as a constitutional matter, which would protect the school from ADA liability.

ii. **Holding for school:** The Supreme Court, in an opinion by Chief Justice Roberts, found unanimously in *favor of the school.* Roberts' opinion held that both the Establishment and Free Exercise Clauses required that in this type of situation, a religious group be given a ministerial exemption, so that government would not interfere with the group's decision to fire one of its ministers. Roberts also concluded that Perich qualified as a "minister."

(1) **Rationale:** Roberts said that "requiring a church to *accept or retain an unwanted minister*, or punishing a church for failing to do so ... *interferes with the internal governance of the church*, depriving the church of control over the selection of those who will *personify its beliefs.*" In addition to violating the Free Exercise Clause,[1] he said, "According the state the power to determine which individuals will minister to the faithful ... violates the Establishment Clause, which *prohibits government involvement in such ecclesiastical decisions.*"

---

1. For a brief discussion of the Free Exercise portion of the opinion, see *infra*, pp. 695-696.

(2) Free-association defense not enough: The EEOC and Perich had claimed that there was no need to hold that the two religion clauses require a ministerial exemption, because a church could adequately defend against a discrimination claim on the basis of the First Amendment *"freedom of association"* (see *supra*, p. 613). But Roberts disagreed. He pointed out that the freedom of association applies equally to religious and secular groups alike. By contrast, the text of the religion clauses shows that the First Amendment "gives *special solicitude to the rights of religious organizations."* Roberts therefore rejected the argument that "the First Amendment analysis should be the same, whether the association in question is a Lutheran church, a labor union, or a social club."

iii. **Perich was a "minister":** Roberts then turned to the issue of whether Perich *qualified as a "minister"* for purposes of the ministerial exception. He declined to specify a "rigid formula" for determining when an employee qualifies as a minister. But he determined that Perich qualified, due to several factors:

❑ By giving Perich the title of "minister," the church was *holding her out* as having a *professional role* distinct from that of *ordinary members* of the congregation;

❑ Perich had had to qualify by undergoing a "significant degree of religious *training*";

❑ She then had to be *elected* to the post of minister by *vote of the congregation*;

❑ Perich's *job duties* reflected "a role in *conveying the church's message and carrying out its mission*"; for instance, she taught religious subjects four days a week, and led her students in prayer three times a day. (The fact that only a small percentage of Perich's typical workday — about 45 minutes — was used for religious duties, with the rest spent on teaching secular subjects, was not dispositive, in view of the religious functions she served and the demanding process by which she had attained the status of minister.)

2. **Truth vs. sincerity:**   The anti-entanglement prong of the Establishment Clause causes courts to *avoid adjudicating the "truth"* of religious beliefs. But courts are sometimes willing to consider the *sincerity* of professed beliefs.

   a. *Ballard:*   The truth/sincerity distinction was made in *U.S. v. Ballard*, 322 U.S. 78 (1944), where the defendants, self-professed *faith healers*, were charged with fraudulently soliciting donations. The Court held that the Free Exercise Clause barred the submission to the jury of the truth or falsity of the defendants' faith healing claims: "Men may believe what they cannot prove. They may not be put to the proof of their religious doctrines or beliefs." However, the Court held, a jury could be required to decide whether the defendants were *sincere* in their claims, that is, whether they genuinely (whether or not reasonably) believed these claims.

H. Entanglement by church involvement in government affairs: The   anti-entanglement principle will also be violated by the converse problem, that of excessive involvement *by the church in affairs of government.*

1. ***Larkin:*** For instance, in ***Larkin v. Grendel's Den, Inc.***, 459 U.S. 116 (1982), the Court struck down a Massachusetts statute prohibiting issuance of a liquor license to any premises located within 500 feet of a church or school if the church or school makes a written objection to the issuance of the license.

    a. Rationale: Giving such a veto provision to churches "enmeshes churches in the exercise of substantial governmental powers," the *Larkin* Court held, and therefore runs afoul of the anti-entanglement principle of the Establishment Clause.

I. Ceremonies and displays: When the government conducts a ***ceremony*** or puts on a ***display***, and the ceremony or display refers to a religious subject, Establishment Clause problems will often result.

1. **Ceremonies:** First, consider ceremonies. The fact that God is ***occasionally referred to*** in a ceremony put on by the government will usually ***not*** cause the ceremony to violate the Establishment Clause.

    a. Legislative chaplain: For instance, the practice of opening each daily session of a state ***legislature*** with a ***prayer*** by a state-paid chaplain does not violate the Establishment Clause, the Court held in *Marsh v. Chambers*, 463 U.S. 783 (1983).

        i. Rationale: The Court relied principally on the theory that such practices have deep ***historic roots***, going back to the First Congress; this fact demonstrated that the congressmen who approved the First Amendment must have believed that use of a chaplain did not violate principles of church-state separation.

        ii. Dissent: But Justice Stevens, one of three dissenters, argued that the Nebraska legislature's choice of a Presbyterian to hold the position of chaplain for sixteen years, probably in order to reflect the state's primary sect, constituted an illegal "preference of one faith over another."

        iii. Distinguished from prayer at school commencement: Recall that it *is* a violation of the Establishment Clause for a school district to sponsor a prayer during ***high school commencement*** ceremonies (see *Lee v. Weisman, supra*, p. 662). What is the constitutional difference between a prayer before the opening of a state legislative session and one before a school commencement? The majority in the school-commencement case distinguished the two as follows: "The atmosphere at the opening of a session of a state legislature where adults are free to enter and leave with little comment and for any number of reasons cannot compare with the constraining potential of the one school event most important for the student to attend." The Court has always been quicker to find Establishment Clause violations in the context of public schools than in other contexts, so the distinction between prayer at a legislative session and prayer during a school commencement is not surprising.

    b. Pledge of Allegiance: What about the Pledge of Allegiance? The Pledge contains the phrase, "One nation, under God, indivisible, with liberty and justice for all." Probably this brief reference to God will not be held (at least by the Rehnquist Court) to be a violation of the Establishment Clause. The Pledge would probably be viewed as a whole, and when so viewed would probably not be found to have the sole purpose of, or the primary effect of, advancing religion.

i. **Tradition:** Also, as *Marsh v. Chambers, supra,* p. 671, shows, the Court seems more inclined to allow references to religious themes when the reference is part of a *long-standing tradition* or *historical practice*. The Pledge certainly seems to qualify on this ground. Similarly, the Court's recent decision in *Van Orden v. Perry, infra,* p. 672 — where the Court upheld a monument of the Ten Commandments on the Texas State Capitol grounds in major part because the monument had stood for 40 years without complaint — reinforces the likelihood that the Court will uphold public use of the Pledge as a long-standing tradition.

2. **Religious displays:** Great controversy can arise when the government either puts on, or makes its property available for private groups to put on, some sort of *display* or presentation that involves religious themes. For instance, suppose the government allows a private religious group to display a copy of the Ten Commandments, a nativity scene, a Hanukkah menorah, or some other symbol that has great religious significance. Does the fact that the government is making its property available for such a display violate the Establishment Clause? The test now seems to be this: Would a reasonable observer seeing the display conclude that the government was *endorsing* religion in general, or endorsing a particular religion? If the answer is "yes," the display violates the Establishment Clause. If the answer is "no," it does not.

a. **Context:** This means that the constitutionality of a given Ten Commandments display, nativity scene, etc., will be a question of fact. The most important single factor seems to be the *context* in which the religious symbol is displayed. If the religious symbol is presented *by itself* in what is clearly a space reserved by the government for its own property and its own messages, the Court is likely to conclude that a "reasonable observer" would believe that the government was endorsing the religious message. Conversely, the presence of *other non-religious symbols nearby,* or the existence of a *sign* indicating that the display was furnished by private parties without governmental approval, or evidence that the religious material was provided for its historical rather than religious value — any of these factors may well be enough to lead a reasonable observer to the conclusion that government was *not* endorsing religion.

b. **Intent:** Government's *intent or motive* in establishing the display is also of vital importance. If the court believes that the government's principal purpose in establishing the display was to *promote or endorse religion* (or some particular religion), this fact by itself will probably lead to a finding of unconstitutionality. *McCreary County v. ACLU,* a Kentucky Ten Commandments case which we'll be reviewing in detail *infra,* p. 674, illustrates how a governmental purpose to advance religion will be fatal.

c. **Five cases:** There have been five cases since 1984 in which the Court has considered whether religiously-oriented displays in public space violate the Establisment Clause. Two involved the Ten Commandments, two involved nativity scenes, and the fifth involved a cross.

d. **The Ten Commandments cases:** Two 2005 companion cases involving public displays of the text of the *Ten Commandments* are the Court's most recent rulings on religiously-oriented displays in public spaces. The two cases went in opposite directions, with one finding a display at the Texas State Capitol to be constitutional, and the other finding a display in two Kentucky courthouses to be unconstitutional. The Texas case was ***Van Orden v. Perry***, 545 U.S. 677 (2005) and the Kentucky one was ***McCreary County v. ACLU of Kentucky***, 545 U.S. 844 (2005).

i. **Two 5-4 decisions:** In each case, the decision was 5-4. Four members of the court (Rehnquist, Scalia, Thomas and Kennedy) believed both displays were constitutional; four other members (Souter, Stevens, O'Connor and Ginsburg) believed both displays were unconstitutional. The swing vote was Justice Breyer, who therefore made a majority for upholding the Texas display and a different majority for striking down the Kentucky one.

ii. **The Texas case (*Van Orden*):** In the Texas case (*Van Orden*), the display was a six-foot high monument containing the text of the King James version of the Ten Commandments. The monument was one of 17 monuments and 21 historical markers installed in 22 acres on the grounds of the Texas Capitol. The monument was contributed to the state in 1961 by Texas branch of the Fraternal Order of Eagles, which during that era contributed similar monuments to state legislatures around America in the hopes of reducing juvenile delinquency. Apparently there was little if any public Establishment-Clause objection to the monument for 40 years, until plaintiff Van Orden, a former lawyer, brought suit.

   (1) **Rehnquist's opinion upholds the display:** Chief Justice Rehnquist, in a plurality opinion joined by Scalia, Kennedy and Thomas, concluded that the monument ***did not violate*** the Establishment Clause. With Justice Breyer's vote concurring in the result, this provided the five votes needed to uphold the display. Rehnquist believed that although the Ten Commandments "are religious," they also "have an undeniable ***historical meaning***," since "Moses was a lawgiver as well as a religious leader." He continued, "Simply having a religious content or promoting a message consistent with a religious doctrine does not run afoul of the Establishment Clause." Texas' "passive use" of the text of the Commandments, placed alongside many other monuments representing "the several strands in the state's political and legal history," did not violate the Establishment Clause.

   (2) **Breyer supplies the fifth vote:** Justice Breyer concurred in the result and thus supplied the needed fifth vote for upholding the Texas display's constitutionality. For Breyer, this was "a borderline case." The Commandments' text had an undeniable religious message. But the display of which they were part conveyed a secular message as well, a message about the historical relation between this religious text and the development of law. To Breyer, the physical setting of the display — among 17 monuments and 21 historical markers, all illustrating the "ideals" of Texas' settlers and later residents — "suggests little or nothing of the sacred[,]" but rather, suggested that the "moral message" of the display was intended to predominate over its religious message.

   (3) **Dissents:** Justices Stevens, Souter, O'Connor and Ginsburg dissented in the Texas case.

      One of the dissents, by Justice Stevens, asserted that the message transmitted by Texas's display was that "this state ***endorses the divine code of the 'Judeo-Christian' God.***" (He noted that the Texas monument displayed the words "I

AM the LORD thy God" in especially large letters.) The Establishment Clause, he said, *"demands religious neutrality* — Government may not exercise a preference for one religious faith over another." The Ten Commandments state the message that "there is one, and only one, God," namely a Judeo-Christian God. Since this message is *"rejected by prominent polytheistic sects*, such as Hinduism, as well as *nontheistic religions*, such as Buddhism," Stevens continued, allowing government to propagate this message "would have the tendency to make nonmonotheists and nonbelievers *'feel like [outsiders] in matters of faith* and [strangers] in the political community.' "

iii. **The Kentucky case (*McCreary County*):**   In the Kentucky case (*McCreary County v. ACLU of Kentucky*), Justice Breyer joined the four dissenters from *Van Orden* to **strike down** two counties' posting of the Ten Commandments. The *history* of that posting — a history that convinced a majority of the Court that government's primary purpose was to endorse religion — was dispositive.

   (1) Facts: The two counties, McCreary and Pulaski, initially ordered large framed copies of the King James version of the Ten Commandments posted on a stand-alone basis in their courthouses. The ACLU sued both counties almost immediately on Establishment Clause grounds. The legislature of each county, acting on legal advice, then ordered the display expanded to add, in smaller frames, various other religiously-oriented portions of historical documents (e.g., the passage from the Declaration of Independence saying that all men are "endowed by their Creator" with inalienable rights).

   The trial court in the ACLU action issued an injunction requiring that the displays be removed. The counties did so, but then installed a new display — the third within a year — consisting of framed copies of the Ten Commandments plus various other historical documents (e.g., the Magna Carta, the Declaration of Independence and the Bill of Rights), each accompanied by a statement about its historical and legal significance.

   (2) Majority strikes down: Justice Souter, writing for himself and for Stevens, O'Connor, Ginsburg and Breyer, concluded that the third display *violated the Establishment Clause*. Souter relied on the *"purpose"* prong of *Lemon v. Kurtzman* (p. 658) — the display was invalid because it was *not supported by any genuine "secular legislative purpose."* Souter quoted a prior holding, that "The First Amendment *mandates governmental neutrality* between religion and religion, and *between religion and nonreligion*[,]" and added that when government acts with the predominant purpose of advancing religion, it "violates that central Establishment Clause value of official religious neutrality[.]"

   Souter then turned to the facts. He looked first at the original display, in which the Ten Commandments were displayed alone. Given the Commandments' status as a "central point of reference in the religious and moral history of Jews and Christians," given the absence of any "context plausibly suggesting a message going beyond an excuse to promote the religious point of view," and given the presence of a pastor who testified at the Pulaski County display ceremony as to the certainty that God existed, any "reasonable observer could only think that the Counties *meant to emphasize and celebrate the Commandments' religious message."*

Souter then considered the second and third displays. As to the third display — the one expressly under litigation — he concluded that the same religious purpose that had motivated the Counties in making the prior displays had continued.

Finally, Souter argued that in close cases, the Establishment Clause should be interpreted in a way that achieves the *"principle of neutrality"*: the framers intended to "guard against the *civic divisiveness* that follows when the Government weighs in on one side of religious debate."

(3) Dissent: Justice Scalia wrote the only dissenting opinion in *McCreary County* (in which Chief Justice Rehnquist and Justice Thomas joined in full and Justice Kennedy in part). Scalia's main objection was to the majority's view that the establishment clause requires *neutrality between religion and nonreligion,* and to what he characterized as the majority's view that *acknowledging society's belief in God* violates this neutrality principle. "Nothing stands behind the Court's assertion that governmental affirmation of the society's belief in God is unconstitutional except the Court's own say-so[.]" Scalia argued that the Court had often violated the no-preference-for-religion neutrality principle, as when it approved property tax exemptions for church property (*Walz v. Tax Comm., supra,* p. 667).

Scalia conceded that the Establishment Clause means, generally, that government cannot *favor one religion over another.* But this principle did *not* prevent government from *acknowledging the idea of a single Creator.* Therefore, he said, the practice of publicly honoring the Ten Commandments, like that of *publicly honoring God*, is "recognized across such a *broad and diverse range of the population* ... that [it] *cannot reasonably be understood as a government endorsement of a particular religious viewpoint."*

e. **The nativity cases:** Before the two Ten Commandments cases were decided, the Court's most important opinions on religious displays were two cases involving *nativity scenes.*

i. **Rhode Island case:** The earlier of the two nativity-scene cases was *Lynch v. Donnelly*, 465 U.S. 668 (1984), involving the city of Pawtucket, Rhode Island.

(1) **Facts:** Pawtucket put up a Christmas display every year in a public park near the city's shopping district. The display included several symbols traditionally associated with Christmas, but not having much, if any, overtly religious significance (e.g., Santa Claus, a reindeer, a Christmas tree, and a banner reading "Seasons Greetings"). The display also included a creche, or nativity scene, depicting the birth of Christ.

(2) **Holding:** A majority of the Court (in a 5-4 vote) concluded that this nativity display did *not* violate any of the three traditional tests, especially when considered "in the context of the Christmas season." There was a secular purpose ("to celebrate the Holiday and to depict the origins of that Holiday"); the pri-

mary effect was not to benefit religion in general, or Christianity in particular (since any advancement of religion was "indirect, remote and incidental," just like exhibition of religious paintings in a government-owned museum); and there was no undue "administrative entanglement" (since the city erected and maintained the display without any contact with religious authorities).

(3) Acknowledgment of holidays: More generally, the majority in *Lynch* believed that the display was allowable because it was merely one of many illustrations of "the Government's *acknowledgment of our religious heritage* and governmental sponsorship of graphic manifestations of that heritage." This display was no different from: (1) federal proclamations making Christmas a national holiday; (2) statutory establishment of "In God We Trust" as our national motto; and (3) the display in government museums of "masterpieces with religious messages."

(4) Dissent: The four dissenters believed that the display violated all three prongs of the test of *Lemon v. Kurtzman* (*supra*, p. 658). As to purpose, the dissenters pointed to evidence that the creche was motivated in part by popular desire to "keep Christ in Christmas." The primary effect of the display was "to place the government's imprimatur of approval on the particular religious beliefs exemplified by the creche" and to convey to minority religious groups and atheists "the message that their views are not similarly worthy of public recognition nor entitled to public support." And, the dissenters argued, significant political divisiveness on the issue had occurred after the suit was filed.

ii. **Pittsburgh case:** But contrast the holding in *Lynch* with the second, later, case involving a nativity scene, *Allegheny County v. American Civil Liberties Union*, 492 U.S. 573 (1989). Here, the Court (again by a 5-4 vote) found that the nativity scene *violated* the Establishment Clause.

(1) Facts: The creche in *Allegheny County* was displayed in the county courthouse during the Christmas season. The creche was owned and put up by a private Catholic group (not by the city itself, as was the case in *Lynch*). In addition to the usual figures of Jesus, Mary, Joseph, shepherds, wise men, etc., the creche contained a banner proclaiming, "Gloria in Excelsis Deo!" ("Glory to God in the Highest"). The creche occupied a prominent position on the Grand Staircase of the courthouse. Unlike the creche in *Lynch*, there were no significant other nearby symbols such as Santa Claus, reindeer, or "Seasons Greetings" banners — the creche stood by itself.

(2) Holding: The five-justice majority believed that this creche violated the Establishment Clause. The test was whether a reasonable observer seeing the display would *believe that the government was endorsing a religious or sectarian message.* Here, there were several factors not present in *Lynch* that would lead an observer to believe that the government was endorsing a Christian message. For instance, there were no other non-religious symbols nearby as there had been in *Lynch* (like the Santa Claus and reindeer), so an observer would not think that the city was merely celebrating the holiday season.

f. Display of cross: The Court's final religious-display case of recent years involved the Ku Klux Klan's attempt to display a *cross* in a state-owned park immediately in front of the Ohio statehouse. By a 7-2 vote, the Court held that the display did ***not*** violate the Establishment Clause. *Capitol Square Review Board v. Pinette*, 515 U.S. 753 (1995).

    i. Facts: The park in question had long been made available to a wide variety of public groups who wanted to conduct expressive activities, or erect unattended displays, there. The question was whether the state could deny the Klan's attempt to put up a cross — which the Court treated as being a religious (as opposed to political) symbol — on the ground that to allow the cross would be a violation of the Establishment Clause.

    ii. 7 members find no violation: Seven Justices believed that it would ***not*** violate the Establishment Clause for the state to allow the cross. But they differed sharply as to the rationale.

    iii. Plurality's view: A 4-Justice plurality, led by Justice Scalia, thought that where the speech was that of a private party rather than the government, the "reasonable observer" test should be ***rejected*** entirely. In the plurality's opinion, only if government ***intentionally "fostered or encouraged"*** the belief that government was endorsing religion, could there be an Establishment Clause violation. So here, where the government had always applied an "equal access" policy toward displays in the park, a policy that was neutral as between religion and non-religion, there was no Establishment Clause violation whether or not a reasonable observer might have (mistakenly) believed that the government was endorsing religion.

    iv. 3-Justice bloc: Another bloc of three Justices, led by O'Connor, believed that the ***"reasonable observer"*** test was the ***correct*** one. Here, a reasonble observer who knew the park's history would have known that the park was essentially open to any private display meeting simple content-neutral permit requirements; therefore, he or she would not have concluded that government was endorsing religion by allowing the cross to be displayed.

g. Synthesis: The law in this "religious display" area is confused and probably still shifting. Here's what we can say:

    i. Government vs. private speech: Where the display is owned and put on by the ***government***, it is of course more likely to be found to be an Establishment Clause violation than if it is put on by a private speaker who is permitted to do so by the government. (But if the display is viewed as a "holiday season" or other "cultural" message rather than a specifically religious message, it can still survive, as the nativity scene in *Lynch* did.)

    ii. Context: ***Context*** remains very important. The presence of non-religious symbols nearby, for instance, makes it more likely that even a usually-religious symbol like like a creche or a copy of the Ten Commandments will be found not to violate the Clause. Thus in *Van Orden, supra*, the fact that a display of the Ten Commandments was only one of 17 monuments and 21 historical markers installed throughout a 22-acre public site helped convince a majority of the Court that a reasonable observer wouldn't conclude that the Ten Commandments display was intended as a governmental endorsement of religion.

    iii. History: The *history* behind the display is important — the longer the display has been around without objection or controversy, the less likely it is to be an Establishment Clause violation.

    iv. "Reasonable observer" test: There remains a bare 5-justice majority in favor of using the *"reasonable observer"* test, by which the Clause is violated when a reasonable observer would believe (even if mistakenly) that government was endorsing religion.

    v. Sign as disclaimer: The government is free to require that any display contain a *sign* or other *disclaimer* to make it clear that the display was placed by private parties; the displayer's free speech rights are not violated where government requires such a disclaimer.

    vi. Close property entirely: Also, the government can avoid constitutional controversies by making the property completely *off-limits* to *all* privately-placed unattended displays, whether religious or not. This is apparently true even where the property is a traditional public forum (e.g., a park) — the government couldn't bar all "live speech" by human beings, but it's entitled to bar all unattended signs or displays.

J. No preference for one sect over others: Just as the Establishment Clause is violated when government prefers religion over non-religion, so is it violated when the government *favors a particular sect over other sects*, or over non-religious interests.

    1. Accommodation vs. favoritism: However, one of the core principles of the Free Exercise Clause is that government must sometimes *"accommodate"* the religious needs of a particular person or group. But government action may sometimes *cross over the line* from "accommodation" into forbidden favoritism. This happened in *Board of Education of Kiryas Joel Village v. Grumet*, 512 U.S. 687 (1994). The case also illustrates that where a state *delegates governmental power* directly to a religious group, a violation of the Establishment Clause is almost certain to be found.

        a. Facts: The *Kiryas Joel* case had its origins when a group of Satmar Hasidim, fundamentalist Jews, moved from Brooklyn to upstate New York, to the Town of Monroe. In 1977, taking advantage of a New York State law that allows groups of residents within a town to form a smaller village, the Satmars formed the Village of Kiryas Joel. The village was drawn to include just the 328 acres owned and inhabited by Satmars. The village has a population of about 8,500 today.

        i. Isolated: The 8,500 Satmars are vigorously religious and deeply insular. They speak Yiddish as their primary language, segregate the sexes outside the home, forbid TV and radio, and dress distinctly. Except for the handicapped children who were the focus of the suit, all children in the village attend private Jewish schools.

        ii. Handicapped children: Under state and federal laws, all *handicapped* children are entitled to special publicly-funded education services. The Satmars wanted to receive these services without having to send their handicapped children to a neighboring district's public schools (where there were almost no Satmar students).

        iii. Special district: The New York Legislature tried to give the Satmars what they wanted, by passing a special statute that provided that "the territory of the Village of Kiryas Joel ... shall be ... a *separate school district.*" The effect of the statute was to allow a locally-elected board of education to open schools, hire teachers, and impose property taxes to fund the operation. The resulting Kiryas Joel Village School District in fact used its powers very narrowly; the only school or program it ever ran was a special-education program for handicapped children, mostly paid for by state funds. At the time the suit was heard by the Court, the new district served only 40 full-time students, of whom two-thirds were Hasidic children who commuted from outside the village.

b. Holding: By a 6-3 vote, the Court held that the establishment of the Kiryas Joel Village School District violated the Establishment Clause. The majority opinion, by Justice Souter, seemed to say that there were two distinct problems with the way the district was created: (1) *religious criteria* were used to *draw the boundary lines* of the district; and (2) the creation of the district was a *special favor* for a particular religious sect, with no assurances that other similarly-situated groups would receive the same benefits.

c. Status of *Lemon* questionable: The *Kiryas Joel* case raises doubts about the continued viability of the *Lemon* three-part test for Establishment Clause violations. The majority opinion did not rely on *Lemon*, and mentioned it only briefly in the form of two "see also" cites. Justice O'Connor, in her concurrence, welcomed this fact, and urged that the Court's jurisprudence be "freed from the *Lemon* test's rigid influence." Even if a majority does not explicitly overrule *Lemon*, something that many think will happen, *Lemon* may simply fade into disuse.

d. Another illustration: *Kiryas Joel* is not the only case in which the Court has found a forbidden preference for one sect over another. The Court also found such an unconstitutional preference in a Minnesota law which originally exempted all religious organizations from registration and reporting requirements applicable to other types of charitable organizations, but which was amended to remove the exemption for any religious organization receiving less than half of its total contributions from members. *Larson v. Valente*, 456 U.S. 228 (1982). One of the first religious groups to be disadvantaged by the amendment was the Unification Church ("Moonies"), who brought the suit giving rise to the Court's decision.

    i. Strict scrutiny: For perhaps the first time in an Establishment Clause case, the Court in *Larson* applied *strict scrutiny* analysis, rather than the three-prong test (*supra*, p. 596). The three-prong test was appropriate in cases where religion as a whole was arguably benefitted *vis-à-vis* non-religion; where *one religion* is *preferred over another*, the more demanding strict scrutiny analysis must be applied, the Court held. Such an inter-denominational preference could be sustained only if it was "justified by a *compelling governmental interest* and ... *closely fitted* to further that interest."

    ii. Result of test: Whether or not Minnesota's asserted interest in guarding against abusive solicitation practices was a compelling one (the Court declined to decide), the means chosen here were *not "closely fitted" to further that interest.* Nothing suggested that the likelihood of solicitation abuse was closely related to the ratio of member contributions to total contributions.

2. **Accommodation found not to be a violation:** In *Kiryas Joel* and *Larson v. Valente*, one religion or sect was accommodated in preference to another, and the accommoation was found to be an Establishment Clause violation. However, where what is being accommodated is not a particular religion or sect, but rather, the ***practice of religion generally***, the Court is much ***less likely*** to find an Establishment Clause violation. For example, the Court recently held that a federal statute requiring accommodation of the ***religious practices of prisoners*** — greater accommodation than given to non-religious practices of prisoners — did not on its face violate the Establishment Clause. See ***Cutter v. Wilkinson***, 544 U.S. 709 (2005).

   a. **RLUIPA:** Congress passed a statute, the Religious Land Use and Institutionalized Persons Act of 2000 (RLUIPA), which says in part that "No government shall impose a substantial burden on the religious exercise of a person residing in or confined to an institution," unless the burden furthers "a compelling governmental interest" and does so by "the least restrictive means."

   b. **Suit by prisoners:** The plaintiffs in *Cutter* were several prisoners in the Ohio State Penal system who belonged to "nonmainstream" religions like Satanist and Wicca. They claimed that Ohio prison officials were violating RLUIPA by denying them religious rights given to members of mainstream religions, such as opportunities for group worship and the right to adhere to the dress mandates of their religion. Ohio defended by claiming that RLUIPA on its face violated the Establishment Clause by improperly advancing religion.

   c. **Court strikes down challenge:** The Court unanimously held that RLUIPA ***did not violate*** the Establishment Clause on its face. Even if RLUIPA gave prisoners' rights beyond what would be required to protect their Free Exercise interests, this was a permissible accommodation because " 'there is room for play in the joints' between the [Free Exercise and Establishment] Clauses ... some space for legislative action neither compelled by the Free Exercise clause nor prohibited by the Establishment Clause." Prisoners are unable to attend to their religious needs without government accommodation, so having government give them that accommodation is not the sort of preference for religion over non-religion that would violate the Establishment Clause, the Court said.

      i. **As-applied challenge:** But it's important to note that the attack on the statute in Cutter was a "facial," not an "as applied," attack. (See *supra*, p. 236, for an explanation of the distinction.) The Court observed that if in a *particular case* RLUIPA caused religious accommodation to override other significant governmental interests, such as security, then on an ***as applied*** basis the statute might still be found to be an unconstitutional preference for religion. In this case, because the state's attack on the statute was a facial one, the state could only win if it showed that there was ***no scenario*** in which the statute could be constitutionally applied; the state had not met this heavy burden.

K. **Financial aid to religious schools:** Probably the most important and sensitive issue in the Establishment Clause area is whether, and to what extent, the government may give ***financial assistance*** to religious schools, or to students at these schools.

1. **Three-prong test:** The Court applies the three-prong test in these financial-assistance cases, and in fact it was in such a case that the test was originally formulated. Thus such a

program must satisfy each of the following requirements in order to avoid violating the Establishment Clause: (1) it must have a ***secular legislative purpose*** (though it may also have a religious purpose, as long as at least one secular purpose exists); (2) its "principal or primary ***effect***" must neither advance nor inhibit religion; and (3) it must not foster "an excessive government ***entanglement*** with religion." Also, as either an additional requirement or as a sub-requirement of (3), the Court has disallowed programs which are likely to be ***"politically divisive."***

2. **Broad themes:** Before we turn to consideration of particular assistance programs, it is worthwhile to summarize some of the broad themes that have characterized the Court's handling of attacks on financial aid schemes.

   a. **Lower vs. higher education:** The Court has been much less likely to sustain programs which aid ***elementary and secondary*** parochial schools, than it has been to uphold those aiding sectarian ***colleges and universities***. This distinction stems from the belief that in the elementary and secondary setting, religious instruction ***permeates every aspect*** of the educational process, whereas in the higher education context, it is possible to identify and support those aspects of the institution which are devoted to purely secular objectives. Most of the discussion which follows relates to elementary and secondary contexts; separate consideration is given to the higher education area beginning *infra*, p. 688.

   b. **Direct vs. indirect aid:** Assistance programs are more likely to be upheld if the aid is given to ***students and their parents***, rather than directly to the school, and each parent or student gets to decide at which school to use the benefit. (See, e.g., *Zelman v. Simmons-Harris*, the tuition-voucher case, *infra*, p. 684, making this distinction.) This distinction is based on the theory that it is easier to ensure that the aid is used to fulfill secular objectives if the parents and students, rather than the school, are given control of the money or items being furnished.

   c. **All students:** A program which by its terms assists ***all students***, both in public and private schools, is much more likely to be sustained than one which is addressed solely to religious-school students. Also, a program which is ***in fact*** utilized by a significant number of students in public schools, or in non-sectarian private ones, is more likely to be upheld than one which, although theoretically available to all, is overwhelmingly used by parochial school pupils. (However, the fact that the overwhelming majority of users of a program are religious schools or their students is not automatically fatal, if the program is theoretically available to all.)

   d. **Secular effect:** All three of these broad principles can be seen as deriving from the basic requirement that the financial assistance have a ***primary effect*** that is ***secular***. For an effect to be secular, the Court has insisted that it be ***clearly separable*** from any religious effects. Also, the ***breadth*** of the ***benefitted class*** (i.e., the extent to which beneficiaries are not just parochial school students) is an important index of secular effect. See Tribe, pp. 1215-16.

3. **Particular programs:** We turn now to consideration of particular programs aiding parochial schools or their students.

4. **Transportation:** A program by which parents were reimbursed for the money spent to ***transport*** their children to school on ***public buses*** was upheld, in *Everson v. Board of Education*, 330 U.S. 1 (1947).

a. **Public school students included:** A key feature of the plan approved in *Everson* was that parents of **public school students** were **included** in the reimbursement scheme. It is highly unlikely that a transportation-reimbursement scheme applicable only to religious-school students would be approved by the Court today. The key difference is that the *Everson* scheme can justly be viewed as supplying the secular benefit of "transportation to one's school," and as supplying that benefit in a way that is completely neutral as between religious and secular institutions.

b. **Advancement of religion:** Of course, the argument can be made that at least some parents who send their children to parochial schools under an *Everson*-like scheme might send them to public schools instead if only transportation to public schools were reimbursed by the state. In this sense, an effect of the scheme is to advance religion. The majority in *Everson* dealt with this argument by asserting that the scheme was neutral as between religion and non-religion. Today, the Court would probably dispose of this argument by saying that any benefit to religion was an **incidental** and remote effect, rather than the "principal" or "primary" one.

5. **Textbooks and other materials:** *Textbooks* may be loaned to parochial school students, as long as: (1) a similar policy is followed with respect to public-school and private-non-parochial students; and (2) the textbooks are themselves secular rather than religiously-oriented. See *Board of Education v. Allen*, 392 U.S. 236 (1968).

   a. **Computers and other non-textbook materials:** Similarly, non-textbook materials and equipment, such as **computers**, **audio-visual equipment,** and the like, may be given or lent to religious schools as long as: (1) the materials are themselves non-religious in nature; (2) the materials are **not diverted** for religious purposes (e.g., computers are not used to run religiously-oriented programs); and (3) **all schools** — religious or not — are eligible for the aid on the **same terms**. *Mitchell v. Helms*, 530 U.S. 793 (2000).

      i. **4 votes for disregarding diversion:** In fact, four members of the Court that decided *Mitchell* believed that even if the non-religious materials *were* diverted for religious use at the school, this would not make any difference. To these four, as long as the government is **evenhanded** in how it treats religious and non-religious schools, there can be no Establishment Clause violation. In other words, these four would not impose requirement (2) above — they would, for instance, allow religious schools to use publicly-funded computers to run religiously-oriented programs.

      ii. **5 members disagree:** But the other five Justices in *Mitchell* disagreed with this extreme view. Justice O'Connor, who contributed the fifth vote needed for the upholding of the program in *Mitchell*, did so even though she thought diversion was impermissible, because she didn't think substantial diversion had actually occurred in the case and she believed that a theoretical risk of diversion or a few isolated actual instances of it did not create a problem.

6. **Salary supplements:** The state may not subsidize parochial education by reimbursing parochial schools for a portion of **teachers' salaries**, even where this reimbursement is theoretically for the teaching of secular subjects. See, e.g., *Lemon v. Kurtzman*, 403 U.S. 602 (1971). Again, the problem is that there is no way to make sure that these funds are not used for religious purposes, at least not without such surveillance of the teachers'

actual conduct that the monitoring itself would constitute excessive entanglement between church and state. *Id.*

7. **Furnishing of teachers:** Suppose the state takes ***public-school teachers*** (i.e., teachers who are on the public payroll and who do most of their teaching in the public schools) and ***sends them into parochial schools*** to teach special subjects. As the result of a major 1997 shift in case law, this will ***no longer be deemed to violate*** the Establishment Clause, if the public-school teachers teach in a secular manner and without curricular interference by the parochial school. ***Agostini v. Felton***, 521 U.S. 203 (1997).

   a. **Rationale:** The 5-Justice majority in *Agostini* made these major points:

      i. **Direct aid not necessarily invalid:** It is not true (as the Court had previously thought it was) that "all government aid that directly aids the educational function of religious schools is invalid."

      ii. **No "symbolic union" problem:** It's also not true that the presence of public-school teachers in parochial school classrooms "will, without more, create the impression of a *'symbolic union'* between church and state."

      iii. **No distinction from sign-language-interpreter situation:** The provision of the educational programs here — remedial courses in basic school subjects, given to those in danger of failing — was "indistinguishable" from the provision of ***sign-language interpreters*** in parochial schools, something that the Court had previously approved.

      iv. **No excessive-entanglement problem:** There was simply no reason to believe that the monitoring needed to ensure that the in-school programs didn't inculcate religion would cause an ***excessive entanglement*** between government and religion. ***Unannounced monthly visits*** by public supervisors would probably be enough to fulfill this need for monitoring, and would not result in any greater "entanglement" than other programs that the Court had previously approved.

   b. **Dissent:** The four ***dissenters*** in *Agostini* strenuously objected. The principal dissent was by Justice Souter.

      i. **Subsidy problem:** First, Souter argued that allowing publicly-funded teachers to teach basic subjects inside the parochial school amounted to a ***"subsidy"*** of the school — the school was relieved of the need to teach core subjects, thus ***freeing up funds*** that could then be used to fulfill the school's religious mission. This violated the "flat ban on subsidization" that, he said, had been an "unwavering rule in Establishment Clause cases."

      ii. **Impression of public endorsement:** Second, he thought that in-school publicly-funded teaching was substantially more likely to give the impression of ***public endorsement*** of religion than such teaching delivered outside the school. "Sharing the teaching responsibilities within a school having religious objectives is far more likely to ***telegraph approval of the school's mission*** than keeping the State's distance would do."

8. **Services:** Publicly-funded ***services*** (e.g., testing and counseling) may be supplied to parochial school students. Apparently the only present limitations on such services are that: (1) they must be ***offered to all schools*** in a way that does not intentionally favor parochial schools; and (2) they must have an exclusively secular content. So if, for instance,

the state offers testing, counseling, remedial education or other specialized services to all non-public schools, with the quantity of services keyed to the size of the school's enrollment, and with the services having no direct religious content, there is apparently no Establishment Clause problem. That seems to be true even if the principal **effect** of the services is to aid religion.

a. **Source of this principle:** This principle — that the presence of a principal effect of aiding religion is not fatal when services are provided — seems to follow from two of the recent cases that we've already discussed, *Agostini v. Felton* (*supra*, p. 683) and *Mitchell v. Helms* (*supra*, p. 682). In *Agostini*, the Court held that the state may supply teachers to teach even basic remedial courses in the parochial schools as long as the curriculum is carefully kept secular. There seems to be no reason why specialized services such as testing and counseling can't also be supplied on this basis. And *Mitchell* establishes that the government may give or lend schools educational equipment and materials subject only to the requirements of even-handedness and secular-content, so this case, too, suggests that services may be furnished to parochial schools on the same basis as to public and non-religious private schools.

9. **Tuition vouchers:** *Tuition vouchers* may be given to parents to enable them to pay religious-school tuition, if the vouchers may also be used in non-religious private schools. In *Zelman v. Simmons-Harris*, 536 U.S. 639 (2002), the most controversial and important Establishment Clause case in years, the Court held by a 5-4 vote that such a tuition voucher plan **did not violate the Clause.** The majority reasoned that any "advancement of a religious message" that the plan facilitated was an "incidental" one that resulted from *"the deliberate choices of numerous individual recipients,"* not from the government. The Court seems to have announced a new approach to cases involving government funding that finds its way to religious institutions — so long as private citizens make individual choices about how to use the funding, the fact that the great majority of the funding ends up being used in religious institutions, for pursuit of religious ends, does not seem to matter.

a. **Facts:** In *Zelman*, the state of Ohio set up a program under which any Cleveland student in kindergarten through 8th grade could receive a voucher of up to $2,250 to attend private school. In the most recent year, 3,700 of the 75,000 students in the Cleveland school district took advantage of the program. Although the program let both religious and non-religious private schools participate, 96% of participating students enrolled in religious schools. The principal purpose of the program seems to have been to enable students in a failing public school system (a federal judge had placed the entire Cleveland system under state supervision on account of its failure to educate students) to afford a private alternative. However, the federal Court of Appeals found the program to violate the Establishment Clause, on the grounds that it had the primary effect of advancing religion.

b. **Majority upholds:** Chief Justice Rehnquist was joined by Justices O'Connor, Scalia, Kennedy and Thomas in upholding the constitutionality of the program.

i. **Reliance on precedent:** The Chief Justice began by reviewing earlier cases that, he said, had distinguished between "government programs that provide aid directly to religious schools" and "programs of true private choice, in which government aid reaches religious schools only as a result of the genuine and independent *choices of private individuals*." Programs falling into this latter category — ones that implement private choices — had been consistently upheld, he said. For instance, in *Mueller v. Allen*, 463 U.S. 388 (1983), the Court rejected an Establishment Clause attack on a Minnesota program that gave tax deductions for certain private school tuition costs, even though 96% of the program's beneficiaries were parents of children in religious schools. In *Mueller*, the Court reasoned that where public funds were made available to religious schools "only as a result of numerous, private choices of individual parents," "no imprimatur of state approval can be deemed to have been conferred on any particular religion, or on religion generally."

  ii. **Private choices here:** Consequently, Rehnquist wrote, the voucher program here was constitutional because it, too, was a "program of *true private choice*," one that was "neutral in all respects toward religion." Rehnquist noted that not only non-parochial private schools, but also public schools from adjacent (non-Cleveland) school districts, were eligible to participate in the voucher program. Therefore, the mere fact that most participating students attended parochial schools did not indicate any preference for religion, especially in view of the fact that 81% of private schools in Ohio were religious schools.

  iii. **Percentage disputed:** Rehnquist also disputed the significance of the fact that 96% of voucher users attended religious schools. The proper way to look at the issue, he said, was to consider what percentage of all students using *any kind of alternative publicly-funded educational program* attended religious schools. If one added to the voucher users those Cleveland children enrolled in "alternative community schools," "alternative magnet schools" and "traditional public schools with [separately funded] tutorial assistance," fewer than 20% of those receiving alternative public funding used that funding to attend religious schools. In sum, the Ohio program permitted "a wide spectrum of individuals" to "exercise genuine choice among options public and private, secular and religious." Such a program of "true private choice" did not have the primary effect of aiding religion, and therefore did not violate the Establishment Clause.

c. **O'Connor concurrence:** Justice O'Connor, in a concurrence, agreed particularly with this last point of Rehnquist's — in deciding whether the program was neutral between religion and non-religion, the Court was required to make "an evaluation of *all reasonable educational options* Ohio provides the Cleveland school system, regardless of whether they are formally made available in the same section of the Ohio Code as the voucher program." By this test, which would include the magnet schools, alternative community schools and the like, the Ohio program met the test of being religiously neutral.

d. **Dissents:** The four dissenters (Stevens, Souter, Ginsburg and Breyer) wrote three dissents. All viewed the majority's opinion as a major and regrettable change to the Court's prior Establishment Clause doctrines, and all warned that this new approach would likely *trigger major social conflicts.*

  i. **Stevens:** In a brief dissent, Justice Stevens warned that "whenever we remove a brick from the wall that was designed to separate religion and government, we *increase the risk of religious strife* and weaken the foundation of our democracy."

ii. **Souter:** Justice Souter warned that the voucher program here gave far more extensive aid to religion than the "isolated and insubstantial" aid allowed by prior decisions. Here, the money would pay for instruction not only in secular subjects but in *religious ones as well*, "in schools that can fairly be characterized as founded to teach religious doctrine and to imbue teaching in all subjects with a religious dimension."

> (1) **Not true private choice:** Souter also rejected the majority's core assertion that the voucher program was merely a neutral implementation of private choices. He said that "the question is whether the private hand is *genuinely free* to send the money in either a secular direction or a religious one." To him, the answer was "no" — the $2,250 cap on tuition reimbursement was *significantly lower than the tuition typically charged* by nonreligious private schools, but fit comfortably with the typical tuition at religious schools in Cleveland (e.g., an average tuition at participating Catholic schools of $1,592). Consequently, it was not surprising that only three secular private schools in Cleveland enrolled more than eight voucher students. "For the overwhelming number of children in the voucher scheme, *the only alternative to the public schools is religious.* And it is entirely irrelevant that the state did not deliberately design the network of private schools for the sake of channeling money into religious institutions."

iii. **Breyer:** Justice Breyer warned that the majority was violating the primary principle behind the court's Establishment Clause cases, the principle of *"avoiding religiously based social conflict."* For instance, he noted that the voucher program here required that no participating school "advocate or foster unlawful behavior or teach hatred of any person or group on the basis of race, ethnicity, national origin, or religion." It is, he said, "difficult to imagine a more divisive activity than the appointment of state officials as referees to determine whether a particular religious doctrine 'teaches hatred or advocates lawlessness.'"

> (1) **Funding of religious teaching:** Furthermore, Breyer pointed out, the vouchers here would be used to *fund primary religious education*. For instance, some of the schools participating in the program had announced that their goals were to "communicate the gospel" and to "provide instruction in religious truths and values." He argued that "history suggests ... that government funding of this kind of religious endeavor is far more contentious than providing funding for secular textbooks, computers, vocational training, or even funding for adults who wish to obtain a college education at a religious university." The "parental choice" aspect of the program, he said, did not cure the problem. For instance, "parental choice cannot help the taxpayer who does not want to finance the religious education of children."

e. **Significance:** *Zelman* suggests that a majority of the Court will henceforth take a significantly less rigorous view of government programs whose benefits flow to religious organizations. So long as the funding program is *facially neutral* as between religious and non-religious organizations, and so long as the program relies upon *individual citizens to make their own decisions* about which organization shall receive the funding, the fact that the vast majority of the total funding directly advances organizations' religious objectives seems not to matter. Here are two examples of how *Zelman* may be interpreted:

❏ Suppose a student wants to use a ***state-funded scholarship*** to study for the priesthood at a religious seminary. Presumably *Zelman* means that so long as the scholarship program is facially neutral — i.e., it allows the funds to be used, at the student's discretion, in both religious and non-religious programs — there's no Establishment Clause problem, even if most students who get such scholarships use them for religious training. (See the discussion of scholarship, Par. 10 below.)

❏ Suppose the federal government adopts a bond program, whereby any organization meeting certain financial criteria can issue ***tax-free bonds to construct buildings***. Suppose further that 90% or more of the buildings so built are houses of worship. As long as the eligibility criteria are facially neutral (i.e., non-religious organizations in theory have an equal opportunity to participate), the fact that the vast majority of the tax-subsidized funds are used to support directly a core mission of worship probably won't matter.

10. **Scholarships for religious study:** Even before *Zelman, supra*, it was clear that a generalized program of awarding ***scholarship money*** or other grants to students would not run afoul of the Establishment Clause, even if some students used the funds to attend religious institutions that would prepare them for a religious calling. Thus in *Witters v. Washington Dept. of Services for the Blind*, 474 U.S. 481 (1986), the Court unanimously held that the Establishment Clause was not violated by a state's grant of funds under a vocational rehabilitation assistance program to a blind student who would use the funds to attend a private Christian school, where he would train to be a "pastor, missionary, or youth director."

   a. **Effect of *Zelman*:** *Zelman* seems to add to this result in *Withers* the further rule that there is no Establishment Clause violation even if the ***vast majority*** of those participating in the scholarship program use the scholarship for religious-education purposes, as long as the program is equally open to those who want to pursue non-religious study.

   b. **Scholarships for ministry-study not required by Free Exercise clause:** By the way, *Witters* and *Zelman* do not mean that a state *must* include scholarships or vouchers for ministry study if the state gives scholarships for study in all other fields. In other words, the mere fact that a state is free under the Establishment clause to give scholarships that will be used for religiously-oriented purposes does *not* mean that it ***violates the Free Exercise clause*** if it excludes ministry studies from a generally-applicable scholarship program.

      i. ***Locke v. Davey***: This result was announced in *Locke v. Davey*, 540 U.S. 712 (2004). There, the state of Washington awarded merit scholarships that could be used in any accredited college, and for any field of study, except the pursuit of a degree in "theology."[2] By a 7-2 vote, the Court concluded that this exclusion of theology studies did not violate the Free Exercise clause. The Court stressed that "there are some state actions permitted by the Establishment Clause but not

---

2. The provision was intended to comply with a state-constitutional prohibition on the provision of public funds used towards degrees that are "devotional in nature or designed to induce religious faith." So a student could use the scholarship to take some theology courses, but could not use the scholarship for a degree in theology, since that would be a "devotional" degree.

required by the Free Exercise Clause," and said that this case fell into that category. For more about *Locke*, see *infra*, p. 690.

11. **Aid to higher education:** Public financial assistance to sectarian *colleges* raises *fewer Establishment Clause problems* than does aid to elementary and secondary schools. Although the Court has applied the usual three-prong test in the aid-to-colleges context, it has found that test to be much more readily met. This has been especially true of the "primary secular effect" and "no excessive entanglement" prongs, which have often tripped up schemes for aiding lower education.

   a. **General subsidies:** For instance, in *Roemer v. Maryland Public Works Bd.*, 426 U.S. 736 (1976), the Court upheld a scheme of subsidies to private colleges, including religious ones, even though the subsidies were not earmarked for particular uses (though they were not permitted to be used for "sectarian purposes.")

      i. **Rationale:** The Court in *Roemer* reasoned that unlike church-related elementary and secondary schools, the colleges performed *"essentially secular educational functions."*

   b. **Construction of chapels:** However, it is possible to imagine programs assisting colleges which might nonetheless violate the Establishment Clause. For instance, a college's use of public funds (paid directly from the government to the college) to *build chapels* would probably be unconstitutional, as would direct governmental assistance to seminaries whose sole function was to train priests or ministers.

III. THE FREE EXERCISE CLAUSE

A. **Introduction:** The First Amendment bars government from making any law *"prohibiting the free exercise"* of religion. The Free Exercise Clause, like the Establishment Clause, applies not only to the federal government but also to the states, via the Fourteenth Amendment.

   1. **No forbidding of belief:** The Free Exercise Clause flatly forbids the outlawing of any religious *belief.*

   2. **Conduct:** The difficult issues arise not in connection with pure beliefs, but in connection with *conduct* that is related to beliefs. Normally, free exercise problems arise when the government, acting in pursuit of *non-religious objectives*, either: (1) forbids or burdens conduct which happens to be dictated by someone's religious belief; or (2) compels or encourages conduct which is forbidden by someone's religious belief.

      Example: The state awards unemployment compensation only to those jobless workers who make themselves available for work Monday through Saturday. Although this rule has a non-religious purpose (making sure that only those whose unemployment is involuntary collect aid), the statute strongly encourages conduct which is violative of the religious beliefs of some persons (e.g., Seventh Day Adventists, whose religion makes Saturday the day of rest). Therefore, the act raises significant free exercise problems. (In fact, the act was held to violate the Free Exercise Clause as applied to Seventh Day Adventists, in *Sherbert v. Verner, infra*, p. 691.)

   3. **General principles:** However, not all statutes that forbid conduct required by religious beliefs or that compel conduct forbidden by religious beliefs are necessarily violative of

the Free Exercise Clause. The Free Exercise analysis depends heavily on the distinction between government action taken with ***intent*** to burden a religious practice, and government action that merely has an ***unintended burdensome effect*** on a religious practice:

a. Intent: Whenever the ***purpose*** of a governmental action is to negatively effect a particular type of conduct ***because*** it is dictated by religion, that act will almost automatically be found to violate the Free Exercise Clause. Such purposeful interference with religion will be ***strictly scrutinized***, and almost never upheld. However, situations where such an illicit motive can be proved rarely arise. For one illustration, see *Church of the Lukumi Babalu Aye, infra.*

b. Burdensome effect: Where the statute is not motivated by an intent to interfere with religiously-related conduct, but the statute nonetheless has that ***effect***, as long as the statute is a rule of ***"general applicability"*** (as opposed to a rule that focuses on religion), an individual's free exercise rights don't entitle him to an exemption from the statute. As the Court put it in the key 1990 case on the subject, "the right of free exercise does not relieve an individual of the obligation to ***comply*** with a ***'valid and neutral law*** of ***general applicability*** on the ground that the law ***proscribes (or prescribes) conduct*** that his religion prescribes (or proscribes).'" *Employment Division v. Smith*, 494 U.S. 872 (1990) (discussed further *infra*, p. 694).

Example: Oregon makes it a crime to use or consume the drug peyote, and refuses to give an exemption to Native Americans whose use of the drug is a central part of their religious rites. The Native Americans argue that the state's failure to give them an exemption from this prohibition violates their free exercise rights. *Held*, for the state: An individual's free exercise rights do not prevent him from being required to obey a "valid and neutral law of general applicability," even though the law forbids conduct that his religion requires. *Employment Div. v. Smith*, *supra* (and *infra*, p. 694).

B. Intent to interfere with religion: As noted, where government takes an action whose ***purpose*** is to forbid or interfere with particular conduct ***because*** the conduct is dictated by a religious belief, the governmental action will be strictly scrutinized and almost always struck down as a violation of the Free Exercise Clause. Cases in this category rarely arise, however.

1. Animal sacrifice case: Virtually the only modern Supreme Court case in which government was shown to have had such an illicit intent to disfavor a particular religion is ***Church of the Lukumi Babalu Aye, Inc. v. Hialeah***, 508 U.S. 520 (1993), involving ***ritual animal sacrifice*** by practitioners of the Santeria religion.

a. The Santeria religion: The plaintiffs in *Lukumi* were members of a church following the Santeria religion. Santeria, found most often in Cuba, is a religion whose members perform ritual sacrifices of chickens, pigeons and other animals as part of rites for birth, marriage and death, for cure of the sick, and at other times. The animal is killed by the cutting of its carotid arteries, and is usually (but not in all instances) cooked and eaten.

b. Government's response: The city of Hialeah, Florida, where the Ps' church was located, enacted a series of ordinances that, taken together, outlawed religious animal sacrifice. One ordinance, for instance, made it unlawful to "sacrifice any animal" within the city limits, and defined "sacrifice" as "to unnecessarily kill, torment, torture, or mutilate an animal in a public or private ritual or ceremony not for the primary purpose of food consumption. ... " The ordinances were written so that their sole effect would be to ban sacrifices by Santeria practitioners; for instance, Kosher slaughter was carefully exempted by defining "sacrifice" so as to exclude slaughter that is "for the primary purpose of food consumption."

    i. Motive: The history behind the ordinances' enactment — such as the supporting statements by Council members, and the public debate concerning the issue — made it clear that the community as a whole *disliked the practice of Santeria*, and wanted to *abolish sacrificial rituals* by Santeria practitioners.

c. Ordinance struck down: *All members* of the Court agreed that the Hialeah ordinances should be struck down as a *violation of the Free Exercise Clause*. Seven Justices believed that the intent of the City Council in enacting the ordinances was to suppress the ritual portion of the Santeria religion, and agreed that governmental action that is intended to disfavor a particular religious practice will almost always violate the Free Exercise Clause.

d. Rationale: Writing for the Court on most points, Justice Kennedy explained that government action that affects religion will be subjected to the *"most rigorous of scrutiny"* (which it will rarely survive) unless the government act is both: (1) *"neutral"*; and (2) of *"general applicability."*

    i. Not "neutral": Here, Kennedy found, the ordinances were clearly *not "neutral"* since they were transparently enacted for the *purpose* of disfavoring a particular religious practice.

    ii. Not "generally applicable": Nor was the ordinance of *"general applicability."* Kennedy seemed to say that the more *"underinclusive"* (see *supra*, p. 238) a governmental action is, the less likely it is to manifest the required "general applicability." Here, the ordinances were very underinclusive. For instance, the city claimed that the ordinance was necessary to protect the public health, since sacrificed animals were frequently not properly disposed of. Yet the city did not regulate the disposal of animals that had been killed by hunters, or the disposal of left-over food by restaurants.

e. Net result: *Lukumi* makes it clear that in those very rare instances where government is shown to have acted for the *purpose* of burdening a particular type of conduct because that conduct is dictated by religion, the governmental act will be subjected to such *strict scrutiny* that it will almost never survive.

f. Not applicable to withholding of rewards rather than giving of punishment: *Lukumi* involved a government-imposed *punishment* of a religiously-motivated practice; the case says that strict scrutiny will be given to that government punishment unless the punishment was both "neutral" and "of general applicability." What if the government disfavors a religious practice not by imposing an affirmative punishment, but rather by *withdrawing a benefit* that is given to otherwise-similar non-religious practices? A 2004 case seems to mean that *Lukumi does not apply* to this "withdrawal of benefits" scenario.

    i. *Locke v. Davey*: The case was *Locke v. Davey*, 540 U.S. 712 (2004) (also discussed *supra*, p. 687), in which the state of Washington gave merit scholarships to all eligible college students, with the one exception that the scholarship could not be used to pursue a degree in "devotional theology" (i.e., training for the ministry).

The Court held that this carve-out of a generally-applicable government benefit did not violate the Free Exercise clause. Justice Scalia (joined by Justice Thomas) argued in dissent that *Lukumi* required that this carve-out be strictly scrutinized, and struck down, as being facially discriminatory towards religion. But the majority responded that *Lukumi **did not apply***, because the state's disfavor of religion here was of a ***"far milder kind"*** than in *Lukumi*,[3] and imposed ***"neither criminal nor civil sanctions** on any type of religious service or right."* Also, majority said, "training someone to lead a congregation is an essentially religious endeavor" that has "no counterpart with respect to other callings or professions"; therefore, *Lukumi* did not require equal treatment of that essentially-religious endeavor.

ii. **Limited scope of *Lukumi*:** So perhaps *Locke* means that *Lukumi* will apply only to criminal or civil ***"sanctions"*** — in essence punishments — that are imposed for the purpose of disfavoring religious practices, not to government conduct that merely withholds some generally-applicable benefit so the benefit cannot be used in connection with a religiously-motivated activity. At the very least, *Locke* seems to mean that *Lukumi* won't apply — and the Free Exercise clause won't be violated — where the government intentionally withdraws funding from an "essentially religious endeavor," like training for the ministry, while funding otherwise-comparable endeavors.

C. **Incidental burdensome effect, and required accommodations:** Now, let us turn to the more usual type of Free Exercise case, that in which governmental action has the ***unintended effect*** of burdening religiously-motivated conduct. In these cases, a person's religion prohibits an act required by the government, or requires/encourages an act that is forbidden by the government. The issue in such cases is, when do free exercise principles require government to grant an ***exemption or accommodation*** from the act that is ordinarily required or forbidden by the government?

1. **1990 shift:** Beginning with a 1990 case, *Employment Div. v. Smith* (*infra*, p. 694), the Court's analysis of these exemption cases underwent a profound shift, making it much harder for the free exercise claim to prevail.

2. **Pre-1990 law:** Prior to 1990, the Court seemed to take a relatively pro-free-exercise approach to this problem of unintended burdens on religion. In general, when a government law had the unintended effect of burdening religious exercise, the Court held (or at least claimed to be holding) that the law could be upheld only if it was the ***least restrictive means*** of accomplishing a ***compelling*** state objective. In other words, the Court purported to give ***"strict scrutiny"*** to the government's insistence on applying its statute even to those whose religious exercise would be burdened by enforcement of the statute. Under the strict scrutiny standard, if the state's objective could be served as well, or almost as well, by granting an ***exemption*** to those whose religious beliefs were burdened by the regulation, ***such an exemption had to be given.***

a. **Accommodation for Sabbath:** The most important case demonstrating this pre-1990 "give an exemption where feasible" approach was ***Sherbert v. Verner***, 374 U.S. 398 (1963). Sherbert, a Seventh Day Adventist, was fired for being unwilling to work

3. For instance, the scholarship could be used at a sectarian college, and could even be used for the taking of a limited number of theology courses, as long as the student was not pursuing a devotional-theology degree.

on Saturdays, her religion's day of rest. All other available jobs required willingness to work on Saturdays. The state refused to give her unemployment compensation benefits, on the grounds that she had declined to accept "suitable work when offered."

i.   **Holding:** The Supreme Court held that the state's refusal to give Mrs. Sherbert an exemption from the "must be willing to work on Saturdays" rule violated her right to the free exercise of her religion.

   (1) **Rationale:** The Court reasoned that South Carolina's policy unduly burdened Sherbert's free exercise of her religion, since it forced her to choose between receiving benefits and following her religion. This choice placed "the same kind of burden upon the free exercise of religion as would a fine imposed against [her] for her Saturday worship." Furthermore, there was a *discriminatory* component to the state's action, since Sunday worshippers were not put to this choice.

   (2) **Strict scrutiny:** But the fact that Sherbert's free exercise rights were burdened was not by itself enough to gain her a victory. Rather, the issue became whether there was a *compelling state interest* justifying the governmental policy, which could *not be satisfied by means placing less of a burden* upon the exercise of religion. In other words, the refusal to give an exemption was to be *"strictly scrutinized."* Here, no showing was made by the state that an *exemption* for Sabbatarians would prevent the state from achieving its objective (assuring that payments go only to those who were involuntarily unemployed).

ii. **Modern Court's view:** Despite the Court's major change of approach in 1990, the ruling and rationale of *Sherbert* — at least when applied to the same *narrow context of unemployment benefits* — might well remain good law.

b. **Compulsory schooling:** Another major illustration of the principle that exemptions must be given where feasible came in a case involving a state *compulsory-schooling* requirement. In *Wisconsin v. Yoder*, 406 U.S. 205 (1972), the Court invalidated Wisconsin's refusal to exempt 14- and 15-year-old Amish students from the requirement of attending school until the age of 16.

i.   **Rationale:** The parents of the Amish students satisfied the Court that it was an essential element of the Amish religion that members be informally taught to earn their living through farming and other rural activities, and that compulsory high school education was at odds with that belief. Applying strict scrutiny, the Court concluded that an exemption must be granted unless the state could show an interest "of the highest order," which could not be served by means other than denial of an exemption.

ii. **Harm not sufficiently great:** The state's interest, of course, was in having all of its citizens be reasonably well-educated, so that they could participate intelligently in political affairs and become economically self-sufficient. The Court implicitly conceded that Amish children who failed to attend high school would not receive the same level of intellectual learning; in other words, the state's objective would not be as fully realized if an exemption were given. But the Court considered it crucial that nearly all Amish children continued to live in the Amish community throughout their lives, and that the informal vocational training they received seemed to prepare them well for that life.

    iii. Significance: Thus the Court in *Yoder* seemed to hold that the state's interest must be read **broadly and flexibly**, not narrowly and rigidly, in determining whether that interest could still be fulfilled if an exemption were given.

c. Other pre-1990 cases go the other way: But even pre-1990, most plaintiffs who sought mandatory exemptions on free-exercise grounds *lost*; *Sherbert* and *Yoder* were among the few exceptions.

    i. Strict scrutiny applied in a non-rigorous way: Sometimes, the religious claimant lost because the Court applied "strict scrutiny" in a relatively **non-rigorous** way, by being quick to find that the governmental interest was "compelling," and by being easily persuaded that requiring the government to give an exemption would badly harm the government's attempt to achieve that compelling interest.

        (1) No exemption for social security taxes: For instance, in *U.S. v. Lee*, 455 U.S. 252 (1982), an Amish employer argued that requiring him to pay **Social Security** taxes violated his free exercise rights, because "the Amish believe it sinful not to provide for their own elderly and therefore are morally opposed to the national social security system." The Court purported to apply strict scrutiny to the government's refusal to give the Amish an exemption, but concluded that the refusal passed muster: the restriction on religious freedom was "essential to accomplish an overriding governmental interest," and that denial of exemptions was "indispensable to [Social Security's] fiscal vitality."

    ii. Strict scrutiny not applied: In other cases, the Court did not even purport to apply strict scrutiny to the government's refusal to give an exemption, on the theory that the case involved a special context in which **greater deference** to government was required.

        (1) Deference to military judgments: For instance, in a case (set forth in the following Example) in which the regulation was imposed by the **military** on its employees, the Court gave **great deference to the military's judgment** about whether granting an exemption would be damaging to the military's interests.

        Example: An Orthodox Jewish Air Force captain asserts a Free Exercise right to wear a yarmulke while on duty, in contravention of an Air Force regulation requiring uniform dress. (A yarmulke is a head-covering that Orthodox Jewish men are required by their religion to wear at all times.) *Held*, for the Air Force: Although a person in military service is not completely without First Amendment rights, "when evaluating whether military needs justify a particular restriction on religiously motivated conduct, courts must give *great deference* to the professional judgment of military authorities concerning the relative importance of a particular military interest."

        Here, the Air Force had made a judgment that the use of **standardized uniforms** "encourages the **subordination of personal preferences and identities** in favor of the **overall group mission**." Even though the rule banning the wearing of religious headgear would cause the plaintiff to violate the tenets of his religion, "the First Amendment does not require the military to accommodate such practices in the face of its view that they would detract from the uniformity sought by the dress regulation." *Goldman v. Weinberger*, 475 U.S. 503 (1986).

    iii. Coercion required: Also, the Court held that the Free Exercise Clause only gets triggered where government in some sense *"coerces"* an individual to do something (or not to do something) against the dictates of his religion. Where the government took an action that *unintentionally happened to make it harder for a person to practice her religion* — but without coercing her into taking or not taking some action as an individual — the Free Exercise Clause *did not apply.*

    Example: The federal government, without intending to affect any religious practice, wants to build a road. The effect will be to destroy Native American ritual grounds.

    Held, there has been no impairment of the Native American plaintiffs' free exercise rights, because the plaintiffs are not being coerced into doing or not doing anything — external reality is simply being changed in a way that makes it harder for them to practice their religion. *Lyng v. Northwest Indian Cemetery Protective Ass'n*, 485 U.S. 439 (1988).

3. The 1990 "generally-applicable rule" case (*Employment Div. v. Smith*): As we've seen, before 1990 individuals sometimes successfully argued that they were entitled to an exemption from a government rule on free exercise grounds, but usually failed. Then, in 1990, the Court made it even *harder* for individuals to use free exercise grounds to win exemptions from *generally-applicable* government rules that *unintentially burden* religious conduct.

In *Employment Division v. Smith*, 494 U.S. 872 (1990), the Court, by a 5-4 vote, held that a generally-applicable religiously-neutral law is automatically *enforceable*, regardless of the degree of burden it causes on an individual's religious beliefs. The majority wrote that "the right of free exercise does not relieve an individual of the obligation to comply with a *valid and neutral law* of *general applicability* on the ground that the law proscribes (or prescribes) conduct that his religion prescribes (or proscribes)."

    a. Facts: In *Smith*, the issue was whether Oregon could *criminalize the possession of the drug peyote*, and refuse to give an exemption to American Indians whose use of the drug is a central part of their religious rites. The majority not only held that Oregon could refuse an exemption, but also held that *no balancing* of the state's interest in its prohibition against the burden on the individual's religious beliefs need be carried out — so long as the ban on peyote was generally applicable, and not motivated by a governmental desire to affect religion, the law was fully enforceable despite the burden on the plaintiffs.

    b. Dissents and concurrences: The other four members of the Court disagreed with this test. In a concurrence by Justice O'Connor, and a dissent by Justice Blackmun (joined by Brennan and Marshall), these four argued that *strict scrutiny* should be applied wherever a generally-applicable law burdened the free exercise of religion. As Justice Blackmun put it, "A state statute that burdens the free exercise of religion ... may stand only if the law in general, and the state's refusal to allow a religious exemption in particular, are justified by a compelling interest that cannot be served by less restrictive means."

c. **Significance:** *Smith* means that *any* generally-applicable regulation, **whether criminal or civil**, and whether it requires conduct or forbids conduct, will be fully enforceable and upheld despite the burden on individuals' religious practices. So the pre-*Smith* traditional strict scrutiny supposedly given to government's refusal to grant an exemption has been **abolished**.

   i. **Other constitutional interests present:** But where the individual's interest in free exercise of religion is combined with a *free speech, freedom of association,* or some other *separate constitutional interest,* the individual has a **better chance of prevailing.** Thus cases like *Wisconsin v. Yoder* (*supra*, p. 692, holding that the state must exempt Amish students from the requirement of attending school) probably remain good law, because in that situation the parents have a strong *substantive due process interest* in controlling the education of their children, in addition to their free exercise interest.

d. **Not applicable to intentional discrimination against religion:** Don't forget that *Smith*, though it makes it dramatically tougher for the plaintiff to win a free exercise challenge to government action, only applies where the government action has the *unintentional effect* of burdening religion. In those rare instances where government acts for the *purpose* of disfavoring a particular religious practice, the most rigorous strict scrutiny will still be applied, and the government action will almost always be struck down. See, e.g., *Church of the Lukumi Babalu Aye, supra*, p. 689, where the Court found that an ordinance forbidding animal sacrifice was exactly such a government action intended to disfavor religion, and thus struck it down.

4. **Anti-discrimination laws, and a group's right to pick its "ministers":** There's one other important limitation on *Smith* that has emerged. *Smith* does *not* apply when the government regulation, even though neutral and generally-applicable on its face, would have the effect of *interfering with the internal decision-making of a religious group* regarding the group's *core faith and mission*. So, for instance, a church will be exempt from a generally-applicable and neutral rule forbidding certain types of *employment discrimination*, if the rule would interfere with the church's right to *select the "ministers"* who will carry out the church's core religious mission. This limitation on *Smith* is illustrated by a 2012 case set forth in the following example.

   Example: Hosanna-Tabor is a Lutheran church that runs a religious school. Perich is a teacher at the school, and has the status of a "minister" within the church and school. As part of her duties, she teaches religious courses and leads students in prayer. During the course of a dispute about whether Perich is to be fired, Perich threatens to make a complaint to the Equal Employment Opportunity Commission (EEOC) that the school has violated the Americans with Disabilities Act by discriminating against her on grounds of her disability. The school fires her, in part because of this threat of litigation. Perich then complains to the EEOC; the EEOC sues the school on Perich's behalf, claiming that the school has violated the ADA's prohibition against retaliation by employers against employees who assert ADA rights. The school defends on the grounds that Perich was a "minister," and that the school's free exercise rights entitle it to a "ministerial exception" to anti-discrimination laws, if the enforcement of such a law would deprive the school of the untrammeled right to choose its ministers. The EEOC (and Perich) counter by saying that the ADA is a "valid and neutral law of general applicability" under *Employment Div. v. Smith*, so the school doesn't have a free exercise right to disregard the statute.

Held, for the school. It's true that the ADA is a "valid and neutral law of general applicability." But *Smith* applies only to government regulation of ***"outward physical acts"*** (such as ingesting peyote). The case does not apply where government is interfering with "an ***internal church decision that affects the faith and mission*** of the church itself." Therefore, *Smith* does not prevent the Court from finding (as it does) that the school is entitled to a ministerial exception that frees it from having to obey the ADA in matters concerning the appointment or retention of ministers. *Hosanna-Tabor Evangelical Lutheran Church and School v. EEOC*, 132 S.Ct. 694 (2012) (also discussed *supra*, p. 668, as to its Establishment Clause implications).

D. Military service and conscientious objection: There are many who hold the religious belief that ***all war is evil***. Since the advent of the selective service system, Congress has always made available to such ***"conscientious objectors"*** an ***exemption from military service***.

   1. Not necessarily required under Free Exercise Clause: However, the Court has ***never*** held that such an exemption is ***required*** by the Free Exercise Clause. In fact, the Court has generally assumed, without deciding, that the exemption is *not* constitutionally required.

   2. Selective conscientious objection: ***"Selective"*** conscientious objectors are those who do not believe that all wars are unjust, but do contend that they should be exempted from service in any ***particular*** war which they believe to be unjust. If such selective conscientious objection is based upon religious beliefs, may Congress constitutionally deny an exemption while granting an exemption for "non-selective" objection? The Court answered ***"yes"*** to this question in *Gillette v. U.S.*, 401 U.S. 437 (1971).

   a. Rationale: The Court conceded that the congressional requirement that conscientious objection be total burdened some types of religious beliefs more than others. But the Court applied the then-familiar principle (abandoned after *Employment Div. v. Smith*, p. 694) that such disparate effect is permissible only if there is an important governmental interest which cannot be achieved by means less burdensome to religious beliefs. Here, the government satisfied this test. One governmental interest was that in ***fairness***; if selective conscientious objection were allowed, there would be a danger that "as between two would-be objectors, [that] objector would succeed who is more articulate, better educated, or better counselled." Also, the government's interest in procuring militarily-necessary manpower might not be fulfillable if selective conscientious objection were permitted.

E. Public health: Another category of regulation sometimes attacked on Free Exercise grounds is that of ***public health*** rules. The individual raising the Free Exercise claim has generally lost when the health or welfare of others was at issue, but has usually won where ***only his own health*** or well-being would be jeopardized by an exemption.

   1. Vaccinations: Thus the Court has held that an individual may be required to ***receive a vaccination*** against disease, even if his religion prohibits such procedures. *Jacobsen v. Massachusetts*, 197 U.S. 11 (1905). This is clearly good law after *Employment Div. v. Smith*, *supra*, p. 694, since vaccination laws are a classic example of a neutral, generally-applicable law, which must be obeyed even when it interferes with a person's religious practices.

2. **Life-saving medical treatment:** Where an adult refuses on religious grounds to receive a *blood transfusion* or other *life-saving medical care*, the issues are complex. If the adult is competent, and there is no issue of contagion, it's not clear whether, even post-*Smith*, he can be forced to submit to such care notwithstanding his free exercise rights — a court might well decide that the absence of potential harm to anyone else, combined with considerations of personal autonomy, dictate respecting the adult's right to decline care. The Supreme Court has never decided such a case.

   a. **Child or parent of minor:** But where the patient is a *child* whose parents object on religious grounds, or the patient is a *parent with minor children*, most courts have *compelled* the treatment, on the theory that the state's interest in safeguarding minors outweighs whatever rights of religious liberty are at stake.

F. **What constitutes a "religious belief":** A Free Exercise claim, to be valid, must of course involve a "religious belief." Thus the courts are forced to consider not only whether a belief is genuinely held, but whether it is "religious." The Supreme Court has never articulated a formal definition of "religious belief" or of "religion." However, several things are clear about how the Court determines the religiosity of a belief:

1. **Not necessarily theistic:** The belief, and the system of beliefs of which it is a part, *need not necessarily recognize a Supreme Being*. That is, non-theistic as well as theistic religions may receive Free Exercise protection. See, e.g., *Torcaso v. Watkins*, 367 U.S. 488 (1961), striking down a state requirement that all holders of public office declare their belief in the existence of God.

2. **Organized vs. unorganized religion:** The Court will try hard to avoid preferring *"organized"* religions (i.e., ones that are well-established, with large numbers of adherents and conventional practices) over ones that are new, unconventional or sparsely-followed.

   a. **Religion practiced by a single person:** In fact, a person's religious beliefs are entitled to the protection of the Free Exercise Clause even if those beliefs are held by a *single person* rather than being part of the teachings of any kind of group or sect. See *Frazee v. Illinois Dept. of Employment Security*, 489 U.S. 829 (1989).

3. **Sincerity:** Obviously, a court should not sustain a Free Exercise claim unless it is convinced that the belief is *genuine*. However, in making this determination the court will strive mightily to avoid considering the "truth" or "reasonableness" of that belief. See *U.S. v. Ballard, supra*, p. 670.

4. **Centrality:** A belief which is claimed to be in conflict with a particular governmental rule must also be *central* to the individual's religion; the government should not be required to grant an exemption from a regulation which merely *inconveniences* a believer. However, as in the case of gauging whether a belief is "sincerely" held, this decision should be based in part on subjective criteria: if an individual genuinely feels that the conflict is with a belief central *for him*, his claim should be upheld even though most members of the same sect would consider the belief to be peripheral. Tribe, p. 1249. See, e.g., *Thomas v. Review Bd. Ind. Empl. Sect. Div.*, 450 U.S. 707 (1981), where a Jehovah's Witness' refusal to work in a munitions factory was held to require an exemption from unem-

ployment compensation rules under the Free Exercise Clause, even though there was evidence that another Jehovah's Witness *was* willing to work in the same factory.

Quiz Yourself on

FREEDOM OF RELIGION *(ENTIRE CHAPTER)*

91. The town of Amity has a religiously diverse population. In October, the mayor announced that he and the City Council believed it would be nice to have some sort of public display celebrating the upcoming holiday season. Therefore, he said, a small area would be set aside in Amity's biggest and most centrally-located park, in which a display could be assembled. He established a "Committee for a Happy Holiday," to which he appointed several eminent local citizens. Anyone else who wished to join the committee was permitted to do so. The purpose of the committee was to design and assemble a display. The committee put together a display consisting of: (1) a crèche or nativity scene, portraying the birth of Christ in the manger; (2) a Christmas tree; (3) a Menorah; (4) a Santa Claus riding reindeer; and (5) a banner reading, "Have a Happy Holiday." There was no instance in which a citizen (whether a member of the committee or not) proposed a figure or item that was rejected.

   (a) You are volunteer counsel to the local branch of the ACLU. Your members wish you to bring suit attacking the constitutionality of this display. What constitutional provision should you base your suit on?

_____

   (b) Will your attack succeed? _____

92. The state of Carginia requires every religious organization operating in the state to register with the state Attorney General, and to submit financial statements, if the institution wishes to be exempt from state property taxes and state income taxes. (An institution is always free to forego these tax advantages, in which case it need not register or submit financial statements.) After numerous small community churches, synagogues and mosques claimed that the paperwork involved was terribly burdensome to them, the registration and financial-statement provisions were amended to grant an exemption for any institution "50% or more of whose financial support derives from donations by persons who consider themselves members of the institution."

   The state legislature considered eliminating the registration/financial-statement requirement altogether, but did not do so because of a fear that groups that solicit donation from non-members are likely to practice fraud, harassment, and other abuses. There is evidence that the legislature was especially concerned about groups that did their fund-raising by ringing doorbells at private homes, such as "Moonies" and Jehovah's Witnesses. A local group of Jehovah's Witnesses gets most of its financial support by selling Bibles door-to-door to non-members. This group has sued to overturn the statutory scheme as a violation of its Establishment Clause rights. Should the court find in favor of the plaintiff? _____

93. The legislature of the state of Largesse was concerned that students in the state's biggest and most financially-troubled city, Bigtown, were not getting a good public-school education. To increase school competition, and to give parents of Bigtown students a choice of schooling options, the Largesse legislature enacted the "Tuition Voucher Plan of 2002." Under this plan, the parents of any elementary- or middle-school student living in Bigtown could attend any licensed private school (including parochial schools) in or near Bigtown, and receive a state voucher worth $2,000 to be used towards the private school's annual tuition. Mostly because the average non-religious private school's annual tuition in Bigtown is $15,000, and the average religious school's annual tuition is just $2,500, about 95% of the students who took advantage of the voucher program in its first year attended religious schools, where they were given intensive instruction in religious subjects (e.g., Roman Catholic catechism) as well as secular subjects. There are no other special programs in Bigtown designed to solve the educational problems that the Largesse legislature has identified. A parent of a public-school attendee, Paul, has sued the state, arguing that the voucher program violates the Establishment Clause. Should the court find in Paul's favor?

_____

94. The religion of Weejun is practiced primarily on a small island in the South Pacific Ocean. A number of adherents have made their homes in the West Coast town of Pacifica. The Weejuns speak their own language, and practice their own rituals in a church located in the town. As part of their rituals, the Weejuns drink a beverage called nectaria, made from fermented nectarines. The beverage is smelly and of quite high alcoholic content. Practitioners sometimes get drunk from using it in their rituals. The Weejuns are, in general, relatively uneducated, of lower income status, and seem quite strange to most non-Weejun residents of Pacifica. For some time, non-Weejun Pacificans had been complaining at Town Council meetings that the Weejuns and their nectaria-based rituals were leading to public drunkenness, and a consequent burdening of the police and lowering of Pacifica's "image." The Town Council then enacted an ordinance whose sole provision was to ban the sale or public use of nectaria. "Public use" was defined to include the use in any gathering of more than three people who were not related to each other and who were not meeting in a private home. Since the Weejun church was a free-standing building, the sole effect of the ordinance was to ban the use of nectaria as part of the Weejun church rituals.

(a) If the members of the Weejun congregation wish to attack the constitutionality of the Pacifica ordinance, what constitutional provision should they rely upon? _____

(b) What test or standard of review should the court apply in evaluating the challenge you referred to in (a)? _____

(c) Is the ordinance constitutional, when judged by that standard of review? _____

95. Practitioners of the religion of Parentism believe that it is up to the parents of the child to carry out that child's education, and that the teaching of the child by strangers (i.e., non-parents) is against God's will. Consequently, each child born to parents who practice Parentism is schooled at home, and no private religious schools following the Parentism religion exist. The state of Gomorra has been worried that students who are taught at home by their parents fail to receive necessary socialization, and frequently don't learn needed skills like cooperation, as well as knowledge of more advanced subjects like trigonometry. Therefore, the state has recently enacted a ban on any kind of home education (though parents are free to send their children to any private or religious school they wish, so long as children from more than one family attend). There is no evidence that the Gomorra regulation was motivated by any particular dislike, or even awareness, of Parentism; in fact, the practitioners of Parentism are so few that state education officials are barely aware that they exist. Priscilla, an adherent of Parentism who has been teaching her child Pamela at home, has applied to the state for an exemption from the no-home-schooling requirement, on the grounds that the ordinance would otherwise violate Priscilla's and Pamela's free exercise rights. Must the state grant an exemption so that Pamela may be schooled at home? _____

96. A central element of the Sharkist religion is to possess and pray to a piece of a fin from a Great White Shark. Because the Great White Shark is a nearly extinct species, and because it has been relentlessly hunted as a source of shark fin soup and other delicacies, the U.S. (acting together with other western nations) has recently enacted a ban on the possession or importing of any fin or other body part from Great White Sharks. When Congress enacted this ban, few if any members of Congress were aware of the existence of the Sharkist religion, which has very few adherents. The federal legislation makes it a felony, punishable by up to five years in prison, to knowingly possess a Great White Shark's fin. Samark, a practitioner of Sharkism, has petitioned the U.S. for an exemption from the ban, contending that the ban violates his free exercise rights. Religious experts estimate that there are fewer than 100 Sharkists in the United States, and that granting them an exemption would have no material effect on the rate at which Great White Sharks are hunted. Must the U.S. grant the exemption? _____

97. The Reverend John Butcher was a self-proclaimed "faith healer." Through programs paid for by his ministry on radio and television, he gave notice to the world that if a person was physically or mentally ill, Butcher would lay hands upon that person and, in most cases, could cure them. Butcher charged a "donation" for each attempt at faith healing, which he said should normally be about equal to one month's wages, payable in advance. Butcher performed dozens of attempted acts of faith healing. Of the first 30 such attempts, 29 ended with the patient/worshipper believing that he or she had not been helped at all; the other one believed that there had been some slight improvement. Butcher's 31st patient, Jones, had cancer; she relied on Butcher's laying on of hands and did not seek medical treatment, which could have cured her. She died of the cancer.

Butcher was prosecuted for the manslaughter of Jones, as well as for financial fraud in her case. The essence of the prosecution was that Butcher did not in fact believe that he had faith healing powers, and purported to have them only as a means to make money. At the trial, the prosecution was permitted to show that 29 of the first 30 patients believed that they had not been helped by Butcher. The judge then charged the jury, "The issue is not whether Butcher's treatments worked, but whether Butcher sincerely believed that they might work. In making this determination of sincerity, you may consider evidence that they did not in fact work, as bearing circumstantially on whether Butcher believed that they might work." Butcher has objected to this charge on the grounds that it infringes upon his free exercise of religion. Is Butcher's argument correct? _____

Answers

91. (a) The Establishment Clause. The Establishment Clause of the First Amendment prohibits any law "respecting an establishment of religion." In a general sense, its purpose is to erect a wall between church and state.

(b) No, probably. The Establishment Clause prevents government from *sponsoring* or *endorsing* one religion over another, or religion over non-religion. A display of religiously-oriented materials at holiday time might indeed be found to constitute an implicit endorsement or sponsorship by the government of religion or of a religious message. In evaluating whether a particular display or ceremony violates the Establishment Clause, the Court generally uses a three-part test (derived from *Lemon v. Kurtzman*). Only if the action satisfies *each* of the following conditions will it be valid: (1) it must have a *secular legislative purpose*; (2) its principal or *primary effect* must neither advance nor inhibit religion; and (3) it must not foster an *excessive governmental entanglement* with religion.

On facts very similar to these, the Court held by a 5-4 vote that the display did *not* violate any of these three tests. *Lynch v. Donnelly*. Here, a court would probably find a secular purpose (to celebrate the holiday, which is a secular government-observed holiday in addition to being one with religious significance). The primary effect of the display would probably not be found to benefit religion in general or Christianity specifically (since the non-religious "holiday spirit" was also being benefitted, and any advancement of religion was somewhat indirect). And there would probably not be found to be undue entanglement between government and religious institutions, since government basically left the space available and allowed citizens to do what they wished without further government intervention. The most important factor would probably be ***context***: here, there were at least some non-religiously-oriented items in the display (e.g., the banner, and the reindeer), so that a reasonable observer would probably not conclude that the display was, overall, a government endorsement of religion. (Observe, however, that *Lynch* was a 5-4 decision, and even a small variation in the items displayed, or in how they came to be displayed, might have resulted in a shift of one vote and thus a change in result.)

92. **Yes.** The facts are similar to those in *Larson v. Valente*. The Court held that this type of scheme benefited one religion or group of religions over another. Therefore, the Court applied ***strict scrutiny***, not the *Lemon* three-prong test. Such a preference of one religious group over others could be sustained only if it was "justified by a compelling governmental interest and … closely fitted to further that interest." Although the state may have an interest in guarding against "abusive solicitation practices," the means selected here are not "closely fitted" to furthering that interest, since there is no reason to believe that the likelihood of solicitation abuse is closely related to the ratio of member contributions to total contributions.

    The conclusion that the legislature has "played favorites" here is buttressed by the evidence that the legislature knew it was disfavoring Jehovah's Witnesses and other residential-doorbell-ringers. If there were evidence that the disfavoring of Jehovah's Witnesses was entirely ***incidental***, perhaps strict scrutiny would not be called for.

93. **No, probably.** The main issue is whether the program here has the "primary effect" of advancing religion (since if it does, it's a violation of the Establishment Clause). The facts here are quite similar to those in *Zelman v. Simmons-Harris*, where a bare majority of the Court held that the program was constitutional because any funding that went to religious education resulted from the "deliberate choices of numerous individual recipients," not from any legislative desire to aid religion. One difference between the facts here and those in *Zelman* is that in *Zelman*, there were other "alternative" educational programs paid for by the state that didn't even arguably aid religion (e.g., special public magnet schools and tutoring programs), and these alternative programs had more participants than the private-school-voucher program — so viewed in the aggregate, the total alternative programs didn't primarily advance religion. Therefore, it's possible that a court would rule that the absence of such alternatives here makes a difference. But probably, the result here would be the same as in *Zelman* — because (a) each parent is making her own decision about whether to use the voucher at a religious or non-religious school, (b) the voucher program is open to students and private-schools regardless of whether they do or don't have a religious affiliation; and (c) there's no evidence that the legislature was intending to advance religion, the program will probably pass muster.

94. **(a) The Free Exercise Clause.** The First Amendment bars government from making any law "prohibiting the free exercise" of religion. The clause can apply to regulations that are directed at religious beliefs or, more commonly, directed at religiously-oriented ***conduct***. Here, we have a regulation that is directed at conduct (the consumption of a particular beverage).

    (b) Strict scrutiny. Where government takes an action whose ***purpose*** is to forbid or interfere with particular conduct ***because*** the conduct is dictated by a religious belief, the government action is strictly scrutinized and almost always struck down. Here, all the evidence is that the Pacifica Town Council was motivated principally by members' dislike of the Weejun religion and its practitioners, not by a generally-applicable dislike of drunkenness. The facts are roughly analogous to those of *Church of the Lukumi Babalu Aye, Inc. v. Hialeah*, where the Court struck down a ban on ritual animal sacrifice on the theory that the ban was motivated by hostility to practitioners of the Santeria religion. When the Court is deciding whether governmental regulation is designed for the purpose of interfering with a particular religious practice, the extent to which the ordinance is of "general applicability" will be considered; here, the ordinance speaks solely of nectaria, not other beverages of equal alcohol content, and the ordinance affects nobody but practitioners of Weejun. Therefore, a court would almost certainly conclude that there was an intent to interfere with the religious practice, not merely an unintended effect upon religion. Consequently, strict scrutiny must be used.

(c) No. Strict scrutiny in the free exercise context, as in other constitutional contexts, means that the regulation will be struck down unless it is *necessary* to achieve a *compelling* governmental interest. The government's interest here in cutting down on public drunkenness might be "compelling," but the means selected are certainly not "necessary" to achieving that end. For instance, the town could simply have banned public drunkenness, or banned all substances of sufficiently high alcohol content that were very likely to produce drunkenness. The ordinance here is extremely underinclusive (it deals with only one source of drunkenness), demonstrating that it is not "drawn in narrow terms" to accomplish the objective.

95. **Yes, probably.** The general rule today is as set forth in *Employment Div. v. Smith*: "the right of free exercise does not relieve an individual of the obligation to comply with a *valid and neutral law* of *general applicability* on the ground that the law proscribes (or prescribes) conduct that his religion prescribes (or proscribes)." Applying this principle would mean that Priscilla is not constitutionally entitled to an exemption. But a pre-*Smith* case that is somewhat on point has never been explicitly overruled post-*Smith*, and would probably be re-affirmed today. That case is *Wisconsin v. Yoder*, where the Court held that a state must exempt Amish teenage students from the requirement of attending school until the age of 16. If the case arose today, the Supreme Court would likely preserve *Yoder* by carving out a narrow exception to *Smith* to allow a free exercise claim by parents who want to home-school their children for religious reasons.

96. **No.** Where government enacts a generally-applicable *criminal prohibition* on a certain type of activity, and government does not intend to burden religious beliefs, government does not have to grant an exemption to those whose religious beliefs or practices are burdened by the prohibition. The facts are analogous to those of *Employment Division v. Smith*, where a state was allowed to refuse to grant American Indians an exemption from the ban on peyote, even though use of the drug was a central part of their religious rites. *Smith* establishes that government does not have to engage in any *balancing* of its interests in its prohibition against the burden on the individual's religious beliefs — so long as the ban is generally applicable, and not motivated by a governmental desire to affect religion, the law is fully enforceable no matter how large the burden on the plaintiff or how small the benefit to the state. Therefore, even though an exemption would not meaningfully interfere with the goal of safeguarding Great White Sharks, no exemption needs to be given.

97. **Unclear.** The facts are analogous to those of *U.S. v. Ballard*, where the defendants were faith healers charged with fraudulently soliciting donations. The Court held that the Free Exercise Clause barred the submission to the jury of the truth or falsity of the defendants' faith healing claims. Here, the prosecution is entitled to prove that Butcher did not in fact believe his claims, but it is not clear that the prosecution should be entitled to show in detail that they were false, as a means of making a circumstantial case that Butcher believed his claims were false — a court might well conclude that, as in *Ballard*, the evidence as to truth or falsity was prejudicial, given that the only ultimate issue properly before the jury was the genuineness of Butcher's belief.

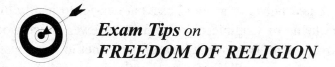

Exam Tips on FREEDOM OF RELIGION

Issues involving freedom of religion are usually easy to spot: the fact pattern has to refer to religion, religious beliefs, church, parochial school, God, prayer, or some symbol commonly associated with religion (e.g., a creche, a Star of David, etc.). So the trick with freedom of religion issues is to analyze them correctly, not to spot them. Here's what to concentrate on:

☛ Of utmost importance: decide whether the issue poses an *Establishment* Clause or a *Free Exercise* Clause problem. A given governmental action will rarely pose the danger of both (though the government will often have a ***choice*** of two actions, each posing the risk of violating a different clause).

    ☞ Here's a tip for deciding which Clause is involved: if government seems to be *favoring* religion generally, or favoring a particular religion over the "rest of society," you probably have an Establishment Clause problem. If government seems to be *disfavoring* a particular person relative to the rest of society, in a way that is related to that person's religious beliefs, then you probably have a Free Exercise Clause problem. Classic illustration of Establishment Clause problem: school prayer. Classic illustration of Free Exercise Clause problem: P can't get unemployment benefits if she doesn't make herself available for Saturday work forbidden by her religion.

☛ In analyzing an ***Establishment Clause*** problem, the first thing to do is to recite the three-part test (which you should cite as the *"Lemon v. Kurtzman"* test):

    ☞ First, the government action must have a ***secular legislative purpose*** (but it's OK if there is ***also*** a religious purpose);

    ☞ The act must have a ***primary secular effect***; and

    ☞ The government action must not involve ***undue entanglement*** of government in religious affairs, or religion in government affairs.

        ☞ Of these three prongs, the one that is most likely to be violated in your fact pattern is probably the "primary secular effect" prong, since a large variety of government programs seem to assist religious groups more than they benefit other groups.

☛ The most common type of Establishment Clause problem that you will see on an exam involves ***religion in the public schools***. Typically, the state gives some sort of financial aid to religious schools or to students who attend religious schools. Here are some rules of thumb in analyzing these:

    ☞ If the program benefits ***all students***, or even all ***private-school*** students (including non-parochial students), the fact that the biggest beneficiaries are religious students is not fatal. (*Example:* Tuition vouchers which can be used to send a student to any private school, religious or non-religious, are allowable — *Zelman v. Simmons-Harris*.)

☞   If the assistance is being rendered to a ***college or university***, it's more likely to pass muster than where it is rendered to a secondary or elementary school.

☞   Loans of ***tangible objects*** (e.g., text books or school buses) are easier to justify than loans of ***personnel***, since the loans of tangible objects involve fewer supervisory/entanglement problems for government. But even a loan of personnel to teach inside the religious school is OK, so long as the religious school authorities don't have any influence over the curriculum or the style of teaching.

☛ A common type of fact pattern involves a school district that makes school premises available ***after hours*** to various groups. The issue becomes, "Must religious groups be excluded?" The correct answer: religious groups typically need ***not*** be excluded, as long as the government does not get entangled with what the group is doing, as by having public officials co-sponsor the activity. In fact, exclusion of religious groups from a program open to other sorts of groups generally violates the religious groups' free exercise rights.

Example: A school district opens elementary school classrooms after hours to various community groups. If religious groups are allowed to participate (even if their programs are worship services), this is not an Establishment Clause program, because the religious groups are just getting equal treatment. (And if the religious groups were excluded, this would violate their free expression rights. *Good News Club*.)

☛ Another common fact pattern occurs where government gives funds to some religious organization for use in some theoretically non-religious "socially beneficial" charitable purpose. (*Example:* Government gives grants to religious and non-religious groups for use in running family planning clinics, legal services clinics, etc.) In this type of fact pattern, use the three-part *Lemon* test. Pay special attention to the risk of entanglement: how does government know that the particular religious organization isn't using the funds to advocate religious doctrine, or to favor its co-religionists? But say that the present Court seems inclined to find that there is no Establishment Clause violation in this type of fact pattern.

☛ A special type of establishment problem is posed where government ***favors one sect*** or religion over another. (*Example:* Government gives tax breaks to certain religions, or gives certain sects free time on government-owned broadcast stations.) This kind of preference is virtually per se violative of the Establishment Clause.

☛ In analyzing ***free exercise*** problems, be on the lookout for two different kinds of scenarios:

☞   In one scenario, P wants to do something that is required by P's religion, and the government blocks him from doing so.

☞   In the other scenario, P doesn't want to do something that is forbidden by her religion, and the government requires her to do so (typically, as a condition to the receipt of some kind of government benefit).

☛ If government's interference with a religious practice or belief is ***intentional*** (i.e., motivated by government's desire to interfere with the religion), the interference is virtually per se illegal. This kind of fact pattern is rare on exams. One example: government bans animal sacrifices, in circumstances showing that government is acting out of dislike of an unpopular minority religion (*Lukumi*, the Santeria Case).

☞ But this principle probably applies only to **serious "sanctions"** — **punishments** — intentionally directed against religion, not to minor withdrawals of generally-applicable government **benefits**. (*Example*: If government funds college scholarships, but doesn't let the scholarship be used for training for the ministry, this is not a Free Exercise violation, because there is no "sanction" or punishment intended here, just avoidance of church-state conflicts. *Locke v. Davey*.)

☛ In the more usual free exercise case, the government's interference with religious practices or beliefs is **unintended** and **incidental**. Here's what to look for in this usual situation:

☞ The key rule is that where government enacts a "**valid and neutral law** of **general applicability**," a person has **no** free exercise right to disobey the law, even if the law forbids (or requires) an action that the person's religion requires (or forbids). In other words, government does not have to give an exemption from the general rule.

Example: Recall *Employment Div. v. Smith*: Oregon can make it a crime to possess or smoke peyote. Native Americans must obey the ban, even though smoking peyote is a core part of their religious rites.

Some additional examples:

❑ Government bans all cruelty to animals, defined to include any death not administered in a painless manner. Assuming that there is no motive to disfavor particular religions, this ban may be applied to groups sacrificing animals as part of a religious ritual, since the ban is a rule of general applicability.

❑ Government bans polygamy. Again, since this is a generally-applicable law that is neutral to religion, government need not give an exemption to groups for whom group polygamy is a religious requirement.

❑ Government requires an autopsy in the event of any death that appears to be "non-natural." Government need not give an exemption in the case of a decedent for whom an autopsy would violate the decedent's religious beliefs.

☞ On the other hand, religious groups *do* have a free exercise right not to have government interfere with the group's **choice of "ministers"** to carry out the group's religious mission. This may require government to grant an exemption from a generally-applicable and neutral rule, such as an anti-discrimination law.

Example: A church fires a minister, after the minister claims that the church has discriminated against her because she is disabled, in violation of the Americans with Disabilities Act (ADA). The church is probably entitled to a "ministerial exception" from the ADA, since the Free Exercise Clause prevents the government from interfering with "an **internal church decision that affects the faith and mission** of the church itself." Cf. *Hosanna-Tabor Evangelical Lutheran Church and School v. EEOC*.

☛ In any free exercise case, be on the lookout for an issue concerning, **"What is a religious belief?"** Here are the key aspects of this issue:

☞ The courts may insist that the belief be **"bona fide."** So the court is permitted to gauge the **"genuineness"** or **"sincerity"** of the individual's belief.

☞   But the court is *not* permitted to gauge the *"truthfulness"* or *"reasonableness"* of the belief. No matter how bizarre or out-of-the-ordinary the belief, only sincerity counts.

☞   Even *unorganized* beliefs, and beliefs practiced by just a *single person*, are protected. Thus the court may not consider that a particular practice is "not traditional" — if it's part of P's own practice of the religion, it doesn't matter that it's a deviation from the general practices of the sect to which P belongs.

CHAPTER 16

JUSTICIABILITY

ChapterScope

In order for a case to be heard by the federal courts, the plaintiff must overcome a series of procedural obstacles that we collectively call the requirements of *"justiciability."* Here is an overview of each of these obstacles:

- **Advisory opinion:** The federal courts may not issue opinions based on *abstract* or *hypothetical* questions. This is known as the prohibition of *"advisory opinions."* It stems from the fact that the Constitution limits federal court jurisdiction only to "cases and controversies."

- **Standing:** The most important single justiciability requirement is that the federal courts may hear a case only when the plaintiff has *"standing"* to assert his claim. By this, we mean that the plaintiff must have a significant *stake* in the controversy.

  - ❑ **Requirement of "injury in fact":** That is, P must show that he has suffered an *"injury in fact."* That is, P must show that *he has himself been injured* in some way by the conduct that he complains of.

  - ❑ **Three requirements:** Generally, there are three standing requirements that the plaintiff must meet: (1) he must show that he has suffered (or is likely to suffer) an *"injury in fact"*; (2) the injury he is suffering must be *concrete* and *"individuated"*; and (3) the action being challenged must be the *"cause in fact"* of the injury.

  - ❑ **Rights of third persons:** A key function of the standing doctrine is that it prevents a litigant from asserting the constitutional rights of *"third persons" not before the court.* (However, there are several exceptions to the rule that P may not assert third-party rights; First Amendment overbreadth is an example.)

- **Mootness:** A case may not be heard by the federal courts if it is *"moot."* A case is moot if *events occurring after the filing* have deprived the litigant of an *ongoing stake* in the controversy.

- **Ripeness:** A case is not yet *"ripe,"* and therefore not yet decidable by a federal court, if it has *not yet become sufficiently concrete* to be easily adjudicated. For instance, if a criminal statute is almost never enforced, P's challenge to the constitutionality of the statute may be found not to be ripe if it is unlikely that the statute will be enforced against P.

- **The 11th Amendment and suits against the states:** The 11th Amendment bars certain types of suits against states. In particular, the amendment bars most types of *damage suits* against the state, including suits where the plaintiff is a citizen either of the defendant's state or some other state.

- **Political questions:** Certain issues are held to involve non-justiciable *"political questions."*

  - ❑ **Commitment to another branch:** For instance, a case will be found to pose a non-justiciable political question if it raises an issue whose determination is clearly committed by the Constitution to *another branch* of the federal government rather than the judiciary. Many issues concerning *impeachment* fall into this category.

❑ **Lack of manageable standards:** Alternatively, an issue may be found to be a non-justiciable political one if there are *"no manageable standards"* to guide the judiciary in deciding that issue.

I. INTRODUCTION

A. Scope: This chapter discusses preconditions which must be satisfied before a federal court will adjudicate a lawsuit, including a suit raising a constitutional claim.

    1. Source of preconditions: Some of these preconditions come from Article III, §2's limitation of federal jurisdiction to "cases and controversies." Others come from non-constitutional discretionary policies implemented by the Supreme Court, sometimes called *"prudential"* considerations. Only if a case satisfies *all* of these preconditions will it be deemed *"justiciable,"* i.e., suitable for being disposed of on the merits.

    2. Summary of topics: The preconditions discussed in this chapter include:

        a. that the suit involve a concrete controversy, so that the court will not be issuing an *"advisory opinion;"*

        b. that the plaintiff have *"standing,"* i.e., an appropriate interest or stake in the matters under suit;

        c. that the suit not be *"moot"* because of events which have occurred following institution of the action;

        d. that the suit be *"ripe,"* i.e., sufficiently well-developed and specific to merit adjudication;

        e. that the suit (or appeal to the Supreme Court) not be one from which the federal courts should *abstain* for the sake of certain discretionary policies (e.g., non-interference with state court proceedings in order to promote federalism); and

        f. that the case not present a non-justiciable *"political question."*

B. Policies served: Most of these requirements for justiciability further one or both of the following policies, implicit within the constitutional requirement of a "case or controversy":

    1. the limitation of federal court jurisdiction to issues presented in an *adversary context* and capable of being resolved by the judiciary; and

    2. the maintenance of the *separation of powers*, by assuring that the federal courts do not intrude into areas reserved for the two other branches of government. See Tribe, p. 67.

II. ADVISORY OPINIONS

A. "Case or controversy" requirement: Article III, §2 of the Constitution limits federal court jurisdiction to "cases" and "controversies." The federal courts are thus prevented from issuing opinions on *abstract* or *hypothetical* questions. An important consequence of this limitation is that federal courts *may not give "advisory opinions,"* that is, opinions which give advice about particular legislative or executive action, when no party is before the court who has suffered or imminently faces specific injury.

Example: Secretary of State Jefferson, on behalf of President Washington, writes to the Supreme Court asking it to give informal advice on various legal issues, such as the rights and duties of the United States under a treaty with France during the 1793 European War.

Held (in a return letter to the President), the Constitution's separation-of-powers principles limit the President, when he wants to solicit opinions, to calling on members of the Executive Branch. Therefore, the Court may not give the requested opinions. *Letter from the Justices to President Washington*, August 8, 1793 (reprinted in Hart and Wechsler, *Federal Courts*, 1973 Ed., pp. 64-66).

1. **Need for focused controversy:** In addition to the separation-of-powers rationale relied on by the Justices in response to Washington's request, the ban on advisory opinions is also frequently justified by the need to have the judiciary decide only *focused, specific conflicts*, in which adversaries *explore every aspect* of the situation. Otherwise, it is feared, the court will not be adequately briefed, and may make an unwise or unduly broad pronouncement which it will then have to revise when confronted with a specific, and real, conflict. (But this problem could probably be overcome if the Court were to assign "friends of the court" or other interested parties to brief and argue the issues, even in the absence of a concrete dispute. See Tribe, p. 74, n. 7.)

2. **"Strict necessity":** The ban on advisory opinions also reflects the general policy of *judicial restraint* in deciding constitutional issues; such issues will not be decided unless *"strictly necessary."* (Most of the other preconditions for justiciability, considered later in this chapter, similarly reflect this policy of avoiding constitutional adjudication whenever possible.)

B. **Declaratory judgments:** A *declaratory judgment* is one in which the court is not requested to award damages or an injunction, but rather, requested to state what the legal effect would be of proposed conduct by one or both of the parties.

1. **Some actions allowed:** The Court has permitted federal court decision or review of at least those declaratory judgment actions which are reasonably *concrete*.

2. **Insufficiently concrete:** But if a declaratory judgment action presents only questions which are unduly *hypothetical* or *abstract*, the federal court may conclude that it is being called upon to issue an illegal advisory opinion, not because the action is for a declaratory judgment, but simply because no specific, concrete controversy exists.

   a. **Criminal statutes:** A plaintiff seeking a declaratory judgment that a *criminal statute* is unconstitutional must generally show *either*: (1) a sometimes-enforced prohibition which *on its face clearly applies* to conduct in which the plaintiff has regularly engaged or will engage; or (2) an *actual threat* that the statute will be enforced *against the plaintiff* (in the case of a statute which on its face does *not* unambiguously cover the plaintiff's conduct). See Tribe, p. 78. If neither showing is made, the declaratory judgment action will be dismissed as being unduly hypothetical.

III. STANDING

A. **Nature of "standing" generally:** When we say that a litigant must have "standing" to assert his claim, we mean that he must have a significant *stake* in the controversy to merit his being the one to litigate it. Thus standing focuses mostly on the *party* asserting the claim, whereas most other elements of justiciability focus upon the nature of the *issue* being litigated. See Tribe, p. 107. The study of standing is thus the study of *what kind of interests in the outcome of a controversy* are sufficient.

1. **Policies behind doctrine:** The requirement of standing reflects principally the policy against allowing federal courts to act like a *"roving commission"* whose purpose is to enforce judges' own views of legality or the interests of "bystanders" in having constitutional or statutory principles adhered to.

2. **Special relevance to constitutional issues:** In most civil actions, the existence of standing is quite clear. The tort plaintiff who alleges personal injury, for instance, and the contract plaintiff who alleges economic damages from a breach, clearly have a sufficiently direct and personal stake in the suit's outcome that they should be permitted to litigate it. But in much *constitutional* litigation, where a plaintiff alleges that the government has acted in an unconstitutional manner, it will be much less clear that the governmental action has affected the plaintiff *more directly* than any other citizen, or that resolution of the dispute in his favor will be of special benefit to him.

   a. **No general interest in constitutional government:** The Court has never been willing to hold that the *generalized interest* of a *citizen* in having his government *behave constitutionally* is a sufficient "stake" to permit the litigation. Therefore, in most of the cases below, the plaintiff tries to show (sometimes successfully, often not) that his interest in the controversy is somehow *more direct* and *individualized* than that of the citizenry at large.

3. **Article III vs. prudential limitations:** The Supreme Court's rules on standing are a blend of: (1) requirements deemed to be imposed by the Article III "case or controversy" requirement; and (2) so-called *"prudential"* considerations, i.e., non-constitutional judgments about what constitutes wise policy in administering the judiciary. The principal consequence of the distinction is that Congress is *not free to override* the Supreme Court as to an element of standing found by the Court to fall within the "case or controversy" requirement, but it *is* free to override the prudential considerations.

4. **Two-part discussion:** Our discussion of standing is divided into two main parts: (1) cases brought by plaintiffs alleging that their rights as *taxpayers* or (less successfully) their rights as *"citizens"* have been infringed; and (2) cases claiming other, usually more individualized, types of injury. The Supreme Court has applied different rules in the two contexts; generally, but not always, the requirements are easier to fulfill for type (2) suits.

5. **Requirement of "injury in fact":** The standing doctrine boils down to just one requirement, in most instances: the requirement that the litigant have suffered an *"injury in fact."*

   a. **"Nexus" requirement in taxpayer cases:** In cases where the plaintiff sues *as a federal taxpayer*, claiming that his taxes are being spent in a way that violates the Constitution or a federal statute, the Court imposes an additional requirement: that there be a certain type of *"nexus"* between the taxpayer's status and the claim sought to be litigated. See *infra*, p. 711.

   b. **"Causation in fact" requirement:** In *non-taxpayer* cases, the modern Court has imposed what might be thought of as a corollary to the "injury in fact" requirement: the injury must be one which was *caused by the act being complained of* (typically a violation of the Constitution or of a federal statute), and there must be a significant possibility that this injury will be *redressed* by giving the litigant the relief he seeks. These two causal aspects may be summarized by saying that the asserted wrongdoing must be the *"cause in fact"* of the injury. See *infra*, p. 716.

6. **Significance:** The standing doctrine tends to keep out of the federal courts three main classes of suits:

   a. **Non-individuated harm:** Cases in which the harm complained of by the plaintiffs is *no different from that suffered by very large numbers of people* not before the court. The prime example is the harm claimed to be suffered by *"citizens" at large* when government does not act according to constitutional or statutory dictates. See, e.g., *Schlesinger v. Reservists to Stop the War, infra*, p. 713.

   b. **"Speculative" future harm:** Cases in which the plaintiff is trying to avoid *future* harm. Plaintiffs can have standing to try to prevent future harm, but the plaintiff must show that the threatened harm is *reasonably likely to occur* in the near future, not merely "*speculative*." This category includes cases in which people try to prevent harm that they fear will be inflicted on them by *government* (e.g., illegal eavesdropping). See, e.g., *Clapper v. Amnesty Int'l, infra*, p. 714.

   c. **Third parties' rights:** Cases where the rights claimed to be violated are those of *third parties* not before the court. (But the general rule against assertion of third parties' rights has numerous exceptions; see *infra*, p. 719.)

B. **Federal taxpayer and citizen suits:** The assertion that the plaintiff's harm is no different from that suffered by lots of others arises most often where the plaintiff is claiming that his rights as a *federal taxpayer* or *federal citizen* have been abridged.

1. **Rule before 1968:** Until the late 1960's, the Supreme Court took a completely hostile view towards actions brought by plaintiffs claiming that their rights as federal *taxpayers* or as federal *citizens* had been abridged. A federal taxpayer could, of course, bring suit on a claim that *his own taxes* had been improperly assessed. But a taxpayer simply had no standing to assert that *taxpayers' funds in general* were being improperly collected or spent. See *Frothingham v. Mellon*, 262 U.S. 447 (1923), reasoning that the plaintiff-taxpayer's "interest in the moneys of the Treasury [is] shared with millions of others [and] is comparatively minute and indeterminable."

2. **Exception in *Flast*:** But in a 1968 case, the Court finally made an exception to *Frothingham*'s general rule that taxpayers do not have standing to attack the validity of government spending. In *Flast v. Cohen*, 392 U.S. 83 (1968), the Court held that a taxpayer may challenge the constitutionality of a federal taxing or spending program if there is a *"logical nexus* between the status [of taxpayer] and the claim."

   a. **What "nexus" requires:** The requisite nexus will be found to exist, the Court held, only where two showings are made: (1) that the statute relies on Congress' power under the *Taxing and Spending Clause* of Article I, §8, rather than being merely "an incidental expenditure of tax funds in the administration of an essentially regulatory [law];" and (2) that the challenged law violates *"specific constitutional limitations"* imposed *on that taxing and spending power*, not simply that the statute is "generally beyond the powers delegated to Congress by Article 1, §8."

   b. **Test satisfied in *Flast*:** The claim in *Flast*, the Court found, *passed* the two-part test. Mrs. Flast's claim was that a federal-aid-to-education act, by giving financial aid to religious schools, violated the First Amendment's Establishment Clause. This Clause, the Court held, operates as a ***"specific constitutional limitation"*** upon Congress' Taxing and Spending powers.

3. **Modern Court's view:** The Burger, Rehnquist and Roberts Courts have never overruled *Flast*. But they have stubbornly refused to allow any broadening whatsoever of the *Flast* exception to *Frothingham*'s general rule against taxpayer actions, and in fact ***no case*** after *Flast* has been able to come within that exception.

    a. **Must be limit on "taxing and spending" power:** Thus the Court has continued to insist that, in a taxpayer action, only those constitutional provisions which act as **"specific"** limitations on the "taxing and spending" power of Congress may be relied upon. *U.S. v. Richardson*, 418 U.S. 166 (1974).

      Example: President George W. Bush, by executive order, sets up the Faith-Based and Community Initiatives Program. Under that program, money supplied by the Executive Branch is used to fund conferences at which the merits of faith-based non-profit social-service programs are extolled by government speakers. The Ps are taxpayers who argue that the purpose and effect of the conferences is for the federal government to promote religion. Congress has not separately authorized any funds for the Faith-Based Program; any funds expended are spent by the Executive Branch from the general (non-earmarked) funds appropriated by Congress for the running of the executive branch.

      Held, the *Flast* exception does not apply, and the Ps therefore do not have standing. The expenditures here were made by the Executive Branch, not by Congress. *Flast* allowed taxpayer standing to attack violations of the Establishment Clause that occur as the result of Congress' use of its Art. I § 8 power to tax and spend for the general welfare. Therefore, *Flast* will be confined to suits alleging Establishment Clause violations that are funded by a ***"specific congressional appropriation*** and undertaken pursuant to an express congressional mandate[.]" *Hein v. Freedom from Religion Foundation*, 551 U.S. 587 (2007).

    b. **Tax credits:** Similarly, where a state gives taxpayers a ***tax credit*** that they can use to contribute to a religious school to cover tuition, a member of the public does ***not*** have taxpayer standing under the *Flast* exception, the Court held by a 5-4 vote. See *Arizona Christian School Tuition Organization v. Winn*, 131 S.Ct. 1436 (2011).

      i. **Rationale:** The majority in *Arizona Christian* reasoned that in the core *Flast* situation, the taxpayer whose tax dollars have been "extracted and spent" knows that he has in some small measure "been ***made to contribute*** to an establishment [of religion] in violation of conscience." But where government merely awards some citizens a tax credit, the other, dissenting, citizens are "allow[ed] to ***retain control over their own funds*** in accordance with their own consciences." The taxpayers who choose to use the tax credit "***spend their own money***, not money the state has collected from [other] taxpayers." So any injury the objectors may suffer is ***not*** ***"fairly traceable to the government."*** Therefore, *Flast* should not apply.

    c. **Significance:** So today, only suits that are virtually ***identical*** to *Flast* — i.e., suits claiming that congressional action taken under the "taxing and spending" power violates the Establishment Clause — may be brought by taxpayers.

    d. Suits by state and local taxpayers: What about federal suits by *state* and *local* taxpayers?

        i. State taxpayers: As to *state taxpayers*, the same no-standing rule applies as to suits by federal taxpayers — "*state taxpayers have no standing* ... to challenge state tax or spending decisions simply by virtue of their status as taxpayers." *DaimlerChrysler Corp. v. Cuno*, 547 U.S. 332 (2006).

        ii. Municipal taxpayer: **M**unicipal taxpayers, on the other hand, clearly *do* have federal-court standing to assert that their tax dollars are being improperly spent. A municipality is viewed as being sufficiently smaller than a state that a municipal taxpayer is deemed to be *directly injured* by an improper expenditure of the town's tax dollars.

4. Citizenship suits: The Court has *never* been willing to recognize standing on the part of individuals *as citizens* to object to unlawful or unconstitutional conduct. This refusal has been based upon the view that one citizen's interest in lawful government is no different from that of any other citizen, and that an individual litigant relying upon citizenship has not shown the *"individualized"* injury-in-fact required for standing. *Schlesinger v. Reservists to Stop the War*, 418 U.S. 208 (1974).

C. Standing not based on taxpayer or citizen status: Somewhat different rules have evolved for actions in which the standing claim is *not* based on taxpayer or citizen status.

1. Summary: The rules presently imposed may be summarized as follows:

    a. Injury in fact: The litigant must have suffered (or be likely to suffer) an *"injury in fact."*

    b. Must be "individuated": The injury suffered must be concrete and *"individuated."* That is, it must not be precisely the same harm as is suffered by an extremely large group of others (so that harms suffered by every "citizen" as the result of, say, violation of the Establishment Clause do not qualify, as noted above). However, the injury in fact need not be *economic*; for instance, damage to environmental conditions where one lives or pursues recreation qualifies.

    c. Causation in fact: The action challenged must be the *"cause in fact"* of the injury. This means both that the challenged action was a "but for" cause of the injury, and that the relief being sought, if granted, has a reasonable likelihood of *redressing* the injury. (No comparable causation requirement is imposed in taxpayer suits.)

    d. No nexus requirement: No requirement of a "nexus" between the injury and the challenged action, comparable to that imposed in taxpayer suits (e.g., *Flast*) is imposed outside the taxpayer context.

We consider each of the above aspects in sequence below: (a) injury in fact (Par. D); (b) "individuated" harm (Par. E); (c) causation in fact (Par. F); and (d) absence of a "nexus" requirement (Par. G).

D. The "injury in fact" requirement: The plaintiff must show that he has suffered or will probably suffer some concrete, "individuated," *"injury in fact."* The most important aspect of this requirement is that if the harm has not yet occurred, there must be a more-than-speculative chance that it will occur.

1. **Non-economic harms:** The harm that the plaintiff complains of need not be *economic* in nature.

> **Example:** An environmental group claims that construction of a recreation area in a national forest will violate federal laws. *Held,* injury to "aesthetic and environmental well-being" can constitute injury in fact. Therefore, the group (whose members use national forests) have standing. *Sierra Club v. Morton,* 405 U.S. 727 (1972).

2. **Must be "actual or imminent," not "speculative":** The "injury in fact" must be *"actual or imminent."* Thus if the threatened harm is too *far in the future,* or its eventual occurrence is too "*speculative,*" the "actual or imminent" element will not be satisfied, and standing will not be found.

> **Example:** The Ps challenge certain federal agency action that, they say, will have the effect of endangering certain species abroad. D (the U.S. government) argues that the Ps do not have standing. The Ps retort that they have in the past, and will again, travel abroad to the habitats of the potentially affected species, in order to observe and study those species.
>
> *Held,* for D. The Ps have not shown the requisite actual or imminent harm. "Such 'someday' intentions — without any description of concrete plans, or indeed any specification of *when* the someday will be — do not support a finding of the 'actual or imminent' injury that our cases require." *Lujan v. Defenders of Wildlife,* 504 U.S. 555 (1992).

> **Note:** In at least one recent case, the Court has said that the threatened harm has to be *"certainly impending."* See *Clapper,* immediately *infra.* It's not clear whether this phrase means anything different than "imminent," but the Court's use of it in *Clapper* seems to mean that if the harm hasn't already occurred, its occurrence has to be not only imminent but highly probable.

   a. **Government surveillance in the war on terror:** The principle that future harms must not be unduly speculative has made it hard for anyone to challenge *federal surveillance programs* enacted as part of the war on terror. For instance, in an important 2013 case involving a special statute allowing intelligence officials to eavesdrop on international phone calls and e-mails, the Court held, 5-4, that the plaintiffs lacked standing because they were unable to show the requisite likelihood that the statute would soon be used to eavesdrop on their own conversations. *Clapper v. Amnesty Int'l USA,* 133 S.Ct. 1138 (2013).

   i. **The statute:** In 2008, Congress amended the Foreign Intelligence Surveillance Act of 1978 (FISA) to add a new section, §1881a, which permits federal intelligence authorities to conduct e-mail and telephone surveillance of *non-citizens* who are believed to be outside of the country, in order to obtain "foreign intelligence information." Congress mainly had in mind surveillance done for *counterterrorism* purposes.

   ii. **The plaintiffs:** The plaintiffs were a loose collection of *U.S. citizens* — including attorneys, reporters, and human-rights workers — who alleged that their work required them to communicate with foreigners that the federal government suspected of having links to terrorist organizations. The plaintiffs said that they reasonably feared that §1881a would be used in the near future to eavesdrop on *conversations between the plaintiffs and these targeted foreigners.* (The plaintiffs conceded that they did not fear being themselves the targets of the surveillance; but they were concerned that the government would target the foreigners, and thereby intercept the plaintiffs' conversations with these foreigners.)

   iii. Majority denies standing: But the Court in *Clapper*, in an opinion by Justice Alito (joined by Roberts, Scalia, Thomas and Kennedy), rejected the plaintiffs' claim that they had standing.

      (1) "Certainly impending": Alito said that prior cases had required that the threatened injury be *"certainly impending."*

      (2) "Speculative": The plaintiffs failed to meet this "certainly impending" requirement, Alito concluded. Because the plaintiffs had *"no actual knowledge"* of what foreign targets the government would choose for surveillance, Alito said, their fear that their own communications would be captured through surveillance targeting others was "necessarily conjectural" and *"highly speculative."*

      (3) Alternative statutory authority: Furthermore, Alito wrote, even if the plaintiffs' fears of having their communications intercepted *had* been sufficiently non-speculative, their worries that this interception would be accomplished by means of *the challenged statute* (§1881a), rather than by use of one of the other possibly-available sources of authority, magnified the speculative element.

      (4) "Avoidance costs" argument rejected: Lastly, Alito rejected the plaintiffs' argument that they had standing because of the *costs they were incurring* in their efforts to *avoid the effects* of the challenged statute (e.g., the cost of traveling abroad for face-to-face meetings instead of telephone calls). The plaintiffs "cannot *manufacture standing* merely by *inflicting harm on themselves* based on their *fears of hypothetical future harm* that is not certainly impending."

   iv. Dissent: Justice Breyer (joined by Ginsburg, Sotomayor and Kagan) *dissented*. Breyer rejected the majority's conclusion that the plaintiffs had shown only "speculative" future harm. He argued that prior case law merely required that there be a *"realistic danger"* that the relevant harm would occur, and that this test was met here.

   v. Significance: *Clapper* will likely make it very hard for anyone to have standing to challenge *secret government conduct*, like that used in national-security surveillance programs — the very secrecy of the methods used by the government makes it hard for the plaintiffs to show how and when these methods will likely be used against them. The consequence may well be that for many kinds of national security programs, *no one has standing* to challenge the program's legality.

E. Harm suffered by many: As long as the litigant (or the group representing him) alleges the requisite "concrete" and "individuated" harm, standing will not be denied merely because there is a *large number* of people suffering the harm.

1. **Citizenship:** But there are limits on how widespread the class may be. Thus the interest of all "citizens" in having their government operate constitutionally and according to statute is so diffuse that actions based on citizenship will not be allowed. See *Schlesinger v. Reservists, supra*, p. 713.

   a. **No interest in avoiding abstract "denigration":** Similarly, *members of a minority group* will not from that membership alone derive standing to litigate against governmental conduct which *denigrates* that minority group. For instance, in *Allen v. Wright*, 468 U.S. 737 (1984) (discussed more extensively *infra*, p. 718), parents of black public school children sued the IRS, claiming that the latter was not effectively carrying out its obligation to ensure that discriminatory private schools do not receive tax-exempt status. The parents' interest in avoiding the "stigmatizing injury" generally caused by racial discrimination was insufficient to establish standing — only those who were *"personally denied equal treatment"* by the challenged discriminatory conduct had standing.

2. **No interest in avoiding "institutional" loss of power:** Similarly, members of a *political body*, such as a *legislature*, do *not* have standing to litigate against an action that they say *takes away the political power of that body*. Thus members of Congress who unsuccessfully voted against a bill allowing line-item vetoes by the President were held not to have standing to litigate the constitutionality of the resulting statute, where their only claim was that the bill "causes a type of *institutional injury* (the diminution of legislative power), which necessarily damages all Members of Congress and both Houses of Congress equally." *Raines v. Byrd*, 117 S. Ct. 2312 (1997).

3. **Organizations and associations:** On the other hand, the Supreme Court is perfectly willing to grant standing to *associations* in some circumstances. An association has standing not only where its own interests are at stake, but in some cases where it is suing solely as a *representative* of its members. An association has standing to sue on behalf of its members if three conditions are met:

   [1] its members would "otherwise have standing to sue *in their own right*";

   [2] the interests the association seeks to protect are "germane to the organization's *purpose*; and

   [3] "neither the claim asserted nor the relief requested requires the participation of *individual members* in the lawsuit."

   Hunt v. Washington Apple Advertising Comm., 432 U.S. 333 (1977).

F. **Causation:** Outside of the taxpayer-suit context, the Court has required that the litigant show that the challenged governmental action *"caused"* the injury of which he complains. This causation requirement has two components; the litigant must show that:

   [1] the challenged action was a *"but for"* cause of the injury, in the sense that the injury *would not have occurred unless the challenged action had taken place*; and

   [2] a favorable decision in the suit will *redress* the injury. (Requirement (2) is called the *"redressability"* requirement.)

   1. **Confusion as to "redressability" standard:** It is not clear whether, to satisfy the redressability requirement, it is sufficient to show that a favorable decision will *probably* redress the harm. Sometimes, the Court has indicated that a *probability* of redress is suffi-

cient; at other times, however, it has suggested that there must be a *virtual certainty* that redress will follow a favorable decision. See Tribe, pp. 129-30.

a. **Potential easier standard:** But the 2007 decision in *Massachusetts v. EPA* (*infra*, p. 718) suggests that in some circumstances, even a *less-than-50/50 chance* that the sought-for relief will redress the problem may be enough, if the severity of the problem is great enough. In that case, Massachusetts tried to require the EPA to regulate U.S. automobile emissions so as to reduce global warming; the majority found that the redressability requirement was met, even though the harm feared by Massachusetts (flooding of its coastal lands) was nearly all yet-to-occur, and even though there was little concrete showing that if the requested relief were granted, the threatened harm would be averted. But *Mass. v. EPA* probably represents merely a weakening of the redressability requirement for the special case of *state-as-plaintiff*, not a general weakening for all plaintiffs.

b. ***Warth v. Seldin:*** A good case illustrating how the Court applies the two causation requirements — the "but for" requirement and "redressability" requirement — is *Warth v. Seldin*, 422 U.S. 490 (1975). The plaintiffs in *Warth* failed to satisfy *either* part of the causation test.

   i. **Facts:** The plaintiffs in *Warth* were a number of parties who claimed to have been injured by the zoning rules of Penfield, New York. They claimed that these rules had been imposed for the purpose of excluding the building of low- and moderate-income housing in the town.

      (1) **Low-income seekers of housing:** For instance, some plaintiffs were low- and moderate-income individuals who had never lived in Penfield, but who alleged that they had sought housing there and *would have moved there had affordable housing been available*; and

   ii. **Standing rejected:** The Supreme Court found that these individuals (like all of the plaintiffs in the case) *lacked standing*.

      (1) **"But for" requirement:** The individuals failed the *"but for"* requirement, because they were unable to show that, had the restrictive zoning practices not existed, there was a *"substantial probability*" that they would have been able to purchase or lease in Penfield." Construction of the appropriate housing would require not merely removal of the zoning laws but also a *third party willing actually to build* the projects, and there was no showing that any third party would indeed have built projects which these particular individual plaintiffs could have afforded.

      (2) **"Redressability" requirement:** Similarly, these plaintiffs failed the *"redressability"* requirement: they couldn't show that if the court awarded the relief being sought — a striking down of the zoning rules — the desired moderate-income projects would in fact likely be built.

2. **Article III basis for cause-in-fact rule:** In *Warth*, the majority did not make it clear whether its entire holding was dictated by the Article III "case or controversy" requirement, or rather, stemmed in part from "prudential" considerations. But in the later case of *Simon v. Eastern Ky. Welfare Rights Organization (EKWRO)*, 426 U.S. 26 (1976), the

Court held that the requirements that the challenged action be the cause of the injury, and that the sought-for relief would remove that injury, are ***imposed by Article III.***

3. **Government allows injury by third party:** *A* plaintiff will generally find it hard to establish the cause-in-fact aspect of standing for a claim that ***government action or inaction*** has caused some ***third party not before the court*** to injure him. The difficulty of establishing standing for such a claim was illustrated when the Court found the cause-in-fact requirement unsatisfied in a case in which ***parents*** of black public school pupils attacked the IRS's ***grant of tax-exempt status*** to ***discriminatory private schools. Allen v. Wright***, 468 U.S. 737 (1984).

   a. **Facts:** In *Wright*, the parents claimed that the tax breaks enabled discriminatory private schools to offer cheaper tuition, thus inducing more parents of white students than would otherwise be the case to withdraw their children from the public schools to place them in these private schools. These withdrawals in turn deprived the black students of their constitutional right to attend integrated public schools, the parents claimed.

   b. **Holding:** But the Court, by a 5-3 vote (with Justice Marshall not participating), concluded that the line of causation from the IRS's conduct to the continued segregation of the public schools was ***so attenuated*** that the latter was ***not*** "fairly traceable" to the former.

      i. **Speculative elements:** For there to have been standing, the majority indicated, the parents would have had to make three showings: (1) that "there were enough racially discriminatory private schools receiving tax exemptions in [plaintiffs'] communities for withdrawal of those exemptions to make an appreciable difference in public-school integration;" (2) that a significant number of schools would, if threatened with loss of the tax exemption, change their policies; and (3) that a significant number of parents of children attending such schools would transfer their children to public school if the exemption were withdrawn. According to the majority, plaintiffs had not alleged any of these three elements.

G. **Special deference when plaintiff is a state acting for its citizens:** When the plaintiff is a *state* acting on behalf of its citizens, the usual rules of standing will apparently be ***relaxed***, as a result of a 5-4 decision by the Court in a case involving global warming. The case, ***Massachusetts v. EPA***, 549 U.S. 497 (2007), seems to mean that the ***individuated-harm*** and ***causation*** requirements are especially likely to be relaxed where the plaintiff is a state suing in an ombudsman-like manner.

1. **Facts:** Massachusetts and ten other states sued the EPA, arguing that the agency was required under a congressional statute to issue regulations that would limit automobile emissions of carbon dioxide and thus reduce global warming. The agency, which under the George W. Bush administration did not want to (or believe that it had authority from Congress to) issue the regulations, argued that the states did not have standing to bring the suit, in part because they had not met the injury-in-fact or causation requirements.

2. **Holding:** The four liberal members of the court (Stevens, Ginsburg, Souter and Breyer) joined with Justice Kennedy to form a majority that concluded that Massachusetts, at least, ***had the requisite standing*** on account of the danger that ***rising sea levels*** would pose to its ***coastal areas.*** The opinion was by Justice Stevens.

   a. State as sovereign: Stevens seemed to be saying that Massachusetts' status in the suit as a *sovereign representing the interests of its citizens* justified some relaxation of the usual standing requirements imposed on private plaintiffs.

     i. Injury in fact: Stevens said that Massachusetts had met the *injury in fact* requirement because global warming had already caused a slight rise in sea level, and the rising seas "have already begun to swallow Massachusetts' coastal land."

     ii. Causation: As to the requirement of causation (that the relief sought might redress the claimed harm), Stevens said, the risk to Massachusetts would be "*reduced to some extent* if [Massachusetts] received the relief [it] seek[s]."

   b. Significance: *Massachusetts v. EPA* seems to mean that states will find it meaningfully easier than private parties to bring federal suits, especially in the environmental area. It is doubtful that a private citizen – even a coastal landowner – would have been found to have standing to attack the EPA's lack of steps to prevent global-warming.

H. Third-party standing: One of the principal functions of the standing doctrine is to implement the general rule that a litigant may normally *not assert the constitutional rights of persons not before the court.* This principle is also sometimes referred to as the rule against assertion of "constitutional *jus tertii*" ("rights of third persons" in Latin).

> **Example:** In *Warth v. Seldin*, 422 U.S. 490 (1975) (other parts of which are discussed *supra*, p. 717), one group of plaintiffs consisted of residents of Rochester who claimed that, because nearby Penfield had refused to allow low- and middle-income housing, their own taxes were higher since Rochester had had to grant tax abatements to encourage construction of more such housing than it otherwise would. The Rochester residents were denied standing; although their higher taxes constituted an "injury in fact," the zoning laws did not apply to them and thus did not violate *their* rights. Their claim thus fell within the general rule that one may not assert the rights of third persons (e.g., those who were excluded from Penfield by the zoning laws) except under special situations, none of which existed here.

   1. Rule is prudential, not constitutional: The general rule against third-party standing is founded upon *discretionary* or *"prudential"* considerations, and is *not mandated by the Article III "case or controversy" requirement.*

     a. Exceptions: Therefore, the Court has been free to develop what has turned out to be a confused patchwork of judge-made *exceptions* to the no-third-party-standing rule.

   2. Relation to overbreadth doctrine: The First Amendment *"overbreadth"* doctrine can be viewed as an exception to the rule against assertion of a third party's rights. Recall that by the overbreadth doctrine (discussed *supra*, p. 483), a party to whom a criminal statute clearly and constitutionally applies may be permitted to argue that the statute is applicable to some types of conduct which, if engaged in by third parties, would be constitutionally protected. In the overbreadth context, the third parties are hypothetical, and the litigant is *also* asserting his *own* constitutional right not to be convicted under a broadly-drawn statute which may chill his (as well as others') freedom of expression.

I. "Prudential" standing: We just saw that the rule against third-party standing is not dictated by the Article III "case or controversy" requirement, and is instead the result of *"prudential"* considerations (i.e., considerations "dictated by prudence"). More generally, the federal courts retain the right refuse to hear *any* case on such prudential-standing grounds, even cases falling outside the pure third-party-standing area.

> **Example:** P is an atheist whose daughter attends a public elementary school that conducts a group recitation of the Pledge of Allegiance. P contends that his First Amendment rights (not his daughter's) are violated by the Pledge, because the Pledge interferes with his right to inculcate in his daughter, free from government interference, his own atheistic beliefs. The case is complicated by the fact that P is divorced from the child's mother, who under California law has the right to make final legal decisions about the daughter's upbringing if the two parents disagree. The mother opposes P's suit.
>
> *Held* (by a 5-3 Supreme Court vote), the prudential standing doctrine should be applied, so that the case will not be heard by the federal courts. The federal courts should generally "leave delicate issues of domestic relations to the state courts." Also, the decision here might have an adverse effect on the non-party daughter's own First Amendment rights; abstention is proper where "prosecution of the lawsuit may have an adverse effect on [a third] person who is the source of the plaintiff's claimed standing." *Elk Grove Unified School Dist. v. Newdow*, 542 U.S. 1 (2004).

IV. MOOTNESS

A. Mootness generally: A case is not justiciable if it is *"moot."* A case is moot if it raised a justiciable controversy at the time the complaint was filed, but *events occurring after the filing* have deprived the litigant of an ongoing stake in the controversy.

> **Example:** P sues D, a state university, claiming that its law school admissions program is racially discriminatory. He is permitted to attend the law school while the case is being litigated. By the time the case arrives at the Supreme Court for review, P is in his final year of law school, and the university says that he will be allowed to graduate.
>
> *Held*, the case is moot, and determination of the legal issues in the suit is no longer necessary. Therefore, the appeal will not be decided. *DeFunis v. Odegaard*, 416 U.S. 312 (1974).

B. Exceptions: There are a number of reasons for which a case which is ostensibly moot will nonetheless be heard. The main ones, each of which is discussed below, are: (1) that the issue is *"capable of repetition, yet evading review"*; (2) that the case seems moot only because the defendant has *voluntarily*, but not necessarily permanently, changed his conduct; and (3) that there are *collateral consequences* to the defendant's action which, when considered, prevent mootness. See Tribe, p. 84.

1. "Capable of repetition, yet evading review": An issue will not be treated as moot if it is *"capable of repetition, yet evading review." Southern Pacific Terminal Co. v. ICC*, 219 U.S. 498 (1911).

> **Example:** P, a pregnant woman, attacks the constitutionality of state anti-abortion laws. She brings the suit as a class action, in which she is the named plaintiff and other pregnant women desiring abortions are unnamed members. By the time the case reaches the Supreme Court, P is no longer pregnant.

Held, the case should not be dismissed as moot. Pregnancy will almost always be completed before the usual appellate process is complete. P herself may become pregnant again, but even if she does not, obviously other women will. The issue is thus "capable of repetition, yet evading review." *Roe v. Wade*, 410 U.S. 113 (1973).

2. **Voluntary cessation by defendant:** If the defendant *voluntarily ceases* the conduct about which the plaintiff is complaining, this will normally *not* be enough to make the case moot. If the plaintiff seeks damages, the cessation will of course be irrelevant to the issue of mootness. But even if the plaintiff seeks an *injunction*, the cessation will not make the case moot, if there is any substantial chance that the defendant might "return to his old ways." See Tribe, p. 89.

3. **Collateral consequences:** In determining whether the plaintiff continues to have a stake in the controversy, all *collateral consequences* of the challenged conduct must be examined. If any of these collateral consequences could be adverse to the plaintiff, the case is not moot. For instance, where a criminal defendant has already *served his sentence*, his attack on the constitutionality of his conviction will not be deemed moot, because of the likelihood of collateral consequences from the conviction, such as loss of the right to vote, and damage to reputation or to employability. See Tribe, p. 92.

V. RIPENESS

A. **Problem generally:** The problem of *ripeness* may be regarded as the opposite of that of mootness. Whereas a case is moot (and therefore not justiciable) because it *no longer* involves an actual controversy, a case will be regarded as not yet ripe (and therefore not yet justiciable) if it has *not yet become sufficiently concrete* to be worthy of adjudication.

1. **Relation to ban on advisory opinions:** The ban on adjudication of unripe matters is closely related to the ban on *advisory opinions (supra*, p. 708). Both doctrines reflect the view, based partly on the constitutional requirement of a "case or controversy," that the federal courts must not render opinions except in situations where there is a well-defined, live controversy, with specific facts, and with either an allegation of past injury or a likelihood of future injury.

2. ***Mitchell* case:** The classic illustration of a matter not yet ripe for adjudication is *United Public Workers v. Mitchell*, 330 U.S. 75 (1947).

    a. **Facts:** The plaintiffs in *Mitchell* were federal civil servants who wished to attack the Hatch Act, which prohibits federal executive-branch employees from involvement in "political management or … political campaigns." The plaintiffs claimed, in essence, that they *desired* to engage in prohibited political activities; however, all but one conceded that they had *not yet done so.*

    b. **Holding:** A majority of the Court held that the claims of those plaintiffs who had not yet violated the Act were *not ripe.*

        i. **Rationale:** The Court reasoned that plaintiffs' claims were so general that they constituted "really an attack on the political expediency" of the statute, "not the presentation of legal issues." It was the province of the legislature, not the judiciary, to make such general determinations of political expediency.

ii. **Specific conduct:** Thus the Court seems to have really been troubled not so much by the fact that the plaintiffs had not yet violated the statute and not yet been subjected to the prescribed punishment (discharge), but rather, by the fact that the plaintiffs were not *adequately specific* as to the precise acts which they wished to carry out. Had the plaintiffs set forth *in detail* what they wished to do, the ripeness doctrine might not have prevented their case from being adjudicated even though these acts had not yet been carried out. See Tribe, p. 79.

B. **Uncertain enforcement of criminal statute:** Ripeness problems also may arise where the plaintiff alleges that he has violated a statute whose constitutionality he attacks, but it is not clear that the statute is *generally enforced*, or that it will be enforced in this particular case. In this situation, the Court has often been reluctant to allow the case to be adjudicated.

1. *Poe v. Ullman:* For instance, in *Poe v. Ullman*, 367 U.S. 497 (1961), two married couples and a physician challenged Connecticut's anti-contraception law. A majority of the Court refused to hear the case on appeal, on the grounds that the statute had been on the books for 80 years with only one reported prosecution and that there was thus not the requisite "clear" threat of prosecution.

2. **Willingness to hear evolution case:** But the Court has not always held that a rarely-enforced statute fails to present a ripe controversy. For instance, in *Epperson v. Arkansas, supra*, p. 664, the anti-evolution statute struck down by the Court had not been enforced in the 40 years of its history, nor was there any showing of a specific threat of enforcement against the plaintiff. See L,K&C, p. 1682, n. 2. The Court's willingness to adjudicate *Epperson* suggests that its refusal to hear *Poe* was an exercise of its *discretion*, not the product of a lack of an Article III "case or controversy." See Hart and Wechsler, *Federal Courts*, p. 657.

C. **Requirement of specific threatened harm:** For a case to be ripe, it is not necessary that the litigant have already suffered harm; it is sufficient that there is a reasonable probability of harm. However, the anticipated harm must be *reasonably specific*.

1. *Laird v. Tatum:* For instance, in *Laird v. Tatum*, 408 U.S. 1 (1972), plaintiffs attacked an Army Intelligence scheme for *gathering data* about persons and activities who had the potential for "civil disorder." Plaintiffs claimed that this surveillance scheme had a "present inhibiting effect" on their activities, even though they had no idea what use, if any, the Army might make of the information being gathered. But the Court, by a 5-4 vote, found that a present "subjective chill" was not enough to make the case ripe; what had to be shown was a *"specific present objective harm"* or a *"threat of specific future harm."*

VI. THE 11TH AMENDMENT, AND SUITS AGAINST STATES

A. **The 11th Amendment:** The 11th Amendment imposes limitations — increasingly important ones in the 1990s — on the jurisdiction of the federal courts.

1. **Text of the Amendment:** That Amendment provides:

The Judicial power of the United States shall not be construed to extend to *any suit in law or equity*, commenced or prosecuted *against one of the United States* by *Citizens of another State*, or by Citizens or Subjects of any *foreign* state.

2. **Facial meaning:** So on its face, the 11th Amendment merely seems to say that one state can't be sued in federal court by a citizen of a different state, or by a foreigner. And in fact, if you were wearing your *Civil Procedure* hat, you might think that this Amendment was simply saying that suits based solely on diversity — rather than on a federal question — could not be brought against a state.

3. **Interpreted more broadly:** But over the years, the Amendment has been interpreted much more broadly than that. We don't have space for a long explication of the Amendment, but here are the highlights of how the Supreme Court has interpreted its scope:

   a. **Suits by citizens of the defendant state:** First, the Amendment is interpreted so as to bar suits by a citizen against his or her *own state*. *Hans v. Louisiana*, 134 U.S. 1 (1890).

   b. **Suits involving federal question:** Second, the Amendment covers *federal question suits*, not just diversity suits. Many scholars believe that the 11th Amendment was intended only to block diversity suits against states, not federal-question suits against them. But this view has not prevailed, and the 11th Amendment is interpreted to block all suits by private citizens against states, whether based on diversity, alienage, or federal question.

   c. **Constitutional embodiment of sovereign immunity:** Third, this broad reading of the limits on suits against states — that a state may not be sued even by its own citizens, and may not be sued even in a case raising a federal question — is now held to be a core *constitutional limitation on federal judicial power*, not just an interpretation of broad "principles" surrounding the 11th Amendment itself. The most important consequence is that *Congress generally cannot overrule this broad reading*, and cannot authorize a state to be sued by its own citizens in federal-question suits. This is the nub of the Court's 1996 ruling in *Seminole Tribe*, discussed in detail *infra*, p. 724.

   d. **Suits in equity:** Finally, the Amendment applies not only to suits "at law," but also to suits "at *equity*." Thus a private citizen cannot sue to have a state enjoined or ordered to do something, any more than she can sue to recover damages. (But as we discuss immediately below, the Amendment does not bar suits against a state *official*, in his private capacity, seeking to enjoin him from violating federal law.)

4. **Exclusions:** There are a number of important exclusions from the coverage of the 11th Amendment:

   a. **Suits against officials for injunctions:** Most important, the 11th Amendment does not prevent suits against *state officials* in which the relief sought is an *injunction* against the *violation of federal law*. This principle was established in *Ex parte Young*, 209 U.S. 123 (1908). The theory behind the principle is that when a state officer's official conduct violates the U.S. Constitution or a federal statute, he is acting without true authority, and his conduct is therefore not really "state conduct" for purposes of the 11th Amendment. See Chemerinsky, §7.5.1.

   b. **Suits against official for money damages:** The Amendment also doesn't bar suits against a *state official* for *money damages*, as long as the damages are to be paid out of the official's own pocket. But where a suit would if successful lead to a state's being ordered to pay damages out of its own pocket, the suit is barred by the Amendment, even if the suit is nominally filed against the official rather than the state itself. Chemerinsky, §7.5.2.

    c. **Suit for injunction against violation of state law:** The 11th Amendment *does* apply to bar injunctions prohibiting state officials from violating *state* (as opposed to federal) law. *Pennhurst State School Hosp. v. Halderman*, 465 U.S. 89 (1984).

    d. **Suits by federal government:** The 11th Amendment does not bar suits *by the federal government* against a state.

    e. **Suits against cities:** The Amendment does not bar suits against *cities*, or other political subdivisions of a state.

    f. **State agencies and other entities:** The caselaw is unclear and inconsistent as to when the Amendment bars suits against state *agencies*, boards and other entities — such as state-owned universities — associated with state government.

    g. **Suits by one state against another:** The Amendment does not bar suits by *one state against another* (as long as the plaintiff state is truly suing for itself rather than merely to protect private interests of individual citizens).

    h. **Suits in state court:** The Amendment only applies in federal courts; it doesn't prevent a private individual from suing a state in *state court*, even to vindicate a federal right. (But, of course, the state court must have jurisdiction over the suit. Some state courts may not have jurisdiction because of the state's enabling statutes; also, some federal statutes that create rights provide for exclusive federal-court jurisdiction in proceedings to enforce those rights, in which case no state-court forum is available.)

        i. **Appellate jurisdiction:** Also, as long as the suit started in state court, nothing in the 11th Amendment prohibits the U.S. Supreme Court from using its *appellate jurisdiction* to review a state-court decision to see if it violates federal law. Chemerinsky, §7.4

    i. **Waiver by state:** The protections of the 11th Amendment can be *waived* by a state — if the state consents to be sued in federal court, the 11th Amendment will no longer stand as a bar. Chemerinsky, §7.6.

    j. **Suits under the post-Civil War Amendments:** If Congress passes a statute pursuant to its power to enforce the *post-Civil War Amendments* (13th, 14th and 15th), and that statute gives private citizens the right to sue a state in federal court, this statute will be enforced, and won't be deemed to violate the 11th Amendment.

5. **Congress' general power to allow suits against the states:** As just noted, where Congress is legislating pursuant to its special powers to enforce the post-Civil War amendments, it may abrogate the 11th Amendment and permit private citizens to sue the states in federal court. But outside this post-Civil War area, ***Congress may not abrogate the 11th Amendment***, no matter how explicitly it tries to do so. This is the somewhat startling holding of ***Seminole Tribe of Florida v. Florida***, 517 U.S. 44 (1996), a major case that significantly hampers Congress' ability to give private citizens the ability to sue states for violations of federal law.

    a. **Facts:** Congress passed a statute, the Indian Gaming Regulatory Act, to govern aspects of gambling operations run by Indian tribes. The IGRA provided that when a state allows non-Indian gambling, the state must also negotiate in good faith with any tribe located in the state to try to reach an agreement permitting the tribe to conduct comparable gambling operations. The statute also provided that if a tribe believed that the state was not negotiating in good faith, the tribe could sue the state in federal court for an order directing the state to negotiate in good faith.

b. Split: The Court, by a 5-4 vote, held that this statute *violated the 11th Amendment*. The split was precisely the same as in *U.S. v. Lopez*, the case restricting Congress' Commerce Clause powers (see *supra*, p. 36).

c. Holding: The majority opinion, by Chief Justice Rehnquist, held that "Even when the Constitution vests in Congress *complete law-making authority over a particular area*, ... the Eleventh Amendment *restricts the judicial power under Article III*, and Article I cannot be used to circumvent the constitutional limitations placed upon federal jurisdiction." So even though Article I gives Congress full authority to "regulate commerce ... with the Indian tribes," Congress cannot allow a tribe to sue a state in federal court.

   i. Rationale: The majority's rationale was that the 11th Amendment *embodies concepts of state sovereignty*. Furthermore, the principle of state sovereignty embodied in the 11th Amendment limits the Article III jurisdiction of the federal courts, and Congress cannot expand those limits just because it wants to.

   ii. Suits based on Commerce Clause: Even though *Seminole* itself involved congressional power based on the Indian Commerce Clause, the decision applies broadly to *all sources of congressional power other than the post-Civil War amendments*. For instance, it clearly applies to congressional action based on the *"regular" Commerce Clause*, a source that probably accounts for a majority of federal statutes enacted over the last 50 years.

d. Dissents: There were two dissents, one by Stevens, the other by Souter (joined by Ginsburg and Breyer). Souter's dissent was the principal one; indeed, at 92 pages it was three times the length of Rehnquist's majority opinion.

   i. Limited view of Amendment: To Souter, all the drafters of the 11th Amendment ever meant to do, and all the Amendment had ever been interpreted as doing, was to prevent suits based *solely on diversity*, i.e. those brought by a state against a non-citizen of that state in circumstances under which no federal question was raised.

   ii. Destructive of ability to protect federal rights: The dissenters believed that the majority's view was not only wrong but *highly destructive of federally-guaranteed rights*. As Stevens put it, the majority's holding *"prevents Congress from providing a federal forum* for a broad range of actions against States, from those sounding in *copyright* and *patent* law, to those concerning *bankruptcy, environmental law*, and the regulation of our vast national economy."

e. Later illustration: A post-*Seminole* decision by the Supreme Court demonstrates the broad impact that *Seminole* is likely to have. In *Florida Prepaid Postsecondary Education Expense Board v. College Savings Bank*, 527 U.S. 627 (1999), the Court held that just as Congress may not abrogate the 11th Amendment when acting under authority of the *commerce* power (the point decided in *Seminole*), Congress may not do so when acting under its *patent* power. Therefore, Congress, no matter how explicitly it tries to do so, ***may not force the state to defend a private patent damage suit in federal court.***

    f.   **Broader significance:** The greatest significance of *Seminole* and *Florida Prepaid* may turn out to be these cases' suggestion of a radically new — and restricted — view of federal power. These cases, taken together with *U.S. v. Lopez*'s limits on the Commerce power (*supra*, p. 36), *New York v. U.S.*'s resurrection of the Tenth Amendment (*supra*, p. 50), *Alden v. Maine*'s recognition of state immunity from state-court suits based on federal rights (*infra*, p. 726), and *Federal Maritime*'s prohibition on certain federal administrative proceedings involving state defendants (*infra*, p. 727), represent the view of a 5-Justice majority that federal power is ***far less extensive than had previously been thought***. As Prof. Tribe has said, "the Court's current dedication to a states' rights doctrine seems to be a rather free-floating cloud that can rain on almost any source of congressional power." *NY Times*, April 1, 1996, p. A1.

6. **States' sovereign immunity from state-court suits based on federal rights:** Just as *Seminole Tribe* says that Congress generally can't authorize federal-court suits against the States, so the doctrine of ***sovereign immunity*** generally prevents Congress from subjecting the states to private suits ***in their own courts, even where the right sued on is federal***. That is the startling result of a 1999 decision, ***Alden v. Maine***, 527 U.S. 706 (1999), decided three years after *Seminole* by the same 5-4 split as in *Seminole*.

    a.   **Facts of *Alden*:** Congress had said that the Fair Labor Standards Act (FLSA), which governs overtime and other wage matters, applies to the states as employers, just as it does to private employers. Congress also said that a state's employees could bring FLSA suits against the state in the state's own courts. In *Alden*, workers employed by the state of Maine did just that, arguing in the Maine courts that they were entitled to certain extra pay for overtime.

    b.   **Struck down:** But in an opinion by Justice Kennedy, the 5-member majority held that Congress had no constitutional authority to force the Maine courts to hear the workers' suit, ***even though that suit was based upon a federal right*** that (even the majority agreed) Congress had authority to confer upon the workers. For a state's immunity from private suits for money damages in the state's own courts was "a ***fundamental aspect of the sovereignty which the states enjoyed before the ratification of the Constitution***, and which they ***retain today.***"

    c.   **Significance:** *Alden* seems to mean that the states now have ***full sovereign immunity from any private suit in the state's own courts seeking damages for the state's violation of federal law.*** For instance, the states as employers are presumably immune to damage suits alleging that they committed ***employment discrimination*** (e.g., discrimination based on age or disability), and the states as market participants are apparently immune from state-court claims that they have violated federal laws governing commerce (e.g., ***trademark*** and ***antitrust*** laws). Coupled with the extensive federal-court 11th Amendment immunity recognized in *Seminole Tribe*, the states now seem to have a large zone in which, as a practical matter, they are completely insulated from congressional attempts to give private individuals a damages remedy for violations of federal rights.

7. **Complaints before federal agencies:** The latest extension of the Court's tendency to limit federal-law-related actions against the states involves federal ***administrative-agency***

proceedings. In a 2002 decision, the Court held that the same principle of state sovereignty cited in *Alden* bars the federal government from ***requiring that states defend*** against private complaints in ***proceedings brought before federal administrative agencies***. *Federal Maritime Comm. v. South Carolina State Ports Auth.*, 535 U.S. 743 (2002).

VII. POLITICAL QUESTIONS

A. **Introduction:** The final aspect of justiciability is the requirement that the case not require decision of what is commonly called a ***"political question."*** The scope of the "political question" doctrine is even less well-defined than the other aspects of justiciability considered above. Also, the doctrine is less important today than it was in prior periods; in only a few cases since 1970 has the Court found an issue to be a non-justiciable political question.

1. **Phrase a misnomer:** The phrase "political question" is something of a misnomer. The Court will not treat as a non-justiciable political question an issue which merely happens to ***involve politics***, even if politically-related issues are at the very heart of the case. Rather, the political question doctrine seems to be a meshing of two sets of principles:

    a. **Separation of powers:** *Separation-of-powers* principles, by which, as a constitutional matter, the Court will not decide matters which it concludes are committed by the Constitution to other branches of government for decision; and

    b. **Prudential concerns:** various ***"prudential"*** considerations, because of which the Court concludes that it is unwise, even if not strictly unconstitutional, for it to decide the case.

2. **General unifying principle:** The factors which lead a court to conclude that an issue is a political question, factors which are discussed in detail below, are not easily summarized into one overarching principle. Perhaps the most useful formulation is that proposed by Tribe; he asserts that in deciding whether an issue is a non-justiciable political question, the court is "determin[ing] whether constitutional provisions which litigants would have judges enforce do in fact ***lend themselves to interpretation as guarantees of enforceable rights***." Tribe, p. 106. (But as Tribe himself concedes, the factors which the courts must consider in making this determination are a diverse blend of constitutional and discretionary considerations. *Id.*)

B. ***Baker v. Carr:*** The modern Court's approach to political questions is set forth most notably in the well-known case of ***Baker v. Carr***, 369 U.S. 186 (1962). That case, which held that the constitutionality of legislative apportionment schemes is not a political question, paved the way for the Court's "one person, one vote" ruling; therefore, the case is discussed more extensively in our treatment of reapportionment, *infra*, p. 730.

1. **Factors:** For now, what is significant is that the Court in *Baker* announced a series of ***factors***, at least one of which (the Court asserted) ***must be present*** in order to make an issue a non-justiciable political question. Each of these factors, the *Baker* Court argued, relates in some way to the ***separation of powers***. The Court listed the following factors:

    a. **Commitment to another branch:** A "textually demonstrable constitutional ***commitment of the issue*** to a ***coordinate political department***" (i.e., to Congress or to the President);

    b. Lack of standards: A "lack of judicially discoverable and manageable *standards* for resolving" the issue;

    c. Unsuitable policy determination: The "impossibility of deciding [the issue] without an initial *policy determination* of a kind clearly for non-judicial discretion";

    d. Lack of respect for other branches: The "impossibility of a court's undertaking independent resolution without expressing *lack of the respect due co-ordinate branches of government*";

    e. Political decision already made: An "unusual need for unquestioning adherence to a *political decision already made*"; and

    f. Multiple pronouncements: The potential for "embarrassment from *multifarious pronouncements* by various departments on one question."

  2. Most significant factors: Here, we will concern ourselves mainly with three of these factors: (1) the "commitment to other branches" factor; (2) the "lack of judicially discoverable and manageable standards" factor; and (3) the "need for a single pronouncement" factor. Additionally, we will consider the existence of a fourth factor not explicitly mentioned in *Baker*, the extent to which the issue raises a controversial question whose adjudication might lead to major, undesirable consequences. Finally, we give separate consideration to the reapportionment cases, which involve more than one of these factors.

C. The "commitment to other branches" strand: As *Baker v. Carr* suggested, the Court will regard as a non-justiciable political question any issue the determination of which is clearly committed by the Constitution to *another branch of government*. The cases decided under this strand have all involved decisions arguably committed to the President or Congress (not decisions arguably committed to the states).

  1. Impeachment: A strong case can be made that the House of Representatives' decision whether to *impeach* the President or other federal officer, and the Senate's decision whether to convict, are *not judicially reviewable* because these decisions are committed to those bodies by the Constitution. If this view is accepted, the Court would not have jurisdiction even to determine whether the grounds upon which, say, the President was convicted fell within the constitutionally-defined category of "high Crimes and Misdemeanors." See *supra*, p. 132.

    a. Majority view: Most commentators believe that impeachment decisions do indeed fall within the "committed to other branches" category, and are therefore non-justiciable political questions. One of the difficulties with a contrary view is that the legitimacy of Supreme Court review of an impeachment conviction might not be apparent to the nation. As one author has noted, if the Senate voted to convict, and the Supreme Court ordered reinstatement, "[o]ur military commanders would have to decide for themselves which President they were bound to obey, the reinstated one or his successor." Black, *Impeachment: A Handbook*, pp. 61-62 (quoted in L,K&C, p. 50).

    b. Senate has sole power to decide what constitutes a "trial": The Court has never had to determine whether Congress' decision to impeach or convict a federal officer is judicially reviewable. But a recent case on a different aspect of impeachment law strongly indicates that most controversies relating to impeachment will be found to fall within the "committed to other branches" category and thus to be non-justiciable political questions. In *Nixon v. U.S.*, 506 U.S. 224 (1993), Walter Nixon, a federal judge whom the House had impeached and the Senate convicted based on bribery charges, challenged the *procedures* used by the Senate. The Senate *delegated to a committee* of senators the job of holding hearings on the accusations against Nixon. The committee then gave the full Senate a transcript of the proceedings, and the Senate voted by more than the required two-thirds majority to convict Nixon.

i. **Argument:** Nixon argued that the Senate, by having a committee rather than the full Senate hear the evidence, violated the requirement of Article I, Section 3, Clause 6 that the Senate "try all impeachments."

ii. **Held non-justiciable:** But the Supreme Court held that Nixon's argument presented a non-justiciable political question. The Court relied mainly on the plain text of the Senate Impeachment Clause, which provides that "the Senate shall have *sole Power* to try all Impeachments." The Court interpreted this reference to "sole Power," along with the history behind the provision, to mean that the Senate, nor the courts, should determine what procedures could validly constitute a "trial." (The Court also reasoned that a "lack of finality" problem dictated that the courts not hear Nixon's claim: "Opening the door of judicial review to the procedures used by the Senate in trying impeachments would 'expose the political life of the country to months, or perhaps years of chaos,'" especially if it were the President who was being impeached.)

2. **Amendment of Constitution:** The process by which *constitutional amendments* are adopted is probably also committed to Congress for final determination, and therefore presents a non-justiciable political question. Thus in *Coleman v. Miller*, 307 U.S. 433 (1939), four members of the Court, concurring, believed that only Congress could determine whether a particular state had ratified a constitutional amendment. (The case is discussed more extensively *infra*, p. 730, because of the Court's reliance on the "lack of judicially manageable standards" strand.)

3. ***Powell v. McCormack:*** The most famous case discussing the "commitment to other branches" strand was one in which the Court concluded that at most only a *limited* commitment of the decision-making authority in question to another branch (Congress) was involved. In ***Powell v. McCormack***, 395 U.S. 486 (1969), Adam Clayton Powell, Jr., who had been elected to Congress from Harlem, successfully challenged the House's refusal to seat him.

a. **Facts:** The House's refusal came after one of its committees found that Powell had dodged the process of the New York courts, had wrongfully diverted House funds, and had made false reports to a House committee. When Powell sued for a declaratory judgment that the refusal to seat him was unconstitutional, the House defended on the grounds that Article I, §5 (which provides that "[e]ach House shall be the Judge of the ... Qualifications of its own Members") gave the House the sole right to determine what qualifications are necessary for membership. Powell, by contrast, argued that that clause merely gives the House the right to determine whether a person possesses the "standing qualifications" expressly set out in the Constitution (Article I, §2's age, citizenship and residence requirements).

b. **Victory for Powell:** The Supreme Court agreed with Powell. Article I, §5 was at most a grant to Congress of the right to determine whether the three standing qualifications set forth in Article I, §2 were satisfied. Therefore, Congress had not been given the right to impose additional qualifications for membership.

    i. Standing qualifications: But, the Court noted, it was still possible that the decision about whether a member met the three standing qualifications *was* committed to Congress, so as to bar the federal courts from reviewing that determination. The Court noted that it was not deciding this issue, which remains undecided to this day. The issue did not arise in *Powell* itself because all parties conceded that Powell met these qualifications.

D. "Lack of judicially manageable standards" strand: A second major factor which may lead the Court to conclude that a case presents a non-justiciable question is that there is a "lack of *judicially discoverable* and *manageable standards* for resolving it."

    1. Guarantee of republican form of government: For instance, the Court has consistently held that claims based upon Article IV, §4 (which provides that "[t]he United States shall guarantee to every State in this Union a *Republican Form of Government*") are non-justiciable political questions.

        a. *Luther v. Borden:*** The best-known case on this so-called *Guaranty Clause* is *Luther v. Borden*, 7 How. 1 (1849). The case grew out of a rebellion by some dissatisfied Rhode Island citizens, and ultimately required the federal courts to decide which of two competing governments was the lawful government of the state. But the Supreme Court declined to make this determination, concluding that the case posed a political question. The decision seems to have been based in part upon the "lack of criteria by which a court could determine which form of government was republican" (as the decision was summarized in the later case of *Baker v. Carr, infra*, p. 731).

    2. War Powers disputes: If the federal courts were called upon to referee a dispute between the President and Congress concerning whether the President had *usurped Congress' war-making powers* by *committing our armed forces to combat* without congressional approval, the "lack of judicially manageable standards" strand might cause the case to be regarded as a political question. For instance, a refusal by the President to bring American troops home from hostilities within 60 days of invocation of the War Powers Resolution of 1973 (see *supra*, p. 140) might fall into this category.

E. The need for a unified voice (especially in foreign affairs): The need for the federal government to speak with a *single, unified voice* has occasionally been a factor in the conclusion that an issue presents a political question. This is more likely to happen in the area of *foreign affairs* than in the domestic area.

    1. Treaty termination: For instance, the Court has refused to decide whether the President can *terminate a treaty* with Taiwan without congressional approval. *Goldwater v. Carter*, 444 U.S. 996 (1979). There was no majority in agreement on why the case was non-justiciable; the four-member plurality may have had the "single voice" rationale in mind when it remarked that the case posed a political question because "it involves the authority of the President in the conduct of our country's foreign relations."

F. Reapportionment: Until 1962, the Court consistently refused to adjudicate claims concerning *legislative apportionment*, on the grounds that they presented political questions. See, e.g., *Colegrove v. Green*, 328 U.S. 549 (1946), in which Justice Frankfurter's plurality opinion declared that "[i]t is hostile to a democratic system to involve the judiciary in the politics of the people. ... [C]ourts ought not to enter this political thicket."

1. ***Baker v. Carr:*** But in ***Baker v. Carr***, 369 U.S. 186 (1962), the Court reversed its course. The challenge in *Baker* was to the apportionment of the Tennessee Assembly, which had not been reapportioned in 60 years, despite a state constitutional requirement that representation be on the basis of population, and despite significant changes in population over the years. The Court concluded that the claim, which was that the malapportionment violated the ***Equal Protection Clause***, did ***not*** present a political question.

   a. **Rationale:** The Court reasoned that not all cases involving "politics" present non-justiciable "political questions." The Court listed a catalogue of factors, at least one of which, it asserted, had always been present in true political-question cases. (See *supra*, p. 727.) The equal protection claim here, the majority concluded, did not involve any of these factors. For instance, the issue had not been "textually ... commit[ted] by the Constitution to another branch of government"; nor were "judicially discoverable and manageable standards for resolving it" lacking.

2. **"One person, one vote" principle (*Reynolds v. Sims*):** The conclusion in *Baker* that apportionment claims do not necessarily present non-justiciable political questions opened the door for numerous challenges to the apportionment of state legislatures and federal congressional districts. In a series of decisions, the Court developed its famous, and simple, "***one person, one vote***" principle. The major case in this line was ***Reynolds v. Sims***, 377 U.S. 533 (1964).

   a. **Facts:** *Reynolds* was a challenge to the apportionment of the Alabama legislature. Therefore, it posed different problems from a case decided shortly before, *Wesberry v. Sanders*, 374 U.S. 1 (1964), a challenge to a state's apportionment of its ***federal congressional districts*** — in *Wesberry*, the Court had been able to dispose of the case by interpreting Article I, §2's requirement that representatives be chosen "by the People of the several States" as requiring that "as nearly as practicable one man's vote in a congressional election is to be worth as much as another's."

   b. **Apportionment struck down:** Nonetheless, the *Reynolds* Court struck down the Alabama apportionment (or rather, malapportionment) scheme. It did so upon an ***equal protection*** theory: the Equal Protection Clause "requires that the seats in ***both houses*** of a bicameral state legislature must be apportioned ***on a population basis***. ... An individual's right to vote for state legislators is unconstitutionally impaired when its weight is in a ***substantial fashion diluted*** when compared with votes of citizens in other parts of the State."

      i. **Rationale:** The Court observed that equal protection generally requires "the uniform treatment of persons standing in the same relation to the governmental action questioned or challenged." Since "legislators represent people, not trees or acres," there was no apparent reason for making one person's vote worth more than another's in the election of those legislators.

      ii. **Some deviations allowed:** The Court in *Reynolds* did ***not*** require ***strict mathematical equality***. "Some deviations" from the equal-population rule would be permissible, if they were directed towards the carrying out of a "rational state policy." But "neither history alone, nor economic or other sorts of group interests, are permissible factors. ... " Furthermore, even pursuit of a "clearly rational state policy" (e.g., "according some legislative representation to political subdivisions") by an apportionment scheme would ***not*** be valid if "population is submerged as the ***controlling consideration...***"

c. Disagreement: Three members of the Court disagreed with the majority's general approach in *Reynolds*.

    i. Harlan's dissent: Only Justice Harlan dissented from the result in *Reynolds*; he argued mainly that the framers of the Equal Protection Clause simply did not intend that Clause to be used to limit the power of the states to apportion their legislatures however they wished.

    ii. Stewart's concurrence: Justice Stewart (joined by Justice Clark) agreed that the Alabama scheme was "completely lacking in rationality." However, he disagreed with the majority's general approach. He did not think that the Equal Protection Clause barred a state's divergence from mathematical equality of votes if this was done for the purpose of providing "effective and balanced representation of all substantial interests." The only limitation imposed by that Clause, he believed, was that a plan "must be such as not to permit the ***systematic frustration of the will of a majority*** of the electorate of the State." That is, so long as a majority was not consistently blocked from electing a majority of the legislators, the scheme must merely be "rational." (For instance, Stewart believed that New York's scheme, reviewed in a companion case, met this standard even though it guaranteed at least one representative to each county, and gave fewer legislators to New York City than it would have been entitled to strictly on the basis of population; Stewart thought that this was a valid attempt to "protect against overcentralization of power.")

d. Justiciability of "one person, one vote" rule: Observe that the existence of "judicially discoverable and manageable standards" for resolving apportionment questions was greatly aided by the Court's selection in *Reynolds* of the "one person, one vote" principle. For instance, had the Court accepted Justice Stewart's more limited rule that there must simply not be "systematic frustration of the will of a majority of the electorate," the Court might have been required to "canvass the actual workings of the floor leadership in the legislative branches, the mechanisms of party control not only over voters in the city government but also over elected representatives — in short, the details of the petty corruption and networks of personal influence that all too often constitute critical sources of power in municipal politics." 20 STAN. L. REV. 247 (quoted in Ely, p. 124). Thus it was "precisely because of considerations of administrability [that the Court] found itself with no perceived alternative but to move to a one person, one vote standard." Ely, p. 124.

3. Other issues: The companion cases to *Reynolds* settled some other issues, in addition to the basic "one person, one vote" principle. Most importantly, *Lucas v. Colorado General Assembly*, 377 U.S. 713 (1964) established that an apportionment scheme that violated the "one person, one vote" rule could not be saved by the fact that it had been ***approved by the voters of the state***. A "citizen's constitutional right can hardly be infringed simply because a majority of the people choose that it be." (Similarly, the fact that the state ***constitution*** apportions one of the two houses on a basis other than population will not make that apportionment valid.)

4. **Local government:** Subsequent cases applied the general "one person, one vote" rule to elections for *local government* bodies. After some initial confusion, the Court settled on the rule that the "one person, one vote" standard applies whenever persons are chosen by popular election to "perform *governmental functions*," whether or not those governmental functions are *"general"* ones. Thus in *Hadley v. Junior College Dist.*, 397 U.S. 50 (1970), the case in which the Court articulated this rule, the Court required an attempt at equal-population apportionment for trustees of a junior college district, obviously not a body of general jurisdiction.

   a. **Special-purpose bodies:** However, the Court noted in *Hadley* that some bodies or officials may have "duties [that] are so far removed from normal governmental activities and [may] so disproportionately affect different groups that a popular election ... might not be required." See *Ball v. James, supra*, p. 357, for an example of such a special-purpose body (a water district) not requiring application of the *Reynolds* principle.

5. **How much equality is required:** In cases following *Reynolds*, the Court was required to decide *how much* deviation from strict mathematical equality is permissible. In doing so, it established a key distinction between *congressional* districting on the one hand, and districting for state and local governmental bodies on the other.

   a. **Congressional districting:** In *congressional* districting, the rule is that *"as nearly as is practicable*, one man's vote in a congressional election is to be worth as much as another's." *Kirkpatrick v. Preisler*, 394 U.S. 526 (1969). States must make a "good-faith effort to achieve *precise mathematical equality*." *Id.*

   b. **State and local apportionment:** By contrast, the Court has been willing to allow *much greater deviation* from mathematical equality in the apportionment of *state legislatures* or *local governmental bodies*.

      i. **"De minimus" category:** First, the Court has established a *"de minimus"* category — deviations below a certain level *need not be supported by any state objective at all*. This category covers *"minor population variations,"* and seems to include all deviations of *less than 10%*.

      ii. **"Legitimate state considerations":** Second, even deviations above this roughly 10% threshold will not cause a state legislative or local governmental apportionment scheme to be invalidated, if the deviations are justified by *"legitimate state considerations." Abate v. Mundt*, 403 U.S. 182 (1971). For instance, in *Mahan v. Howell*, 410 U.S. 315 (1973), the Court approved an apportionment of one house of the Virginia Legislature having a maximum variation of 16.4% from population equality; this deviation was justified by the state's policy of "maintaining the *integrity of political subdivision lines*."

6. **Gerrymandering:** The *Reynolds* "one person, one vote" formulation says nothing about *how the district lines are to be drawn*; all that standard requires is that the districts end up with equal numbers of voters in each. But "one person, one vote" by itself leaves room for a maneuver which may have an even more dramatic ability to dilute some voters' strength: the *gerrymander*.

   a. **Gerrymander defined:** The gerrymander is a device by which the strength of a particular voting bloc is curtailed by restricting its members to carefully- and artificially-constructed districts. (For an illustration of a gerrymander, see *supra*, p. 313.)

b. Justiciable: A bare majority of the Court continues to hold that claims of unconstitutional gerrymandering are *justiciable*.

    i. *Davis v. Bandemer*: In *Davis v. Bandemer*, 478 U.S. 109 (1986), by a 6-3 vote the Court held that there were indeed "judicially discernible and manageable standards by which political gerrymander cases [may] be decided." Such cases involve the adequacy of representation, and are therefore no different in a general sense from claims involving population apportionment, found to be justiciable in the Reynods "one person, one vote" decision. (The six Justices in the majority split sharply into two camps with regard to what the substantive standards should be for deciding whether a political gerrymander violated the Equal Protection clause.)

    ii. *Vieth v. Jubelirer* affirms this result: Then, in 2004, an even narrower (5-Justice) majority of the Court affirmed *Bandemer*'s ruling that political gerrymander cases could theoretically be justiciable. In ***Vieth v. Jubelirer***, 541 U.S. 267 (2004), five Justices concluded that although it is hard to figure out a standard for determining which gerrymanders are so extreme as to violate the Constitution, the Court should not hold gerrymander cases to be categorically non-justiciable. But this five-justice majority for the proposition that gerrymander cases may be justiciable was a very weak one; for instance, one of the five, Justice Kennedy, said that he would use "great caution" in even approaching such cases, that he did not at present know of a rationale or standard for deciding such cases, and that he was merely voting in *Vieth* "not [to] *foreclose all possibility*" of judicial relief" if an appropriate standard could be found in the future.

        (1) 4-Justice dissent argues for nonjusticiability: Four Justices in *Vieth* pointed out that in the almost two decades following *Bandemer*, "no judicially discernible and manageable standards for adjudicating political gerrymandering claims have emerged." Therefore, these four said, "we must conclude that political gerrymandering claims are *nonjusticiable* and that *Bandemer* was wrongly decided[.]" When these four votes are added to Justice Kennedy's view that no acceptable rationale for deciding such cases has emerged yet, a majority of the *Vieth* Court could not see any concrete circumstance in which they would vote to award relief on a gerrymandering claim.

    iii. Nearly impossible to win: In any event, even though as noted a bare majority of the Court continues to view partisan gerrymandering cases as being theoretically justiciable, it has proven *virtually impossible for plaintiffs to win* such cases. For instance, in both *Bandemer* and *Vieth*, the plaintiffs failed to convince the Supreme Court that the gerrymandered districting plans there violated the constitution. See *supra*, p. 313, for more about the Court's fierce internal disagreements about what the substantive standard for judging partisan gerrymandering claims should be.

Quiz Yourself on

JUSTICIABILITY (ENTIRE CHAPTER)

98. The President, in an attempt to restore democracy in Haiti, dispatched American troops to that island without a congressional declaration of war. The troops have now remained there for 60 days, still without a congressional declaration. Their expenses have been paid for out of the general Defense Department budget, appropriated by Congress before the troops were sent and without the expectation that they would be sent. Paul, a U.S. citizen and taxpayer, has sued the President seeking an injunction requiring the President to withdraw the troops. The substance of Paul's suit is that only Congress has the power to declare war, and that the President's action amounts to an illegal declaration of war. Paul further asserts that his federal tax dollars are being unconstitutionally spent to support this illegal action.

    (a) If you are the President's lawyer, what is the first defense you should assert? _____

    (b) Will this defense prevail? _____

99. Same basic facts as above question. Now, however, assume that Paul asserts that he has standing to pursue his claim in federal court, because he is a citizen of the United States, and his right to have his government not behave in an unconstitutional manner has been abridged. Is Paul correct? _____

100. A federal statute places restrictions on the extent to which private companies may be permitted by the U.S. government to engage in logging in national forests. Penzel, a private individual, sues the U.S. Secretary of the Interior. His suit contends that the Secretary has administered regulations on logging in a way that contravenes the statute. The suit contends that the effect will be to allow more logging in the forests than permitted by statute. Penzel asserts that he uses a particular national forest for a one-week hike twice per year, and that the unauthorized logging affects a part of the forest that he expects to hike in during the next year. At least four million hikers each year will cross through parts of federal forests that are likely to have been affected by the allegedly excessive logging. The Secretary asserts that Penzel lacks standing to make this claim. Does Penzel have standing? _____

101. Same facts as prior question. Now, however, assume that the plaintiff is Friends of the National Forests, Inc. (FNF), a non-profit corporation whose members are users and lovers of the national forests. No individual plaintiffs are named. Does FNF have standing to pursue the suit? _____

102. George Brensteiner was the owner of the New York Strikers of the National Soccer League. Brensteiner's existing stadium was about to be demolished, and he needed to pick a new site for a stadium that he would build. After some preliminary investigation, Brensteiner announced that there were three "finalist sites," of which one was Yonkers, New York. Brensteiner applied for clearances from the federal Environmental Protection Agency (EPA) for all three sites. He received quick clearances for the other two. As to Yonkers, the local EPA administrator covering Yonkers determined that the proposed stadium would be on a protected wetland, and that the stadium could not be built unless Brensteiner first filed an Environmental Impact Statement (EIS) showing that the wetlands would not be damaged. Brensteiner then announced, "Because of the expense of preparing an EIS for the Yonkers site, I have selected one of the other sites as the winner, namely, Rutherford, New Jersey." Brensteiner acquired land in Rutherford, and quickly completed about 10% of the construction. At that moment, Steve, a Yonkers resident, brought suit against the EPA. Steve's suit argued that the EPA's requirement of an EIS for the Yonkers site was in violation of federal statutes, and that the effect of this violation was to deprive him, Steve, of easy access to a soccer stadium (in Yonkers) in which to view Strikers games. Steve's suit asked for a declaratory judgment that an EIS was not required for the Yonkers site. The EPA has defended on the grounds that Steve lacks standing. Is the EPA's contention correct? _____

103. Fred, who is black, is a police officer on the force of the town of Suburbia. Suburbia's population is 30% black, but Fred is the only black out of 15 officers on the force. Fred has sued the department, arguing that the department's failure to hire more black patrol officers is intentional, and constitutes a violation of the Equal Protection Clause. Fred asserts that this failure to hire additional black officers harms him, by making him racially isolated on the force and leading to a department that is generally insensitive to the concerns of the minority community, thus making Fred's own working conditions less attractive. Does Fred have standing to bring this suit? _____

104. A local school district allows non-profit community groups to use classrooms at the district's public high school at night. The Old Christians Association (OCA), a group of senior citizens who want to pray together, applied for a room. The school district turned them down on the grounds that to allow them to use the room would constitute an unconstitutional establishment of religion. The OCA began a suit in federal district court against the school board, asserting that the denial of a room violated their free exercise rights. After the suit was begun, the school board issued a statement reversing its policy against allowing religious groups to use classrooms, and granted the OCA's permit request. The OCA would like to continue with the suit, so that they may obtain a judicial opinion in their favor that can be cited as precedent in other school districts.

    (a) What defense should the school board defendant raise? _____

    (b) Will this defense succeed? _____

105. Pintard is a 52-year-old trooper in the police department of the State of New Spain, and is a resident of that state. New Spain has fired him because, in the department's judgment, no one over the age of 50 is physically fit enough to carry out the duties of state trooper. A federal statute, the Federal Age Discrimination Act, applies to all employees and forbids firing on account of age. Pintard has sued the state of New Spain for damages. (He does not want to be reinstated, because he has found a new job.)

    (a) What defense should the state raise? _____

    (b) Will this defense succeed? _____

106. The state of Caledonia was running short of funds, due to a budget crisis. To save money, the Governor ordered that only one copy be purchased of any personal-computer software package needed by the state government, and that staff members make copies. A staffer made 2,000 copies of the "PC-Word" word-processing package (published by PC Word Corp., a Caledonia company), and distributed these to each state office, where they were used. The retail value of each copy of PC Word is $295. PC Word Corp. has sued the state in federal court for the district of Caledonia, alleging that the state has violated the federal copyright act and seeking money damages ($295 x 2,000). Assume that the federal copyright act expressly allows a state to be sued in federal court (whether by its own citizen or by a citizen of another state).

    (a) What defense should Caledonia raise? _____

    (b) Will this defense succeed? _____

107. Jose won a U.S. congressional seat from a district located in New York City, in a close race against Martin. The House routinely determined that Jose met the constitutional requirements to be seated (that he was at least 25 years old, a U.S. citizen, and a resident of the state from which he had been elected). Martin then brought a federal district court suit against the House of Representatives and Jose, seeking to have Jose ruled unqualified to sit in the House. The essence of Martin's suit was that Jose really "inhabits" (as that term is used in Art. I, §2, second sentence) not the state of New York but rather, the State of Pennsylvania. Martin has come forward with evidence from voting records, state income tax filings, and other documents strongly suggesting that Jose spends the vast bulk of his time in, and considers himself a resident of, Pennsylvania.

    (a) What defense should Jose raise to these proceedings? _____

    (b) Will this defense succeed? _____

Answers

98. (a) That Paul lacks standing.

    (b) Yes. As a general matter, federal taxpayers do not have standing to assert that taxpayers' funds in general are being improperly spent. There is an extremely narrow exception if plaintiff is able to show: (1) that the federal action complained of is an exercise of Congress' power under the Taxing and Spending Clause; and (2) that the challenged action violates some specific constitutional limitation imposed on the taxing and spending power. *Flast v. Cohen.* It is highly unlikely that Paul can satisfy either of these requirements for the exception. The President's dispatch of troops presumably relies upon his Commander in Chief powers, and certainly does not rely upon Congress' taxing and spending power. Furthermore, the requirement that only Congress may declare war is not a specific constitutional limitation on the taxing and spending power, merely an unrelated constitutional limit. Therefore, the general rule that there is no taxpayer standing would apply.

99. No. The Supreme Court has never been willing to recognize standing on the part of individuals *as citizens* to object to unlawful or unconstitutional conduct. This refusal is based on the view that one citizen's interest in lawful government is no different from that of any other citizen, and that an individual litigant relying upon citizenship has not shown the *"individualized"* injury-in-fact required for standing. See, e.g., *Schlesinger v. Reservists to Stop the War.*

100. Yes, probably. A federal-court plaintiff must show some concrete, *"individuated,"* "injury in fact." But this harm need *not* be *economic* in nature; harms to a person's esthetic enjoyment of nature, for example, will suffice. See, e.g., *Sierra Club v. Morton* (giving people who use national forests standing to protest construction of recreation area in the national forest). The threatened harm must be "actual or imminent." Since Penzel asserts that he will walk within one of the affected areas within the next year, the "imminence" requirement is probably satisfied. The fact that there are a large number of people suffering or likely to suffer the same harm as alleged by the plaintiff does not by itself remove standing from the plaintiff.

101. Yes. An association or organization has standing not only where its own interests are at stake, but in some cases where it is suing solely as a *representative* of its members. An association has standing to sue on behalf of its members if three conditions are met: (1) its members would otherwise have standing to sue *in their own right*; (2) the interests the association seeks to protect are *germane* to the organization's *purpose*; and (3) neither the claim asserted nor the relief requested requires the participation of *individual members* in the lawsuit. *Hunt v. Washington Apple Advertising Comm.* Here, all three of these requirements seem to be met: the prior question illustrates that individual forest-lovers would have standing; protection of the forests certainly is the core purpose of the organization; and there seems to be no reason why individuals rather than the organization need to participate in the lawsuit.

102. Yes, probably. One of the requirements for standing is that the challenged action must be the *"cause-in-fact"* of the injury. A sub-aspect of the "cause in fact" requirement is that the litigant must show that the relief being sought, if granted, has a reasonable likelihood of *redressing* the injury. The problem here is that even if the EPA was completely wrong in the first instance, it is far from clear that a victory by the plaintiff will result in the stadium being built in Yonkers rather than Rutherford. The ultimate decision is up to Brensteiner. Since Brensteiner has already bought the property in Rutherford and commenced construction, it is very unlikely that a declaratory judgment that the EPA should not have required an EIS for Yonkers will cause Brensteiner to stop construction and start it instead in Yonkers. Therefore, even though the other requirements of standing are met (Steve's loss of the ability to watch Strikers games near his house is certainly an "injury-in-fact" that is sufficiently concrete, individuated and imminent), the fact that victory in the suit will not redress the harm is fatal to Steve's standing. See, e.g., *Simon v. Eastern Ky. Welfare Rights Organization* (where IRS rules reduced the amount of free medical care that hospitals must donate to the poor in order to get tax breaks, a suit by poor people attacking those rules does not have standing, because the hospitals might not give the free medical care even if the rules were struck down).

103. **No, probably.** As a general rule, a litigant may normally not assert the constitutional rights of ***third persons not now before the court***. This is the rule of constitutional *"jus tertii."* Fred may have been injured "in fact" by the absence of other blacks on the force. But the Equal Protection Clause protects only those applicants who would have been hired had there not been intentional discrimination. Since Fred was not part of this group, the fact that he may have suffered some incidental injury is not enough to give him standing — he must assert that the challenged governmental action violates ***his*** rights, not the rights of some other person not now before the court. (There are some important exceptions to the rule against third-party standing, such as where there is some legal restriction preventing the third party from exercising his own constitutional rights. But here, black applicants whom the department intentionally declined to hire because of their race clearly could bring their own suit, so neither this nor any of the other exceptions to the rule against third-party standing applies.)

104. **(a) That the action is now moot.** A case is moot if it raised a justiciable controversy at the time the complaint was filed, but ***events occurring after the filing*** have deprived the litigant of an ongoing stake in the controversy.

(b) Yes. Where the intervening event is the defendant's ***voluntary*** cessation of the conduct complained of, this may or may not be enough to render the case moot. If the facts show that the conduct claimed to be illegal is ***very unlikely*** to recur, then the voluntary cessation usually ***is*** enough to make the case moot. That is probably what the court would find to be the situation here. Therefore, the OCA's desire to obtain a favorable decision that it may use as precedent elsewhere will not be enough to give it an ongoing stake in the controversy, and the action will be dismissed.

105. **(a) The Eleventh Amendment.** The Eleventh Amendment excludes from the federal judicial power any suit "against any one of the States by Citizens of another State or by Citizens or Subjects of any Foreign State."

(b) Yes. Although on its face the Eleventh Amendment does not seem to prohibit federal-court suits against a state by a citizen of that state, the amendment has been interpreted to ban these suits as well as those by a citizen of one state against another state. See *Hans v. Louisiana*. The Eleventh Amendment applies only to suits for damages (as opposed to suits for injunctions), but the facts make it clear that money damage relief is what is sought here. Therefore, the Eleventh Amendment defense will be successful.

106. **(a) The Eleventh Amendment.**

(b) Yes. *Seminole Tribe v. Florida* holds that except with respect to suits brought under federal statutes supported by Congress' power to enforce the post-Civil War Amendments, Congress cannot remove the state immunity provided by the Eleventh Amendment. Therefore, even though Congress has clearly said that a state may be sued for damages for violating the copyright act, this statement of congressional intent is without effect, and the Eleventh Amendment applies to bar the suit. (But PC Word Corp. could get an *injunction* against the governor prohibiting further violations, since the Eleventh Amendment does not apply to injunction suits against state officials; see *Ex parte Young*.)

107. (a) That the issue posed here is a **non-justiciable political question.**

(b) Yes, probably. The Court will regard as a non-justiciable political question any issue whose determination is committed by the Constitution to **another branch** of government (i.e., the executive or the legislative). There is an excellent chance that the Court will conclude that the decision about whether a person elected to Congress meets the three standing requirements is committed by the Constitution to the House itself. The Court would point to Art. I, §5, which provides that "each House shall be the Judge of the Elections, Returns and Qualifications of its own members. ... " In *Powell v. McCormack*, the Court held that the issue of whether the House could refuse to seat a Congressman who met the three standing requirements but who had, in the House's opinion, committed other infractions, was **not** committed by the Constitution to the House, and could be heard by the Court. But it seems probable that a suit involving the narrow issue of whether a person met all of the three requirements expressly listed in Art. I, §2 is committed to the House and is thus non-justiciable (though the Court has never explicitly decided that question).

Exam Tips *on* JUSTICIABILITY

Justiciability questions are pervasive and often hidden. Typically, your fact pattern will **not** contain the key words "standing," "ripe," "moot," "abstain," "political question," etc. — it will be up to you to spot these issues. Worse, these issues can be hidden in absolutely **any type** of fact pattern, so you can't let your guard down for a moment. Here are some specifics to watch for:

☛ Here's a brief checklist of justiciability issues:

(1) *advisory opinions;*

(2) *standing;*

(3) *mootness;*

(4) *ripeness;*

(5) *11th Amendment's* ban on certain *suits against the states;*

(6) *abstention;* and

(7) *political questions.*

☛ "Advisory opinion" problems usually arise on exams where a *state court* issues an advisory opinion (as allowed by the procedures of most states), and the loser seeks review in the U.S. Supreme Court. Typically, you'll say that even if the state court advisory opinion is based on federal law, the Supreme Court cannot hear the issue because there is no true "case or controversy" as required by Article III.

☛ The overwhelmingly most important aspect of justicability on exams is *"standing."* For *every claim* asserted anywhere on your exam, ask yourself, "Has P suffered, or is she about to suffer, a ***concrete, individualized harm***, that would be ***redressed*** by a favorable result in the lawsuit?" Unless the answer is "yes," there's probably no standing.

☞ Here's a checklist for standing, with the five individual elements broken out::

    ☞ P must have suffered an ***"injury-in-fact,"*** or be ***likely*** to suffer one reasonably ***soon***;

    ☞ P's harm must be ***concrete***, not abstract;

    ☞ P's harm must be ***"individuated,"*** i.e., not the same as that suffered by every other citizen or taxpayer;

    ☞ The action that P is complaining about must have been the ***"but for" cause*** of P's harm; and

    ☞ A favorable decision in the suit must be likely to ***redress*** the injury to P.

☞ One common fact pattern: P has a contract with the government, and some statute or rule would prevent (or dissuade) the government from honoring the contract. Here, there's usually standing because P is likely to suffer an "injury in fact" from losing the benefit of the contract. (*Example:* P has a contract to build a school for state X; a federal statute would withdraw funds that X was expecting to receive and pay over to P. In this situation, P has standing.)

☞ Remember that P need not have already suffered the harm. But if not, the threatened harm needs to be pretty ***imminent*** and pretty likely — some small chance of harm at some indefinite future time won't suffice. (*Example:* A first-year law student doesn't have standing to challenge a state's Continuing Legal Education requirement, because that requirement won't apply to her for several years.)

    ☞ Be on the lookout for a fact pattern where the plaintiff is contending that the ***government*** is likely to take some adverse action against him in the future. If the government's procedures are shrouded in ***secrecy***, it will be difficult for the plaintiff to prove the ***requisite likelihood*** that the government will really take the feared action soon.

    Example: P has email contacts with two foreign terror suspects, X and Y, and is afraid that the National Security Agency will intercept these emails under a statute letting the agency do surveillance on terror-related emails. If P can't show how the NSA chooses its surveillance targets and thus whether X and Y have been targeted, P won't have standing to challenge the constitutionality of the surveillance. (Cite to *Clapper v. Amnesty Int'l.*)

☞ An ***organization*** will generally be allowed to sue ***on behalf of its members***, if the members would individually have standing, and if the suit is ***related*** to the organization's ***purposes***. Most organization-based suits you'll see on an exam will ***satisfy*** these conditions.

☞ If P is asserting rights as a ***federal "taxpayer"*** or as a ***"citizen,"*** and P is not part of the transaction in question, probably P does ***not*** have standing. Three special cases:

☞ If P is a *state* taxpayer challenging a state expenditure, then probably all that's required for standing is that there be a "direct expenditure of funds" by the state. Normally, this will be satisfied in your fact pattern.

☞ If P is a federal taxpayer who is challenging the *tax itself*, which P would have to pay unless the suit succeeds, P has standing.

☞ If P is a federal taxpayer or citizen challenging a federal expenditure that *directly violates some constitutional guarantee*, P may have standing. Probably, this exception only applies to federal expenditures that violate the First Amendment's *Establishment Clause* (e.g., the federal government pays money to private schools to be used in furthering their religious message).

☞ Regardless of whether P has standing on her own, P will *not* usually be allowed to assert the rights of *third persons* not then before the court. You can refer to this as the rule against *"jus tertii"* to sound erudite. There are three important exceptions:

☞ In free-expression cases, litigants get to use the First Amendment *overbreadth* doctrine. This lets P say, in effect, "This statute blocks expressive conduct of mine that may constitutionally be proscribed, but it also could be interpreted to block expressive conduct or speech on the part of others not present, for whom it would violate their free speech rights."

☞ The litigant can assert the third party's rights if these rights would be impaired, and it's legally or practically *difficult* for the third party to be present in the suit. (*Example:* Vendors are often permitted to assert the rights of their customers, who would each individually have too little at stake to sue.)

☞ Associations get to assert their members' rights, as noted above.

☛ You can spot a *mootness* problem by the fact that P "doesn't really seem to have a problem anymore." (*Example:* P has been kept out of a public university by an allegedly discriminatory policy; if the university then allows P to enroll, the case has become moot.)

☞ Before you conclude that P doesn't really have a problem anymore, look for *"collateral consequences."* Most common: the litigant (he can either be P or D) has been *convicted*, then paroled or discharged — there will still be collateral consequences to him from having a conviction on the books (e.g., job or voting problems), so the case is not moot.

☞ Look for issues that are "capable of *repetition*, yet evading review." This happens where P is one of a series of similarly-situated people, each of whom would face the same problem that would always turn out to be moot. Classic illustration: P is a pregnant woman seeking to overturn restrictions on abortion; she's no longer pregnant by the time the suit gets heard, but all other pregnant women similarly situated would have the same problem, so a court will hear the case now. Another illustration: a political group is prevented from doing something until "after the election"; the election is now over, but other political groups, or this very group, would be likely to face the same mootness problem in a future context.

☛ You can spot a *ripeness* problem by looking for a situation that's *"too early"* or *"not con-*

crete enough."

☞ Classic illustration of ripeness: there's a criminal statute on the books that P wants to violate or has violated, but there's very little risk that the statute will in fact be enforced against P. (In this scenario, P is generally seeking a declaratory judgment that the statute is unconstitutional.) This type of problem is especially acute where P *hasn't committed* the violation yet, and we're not sure that he will. (*Example:* A statute prevents people from distributing literature on private property, including shopping centers. P says he wants to do this kind of distribution, but hasn't done it yet, and it's not even clear that the owner will object or that the police will arrest. P's case is probably unripe.)

☞ Another type of scenario: the risk is too *abstract*. (*Example:* A state keeps a secret file on citizens; P, one of the monitored citizens, claims that his First Amendment rights are being "chilled." The Court will probably hold that any chilling problem is too speculative and abstract, and the case unripe, unless P can show what activity he is being dissuaded from engaging in.)

☛ Whenever a suit is brought in federal court by a *private citizen* against a *state*, there's a good chance that the suit is blocked by the *11th Amendment*. This is true whether P is a citizen of the defendant state or of some other state. (*Example:* P, a citizen of state D, is injured when a state D employee runs him over while the employee is on the job. P sues state D in federal court for damages. The suit will be blocked by the 11th Amendment.)

☞ Some *exceptions* to the 11th Amendment:

☞ Suits against a state by *another state* or by the *federal government*;

☞ Suits against *counties*, *cities*, or anything but the state itself.

☞ Suits for an *injunction* against state *officials* directing them to *cease violating federal law*. (But a suit to force a state official to obey *state* law *is* covered by the 11th Amendment and thus not allowed in federal court.)

☞ Keep in mind that *Congress generally can't change* this "no federal-court suits against the states" law, even if it wants to. Cite to the *Seminole Tribe* case on this point. (*Example:* Congress passes a statute saying any state can be sued by private citizens for violating federal environmental-protection laws. This statute won't have any effect, and the federal court won't be allowed to hear a private suit against a state for damages for environmental violations.)

☞ But also remember that Congress *can* provide for federal-court suits by private citizens when the right being sued on stems from Congress' power to enforce the *post-Civil War Amendments*. (*Example:* Congress passes a broad statute banning racial and gender discrimination in employment, and says that workers can sue states in federal court for violations. The 11th Amendment won't block such suits, because Congress has the power to say that the Amendment won't apply to suits brought under federal statutes passed under Congress' authority to enforce the 14th Amendment.)

☞ If the question involves a private damages suit brought on a congressionally-guaranteed right, but brought *against a state in its own courts*, remember that the newly-recognized constitutional doctrine of *sovereign immunity* (the *Alden v. Maine* case) means that the state *doesn't have to hear the case.*

☛ Be alert to possible non-justiciable *"political questions."* Remember that there are two different ways a question can become a non-justiciable political one:

   ☞ First, this can happen where, at least arguably, the Constitution gives the problem to the *executive* or *legislative* branch to resolve, rather than to the judiciary. Classic illustration: anything to do with the procedures or grounds for *impeachment*. Another illustration: a federal court is asked to overrule Congress' decision that P doesn't satisfy the age, citizenship or residency requirement for Senators and Representatives.

   ☞ Second, a question can be a non-justiciable political one because there are *no "manageable standards"* to guide the judiciary in deciding. This type of fact pattern is relatively rare. (*Example:* P claims that a particular tax is so burdensome that it amounts to an uncompensated "taking" in violation of the Fifth Amendment. This issue is a non-justiciable political one, because no standards exist to tell the Court how to decide.)

      ☞ One area that you might think would fall into this "no manageable standards" category — *reapportionment* — doesn't. The Court has decided that the "one person, one vote" principle applies to virtually all federal and state elections, and that this principle can be successfully applied by the judiciary.

ESSAY EXAM
QUESTIONS AND ANSWERS

The following Essay Questions are taken from the Constitutional Law volume of *Siegel's Essay & Multiple Choice Questions & Answers*, a series written by Brian Siegel and published by Wolters Kluwer Law & Business. The full volume contains 27 essays (with model answers), as well as 128 multiple-choice questions. (The majority of the essay questions were originally asked on the California Bar Exam, and are copyright the California Board of Bar Examiners, reprinted by permission.) The book is available from your bookstore, or by clicking on "Education" at www.wolterskluwerlb.com.

QUESTION 1: City, a municipality of State X, has a permit ordinance that prohibits making speeches in the City-owned city park without first obtaining a permit from City's police chief. The ordinance authorizes the police chief to establish permit application procedures, and to grant or deny permits based upon the chief's "overall assessment of the good of the community." The ordinance also provides that denial of a permit may be appealed to the city council.

On Tuesday, Tom applied to Dan, City's police chief, for a permit to speak in the city park the following Saturday. Tom gave Dan his name and local address, but Dan denied Tom's application for a permit because Tom refused Dan's request for a summary of what he intended to say in his speech. When Tom told Dan that he intended to make his speech anyway, Dan immediately gave Tom's name and address to the city attorney of City.

The city attorney did nothing about the matter until Friday, when, without notice to Tom, he made application on behalf of City to a State X court of general jurisdiction for a temporary restraining order preventing Tom from speaking in the city park without a permit. The State X court issued an ex-parte temporary restraining order and an order to show cause, answerable in five days, directed to Tom. The orders were served on Tom in the city park on Saturday as he was about to speak. Despite the temporary restraining order, Tom spoke to about twenty mildly interested persons who were then in the park for various other reasons.

The essence of Tom's speech was that the federal government, "aided and abetted" by City's government, was "leading America to destruction," and that "those who would survive will eventually have to fight in the streets of City to regain their liberties." Tom urged the audience to "stockpile weapons" and to "start thinking about forming guerrilla units to take back freedom from the government."

Tom was arrested and charged in the State X court which had issued the temporary restraining order with **(a)** speaking in the city park without a permit, a misdemeanor, **(b)** contempt of court for violating the temporary restraining order, and **(c)** violation of the State X criminal advocacy statute prohibiting "advocating insurrection against local, state, or the federal governments," a felony.

Five years ago, the State X Supreme Court construed the criminal advocacy statute as applying only to advocacy that is not protected by the United States Constitution.

A week after Tom's speech, in a case unrelated to the charges against Tom, the State X Supreme Court construed City's permit ordinance as authorizing the City police chief to consider "only the time, place and manner of the proposed speech, and not its content" in passing upon permit applications.

What rights guaranteed by the United States Constitution should Tom assert in defense to the charges brought against him, and how should the court rule? Discuss.

QUESTION 2: County School Board (Board) cancelled the remedial reading program in County's public schools. At the same time, Board increased funding for drama arts workshops provided for seniors in the public high schools of County. Such increased funding is about 15% of the cost of the remedial reading program.

Racial minorities comprise 10% of the County population and 50% of the students enrolled in the remedial reading program. "AB" is an organization consisting of the parents of these minority students.

Some students are enrolled in the remedial reading program because of learning disabilities or other handicaps adversely affecting reading skills. "CD" is an organization of the parents of these students.

AB objected to the cancellation of the remedial reading program on the ground that the program's termination would disproportionately affect their children adversely. CD objected to the program's termination on the ground that such action would effectively end public education for their children.

In recommending termination of the program, the Board's director had stated: "This action is a necessary economy measure. We have other educational programs, such as pre-college math, which are educationally more important. Handicapped students will simply have to be served sometime in the future when we again have sufficient financial resources. We will, even then, have to target the program so that it helps handicapped children, not children of racial minorities who just need to improve their skills in the English language." Board's actions were based on its director's recommendations.

AB and CD filed suit against Board in federal court, asserting that termination of the remedial reading program violated the constitutional right of the parents and the children represented by those organizations, and asking that Board be ordered to reinstate the program. While the suit was pending, Congress enacted a federal statute requiring school boards of all state political subdivisions to provide remedial reading courses. In passing this legislation, Congress relied upon findings derived through congressional hearings that adults without reading skills inhibit production, sales and travel in interstate commerce.

Assume that both AB and CD have standing to assert their claims.

1. Is the federal statute constitutional? Discuss.

2. If the court rules that the federal statute is unconstitutional:

   A. What issues under the U.S. Constitution should AB raise against the actions of Board? How should they be decided? Discuss.

   B. What issues under the U.S. Constitution should CD raise against the actions of Board? How should they be decided? Discuss.

QUESTION 3: The legislature of State A recently passed a law requiring drivers of trucks carrying explosives on roads in State A to have "Special Driving Permits." These permits are to be issued only after rigorous physical examinations and driving tests. The State A law also provides that only permits issued by State A are acceptable for truck drivers; permits issued by certain other states, all of which have less stringent requirements, are not acceptable. Under the State A law, permits cannot be issued to persons under 30 or over 60 years of age, because statistical studies have shown that drivers in these categories have higher accident frequencies.

Assume that a federal law prohibits employers from discriminating against employees on the basis of age.

Ned, who is 62 years old, is a driver for Ajax, a truck company engaged in the interstate transportation of dynamite for construction projects in various states, including State A. Ned would normally be assigned to drive dynamite shipments from Ajax's headquarters in State B, into State A, but he cannot obtain a Special Driving Permit from State A. Ned would be able to satisfy both the physical examination and driving test requirements of the State A law, but is barred solely because of his age. Ned has a driver's permit issued by State B qualifying him to drive trucks carrying explosives. As a consequence of the State A law, Ajax has been obliged to revise its normal driver assignment policy to schedule Ned on routes which do not require ingress into State A.

Ajax and Ned have brought suit in the United States District Court in State A against the appropriate State A officials, seeking to have the State A law declared invalid. The defendants have moved to have the case dismissed on the grounds that (1) the plaintiffs lack standing, and (2) State A courts have not yet ruled upon the validity of the new law.

1. How should the court rule on the motion for dismissal? Discuss.

2. Assume the motion for dismissal is denied. What rights arising under the United States Constitution should Ajax and Ned urge in support of their claims that the State A law is invalid, and what result should follow? Discuss.

ANSWERS

SAMPLE ANSWER TO QUESTION 1:

(a) The misdemeanor charge:

Tom ("T") could initially contend that the misdemeanor charge should be dismissed because it was based upon a statute which was overly broad on its face (i.e., the entity charged with enforcing the law had virtually total discretion in determining whether or not it should be applied to a particular situation). Such enactments cannot serve as the basis for governmental action; *Lovell v. Griffin*, 303 U.S. 444 (1938). Since the statutory standard to be utilized in granting licenses or not is highly subjective in nature (i.e., the "overall community good"), T would argue that it was constitutionally defective. While it would be difficult for City to argue that the test for determining if licenses should be granted or not is adequate, it could assert that where the defendant should have anticipated a constitutionally curative construction, an overly broad enactment may serve as the basis for governmental action; *Shuttlesworth v. Birmingham*, 394 U.S. 147 (1969). Since the State X Supreme Court had made a proper narrowing interpretation of the criminal advocacy statute five years earlier, T should have foreseen that a constitutionally proper interpretation of the misdemeanor statute would also be rendered when it was judicially reviewed.

T could respond, however, that he could *not* foresee a constitutionally curative interpretation of the licensing ordinance because it appeared to be plain on its face (i.e., it would have been very difficult to anticipate that the requirement for speaking would be almost completely repudiated and the factors of time, place and manner of speech substituted in lieu thereof).

Alternatively, T could argue that, even if a proper narrowing interpretation could have been anticipated, a law which is unconstitutionally applied (i.e., the permit was rejected for T's failure to disclose the content; not time, place or manner considerations) cannot serve as the basis for a criminal conviction where no adequate opportunity for review is available. T would assert that this standard was satisfied because (1) there was no provision for independent review by a judicial body (any appeal was to be heard by the city council, presumably the same entity which enacted the law), and (2) the facts are unclear as to how often the city council met (if it was not until after T's projected speaking date, no timely appeal to that body could possibly be taken). While City could contend in rebuttal that T waived any potential constitutional defect in the prescribed review procedure by neglecting to contest the police chief's decision to deny T's request for a permit before the city council, a procedure which requires appeal to a legislative branch of local government is probably inadequate.

In summary, the prosecution of T for violation of the licensing ordinance will probably *not* be successful.

(b) The contempt of court decree:

Ex-parte orders are ordinarily not appropriate unless there was a need to act immediately and there was no opportunity to give the opposing party notice. Since the attorney for City was apparently aware of T's prospective speech on Tuesday (the facts indicate that Dan "immediately" gave the City attorney T's name and address), T probably should have been given an opportunity to contest the issuance of an injunction. While even an improper court order must ordinarily be obeyed, where an ex-parte injunction is deliberately sought and served in such a manner as to preclude effective judicial review (as was the case in this instance since City's attorney served the order upon T just as he was beginning to speak), it may be attackable in a subsequent proceeding; *Walker v. Birmingham*, 388 U.S. 307 (1967). However, since T's speech had not been preceded by extensive publicity, it would not have greatly burdened him to have sought appellate review of the injunction. Thus, a conviction for contempt would appear to be proper.

(c) The felony charge:

While the advocacy of ideas is protected by the First Amendment (applicable to the states via the Fourteenth Amendment), speech made for the purpose of inciting immediate unlawful conduct and which is likely to incite such action may be proscribed; *Brandenburg v. Ohio*, 395 U.S. 444 (1969). T could contend that the felony charges must be dismissed because (1) the statute in question is too vague (i.e., a person of ordinary intelligence could not determine what words constituted "advocating insurrection"), and (2) alternatively, the above cited standard is not satisfied in this instance because (i) while he advocated that the listeners "stockpile weapons" be never suggested that this be done illegally (in most states, various types of firearms can be purchased in a lawful manner), (ii) even if his words could be construed as urging illegal conduct, it wouldn't be done imminently (i.e., it would take time to aggregate these weapons), and (iii) there was little likelihood that the listeners would respond to T's speech, since they were (a) in the park for "various other reasons," and (b) only mildly interested in T's speech. Finally, T's comment to "begin thinking about forming guerilla units" obviously does not contemplate immediate unlawful conduct.

While City could respond to T's vagueness assertion by pointing out that the statute had received a constitutionally curative interpretation, there appears to be no successful rebuttal to T's argument that the *Brandenburg* test is not met. Thus, the felony charge should be dismissed.

SAMPLE ANSWER TO QUESTION 2:

1. *Is the federal statute constitutional?*

Board's strongest argument is that the statute violates the Tenth Amendment, on the theory that Congress may not compel a local school board to provide remedial reading courses. Under *Printz v. U.S. & Mack v. U.S.*, 521 U.S. 898 (1997), Congress may not compel a state or local government's executive branch (which includes local school boards) to perform tasks or functions, even doing background checks on gun purchasers. A court would probably conclude that requiring particular courses in public schools is a comparable over-reaching of congressional power. Therefore, the statute will probably be held unconstitutional under *Printz/Mack*.

As a second argument, Board can contend that even if the statute was valid under the Tenth Amendment, it would be invalid under the Commerce Clause. Under Article I, Section 8 (Clause 3), of the Constitution, Congress has the right to regulate interstate commerce. There are three broad categories of activities that Congress can constitutionally regulate under its commerce power: (1) "channels" of interstate commerce; (2) "instrumentalities" of interstate commerce; and (3) those activities having a "substantial effect" on interstate commerce. *U.S. v. Lopez;* 514 U.S. 549 (1995). The federal statute falls under the third category, since it has no effect on the channels or instrumentalities of interstate commerce. Since the activity being regulated (education) is non-commercial, there must be an *obvious connection* between the activity and interstate commerce. While Congress did make legislative findings linking the regulated activity to interstate commerce, the Court no longer finds this dispositive on the constitutionality of commerce clause regulations. *Lopez*. Here, there is no jurisdictional nexus between the regulations and interstate commerce; i.e., the regulation equally affects those people traveling in, and those not traveling in, interstate commerce.

Therefore, there is no "obvious connection" between the regulation and interstate commerce, and it is likely that under *U.S. v. Lopez* the legislation will be held unconstitutional.

2A. *Assuming the federal statute is unconstitutional, what issues should the AB group raise against Board?*

The AB group would raise equal protection and due process objections to the Board's action.

In determining whether a law which is neutral on its face (such as the present legislation, which discontinues **all** remedial reading programs) has a discriminatory purpose, a court may consider any pertinent data (including the statements made by the Board's director). If purposeful discrimination could be shown, the County's actions would have to satisfy the strict scrutiny standard (i.e., a compelling state interest is furthered by the governmental conduct, and there is no less burdensome means of satisfying that objective). Since the termination of the program has a disproportionately adverse racial impact (while racial minorities comprise 10% of the County's population, they constitute 50% of the number of students enrolled in the program), Board would have the burden of proving that its actions were **not** racially motivated.

Board could argue that (1) its action was dictated by financial necessity, and (2) the effect of the program's termination also impacts upon non-minority students. In rebuttal, the AB group could contend that Board's purposeful discrimination is proven by the facts that (1) there were **increased** monies available for the drama arts workshops (however, the total of this amount was only 15% of the funds which had been available for the remedial reading program), and (2) the director indicated handicapped students would receive preference over minority students if adequate funding subsequently became available (although this could be defended by the fact that the latter group would completely fail to learn to read if their regular studies were not supplemented by the remedial program). Without data as to Board's financial situation, it is impossible to determine if the cessation of the program was "a necessary economy measure" or racially inspired. Assuming the court found that it was not, then County would only have to show that the program's termination had a reasonable relationship to a constitutional purpose to sustain its action. This would seem to be established by the County's showing that monetary pressures compelled cessation of the remedial reading program.

The AB group could alternatively contend that the program's closure violated their substantive due process rights. Under the Fourteenth Amendment, one cannot be deprived of fundamental "liberties" (i.e., rights recognized as essential to the orderly pursuit of happiness). The right to possess reasonably adequate reading skills is arguably "fundamental," since a failure to read proficiently inevitably results in lower paying jobs and an overall diminished ability to enjoy life. While the Supreme Court has held that there is no fundamental right to an equally financed education (i.e., all school districts within a particular county do not have to expend an equal dollar amount per child; *San Antonio School District v. Rodriguez*), it has never held that a school district can offer less than an adequate education.

Again, more facts are necessary to determine if, without the program, children of the AB group would be literate. If not, continuation of the program probably is a fundamental right, and therefore the strict scrutiny test would be applicable (i.e., Board would have to show that discontinuing the remedial reading program was virtually the only means of meeting its budgetary crisis). However, if the AB group would receive an adequate education without the program, Board's action would only have to have a reasonable relationship to a constitutional purpose. This would seem to be present in this case, since any good faith decision with respect to how a limited amount of education money is apportioned would be reasonable.

2B. *Assuming the federal statute is unconstitutional, what issues would the CD group raise against Board?*

The CD group would also raise the substantive due process argument described above (i.e., that the right to receive adequate reading skills is a "fundamental" one, and therefore cessation of the program is subject to a strict scrutiny analysis). The facts indicate that, given their innate learning disabilities, this group would not acquire adequate reading skills without the program. Since it is unlikely that Board could show that other programs are more important than minimal reading proficiency, it is highly doubtful that (1) cancellation of the program served a compelling state interest, and (2) there was no less burdensome means available to Board of satisfying its financial constraints. In summary, the substantive due process argument of the CD group should be successful.

Alternatively, the CD group would contend that their equal protection rights were violated. There is no case law supporting the proposition that educationally handicapped students are a "suspect" or "quasi-suspect" group. Since (1) there has probably been no history of purposeful unequal treatment with respect to educationally handicapped persons, and (2) their handicaps are (presumably) not unalterable, it appears to be doubtful that the CD group would be classified as "suspect" or "quasi-suspect." Since the program's cessation would probably meet the rational relationship test, CD's equal protection argument should be unsuccessful.

SAMPLE ANSWER TO QUESTION 3:

1. The Motion for Dismissal:

Abstention:

A U.S. District Court may abstain from hearing a case which challenges the constitutionality of an ambiguous non-federal statute if the alleged defect might be cured by a narrowing interpretation by a state court. While State A might contend that abstention is appropriate in this instance because no state court has yet construed the statute in question, Ajax and Ned ("Plaintiffs") could probably successfully argue in rebuttal that a curative construction is unlikely since both the (1) 30-60 year parameters, and (2) specific testing requirements, leave virtually no room for a constitutionally valid interpretation.

2. The rights of the Constitution versus State A law:

Standing:

Article III of the Constitution requires that to have standing in federal court, a plaintiff must show a direct and immediate personal injury which is traceable to the challenged action; *Simon v. Eastern Kentucky Welfare Rights Organization*, 426 U.S 26 (1976). State X might contend that Ned has suffered no injury since he has not been terminated from his employment, nor is there any indication that he is receiving less compensation than he had made prior to the State A enactment. Ajax arguably lacks standing because it apparently has other drivers who are capable of obtaining the "Special Driving Permits." Assuming, however, (1) Ned's re-assignment (a) to other routes ultimately results in lessened compensation (of any amount) for him, or, (b) is disadvantageous for any other reason (i.e., the substituted routes are more physically demanding because they are longer and/or more dangerous), and (2) altering driving assignments to. comply with State A law could result in some drivers deciding to leave Ajax's employ, the Plaintiffs probably have standing.

The State A Statute:

Pursuant to the Tenth Amendment, a state may ordinarily enact legislation which is aimed at promoting the health, safety or welfare of its citizenry. Since the legislation in question is obviously aimed at decreasing the possibility of accidents involving explosive-carrying trucks, it would be constitutionally valid (unless it contravenes some federal interest).

Supremacy Clause:

Where a state statute conflicts with the language of, or purposes sought to be achieved by, a federal statute, the former enactment will be invalid under the Supremacy Clause.

Plaintiffs will contend that the State A statute is inconsistent with the purposes sought to be achieved by the federal law because it would induce age discrimination (i.e., to avoid being obliged to juggle schedules to circumvent State A, employers would (a) hire drivers within State A's age parameters, and (b) be more likely to terminate employees who could not travel within State A). However, State A could argue in rebuttal that (1) Plaintiffs' argument is premised on speculative secondary effects of its law, and (2) it is unlikely that Congress intended to preempt state legislation which was based upon bona fide occupational qualifications (statistical studies support State A's age restrictions). Unless there is clear legislative history that Congress intended to totally preclude age as a consideration for employment, Plaintiffs probably would not succeed on this argument.

Equal Protection Clause:

Since the elderly have not historically been subjected to purposeful unequal treatment or relegated to a position of political powerlessness, the strict scrutiny standard would probably not apply; *Massachusetts Board of Retirement v. Murgia*, 427 U.S. 307 (1976).

Plaintiffs might nevertheless contend that the rational relationship test (i.e., there must be a rational relationship between the classification drawn by the statute and the governmental object sought to be achieved) is not satisfied. This is because (1) the physical examination and driving test measure more accurately one's ability to drive safely than strict biological age, and (2) persons with perfect driving records could be excluded as a consequence of the statute, while others with negative driving histories might nevertheless qualify for a Special Driving Permit ("SDP"). However, since the classification (1) need only be rational (i.e., maybe drivers over 60 are more prone to heart attacks), and (2) is supported by empirical data, State A would probably prevail on this issue too.

Dormant Interstate Commerce Clause:

State legislation which unduly burdens interstate commerce (i.e., the interference with interstate commerce resulting from the local regulation outweighs the interest sought to be protected by the law) is invalid; *Bibb v. Navajo Freight Lines, Inc.*, 359 U.S. 520 (1959). Plaintiffs could contend that the State A statute imposes a substantial burden upon interstate commerce, since interstate trucking companies will now be obliged (probably at substantial inconvenience and expense) to avoid State A or be compelled to hire additional employees who can acquire a SDP. State A, however, could argue in rebuttal that it has a strong interest in the legislation (i.e., the desire to avoid catastrophic explosions which have a potential for causing great loss of lives and property).

Assuming State A could show that most truck companies have drivers within their employ who qualify for a SDP (and therefore the statute merely results in the inconvenience of having to alter job assignments), it would again prevail.

Due Process:

Where a state statute irrebuttably presumes that certain facts exist which result in an adverse classification, the denial of an opportunity to challenge that presumption violates an individual's Fourteenth Amendment's due process right to demonstrate that the fact presumed is not true in his/her case, some Supreme Court cases suggest. See, e.g., *Vlandis v. Kline*, 412 U.S. 441 (1973). Thus, Plaintiffs' could argue that the irrebuttable presumption that persons over 60 are more prone to accidents than others is invalid (especially since Ned was capable of satisfying the physical examination and driving test requirements of State A). However, State A could probably successfully contend in rebuttal that (1) the irrebuttable-presumption cases like *Vlandis* are probably no longer good law; (2) there is no "property" interest in private employment, and (3) statistical studies (which were presumably methodologically sound) have established that drivers over 60 have a higher incidence of accidents than others, so the classification is certainly rational, which is all that is required by either due process or equal protection.

In summary, it is unlikely that Plaintiffs would be able to invalidate the State A statute.

TABLE OF CASES

Principal discussion of a case
is indicated by page numbers in *italics*.

Abate v. Mundt *733*

Abington School District v. Schempp 656, *661*

Abood v. Detroit Board of Education 614, 615

Abrams v. U.S. 504, 510, *511*

ACLU v. Reno 567

Adarand Constructors, Inc. v. Pena *320–323*, 351, 407

Adkins v. Children's Hospital 168, 169

Agency for Int'l Dev. v. Alliance for Open Soc'y Int'l, Inc.
626, 644, 654

Agins v. Tiburon 417

Agostini v. Felton *683*

Akron v. Akron Center For Reproductive Health 185

Alaska Hire case 118

Alden v. Maine 56, *726*, 743

Allegheny County v. American Civil
Liberties Union 676

Allen v. Wright 716, *718*

Allgeyer v. Louisiana 166

Allied Structural Steel Co. v. Spannaus *430*

Alvarez, U.S. v. 509, *574–576*, 651

Ambach v. Norwick 353, *355–355*, 364

Amer. Library Ass'n., Inc., U.S. v. 556

American Party of Texas v. White 393

American Trucking Assoc. v. Scheiner 112

Anderson v. Martin 275

Apodaca v. Oregon 164

Arizona Christian School Tuition Organization v.
Winn 712

Arizona Free Enterprise Club's Freedom Club
PAC v. Bennett 596–597

Arkansas Educational Television Comm'n v.
Forbes 553, 555, 556

Arkansas Writer's Project, Inc. v. Ragland 628

Arlington Heights v. Metropolitan Housing Corp. 268

Arnett v. Kennedy 520

Ashcroft v. ACLU *548–549*, 568, 652

Ashcroft v. Free Speech Coalition 580

Associated Press v. Walker 570

Bailey v. Drexel Furniture Co. 68, 69

Baird v. State Bar of Arizona 624

Baker v. Carr 727, 728, 730, *731*

Bakke, Univ. of California v., see University of
California Regents v. Bakke

Baldwin v. G.A.F. Selig, Inc. *92*

Baldwin v. Montana Fish and Game Comm'n 118

Ball v. James 386, 403, 733

Ballard, U.S. v. 670, 697, 702

Barnes v. Glen Theatre, Inc. 568

Barron v. The Mayor and City Council of Baltimore ... 162

Barrows v. Jackson 458

Bartnicki v. Vopper 637–638

Bates v. State Bar of Arizona *584*

Batson v. Kentucky 270, 345

Belle Terre v. Borass 198, 217

Bellotti v. Baird 185

Bernal v. Fainter 355

Bethel School District No. 403 v. Fraser 607

Bibb v. Navajo Freight Lines, Inc. 91

Blum v. Yaretsky 456, 459

BMW of North America v. Gore 229

Board of Curators v. Horowitz 237

Board of Directors of Rotary Int'l v. Rotary
Club of Duarte 614

Board of Education of Kiryas Joel v.
Grumet 658, *678–679*, 680

Board of Education v. Allen 682

Board of Education v. Dowell 281

Board of Education v. Mergens 659

Board of Education v. Pico 213, *606–607*

Board of Regents of the University of Wisconsin
System v. Southworth *615*

Board of Regents v. Roth 216, *224–226*

Board of Trustees of SUNY v. Fox 587

Board of Trustees of Univ. of Alabama v.
Garrett 490, 491–492, 494

Boddie v. Connecticut 396

Boerne, City of v. Flores 477, 483, 486, *487–489*,
490, 495, 497

Bolger v. Youngs Drug Products Corp. 590

Bolling v. Sharpe 251, 278

Bond v. Floyd 516

Boos v. Barry 506

Boumediene v. Bush 138, *139–141*

Bowen v. Kendrick 668

Bowers v. Hardwick *201–202*, 202, 203, 216, 383

Bowsher v. Synar 146–147, 155

Boy Scouts of America v. Dale *616–617*

Brandenburg v. Ohio 510, 513, 514, 515–516, 518, 525,
536, 618

Branti v. Finkel 619

Branzburg v. Hayes 627, *634–636*, 645

Brentwood Academy v. Tenn. Secondary School
Athletic Assoc. *463, 465*

Broadrick v. Oklahoma *521–521*

Brockett v. Spokane Arcades, Inc. 577, 578

Brown v. Board of Education 11, *277–279*, 282, 285
Brown v. Board of Education (Brown II)..................... 279
Brown v. Entertainment Merchants Ass'n................... 580
Brown, U.S. v. 442, 446
Buck v. Bell 174
Buckley v. Valeo 142, 143, *593–595*, 623
Burdick v. Takushi.. 386, 388
Burton v. Wilmington Parking
      Authority 459, 460, 467, 468
Bush v. Gore... *389–390*
Bush v. Vera 330, 331
Butler, U.S. v. *71*

C & A Carbone, Inc. v. Clarkstown........................... 97, 98
Caban v. Mohammed... 344
Cabell v. Chavez-Salido 354, 355
Calder v. Bull... 440
Califano v. Goldfarb 287
Califano v. Jobst 199
Califano v. Webster 287, 338, 342
California Medical Assn. v. FEC................................. 597
Caperton v. A.T. Massey Coal Co...................... *230–231*
Capitol Square Review Board v. Pinette 677
Carey v. Population Services Int'l...................... 176, *196*
Carolene Products Co., U.S. v. 169, 271, 362
Carter v. Carter Coal Co.. *32, 53*
Castle Rock v. Gonzales.............................. *215–216*, 245
Central Hudson Gas v. Public Service
      Commission.................... 583, 585, 587, 592
Champion v. Ames 30
Chaplinsky v. New Hampshire............. *533*, 567, 569, 576
Christian Legal Society Chapter v.
      Martinez *554–554*, 556
Church of the Lukumi Babalu Aye, Inc. v. Hialeah 689,
      689–690, 690, 695, 701
Citizens United v. Federal Election
      Comm. 594, 597, 600, *600–603*
City of — see city name
Civil Rights Cases... *450–452*
Clapper v. Amnesty Int'l USA 711, *714–715*, 740
Clark v. Community For Creative
      Non-Violence 528, *560*
Clark v. Jeter... 359
Cleburne, City of v. Cleburne Living
      Center 261, 262, 263, *360–362*
Cleveland Bd. of Ed. v. Loudermill................ 228, *236*
Clinton v. Jones 150
Clinton v. New York...................................... *131–132*
Cohen v. California..................... 503, *536*, 544, 567, 649
Cohen v. Cowles Media Co. 627
Cohens v. Virginia 11
Cole v. Richardson.. 619, 644
Colegrove v. Green 730
Coleman v. Court of Appeals of Maryland 344
Coleman v. Miller.. 729

Collin v. Smith... 540
Colorado Republican Federal Campaign Committee v.
      Federal Election Commission ("Colorado Repub-
      lican I").. 603
Comstock, U.S. v. 23
Connally v. General Construction Co............................ 522
Connick v. Myers... *620*, 644
Consolidated Edison v. Public Serv.
      Commission.. 507, 524
Cooley v. Bd. of Wardens of the Port of
      Philadelphia..................................... *87*, 95, 109
Cooper v. Aaron.. 11, 279
Cornelius v. NAACP Legal Defense and
      Educational Fund........................... 550, 555, 556
Cox Broadcasting Corp. v. Cohn............................... 637
Cox v. Louisiana 534, 567
Cox v. New Hampshire... 531
Craig v. Boren............... 250, 256, 286, 288, 289, 336, 343
Crawford v. Los Angeles Board of Education...... 284, 285
Crawford v. Marion County Election Board *386–388*
Crist v. Bretz.. 163
Cruzan v. Missouri Department of
      Health *205–207*, 208, 221
Curtis Pub. Co. v. Butts 570
Curtiss-Wright Export Corp., U.S. v. 136
Cutter v. Wilkinson... 667, *680*

DaimlerChrysler Corp. v. Cuno................................... 713
Dames & Moore v. Regan 129, 155
Dandridge v. Williams.............................. 382, 399, 404
Darby, U.S. v. *35–36*
Davis v. Bandemer... 734
Davis v. F.E.C.. *596*
DeFunis v. Odegaard 720
Dean Milk Co. v. City of Madison 89, 93, 111
Debs v. U.S.. 511
Dennis v. U.S... 515
District Attorney's Office for the Third
      Judicial District v. Osborne................ *233–233*
District of Columbia v. Heller............................. *432–440*
Dolan v. City of Tigard........................... *422–423*, 424
Douglas v. California... 395, 400
Duke Power v. Carolina Environmental
      Study Group, Inc. 170
Dun & Bradstreet, Inc. v. Greenmoss
      Builders, Inc. 572, *572–573*
Duncan v. Louisiana 163
Dunn v. Blumstein 386, 399

Edenfield v. Fane 584, 585, 587, 588
Edmonson v. Leesville Concrete Co.......................... 463
Edwards v. Aguillard 665, 666
Edwards v. California 95
Eichman, U.S. v. 562
Eisenstadt v. Baird.. 176

El Paso v. Simmons 428

Election Law Case 143

Elfbrandt v. Russell 618

Elk Grove Unified School Dist. v. Newdow 720

Employment Division v. Smith ... 487, *689, 694–695*, 696,
  702, 705

Energy Reserves Group, Inc. v. Kansas Power
  and Light Co. 431

Engel v. Vitale 661

Epperson v. Arkansas 605, *664–665*, 666, 722

Erie v. Pap's A.M. *545–546*, 578

Evans v. Abney 455, *459*

Evans v. Newton *455, 459*

Everson v. Board of Education 657, 681

Evitts v. Lucey 232

Ex parte — see name of party

Exxon Corp. v. Eagerton 431, 445

Exxon Corp. v. Governor of Maryland *94–95*

Farber, In re 636

FCC v. League of Women Voters 626, 641

FCC v. Pacifica Foundation 547, 549, 640

FEC v. National Conservative Political Action
  Committee 597

Federal Election Comm. v. Wisconsin Right
  to Life 597, *600–603*

Federal Maritime Comm. v. South Carolina State Ports
  Auth. 726, 727

Feiner v. New York 535

First English Evangelical Lutheran Church v.
  Los Angeles County 417

First National Bank of Boston v. Bellotti 604

Fisher v. Univ. of Texas 293, 297, *300–305*,
  305–306, 313, 351, 352, 353, 408

Flagg Bros., Inc. v. Brooks 455, *456–456*, 463, 464

Flast v. Cohen 711, 737

Florida Lime & Avocado Growers v. Paul 105

Florida Prepaid Postsecondary Education Expense
  Board v. College Savings Bank *725*

Foley v. Connelie 355

Fordice, U.S. v. 284

Forsyth County v. The Nationalist Movement 530

44 Liquormart v. Rhode Island 589, *589*, 592

Frazee v. Illinois Dept. of Employment Security 697

Free Enterprise Fund v. Public Company
  Accounting Oversight Board 144, 145

Frisby v. Schultz 532, 550, 551

Frohwerk v. U.S. 511

Frontiero v. Richardson 336, 357

Frothingham v. Mellon 711

Gade v. National Solid Wastes Management 105

Gannett Co. v. DePasquale 634, *639*

Garcetti v. Ceballos 620, *621–622*, 644

Garcia v. San Antonio Metropolitan Transit
  Authority *54–56*, 56, 59, 62, 117

Garner v. Louisiana.. 535

Geduldig v. Aiello.. 344–345

Gentile v. State Bar of Nevada 633, 645

Georgia v. McCollum 463

Georgia, U.S. v. 68, 493

Gertz v. Robert Welch, Inc. 571, *572–573*, 591

Gibbons v. Ogden 28–29, *85*

Gillette v. U.S. 696

Gitlow v. New York.. 513, 515

Globe Newspapers v. Superior Court 640

Goesaert v. Cleary.. 336

Goldberg v. Kelly 224, 227, 228, 237, 400

Goldblatt v. Hempstead 419, 444

Goldman v. Weinberger.. *694*

Goldwater v. Carter 730

Gonzales v. Carhart...... 176, 178, 184, 185, 186, 188, 189,
  190–195, 195, 196, 220, 242

Gonzales v. Raich 35, 38, *42–44*, 51, 61, 63

Good News Club v. Milford Central School 659–660

Goss v. Board of Education 280

Goss v. Lopez 226, 237

Graham v. Richardson 354, 357

Gratz v. Bollinger 292, 293, 294, *298–299*,
  305–306, 352, 408

Graves v. New York ex rel. O'Keefe.......................... 116

Greater New Orleans Broadcasting Assoc., Inc.
  v. U.S. 588

Green v. County School Board.................................. 280

Greenholtz v. Inmates 232

Greer v. Spock 555

Gregory v. Ashcroft 263

Griffin v. County School Board.................................. 280

Griffin v. Illinois.................................... *395–395*, 400

Griffiths, In re 354

Griswold v. Connecticut 173, *174–176*, 216, 219

Grutter v. Bollinger............. 273, 290, 292, 293, *294–298*,
  305–306, 318, 319, 324, 334, 351, 408

Guest, U.S. v. 451, 470, *472*, 476

H.L. v. Matheson 186

Hadley v. Junior College Dist..................................... 733

Hague v. CIO 527, 551

Hamdan v. Rumsfeld *130*, 154

Hamdi v. Rumsfeld *233–236*

Hamling v. U.S. 581, 582

Hammer v. Dagenhart................................. *30–31*, 31, 35

Hampton v. Mow Sun Wong 214, 356

Hans v. Louisiana 723, 738

Harlow v. Fitzgerald 149, 155

Harper v. Virginia Bd. of Elections 379, *385–385*

Harris v. McRae 187

Hawker v. New York.. 442

Hazelwood School District v. Kuhlmeier 607

Heart of Atlanta Motel v. U.S. 37
Hein v. Freedom from Religion Foundation 712
Hernandez v. Texas 265
Hess v. Indiana 517
Hicklin v. Orbeck 118
Hill v. Colorado *532–532*
Hines v. Davidowitz 105
Hipolite Egg Co. v. U.S. 30
Hodgson v. Minnesota 186
Holder v. Humanitarian Law Project 517–518
Hollingsworth v. Perry 369
Home Building & Loan Ass'n v. Blaisdell 429
Hood, H.P. & Sons v. DuMond 96
Hosanna-Tabor Evangelical Lutheran Church
      and School v. EEOC *668–670, 695–696,* 705
Houston E. & W. Texas Railway Co. v. U.S. 29, 31
Hudgens v. NLRB *454,* 557
Hughes v. Alexandria Scrap Corp. 100, 111
Hughes v. Oklahoma 96
Humphrey's Executor v. U.S. 144
Hunt v. Washington Apple Advertising
      Commission *93,* 716, 737
Hunter v. Erickson 276, 284
Hunter v. Underwood 268
Hurley v. Irish-American Gay, Lesbian,
      and Bisexual Group of Boston 615
Hustler Magazine v. Falwell 573

Immigration and Naturalization Service (INS)
      v. Chadha *133–134,* 135, 154, 155
In re — see name of party
International Society for Krishna Consciousness
      v. Lee 78, 552, 553, 555, 568

J.E.B. v. Alabama 270, 345
Jackson v. Metropolitan Edison Co. 455, *462,* 464
Jacobellis v. Ohio 577
Jacobsen v. Massachusetts 696
James v. Valtierra 399
Jenkins v. Georgia 581
Jenness v. Fortson 393
Johnson v. California 276, *333–334*
Johnson v. Maryland 117
Jones v. Alfred H. Mayer Co. 451, 470, *474–475,* 495

Kassel v. Consolidated Freightways Corp. 90, 91
Katzenbach v. McClung 37, 41
Katzenbach v. Morgan 488
Kelley v. Johnson 221
Kelo v. New London 425, *426–427,* 447
Keyes v. School District 1 .... *282–283*
Keystone Bituminous Coal Ass'n v. DeBenedictis 416
Kimel v. Florida Bd. of Regents *490–491,* 492
Kirkpatrick v. Preisler 733
Klein, U.S. v. 14

Knight Co., E.C., U.S. v. 32
Koontz v. St. Johns River Water Mgmt. Dist. 421, *423–424,* 424
Korematsu v. U.S. 274
Kovacs v. Cooper 504, 531
Kramer v. Union Free School District No. 15 385
Kras, U.S. v. 396

Ladue, City of, v. Gilleo 529
Laird v. Tatum 722
Landmark Communications, Inc. v. Virginia 637
Larkin v. Grendel's Den, Inc. 671
Larson v. Valente 679, 680, 701
Law Students Research Council v. Wadmond 624
Lawrence v. Texas 176, *201–205,* 217, 219,
      220, 242, 366, 370, 372, 383
League of United Latin American Citizens
      v. Perry 274, 331
Leathers v. Medlock 628
Lebron v. National Railroad Passenger Corp. 450
Lee v. Weisman *662,* 671
Lee, U.S. v. 693
Lehman v. Shaker Heights 531, 556
Lemon v. Kurtzman *658,* 661, 665, 668, 676, 679, 682–683, 700, 703
Levy v. Louisiana 382
Lindsey v. Normet 400
Linmark Associates, Inc., v. Willingboro 583
Little v. Streater 394, 396
Lochner v. New York *166–169,* 214, 586
Locke v. Davey 687, 688, *690,* 705
Lopez, U.S. v. *38–41,* 51, 53, 63, 725, 726
Loretto v. Teleprompter Manhattan CATV Corp. 415–416
Lorillard Tobacco Co. v. Reilly 588, 590
Los Angeles v. Taxpayers For Vincent 557
Lovell v. Griffin 530, 566
Lovett, U.S. v. 441
Loving v. Virginia 275, 277
Lubin v. Panish 393
Lucas v. Colorado General Assembly 732
Lucas v. South Carolina Coastal Council *417–419,* 420
Lugar v. Edmondson Oil Co. 462
Lujan v. Defenders of Wildlife 714
Luther v. Borden 730
Lynch v. Donnelly 663, 675–678, 700
Lynch v. U.S. 427
Lyng v. Castillo 272
Lyng v. Northwest Indian Cemetery
      Protective Ass'n 694

M.L.B. v. S.L.J. 396
Mahan v. Howell 733
Maher v. Roe 186
Malloy v. Hogan 164
Marbury v. Madison *8–10,* 56, 151, 488

Marsh v. Alabama.............................. *454*, 457
Marsh v. Chambers................................... 671
Marston v. Lewis..................................... 386
Martin v. Hunter's Lessee............................ 10
Martin v. Struthers.................................. 533
Massachusetts Bd. of Retirement v.
       Murgia............... 254, *262*, 263, 264, 491
Massachusetts v. EPA................ 717, 718–719
Masses Publishing Co. v. Patten............... 512, 515
Mathews v. Eldridge............. 227–228, 234, 236
Matthews v. Diaz.................................... 356
McCardle, Ex parte............................. 13–14
McCollum v. Board of Education........... 658–659, 660
McConnell v. Federal Election Comm. *597–600*, 600, 603
McCreary County v. ACLU of Kentucky... 672, 673, *674–675*
McCulloch v. Maryland...... *21–23*, 49, 115, 117, 122, 472
McDermott v. Wisconsin.............................. 106
McDonald v. Board of Election....................... 259
McDonald v. City of Chicago....... 163, *437–438*, 438, 439
McGowan v. Maryland................................. 666
McKane v. Durston................................... 232
Meachum v. Fano..................................... 231
Memorial Hospital v. Maricopa County............ 398, 404
Metro Broadcasting, Inc. v. FCC..................... 320
Metromedia, Inc. v. San Diego............. 528, 551, 557
Metropolitan Life Ins. Co. v. Ward.................. 257
Meyer v. Nebraska............. 173, 213, 223, 605
Michael H. v. Gerald D.............................. 200
Michael M. v. Superior Court.............. 253, 288, 338
Milkovich v. Lorain Journal Co...................... 573
Miller v. California............ *577–578*, 578, 581, 591
Miller v. Johnson................................ *329–331*
Miller v. Schoene................................... 419
Miller, U.S. v...................................... 434
Milliken v. Bradley................................. 283
Minneapolis Star & Tribune Co. v.
       Minnesota Comm'r of Revenue........... 507, 627
Minnesota v. Clover Leaf Creamery Co........... *100*, 262
Mississippi University for Women v. Hogan.......... 337
Mistretta v. U.S.................................... 135
Mitchell v. Helms............................... *682*, 684
Moore v. East Cleveland.......... *197–198*, 217, 243, 419
Moose Lodge No. 107 v. Irvis.................. 461, 468
Morrison v. Olson............. 135, 142, 145
Morrison, U.S. v........... 38, *41–42*, 51, 53, 63, *473*, 495
Morse v. Frederick.............................. 608–609
Mueller v. Allen.................................... 685
Mugler v. Kansas.................................... 166
Muller v. Oregon.................................... 168
Munn v. Illinois.................................... 165

NAACP v. Alabama.................................... 614
NAACP v. Button............................ 584, *609*, 613
National Endowment for the Arts v. Finley.......... 612

National League of Cities v. Usery................ *54–54*, 62
Near v. Minnesota............................. 530, *629*
Nebbia v. New York.................................. 169
Nebraska Press Association v. Stuart ... *632–634*, 639, 645
New York Times Co. v. Sullivan.. *569–572*, 573, 583, 651
New York Times Co. v. U.S.......................... 630
New York v. Ferber.................... 545, *580*, 580
New York v. U.S. (326 U.S. 572, 1946).............. 116
New York v. U.S. (505 U.S. 144, 1992)............. 54,
      56–58, 62, 64, 726
N.F.I.B. v. Sebelius.. 38, *44–51*, 52, 53, 58, 61, 62, 63, 66,
      67–70, *72–77*, 81, 82
Nguyen v. INS.............................. *338–339*, 344
Nixon v. Administrator of General Services 153
Nixon v. Fitzgerald.......................... 149, 155
Nixon v. Shrink Missouri Government PAC........... 604
Nixon v. U.S.............................. 148, 728
Nixon, U.S. v................... 149, *150–152*
NLRB v. Jones & Laughlin Steel Corp. 33–34
Nollan v. California Coastal Commission 416, 421, 424
Northwest Austin Municipal Util. Dist. v. Holder........ 483

O'Brien, U.S. v.............................. *558*, 560
Ogden v. Saunders.................................. 429
Ohralik v. Ohio State Bar Ass'n.................... 584
Oregon Waste Systems, Inc. v. Dep't of
      Environmental Quality....................... 100
Orr v. Orr... 286
Ortwein v. Schwab.................................. 396
Osborne v. Ohio......................... 579, 580, 591

Pacific Gas & Electric Co. v. State Energy
      Comm'n.................................. 106, 107
Palazzolo v. Rhode Island.......................... 425
Palmore v. Sidoti.............................. 276, 349
Parents Involved in Community Schools v.
      Seattle School District No. 1 273, 275, 285, *306–313*, 352, 408
Paris Adult Theatre I v. Slaton.............. 578, 579
Paul v. Davis......................... 225, *226–226*
Pell v. Procunier.................................. 639
Penn Central Transportation Co. v. New York City..... 420
Pennhurst State School Hosp. v. Halderman.............. 724
Pennsylvania Coal Co. v. Mahon..................... 416
Pennsylvania v. Finley............................. 232
Pentagon Papers Case............................... 631
People v. (See opposing party)
Perry Education Ass'n v. Perry Local Educators' Ass'n....
      556
Perry v. Sindermann....................... *224–225*, 239
Personnel Administrator of Massachusetts v.
      Feeney.................................. *269–269*, 343
Philadelphia Newspapers, Inc. v. Hepps............. 572
Philadelphia, City of, v. New Jersey........... *98–100*, 111
Philip Morris USA v. Williams...................... 229

Pierce v. Society of Sisters *173*, 198, 220

Pike v. Bruce Church, Inc. 89, 97

Pittsburgh Press Co. v. Human Relations Commission 586

Planned Parenthood of Missouri v. Danforth 184, 188

Planned Parenthood of Southeastern Pennsylvania
       v. Casey *178–184*, 185, 186, 188, 195,
       196, 203, 219, 242

Playboy Entertainment Group, Inc., U.S. v. 642

Pleasant Grove City v. Summum 610, *612–613*

Plessy v. Ferguson *277*

Plyler v. Doe 354, *356–359*, 364, 381

Poe v. Ullman 175, 722

Powell v. McCormack 24, 729, 739

Press Enterprise Co. v. Superior Court 639

Price, U.S. v. 474

Primus, In re. *584*, 609

Printz v. U.S. 54, 56, *58–59*

Progressive, Inc., U.S. v. 631

Prudential Insurance Co. v. Benjamin 109

Pruneyard Shopping Center v. Robins 557

Quill Corp. v. North Dakota 103–104

Quilloin v. Walcott 200

R.A.V. v. City of St. Paul 504, 506, 540, *541–543*, 567

Railway Express Agency v. New York 255, 257

Raines v. Byrd 716

Randall v. Sorrell 595

Rankin v. McPherson 621, 644

Red Lion Broadcasting Co. v. FCC 640

Reed v. Reed 336

Reeves v. Stake 100, 111

Regents of Univ. of Calif. v. Bakke,
       see University of California Regents v. Bakke

Reid v. Covert 78

Reidel, U.S. v. 579

Reitman v. Mulkey 460

Rendell-Baker v. Kohn 457, 462, 466

Reno v. American Civil Liberties Union *547–548*

Reno v. Condon 52, 64

Republican Party of Minn. v. White 605

Reynolds v. Sims 390, *731–732*, 733

Rice v. Cayetano 390

Richardson v. Ramirez 388

Richardson, U.S. v. 712

Richmond Newspapers, Inc. v. Virginia 638, *639–640*

Richmond v. J.A. Croson Co. 265, 286, 290–293,
       313–319, 320, 326, 332, 350, 407

Riegel v. Medtronic 107, 108

Roberts v. United States Jaycees 614, 617

Roe v. Wade 173, 174, *176–178*, 179, 196, 721

Roemer v. Maryland Public Works Bd. 688

Rogers v. Lodge 267, 271

Rome, City of v. U.S. 477–478, 479, 481

Romer v. Evans 203, 261, 262, 263, 366, *366–368*, 370,
       372

Rosenberger v. University of
       Virginia 507, 553, *554*, 610, 611, *660*

Rosenbloom v. Metromedia, Inc. 572

Ross v. Moffitt 395

Rostker v. Goldberg *289–289*, 338

Roth v. U.S. 576–578

Rowan v. Post Office Dept. 532

Rubin v. Coors Brewing Co. 588

Rumsfeld v. FAIR 77, *616*, 647

Rust v. Sullivan *187–188*, 610, *625–626*

Rutan v. Republican Party of Illinois 619

Saenz v. Roe 399, *413–414*, 444, 446

St. Amant v. Thompson 570

Salerno, U.S. v. 252

San Antonio Ind. School Dist. v.
       Rodriguez 358, *380–383*, 399

Sandin v. Conner 231, 232

Santa Fe Independent School Dist. v. Doe *663–664*

Saxbe v. Washington Post Co. 639

Scales v. U.S. 517

Schaumburg v. Citizens For Better Environment 533

Schechter Poultry Corp. v. U.S. 31–32

Schenck v. U.S. 510

Schlesinger v. Reservists to Stop
       the War 711, 713, 716, 737

Schneider v. State 504, 527, 550

Schware v. Board of Bar Examiners 214

Seminole Tribe of Florida v. Florida 56, 490, 723, *724–*
       726, 726, 738

Shapiro v. Thompson 214, 379, *397–398*, 399

Sharpnack, U.S. v. 117

Shaw v. Hunt 329, 330

Shaw v. Reno *329*, 331

Shelby County v. Holder *479–486*

Shelley v. Kraemer *457–459*, 468

Sheppard v. Maxwell 632

Sherbert v. Verner 667, 688, *691–692*

Sierra Club v. Morton 714, 737

Simon v. Eastern Ky. Welfare Rights
       Organization 717, 738

Skinner v. Oklahoma *173*, 382

Slaughterhouse Cases 165, *412–413*

Smith v. Allwright 453

Smith v. California 582

Smith v. Daily Mail Publishing Co. 637

Snyder v. Phelps 504, 525, *538–539*, 574, 647

Sorrell v. IMS Health Inc. 588

Sosna v. Iowa 398

South Carolina State Highway Dept. v.
       Barnwell Bros., Inc. 90

South Carolina v. Katzenbach 471, *478–479*, 483, 484

South Dakota v. Dole 62, 72, 74, 75

South-Central Timber Development, Inc.
v. Wunnicke 101
Southeastern Promotions, Ltd. v. Conrad 552
Southern Pacific Terminal Co. v. ICC 720
Spence v. Washington 508
Stanley v. Georgia 20, 201, 213, *579–579*, 580, 591
State Farm Mut. Automobile Insur. Co. v. Campbell... 229
Stenberg v. Carhart *189–190*
Stevens, U.S. v. 509, *580*
Strauder v. West Virginia 266
Stromberg v. California 522, 557
Sugarman v. Dougall 354
Supreme Court of New Hampshire v. Piper 119, 122
Swann v. Charlotte-Mecklenburg Board
of Education *280–281*, 292
Swift & Co. v. U.S. 29, 34

Tahoe-Sierra Preservation Council, Inc. v.
Tahoe Regional Planning Agency *418*
Tancil v. Woolls 276
Tennessee v. Lane *492*, 494
Terminiello v. Chicago 534
Terry v. Adams 453
Texas Monthly, Inc. v. Bullock 658, 667
Texas v. Johnson *560*
Thomas v. Review Bd. Ind. Empl. Sect. Div. 697
Thompson v. Western States Medical Center 587
Thornhill v. Alabama 519
Thornton v. Caldor, Inc. *666*
Time, Inc. v. Firestone 571
Timmons v. Twin Cities Area New Party 393
Tinker v. Des Moines School District 568, 605
Toomer v. Witsell 118
Torcaso v. Watkins 697
Trimble v. Gordon 363, 365
Troxel v. Granville *198–199*, 220
Turner Broadcasting System Inc. v. FCC (Turner II)... 641
Turner Broadcasting System, Inc. v. FCC (Turner I)... 641

U.S. Dep't of Agric. v. Moreno.... *260*, 262, 263, 372, 373
U.S. Postal Service v. Greenburgh Civic Assns. 532
U.S. R.R. Retirement Bd. v. Fritz *258–259*
U.S. Term Limits v. Thornton *24–25*
U.S. Trust Co. v. New Jersey *428–428*, 431, 445
U.S. v. Windsor 261
United Building and Constr. Trades Council v.
Camden 102, *119*
United Haulers Ass'n v. Oneida-Herkimer
Solid Waste Management Auth. 97, 101
United Public Workers v. Mitchell 721
United States v. — see opposing party
University of California Regents v. Bakke... 272, 293–294

Van Orden v. Perry 672, *673–674*, 677
Vieth v. Jubelirer *328–328*, *734*

Virginia Board of Elections v. Hamm 276
Virginia Pharmacy Board v. Virginia
Consumer Council 503, 505, *582–583*, 585
Virginia v. Black 541, 544
Virginia v. Tennessee 121
Virginia, U.S. v. 289, 335, 337, 338, *339–342*,
350, 351, 408
Vitek v. Jones 232

Walker v. Birmingham 629
Wallace v. Jaffree *662*, 666
Walz v. Tax Commission 667, 675
Ward v. Rock Against Racism *528*, 528, 531
Warth v. Seldin *717*, 719
Washington v. Davis *267*, 559
Washington v. Glucksberg 205, *209–213*, 221
Washington v. Seattle School Dist. No. 1 284–285
Watchtower Bible and Tract Soc. of N.Y.
v. Village of Stratton 567
Watts v. U.S. 517
Webster v. Reproductive Health Services 187
Wengler v. Druggist's Mutual Ins. Co. 288, 337
Wesberry v. Sanders 731
West Coast Hotel v. Parrish 169
West Virginia State Bd. of Educ. v. Barnette 213, 605
Whalen v. Roe 171
White Primary Cases *453*, 457
Whitney v. California *514–514*, 515–516
Wickard v. Filburn.... 34–35, 37, 39, 43, 44, 47, 49, 51, 61
Widmar v. Vincent 505, 524, 659
Wilkinson v. Austin 232
Williams v. Rhodes 392–393, 404
Williamson v. Lee Optical Co. 170, 406
Willson v. The Black Bird Creek Marsh Co. 86–88
Windsor, U.S. v.... 199, 200, 205, 221, 242, 243, 262, 263,
366, *368–379*, 402, 406
Wisconsin v. Mitchell 541, 543
Wisconsin v. Yoder 692, 695, 702
Witters v. Washington Dep't of Services for the Blind 687
Woods v. Miller Co. 77
Wyeth v. Levine 108
Wygant v. Jackson Bd. of Ed. 326

Yick Wo v. Hopkins 265, 267
Young v. American Mini Theatres 549
Young, Ex parte 723, 739
Youngberg v. Romeo *213*
Youngstown Sheet & Tube Co. v.
Sawyer *128–129*, 135, 136

Zablocki v. Redhail *199–200*, 243
Zelman v. Simmons-Harris 681, *684–687*, 701, 703
Zorach v. Clauson 659
Zurcher v. Stanford Daily 627, 636

SUBJECT MATTER INDEX

ABORTION
Clinics, performance by
    Standards for, 189
Consent to, 181, 182, 184, 186
    By parents, 182, 185, 186
    By spouse, 184
Counseling, restrictions on, 187, 188
Free speech concerning, 532
Hospitals, 189
    Casey, effect on hospitalization, 189
Informed consent, 181, 185
    Regulations discouraging abortion, 181, 188
Minors, 182, 185, 186
    Immature, 186
    Mature or emancipated, 185
Notice and consultation, 181, 182, 186
    By spouse, 181
    To parents, 182, 186
Partial birth method, 189-195
Planned Parenthood v. Casey, 178, 184
    Undue burden standard, 180
Procedures for, 188
Public facilities, 187
    Ban on use of, 187
Public funding of, 186, 188
    Counseling about abortions, 187, 188
    Medically-necessary abortions, 187
    Refusal of in non-therapeutic abortions, 186, 187
    Webster, effect of, 187
Right to privacy rationale, 177-178
Roe v. Wade case, 176
    First, second, third trimesters, 177
    Holding, 177
    Limitations on legislature, 176
    Planned Parenthood v. Casey, effect of, 178, 181
    Post-Roe developments, 178, 188
    Rationale, 177, 178
    Types of abortion allowed, 188
Types of procedures allowed, 188
Undue burden standard, 180, 181, 185, 189

ADMISSIONS
Use of race in, 293-306

ADULT SEXUAL RELATIONS
See EQUAL PROTECTION

ADVISORY OPINIONS
Generally, 708-709

AFFIRMATIVE ACTION
See EQUAL PROTECTION

AFFORDABLE CARE ACT
Commerce power as basis for, 46-50
Taxing power as basis for, 68-69

ALIENAGE
See EQUAL PROTECTION

ANCESTRY
As proxy for race under post-Civil War Amendments, 266

"AS APPLIED" ATTACKS, 252

ASSOCIATION, FREEDOM OF
See FREEDOM OF ASSOCIATION

BILL OF RIGHTS
Application to states, 161-164
    Selective incorporation approach, 162
Total incorporation approach, 163

BILLS OF ATTAINDER
Generally, 441-442
"Punishment" defined, 442
Rationale for ban on, 442

BIRTH CONTROL
Generally, 174-176
Regulation of, following *Roe v. Wade*, 196-197
Use by minors, 197

CABLE TV
Free speech and, 546

CHILD PORNOGRAPHY, 579, 580

CHILD-REARING
Parent's substantive due process right to control, 198-199

CIVIL RIGHTS LAWS
"Color of law," actions taken under, 470
Commerce Clause as support for, 36-38
Congress' power to modify constitutional rights given
    by, 476, 486-489
Congressional enforcement of, 469-497
    Private conduct, Congress' power to reach, 471-476
Public accommodations, 471
Repeal of as state action, 460
Thirteenth Amendment, laws passed under authority of, 474-476
Voting rights, 471

COMA
Rights of patient in, 205-208

COMMERCE CLAUSE
See INTERSTATE COMMERCE

COMMERCIAL SPEECH
See FREEDOM OF SPEECH

CONGRESS' POWERS
Appointment and removal of federal officers, 141-148
Commerce, *See* INTERSTATE COMMERCE
Commitment of the armed forces, 137-138
Enforcement of civil rights laws, 469-497
Enumerated powers of, 79
Executive officers, right to remove, 146-148
Legislative veto, 132-134
Modification of constitutional rights, 486-494
Removal of executive officers, 147-148
Removal of federal officers, 146-147
Specific powers of, 20
Substantive scope of constitutional rights, modification
    of, 486-489
Use of "Necessary and Proper" Clause, 21-22

CONSCIENTIOUS OBJECTION
See FREE EXERCISE CLAUSE

CONSTITUTIONAL RIGHTS
Congress' inability to modify substantive content of, 486-489
Congress' power to remedy violations of, 477-486

CONTRACT CLAUSE
Generally, 427-432
Deferential standard, 431
Distinction between public and private contracts, 431
Incidental effect on contract, 431
Private contracts, application to, 428-430
Public agreements, application to, 428

CROSS BURNING, 541-543

DECLARATORY JUDGMENT
As advisory opinion, 709

DEFAMATION
Generally, 569-574
Damages for, types of, 571
Falsity, burden of proving, 572
Non-media defendants, 572
Opinion, 573
"Private figures", 571
"Public figures", 570
Public interest, statements having no, 572

DEFENSE OF MARRIAGE ACT
Partial invalidation of, 368-379

DIVERSITY
As compelling governmental interest, 296

DNA TESTING
Prisoner's due process right to, 232-233

DORMANT COMMERCE CLAUSE
Generally, 84-104
Local processing requirements, 96
Modern test for, 88
State barriers to outgoing trade, 95

DUE PROCESS OF LAW
Generally, 159-237
Abortion, 176, 184
    See also ABORTION, 176
Child visitation, 198-199
Child-rearing, 198-199
Civil litigation, 228-231
Criminal defendant's right to, 231-233
DNA testing
    Prisoner's right to, 232-233
Economic regulation, 168-171
    Hypothesizing of legislative objectives, 170
    Modern approach to, 168-171
    Pre-1934 approach, 164-168
    Summary of modern approach, 170-171
Enemy combatants, detention of, 233-236
Family relations, 197-200
    Child-raising, 198
    Marriage, 199-200
    Zoning and the "non-nuclear" family, 197-198
Freedom of inquiry, 213
Fundamental rights, 172, 216
Homosexuality, 200-205
Incorporation of Bill of Rights, 159-164

Judicial bias as violation of, 230-231
Marriage, right of, 199-200
Mentally retarded, rights of, 213
Motorcycle helmet rules, 213
Natural father, rights of, 200
Non-economic rights, 172-217
    Birth control use, 174-176, 196-197
    Early cases, 173-174
Occupation, right to engage in, 214
"Penumbra" theory, 174
Prisoners, rights of, 231-233
Privately-imposed harm, no right of protection, 214-216
Procedural due process, 222-237
    Early view, 223
    Governmental regularity *per se*, 222
    Legislature's right to limit procedures, 236-237
    "Liberty" definition narrowed, 226
    Protection from third-party harm, as property
        interest, 214-216
    Rationales for, 237
    Reputation, interest in, 226
    Students, rights of, 226, 237
    Tenured employees, 224-226, 228
    Welfare benefits, 224, 227
    What process is due, 227-237
Punitive damages, 229
Purposeful discrimination, 266
    In administration, 266
Reputation, no protected right in, 226
Retroactivity as violation of, 432
Right to die, 205-213
    Children, 208
    "Clear and convincing" standard, 206
    Health-care proxy, 208
    Incompetent patient, 207
    Living will, 207
    Substituted judgment of family, 206
    Suicide, 208-213
Sexual privacy, 176
Sexuality, 200-205
Substantive due process, 164-217
    Early history of, 164-168
    Maximum-hour laws, 168
    Minimum wage laws, 168
    Protection of non-economic rights
        Generally, 172-217
Two-tier standard of review, 172
Visitation rights, 198-199

ECONOMIC AND SOCIAL REGULATION
See EQUAL PROTECTION

EDUCATION
Denial of as equal protection violation, 380
Illegal aliens, 356

ELECTION DISTRICTS
See VOTING RIGHTS

ELEVENTH AMENDMENT
Generally, 722-726
Administrative agencies and, 726-727
Age discrimination and, 490-491
Broad interpretation of amendment, 723
Court access and, 492
Disability discrimination and, 491-492

Exclusions, 723-724
Facial meaning, 723
Heightened scrutiny and, 492
Patent suits, states' immunity from, 725
State-court suits and, 726
Suits against state official, 723
Suits against states, Congress' general power to allow, 724-726
Text of, 722
Three-step analysis for overcoming, 493

EQUAL PROTECTION
Generally, 249-401
Admissions, use of race in, 293-306
Adoption, 276-277
Affirmative action, 285-334
    Alimony, 286
    Attempt to remedy past discrimination, 287
    Congressionally imposed, 320-323
    Harm to members of minority from, 332
    Hiring, 323, 324
    Housing, 332
    Lay-offs, 325
    Minority set-asides, 313-319
        Congressionally imposed, 320-323
    Promotion preferences, 326
    Quotas, use of, 291, 319, 325, 332
    Racial classifications, benign use of, 290-292
    Separation desired by minorities, 332
    Sex discrimination remedied, 342-343
    Sex-based classes, 286, 334
        Intermediate scrutiny rigorously applied, 335
        Single-sex education, 339-342
        Stereotypes or generalizations, 339-342
    Standard of review for, 273
    Strict scrutiny, required, 272
    To cure racial discrimination generally, 290-334
    Voluntary plans by public employers, 326
Alienage, 353-359
    Education of illegal aliens, 356-359
    Exceptions to strict scrutiny of, 354-355
    Federal government's right to classify based on, 355-356
    Strict scrutiny applied, 354
Animus toward unpopular groups, 260-261
    Anti-gay laws, 260-261
    Out-of-staters, discrimination against, 262
Ballots, see Voting Rights, this entry
Child custody, 276
Courts, access to, 394-396
    Civil litigation, 395-396
    Counsel during appeal, 395
    Transcripts on appeal, 395
Desegregation
    As type of affirmative action, 292-293
    Busing to accomplish, 281, 284-285
    Closing of public schools, 280
    De facto/de jure distinction, 267, 280, 282, 293
    Ending court supervision, 285
    "Freedom of choice", 280
    Harm to minority members from, 332
    In the North, 282
    Interdistrict remedies, 283-284
Diversity as compelling interest, 296
Economic and social regulation, 256-263

Hypothetical legislative objectives, 257-259
    Means-end link, 262, 263
    Objective of legislature, 256
    "One step at a time", 257
Education, right to, 380-383
Federal government, application to, 251
Fundamental rights, 379-401
    Access to courts as, 394-396
    Ballot access as, 390-394
    Education as, 380-383
    Right to travel as, 396-399
    Voting rights as, 383-390
Hiring, 323-326, 333
Historical overview, 249
Homosexuals, singling out of, 260-261
Illegitimacy, 359
Jury selection, 270
Mentally ill, discrimination against, 361-362
Mentally retarded, discrimination against, 261, 360
"Mere-rationality" review, 255
"Mere-rationality" standard, 256-263
Middle-level review, 256, 362-363
    Close means-end fit required, 362
    General principles of, 362
    Hypothesizing of state purpose, 362
    Mental illness, 361
    Mental retardation, not applicable to, 360-361
Objective of legislature, significance of, 253
"One step at a time" reform, 257, 261
Operation of the Clause, generally, 251-256
Over-inclusive classification, 254-255
Partisan gerrymanders, 327-328
Political process, race used in, 275-276
Poll tax as violation of, 54, 384
Private conduct
    Congress' power to reach, 471-474
Public school admissions based on race, 306-313
Purposeful discrimination, 266-271
    Circumstantial evidence used to prove, 267
    Dual motives, 268
    Facially discriminatory statute, 266
    Must be cause of conduct, 269
    Passage of time, 269
    Proving, 267
    Sex discrimination, 344
    Statistics used to prove, 270-271
Racial discrimination, 265-285
    Adoption, 276
    Child custody, 276
    Establishment-of-religion defense against claim of, 688
    Law enforcement operations, 333
    Racially restrictive covenants, 457-459
    Voting, 383-390
Remedial powers of Congress, 477-494
Segregation, 277-285
    See also "Desegregation" under this main heading
    Prison-cell assignments, 333-334
    Remedies to combat, 277-285
    "Separate but equal" doctrine, 277
"Separate but equal" treatment, 274-275
Sex discrimination, 285-290, 334-345
    Alimony, 286
    Attempt to remedy past discrimination, 287

Bathrooms and locker rooms, 345
Discriminatory purpose required, 343-345
Draft registration, 289-290
Intermediate scrutiny of, 336-337
Statutory rape, 288-289
Veterans' preference as, 269
Special traits pertaining to one race, 275
States, violation of by, 489-494
Stereotypes, significance of, 272
Strict scrutiny, 255, 271-276
How much, 276
How strict, 272-277
Immutability, significance of, 271
Other requirements for, 271-272
Purposeful discrimination required for, 266-271
Stereotypes, significance, 272
Surviving strict scrutiny, chances of, 273
Suspect classifications, 265-272
See also SUSPECT CLASSIFICATIONS
Travel, right to, 396-399
Medical benefits, residency requirements for, 398
Welfare benefits, residency rules for, 397-398
Two-tier model, 255-256
Under-inclusive classification, 254
Voting rights, 268, 383-390, 399
Ballot access, 390-394
Ballot counting procedures, 389-390
Duration-of-residence requirements, 386
Felons, denial of vote to, 388
Partisan gerrymanders, 327-328
Standards for judging cases alleging violations of, 326-331
Warren Court's view, 250
Wealth, classifications based on, 266, 399-401
Housing, 400
Welfare benefits, 399
Welfare benefits, 399

ESTABLISHMENT CLAUSE
Generally, 657-688
Ceremonies and displays, 671-678
Cross, display of, 677
Entanglement of church and state, 670-671
Free Exercise Clause, relation to, 656-657
Funding of student activities, 660
Graduation ceremony, 662-663, 671
Holidays, celebration of, 672-676
Interdenominational preferences, 678-679
Legislative chaplain, 671
Military chaplains, 667
Ministerial exception from government regulation, 668-670
Nativity scene, display of, 672-676
Parochial schools aid to, 680-688
Equipment, 682
Higher education, 688
Salary supplements, 682
Scholarships for religious study, 687
Services, furnishing of, 683-684
Teachers, furnishing of, 683
Textbooks and other materials, 682
Three-prong test for, 680
Transportation, 681
Pledge of Allegiance, 663, 671
Prayer-reading in public schools, 661-664

Preference among denominations, 678-679
Prisoners, accommodation of, 680
Public schools, 658-666
Anti-evolution laws, 664
Facilities use by student groups, 659-660
Graduation ceremony, 662-663, 671
Modification of curriculum, 664-666
Moment of silence, 661-662
Prayer reading, 661-663
Religious instruction, 658-661
Tuition vouchers, 684-687
Religious displays, 672-678
Sabbath, right not to work on, 666, 691-692
Secular purpose required, 666
Sincerity of religious belief, 670
Single test, future possibility, 658
Specific prohibitions, 657-658
Sunday closing laws, 666
Ten Commandments, display of, 672-675
Three-prong test for, 658
Tuition vouchers, 684-687

***EX POST FACTO* LAWS**, 440-441

EXECUTIVE AGREEMENTS, 78, 136

EXECUTIVE POWERS
See also IMMUNITIES
Appointment of officials by President, 141-143
Commitment of the armed forces, 137-138
Executive privilege, 150-153
Legislative veto
Invalidated, 132-134
"Line item" veto
Invalidated, 131-132
No right to make laws, 128-129
Pocket veto, 130
Right to remove appointees, 143-146
Veto power, 130-134

EXECUTIVE PRIVILEGE, 150-153

FACIAL ATTACKS ON STATUTES, 252

FALSE STATEMENTS
Government power to ban, 574-576

FEDERAL COURTS
Powers of, 79

FEDERALISM, 19-21

FIFTEENTH AMENDMENT, 390

FIRST AMENDMENT
See FREEDOM OF SPEECH, FREEDOM OF ASSOCIATION, FREEDOM OF THE PRESS, FREEDOM OF RELIGION

FOREIGN AFFAIRS
Commitment of the armed forces, 137-138
Federal government's power over, 21, 79

FOURTEENTH AMENDMENT
See DUE PROCESS OF LAW, EQUAL PROTECTION, IMMUNITIES
Congress' remedial powers under, 476-494

FREE EXERCISE CLAUSE
Generally, 688-698
Animal sacrifice, 689-690

Centrality of belief, 697
Conflict with criminal statute, 694-695
Conscientious objection, 696
Drugs, 694-695
Establishment Clause, relation to, 656-657
Intent to interfere with religion, 689-690
Life-saving medical treatment, 697
Military service, relation to, 696
Ministerial exception from regulation, 695-696
Nativity Scene, right to display, 672-676
Public health objectives as interference with, 696
Religious belief, definition of, 697-698
Sabbath, accommodation for, 691-692
Sacrifice of animals, 689-690
Scholarships for ministry study, 687, 690
Sincerity of belief, 697

FREEDOM OF ASSOCIATION
Generally, 613-626
Bar membership restrictions, 623-624
Campaign spending, compulsory disclosure of, 623
Compulsory disclosure, 622-623
Campaign contributions, disclosure of, 623
Compulsory financial support, 614-615
Denial of public jobs or benefits, 618-622
Loyalty oaths, 619-620
Patronage dismissals and hirings, 618
Speech critical of superiors, 620-622
Discrimination by private groups, 614
Illegal groups, 618
Legal services furnished by lay groups, 609
Loyalty oaths, 619-620
Membership, interference with, 616-618
Right not to associate, 614-618
Social association, no general right, 613
Strict scrutiny of interferences with, 613

FREEDOM OF EXPRESSION
See FREEDOM OF SPEECH, FREEDOM OF
ASSOCIATION

FREEDOM OF RELIGION
Generally, 655-698
Religious belief, definition of, 697-698
See also ESTABLISHMENT CLAUSE, FREE EXERCISE
CLAUSE

FREEDOM OF SPEECH
Abortion clinics, women visiting, 532
Accountant, solicitation by as protected speech, 584
Advocacy of illegal acts, 509-522
"Clear and present danger" test for, 510-512
Incitement required, 516
Modern standard for, 515-519
Statutes directly proscribing speech, 513-514
Audience's right to information, 583
Broadcast ads, regulation of, 597-603
Broadcasting
See also "Media" under this main heading
Phone, cable and computer systems distinguished, 546-
549
Special rules applicable to, 546
Cable TV, 546
Campus speech, regulation of, 544
Canvassing and soliciting, 532-533
Anonymously, 533

In public places, 533
Mailboxes, 532
Visits to home, 533
Captive audience, 531-532, 537
"Clear and present danger" test, 510-512
Commercial speech, 582-590
Current status of, 586-590
"For Sale" signs banned, 583
Harmful products, advertising of, 588-589
Constitutionally-protected products, 590
Vice products, 588-589
Internal consistency required in regulation of, 587
Lawyers, regulation of speech of, 584
Misleading statements, 586
Protection curtailed, 585-586
Protection first given to, 582
"Reasonably tailored means", 587
Communicative impact
Regulation aimed at speech, 504-507
Compelled speech, 614-618
Computer-generated images, 580
Conduct distinguished from speech, 528
Confidential information, disclosure of, 636-638
Content-neutrality generally required, 542, 553-554
Corporate political expression, 604
Crime, disclosure of information obtained by, 637-638
Criminal trials, access to, 639
Cross burning, 541-543
Defamation, 569-574
See also DEFAMATION
Draft resistance, 558-559
Draft-card burning, 558-559
Drug use, advocacy of in schools, 608
Emotional distress, intentional infliction of, 573
Fairgrounds, 533
False statements of fact
Government's right to ban, 574-576
"Fighting words" doctrine, 533-536, 541, 542
Flag desecration and misuse, 560
Constitutional amendment, need for, 562
Federal statute, 562
Gag order to preserve fair trial, 632-634
Government as speaker or funder of speech, 610-612
Display of privately-donated monument, 612-613
Government employees, speech by, 620-622
Hair and clothing regulation, 560
"Hate speech," regulation of, 540-544
Penalty-enhancement statutes, 543
Hostile audience, 533-536
Anger by audience not sufficient, 535
Crowd-control required, 534
Indecency, regulation of, 544-546, 546-549
Internet, 547-549
Secondary-effects doctrine, 545-546
Intentional infliction of emotional distress, 537-539, 573
Internet, 547-549
Internet connections in libraries, 556
Intimidation as non-protected activity, 543-544
Issue ads, 597-603
Jails, 555
Lawyers, comments by, 633
Lawyers, commercial speech by, 584
Legal services furnished by lay groups, 609

Licensing requirements, 529-531
Loudspeakers, 531
Media, 627-642
    Access to jails, 638
    Access to pre-trial proceedings, 639
    Broadcast media, 640-642
    Criminal trials, right of access to, 639
    Editorializing by public broadcasters, 641
    Ex parte search warrants, 636
    Government demands for information held by, 634-636
    Grand jury subpoenas, 634
    Prior restraints, 629-634
    Right of access to government-held information, 638-
        640
    Shield laws, 636
    Special role for the press, 627
Mental anguish to listeners, 540
Military bases, 555
Military honors, lying about, 574-576
Minors, protection of, 589-590
Monument, government display of, 612-613
Non-communicative impact aimed at speech, 503, 507
Nude dancing, 545-546
Obscenity, 576-582
    See also OBSCENITY
Offensive words, 536-544
Opinion, statements of, 573
Outside speeches and articles, ban on payment for, 622
Overbreadth
    See OVERBREADTH
Political campaign spending
    Constitutional limits, 593
    Contributions by individuals, 593, 604
    Contributions to and by Political Action
        Committees, 595
    Corporate political expression, 604
    Expenditures by individuals, 594
    General rules governing, 593
    Limits on total campaign spending, 594
    Political parties, regulation of, 603
    Soft-money donations, 597
    Spending by millionaire's opponent, 595
    Spending by political parties, 597, 603
    Spending of candidateÕs own money, 594
Pornography
    Child pornography, 579-580
Pre-trial proceedings, access to, 639
Prior restraints, 530, 629-634
    Distinguished from subsequent punishment, 629, 633
    Gag orders to preserve fair trial, 632-634
    Receipt of stolen goods as exception to, 631
    Strict scrutiny of, 630
    Threat of H-bomb, 631
Private places, 508, 527, 551
    Right of access to, 557
Public forum, 507, 527, 549-557
    Designated public forum, 552
    Jails, 555
    Military bases, 555
    Non-public forums, 552-557
    Schools
        School mail system, 556
    Semi-public forums, 550

Significant state interest required for regulation, 550
    True public forums, 551
    Workplace, governmental, 556
Religious speech, 507
School mail system, 556
Schools, 605-609
    Protest in, 559
    Students, speech by, 607
    Teaching materials, choice of, 606-607
Secondary-effects doctrine, 545-546
Secret information, disclosure of, 636-638
Shopping centers, 557
Sleeping in park, 560
Sound equipment, regulation of, 531
Students, speech by, 607
Subject matter forbidden, 507
Subversive advocacy, 509-522
    See also "Advocacy of illegal conduct" under this main
        heading
Symbolic expression, 557-562
Taxation as violation of, 507
"Time, place and manner" regulations, 526-557
    General test for validity, 527
"Unprotected categories" approach, 504-507
Vagueness
    See VAGUENESS
Value, some speech having less than others, 507, 544
Viewpoint neutrality, 79, 553
Workplace, 556

FUNDAMENTAL RIGHTS
See DUE PROCESS OF LAW

GAY MARRIAGE
Equal protection analysis of, 260-261, 368-379
Substantive due process analysis of, 204-205

GERRYMANDERING
See VOTING RIGHTS

GOVERNMENTAL MOTIVE
Commerce Clause cases, irrelevant in, 36
Discriminatory intent, 266-271
Generally not inquired into, 23
In freedom of speech cases, 505, 507

HABEAS CORPUS, 138-141

"HATE SPEECH"
See also FREEDOM OF SPEECH
Regulation of as First Amendment violation, 540-544

HEALTH CARE ACT
Constitutionality of federal, 44-51

HIRING
Equal protection and, 323-326, 333

HOMOSEXUALITY
See also DUE PROCESS OF LAW, GAY MARRIAGE, and
    SEXUALITY
Animus toward unpopular groups, 260-261
Fundamental right not found, 201
Gay marriage, 200-205, 260-261
Substantive due process protection of, 200-205

ILLEGITIMACY
See also EQUAL PROTECTION
    Generally, 359

IMMUNITIES
Civil immunity of presidential assistants, 149-150
Civil liability of President for official acts, 149
Civil liability of President for unofficial acts, 150
Criminal prosecution of executive officials, 150
Federal immunity from state regulation, 117
From taxation, 115-117
    Federal immunity from state regulation, 115-116
    State immunity from federal taxation, 116-117
Of Congress, 149
Of executive, 149-150

IMPEACHMENT
Generally, 147-148
Congress' demand for materials pursuant to, 152
Criminal liability following, 148
"High crimes and misdemeanors," meaning of, 147
Reviewability of by the courts, 148, 729

INDEPENDENT AND ADEQUATE STATE GROUNDS
Supreme Court review obviated by, 11-12

INTERMEDIATE SCRUTINY
See EQUAL PROTECTION

INTERNET
Indecency on, regulation of, 547-549

INTERSTATE COMMERCE
Channels of interstate commerce, 52
Congress' power over, 53-59
    "Activity" required for, 47
    Child labor, 30
    Civil rights legislation, 36-38
    "Cumulative effect" theory, 34-35
    "Current of commerce" theory, 29, 31
    "Direct logical relationship" to required, 32
    Early cases, 27-31
    Findings by Congress, significance of, 37
    Forced purchase of good or service, 44-51
    Insurance, forced purchase of, 44-51
    Intrastate activities, regulation of, 30, 33-34, 42-44
    Limits on, 38-52
    Marijuana cultivation, 42-44
    Modern trend, generally, 33-38
    Non-commercial activities, regulation of, 42-44, 51
    Police-power regulations, 30-31, 35-36
    "Substantial economic effect" on, 29, 33-34
    Tenth Amendment as limit on, 53-59
    Violence against women, 41-42
Instrumentalities of interstate commerce, 52
Outgoing trade, barriers to, 100
Relocation, pressures inducing, 96
State as purchaser or subsidizer, 100-102
State regulation of, 84-102
    Balancing test, 89
    Congress' power to reverse, 84
    Congress' silence, general effect of, 85
    Contradictory standards, 90
    Cumulative burdens, 90-91, 103-104
    Discrimination, 88, 90, 91, 93-95, 99
    Disproportionately burdensome to, 94, 102
    Environmental rules, 98-100
    Health objectives, 92
    Incoming trade, barriers to, 91-95
    Less-restrictive alternatives, 89, 93
    Local matters, 86-88, 89, 95
    Local-processing requirements, 96
    "Market participant," state as, 100-102, 119-120
    Means-end fit, 88
    Migration by individuals, 95
    Modern approach, 88
    Natural resources, embargo of, 96
    Need for "legitimate state end", 88
    Outgoing trade, barriers to, 95-96
    Protectionism, 92
    Purchaser or subsidizer, state acting as, 100-102
    Taxation, 102-104
    Transportation, 89-91
"Substantially affecting" commerce, 53

INTERSTATE COMPACTS, 121

JUDGES
Campaign speech by, regulation of, 605

JUDICIAL BRANCH
Bias by judge as due process violation, 230-231
Congress' control of federal judicial power, 12-14
Separation of powers involving, 135
Speech by judges, regulation of, 605
Supreme Court's powers, 8-14

JUDICIAL REVIEW
Legitimacy of, 8-12

JUSTICIABILITY, 707-734
See also ADVISORY OPINION, ELEVENTH
        AMENDMENT, MOOTNESS, POLITICAL
        QUESTIONS, RIPENESS and STANDING

LEGISLATIVE VETO
Invalidated, 132-134

LESS RESTRICTIVE ALTERNATIVES
Access to criminal trials, 639
Compulsory disclosure of associational ties, 622
Interstate Commerce, 89, 93
State regulation of commerce, 89, 93

LIBERTY OF CONTRACT, 166

"LINE ITEM" VETO
Invalidated, 131-132

MARRIAGE
As fundamental right, 199
By homosexuals, 204-205, 368-379
By persons owing child support, 199

MEDICAL TREATMENT
Right to refuse, 205-208

"MERE-RATIONALITY" TEST
See EQUAL PROTECTION

MIDDLE-LEVEL SCRUTINY
See EQUAL PROTECTION

MILITARY COMMISSIONS
President's power to establish, 138-141

MILITARY HONORS
Government's right to punish lies about, 574-576

MOOTNESS
Generally, 720-721
"Capable of repetition, yet evading review", 720
Class actions, 720

Collateral consequences, 721
Voluntary cessation by defendant, 721

MORATORIUM
On development, as taking, 417

MOTIVE
See GOVERNMENTAL MOTIVE

NECESSARY AND PROPER CLAUSE
Broad reading given to, 22
Must be incidental to enumerated power, 48

OBSCENITY
Generally, 576-582
Child pornography, possession of, 579, 580
Children as audience, 579
Children as photographic subjects, 580
Community standards, 578, 581
Pictures, book without, 581
Private possession by adults, 579, 580
Scienter required, 582

OPINION
Statement of as defamation, 573

OVERBREADTH
Generally, 519-522
As exception to rule against third-party standing, 719
Canvassing and soliciting, 532
Communist-control statutes, 515
Defined, 519
Rationale for, 520
Substantial overbreadth now required, 520-521

PARADES
Government interference with participation in, 615

"PARTIAL BIRTH" ABORTION, 189

PERMIT
Requirement of as free-speech violation, 529-531

PLEDGE OF ALLEGIANCE
As violation of Establishment Clause, 671

POLITICAL QUESTIONS
Generally, 727-734
Commitment to other branches, 728-730
Factors giving rise to, 727
Gerrymandering, 733
Impeachment, 728
Judicially manageable standards, lack of, 730
Reapportionment, 730-734
Republican form of government, guarantee of, 730
War Powers disputes, 730

PREEMPTION
Generally, 104-109
Conflicts preemption, 106-107
Consent by Congress to state laws, 108-109
Express preemption, 104
Field preemption, 105
Implied preemption, 104-108

PRESIDENT
See EXECUTIVE POWER

PRIVACY, RIGHT OF, 172
See also DUE PROCESS OF LAW

PRIVATE CONDUCT
Congress' power to reach under 14th Amendment, 471-474

PRIVILEGES AND IMMUNITIES
Of national citizenship (14th Amendment), 399, 412-414
    Recent expanded view of, 413
    Right to travel, 413
Of state citizenship (Art. IV), 118-121
    Discrimination, test for, 102, 119
    Equal protection, distinguished from, 120
    "Fundamental rights," limitation to, 118
    Market participant, no exception for, 119-120
    Municipal residence, discrimination based on, 120
Practice of law, right to, 119

PUBLIC FORUM
See FREEDOM OF SPEECH, Public forum

PUNITIVE DAMAGES
See DUE PROCESS OF LAW, Punitive damages

QUOTAS
Ban on in admissions, 296, 298
Defined, 291-292

RACIAL CLASSIFICATIONS AND QUOTAS
See also EQUAL PROTECTION and QUOTAS
Minority set-asides by states and cities, 313-319

REAPPORTIONMENT
Generally, 730-734
Equality, permissible deviation from, 733
Gerrymandering, 733
Local government bodies, 733
"One person, one vote" principle, 731

RELIGION, FREEDOM OF
See ESTABLISHMENT CLAUSE and FREE EXERCISE
    CLAUSE

RETROACTIVITY
Contract Clause as restriction on, 431-432
Ex post facto rule as restriction on, 440-441
Taking Clause as restriction on, 414

RIGHT OF INTERSTATE MIGRATION
See RIGHT TO TRAVEL, EQUAL PROTECTION

RIGHT TO DIE
See also DUE PROCESS OF LAW, "Right to die"
    Generally, 205-213
Children, 208
"Clear and convincing" standard, 206
Health care proxy, 208
Incompetent patient, 207
Living will, 207
Substituted judgment of family, 206
Suicide, 208-213

RIGHT TO TRAVEL
See also EQUAL PROTECTION
    Generally, 396-399
Protected under 14th Amendment Privileges or Immunities
    Clause, 399, 413-414

RIPENESS
Generally, 721-722
Criminal statute, uncertain enforcement of, 722
Specific threatened harm, 722

SAME-SEX MARRIAGE
Equal protection analysis of, 261, 368-379
Substantive due process analysis of, 204-205

SECOND AMENDMENT, 432-440
Handgun ban and, 435, 439
Standard of review for, 438
Types of weapons covered, 439
Unloaded guns, requirement of, 435

SECONDARY-EFFECTS DOCTRINE
In free-speech cases, 545-546

SEGREGATION
See EQUAL PROTECTION

SEPARATION OF POWERS
Generally, 127-153
Appointment of federal officers, 141-143
Commitment of the armed forces, 137-138
Executive immunity, 149-150
Executive privilege, 150-153
Habeas corpus and, 140
Impeachment, 147-148
Judicial branch, undue delegation to, 135
President's power, *see* EXECUTIVE POWER
President's veto power, 130-134
    Legislative veto, 132-134
    "Line item" veto, 131-132
    Pocket veto, 130
Removal of appointees, 143-148
    By Congress, 146-148
    By President, 143-146
Special prosecutor, 134

SEX DISCRIMINATION
See also EQUAL PROTECTION
Affirmative action to cure, 286-290

SEXUALITY
Consensual sexual activity
    Homosexual conduct, change in Court attitude
        towards, 260-261
Equal protection and, 383
Privacy right, two strands to, 202
Substantive due process protection of, 200-205

SOVEREIGN IMMUNITY
Of states before federal administrative agencies, 726
Of states in their own courts, 726

SPEECH AND DEBATE CLAUSE, 149

SPENDING POWER
Generally, 70-77
Coercion of states as limit on, 72-75
Conditions set on use of federal funds, 71-75
Distinct enumerated power, existence as, 70-77
"General welfare" requirement, 77
Regulation, attempt to use for, 71

STANDING
Generally, 709-719
"Actual or imminent harm" requirement, 714
Causation requirement, 716-718
    Constitutional basis for, 717
"Certainly impending" requirement, 714-715
Citizenship suits, 713
Constitutional vs. prudential limitations, 710

Federal taxpayer suits, 711-713
Harm suffered by many, 715
"Injury in fact" requirement, 713
"Institutional" loss of power, 716
Minorities, denigration of, 716
Nexus requirement for taxpayer suits, 711
Non-economic harms, 714
Organizations and associations, 716
Prudential standing, 719-720
Rationale behind doctrine, 710
State as plaintiff, 718-719
Suits not based on taxpayer or citizenship status, 713-718
Tax breaks for discriminatory private schools, 718
Taxpayers' standing, 711-713
Third-party standing, 719

STATE ACTION
Generally, 449-465
Acquiescence by state, 464
Civil rights laws, repeal of, 460
Commandment by state, 457-459
Company towns and shopping centers, 453
Early interpretations of, 450-452
Electoral process as constituting, 453
Encouragement by state, 459
Entanglement by state, 461-465
Entwinement between state and private actor, 463-464
Final act, by state, 465
Funding by state, 462
"Government entity" defined, 449
Involvement of state, 457-465
Joint participation by state as private actor, 462-463
Licensing by state, 461
Modern approach to, 452
Monopoly, grant of by state, 462
"Nexus" doctrine, 457-465
Parks and recreation, operation of, 455
Private school, operation of, 457
"Public function" approach, 453-457
Racially-restrictive covenants, 457-459
Recognition by state of private actor's role, 465
State "exclusivity" requirement, 455
"Symbiosis" between state and private actor, 460
Utility, operation of, 455
Warehouseman's lien as, 456

STRICT SCRUTINY
See EQUAL PROTECTION

SUBSTANTIVE DUE PROCESS
See DUE PROCESS OF LAW

SUICIDE
See DUE PROCESS OF LAW, RIGHT TO DIE

SUPREMACY CLAUSE
See PREEMPTION

SUPREME COURT'S AUTHORITY
Generally, 8-15
Certiorari, 15
    Grounds for grant of, 15
Congress' control of, 12-14
Jurisdiction of Court today, 15
Review of state court decisions, 10-12
    Independent and adequate state grounds, 11-12
Right to judge statute's constitutionality, 8-10

SUSPECT CLASSIFICATIONS
Generally, 265-272
National origin, 265
Purposeful discrimination required, 266-271
Race, 265
Wealth as, 266, 399-401

SUSPENSION CLAUSE
Habeas corpus and, 138

TAKING CLAUSE
Generally, 414-427
Denial of all economically viable use, 416
Diminution in value, 416
Economic development as basis for taking, 425-427
Landmark preservation, 420
Moratorium on development as taking, 417
Notice, owner who takes with, 425
Physical occupation, 415-416
"Prevention of harm" or "noxious use" rationale, 418-419
"Public use" required, 425
States subject to, 415
Taking distinguished from regulation, 415-425
Temporary delay as taking, 417
Zoning regulations, 419

TAXATION
Apportionment of direct taxes, 66
Cumulative burdens, 103-104
Based on content, 628
Exports not taxable, 66
Federal government's power of, 65-70
Immunities from, 115-117
Penalty as falling within Congress' power to tax, 68-70
Regulatory effect of, 66-70
States, power of, 102-104
Burdensome but facially neutral schemes, 103
Discrimination against commerce, 103
Minimum contacts required, 102

TAXPAYERS
Standing of to bring federal suit, 711-713

TEN COMMANDMENTS
Display of as Establishment Clause violation, 672-675

TENTH AMENDMENT
Impairment of state's essential functions, 54-59
Law-making mechanisms, use of states', 56-59
Insignificant as general rule, 36, 54
Procedural safeguards protecting, 55

TERM LIMITS, 24-25

THIRTEENTH AMENDMENT
Congress' power to enforce, 474-476
Private conduct reachable under, 474-475

Purposeful discrimination required, 475
Self-executing scope of, 475

TREATY POWER
Generally, 78
Executive agreements, 78, 136

TUITION VOUCHERS
Establishment Clause and, 684-687

VAGUENESS
Generally, 522
Canvassing and soliciting, 532
Use of to invalidate denials of public jobs or benefits, 618

VISITATION RIGHTS
Parent's substantive due process right to control, 198-199

VOTING RIGHTS
See also FREEDOM OF SPEECH, "Political campaign
spending," FIFTEENTH AMENDMENT, and
VOTING RIGHTS ACT
As being fundamentally right, 384
Ballot access, 390-394
Candidate eligibility rules, 391
Discriminatory purpose required, 267-268
Drawing of election districts, 326-331, 733-734
Duration-of-residence requirements, 386
Election districts, drawing of, 326-331
Election districts, racially motivated, 329-331
Electoral process as state action, 453
Felons, denial of voting rights to, 388
Filing fees payable by candidates, 393
Gerrymandering, 326-331, 733
Minor parties, 391-393
Partisan gerrymanders, 327-328
Poll tax, 54, 384
Statutory protection of, 469-471
Voter identification requirements, 386-388
Voter qualifications, 384-389
Voting Rights Act, 273, 477-486

VOTING RIGHTS ACT
Congressional enforcement of voting rights in, 477, 478-486

WAR POWERS
Generally, 77, 136
Commitment of the armed forces, 137-138
Power to establish military commissions, 138-141
Regulation of private behavior and, 77

WEALTH CLASSIFICATIONS
See EQUAL PROTECTION